vegetables, herbs & fruit

vegetables, herbs & fruit

AN ILLUSTRATED ENCYCLOPEDIA

MATTHEW BIGGS, JEKKA MCVICAR
AND BOB FLOWERDEW

FIREFLY BOOKS

A FIREFLY BOOK

Published by Firefly Books Ltd. 2013

First printing

Publisher Cataloging-in-Publication Data (U.S.)

A CIP record of this book is available from Library of
Congress

**Library and Archives Canada Cataloguing in
Publication**

A CIP record of this book is available from Library and
Archives Canada

Published in the United States by
Firefly Books (U.S.) Inc.
P.O. Box 1338, Ellicott Station
Buffalo, New York 14205

Published in Canada by
Firefly Books Ltd.
66 Leek Crescent
Richmond Hill, Ontario L4B 1H1

Cover design by Interrobang Graphic Design Inc.

Printed in Singapore

To Henry John William
and Chloe Elizabeth
—*Matthew Biggs*

To Mac, Hannah, and Alistair
—*Jekka McVicar*

To all those who helped
make our glorious fruits from
such humble beginnings
—*Bob Flowerdew*

Much of the material in this book is taken from
Matthew Biggs's *Complete Book of Vegetables*, Jekka's
Complete Herb Book, and Bob Flowerdew's *Complete Fruit
Book*, first published in 1997, 1994, and 1995 respectively.

Permissions acknowledgments appear on page 639

Cover images
Front (clockwise from top left): © shutterstock.com/
Anastasiya Smirnova; heinteh; maryo; Mazzzur
Back (top to bottom): © shutterstock.com/
Artography; liza1979; VojtechVlk; Zigzag Mountain Art

IMPORTANT NOTICE

CONTENTS

INTRODUCTION

A flourishing, productive garden, containing vegetables, herbs, and fruit plants, is a testament to diligent, imaginative gardening and a promise of a delicious harvest to come. The range of color, texture, scent, and flavor offered by these plants is unrivaled, and there is space in any garden—even in a window box—for a selection of edible and useful plants.

Vegetables, herbs, and fruit have always been essential to humanity. They are the basis of the food chain—even for meat-eaters—and are a vital component in creating tempting, palatable meals, as well as providing unique flavoring and aromas. All are health-giving, providing essential vitamins and minerals for a balanced diet, and many herbs have the added dimension of being used medicinally.

Vegetables and herbs can be widely defined. Vegetables are those plants where a part, such as the leaf, stem, or root, can be used for food. Herbs, similarly, are those plants that are used for food, medicine, scent, or flavor. Fruits tend to be the sweet, juicy parts of the plants, containing the seed. There is considerable overlap between the three types of plant—one further distinction is that fruits are generally sweet, or used in sweet dishes, while vegetables are savory, although this is by no means clear-cut.

For centuries throughout the world, productive gardens have been the focal point of family and community survival. Our earliest diet as hunter-gatherers must have included a wide range of seeds, fruits, nuts, roots, leaves, and any moving thing we could catch. Gradually, over millennia, we learned which plants could be eaten and how to prepare them—as with the discovery that eddoes were edible only after washing several times and cooking to remove the injurious calcium oxalate crystals. Fruit trees and bushes sprang up at the camp sites of nomadic people and were waiting for them when they returned, growing prolifically on their fertile waste heaps.

Vegetables and herbs were collected from the surrounding countryside, and gradually were domesticated. Cultivated wheat and barley have been found dating from 8000 to 7000 B.C., and peas from 6500 B.C., while rice was recorded as a staple in China by 2800 B.C.

With domestication came early selection of plants for beneficial characteristics such as yield, disease resistance, and ease of germination. These were the first cultivated varieties, or "cultivars." This selection has continued extensively and by the eighteenth century in Europe, seed selection had become a fine art in the hands of skilled gardeners. Gregor Mendel's work with peas in 1855–1864 in his monastery garden at Brno in Moravia yielded one of the most significant discoveries, leading to the development of hybrids and scientific selection. Most development has centered on the major food crops. Minor crops, such as sea kale, have changed very little, apart from the selection of a few cultivars. Others, like many fruits, are similar to their wild relatives, but have fleshier, sweeter edible parts. Herbs have in general had less intensive work done on selection; many of the

The Frugal Meal by Jozef Israels, 1824–1911

most popular and useful herbs are the same as or closely related to plants found in the wild.

Food plants have spread around the world in waves, from the Roman Empire, which took fruits such as peaches, plums, grapes, and figs from the Mediterranean and North Africa to northern Europe, to the exportation of plants such as potatoes and maize from the New World in the fifteenth century. In between, monasteries guarded fruits, vegetables, and herbs for their own use and for their medicinal value. During the famine and winter dearth of the Middle Ages and beyond, the commonplace scurvy and vitamin deficiencies would have seemed to many people almost miraculously cured by monks' potions containing little more than preserved fruits, vegetables, or herbs full of nutrients and vitamin C. In 1597 John Gerard wrote his *Herball*, detailing numerous plants and their uses, and giving practical advice on how to use them.

Productive gardening developed on several levels. The rich became plant collectors and used the latest technology to overwinter exotic plants in hothouses and stove houses. Doctors followed on in the traditions of the monasteries and had physic gardens of medicinal herbs. Villagers had cottage gardens filled with fruit trees and bushes, underplanted with vegetables and herbs.

In the twentieth century, the expense of labor and decrease in the amount of land available meant that productive gardening declined. Home food production revived during World War II, but the availability of ready-made foods afterward again hit edible gardening at home. The later years of the century saw a reaction against the blandness and cost of mass-produced food.

A well-kept vegetable garden is a source of pride.

The Vegetable Garden, Coombe, **by Paul Riley, 1988**

There was also an increasing awareness of the infinite variety of herbs, and their use in herbalism, cosmetics, and cooking all over the world.

The wider realization that we had polluted our environment and destroyed much of the ecology of our farms, countryside, and gardens was to bring about a real revolution.

A mass revulsion against chemical-based methods was mirrored in the rise of organic production and the slowly improving availability of better foods. Vegetarianism also increased as many people turned away from meat, in part because of factory farming. These trends mean that there is an increased demand for fruits and vegetables, often organically produced or with a fuller flavor, and grocery stores now offer a huge range all year round.

But there is also a move by people toward growing their own. The health benefits, ecology, and economy of gardening appeal to a greener generation. An increased awareness of alternative medicine, including herbalism and aromatherapy, have revived interest in a range of herbs. With food processors, juicers, and freezers, it is

easier than ever to store and preserve what we harvest. In addition, the genetic richness represented by the huge range of food plants has been recognized and organizations such as the Henry Doubleday Research Association in the U.K., Seed Savers in the U.S., and Seed Savers International are working to safeguard and make available the old and rare varieties.

The availability of different gardening techniques also offers great opportunities at home. Dwarfing fruit rootstocks, varieties that store well or resist disease, glass or plastic cover, and controlled heating in greenhouses give us the opportunity to grow a huge variety of crops, even in a small garden. The earlier and later seasons, combined with gardening under cover, also mean that we can be planting and harvesting for a larger proportion of the year.

This book is intended to guide the reader in choosing which vegetables, herbs, and fruit to grow, and then in producing a crop successfully. The vegetable and herb sections are arranged alphabetically by the botanical Latin name. The fruit section is grouped into five chapters covering different types of fruit plants—Orchard Fruits; Soft, Bush, and Cane Fruits; Tender Fruits; Shrub and Flower Garden Fruits; and Nuts—according to how they are usually grown in temperate gardens.

Under each plant, after a brief introduction covering origins and history, the most useful and recommended varieties are given, followed by details of cultivation, including propagation, growing under glass and in containers, a maintenance calendar, pruning and training (if needed), dealing with pests and diseases, companion planting, and harvesting and storing. Information and ideas are given for using the plant, including recipes and medicinal and cosmetic uses. If any part of the plant is toxic or harmful in any way, a detailed warning is given. If the plant is of particular ornamental or wildlife value in the garden, this is indicated. Hardy, half-hardy, and tender plants are covered, with detailed growing guidelines for the best results in a temperate climate. The fruit and vegetable sections cover some of the more exotic tropical and subtropical crops that can, with variable success, be grown under cover.

The end of the book covers the practical aspects of making a productive garden, including planning your plot and preparing the soil, creating an ornamental edible garden, crop rotation, pollination, propagation, protected cropping and growing in containers, maintenance, companion planting, and pests, diseases, and weeds. A yearly calendar details the tasks in the productive garden season by season, although precise dates for these will vary according to frost times in different regions.

There is nothing more satisfying to the soul, eye, and stomach than a garden well stocked with produce. This book will help you to grow what you want with confidence, and perhaps to experiment and try out new plants and flavors.

A Note on Botanical Names

While common names are widely used, one plant may have several common names, or a common name in different parts of the world refers to different plants. Botanical names are vital for clearly identifying plants. The system of botanical names used today is known as the Binomial System and was devised by the eigteenth-century Swedish botanist Carl Linnaeus (1707–1778). In this system, each plant is classified by using two words in Latin form. The first word is the name of the genus (e.g., *Thymus*) and the second the specific epithet (e.g., *vulgaris*): together they provide a universally known name (e.g., *Thymus vulgaris*).

The Linnaean system of plant classification has been developed so that the entire plant kingdom is divided into a multibranched family tree according to each plant's botanical characteristics. Plants are gathered into particular families according to the structure of their flowers, fruits, or seeds. A family may contain one genus or many. The Asteraceae family, for example, contains over 800 genera, including *Achillea*, *Arnica*, and *Artemisia* to name a few, and over 13,000 species.

Plants are cultivated for the garden from the wild to improve their leaf or their flower or their root. This can be done either by selection from seedlings or by spotting a mutation. Such plants are known as cultivars (a combination of "cultivated varieties"). Propagation from these varieties is normally done by cuttings or division. Cultivars are given vernacular names, which are printed within quotes, e.g., *Thymus* 'Doone Valley,' to distinguish them from wild varieties in Latin form appearing in italics, i.e., *Thymus pulegioides*. Sexual crosses between species, usually of the same genus, are known as hybrids, and are indicated by a multiplication sign, e.g., *Thymus* x *citriodorus*.

Finally, a problem that seems to be getting worse: Many plants are undergoing reclassification, and long-established names are being changed. This is the result of scientific studies and research whereby it is found either that a plant has been incorrectly identified or that its classification has changed. This book uses the latest information available. Where there has been a recent change in the botanical name, this is shown in brackets.

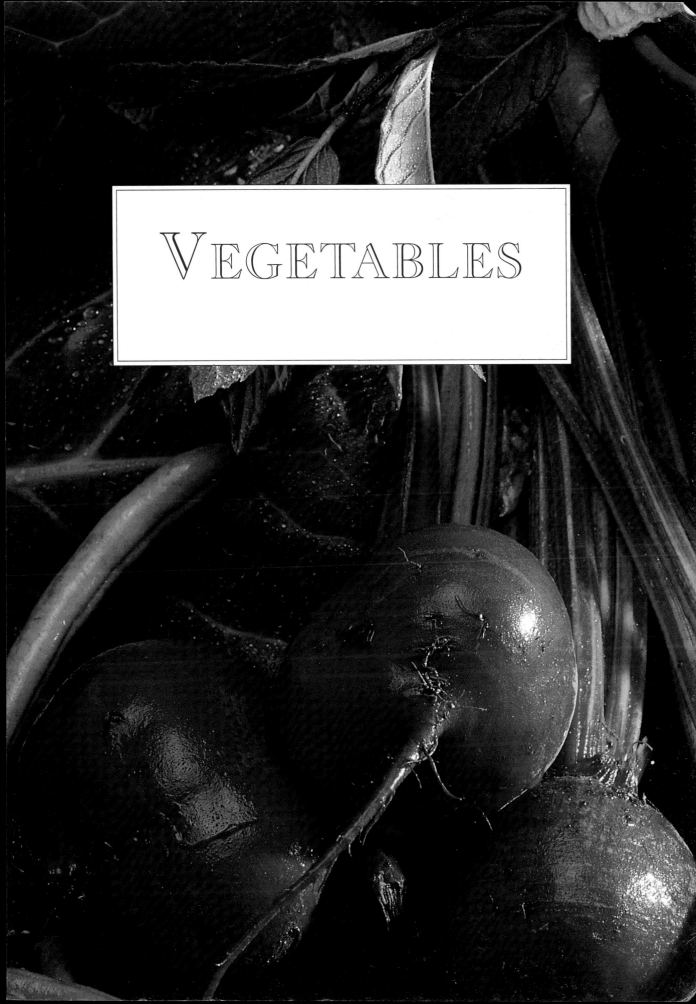

VEGETABLES

Abelmoschus esculentus (syn. *Hibiscus esculentus*). *Malvaceae*

OKRA

Also known as Lady's Fingers, Bhindi, Gumbo. Annual grown for its edible pods.
Tender. Value: rich in calcium, iron, potassium, vitamin C, and fiber.

The red forms lose their strong coloration when cooked.

The okra, a close relative of the ornamental hibiscus, with slender edible pods, has been cultivated for centuries. It is thought to have originated in northern Africa around the upper Nile and Ethiopia, spreading eastward to Saudi Arabia and to India. One of the earliest records of it—growing in Egypt—describes the plant, its cultivation, and uses. It was introduced to the Caribbean and southern North America by slaves who brought the crop from Africa; the name "gumbo" comes from a Portuguese corruption of the plant's Angolan common name.

VARIETIES

'**Annie Oakley II**' is a hybrid that produces 2 to 3 times more than old varieties and grows well in cooler northern gardens. Harvest in just 48 days. '**Burgundy**' grows about 5 ft. tall, with wonderful rich red pods, which are excellent in salads. The color, however, is lost on cooking. This tolerates cooler growing conditions than most. '**Cajun Delight Hybrid**' was an All-America Selections winner in 1997. Its tender flavorful pods mature early. Good for northern gardens. '**Clemson Spineless**' is a popular, reliable variety with high yields of dark, fleshy pods over a long period. It grows well under cover. '**Dwarf Green Long Pod**' is only about 3 ft. tall, but

crops well, producing dark green, spineless pods. '**Mammoth Spineless Long Pod**' is vigorous and high yielding with pods that stay tender for a long time. It is excellent fresh or bottled. '**Red Velvet,**' another spectacular red variety, is vigorous, reaching 4–5 ft.

A defoliated plant with several upward-pointing fruits

'**Star of David Heirloom**' is an Israeli variety growing to 6–8 ft. tall, well flavored, and high yielding. The pods grow to 9 in. long, but are better eaten when small.

CULTIVATION

A garden plant for the tropics and warm temperate zones, okra can be tried outdoors in cooler zones during hot summers, although success is more likely if sown under cover. **Zones 4–11.**

Propagation
Soak the seeds in warm water for 24 hours before planting. A friend of mine who gardens in Memphis, Tennessee, has been successful with several other methods that reduce germination time from 15 to 5 days: soak the seed in

bleach for 45–60 minutes, rinse, then plant; pour boiling water over seed, soak overnight, then plant; or place 3 seeds in each section of an ice-cube tray, allow to freeze for a few hours, then plant.

When soil temperatures are about 60°F, sow seeds in rows about 24 in. apart, leaving the same distance between plants. Alternatively, sow in "hills" 8–12 in. apart, thinning to leave the strongest seedling. Plant seedlings grown in trays or packs into 3-in. pots when they are large enough to handle and later harden them off, ready for transplanting when they are about 4–6 in. tall.

Growing
Okra needs a rich, fertile, well-drained soil, so incorporate organic matter several weeks before sowing. Put a stake in place before transplanting and tie in the plant as it grows, pinching out the growing tip on the main stems when plants are around 9–12 in. tall to encourage bushy growth. Apply a general liquid fertilizer until plants become established, then change to a liquid high-potash feed every 2 weeks or scatter sulfate of potash around the plant base.

In cool temperate conditions, warm the soil for several days before planting outdoors, spacing plants 24 in. apart once the danger of frost has passed.

Maintenance

Spring Sow seeds under cover or outdoors in warmer zones when the soil is warm enough. Pinch out the growth tips as they appear.
Summer Water, feed, and tie in plants to their supporting stakes. Keep crops weed-free. Harvest young pods.
Fall Protect outdoor crops in cooler zones to extend the cropping season.
Winter Prepare the ground for the following season.

Protected Cropping

In cooler zones, plant okra in heated greenhouses or plastic tunnels from early spring, waiting until midspring if heat is not provided. Plant them about 24 in. apart in beds or borders. Insert a supporting stake before planting.

Temperatures should be a minimum of 70°F with moderate humidity. Feed plants every 2 weeks with a liquid general fertilizer, changing to a high-potash fertilizer once they are established.

Container Growing

Okra can be grown in 10 in. pots or growing bags, in peat-substitute potting mix, under cover or outdoors. Water regularly and feed every 2 weeks with a high-potash liquid fertilizer during the growing season.

Harvesting and Storing

Harvest with a sharp knife or scissors while seed pods are young, picking regularly for a constant supply of new pods. Handle gently: the soft skin marks easily. Pods keep for up to 10 days wrapped in a plastic bag in the crisper in the refrigerator.

Pests and Diseases

Precautions should be taken against heavy infestations of **aphids**, which weaken and distort growth, and **powdery mildew**, which stunts growth and, in severe cases, causes death. This is more of a problem when plants are underwatered. **Whitefly** can cause yellowing, stickiness, and mold formation on the leaves. They form clusters on the leaf undersides and fly into the air when the foliage is disturbed.

COMPANION PLANTING

Okra flourishes when it is grown with melons and cucumbers, as it enjoys the same conditions.

Growing in Brazil, bright yellow flowers are followed by the developing pods.

CULINARY

Okra is used in soups, stews, and curries, can be sautéed or fried and eaten to accompany meat or poultry. To deep-fry, remove the stalks, trim around the "cone" near the base, simmer for about 10 minutes, drain and dry each pod, then deep-fry until crisp. In the Middle East, pods are soaked in lemon juice and salt, then fried and eaten as a vegetable. In Indian cooking, bhindi is used as a vegetable or as a bhagee to accompany curries.

Okra should not be cooked in iron, brass, or copper pans, otherwise it will discolor.

Overcooked, the pods become very slimy. Any "gluey" texture can be overcome by adding a little lemon juice to the pan and the fine, velvety covering over the pod can easily be removed by scrubbing the pod gently under running water.

Okra can also be eaten raw in salads or used as a "dip." Wash pods, carefully trimming off the ends. To reduce stickiness, soak them for about 30 minutes in water with a dash of lemon juice, then drain, rinse, and dry. Okra seed oil is also used in cooking.

Gumbo
Serves 4

This spicy Creole dish is known for its good use of okra.

3 cups okra
1 tablespoon olive oil
2½ cups home-cooked ham, diced
½ cup onion, finely sliced
½ cup celery, chopped
1 red bell pepper, seeded and chopped
½ tablespoon tomato paste
1½ cups tomatoes, skinned and chopped
1 dried chile, chopped small
Salt and freshly ground black pepper

Trim the stalk ends of the okra to expose the seeds, then soak for 30 minutes in acidulated water.

In the meantime, heat the oil and gently cook the ham, onion, celery, and pepper until the onion begins to color. Add the tomato paste and the tomatoes, mix in well, and cook over a high heat for a minute or so.

Stir in the drained okra and seasonings. Cover and cook gently until stewed. Add a little water if the mixture gets dry.

Serve with plain broiled chicken.

Gumbo

MEDICINAL

The mucilage from okra is effectively used as a demulcent, soothing inflammation.

In India, infusions of the pods are used to treat urino-genital problems as well as chest infections.

Okra is also added to artificial blood plasma products.

Allium cepa. Alliaceae

ONION

Biennial; grown as annual for swollen bulbs. Half hardy. Value: small amounts of most vitamins and minerals.

A vegetable of antiquity, the onion was cultivated by the Egyptians not only as food, but also to place in the thorax, pelvis, or near the eyes during mummification. Pliny recorded six varieties in ancient Rome. The onion was highly regarded for its antiseptic properties, but many other legends became attached to it. In parts of Ireland it was said to cure baldness: "Rub the sap mixed with honey into a bald patch, keep on rubbing until the spot gets red. This concoction if properly applied would grow hair on a duck's egg." Many varieties have been bred over the centuries; some, like 'The Kelsae,' are famous for their size, while newer varieties have incorporated hardiness, disease resistance, and color.

'First Early'

VARIETIES

Varieties of *Allium cepa* fall into groups according to color, shape, and use. The bulb or common onion has brown, yellow, or red skin and is round, elongated, or flattened. (Grouped with these are Japanese onions, a type of the perennial *Allium fistulosum*, which are grown as an annual for over-wintering.) Bunching onions or scallions are harvested small, and pickling varieties (also known as "silverskin," "mini" or "button" onions) are allowed to grow larger.

Bulb or Common Onions
'Ailsa Craig,' an old favorite, is a large variety, round and straw-colored with a mild flavor. **'Buffalo'** is high yielding, for sowing in summer and harvesting the following year. The round, firm bulbs are well flavored. **Chippolini** are small, round, and flattened old-fashioned Italian onions that are used for boiling and for creamed onions. **'Red Baron'** is a gorgeous dark-red-skinned onion with a strong flavor and red outer flesh to each ring. Good for storing. **'Senshyu Semiglobe Yellow'** is a Japanese onion with a deep yellow skin. **'Sturon,'** an old, high-yielding variety, has straw-colored skin and an

excellent resistance to running to seed. **'Stuttgarter Giant'** is a reliable variety with flattened bulbs and a mild flavor. A good keeper and slow to bolt. **'Super Star,'** a hybrid All-America Selections Winner, is a day-neutral variety, so it grows well throughout North America. Uniform, large, white onions are mild, but do not store well. **'The Kelsae,'** a large, round onion with mild flesh, does not store well. **'Torpedo'** is a spindle-shaped onion that is mild-flavored, but does not store well. **'Walla Walla Sweet'** is a long-day West Coast classic that may be sown in spring, or in fall where winter temperatures do not drop below -10°F. Fall-

'Torpedo,' or 'Red Italian'

sown seeds grow to form huge and exceptionally sweet bulbs. **'Yellow Granex Hybrid 33'** is the variety grown in Georgia and sold as the famous Vidalia sweet onion. Very sweet, with light-yellow flesh, this short-day southern onion requires up to 125 days to mature.

Bunching Onions or Scallions
'Ishikura,' a cross between a leek and coarse chives, is prolific, tender, and a rapid grower with upright, white stems and dark green leaves. It can be left in the ground to thicken and still retains its taste. **'Red Baron'** offers consistent red color from the base to its lower leaves, regardless of weather. It may be sown continuously for spring and summer harvest. **'Redmate'** is a colorful

Spring onions add bite to salads.

CULTIVATION

Onions require an open, sunny site, fertile soil, and free drainage. "Sets" (immature bulbs that have been specifically grown for planting) are more tolerant than seedlings and do not need a fine soil or such high levels of fertility. Pickling onions tolerate poorer soil than other types. Rotate crops annually.

Two distinct types of onion are grown in North America: long-day types require extended periods of summer sunlight to form bulbs and so are grown in the northern U.S. and Canada. Short-day onions mature only in the shorter summer days of the South. Because they require a longer growing period the latter are usually sown in fall and overwintered. Zones 3–11.

Propagation

Onion sets have several advantages over seed. They are quick to mature, are better in cooler areas with shorter growing seasons, they grow well in poorer soils, and are not attacked by onion fly or mildew. They are easy to grow and mature earlier, but are more expensive and prone to run

'Sturon' drying. Check stored onions regularly, removing any that are diseased or damaged

to seed. (Buying modern varieties and heat-treated sets about ¾ in. in diameter reduces that risk.) There is a greater choice of varieties when growing from seed. If planting is delayed, spread out sets in a cool, well-lit place to prevent premature sprouting. It is possible to save your own sets from bulbs grown the previous year. Plant onion sets when the soil warms from late winter to midspring. Sets that have been heat-treated should not be planted until late spring. Plant in shallow drills or push them gently into the soil until only the tips are above the surface. For medium-sized onions, plant 2 in. apart in rows 10 in. apart; for larger onions space sets 4 in. apart in the rows.

Sow seed indoors in late winter at 50–60°F in seed trays, pots, or packs (about 6 seeds in each pack). Harden off the seedlings by gradually increasing ventilation, then plant out in early spring when the seedlings have 2 true leaves. When transplanting those raised in packs and pots, ensure that the roots fall down into the planting hole and that the base of the bulb is about ½ in. below the surface.

Onions can also be sown outdoors in a seedbed in early to midspring in cool temperate zones. Use cloches or row covers to ensure the soil is warm, as cold, wet soil

leads to poor germination and disease. Use treated seed to protect against fungal disease.

When the soil is moist and crumbly, rake in a general fertilizer about 2 weeks before sowing and walk over the plot to create a firm seedbed, then sow onions ½–¾ in. deep in rows 12 in. apart. Once they germinate, thin to 1–1½ in. apart for medium-sized onions and 3–4 in. for large onions. Thin when the soil is moist to deter onion fly. Plant multisown blocks 10–12 in. apart. Plant firmly.

Sowing times for Japanese onions are critical; sown too early, they run to seed; sown too late, they are too weak to survive the winter. To cover for losses over winter, sow seeds about 1 in. apart in rows 12 in. apart. Top-dress with nitrogen in midwinter.

Sow pickling onions in spring, either broadcast or in drills the width of a hoe and about 4 in. apart. Thin according to the size of onions required and harvest them when the leaves have died back.

Sow bunching onions or scallions thinly, watering the drills before sowing in dry weather. Rows should be 4 in. apart; thin to a final spacing of ½–1 in. when the seedlings are large enough to handle for good-sized onions. For a regular supply, sow at 2–3 week intervals through late spring and

variety that is red toward the base, ideal for livening up salads. It can be thinned to 3 in. apart for mild bulb onions. **'Southport White Bunching'** produces a mild white scallion that matures quickly and can be sown spring through summer. Stems are bright white with strong tips. **'White Lisbon'** is tasty, popular, and reliable. It is fast-growing and very hardy.

Pickling Onions
'Brown Pickling SY300' is a pale brown-skinned early variety. It stores well and remains firm when pickled. **'White Paris'** is a popular "cocktail" onion, which grows rapidly and thrives in poor soil. Sow from midspring and dig when about the size of your thumbnail. **'Purplette'** produces a very attractive small burgundy bulb with a pastel pink color even when cooked or pickled.

Onions for pickling should be peeled thoroughly before storing

'Senshyu', a very attractive and reliable variety

early summer, watering well during dry weather.

Growing

Dig thoroughly during early winter, incorporating liberal quantities of well-rotted manure or compost if needed. Do not grow on freshly manured ground. Lime acid soils. Before planting, rake the surface level, removing any debris and adding a general granular fertilizer to it at 2 oz. per square yard. In summer pull back the earth or mulch from around the bulb to expose it to the sun.

Maintenance

Spring Plant sets or seeds. Keep weed-free, particularly in the early stages of growth.
Summer Mulch to reduce water loss and weeds. Watering is only vital during drought.
Fall Dig early fall.
Winter Push back any sets that have been lifted by frost or birds.

Protected Cropping

Onions do not need protection, although early sowings in cold weather and overwintering onions benefit from cloching or from frost fabric in very cold or wet weather.

Early sowings of bunching onions or scallions can be made in late summer or early fall and protected with cloches during severe weather for harvesting the following spring.

Container Growing

Bulb onions can be grown in containers, but yields will be small and not really worth the trouble.

Harvesting and Storing

Harvesting commences when the tops bend over naturally and the leaves begin to dry out. Do not bend the leaves over. Allow the bulbs and leaves to dry out while still in the ground during fine weather; wait until the dried foliage rustles before digging. In adverse weather, spread out the bulbs on sacking or in trays in cold frames, cloches, or a shed, turning them regularly. Handle bulbs carefully to avoid damage and disease. Before storing, be sure to remove any

damaged, soft, spotted, or thick-necked onions and use them immediately. Onions can be stored in trays, net bags, or hose, or tied to a length of cord as onion ropes in a cool place.

Harvest bunching onions or scallions before the bases swell. During dry weather, water before harvesting to make pulling easier.

Making an Onion Rope

Storing onions on a rope enables the air to circulate, reducing the possibility of diseases. It is attractive and a convenient method of storage. You can braid the stems to form a rope as with garlic, but they are usually too short and are better tied to raffia or strong string.

Firmly tie in 2 onions at the base, then wind the leaves of each onion firmly around the string, with each bulb just resting on the onions below. When you reach the top of the string, tie a firm knot around the bulbs at the top, then hang them up to dry. Cut onions from the rope as they are needed.

Pests and Diseases

If **birds** are a nuisance, protect plants with black thread or netting.

The larvae of **onion fly** tunnel into bulbs, causing the stems to wilt and become yellow. Seedlings and small plants may die. Cultivate the ground thoroughly over winter; grow under fabric; grow sets. Remove and destroy affected plants and rotate crops.

White rot can be a problem, particularly on salad onions. White mold like cotton balls, dotted with tiny, black spots, appears around the base. Leaves turn yellow and die. It is almost impossible to eradicate. Remove affected onions with as much of the soil around them as possible, dispose of plants and any debris—do not put them on the compost pile. Do not grow onions or their relatives on the area for 8 years. 'Norstar' has some resistance.

When attacked by **stem eelworm**, bulbs become distorted, crack, soften, then die. Grow plants from seed; rotate crops; in severe cases do not grow in the same place again. Dispose of plant debris thoroughly and remove any affected plants.

COMPANION PLANTING

Parsley sown with onions is said to keep onion fly away.

MEDICINAL

Used as an antiseptic and diuretic, the juice is good for coughs and colds. The bulbs and stems were applied as poultices to carbuncles.

The traditional way of storing onions is also highly decorative.

CULINARY

So indispensable are onions for flavoring sauces, stocks, stews, and casseroles that there is hardly a recipe that does not start with some variant of "fry [or sauté or sweat] the onion in the oil or fat until soft . . ." They also make a delicious vegetable or garnish in their own right: roasted or boiled whole, cut into rings, battered, and deep-fried, or sliced and slowly softened into a meltingly sweet "marmalade." Finely chopped raw onion adds zing to dishes like rice salad; you can also use the thinnings to flavor salads.

Bunching onions are perfect for salads, pastas, soups, and quiches. In France they are chopped, sautéed in butter, and added to chicken consommé with vermicelli.

Pickled onions are an excellent accompaniment to bread, strong cheese and pickled beet—the traditional "Plowman's Lunch." Besides being pickled, pickling varieties can be used fresh in salads and stir-fries, added to stews, or else threaded on to kabob skewers for barbecuing.

Onion and Walnut Muffins
Makes 20

This wonderful recipe comes from chef Wally Malouf's *Hudson Valley Cookbook.*

1 large onion
2 sticks unsalted butter, melted
2 large eggs
6 tablespoons sugar
1 teaspoon sea salt
1 teaspoon baking powder
2½ cups shelled walnuts, coarsely crushed
3 cups all-purpose flour

Preheat the oven to 425°F. Peel the onion, cut it into quarters and puree it finely in a food processor. Measure the puree to achieve 8 oz. Beat together the butter, eggs, and sugar and add the onion puree. Stir in the remaining ingredients one by one and mix thoroughly. Fill muffin tins almost full. Bake them for 20 minutes, or until they are puffed and well browned. Serve warm.

Onion and Walnut Muffins

Onion Tart
Serves 4

This Alsatian dish is full of flavor and very filling. Enjoy it with a simple fresh green salad.

½ cup olive oil
4 cups onions, sliced into rings
1 cup bacon, diced
1 cup heavy cream
3 eggs, lightly beaten
Salt and freshly ground black pepper
Shortcrust pastry to line a 8–9 in. tart tin

In a heavy pan, heat the oil and sauté the onions until soft but not browned. Drain well on paper towels. Add the bacon to the pan and cook briskly for a couple of minutes, then drain off the fat. Next, mix the cream and the eggs and season well. Then stir in the onions and the bacon and fill the piecrust.

Bake in a preheated oven at 425°F for 10–15 minutes, turning the heat down to 375°F for an additional 15 minutes, or until the filling is set. Serve warm.

Onion Tart

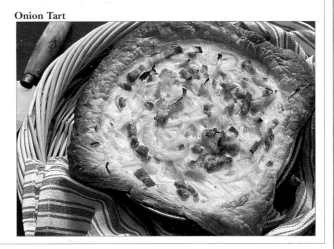

Allium cepa Aggregatum Group. *Alliaceae*

SHALLOT

Small onion, grown as an annual, forming several new bulbs. Hardy. Value: small amounts of most vitamins and minerals.

Shallots are hardy, mature rapidly, are good for colder zones, tolerate heat and will grow on poorer soils than common onions. Sets are more expensive than seed and are inclined to bolt unless they are heat-treated; buy virus-free stock which is higher-yielding and vigorous, or save healthy bulbs of your own for the following year.

VARIETIES

'**Ambition**' is a brown shallot with good bolt-resistance. '**Bonilla**' is a high-yielding, good storing shallot with straw yellow skin and clean white flesh. '**Dutch Yellow**' yield a good quantity of firm bulbs with creamy yellow flesh and a pungent flavor. '**Golden Snowshoe**' is an heirloom variety from Germany that is hardy to well below zero. '**Gray**' is reputed to have the best taste of all. '**Hative de Niort**' is an extremely attractive variety with elongated, pear-shaped bulbs, dark brown skins, and white flesh. '**Matador**' is a brown shallot that stores exceptionally well. '**Pikant**' is prolific and resistant to bolting. Its skin is dark reddish-brown, the flesh strongly-flavored and firm. '**Prisma**' is a torpedo-shaped, purple shallot with a red interior. Stores well. '**Red Potato Onion**' is extremely hardy, with bronze-red skin and pink flesh that keeps well. '**Red Sun**' has golden skin and red interior. '**Sante**' is large and round with brown skin and pinkish-white flesh which is packed with flavor. Yields are high and it stores well. However, it is inclined to bolt and should only be planted from mid- to late-spring when conditions improve.

CULTIVATION

Propagation

The ideal size for sets is about ¾ in. diameter, which will result in a high yield of good-sized shallots; larger sets will produce a greater number of smaller shallots.

Plant from late winter or early spring, as soon as soil conditions are suitable. Shallots can also be planted from late fall to midwinter for early crops. Cover the soil with cloches, frost fabric, or crop covers about 2 weeks before planting to warm the soil. If the weather is unfavorable, bulbs can be planted in 4-in. pots of potting mix and transplanted when conditions improve.

Space sets 9 in. apart with 12–15 in. between the rows. Make small holes with a trowel rather than pushing bulbs into the ground (the compaction this causes, particularly in heavier soils, can act as a barrier to young roots). Leave the tips of the bulbs just above the soil. Alternatively, plant in drills, ½ in. deep, 7 in. apart, then cover with soil.

F_1 hybrids that are grown from seed produce one bulb, rather than several. From early to midspring, as soon as soil conditions allow, sow seed thinly ½ in. deep in broad drills the width of a hoe, thinning until there is 1–2 in. around each plant. If spaced farther apart, clusters of bulbs are more likely to form.

Undersized shallots can be grown for their leaves, or you can pick a few leaves from those being grown for bulbs. Plant from fall to spring under cloches in mild areas for earlier crops, in seed trays or pots of potting mix under cover and outdoors when the soil becomes workable. Each bulb should be about 1 in. apart. **Zones 3–11.**

Growing

Shallots flourish in a sheltered, sunny position on moist, free-draining soil, preferably one that has been manured for the previous crop.

Alternatively, double dig the area in early fall, incorporating plenty of well-rotted organic matter

Shallots are small and mild enough to be added whole to casseroles.

Unlike onions, shallots develop in small clusters.

into the lower spit.

Before planting, level the soil and rake in a general fertilizer at 4 oz. per square yard. If you are sowing sets, a rough tilth will suffice, but seeds need a seedbed of a finer texture.

Water during dry periods and keep crops weed-free, particularly while becoming established. Use an onion hoe with care, as damaged bulbs cannot be stored.

Maintenance
Spring Plant sets when soil conditions allow. Sow seed when the soil warms up.
Summer Keep crops weed-free. Water during dry periods.
Fall Dig in well-rotted organic matter if needed. Plant sets for early crops.
Winter Plant sets from late winter onward.

Protected Cropping
Shallots are extremely hardy, but benefit from temporary protection under cloches or frost fabric in periods of severe winter weather, particularly if the soil is poorly drained.

Container Growing
Shallots will grow in large pots or containers of soil-based potting mix. Add slow-release fertilizer to the mix and put a good layer of broken pottery or Styrofoam in the bottom of the pot for drainage. Keep plants well watered in dry periods.

Harvesting and Storing
From midsummer onward, as the leaves die back, carefully dig the bulbs and in dry weather leave them on the surface for about a week to dry out; otherwise dry them as onions. Do not cut off the green foliage as this may cause fungal infection, spoiling the bulbs for storage. Break up the bulbs in each clump, remove any soil and loose leaves, then store them in a dry, cool, well-ventilated place. Store on slatted trays, in net bags or in old hose. Shallots grown for their foliage should be harvested when the leaves are about 4 in. high.

Pests and Diseases
Shallots are usually free of pests and diseases. **Bolting** may be a problem in early plantings or if temperatures fluctuate. Use resistant varieties for early plantings.
Bulbs infected with **virus** are stunted and yields are poor. Use disease-free stock. If **mildew** is a problem, treat as for onions.

Birds can be a nuisance, pulling sets from the ground. Sprinkling a layer of fine soil over the tips can help; otherwise protect the crop with bird wire or similar bird scarers.

Bulbs lifted by **frost** should be carefully replanted immediately.

Wireworms and **onion fly** should be treated in the same way as for onions.

COMPANION PLANTING

Shallots make good companions for apples and strawberry plants; storing sulfur, they are believed to have a fungicidal effect.

CULINARY

Shallots have a milder taste than onions; generally, the yellow-skinned varieties are larger and keep better, while red types are smaller and have the best flavor. The bulbs can be eaten raw or pickled and the leaves used like scallions.

Shallots can be finely chopped and added to fried steak just before serving. Do not brown them, as it makes them bitter. Béarnaise sauce is made by reducing shallots and herbs in wine vinegar before thickening with egg and butter.

Shallots keep better than ordinary onions.

Allium porrum. Alliaceae

LEEK

Biennial grown as annual for blanched leaf bases. Hardy. Value: good source of potassium and iron, smaller amounts of beta carotene, and vitamin C, particularly in green leaves.

The Bible mentions "the cucumbers, and the melons, and the leeks, and the onions and the garlic" that grew in Egypt, where the leek was held as a sacred plant and to swear by the leek was the equivalent to swearing by one of the gods. This ancient crop still stirs passions. Giant leek contests have been held in pubs and clubs throughout the northeast of England since the mid-1880s. At one show in 1895, W. Robson was awarded a second prize of £1 and a sheep's heart; now the world championships have a first prize of over £1,300 ($2,000). Alongside the daffodil, the leek is one of the national symbols of Wales. Currently the European Union produces over 7 million tons per year and France is the chief grower.

VARIETIES

Older varieties are divided into two main groups, long thin and short stout types. In many modern cultivars, such differences are less obvious. There are also early, midseason, and late varieties. **'King Richard'** is a high-yielding, mild-tasting, early variety with a long shank. Good for growing at close spacing for "mini leeks."

'American Flag' is an old favorite that produces hardy and sweet 9-in.-long leeks. **'Autumn Mammoth 2— Argenta'** matures in late fall and can be harvested until midspring. A high-yielding leek with a medium shank length and thick stems. **'Leekool'** will produce heavy crops of dark blue-green leaves atop white shanks, even from direct sowing. **'Rikor'** is a new early and vigorous variety for baby leeks from direct sowing. **'Laura'** is an extra hardy leek for overwintering. Its upright leaves are deep blue.

CULTIVATION

Leeks flourish in a sunny, sheltered site on well-drained, neutral to slightly acid soil. **Zones 5–10.**

Propagation
Leeks need a minimum soil or potting mix temperature of at least 45°F to germinate, so you will achieve more consistent results, particularly with early crops, when they are sown under cover. For rapid germination, sow early varieties indoors during late winter at 55–60°F in trays, pots, or packs of potting mix. Repot those grown in trays or pots, spacing them about 2 in. apart, when 2 true leaves are produced or when they begin to bend over. Harden off gradually before planting out in late spring.

Leeks can also be sown in unheated greenhouses, in cold frames, or under cloches. Sow seeds from late winter to early spring, pot up, harden off, and transplant in late spring.

Although all varieties are suitable, later sowings of midseason and later types are particularly successful in seedbeds. Warm the soil using cloches, black plastic, or frost fabric and rake the seedbed to a fine tilth. Sow thinly in rows 6 in. apart and 1 in. deep, providing protection during cold spells. They can also be sown directly in the vegetable plot, 1 in. deep in rows 12 in. apart, thinning when seedlings have 2 or 3 leaves.

Sowing seeds in packs—either in pairs or singly—keeping the most vigorous of the 2, and multisowing 3–5 per cell, avoids the necessity of "pricking out" or thinning.

Growing
Fertile, moisture-retentive soil is essential, so dig in plenty of organic matter the winter before planting, particularly on light soils. On heavy soils, add organic matter and sharp sand to improve drainage as crops are poor on heavy or waterlogged soil. Rake, level, and firm the soil before planting in spring. As they are a long-term, high-nitrogen crop, apply a general fertilizer, fish, blood, and bone, or ammonium sulfate at 2–3 oz. per square yard 1–2 weeks before planting.

A fine display of leeks grown in a deep raised bed for showing

Leek flowers are invaluable for attracting beneficial insects

Transplant leeks when they are 6–8 in. tall. Trim the leaf tips back if they drag on the ground, but not the roots, as is often recommended. If the soil is dry, water the area thoroughly before planting. Planting 6 in. apart in rows 12 in. apart provides a high yield of moderately sized leeks. Planting them 3–4 in. apart in rows gives a high yield of slim leeks. A spacing of 6–7 in. each way provides a reasonable crop of medium-sized leeks. Leeks grown in packs should be planted 9 in. apart each way.

There are 2 methods of planting to ensure well-blanched stems. I find the first method better, as deeply planted leeks are more drought-resistant and soil is less likely to fall down between the leaves. Make a hole 6–8 in. deep with a dibble, drop the plant into it and fill the hole with water (this washes some soil into the bottom of the hole), but do not fill any further.

Alternatively, plant leeks 3 in. deep and several times through the season pull the earth up around the stems, 2–3 in. at a time, with a draw hoe. Stop earthing up when the plants reach maturity and make sure that the soil does not fall down between the leaves. Earthing up is easier on light soil.

Whichever method you use, after planting, water gently with a seaweed-based fertilizer. If there is a dry period after planting, water leeks daily until the plants are well established and thereafter only during drought conditions. Hand weed or hoe carefully to keep down weeds, using an onion hoe around younger plants to avoid any damage. In poorer soils, feed weekly in summer with a liquid seaweed or comfrey fertilizer.

Maintenance

Spring Repot leeks grown under glass; sow seed outdoors.
Summer Transplant seedlings, water, and feed. Keep crops weed-free by hoeing or mulching.
Fall Harvest crops as required.
Winter Harvest mid- and late-season crops. Sow seed under glass in late winter.

Protected Cropping

Apart from early sowings in the greenhouse or cold frame or under cloches and frost fabric, leeks are an extremely hardy outdoor crop.

Harvesting and Storing

Early varieties are ready for digging from early to midfall, midseason types from early to midwinter and lates from early to midspring. Dig leeks carefully with a garden fork and ensure that you dispose of any leaf debris to reduce the risk of disease in the future. Late varieties taking up space in the vegetable garden that is needed for spring planting can be stored for several weeks in a shallow, angled trench 6–8 in. deep; cover them lightly with soil and leave the tops exposed. If inclement weather is likely to hinder harvest, they can be dug and packed closely together in a cold frame. The top should be raised to provide ventilation on warmer days.

PESTS AND DISEASES

Leeks share many diseases with their close relatives, onions. **Leek rust** appears as orange pustules on the leaves during summer and is worse in wet seasons. Foliage developing later in the season is healthy. Feed with high-potash fertilizer, remove infected plants and debris. Improve drainage; do not plant leeks on the site for 4 to 5 years; grow

Leeks grown in tile drains for early digging

partially resistant varieties like 'Autumn Mammoth,' 'Titan' or 'Gennevilliers-Splendid.' **Slugs** can be damaging. Collect them at night, use biological control, set traps or use aluminum sulfate pellets. Mature leeks usually survive slug damage. **Stem wireworm** causes swelling at the base and distorted leaves. Destroy affected plants immediately and rotate crops. **Leaf rot** is common during periods of high humidity, particularly on high-nitrogen soils. White spots appear on the leaf tips, followed by shrivelling leaf tips. Spray with fungicide, increase the spacing between plants to improve air circulation and apply high-potash fertilizer.

COMPANION PLANTING

Leeks grow well with celery. When planted with onions and carrots they discourage onion and carrot fly. Grow leeks in your rotation program alongside garlic, onions, and shallots. Leeks are a useful crop after early potatoes and if they are grown at a 12 in. spacing, their upright growth makes them ideal for intercropping with lettuces like 'Tom Thumb,' land cress, or winter purslane.

Some leeks are ideal for the ornamental border.

CULINARY

Leeks can be boiled, baked, or steamed, made into terrines, added to pasta dishes, or cooked in casseroles. They are a useful addition to soups and an important ingredient in "Cock-a-leekie" soup and in French vichyssoise. Braise in stock with a little wine added and bake in a medium oven. Partially cook trimmed leeks in boiling water, drain well, and roll in slices of good country ham and lay them in a dish; cover with a well-seasoned cheese sauce and bake in a hot oven until well browned. Use young leeks raw as a substitute for scallions in salads.

Leek and Ricotta Pie
Serves 4

4 largish leeks, trimmed
2 tablespoons olive oil
2 cloves garlic, finely chopped
1 cup ricotta
2 tablespoons pine nuts
3 tablespoons raisins, softened
  in warm water
1 egg
Salt and freshly ground black
  pepper

For the pastry:
1 stick butter
2 cups all-purpose flour
3 tablespoons water
Pinch salt

Make the pastry by crumbling the butter into the flour and then adding water to make a dough. Add the salt and sprinkle with flour. Wrap in plastic wrap and chill in the refrigerator for 30 minutes.

Roughly chop the leeks. Steam gently for about 10 minutes and drain well.

Preheat the oven to 375°F. In a heavy sauté pan heat the oil and gently fry the garlic. Then add the leeks and stir to coat well with oil; allow them to cook for about 5 minutes, stirring occasionally.

Remove from the heat. In a bowl mix the ricotta with the pine nuts and raisins, and bind with the egg. Add the leeks, mix well, and season.

Gently roll out the pastry to fit a 8 in. quiche tin. Prick the base and bake blind for 10–15 minutes. Fill the tart with the leek and ricotta mixture and continue baking for 30 minutes.

Serve the pie with a green salad.

Leeks wrapped in country ham and baked with a covering of cheese sauce

Barbarea verna. Brassicaceae

LAND CRESS

Also known as American cress. Biennial or short-lived perennial grown as annual for young leaves. Hardy.
Value: low in calories, good source of iron, calcium, beta carotene, and vitamin C.

The genus *Barbarea* was known as *herba Sanctae Barbarae,* the "herb of St. Barbara," patron saint of miners and artillerymen and protectress from thunderstorms! Land cress is a fast-growing, hardy biennial with a rosette of deeply lobed, shiny leaves and yellow flowers. Native to southwestern Europe, it has been grown as a salad crop since the seventeenth century; by the eighteenth century, extensive cultivation had died out in England, although plants became naturalized and are still common in the wild. In America it is still a popular annual crop. The peppery-tasting leaves make a fine substitute for watercress—and are a good deal more practical for most gardeners to grow.

CULTIVATION

Land cress grows in wet, shady conditions, but is best in moist fertile soil; in summer plant in light shade, under deciduous trees.
Zones 3–9.

Propagation
Sow as soon as the soil becomes workable, in early spring to early summer for a summer crop and in mid- to late summer for fall to spring crops. Sow in seed trays or packs for transplanting when large enough to handle, or in drills ½ in. deep, thinning the seedlings to 6–8 in. Germination takes about 3 weeks in spring but in midsummer half that time. If a few plants are left to run to seed in late spring to early summer the following year, they will seed freely; transplant seedlings into rows and water well.

Growing
Before sowing, dig in well-rotted manure or compost. Transplant seedlings sown in late summer under glass. In heat and drought they run to seed, so water often. Pick flower stalks as they appear.

Maintenance
Spring Sow seed, water well.
Summer Water as necessary so plants do not run to seed.
Fall Sow winter crops and transplant plantlets under glass.
Winter Prepare beds for spring sowing; harvest protected crops.

Protected Cropping
Improve the quality of fall and winter crops by growing in an unheated greenhouse or cold frame, or under cloches.

Container Growing
Grow in moisture-retentive, peat-substitute potting mix, water well and feed with a dilute general liquid fertilizer every 3 weeks.

Harvesting
Harvest after 7 weeks when plants are 3–4 in. long. Pick or cut the tender young leaves about 1 in. above ground. Do not harvest heavily until the plant is established. Soak in water to loosen dirt, then wash it off.

Pests and Diseases
Flea beetle may affect plants; dust seedlings with rotenone or grow under fabric.

COMPANION PLANTING

Makes a good edging plant for borders. Can be grown between taller crops, e.g., grains and brassicas.

CULINARY

Use its peppery-tasting leaves as a watercress substitute—as a garnish, in salads and sandwiches. Or cook them like spinach and make into soup. Good in rice, pasta salads, and stir-fries.

Cress, Anchovy, and Barley Salad
Serves 4

1½ cups pearl barley
4 tablespoons virgin olive oil
2 tablespoons white wine vinegar
2 tablespoons finely chopped dill
Salt and freshly ground pepper
4 anchovy fillets, roughly chopped
12-oz. cress, washed and dried
1 cucumber, diced

Cook the barley in boiling water until tender and drain. Set aside. Make the dressing: mix the oil and vinegar with the dill and seasoning. In a separate bowl, mix the barley with the anchovies, add the cress and cucumber, and pour on the dressing. Toss well.

Plants flower in early spring.

Allium sativum. Alliaceae

GARLIC

Perennial grown as annual for strongly aromatic bulbs. Half hardy. Value: contains small quantities of vitamins and minerals.

Prized throughout the world for its culinary and medicinal properties, garlic, now known only as a cultivated plant, is thought to have originated in western Asia. It has been grown since Egyptian times and for centuries in China and India. Its reputation as a cure-all has been endorsed by modern science. The Egyptians placed it in their tombs and gave it to the slaves who built the pyramids to ward off infection, while Hippocrates prescribed it for uterine tumors. In medieval Europe it was hung outside doors to deter witches. Today almost 3 million tons per annum are produced globally.

VARIETIES

Buy garlic cloves that are compatible with the climate and day length in your area. **'Bavarian Purple'** is a strong-flavored garlic that produces up to eight cloves per head. **'California Late'** is very reliable in Mediterranean conditions. It keeps well. **'Elephant'** garlic is sweet and mild; bulbs up to 4 in. in diameter. **'Spanish Roja'** is a midseason variety, and perhaps the most popular hardneck type with a true garlic flavor.

Allium sativum var. *ophioscordon* is sold as **'Rocambole'** and is also called "Serpent Garlic" on account of its coiled, bulbil-producing stem. The bulbs are red in color. **'Premium Northern White,'** an heirloom from Germany, may be the most cold-hardy garlic of all. '**Music**' outscored every other garlic in productivity trials at Michigan State University. Big cloves with a blush of pink.

CULTIVATION

Propagation
Garlic is usually grown from healthy, plump bulb segments ("cloves") saved from a previous crop. Where possible, buy nematode- and virus-resistant stock.

Plant cloves, a minimum of $\frac{1}{2}$ in. diameter, in late fall or early spring, at a depth of 1 in. and 4 in. apart, with the rows 6–8 in. apart.

Garlic is surprisingly hardy and needs a cold, dormant period of 1 or 2 months when temperatures are 32–50°F to yield decent-sized bulbs; for this reason it is generally better planted in late fall. A long growing period is also beneficial for the ripening process.

In areas with heavy soil, cloves can be planted any time in winter in pots or packs containing loam-based potting mix with added sharp sand, and can be planted out as soon as soil conditions are favorable. Plant cloves vertically with the flattened base plate at the bottom, twice the depth of the clove with at least 1 in. of soil above the tip. On good soils, planting up to 4 in. deep increases the yield. When planting, you should handle the cloves lightly: do not press them into the soil, as this reduces root development. The amount of leaf growth dictates the size of the mature bulb which develops during long summer days. Zones 3–10.

Growing
Garlic favors an open, sunny position on light, well-drained soil. On heavier soil, grow in ridges or improve the drainage by working sharp sand or grit in to the topsoil.

Garlic is less successful in areas of heavy rainfall. On poor soils, it is beneficial to rake in a general fertilizer about 10 days before planting. Garlic can be grown on soil manured for the previous crop as well as limed acid soils.

Rotate the crop and do not grow in sites where onions have been planted the previous year. Keep the bulbs weed-free throughout the growing season.

Maintenance
Spring Mulch to suppress weeds. Water if necessary.
Summer Keep weed-free.
Fall Plant cloves.
Winter Plant cloves in containers for planting out in spring.

Protected Cropping
Garlic can be grown in an unheated greenhouse for an early crop.

Container Growing
Garlic can be grown in pots, window boxes, or containers, in a moisture-retentive, free-draining potting mix. Water

Plump garlic cloves

regularly to produce decent-sized bulbs and place the container in a sunny position to allow the bulbs to develop.

Harvesting and Storing
From mid- to late summer, as soon as the leaves and stems begin to yellow, dig the bulbs carefully with a fork and allow them to dry off in the sun. Delaying harvest causes the bulbs to shrivel and increases the possibility of disease during storage. Handle them delicately as they are easily bruised.

In inclement weather, dry them under cover on trays. Store them in cool, dry conditions indoors or in a shed or garage. Hang them in bunches tied by the leaves, in string bags, or braid the stems together. Plants that have gone to seed can still produce usable bulbs for the kitchen.

PESTS AND DISEASES

Onion flies lay their eggs around the base of garlic, the larvae tunnel into the bulb and the plant turns yellow and dies. Rotate crops, dig the plot over winter, grow under crop covers, and apply chemicals to the soil before sowing.

Downy mildew is a common problem in wet seasons. Gray patches appear on the leaves. **White rot**, a gray fungus on the roots, turns the leaves yellow. Dig and destroy infected plants, and do not grow garlic, onions, or shallots on the site for 8 years.

Stem and bulb wireworm: seedlings become blunted, bloated and distorted, and stems rot. Dig and destroy affected plants. Rotate crops.

Planting garlic in Thailand

COMPANION PLANTING

Planted beside rose bushes, garlic controls greenfly. Good companions are lettuce, beet, summer savory, Swiss chard, and strawberries. It should not be planted with peas and beans.

MEDICINAL

Garlic has powerful antiviral, antibacterial, and antifungal properties, and is effective for digestive complaints, bowel disorders, and insect stings. It contains two chemicals that combine to form the bactericide allicin, which gives it the characteristic odor. Modern herbalists believe a cold will be cured by rubbing garlic on the soles of feet. (What a combination of odors!) Current research indicates its ability to reduce blood cholesterol levels and the chance of heart attack. There is also a lower incidence of colonic and other types of cancer where it is part of the daily diet.

CULINARY

Garlic is used almost exclusively as a seasoning in a range of dishes from curries and stews to pasta. For the daring, the whole immature plants can be added to salads.

La Gasconnade
Serves 6–8

Jeanne Strang gives this recipe from Gascony in *Goose Fat and Garlic*:

1 leg lamb
12 anchovy fillets
1 lb. garlic
³⁄₄ cup bouillon

The *gigot* (lamb) is spiked not only with the usual few cloves of garlic but with anchovy fillets as well. You will need to cut them into small pieces in order to slide them into the slits in the meat.

Lay the fillets across the top of the roast. During the cooking they will melt over the meat and give it the same effect as if it were roasted revolving on a spit.

Cook the lamb in a pre-heated oven, 450°F for 20 minutes, then reduce the heat to 350°F. Allow to cook for 15 minutes per pound from start to finish.

While the lamb is cooking, peel the rest of the garlic and blanch in boiling water until the cloves are almost cooked, then throw them into cold water for 20 seconds and drain. Heat the bouillon in a saucepan, add any pan juices and the garlic, and reduce the sauce until it is nearly a puree. Serve as a garnish to the *gigot*.

Pistou
This is a version of the classic garlic and basil butter, which is extremely good over pasta and which the Italians eat with fish. For ¼ cup butter, have 2 plump cloves garlic, 5–6 sprigs of fresh basil, 2 tablespoons Parmesan, and a pinch of salt. Pound the garlic in a mortar, tear the basil leaves roughly, then add to the garlic with the butter and cheese. Pound to mix.

Aïoli
Mayonnaise flavored with garlic enriches many delicious soups and stews such as bouillabaisse. Pound 2 cloves of garlic in a mortar, stir in the yolks of 2 eggs, pour into a blender and add 1 cup of oil drop by drop at first, faster as the mixture begins to thicken.

La Gasconnade

Alpinia galanga (syn. *Langaas galanga*). *Zingiberaceae*

GREATER GALANGAL

Also known as Galangal Languas, Siamese Ginger. Herbaceous perennial; rhizomatous rootstock used as flavoring. Tender. Value: negligible nutritive value.

Two species, greater and lesser galangal, have been grown for centuries for their pungent, aromatic roots, which are used as spices and medicinally. The earliest records date from around A.D. 550, while Marco Polo noted its cultivation in southern China and Java in the thirteenth century. In the Middle Ages it was known as "galangale," a name also used for the roots of sweet sedge, whose violet-scented rhizomes are used in perfumery.

The word *galangal* came from the Chinese, meaning "a mild ginger from Ko," a region of the Canton province. It is an essential ingredient of many Malaysian and Thai dishes. The spicy rhizomes have a somewhat different use in the Middle East, where they have been used to "spike" horses!

CULTIVATION

The plant is a herbaceous perennial with pale orange-flushed cream bulbous rhizomes. Stems grow to 6 ft. tall, with dark green lance-shaped leaves to 20 in. long. Flowers are pale green and white with pink markings; the fruit a round red capsule. There are many different races in cultivation, including types with red and white rhizomes. Lesser galangal is regarded as superior as it is more pungent and aromatic, but is uncommon in cultivation.

Propagation
Sow fresh seed in pots of peat-lite mix at 68°F. Keep the potting mix moist using tepid water and transplant seedlings when they are large enough to handle. In tropical and subtropical regions they can be sown outdoors in a seedbed (for ground preparation, see "Growing").

Divide rhizomes in spring when the young shoots are about 1 in. long. Remove young, vigorous sections from the perimeter of the clump using a sharp knife, dust the cuts with fungicide, and transplant just below the soil or potting mix surface. Soak thoroughly with tepid water and maintain high humidity and temperatures.

Growing
Galangal grows outdoors in tropical or subtropical zones, thriving in sunshine or partial shade. It needs a rich, free-draining soil, so dig in plenty of well-rotted compost and allow the ground to settle for a few weeks before planting. Allow 36 in. between plants. Keep crops weed-free and water during dry periods. Mulch with well-rotted compost when plants are well established.

Container Growing
Plants can be grown in containers under cover in a potting mix of 2 parts each of loam and leaf mold, 1 part horticultural grit or sharp sand, and 3 parts medium-grade bark. Repot and divide in spring when the rhizomes outgrow their allotted space.

Protected Cropping
In temperate zones, plants can be grown in a heated plastic tunnel or greenhouse in bright filtered light, with a minimum temperature of 58°F. Maintain high humidity by misting plants with tepid water and "damping down" paths. Prepare borders as for "Growing" and allow 36 in. between plants. Keep the potting mix constantly moist with tepid water and reduce watering in lower temperatures. After flowering, reduce watering as the foliage gradually becomes yellow and dies back. The potting mix should remain slightly moist throughout the dormant period. Increase watering when new shoots emerge the following spring.

Feed regularly with a liquid general fertilizer every 2 weeks while the plant is actively growing. Mulch plants grown in borders annually in spring with well-rotted manure.

Harvesting and Storing

Rhizomes are ready to harvest after 3–4 years. Dig plants toward the end of the growing season and remove mature rhizomes, retaining younger ones for transplanting. It is a good idea to divide and replant a few each year to ensure a constant supply.

Galangal are better used immediately after harvest but will keep for at least a week in a cool place. Alternatively, they can be frozen whole in a plastic bag and segments removed as required. Keep dried roots in airtight containers in a cool dark place.

PESTS AND DISEASES

Red spider mite can be a problem under glass. Check plants regularly, as small infestations are easily controlled. Speckling, mottling, and bronzing of the leaf surface are the usual symptoms; in later stages, fine webbing appears on leaves and stems. They prefer hot, dry conditions. Control by maintaining high humidity or spray with rotenone or a similar insecticide.

MEDICINAL

Plants contain cineol, an aromatic, antiseptic substance. The essential oil acts as a decongestant and respiratory germicide and digestive aid. In India it is used as a breath purifier and deodorant, and a paste is made from the rhizomes to treat skin infections. It is also said to be an aphrodisiac. Infusions are taken after childbirth.

CULINARY

Before use scrape or peel off the skin. The raw chopped or ground root is used in Malaysian and Indonesian dishes with tofu, meat, poultry, fish, curries, and sauces. It is also used as a marinade to flavor barbecued chicken. The fruits are a substitute for cardamom, the buds can be pickled, and the flowers are eaten raw with vegetables or pickles in parts of Java. In Thai cooking it is preferred to ginger. In medieval England a sauce was made from bread crusts, galangal, cinnamon, and ginger pulverized and moistened with stock. It was heated with a dash of vinegar and strained over fish or meat.

Galangal Soup
Serves 4

There are many variations on this soup, the recipe for which comes from Vietnam. First, make a stock from the following:

4 cups water
1 chicken carcass
4 bulbs lemon grass, bruised
5 in. galangal, peeled and sliced
1 onion, roughly sliced
2 dried red chilies
6 kaffir lime leaves
Salt and freshly ground black pepper

Then strain the stock through some fine muslin. Reheat in a heavy saucepan, adding the meat from the chicken carcass, chopped finely, together with 1 tablespoon of fish sauce and 4 tablespoons of lime juice. Simmer for 5 minutes and then add 1 cup shiitake mushrooms, left whole. Simmer for an additional 3 minutes before stirring in ½ cup thick coconut milk. Do not allow to reboil. Check the seasoning. Serve hot.

OTHER USES

Roots of lesser galangal are used in Russia for flavoring tea and a liqueur called Nastoika. The rhizomes produce a yellow or yellow-green dye.

Kaempferia galanga
(Chinese keys)

The rhizomes, common in the markets of southeast Asia, produce a distinctive cluster of fingerlike roots, which are pale brown with bright yellow flesh and a pungent aroma. They have a very strong taste and should be used sparingly in green curry paste, sauces, soups, and curries.

The rhizomes may be eaten raw when young, or steamed and eaten as a vegetable. Young shoots are cooked as a vegetable, pickled or eaten raw.

Chinese keys are used as a carminative, stomachic, expectorant, analgesic, and to treat dandruff and sore throats.

Apium graveolens var. *dulce. Apiaceae*

CELERY

Biennial grown as annual for fleshy leaf stems and leaves. Hardy. Value: low in carbohydrate and calories, high in potassium.

The species is a biennial plant, native to Europe and Asia. It is usually found on marshy ground by rivers, particularly where the water is slightly saline. Its Latin generic name *Apium* is derived from the Celtic *apon*, water, referring to its favored habitat, while *graveolens* means heavily scented, alluding to its aroma. The stems of the wild plant are very bitter, distinguishing it from *var. dulce*—meaning sweet or pleasant—from which the culinary varieties have been bred. Celery became popular in Italy in the seventeenth century and during the following 200 years spread throughout Europe to North America. "Trench celery" (so called from the method used for blanching the stems) is very hardy and is harvested from late fall to early spring, while the more recently developed self-blanching and American green types have a shorter growing season and are less hardy, cropping from midsummer until midfall. Less succulent, but full of flavor, is the smaller-stemmed "cutting celery."

VARIETIES

Trench celery
This is grouped into white, pink, and the hardier red varieties:
'Giant Pink' is a hardy variety harvested from mid- to late winter. The crisp, pale pink stalks blanch easily. **'Giant Red'** is hardy and vigorous; the outer stalks turn shell-pink when blanched. **'Giant White'** is an old, tall, white celery variety with crisp stems and a solid, well-flavored heart. It needs good growing conditions to flourish.
'Hopkins Fenlander' is a late-maturing green celery with sticks of medium length and free from string. It has a good flavor. **'Standard Bearer'** red celery has the reputation of being the latest of all to reach maturity.

Self-blanching and American green celery varieties
These include: **'Celebrity,'** an early-maturing variety, has crisp, long stems and a nutty-flavored heart. It has good bolting resistance and is one of the least stringy self-blanching varieties. **'Golden Self Blanching'** is compact

American green varieties do not need blanching.

with firm golden-yellow hearts that are crisp and tasty. Does not become stringy. **'Greensleeves,'** a green variety, produces tasty green sticks. **'Ivory Tower'** has long white "stringless" crisp stems. **'Lathom Self Blanching'** is a vigorous, well-flavored, early variety with crisp stems. **'Tall Utah Triumph'** has long tender green stems. It crops from late summer to early fall but the season can be extended by growing under cloches.

Leaf, cutting, or soup celery
This produces leaves and stems over a long period and is very hardy. It is usually sold as seed mixes, but cultivars are available: **'Tango'** is an early variety with good resistance to fusarium. Stalks are sweet and crunchy. **'Ventura'** is an

Celery maturing under glass

A healthy, well-grown row of celery is a tempting proposition.

early Utah type that has well-developed hearts and good upright growth. *Apium graveolens*, known as smallage or wild celery, is similar in appearance to cutting celery. It tastes bitter and has medicinal rather than culinary uses.

CULTIVATION

Celery is a crop for cool temperate conditions, flourishing at 59–70°F on an open site. It requires rich, fertile soil that is constantly moist, yet well drained, and has a pH of 6.5–7.5. Lime acid soils before planting if needed. **Zones 5–10.**

Propagation

Sow celery from mid- to late spring, in trays of moist seed potting mix, scattering the seed thinly over the surface; do not cover it with potting mix, as light is needed for germination. Keep the tray in a propagator or in a greenhouse at 55–60°F; germination can take several weeks, so be as patient as possible.

When 2 true leaves appear, transplant the seedlings into trays of moist seed potting mix about 2½ in. apart or individually into 3-in. pots and allow them to establish. Harden off before planting outdoors from late spring to early summer when they have five to seven true leaves.

Low temperatures after germination sometimes cause bolting later in life; temperatures should not fall below 50°F for longer than 12 hours until the seedlings have become established. They are particularly sensitive at transplanting size, so cover them with cloches and do not try to slow down the growth of advanced seedlings by putting them outdoors. It is much better to trim plants back to about 3 in. with sharp scissors and keep them in the warmth until outdoor temperatures are satisfactory. Cutting back also seems to lead to more successful transplanting. Planting in packs of seed potting mix lessens transplanting shock, which can also result in bolting. If you are unable to provide the necessary conditions, plantlets can always be bought.

Celery can also be sown in situ but germination is usually erratic and it is not worth the trouble. Celery's low germination rate can be improved by "fluid sowing." If possible, use treated seed to control celery leaf spot. Several sowings at 3-week intervals lengthens the harvesting season.

Sow cutting celery in trays of seed potting mix from late spring to late summer before hardening off and planting out 6 in. apart each way. Alternatively, multisow in packs, about 6–8 seeds in each, and plant each pack group 8 in. apart. Leave a few plants to run to seed the following year, then transplant self-sown seedlings at the recommended spacing.

Growing

The planting method is different for "trench celery" and self-blanching types. "Trenching" celery can only be done in temperate regions where the climate allows overwintering. Dig a trench 15–20 in. wide and 12 in. deep in late fall or early spring and incorporate as much well-rotted manure or compost as you can find. If more than one trench is needed, their centers should be 4 ft. apart. Trench celery can also be grown by filling in the trench to a depth of about 3–4 in. and leaving the remaining soil alongside for earthing up. A week or 10 days before planting, rake in a balanced general fertilizer at rate of 2–3 oz. per square yard into the bottom of the trench. Celery is easier to manage when planted in single rows with plants 12–18 in. apart. If you plant in double rows, set the plants 9 in. apart in pairs, rather than staggered. This makes blanching easier. Water thoroughly after planting.

Blanch by earthing up plants when they are about 12 in. high. Before you start, tie the stems loosely, just below the leaves, using raffia

Where space is limited, celery can be grown in deep containers.

or soft string and make sure the soil is moist, watering if necessary (or hill up after rain). Draw soil up the stems about 3 in. at a time, repeating this 2 or 3 times at 3-week intervals until only the tops of plants are exposed. Do not hill up higher than the leaves, neither should you let soil fall into the heart of the plant. If heavy frosts are forecast in winter, place hay, straw, or other protective material over plants to keep in good condition for as long as possible.

Plants can also be blanched with "collars." Use 9–10 in. strips of thick paper like newspaper, corrugated cardboard, brown wrapping paper, or thick black plastic. (Ideally this should be lined with paper to prevent sweating.) I have also seen tile drainpipes and plastic guttering being used to good effect.

Begin blanching when plants are about 12 in. high, tying the collar quite loosely around the plant to give it room to expand and leaving about one-third of the plant exposed. Further collars can be added every 2 to 3 weeks as the plants grow.

Remember to unwrap them periodically to remove any slugs hiding beneath. If collars are used in exposed sites, support them by staking. Cover the top of the stake with a flower pot, film canister, or table tennis ball to avoid inflicting any damage to your eyes.

Labor-saving self-blanching types do not need earthing up. They also tolerate a wider range of soils, and are particularly good where the ground is heavy and trenching or waterlogging would be a problem. They are, however, shallow-rooted and should be fed and watered regularly throughout the growing season. Self-blanching celery is planted at ground level. Dig in generous amounts of well-rotted organic matter in spring before planting. The spacing varies according to your requirements and plants should be arranged in a square pattern, not staggered rows. Spacing about 6 in. apart gives a high yield of very tender, small-stemmed sticks; 11 in. apart each way, the optimum spacing, gives high yields of longer, well-blanched sticks and 9 in. apart each way gives moderate stem growth. Plant with the crown at soil level and put straw around the outer plants when they mature to help blanching.

For good-quality crops celery must be watered copiously throughout the growing season and the soil should not be allowed to dry out. Apply up to 5 gallons per square yard per week during dry periods. Mulching with straw or compost once plants have established conserves moisture and suppresses weeds. Feed with a granular or liquid general fertilizer about 4–6 weeks after transplanting. Rotate crops, but do not plant next to parsnip, as both are attacked by celery fly. Avoid anything that checks plant growth throughout the season as this can cause bolting, so transplant the seedlings when the soil is warm, water and feed them regularly, and always mulch or hoe around the plants very carefully.

Maintenance
Spring Prepare the ground for planting. Sow seed and plant earlier crops out under cloches.
Summer Plant out in early summer, keep soil moist, and weed regularly. Check for pests and diseases.
Fall Harvest with care using a garden fork.
Winter Cover with straw, hay, or similar materials to allow harvest to continue during heavy frosts.

Protected Cropping
Protect newly transplanted plantlets with cloches or horticultural fleece for several weeks after planting, until they become established. This is particularly necessary in cooler conditions.

Harvesting and Storing
Dig celery carefully with a garden fork, easing the roots from the ground. Hay, straw, or other protective material placed over trenches assists digging in frosty weather.

Self-blanching celery can be harvested from midsummer to early fall. Before the first frosts, dig and store any remaining plants and put them in a cool, frost-free shed. They will keep for several weeks.

Harvest cutting celery regularly from about 5 weeks after planting.

Lush leaves top celery stems.

MEDICINAL

Cultivated varieties are said to be beneficial in the treatment of rheumatism and as a diuretic.

The dense foliage of maturing celery suppresses weed growth.

PESTS AND DISEASES

Celery leaf miner or **celery fly larvae** tunnel through the leaves leaving brown blisters. Severe attacks check growth. Grow under crop covers, pinch out affected leaves, do not plant seedlings that have affected leaves, or spray with systemic insecticide at the first signs of attack. Do not plant near parsnips as they can be affected.

Slugs are a major problem, particularly on heavy soil. Use biological control, traps, hand pick, or use aluminum-sulfate-based slug pellets.

Carrot fly attack the roots and stem bases, stunting growth. Rake insecticide into the soil before planting, grow under fabric or put fine mesh netting barriers 18–30 in. high around the crop before or straight after transplanting.

Celery leaf spot shows as brown spots on older leaves, spreading to younger ones. Severe attacks can stunt growth; use treated seed or spray with fungicide.

Celery pale leaf spot (early blight) appears as tiny yellow spots on the leaf surfaces with accompanying gray mold in damp conditions. This disease spreads rapidly. Spray with Bordeaux mixture or similar fungicide. Destroy any plant debris at the end of the season.

COMPANION PLANTING

Celery helps brassicas by deterring damaging butterflies. It grows well with beans, tomatoes, and particularly leeks. If left to flower, celery attracts beneficial insects.

CULINARY

Usually eaten raw rather than cooked, celery adds welcome crunchiness to salads, particularly in winter months. It is a key ingredient of Waldorf Salad, made with equal quantities of chopped red-skinned apples and celery, combined with walnuts and bound with mayonnaise.

Celery goes well with cheese—sticks filled with cream cheese or pâté are an appetizing "nibble." The "heart" is particularly tasty. Cook celery in soups and stews, or stir-fry. Braise hearts by simmering in boiling water for 10 minutes, then cook in a covered dish for 45 minutes in a low oven to accompany roasts.

Add leaves, like parsley, to meat dishes. Fresh or dried leaves flavor soups and stuffings. Cutting celery is a flavoring for salads, soups and stews; the seeds can also be used.

Celery will stay fresh in a plastic bag in the refrigerator for up to 3 days. Do not stand in water for long, or the freshness is lost.

Freeze celery by washing and cutting the sticks into 1-in. lengths, blanch for 3 minutes, cool, drain, and pack into plastic bags. Use frozen celery only in cooked dishes.

Celery and Zucchini with Blue Cheese Dip
Serves 4

2 tablespoons olive oil
1 teaspoon chili powder
$\frac{1}{2}$ teaspoon paprika
1 clove garlic, crushed
4 basil leaves, roughly chopped
4 zucchini, sliced lengthwise into quarters
4 stalks celery, cut into 3-in. lengths
Chives, to garnish

For the dip:
4 tablespoons cottage cheese
2 tablespoons crumbled blue cheese
4 tablespoons yogurt
Salt and freshly ground pepper

In a heavy sauté pan over a gentle heat, mix the oil with the chili powder, paprika, garlic, and basil. Turn up the heat and fry the zucchini, cut side down, until browned, and turn to brown the other side.

In a small bowl mix together all the dip ingredients. On four small plates, arrange a fan of alternating zucchini and celery sticks and fill the center with the dip. Garnish with finely snipped chives and serve.

Apium graveolens var. r*apaceum. Apiaceae*

CELERIAC

(Celery Root) Biennial usually grown as annual for edible root. Hardy. Value: rich in potassium; moderate amounts of vitamin C.

If you have never grown this vegetable, do so immediately; it is absolutely delicious. This swollen-stemmed relative of celery has long been popular in Europe. It was introduced to Britain in the early eighteenth century by the writer and seedsman Stephen Switzer, who brought seed from Alexandria and wrote about the vegetable in his book *Growing Foreign Kitchen Vegetables*. It is an excellent, versatile winter vegetable, hardier and more disease-resistant than celery, but with similar flavor and aroma.

VARIETIES

The lowest part of the stem, known as the "bulb," is eaten; the roots that grow below are removed.

'Iram' is a medium-sized bulb, with few sideshoots. It stores well and the flesh remains white when cooked. 'Marble Ball,' a well-known variety, is medium-sized, globular, and strongly flavored. It stores well. 'Alabaster' is a high-yielding variety with upright foliage, round bulbs, and good resistance to running to seed. 'Tellus' is a quick-growing variety which remains white after boiling. It has firm flesh and a smoother skin than many varieties. 'Balder' has a good flavor with round, medium-sized roots, which are excellent when cooked or raw. The bulb of 'Brilliant' is smooth with white flesh and does not discolor. 'Monarch' is a popular variety with smooth skin and succulent flesh. 'Regent' produces large, firm roots with white flesh. It does not discolor when cooked.

CULTIVATION

Propagation
Celeriac needs a long growing season. Sow in late winter to early spring in a propagator at 65°F or in mid- to late spring in a cold greenhouse, under cloches, or in a cold frame. Plant seeds in peat-lite mix either several to a pot or in seed boxes or packs. Germination is notoriously erratic. Repot strong seedlings when they are about ½ in. tall and large enough to handle. Plant them into single 3-in. pots, packs, or in seed trays at 2-in. intervals, keeping the temperature at 55–60°F. Harden off when the weather becomes warm in late spring and plant outdoors once there is no danger of frost.

Celeriac is sensitive to cold at the transplanting stage; do not try to slow the growth of fast-growing seedlings by lowering the temperature, as this will encourage them to run to seed later in the season. Maintain the temperature and cut off the tops of the plants with sharp scissors to 3 in.—the ideal size for transplanting. **Zones 4–10.**

Growing
Celeriac needs rich, fertile, moisture-retentive soil and is ideal for damper parts of the garden. In fall, incorporate as much well-rotted manure or compost as possible. Space plants 12–15 in. apart each way. Do not bury the crowns; they should be planted at ground level. Plant firmly and water thoroughly and continually. In midsummer, remove the outer leaves to expose the crown and encourage the bulb to develop, and remove sideshoots if they appear.

Maintenance
Spring Plant out seedlings—harden off. Keep weed free.
Summer Water in dry weather. Mulch to conserve moisture; feed weekly with a liquid manure, particularly in poorer soils.
Fall Begin harvesting. Cover with straw.
Winter Prepare ground. Sow seeds under glass.

Protected Cropping
Celeriac benefits from protection only when it is at the seedling stage.

Celeriac 'Iram'

Harvesting and Storing

Celeriac can be harvested throughout the winter. Harvest when the plants are 3–5 in. diameter, although they can be dug when larger with no loss of flavor. Ideally they should remain in the ground until required. Before the onset of severe winter weather, protect plants with a layer of straw, hay, or with frost fabric to prevent the ground from freezing. If the soil is heavy, the site exposed or needed for another crop, dig and remove the outer leaves keeping the central tuft attached; cut off the roots and store in a cool shed in boxes of damp peat-lite mix or sand.

Alternatively, dig and "heel in" or transplant the crop in another part of the garden, laying them close together in a trench and covering the bulbs with soil. They last for several weeks when stored in this manner.

Bulbs can be frozen; cut into cubes, blanch for 3 minutes, dry, store in plastic bags, and put in the freezer. They will keep for a week in the salad drawer of the refrigerator.

PESTS AND DISEASES

Celeriac has the same problems as celery. Protect against **slugs**; use aluminum sulfate-based slug pellets, pick off slugs at night, and encourage natural predators. **Slugs** congregate under lettuce leaves or wet paper; pick off and destroy. **Carrot fly** is often a pest when established on carrots. Rake insecticide into the soil before planting. Grow under crop covers or place a barrier 2½ ft. high of fine netting or plastic, erected before or just after sowing. **Celery fly** is less of a problem than on celery. Pick off any brown, blistered leaflets or grow under frost fabric.

COMPANION PLANTING

Celeriac grows well where legumes have been planted the previous year and benefits from being placed alongside beans, brassicas, leeks, tomatoes, and onions.

MEDICINAL

Celeriac oil has a calming effect and is a traditional remedy for skin complaints and rheumatism. It is also said to restore sexual potency after illness! Celeriac is rich in calcium, phosphorus, and vitamin C.

WARNING

Celeriac is a diuretic. Pregnant women and those with a kidney disorder should avoid eating it in large quantities.

CULINARY

Containing only 14 calories per 4 oz., celeriac is excellent for anyone on a diet.

Scrub the bulb well to remove dirt before peeling. It discolors rapidly when cut; put immediately into acidulated water. Shredded celeriac can be added raw to winter salads. Alternatively, blanch the slices or cubes in boiling water for a few seconds beforehand. In France it is cut into cubes and mixed with mayonnaise and Dijon mustard to make *Céleri-rave rémoulade*.

The bulb adds flavor to soups or stews and is good with lamb or beef; pureed or seasoned with pepper, salt and butter, it is an ideal accompaniment for stronger-flavored game.

The leaves are strongly flavored and can be used sparingly to garnish salads or dried for use in cooking. The stems can be cooked and eaten like sea kale.

Celeriac can be made into delicious "fries": boil a whole, peeled root in salted water until just tender and then cut into sticks and fry in a mixture of butter and oil until lightly browned. These fries make an excellent accompaniment to game or plain broiled steaks.

Boiled and sliced, celeriac can be covered with a cheese sauce well flavored with French mustard. It also makes an excellent soup.

Monkfish with Celeriac
Serves 4

1½ lb. monkfish, cut into chunks
1 large onion, finely sliced
1 carrot, peeled and cut into julienne strips
½ cup celeriac, cut into julienne strips
1 stick butter
1 tablespoon flour
2 teaspoons French mustard
2 tablespoons yogurt
1 tablespoon heavy cream
Salt and freshly ground black pepper

Season the monkfish and prepare the vegetables. Heat half the butter in a heavy sauté pan and cook the monkfish gently for about 7–8 minutes, turning it until just tender. Remove from the pan and keep warm. Using the rest of the butter, add the vegetables to the pan and sauté until soft. Stir in the flour and cook for a couple of minutes; then add the mustard, yogurt, and cream. Stir well and heat through gently. Put the fish pieces in, stir to coat well, and serve piping hot.

Asparagus officinalis. Asparagaceae

ASPARAGUS

Long-lived perennial grown for slender young shoots and ornamental foliage. Half hardy. Value: high in potassium and folic acid, moderate source of beta carotene and vitamin E.

The genus *Asparagus* provides us with a range of robust foliage houseplants and one of the world's most desirable vegetables. The delicious taste, succulent texture, and suggestive shape of the emergent shoots combine to create an eating experience verging on the decadent that has been celebrated for over 2,000 years. Pliny the Elder describes cultivation methods used by the Romans for producing plants with blanched stems, and mentions a cultivar of which three "spears" weighed a pound. These spears were once believed to arise from rams' horns buried in the soil. Wild asparagus grows in Europe, Asia, and northwest Africa, in habitats including dry meadows, sand dunes, limestone cliffs, and volcanic hillsides.

VARIETIES

'Connover's Colossal,' an early, heavy-cropping old variety producing large tasty spears, is suitable for light soils and freezes well. 'Franklin' is heavy-cropping with thick spears. A few can be harvested from 2-year-old crowns. 'Jersey Giant' is a hybrid resistant to most diseases, producing top-quality spears. 'Jersey Knight' is similar to 'Jersey Giant,' but 99 percent of the plants are male for heavier cropping. 'Martha Washington,' an established favorite, crops heavily, has long spears and is rust-resistant.

The fall fruits of 'Connover's Colossal.' Although the ripe fruits of female varieties are attractive, they tend to germinate more freely.

CULTIVATION

Asparagus thrives in an open, sheltered position on well-drained soil. A bed can be productive for up to 20 years, so thorough preparation is essential. **Zones 3–8.**

Propagation
Asparagus can be grown from seed, although it is easier and less time-consuming to plant crowns. Soak seed for 2 days before sowing in midspring, 1 in. deep in drills 18 in. apart. Thin seedlings when they are 3 in. tall until they are 6 in. apart. Alternatively, sow indoors in late winter at 55–60°F directly into packs,

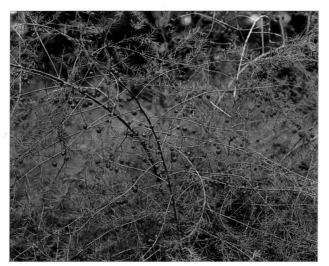

pots, or trays. Repot, harden off, and plant outdoors in early summer. Male plants are the more productive, so the following year, remove any females (identifiable by their fruits) before they shed their fruits. Transplant the remaining male crowns into their permanent position in midspring the following year.

Growing
The fall or winter before planting, dig in plenty of well-rotted organic matter; lime acid soil to create a pH of 6.5–7.5. It is vital to remove perennial weeds. Fork over the soil 1 or 2 weeks before planting and rake in a general fertilizer at approximately 3 oz. per square yard.

One-year-old crowns establish quickly; 2- and 3-year-old crowns tend to suffer from a growth check after transplanting. Plant in midspring, once the soil is warm. The roots dry out quickly and are easily damaged, so cover with burlap until ready to plant, then handle with care.

Either plant in single rows with the crowns 12–18 in. apart or in beds with 2 or 3 rows 12 in. apart. For several beds, set them 3 ft. apart. Before planting dig a trench 12 in. by 8 in. and make a 4 in. mound of soil in the base; plant crowns along the top, spreading out the roots, and cover them with 2 in. of sifted soil. As the stems grow, gradually cover with soil; by fall, the trench should be filled with soil. Keep beds weed-free by hand weeding or hoeing carefully to avoid damaging the shallow roots. On more exposed sites, support the "ferns" when windy to avoid damage to the crown, and water during dry weather.

After harvesting, apply a general fertilizer to nurture stem growth and build up the plants for the following year. In fall, when stems have turned yellow, cut back to within 1–2 in. of the

Cutting off asparagus roots

surface and tidy up the bed. Ferns can be shredded and composted. Each spring apply a general fertilizer as growth begins. Mulching with manure has little value beyond suppressing weeds and conserving moisture.

Maintenance

Spring Sow seed and plant crowns. Harvest late spring. *Summer* Keep weed-free and water as necessary. Stop harvesting by midsummer. *Fall* Cut back yellowing ferns and tidy beds. *Winter* Prepare new beds: mix in organic matter and remove perennial weeds.

Protected Cropping

Protect the crowns from late frosts with frost fabric or cloches.

Harvesting and Storing

However tempting, do not cut spears until the third year after planting (except possibly with 'Franklin'). Harvesting lasts for 6 weeks in the first year and 8 weeks in subsequent years. Do not harvest after midsummer: it can result in thin spears the following year. When spears are 4–7 in. long, cut them obliquely about 1–2 in. below the surface with a sharp knife or a serrated asparagus knife.

Pests and Diseases

The black and yellow adults and small grayish larvae of **asparagus beetles** appear from late summer, stripping stems and foliage.

COMPANION PLANTING

Where growing conditions allow, asparagus is compatible with tomatoes, parsley, and basil.

MEDICINAL

Asparagus is used to treat rheumatism, gout, and cystitis. Anyone who lacks the enzyme to break down asparagin produces urine with a strong odor—a disconcerting but harmless phenomenon.

WARNING

The berries are poisonous.

CULINARY

Asparagus spears should be used as fresh as possible, preferably within an hour of harvesting. They can be refrigerated in a plastic bag for up to 3 days. To freeze, tie into bundles and blanch thick spears for 4 minutes, thin for 2. Freeze in a plastic container.

Asparagus is best eaten steamed or boiled and served hot with butter. Also good cold with vinaigrette, Parmesan cheese, or mayonnaise. Asparagus tips can be added to salads and pizza toppings.

To boil, wash spears, peel away the skin below the tips, and soak in cold water until all have been prepared. Sort into stalks of even length (perhaps 20 stalks if thin varieties and 6–8 if thicker-stemmed), and tie with soft string or raffia, one close to the base and another just below the tip. Stand bundles upright in boiling salted water, with the tips above water level. Cover and boil gently for 10–15 minutes until al dente, then drain and serve. Don't overcook: the tips should be firm, and the spears should not bend when held at the base. The water can be used in soup.

Asparagus Risotto
Serves 4

6 morels, fresh or dried
1 big bunch thin asparagus,
  cut into 1 in. pieces
1 tablespoon unsalted butter
1¹/₂ tablespoons olive oil
2 red onions, finely chopped
1¹/₂ cups arborio rice
2 cups chicken stock, boiling
1 tablespoon fresh marjoram (or
  1 teaspoon dried)
2 tablespoons mascarpone
Salt and freshly ground black
  pepper
Freshly shredded Parmesan
  (optional)

Soak fresh morels in salted water for 10 minutes and wash thoroughly. Pat dry and cut each into several pieces. If using dried morels, soak in warm water for 30 minutes before cutting up.

Blanch the asparagus in boiling water for 1 minute, drain and set aside.

Heat the butter and oil in a heavy-bottomed pan and sauté the onion and morels until soft. Stir in the rice and coat it well with the oil and butter. Pour in a cup of the stock and the marjoram and cook over a low heat, stirring frequently, until the liquid is absorbed. Add more cupfuls of stock one at a time and continue cooking until the rice is just tender and the consistency is creamy. Stir in the asparagus and the mascarpone and season well. Serve with Parmesan.

Asparagus Risotto

Beta vulgaris subsp. *cicla. Chenopodiaceae*

SWISS CHARD

Also known as Silver Chard, Silver Beet, Seakale Beet. Biennial grown as annual for leaves and midribs. Hardy. Value: high in sodium, potassium, iron, and an exceptional source of beta carotene, the precursor of vitamin A.

Perpetual spinach is highly resistant to bolting.

The umbrella name "leaf beet" includes Swiss chard and also encompasses perpetual spinach or spinach beet. (The "true" spinach and New Zealand spinach both belong to other genera.) A close relative of the beet, leaf beet is an ancient vegetable cultivated for its attractive, tasty leaves. Native to the Mediterranean, it was well known to the Greeks, who also ate its roots with mustard, lentils, and beans. Aristotle wrote of red chard in the fourth century B.C., and Theophrastus recorded both light and dark green varieties. The Romans introduced it to central and northern Europe and from there it slowly spread, reaching the Far East in the Middle Ages and China in the seventeenth century. The name "chard" comes from the French *carde* and derives from the resemblance of the leaf stalks to those of globe artichokes and cardoons. In 1597 John Gerard wrote in his *Herball*, ". . . it grew with me to the height of eight cubits and did bring forth his rough seeds very plentifully." If the measurement is correct, his Swiss chard would be approximately twelve feet tall. I wonder where that variety is today—was his yardstick wrongly calibrated, or had it simply bolted?

CULTIVATION

Although they tolerate a wide range of soils, the best growing conditions are sunny or lightly shaded positions in rich, moisture-retentive, free-draining soil. On impoverished soils, bolting can be a problem, so dig in plenty of well-rotted organic matter the winter before planting. The ideal pH is 6.5–7.5 and acid soils should be limed.

The ideal growing temperature is 60–65°F, although the range of tolerance is remarkably broad. They survive in winter temperatures down to about 7°F and are more tolerant of higher summer temperatures than true spinach, which is inclined to bolt. **Zones 3–10.**

Propagation
For a constant supply throughout the year, make 2 sowings, one in midspring for a summer harvest and another in mid- to late summer. The later crop usually has a lower yield.

Sow 3–4 seeds in hills 9 in. apart, in drills ½–¾ in. deep. Swiss chard needs 18 in. between the rows, and perpetual spinach 15 in. Thin seedlings when large enough to handle to leave the strongest seedling.

VARIETIES

Swiss chard has broad red or white leaf stems and midribs. **'Fordhook Giant'** has huge, glossy green leaves with white veins and stems. It is tasty and high yielding, producing bumper crops even at high temperatures. **'Lucullus'** is vigorous and crops heavily, producing pale yellow-green leaves with fleshy midribs. Tolerant of high temperatures, it does not bolt. **'Rhubarb Chard' ('Ruby Chard')** is noted for its magnificent bright crimson

The bright stems of 'Ruby Chard' are spectacular.

leaf stalks and dark green puckered leaves. Ideal for the ornamental border or "potager," it needs growing with care, as it is prone to bolting. **'Vulcan'** is another cultivar with beautiful red stems and dark green, sweet-tasting leaves.

'Perpetual Spinach,' or spinach beet, is similar but smaller, with narrower stems, dark, fleshy leaves and is very resistant to bolting. **'Erbette,'** an Italian variety, is well flavored and has an excellent texture. It is good as a cut-and-come-again crop.

Alternatively, sow in packs or trays and transplant to their final spacing when they are large enough to handle. Swiss chard is particularly successful as a cut-and-come-again crop. Prepare the seedbed thoroughly and broadcast or sow seed in drills the width of a hoe.

Growing
Keep crops weed-free by hoeing or, preferably, mulching with well-rotted organic matter, and keep the soil continually moist. In dry conditions, plants will need 2–3 gallons per week, but are surprisingly drought-tolerant. A dressing of general granular or liquid fertilizer can be given to plants needing a boost.

Maintenance
Spring Sow the first crop in midspring in hills; thin, leaving a strong seedling.
Summer Weed, water, and feed as necessary. Sow a second crop in mid- to late summer. Harvest as needed.
Fall Protect with cloches or row covers in late fall for good-quality growth.
Winter Dig over the area where the following year's crop is to be planted. Harvest overwintering crops.

Protected Cropping
Although they are hardy enough to withstand winters outdoors, plants protected in cloches, cold frames, row covers or frost fabric produce better crops of higher-quality leaves.

Container Growing
Swiss chard can be grown in containers and makes a fine ornamental feature. Either transplant seedlings or sow directly into loam-based potting mix or garden soil, with added organic matter.

Harvesting and Storing
Seeds sown in midspring are ready to harvest from early to midsummer. Harvest the outer leaves first, working toward the center of the plant and cutting at the base of each stem: snapping them off is likely to disturb the roots. Choose firm leaves and discard any that are damaged or wilted. Pick regularly to ensure a constant supply of tender regrowth, so harvest even if you are unable to use them—they are certain to be welcomed by friends.

They can also be grown as cut-and-come-again crops from seedling stage through to maturity. Cut seedlings when about 2 in. tall. After 2 or 3 crops have been harvested, allow them to regrow to about 5 in. Semimature plants are harvested leaf by leaf and mature plants can be cut about 1 in. above the ground; from this, new growth appears.

Swiss chard and perpetual spinach are best eaten straight from the plant. Leaves (minus the stalks) keep in the refrigerator in the crisper or in plastic bags for 2–3 days.

Swiss chard is highly productive.

PESTS AND DISEASES

They are relatively trouble-free, although beware of **downy mildew** when dense patches of seedlings are sown for cut-and-come-again crops. It appears as brown patches on leaves.

Birds sometimes attack seedlings, so protect crops; growing plants under brassicas or beans also gives them some protection.

COMPANION PLANTING

They grow well with all beans except string beans, and flourish with brassicas, onions, and lettuce. Herbs like sage, thyme, mint, dill, hyssop, rosemary, and garlic are also compatible.

MEDICINAL

Leaves are vitamin- and mineral-rich with high levels of iron and magnesium. In folk medicine the juice is used as a decongestant; the leaves are said to neutralize acid and have a purgative effect. Beware of eating it in large quantities!

CULINARY

Perpetual spinach can be lightly boiled, steamed, or eaten raw. Swiss chard takes longer to cook: try it steamed, served with butter or sorrel. Soup can be made from the leaves and its midribs cooked and served like asparagus, or added to pork pies. 'Rhubarb Chard' tastes milder than white-stemmed varieties.

Spinach Beet Fritters
Serves 4

These robust fritters go well with salmon or cod.

1½ lb. spinach beet, well washed
Pat of butter
2 large eggs, separated
1 tablespoon shredded Parmesan
1 teaspoon shredded lemon peel
Olive oil, for frying
Salt and freshly ground black pepper
Pinch of nutmeg

Prepare the leaves, removing the midribs, and chop roughly. Cook in the water that clings to the leaves until wilted—2–3 minutes—and drain well. Chop finely and return to the pan with the butter, cooking until all the liquid evaporates. Allow to cool for 5 minutes and stir in the egg yolks, Parmesan, and lemon peel. When almost cold, fold in the stiffly beaten egg whites and season with salt, pepper, and nutmeg to taste.

Drop spoonfuls into hot oil, heated in a heavy sauté pan, and cook for a minute or two, turning halfway. Drain well and serve hot.

Beta vulgaris subsp. *vulgaris. Chenopodiaceae*

BEET

Also known as Beetroot. Biennial grown as annual for swollen root and young leaves. Hardy. Value: slightly higher in carbohydrate than most vegetables, good source of folic acid and potassium.

Beet is a form of the maritime sea beet that has been selected over many centuries for its edible roots. From the same origin come mangold (a cattle fodder), the beet used for commercial sugar production, and Swiss chard. Grown since Assyrian times, the vegetable was highly esteemed by the ancient Greeks and was used in offerings to Apollo. There were many Roman recipes for beet, which they regarded more highly than the greatly revered cabbage. It appeared in fourteenth-century English recipes and was first described as the beet we know today in Germany in 1558, although it was a rarity at that time in northern Europe. The typical red coloration comes from its cell sap, but there are also varieties in other colors.

VARIETIES

Beets are grouped according to shape—round or globe-shaped, tapered or long, and flat or oval. To reduce the amount of thinning needed, breeders have introduced "monogerm" varieties.

Globe
'Boltardy' is a delicious, well-textured, smooth-skinned variety, an excellent early cropper as it is very resistant to bolting, and good in containers. **'Detroit 2 Little Ball'** produces deep red, smooth-skinned "baby beet," which are ideal for pickling, bottling or freezing. A good crop for late sowing and for storing. **'Detroit 2 Dark Red'**

'Burpee's Golden' is an especially tasty variety.

has dark red flesh, a good flavor and stores well. **'Monogram'** is dark red, well-flavored and vigorous, with smooth skin and rich red flesh. It is a "monogerm" variety. **'Monopoly'** is also a "monogerm" and is resistant to bolting, with a good color and rough skin. **'Regala'** has very dark roots and is quite

small, even at maturity. An excellent variety for containers, and resistant to bolting. **'Warrior'** is a new hybrid with deep red color both inside and out. The roots are smooth, tender, and delicious.

Tapered
'Cheltenham Green Top' is a tasty, old variety with rough skin and long roots. It stores well. **'Cheltenham Mono'** is a tasty, medium-sized "monogerm" which is resistant to bolting, good for slicing, and stores well.

Others
'Albina Vereduna' (**'Snowhite'**) is a wonderful globe-shaped white variety, with smooth skin and sweet flesh; it has the advantage that it does not stain. The curly leaves can be used as "greens" and are full of vitamins. It does not store

well and is prone to bolting. **'Barbabietola di Chioggia'** is a mild, traditional Italian variety. Sliced, it reveals unusual white internal "rings." It gives an exotic look to salads, certain to provoke comment. When cooked, it becomes pale pink. Sow from midspring. **'Burpee's Golden'** has beautiful orange skin and tasty yellow flesh; it is better harvested when small. It looks great in salads, keeps its color when cooked, does not bleed when cut and the leaves can be used as "greens." It stores well and has good bolting resistance. **'Egyptian Turnip Rooted'** (**'D'Egypte,' 'Egyptian Flat'**) has smooth roots with deep red, delicious flesh. An American introduction, it was first grown around Boston about 1869. **'Forono'** is very tasty, with large, cylindrical roots, smooth skin, and good color. Slow to go woody, it is ideal for slicing, for summer salads, and stores well. Susceptible to bolting, it should be sown from midspring. **'Cylindrica'** has sweet-tasting, dark, oval roots with excellent keeping qualities and good flavor. Because of its shape, it is perfect for slicing and cooks well. Harvest when young.

Varieties of "mini vegetables" include **'Kestrel,' 'Action,'** and **'Avenger.'**

'Cylindrica' is ideal for slicing

'Boltardy' is a reliable variety.

CULTIVATION

Propagation

In most varieties each "seed" is a corky fruit containing 2 or 3 seeds, so a considerable amount of thinning is required. "Monogerm" varieties, each containing a single seed, reduce such a work load. They also contain a natural inhibitor that slows or even prevents germination. Remove this by soaking seeds or washing them in running water for ½–1 hour before sowing.

At soil temperatures below 45°F germination is slow and erratic. To overcome this, sow early crops in packs, "fluid sow" or sow in drills or hills after warming the soil with cloches. These can be left in place after sowing until the weather warms tip. Use bolting-resistant varieties until midspring; after that, any variety can be used.

Sow the first crops under cloches from late winter to early spring ½–¾ in. deep and 1 in. apart with 9 in. between rows. Thin to a final spacing of 4 in. between plants. Alternatively sow 2–3 seeds at hills 4 in. apart, thinning to leave the strongest seedling when the first true leaf appears. "Round" varieties can be "multisown" in a cool greenhouse planting three seeds per pack, thinning to 4–5 seedlings, then planting the packs 4 in. apart when about 2 in. high. Early crops can also be sown thinly in broad flat drills ½–¾ in. deep, in a similar way to peas. Thin as soon as seedlings are touching and keep thinning as plants grow: those large enough can be used whole. If you grow beets under frost fabric or a similar cover (put in place once the seedlings have established), yields can be increased by up to 50 percent. Remove protection 4–6 weeks after sowing. From midspring, if the weather is warm seeds can be sown without the protection of cloches, thinning to 3–4 in. apart.

Beets grown for pickling need to be about 2 in. in diameter. Sowing in rows 3 in. apart, thinning plants to 2½ in. apart will give you the correct size.

From late spring to early summer sow the main crop, using any round or long variety. Harvest throughout the summer and for winter storing. Sow in drills or at hills, thinning to leave a final spacing of 3 in. apart in rows 8 in. apart or 5–6 in. in and between the rows.

For a constant supply of beets, sow round cultivars under glass from late winter at 4-week intervals for midspring crops; and for a late fall crop sow from early to midsummer in mild areas (for digging during winter, thin to 4 in.).

For winter storage sow in late May, early June. **Zones 3–9.**

Growing

Beets need an open site with fertile, well-drained light soil that has been manured for the previous crop. The pH should be 6.5–7.5, so acid soils will need liming. Fall-maturing varieties tolerate heavier conditions and long-rooted varieties require a deeper soil. The best quality grow in moderate temperatures around 61°F.

Scatter a slow-release general fertilizer at 2–3 oz. per square yard 2–3 weeks before sowing, raking the seedbed to a fine tilth.

For good-quality beet, it is important to avoid any check in growth; at the onset of drought, water at a rate of 2½ gal. per square yard every 2 weeks. Do not overwater, as this results in excessive leaf growth and small roots. If watering is neglected, yields are low, roots become woody, and when it rains or you water suddenly, the roots will split. Keep weed-free and hoe with care as damage causes the roots to bleed: use an onion hoe or mulch around the plants. Mulching with a 2 in. layer of well-rotted compost or spent mushroom compost will conserve moisture.

Maintenance

Spring Sow early crops under glass or cloches. Midspring crops can be sown without protection.
Summer Sow successively every month, harvest earlier crops, keep the plot weed-free, and water as required. Sow main crops.
Fall Dig later crops and those for storage.
Winter In mild areas leave overwintering crops outdoors and protect with hay, straw, or similar materials. Alternatively, dig and store indoors.

Protected Cropping

Grow early crops under glass in packs and transplant under cloches. Alternatively, grow under cloches or crop covers and remove these about 6 weeks after sowing.

Container Growing

Unless growing for exhibition, grow only globe varieties in containers—about 8 in. deep—or troughs or growing bags. Sow seed thinly ½–¾ in. deep from midspring to midsummer, thinning to 4–5 in. apart. Water regularly, harvest when the size of a tennis ball, and keep weed-free.

Harvesting and Storing

Beets take 60–90 days to mature. They must always be harvested before they becomes woody and inedible. Harvest salad beet from late spring to midfall and main-crop varieties from midsummer onward. Early varieties are best harvested when the size of a golf ball; when later crops reach that size, dig every other plant and use for cooking, leaving the rest for digging when they reach cricket ball–size.

'Red Ace' is a vigorous grower.

Dig roots carefully with a fork, shake off soil, and twist off the leaves. Do not cut off the leaves: it causes bleeding and makes a terrible mess! Use any damaged roots immediately. Dig beet for storage by midfall and put in stout boxes of moist peat substitute, sand, or sawdust, leaving a gap between each root. Store in a cool, frost-free shed or garage. Roots should keep until midspring the following year but check regularly and remove any that deteriorate. The long-rooted types are traditionally grown for storage, but most varieties store successfully.

In mild areas and on well-drained soil they can be left over winter, but need a dense protective covering of straw or similar material before the frosts. This also makes digging easier.

PESTS AND DISEASES

Beets are generally trouble-free but may suffer from the following problems:

Black bean aphid forms dense colonies on the leaves. Yellow blotches between the veins, the symptom of manganese deficiency, appear on older leaves first and can be a problem on extremely alkaline soil.

Rough patches on the surface of the root and waterlogged brown patches and rings at its center are a sign of **boron deficiency**. There may also be corky "growths" on the shoots and leaf stalks.

Make sure that beet seedlings are protected against **birds**.

Slugs make holes in leaves. The problem is worse in damp conditions.

COMPANION PLANTING

Beets flourish in the company of kohlrabi, carrots, cucumber, lettuce, onions, brassicas, and most beans (not string beans). Dill or fennel planted nearby attracts predators. Because they combine well with so many other crops and small roots mature within 9–13 weeks, beets are good for intercropping and useful catch-crops.

OTHER USES

The foliage is attractive and ideal for inclusion in an ornamental border, particularly varieties like 'Bull's Blood.' The leaf mineral content is 25 percent magnesium, making it useful on the compost pile.

MEDICINAL

Used in folk medicine as a blood tonic for gastritis, piles, and constipation; mildly cardio-tonic. Recent research has shown that drinking at least one glass of raw beet juice a day helps control cancer.

WARNING

The sap stains very badly and is difficult to remove from clothing and skin.

CULINARY

The roots are eaten raw—try them shredded as a crudité—or cooked and served fresh or pickled. Young "tops" can be cooked like spinach and used as "greens."

They add color and flavor to salads, particularly the red, yellow, white, and bicolored varieties. Bean and beet salad is particularly tasty. Wash in cold water, keeping root and stems intact: do not "top and tail" or damage the skin, as bleeding causes loss of flavor and color. Boil for up to 2 hours in saltwater, depending on the size, then carefully rub off the skin. It is delicious served hot as a vegetable, otherwise cool for pickling or for a fresh salad.

Beets can also be baked, and are the basis for borscht soup when cooked with white stock. They also make excellent chutney.

Freeze small beets that are no more than 2 in. across. Wash and boil, skin and cool, then cut roots into slices or cubes and freeze in a rigid container. You should use within 6 months.

In a plastic bag or the crisper in the refrigerator, they stay fresh for up to 2 weeks.

Spicy Beet Salad
Serves 4

$1^1/_2$ lb. beets, washed and trimmed
Juice of half a lemon
$^1/_2$ teaspoon cumin
$^1/_2$ teaspoon cinnamon
$^1/_2$ teaspoon paprika
1 tablespoon orange-flower water
2 tablespoons olive oil
Salt and freshly ground black pepper
2 tablespoons chopped parsley
Lettuce (mixed field greens)

Cook the beets in a steamer for 20 or 30 minutes until tender. Peel and slice them when cool, reserving the liquid that accumulates on the plate.

Toss them in lemon juice and coat with the spices, orange-flower water, and olive oil, together with the liquid. Season, cover and chill. To serve, toss with the parsley and arrange on individual plates on a bed of lettuce leaves.

Spicy Beet Salad

Brassica oleracea Gemmifera Group. *Brassicaceae*

BRUSSELS SPROUT

**Biennial grown as annual for leafy buds and "tops."
Hardy. Value: excellent source of vitamin C, rich in beta
carotene, folic acid, vitamin E, and potassium.**

First recorded as a spontaneous sport from a cabbage plant found in the Brussels region of Belgium around 1750, this vegetable had reached England and France by 1800. The Brussels version may not have been the first occurrence: a plant described as "*Brassica capitata polycephalos*" (a many-headed brassica with knoblike heads) was illustrated in D'Alechaps's *Historia Generalis Plantarum* in 1587. A stalwart among winter vegetables in cool temperate zones, sprouts are extremely hardy and crop heavily, but are rather fussy to prepare. As with all vegetables, homegrown ones taste far better than those bought from a store. If you have never eaten sprouts harvested fresh from the garden, try them: they are absolutely delicious.

Harvest the buttons while firm.

VARIETIES

Sprouts are divided into early, midseason, and late varieties, harvested from early to midfall, midfall to midwinter, and midwinter to early spring respectively. "Earlies" are shorter and faster-growing than the hardier "lates," which are taller with higher yields. To extend the season, grow one variety from each group if you have space; alternatively, grow midseason and late types for midwinter to early spring crops, when other vegetables are scarce.

Although older open-pollinated varieties are very tasty, it is generally accepted that the modern, compact F_1 hybrids are a better buy. They produce a heavy crop of uniform "buttons" all the way up the stem, which remain in good condition for a long period without "blowing;" plants are also less likely to fall over.

'**Citadel**' (midseason) produces moderately sized dark green sprouts which freeze well. '**Falstaff**' is a vigorous, high-yielding red cultivar with tasty "buttons." The red coloration disappears when boiled, so steaming is a better method of cooking. The Dutch import '**Harley**' produces delicious firm sprouts that detach easily from the stalk. The plants are hardy and resistant to fusarium disease.

'**Oliver**' (very early) is a high-yielding variety producing large tasty sprouts. Good resistance to powdery mildew. '**Peer Gynt**' (early to midseason) produces medium-sized sprouts. Lower "buttons" have a tendency not to open if mature sprouts are left on the plant. Harvest regularly. '**Rubine**,' a red form, is worth a place in an ornamental border and produces small crops of tasty sprouts. '**Trafalgar**' is a late-season, English-bred variety that produces good-tasting elongated sprouts on a tall and hardy plant. '**Widgeon**' (midseason) is a good-flavored variety producing moderately sized sprouts.

'Rubine,' a magnificent red variety, is an excellent ornamental plant.

'Oliver' in full crop

CULTIVATION

Sprouts need a sheltered, sunny spot; wind rock can be a problem in exposed sites. Soil should be moisture-retentive yet free-draining, with a pH of 6.5.

Propagation

Sow early varieties from late winter to early spring, midseason varieties from mid- to late spring and late varieties from midspring. Sow seeds thinly, ³/₄ in. deep in a half tray of moist potting mix and put them in an unheated greenhouse, cold frame, or sheltered spot outdoors to germinate. Transplant seedlings when they are large enough to handle into a larger seed tray, in potting mix, about 1¹/₂–2 in. apart.

Sowing in packs reduces root disturbance when transplanting. Put 2 seeds in each pack and retain the strongest after germination. Sow early varieties from late winter in a propagator at 50–55°F; and transplant them into their permanent position after hardening off. Taller varieties are prone to falling over when grown in packs, but when planted deeply, a long taproot develops.

The previous two methods are preferable to sowing in a seedbed, which takes up space that could be used for other crops, and leaves seedlings vulnerable to pests and diseases; I do not recommend it. If necessary, warm the soil with cloches or black plastic. Protect earlier sowings from cold weather; later sowings can be made without shelter. Water before sowing if the soil is dry. Level, firm, and rake the seedbed to a fine tilth before sowing seed thinly, ³/₄ in. deep in rows

8 in. apart, thinning seedlings to 3–4 in. apart when they are large enough to handle. Transplant into their final position when they are about 4–6 in. tall.

Gradually harden off those grown under cover before planting them in their final positions.

Growing

Dig in plenty of well-rotted manure or compost several months before planting, particularly on light, poor, or heavy soils. The ground should not be freshly manured, as excessive nitrogen causes sprouts to "blow."

Plant earlier, smaller varieties about 2 ft. apart each way, those of moderate size 2¹/₂ ft. apart and taller varieties 3 ft. apart. Wider spacing encourages larger sprouts, improves air circulation, and reduces fungal problems, while closer spacing means smaller, compact "buttons" that will mature at the same time.

Plant with the lowest leaves just above the soil surface. Tug a leaf—if the whole plant moves it has not been planted firmly enough. On light soils,

make a drill 3–4 in. deep, plant sprouts in the bottom, and refill it with soil. The extra support makes the plants more stable. Water immediately after transplanting for 3–4 weeks until plants have become established and, if available, mulch with straw to a depth of 2–3 in.

Keep the beds weed-free. Watering is not normally needed once plants are established except during drought, when each plant can be given up to 2 cups of water per day to maintain the constant growth necessary for good cropping. Remove any diseased or yellowing leaves as they appear. Earthing up around the stem base to a depth of 3–5 in. provides extra support against winter winds, although tall varieties will usually need staking. In exposed gardens, even dwarf varieties need staking.

"Stopping" by removing the growing point is only beneficial for fall-maturing F_1 cultivars being grown for freezing. Plants can be stopped when lowest sprouts reach ¹/₂ in. diameter, to encourage

Brussels sprouts in the snow, proving their hardiness.

'Falstaff'—what would Shakespeare have thought?

even development of sprouts on the stem. When left unstopped, sprouts can be picked over a longer period.

Grow sprouts on a 3- or 4-year rotation, preferably following peas and beans (where they benefit from the nitrogen left in the soil). In late summer, feeding with a liquid high-potash fertilizer gives plants a useful boost. Plant small lettuces like 'Little Gem' between sprouts for summer and fall cropping, and winter purslane or land cress for early winter crops.

Dig plants immediately after harvesting, put leaves on the compost pile, and shred the stems.

Maintenance
Spring Sow outdoors in seedbeds, thin, and keep weed-free.
Summer Transplant outdoors and water during drought.
Fall Harvest early varieties; stake tall varieties if needed.
Winter Sow early varieties indoors. Harvest later crops.

Protected Cropping
Earlier sowings made outdoors in a seedbed should be protected with cloches or frost fabric. Continued protection

with row covers provides a physical barrier against pests such as cabbage root fly, flea beetle, aphids, and birds.

Harvesting and Storing
Pick sprouts when those at the base are walnut-sized and tightly closed. Snap them off with a sharp downward tug or cut with a knife, removing "blown" sprouts and any yellow, diseased leaves. When harvest is over, the tops can be cooked as cabbage. During severe winter weather, dig a few plants to hang in a shed where they can be easily harvested. They will last for several weeks.

PESTS AND DISEASES

Sprouts are very robust yet subject to the usual brassica problems.

Downy mildew shows as yellow patches on the leaves, with patches of fluffy mold on the underside in humid conditions. Remove all affected leaves or spray with fungicide. If downy mildew appears on seedlings, improve ventilation and increase spacing.

Powdery mildew is a white powdery deposit over shoots, stems, and leaves. In severe cases, plants become yellow and die. It is more of a problem when plants are dry at the roots. Water and mulch, remove diseased leaves, and spray with fungicide.

Clubroot, affecting members of the family Brassicaceae, is a disease to be avoided at all costs. Roots swell and distort, young plants wilt on hot days but recover overnight, growth is stunted and crops ruined. It is more of a problem on poorly drained, acid soils. Spores remain in the soil for up to 20 years. Never buy

brassicas from unknown sources: grow them yourself. Repotting plants into 4–6 in. pots allows the roots to become established before they are planted out, which lessens the effects of clubroot. Improve drainage; lime acid soils to create a neutral pH. Earthing up often encourages new roots to form and reduces the effects. Remove all diseased plants, with the whole root system if possible, and destroy them.

Ringspot is worse in cool wet seasons and on well-manured land. It is most evident on older leaves as round brown spots with dark centers. Remove and burn any affected plants and rotate crops.

COMPANION PLANTING

When planted among maturing onions, sprouts benefit from their root residues and the firm soil.

CULINARY

Steam or boil sprouts briskly for the minimum time required to cook through—they should not turn mushy. Small sprouts can be shredded in salads—'Rubine' and 'Falstaff' are particularly attractive.

They can be stored for up to 3 days in a plastic bag in the refrigerator. Freeze sprouts only if they are small. Blanch for 3 minutes, cool, and drain before drying and packing them into plastic bags.

Stir-fried Sprouts
Serves 4
This can look quite spectacular made with a red variety such as 'Falstaff' or 'Rubine.'

2 tablespoons vegetable oil
2 tablespoons soy sauce
1 lb. Brussels sprouts, prepared and finely sliced
2 tablespoons hazelnuts, roughly ground
Salt and freshly ground black pepper

Heat the oil in a wok, stir in the soy sauce, and, over a high heat, cook the sprouts for 2–3 minutes. Sprinkle with the hazelnuts. Season and serve.

Stir-fried Sprouts

Brassica napus Napobrassica Group. *Brassicaceae*

RUTABAGA

Also known as Swede, Swedish Turnip. Biennial grown as annual for swollen root and young leaves. Hardy.
Value: small amounts of niacin (vitamin B) and vitamin C, low in calories and carbohydrate.

Rutabaga is one of the hardiest of all root crops and is the perfect winter vegetable for cool temperate zones. Its alternative name, "Swedish turnip," indicates its origins. Eaten in France and southern Europe in the sixteenth century, it came to Britain from Holland in 1755 and rapidly became popular as the "turnip-rooted cabbage." Along with the turnip, it was first used as winter fodder for sheep and cattle, improving milk production during a traditionally lean period. During times of famine, rutabaga was eaten by country folk and still has the reputation among many as "peasant food."

To despise it is your loss; it is robust, undemanding, and one of the easiest vegetables to grow. New varieties are disease-resistant, tasty, and a wonderful accompaniment to sprouts as a winter vegetable—particularly when mashed with butter, cream, and spices.

CULTIVATION

Propagation

Rutabaga needs a long growing season and should be sown from early spring in cooler zones to early summer where temperatures are warmer and germination and growth are rapid. Sow in drills ¾ in. deep and 16–18 in. apart, thinning seedlings to 9–12 in. Thin when they are no more than 1 in. high, when the first true leaves appear, to ensure that the roots develop properly. Firm the soil after thinning. **Zones 3–7.**

Growing

Rutabaga prefers a sheltered and open site in fertile, well-drained, but moisture-retentive soil. Good drainage is essential. Summer sowings can be made in moderate shade, provided they receive sufficient moisture. Rutabaga prefers a pH of 5.5–7.0, so very acid soil will need liming. If the ground has not been manured for the previous crop, double dig in the fall, incorporate plenty of well-rotted organic matter and allow the soil to "weather" over winter. About a week prior to sowing, remove any weeds or debris and rake general fertilizer into the soil at 2 oz. per square yard. In common with other brassicas, rutabaga grow poorly on loose soil, so rake the soil to a fine tilth and firm it with the head of a rake or by carefully treading. If the soil is dry, water thoroughly before sowing and stand on a planting board to avoid compacting the soil. Mark each row with stakes, and label and date the crop.

VARIETIES

'**Acme**' has round roots with pale purple skin. Its tops are prone to powdery mildew. '**Marian**' is purple with yellow flesh, very tasty and quick-growing. It produces large roots and has good resistance to clubroot and powdery mildew. '**American Purple Top,**' a classic old variety, is still one of the best. Early to mature, the roots are yellow, fine-textured, and very sweet. '**Joan**' is a recent introduction that offers sweeter flesh than most yellow varieties. '**Gilfeather,**' grown for over 100 years in New England, is a large, white, top-shaped rutabaga with mild sweet flesh.

Correct spacing between plants is vital for vigorous growth.

Keep crops weed-free by hand weeding and careful hoeing. Rutabaga need a constant supply of water throughout the growing season, otherwise they tend to run to seed or produce small, woody roots. Sudden watering or rain after a period of drought causes the roots to split, so they will need up to 2 gallons per square yard per week in dry periods. This improves the size and quality but usually reduces the flavor.

Rotate rutabaga with other brassicas.

Rutabaga greens can be blanched for eating raw as a winter salad vegetable. Dig a few roots in early to midwinter, cut back the leaves and plant the roots under the greenhouse benches, or stand them upright in boxes or wooden trays filled with peat substitute, humus-rich garden soil or with a thick layer of straw. Cover with overturned boxes or black plastic to exclude the light and put them in a cellar, garage, or shed. After 3–4 weeks shoots will appear and can be cut when they are 4–5 in. long.

Maintenance

Spring Warm soil under cloches for early sowings.
Summer Water crops and keep weed-free.
Fall Harvest early varieties.
Winter Dig and store crops before severe weather starts.

Protected Cropping

Cover ground with cloches, crop covers, or black plastic for 2–3 weeks in late winter to early spring to warm the ground before sowing early crops. Seedlings should be protected until they are well established.

Harvesting and Storing

Harvest begins any time from early to midfall. Rutabaga are extremely hardy and can be left in the ground until needed, although it is advisable not to leave them for too long or they will become woody. Dig when they are about the

size of a grapefruit. They can be stored in boxes in a garage or cool shed. Twist off the leaves and place roots between layers of peat substitute, sawdust, or sand in a stout box.

Smaller rutabaga are more tasty and succulent, so begin digging as soon as the roots are large enough to use, before they reach their maximum size.

Pests and Diseases

Rutabaga are affected by the same problems as turnips.

Powdery mildew is common. It appears as a white powdery deposit over shoots, stems and leaves, causing stunted growth. In severe cases leaves become yellow and die. It is more of a problem when plants are dry at the roots and if it is cold at night and warm and dry in the day.

Rutabaga are susceptible to **clubroot**—a disease to be avoided at all costs. Roots swell and distort, young plants wilt on hot days but recover overnight, growth is stunted and crops ruined. It is more of a problem on poorly drained, acid soils. Spores remain in the soil for up to 20 years.

Flea beetles are ⅛ in. long and black with yellow stripes. They nibble leaves of seedlings, checking growth.

'Acme,' showing its subtle color and extensive taproots.

COMPANION PLANTING

They grow well with peas.

MEDICINAL

Rutabagas have been used in folk medicine for the treatment of coughs, kidney stones, and whooping cough, although their efficacy has not been recorded.

CULINARY

Rutabaga can be sliced or cubed and roasted like parsnips, or added to casseroles and stews.

Otherwise, they are delicious mashed with potatoes and served with meat or fish.

To boil, peel off the outer "skin," cut into slices or cubes, and boil for 30 minutes. Drain thoroughly before serving.

Neeps, Tatties, and Haggis

Neeps
Serves 4

This is the traditional accompaniment for haggis and tatties (mashed potatoes), washed down with plenty of whisky, on Burns Night in Scotland.

1½ lb. rutabaga
Salt and black pepper
Pinch nutmeg
Butter or olive oil

Clean the rutabaga, cut them up, and boil in enough water to prevent them from burning until tender. Process in a blender or put through a sieve, discarding the juices. Season, and reheat with either butter or olive oil.

Brassica rapa Rapifera Group. *Brassicaceae*

TURNIP

Biennial grown as an annual for globular, swollen root and young leaves. Hardy.
Value: low in calories and carbohydrate; small amounts of vitamins and minerals.

This ancient root crop was known to Theophrastus in 400 B.C. and many early varieties were given Greek place names. Pliny listed twelve distinct types under *rapa* and *napus*—which became *naep* in Anglo-Saxon, and together with the word *turn* (meaning "made round"), gave us the common name. Introduced to Canada in 1541, the turnip was brought to Virginia by the colonists in 1609 and was rapidly adopted by the native Americans. In Britain they have found a role in folklore. In Northern Ireland, turnips were made into lamps for Halloween (October 31), and in the Shetland Islands of Scotland slices were shaped into letters and put into a tub of water for young revelers to retrieve with their mouths; they usually tried to pick the initial of someone they loved.

VARIETIES

Turnips are simple to grow and tasty. The leaves (turnip greens) are also delicious.

Earlies
'Purple Top Milan' produces flattish roots with purple markings and white flesh. Tender when young, early maturing, and good for overwintering, it has an excellent flavor. **'Purple Top White Globe'** (**'Veitch's Red Globe'**) is an attractive old cultivar with round or slightly flattened roots. It is reddish-purple above ground and white below. **'Snowball'** is a delicately flavored, fast-maturing white

variety with cut leaves. **'Tokyo Cross'** is an excellent F$_1$ hybrid that produces small tasty white globes and matures rapidly, in about 35–40 days. A "mini vegetable" that is also tasty when larger, it is suitable as a late summer to early fall crop.

'Purple Top Milan'

'Tokyo Cross' is reliable and has an unusual flavor.

Main-crops
'Golden Ball' (**'Golden Perfection'** or **'Orange Jelly'**) is a small, round yellow variety that should be grown quickly to keep the flesh succulent. Tasty, hardy, and excellent for storing. **'Hakurei'** is a new white "salad" turnip offering a sweet taste even when raw. **'Gilfeather'** is a well-respected heirloom variety with white, sweet flesh.

CULTIVATION

Turnips flourish at about 68°F and prefer a sheltered, open site in light, fertile, well-drained, but moisture-retentive soil. Summer sowings can be made in moderate shade provided they receive sufficient moisture. Turnips prefer a pH of 5.5–7.0; very acid soil will need liming. **Zones 3–9.**

Propagation
Sow early turnips in midspring, as soon as the ground is workable, or in late winter or early spring under cloches or row covers.
  Prepare the seedbed carefully and sow early turnips thinly in drills about ³⁄₄–1 in. deep, in rows 9 in. apart. Then thin to a final spacing of 4–5 in. They can also be grown in a grid pattern: mark 5-in. squares in the ground with a stick and sow 3 seeds where the hills cross, thinning after germination to leave the strongest seedling.
  Sow main-crop varieties from mid- to late summer in drills ³⁄₄ in. deep and 12 in. apart, thinning to 6–9 in. apart. It is important to thin seedlings when no more than ³⁄₄ in. high, when the first true leaves appear, to ensure the roots develop properly. Firm the soil after thinning; do not thin turnips grown for greens.
  When growing for their greens, prepare the seedbed and broadcast seed over a small area or sow thinly in rows 4–6 in. apart as soon as soil conditions allow. Sow early cultivars in spring for summer cropping and hardy varieties in late summer or early fall. Small seedlings of main crops overwinter and grow rapidly in spring, making them a useful early crop, particularly when covered with cloches or row covers. To ensure a

'Snowball,' a popular variety.

prolonged harvest, make successional sowings of "earlies" from early spring until early summer.

Growing

If the ground has not been manured for the previous crop, double dig in fall, working plenty of well-rotted organic matter into the soil and allowing it to weather over winter. About a week to 10 days before sowing, remove any weeds or debris and rake general fertilizer into the soil at 2 oz. per square yard. In common with other brassicas, turnips grow poorly on loose soil, so rake the soil to a fine tilth and firm it with the head of a rake or by carefully treading. If the soil is dry, water thoroughly before sowing and stand on a planting board to avoid compacting the soil. Mark each row with stakes, and label and date the crop.

Keep crops weed-free by hand weeding or careful hoeing. Turnips must have a constant supply of water throughout the growing season, otherwise they tend to run to seed or produce small woody roots, while sudden watering or rain after a period of drought causes them to split. They will need up to 2 gallons per square yard per week during dry periods. This improves the size and quality of the crop, but usually reduces the flavor.

Turnips should be rotated with other brassicas.

Maintenance

Spring Prepare seedbed, sow early varieties under cloches. *Summer* Sow earlies every 2–3 weeks for successional cropping. Keep crops weed-free and water as necessary. From mid- to late summer, sow main-crop varieties. *Fall* Sow "earlies" under cloches mid- to late fall. Thin main-crop varieties. *Winter* Harvest and store main-crop turnips.

Protected Cropping

Cover ground with cloches, row covers, or black plastic for 2–3 weeks in late winter to early spring to warm the ground before sowing early crops. In late summer protect sowings of early cultivars. Main-crop turnips grown for their greens can be grown under cloches after sowing in fall and picked during winter.

Container Growing

Fast-maturing early varieties grow well in large containers of well-drained, soil-based potting mix with added organic matter. Water crops well.

Harvesting and Storing

Harvest early varieties when young and tender. Gather those to be eaten raw when they are the size of a golf ball; any time up to tennis ball–size if they are to be cooked. Hand pull them in the same way as radishes.

Main-crop turnips that are dug in midfall for winter use are much larger, hardier, and slower to mature. To keep the flavor, harvest at maturity as they soon become woody and unpalatable. Turnips can be left in the soil and dug as required using a garden fork. Keep them in a cool place and use within a few days. In cold, wet zones, roots are better harvested to prevent deterioration. Twist off the leaves, remove any soil, put the roots between layers of dry peat-lite mix, sawdust, or sand in a box, then store in a cool shed.

Turnips grown for their greens can be harvested when about 4–6 in. high, cutting about 1 in. above ground level. Keep soil moist and they will resprout several times before finally running to seed.

Pests and Diseases

Flea beetle, $\frac{1}{8}$ in. long and black with yellow stripes, nibbles holes in leaves of seedlings, checking growth. Large infestations of **mealy aphid** may kill young plants or cause black "sooty mold" on leaves. **Cabbage root fly larvae** feed on roots; transplanted brassicas are particularly vulnerable. **Powdery mildew,** a white deposit over shoots, stems and leaves, causes stunted growth. In severe cases leaves yellow and die.

COMPANION PLANTING

Growing with peas deters aphids. Turnips are useful for intercropping between taller crops and for catch-cropping.

MEDICINAL

The liquor from turnips sprinkled with brown sugar was used in folk medicine to cure colds.

Glazed Turnips

CULINARY

Eat early turnips raw in salads or boiled, tossed in butter and chopped parsley.

Peel main-crop turnips before cooking. They are good mashed, roasted, and in casseroles and soups.

Glazed Turnips
Use small young turnips. Scrub them and cut into $\frac{1}{2}$ in. dice (or use whole). Drop into boiling water for 3 minutes. Drain. Melt a little butter and olive oil in a sauté pan, add the turnips, sprinkled with a little sugar, and fry over a high heat, stirring constantly, until browned and caramelized. This is particularly delicious with the 'Snowball' variety.

Turnip Greens
Wash well, removing stringy stalks. Chop roughly into manageable pieces. Steam over boiling water until just tender. Serve warm, tossed in olive oil and lemon juice vinaigrette, sprinkled with a finely chopped garlic clove. Or cook like spinach: put the washed leaves in a pan, add salt, pepper, and a small pat of butter, and steam for 10 minutes in only the water remaining on the leaves. Drain thoroughly and serve immediately.

Brassica oleracea Acephela Group. *Brassicaceae*

KALE

Also known as Collards, Borecole, Colewort, Sprouts. Biennial grown as annual for young leaves and shoots. Hardy. Value: good source of calcium, iron, beta carotene, vitamins E and C.

Kales are exceptionally robust, making an ideal winter crop. In addition, they are untroubled by common brassica problems. A type of primitive cabbage, kales are among the earliest cultivated brassicas (the Romans grew several types), with many similarities to the wild *Brassica oleracea* on the western coasts of Europe. The Celtic "kale" derives from "coles" or "caulis" used by the Greeks and Romans to describe brassicas; the German *Kohl* has the same origin. First recorded in North America by 1669, kales are thought to have been introduced much earlier.

VARIETIES

Varieties are classified into groups, including the true kale, Siberian kale, and "collards." These are popular in the southern states and other warm climates.

Kales vary in height from dwarf types, about 12–16 in. high, to tall varieties growing to 3 ft. and spreading to 24 in. The novelty **'Jersey Kale'** ("Walking Stick Cabbage") is grown for its straight stems to 7 ft., which can be dried and made into walking sticks.

'Siberian Kale,' 'Rape Kale' or 'Curled Kitchen Kale' (Brassica nalpus *Pabularia Group*) This is a relative of the rutabaga, grown for the leaves, not the roots. It is variable in form and color, with broader leaves than kale, which are sometimes curled or frilled. This must be sown in situ, not transplanted, cropping when true kales have finished. **'Hungry Gap'** is a late variety, cropping mid- to late spring. **'Laciniato,'** an Italian variety, has deeply cut flat leaves. **'Ragged Jack'** has pink-tinged leaves and midribs. **'Red Russian'** has green-red frilly leaves; excellent flavor. **'True Siberian'** is fast-growing, with blue-green frilly leaves. Can harvest continually throughout winter.

Kale (Scotch Kale, Curly-leaved Kale, or Borecole)
True kale usually has dark green or glaucous leaves with heavily frilled margins. **'Darkibor'** is exceptionally hardy with dark green curled leaves. **'Dwarf Blue Curled Scotch' ('Dwarf Blue Curled Vates')** is low-growing, with glaucous leaves, extremely hardy, and slow to bolt. **'Dwarf Green Curled'** is compact, hardy, and easy to grow; ideal for the small garden or windswept sites. **'Pentland Brig,'** a cross between curly and plain-leaved kale, is grown for the young leaves, sideshoots, and immature flower heads (which are cooked like broccoli). An excellent vegetable. **'Tall Green Curled' ('Tall Scotch Curled')** is excellent for freezing and shows good resistance to clubroot and cabbage root fly. **'Thousand Head'** is a plain-leaved, tall, old variety and exceptionally

The stout stem of curly-leaved kale, topped by its leaves, makes it look like a miniature tree.

'Ragged Jack' is appropriately named, its leaves an interesting contrast to curly-leaved kale.

hardy. For harvesting through winter and spring.

Collards (or Greens)
These have smooth, thinner leaves than true kale, taste milder, and are more heat-tolerant. **'Champion'** has dark green, cabbagelike leaves, and is hardy, with good resistance to bolting. **'Georgia'** has glaucous, white-veined leaves; it tolerates poor soil and extreme heat. **'Redbor'** offers not only a rich and sweet flavor, but is a great ornamental in the garden, as it displays large, deep purple-red leaves. It is high in nutrition too. **'Winterbor'** is similar to **'Redbor'** in a greenish-blue shade. Its flavor sweetens in cold weather. **'Toscano'** is a fast-maturing small kale of the dinosaur type with extra-dark savoyed leaves.

CULTIVATION

Propagation
Sow in early spring in trays of moist seed potting mix or packs, or outdoors in seedbeds in milder areas, for summer crops. Sow from late spring for fall and winter crops. Alternatively, sow thinly in drills ½ in. deep in situ, gradually thinning to final spacing, or

sow 3 seeds in hills at the final spacing, thinning to leave the strongest seedling. When 4–6 in. high, water the rows the day before, then transplant in the early evening, keeping the lowest leaves just above the soil surface. Water well with liquid seaweed after planting and until they become established. The final spacing for dwarf varieties should be 18 in. apart, with taller types 24–30 in. apart.

Collards are sown in late spring in areas with cool summers and in late summer in hotter zones.

Sow Siberian kale thinly in early summer, in situ, in drills 18 in. apart, thinning when large enough to handle to a final spacing of 18 in. apart. **Zones 3–9.**

Growing

Kales are very hardy: some survive temperatures down to 5°F; others tolerate high summer temperatures. They grow in poorer soils than most brassicas, but flourish in a sunny position on well-drained soil with moderate nitrogen levels. Excessive nitrogen encourages soft growth, making plants prone to damage. Lime acid soils.

Prepare the seedbed when the soil is moist. Lightly fork the surface, remove any weeds, then firm (but do not compact) the soil.

Overwintering crops need top-dressing with high-nitrogen liquid or granular fertilizer at 2 oz. per square yard in spring to encourage sideshoots.

Keep crops weed-free, water thoroughly before the onset of dry weather, mulch with a 2 in. layer of organic matter, and in fall, firm or hill up around the base of taller plants to prevent wind rock. On more exposed sites, they may need staking.

Kales are good where peas, early potatoes, or very early crops have been grown. Rotate with brassicas.

'Tall Green Curled'

Maintenance

Spring Sow early crops under cover; in midspring sow in trays or packs, or outdoors in a seedbed. *Summer* Transplant seedlings, feed and water well during dry spells. Keep weed-free. Harvest regularly. *Fall* Firm around plant bases; stake if necessary. *Winter* Harvest regularly.

Protected Cropping

Make early sowings as a cut-and-come-again crop in the greenhouse border or in mild areas outdoors under cloches, from mid- to late winter. Sow in drills the width of a hoe, broadcast thinly, or sow sparingly in drills, thinning to 3 in. apart.

Sow kale under cover in mid- to late winter for transplanting from midspring onward when soil conditions are suitable.

Harvesting and Storing

Harvest by removing young leaves with a knife when they are 4–5 in. long. Cut from several plants for an adequate picking.

Harvest regularly for constant young growth and a long cropping season; older shoots become bitter and tough. Harvest early sowings of cut-and-come-again crops when about 2–3 in. high, or thin to 4 in. and harvest when 5–6 in. high.

Pests and Diseases

Kale is resistant to cabbage root fly and clubroot, and is usually ignored by pigeons. Take necessary precautions against **whitefly, cabbage caterpillar,** and **flea beetle.** Caterpillars eat irregular holes in the leaves: check regularly for eggs, squashing them. Beware of infestations of **cabbage aphids,** which check growth and may kill young plants.

COMPANION PLANTING

Kale can be planted with corn and peas.

CULINARY

Young leaves of later varieties taste better after being frosted.

Wash well and boil in 1 in. of water for 8 minutes at most. Serve with butter or white sauce—an excellent accompaniment for poached eggs, fried fish, bacon, and other fatty meats. Kale is also good with plain fish dishes such as salmon or cod. In parts of North America kale is served with hog jowls, and the juice is eaten with hot corn bread.

Kale can also be used in salads, soups, and stews; it can be creamed or braised with onions, parsley, spices, and bacon or ham.

Before freezing, blanch young shoots for 1 minute, then cool, drain, and chop. Stays fresh for 3 days in the refrigerator in a plastic bag.

Stir-fried Kale
Serves 4

1½ lb. young kale
3 tablespoons peanut or olive oil
Salt and freshly ground black pepper
Juice of half a lemon

Thoroughly wash and dry the kale in a salad spinner. Chop it roughly. Pour the oil in a wok or heavy sauté pan over a high heat and, when the oil is steaming, toss in the kale and cook for 3 minutes, stirring constantly. Season and add the lemon juice, adding shavings of lemon peel for decoration if you wish. Serve piping hot with stews or roasted meats.

Stir-fried Kale

Brassica oleracea Botrytis Group. *Brassicaceae*

CAULIFLOWER

Annual or perennial grown for immature flower heads. Hardy or half hardy.
Value: good source of vitamin C, traces of most other vitamins.

Cauliflowers are believed to have originated in Cyprus and the oldest record dates from the sixth century B.C. One thousand years later they were still widely grown there, being known in England as "Cyprus coleworts." A Jewish-Italian traveler wrote from Cyprus in 1593 that cabbages and cauliflowers were to be found growing in profusion, and, "For a quattrino one can get more almost than one can carry." Gerard in his *Herball* of 1597 calls them "Cole flowery." Moorish scholars in twelfth-century Spain described three varieties as introductions from Syria, where cauliflowers had been grown for over a thousand years and were much developed by the Arabs. Even in 1699, John Evelyn suggested that the best seed came from Aleppo (now Halab, in northern Syria). Cultivation methods improved after 1700, and by the end of the eighteenth century the cauliflower was highly regarded throughout Europe. Dr. Johnson is said to have remarked, "Of all the flowers in the garden, I like the cauliflower." But Mark Twain wrote disdainfully, "Cauliflower is nothing but cabbage with a college education." This, of course, is a matter of opinion.

A robust variety for fall harvest

VARIETIES

There are four main groups for spring, summer, fall, and winter, but many overlap the seasons.

'All the Year Round' is sown in late fall or spring for spring or summer harvest. Produces good-quality white heads. Excellent for successional sowing. **'Alverda'** has yellow-green heads. Sow late spring to midsummer for fall cropping. **'Autumn Giant 3'** has beautiful white, firm heads. Excellent for late fall and winter cropping. **'Early Snowball'** is dwarf and compact, growing well in mild zones. Heads do not discolor in bad weather. **'Minaret'** has small, tasty, lime-green florets. Crops in late fall. **'Purple Cape'** is a hardy overwintering purple type cropping from late winter to midspring. Good raw or cooked; the head turns green when cooked. **'Snowball Self Blanching'** is high yielding, and the leaves naturally blanch the curds. **'Snowcap'** is a very late variety, for harvest in mid- to late winter. **'Snow Crown'** is an old favorite that produces large creamy white heads, and is more tolerant of bad weather. **'Veitch's Autumn Giant'** is a huge plant with large leaves and massive heads to 12 in. in diameter. Very tasty; stores well. **'Violet Queen'** needs no blanching to produce small heads of intriguing purple (that turn pale green when cooked). This broccoli relative may be planted as close as one foot apart in the garden. **'Walcheren Winter 3—Armardo April'** is an overwintering variety. Hardy, frost-resistant and tasty. **'Walcheren Winter 4—Markanta'** is one of the hardiest of all overwintering varieties, with pure white heads. **'White Rock'** produces plenty of leaves to protect the head. It is a very versatile variety.

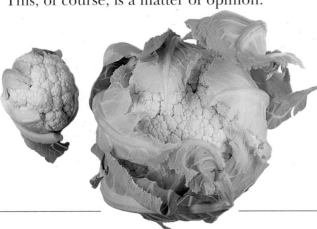

CULTIVATION

Propagation

Start off crops as described in "Protected Cropping" (see page 54). Plants are ready for transplanting when they have 5–6 leaves; water before moving and retain as much soil as possible around the roots.

Sow successively to ensure regular cropping all year round.

In mild areas, sow early summer crops in midfall and leave them to overwinter under cover. Harden off in late winter, transplant from midspring as soon as the soil is workable and warm. Space plants 20 in. apart with 24 in. between the rows or with 20 in. between the rows and plants. Protect with crop covers until established.

Sow summer cauliflowers in early spring under cover or in a seedbed outdoors if the soil is warm and workable, for transplanting in midspring and harvesting from midsummer to fall. Spacing as above.

Sow early fall cauliflowers in midspring for transplanting in early summer and harvesting from late summer to early fall. Space 21 in. apart in and between rows, or 20 in. between plants and 24 in. between rows.

Sow fall cauliflowers in late spring for transplanting in midsummer and harvesting from mid- to late fall. Space plants 24 in. apart in and between rows.

If you have available space, sow overwintering cauliflowers, but remember that they can be in the ground for almost a year. Sow in seedbeds outdoors and transplant in midsummer. Winter cauliflowers for harvesting from midwinter to early spring should be 26 in. apart each way; those for cutting from midspring to early summer should be spaced 24 in. apart in and

Commercially grown cauliflowers harvested from Britain's Fenlands.

between the rows. Most varieties need frost protection to avoid damage to the heads. **Zones 3–9.**

Growing

Cauliflowers need a sheltered sunny site on deep, moisture-retentive, free-draining soil with a pH of 6.5–7.5. Dig in plenty of well-rotted organic matter in fall before planting and lime acid soils where necessary.

Avoid planting over-wintering types in frost pockets. Rake over the area before planting: the ground should be firm, but not compacted.

Keep plants well watered from germination to harvest, as checks in growth spoil the quality of the heads. They need at least 4 gallons per square yard every 2 weeks.

Cauliflowers also need moderate nitrogen levels, although excessive amounts encourage soft leafy growth. Overwintering cauliflowers require low nitrogen levels, or they will be too soft to survive colder weather.

Keep crops weed-free with regular hoeing or mulching. Bend a few leaves over the heads of summer varieties to protect them from sunshine; do the same with winter crops to protect plants from frost and snow. Leaves can be easily tied in place with garden twine.

If the weather is hot and dry, mist plants every now and then to maintain humidity and cool temperatures. Unwrap heads occasionally to check for hiding pests. After cutting the head, feed with a general liquid fertilizer or scatter a granular general fertilizer at $\frac{1}{2}$ oz. per square yard to encourage the sideshoots to grow.

Rotate crops.

The dark florets of 'Purple Cape' do not affect the taste.

A mass of leaves hug the developing curds.

Ventilate on warm days, then harden off and transplant as required.

Harvesting and Storing

Harvest cauliflowers successively while they are small, rather than waiting until they all mature. If the heads become brown or if florets start to separate, it is too late: they should be cut. Harvest in the morning, except in frosty conditions when you should wait until midday.

Cauliflowers can be stored for up to 3 weeks by digging whole plants, shaking the soil off the roots, and hanging them upside down in a cool shed; mist the heads occasionally to maintain freshness.

Freeze tight heads only. To prepare, divide into sprigs, blanch for 3 minutes in water with a squeeze of lemon juice. Cool, drain, pack carefully, and freeze in plastic bags.

Cauliflowers will store, wrapped, in the crisper in the refrigerator for up to one week.

PESTS AND DISEASES

Beware of **clubroot**, **cabbage root fly**, **caterpillars,** and **birds**.

COMPANION PLANTING

Plant with rosemary, thyme, sage, onions, garlic, beets, and chards.

MEDICINAL

This is another vegetable reputedly good for reducing the risk of cancer, especially of the colon and stomach.

Maintenance

Spring Sow early crops under glass and outdoors in seedbeds. Keep well watered and weed-free. Transplant.
Summer Sow indoors or outdoors in seedbeds. Transplant, harvest.
Fall In mild areas, sow overwintering crops. Harvest.
Winter Prepare ground for the following year. Harvest.

Protected Cropping

Sow under a cold frame or under cloches and thin after germination to about 2 in., or sow 2–3 seeds in hills at the required spacing and thin to leave the strongest seedling. Grow on in the seedbed or transplant into small pots or packs. Alternatively, sow directly in small pots or packs and germinate in a propagator or an unheated greenhouse according to the time of year. Repot when they are large enough to handle.

'All Year Round,' a popular commercial variety

CULINARY

Separate into florets, boil or steam, and serve with cheese or white sauce and grated nutmeg or flaked almonds. Alternatively, dip in batter, fry, and eat as fritters.

Sprigs can be served raw with mayonnaise and other dips, or added to soups, soufflés, and pickles.

Cauliflower with Chilies and Black Mustard Seeds
Serves 4

In Indian cuisine, cauliflower can be cooked into curries, but it is more often served dry, as in this recipe from southern India, given to me by the chef at Madras' Chola Hotel. For this dish, buy the washed or white dahl.

5 tablespoons vegetable oil
½ teaspoon asafetida
1 teaspoon whole black mustard seeds
1 teaspoon urad dhal (lentils)
2 dried hot red chilies, whole
6 fresh hot green chilies, whole
1½ lb. cauliflower, broken into bite-sized florets
Salt
2 tablespoons fresh coconut, shredded

Either use a *karhari* or a heavy sauté pan. Heat the oil over high heat and add the asafetida, then the mustard seeds. When the seeds pop, add the dhal; this will turn red, at which point add the chilies and cook until the red ones start to darken. Then stir in the cauliflower and cook for a minute or so. Add a tablespoon of water, season with salt, and keep stirring, adding more water as necessary; you will probably need to cook for 4–5 minutes, using 4–5 tablespoons water. At this point, turn the heat down and cook, covered, for an additional 5 minutes, until all the liquid has evaporated. Take care not to let the cauliflower burn.

Stir in the coconut and serve, discarding the chilies unless you like really hot food.

Cauliflower with Chilies and Black Mustard Seeds

Cauliflower Soufflé
Serves 4

1 lb. cauliflower florets
1 tablespoon butter
1 tablespoon all-purpose flour
½ cup milk
3 large eggs, separated
4 tablespoons cheddar, shredded
Pinch of nutmeg
Salt and freshly ground pepper

Steam or boil the cauliflower in salted water until just tender. Drain and dice finely. Keep warm. In a heavy saucepan, make a roux from the butter and flour and cook for 1 minute. Stir in the milk and bring to a boil, stirring constantly, to thicken the sauce. Then remove from the heat and stir in the egg yolks. Beat well and add the cheddar and cauliflower, seasoning well. Whisk the egg whites until stiff, then, using a metal spoon, fold into the cauliflower mixture.

Pour into a buttered soufflé dish and cook on the middle shelf of a preheated oven at 375°F, until the top is gloriously browned.

This should take about 30–35 minutes. Serve the soufflé immediately.

Brassica oleracea Capitata Group. *Brassicaceae.*

CABBAGE

Biennial grown as annual for leaves and hearts. Half hardy/hardy. Value: rich in beta carotene and vitamin C—especially green varieties and outer leaves; outer leaves contain vitamin E.

The overwintering cabbage 'January King' will survive even the harshest winters.

The Latin *Brassica* comes from *bresic*, the Celtic word for cabbage, a plant cultivated for centuries in the eastern Mediterranean and Asia Minor. The Romans believed that cabbages rose from Jupiter's sweat as he labored to explain two contradicting oracles—esteeming wild and cultivated cabbages as a cure-all as well as recommending them to prevent unseemly drunkenness.

Many varieties have been developed over the centuries. Heat-tolerant types were bred in southern Europe, while many hard-headed varieties were introduced by the Celts and Scandinavians. White cabbages appeared after A.D. 814 and German literature records the cultivation of red cabbages in 1150; in the sixteenth century Estienne and Liébault believed these were made by watering cabbages with red wine or by growing them in hot places. By the thirteenth century "headed cabbage" was well known, and three kinds of "Savoy" were mentioned in a German herbal of 1543.

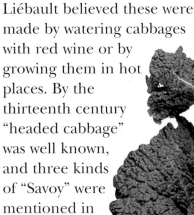

VARIETIES

Cabbages are usually grouped according to the season when they are harvested. They range from fairly loose-leaved heads of pointed or conical shape to rounded "ball" shapes with varying degrees of densely packed leaves.

Spring
Spring cabbages traditionally have pointed heads, but there are now round-headed types. For "spring greens," use their immature leaves or choose a leafy variety bred for this purpose. **'Offenham 1 Myatts Offenham Compacta'** is a tasty, very early spring cabbage and has dark green leaves. **'Pixie'** is another very early spring cabbage, with compact, tight hearts. It is ideal for small gardens.

Early summer/summer
Varieties that harvest in early summer usually have pointed heads. **'Derby Day'** is an excellent "ball-head" cabbage for harvesting from early summer. **'Hispi'** is reliable, with pointed heads of good quality and taste. Maturing rapidly, it is ideal for close spacing. **'Ruby Ball'** is an ornamental and colorful red cabbage, very reliable and particularly excellent for use in salads.

Late summer/fall
Late summer and fall cabbage varieties generally have round or "ball" heads. **'Golden Acre,'** a ball-headed variety, is compact and sweet-tasting with round gray-green heads. It tolerates close spacing, is high yielding, and grows well on poorer soils. **'Stonehead'** has a tightly packed head and is early-maturing. It is resistant to yellow and black rot. **'Early Jersey Wakefield'** is one the best-tasting cabbages, the heads, small and pointed, mature in only

2 months from planting. The All-America Selections Winner **'Dynamo'** is good in small gardens—or even containers. Its deep bluish-green 4-in. heads are produced on small plants. For big cabbage, **'Tropic Giant'** produces heads up to 1 ft. across and weighing as much as 15 lb.

Winter/winter storage
Winter cabbages are usually ball- or drum-headed. The white-leaved Dutch cabbage (used primarily for coleslaw) matures from mid- to late fall and can be cut for storage or left to stand in mild conditions. The extremely hardy, tasty, and attractive Savoy types with puckered green leaves mature from midfall to late winter. **'January King 3'** is an excellent drumhead Savoy type, extremely hardy and frost-resistant, maturing in midfall to early winter.

CULTIVATION

Propagation
Seeds sown in trays, packs, or seedbeds will be ready for transplanting about 5 weeks after sowing. Spacings can be modified according to the size of "head" required. Closer spacing means a smaller head while wider spacing produces slightly larger heads.

Sow spring cabbage from mid- to late summer; transplant from early to midfall. Space 10–12 in. apart in and between the rows. Protect with cloches or crop covers over winter to encourage earlier cropping. For "spring greens," grow suitable varieties with 10 in. in and between the plants, or space spring cabbage plants 4–6 in. apart and harvest when immature.

Sow cabbages for summer and fall harvest successively, with "earlies" and "lates" for an extended cropping season (see "Varieties"). You should make the first sowings in a propagator or heated glasshouse at 55–60°F from late winter to early spring, repot and transplant in mid- to late spring. Follow these with sowings in cold frames or a seedbed under cloches or crop covers. Make further sowings without protection until late spring.

Transplant from early to midsummer, spacing plants 14–20 in. apart, depending on the size of head you require.

Sow winter-maturing varieties successively from mid- to late spring under cover or outdoors for transplanting from early to midsummer. Space about 18 in. apart. **Zones 3–9.**

Growing
Cabbages flourish at around 59–68°F and should not be transplanted at temperatures above 77°F, while some overwintering varieties survive temperatures down to 14°F.

Cabbages need a rich, fertile, moisture-retentive soil with a pH of 5.5–7.0. Dig in plenty of well-rotted organic matter several weeks before planting and lime the soil if necessary. Rake the soil level before planting and ensure that it is firm but not compacted.

Do not fertilize spring cabbages after planting, as this encourages soft growth and the nutrients are washed away by winter rains. Wait until early to midspring and scatter a general granular fertilizer around the plants, or liquid feed.

Summer, fall, and winter cabbages need a dressing of

A cross section of this red cabbage is bizarrely beautiful.

'Ruby Ball,' a particularly attractive and tasty red cabbage

'Stonehead,' a reliable early variety

fertilizer after transplanting and will benefit from an additional granular or liquid feed in the growing season.

To increase stability, hill up spring and winter cabbages as they grow.

Provided growing conditions are good and plants healthy, you can produce a second harvest from spring or early summer varieties. After cutting the head, cut a cross shape ½ in. deep in the stump, which will sprout a cluster of smaller cabbages.

Keep cabbages moist and weed-free with regular hoeing, hand weeding, or mulching. Rotate cabbages with other brassicas.

Maintenance

Spring Sow and transplant summer, fall, and winter cabbage. Harvest.
Summer Sow spring cabbage. Harvest.
Fall Transplant spring cabbage. Harvest.
Winter Sow summer cabbages in mild regions. Harvest.

Harvesting and Storing

Spring cabbages are ready to harvest from mid- to late spring. Summer and fall varieties are ready to harvest from midsummer to midfall. Winter types can be harvested from late fall to midspring.

Spring and summer varieties are eaten immediately after harvest. Dutch winter white cabbages and some red cabbages can be dug for storing indoors. Choose those that are healthy and undamaged and dig them up before the first frosts for storage in a cool, slightly humid, frost-free place. Remove the loose outer leaves and stand the heads on a slatted shelf or a layer of straw on the shed floor. Alternatively, suspend them in nets.

They can also be stored in a spare cold frame if it is well ventilated to discourage rotting. They should store for up to 5 months.

Spacing between cabbages directly determines the size of "head."

Freeze only the best quality fresh crisp heads. Wash, shred coarsely, blanch for about 1 minute, and pack into plastic bags or rigid plastic containers.

Wrapped in plastic wrap in the refrigerator, cabbages stay fresh for about a week.

PESTS AND DISEASES

Cabbages suffer from the common brassica problems, including **cabbage root fly**, **clubroot**, **aphids,** and **birds**.

COMPANION PLANTING

Cabbages thrive in the company of herbs like dill, mints, rosemary, sage, thyme, and chamomile. They also grow well with many other vegetables including onions, garlic, peas, celery, potatoes, fava beans, and beets.

Like all brassicas, they benefit from the nitrogen left in the soil after legumes have been grown. The belief that they do not grow well with vines, oregano, and cyclamen stems from Classical times. In the 16th century, it was well known that "Vineyards where Coleworts grow, doe yeeld the worser Wines."

MEDICINAL

Eating cabbage is said to reduce the risk of colonic cancer, stimulate the immune system, and kill bacteria. Drinking the juice is alleged to prevent and heal ulcers.

Some active principles are partly destroyed on cooking, so cabbage is much more nutritious eaten raw.

According to folklore, placing heated cabbage leaves on the soles of the feet reduces fever; placed on a septic wound, they draw out pus or a splinter.

CULINARY

Traditionally cabbage is cooked by boiling— preferably as briefly as possible—in a small amount of water, to preserve the nutrients. Add the cabbage to boiling water, which should not stop boiling while you place the younger leaves from the heart on top of the older leaves below. Cover, cook briefly for 3 minutes, then drain. Or steam for about 6–8 minutes.

Stir-frying is an almost equally rapid method; alternatively, bake, braise, or stuff. Use as a substitute for vine leaves in dolmades.

Eat shredded white or red cabbage raw in salads. Coleslaw is a mixture of shredded cabbage, carrot, apple, and celery with French dressing or a mayonnaise/sour cream blend; its name derives from *cole*, the old name for cabbage, and the Dutch *slaw*, meaning salad.

Pickle red cabbage in vinegar and white cabbage in brine (as sauerkraut).

Czemona Kapusta
Serves 6

The Poles and Czechs are extremely keen on red cabbage. This dish combines subtle flavors to make a refreshing change from our usual ways of cooking the vegetable.

5 cups red cabbage, finely sliced
1 teaspoon salt
1 tablespoon butter
1 tablespoon all-purpose flour
½ cup red wine
2 teaspoons sugar
Pinch ground cloves
Pinch cinnamon
Freshly ground black pepper

Colcannon

Put the cabbage in a colander and sprinkle with salt; leave for 15 minutes and then rinse well under cold water. Transfer to a heavy pan of boiling water and simmer gently until the cabbage is just cooked. Drain and keep warm. Reserve a little of the liquid.

Heat the butter in a saucepan over a medium heat and mix in the flour to make a roux. Cook for 2 minutes without burning. Dilute with the cooking liquid to make a thick sauce and stir in the cabbage. Season and add the red wine, sugar, cloves, and cinnamon. Mix well and simmer for 5 more minutes. Serve.

Colcannon
Serves 4

Probably the most famous Irish dish, some believe this was traditionally made with kale but today it is commonly made with cabbage. Use a Savoy.

2½ cups potatoes, peeled and cooked
1 leek, cleaned, sliced and cooked in a little cream or milk
2½ cups cabbage, sliced and cooked
4 tablespoons butter
Salt and freshly ground black pepper

Mash the potatoes and season them before stirring in the slices of leek and juices in which they were cooked. Then add the cabbage and mix thoroughly over a low heat. Arrange on a warmed serving dish and make a hole in the center. Keep warm. Partly melt the butter, season, and pour it into the cavity. Serve immediately, piping hot.

Czerwona Kapusta

Brassica oleracea Gongylodes Group. *Brassicaceae*

KOHLRABI

Biennial grown as annual for rounded, swollen roots. Hardy.
Value: rich in vitamin C, traces of minerals.

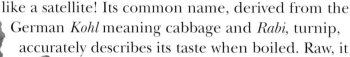

This odd-looking vegetable with a distinctive name has a rounded, swollen stem, which, with the leaves removed, looks like a satellite! Its common name, derived from the German *Kohl* meaning cabbage and *Rabi*, turnip, accurately describes its taste when boiled. Raw, it has a fresh, nutty flavor. Found in northern Europe in the fifteenth century, it may already have existed for centuries, as a similar-sounding vegetable was described by Pliny around A.D. 70. This highly nutritious, tasty vegetable is more drought-resistant than most brassicas, succeeding where rutabaga and turnips fail. It deserves to be more widely grown and eaten.

VARIETIES

'Azur Star,' a very early variety, has attractive deep blue skin and is resistant to bolting. 'Green Vienna,' an early-maturing variety, is green-skinned with white flesh. 'Lanro' is a white-fleshed, green-skinned variety that does not deteriorate when harvested after maturity. 'Purple Vienna' is purple-skinned with white flesh, for late sowing and winter harvesting. 'Rowel' is juicy and sweet, with green skin, white flesh, and a crisp texture. It does not become woody if allowed to grow larger than a tennis ball. 'Trero' is sweet, uniform, vigorous and slow to become "woody." 'White Vienna' has pale green skin and is delicately flavored. Other varieties are especially well suited to growing as "mini-vegetables."

'Purple Vienna,' bizarrely shaped

CULTIVATION

Propagation

As a general rule, green varieties are sown from midspring to midsummer for summer crops and the hardier purple-skinned types from midsummer to midfall for winter use. Sow successively for a regular harvest.

Early sowings in seed or multipurpose potting mix in a propagator at 55–65°F can be made during midwinter to early spring. Transplant after hardening off in midspring when they are no more than 2 in. high; if you let them grow taller or sow seed when soil temperatures are below 50°F, they are liable to run to seed. Protect with cloches or frost fabric until the plants are established.

Water the drills before sowing and sow later crops thinly in drills ½ in. deep in rows 12 in. apart. Thin seedlings when they are about 1 in. high and the first true leaves appear, to a final spacing 6–8 in. apart. Prompt thinning is vital, as growth is easily checked. Alternatively, plant 3 seeds together in hills 6 in. apart and thin to leave the strongest seedling. Kohlrabi can also be grown successfully in packs and then transplanted at their final spacing.

Kohlrabi grown as a "mini-vegetable" is ideal for the small garden. Sow cultivars like 'Rolano,' 'Logo,' 'Korist,' and 'Kolibra' and thin to about 1 in. apart between the plants and rows. Harvest after 9–10 weeks when about the size of golf balls. **Zones 3–9.**

Growing

The ideal situation is a sunny position on light, fertile, humus-rich, well-drained soil. Incorporate organic matter the winter before planting if necessary and lime acid soils to create a pH of 6–7. The ground must be firm before planting, as (in common with other brassicas) kohlrabi does not grow well on loose soil. Lightly fork the area, removing any debris, then gently tread down the surface or firm it with the head of a rake. Finally, rake in a general fertilizer at 3 oz. per square yard and level. Kohlrabi must receive a constant supply of water throughout the season. This is because if growth is checked they can become "woody." During drought periods, they need up to 2 gallons per square yard of water per week. If growth slows down, liquid feed with a high-nitrogen fertilizer. Keep crops weed-free and mulch with compost to suppress weeds and retain moisture.

Rotate kohlrabi with brassicas.

Maintenance
Spring Prepare the seedbed and sow seed in situ under cloches.
Summer Sow regularly for successional cropping. Sow hardier purple varieties later in the season. Weed and water as necessary.
Fall Sow in midfall and protect with cloches for early winter harvest.
Winter From late winter, sow early crops in packs or trays. Prepare the ground for outdoor sowings.

Protected Cropping
Early and late outdoor crops should be protected with cloches or crop covers.

Container Growing
Kohlrabi are ideal for containers, particularly when grown as "mini-vegetables." Plant in a loam-based potting mix with a moderate fertilizer content and maintain a regular supply of water. Feed every 2–3 weeks with a general liquid fertilizer.

Harvesting and Storing
Kohlrabi matures rapidly and is ready for harvest 2 months after sowing. Dig when plants are somewhere in size between a golf ball and a tennis ball. Larger "bulbs" tend to become woody and unpalatable, but this is less of a problem with newer cultivars.

Harvest as required. In particularly severe weather, they can be dug and stored in boxes of sand or sawdust. Remove the outer leaves, retaining the central tuft of leaves to keep them fresh. Some flavor tends to be lost during storage.

'Rowel' is best harvested when small.

CULINARY

There is no need to peel tiny kohlrabi, but peel off the tough outer skin of older globes before cooking. Young ones can be trimmed, scrubbed, and boiled whole or sliced for 20–30 minutes, then drained, peeled, and served with melted butter, white sauce, or mashed.

Boiled kohlrabi can be made into fritters by frying with egg and bread crumbs. Add kohlrabi to soups and stews, serve stuffed, cook like celeriac, or eat in a cheese sauce. It complements basil and is excellent steamed.

Kohlrabi globes can also be eaten raw, shredded, or sliced into salads, and the leaves are good boiled.

Kohlrabi sautéed in butter

PESTS AND DISEASES

As it matures quickly, kohlrabi is untroubled by many of the usual brassica problems, including clubroot.

Birds can cause severe damage, particularly to young plants. You should protect crops with netting, cages, humming wire, or with bird scarers.

Flea beetles—⅛ in. long and black with yellow stripes—nibble holes in leaves of seedlings, checking growth. Dust plants and the surrounding soil thoroughly with rotenore or insecticide when symptoms appear. They can also be controlled by brushing a yellow sticky trap or piece of wood covered in glue along the tops of the plants: the insects jump out, stick to the glue, and can be disposed of.

Cabbage root fly larvae cause stunted growth, wilting and death. Protect the seedlings when transplanting with 5 in. squares of plastic, cardboard, or rubberized carpet underlay, slit from edge to center and fitted around the stems. This stops adults from laying eggs.

COMPANION PLANTING

Kohlrabi grows well with beets and onions.

Brassica oleracea Italica Group. *Brassicaceae*

BROCCOLI

Also known as Sprouting Broccoli, Heading Broccoli, Calabrese. Perennial or annual grown for immature flower heads. Hardy or half hardy. High in beta carotene, vitamin C, folic acid, and iron. Moderate levels of calcium.

Said to have originated in the eastern Mediterranean, early forms of broccoli were highly esteemed by the Romans and described by Pliny in the first century A.D. It spread from Italy to northern Europe, arriving in England in the eighteenth century. Philip Miller in his *Gardener's Dictionary* of 1724 called it "Sprout Cauliflower" or "Italian Asparagus."

Broccoli is an Italian word, derived from the Latin *brachium*, meaning "arm" or "branch." Calabrese, a similar plant with the same botanical origin, grown for its larger immature flower heads, also takes its name from the Italian—meaning "from Calabria." This delicious vegetable was introduced to France by Catherine de Medici in 1560 and spread from there to the rest of Europe. "Green broccoli" was first mentioned in American literature in 1806, but was certainly in cultivation long before that. It is said to have been introduced by Italian settlers and is extensively grown around New York and Boston.

Heading broccoli should be eaten before the buds turn yellow and flowers emerge.

VARIETIES

Old varieties of perennial broccoli are still available; outstanding among them all is **'Nine Star,'** a multiheaded variety with small white heads. Cropping improves if unused heads are removed before they go to seed.

Sprouting broccoli
This excellent winter vegetable produces a succession of small flower heads for cropping over a long season from early winter to late spring in mild winter regions. It is an excellent crop for poor soils. "Purple" varieties are hardier than the "white," which have a better taste, crop later, but tend to be less productive.

'Christmas Purple Sprouting' appears early during good weather, ready for your Christmas dinner! **'Purple Sprouting'** crops heavily from early to midspring. **'Purple Sprouting Early'** is easy, prolific, and extremely hardy. Ready for harvesting from late winter. **'Purple Sprouting Late'** is similar, but ready for picking from midspring. **'White Sprouting'** is delicious, with shoots like tiny cauliflowers. **'White Sprouting Early'** is the white equivalent of **'Purple Sprouting.'** **'White Sprouting Late'** is ready to harvest from midspring.

Heading broccoli
Also known as American, Italian, or green sprouting broccoli, this produces a large central flower head surrounded by smaller sideshoots, which develop after the main head has been harvested. Maturing about 3 months after sowing, it crops from summer until the onset of the first frosts.

'Broccoletto' is quick-maturing and sweet, with a single head. **'Early Emerald Hybrid'** produces rich green-blue heads over a season. **'Gallant'** produces very tight florets that have great holding ability in the garden for a long harvest. It produces several mild-tasting heads per plant. **'Green Comet'** is early with a large dark-green flower-head and masses of side-shoots. **'Green Sprouting,'** an old Italian variety, matures early. **'Packman'** produces some of the largest heads of all broccoli varieties. This early variety grows well under hot conditions. **'DeCicco,'** an old Italian variety for spring or fall cropping, produces heads over a long period. Tasty, tender and freezes well. **'Romanesco'** is tender with an excellent flavor and lime-green heads. Steam and serve it like asparagus.

CULTIVATION

Propagation

Prepare the seedbed for sprouting broccoli by raking the soil to a fine texture. Sow over several weeks from mid- to late spring, planting the earlier varieties first. Sow thinly in drills in a seedbed, 12 in. apart and ½ in. deep, thinning to 6 in. apart before transplanting at their final spacing. Alternatively, sow 2–3 seeds in hills 6 in. apart, thinning to leave the strongest seedling.

For early spring crops, sow early maturing cultivars indoors in trays from late summer to early fall. Transplant seedlings when they are about 5 in. tall into a unheated greenhouse or cold frame. Harden off and transplant outdoors from late winter to midspring. Alternatively, sow 2 seeds per pack and thin to leave the stronger seedling. The final spacing for plants should be about 27–30 in. apart in and between the rows. It is worth noting that they take up a lot of space and have a long growing season.

Heading broccoli can be sown successively from midspring to midsummer for cropping from early summer to fall. It does not transplant well and is better sown in situ. Sow 2–3 seeds at hills, thinning to leave the strongest seedling. Close spacing suppresses sideshoots and encourages small terminal spears to form, which are useful for freezing. Wider spacing means higher yields. While

The popular and prolific 'Purple Sprouting' broccoli

Heading broccoli 'Romanesco' is outstanding for its unusual lime-green florets.

they can be as close as 3 in. apart with 24 in. between rows, the optimum spacing is 6 in. apart with 12 in. between the rows. **Zones 3–10.**

Growing

Sprouting broccoli thrives in a warm, sunny position. Soil should be deep, moisture-retentive and free-draining. Nitrogen levels should be moderate; excessive amounts encourage soft, leafy growth. You should avoid shallow or sandy soils and windy sites.

Sprouting broccoli tends to be top-heavy, so hill up around the stem to a depth of 3–5 in. to prevent wind rock, or stake larger varieties. Firm stems loosened by wind or frost.

Keep crops weed-free with regular hoeing or mulch with a 2 in. layer of organic matter. Water crops regularly before the onset of dry weather: do not let them dry out. Heading broccoli needs at least 4 gallons per square yard every 2 weeks, although a single thorough watering 2–3 weeks before harvesting is a useful option for those under watering restrictions!

Feed with a general liquid fertilizer, or scatter and water in ½ oz. per square yard of granular fertilizer after the main head has been removed to encourage the sideshoots to grow.

Maintenance

Spring Sow early broccoli indoors and later crops in seedbeds. Sow heading broccoli.
Summer Water crops and keep weed-free. Feed calabrese after harvesting the terminal bud.
Fall Harvest calabrese and remove and dispose of crop debris.
Winter Harvest sprouting broccoli.

Harvesting and Storing

Cut sprouting broccoli when the heads have formed, well before the flowers open, when the stems are 6–8 in. long. Regular harvesting is essential, as this encourages sideshoot formation and should ensure a 6–8 week harvest. Never strip the plant completely, or let it flower, as this stops the sideshoots forming and makes existing "spears" woody and tasteless.

Sprouting broccoli can be stored in a plastic bag in the refrigerator. It will keep for about 3 days.

To freeze, soak in salted water for 15 minutes, rinse and dry. Blanch for 3–4 minutes, cool, and drain. Pack it in containers and then freeze.

Cut the mature central heads of heading broccoli with a sharp knife, while still firm and the buds tight. This encourages growth of sideshoots in 2–3 weeks. Pick as the sprouting variety.

Heading broccoli can be stored in the refrigerator for up to 5 days, and freezes well.

PESTS AND DISEASES

Pollen beetle, pigeons, and **mealy aphids** are frequently a problem.

Check regularly for **caterpillars**.

COMPANION PLANTING

Plant with rosemary, thyme, sage, onions, garlic, beets, and chards.

Broccoli makes a magnificent plant for the potager.

CULINARY

Remove any tough leaves attached to the stalks and wash florets carefully in cold water before cooking. For the best flavor cook immediately after picking in boiling salted water for 10 minutes, or steam by standing spears upright in 2 in. of gently boiling water for 15 minutes with the pan covered. Drain carefully and serve hot with white, hollandaise, or béarnaise sauce, melted butter, or vinaigrette. An Italian cookbook recommends braising heading broccoli in white wine or sautéing it in oil and sprinkling with shredded Parmesan cheese. In Sicily it is braised with anchovies, olives, and red wine. Broccoli fritters are dipped in batter, then deep-fried.

Stir-fried florets can be blanched for 1 minute and fried with squid and shellfish. On a more mundane but practical level, broccoli and calabrese can be used as a fine substitute in cauliflower cheese.

Penne with Broccoli, Mascarpone, and Dolcelatte
Serves 4

3 cups broccoli florets
³/₄ cup mascarpone
1 cup dolcelatte
2 tablespoons crème fraîche
1 tablespoon balsamic vinegar
1 tablespoon dry, white wine
3¹/₂ cups penne
2 tablespoons capers
4 tablespoons black olives
1 tablespoon hazelnuts, crushed
Salt and freshly ground black pepper

Steam the broccoli florets over a pan of boiling water for 2–3 minutes. Run under cold water and set aside. In a heavy pan, gently heat the mascarpone, dolcelatte, crème fraîche, vinegar, and wine. Add the broccoli florets. Cook the pasta until it is just tender and drain well. Add the hot sauce, sprinkle with the capers, olives, and hazelnuts, and toss well. Adjust the seasoning and serve.

Brassica rapa Pekinensis Group. *Brassicaceae*

CHINESE CABBAGE

Also known as Napa Cabbage, Celery Cabbage, Pe Tsai, Peking Cabbage. Annual or biennial grown as annual for edible leaves, stems, and flowering shoots. Half hardy. Value: moderate folic acid and vitamin C levels.

Chinese cabbage was first recorded in China around the fifth century A.D. and has never been found in the wild. It is thought to have been a spontaneous cross in cultivation between the bok choy and the turnip. Taken to the East Indies and Malaya by Chinese traders and settlers who established communities and maintained their own culture, in the 1400s Chinese cabbage could be found in the Chinese colony in Malacca.

By 1751 European missionaries had sent seeds back home, but the vegetable was regarded as little more than a curiosity. Another attempt at introduction was made by a French horticulturalist in 1845, but the supply became exhausted and the seed was lost. In 1970 the first large-scale commercial crop was produced by the Israelis and distributed in Europe; about the same time it was marketed in the United States as the Napa cabbage, after the valley in California where it was grown. It has become a moderately popular vegetable in the West.

VARIETIES

There are many groups, but three have become popular: the "tall cylindrical," the "hearted" or "barrel-shaped," and the "loose-headed."

The cylindrical type has long, upright leaves and forms a compact head, which can be loosely tied to blanch the inner leaves. It is slow-growing, takes about 70 days from sowing to harvest and is most susceptible to bolting. This type is sweet and stores well.

Hearted types have compact, barrel-shaped heads with tightly wrapped leaves and a dense heart. They mature after about 55 days and are generally slow to bolt.

Loose-headed types are lax and open-headed, often with textured leaves. The "self-blanching" ones have creamy centers, beautifully textured leaves, and look good in salads. They are less liable to bolt than headed types. **'China Express'** is a mild, sweet, and very crisp Napa type cabbage with good bolt resistance. Heads reach up to 5 pounds. **'Greenwich'** is a tasty new Michihili type cabbage with firm narrow heads of green savoyed leaves. **'Jade Pagoda'** is cylindrical with a firm, crisp head. It takes about 65 days to mature and is cold-tolerant. **'Joi Choi'** is a very fast maturing Pac Choi type cabbage, forming full 11-in.-long stalks in just 45 days. Juicy and mild with a hint of mustard. **'Kasumi,'** a barrel type, has a compact head and is resistant to bolting. **'Ruffles'** is delicious and early-maturing, with lax, pale green heads and a creamy white heart. Early sowings are liable to bolt. **'Shantung'** has a spreading habit, with tender, light green leaves.

Chinese cabbage ready for picking, showing its open habit

CULTIVATION

Propagation

A cool-weather crop, Chinese cabbage is more likely to bolt in late spring and summer. Use resistant varieties or sow after midsummer. The chance of bolting increases if young plants are subjected to low temperatures or dry conditions, or suffer from transplanting check.

Sow the main crop in situ from mid- to late summer, 2–3 seeds per hill, spaced 12–14 in. apart in and between the rows. Thin to leave the strongest seedling.

Alternatively, sow sparingly in drills and thin to the final spacing.

Otherwise it can be sown in packs or pots, transplanting carefully to avoid root disturbance when there are 4–6 leaves. If the soil is dry, water thoroughly.

Broadcast or sow loose-headed types as cut-and-come-again seedlings. Make first sowings in a cold greenhouse or cold frame in early spring, sow outdoors under cloches or frost fabric as the weather improves and the soil becomes workable. Summer sowings tend to grow too rapidly and become "tough," unless it is a cool summer. Make the last sowing under cover in early fall.

Cut seedlings when they have reached a few inches tall, leaving them to resprout.

Seeds can also be sprouted, as for alfalfa. **Zones 3–10.**

Growing

Chinese cabbage needs a deep, moisture-retentive, free-draining soil with plenty of organic matter. Excessively light, heavy, or poor soils should be avoided unless they are improved by incorporating organic matter or grit. Alternatively, grow in raised beds or on ridges. Dig the soil thoroughly before planting; acid soils should be limed, as the ideal pH is 6.5–7.0. Slightly more alkaline soils are advisable where there is a risk of clubroot.

Chinese cabbage prefers an open site, but tolerates some shade in midsummer.

Water crops thoroughly throughout the growing season; do not let them dry out. They are shallow-rooted and so need water little and often. Mulching is also advisable. Erratic watering can result in damage to the developing head, encouraging rots. Scatter general fertilizer around the base of transplants or feed with a general liquid fertilizer as necessary to boost growth—this is particularly important on poorer soils. Keep crops weed-free.

In late summer, tie up the leaves of hearting varieties with soft twine or raffia. (With self-hearting varieties, this is unnecessary.)

Rotate Chinese cabbage with other brassicas.

Maintenance

Spring Sow early cut-and-come-again seedling crops under cover. Sow later crops outdoors.
Summer Sow in drills from mid- to late summer. Water a little and often, mulch, and keep weed-free. Harvest.
Fall Sow quick-maturing varieties or cut-and-come-again crops outdoors; sow later crops under cover. Harvest.
Winter Harvest cut-and-come-again crops grown under cover.

Protected Cropping

Earlier crops can be achieved by sowing bolting resistant cultivars from late spring to early summer. They need temperatures of 68–77°F for the first 3 weeks after germination to prevent bolting. Harden off,

Thai workers in evening light, harvesting crops grown on raised beds.

transplant, then protect the plants with cloches or with crop covers.

Late summer-sown crops should be transplanted under cover. Space plants about 5 in. apart and grow them as a semimature cut-and-come-again crop.

Container Growing

The fast-growing varieties give the best results. Use a 10-in. pot or container and loam-based potting mix with added organic matter and a thick basal layer of drainage material. Sow seeds ½ in. deep and ¾ in. apart in shallow pots or packs in midspring. Transplant seedlings singly into pots when they have 3–4 leaves.

Harvesting and Storing

In fall, cold-tolerant varieties stand outside for several weeks provided it is dry. Protect from wet and cold using cloches. Dig developing crops and replant in cold frames, or uproot and lay plants on straw, hay, or similar, covering them with the same material if temperatures fall below freezing. Ventilate on warm days.

Harvest as cut-and-come-again seedlings, semimature or mature plants, and for the flowering shoots. Cut seedlings when they are 1–2 in. tall. Semimature or mature plants can be cut with a sharp knife about 1 in. above the ground and will then resprout; after several harvests they will send up a flower head. Harvest the flowering shoots when they are young, before the flowers open.

Harvest mature heads when they are firm.

Chinese cabbage keeps in the crisper in the refrigerator for several weeks. Wash thoroughly before storing. Heads can be stored in a cool, frost-free shed or cellar for up to 3 months. When storing, check plants every 3–4 weeks and remove any diseased or damaged leaves immediately.

PESTS AND DISEASES

Chinese cabbage can be affected by any of the usual brassica pests and diseases. You should take precautions in particular against **flea beetle, slugs, snails, caterpillars, clubroot,** and **powdery mildew.** Crops grow well under frost fabric or fine netting.

COMPANION PLANTING

Plant with garlic and dill to discourage caterpillars. Main crops are ideal after peas, early potatoes, and fava beans; late crops are good companions for Brussels sprouts. It is good for cropping between slower-growing vegetables.

Chinese cabbages are sometimes grown as sacrificial crops so that slugs, flea beetles, and aphids are attracted to them rather than other crops. Sometimes they are used among corn, as they attract corn worms.

Chinese cabbage crop growing near Kanchanaburi, Thailand

WARNING

To minimize the risk of listeria, you should never store Chinese cabbage in plastic bags.

CULINARY

Cook Chinese cabbage only lightly to retain the flavor and nutrients. Steam, boil quickly, stir-fry—or eat raw. (Seedlings are better cooked.) Leaves blend well in raw salads of lettuce, green pepper, celery, and tomato. They also make a delicious warm salad, stir-fried and mixed with orange. Otherwise use in soups, cook with fish, meat, poultry, and use in stuffing.

Outer stalks can be shredded, cooked like celery, and tossed in butter. In Korea, China, and Japan heads are used to make fermented and salted pickles.

Sweet and Sour Chinese Cabbage

Serves 4

2 tablespoons olive oil
1 onion or several shallots, sliced
2 tablespoons white wine vinegar
2 teaspoons sugar
6 tablespoons chopped tomatoes in their juices
4 cups Chinese cabbage, finely shredded

Salt and freshly ground black pepper

Heat the oil in a heavy-bottomed pan and cook the onion until soft. Stir in the vinegar, sugar, and tomatoes and blend well. Add the Chinese cabbage and seasoning. Cook for 10 minutes with the lid on, stirring occasionally, until the cabbage is tender. Serve hot.

Sweet and Sour Chinese Cabbage

Capsicum annuum. Solanaceae

Sweet Pepper & Hot Pepper

Also known as Bell Pepper, Capsicum, Pimento, Chili Pepper. Annuals and short-lived perennials grown for edible fruits. Half hardy. Value: very rich in vitamin C and beta carotene.

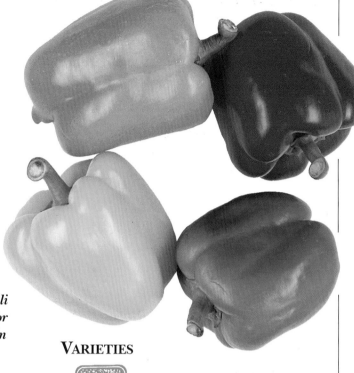

Both sweet and hot peppers come from one wild species that is native to Central and South America. It is thought that the hot types were the first to be cultivated; seeds have been found in Mexican settlements dating from 7000 B.C., and the Aztecs are known to have grown them extensively. They are one of the discoveries made in the New World by Columbus. He thought he had discovered black pepper, which at the time was extremely expensive, and used the name "pepper" for this new fiery spice.

Chili peppers are notorious for their fieriness. Their heat is caused by the alkaloid capsaicin, which is measured in Scoville units. Mild chilies are around 600 units. Beware the 'Habanero' types, measured at between 200,000 and 350,000 units!

Peppers will keep for 14 days.

Varieties

The larger, bell-shaped, mild-tasting sweet peppers eaten as vegetables are members of the *Capsicum annuum* Grossum Group. Green when immature, different cultivars ripen to yellow, orange, red, or "black."

The smaller, hotter chilies used for flavoring are classed in the *C. a.* Longum Group.

Sweet peppers

'Big Bertha' is one of the largest bell peppers, growing to 7 in. long by 4 in. wide. Excellent for growing in cooler zones and for stuffing. **'Californian Wonder'** has a mild flavor, is good for stuffing, and crops well over a long period. **'Calwonder Wonder Early'** grows well in short seasons. Prolific. **'Gypsy'** is an early cropper with slightly tapered fruits. Resistant to tobacco mosaic virus. **'Red Skin'** is compact and ideal for pots and growing bags. **'Sweet Chocolate'** is an unusual chocolate-brown color. Good when frozen whole.

Chili peppers

'Anaheim' produces tapered, moderately hot fruits over a long period. **'Cayenne Long Slim'** is a hot pepper much used for flavoring. When kept for longer periods it becomes hotter. **'Garden Salsa'** produces 8–9-in.-long, mildly hot peppers that can be picked green or red for making salsa. The moderately hot yellow fruits of **'Hungarian Yellow Wax Hot'** ripen to become crimson. Good for growing in cool areas. **'Jalapeno'** is extremely hot and can be harvested over a long period. **'Large Red Cherry'** is extremely hot, with flattened fruits ripening to cherry red. Good for drying and ideal in curries, pickles, and sauces. **'Red Chili'** is a high-yielding extremely hot variety, for pickling or drying. Fruits are narrow and tapered. **'Ring of Fire'** is, not surprisingly, hot-fruited. Early cropping, producing short, thin cayenne-type peppers. **'Serrano'** is extremely hot with orange-red fruits. It is prolific and can be dried. **'Tabasco Habanero'**—as the name suggests—is lethal!

CULTIVATION

Propagation

Sow seed indoors from mid-to late spring in trays, packs, or pots of moist potting mix at 70°F. Lower temperature gradually after germination. Transplant into 3–3½ in. pots when 3 true leaves appear, repotting again into 4–5 in. pots when sufficient roots have been formed. Move plants into their final position when about 4 in. high and the first flowers appear. Harden off outdoor crops in cool temperate zones and transplant in late spring to early summer when the soil is warm and there is no danger of frost.

Space standard varieties 15–18 in. apart; dwarf varieties should be spaced 12 in. apart. **Zones 4–11.**

Growing

Chilies benefit from protection with cloches or fabric but tend to be more tolerant than sweet peppers of fluctuating temperatures and high or low rainfall and grow in marginally less fertile soil. Blossom drops when night temperatures fall below 60°F. Soil should be moisture-retentive and free-draining on ground manured for the previous crop. Alternatively, dig in plenty of well-rotted organic matter in fall or winter prior to planting. Rake in a granular general fertilizer at 4 oz. per square yard before planting.

Keep the soil moist and weed-free; mulching is recommended. Feed with a general liquid fertilizer if plants need a boost. Excessive nitrogen can result in flower drop.

If branches are weak and thin, when the plant is about 12 in. tall remove the growth tips from the stems to encourage branching. Normally, they branch naturally. Support with a trellis if necessary.

Maintenance

Spring Sow seeds under cover. Transplant when the danger of frost is passed or grow in an unheated greenhouse.
Summer Keep crops weed-free; damp down the glasshouse in warm weather. Harvest.
Fall Cover outdoor crops where necessary. Harvest.
Winter Prepare the ground for outdoor crops.

Protected Cropping

Crops can be grown under glass, row covers, cold frames, or cloches in cool zones. In greenhouse borders, prepare the soil as directed under "Growing." Keep it moist but not waterlogged and mist with tepid water to maintain humidity and help fruit set.

Sow in midspring for growing in a greenhouse and in late spring for crops under cloches. Ventilate well during hot weather. If you are growing dwarf varieties on a sunny windowsill, you should turn pots daily to ensure even growth.

Plants grown under cloches may outgrow their space: rigid cloches can be turned vertically and supported with trellis. Alternatively, use plastic sheeting.

Peppers have the luxury of a choice of colors: here they are "black."

Container Growing

Grow under cover or outdoors. Plant in 8–10 in. pots of loam-based potting mix with moderate fertilizer levels or in growing bags. Dwarf varieties can be grown successfully in pots on potting mix, moist but not waterlogged, and misted with tepid water, particularly during flowering to assist fruit set.

Water frequently in warm weather, less at other times.

Harvesting and Storing

Harvest with scissors or pruning shears when sweet peppers or chilies are green, or leave on the plant for 2–3 weeks to ripen and change color. Picking them when they are green increases the yield.

Peppers may be stored in a cool, humid place for up to 14 days at temperatures of 55–58°F.

Toward the end of the season, uproot plants and hang them by the roots in a frost-free shed or greenhouse; fruits will continue to ripen for several months.

The heat of chilies increases with the maturity of the fruit. Fresh chilies keep for up to 3 weeks in the refrigerator in a paper bag. Or store them in an airtight jar in a dark cupboard.

Chilies can either be dried and used whole or ground into powder.

Both sweet peppers and chilies freeze successfully.

Sweet peppers are best grown under glass in cool zones.

Chilies become hotter as they mature.

PESTS AND DISEASES

Red spider mite can be a nuisance under cover. Slugs can damage seedlings, stems, leaves, and fruits. Remove any decaying flowers or foliage immediately.

COMPANION PLANTING

The capsicum family grows well with basil, okra, and tomatoes.

MEDICINAL

Capsaicin increases the blood flow and is used in muscle liniments. It is said to help the body metabolize alcohol, acts as expectorant, and prevents and alleviates bronchitis and emphysema. Ten to 20 drops of red-hot chili sauce in a glass of water daily (or hot spicy meals 3 times a week) can keep airways free of congestion, preventing or treating chronic bronchitis and colds. It stimulates endorphins, killing pain, and inducing a sense of well-being.

WARNING

Ventilate the kitchen when using chilies. Wear rubber gloves to handle them and always avoid touching your eyes or other sensitive areas after handling.

CULINARY

Sweet peppers add both color and taste to the table. They can be eaten raw in salads, roasted or barbecued, fried or stir-fried, stuffed with rice, fish or meat mixtures, and used in countless casseroles and rice dishes.

Chilies are used in chili con carne, curries, and hotpots. Removing the internal ribs and seeds reduces the heat intensity.

Paprika is the dried and powdered fruits of sweet peppers. Cayenne pepper is dried and ground powder made from chilies.

If chili is too strong, it can cause intestinal burning. Rice, bread, and beans are a good antidote. By coating the tongue, the fat content of yogurt and milk soothes a chili-burned mouth. Water only makes things worse.

If you're uninitiated at eating chili peppers, start with small doses and build up tolerance of heat. Excessively hot peppers can cause jaloproctitis or perianal discomfiture.

Mrs. Krause's Pepper Hash
Serves 6

William Woys Weaver in *Pennsylvania Dutch Country Cooking* quotes this recipe from Mrs. Eugene F. Krause of Bethlehem, who lived in the early part of the century and was renowned for her peppery hashes.

6 green bell peppers, seeded and finely chopped
6 red bell peppers, seeded and finely chopped
4 onions, finely chopped
2 small pods hot chili peppers, seeded and finely chopped
1½ tablespoons celery seeds
1 cup cider vinegar
1¼ cups brown sugar
1½ teaspoons sea salt

Combine the peppers, onions, hot chili peppers, and celery seeds in a nonreactive preserving pan. Heat the vinegar in a nonreactive pan and dissolve the sugar and salt in it. Bring to a fast boil, then pour over the pepper mixture. Then cook over a medium heat for 15 minutes, or until the peppers begin to discolor.

Pack into hot sterilized preserving jars, seal, and place in a 15-minute water bath. Let the pepper hash mature in the jars for 2 weeks before using.

Duvec
Serves 4

This is a Croatian recipe with subtle flavors. It makes an excellent one-dish supper and uses up leftovers as well.

1 onion, finely sliced
2 tablespoons olive oil
2 cloves garlic, crushed
3 cups red, green, or yellow sweet peppers, seeded and diced
1½ cups tomatoes, peeled and seeded
½ cup rice, cooked
5 cups leftover cooked meat
1 cup stock
Salt and freshly ground black pepper

Cook the onion in the oil in a heavy pan over medium heat until softened. Grease an ovenproof dish and put in a layer of onion and garlic, followed by one of peppers, then one of tomatoes, one of rice and bite-sized pieces of meat. Repeat the layers until all the ingredients are used up, seasoning as you go.

Pour in the stock, cover, and bake in a preheated oven at 350°F for about 45 minutes. Remove the cover and continue cooking for an additional 15 minutes. Serve.

Mrs. Krause's Pepper Hash

Cicer arietinum. Papilionaceae

CHICKPEA

Also known as Dhall, Egyptian Pea, Garbanzo, Gram. Annual grown for seed sprouts, seeds, young shoots and leaves. Tender. Value: high in protein, phosphorus, potassium, most B vitamins, iron, and dietary fiber.

Chickpeas originated in the northern regions of the fertile crescent. Evidence of their ancient use as a domesticated crop was found at a site in Jericho and dated to around 6500 B.C. Seeds excavated in Greece indicate that the chickpea must have been introduced to Europe with the first food crops arriving from the Near East. Today it is cultivated worldwide in subtropical or Mediterranean climates as a cool-season crop, needing about 4–6 months of moderately warm, dry conditions to flourish. It is the world's third most important pulse after peas and beans, and 80 percent of the crop is produced in India. It is eaten fresh or dried, made into flour, used as a coffee substitute, and grown as a fodder crop. The plant grows about twelve inches tall, with compound leaves of up to eight toothed leaflets. Its tiny white or blue flowers are followed by a small flat pod containing one or two round seeds, each with a small "beak"—hence the common name "chickpea."

$2\frac{1}{2}$–4 in. deep with the rows 20 in. apart, thinning to 10 in between plants after germination. Alternatively, sow 3–4 seeds in hills 10 in. apart and thin to leave the strongest seedling. **Zones 5–11.**

Growing
Dig over the area thoroughly before planting, adding organic matter to poor soils. Rake over the area to create a fine tilth and water well before sowing if the seedbed is dry. Alternatively, soak the seeds for an hour. Keep crops weed-free during the early stages; as plants mature, their spreading habit naturally stifles weed growth. Chickpeas are drought-tolerant, but watering just before flowering and as the peas begin to swell improves productivity. Rotate with other legumes and leave the roots in the ground after harvest to provide nitrogen for the following crop.

VARIETIES

The smooth-seeded "Kabuli" race is dominant throughout the Mediterranean and Near East and the wrinkled-seeded "Desai" type in Ethiopia, Afghanistan, and India. The following are Indian cultivars: **'Annegeri'** is a semispreading high-yielding variety with yellowish-brown seeds. It is deep-rooting and needs good soil, but a coarse tilth is adequate. **'Avrodhi'** has medium-sized brown seeds and is wilt-resistant. **'Bheema,'** a semispreading variety, has large, light brown smooth seeds and is suitable for drought-prone or low-rainfall areas.

CULTIVATION

Chickpeas need a light, fertile, well-drained soil in full sun.

Propagation
Seeds can be broadcast or sown in drills during winter in Mediterranean regions or after the rains in subtropical climates. Broadcasting is very simple. Prepare the soil using the "stale seedbed" method, raking and leveling, allowing the weeds to germinate and hoeing them off before sowing. Then scatter the seed evenly, raking the soil twice—first in one direction, then again at 90 degrees to ensure even coverage. Chickpeas can also be sown in drills

Chickpea in pod, showing the head and small "beak"

A lilac-flowered variety, growing in the U.S.

Maintenance

Spring Dig over the planting area, adding organic matter where needed.
Summer Keep crops weed-free. Water in prolonged drought, just before flowering and as the peas swell.
Fall Harvest crops.
Winter Dig over the planting area, adding organic matter where needed.

Protected Cropping

In cooler zones, sow seeds in early spring into small pots of moist seed potting mix in a greenhouse or on a windowsill. Harden off in late spring and plant outdoors once there is no danger of frost. Growing crops in cloches or plastic tunnels increases the yield.

Container Growing

They can be grown in containers, but seed production levels do not make them a worthwhile proposition as a crop plant.

Harvesting and Storing

Crops are ready after about 4–6 months. Harvest when leaves and pods turn brown; don't leave it too long, or the seeds will be lost when the pods split. Cut the stems at the base and tie them together before drying upside down in a dry, warm place. Collect the dry seeds and store in airtight jars. Peas can also be harvested fresh for cooking, but fresh ones deteriorate rapidly and should be used as soon as possible.

Sprouting Seeds

Always buy untreated chickpeas for sprouting, as seed sold for sowing is often treated with chemical dressings. Soak seeds overnight or for several hours in boiling water, tip into a sieve, and rinse. Put several layers of moist paper towels or blotting paper in the base of a jar and cover with a layer of seed. Cut a square from pantyhose or piece of muslin and cover the top, securing with an elastic band. Place in a bright position, away from direct sunshine, maintaining constant temperatures around 68°F. Rinse the seed 3–4 times a day by filling the jar with water and pouring off again. Harvest after 3–4 days when the sprouts are about ½ in. long.

Pests and Diseases

Plants can suffer from **root rot.** They turn black and finally dry up, leaves fall and the stems dry out. Ensure the soil is well drained and destroy affected crops immediately. The acidic secretions from the glandular hairs are a good defense against most pests.
Gram pod borer caterpillars feed on the crop from seedlings to maturity, damaging seedpods and the immature seeds. Spray with pyrethrum.

CULINARY

With a protein content of 20 percent, chickpeas are an important meat substitute and good for children and expectant and nursing mothers. Chickpeas are used fresh or dried. They are ground into "gram flour" (used in vegan cooking), and the ground meal is mixed with wheat and used for chapatis. Whole chickpeas are fried, roasted (to eat as a snack), and boiled. To make hummus, grind boiled chickpeas into a paste, mix with olive or sesame oil, flavor with lemon and garlic, and eat on pita bread or crackers.

Chickpeas are also used to make "dhall" and are found in spicy side dishes, vegetable curries, and soups. The young shoots and leaves are used as a vegetable and cooked like spinach—boiled in soups, added to curries, or fried with spices.

Pureed Chickpeas
Serves 4

1 cup dried chickpeas, soaked
  overnight
2 tablespoons olive oil
1 onion, sliced finely
3 garlic cloves, crushed
³/₄ cup tomatoes, peeled, seeded,
  and chopped
Salt and freshly ground black
  pepper

Drain the chickpeas, put in a heavy-bottomed saucepan, cover with fresh water and cook until tender. This will take up to 1½ hours, depending on the age of the chickpeas. Drain. Puree in a food processor.

Heat the oil in a sauté pan, and sauté the onion until softened, add the garlic and cook for 30 seconds longer. Add the tomatoes and simmer for 5 minutes before adding the chickpea puree. Season well and serve immediately.

Cichorium endivia. Asteraceae

CHICORY

Also known as Escarole, Batavian Endive, Grumolo. Annual or biennial grown as annual for blanched hearts and leaves. Value: rich in iron, potassium, and beta carotene; moderate vitamin A and B complex.

The origins of this plant are obscure, but it was certainly eaten by the Egyptians long before the birth of Christ and is one of the bitter herbs used at Passover. Mentioned by Ovid, Horace, Pliny, and Dioscorides, it was highly valued by the Greeks and Romans as a cultivated plant. It was introduced to England, Germany, Holland, and France around 1548 and was described by several writers. The French at first used it primarily as a medicinal plant—to "comfort the weake and feeble stomack" and to help gouty limbs and sore eyes. European colonists took it to America in 1806 and created a confusion that persists in transatlantic cookbooks to this day. The French name of *chicorée frisée*—"curly chicory"—must have traveled with it to the U.S., where it is sometimes called "frisée." Even more confusingly, its forced 'Witloof' cousin, known as "Belgian endive" in America and *endive* in France, is known as "chicory" in Britain.

VARIETIES

There are two types. The Batavian, scarole, or escarole has large, broad leaves and is an upright plant. Curly, or fringed chicory is a really pretty plant, with a low rosette of delicately serrated leaves. Curled varieties are generally used for summer cropping; the more robust broad-leaved types tolerate cold, are disease-resistant, and grow well in winter.

   '**Broad Leaved Batavian**' has tightly packed heads of broad, deep green leaves which become creamy-white when blanched. '**En Cornet de Bordeaux**,' an old variety, is very tasty, extremely hardy and blanches well. '**Green Curled Ruffec**,' a curly type, is easily blanched and makes a good garnish. Very hardy and cold resistant. '**Green Curled**' ('**Moss Curled**') produces compact heads of dark green, fringed leaves. '**Ione**' has light green finely cut leaves, with a creamy heart and mild taste. '**Limnos**' is a vigorous variety which is slow to bolt with broad upright leaves and a yellow heart. '**Riecia Pancalieri**' has very curly leaves with white, rose-tinged midribs. '**Salad King**' is prolific and extremely hardy, with large, dark green, finely cut leaves. '**Sanda**' is vigorous and resistant to tip burn, cold, and bolting. '**Scarola Verde**' is broad-leaved with a large

Frisée leaves are slightly bitter.

Chicory needs an open site.

head and green and white leaves. It may bolt in heat. '**Très Fine Maraîchère**' ('**Coquette**') has finely cut curled leaves. Mild and delicious, it grows well in most soils. '**Wallone Frisée Weschelkopf**' ('**Wallone**') has a large, tightly packed head with finely cut leaves. Vigorous and hardy.

CULTIVATION

Propagation
Sow thinly, ½ in. deep in situ or in a seedbed, pots, or packs to transplant. Allow 12–15 in. between plants and rows.

   Chicory germinates best at 68–72°F. Sow early crops under cover and shade summer crops.

   Sow from early to midsummer for fall crops, in late summer for winter crops, using curled or hardy Batavian types. Sow all year round for cut-and-come-again seedlings or semimature leaves, making early and late sowings under glass. **Zones 3–9.**

Growing
Chicory needs an open site, although slimmer crops tolerate a little shade. Soils should be light, moderately

rich, and free-draining; this is particularly important for winter crops. If necessary, dig in plenty of well-rotted organic matter before planting. Excess nitrogen encourages lush growth and makes plants prone to fungal diseases.

Chicory is a cool-season crop, flourishing between 50–68°F, yet it withstands light frosts; hardier cultivars withstand temperatures down to 15°F. Higher temperatures tend to encourage bitterness, although "curled" types are heat-tolerant. Young plants tend to bolt if temperatures fall below 41°F for long. Keep crops weed-free; mulch and water thoroughly during dry weather, as dryness at the roots can cause bolting. Use a general liquid fertilizer to boost growth if necessary.

Blanch to reduce bitterness and make leaves more tender. Many newer cultivars have tight heads and some blanching occurs naturally. Damp leaves are likely to rot, so choose a dry period or dry plants under cloches for 2–3 days. Draw the outer leaves together and tie with raffia 2–3 weeks before harvest, placing a tile, piece of cardboard, or dinner plate over the center of the plant, and covering with a cloche to keep off the rain. Alternatively, cover the

Fringed frisée is attractive.

whole plant with a bucket or a flower pot with its drainage holes covered. Blanching takes about 10 days. Blanch a few at a time; they rapidly deteriorate afterward.

Maintenance
Spring Sow early crops under glass or cloches. Harvest late crops under cover.
Summer Sow curly varieties outdoors in seedbeds for transplanting, or in situ. Keep early-sown crops weed-free and moist. Harvest.
Fall Sow outdoors and under cover. Harvest.
Winter Sow under cover and harvest.

Protected Cropping
Sow hardy cultivars under cover in trays or packs at 68°F in midspring for early summer crops and maintain a minimum temperature of 39°F after germination for 3 weeks after transplanting to prevent bolting.

For winter and early spring crops, transplant in early fall from seed trays or packs under cover. Sow cut-and-come-again crops under cover in early spring, and in early fall.

Chicory grows better than lettuce in low light and is also a useful crop for the greenhouse in winter.

Container Growing
Sow directly or transplant into large containers of loam-based potting mix with added well-rotted organic matter. Keep potting mix moist and weed-free. Use a general liquid fertilizer to boost growth if necessary.

The more tolerant 'Batavian'

Harvesting and Storing
Harvest chicory from 7 weeks after sowing, depending on cultivar and season.

Cut-and-come-again seedlings may be ready from 5 weeks. With some cultivars, only one or two cuts may be possible before they run to seed. Pick individual leaves as needed or harvest them using a sharp knife about ¾ in. above the ground, leaving the root to resprout.

The whole plant can be dug in fall and put in a cool, dark place to blanch.

Leaves do not store well and are better eaten fresh. They last about 3 days in a plastic bag in the crisper in the refrigerator.

PESTS AND DISEASES

Protect plants from **slugs** and control **aphids**.

Keep winter crops well watered and mulched to prevent tip burn.

COMPANION PLANTING

Chicory is good for inter-sowing and intercropping.

CULINARY

Chicory is used mainly in salads with—or instead of—lettuce and other greens; the slightly bitter taste and crisp texture gives it more of a "bite" than the usual lettuce combinations. It suits strongly flavored dressings. Crisp bacon pieces or croutons are often included. With mature chicory, use the inner leaves for salads; the outer ones can be cooked as greens. Chicory can also be braised. Try serving it shredded and dressed with hot crushed garlic, anchovy fillets, and a little olive oil and butter.

Warm Red and Yellow Pepper Salad
Serves 6

The slightly bitter taste of curly chicory (escarole or frisée) is ideal combined with other lettuces such as corn salad or watercress in winter months. The sweetness of the peppers in this dish happily complements the chicory.

1 large head chicory, washed roughly chopped
Big bunch corn salad, washed
2 large red bell peppers
3 tablespoons olive oil
3 cloves garlic, crushed
1 tablespoon fresh herbs
Salt and freshly ground black pepper

For the dressing:
3 tablespoons extra-virgin olive oil
1 tablespoon white wine vinegar
Salt and freshly ground black pepper

Arrange the lettuces in a large bowl. Core and seed the bell peppers and cut them into thin strips. Heat the oil in a heavy pan and sauté the peppers, stirring constantly. Add the garlic after 5 minutes and cook for an additional minute.

Add the peppers to the salad. Make the dressing and toss in the herbs and seasoning. Serve the salad alongside plain broiled fish or chicken.

Cichonum intybus. Asteraceae

ENDIVE

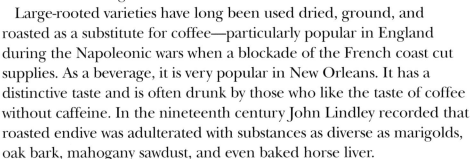

Also known as Witloof, Chicory, Succory, Sugarloaf Chicory, Radicchio. Hardy perennial grown as annual for blanched leaves or root. Very hardy.
Value: moderate levels of potassium.

A native of Europe through to central Russia and western Asia, endive has been cultivated for centuries. Pliny tells us that *cichorium* is a Greek adaptation of the Egyptian name; he also noted its medicinal use as a purgative and the blanching of leaves for salads.

Large-rooted varieties have long been used dried, ground, and roasted as a substitute for coffee—particularly popular in England during the Napoleonic wars when a blockade of the French coast cut supplies. As a beverage, it is very popular in New Orleans. It has a distinctive taste and is often drunk by those who like the taste of coffee without caffeine. In the nineteenth century John Lindley recorded that roasted endive was adulterated with substances as diverse as marigolds, oak bark, mahogany sawdust, and even baked horse liver.

Gibault, in his *Histoire des Legumes* of 1912, tells of the accidental discovery in the 1840s that the Witloof variety could be blanched. The head gardener at Brussels Botanic Gardens wanted to bring on winter endive in frames. He lifted several roots, chopped off the foliage, and planted them. Soon small, tight shoots emerged through the soil. Next season he did the same. He kept his find a secret, but when he died his widow told her gardener, who passed it on and the technique is now widely practiced. Perhaps it is due to this Brussels connection that Witloof is known in the U.S. as "Belgian endive."

"sugarloaf" types produce large-hearted lettucelike heads for fall harvest.
'**Brussels Widoof**' ('**Witloof de Brussels**') is one of the most famous forcing types which is also grown for its root.
'**Ceriolo**' is nonforcing and very cold-hardy with rounded leaves. Store the roots of '**Flash**' in the refrigerator or root cellar and pot up to force any time during the winter months.
'**Rollelof**' is a Dutch variety that produces mild bright red heads with white ribs '**Rossa di Treviso**,' another radicchio, has crisp, green leaves that become deep red and veined with white in cooler conditions. Tolerates light frost. Dates back to the 16th century. '**Rossa di Verona**' is a radicchio with a spreading habit that withstands considerable frost. '**Sugarhat**' is a nonforcing sugarloaf variety that has sweet leaves.
'**Witloof Zoom**,' a forcing endive, produces tightly packed, high-quality leaves.

CULTIVATION

Propagation
Sow seed of forcing varieties thinly in late spring to early summer in drills ½ in. deep and 9–12 in. apart. Thin

"Red chicory," or "radicchio"

VARIETIES

Endive has a distinctive, slightly bitter flavor. Most varieties are hardy and make a good winter crop with colorful, attractive leaves. There are three types.

"Forcing" endives like 'Witloof' (that is, whiteleaf) produce plump, leafy heads (known as "chicons") when blanched. "Red endive" or "radicchio" includes older cultivars, which responded to the reduced day length and lower temperatures of fall by turning from green to red; newer cultivars are naturally red and heart earlier. "Nonforcing" or

Some varieties are very pretty.

Sugarloaf' (nonforcing variety)

when the first true leaves appear to 8 in. apart.

Sow early radicchio under cover in seed trays and packs before hardening off and transplanting from midspring for summer harvest, using early maturing types first. Sow for fall harvest from early to midsummer, and in mid- to late summer for transplanting under cover in fall and cropping over winter. Thin to 9–15 in. in and between the rows.

Nonforcing or sugarloaf types can be broadcast or sown in broad drills under cover in late winter in mild regions. When the soil warms and the weather improves, sow successively outdoors until late summer. Sow the final crop during early fall under cover.

Thin to a final spacing of 9–12 in. in and between the rows. For a semimature cut-and-come-again winter crop, sow seed from mid- to late summer and transplant indoors in fall. **Zones 3–9.**

Growing

Endives prefer an open, sunny site, but tolerate a little shade. Soil should be fertile and free-draining, with organic matter added for the previous crop: avoid recently manured ground, as this causes the roots to fork.

Radicchio tolerates most soils except gravel or very heavy clay. The ideal pH is 5.5–7. Rake soil to a fine texture before sowing. Apply a general balanced fertilizer at 1 oz. per square yard.

Keep weed-free with regular hoeing or mulching. Water thoroughly during dry weather to prevent bolting.

Force appropriate varieties in situ if soil is light and winters are mild. In late fall to early winter, cut back the leaves to 1 in. above ground level. Form a ridge of friable soil 6–8 in. high over the stumps and cover with straw or leaf mold. After about 8–12 weeks, when the tips are appearing, remove the soil and cut the heads off at about 1 in. above the neck. Keep the compost moist while the "chicons" are growing.

Maintenance

Spring Sow early radicchio under cover, transplant from midspring. Sow sugarloaf types as cut-and-come-again crops.

Summer Harvest early radicchio and sow main-crop. Sow sugarloaf outdoors for cut-and-come-again and fall main crop.

Fall Harvest radicchio crops sown early to midsummer; sow late crops for winter. Harvest forcing types or force outdoors.

Winter Force roots indoors successively until spring. Sow sugarloaf indoors.

Protected Cropping

Nonforcing varieties can be grown under glass, for early or late crops.

In fall, cover outdoor crops of radicchio with cloches, fabric, or the like to extend the growing season.

Container Growing

All endives can be grown in large containers or beds of loam-based potting mix.

Forcing

Force "chicons" indoors if soil is heavy, if winters are severe, or for earlier crops. In mid- to late fall when the foliage dies down, dig roots

carefully, discard any forked or damaged ones and keep those that are at least 1½–2 in. in diameter at the top.

Cut off the remaining leaves to within ½ in. of the crown, trim back the side and main roots to about 8–9 in. Pack horizontally in boxes of dry sand, peat substitute, or sawdust and store in a cool, frost-free place.

For forcing, remove a few roots from storage at a time.

Plant about 5 to 6 roots in a 9-in. pot of sand or light soil, ensuring that ½ in. of the crown is above the surface. Surround the roots with moist peat or potting mix, leaving the crown exposed above ground.

Water sparingly and cover with a black plastic bag, an empty flower pot with the holes blocked up, or an empty box. Maintain temperatures of 50–60°F. They can also be blanched in a dark cellar or shed or under greenhouse benches (see "Growing," page 77).

The blanched "chicons" should be ready for cutting within 4 weeks, depending on the temperature.

Roots may resprout, producing several smaller shoots, which can then be blanched.

Harvesting and Storing

Harvest endives grown for roots after the first frost.

Cut heads of mature sugarloaf varieties with a sharp knife 1 in. above the soil in late fall; use immediately or store in a frost-free place.

Allow the plants to resprout as a cut-and-come-again crop under cloches.

Pick radicchio leaves as required, taking care not to overharvest, as this weakens plants. Alternatively, cut the whole head and leave the roots to resprout.

"Chicons" can be stored in the refrigerator, wrapped in foil or paper to prevent them from becoming bitter. Nonforcing endive will stay fresh for up to 1 month.

PESTS AND DISEASES

Seldom troubled by pests and diseases, crops can still rot outdoors in cold weather.

COMPANION PLANTING

The blue flowers of endive are attractive in a ornamental border.

MEDICINAL

Endive is said to be a digestive, diuretic, and laxative, reducing inflammation. A liver and gall bladder tonic, it is used for rheumatism, gout and hemorrhoids. Culpeper suggests its use "for swooning and passions of the heart."

'Witloof' plants grown in the dark in stacked wooden racks to blanch for use as a vegetable

CULINARY

All types of endive make a wonderful winter salad, particularly if you mix the colors of red, green, and white. Add tomatoes or a sweet dressing to take away some of the bitter taste. Homegrown chicons stored in the dark tend to be less bitter.

For a delicious light supper dish, pour a robust dressing (made with lemon juice rather than vinegar) over the leaves, add some anchovy fillets, crumbled hard-boiled eggs, and top with a handful of Kalamata olives.

As an accompaniment to cold meat and game, eat with sliced oranges, onion, and chopped walnuts. With roasted meats, braise endive with butter, lemon juice, and cream. Radicchio can also be braised, but loses its color.

To make a coffee substitute, dry roots immediately after harvest and grind.

Endive with Ham and Cheese Sauce
Serves 4

4 heads endive
8 slices smoked country ham
2 tablespoons butter
2 tablespoons all-purpose flour
2 teaspoons Dijon mustard
1/2 cup milk
Enough light cream to mix to a smooth consistency
4 tablespoons Gruyère cheese
Salt and freshly ground black pepper

Bring a pan of salted water to a boil and drop in the endive heads. Allow to blanch for 5 minutes, drain and gently squeeze as much water as you can out of them. Cut each

Endive with Ham and Cheese Sauce

endive in half and wrap in a slice of the ham. Then arrange in one layer in an ovenproof dish.

Preheat the oven to 400°F. Make the cheese sauce: melt the butter in a heavy pan and stir in the flour. Cook for 2 minutes, then stir in the mustard. Pour in the milk gradually, stirring vigorously as the sauce thickens, then add the cream and cheese. Stir over a gentle heat for 5 minutes to let the cheese melt. Season to taste.

Pour the cheese sauce over the endives wrapped in ham and cook in the oven for 20 minutes until nicely browned. Serve immediately.

Braised Endive
Serves 4

The French, especially in the southwest and in Provence, braise endive and serve it with roasted meats such as lamb and beef.

2 tablespoons butter
1 red onion, finely chopped
2 slices bacon, diced
4 heads endive, trimmed
1/2 cup chicken stock and white wine combined
Juice of half a lemon

Salt and freshly ground black pepper

Liberally coat the sides and bottom of a heavy, lidded casserole with half the butter and heat the remaining butter in a small pan over a medium flame. Gently fry the onion and bacon, and set aside.

Arrange the endives in the casserole. Add some of the stock and white wine, season with salt and pepper, and cover. Allow to sweat over a low heat until just changing color. Roll them over and cook on the other side.

Add a little more liquid as required. The liquid should evaporate from the endives, so that they are browned and tender (you may have to remove the lid for a short while). Add the onion and bacon and quickly heat up. Drizzle with the lemon juice, season, and serve immediately.

Colocasia esculenta var. *esculenta. Araceae*

DASHEEN

Also known as Elephant's Ear, Arvi Leaves, West Indian Kale, Taro. Herbaceous perennial grown for its edible leaves, shoots, and tubers. Tender. Value: tuber rich in starch; leaves high in vitamin A, good source of B$_2$.

In cultivation for around 7,000 years, dasheen is said to have been first grown in India on terraces where rice now flourishes. The common name derives from "*de Chine*" (from China): the root was imported from southeast Asia following a competition organized by the Royal Geographical Society to find a cheap food source for the slaves on West Indian sugar plantations.

Growing in Paradise Park, Hawaii: the angle of the leaves allows accumulated water to be poured away

VARIETIES

Dasheen have a cylindrical main tuber with fibrous roots and a few side tubers. The upright stems up to 6 ft. tall are topped with large, heart-shaped leaves with prominent ribs on the underside. Cultivated types rarely flower and are grouped by the color of their flesh, ranging from pink to yellow, and leaf stems of green, pinkish purple, to almost black.

CULTIVATION

Propagation
Dasheen are propagated from "tops" with a small section of tuber, small side tubers or "suckers." Plant 24 in. apart with 40 in. between rows, or 2–3 ft. apart; add general fertilizer to the hole before planting. **Zones 9–11.**

Growing
Dasheen tolerate quite heavy, fertile, moisture-retentive soil rich in organic matter with a pH of 5.5–6.5. Dig in compost or well-rotted manure if necessary. As dasheen need plenty of water and tolerate waterlogging, they are ideal for areas by streams and rivers. Where the water table is high, mound or ridge planting is advised. Irrigate heavily during dry weather.

In well-manured soil, a second crop can be planted between the rows 12 weeks before the main crop is harvested.

Maintenance
Spring Plant presprouted tubers with protection.
Summer Keep crops well fed and watered and weed-free.
Fall Harvest crops.
Winter Prepare for the following year.

Protected Cropping
Plant presprouted tubers in spring into greenhouse borders. Keep temperatures around 70°F, and maintain high humidity by misting plants with soft tepid water or damping down the greenhouse floor. Do not worry about overwatering.

Feed every 3–4 weeks with a high-potash fertilizer; extra nitrogen may be needed if growth slows.

The true flowers are enclosed within the larger spathe.

Container Growing

Dasheen can be grown as a "novelty" crop in 8–12 in. pots of peat-substitute potting mix. Soak thoroughly after planting and stand the pot in a shallow tray of tepid water throughout the growing season. Treat as directed in "Protected Cropping."

PESTS AND DISEASES

Taro leaf blight causes circular water-soaked spots on leaves followed by collapse of the plant. Those grown under glass are susceptible to **aphids**. **Red spider mite** and **downy mildew** can also be a problem. Take the necessary precautions.

Dasheen is an important food crop in the humid tropics—seen here in Hawaii.

CULINARY

Tubers can be roasted, baked, or boiled, served with spicy sauces and in stews. Larger tubers, which tend to be dry and coarse, should be braised and cooked slowly.

Leaves (with midrib removed) can be stuffed, boiled, or steamed and eaten with a pat of butter. Avoid particularly large leaves; they are often tough. In the West Indies, Callaloo Soup is made from dasheen leaves, okra, crab meat, and coconut milk. Young blanched shoots can be eaten like asparagus.

Palusima

This is a Western Samoan or Polynesian dish.

Allow about 7 oz. dasheen per person. Peel and chop roughly, then parboil in plain salted water for 5–10 minutes. Drain, then boil until reduced in coconut milk (enough to come to half the height of the dasheen in the pan) until thickish. Mash.

Stuff the mashed dasheen into parboiled leaves and secure with a toothpick. (Alternatively, wrap it in banana leaves, or even spinach or cabbage.) Bake for 15 minutes in a lightly greased dish in a preheated oven at 350°F. Serve with any good white fish such as cod.

Palusima

Harvesting and Storing

Dasheen take 7–11 months to mature. Harvest by digging the main tuber, saving some side tubers for eating and others for replanting. Undamaged tubers can be dried and stored for 4 weeks; washed leaves keep for several days in the refrigerator.

WARNING

Although selection has, over the years, reduced calcium oxalate levels in the skin of dasheen, it is extremely important to wear gloves or to cover the hands with a layer of cooking oil. This prevents skin irritation when peeling the vegetables.

Always make sure dasheen are cooked thoroughly before eating.

Colocasia esculenta var. *antiquorum. Araceae*

EDDOE

Perennial grown as annual for edible tubers. Tender. Value: rich in starch, magnesium, potassium, and vitamin C.

This variety of taro, native of India and southeast Asia, was first recorded by the Chinese 2,000 years ago. It is now grown throughout the humid tropics. Eddoes flourish in moist soil alongside rivers and streams. The central tuber is surrounded by clusters of smaller tubers that are harvested, making it different from the single-tubered dasheen. The brown, hairy tubers can weigh up to five pounds, and when sliced reveal flesh that is usually white but can also be yellow, pink, or orange. Their taste is similar to a garden potato but with an attractive nutty flavor. Tubers should never be eaten raw, as all varieties contain calcium oxalate crystals, a skin irritant.

VARIETIES

'Euchlora' has dark green leaves with violet margins and leaf stems. 'Fontanesii' produces leaf stems which are dark red-purple or violet. Its leaf blades are dark green with violet veins and margin.

CULTIVATION

Propagation
In the humid tropics, eddoes can be planted any time. In temperate zones they must be grown under glass or polyethylene at a minimum temperature of 70°F, and planted in spring. Plant small tubers or a tuber section containing some dormant buds in individual holes 25–30 in. apart. Cuttings consisting of the top

Eddoe cultivation

of a tuber with several leaves and a growth point can be planted directly into the soil and will establish rapidly. Add general fertilizer to the planting hole. **Zones 9–11.**

Growing
Eddoes need humus-rich, slightly acid, moisture retentive soil, in sunshine or partial shade. Cultivate the soil before planting and remove any weeds.

Maintenance
Spring Plant tubers if protected cropping. *Summer* Feed every 3–4 weeks with a high potash fertilizer; additional nitrogen may be needed. During drier periods, irrigate as needed to ensure swelling of the tubers and hill up. Keep weed-free. *Fall* Harvest as required. *Winter* Prepare beds for the following year's crop if growing in a greenhouse.

Protected Cropping
If you have space in a greenhouse or polyethylene tunnel, it is worth trying to grow eddoes. Plant presprouted tubers in spring into growing bags or 8–12-in. pots containing peat-lite mix. Maintain heat and high humidity: damp down the greenhouse floor or mist plants with soft tepid water.

Harvesting and Storing
Eddoes take between 5 and 6 months to mature. Harvest when the stems begin to turn yellow and die back. Dig the tubers carefully with a garden fork; select some for eating and save others for replanting. If they are undamaged and dried carefully, tubers can be stored for several months.

Health
The starch grains in tubers are among the smallest found in the plant kingdom, making them easy to digest.

Eddoe Soup

CULINARY

Tubers can be boiled, baked, roasted, pureed, and made into soup. They can also be fried.

PESTS AND DISEASES

Eddoes grown outdoors are generally problem-free but when grown under glass they are susceptible to **aphids** and **fungal leaf spots; red spider mite** can also be a problem, particularly when humidity is low. **Downy mildew** can attack tubers after they have been lifted so it is important to ensure that they are dried well before being stored. Dispose of infected tubers and do not use them for propagation.

WARNING

When handling and peeling eddoes, be sure to wear gloves or cover the hands with a layer of cooking oil to prevent a nasty rash.

Cucumis sativus. Cucurbitaceae

CUCUMBER

Climbing or scrambling annual, grown for elongated or round succulent fruits. Tender.
Value: moderate potassium and small amounts of beta carotene.

The wild species from central Asia is now rare in nature, yet the world-renowned salad crop has been cultivated for centuries. The first record was in Mesopotamia around 2000 B.C. in the earliest known vegetable garden, and cucumbers were grown in India a thousand years later. The Romans in the first century A.D. cultivated them in baskets or raised beds mounted on wheels so they could be moved around "as the sun moved through the heavens." When the day cooled, they were moved back under frames or into cucumber houses glazed with oiled cloth known as *specularia*. Tiberius found them tasty and was said to have eaten them every day of the year.

Early varieties were quite bitter and were boiled and served with oil, vinegar, and honey. They were a common ingredient in soups, stews, and as a cooked vegetable until the nineteenth century. Eighteenth-century English recipes include cucumbers stuffed with partly cooked pigeons (with head and feathers left on: the idea was to make the head appear attached to the cucumber); the whole was then cooked in broth and the heads garnished with barberries. Cooks in Georgian England must have had a rather bizarre sense of humor!

Columbus introduced cucumbers to the New World. They are recorded as being planted in Haiti in 1494 and grown by English settlers in Virginia in 1609. About the same time, French writers Estienne and Liébault warned: "Beware that your seed be not olde, for if it be 3 years olde, will bring forth radishes." Obviously their soil was as fertile as their imagination.

The smooth-skinned types can grow to well over 12 in.

VARIETIES

Your seed catalog will give an idea of the huge number of cultivars to choose from. There are "greenhouse cucumbers" (although many indoor varieties can grow outdoors in a sheltered position in cooler zones and grow outdoors in warm zones); "row" or outdoor types, which need protection as seedlings but can be grown outdoors in cool temperate zones; pickling cucumbers or gherkins; round varieties; Japanese climbing and bushy types.

Greenhouse or indoor cucumbers
'Crystal Apple,' a small, yellow, round cucumber, is prolific and easy to grow. For the unheated greenhouse or outdoors. **'Telegraph'** is a popular, reliable variety with smooth skin and good-sized fruits. **'Telegraph Improved'** is tasty and prolific with long fruits. **'Yamato'** produces delicious long thin fruits.

Outdoor or row cucumbers
'Burpless Tasty Green' is tender, tasty, and crisp, resistant to mildew and tolerant of heat. **'Chicago Pickling'** is high yielding and disease-resistant. **'Crystal Lemon'** fruits are tangy and the size of a

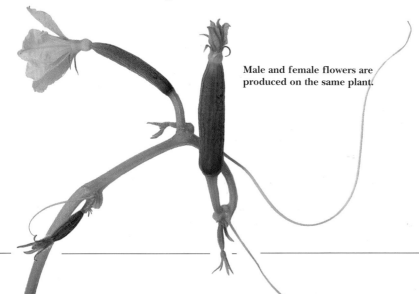

Male and female flowers are produced on the same plant.

lemon. They are perfect for pickling, slicing, or stuffing.

For a garden oddity, try **'De Bouenil,'** an all-white cucumber. When picked young they can be sliced in salads. Larger fruit are good for pickle-making. **'Long Green Improved'** is a robust, highly productive, and reliable variety with large, tasty fruits. It can be also used for pickling. **'Marketmore'** is smooth, tasty, and excellent for cooler conditions. It is resistant to powdery and downy mildew. **'Boothby Blond'** has been grown for generations by the Boothby family of Maine, but it is not commercially available. Many older varieties were grown from seed saved from the previous year's crop.

Pickling cucumbers or gherkins **'Gherkin'** is fast-growing, with masses of small prickly fruits. **'H-19 Little Leaf'** is a totally unique cucumber with small, blocky fruit growing on compact, little-leaved bushes. Fruit is good for fresh-eating or pickling. **'County Fair'** is never bitter; the 3-in. cukes are borne on vigorous bushy plants. **'National Pickling'** is short, blunt-ended with small, smooth fruits. It is vigorous and heavy yielding. It was introduced in 1929 by the National Pickle Packers Association in Britain. **'Vert de Massy Cornichon'** is very tasty. Pickle when small, or allow to reach maturity.

CULTIVATION

Propagation

When growing outdoor cucumbers, sow 2 seeds edgewise ½–¾ in. deep in a 2–3 in. pot from midspring. Place in a propagator or heated greenhouse at 68°F. Retain the stronger seedling after germination, keep moist with tepid water and tie up small sticks. Feed with a general liquid fertilizer to boost growth.

Give plants plenty of light and harden off before transplanting with care to avoid checks, when the danger of frost has passed. Allow 36 in. between plants. Protect with cloches or frost fabric until established.

Sow successionally to extend the cropping season.

Alternatively, pregerminate or sow 2–3 seeds, ½–¾ in. deep in situ under jelly jars or cloches from late spring to early summer when the soil temperature is around 68°F. Thin to leave the strongest seedling.

The latter method is preferable, as cucumbers do not transplant well. **Zones 3–11.**

Growing

"Row" cucumbers need rich, fertile, well-drained soil in a sunny, sheltered position. A few weeks before planting, dig out holes or longer rows at least 18 in. wide and 12 in. deep. Half-fill with well-rotted manure or good garden compost, then return the excavated soil, mounding it to about 6 in. above ground level.

Better fruits are obtained when plants are grown against supports, although traditionally they are left to trail over the ground.

Once plants have produced 5–6 leaves, pinch out growing points of the stems, allow 2 laterals to form and pinch out the growing tips again. Row cucumbers are insect-pollinated, so do not remove male flowers as you would with greenhouse cultivars.

Grow gherkins like row cucumbers, or train them up some netting.

Train Japanese cultivars up trellis, stake tripods, wire, or nylon netting. Nip out the growing point when stems reach the top of the support. Water regularly; feed with a high-potash fertilizer every 2 weeks when fruits are forming.

Keep crops weed-free and the soil moist.

Light-shading is essential, as with these 'Telegraph' types.

Maintenance

Spring Sow under cover from midspring.
Summer Plant row cucumbers outdoors once frost is past. Maintain high temperatures and humidity indoors. Train and harvest.
Fall Harvest.
Winter Store in a cool place.

Protected Cropping

Sow under cover or in a propagator from midspring at 70–75°F. To avoid erratic germination, seeds can be pregerminated on moist paper towels in a covered plastic container, then placed in an airing cupboard or propagator. After about 3 days, when the seeds have germinated, sow in 3-in. pots of seed potting mix.

Sow from late spring if no heat can be provided. Fill 3½-in. pots with potting mix and press the seed down edgewise into each pot about ½ in. deep.

Greenhouse cucumbers need a humid atmosphere and temperatures around 70°F. Soils should be rich, moisture-retentive and free-draining, so incorporate well-rotted organic matter if you are planting in the greenhouse border. Even better, grow in 10-in. pots of soil-based potting mix with added organic matter, in growing bags, or in untreated straw bales with a bed of compost in the center.

'Boothby Blond'

Insert a stake at the base of the plant and tie it into the roof structure of the greenhouse. Tie in the main stem and remove the growth tip when it reaches the roof, pinching out the laterals 2 leaves beyond each fruit.

Greenhouse cucumbers should not be pollinated or they become bitter: remove male flowers. Female flowers are identified by the swelling behind each one. Or choose "all-female" cultivars.

Mist plants regularly with tepid water and keep the potting mix moist with tepid water. Feed every 2 weeks with high-potash fertilizer once fruits begin to swell.

Outdoor cucumbers can be grown in cold frames or a cold greenhouse in cooler zones. They are better trained above the ground. Ventilate well on warm days and mist regularly.

Container Growing
Sow indoor types in pots or growing bags (see "Protected Cropping"). Smooth-skinned varieties can be grown in a growing bag or container 12 in. wide by 8 in. deep in a sunny position outdoors. Sow 3 seeds 1 in. deep in late spring or early summer.

Thin out to leave the strongest seedling; pinch out growing tips when the plant develops 6–7 leaves. Train the sideshoots on netting or trellis. Keep soil moist. Feed with high-potash fertilizer when fruits form. 'Bush Champion' is ideal.

Harvesting and Storing
Fruits should never be harvested until they are fully ripe, and the 16th-century practice of leaving fruit on until they were mottled brown and yellow with a rich flavor may be to your taste.

Outdoor cucumbers crop midsummer to early fall: cut with a sharp knife when they are large enough to use. For maximum yields, you should pick fruit regularly.

Cucumbers last for several days in the crisper in the refrigerator. Cover the cut end with plastic wrap and use as rapidly as possible. Or stand it stalk end down in a tall jug with a little water in the bottom. Like squash, they can be stored in nets in a cool place.

PESTS AND DISEASES

Red spider mite, aphids, slugs, and **powdery mildew** can be troublesome.

Cucumber mosaic virus shows as mottled, distorted leaves. Burn young infected plants and leaves from older plants. Older plants may recover, although yields will be lower.

COMPANION PLANTING

Row cucumbers thrive in the shade of corn or sunflowers, and grow well with peas and beans, beets, or carrots.

Climbing cucumbers flourish scrambling over corn and beans.

MEDICINAL

Cucumbers were used by the Romans against scorpion bites, bad eyesight, and to scare away mice.

Wives wishing for children wore cucumbers tied around their waists, and they were carried by midwives and thrown away once the child was born.

CULINARY

Eat while the stalk end is still firm. Some people remain adamant that peeled cucumbers are best: others think the flavor and appearance of the skin enhances the vegetable.

They are frequently sliced and eaten in salads, and are good in sandwiches with salmon. Mix with yogurt and mint as a side dish to Middle Eastern dishes or curries. Make into a delicious cold soup.

To eat them as a vegetable, peel, seed, dice, and stew them in a little water and butter for 20 minutes, until soft. Thicken with cream and serve with mild- or rich-flavored fish.

Cucumber and Cream Cheese Mousse

Cucumber and Cream Cheese Mousse
Serves 4

Half a cucumber, in chunks
1¼ cups cream cheese
1–2 tablespoons mint leaves
2 teaspoons white wine vinegar
2½ teaspoons unflavored gelatin
½ cup vegetable stock
Salt and freshly ground black pepper
Radicchio leaves and sprigs of mint, to serve

Put the cucumber into a blender with the cream cheese, mint, and vinegar and puree until smooth. Dissolve the gelatin in a little stock over a low heat. Allow to cool, then stir in the rest of the stock. Add this to the cream cheese, season, and blend.

Chill for at least 2 hours before serving, arranged individually with radicchio leaves and garnished with a few fine slices of cucumber and sprigs of mint.

Crambe maritima. Brassicaceae

SEA KALE

*Perennial grown for its blanched young shoots. Hardy.
Value: an excellent source of vitamin C.*

Found on the seashores of northern Europe, the Baltic, and the Black Seas, sea kale was harvested from the wild and sold in markets long before it came into cultivation. In Britain in Victorian times it was seen as an aristocrat of the vegetable garden and widely cultivated by armies of gardeners in the enormous kitchen gardens attached to great houses. Today it is rarely grown, perhaps because the scale on which it was forced for Victorian tables gave it a reputation for being labor-intensive. However, it is easy to grow at home, and quite delicious; so it is high time it experienced a revival!

Sea kale exposed to the sea breeze

VARIETIES

'Lily White' crops heavily, has a good flavor and pale stems. Unnamed selections of the wild species are also available from nurseries.

Sea kale flowers in summer and is sweetly scented.

CULTIVATION

Propagation
Sea kale can be grown from seed, but it is usually propagated from crowns or root cuttings from the side roots, taken in fall after the leaves have died back. These are called "thongs." Buy them from a nursery or select roots that are pencil-thick and 3–6 in. long. Make a straight cut across the top of the root and an angled cut at the base (so top and bottom are distinguishable). Store in sand until planting. **Zones 4–9.**

Growing
Sea kale needs a sunny position on deep, rich, well-drained light soil with a pH of around neutral. The winter before planting, dig in some well-rotted compost; on heavier soils, add sharp sand or grit, or plant on a raised bed.

Sea kale should crop for about 5–7 years before it needs replacing, so it is vital to prepare the ground thoroughly. Two weeks prior to planting, rake in a general fertilizer. Before planting, in early spring, rub off all the buds to leave the single strongest bud and plant thongs or crowns 18 in. apart, covered with 1–2 in. of soil.

Water regularly, feed occasionally, remove flower stems as they appear and keep weed-free. In fall, cut down the yellowing foliage. From late fall until midwinter, cover the crowns with a bucket, flower pot (cover the drainage holes), or sea kale forcer and surround with manure, straw, or leaf mold.

Stop harvesting in late spring, rake in a general fertilizer, and mulch with well-rotted manure or compost. Keep the beds weed-free and water well in dry periods. Delaying harvest until the second year lets plants become established.

Maintenance
Spring Force crops outdoors.
Summer Water in dry weather, feed occasionally, and keep weed-free.
Fall Remove the yellowing foliage.
Winter Dig crowns for forcing.

Protected Cropping
For an early crop, dig crowns after leaves die back, trim the main root to 6 in., and remove the sideshoots; plant 4 in. apart in boxes or 3 per 9-in. pot filled with rich soil from the sea kale bed or loam-based potting mix with a high fertilizer content. Cover with overturned pots, black plastic, or anything

Sea kale, after blanching, looks like a bizarrely twisted sculpture.

opaque. Keep the potting mix moist. They should be ready in 5–6 weeks at temperatures of 48–55°F; from 60–70°F they will be ready earlier. Keep them in a cellar, boiler room, or under the greenhouse benches and maintain a constant supply by lifting crowns regularly. In frosty weather dig and store crowns in moist sand until required. Dispose of exhausted crowns after use.

Harvesting and Storing
When blanched sprouts are 3–8 in. long, remove the soil from around the shoots and cut through the stems with a sharp knife, removing a tiny sliver of root. Crops forced outdoors can be harvested in late fall to early spring. After harvesting, discard the exhausted roots of those forced indoors.

PESTS AND DISEASES

Do not plant in beds infected with **clubroot. Flea beetle** make round holes in the leaves; dust seedlings with rotenone.

OTHER USES

Sea kale is attractive in a flower border. It forms a compact rosette of large, wavy-edged, glaucous leaves, with large bunches of white, honey-scented flowers towering above the foliage in summer.

CULINARY

Better eaten fresh, sea kale lasts for 2–3 days in the crisper in the refrigerator.

Wash stems and tie them into bundles using raffia and steam or lightly boil them until tender— overcooking toughens the stems and makes them less palatable.

Victorians served sea kale on toast, drenched in white sauce or melted butter.

Sea kale is also delicious served as a starter with béchamel or hollandaise sauce, or covered in lemon-flavored melted butter.

Young flowering shoots can be eaten once they are lightly boiled.

Sea Kale Gratinée
Serves 4

This is excellent served with baked ham.

1½ lb. well-washed sea kale

For the béchamel sauce:
2 tablespoons butter
2 tablespoons flour
1 teaspoon French mustard
½ cup milk or crème fraîche
4 tablespoons good strong cheddar cheese
Salt and freshly ground black pepper

Rinse the sea kale well, tie into bundles and cook until al dente in boiling salted water. Drain well. Arrange in an ovenproof dish.

Make the béchamel sauce, flavoring with the cheddar cheese. Pour the sauce over the sea kale and bake in a preheated oven at 400°F for 15 minutes. Serve hot.

Sea kale with traditional terra-cotta forcing jars

Cucurbita maxima, Cucurbita moschata and *Cucurbita pepo. Cucurbitaceae*

PUMPKIN & SQUASH

SUMMER SQUASH, WINTER SQUASH, ZUCCHINI, MARROW, POTIRON

Annuals grown for edible fruits, often colorful, which can be extremely large
Tender. Value: high in beta-carotene, moderate amounts of vitamin C, and folic

On the coast of Coromandel
Where the early pumpkins blow
In the middle of the woods
Lived the Yonghy-Bonghy-Bo . . .
Edward Lear (1812–88)

The name "pumpkin" appeared in the 17th century, shortly before Perrault wrote Cinderella, the tale about a poor girl whose fairy godmother turned a pumpkin into a golden coach that took her to a fabulous ball. "Pumpkin" comes from the Greek word for melon—*pepon,* or "cooked by the sun"—while one French name, *potiron,* means "large mushroom," from the Arabic for morel mushrooms. "Squash" is an abbreviation of the Native American word *askutasquash*, meaning "eaten raw or uncooked."

The squashes originated in the Americas and are believed to have been cultivated for between five and ten thousand years. Wild forms were originally gathered for their seeds and were only later found to have sweet flesh. Many varieties arrived in Europe soon after the discovery of the New World in the sixteenth century. Not only were they eaten, but the seeds were pounded into a meal and applied to the face, to bleach freckles and other blemishes. Estienne and Liébault wrote in 1570: "To make pompions keep long and not spoiled or rotted, you must sprinkle them with the juice of a houseleek." In the seventeenth century they were mashed to bulk up bread, or boiled and heavily buttered.

This group contains a wealth of edible and outstandingly ornamental fruits. One of the most beautiful sights in the kitchen garden is pumpkins ripening in golden sunshine during the fall.

Winter squash

'Little Gem' comes from the same group as the summer squash, but grows round rather than long.

VARIETIES

Members of the genus *Cucurbita* are bushy or trailing annuals—sometimes extremely vigorous plants—bearing a wide range of edible and/or ornamental fruit. The fruits from all of these species are often grouped together according to their shape or time of harvest—crookneck, summer squash, winter squash, and so on; in practice categories overlap and some are multipurpose, being served differently when young and when mature. Additional confusion arises because of local variation in what is grown and what it is called. Here they are classed according to species.

The *Cucurbita maxima* group has large, variable fruits and includes most traditional pumpkins and winter squashes, containing several ornamentals like the banana, buttercup, hubbard, and turban types. They tend to have hard skins when mature, and keep well; the yellow flesh needs cooking. They flourish in low humidity from 68–80°F, though some tolerate cooler conditions. **'Atlantic Giant'** is not for the faint-hearted—it can grow to 700 lb. **'Banana Pink'** is long, broad, and curved, with pale pink skin. **'Big Max'** is a massive pumpkin with rough red-orange skin and bright flesh. It is excellent for pies, exhibitions, and as a "giant" vegetable. **'Buttercup'** is delicious with firm, dense, sweet flesh. The skin is dark green with pale narrow stripes. Good for soups, roasting, and pumpkin pie. **'Crown Prince'** is small fruited with tender orange flesh. Tasty and keeps well.

Cut open the slate-gray **'Sweet Meat'** to reveal a sweet, golden yellow flesh. **'Turk's Turban'** (**'Turk's Cap'**), a wonderful ornamental squash, is orange with cream and green markings. The name aptly describes the shape. **'Warted Hubbard'** is a small, round fruit with extraordinary dark green warty skin and orange-yellow flesh. It keeps well. **'Dulong Qui'** is an Australian native that looks like a gray, flattened pumpkin. The golden-yellow flesh is dry and sweet.

Cucurbita pepo embraces summer squashes (including zucchini and their larger version, the marrow), nonkeeping winter pumpkins, and ornamental gourds such as custard squash, plus straight and crook-necked types. The fruits are usually soft-skinned, especially when young, and may be served raw when small. One variety, **'Little Gem,'** is slow to mature, taking about 4 months. It may not be suitable for growing in cooler zones.

'Crown Prince' looks pale besides its brighter counterparts.

'Crown of Thorns'

Summer Squash
'Early Golden Summer Crookneck' is an early cropper with bright yellow fruits, excellent for eating. Harvest when 4 in. long. **'Early Prolific Straight Neck'** is lemon-yellow with finely textured thick flesh. **'Vegetable Spaghetti'** (**'Spaghetti Squash'**) is pale yellow when mature. Boil or bake fruits whole; scoop out the flesh inside and it looks like spaghetti. **'White Patty Pan'** (**'White Bush Scallop'**) has an unusual flattened shape with a scalloped edge. It is better harvested and cooked whole when about 3 in. in diameter. It is bushy and ideal for small gardens. **'Yellow Bush Scallop'** is an old variety with coarse, pale yellow flesh and a bright yellow skin.

Marrow
This elongated type of summer squash has long been popular. **'Long Green Trailing'** is a prolific, long-fruited variety that is dark green with pale stripes. **'Tiger Cross,'** an early green bush type, crops well, and has good-quality fruits. Resistant to cucumber mosaic virus. **'Caserta'** is an All America Selections winner that produces light-green, thin-skinned striped fruit with a firm creamy flesh.

Zucchini
Varieties of marrow bred for picking small, the following are all bush types and ideal for the smaller garden.

autumn decoration. **'Small Sugar'** has rounded orange fruits growing to 7½ in. diameter. The flesh is tender, yellow, and excellent for pies. It matures from late fall.

Cucurbita moschata includes the early butternut, butternut, Kentucky Field, and crookneck squashes, harvested in fall and winter. They are large, rounded, and usually have smooth, tough skin. Possibly one of the earliest species in cultivation, they are widely found in the tropics. Particularly heat-tolerant.

'Butternut' has pale tan, stocky, club-shaped fruits with bright orange flesh. It stores well and succeeds in cooler zones. **'Early Butternut'** is a curved, narrow fruit with a swollen tip. This bush variety matures rapidly and keeps well. **'Kentucky Field'** (**'Large Cheese'**) is flattened with faintly ribbed, pale cream-colored skin.

'Snackjack' is a small, uniform, bright orange, 2-lb. pumpkin that's well suited for carving. In addition, its seeds are hull-less. Clean and roast them for a snack that tastes much like sunflower seeds. **'Waltham Butternut'** has a smooth, pale tan skin, yellow-orange flesh and a nutty taste. It is very good for storing and yields extremely well.

CULTIVATION

Propagation
Sow in situ or in pots in cooler zones, as seeds do not germinate if the soil is below 56°F.

From mid- to late spring, soak the seeds overnight, then sow one seed edgewise, about 1 in. deep in a 3 in. pot or pack of moist multipurpose or seed potting mix, and place in a propagator or on a warm windowsill, preferably at 68–77°F. After germination transplant the seedlings when they are large enough to handle into 5-in. pots, taking care not to damage the roots. Keep potting mix moist but not waterlogged. Harden off gradually and transplant from late spring to early summer when the danger of frost has passed. Protect with cloches until the plants are established.

Alternatively, sow in situ

'Ambassador' is high yielding with dark green fruit and crops over a long period. **'Defender'** produces high yields of midgreen fruits. Harvest regularly. Resistant to cucumber mosaic virus. **'De Nice à Fruit Rond,'** a round variety, should be picked when the size of a golf ball. Delicious flavor. **'Gold Rush,'** a compact bush with yellow fruits, crops over a long period. **'Spacemiser'** is a compact and prolific gourmet variety. **'Supremo'** produces very tasty, dark green fruit.

Winter squash
These usually have white or pale yellow flesh, whereas pumpkins have coarse, orange flesh. **'Ebony Acorn'** (**'Table Queen'**) is an ancient early-cropping variety with thin, dark green skin and pale yellow, sweet flesh. It is a semi-bush, and is good for baking. **'Jack be Little'** is a miniature pumpkin with deep ribbed fruits about 2–3 in. in diameter and orange skin. It is edible, but is more attractive simply as an

The high-yielding 'Gold Rush'

when the soil is warm and workable and there is no danger of frost, from late spring to early summer.

Dig out a hole at least 12–18 in. square and half-fill with well-rotted manure 7–10 days before planting. Sow 2–3 seeds 1 in. deep in the center of the mound and cover with a jelly jar or cut the base from a plastic bottle and use as a crop cover. After germination, thin to leave the strongest seedling, remove the cover and mark the position with a stack so you know where to water the plant among the mass of stems. Alternatively, prepare the ground as described and transplant seedlings.

Space cultivars according to their vigor. Sow bush varieties on mounds or ridges, 24–36 in. apart with 36–48 in. between rows. Trailing varieties should be 48–72 in. apart with 6–12 ft. between rows. **Zones 3–11.**

Growing

Pumpkins and squashes need a sunny position in rich, moisture-retentive soil with plenty of well-rotted organic matter and a pH of 5.5–6.8.

It is a good idea to plant through a black plastic mulch laid over the soil with the edges buried to hold it in place. This warms the soil, suppresses weeds, conserves moisture, and protects ripening fruit.

A thick layer of straw or frost fabric are useful alternatives, or you can lay

Outstandingly strange-looking, 'Turk's Turban' will store for several months.

The 'White Patty Pan' looks like a flying saucer.

the ripening fruit on a roof tile, a piece of wood, or similar to protect it from the soil and prevent rotting.

Hand-pollination is recommended, particularly in cold weather when insect activity is reduced. Female flowers have a small swelling, the embryonic squash, immediately behind the petals, while male flowers have only a thin stalk.

When the weather is dry, remove a mature male flower, fold back or remove the petals and dust pollen on to the stigma of the female flowers. Alternatively, transfer the pollen with a fine paintbrush. Periods of hot weather can reduce the ratio of female to male flowers.

Plants need copious amounts of food and water, particularly when flowers and fruits are forming, up to 2 gallons of water per week, but they should never be allowed to become waterlogged.

Feed with a liquid general fertilizer every 2 weeks. Plants grown with a black plastic mulch also need an occasional foliar feed to boost growth.

Pinch out tips of main shoots of trailing varieties when they reach 2 ft. to encourage branching and trim back those that outgrow their position.

Trailing types can also be trained over trellis or supports. Where space is limited, you can push a circle of pegs into the soil and trail the stems around the pegs.

To guarantee large fruits, allow only 2–3 to develop on each plant.

Keep crops weed-free.

Maintenance

Spring Sow seeds under glass or outdoors.
Summer Feed and water copiously; keep crops weed-free. Harvest zucchini and marrows.
Autumn Harvest pumpkins and winter squashes, allow to ripen and protect from frost.
Winter Store winter squashes until midwinter or later.

Protected Cropping

In cooler zones or to advance growth, sow seed indoors, and transplant. Protect with cloches or crop covers until they are well established. Use bush varieties for earlier crops.

Container Growing

Zucchini, marrows, bush varieties of other squashes, and those that are moderately vigorous can be grown in growing bags or containers that are at least 14 in. by 12 in. deep. Use a loam-based potting mix with additional well-rotted organic matter. Sow indoors to transplant later or sow directly outdoors. Keep plants well watered and do not allow the potting mix to dry out.

Plants can be grown up strong stakes 6½ ft. tall. Pinch out growing points when stems reach the top; tie the main stem and side shoots firmly to the supporting stakes.

Hand-pollinate for successful cropping.

Harvesting and Storing

Pick zucchini and summer squashes when they are about 4 in. long and still young and tender. Marrows are harvested when they have reached full size. Push your thumbnail gently into the skin near the stalk; if it goes in easily then the marrow is ready for harvest. Cut them from the stem leaving a short stalk on the fruit and handle with care to avoid bruising. Harvest regularly for continual cropping. They can be stored in a cool place for about 8 weeks.

Zucchini can be kept in a plastic bag in the refrigerator and will stay fresh for about a week.

Zucchini are suitable for freezing. Cut into ½ in. slices, blanch for 2 minutes, cool, drain, and dry. Freeze in plastic bags. Flesh of winter squashes and pumpkins can be cooked and then frozen without any loss of flavor.

Toward the end of the growing season, remove any foliage that shades the fruits. Harvest pumpkins and winter squashes from late summer to fall, though they must be brought into storage before the first heavy frosts. On maturity, the foliage rapidly dies, the skin hardens, and the stem starts to crack.

After harvest, leave them outdoors for about 14 days as cold weather improves the taste and sugar content, hardening the skin and sealing the stem. Protect from heavy frost with burlap, straw, or the like.

In cooler zones they can be ripened in a greenhouse or on a sunny windowsill. Pumpkins will last until midwinter when stored in a frost-free shed.

Store winter squashes at a minimum temperature of 50°F; they last for up to 6 months, but may deteriorate earlier. Some Japanese varieties will last even longer.

Marrows are traditionally allowed to trail, but can also be grown on frames.

The edible flowers of the marrow

COMPANION PLANTING

Grow zucchini and marrow alongside corn for support and shade, and with legumes, which provide essential nitrogen.

PESTS AND DISEASES

If fruits show signs of withering, water and feed more often.

Aphids, powdery and downy mildew, and **slugs** can be a problem.

Cucumber mosaic virus causes yellow mottling and puckering of the leaves and rotting of the fruit. Destroy infected plants immediately and control **aphids,** which transmit this virus.

CULINARY

Flowers of all varieties can be used in salads or stuffed with rice or minced meat and fried in batter. Prepare the meat, rice, and batter before picking the flowers, as they wilt quickly. They can also be pureed and made into soup. Young shoots are steamed or boiled. Pumpkin flesh is used for pies; their seeds are deep-fried in oil, salted and are known as "pepitos."

The fruits can be stuffed, steamed, stir-fried, added to curries, or made into spreads or pickles.

Zucchini Omelet
Serves 2

A particularly pretty omelet can be made with young zucchini; use a mixture of yellow and green ones to good effect.

5 eggs
Salt and freshly ground black
*   pepper*
2 cups zucchini
4 tablespoons olive oil
1 tablespoon fresh basil leaves
*   (purple for preference)*
1 tablespoon fresh thyme leaves

Whisk the eggs with salt and pepper and set aside. Cut the zucchini in coarse dice. Heat half the oil and sauté the zucchini for a couple of minutes. Then remove from the heat.

In an omelet pan, heat the balance of the oil and pour in the eggs, zucchini, and herbs. Stir gently over a low heat while the omelet sets. Turn it onto a plate and slide back into the pan to cook the second side for a minute or so until nicely browned. Serve as a refreshing Sunday supper dish.

Pumpkin Kibbeh
Serves 4

A centerpiece of many Middle Eastern meals, these "balls" should be served warm, rather than hot. This recipe was given to me by Arto der Haroutunian.

1¹⁄₂ cups freshly boiled
*   pumpkin flesh*
2¹⁄₂ cups bulgar wheat
1¹⁄₄ cups all-purpose flour
1 onion, finely chopped
Salt and freshly ground black
*   pepper*

For the filling:
2 shallots, finely chopped
Oil for frying
2¹⁄₂ cups spinach, washed
1 cup cooked chickpeas,
*   drained*
¹⁄₂ cup chopped walnuts
¹⁄₂ cup dried apricots
¹⁄₄ teaspoon sumac
*   (from Middle Eastern*
*   specialty stores)*
1 tablespoon lemon juice
Salt and freshly ground black
*   pepper*

In a large bowl, puree the pumpkin using a fork. Sieve the bulgar and flour into the bowl and mix in the onion and seasoning. Leave in a cool place for 10–15 minutes. If the dough is too hard to handle, you may need to add a tablespoon of water and knead well.

To make the filling, sauté the shallots in the oil until they just turn brown. Mix in the spinach and allow to wilt, stirring constantly. Then add the rest of the ingredients, mixing well.

Make the kibbehs with wet hands to prevent the mixture from sticking. Form the bulgar and pumpkin mixture into oval patties— they should be about 3 in. long and just big enough to stuff. Create an opening at one end; fill each kibbeh with the spinach and apricot stuffing. Using your fingers, seal up the ends.

Fry the kibbehs in hot oil for a couple of minutes on each side and drain on paper towels. There should

Acorn Squash with Balsamic Vinegar

be enough to make between 20 and 24 kibbehs.

Acorn Squash with Balsamic Vinegar

Allow 4 oz. of acorn squash per person. Cut in half and remove the seeds and fibers. Place in a buttered, ovenproof dish and add 1 tablespoon balsamic vinegar, 2 tablespoons honey, and 1 tablespoon lemon juice for each serving. Cook in a preheated oven at 350°F for 40 minutes, turning over halfway through the cooking time.

Custard Marrow with Bacon and Cheese

4 cups custard marrow
2 tablespoons butter
1 small onion, finely sliced
3 oz. bacon, diced
¹⁄₄ cup crème fraîche
Salt and freshly ground black
*   pepper*
4 tablespoons shredded mature
*   cheddar cheese*

Cut the custard marrow into a rough dice and steam it until just tender. Remove from the heat and keep warm. Make a sauce by heating the butter and

cooking the onion until softened. Add the bacon and continue cooking for 5 minutes, stirring from time to time. Mix in the crème fraîche, the custard marrow, and seasoning and pour into a greased ovenproof dish. Top with the cheese and cook in a preheated oven at 425°F for 15 minutes.

OTHER USES

Pumpkins are hollowed out and made into Halloween jack-o'-lanterns. Mature marrows can be used for wine making.

MEDICINAL

In Ethiopia seeds from squashes are used as laxatives and purgatives; they are used worldwide to expel intestinal worms. Eating winter squash and pumpkin is said to reduce the risk of cancer.

Cynara cardunculus. Asteraceae

CARDOON

Also known as Cardon. Perennial grown as annual for "heart" and blanched leaf midribs. Half hardy. Value: rich in potassium.

This close relative of the globe artichoke is found in the wild through much of the Mediterranean and North Africa. Cultivated versions are valued as a vegetable and in the ornamental garden. When grown as a food crop, the stems are blanched in the fall in a similar manner to celery. Its delights have been enjoyed for centuries; it was grown before the birth of Christ and was esteemed by the Romans, who paid high prices for it in their markets as an ingredient for stews and salads. Cardoons reached England by 1658 and North America by the following century, but never established themselves as a major crop despite their popularity in Europe. Today they are more likely to be found in the herbaceous border, where the bold angular foliage and tall candelabras of thistlelike purple flowers are outstanding.

VARIETIES

'Gigante di Romagna' is a reliable variety with long stalks. 'Plein Blanc Inerma Ameliora' grows to 4 ft. tall, with white ribs that are well textured and tasty. 'Tours' is a large and vigorous variety. Beware of the large spines and protect yourself accordingly!

Cardoons make fine ornamentals

CULTIVATION

Cardoons need a sunny, sheltered site on light, fertile, well-drained soil. **Zones 3–10.**

Propagation
Sow in situ in midspring, planting 3–4 seeds 1 in. deep in hills 20 in. apart with 5 ft. between rows. Thin after germination to retain the strongest seedling. In cooler zones or if spring is late and the soil is yet to warm up, sow indoors. Place 3 seeds in 3-in. pots or packs of moist seed potting mix in a propagator or greenhouse at 55°F. Thin, leaving the strongest seedling, then harden off before planting outdoors in mid- to late spring, when there is no danger of frost. Water well after planting and protect from scorching sunshine until they have established.

Growing
The fall or early spring before seed sowing or planting out seedlings, double dig the site, adding well-rotted organic matter. Alternatively, plant in trenches 15–20 in. wide and 12 in. deep; dig these in late fall or early spring, incorporating plenty of rotted manure or compost into the base and refilling to 3–4 in. below the surface. Leave the remaining soil alongside for earthing up. Before planting, rake in general fertilizer at 2 oz./sq. yd.

In late summer to early fall, on a day when the leaves and hearts are dry, begin blanching: pull stems into a large bunch (wear long sleeves and gloves for protection), and tie with raffia or soft string just below the leaves. Wrap cardoons with "collars" of newspaper, corrugated cardboard, brown wrapping paper, or black plastic tied firmly around the stems. Tile drainpipes and plastic guttering are just as effective at excluding the light. Support collars with a stake, particularly on exposed sites. Alternatively, cardoons can be earthed up. Cover stems with dry hay, or straw held firmly at several points with twine and cover with soil, banked at an angle of 45 degrees. The first method is easier, cleaner, and quicker.

Cardoons need a regular water supply from early summer to early fall, and liquid general fertilizer every 2 weeks. Keep weed-free by hand weeding, hoeing, or, preferably, mulching with a 2-in. layer of organic matter once plants are established.

Maintenance
Spring Sow seeds in situ or under glass.
Summer Feed and water regularly. Keep weed-free.
Fall Harvest crops using a sharp knife. Prepare the planting bed.
Winter Store in a cool, dry place until required.

The flower heads are similar to those of globe artichokes

Protected Cropping
Protect transplants or seedlings under cloches or frost fabric if late spring frosts are forecast.

Container Growing
Grow in large containers of loam-based potting mix with added organic matter or in free-draining, moisture-retentive soil. Allow plenty of room for leaves to grow. Water and feed regularly: do not let the potting mix dry out. Blanch using "collars."

Harvesting and Storing
Blanching takes about 3–4 weeks. When ready to harvest, lift plants with a garden fork, trim off roots, and remove outer leaves. Cardoons can remain in the ground until needed, but protect with hay, straw, or other insulating material in moderate frosts. If hard frosts are expected, lift and store in a cool shed or cellar.

Pests and Diseases
Cardoons are robust and have few problems. They can be affected by **powdery mildew**, which is worse when plants are dry at the roots and if nights are cold and days warm and dry.

Mice will eat the seeds. An old remedy is to dip the seeds in paraffin; otherwise buy humane traps or a cat!

CULINARY

The leaf midribs and thinly sliced hearts are eaten raw in salads, in soups and stews, or as an alternative to fennel or celery. They can be boiled in salted water with a squeeze of lemon juice for about 30 minutes until tender. Once cardoons are cut, drop them into water with a squeeze of lemon juice, as the cut surfaces tend to blacken.

The dried flowers are used as a substitute for rennet in Spain and some parts of South America.

Lamb Tagine with Cardoons
Serves 4

Tagines (or stews) are popular in northern Africa. Cardoons give this traditional Moroccan dish a rich flavor.

1½ lb. lamb fillet, cubed
3 cloves garlic, crushed
1 teaspoon ground ginger
Pinch saffron
¼ teaspoon turmeric
2–3 tablespoons vegetable oil
2 tablespoons cilantro, chopped
1 onion, peeled and sliced
1½–2 lb. cardoons, cleaned and sliced into 2-in. pieces
2 preserved lemons, quartered
4 tablespoons black olives
Juice of 2 lemons
Salt and freshly ground black pepper

Put the lamb, garlic, ginger, saffron, turmeric, oil, chopped cilantro, and onion in a heavy pan and mix well. Add a cup or two of water and bring to a boil.

Skim and then simmer, covered, for 1 hour, adding more water if necessary, to just cook the lamb. Then add the cardoons and enough water to cover them (this is important), and continue cooking for an additional 30–40 minutes.

Stir in the preserved lemon quarters and the olives and enough lemon juice to taste, and ensure the tagine is well mixed. Taste and adjust the seasoning before serving piping hot.

Lamb Tangine with Cardoons

Cynara scolymus. Asteraceae

GLOBE ARTICHOKE

Also known as French Artichoke, Green Artichoke. Tall, upright perennial grown for edible flower buds. Half hardy. Value: 85% water; half carbohydrate indigestible inulin, turning to fructose in storage; moderate iodine and iron content.

Originating in the Mediterranean, globe artichokes were grown by the Greeks and Romans, who regarded them as a delicacy. The common name comes from the Italian *articoclos*, deriving from *cocali*, or pinecone—an apt description of the appearance of the flower bud. Artichokes waned in popularity in the Dark Ages, but were restored to favor when Catherine de Medici introduced them to France in the sixteenth century. From there they spread around the world. Globe artichokes reached the United States in 1806, traveling with French and Spanish settlers.

In Italy, its bitter principle flavors the aperitif *cynar*, which is as popular as vermouth and definitely an acquired taste!

Growing to about 4–5 ft. tall, with a 3-ft. spread, attractive leaves and large thistlelike flowers, globe artichokes always look wonderful in a flower border and make excellent dual-purpose plants.

VARIETIES

'Green Globe' has large green heads with thick, fleshy scales. It needs winter protection in cooler zones. **'Imperial Star'** is a heavy producing variety, producing large, tender globes in just 80 to 90 days. **'Gros Camus de Bretagne'** is only suitable for warmer zones, but it is worth growing for its large, well-flavored heads. **'Purple Sicilian'** has small, deep, purple-colored artichokes that are excellent for eating raw when they are very young. This variety is not frost-hardy. **'Vert de Laon'** is hardy with an excellent flavor. **'Violetta di Chioggia,'** a purple-headed variety, is excellent in a flower border.

CULTIVATION

Artichokes need an open, sheltered site on light, fertile, well-drained soil.

Propagation

Artichokes can be grown from seed or divided, but are sometimes propagated from rooted "suckers"— shoots arising from the plant's root system. Suckers can be bought or removed from established plants in midspring in mild-winter zones. They should be

An immature flower head, just before harvesting

healthy, about 8–9 in. long and well rooted, with at least 2 shoots. Clear soil from around the roots of the parent plant and remove them with a sharp knife, cutting close to the main stem between the sticker and parent plant. Alternatively, divide established plants in spring by lifting the roots and easing them apart with two garden forks, a spade, or an old knife and replanting the sections; these too should have at least 2 shoots and a good root system. To keep your stocks vigorous and productive, renew the oldest one-third of your plants every year. This extends the cropping season, too, as mature plants are ready for harvest in late spring to early summer and young plants in late summer.

You can grow from seed and select the best plants, but this is time-consuming, uses valuable space, and is not recommended; it is far better to grow proven, named cultivars. If you have the time and inclination, sow seeds in trays of moist seed potting mix in an unheated greenhouse during late winter or outdoors in early spring. Thin to leave the strongest seedlings and harden off before planting out at their final spacing in late spring. Once flower buds have been produced, retain the best plants for harvest and for future propagation, discarding the rest.

Growing

If necessary, improve the soil by digging in plenty of well-rotted organic matter in spring or fall before planting. This prevents summer drought and winter waterlogging, conditions that globe artichokes dislike. Before planting, rake in general fertilizer at 2 oz./sq. yd.

Plant suckers or divisions 2 ft. apart with 2–2½ ft. between each row, trimming the leaves back to 5 in., which helps to reduce water loss, and shading them from full sun until they are established. Water thoroughly after planting and during periods of dry weather, applying a high-potash liquid fertilizer every 2 weeks when the plants are actively growing.

Keep the beds weed-free and mulch with organic matter in spring. In mild zones where artichokes can be overwintered, protect plants by earthing up with soil, then covering them with a thick layer of straw, hay, or other organic insulation if heavy frosts are forecast. Remove the covering in spring.

Maintenance

Spring Divide or remove suckers from existing plants and replant.
Summer Keep weed-free and water thoroughly during drought.
Fall In areas with moderate temperatures, retain leaves and stems as frost protection.
Winter If severe frost is forecast, remove the decayed leaves, earth up, and protect plants with insulating material. Remove the materials in spring before growth begins.

Harvesting and Storing

Each flowering stem normally produces one large artichoke at the tip and several smaller ones below. A few flower heads will be produced in the first year; these are best removed so that the energy goes into establishing the plant, but if you cannot resist the

Globe artichoke flowers, which are closely related to the cotton thistle, are attractive to pollinating insects.

temptation, harvest in late summer. In the second and third years more stems will be produced and are ready for cutting in midsummer. Harvest when the scales are tightly closed, removing the terminal bud first with 2–3 in. of stem, then the remaining side buds as they grow large enough. Alternatively, remove the lower artichokes for eating when they are about 1½ in. long.

Once the scales begin to open, globe artichokes become inedible.

Pests and Diseases

Slugs attack young shoots and leaves—the problem is worse in damp conditions. Keep the area free of plant debris, use biological controls, scatter aluminum-sulfate-based slug pellets around plants, or make traps from plastic cartons half-buried in the ground and filled with milk or beer. Lay roof tiles, newspaper, old lettuce leaves, or other tempting vegetation on the ground and hand pick slugs regularly from underneath them. Or put a barrier of grit around plants, or attract natural predators such as birds to the garden. **Lettuce root aphids** can be a problem. Creamy yellow aphids appear on the roots during summer, sucking sap and weakening plants. Water well in dry weather; apply systemic insecticide.

MEDICINAL

Artichokes are highly nutritious and are especially good for the liver, aiding detoxification and regeneration. They reduce blood sugar and cholesterol levels, stimulating the gallbladder and helping the metabolism of fat. Artichoke is also a diuretic and used to treat hepatitis and jaundice. It was used in folk medicine as a contraceptive and aphrodisiac, but its potency is not recorded!

Globe artichokes grow to 5 ft. high

CULINARY

Artichokes can be stored for up to a week in a plastic bag in the refrigerator.

The edible parts are the fleshy base of the outer scales, the central "heart," and the bottom of the artichoke itself. Wash the artichoke thoroughly before use and sprinkle any cut parts with lemon juice to prevent them from turning black. Boil artichokes in a nonmetallic pan of salted water with lemon juice for 30–45 minutes until soft. Check if they are ready by pushing a knife through the heart, or try a basal leaf to check it for tenderness.

Eat artichokes by hand, pulling off the leaves one by one and dipping the base in mayonnaise, hollandaise, lemon sauce, melted butter, or plain yogurt before scraping off the fleshy leaf base between your teeth. Pull off the hairy central "choke," or remove it with a spoon, and then eat the fleshy heart.

Bottoms can be a garnish for roasts, filled with vegetables or sauces. Cook "Cypriot-style" with oil, red wine, and cilantro seeds, or toss in oil and lemon dressing for an hors d'oeuvre. Make a salad of cubed artichoke bottoms and new potatoes (leftovers are suitable) and season well. Toss in mayonnaise and crumble over finely chopped hard-boiled egg and good-quality black olives. Sprinkle with chives and Italian parsley. Whole baby artichokes can be battered and deep-fried or cooked in oil. Eat them cold with vinaigrette.

A seventeenth-century herbalist and apothecary wrote that even the youngest housewife knew how to cook artichokes and serve them with melted butter, seasoned with vinegar and pepper. Florence White, a founder of the English Folk Cookery Association and member of the American Home Economics Association, gives a recipe for artichokes in *Good Things in England* (1929) from the time of Queen Anne:

A Tart of Artichoke Bottoms

"Line a dish with fine pastry. Put in the artichoke bottoms, with a little finely minced onion and some finely minced sweet herbs. Season with salt, pepper and nutmeg. Add some butter in tiny pieces. Cover with pastry and bake in a quick oven. When cooked, put into the tart a little white sauce thickened with yolk of egg and sharpened with tarragon vinegar."

Risotto with Artichokes
Serves 6

Rose Gray and Ruth Rogers give this recipe in their wonderful *River Café Cookbook*:

8 small globe artichokes, prepared and trimmed (chokes removed if at all prickly)
2 garlic cloves, peeled and finely chopped
3 tablespoons olive oil
Sea salt and freshly ground black pepper
4 cups chicken stock
1 stick butter
1 medium red onion, very finely chopped
1½ cups risotto rice
¼ cup extra dry white vermouth
1¼ cups Parmesan, freshly shredded

Cut the artichokes in half and slice as thinly as possible. Fry gently with the garlic in 1 tablespoon of the olive oil for 5 minutes, stirring continuously, then add ½ cup of water and salt and pepper and simmer until the water has evaporated. Set aside.

Heat the chicken stock and check for seasoning. Melt 1 tablespoon of the butter in the remaining oil in a large heavy-bottomed saucepan and gently cook the onion until soft, about 15–20 minutes. Add the rice and, off the heat, stir for a minute until the rice becomes totally coated. Return to the heat, add 2 or so ladlefuls of hot stock—just enough to cover the rice— and simmer, stirring, until the rice has absorbed nearly all the liquid. Add more stock as the liquid is absorbed. After about 15–20 minutes, nearly all the stock will have been absorbed by the rice; each grain will have a creamy coating, but will remain al dente.

Add the remaining butter in small pieces, then gently mix in the vermouth, Parmesan, and artichokes, being careful not to overstir.

Risotto with Artichokes

Eruca vesicaria subsp. *sativa. Brassicaceae*

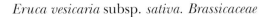

ARUGULA

Rocket Salad, Roquette, Italian Cress, Rucola.
Annual grown for tender edible leaves. Hardy.
Value: high in potassium and vitamin C.

Arugula has been cultivated since Roman times and is native to the Mediterranean and Eastern Asia, though it grows in many areas after "escaping" from gardens. *Eruca* means "downy-stemmed;" *vesicaria*, "bladderlike," describes the slender seed pods. Introduced to North America by Italian settlers, the spicy leaves were particularly popular in Elizabethan England.

Flowering rocket in the herb garden

SPECIES

Eruca vesicaria subsp. *sativa,* an erect plant growing to 36 in., has hairy stems, broadly toothed leaves and cross-shaped, creamy flowers with attractive purple veins. Cultivated plants, a separate subspecies, are larger than their wild counterparts and have paler flowers.

CULTIVATION

Propagation
Sow seed successively every 2–3 weeks, from midspring to early summer, in drills ½ in. deep and 12 in. apart. Thin when large enough to handle until 6 in. apart. Arugula germinates at fairly low temperatures. In warmer zones sow in winter or early spring. **Zones 3–9.**

Growing
Arugula needs rich, moisture-retentive soil in partial shade. It may need extra shading in hot weather, otherwise it produces less-palatable leaves. Keep weed-free and water regularly.

Maintenance
Spring Sow seeds from midspring; thin when large enough to handle.
Summer Continue sowing until midsummer. Water and feed as necessary. Harvest regularly to encourage tender growth and keep from bolting.
Fall Harvest, prepare the ground for the following year's sowing and sow seeds for protected crops.
Winter Harvest winter crops.

Protected Cropping
Although hardy, protect against severe frosts with cloches. Sow fall/winter crops from late summer in a cool greenhouse, cold frame, or under cloches.

Container Growing
Arugula is not the perfect plant for pots, but it can be grown in a soil-based potting mix with low fertilizer levels with added peat-lite mix. Sow seed in situ. Water thoroughly.

Harvesting
Plants are ready to harvest after 6–8 weeks. Pick frequently to encourage a regular supply of good-quality leaves and to prevent plants from running to seed in hot weather. Discard any damaged leaves. Either pull leaves as required or treat as a "cut and come again" crop, cutting the plant 1 in. above the ground.

Pests and Diseases
Arugula is usually trouble-free, but **black flea beetle** can damage seedlings. Treat and protect accordingly.

MEDICINAL

Young leaves are said to be a good tonic and are used in cough medicine. Dioscorides described it as "a digestive and good for ye belly."

CULINARY

The increasingly popular leaves are delicious in salads—younger leaves are milder. They can be lightly boiled or steamed, added to sauces, stir-fried, sautéed in olive oil and tossed with pasta. The flowers are edible and can decorate salads.

Penne with Sausage and Arugula
Serves 4

3½ cups penne
2 tablespoons olive oil
4½ cups sausages, cut into bite-sized pieces
1 red onion, thinly sliced
2 tablespoons dry white wine
12 cherry tomatoes, halved
3½ cups arugula leaves, washed and shredded
Salt and freshly ground black pepper
½ cup Parmesan, freshly shredded

Bring a pan of salted water to a boil and cook the penne. Meanwhile, heat the oil in a large sauté pan, add the merguez and onion and fry for 2–3 minutes. Add the wine and simmer for 10 minutes. Then add the tomatoes. When the pasta is cooked, drain well and toss in the sauce with the arugula. Mix well, season, and serve at once with Parmesan.

Daucus carota complex *sativus. Apiaceae*

CARROT

Swollen-rooted biennial grown as annual for edible orange-red roots. Hardy/half hardy. Value: extremely rich in beta carotene (vitamin A), small amounts of vitamin E.

Though there are white, yellow, purple, and violet carrots, most of us are more familiar with orange carrots, which have been known only since the eighteenth century. Domestication is thought to have occurred around the Mediterranean, Iran, and the Balkans. The Greeks cultivated them for medicinal uses, valuing them as a stomach tonic. In Roman and early medieval times, carrots were branched, like the roots of wild types; the conical-rooted varieties seem to have originated in Asia Minor around A.D. 1000. Moorish invaders took them to Spain in the twelfth century; they reached northwest Europe by the fourteenth and England in the fifteenth century. Gerard mentions only one yellow variety, purple ones being most popular—even though when cooked they turned a nasty brown color.

The Elizabethans and early Stuarts used the flowers, fruit, and leaves as fashion accessories for hats and dresses, and carrot tops were highly valued as a substitute for feathers, particularly when they colored up in the fall.

European explorers took the carrot across the Atlantic soon after the discovery of the New World, and it was growing on Margarita Island off the coast of Venezuela in 1565, arriving in Brazil before the middle of the seventeenth century. The Pilgrims took it to North America and it was grown by early colonists in Jamestown, Virginia, in 1609. Said to make you see well in the dark and to make your hair curly, it is now highly valued as a rich source of vitamin A.

'Sweetheart' produces good, uniform roots and is ideal for early cropping.

VARIETIES

There are several groups of carrots, and the names indicate the root shape and time of maturity. With successional sowing it is possible to harvest carrots for up to 9 months of the year and still have supplies in store.

Paris Market types
These have small, round or square roots and are ideal for difficult, shallow, heavy, or stony soils. Fast-maturing for early crops. **'Little Finger'** is blunt-tipped with extremely sweet, bright orange round roots. **'Parmex,'** an early-maturing round carrot, is excellent for heavy, stony, or shallow soil.

Nantes types
These carrots are broader and longer. Mainly for forcing and early crops. **'Newmarket'** are good-quality, sweet-tasting, tender carrots.

Chantenay types
This group is stump-rooted and slightly tapered. A main crop for summer. **'Red Cored-2'** is a richly colored carrot with an excellent flavor and small core.

Berlicum types
These are cylindrical and stump-rooted, a late crop for storing. **'Camberly'** produces a high-quality, deep orange root with a smooth skin. **'Ingot'** is extremely tasty. Particularly high in beta carotene and vitamin C.

Fall King types
These are large and late-maturing. For winter use and storing. **'Autumn King'** is robust, substantial, and well colored.

Other carrots worth growing are **'Flyaway'** and **'Juared,'** also known as **'Juwarot.'** This is a medium to late variety, extremely rich in vitamin A and ideal for winter storage.

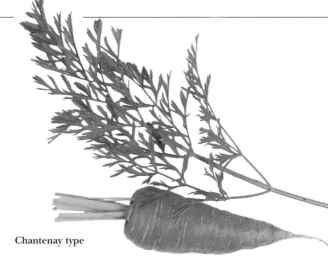

Chantenay type

'Juared' has approximately double the quantity of vitamin A than regular varieties, and is ideal for juicing

CULTIVATION

Propagation
Germination is poor at soil temperatures below 45°F: warm the soil before sowing early crops. Another option is available for the small Paris Market varieties—sow 3–4 seeds per pack and plant out after hardening off in midspring.

Carrot seed is very small and is easier to sow when mixed with sand or "fluid sown." Sow sparingly to reduce thinning and associated problems with carrot fly.

Seeds should be in drills ¾ in. deep in rows 6 in. apart; allow 4 in. between plants in the rows for early crops and 1½–2¼ in. apart for main crops, depending on the size of roots you require.

Sow all but the Berlicum and Fall King types from mid- to late spring for cropping from late summer to early fall.

Sow Chantenay, Fall King, and Berlicum types from mid- to late spring for mid-to late fall crops.

Sow Fall King and Berlicum types in late spring for mid- to late winter harvesting.
Zones 3–10.

Growing
Early carrots need an open, sheltered position; main crops are less fussy. Soils should be deep, light, and free-draining, warming early in spring, and with a pH of 6.5–7.5. Carrots are the ideal crop for light sandy soils—you should be able to push your index finger right down into the seedbed. Avoid walking on prepared ground to ensure maximum root growth.

Dig in plenty of well-rotted organic matter in the fall before planting. On heavy or stony soils, grow round or short-rooted varieties, or plant in raised beds or containers.

Rake the seedbed to a fine texture about 3 weeks before sowing and use the "stale seedbed" method, allowing the weeds to germinate and hoeing off before sowing.

Keep crops weed-free at first by mulching, hand weeding, or careful hoeing to avoid damaging the roots. In later stages of growth the foliage canopy will suppress weed growth.

Keep the soil moist to avoid root splitting and bolting. Water at a rate of 3–5 gallons/sq. yd. every 2–3 weeks, taking particular care with beds surrounded by barriers as a protection against carrot fly, as these create an artificial rain-shadow.

Maintenance
Spring Sow crops successively from midspring when the soil is workable.
Summer Harvest early crops, sow main crops. Keep well watered.
Fall Sow under cover for a midspring crop. Harvest.
Winter Harvest and store.

'Autumn King' ready for lifting

Protected Cropping

Sow Nantes types in an unheated greenhouse, or under cloches or row covers in midfall for a midspring crop. Sow Paris Market, Nantes, and Amsterdam Forcing in midspring for early to midsummer crops.

Container Growing

Choose short-rooted or round varieties for containers, window boxes, or growing bags. Sow in loam-based potting mix; keep moist throughout the growing season.

Harvesting and Storing

Early cultivars are ready to harvest after around 8 weeks and main crops from 10 weeks. In light soils, roots can be pulled straight from the ground, but on heavier

'Early Nantes' to the left; Autumn King' center and right

soils they should be eased out with a garden fork. Water the soil beforehand if it is dry.

On good soils, main-crop carrots can be left in the ground until required. Cover with a thick layer of straw, hay, or similar material before the onset of inclement weather to make lifting easier.

Alternatively, dig roots, cut or twist off foliage, and store healthy roots in boxes of sand in a cool, dry, frost-free place for up to 5 months. Check regularly and remove any that are damaged.

Freeze finger-sized carrots in plastic bags. Top and tail, wash, and blanch for 5 minutes. Cool and rub off the skins.

Carrots will stay fresh for about 2 weeks in a cool room or in a plastic bag in the refrigerator.

PESTS AND DISEASES

Carrot fly is the most serious problem. Attracted by the smell of the juice from the root, their larvae tunnel into the roots, making them

inedible. Leaves turn bronze. Sow resistant cultivars, sow sparingly to avoid thinning, thin on a damp overcast day (or water before and after), pinch off the tops of thinnings just above the soil level and dispose of them in the compost pile. Lift and dispose of affected roots immediately. Lift "earlies" by early fall and main crops by midfall.

Since these pests do not fly very high, grow carrots under fabric or film, or surround with a barrier of fine netting or fabric 24 in. high, or grow in raised beds or boxes.

Root and leaf aphids can also be a problem.

COMPANION PLANTING

Intercropping carrots with onions reduces carrot fly

attacks; leeks and salsify have also been used with some success.

Mixing with seeds of annual flowers also seems to discourage carrot fly.

Carrots grow well with lettuce, radishes, and tomatoes, and encourage peas to grow. They dislike anise and dill.

If left to flower, carrots attract hoverflies and other beneficial predatory insects to the garden.

MEDICINAL

Reputed to be therapeutic against asthma, general nervousness, dropsy, and skin disorders.

Recent research suggests that high intake of beta carotene slows cancerous growths. Beet and carrot juice is reported to prevent diarrhea.

A bunch of carrots just waiting for Peter Rabbit to swipe them!

Carrot Juice

CULINARY

For eating raw, harvest young for maximum sweetness. Older carrots need to be peeled and the hard core discarded. Shredded, they can be made into salads and are especially good mixed with raisins and a little chopped onion and then tossed in a good French dressing or mayonnaise thinned with a little virgin olive oil.

Try freshly plucked baby carrots, rinsed under the tap, topped and tailed, very lightly boiled in as little water as possible, then sprinkled with chopped parsley, a little sugar, and freshly ground black pepper, or just a pat of butter. Add a sprinkling of sugar, a tablespoon of butter, and a pinch of salt, cover and gently steam until tender. Cook in a cream sauce seasoned with tarragon, nutmeg, and dill, or steam with mint leaves.

Cut into sticks as raw snacks, slice for stews and casseroles, pickle, stir-fry, and use for jellies, wine, and carrot cake. Carrots are an essential ingredient in stocks, soups, and many sauces.

Balkali Havuçi
Serves 4

Serve this Armenian-Turkish dish with pilaf and salad; it can be topped with a dollop of yogurt.

3 cups fava beans, shelled
1 cup water
1 onion, chopped
2 cloves garlic, finely chopped
2 carrots, cut into rings 1 in. thick
2 tablespoons dill or mint, chopped
1 teaspoon salt
Freshly ground black pepper
Pinch sugar
3 tablespoons virgin olive oil

Rinse the beans. Put the water into a large saucepan and bring to a boil; add the onion and beans, bring to a boil, cover, and simmer until tender.

Stir in the remaining ingredients and cook until the vegetables are just tender, about 20 minutes more. Serve hot with chunks of good bread as a starter.

Carrot and Raisin Cookies

Carrot and Raisin Cake
Makes 1 cake or approx. 40 cookies

This spicy dough mixture can also be used to make cookies, in which case drop heaped tablespoonfuls of dough onto a lightly greased cookie sheet 2 in. apart and bake for 12–15 minutes until golden. Cool on a rack and store in the refrigerator.

3¹/₂ cups all-purpose flour
2 teaspoons baking powder
1 teaspoon cinnamon
Pinch mace
Pinch salt
2 heaped tablespoons seedless raisins
³/₄ cup carrots, shredded
Shredded zest of half an orange
2 tablespoons orange juice
1 stick butter
³/₄ cup brown sugar
2 large eggs

Preheat the oven to 350°F. Sift the flour, baking powder, spices, and salt into a large bowl and set aside. Mix the raisins, carrots, and orange zest and juice and set aside. Cream the butter and sugar thoroughly in a mixer and beat until light. Add the eggs, one at a time, with the blender on slow. Combine the batter with the flour and carrot mixtures and blend well.

Pour into a greased and lined 8-in. cake pan and bake for 40–60 minutes. Test with a skewer to ensure the cake is cooked and allow to cool in the pan for 15 minutes before turning out on a wire rack.

Balkali Havuçi

Dioscorea alata. Dioscoreaceae

YAM

Also known as Greater Yam, Asiatic Yam, White Yam, Winged Yam, Water Yam.
Twining climber grown for large edible tubers. Tender.
Value: rich in carbohydrate and potassium, small amounts of B vitamins.

Yams maturing in paddy fields in Luzon, Philippines

The "greater yam" is believed to have originated in east Asia and is widely cultivated as a staple crop throughout the humid tropics. It was said to have reached Madagascar by A.D. 1000, and by the 16th century Portuguese and Spanish traders had taken it to West Africa and the New World, often as a food on slave-trading ships. Christopher Columbus knew of the plant as *nyame,* and the tubers were regularly used for ships' supplies because they stored for several months without deteriorating and were easy to handle. There are hundreds of different forms, producing tubers with an average weight of 8–22 lb., although specimens with massive tubers up to 136 lb. have been recorded.

VARIETIES

Dioscorea alata has square, 4-winged or angled twining stems with pointed, heart-shaped leaves. Small bulbils are often produced on the stems. The tubers are brown on the outside with white flesh, vary in size, and are usually produced singly. There are a great number of cultivars that vary in the color and shape of the stems, leaves, and tubers.

'White Lisbon,' one of the most widely grown, is high-yielding, shallow-rooted, and tasty; it will store for up to 6 months. **'Belep,' 'Lupias,' 'Kinbayo,'** and **'Pyramid'** are also high yielding.

Propagation
Yams are usually planted on banks, mounds, or ridges at the end of the dry season while they are still dormant, as they need the long rainy season to develop. Small tubers, bulbils, or sections with 2–3 buds or "eyes" taken from the tops of larger tubers are used for propagation. The latter are preferable, as they sprout quickly and produce higher-yielding plants. They can be "sprouted" in a shady position before planting 6 in. deep and 12–36 in. apart on mounds 48 in. across or ridges 48 in. apart. Spacing depends on the site, soil, and variety. **Zones 8–11.**

Growing
Yams need a humid, tropical climate, 60–70 in. of rain in a 6–12 month growing season, and a site in sun or partial shade. Soils must be rich, moisture-retentive and free-draining, as yams can survive drought but not waterlogging.

Dig in plenty of well-rotted organic matter before planting and grow plants up trellising, arbors, poles, or netting at least 72 in. high, or allow them to grow into surrounding trees.

Keep crops weed-free. Tropical crops do not grow well below 68°F. Growth increases with temperature, and the crucial time for rain is 14 to 20 weeks after planting, when food reserves are nearly depleted and the shoots are growing rapidly.

Maintenance
Spring Increase watering as new shoots appear when growing under cover.
Summer Maintain high temperatures and humidity.
Fall Reduce watering as stems turn yellow.
Winter Keep compost slightly moist.

Protected Cropping
If you are able to provide an environment and cultural conditions similar to those described under "Growing," yams can be grown indoors. The minimum temperature for active growth is 68°F; damp down greenhouse paths and mist with tepid water during summer, and

Yams drying in the sun

reduce watering during the resting season as the stems die back, gradually increasing the amount in spring when plants resume active growth.

Harvesting and Storing
Depending on the variety and weather conditions, tubers are ready to harvest from 7–12 months after planting as the leaves and stems die back. Lift them carefully, as damaged tubers cannot be stored.

Tubers are normally dried on a shaded vertical frame or in an open-sided shed before being stored in a dark, cool, airy place where they can last for several months. Do not store yams at temperatures below 50°F.

PESTS AND DISEASES

Leaf spot appears as brown or black spots on stems and leaves. **Storage rot** can be a serious problem and **yam beetles** feed on tubers and damage the shoots of newly planted sets. **Scale insect** also causes problems.

Yams need to be well spaced to flourish

COMPANION PLANTING

Grows well with taro, ginger, maize, okra, and cucurbits.

MEDICINAL

Yams have been used as a diuretic and expectorant.

WARNING

All yams except *Dioscorea esculenta* contain a toxin, dioscorine, which is destroyed by thorough cooking.

CULINARY

Yam can be peeled and then boiled, mashed, roasted, and fried in oil. In West Africa, they are pounded into *fufu* in a similar way to manioc, and are added to a thick soup made of spices, meat, oil, fish, and vegetables. Yams are tasty cooked with palm oil, candied, casseroled with orange juice, or curried.

They can be peeled and boiled in water with a pinch of salt, then brushed with melted butter and broiled or barbecued until brown; serve with more butter.

In China they are mashed with lotus root, wrapped in lotus leaves and steamed.

They can also be peeled, rubbed with oil, and baked at 350°F for 1½ hours, then slit like a baked potato and eaten with seasoned butter or a similar filling.

Yellow Yam Salad
Serves 6

3 lb. yellow yams
1 large onion, sliced
3 tablespoons chopped chives
1 green bell pepper, seeded and diced
8 tablespoons mayonnaise
½ teaspoon cayenne pepper
Salt and freshly ground black pepper
4 hard-boiled eggs, chopped
1 tablespoon black olives, pitted and sliced

Clean the yams and cook in boiling salted water until tender but firm. Drain and allow to cool slightly, then cut into cubes. Add the onions, chives, and bell pepper and mix well.

Season the mayonnaise with the cayenne, salt, and black pepper and stir into the yam mixture, folding in the eggs and olives carefully.

Check the seasoning. Chill for an hour before serving.

Foeniculum vulgare var. *dulce. Apiaceae*

FLORENCE FENNEL

Also known as Sweet Fennel, Finocchio. Biennial or perennial grown as annual for pungent swollen leaf bases, leaves, and seeds. Half hardy. Value: good source of potassium; small amounts of beta carotene.

This outstanding vegetable with a strong aniseed flavor, swollen leaf bases (known as "bulbs") the texture of tender celery, and delicate feathery leaves has been cultivated for centuries as an ornamental vegetable. Its close relative, wild fennel, which lacks the swollen base, is used as an herb. When Portuguese explorers first landed on Madeira in 1418, they found the air fragrant with the aroma of wild fennel, so the city of Funchal was named after *funcho*, the Portuguese name for the plant. Florence fennel was popular with the Greeks and Romans, whose soldiers ate it to maintain good health—while the ladies used it to ward off obesity. In medieval times, seeds were eaten during Lent to alleviate hunger, and dieters still chew raw stalks to suppress their appetite. The first records of its cultivation in England date from the early eighteenth century, when the 3rd Earl of Peterborough cultivated and ate it as a dessert.

In 1824 Thomas Jefferson received seeds from the American consul in Livorno and sowed them in his garden in Virginia. He enthused: "Fennel is beyond every other vegetable, delicious . . . perfectly white. No vegetable equals it in flavor." However, it has become a weed in those countries where conditions are particularly favorable.

VARIETIES

'**Fino**' ('**Zefa Fino**') is particularly vigorous and ornamental, looking good in a flower border. It is resistant to bolting. '**Herald**,' an old Italian variety, forms plump, sweet bulbs, is resistant to bolting, and is ideal for early and successional sowing.

'**Perfection**,' a French variety, has medium-sized bulbs and a delicate aniseed flavor. Resistant to bolting, it is ideal for early sowing. '**Sirio**,' again from Italy, is compact with large, sweet white bulbs, and matures rapidly. '**Sweet Florence**' is moderately sized and should be sown from midspring to late summer. '**Tardo**' ('**Zefa Tardo**') is an early cropping, bolting-resistant variety.

'**Sweet Florence**,' showing its developing bulbs and light, feathery foliage

CULTIVATION

Propagation
Fennel thrives in a warm climate and is inclined to bolt prematurely if growth is checked by cold, drought, or transplanting. For early sowings choose cultivars that are bolt-resistant.

Grow successively from late spring to late summer for summer and fall crops. Sow thinly in drills ½ in. deep and 18–20 in. apart, thinning when seedlings are large enough to handle to a final spacing of 9–12 in. apart.

Where possible, fennel is better sown in situ to reduce problems with bolting. Packs are preferred for plants started under cover. Growing in trays is fine if transplants are treated carefully enough. **Zones 4–10.**

Growing
Fennel flourishes in temperate to subtropical climates, though mature plants can withstand light frosts. The largest bulbs are formed during warm, sunny summers. Plants should be grown as rapidly as possible, so incorporate a slow-release general fertilizer into the soil before planting at

1–2 oz./sq. yd. Plants need a sunny, warm, sheltered position and well-drained, moisture-retentive, slightly alkaline soil. A light, sandy soil with well-rotted organic matter dug in the winter before planting is ideal. Stony soils and heavy clays should be avoided. Never allow the soil to dry out; mulch in spring and hand weed around bulbs to avoid damage.

When the stem bases start to swell, earth up to half their height to blanch and sweeten the bulbs. Or tie cardboard "collars" around the base.

Maintenance

Spring Sow early crops under cover. Warm the soil with cloches before sowing early crops outdoors.
Summer Keep the soil constantly moist and weed-free. Harvest mature bulbs.
Fall Cover later crops to prolong the growing season.
Winter Transplant later sowings for an early winter crop.

Protected Cropping

Cover early outdoor crops with cloches. Sow from midspring, in packs or trays of seed potting mix at 60°F. Repot seedlings grown in trays when very small, with a maximum of 4 leaves, into 3-in. peat pots. Transplant in

Mature plant ready for harvest

The bulb is made up of swollen, overlapping leaf bases.

the pots a month after hardening off.

Harden off and plant out those grown in packs at a similar size. Late sowings can be made for transplanting under cover in early winter. Plants do not always produce "bulbs," but leaves and stems can be used in cooking.

Container Growing

Grow single plants in a container at least 10 in. wide by 12 in. deep containing loam-based potting mix with added sharp sand. Apply a general liquid fertilizer monthly from late spring to late summer.

Harvesting and Storing

Harvest about 15 weeks after sowing or 2–4 weeks after earthing up, when the bulbs are plump, about 2–3 in. across and slightly larger than a tennis ball. Cut the bulb with a sharp knife, just above the ground, and the stump should resprout, producing small sprigs of ferny foliage. Bulbs do not store and should be eaten when they are fresh.

Leaves can be harvested throughout summer and used fresh in salads, or deep-frozen.

Pests and Diseases

Slugs can damage young plants. Lack of water, fluctuating temperatures, and transplanting check can cause bolting.

COMPANION PLANTING

Allow a few plants to flower; they are extremely attractive to a large number of beneficial insects that prey on garden pests.

Fennel has a detrimental effect on beans, kohlrabi, and tomatoes.

MEDICINAL

An infusion eases flatulence, colic, urinary disorders, and constipation. Recent research indicates that fennel reduces the effects of alcohol.

Use in an eye bath or as a compress to reduce inflammation.

Chew to sweeten breath or infuse as a mouthwash or gargle for gum disease and sore throats, and to alleviate hunger and ease indigestion.

WARNING

Do not take excessive doses of the oil; it should not be given to pregnant women.

CULINARY

Use bulbs as you would celery, removing green stalks and outer leaves. For salads, slice inner leaf stalks and chill before serving. (To ensure bulbs are crisp, slice and place in a bowl of water and ice cubes in the refrigerator for an hour.)

Fennel can be parboiled with leeks and is suitable for egg and fish dishes. Steam, broil, or boil and serve with cheese sauce or butter. Infuse fresh leaves in oil or vinegar, add to a bouquet garni, or snip as a garnish over soups or salads. Gives characteristic flavor to *finocchiona*, an Italian salami, and the French liqueur *fenouillette*.

Fennel Sautéed with Peas and Bell Peppers
Serves 4

2 tablespoons olive oil
2 red bell peppers, seeded and cut into thin strips
8 cups fennel, trimmed and finely sliced
2 cloves garlic, crushed
1 cup peas
Salt and freshly ground black pepper

In a wok or heavy-based sauté pan, heat the oil, add the peppers and fennel, and cook for 10–15 minutes over a moderate heat, stirring occasionally. Add the garlic and peas and continue cooking for 2 minutes. Season and serve.

Glycine max (syn. *Glycine soja*). *Leguminosae*

SOYBEAN

Also known as Soya Bean. Annual grown for seed sprouts and seeds. Half hardy.
Value: rich in potassium, protein, fiber, vitamin E, vitamin B, and iron.
Seed sprouts are rich in vitamin C.

One of the most nutritious of all vegetables, this native of Asia is thought to have been the plant that the Chinese emperor Shen Nung used to introduce people to the art of cultivation. It is mentioned in his *Materia Medica* around 2900 B.C. Soybeans were first known in Europe through Engelbert Kaempfer, physician to the governor of the Dutch East India company on an island off Japan, 1690–1692. The Japanese guarded their culture, but by bribing the guards Kaempfer was able to get his botanical specimens. Benjamin Franklin sent seeds back to the U.S. from France in the late eighteenth century. In 1829 soybean was being grown in Cambridge, Massachusetts, where it was considered a luxury. One of the first Americans interested in soybeans was Henry Ford, who saw their potential for manufactured goods and is said to have eaten them at every meal, had a suit made from "soy fabric," and sponsored a sixteen-course soybean dinner at the 1934 "Century of Progress" show in Chicago.

VARIETIES

Glycine max is an herb, usually with trilobed leaves and white to pale violet flowers. The pods, containing 2–4 seeds, are mainly on the lower parts of the stem. **'Black Jet'** is early-maturing; the seeds have a good flavor and it is ideal for a short growing season. **'Fiskeby V'** has yellow beans and is very hardy. **'Hakucho Early,'** an early dwarf Japanese variety, produces 3 small seeds per pod but is high-yielding. **'Lammer's Black'** is the best bean for short seasons, producing heavy crops of thin-skinned, tasty seeds.

Perhaps the earliest green soybean is the 2-foot-tall **'Envy,'** good for fresh shelling or drying. **'Butterbean'** is said to be the finest tasting of all.

Immature soy bean pods on plant

CULTIVATION

Propagation
Sow when danger of frost has passed and the soil has warmed. Sow 2–3 seeds 1 in. deep in heavy soil and 1½ in. deep in lighter soils in hills 3–4 in. apart with 18–24 in. between rows. After germination, thin, leaving the strongest seedling. Alternatively, sow thinly and thin to the final spacing when large enough. **Zones 4–10.**

Sprouting Seed
Seeds can also be sprouted. Use untreated seed and remove any that are damaged or moldy. Soak overnight in cold water. The following morning rinse them thoroughly. Put a layer of moist paper towels over the base of a flat-bottomed bowl, tray, or "seed sprouter." Spread over a layer of soybeans ½ in. deep and cover with plastic wrap. Exclude light by putting the bowl in a dark cupboard or wrapping it in newspaper or aluminum foil. Temperatures should be 68–75°F. Check that the absorbent layer stays damp, rinsing morning and night. They should be ready to harvest in 4–10 days when shoots are 1–2 in. long. Remove sprouts from the shell, and rinse well before eating.

Growing
Soybeans flourish in an open site with rich, free-draining soil and a pH of 5.7–6.2, although there are now cultivars to suit most soils. Where necessary, lime soils and dig in well-rotted organic matter before planting. They are not frost hardy; they prefer 68–75°F; exceeding 100°F may retard growth.
Keep plants well watered during drought and early stages of growth. Remove weeds regularly, or suppress by mulching in spring.

Maintenance
Spring Sow seeds under cover or outdoors when there is no danger of frost. *Summer* Keep crops weed-free. Water during drought. *Fall* Harvest before the pods are completely ripe. *Winter* Hang in bunches in a cool shed and collect seed when the pods open.

Protected Cropping
In cooler zones, sow seeds in pots, packs, or trays of seed potting mix, planting out when the soil is warm. Harden off before transplanting and protect under cloches until established. In cooler zones, sow crops in a heated greenhouse.

A soybean crop in Kansas, planted to match the field contours

Container Growing

This is only worth growing in containers as a "novelty" crop. Use 8–10 in. pots and loam-based potting mix with moderate fertilizer levels, adding well-rotted organic matter. Keep well watered and weed-free.

Harvesting and Storing

Soy needs a hot summer and fine fall for the seeds to ripen. Harvesting should be carefully timed so that the seeds are ripe but the pods have not yet split. If conditions are unfavorable, pull up plants when the pods turn yellow and hang up to ripen in a dry place.

Do not harvest when plants are wet, as the seeds are easily bruised. Harvest for green beans as soon as pods are plump and the seeds are almost full size.

PESTS AND DISEASES

Fungal diseases can be a problem if plants are harvested when wet and pods are bruised or broken.

OTHER USES

Soy oil is used in a range of products including ice cream, margarine, soaps, and paint; milk substitute is made from the crushed beans, and fermented they make soy sauce, tofu, and Worcestershire sauce. Also an ingredient in firefighting foam and meat substitute. A valuable plant indeed!

MEDICINAL

Said to control blood sugar levels, lower cholesterol, regulate the bowels, and relieve constipation.

WARNING

Soybeans should be cooked before drying; they can cause stomach upset.

CULINARY

Used mainly when green or sprouted for salads or stir-fries. Remove the shell by plunging into boiling salted water for 5 minutes, then allow to cool and squeeze out the seeds. Cook for 15 minutes, then sauté with butter. Juvenile pods can be cooked and eaten whole.

Soak dried beans before eating. For a shortcut you can cover with water in a kettle, boil for 2 minutes, allow to stand for one hour, then cook until tender.

Soybean and Walnut Croquettes
Serves 4

1 cup soybeans, soaked and well rinsed
1 onion, finely chopped
1 clove garlic, crushed
1 tablespoon butter
1 cup walnuts, pulverized in the food processor
1/2 teaspoon dried thyme
1/2 cup whole-wheat bread crumbs
1 tablespoon tomato puree
2 tablespoons chopped parsley
1/2 teaspoon grand mace
1 egg
Salt and freshly ground black pepper
Whole-wheat flour
1 beaten egg
Dried bread crumbs
Oil for shallow frying

Cook the beans until very tender, drain, then mash with a fork, enough to break them up. Fry the onion and garlic in the butter for 10 minutes, then remove from the heat and stir in the beans. Add the walnuts, thyme, bread crumbs, tomato puree, parsley, mace, and egg. (You may need to add more liquid; otherwise use fewer bread crumbs.) Mix well and season to taste. Shape into small croquettes, then roll in the flour, dip into the egg, and roll in the crumbs. Fry in hot oil until crisp and drain on paper towels. Serve hot. These go particularly well with a spicy tomato sauce.

Helianthus tuberosus. Asteraceae

JERUSALEM ARTICHOKE

Also known as Girasole, Sunchoke. Tall perennial grown as annual for edible tubers. Hardy. Value: high in carbohydrate but mostly inulin, turning to fructose in storage; moderate vitamin B_1, B_5, low in calories.

This vegetable is not from Jerusalem, nor is it any relative of the globe artichoke. "Jerusalem" is said to be a corruption of the Italian *girasole* or "sunflower"—a close relative; the nutty-flavored tubers were thought to taste similar to globe artichokes, hence the adoption of that name. Frost-hardy, these tall, upright perennials are native to North America, where they grow in damp places. The tubers contain a carbohydrate that causes flatulence; in 1621 John Goodyear wrote that "they stirre and cause a filthie loathsome wind within the bodie." In the 1920s they were a commercial source of fructose and were expected to replace beet and cane as a source of sugar.

VARIETIES

'**Dwarf Sunray**' is a short-stemmed, crisp, tender variety that does not need peeling. It flowers freely and is good for an ornamental border. '**Fuseau**' has long, smooth, white tubers. Plants are compact, reaching 5–6 ft. It is a traditional French variety. '**Stampede**' is a quick-maturing variety with large tubers. '**Jacks Copperclad**' has dark coppery-purple tubers and small pretty sunflowers. Plants are tall, reaching 10 ft. It is high yielding and has an excellent taste. '**Mulles Rose**' has large white tubers with rose-purple fleshed eyes. It is

easy to grow and extremely tolerant of cold conditions. '**Stampede**' is an extra-early variety, producing large, white tubers in just 90 days, one month earlier than many common varieties. The tubers of '**Sun Choke**' have a fresh nutty flavor, and are excellent raw in salads, cooked or creamed.

CULTIVATION

Jerusalem artichokes prefer a sunny position, but will grow in shade. They tolerate most soils, though tubers are small on poor ground; the best are grown on sandy, moisture-retentive soil.

They will grow in heavy clay provided it is not extremely acid or subject to winter waterlogging. The fibrous root system makes them useful for breaking up uncultivated ground. The tall stems make excellent temporary screens or windbreaks in sheltered

areas, but need staking in more exposed sites. **Zones 4–11.**

Propagation
Tubers bought from the market can be used for planting. Choose tubers the size of chicken eggs and plant from early to late spring, when the soil becomes workable, 4–6 in. deep, 12 in. apart and 3 ft. between rows; cover the tubers carefully. During harvest, save a few tubers to replant or leave some in the soil for the following year.

Growing
Incorporate organic matter in fall or early winter before planting. Hill up the base of stems to improve stability when plants are 12 in. high. Water during dry weather.
　Remove flower buds as they appear. Shorten stems to 5–6 ft. in late summer to stop them from being blown over; on windy sites they may also need staking. On poor soil, feed with liquid general fertilizer every 2–3 weeks.

Maintenance
Spring Plant tubers.
Summer Keep weed-free, water, and stake if necessary. Remove flower buds.

Jerusalem artichoke stems can make effective windbreaks.

Fall Cut back stems and begin harvesting.
Winter Save tubers for next year's crop.

Harvesting and Storing

In fall, as the foliage turns yellow, cut back stems to within 3–6 in. of the ground. Use the cut stems as a mulch to protect the soil from frost, making lifting easier; alternatively, cover with straw. Lift tubers from late fall to midwinter. They keep better in the ground, but in cold zones or on heavy ground, lift in early winter and store for up to 5 months in a cool cellar in moist peat substitute or sand.

Pests and Diseases

Slugs tend to hollow out tubers. Set traps, aluminum sulfate pellets, or pick off manually.

Sclerotinia rot causes stem bases to become covered with fluffy white mold. Lift and burn diseased plants; water healthy plants with fungicide.

Cutworms eat stems at ground level; damaged plants wilt. Keep crops weed-free, cultivate well, or scatter an appropriate insecticide in the soil before planting.

MEDICINAL

The carbohydrate inulin is difficult to digest; tubers are low calorie and suitable for diabetics.

WARNING

Jerusalem artichokes can become an invasive weed. After harvesting, lift even the smallest tuber from the ground.

Artichoke Soup

CULINARY

Artichokes are versatile vegetables when the weather is cold: they can be kept in the ground until you want to cook them and then dug up root by root. Fresh tubers have a better flavor, but they become more digestible if stored; they will keep in a plastic bag in the crisper in the refrigerator for up to 2 weeks.

There is no need to peel them painstakingly unless you want a very smooth, creamy-white puree—the vitamins are, after all, just below the skin. (If you do want them peeled, steaming or boiling knobbly varieties makes the job easier.) To serve as a vegetable, scrub tubers immediately after lifting, boil for 20–25 minutes in their skins in water with a teaspoon of vinegar, and peel before serving if desired. The addition of a little grated nutmeg always does wonders in bringing out the unusual flavor.

To make rissoles, form boiled, mashed artichokes into flat cakes and deep-fry. Jerusalem artichokes can also be fried, baked, roasted, or stewed—or eaten raw.

Artichokes gratinéed in a sauce made with good, strong cheddar make an excellent accompaniment to plain meat dishes such as baked ham or roast lamb. Parboil the artichokes and drain when they are just tender. Roughly slice and layer into a dish. Top with a béchamel sauce flavored with French mustard and well-matured cheese and bake in a hot oven at 400°F until browned.

Artichoke Soup
Serves 4

2½ cups Jerusalem artichokes
2 tablespoons olive oil
2 large onions, sliced
1 large garlic clove, crushed
2 cups chicken stock
Strip of orange peel
Salt and finely ground black
  pepper
4 tablespoons heavy cream

Scrub the artichokes, discard any hard knobs, and roughly chop. Heat the oil in a heavy-based pan and add the onions. Cook until translucent, add the garlic, continue cooking for a couple of minutes, and add the artichokes. Toss well to coat with oil and pour in the chicken stock. Bring to a boil, add the orange peel, and season. Cover and simmer for 15–20 minutes, until cooked. Remove from the heat, discard the peel, and blend in a food processor. Return to the pan, adjust the seasoning, stir in the cream, and serve.

Ipomoea batatas. Convolvulaceae

SWEET POTATO

Also known as Kumara, Louisiana Yam, Yellow Yam. Trailing perennials grown as annuals for starchy tubers and leaves. Tender. Value: excellent source of beta carotene, rich in carbohydrate, moderate potassium, and vitamins B and C. Yellow and orange types rich in vitamin A.

The "sweet potato" is unrelated to the "Irish" potato but is a relative of the bindweed, in the morning glory family. It was cultivated in prehistoric Peru and is now found throughout the tropics; it is also a "staple" crop in Polynesia. Its arrival there is a mystery; some suggest it was taken there by Polynesians who visited South America, others think it arrived on vines clinging to logs swept out to sea. It was cultivated in Polynesia before 1250 and reached New Zealand by the fourteenth century. Captain Cook and Sir Joseph Banks found the Maoris of the North Island growing it when they

landed in 1769. It was grown in Virginia by 1648. Columbus introduced it to Spain and it was widely cultivated by the mid-sixteenth century, predating the "Irish" potato by nearly half a century. It reached England via the Canary Islands about the same time and was the "common potato" in Elizabethan times, some even holding it to be an aphrodisiac.

VARIETIES

There are hundreds of sweet potato varieties worldwide. They are classified under three groups: dry and mealy-fleshed, soft and moist-fleshed, and coarse-fleshed types used as animal feed. White or pale types are floury with a chestnut-caramel flavor, while yellow and orange varieties are sweet and watery.

'Centennial' is vigorous, growing to 16 ft., with bright copper-orange skin and deep orange flesh. Prolific with high-quality tubers, it grows well in short seasons. 'Jewel,' a vigorous, high-yielding variety, has excellent quality copper-colored tubers with moist white flesh. Stores well and disease-resistant. 'Porto Rico Bush' has deep orange, sweet flesh. Excellent for baking. Does not need much space. 'Tokatoka Gold' is large, rounded and smooth-textured. Popular in New Zealand. 'Vardaman' does not "vine," has golden-yellow skin and deep red-orange flesh. High yielding.

CULTIVATION

Propagation
Take cuttings from healthy shoots 8–10 in. long. Cut just below a leaf joint, remove basal leaves.

Alternatively, pack several healthy tubers in a tray of moist potting mix and sharp sand, vermiculite, or perlite in a warm greenhouse, or plant into hotbeds. When shoots reach 9–12 in., cut them off 2 in. above the soil and take the cuttings as described above. Three potatoes should produce about 24 cuttings, enough for a 25-ft. row.

In the humid tropics and subtropics, cuttings are rooted in situ at the start of the rainy season. Plant on ridges 6–12 in. high and 3–4½ ft. apart. Just below the ridge top, insert cuttings 9–12 in. apart, leaving half of the stem exposed.

Or, instead of cuttings, plant small tubers 3–4 in. deep along the top of the ridge. On sandy, free-draining soil, plant cuttings and tubers on level ground. **Zones 5–11.**

Growing
Sweet potatoes thrive in a tropical or subtropical climate with an annual temperature of 70–77°F. Light frost kills leaves and damages tubers.

Ideal annual rainfall is 30–50 in., with wet weather in the growing period and dry conditions for the tubers to ripen. Tuber production is fastest and sugar

Large-scale sweet potato crop in North Carolina

production highest when day length exceeds 14 hours.

Soils should be moisture-retentive and free-draining with a pH of 5.5–6.5. If necessary, dig in well-rotted organic matter before planting. Watering is rarely needed if planted at the start of the rainy season.

Excessive nitrogen encourages stems to develop rather than tubers. Once established, scatter a high-potash granular fertilizer around plants. Occasionally lift vines from the ground to prevent rooting at the leaf joints. Rotate crops.

Maintenance

Spring Take cuttings under cover, keep warm and moist.
Summer Keep cuttings weed-free, water well, and feed. Prune as necessary.
Fall Harvest. Save some tubers for the next crop.
Winter Keep compost slightly moist.

Protected Cropping

Grow under cover in cool temperate zones at a minimum temperature of 77°F.

Take cuttings as normal from healthy shoots of mature plants, and insert about 4 cuttings around the outside of a 6-in. pot filled with potting mix. Keep moist with tepid water. Transplant into a green-house border once a good root system has formed. Mist regularly. Prune stems longer than 24 in. to encourage sideshoots and also from late winter to thin out congested growth.

Container Growing

Grow in pots or containers 12 in. deep and 15 in. wide using loam-based potting mix with moderate fertilizer levels. Provide supports.

Harvesting and Storing

In good conditions, tubers ripen in 4–5 months. Lift when slightly immature; otherwise wait until vines begin to yellow. Lift

The flower is similar to that of the morning glory

carefully to avoid bruising. Use fresh or store once dried in a cool dark place for up to a week.

Pests and Diseases

Leaves can suffer from **leaf spot** and **sooty mold**. **Black rot** appears at the base of the stem and brown rots on the tuber. Check stored tubers regularly. Also susceptible to **whitefly** or **red spider mite** under cover.

Medicinal

Sweet potatoes and their leaves contain antibacterial and fungicidal substances and are used in folk medicine. In Shakespeare's day they were sold in crystallized slices with sea holly ("eringo") as an aphrodisiac. In *The Merry Wives of Windsor*, Falstaff cries: "Let the sky rain potatoes . . . hail kissing-comforts and snow eringoes." The Empress Josephine introduced sweet potatoes to her companions, who were soon serving them to stimulate the passion of their lovers. The results are not recorded!

Culinary

A sweet potato contains roughly one and a half times the calories and vitamin C of the "Irish" potato. Before cooking, wash carefully and peel or cook whole. Parboil and cut into "chips," grate raw and make into fritters or roast with a joint of meat.

Glazed with butter, brown sugar, and orange juice, sweet potatoes accompany Thanksgiving dinner. In Latin America and the Caribbean they are used in spiced puddings, casseroles, soufflés, and sweetmeats. The leaves can be steamed.

Tzimmes
Serves 4

This one-pot meal is based on Olga Phklebin's recipe from *Russian Cooking* but adapted to our ingredients.

1–2 sweet potatoes, depending on size
2 large potatoes
Olive oil
2 lb. stewing steak, cubed
1 large onion, chopped
2 carrots, chopped
2¼ cups vegetable stock
3 tablespoons honey
½ teaspoon ground cinnamon
1 tablespoon all-purpose flour
Chopped parsley, to garnish
Salt and freshly ground black pepper

Peel all of the potatoes and cut roughly. Heat the oil in a heavy pan and sauté the meat well to brown it on all sides. Remove from the pan and keep warm. Brown the onion, adding the carrots and the meat and sufficient stock to cover. Season with salt and pepper and bring to a boil, then simmer for 45 minutes.

Stir in the potatoes, the honey, cinnamon, and more seasoning if required. Bring back to a boil and simmer for 45 more minutes, covered. (If the stew is too liquid, allow it to boil fast at this stage.) Remove 5 tablespoons of the stock and mix with the flour. Pour this back into the pot, return to a boil, and cook for another 30 minutes, or until the meat is tender and the potatoes are cooked. Sprinkle with parsley and serve with a green salad.

Lactuca sativa. Asteraceae

LETTUCE

***Annual grown for edible leaves. Half hardy to hardy.
Value: rich in beta carotene, particularly outer leaves.***

The garden lettuce is believed to be a selected form of the bitter-leaved wild species *Lactuca serriola*, which is found throughout Europe, Asia, and North Africa. The ancient Egyptians were said to have been the first to cultivate lettuces and there are examples of tomb wall paintings depicting a form of Cos lettuce, which is said to have originated on the Greek island of the same name. They believed it was an aphrodisiac and also used its white sap and leaves in a concoction alongside fresh beef, frankincense, and juniper berries as a remedy for stomachache. The Romans, too, attributed medicinal properties to the lettuce and the emperor Augustus erected an altar and statue in its honor; they believed that it upheld morals, temperance, and chastity. The Romans were said to have introduced it to Britain with their conquering armies and even after many centuries it is still regarded as the foundation of a good salad.

Romaine lettuce

'Lollo Rossa'

VARIETIES

The many cultivars are divided into three main categories—heading, leaf, and romaine types. They can be grown all year round, and many modern cultivars are disease-resistant.

Head Lettuce
More tolerant of drought and drier soils than the other kinds, this group includes Butterhead types, with soft, buttery-textured leaves, which are usually grown in summer, and Crisphead types, which have crisp leaves forming compact hearts.

Butterhead: **'All Year Round'** is tasty and compact with pale green leaves. It is slow to bolt and hardy. **'Avondefiance'** is an excellent, high-yielding, dark green lettuce that withstands drought and high temperatures. It is ideal for summer crops, particularly those sown from mid- to late summer, and is resistant to root aphid and downy mildew. **'Buttercrunch'** has compact, crisp, dark green heads and a beautiful "buttery" heart. Slow to bolt and heat-resistant. **'Esmerelda'** offers strong disease resistance and crisp, sweet, light green heads that weigh in at one pound each. **'Kwiek,'** a large-headed variety for winter cropping, is downy mildew-resistant. Sow in late summer for harvesting in midwinter or force as an early spring crop. **'Optima'** is one of the darkest of all Boston-type lettuces. The thick leaves tolerate high heat, and the plants resist bolting even when temperatures reach 90°F. Resists several diseases. The outer leaves of **'Sangria'**

'Lobioits Green' combines well with sorrel and can be made into soups

'Oak Leaf,' an old variety, has several different color forms

are tinged red, the inner a pale green. Has some resistance to mildew and mosaic virus. For heat tolerance, no lettuce beats **'Sierra.'** Its deep green, open head stays crisp, sweet, and solid long after other butterheads have bolted. **'Valdor,'** which has firm, dark green hearts, is a

excellent for summer cropping and is resistant to tip burn. **'Webb's Wonderful'** is extremely popular, and rightly so. It is a good-quality lettuce that lasts well at maturity.

Salad Bowl or Leaf Lettuce
These are loose-leaved varieties that sometimes form an insignificant heart. Cut to resprout, or remove single leaves as needed. They stand longer before bolting than other types and can be grown at any time of year; however, growth is slower in winter.

'Grand Rapids' has crinkled pale green leaves and is resistant to tip burn. **'Lollo Blonda'** is similar to 'Lollo Rossa,' but with fresh pale green leaves and some

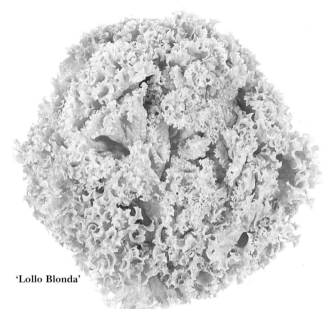

'Lollo Blonda'

'Rosa Pablo,' showing its tightly packed habit

of the first leaf lettuces with masses of green, deeply lobed leaves that are crisp but tender. Good resistance to bolting.

Romaine or Cos
These flourish in humus-rich, moist soil, take longer to mature than other varieties and are better in cooler weather. Some can overwinter outdoors or be grown as leaf lettuce if closely spaced. They are generally very tasty.

'Lobjoits Green' is a large, good-quality, tasty old variety which is deep green and crisp. It can be grown as closely as leaf lettuce. Subject to tip burn. **'Little**

Gem' is a compact, quick-maturing, semi-romaine with a firm, sweet heart. Good as a catch crop, for early crops under cover, and for small gardens. It has remained a popular variety since the late 19th century. **'Red Riding Hood'** is an open-hearted romaine-type lettuce that grows very well in warm zones. It makes large, red butterheads even in the heat of summer. **'Valmaine'** is good for growing as a "cut and come again" or for close planting and use as leaf lettuce. **'Winter Density'** is very sweet-tasting and good for overwintering outdoors or for sowings under cover.

hardy lettuce for overwintering outdoors.
Crisphead: **'Iceberg'** has very crisp tender leaves with large ice-white hearts, ideal for spring or summer sowing. The heart has the best-quality leaves. **'Malika'** grows very rapidly and should be harvested soon after it matures. It has some resistance to "tip burn" and lettuce mosaic virus. **'Premier Great Lakes'** is large, crisp and rapidly maturing. Heat- and tip-burn-resistant. **'Saladin'** is

resistance to lettuce root aphid. '**Lollo Rossa**' adds color to salads. The leaves are tinged red with serrated, wavy margins. Good mixed with romaine or iceberg lettuces and attractive as an edging plant in the flower border or vegetable plot. **'Oak Leaf'** has several different color forms, from pale green to brown. It dates from the late 18th century and is tasty and ornamental. **'Red Salad Bowl'** has bronze-green to crimson leaves. **'Ruby'** is crinkled and pale green with deep red tints. Has good heat resistance. **'Salad Bowl'** was one

'Webb's Wonderful'

CULTIVATION

Propagation

Germination is poor, particularly with Butterhead types, if soil temperatures exceed 77°F, with the critical period being a few hours after planting. During hot weather sow in late afternoon or evening, when soil temperatures are lower, water after sowing to reduce soil temperature, shade before and after sowing, germinate in trays or packs in a cool place, and transplant, or fluid sow. Lettuces do not transplant well in dry soil and hot weather; where possible, summer sowings are better made in situ or in packs.

Sow thinly in drills ½–¾ in. deep; seeds sown too deeply are slow or fail to germinate. Thin to the final spacing when plants are large enough to handle (overcrowding checks growth and can cause bolting). In cool weather, thinnings can be transplanted if lifted with care to avoid root damage.

Sow those grown in trays or packs in loam-based potting compost to maintain strong growth and harden off before transplanting when they have 4 to 5 true leaves. Do not transplant when the weather is hot and dry, unless shading can be provided, and do not plant them too deeply.

Sow summer crops from midspring to midsummer. Sow winter-hardy varieties from late summer to early fall, thinning to the final spacing in spring.

As they do not last long after maturity, maintain a continuous supply of lettuce by sowing successively, about every 2 weeks, just as the seedlings from the previous sowing appear.

Thin when the seedlings are large enough to handle, where possible staggering them in a triangular pattern to make optimum use of the area.

Space small lettuces 8 in. apart in and between the rows, Butterheads with about 11 in. in and between the rows, or 10 in. apart in rows 12 in. apart. Crispheads should be planted 15 in. apart or 12 in. apart with the rows 15 in. apart. Plant Salad Bowl or romaine about 14 in. apart in and between the rows.

Leaf lettuce can also be grown as "cut and come again" seedlings providing 2 or 3 harvests before bolting:

'All Year Round'—ironically, for sowing only from spring to fall

summer crops tend to run to seed more rapidly. Make sure you sow thinly.

Romaine varieties like 'Lobjoits Green' can be grown as leaf lettuce. Sow in rows 5 in. apart, thinning to 1 in. Sow weekly from late spring to early summer and again in 3 consecutive weeks from late summer. This technique was developed at Horticulture Research International, Wellesbourne, U.K. **Zones 3–11.**

Growing

Lettuce prefers cool growing conditions, 50–68°F, and needs an open, sunny site on light, rich, moisture-retentive soil, with a pH of around neutral.

It struggles on dry or impoverished soil, so dig in plenty of well-rotted organic matter the fall before sowing or grow on ground manured for the previous crop. Lightly fork in a base dressing of general fertilizer at 2 oz./sq. yd. about 10 days before sowing and create a seedbed by raking to a fine tilth.

Hoe and hand weed regularly to remove weeds. A constant supply of moisture is vital for success. Lettuce needs 4 gallons/sq. yd. per week in dry weather. Water in the mornings on sunny days so that the water on the leaves evaporates quickly, reducing the risk of disease. If water is scarce, apply only on the last 7–10 days before harvest.

Boost growth of winter-hardy outdoor crops with a liquid general fertilizer in midspring and use the same treatment for slow-growing crops at any time of year.

Rotate crops every 2 years to avoid the buildup of pests and diseases.

Maintenance

Spring Sow crops under glass or outdoors under cloches in early spring. Sow later crops outdoors. Harvest early crops.
Summer Sow successively and harvest overwintered crops. Keep crops weed-free, water as needed. Harvest.
Fall Sow and protect crops under cloches. Harvest.
Winter Sow crops under cover. Harvest.

Protected Cropping

Sow from late winter to early spring in packs or trays for transplanting under cloches or cold frames from mid- to late spring. Alternatively,

It is worth growing the attractive 'Sangria' in ornamental borders.

they can be sown in situ in cold frames or under cloches for growing on or transplanting outdoors in a protected part of the garden and covered with floating cloches.

Protect late spring and summer transplants under cloches until they become established and protect late summer sowings under cloches to maintain the quality of fall crops.

Grow hardier varieties under floating cloches or in a greenhouse or a cold frame over winter, ideally with a gentle heat around 45°F.

Sow from late summer to midfall for transplanting. Earlier sowings can be made outdoors in a seedbed for transplanting; others can be sown in packs or seed trays. Ventilate well to avoid disease problems.

Harvest from late fall to midspring. Cover outdoor winter-hardy crops with glass or floating cloches in mild winter regions to ensure a good-quality crop and provide protection during severe weather.

Sow early crops of "cut and come again" seedlings under cover in late winter or spring, and also from midfall.

Container Growing
Compact varieties are suitable for growing in pots,

containers, and window boxes. Use a soil-based potting mix, mix in a slow-release granular fertilizer and water regularly. Sow either in situ or in packs for transplanting.

Harvesting and Storing
Summer main-crop lettuce is ready to harvest from early summer to midfall, around 12 weeks after sowing. Romaine stands for quite a time in cool weather but Butterheads deteriorate within a few days of maturity. Crispheads last for about 10 days before deteriorating. Leaf lettuces can be picked over a long period. Harvest hardy overwintered outdoor crops from late spring to early summer.

Harvest "cut and come again" seedlings about 4 weeks after sowing and romaine types grown as leaf lettuce about 1 in. above the ground when they are 3–5 in. high. A second crop can be harvested from 3 to 8 weeks later, depending on the growing conditions.

Cut mature lettuces at the base just below the lower leaves. Do not squeeze hearting lettuces to check if they are ready for harvesting as this can damage the leaves: press them gently but firmly with the back of your hand. Pull single leaves from leaf lettuce as required or cut 1 in. above the base and allow to resprout.

Growing lettuce under black plastic sheeting warms the soil, suppresses weeds, and conserves moisture.

Store lettuce in the refrigerator in the crisper or a plastic bag for up to 6 days. Romaine lettuce stores the longest.

PESTS AND DISEASES

Root aphids appear in clusters on the roots and are usually covered in a white powdery wax. The symptoms are stunted growth and yellowing leaves; plants may collapse in hot weather. They are less of a problem in cool, damp conditions. Pick and destroy affected plants or grow resistant varieties.

Aphids can also be a problem.

Leaf tips become brown and dry when affected by "tip burn," caused by sudden water loss in warm weather. Water well and shade if necessary; do not allow lettuces to grow excessively large; grow resistant varieties where possible.

Botrytis or **gray mold** can be a problem in cool, damp conditions. Do not plant seedlings too deeply, handle transplants carefully to avoid damage, thin early, remove diseased material, improve ventilation, and spray with systemic or copper-based fungicide. Grow resistant varieties.

Bolting or running to seed is caused by check during transplanting, drought, temperatures over 70°F, or long days; otherwise lettuces will only bolt after hearting. Grow resistant varieties or leaf lettuce.

Blackbirds and **sparrows** can damage seedlings. Grow under row covers, tie thread between bamboo canes, use bird wire or other deterrents.

Lettuce mosaic virus causes the leaves to become puckered and mottled, veins become transparent, and growth is stunted. More of a problem on overwintering crops. Destroy those that are affected, control aphids, and grow resistant varieties.

'Webb's Wonderful,' a large-hearted lettuce, grows well in hot summers.

COMPANION PLANTING

Lettuce grows well with cucumbers, onions, radishes, and carrots. Dill and chervil protect them from aphids.

MEDICINAL

Lettuce is used as a mild sedative and narcotic, and lettuce soup is reported to be effective in treating nervous tension and insomnia. Lettuce sap dissolved in wine is said to make a good painkiller.

Lettuce soothes inflammation—lotions for the treatment of sunburn and rough skin are made from its extracts.

It can also be used as a poultice on bruises or taken internally for stomach ulcers and for irritable bowel syndrome.

It is also antispasmodic and can be used to soothe coughs and bronchial problems; it is reputed to cool the ardor.

CULINARY

Wash leaves thoroughly before use. Use fresh or wilted in salads, braise with butter and flavor with nutmeg or braise with peas and shallots and serve with butter. Stir-fry with onions and mushrooms, steam and add to chicken soup or make cream of lettuce soup and garnish with hard-boiled eggs and a sprinkling of curry powder. Stalks can be sliced and steamed.

Braised Lettuce
Serves 4

Romaine lettuces all seem to bolt at the same time, and braising them is a nice change from the usual salad.

4–5 lettuces, trimmed
A little oil or butter
½ cup bacon, roughly diced
1 carrot, roughly diced
1 red onion, sliced
¾ cup well-flavored vegetable stock
2 tablespoons chopped thyme and parsley
Salt and freshly ground black pepper

In a saucepan of salted water, cook the lettuces for 5 minutes. Drain and refresh in cold water. Drain again and remove as much liquid as possible.

Preheat the oven to 350°F. Grease an ovenproof dish and sprinkle the base with the bacon, carrot, onion, and seasoning. Arrange the lettuces neatly in the dish and pour in the stock. Cover with buttered paper and braise in the oven for 30–40 minutes.

Remove the lettuces and other ingredients and keep hot. Then reduce the cooking liquid and pour it over the vegetables. Sprinkle with the fresh herbs and serve.

Braised Lettuce

Lactuca sativa var. *augustana*. Asteraceae

CELTUCE

Also known as Stem Lettuce, Asparagus Lettuce, Chinese Lettuce. Annual grown for edible leaves. Value: little nutritive value; low in carbohydrate and calories; a source of potassium.

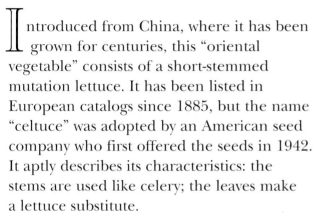

Introduced from China, where it has been grown for centuries, this "oriental vegetable" consists of a short-stemmed mutation lettuce. It has been listed in European catalogs since 1885, but the name "celtuce" was adopted by an American seed company who first offered the seeds in 1942. It aptly describes its characteristics: the stems are used like celery; the leaves make a lettuce substitute.

VARIETIES

'Zulu' is a new variety for cooler zones, with narrow, dull-textured leaves. Others are sold in seed mixes of broad, dull, glossy, or red-leaved varieties.

CULTIVATION

Celtuce needs well-drained, rich, fertile soil, with a pH of 6.5–7.5, around neutral. Celtuce tolerates a range of temperatures from light frosts to over 80°F. It tends to bolt prematurely in extremely hot conditions, but is still more heat-resistant than lettuce. Grow celtuce as a winter crop in mild zones.
Zones 4–10.

Propagation

For successional cropping, sow every 2 weeks from midspring until midsummer in drills 1/2 in. deep and 12 in. apart. When large enough to handle, thin to 3 1/2 in.

Germination is poor in temperatures above 80°F. In hot summers, sow in seed trays or packs in a cool, partially shaded position. Packs tend to produce better plants than seed trays; weak seedlings rarely produce good stems. Transplant when 3–4 leaves have been produced, generally after 3–4 weeks. Mulch after planting to conserve moisture and suppress weeds; the shallow roots are very easily damaged by hoeing.

Growing

In poor soils add copious amounts of organic matter the winter before planting. Celtuce grows well on light soil, but develops a stronger root system and more robust plants on heavier soils.

Water well as leaves develop to keep them tender. As the stems develop, reduce watering, but take care to keep the supply steady: if the soil becomes too wet or too dry, the stems may crack. Feed with a liquid general fertilizer every 3 weeks.

Maintenance

Spring Sow seed.
Summer Water and remove weeds.
Fall Transplant seedlings for winter crops.
Winter Grow under cover; harvest mature crops.

Protected Cropping

Grow in cloches, unheated greenhouses, tunnels, or under frost fabric to extend the season. Raise early crops by sowing and planting under cover in early spring and late crops by transplanting summer-sown seedlings under cover in fall.

Container Growing

Sow in containers or pots in a loam-based potting mix with moderate levels of added fertilizer.

Harvesting and Storing

Harvest 3–4 months after sowing, when 12 in. high and 1 in. diameter. Cut the stalks and pull up the plant or cut it off at ground level. Trim the leaves from the stem but do not touch the top rosette of leaves in order to keep the stem fresh.

Celtuce stems can be kept for a few weeks in cool conditions.

PESTS AND DISEASES

Celtuce is susceptible to the same problems as lettuce. Pick off **slugs**, set traps or use aluminum sulfate pellets. **Downy mildew** is worse in cool, damp conditions: treat with fungicide, and remove infected plants and debris at the end of the season.

COMPANION PLANTING

Plant with chervil and dill to protect from aphids. Interplant between slower-growing crops such as cauliflower, self-blanching celery, or Chinese chives.

CULINARY

Celtuce is excellent raw and cooked. Prepare the stems by peeling off the outer layer. Cut into thin slices for salads or into larger pieces for cooking. Cook lightly, no more than 4 minutes. Stir-fry with white meat, poultry, fish, other vegetables, or on its own seasoned with garlic, chili powder, pepper, soy, or oyster sauce.

Lagenaria siceraria. Cucurbitaceae

BOTTLE GOURD

*Also known as Doodhi, Calabash Gourd, White-flowered Gourd, Trumpet Gourd.
Vigorous annual climber grown for edible young fruits, shoots, and seeds. Tender.
Value: little nutritive value; a moderate source of vitamin C, small quantities of
B vitamins, and protein.*

Early evidence for the cultivation of this versatile tropical
gourd comes from South America around 7000 B.C., though
it is thought to have originated in Africa south of the Sahara or in
India. Some sources suggest that it may have dispersed naturally
by floating on oceanic currents from one continent to another:
experiments have found that seed will germinate after
surviving over seven months in seawater. One of the
earliest crops cultivated in the tropics, these gourds with
their narrow necks have developed in many shapes and
sizes, some reaching up to 6 ft. long. The young fruits
are edible, but mature shells become extremely
hard when dried and have been used to make bottles,
kitchen utensils, musical instruments, floats for fishing
nets, and even gunpowder flasks. In the past *lagenaria*
leaves were used as a protective charm when
elephant hunting.

VARIETIES

Lagenaria sicerana is a
vigorous annual, climbing
or scrambling by means of
tendrils to more than 30 ft.
The leaves are broad and
oval with wavy margins. Its
solitary, fragrant, white
flowers open in the
evenings. Its fruits are pale
green to cream or yellow,
with a narrow "neck," and
contain white, spongy flesh
and flat cream-colored
seeds. The names of
selected forms (like "bottle,"
"trumpet," "club" or
"powderhorn" gourd) relate
to their use and appearance.

CULTIVATION

They flourish in warm
conditions, around 68–86°F
and plenty of sunshine, but
will grow outdoors in warm
temperate zones where
humidity levels are
moderate to high. Plants
need to be trained over
supporting structures. **Zones
4–11.**

Propagation
Soak seeds overnight in
tepid water before sowing
on mounds of soil about
12 in. apart, containing
copious amounts of well-
rotted manure. Plant 3
seeds, edgewise, and thin to
leave the strongest seedling.
Seeds can be sown in a
nursery bed and
transplanted when they have
2 to 3 leaves. Seeds are
usually sown at the start of
the rainy season.

Growing
Gourds need fertile, well-
drained soil, preferably with
a pH of 7. Add a granular
general fertilizer to the
planting hole or scatter it
around the germinated
seedling. Train the stems
into trees, or over fences,
arbors, or frames covered
with 6 in. mesh netting.
Erect stakes or trellis on the
beds or among the groups
of mounds. Alternatively,
grow plants in beds
48–72 in. square, planting a
seedling at each corner and
training toward the center.
Pinch out the terminal
shoots when they are
1¼–1½ in. long to
encourage branching. The
best yields are obtained in
warm-climate zones with
rainfall around 28–48 in.
per annum, but they grow
well in drier regions if they
are kept well watered. Feed
with a high-nitrogen
fertilizer every 3 weeks
during the growing season,
keep crops weed-free and
mulch with a layer of
organic matter.

Plants can grow extremely
rapidly in hot weather:
2 ft. in 24 hours has been
recorded. Where conditions
are suitable they can be
grown all year round. To
grow outdoors in cooler

zones, harden off under cloches or cold frames and plant in a sheltered, sunny position when the danger of frost has passed.

The chance of success is greater in hot summers; they should reach edible size, though they rarely have a long enough season to mature fully.

Maintenance

Spring Sow seeds under glass in warm conditions. *Summer* Train vines over trellis or netting. Water regularly, feed as necessary. Damp down the greenhouse to maintain humidity and harvest young fruits. *Fall* In cooler zones harvest mature gourds for preserving, before the onset of the first frosts.

Protected Cropping

In cool temperate zones, sow seeds 6–8 weeks before the anticipated planting out time. Sow 2–3 seeds in a 6-in. pot of peat-lite mix in late winter or early spring at 70–75°F.

Germination takes 3–5 days. If the ideal temperatures cannot be achieved and maintained, delay sowing until mid- to late spring. Transplant when seedlings are 4–6 in. high. They will grow at temperatures down to 50°F, but flourish at high temperatures and in humid conditions in bright filtered light.

Damp down the greenhouse floor at least twice a day, depending on outside weather conditions. Dig in plenty of well-rotted manure and horticultural grit or sharp sand into the greenhouse border, or grow in containers. Keep the potting mix constantly moist using tepid water and feed with a liquid general fertilizer every 2 weeks.

Train up a trellis, wires, or netting. Flowers will appear from early summer and only 1 or 2 should be allowed to grow to maturity.

Gourds growing in a Cypriot village garden

Container Growing

Repot as plants grow until they are in 12 in. pots, or grow in large containers of loam-based potting mix with added organic matter and horticultural grit or sharp sand to improve drainage. Keep the potting mix moist, with tepid water. Growth is better restricted when they are grown in pots and is preferable in the greenhouse border, increasing the chance of successful fruiting.

Stop the shoot tips when the stems are 5 ft. long and train the side stems along a wire. (It is worth noting that even with this method, plants still need a considerable amount of space.) Hand-pollination ensures a good crop. (Male and female flowers are on the same plant: females are recognized by the ovary at the back of the flower, covered in glandular hairs.) Once a flower has formed, allow 2 more leaves to appear, then pinch out the growing tip. If it is a male flower or a fruit is not going to form, cut the stem back to the first leaf. A replacement will be formed.

Harvesting and Storing

Vines begin to fruit 3–4 months after planting. Harvest immature fruits when a few inches long, 70–90 days after sowing. Mature fruits can be harvested and dried slowly as ornaments.

Pests and Diseases

This very robust plant is rarely troubled by disease. **Whitefly** can occasionally be a problem when plants are grown under cover. In warm, humid zones, **anthracnose** appears as pinhead-sized, water-soaked lesions on the fruits, combining to form a small black mass. **Fruit rot** can also be a problem. Spray with Bordeaux compound and remove badly affected leaves. Harvest fruits carefully to avoid damage.

MEDICINAL USES

The fruit pulp around seeds is emetic and purgative and is sometimes given to horses! Juice from the fruit treats baldness; mixed with lime juice, it is used for pimples; boiled with oil, it is used for rheumatism. Seeds and roots are used to treat dropsy and the seed oil used externally for headaches.

CULINARY

Young fruits, which are rich in pectin, are popular in tropical Africa and Asia. They have a mild, somewhat bland taste, are peeled before eating, and any large seeds are removed. They can be cubed or sliced, sautéed with spices to accompany curries and other Indian dishes, and added to stews or curries. Young shoots and leaves can be steamed or lightly boiled. Seeds are used in soups in Africa and are boiled in salt water and eaten as an appetizer in India. The seed oil is used for cooking.

Lens culinaris. Leguminosae

LENTIL

Also known as Split Pea, Masur.
Annual herb grown for edible, flattened seeds. Tender.
Value: rich in protein, fiber, iron, carbohydrate, zinc, and
B vitamins.

Presumed to be native to southwestern Europe and temperate Asia, lentils are one of the oldest cultivated crop plants. Carbonized seeds found in Neolithic villages in the Middle East date to 7000–6000 B.C., and it is believed that they were domesticated long before that. By 2200 B.C. plants appeared in Egyptian tombs; they are referred to in the Bible as the "mess of pottage" for which Esau traded his birthright (Genesis 25:30, 34). The English "lens," describing the glass in optical instruments, comes from their Latin name— its cross section resembles a lentil seed. Christian "Lent" has the same origin, as lentils were traditionally eaten during the fast.

Grown throughout the world, lentils have become naturalized in drier areas of the tropics. Because of their relatively high drought tolerance, they are suitable for semi-arid regions. The quick-maturing plant is rarely more than 18 in. tall and has branched stems forming a small bush. The white to rose and violet flowers lead to 2–3 seeded pods.

VARIETIES

Lentils have been selected over many centuries for their size and color. Today many different races and cultivars exist. Two main races predominate: the larger, round-seeded types usually grown in Europe and North America, and the smaller, flatter-seeded types common in the East.

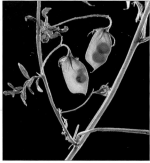
'Lentille du Puy,' a small seed French variety, in unripe pod

'Lentille du Puy,' ready for harvest

Frequently encountered is the **split red** or **Persian lentil**, which is extremely tender and quick to cook.

Among round-seeded types grown in Europe, the **'Lentille du Puy,'** a tiny green form, is the tastiest and tenderest. Similar but coarser is the **lentille blonde** or **yellow lentil** commonly grown in northern France, while **German** or **brown lentils** are coarser still and need lengthy cooking to make them tender. Of varieties grown in North America, **'O'Odham'** has flat gray-brown to tan-colored seeds and **'Tarahumara Pinks'** from Mexico has mottled seeds and thrives in semi-arid conditions.

CULTIVATION

Propagation
Prepare the seedbed by removing any debris from the soil surface and raking to a moderate texture. Sow in spring when the soil is warm in drills 1 in. deep, thinning seedlings to 8–12 in. apart with 18 in. between rows. They can also be broadcast and then thinned after germination to 8–12 in. apart.
Zones 5–11.

Growing
Lentils are not frost-hardy but flourish in a range of climatic conditions. They prefer a warm, sunny, sheltered position on light, free-draining, moisture-retentive soil. Sandy soils with added well-rotted organic matter are ideal, though equally good crops are grown on silty soil. Keep crops weed-free and irrigate if necessary during periods of prolonged drought. Excessive watering can lead to over-production of leaves and poor cropping.

Lentils can be grown as a "novelty" crop in cool temperate zones, but yields are not high enough to make it worthwhile on a large scale.

Growing in Idaho

Maintenance

Spring Prepare the seedbed and sow when soil is warm.
Summer Keep crops weed-free and irrigate if necessary.
Fall Harvest before the seeds split.
Winter Store seeds or pods in a cool dry place, for use as required.

Protected Cropping

In cool temperate zones sow seeds in spring in trays, pots, or packs of seed potting mix. Keep potting mix moist and repot when seedlings are large enough to handle. Harden off before planting outdoors when the soil is warm and workable and there is no danger of frosts. Protect plants under cloches until they are properly established.

Container Growing

Grow in containers of soil-based potting mix with moderate fertilizer levels. Water well and keep weed-free. To avoid the need for transplanting, seeds can be sown in a container that is then moved outdoors into a sunny spot after they have germinated.

Harvesting and Storing

Lentils take about 90 days to reach maturity. Harvest as foliage begins to yellow, before the pods split and the seeds are shed. Lift the whole plant and lay on trays or mats in the sunshine to air-dry or put them in an airy shed. When the pods dry and split, remove the seed and store in a cool, dry place.

CULINARY

As their protein content is about 25 percent, lentils are an important meat substitute. They also have the lowest fat content of any protein-rich food.

Soak overnight, drain and replace the water. Boil rapidly for 10 minutes, then simmer for 25 minutes until tender. Use in soups, thick broth, or grind into flour.

Lentils are commonly used for "dhal." Seeds are moistened with water and oil and dried before milling 2–3 times, each time separating the "chaff" from the meal.

Puy Lentils with Roasted Sweet Peppers and Goat's Cheese
Serves 4

3 red bell peppers
³/₄ cup lentilles du Puy
1 red onion
1 carrot
Sprig each of parsley, marjoram, and thyme
2 tablespoons sun-dried tomatoes, chopped
1 cup crumbled goat's cheese
1 tablespoon freshly chopped herbs

for the dressing:
4 tablespoons extra-virgin olive oil
1¹/₂ tablespoons lemon juice
Salt and freshly ground black pepper

Roast the peppers on a baking sheet in a preheated oven at 475°F for 30 minutes. Put them into a plastic bag and set aside. When cooled, seed and peel the peppers, then cut into strips. Set aside.

Wash the Puy lentils thoroughly and cook them, covered, with the whole onion, carrot, and herbs. These lentils cook faster than other types and should be done in 15 minutes. Drain. Roughly chop the onion and add back into the lentils. Discard the carrot and herbs. While still warm, add the tomatoes and goat's cheese and stir gently. Season.

Make the dressing and toss the lentil mixture in it. Arrange the lentils with the slices of red pepper on individual plates. Sprinkle with the herbs and serve.

PESTS AND DISEASES

Lentils suffer from few pests and diseases. **Leaf rust** can occur; burn plants after harvest and use treated seed.

COMPANION PLANTING

Lentils can be grown as a "green manure."

OTHER USES

Dried leaves and stems are used as forage crops.

Lentils have also been used as a source of commercial starch in the textile and printing industries, the by-products being used as cattle feed. Plants are used fresh or dried as hay and fodder.

WARNING

Never eat lentils raw.

Lotus tetragonolobus (syn. *Tetragonolobus purpureus*). *Papilionaceae*

WINGED BEAN

Also known as Asparagus Pea. Sprawling annual winged bean, ornamental but grown for edible pods. Half hardy. Value: small amounts of protein, carbohydrate, fiber, and iron.

A wildflower of open fields and wasteland in Mediterranean countries, this plant may have arrived in Britain with imported grain. It has since become naturalized. Gerard records its cultivation before 1569 for its dark crimson, pea-like flowers; only later were its edible merits discovered, but it has never gained widespread popularity. The 1807 edition of Miller's *Gardener's Dictionary* notes: "formerly cultivated as an esculent plant, for the green pods . . . it is now chiefly cultivated in flower gardens for ornament."

The prominent winged pods illustrate the plant's name

CULTIVATION

Propagation
Sow seed outdoors from mid- to late spring, once the soil warms and frosts are over. Drills should be ¾ in. deep and 15 in. apart; thin to 8–12 in. apart once they are large enough to handle. In cooler areas, sow under cloches or in the greenhouse in trays or packs of moist seed potting mix. Harden off and transplant outdoors when plants are 2 in. tall, spacing them about 8–12 in. apart. **Zones 4–11.**

Growing
Winged beans flourish in an open, sheltered, sunny site on light, rich, free-draining soil. Keep weed-free and water as required.

As they are lax in habit, growing up pea sticks or a similar support saves space and makes harvesting easier. Rotate them with other legumes.

Maintenance
Spring Sow seed in mid- to late spring.
Summer Harvest regularly.
Fall Harvest until early fall.
Winter Prepare ground for the following year's crop.

Protected Cropping
In cooler areas sow under glass for transplanting later.

Harvesting and Storing
Harvest from midsummer to early fall, when pods are 1 in. long. Pick regularly to prolong the harvest. Longer, older pods are "stringy" and inedible. Pods that do not bend easily are unsuitable for eating. Harvesting is easier in the evening, when the leaves close and the small green pods are more visible.

Pests and Diseases
Protect crops from **birds** using bird wire or similar bird scarers. They can also suffer from **downy and powdery mildew**.

CULINARY

The subtle flavor is similar to asparagus. Wash the pods, "top and tail" if necessary, then steam for up to 5 minutes (check them after about 3 minutes, as they need only light cooking). Drain well before eating. Mix with butter and cream or serve on toast. Alternatively, cook in butter until tender, drain, and serve.

Winged bean flowers are blood-red and tiny

Lycopersicon esculentum. Solanaceae

TOMATO

lso known as Love Apple. Short-lived perennial grown as annual for fleshy, succulent berry. Half hardy. Value: rich in beta carotene and vitamin C; some vitamin B.

The wild species is believed to have originated in the Andean regions of north and central South America, spreading to Central and North America along with corn during human migrations over 2,000 years ago. The fruits had been cultivated in Mexico for centuries when European explorers found them growing under local names including *tomati, tomatl, tumatle,* and *tomatas.* When they were first brought to Europe around 1523, tomatoes were considered to be poisonous, due to their strong odor and bright white, red, and yellow berries, and were grown only as ornamentals. Dodoens in his *Historie of Plants* of 1578 records, "This is a strange plant and not found in this country, except in the gardens of some herborists . . . and is dangerous to be used."

In Europe, it was first used for food in Italy. Like many vegetable introductions from the New World, it was considered to be an aphrodisiac. The Italian name *pommi dei mori* was corrupted during translation to the French *pomme d'amour* or "apple of love," as it was thought to excite the passions. Not all believed it to have this effect. Estienne and Liébault wrote that tomatoes were boiled or fried, but gave rise to wind, choler, and "infinite obstructions"—hardly an inducement to romance!

The use of tomatoes by North American settlers was not recorded until the late 1700s, but they were regularly used as food by Italian immigrants to New England and French settlers living in New Orleans, who were making ketchup by 1779. Thomas Jefferson was certainly growing them in his garden in 1781 and they were introduced to Philadelphia eight years later.

'Tigerella' is unusual but worth growing for its flavor.

VARIETIES

Most greenhouse varieties are "indeterminate," with a main stem that can become several yards long—these are usually grown on stakes. Most of those grown outdoors are bush types that do not need supporting and can be grown under crop covers or cloches. Low-yielding, dwarf varieties are good for pots or window boxes.

As you will see from any seed catalog, there are hundreds of tomato varieties. Those for cultivation under cover in a cold greenhouse and outdoor varieties are generally interchangeable. They range in size from the large, ribbed, "beefsteak" types to small "cherry," "pear-shaped," and "currant," tomatoes in a great range of colors, including mottled, dark skinned, pink, and yellow.

'Ailsa Craig' grows well indoors and outdoors. It is a reliable, tasty, heavy-cropping variety. **'Alicante,'** another indoor/outdoor variety, crops heavily, producing smooth tasty fruit. Early maturing, it grows well in growing bags.

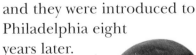

'Brandywine' can weigh up to 1 lb. each

red-and-yellow striped fruit of **'Big Rainbow'** taste as good as they look. **'Black Plum'** is a Russian variety found in specialist lists. The fruit are elongated, about 3 in. long and deep mahogany to brown. **'Brandywine'** is a delicious old variety; the fruit can become quite sizable. The skin is rosy pink or tinged slightly purplish-red. Better in cooler zones. **'Cherry Belle,'** a tasty little "cherry" tomato, is of good quality and high yielding. It has resistance to tobacco mosaic virus. **'Delicious'** is a large beefsteak variety with fruits weighing up to 1 lb. They are tasty, succulent, and store well. **'Dombito,'** also a beefsteak, is delicious, crops well, and has resistance to tobacco mosaic virus and fusarium wilt. **'Gardener's Delight'** is extremely popular, producing long trusses of delicious, sweet, "cherry" tomatoes over a long period. Grows indoors and outdoors, is ideal for containers and generally trouble-free. **'Green Grape'** produces unusual one-inch yellow-green fruit on compact plants. These tiny tomatoes are very sweet and juicy. **'Green Zebra'** is a tasty tomato with unusual green fruits and yellow stripes. **'Marmande Super'** is a delicious outdoor variety with deep red ribbed fruits. Early cropping and resistant to fusarium and verticillium wilt. **'Moneymaker'** is a famous old variety for indoors and

outdoors. The succulent scarlet fruits are full of flavor. **'Moreton Hybrid'** is an esteemed American hybrid offering tangy old-fashioned flavor in medium-sized fruit that grow on reliable and disease resistant plants. A frequent winner of tomato taste judgings, **'Persimmon'** is an heirloom variety that produces large, orange tomatoes in just 80 days. **'Roma VF'** is an outdoor bush "plum" tomato for paste, ketchup, bottling, soups, or juice. It crops heavily and has high resistance to fusarium and verticillium wilt. It sometimes needs supporting. **'San Marzano,'** another Italian tomato, is good for soups, sauces, or garnishing salads. Crops heavily. **'Shirley'** is grown commercially and has good quality, tender, tasty fruit. Withstanding lower temperatures than most types, it does not suffer from "greenback" and is highly resistant to tobacco mosaic virus, leaf mold, and fusarium. An ideal tomato for organic growers. **'Siberia Tomato'** crops extremely early, around seven weeks from transplanting. This bush variety sets fruit at temperatures down to 38°F, producing clusters of bright red berries. **'Super Beefsteak'** is a huge old fleshy variety whose fruits are at least 1 lb. in weight. Has resistance to wilt and root knot nematodes. **'Tigerella'** produces tasty,

small orange-red fruits with pale stripes. Crops well over a long period. **'Tiny Tim'** is compact, bushy and ideal for pots, window boxes and hanging baskets. Fruits are cherry-sized and tasty. **'Tumbler'** was bred for hanging baskets. It has flexible, hanging stems, the bright red fruits ripen quickly and are sweet to the taste. **'Yellow Pearshaped'** are well described by their name. The dense clusters of fruit are sweet-tasting and have few seeds. Plants are vigorous and high yielding. **'Yellow Perfection'** is prolific with bright yellow fruits, early cropping and tasty. An excellent tomato.

Modern greenhouse varieties such as **'Aromata,'** **'Moravi,'** and **'Merlot'** are significantly disease-resistant compared with older sorts.

CULTIVATION

Propagation

A minimum temperature of 60°F is needed for germination, but seedlings can tolerate lower night temperatures if those during the day are above this level.

In cool zones, for growing in heated greenhouses, sow from midwinter. For growing outdoors or in an unheated greenhouse, sow seed indoors ¾ in. deep in trays of seed potting mix, 6–8 weeks before the last frost is due, or sow 2–3 seeds in 3-in. pots or packs, thinning to leave the strongest seedling.
Zones 3–11.

The popular and prolific 'Gardener's Delight'

Transplant tray- or pack-grown seedlings into 3-in. pots when 2–3 leaves have formed, keeping the plants in a light, well-ventilated position. Harden off carefully and plant out when there is no danger of frost and air temperatures are at least 45°F with soil temperatures at a minimum of 50°F.

Transplant, with the first true leaves just above the soil level, when the flowers on the first truss appear. Do not worry if your plants have become spindly; planting them deeply stimulates the formation of roots on the buried stems, making the plants more stable.

Tomatoes can also be fluid-sown from midspring in situ or in a cold frame for transplanting after warming the soil. Germinate on moist paper towels at 70°F, sowing when the rootlets are a maximum of ¼ in. long (see advice on fluid sowing). Sow outdoors in drills and thin to leave the strongest seedling or in hills at their final spacing. Cover the drills with potting mix and protect them with cloches until the first flowers appear.

When sowing in cold frames, sow seed in rows 5–6 in. apart, thinning to 4–5 in. apart in the rows. Transplant carefully when the plants are 6–8 in. tall.

Alternatively, buy plants grown individually in pots rather than packed in boxes or trays, using a reliable supplier.

Plant "staking" types 15–18 in. apart, or in double rows with 36 in. between each pair of rows. Bush types should be planted 18–24 in. apart and dwarf cultivars 10–12 in. apart, depending on the variety.

Closer spacing produces earlier crops; wider spacing generally produces slightly higher yields.

Growing

Outdoor tomatoes need a warm, sheltered position, preferably against a sunny wall, in a moisture-retentive, well-drained soil. Add well-rotted organic matter where necessary and lime acid soils to create a pH of 5.5–7. If tomatoes are grown in very rich soil or are fed with too much nitrogen they produce excessive leaf growth at the expense of flowers and fruit. Fruit will not set at night temperatures below 55°F and day temperatures above 90°F. Night temperatures around 76°F may well cause blossom to drop.

Tomatoes should be fed with a liquid general fertilizer until established, then with a high-potash fertilizer to encourage flowering and fruiting. Excessive feeding and watering spoils the flavor.

Keep crops weed-free by hoeing and hand weeding, taking care not to damage the stems, or mulch with a layer of organic matter.

Plum tomatoes, grown primarily for cooking and tomato paste because of their fuller flavor

Keep them constantly moist but not waterlogged; erratic watering causes the fruit to split and also encourages "blossom end rot," particularly when plants are grown in containers or growing bags. Use tepid water. In dry conditions or when the first flowers appear they need about 2 gallons of water each week.

Careful watering and feeding is essential, particularly near harvest time to ensure that the fruits are not excessively watery and have a good flavor. Feed with tomato fertilizer according to the manufacturer's instructions.

Indeterminates need supporting with stakes, strings, or a frame. Using a sharp knife or by pinching between the finger and thumb, remove sideshoots when they appear and "stop" plants by removing the growing tip 2–3 leaves above the top truss when 3–5 trusses have been formed or when the plant has reached the top of the support. The number of trusses on each plant depends on the growing season: in shorter growing seasons, leave fewer trusses. Remove any leaves below the lowest truss to encourage good air circulation.

In seasons when ripening is slow, remove some of the leaves near to the trusses with a sharp knife, exposing fruits to the sunshine.

To keep the fruit clean and stop fruit from rotting, grow bush tomatoes on a mulch of straw, glass clippings, or crop covers laid over the soil. Black polyethylene or even a split garbage bag (with the edges anchored by burying them in the soil) absorbs heat, warms the soil, conserves moisture, and helps fruit to ripen.

Rotate crops annually.

'Pearshaped' and currant tomatoes

Maintenance
Spring Sow crops under cover and, later, outdoors. *Summer* Keep crops watered, fed and weed-free. Shade and ventilate as necessary. Remove sideshoots. Harvest. *Fall* Ripen late outdoor crops under cloches or indoors.

Protected Cropping
In cooler zones, more reliable harvests can be achieved by growing tomatoes in an unheated greenhouse or polyethylene tunnels. Rotate crops to avoid the buildup of pests and diseases and sterilize or replace the soil every 2–3 years. Or use containers. To assist pollination and fruit set, particularly of plants grown indoors, mist occasionally and tap the trusses once the flowers have formed; do this around midday if possible. (It is not so important for outdoor crops, as wind movement assists pollination.) Shade greenhouses before the heat of summer and ventilate well in warm conditions.

A fairly recent innovation is the "Wall-o-Water," a series of connected plastic tubes filled with water that absorbs heat during the day and warms by radiated heat at night. This is reusable and offers protection down to 16°F, extending the growing season and warming the soil. Adding roughly 1 part bleach to 500 parts water will prevent the formation of algae on the inside of the tubes.

Protect newly planted outdoor tomatoes with cloches or floating crop covers until they become established. Once the first flowers are pushing against the cover, make slits along the center; about 7–10 days later slit the remainder of the cover and leave as a shelter alongside the plants. "Indeterminate" varieties can then be tied to stakes.

Container Growing
Tomatoes are excellent for containers, pots, or growing bags, indoors or outside where they can be included in "edible" displays in window boxes, pots, and hanging baskets.

Grow in 9-in. pots of loam-based potting mix with high fertilizer levels. For requirements see "Growing" and "Protected Cropping." Bushy varieties are ideal.

Plants in containers dry out rapidly, so careful feeding and watering is essential. Water regularly and remember to label your plants.

Harvesting and Storing
Harvest fruits as they ripen, about 7–8 weeks after planting for bush types and 10–12 weeks for indeterminate varieties. Lift and break the stem at the "joint" just above the fruit. Outdoor crops should be harvested before the first frosts. Toward the end of the season, indeterminate varieties with unripe fruit can be lifted by the roots and hung upside down in a frost-free shed to ripen. Alternatively, they can be detached from their support, laid on straw and covered with cloches or put in a drawer or a paper bag with a ripe banana or apple (the ethylene these produce ripens the fruit). Bush and dwarf types can be ripened under cloches.

Tomatoes can be cooked and bottled in airtight jars. To freeze, skin and core when ripe, simmer for 5 minutes, then sieve, cool, and pack in a rigid container.

Tomatoes stay fresh for about a week in a plastic bag or the crisper in the refrigerator. To retain flavor they are better stored at 60°F

Dry large "meaty" tomatoes in the sun or in the oven. Cut into halves or thirds and put skin side down on a tray and cover with a gauze frame as a protection from insects. Ideal drying conditions are in warm, dry, windy weather, but they should be brought indoors at night if dew is likely to form. Humid conditions are not suitable for outdoor drying. Oven-dry just below 145°F until tomatoes are dried

but flexible. Stored in airtight containers in a cool place, they can last for up to 9 months. Before use put the tomatoes in boiling water or a 50-50 mix of boiling water and vinegar and allow them to stand until soft. Drain and marinate for several hours in olive oil with added garlic to suit your taste. They last in the marinade for about a month and are excellent with pasta and tomato sauce.

Pests and Diseases
Blossom end rot appears as a hard, dark flattened patch at the end of the fruit away from the stalk. This indicates a deficiency in calcium, usually caused by erratic watering. It is often a problem with plants grown in growing bags. Water and feed regularly, particularly during hot

weather. Erratic watering causes fruit to split, which may also happen with sudden growth after overcast weather. Pick and use split fruits immediately.

"**Greenback,**" hard, green patches appearing near the stalk, caused by sun scorch and overheating, is more of a problem with plants growing under glass. Sometimes this becomes an internal condition known as "**whitewall.**" Shade and ventilate well, water regularly, and feed with a high-potash liquid fertilizer.

Curled leaves are caused by extreme temperature fluctuations between day and night. It is often a problem in greenhouses: shade, ventilate, and damp down. Close ventilation before temperatures drop.

Whitefly, aphids, and **red spider mite** can be a problem, as can potato blight in wet summers: dark blotches with lighter margins appear on the leaves. Spray with a copper fungicide before fruit set.

Plants with **verticillium wilt** droop during the day and usually recover overnight. Lower leaves turn yellow and cut stems have brown markings on the inside. Do not plant when the soil is cold; drench with a spray-strength solution of systemic fungicide, mist regularly, and shade. Mounding moist potting mix around the stem encourages the formation of a secondary root system. The symptoms and control of **fusarium wilt** are similar.

Tobacco mosaic and other viruses show as mottling on the leaves, some of which may be misshapen; inside the fruit is browned and pitted and growth is stunted. Dispose of affected plants, wash your hands, and sterilize tools by passing them through a flame. Grow the following year's plants in sterilized potting mix or in growing bags.

The **tomato hornworm** is a large (3½ to 4 in. when

mature) pale green or brown caterpillar with white and black markings that feeds on the leaves of tomatoes and related plants. It has 8 V-shaped markings down each side. Hand picking or snipping the hornworms in half with scissors gives good control.

The symptoms of **magnesium deficiency** are yellowing between the leaf veins, older leaves being affected first. Spray, drench, or scatter magnesium sulfate around the base. Where possible, grow disease-resistant varieties.

COMPANION PLANTING

Grow with French marigolds to deter whitefly. Tomatoes grow well with basil, parsley, alliums, nasturtiums, and asparagus.

MEDICINAL

Tomatoes are believed to reduce the risk of cancer and appendicitis.

In American herbal medicine tomatoes have been used to treat dyspepsia and liver and kidney complaints, and are also said to cure constipation.

WARNING

Some doctors believe that tomatoes aggravate arthritis and may be responsible for food allergies. The leaves and stems are poisonous.

Cherry tomatoes underplanted with thyme

CULINARY

In salads, tomatoes are particularly good with mozzarella, basil, olive oil, and seasoning. They are also good with chives. Some people prefer to peel them first, by immersing in boiled water for 1 minute to loosen the skins. Use in soups, stews, sauces, pasta, and omelets. Gazpacho is a spicy cold soup of tomatoes, sweet peppers, cucumbers, and onions and is delicious.

Tomatoes are wonderful broiled: cut them in half and cover the cut surface with olive oil, pepper, and sugar. Grill for 5 minutes. Alternatively, glaze them with wine and brown sugar and broil.

Use them in a BLT, or have "currant" and "cherry" varieties as a snack.

Use larger "beefsteak" varieties as a garnish with steak or hollow out and stuff with shrimp, potato salad, cold salmon, cottage cheese, or mashed curried egg. Serve hot or cold.

Green tomatoes can be sliced, dipped in batter and then bread crumbs, and fried in hot oil, or made into chutney or jam. They can also be added to orange marmalade.

Tomato and red onion salad

Stuffed Tomatoes
Serves 4

In times gone by Catholics all over Europe ate these on fast days, when meat was not allowed.

4 large ripe tomatoes
6 cups white bread crumbs (day-old bread)
½ cup milk
2 eggs, lightly beaten
2 tablespoons chopped basil
2 tablespoons finely chopped parsley
2 cloves garlic, finely crushed
1 onion, finely chopped
2 tablespoons toasted bread crumbs
5–6 tablespoons shredded Gruyère
Olive oil
Salt and freshly ground black pepper

Remove a slice from the top of each tomato and scoop out the pulp. Season the insides of the tomatoes with salt and pepper, and arrange in a greased baking dish.

Preheat the oven to 350°F. To make the stuffing, combine the white bread crumbs with the milk and eggs in a bowl and add the garlic, herbs, and onions. Season with salt and pepper and fill the tomatoes.

Sprinkle with the toasted bread crumbs and Gruyère and drizzle with a little olive oil to prevent burning. Bake until the tomatoes are tender, about 30 minutes.

Manihot esculenta (syn. *M. utilissima*). *Euphorbiaceae*

CASSAVA

Also known as Tapioca, Yucca, Manioc.
Tall herbaceous perennial grown for edible tubers and leaves. Tender. Value: mainly starch; small amounts of vitamin B, C, and protein.

O ne of the most important food crops in the humid tropics, cassava is believed to have been cultivated since at least 2500 B.C. Unknown as a wild plant, it may have originated in equatorial South America in the Andean foothills, the Amazon basin, or regions of savannah vegetation. The earliest archaeological records, from coastal Peru, date from 1000 B.C. Tubers contain highly toxic cyanide, which is removed by cooking; accounts tell of starving European explorers eating raw manioc and dying at the moment they thought sustenance had been found. The indigenous Indians tipped their arrows and blowpipe darts with its toxic sap; Arawak Indians committed suicide by biting into uncooked tubers rather than be tortured by the conquistadores.

The Portuguese brought the crop to West Africa and it quickly spread, reaching Sri Lanka in 1786, India in 1794, and Java by 1835. An estimated 62 million tons of cassava is produced annually, much of it in West Africa, where it is eaten as *fufu*.

Mature cassava plants, Thailand

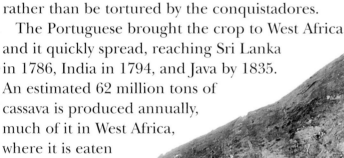

VARIETIES

Manihot esculenta is tall and branched, its stems becoming woody with age. The leaves are long-stalked, with 5–9 lobes; toxic latex is present in all parts of the plant. The swollen tubers are cylindrical or tapering, forming a cluster just below the soil surface, and weigh 11–22 lb.

There are two types. **"White cassava"** is sweet and soft, and used as a source of starch; **"yellow"** varieties are bitter and usually grown as a vegetable. The more primitive bitter varieties contain larger quantities of cyanide, which is washed out by boiling in several changes of water before cooking. In recent selections of "sweet" varieties, most of the toxin is in the skin, and tubers are edible after simple cooking.

There are well over 100 different forms with local names. **'Nandeeba,'** quick to mature, and **'Macapera,'** used for boiling, are both from Brazil.

Propagation
Take cuttings from mature stems 6–12 in. long; plant 4 ft. apart in rows 3 ft. apart or "pits" 3–3½ ft. square in a grid pattern. Planting cuttings upright, leaving the top 2 in. exposed, gives best results. Plant cuttings at the start of the rainy season. **Zones 9–11.**

Growing
Cassava flourishes where the warm rainy season is followed by a dry period. It has good resistance to drought; in a constantly wet climate, there is excessive

stem growth and tuber formation is poor. Soils should be deep, rich, and free-draining. It is often grown on ridges or mounds as it dislikes waterlogging. Dig deeply before planting, adding well-rotted organic matter. Hill up as necessary. Cassava is a heavy feeder and cannot usually be grown for more than 3 years on the same ground.

Maintenance
Spring Dig in organic matter before planting.
Summer Plant cuttings at the start of the rainy season.
Fall Keep weed-free.
Winter Harvest at maturity.

Protected Cropping
In cool temperate zones, plants can be grown as a "novelty crop" in a hothouse. Prepare the borders and cultivate as for "Growing." Water well during the growing season and reduce watering during winter.

Harvesting and Storing
Varieties are harvested from 8 months to 2 years after planting, depending on the locality and variety. Harvest when plants have flowered and the leaves are yellow. Lift the whole plant and carefully remove the tubers. They store for up to 2 years in the ground, but should be used within 4–5 days of lifting.

PESTS AND DISEASES

Whitefly and **fungal diseases** can be a problem. **Bacterial diseases**, **scale** and **cassava mosaic** are a severe problem in Africa.

Plants are highly resistant to locusts.

Harvesting cassava plants in Indonesia

OTHER USES

Cassava is also a source of starch for the manufacture of fiberboard, textiles, adhesives, and paper.

WARNING

All parts of the plant contain toxic latex. Prepare tubers thoroughly before eating. Inhabitants of Guyana take chilies steeped in rum as an antidote to yucca poisoning, but do not rely on it!

CULINARY

The fresh root is equivalent in starch to one-third of its weight in rice and half in bread, but its nutritional value is unbalanced; high consumption can lead to protein deficiency.

Wash thoroughly and remove the skin and rind with a sharp knife or potato peeler. Boil in several changes of water and allow to dry before cooking.

It can be eaten mashed or boiled as a vegetable or made into dumplings and cakes. Mix with coconut and sugar to make cookies. The juice from shredded cassava is boiled down and flavored with cinnamon, cloves, and brown sugar to make "cassareep," a powerful antiseptic and essential to the West Indian dish pepperpot. Tapioca flour is made from ground chips.

In Africa the fresh root is washed, peeled, boiled, and pounded with a wooden pestle to make *fufu*. Cook cassava chunks in boiling water for 45–50 minutes, drain, cool, pound into dough, and shape into egg-sized balls to add to soups and stews as a traditional African accompaniment.

Roots of "sweet" varieties can be roasted like sweet potato, baked, or fried.

Young leaves can be boiled or steamed and eaten with a pat of butter.

Cassava Chips (Singkong)

These thin, crispy wafers are perfect served as a snack or as a garnish. Allow 10 oz. per person to accompany a plain meat course.

Slice the cassava very thinly and allow to dry. Heat some peanut or vegetable oil (don't let it smoke) in a wok or a deep pan. Deep fry 1–3 slices at a time by immediately submerging each below the surface of the oil. Remove quickly from the heat and drain well on layers of paper towels.

Cooked singkong can be stored in an airtight container for several weeks, but is best served at once.

Medicago sativa. Papilionacae

ALFALFA

Also known as Lucerne, Purple Medick. Grown as annual or short-lived perennial for seed sprouts and young leaf shoots. Hardy. Value: good source of iron and protein.

"Medick" comes from the Latin *Herba medica*, the Median or Persian herb, imported to Greece after Darius found it in the kingdom of the Medes. It was a vital fodder crop of ancient civilizations in the Near East and Mediterranean, and known in Britain by 1757. Today, alfalfa is valued by gardeners as a green manure as well as a nutritious vegetable. Its blooms in the wildflower meadow are rich in nectar, while the leaves are a commercial source of chlorophyll.

VARIETIES

The species *Medicago sativa* is a fast-growing evergreen legume with cloverlike leaves; growing ultimately to 3.5 ft., it has spikes of violet and blue flowers. It produces quality crops on poor soils, as it is highly effective at fixing nitrogen in the root nodules.

Penetrating up to 20 ft. into the ground, the roots draw up nutrients and aerate the soil. Agricultural varieties are available. If you want to sprout alfalfa seeds, buy untreated seed; that sold for sowing as a crop is usually chemically treated.

CULTIVATION

Alfalfa can be grown as a short-lived perennial, a cut-and-come-again crop, or as seed sprouts. It tolerates low rainfall and can be grown in any soil, in temperate to sub-tropical conditions, or at altitude in the tropics. **Zones 3–9.**

Propagation
Sow in spring or from late summer to fall. Thin those grown as perennials to 10 in. apart when large enough to handle. Sow cut-and-come-again crops, spaced evenly, by broadcasting or in shallow drills 4–5 in. wide.

Growing
Prepare seedbeds in winter, fork the area, remove debris and stones, and rake level. Keep weed-free until established. Cut perennials to within a few inches of the base after flowering and renew every 3–4 years, as old plants become straggly.

Maintenance
Spring Sow seed outdoors.
Summer Harvest young shoots from perennials.
Fall Sow protected crops.
Winter Prepare seedbed.

Protected Cropping
Sow under cloches, frost fabric, or glass in late summer to fall for winter cropping.

Container Growing
Sow cut-and-come-again crops in a bright open position in a loam-based potting mix with low fertilizer levels; water pots regularly.

Harvesting
Harvest cut-and-come-again crops when about 2 in. long, a few weeks after sowing. Cut back plants regularly to encourage new growth; they provide young growths for 4–5 years.

Sprouting Seeds
To sprout alfalfa, soak seeds overnight or for several hours, tip seeds into a sieve, and rinse. Put several layers of moist paper towels or blotting paper in the base of a jar and cover with a ¼ in. layer of seed. Cut a square from pantyhose or piece of muslin to cover the top, securing with a band. Place in a bright position, away from direct sun, maintaining constant temperatures around 68°F. Rinse seed daily by filling the jar with water and pouring off again. Harvest shoots after 3–7 days, when they have nearly filled the jar. Wash and dry sprouts and use as required; do not store more than 2 days.

Pests and Diseases
Rabbits can be a problem.

CULINARY

Young shoot tips and sprouted seeds can be used raw in salads or cooked lightly.

For a tasty salad, try it with hard-boiled eggs (1 per person), anchovies, and capers served on a bed of chicory and radicchio leaves. To stir-fry, pour a little oil in a pan, add the alfalfa, and stir briskly for 2 minutes; serve immediately.

COMPANION PLANTING

Alfalfa accumulates phosphorus, potassium, iron, and magnesium; it keeps grass green longer in drought.

MEDICINAL

An infusion of young leaves in water is used to increase vitality, appetite, and weight. The young shoots, rich in minerals and vitamin B, are highly nutritious and the seeds appear to reduce cholesterol levels.

Momordica charantia. Cucurbitaceae

BITTER GOURD

Also known as Karela, Balsam Pear, Bitter Cucumber, Momordica. Annual climber grown for edible fruits and leaves. Tender. Value: fruit a good source of iron, ascorbic acid, and vitamin C; leaves and young shoots contain traces of minerals.

This strange-looking fruit with skin the texture of a crocodile's has been grown throughout the humid tropics for centuries. Rudyard Kipling's description in Mowgli's "Song Against People" conveys the plant's vigor (it climbs to 12 ft.):

> *I will let loose against you the feet footed vines,*
> *I will call in the Jungle to stamp out your lines.*
> *The roofs shall fade before it, the house-beams shall fall;*
> *And the Karela shall cover it all.*

The strongly vanilla-scented flowers are followed by the elongated fruit. When ripe, it splits at the tip into three sections, exposing brown or white flattened seeds surrounded by blood-red pulp. The fruit is better eaten young.

The odd-looking, slender fruit have a blistered, puckered skin

CULTIVATION

Male and female flowers are borne on the same plant. Male flowers are 2–4 in. long; females are similar, but with a slender basal bract. The fruit can grow up to 10 in. and ripens to become orange-yellow, though a white variety is grown in India and eastern Asia. **Zones 8–11.**

Propagation
In humid tropical climates sow at the start of the rainy season, placing 2–3 seeds outdoors in hills 36 in. apart, in and between the rows. Thin after germination, leaving the strongest seedling. Water plants as necessary.

The first flowers appear 30 to 35 days after sowing. In temperate zones, sow seed in early spring under glass at 68°F in peat-lite mix. Keep the potting mix moist with tepid water and repot as necessary when the roots become visible through the drainage holes.

Growing
Bitter gourds flourish in moderate to high temperatures with sunshine and high humidity. Plant in beds or mounds of rich, moisture-retentive, free-draining soil. Dig in plenty of well-rotted manure or similar organic matter before sowing.

Pinch out the terminal shoots when they are 1¼–1½ in. long to encourage branching, then train the stems into trees, or over fences, arbors, trellis, or frames covered with 6 in. mesh netting. Keep plants constantly moist and weed-free throughout the growing season.

Maintenance

Spring Sow seed under glass in peat-lite mix.

Summer Keep plants well fed and watered.

Fall When cropping finishes add leaves and stems to your compost pile.

Winter Prepare the greenhouse border for the following year's crop.

Container Growing

Plants can be grown indoors in containers containing a rich, well-drained potting mixture of equal parts loam-based potting mix and well-rotted organic matter with added peat and grit.

Keep the potting mix moist with tepid water and feed every 2 weeks with a liquid general fertilizer.

Protected Cropping

Grow under cover in temperate zones. Plants need hot, humid conditions in bright light. To prepare the soil for growing plants in the greenhouse border, see "Growing."

Growth is better restricted in borders and containers. Stop the shoot tips when the main stems are 5 ft. long, training the lateral stems along wires or trellis.

Once a flower has formed, allow 2 more leaves to appear, then pinch out the growing tip. If it is a male flower or a flower does not form, cut the stem back to the first leaf to allow a replacement to form. Flowers should be hand pollinated.

You should damp down the greenhouse floor regularly during hot weather.

Harvesting and Storing

The first fruits appear about 2 months after sowing and should be harvested when they are about 1 in. long and are yellow-green in color. They can be eaten when longer.

Fruits can be kept in a cool dark place for several days or stored in the crisper in the refrigerator for 4 weeks. Gourds can also be sliced and dried for use out of season.

Ripe fruit showing crimson seeds

PESTS AND DISEASES

Fruit fly is common; spray with contact insecticide or protect the fruits with a piece of paper wrapped round the fruit and tied with string round the stalk. **Red spider mite** is a common pest under cover. Leaves become mottled and bronzed. Check plants regularly; small infestations are easily controlled—isolate young plants. The mites prefer hot, dry conditions, so keep humidity high. Spray with rotenore.

MEDICINAL

The fruits are said to be tonic, stomachic, and carminative and are a herbal remedy for rheumatism, gout, and diseases of the liver and spleen. In Brazil, the seeds are used as an anthelmintic. Its fruits, leaves, and roots are used in India and Puerto Rico for diabetes. In India, leaves are applied to burns and as a poultice for headaches and the roots used to treat hemorrhoids. In Malaya they are used as a poultice for elephants with sore eyes.

CULINARY

Remove the seeds from mature fruit, and remove any bitterness by salting. Young fruits do not need to be salted.

Gourds are ideal diced in curries, stir-fries, or pickles; stuffed with meat, shrimps, spices, and onions and fried; or added to meat and fish dishes. Mature fruits can be parboiled before adding to a dish or cooked like zucchini and eaten as a vegetable.

Young shoots and leaves are cooked like spinach.

Pelecing Peria
Serves 4

Sri Owen gives this recipe in her marvelous book, *Indonesian Food and Cookery.* Some of the ingredients need determination to track down, but it is worth the trouble.

3–4 bitter gourds (peria)
Salt
6 cabé rawit (or hot red chilies)
3 candlenuts
2 cloves garlic
1 piece terasi (shrimp paste, available at Thai shops)
1 tablespoon vegetable oil
Juice of 1 lime

Cut the gourd lengthwise in half, take out the seeds, and then slice like cucumbers. Put the slices into a colander, sprinkle liberally with salt and leave for at least 30 minutes. Wash under cold running water before boiling for 3 minutes with a little salt.

Pound the cabé rawit, candlenuts, garlic, and terasi in a mortar until smooth. Heat the oil in a wok or sauté pan and fry for about 1 minute. Add the gourd and stir-fry for 2 minutes; season with salt and lime juice. Serve hot or cold.

Oxalis tuberosa. Oxalidaceae

OCA

Also known as Iribia, Cuiba, New Zealand Yam. Perennial grown for tubers. Half hardy. Value: about 85% water; some carbohydrates; small amounts of protein.

This is common in the high-altitude Andes from Venezuela to northern Argentina, where it is second only to the potato in popularity. At the northern end of Lake Titicaca, more than 150 steep terraces dating from the Incas are still cultivated. Oca is grown in New Zealand, where it was introduced from Chile in 1869. Today it is rarely found in European or American gardens, though it was once grown as a potato substitute. Tubers form in fall when day lengths are less than nine hours.

VARIETIES

Oxalis tuberosa is bushy to 10 in. tall, with trilobed leaves and orange-yellow flowers. It produces small tubers 2–4 in. long that are yellow, white, pink, black, or piebald.

CULTIVATION

Propagation
Plant single tubers or slice into several sections, each with an "eye" or dormant bud, and dust the cut surfaces with fungicide.

Plant 5 in. deep and 1 ft. apart with 1 ft. between rows. In frost-free zones plant in midspring; in cooler areas propagate under cover in 5–8-in. pots of potting mix before planting out once frosts have passed. **Zones 7–9.**

Growing
Oca flourish in deep fertile soils, so incorporate organic matter before planting. Earthing up before planting increases the yield.

Maintenance
Spring Plant tubers.
Summer Water as necessary.

Exposed tubers, New Zealand

Fall Tubers can be lifted when needed.
Winter Store tubers in sand.

Protected Cropping
Where early or late frosts are likely, grow under cover to extend the harvest season. Plant in midspring in greenhouse borders. Harvest from midfall to early winter. Extend outdoor cropping by protecting with crop covers or cloches.

Container Growing
Oca grow well in containers, although yields are lower. Tubers should be planted in spring in 12-in. pots in loam-based potting mix with moderate fertilizer levels, with added organic matter.

Regular watering is vital, particularly as tubers begin to form. Allow the potting mix surface to dry out before rewatering. An occasional feed with liquid fertilizer helps to boost growth.

Harvesting and Storing
About 8 months after planting, check to see if the tubers are mature, then lift carefully. Undamaged tubers can be stored in boxes of sand in a dry, frost-free place.

Pests and Diseases
Slugs are often a problem.

COMPANION PLANTING

Oca grow well with potatoes and can be grown under runner beans, corn, or crops of a similar height.

WARNING

Prepare tubers correctly before eating to remove calcium oxalate crystals.

CULINARY

Tubers have been selected over the centuries for flavor and reduced levels of calcium oxalate crystals, which otherwise render them inedible. Leave them for a few days to become soft before eating. In South America they are dried in the sun until floury and less acid. If dried for several weeks, they become sweet, tasting similar to dried figs.

The acidity can be removed by boiling in several changes of water. The flavor of tubers even improves once frozen.

Oca can be eaten raw, roasted, boiled and candied like sweet potato, and added to soups and stews. Use leaves and young shoots in salads or cook them like sorrel.

Oca and Bacon

Clean 1 lb. oca and cut into cubes. Boil in salted water until just tender; drain and combine with ½ lb. diced, cooked bacon. Coat with mayonnaise, sprinkle over fresh chives, and season. Serve warm.

Pastinaca sativa. Apiaceae

PARSNIP

Biennial grown as annual for edible root. Hardy.
Value: some carbohydrate, moderate vitamin E,
smaller amounts of vitamins C and B.

This ancient vegetable is thought to have originated around the eastern Mediterranean. Exactly when it was introduced into cultivation is uncertain, as references to parsnips and carrots seem interchangeable in Greek and Roman literature: Pliny used the word *pastinaca* in the first century A.D. when referring to both. Tiberius Caesar was said to have imported parsnips from Germany, where they flourished along the Rhine—though it is possible that the Celts brought them back from their forays to the east long before that. In the Middle Ages, the roots were valued medicinally for treating problems as diverse as toothache, swollen testicles, and stomachache. In sixteenth-century Europe parsnips were used as animal fodder, and the country name of "madneps" or "madde neaps" reflects the fear that delirium and madness would be brought about by eating the roots.

Introduced to North America by early settlers, they were grown in Virginia by 1609 and were soon accepted by Native Americans, who readily took up parsnip growing. They were used as a sweetener nineteenth the development of sugar beet in the 19th century; the juices were evaporated and the brown residue used as honey. Parsnip wine was considered by some to be equal in quality to Malmsey, and parsnip beer was often drunk in Ireland. In Italy pigs bred for the best-quality Parma ham are fed on parsnips.

VARIETIES

Roots are "bulbous" (stocky, with rounded shoulders), "wedge" types (broad and long-rooted), or "bayonet" (similar, but long and narrow in shape).

'Avonresister' is small with bulbous roots and excellent resistance to canker and bruising. It is sweet-tasting, performs well on poorer soil, and grows rapidly. Smooth skins characterize

'Cobham Improved Marrow,' a half-long variety that produces 8-in.-long roots with a very high sugar content, and good resistance to canker. 'Exhibition Long' is extra-long, with an excellent flavor. 'Gladiator' produces large, vigorous, well-shaped, and fine-flavored roots with good canker resistance. 'Javelin' is wedge- or bayonet-shaped, high yielding, and canker-resistant; "fanging" rarely occurs. 'Lancer' produces long, slender, supersweet roots with resistance to canker. 'Hollow Crown' has fine, mild, tender flesh and crops well. 'Student' has long, slender roots and is very tasty. It originated around 1810 from a wild parsnip found in the grounds of the Royal Agricultural College, Cirencester, England. 'Tender and True' is an old variety. Very tasty, tender, and sweet, it has very little core. 'White Gem' has wedge-shaped to bulbous smooth roots, with delicious flesh and good canker resistance. It is ideal for heavier soils.

Parsnips cultivated commercially are also rotated; here they are seen growing in Devon, England.

CULTIVATION

Propagation

Parsnip seed must always be sown fresh, as it rapidly loses the ability to germinate. Seeds are also renowned for erratic, slow germination in the cold, wet conditions that often prevail early in the year when they are traditionally sown.

To avoid poor germination, sow later, from mid- to late spring, depending on the weather and soil conditions, when the ground is workable and temperatures are higher than 45°F.

Warm the soil with cloches or frost fabric a few weeks before sowing. Rake in a granular general fertilizer at 2 oz./sq. yd. 1–2 weeks before sowing. Rake the seedbed to a fine texture before sowing.

Sow in situ on a still day so the light, papery seeds are not blown away. In dry conditions, water drills before sowing 2–3 seeds at the recommended final spacing in hills, thinning to leave the strongest seedling after germination. Sow radishes between the stations to act as a marker crop indicating where slower-germinating parsnip seeds are sown.

Alternatively, sow thinly in drills ¼ to ½ in. deep, sowing shorter-rooted varieties in rows 6–8 in. apart, thinning to 2–4 in., and larger types in rows 12 in. apart, thinning to 5–8 in.

In stony soil make a hole up to 36 × 6 in., fill with finely sieved soil or potting mix, sow 2–3 seeds in the center of the hole, and thin to leave the strongest seedling. Grow short-rooted varieties in shallow soils. **Zones 3–7.**

Growing

Parsnips thrive in an open or lightly shaded site on light, free-draining, stone-free soil that was manured the previous year.

Traditionally, parsnips are not grown on freshly manured soil as this causes "fanging," or forking of the roots; however, recent research has not supported this. Dig the plot and add plenty of well-rotted organic matter in fall or early winter the previous year. Deep digging is particularly important when growing long-rooted varieties.

The ideal pH is 6.5–7.0; lime where necessary, as roots grown in acid soil are prone to canker. Rotate with other roots.

Keep crops weed-free, by hoeing or hand weeding carefully to avoid damaging the roots, or by mulching with well-rotted organic matter. Do not let the soil dry out, as erratic watering causes roots to split. Water at 3–4 gallons/sq. yd. every 2 weeks during dry weather when the roots are swelling.

Maintenance

Spring Rake the seedbed to a fine tilth, apply general fertilizer, sow seed in packs, "fluid sow," or sow in situ when the soil is warm.
Summer Keep crops weed-free by mulching, hand weeding, or careful hoeing.
Fall Harvest crops.
Winter Cover crops with straw or hay before the onset of inclement weather. Dig the soil for the following year's crop.

'Hollow Crown Improved' dug and washed, ready for use

Wild parsnip bears little resemblance to its cultivated counterparts and is less tasty.

Protected Cropping

Possible germination problems can be avoided by pregerminating and fluid-sowing seed, or by sowing in packs under cover and transplanting before the tap root starts to develop.

Container Growing

Shorter-rooted varieties can be grown in large containers of loam-based potting mix. Longer types are grown in large barrels, making a deep hole in the potting mix as described above for stony soil. Make sure that containers are well drained.

Harvesting and Storing

Parsnips are a long-term crop and occupy the ground for around 8 months—a factor worth bearing in mind if your garden is small. Roots are extremely hardy and can remain in the ground until required.

Harvest from midfall onward, covering plants with straw, hay, or burlap for ease of lifting in frosty weather. Make sure you dig them carefully with a fork to avoid root damage.

Dig all your roots by late winter and store them in boxes of moist sand, peat substitute, or wood shavings in a cool shed.

Parsnips have a better flavor when they have been

exposed for a few weeks to temperatures around freezing point. (This changes stored starch to sugar, increasing sweetness and improving the flavor.) Stored in a plastic bag in the refrigerator, they remain fresh for up to 2 weeks.

Wash, trim, and peel roots, then cube and blanch in boiling water for 5 minutes before freezing them in plastic bags.

PESTS AND DISEASES

Parsnip canker is a black, purple or orange-brown rot, often starting in the crown, which can be a problem during drought, when the crown is damaged or the soil is too rich. There is no chemical control. Sow crops later, improve drainage, keep the pH around neutral, rotate crops, and sow canker-resistant varieties. **Carrot fly** can also be a problem.

COMPANION PLANTING

Sow rapidly germinating radish and lettuces between rows. Parsnips grow well alongside peas and lettuce, providing they are not in the shade.

Plant next to carrots and leave a few to flower the following year as they attract beneficial insects.

MEDICINAL

In Roman times, parsnip seeds and roots were regarded as an aphrodisiac.

CULINARY

In 17th-century England there are records of parsnip bread and "sweet and delicate parsnip cakes." They were often eaten with salt fish and were a staple during Lent.

Scrub rather than peel parsnips, and use boiled, baked, mashed, or roasted with beef, pork, or chicken. They combine particularly well with carrots.

Parsnips can be lightly cooked and eaten cold. Parboil and fry like potatoes or slice into rings, dip in batter, and eat as fritters. Grate into salads or add chopped and peeled to casseroles or soups. Or parboil, drain, then stew in butter and garnish with parsley. They are also good parboiled, then broiled with a sprinkling of Parmesan. Try steaming them whole, slicing them lengthways and pan-glazing with butter, brown sugar, and nutmeg, or garnishing them with chopped walnuts and a dash of sweet sherry.

Puree of Parsnips

Boil some parsnips and mix them with an equal quantity of mashed potatoes, plenty of salt and freshly ground black pepper, a little shredded orange rind, a splash of heavy cream, and enough butter to make a smooth dish. Sprinkle with chopped Italian parsley and serve piping hot. (Pureed parsnips are also wonderful combined with carrots and seasoned with nutmeg.)

Curried Parsnip Soup
Serves 4–6

2 lb. parsnips
1 large onion, sliced
1 tablespoon butter
2 cloves garlic, crushed
1 teaspoon curry powder
1 14-oz. can chopped tomatoes
4 cups vegetable stock
1 bay leaf
Sprig each of thyme and parsley
4–6 teaspoons yogurt
Salt and freshly ground black pepper
Chopped parsley, to garnish

Clean the parsnips and peel if old. Chop them roughly. Add the onion to a large soup pot with the butter and garlic and sauté over a medium heat until lightly browned (this helps to give the flavor of Indian cuisine). Stir in the curry powder and continue to cook for 1 minute, stirring constantly.

Then add the parsnips and stir, coating them well in the curry and onion mixture, and add the tomatoes, stock, and herbs. Stir thoroughly. Season, bring to a boil and simmer, covered, for about 15–20 minutes, until the parsnips are tender.

Remove the herbs. Then puree the soup, adjust the seasoning, and garnish with yogurt and parsley. This is delicious served with crusty bread.

Curried Parsnip Soup

Petroselinum crispum var. *tuberosum. Apiaceae*

HAMBURG PARSLEY

The leaves look similar to those of Italian parsley

Also known as Parsley Root, Turnip-rooted Parsley. Swollen-rooted biennial, usually grown as annual for roots and leaves. Hardy. Value: root contains starch and sugar; leaves high in beta carotene, vitamin C, and iron.

Hamburg parsley is an excellent dual-purpose vegetable. The tapering white root looks and tastes similar to parsnip and can be eaten cooked or raw. The finely cut, flat, dark green leaves resemble parsley; they are coarser in texture, but contribute a parsley flavor and can be used as garnish. As an added bonus it grows in partial shade, is very hardy, and an ideal winter vegetable.

Popular in central Europe and in Germany, it is one of several vegetables and herbs known as *Suppengrun,* or "soup greens," which are added to the water when beef or poultry is boiled and later used for making sauce or soup. Introduced from Holland to England in the eighteenth century, this versatile vegetable enjoyed only a relatively brief period of popularity. It should certainly be more widely grown by America's gardeners.

CULTIVATION

Hamburg parsley needs a long growing season to develop good-sized roots. Grow it in moisture-retentive soil in an open or semishaded position.

Propagation
As seeds are sown early in the year, it may be necessary to cover the bed with cloches or crop covers before sowing to warm up the soil. Sow from early to midspring in drills 1 ½ in. deep and 10–12 in. apart, thinning seedlings to a final spacing of 9 in.

They can also be sown in hills, planting 3–4 seeds in groups 9 in. apart. Thin to leave the strongest seedling when they are large enough to handle.

Seeds can also be sown in packs, but should be planted in their final position before the taproot begins to form. To extend the harvesting season, make a second sowing in midsummer, which will provide crops early the following year. **Zones 4–9.**

Growing
Dig in plenty of well-rotted organic matter the fall before planting or plant in an area where the soil has been manured for the previous crop.

Rake the soil finely before sowing. Germination is often slow and it is important that the seedbed is kept free of weeds, particularly in the early stages.

Use a hoe with care as the plants become established to avoid damaging the roots. Mulching established plants is a sensible option as this stifles weed growth and conserves moisture. A 1-in. layer of well-rotted compost will perform the task perfectly. Root splitting can occur if plants are watered after the soil has dried out, so water thoroughly and regularly during dry periods to maintain steady growth.

Maintenance
Spring Sow seeds outdoors, warming the soil if necessary. Seeds can also be sown in packs.
Summer Keep crops weed-free, water during drought, and make a second sowing in midsummer for early crops the following year.
Fall Harvest as required.
Winter Cover crops with hay or similar protection to make lifting easier in severe weather.

Container Growing
Hamburg parsley can be grown in containers if they are deep enough not to dry out rapidly and provide sufficient space for the roots to form. Regular watering is vital and plants should also be kept out of scorching, bright sunshine.

Harvesting and Storing
This is such a hardy vegetable that it can remain in the ground until required any time from early fall to

midspring. When frosts are forecast, cover with straw, hay, or a similar material to make lifting easier. After removing the foliage, store in a box of sand or peat substitute in a cool shed or garage; some of the flavor is lost when roots are stored in this way, so they are better left in the ground if possible.

PESTS AND DISEASES

This tough vegetable is generally trouble-free, but it can suffer from **parsnip canker**. This appears as dark patches on the root. Control is impossible, but the following measures will help. Dig up and dispose of affected plants immediately, ensure that the soil is well drained, rotate crops, and maintain the soil at a pH around neutral.

Hamburg parsley, showing its small parsniplike roots

COMPANION PLANTING

When hill-sowing, fill the spaces by planting 'Tom Thumb' or a similar lettuce variety. Sowing radishes between hills is also useful because their rapid germination indicates the position of the Hamburg parsley and prevents you accidentally removing any newly germinated seedlings when weeding.

WARNING

Hamburg parsley should not be eaten in large amounts by expectant mothers or those with kidney problems.

CULINARY

The flavor reminiscent of celeriac, Hamburg parsley is frequently used in Eastern European cooking.

Prepare for cooking by removing the leaves and fine roots, then gently scrubbing to remove the soil: don't peel or scrape. Try Hamburg parsley sliced, cubed, and cooked like parsnips (sprinkle cut areas with lemon juice to prevent discoloration). It is delicious roasted, sautéed, or fried, as well as boiled, steamed, or added to soups and stews. It can also be shredded raw in winter salads.

Dried roots can be used as a flavoring. Dry them on a shallow baking tray in an oven heated to 170°F; allow to cool before storing in an airtight jar, in a dark place. Wash the leaves and use as flavoring or garnish.

Croatian Hamburg Parsley Soup
Serves 8

1 lb. Hamburg parsley
1 turnip, peeled
1 large onion, peeled
1 good-sized leek, cleaned
½ stick butter
10 cups vegetable stock
Salt and freshly ground black pepper
4 tablespoons sour cream
2 tablespoons each chives and dill
4 tablespoons croutons

Chop all the vegetables coarsely. Heat the butter in a heavy-bottomed pan and sauté the vegetables until softened. Stir to prevent burning. Add the stock, season with salt and pepper, and simmer until the vegetables are tender.

Puree and return to the pan. Stir in the sour cream and the herbs, allow to heat through again, and adjust the seasoning. Do not allow to boil. Serve piping hot, with croutons.

MEDICINAL

The leaves are a good source of vitamins A and C and contain similar properties to traditional garnishing parsley. They reduce inflammation, are used for urological conditions like cystitis and kidney stones, and help indigestion, arthritis, and rheumatism. After childbirth the leaves encourage lactation; the roots and seeds promote uterine contractions. The leaves are also an excellent breath freshener—powerful enough to counter the effects of garlic!

Phaseolus aureus. Papilionaceae

MUNG BEAN

Also known as Green Gram, Golden Gram. Annual grown for its seed sprouts and seeds. Tender. Value: sprouts: rich in vitamins, iron, iodine, potassium, calcium; seeds: rich in minerals, protein, and vitamins.

Growing

Mung beans flourish on rich, deep, well-drained soils and dislike clay. Add organic matter if necessary and lime to create a pH of 5.5–7.0. Water well throughout the growing season. Ideal growing conditions are temperatures of 86–97°F with moderate rainfall.

Sprouting Seeds

Use untreated seeds for sprouting, as those treated with fungicide are poisonous. Remove any that are discolored, moldy, or damaged. Soak them overnight in cold water and the following morning, rinse in a sieve. Place a layer of moist paper towels or damp flannel over the base of a flat-bottomed tray or "seed sprouter," then spread a layer of mung beans about ½ in. deep over the surface. Cover the container with plastic wrap and put the bowl in a dark cupboard, or wrap it to exclude light.

Temperatures of 55–70°F should be maintained for rapid growth. Rinse the sprouts daily, morning and night.

Make a "seed sprouter" from a large yogurt container or ice cream container with holes punched in the bottom and use the lid as a drip tray.

VARIETIES

Phaseolus aureus is a sparsely leaved annual that grows to 3 ft. with yellow flowers and small, slender pods containing up to 15 olive, brown, or mottled seeds.

CULTIVATION

Propagation

Rake in a general fertilizer at 2 oz./sq. yd. about 10 days before sowing. Seeds can be broadcast or sown in drills on a well-prepared seedbed, thinning to 8–12 in. apart with 16–20 in. between the rows.
Zones 4–11.

This major Indian pulse crop was introduced to Indonesia and southern China many centuries ago and is grown throughout the tropics and subtropics, being sown toward the end of the wet season to ripen during the dry season. The leaves and stems are used to make hay and silage and the seeds are used for cattle feed. Mung beans came to prominence in the West with an increased interest in Asian cuisine: bean sprouts are an easy-to-grow major crop. Among other uses, their flour is a soap substitute and they serve as a replacement for soybeans in the manufacture of ketchup.

Young crop growing in a field in Thailand

Seed sprouts make great stir-fries.

This makes for easier daily rinsing of the seedlings.

Maintenance
Outdoors Broadcast or sow seed in drills; water when needed, as the soil dries out. Harvest before the pods split. *Sprouting* Keep seeds moist. Harvest regularly.

Harvesting and Storing
Harvest shoots from 3 days onward, when they are about 1–2 in. long. If the seed coats remain attached to the sprouts, soak them in water, then top and tail, removing the seed and shoot tip. Store in the refrigerator. When growing for seed, gather before they split to prevent the seeds being lost.

Pests and Diseases
Powdery mildew is a problem when plants are dry at the roots. Mulch and water regularly, remove diseased leaves immediately, spray with a systemic fungicide or bicarbonate of soda, and destroy plant debris at the end of the season.

MEDICINAL

The seeds are said to have a cooling and astringent effect on fever and an infusion is used as a diuretic when treating beriberi. In Malaya it is prescribed for vertigo.

WARNING

Do not let bean sprouts become waterlogged, as they rapidly become moldy.

CULINARY

Bean sprouts can be eaten raw in salads with a suitable dressing or lightly cooked for about 2 minutes only in slightly salted water. (Be warned: overcooked shoots lose their taste.)

To stir-fry, use only a little oil and stir briskly for about 2 minutes. In Asian cooking, bean sprouts combine well with other vegetables, eggs, red meat, chicken, and fish and can be used to stuff savory pancakes, egg rolls, and tortillas.

Stir-fried Mung Beans
Serves 2

8-oz. bag mung beans
Peanut oil, for frying
2 cloves garlic, crushed
3/4 cup chicken stock
1 tablespoon light soy sauce
1 heaped teaspoon cornstarch
2–3 scallions, roughly chopped

Rinse the mung beans well. Heat the oil and the garlic in a wok, then add the mung beans. Fry for 1 minute, stirring constantly.

Add chicken stock and cook until the beans are tender and the liquid has evaporated. Then stir in the soy sauce and the cornstarch. Cook for 2 minutes more.

Garnish with scallions and serve with rice.

Dried beans just before soaking

Phaseolus coccineus. Papilionaceae

RUNNER BEAN

Also known as Scarlet Runner. Perennial climber grown as annual in temperate climates for edible pods and seeds. Half hardy. Value: moderate levels of iron, vitamin C, and beta carotene.

A native of Mexico, the runner bean has been known as a food crop for more than 2,200 years. In the late sixteenth century, Gerard's *Herball* mentions it as an ornamental introduced by the plant collector John Tradescant the Elder: "Ladies did not . . . disdain to put the flowers in their nosegays and garlands," and in the garden it was grown around gazebos and arbors. Vilmorin Andrieux commented in 1885: "In small gardens they are often trained over wire or woodwork, so as to form summer houses or coverings for walks." Philip Miller, keeper of Chelsea Physic Garden, is credited with being the first gardener to cook them.

It was the fashion in seventeenth-century England to experiment with soaking seeds. Mr. Gifford, minister of Montacute in Somerset, noted in his diary: "May 10th 1679, I steep'd runner beans in sack five days, then I put them in sallet-oyle five days, then in brandy four days and about noon set them in an hot bed against a south wall casting all liquor wherein they had been infused negligently about the holes, within three hours space, eight of the nine came up, and were a foot high with all their leaves, and on the morrow a foot more in height . . . and in a week were podded and full ripe." You could try this for yourself—or perhaps you would prefer to stick to today's more conventional methods!

VARIETIES

Older cultivars were rather stringy unless eaten young; newer varieties are "stringless." Besides the traditional tall-growing climbers, there is also a choice of dwarf varieties that do not need supporting and are ideal for smaller gardens, early crops under cloches, and exposed sites.

Non-stringless types
'Enorma' is equally ornamental, with red flowers. It has long pods and is very tasty. **'Painted Lady,'** a variety grown since the 19th century, has delicate red and white flowers and long pods.

Stringless types
'Butler' is vigorous and prolific, with tender pods. **'Desiree'** has white flowers and seeds, and is high-yielding and tasty. **'Kelvedon Marvel'** is tasty, matures early, and crops heavily. It can also be grown along the ground. **'Polestar'** crops heavily with long, well-flavored pods. **'Red Knight,'** with red flowers, crops heavily and is excellent for freezing; it is disease-resistant. **'Red Rum'** is very early, high yielding, tasty, and resistant to halo blight. It can also grow along the ground. **'Scarlet Emperor'** is a traditional variety with scarlet flowers and tasty pods.

Dwarf varieties
'Hammonds Dwarf Scarlet' is ideal for the small garden. Pods are easy to harvest.

Supports must be strong to take the weight of the heavy vines

Tops may need to be pinched out. **'Pickwick'** is red-flowered, producing early heavy crops of juicy pods. No support needed. **'Dwarf Bees'** is an oddity: a true bush runner bean with masses of brilliant scarlet-orange blossom.

CULTIVATION

Propagation
Runner beans are not frost-tolerant and need a minimum soil temperature of 50°F to germinate. Sow from late spring to early summer 2–3 in. deep, 6 in. apart in double rows 24 in. apart. To shelter pollinating insects they are better grown in blocks or several short rows rather than a single long one. Allow 3–5 ft. between rows for ease of harvesting, depending on the cultivar.

Climbing types can be encouraged to bush by pinching out the main stems when they are around 10 in.; the sideshoots can be pinched out at the second leaf joint for a bushy plant that does not need staking.

Seed sown outdoors crops in about 14–16 weeks, depending on climatic and cultural conditions.
Zones 4–10.

Growing
Runner beans are not frost-hardy and are less successful in cooler zones unless you have a suitable microclimate. They flourish between 57–85°F, needing a warm, sheltered position to minimize wind damage and encourage pollinating insects.

Soil should be deep, fertile, and moisture-retentive. Dig a trench at least 12 in. deep and 24 in. wide in late fall to early winter before planting, adding plenty of well-rotted organic matter to the backfill. Before sowing, rake in 2–3 oz./sq. yd. of granular general fertilizer.

Keep crops weed-free during early stages of growth. Mulch after germination or after transplanting. Watering is essential for good bud set: the traditional method of spraying flowers has little effect. As the first buds are forming and again as the first flowers are fully open plants need 1–2 gallons/sq. yd. Crops should be rotated.

Climbers can be up to 10 ft. tall or more, and a good sturdy support should be in place before sowing or transplanting. Traditionally, a "teepee" of stakes, or a longer row of crossed stakes, was used; these may need supporting strings at the end of each row, like tent guy ropes. You can improvise: I once saw a wonderful structure like a V-shaped frame designed so the beans would hang down and make picking easier. Use strong wooden stakes, steel tubes, or make frameworks of netting. There should be one stake or length of strong twine for each plant.

Maintenance
Spring Sow crops under cover or outdoors in late spring. Erect supports.
Summer Keep crops weed-free and well watered. Harvest regularly.

'Pickwick' is stringless.

Fall Continue harvesting until the first frosts.
Winter Prepare the soil for the following year's crop.

Protected Cropping
For earlier crops and in cooler zones, sow in boxes or pots of seed potting mix under cover from midspring, harden off, and plant out from late spring. Protect indoor and outdoor crops with cloches or crop covers until they are established.

Container Growing
Runner beans can be grown in containers at least 8 in. wide by 10 in. deep, depending on the vigor of the cultivar.

Sow seeds 2 in. deep and 4–5 in. apart indoors in late spring, moving the container outdoors into a sunny site. Water frequently in warm weather, less often at other times. Feed with liquid general fertilizer if plants need a boost.

Stake tall varieties, pinching out growing points when plants reach top of supports. Otherwise use dwarf varieties.

Harvesting and Storing
Harvest from midsummer to midfall. Regular picking is essential to ensure regular cropping and high yields, and to avoid "stringiness."

Runner beans freeze well.

The seeds of 'Painted Lady' are a pink/brown color

Beans growing over a frame

PESTS AND DISEASES

Slugs, **black bean aphid,** and **red spider mite** may be troublesome.

Gray mold *(Botrytis)* and **halo blight** may cause problems in wet or humid weather. **Mice** may eat seeds.

Root rots may kill plants in wet or poorly drained soils. Rotate.

COMPANION PLANTING

Runner beans are compatible with all but the *Allium* family.

Grow with corn to protect it from corn army worms. Nitrogen-fixing bacteria in the roots improve soil fertility. After harvesting, cut off tops, leave roots in the soil, or add to compost piles. They thrive with brassicas; Brussels sprout transplants are sheltered and grow on once beans die back.

Late in the season, their shade can benefit celery and salad crops if enough water is available.

CULINARY

Wash, top and tail, pull off stringy edges, slice diagonally, and boil for 5–7 minutes. Drain and serve with a pat of butter. Alternatively, cook whole and slice after cooking.

Runner Bean Chutney
Makes 3 lb.

Clare Walker and Gill Coleman give this recipe in *The Home Gardener's Cookbook*:

6 cups runner beans
2 cups onions, peeled and finely chopped
³/₄ cup water
1 tablespoon salt
1 tablespoon mustard seeds
¹/₂ cup sultanas
1¹/₂ teaspoons ground ginger
1 teaspoon turmeric
6 dried red chilies, left whole
2 cups spiced vinegar
2¹/₄ cups demerara sugar

Wipe, top and tail, and string the beans and cut them into small slices. Place in a preserving pan with the onions. Add the water, salt, and mustard seeds and simmer gently for 20–25 minutes until the beans are just tender.

Then add the sultanas, ginger, turmeric, chilies, and spiced vinegar, bring to a boil and simmer for 30 minutes, or until the mixture is fairly thick.

Stir in the sugar, allow to dissolve, then boil steadily for about 20 minutes until the chutney is thick. Remove the chilies if desired. Pour into warm, dry jars, cover with thick plastic, and seal with a lid. Label and store in a cool, dry place for at least 3 months before using.

Runner Bean Chutney

Phaseolus vulgaris. Papilionaceae

STRING BEAN

Also known as Common, Kidney, Bush, Pole, Snap, French, Green, Wax Bean; Haricot;
Baked Bean; Flageolet; Haricot Vert.
Annual grown for edible pods and beans. Half hardy.
Value: moderate potassium, folic acid, and beta carotene. Very rich in protein.

Evidence of the wild form, found in Mexico, Guatemala, and parts of the Andes, has been discovered in Peruvian settlements from 8000 B.C. Both bush and climbing varieties were introduced to Europe during the Spanish conquest in the early 16th century, though the dwarf varieties did not become popular for two more centuries. They were first referred to as "kidney beans" by the English in 1551, alluding to the shape of their seeds.

Gerard in his *Herball* calls them "sperage" beans and "long peason," while Parkinson wrote: "Kidney beans boiled in water and stewed with butter were esteemed more savory . . . than the common broad bean and were a dish more oftentimes at rich men's tables than at the poor." Another writer commented in 1681: "It is a plant lately brought into use among us and not yet sufficiently known."

In Europe, "haricot vert" was used in ships' stores in voyages of exploration during the early 1500s. When European colonists first explored the Americas, they found climbing beans planted with corn, providing starch and protein for indigenous tribes.

Beans are self-pollinating, so close spacing provides higher yields

VARIETIES

This group of beans contains considerable variety. Plants are dwarf (ideal for the smaller garden or containers) or climbing, pods are flat, oval, or round in cross section and are green, yellow (waxpods), purple, or marbled. The seeds are colorful and often mottled. As well as being grown for the immature pods, eaten whole, the seeds may be allowed to swell and ripen; seeds are eaten fresh as "flageolets," or dried and known as "haricots."

Pole Beans
'**Borlotto Lingua di Fuoco**' is an ornamental "fire tongue" form, with red-marked green pods. '**Corona d'Oro**' is high yielding with rounded, tender, golden-yellow pods.

'**Emerite**' is one of the most productive of all pole beans. '**Kwintus**' produces tender, tasty pods. '**Musica**' can be sown early and is full of flavor. '**Romano,**' an old variety, is tender, tasty, and prolific. Excellent for freezing. '**Trionfo Violetto**' is an heirloom variety, and one of the prettiest. The long stringless beans are produced on plants with purple leaves and lavender flowers.

Dwarf or bush types
'**Annabel**' is high yielding, round, and tasty—perfect for the patio. The legendary Blue Lakes, known for their sweet, beany flavor, are now available in compact bush form as '**Bush Blue Lake.**' '**Chevrier Vert,**' a classic French flageolet from 1880, is tasty and tender. '**Masai**' has long thin pods, is robust, early, and high yielding, with good disease and cold tolerance. '**Purple Queen**' is delicious, producing heavy yields of glossy purple pods.

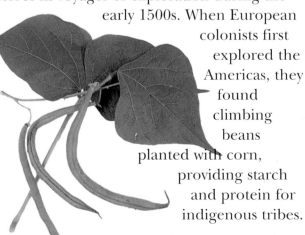

'Royalty,' ideal for the "potager"

'**Royal Burgundy**' germinates well in cold soil and has tasty, dark green pods. Resistant to pea and bean weevil. Freezes well. '**Royalty**' crops heavily. Delicately flavored dark purple pods that turn green when cooked. The dark green pods of '**Sprite**' freeze well. '**Nickel**' is a new breed of longstanding filet beans.

CULTIVATION

Propagation
String beans dislike cold wet soils and are inclined to rot; for successful germination, do not sow until the soil is a minimum of 50°F. For early sowings or in cold weather warm the soil first with cloches or black plastic 3–4 weeks before sowing.

Sow successively from midspring to early summer in staggered drills 1½–2 in. deep with 9 in. between the rows and plants for optimum yields.

Pole beans should be in double rows 6 in. apart with 2 ft. between rows.
Zones 4–11.

Growing
String beans flourish in a sheltered, sunny site on a light, free-draining, fertile soil where organic matter was added for the previous crop. Alternatively, dig in

plenty of well-rotted organic matter in late fall or winter before planting.

The plants need a pH of 6.5–7.0; lime acid soils if necessary. Rake the soil to a medium tilth about 10–14 days before sowing, incorporating a balanced granular fertilizer at 1–2 oz./sq. yd.

Keep crops weed-free or mulch when the soil is moist. Hill up round the base of the stems for added support and push twigs under mature bush varieties to keep pods off the soil, or support plants with pea sticks. Support pole beans in the same way as runner beans.

Keep well watered during drought; plants are particularly sensitive to water stress when the flowers start to open and as pods swell. Apply 3–4 gallons/sq. yd. per week.

Maintenance
Spring Sow early crops under cover or outdoors in late spring. Support climbers. Transplant when 2–3 in. tall.
Summer Keep crops weed-free, mulch, water in drought. Harvest regularly.
Fall Continue harvesting until the first frosts. Protect later crops with cloches or frost fabric.
Winter Prepare the soil for the following year's crop.

Protected Cropping
For earlier crops and in cooler zones, sow in boxes, packs, or pots of seed potting mix under cover from midspring. Warm the soil before transplanting. Harden off and plant out from late spring, depending on the weather and soil conditions. Protect crops sown indoors or in situ with cloches, crop covers, or with frost fabric until established.

For very early harvest, sow in pots in a heated greenhouse at

60°F from late winter. Sow 4 seeds near the edge of a 9–10-in. pot containing loam-based potting mix with moderate fertilizer levels.

Seeds can also be pregerminated on moist paper towels in an airing cupboard or similar. Keep moist with tepid water, ventilate in warm weather, harvest in late spring.

Container Growing
String beans can be grown in containers that are at least 8 in. wide by 10 in. deep.

Sow seeds 1½–2 in. deep indoors in midspring, moving the container outdoors into a sheltered, sunny site. Feed with liquid general fertilizer if necessary.

Stake pole beans; pinch out growing points when plants reach the top of supports.

Harvesting and Storing
Plants are self-pollinating, so expect a good harvest. Pick when pods are about 4 in. long, when they snap easily, before the seeds are visible. Pick regularly for maximum yields. Cut them with a pair of scissors or hold the stems as you pull the pods to avoid uprooting the plant.

For dried or haricot beans, leave pods until they mature, sever the plant at the base, and dry indoors. When pods begin to split, shell the beans and dry on paper for several days. Store in an airtight container.

String beans freeze well. Wash and trim young pods, blanch for 3 minutes, and freeze in plastic bags or

Climbing string beans

rigid containers. You should use within 12 months.

They keep in a plastic bag in the refrigerator for up to a week and last about 4 days in a cool kitchen.

PESTS AND DISEASES

Slugs, **black bean aphid,** and **red spider mite** can be troublesome. **Gray mold** (*Botrytis*) and **halo blight** may be problems in wet or humid weather. **Mice** may eat seeds. **Root rots** can kill plants in wet or poorly drained soils. Rotate crops.

COMPANION PLANTING

String beans do well with celery, corn, cucurbits, and melons. Intercrop with brassicas.

MEDICINAL

One cup of beans a day is said to lower cholesterol by about 12 percent.

String Bean, Roquefort, and Walnut Salad

CULINARY

String beans, fresh from the garden, have such a delicate flavor that they hardly need more than boiling in water and serving as an accompaniment to meat and other dishes. Wash, top and tail pods, and cook whole in boiling salted water for 5–7 minutes, preferably within an hour of harvesting. Cut large flat-podded types into 1-in. slices.

Alternatively, serve cold in salads or try them stir-fried with other vegetables.

For haricot beans, place fresh beans in cold water, bring to a boil, remove from the heat, and allow to stand for an hour. Drain and serve as a hot vegetable or in vinaigrette as a salad.

String Bean, Roquefort, and Walnut Salad
Serves 4

1³/₄ cups string beans, topped and tailed
2 cups Roquefort cheese
1 cup walnuts
1 small radicchio
2 little gem lettuces
3 tablespoons extra-virgin olive oil
1 tablespoon balsamic vinegar
1 clove garlic, crushed
Salt and freshly ground black pepper

Wash the beans and steam them over a pan of boiling water until just crunchy. Keep warm. Crumble the Roquefort and lightly crush the walnuts. Wash the lettuces. Make a dressing with the remaining ingredients.

Arrange the lettuces in a large bowl, top with the beans, walnuts, and cheese, and pour over the dressing. Toss and serve while the beans are still warm.

Red Chili Beef
Serves 4

3 or 4 ancho chilies
1–2 small red chilies, dried
1 tablespoon ground cumin
3 tablespoons vegetable oil
2 onions, finely sliced
3 cloves garlic, finely crushed
1¹/₂ lb. ground beef
2 cups cooked red kidney beans
2 tablespoons tomato puree
Salt and freshly ground black pepper
³/₄ cup good beef stock

Infuse the ancho chilies in hot water to soften them. Remove the stems and push the flesh through a fine sieve. Set aside. Then finely chop and seed the dried chilies.

Put the cumin into a heavy frying pan over a medium heat and toast until the fragrance comes out, taking care not to burn it. Set aside.

Heat the oil in a large, heavy saucepan and cook the onions and garlic until just colored. Add the meat and brown well. Add both sorts of chili, the kidney beans, tomato puree, and salt and pepper. Mix well.

Pour in the stock and cook for 40 minutes, covered, adding a little extra liquid if necessary. Serve hot with plainly cooked rice.

Pisum sativum. Papilionaceae

PEA

Also known as Garden Pea, English Pea. Climbing or scrambling annual grown for seeds, pods and shoot tips. Half hardy. Value: good source of protein, carbohydrates, fiber, iron, and vitamin C.

'Early Onward,' a robust, prolific variety

Like many legumes, peas are an ancient food crop. The earliest records are of smooth-skinned types found in Mediterranean and European excavations dating from 7000 B.C. The Greeks and Romans cultivated and ate peas in abundance, and it was the Romans who were said to have introduced them to Britain. In classical Greece they were known as *pison*, which was translated in English to "peason"; by the reign of Charles I they became "pease," and this was shortened to "pea" in the eighteenth century. During the reign of Elizabeth I, types seen as "fit dainties for ladies, they come so far, and cost so dear" were imported from Holland.

In England, "pease pudding," made from dried peas, butter, and eggs, was traditionally eaten with pork and boiled bacon. It was obviously quite versatile, as evidenced in the nursery rhyme that begins "Pease pudding hot, pease pudding cold, pease pudding in the pot nine days old." Peas were eaten dried or ground until the sixteenth century, when Italian gardeners developed tender varieties for cooking and eating when fresh. It wasn't until the following century that this practice was accepted by the wealthy and fashionable.

Peas were the favorite vegetable of Thomas Jefferson, who held an annual competition among his friends to grow the first peas of the season. The winner had the privilege of inviting others in the group to dinner to celebrate their arrival. The invitations that were issued read, "Come tonight, the peas are ready!"

some descriptions refer to the pea itself, or to the pod.

Earlier varieties are lower-growing than later types, which are taller and higher-yielding. Smooth-seeded types are hardy and are used for early and late crops. Wrinkle-seeded varieties are less hardy and generally sweeter. "Petit pois" are small and well flavored. "Semi-leafless" peas have more tendrils than leaves, becoming intertwined and self-supporting as they grow.

"Sugar peas," "snap peas," or "mangetout"—varieties of *Pisum sativum* var. *macrocarpon*—are grown for their edible immature pods; of these, the "Sugar Snap" type are particularly succulent and sweet. Some varieties can be allowed to mature and the peas eaten.

Early Peas
'Early Onward' is a heavy cropper, with large blunt pods and wrinkled seeds. 'Feltham First' is an excellent early round-seeded variety with large, well-filled pods. 'Prince Albert' is early and vigorous, producing bumper crops.

Main-crop peas
'Alderman' is an heirloom that will easily climb an 8-ft. trellis. 'Green Arrow' is disease resistant, producing gigantic pods that contain up to 11 tender peas each. 'Hurst Green Shaft' is sweet-tasting and heavy-cropping, maturing over a long period.

VARIETIES

Peas are usually listed according to the timing of the crop—early, second early (or early main crop), and main-crop types—but

A row of peas sitting snugly in the pod

'Feltham First,' an early type, can be grown up pea sticks or netting.

Wrinkle-seeded. Downy mildew– and fusarium-resistant. **'Knight'** is one of the earliest large-podded peas. The small plants are loaded with huge pods full of sweet, tender peas. The unique **'Novella'** plants are semi-leafless, which allows them to put more energy into pod production. Three-inch pods are born on 3-ft. plants that need no staking.

Sugar peas
Extra-sweet **'Sugar Lace'** peas grow on semi-leafless plants and need no trellising. **'Oregon Sugar Pod'** is sweet and tasty; harvest as the peas form. Fusarium-resistant. **'Sugar Snap'** produces succulent, sweet edible pods or can be grown on for peas. Very sweet. Fusarium-resistant.

CULTIVATION

Propagation
Germination is erratic and poor on cold soils; do not sow outdoors when soil temperatures are below 50°F.

Sow earlies or second earlies successionally every 14–28 days from midspring to midsummer. Avoid excessively hot times; these can affect germination.

According to the growing conditions, earlies mature

after about 12 weeks, second earlies (or early main crop) take 1–2 weeks longer, and main crops take another 1–2 weeks longer again. As an alternative option, sow groups of earlies, second earlies and main crops in mid- to late spring; the length of time taken for each type to reach maturity will give you a harvest over several weeks.

In midsummer, with at least 12 weeks before the first frosts are expected, sow an early cultivar for harvesting in fall, and where winters are mild, sow earlies in mid- to late fall for overwintering. Cloche protection may be necessary later in the season.

Peas can be sown in single V-shaped furrows 1–2 in. deep and 2 in. apart, double rows 9 in. apart or broad or flat drills 10 in. wide.

The distance between the rows or pairs of rows should equal the ultimate height of the plant.

Peas can also be sown in strips 3 rows wide with the seeds 4½ in. apart in and between the rows and with 18 in. between the strips.

They can also be sown in blocks 36–48 in. wide with seeds 2–3 in. apart.

Yields are higher when plants are supported. Use pea sticks made from brushwood or netting. Place supports down one side of a single row, on either side or down the center of wide drills and around the outside of blocks of plants. **Zones 3–7.**

Growing
Peas are a cool-season crop flourishing at 55–65°F, so crops will be higher in cooler summer temperatures. They do not tolerate drought, excessive temperatures, or waterlogged soil. Peas should be grown in an open, sheltered position on moisture-retentive, deep, free-draining soil with a pH of 5.5–7.0.

Incorporate plenty of organic matter in the fall or

winter prior to sowing or plant where the ground was manured for the previous year's crop.

Keep crops weed-free by hoeing, hand weeding, or mulching (which also keeps the roots cool and moist). Hill up overwintering and early crops to provide extra support.

Unless there are drought conditions, established plants do not need watering until the flowers appear, then, for a good harvest, they will need 4 gallons/sq. yd. each week until the harvest is complete.

Maintenance
Spring Sow early main crops.
Summer Sow main crops early in the season. Harvest, keep weed-free and water. Sow earlies for fall harvest.
Fall Sow early overwintering crops under cover. Prepare the ground for the following year.
Winter Sow early crops under cover.

Protected Cropping
Warm the soil before sowing treated seed in spring. Sow the seed of dwarf cultivars under cover in early spring, removing the covers when the plants need supporting.

Early spring and late fall

sowings can be made under cover, as flowers and pods cannot withstand frost.

Container Growing
Sow early dwarf varieties successionally through the season in large containers of loam-based potting mix with moderate fertilizer levels. Provide support and keep weed-free and well watered.

Harvesting and Storing
Harvest early types from late spring to early summer and main crops from midsummer to early fall. Pick regularly to ensure a high yield when the pods are swollen. Harvest those grown for their pods when the peas are just forming.

If peas are to be dried, leave them on the plant as long as possible, lifting just before the seeds are shed; hang in a cool airy place or spread the pods out on trays to dry until they split and the peas can be harvested. Store in airtight containers.

Freeze young peas of any variety. Shell and blanch for 1 minute. Allow to drain and cool, and freeze in plastic bags or containers. Use within 12 months.

Peas in a plastic bag in the refrigerator stay fresh for up to 3 days.

Evening light illuminating the foliage of young peas

Peas are one of the most popular frozen vegetables.

Pests and Diseases
Birds can be a problem: net crops.

Pea moths are common, their larvae eating the peas. Protect with crop covers at flower bud stage. Fall, early, and midsummer sowings often avoid problems; spray with pyrethrin-based insecticide 10 days after flowers open.

Pea thrips attack developing pods, making pods distorted and silvery; peas do not develop. Spray with rotenore or pyrethrum.

Mice may also be troublesome, eating seeds, particularly with over-wintered crops; trap them.

Powdery mildew, **downy mildew,** and **fusarium wilt** can be a problem: sow resistant varieties.

COMPANION PLANTING

Peas grow well with other legumes, root crops, potatoes, cucurbits, and corn.

MEDICINAL

Peas are said to reduce fertility, prevent appendicitis, lower blood cholesterol, and control blood sugar levels.

CULINARY

Garden peas are eaten fresh or dried. When small and tender, they can be eaten raw in salads.

Peas are traditionally boiled or steamed with a sprig of mint. Eat with butter, salt and pepper, or herbs. Serve in a cream sauce with pearl onions, with celery, orange, carrots, wine, or lemon sauce.

Snap peas should be boiled for 3 minutes (or steamed), tossed in butter and served.

Young shoot tips can be cooked and eaten.

Pea and Pear Soup
Serves 4

An unusual combination and very refreshing in summertime when there is a glut of peas.

2¹/₂ cups peas, shelled
6–7 pears, very ripe, unpeeled
3¹/₂ cups chicken stock
Pinch cayenne pepper
2 tablespoons finely chopped fresh mint
Salt and freshly ground black pepper

Cook the peas in lightly salted water for 5 minutes or so. Drain. Quarter and core the pears. Puree them in a blender with the peas, the stock, and the cayenne. Pour into a saucepan and stir in the mint and seasoning. Heat through and serve.

Pasta and Snap Pea Salad

Pasta and Snap Pea Salad
Serves 4

Snap peas or sugar peas from the garden are completely different from the tired beasts bought in the store. The quicker they are cooked, the better they taste.

4 cups pasta—penne or fusilli
4 tablespoons olive oil
3 cups snap peas, topped and tailed
1 small onion, finely sliced
2 cloves garlic, crushed
1¹/₄ cups tuna, drained and flaked
2 tablespoons heavy cream
2 tablespoons Italian parsley
Salt and freshly ground black pepper

Cook the pasta in boiling salted water for 10 minutes, or until al dente, and drain. Drizzle over 1 tablespoon of the oil and toss well. Allow to cool.

Meanwhile, cook the snap peas in a steamer for 2–3 minutes; they should remain crunchy. In a separate pan, heat the oil and sauté the onion for a couple of minutes, then add the garlic and continue cooking for 1 minute. Remove from the heat and allow to cool.

Put the pasta into a large serving bowl and mix in all the ingredients. Taste for seasoning and serve.

Pea and Pear Soup

Portulaca oleracea subsp. *sativa. Portulacaceae*

PURSLANE

Also known as Summer Purslane. Annual grown for succulent shoot tips, stems, and leaves. Half hardy. Value: rich in beta carotene, folic acid, vitamin C; contains useful amounts of essential fatty acids.

Purslane has been grown for centuries in China, India, and Egypt, and is now widespread in the warm, temperate, and tropical regions of the world. It was once believed to protect against evil spirits and "blastings by lightning or planets and burning of gunpowder." Its name in Malawi translates as "buttocks of the wife of a chief," referring to the plant's succulent, rounded leaves and juicy stems! The cultivated form has an erect habit and larger leaves than the wild species.

VARIETIES

Portulaca oleracea **var.** *sativa* is a vigorous, upright annual growing to 18 in. tall with thick, succulent stems, spoon-shaped leaves and bright yellow flowers.

P. o. **var.** *aurea* is a yellow-leaved, less hardy form. It is more succulent, but has less flavor. Attractive in salads and as an ornamental.

CULTIVATION

Propagation
Sow in seed trays indoors in late spring and transplant seedlings into packs when large enough to handle. Harden off and plant when there is no danger of frost, 6 in. apart. In frost-free zones or for later crops, sow directly, thinning to 6 in. apart. Sow in late spring for a summer crop and in late summer for fall cropping. **Zones 3–11.**

Mature purslane plant in flower

Growing
Easily cultivated, purslane thrives in a sunny, warm, sheltered site on light, well-drained soil. Add organic matter and sand to improve drainage if needed. Remove flowers as they appear.

Maintenance
Spring Sow protected crops, or in situ once the danger of frost is passed.
Summer Keep plants weed-free and water as necessary. Harvest regularly.
Fall Cut back mature plants to allow regrowth.
Winter In late winter sow early crops under glass.

Protected Cropping
To extend the season, sow in early to midspring and early to midfall under cover. Make earlier and late summer sowings under cover as a cut-and-come-again crop.

Container Growing
Plant seedlings or sow seed in pots or containers when there is no danger of frost, using a soil-based potting mix with a low fertilizer content. Water regularly.

Harvesting
Pick young shoot tips, stems and leaves when about 1½–2 in. long. Cut-and-come-again crops are ready to harvest after about 5 weeks. Regular picking encourages young growth. As older plants deteriorate toward the end of the growing season, cut them back to within 2 in. of the ground and water well, and they should resprout.

Pests and Diseases
Purslane is prone to **slug** damage, particularly when young. **Damping off** can be a problem if sown at low temperatures or in cold soil.

Medicinal
A traditional remedy for dry coughs, swollen gums, and, infused in water, for blood disorders. Research indicates that its high levels of fatty acids can prevent heart attacks and stimulate the body's immune system.

CULINARY

Wash thoroughly; growing close to the ground, leaves can be gritty. It can be lightly cooked, although the taste is not memorable. Older leaves can be pickled.

Purslane Salad
Serves 4

Use young buds and stems as well as the leaves.

4 ripe nectarines or peaches
Hazelnut oil
Handful of purslane
15 hazelnuts, toasted
½ teaspoon of coriander seeds, freshly crushed

Slice the nectarines or peaches and arrange on a plate brushed with hazelnut oil. Add the purslane leaves. Trickle over a little more oil, sprinkle with the chopped nuts, and season with crushed coriander.

WARNING

Expectant mothers and those with digestive disorders should not eat purslane in large quantities.

Raphanus sativus. Brassicaceae

RADISH

Annual or biennial grown for edible swollen roots, seed pods, and leaves. Hardy. Value: low in calories, moderate vitamin C, small amounts of iron and protein.

Thought to be native to Asia, yet domesticated in the Mediterranean, this reliable little salad vegetable has been in cultivation for centuries. Depicted in the pyramid of Cheops, it was cultivated by the Egyptians in 2780 B.C. and Herodotus noted that laborers working on the pyramids received "radishes, onions, and garlic" as their rations. By 500 B.C. it was grown in China, reaching Japan 200 years later. Pliny records that "models of turnips, beets, and radishes were dedicated to Apollo in the temple at Delphi, turnips made of lead, beets of silver, and radishes of gold," while Horace wrote of "lettuces and radishes such as excite the languid stomach." John Evelyn, too, wrote: "Radishes are eaten alone with salt only, as conveying their pepper in them." The fiery flavor is due to the presence of mustard oil. Although radishes are usually red, there are also black, purple, yellow, and green-skinned types.

VARIETIES

The fast-growing salad types are ready to harvest in about 4 weeks. Larger, slow-growing types, often with long cylindrical roots, include large overwintering varieties and the Asian varieties known as "mooli" or "daikon."

Salad and overwintering radishes
'**Cherry Belle**' is round, with crisp, white, mild flesh. Tolerant of poorer soils, it is slow to go woody and keeps well. Harvest 3 weeks after sowing. The uniform roots of '**Cherriette**' are smooth and sweet with just enough bite. '**China Rose**' is a well-flavored winter variety with bright red roots and white flesh. '**D'Avignon**' is rose-colored with a white tip, crunchy and extremely hot. '**18 Day**' is a fast-growing French Breakfast type, crisp and mild. '**French Breakfast 3**' is long, mild, sweet, and tender. Harvest at maturity or it becomes hot and woody. '**Scarlet Globe**' is justifiably popular for its mild flavor and good quality. Can be sown early under cover. '**Long Black Spanish**,' a winter variety, has wonderful dark skin and is extremely hot. '**Munchen Bier**' is grown for its tasty

'**Round Black Spanish**'

green pods, which are eaten raw or stir-fried. '**Round Black Spanish**' is similar to '**Long Black Spanish,**' but globe-shaped.

Mooli or daikon
"**Mooli**" and "**daikon**" are general terms for a group of long, white radishes (*Raphanus sativus* var. *longipinnatus*) that need cool temperatures and short day lengths to flourish.
'**April Cross**' is crisp, juicy, and mild. '**Long White Icicle**' is tender with a pungent, almost nutty taste. The skin of '**Mantanghong**' is white and green, but the inner flesh is a bright magenta. '**Mino Early**' is a large Japanese variety. '**Summer Cross Hybrid**' is fast-growing and ready to harvest when 6 in. long.

CULTIVATION

Propagation
Radishes are one of the easiest and quickest vegetables to grow. Sow successively every 2 weeks from when the soil becomes workable in early to midspring to early fall. Sow thinly in drills $1/2$ in. deep and 6 in. apart, thinning to 1 in. apart about 10 days after they appear. Alternatively, broadcast seed and thin to 1 in. apart. Radishes dislike being overcrowded.

In mild-winter zones, sow overwintering radishes in summer, ¾ in. deep in furrows 9–12 in. apart; depending on the cultivar, thin to 6–9 in. Sow mooli/daikon from mid- to late summer.

Small radishes can be grown as cut-and-come-again seedlings. Harvest when 2–3 in. tall; if you allow them to grow to 8–9 in., the leaves can be cooked like spinach. **Zones 3–9.**

Growing

As radishes are a cool-weather crop, grow earlier and later crops in an open site, but plant summer crops in light shade, surrounded by taller plants. They flourish in a light, moisture-retentive, free-draining soil which was manured for the previous crop, with a pH of 6.5–7.5. Dig the ground thoroughly before preparing the seedbed and remove any stones, particularly when growing longer-rooted varieties.

Rake a slow-release granular fertilizer into the seedbed at 1 oz./sq. yd. before sowing the first crops and before planting winter varieties.

Rapid growth is essential for tasty, tender roots, so supply plenty of water and do not let the seedbed dry out. Overwatering encourages the production of leaves rather than roots and erratic watering causes roots to become woody or split. During drought, water weekly at 2 gallons/sq. yd. Hoe and hand weed regularly.

Maintenance

Spring Sow crops outdoors when soil conditions allow.
Summer Sow successionally; keep crops well watered and weed-free. Sow winter crops.
Fall Grow later crops under cover.
Winter Harvest over-wintering crops. Sow early crops under cover.

Protected Cropping

Grow early and late crops of summer varieties under cloches to extend the cropping season. Ventilate and water thoroughly.

Grow summer crops under floating cloches to protect them.

Radishes' pretty exterior belies their fiery taste.

Container Growing

Radishes are easily grown in containers. These should be 6–12 in. wide by 8 in. deep. Use a loam-based potting mix or free-draining, moisture-retentive garden soil. Water well and liquid feed with general fertilizer if necessary. They can also be sown in growing bags, thinning until they are 1–2 in. apart.

Harvesting and Storing

Pull immediately after they mature, in 8 to 10 weeks, otherwise they will become woody or run to seed.

Later crops can be stored. Twist off leaves and store in boxes of dry sand or sawdust in a frost-free place. Overwintering types can be left in the ground and lifted as needed. Protect with straw or hay. For ease of lifting, these can be allowed to grow over 15 in. long without being coarse.

Kept in a plastic bag in the refrigerator, radishes stay fresh for about a week.

Pests and Diseases
Flea beetle, cabbage fly, and **slugs** can be a problem.

COMPANION PLANTING

Radishes grow well with chervil, peas, and lettuce, and thrive with nasturtium and mustard.

Because of their rapid growth, radishes make an excellent "indicator crop." Sown in the same row as slow-germinating crops like parsnips or parsley, they mark where the main crop has been sown, make weeding easier, and can be harvested without disturbing the developing plants.

MEDICINAL

Radishes can be eaten to relieve indigestion and flatulence, and can be taken as a tonic herb and an expectorant.

'Long Black Spanish'

'Cherry Belle,' picked and packed

Radish and Scallop Soup

CULINARY

Radishes are usually eaten raw, whole, shredded, or sliced into salads. Alternatively, wash and trim the root, remove the leaves and all but the bottom 1 in. of stalk to use as a "handle," and enjoy it with rough bread, creamy butter, salt, cheese, and a pint of good ale! (In Germany, you'll find them on the bar instead of peanuts.) They can also be sliced and used instead of onions in hamburgers.

Seedling leaves are eaten raw and older leaves are cooked like spinach.

Long white summer radishes and winter radishes can be eaten raw but are usually cooked and added to casseroles, stews, or curries.

Winter varieties are also pickled. Peel, then cube or slice in slightly salted water for about 10 minutes. Drain thoroughly and serve tossed in butter.

Thin slices of winter varieties or larger summer types can be stir-fried.

For extra crispness, put them into a bowl of water with a few ice cubes for a couple of hours.

Slice radishes and tangerines, mandarins, or oranges into small pieces, sprinkle lightly with salt, chopped fennel leaves, and lemon juice. This interesting recipe is an acquired taste!

To make a "radish rose," remove the stalk and make a number of vertical cuts from the stalk almost to the root. Place in iced water for 30 minutes; the petals open.

Immature green seed pods can be eaten raw, cooked, or pickled. Pick when crisp and green. Scrape or peel and top and tail mooli or daikon before use. In India they are eaten cooked or raw. In Japan shredded mooli is a traditional accompaniment to sashimi (raw fish) and is eaten with sushi.

As with summer radishes, a thin slice makes an excellent mustard substitute with a roast beef sandwich.

Radish and Scallop Soup
Serves 4

2 bunches radishes, topped and tailed
10 scallops, trimmed
2 scallions, chopped
2 tablespoons butter
2 cups fish stock and milk combined
2 bay leaves
Pinch cayenne pepper
1 tablespoon parsley
4 tablespoons heavy cream

First wash the radishes thoroughly and cut them into small dice. Then cut the scallops in half and set to one side.

In a soup pot, cook the scallions in the butter until soft, and then add the scallops. Cook them for 30 seconds on each side over a gentle heat and then add the radishes.

Add the stock and milk mixture. Add the bay leaves, cayenne, and parsley and cook for 15 minutes over a gentle heat, just simmering.

Remove the soup from the heat. Take the scallops out of the soup with a slotted spoon; cut them into slivers and return them to the pan. Last, stir in the parsley and the cream and serve immediately.

Rheum x cultorum. Polygonaceae

RHUBARB

Pieplant. Large perennial herb grown for pink edible stems. Half hardy. Value: very low in calories, contains small amounts of vitamins.

The earliest records of rhubarb date from China in 2700 B.C., and there are references to its cultivation in Europe in the early 1700s. It was originally grown for its medicinal use as a powerful purgative; the annual value of imports to England for this purpose was once estimated to be £200,000. It was first mentioned as a food plant in 1778 by the French, for making tarts and pies. Rhubarb was introduced to Maine from Europe around 1790; from there it spread to market gardeners in New England and Massachusetts. Forcing and blanching were discovered by chance at the Chelsea Physic Garden in 1817 after crowns were covered in debris when a ditch was cleared!

VARIETIES

A greater range of cultivars is to be found in specialist nurseries. **'Crimson Red'** has a distinctive sweet yet sharp flavor. **'Early Champagne'** (**'Early Red'**) produces long, delicious scarlet stalks that are excellent for wine making and early forcing. **'Glaskin's Perpetual'** is vigorous and tasty, and crops over a long period. '**MacDonald**' plants are very prolific, producing very vigorous and tender light red stalks. The stalks of '**Tilden**' are thick and deep red. **'Timperley Early'** is very early, vigorous, and suitable for forcing. **'Valentine'** is hardy and vigorous with tender, rose-colored stalks. Perfect for pies and jams, it has a wonderful flavor. **'Victoria,'** a reliable old variety, is variable in size. Harvest from late spring.

Rhubarb forced using traditional terra-cotta jars

CULTIVATION

Propagation
Rhubarb can be grown from seed, but the results are invariably poor. It is better to lift and divide mature crowns of known varieties or buy virus-free plants from a reputable nursery.

Plants should be divided every 2 or 3 years; if plants are any older, take divisions from the outer margins. Lift dormant crowns in winter after the leaves have died back and divide with a spade or knife. Each "set" should be about 4 in. across with plenty of fibrous roots and at least one bud.

Plants tend to establish more rapidly if transplanted into 10-in. pots of multi-purpose potting mix for 3 months prior to planting out. Transplant, 2½–3 ft. apart, from late fall (the best time) to early spring, with the bud tip covered by 1 in. of soil. Plant cultivars that have large buds with the buds slightly above ground to prevent rotting. Plants remain productive for several seasons; their decline is marked by the production of masses of thin stalks.

Alternatively, sow in drills about 1 in. deep and 12 in. apart, thinning to 6 in. Plant out the strongest in fall or the following spring.
Zones 3–7.

Growing
Rhubarb flourishes in an open, sunny position in deep, fertile, well-drained soil with a pH of 5.0–6.0. It is ideal for cool temperate zones. It is very hungry, with deep roots, so ensure that the soil contains well-rotted manure or compost. On very heavy soils, plant on ridges or raised beds.

Mulch plants every winter with a good, thick layer of well-rotted compost or manure. Do not allow them to flower unless you wish to save the seed, as this affects cropping the following year. Keep weed-free and watered, removing dead leaves instantly. In early spring, scatter a balanced general fertilizer around the crowns.

Maintenance
Spring Force early crops under a bucket or similar.
Summer Harvest stems.
Fall When stems die back remove all plant debris.
Winter Mulch with well-rotted compost or manure.

'Timperley Early,' a popular variety for gardeners

Protected Cropping

For early crops lift a few crowns in late fall, leave them above ground and let them be frosted, then bring indoors into a cool place for forcing. Put in a large container packed with soil or plant under greenhouse benches. Exclude light with an upside-down box or bucket 15–18 in. high to allow for stem growth. They can also be forced in garbage bags. Keep potting mix moist. Dispose of exhausted forced crowns after harvest.

Alternatively, from late winter, cover in situ with a 6-in. layer of straw or with an overturned bucket, trash can, or blanching pot covered with straw or strawy manure. Harvest in early to midspring. Do not harvest from a crown for at least 2 years after forcing.

Harvesting and Storing

Do not harvest until 12–18 months after planting, taking only a few "sticks" in the second season and more in later years. Cropping can last from early spring to mid-summer. To harvest, hold the stems near the base and twist off. Avoid breaking the stems, as it can cause fungal problems. Do not overpick; it can weaken the plant.

To freeze, chop the stems into sections and place on an open tray, freeze for 1 hour before packing into plastic bags. This prevents the sections from sticking together. They can be stored for up to a year.

PESTS AND DISEASES

Honey fungus may appear as white streaks in dead crown tissue; brown toadstools appear around the base. Dig out and burn diseased roots.

Crown rot damages terminal buds and makes stems spindly. Dig out and burn badly infected plants. Do not replant in the area.

Virus disease has no cure. Dig up and burn.

COMPANION PLANTING

Rhubarb is reported to control red spider mite. A traditional remedy suggests putting rhubarb in planting holes to control clubroot. An infusion of leaves is effective as an aphicide and to check blackspot on roses.

CULINARY

Forced rhubarb is tender and needs less sugar. Cook stems slowly with sugar. Very little or no water is required; do not overcook them. Avoid using aluminum pans.

Rhubarb can be stewed for fruit pies, bottling or preserving, fools, mousses, and rhubarb crumble, which is delicious. The flavor can be improved by adding orange juice, marmalade, or cinnamon. It can also be pureed with apple. Claudia Roden's *Middle Eastern Food* demonstrates that it is unexpectedly wonderful stewed with beef or lamb in Persian *khoresh*.

Preserved Rhubarb

18 cups rhubarb
14 cups preserving sugar
Juice and shredded peel of 2 lemons
1/2 cup blanched almonds

Cut the rhubarb into 1 in. lengths and cook gently in a preserving pan until the juices start to run. Add the sugar, lemon juice and peel, and the almonds. Stir until the sugar dissolves, then boil until a good color and thickened. Put into sterilized jars and seal.

Rhubarb Sorbet
Serves 4

2 cups rhubarb
1/2 cup superfine sugar
Juice of half a lemon

Cut the rhubarb into 1 in. lengths and put into a heavy-bottomed pan. Add 1/4 cup water. Warm gently until the juices run, then stir in the sugar and lemon juice and simmer, covered, until tender. Freeze, whisking several times as it freezes to break up the ice crystals. If you use an ice cream maker, churn until smooth. Remove from the freezer and place in the refrigerator 15 minutes before serving.

Rhubarb Sorbet

MEDICINAL

Rhubarb is an astringent, stomachic, and potent laxative. Dioscorides recommended it for chest, stomach, and liver complaints, and ringworm. By the 16th century, in Western Europe, it was taken as an infusion with parsley as a cure for venereal disease.

WARNING

Do not eat the leaves, which are extremely poisonous!

Nasturtium officinale. Cruciferae

WATERCRESS

Also known as Summer Watercress. Usually aquatic perennial grown for pungent, edible leaves and stems. Hardy. Value: excellent source of beta carotene, vitamins C and E, calcium, iron, and iodine.

This highly nutritious aquatic herb, a native of Europe, North Africa, and Asia, has been cultivated as a salad plant since Roman times and is grown throughout the world's temperate zones. It has become a weed in North America and New Zealand. Pliny records the Latin derivation of its original generic name as *Nasus tortus*, meaning "writhing nose"—referring to its spicy taste and pungent odor; *officinale* is often applied to plants with medicinal uses. Watercress was listed as an aphrodisiac in Dioscorides's *Materia Medica* of A.D. 77.

It was mentioned in early Irish poetry around the twelfth century—"Well of Traigh Dha Bhan, Lovely is your pure-topped cress" and "Watercress, little green-topped one, on the brink of the blackbirds' well . . ." Early references to the shamrock are believed to mean watercress. Evidence to support this comes from Ireland's County Meath and Shamrock Well, whose watercress was still remembered in the 1940s as "the finest in the district." Watercress was also known in Ireland as "St Patrick's Cabbage." The first records of commercial cultivation are from Germany around 1750, France between 1800 and 1811, and near Gravesend in England, around 1808.

Growing

Plants grown in the garden need a bright, sheltered position away from direct sunshine; never allow it to dry out, or plants run to seed. As a cool-season crop, watercress grows most actively in spring and fall, and during the winter in warmer zones.

Occasional feeding with a dilute high-nitrogen liquid fertilizer or liquid seaweed may be needed. Do not grow in stagnant or still water.

Maintenance

Spring Take cuttings or sow seed mid- to late spring. *Summer* Do not let potting-mix-grown plants dry out. Keep weed-free. Harvest as needed. Remove flower heads as they appear. *Fall* Continue to harvest. *Winter* Protect with cloches for continuous growth.

Protected Cropping

Cover plants with cloches, frost fabric, or crop covers before the first frosts. Make a watercress bed in an unheated greenhouse over winter, or grow in pots.

Container Growing

Grow in large pots or containers of moist peat-lite

CULTIVATION

Found in and alongside fast-flowing rivers and streams, watercress has fleshy, glossy leaves on long stalks with 5 to 10 leaflets. Its long stems creep or float on the surface and root easily. Small whitish-green flowers appear in flat-topped clusters from midspring to early fall.

The best watercress is grown in pure, fast-flowing chalk or limestone streams with slightly alkaline water. This avoids the risk of contamination from pollution, which can cause upset stomach. **Zones 3–8.**

Propagation

The easiest way to propagate watercress is from shop-bought material. Cuttings 4 in. long take only about a week to root when placed in a glass of water.

If you live by a fast-flowing stream, plant rooted cuttings 6 in. apart in the banks. Firm well to prevent them from being dislodged.

To grow watercress in the garden, dig a trench 2 ft. wide and 12 in. deep and put a 6-in. layer of well-rotted farmyard manure or compost into the base. (Do not use sheep manure as it can carry dangerous liver fluke.) Mix in a little ground limestone if your soil is not alkaline, then cover with 3–4 in. of soil. Plant cuttings 6 in. apart in midspring.

Alternatively, in spring, mark out an area and dig in well-rotted organic matter and ground limestone, firm and soak with water before scattering seed thinly on the surface. Water daily.

Seeds can also be sown indoors from mid- to late spring, in a propagator or trays of peat-lite seed mix on a windowsill. Cover the seeds with $1/8$ in. of potting mix and keep it constantly moist at around 50–60°F.

Transplant 3–4 seedlings into a 3-in. pot when large enough to handle, then plant out 4–6 in. apart from midspring onward. When plants deteriorate, replace them with fresh cuttings.

Wild watercress by a fast-flowing stream, Guernsey

mix, with a layer of gravel in the base, spacing 4–6 in. apart. Keep potting mix moist by standing the pot in a bowl of water that is replaced daily. Grow plants on a bright windowsill, but away from direct sunshine.

Harvesting and Storing

Younger leaves near the stem tips have the best flavor. Harvest lightly during the first season and annually toward the fall if plants are to be overwintered in a mild-winter zone, cutting regularly for a constant supply of bushy shoots.

Use leaves fresh or store in the crisper in the refrigerator for 2–3 days.

PESTS AND DISEASES

Watercress is rarely troubled, but **caterpillars** of cabbage white butterfly may cause problems.

MEDICINAL

Watercress has been valued for its medicinal qualities since antiquity. It has been eaten to cure rheumatism, and used as a diuretic and as an expectorant for catarrh, colds, and bronchitis; it is a stimulant, a digestive, and a tonic to promote appetite, counteract anemia, and also to lower blood-sugar levels in diabetics.

Externally it is a hair tonic. Rubbed on the skin it is said to remove rashes. Culpeper recommended the bruised leaves or juice for clearing spots and freckles and a poultice was said to heal glandular tumors and lymphatic swellings.

Traditionally it was taken as a spring tonic. In the past, in isolated parts of the British Isles where the diet was predominantly shellfish and salt meat, it was often grown to prevent scurvy, and was so mentioned by Philip Miller in his *Gardener's Dictionary* of 1731.

Unless harvested regularly, watercress develops small white flowers. Once flowered, the leaves are less tender.

CULINARY

As with its relative the radish, the hot, spicy taste of watercress comes from mustard oil. Remove discolored leaves and wash thoroughly, shaking off excess water. Eat in salads and stir-fries, or puree to make chilled soup. It makes a perfect garnish for sandwiches. Chop finely and add to butter, mashed potatoes, dumplings, or a white sauce. Or sauté in butter for 10 minutes and serve as a vegetable.

Among her many tastebud-tingling recipes, Jane Grigson suggests cutting orange segments into quarters and mixing with watercress, olive oil vinaigrette, and black pepper; add walnuts or black olives and eat as a salad with ham, duck, or veal.

Salmon with Watercress Sauce
Serves 6

6 salmon fillets, trimmed
4 tablespoons butter
4 tablespoons finely chopped shallots
2 large bunches watercress, plus sprigs to garnish
1/2 cup heavy cream
Salt and freshly ground black pepper

WARNING

Do not gather from streams if sheep are grazing nearby, as there is a risk of liver fluke. Fluke can be destroyed by thorough cooking.

Steam the salmon fillets, until cooked; this should take 10 minutes or so.

Meanwhile, prepare the sauce by melting the butter in a heavy frying pan and sautéing the shallots until softened. Add the watercress and, constantly stirring, allow the watercress to wilt for about 2 minutes; it should retain its bright green color. Stir in the cream and seasoning and bring to a boil. Remove from the heat and blend in a food processor until smooth. Then reheat gently.

Arrange the salmon fillets in the center of individual plates and spoon sauce over each, garnishing with a little fresh watercress.

Crithmum maritimum. Apiaceae

SAMPHIRE

Also known as Rock Samphire, Sea Fennel, Sea Samphire. Low-growing maritime perennial. Half hardy. Value: good source of iron and vitamin C; moderate iodine.

Rock samphire is found on the shores and cliffs of Europe. Its name comes from "sampiere," a contraction of the French *herbe de St. Pierre*—the fisherman saint's herb. Collected from the wild for centuries, by the English Tudor period it was widely cultivated in gardens. William Turner wrote: "Creta marina groweth much in rockes and cliffes beside Dover." This precarious habitat is mentioned in *King Lear*, where harvesters dangle over the cliffs from a rope. Robert Turner in 1664 described similar dangerous activities on the 600-foot cliffs of the Isle of Wight: "yet many adventure it though they buy their sauce with the price of their lives." Samphire harvests were sent in casks of seawater to London, where wholesalers paid four shillings a bushel—but for the privilege of collecting it, the lord of the manor exacted an annual rent.

VARIETIES

Crithmum maritimum has a woody base, with stems to 2 ft. and lobed gray-green leaflets. The white-cream flowers, in flat clusters, are followed by small oval fruits. The leaves have an aromatic odor which has been likened to the smell of furniture polish!

CULTIVATION

Propagation
Plants are propagated from fresh seed sown in the fall or spring in a sheltered position. Transplant when large enough to handle, or divide plants in spring. **Zones 6–9.**

Growing
Its natural habitat is in sand; if you create a satisfactory habitat in a coastal garden, natural colonies may form. Plants often inhabit dry stone walls. They flourish in well-drained, sandy or gritty soil,

Samphire flourishes in sea spray

which is constantly moist and protected from full heat. An open east- or south-facing position is ideal. Mulch with seaweed or burn seaweed and scatter with the sodium-rich debris. If possible, water with seawater or sea salt solution.

Maintenance
Spring Sow seed in gritty potting mix or in shallow drills.
Summer Keep soil moist with a saline solution. Harvest.
Fall Harvest. Protect crops during colder weather.
Winter Mulch with straw or leaves.

Protected Cropping
As a succulent plant, rock samphire needs frost protection. Cover with leaves, straw, or cloches.

Container Growing
Grow in containers of gritty, loam-based potting mix.

Water regularly in summer; in cooler zones, bring plants indoors during the winter.

Harvesting and Storing
Harvest young shoots and leaves by cutting or pulling. Young spring growth is the most tender. Do not harvest excessively from each plant. Best eaten immediately after harvesting, but will last for up to 2 days in the refrigerator.

Pests and Diseases
Usually trouble-free.

CULINARY

Wash thoroughly in running water before use.
  Tender young shoots and leaves can be eaten fresh or cooked as a vegetable. They are added raw to salads or dressed with oil and lemon juice as an hors d'oeuvre.
  Pickle young shoots, leaves, and stems by filling a jar with samphire cut into 1-in. lengths, add peppercorns, a little shredded horseradish, and a boiling mixture of equal parts dry cider and vinegar, and infuse for an hour before sealing. Pickled, it is used as a garnish and as a caper substitute.
  In Italy it is known as "Roscano."

MEDICINAL

John Evelyn noted "its excellent vertues and effects against the Spleen. Cleansing the Passages and sharpning appetite." It was also recommended as a kidney, bladder, and general tonic and as a treatment for "stones." It is said to be a diuretic, to improve digestion and has been used to encourage weight loss.

Scorzonera hispanica. Asteraceae

SCORZONERA

Also known as False Salsify, Spanish Salsify.
Grown as biennial for shoots, flower buds, and flowers; as annual for cylindrical tapering roots. Hardy. Value: contains indigestible carbohydrate inulin, which, when converted to fructose in storage, increases calorific content (27 calories per 100 g); small amounts of vitamins and minerals.

Scorzonera is very similar to salsify, though scorzonera is perennial, not biennial; its skin is darker, the roots narrower, and the flavor is not as strong. The name scorzonera may have come from the French "*scorzon,*" or serpent, as the root was used in Spain to cure snake bites. Another interpretation suggests it comes from the Italian "*scorza,*" bark, and "*nera,*" black, describing the roots. Native to central and southern Europe through to Russia and Siberia, scorzonera was known by the Greeks and Romans, who took little interest in its cultivation; it arrived in England by 1560 and in North America by 1806. It is widely grown in Europe as an excellent winter vegetable. The leaves have been used as food for silkworms.

If allowed to grow, the bright yellow flowers make ideal ornamentals.

VARIETIES

'Duplex' produces long tasty roots. 'Flandria Scorzonera' has long roots, growing to 12 in., with strongly flavored flesh. 'Habil' is long-rooted with a delicious flavor. 'Lange Jan' ('Long John') has long, tapering, dark brown roots. 'Long Black' is similar, but with black roots. 'Russian Giant' lives up to its name with long roots and a subtle, delicate flavor.

CULTIVATION

Propagation
Sow fresh seed in situ from mid- to late spring, in drills ½–¾ in. deep with rows 6 in. apart. Alternatively, sow 2 or 3 seeds in hills 6 in. apart, thinning to leave the strongest seedling when large enough to handle. Or sow in late summer for use early the following fall. **Zones 5–10.**

Growing
It flourishes in a sunny position on a deep, light, well-drained soil that should have been manured for a previous crop. Do not grow on freshly manured or stony ground, as this causes "forking." A pH of 6.0–7.5 is ideal, so lime the soil if necessary. On heavy or stony soils, fill a narrow trench about 12 in. deep with finely sieved soil or free-draining potting mix so that the roots grow straight. Dig the soil deeply and rake in 2–3 oz./sq. yd. general balanced fertilizer 10 days before sowing.

Remove weeds around the plants by hand, as roots bleed easily when damaged by a hoe. Mulching once the roots have established helps to smother weeds, conserves moisture, and reduces the risk of bolting during dry weather. Water at a rate of 3–5 gallons/sq. yd. per week.

Roots can be left in the ground to produce "chards"

'Russian Giant,' one of the more commonly grown varieties

Scorzonera tends to be neglected by American gardeners, but is often found growing in Mediterranean countries

PESTS AND DISEASES

Scorzonera rarely suffers from problems but may develop "**white blister**," which looks like glistening paint splashes. Affected plants become distorted.

COMPANION PLANTING

Scorzonera repels carrot root fly and the flowers attract beneficial insects.

MEDICINAL

The name derived from the Spanish reflects its reputation as an antidote to snake venom—" . . . and especially to cure the bitings of vipers (of which there may be very many in Spaine and other hot countries)," wrote Gerard in his *Herball* of 1636. This has not been proven.

(edible shoots) the following spring. In the fall, cut off old leaves, leaving ½–1 in. above the soil. Hill up the roots to a depth of about 6 in. so the developing shoots are blanched during the winter. In late spring, scrape away the soil and harvest when the shoots are 5–6 in. long. They can also be blanched by covering to a similar depth with straw or leaves in early spring. Roots too small to harvest in the first year can be left to mature the following year.

Maintenance
Spring Sow thinly, from mid- to late spring. Thin when large enough to handle.
Summer Keep crops weed-free and water thoroughly as needed to keep soil moist.
Fall Leave roots in the ground and lift carefully with a fork as needed.
Winter Continue harvesting. Prepare the ground for the next crop in mild-winter regions.

Protected Cropping
Scorzonera is hardy, but protection with straw or cloches before the onset of severe weather makes lifting much easier.

Container Growing
In shallow or stony soils plants can be grown in deep containers of loam-based potting mix. Water regularly.

Harvesting and Storing
Plants need at least 4 months to reach maturity and are ready to harvest from midfall to midspring. In a good year the roots may grow to 16 in., but are more often about 8 in. long.

Roots can either be left in the ground until needed or lifted—with care, as they are easily damaged. Clean and store in boxes of sand or sawdust in a cool place. They last up to 1 week in the refrigerator.

Mature plants flower in spring or summer of the second year. The buds can be harvested with about 3 in. of stem.

If, while lifting, you see that your crop has many forked roots, the remaining plants can be kept for their young shoots and buds.

CULINARY

Roots can be baked, pureed, dipped in batter, sautéed and made into croquettes and fritters, deep-fried or served au gratin with cheese and bread crumbs.

Boiling allows you to appreciate the flavor fully. The roots discolor when cut, so drop into water with a dash of lemon juice, then boil for 25 minutes in salted water with a tablespoon of flour added. Peel after boiling as you would a hard-boiled egg. Toss with melted butter and chopped parsley. Young "chards" can be served raw in salads. The flower stalks are considered tastier than those of salsify.

Sautéed Scorzonera
Allow 1 cup per person of cleaned scorzonera; it should not be peeled. Chop roughly and cook in a heavy sauté pan in a little extra-virgin olive oil until al dente, turning to cook every side. Drain on paper towels and sprinkle with lemon juice mixed with 1 crushed garlic clove and 1 tablespoon finely chopped Italian parsley.

Sautéed Scorzonera

Sechium edule. Cucurbitaceae

CHAYOTE

Also known as Choko, Chow Chow, Christophine. Vigorous, scrambling, tuberous rooted perennial, grown for edible fruit and seed. Tender. Value: 90% water; low in calories; some vitamin C.

In good conditions, this climber spreads to fifty feet and produces huge tubers. It originated in central America; "chayote" comes from the Aztec *chayotl*, while in the West Indies it is called "christophine" after Columbus, who reputedly introduced it to the islands. The pear-shaped fruits contain a single nutty-flavored seed, much prized by cooks.

VARIETIES

'Ivory White' is a small, pale-skinned variety.

CULTIVATION

Chayote needs rich, fertile, well-drained soil. **Zones 8–11.**

Propagation
Propagate cultivars from soft tip cuttings in spring at 65°F. Alternatively, plant the whole fruit laid on its side, at a slight angle, with the narrow end protruding from the soil.

Growing
Grow on mounds 12–14 in. high and 3 x 3 ft. apart; cover a shovel full of well-rotted manure with 6 in. of soil. Lightly mulch.

Alternatively, grow on beds 9 ft. square; dig in organic matter, plant seeds in the corners, and grow vines toward the center. Or, plant in 3 ft. wide ridges. Train the stems into trees or over trellising, fences, or 6 in. mesh netting. Water regularly in dry weather; optimum growth is during the wet season. A day length of just over 12 hours is required for flowering.

In the humid tropics, it grows better in moderate temperatures at altitude.

Maintenance
Spring Sow seed or take cuttings.
Summer Feed and water.
Fall Harvest.
Winter Store fruit for next year's crop.

Protected Cropping
In cool temperate regions, grow under glass in bright light with moderate temperatures and humidity. In warmer areas, start off indoors and plant when the danger of frost has passed. Grow in the greenhouse border or in containers.

Container Growing
Propagate in spring from seed or cuttings. Repot into loam-based potting mix with a high fertilizer content, add well-rotted manure and grit for drainage. Water well, feed twice a month with general liquid fertilizer and, once established, with a high-potash fertilizer. Train onto a trellis.

Harvesting and Storing
In tropical climates, plants last for several years, fruiting from 3 to 4 months after sowing, all year round. Harvest by cutting the stalk above the fruit with a knife. Fruit reaches its maximum size 25–30 days after fruit set. It will keep up to 3 months in a cool place.

Pests and Diseases
Root knot nematode causes wilting; **powdery mildew** can appear on leaves and stems; and **red spider mite** affects plants grown under glass.

MEDICINAL

Chayote is good for stomach ulcers. It contains some trace elements.

CULINARY

This versatile vegetable can be made into soups, boiled, candied, pureed (spiced with chili powder) or added to stews, curries, and chutneys. Its seeds can be cooked in butter, the young leaves cooked like spinach, and the tuber eaten when young. Its flesh stays firm after cooking. It makes a good substitute for avocado in a salad and is ideal for those on a diet.

For a stuffing, try a well-flavored bolognese sauce; add boiled chayote flesh and stuff back into halved chayote shells. Sprinkle with cheddar and bake for 30 minutes in an oven preheated to 350°F.

Chayote in Red Wine
Serves 6

Jane Grigson gives a recipe for this pudding.

6 pear-sized chayotes, peeled and left whole
³/₄ cup sugar
1 cup water
¹/₂ cup red wine
2 in. cinnamon stick
4 cloves
Lemon juice
Whipped cream (sweetened with confectioners' sugar)

Use a pan that will hold the chayotes in a single layer. Put the sugar and water on to dissolve and simmer for 2 minutes. Carefully add the chayotes, then the wine and spices.

Cover and simmer until tender. Remove the chayotes to a bowl and arrange upright like pears. Reduce the liquid until syrupy and add a little lemon juice to bring out the flavor. Strain the juice over the chayotes and serve with whipped cream.

Chayote in Red Wine

Stachys affinis. Lamiaceae

CHINESE ARTICHOKE

Also known as Japanese Artichoke, Crosne. Dwarf herbaceous perennial grown as annual for edible tubers. Hardy. Value: very high in potassium.

From the same family as mint, lavender, and many other herbs, Chinese artichokes are not grown for their aromatic foliage but for the small, ridged tubers at the tips of creeping underground stems. A native of Japan and China, it has rough, oval leaves and white to pale pink flowers that appear in small spikes. It was introduced from Peking to France by a physician in the late nineteenth century. It has never been hugely popular, probably because a large area is needed for decent quantities, but it is worth trying, if only as a "novelty" crop.

CULTIVATION

Chinese artichokes flourish in an open, sunny site on light, fertile yet moisture-retentive soil. **Zones 5–10.**

Propagation
For early crops, sprout the tubers in shallow trays or pots of potting mix in a moderately warm room, then plant out when soil is warm. Increase your stock by planting tubers individually in small pots of soil-based potting mix with added organic matter, transplanting as required. Place in 8–9-in. pots for the rest of the growing season. Feed and water regularly.

Growing
In spring, plant the tubers vertically 1½–3 in. deep; on light soils up to 6 in. deep. Plant large tubers only, 12 in. apart each way or 8 in.

apart in rows 16 in. apart. When 1–2 ft. high, hill up around the stems to about 3 in. Keep weed-free at first; as the plants mature, the leaf canopy naturally suppresses weed growth. Feed with a liquid general fertilizer every 2 weeks and remove flowering spikes to concentrate energy into fattening the tubers. Trim back the foliage. Rampant growth makes Chinese artichokes an ideal low-maintenance crop for a spare corner of the garden.

Maintenance
Spring Plant tubers when the soil has warmed.
Summer Keep crops weed-free; water and feed.
Fall Harvest after the first frosts, or about 5 months.
Winter Protect crops with burlap or straw to enable harvesting to continue.

Harvesting and Storing
Harvest as required from midfall to early spring, after the foliage has died back or when plants have been in

A mass of tubers

the ground 5–7 months. Lift them just before use as they quickly shrivel. When forking through the ground during the final harvest, you should remove even the smallest tubers or they will rapidly become weeds.

PESTS AND DISEASES

Chinese artichokes are usually pest-free, but you should take precautions against **lettuce root aphid**, which can cause wilting.

CULINARY

The tubers have a delicate, nutty flavor. Only about 2 in. long, they are rather tricky to cook. Boiling is simplest, but they can also be fried, stir-fried, roasted, added to soup, or eaten raw in salads.

Creamed Chinese Artichokes
Serves 4

Jane Grigson, in her *Vegetable Book*, quotes this recipe from *La Cuisine de Madame Saint-Ange*.

2½ cups Chinese artichokes
1 tablespoon butter
½ teaspoon lemon juice
1 cup heavy cream
Salt and freshly ground white
   pepper
Pinch of nutmeg
Heavy cream, to serve

Boil the artichokes for about 5 minutes, drain, add the butter and lemon juice, and cook gently for 5–7 minutes. Bring the cream to a boil, then add it to the artichokes, stirring in well. Season. Cover and leave for 15 minutes over a moderate heat, until the cream has reduced by a quarter. Just before serving, stir in 3 spoonfuls of heavy cream and quickly remove from the heat.

Solanum melongena. Solanaceae

EGGPLANT

Also known as Aubergine, Brinjal, Garden Egg, Guinea Squash, Pea Aubergine. Short-lived perennial grown as annual for fruits. Tender. Value: small amounts of most vitamins and minerals; very low in calories, with 3% carbohydrate and 1% protein.

Aubergine flowers reveal the family likeness to the potato

This glossy-skinned fruit was known to sixteenth-century Spaniards as the "apple of love." In contrast, many botanists of the time called it *mala insana* or "mad apple," because of its alleged effects. The Chinese first cultivated eggplants in the fifth century B.C. and they have been grown in India for centuries, yet they were unknown to the Greeks and Romans. Moorish invaders introduced them to Spain and the Spaniards later took them to the New World. "Aubergine" is a corruption of the Arabic name *al-badingan*.

VARIETIES

Fruits vary in shape from large, purple-skinned types to small, rounded white fruits 2 in. in diameter. Most modern F$_1$ hybrids are bushy and grow about 3 ft. tall. Unlike older varieties, they are almost spineless. **'Bambino'** is a small variety, grown as a "mini vegetable." **'Black Beauty'** produces dark purple fruits of

good quality over a long period. It is high yielding. **'Black Enorma'** has monstrous, dark, almost spherical fruit. Regular harvesting is advisable and a stout supporting stake is recommended, too! **'Easter Egg,'** despite its name, is not chocolate-colored and sweet, but white, about the size of a large egg. It should be harvested when it is about 5 in. long. It ripens after 2 months in good growing conditions. **'Florida Market'** is oval, glossy purple-black, and ideal for warm zones. Cropping over a long period, the fruits are rot-resistant and tasty. **'Green Tiger'** is a very popular Thai variety. The 3–4 ft. tall plants bear clusters of 1–2 in.-round, pale green fruit. **'Long Purple'** produces good yields of dark purple fruits about 6 in. long. **'Moneymaker'** is a superb early variety with tasty fruits. Tolerant of lower temperatures, it can be grown indoors as well as outside. **'Short Tom'** is a small, early cropping variety. The fruits can be harvested when they are small or allowed to grow larger. It is

ideal for containers. **'Violette di Firenze'** needs warmth to ripen fully. The unusual yet very attractive dark mauve fruits make this an ideal plant for growing in a "potager."

CULTIVATION

Eggplants need long, hot summers, and are the ideal crop for warm zones. In cooler regions, they will grow outside, but better harvests come from those protected indoors. Constant temperatures between 75–86°F with moderate to high humidity are needed for optimum flower and fruit production. Below 68°F growth is often stalled. **Zones 4–11.**

Propagation
Temperatures of 58–70°F are needed for good germination. Sow seed in early spring, in trays, pots, or packs of moist seed potting mix in a propagator or warm greenhouse or on a windowsill. Soaking seed in warm water for 24 hours

before sowing helps germination. When 3 leaves appear, repot plants grown in seed trays into 2–3 in. pots, repotting as required until they are ready to plant outdoors or under cover. If you are growing eggplants outdoors, sow seeds 10–12 weeks before the last frosts are expected.

Growing
Eggplants flourish in a sunny, sheltered position on fertile, well-drained soil. Before planting, fork in a slow-release general fertilizer at 1–2 oz./sq. yd., improve the soil with the addition of organic matter, and, in cooler zones, warm the soil before planting and leave the cloches in place until the plants are established for 2–3 weeks, allowing them to "harden off" before removing the cloches.

Space plants 20–24 in. apart. Pinch out the growth tip when plants are 16 in. tall, or 9–12 in. for smaller varieties. Stake the main stem or support branches with string if necessary as fruit begins to mature. Mulch outdoor plants to conserve moisture and suppress weeds.

Feed plants with a liquid general fertilizer until they are established, then water with a high-potash liquid feed every 10 days once the first fruits are formed. When the flowers begin to open a light spray with tepid water helps pollination; for large, high-quality fruits, allow only 4–5 to form on each plant, after which any new sideshoots should be removed.

Maintenance

Spring Sow seeds under glass.
Summer Once frosts are over, transplant outdoors. Retain 4–6 fruits per plant, harvesting as they mature.
Fall Protect outdoor crops from early frosts.
Winter Order seed for the following growing season.

Protected Cropping

When growing plants indoors, mist them regularly with tepid water or "damp down" the paths on hot days. Keep the potting mix moist throughout the growing season but take care to avoid waterlogging.

Container Growing

Eggplants can be grown in 8–12-in. pots or in growing bags. Keep temperatures around 58–65°F; water regularly, keep the potting mix moist and feed with a half-strength high-potash fertilizer every other watering.

Harvesting and Storing

Harvest when the skin is shiny: overripe fruits have dull skin and are horribly bitter. Using a knife, cut the fruit stalks close to the stem. They will keep for 2 weeks in a cool, humid place or in the refrigerator.

PESTS AND DISEASES

Eggplants are susceptible to the typical problems of crops grown under glass.

Check plants for **aphids**, **whitefly** and **red spider mite**. **Powdery mildew** can stunt growth, and in severe cases leaves become yellow and die. **Verticillium wilt** turns lower leaves yellow; plants wilt but recover overnight.

COMPANION PLANTING

Eggplants flourish alongside thyme, tarragon, and peas.

MEDICINAL

In Indian herbal medicine white varieties are used to treat diabetes and as a carminative. The Sanskrit *vatin-ganah* means "antiwind vegetable." *Kama Sutra* prescribes it in a concoction for "enlarging the male organ for a period of 1 month." Neither claim has been proven!

WARNING

Always remove the fruit's bitter taste, as it irritates the mucous membranes.

'Violette di Firenze,' beautiful and unusual

CULINARY

The large "berries" contain a bitter quality in the flesh. Slice large varieties, sprinkle with salt, and let sit for 30 minutes to leach out the bitterness before rinsing. Small and newer varieties do not need this treatment. Rub cut surfaces with lemon juice to prevent discoloration.

Eggplants can be made into soups, pureed, stewed, stuffed, fried, and pickled. Slices can be dipped in batter to make fritters, or drizzled with olive oil and broiled or roasted. In the Middle East the skin is burned off over a naked flame, giving the flesh a smoky flavor.

In Provence the vegetable stew ratatouille is made from eggplants, garlic, peppers, zucchini, onions, and coriander seeds, all cooked in olive oil. The Greek moussaka contains ground meat and eggplants.

In the Caribbean small white varieties are stewed in coconut milk and sweet spices. Asian eggplants have a sweetness that does not suit European cooking; use them in stir-fries.

Sautéed Eggplants with Mozzarella
Serves 4

This dish goes well with plain meats.

4 small, long, thin eggplants
1 clove garlic, crushed
1 tablespoon chopped parsley
Salt and freshly ground black pepper
¹/₄ cup toasted bread crumbs
3 tablespoons olive oil
1 cup buffalo mozzarella, cut into ¹/₄-in. slices

Preheat the oven to 350°F. Cut the eggplants in half lengthwise. Score the flesh deeply, but do not cut the skin. Arrange in a shallow pan, skin side down. Mix the garlic, parsley, salt and pepper, the bread crumbs, and half the olive oil and press this into the scored eggplants. Drizzle with the rest of the oil and bake in the oven until tender, about 20 minutes.

Raise the heat to 400°F and, as the oven warms, arrange the mozzarella on top of the eggplants. Return to the oven for 5 minutes. Serve this dish as soon as the mozzarella melts.

Solanum tuberosum. Solanaceae

POTATO

Also known as Common Potato, Irish Potato. Perennial, grown as annual for edible starchy tubers. Half hardy. Value: rich in carbohydrates, magnesium, potassium; moderate amounts of vitamins B and C.

Then a sentimental passion of a vegetable fashion must excite your languid spleen.
An attachment à la Plato for a bashful young potato or a not too French French bean.
—Sir William Gilbert (1836–1911)

The world's fourth most important food crop after wheat, corn, and rice, the potato is a nutritious starchy staple grown throughout temperate zones. Hundreds of varieties have been developed since 5000 B.C., when potatoes were first cultivated in Chile and Peru. The name derives from *batatas,* the Carib Indian name for the sweet potato, or from *papa* or *patata,* as it was called by South American Indians.

The Spaniards introduced potatoes to Europe in the sixteenth century and Sir John Hawkins is reputed to have brought them to England in 1563. Extensive cultivation did not start until Sir Francis Drake brought back more in 1586, after battling with the Spaniards in the Caribbean. Sir Walter Raleigh introduced them to Ireland and later presented some to Elizabeth I. Her cook is said to have discarded the tubers and cooked the leaves, which did not help its popularity!

In England and Germany potatoes were considered a curiosity; in France they were believed to cause leprosy and fever. However, in 1773 the French scientist Antoine Parmentier wrote a thesis extolling the potato's virtues as a famine food after eating them while a prisoner of war in Prussia. He established soup kitchens to feed the malnourished; potato soup is now known as

Potage Parmentier, and there is also Omelette Parmentier. He created "French fries," which were served at a dinner honoring Benjamin Franklin, who was unimpressed; it was Thomas Jefferson who introduced French fries to America at a White House dinner.

Parmentier presented a bouquet of potato flowers to Louis XVI, who is said to have worn one in his buttonhole. Marie Antoinette wore them in her hair, which made it highly fashionable. By the early nineteenth century, the potato had become a staple in France.

Ireland's climate and plentiful rain produced large crops. Potatoes were propagated from small tubers that were passed from one household to another, so the whole crop came from a few original plants. These were susceptible to potato blight, and devastating crop failure in the 1840s resulted in the deaths of more than 1.5 million people. Almost a million others emigrated to North America.

During the Civil War, potatoes were sent to the prisons and front lines. By eating the potatoes in their skins, soldiers received adequate supplies of vitamin C. The common name "spud" came from a tool that was once used to weed the potato patch.

VARIETIES

Potatoes are classified as "first early," "second early" (or "midcrop"), and main-crop varieties. Early and second early varieties grow rapidly, taking up less space for a shorter time than main crops, so are better for small gardens. Yields are usually lower. They are also unaffected by some of the diseases afflicting main crops. Second earlies are planted about a month after earlies. Main crop are for immediate consumption or for storage over the winter.

Potatoes come in a huge range of shapes, sizes, colors, and textures. The skin may be red, yellow, purple, or white and the flesh pale cream or yellow, mottled, or blue. Their texture may be waxy or floury and shapes variously knobbly, round, and oval. Because of government legislation, some old varieties are available only from specialists, though many suppliers have a good range for sale. Make sure to choose varieties recommended for your area.

'**Yukon Gold**' is an early round tuber with thin yellow skin and a bright yellow flesh. '**Russian Banana**' is the most popular of the fingerling types. It has a waxy texture, with light yellow flesh. The plants are resistant to scab. '**Rose Gold**' tubers have rosy red skin covering a bright yellow flesh. This Canadian development is perfect for new potatoes. Their waxy flesh is good boiled, roasted, or baked. '**Kennebec**' has been a Maine standard for years. Some say it's the perfect potato. Great yield, good taste, and fantastic storage ability make it a must for every garden. Plants resist drought and disease.

The good-sized, smooth, white fleshed tubers of '**Superior**' taste great fresh out of the ground, and store well too. '**All Blue**' sets the standard for blue potatoes. Both skin and flesh are purple/blue. The

'King Edward,' an old variety

smooth oval tubers store well. They make a great potato salad.

'**Purple Viking**' has dark purple skin over bright white flesh. Excellent flavor and keeping quality. '**Russet Nugget**' is a large russet type reaching 5 in. long. Good for baking.

'**Chippewa**' is a good choice for heavy soils in Northern states. The medium-sized white potatoes are very flavorful. '**Viking**' is a very early variety that will produce small, new potatoes in as little as 70 days. The rich red skin of '**Rosy Gold**' covers a deep yellow flesh. The potato flesh is mildly dry and good for baking.

'Pink Fir Apple'

'**Red Sangria**' is an early variety with red skin and pure white flesh. Plants produce a good crop of round tubers that store well. '**Onaway**' is an old fashioned round, white-fleshed potato that's well suited for boiling and baking. '**Irish Cobbler**' is an old favorite. Though productive, this medium sized white potato has little disease resistance. '**Katahdin**' produces medium-sized, oval tubers. The plants are resistant to disease and well suited to small gardens.

The crisp white flesh of '**Caribe**' is covered by a beautiful purple skin. The small oblong potatoes are good for baking, boiling, or frying.

'**Island Sunshine**' are beautiful golden-fleshed potatoes that were originally grown on Prince Edward Island. They have an exquisite flavor when boiled.

Sprouting seed potatoes

Potato crop in Oregon

CULTIVATION

Propagation

Potatoes are normally grown from small tubers known as "seed potatoes." Buy "certified" virus-free stock from a reputable supplier to be certain of obtaining a good-quality crop.

These are "sprouted" (or "chitted") about 6 weeks before planting to extend the growing season, which is particularly useful for early cultivars and in cooler zones. It is worth chitting second earlies and main crops if they are to be planted late. Put a single layer of potatoes in a shallow tray or egg box with the "rose end" (where most of the "eyes" or dormant buds are concentrated) upwards, then put the tray in a light, cool, frost-free place to encourage growth. At 45°F it takes about 6 weeks for shoots about 1 in. long to form. At this stage, they are ready for planting. They can be planted when the shoots are longer, but need handling with care, as they are easily broken off. For a smaller crop but larger potatoes, leave 3 shoots per tuber on earlies; otherwise leave all of the shoots for a higher yield.

Plant earlies from midspring and main crops from late spring, when there is no longer any danger of hard frosts and soil temperatures are 45°F.

Make trenches or individual holes 3–6 in. deep, depending on the size of the tuber. Plant them upright with the shoots at the top and cover with at least 1 in. of soil. Take care not to damage the shoots. Earlies can be planted a little deeper to give more protection from cooler weather. Ideally the rows should face north-south so that both sides of the row receive sunshine.

Plant earlies 12–15 in. apart with 15–20 in. between the rows and main crops 15 in. apart with 30 in. between the rows. Alternatively, plant earlies 14 in. apart and second earlies and main crops 12–15 in. apart in and between the rows. Spacing can be varied according to the size of the tubers and also to their subsequent cropping potential.

While the traditional method of propagation is very common, seed is also available, which is easy to handle and produces healthy crops. Seeds are sown indoors before repotting, hardening off, and transplanting. "Plantlets" produced by tissue culture are also available; these are healthy, virus-free, and vigorous. These, too, will need growing on before hardening off and then transplanting.

Cutting large potatoes in half is not recommended, nor is the method I once saw being used—hollowing the tubers to leave a thin layer of flesh, then planting the skins only! **Zones 3–8.**

Growing

Potatoes flourish in an open, sunny, frost-free site on deep, rich, fertile, well-drained soil. They grow better in cool seasons, when temperatures are between 61–64°F, and are tolerant of most soils. Lighter soils are better for growing earlies. Add organic matter to sandy soils. Alkaline soils or heavy liming encourages scab. Grow resistant varieties and lime acid soils gradually to create a pH of 5–6, or cultivate in raised beds or containers. If necessary, dig in plenty of well-rotted organic matter in the fall, then rake to a rough tilth 10 days before planting, adding a general granular fertilizer at 3–4 oz./sq. yd.

Potatoes are an excellent crop for new or neglected gardens; while the crop may not be large, the root system breaks up the soil and improves its structure. Keep crops weed-free until they are established, when the dense canopy of foliage suppresses weeds.

Potatoes are "hilled up"; this prevents exposure to light, which makes them green and inedible, and also disturbs germinating weeds. When the plants are about 8–9 in. tall, use a rake or spade to draw loose soil carefully around the stems to a depth of 4–6 in. Alternatively, begin hilling up in stages when the plants are about 4 in. tall, adding soil every 2–3 weeks.

To avoid having to hill up, plant small tubers about 5 in. deep and 9–10 in. apart on level ground. Wide spacing means tubers are not forced to the surface, yet still produce a moderate crop.

Potatoes need at least 20 in. of rainfall over the growing season for a good crop. During dry weather water earlies every 12–14 days at 3–4 gallons/sq. yd. Except when there are drought conditions, do not water main crops until the tubers are the size of marbles (check their development by scraping back the soil below a plant).

Planting 'Baillie'

At this point, a single, thorough soaking with at least 5 gallons/sq. yd. encourages the tubers to swell, increases the yield, and makes them less prone to scab.

Potatoes need a constant supply of water; erratic watering causes malformed, hollow, or split potatoes.

An organic liquid feed or nitrogenous top dressing helps plants to become established during the early stages of growth.

Early potatoes can be grown under black plastic, which also makes hilling up unnecessary. Prepare the soil, lay a sheet of black polyethylene over the area, anchor the edges by covering with soil, and plant your potatoes through crosses cut in the polyethylene. Alternatively, plant the potatoes, cover them with plastic, and when the foliage appears, make a cut in the polyethylene and pull through.

Where early frosts and windy conditions do not occur and the ground is excessively weedy or wireworm is a problem, potatoes can be grown in a bed of potting mix and straw. Clear the ground and cover the soil with a good layer of well-rotted manure or compost. Space the potatoes as required and cover them with a 2–3 in. layer of straw or hay, adding more as the potatoes grow, to a maximum of 6 in. At this point, spread a 3–4-in. layer of lawn clippings over the area to exclude light from the developing tubers.

Rotate earlies every 3 years and main crops every 5 years.

Maintenance
Spring Chit potatoes before planting.
Summer Keep crops weed-free and water as necessary. Harvest and use or store.
Fall Plant winter crops under cover. Prepare the soil for the following year.
Winter Harvest winter crops.

Protected Cropping
To advance early crops and protect them from frost, cover early potatoes with cloches or floating crop covers, anchored by burying the edges under the soil. When the shoots appear, cut holes in the plastic and pull the foliage through. After 3–4 weeks cut the cover, leaving it in place to allow the potatoes to become acclimatized.

Protect the foliage and stems ("haulm") from heavy frosts by covering them at night with a layer of straw, hay, or newspaper, or a thin layer of soil. Light frosts do not generally cause problems.

For winter crops of new potatoes, in warm zones, plant earlies in midsummer and cover with cloches in the fall. Alternatively, grow them in the borders of a frost-free greenhouse at 45–50°F. Provide warmth if necessary.

Container Growing
Potatoes can be grown in any container if it is at least 12 in. wide and deep and has drainage holes. It is possible to buy a potato barrel for this purpose—some models have sliding panels for ease of harvesting—but an old trash can, flower pot, or something similar is just as good. Potatoes can also be grown in black garbage bags! Wider containers can of course hold more potatoes.

Potatoes growing in a compost pile

Place a 4–5-in. layer of compost or good garden soil in a container, stand 2–3 chitted potatoes on the surface, and cover with a layer of compost about 4–6 in. deep. When the shoots are about 6 in. tall, cover with another 4–6-in. layer of compost, leaving the tips showing. Continue hilling up until the shoots are 2–3 in. below the rim of the container.

Winter crops of first earlies can also be grown in containers. Plant in midsummer for harvesting at Christmas in mild-winter zones. Cover the "haulms" in frosty weather or grow under glass.

Be sure to keep crops well fed and watered.

Harvesting and Storing
Earlies are ready to harvest from early to midsummer, second earlies from late summer to early fall, and main crops mature from early to midfall.

Harvest earlies when they are about the size of an egg: their readiness is often indicated by the flowers opening. Remove some soil from the side of a ridge and check them for size before lifting the root. Insert a flat-tined fork into the base of the ridge and lift the whole plant, bringing the new potatoes up to the surface.

Harvest those grown under black poleythylene by folding back the sheeting: the crop of potatoes will be lying on the surface. Collect as required.

Scrape away potting mix from those grown in containers to check their size before harvesting them.

Leave healthy main-crop potatoes in the soil for as long as possible, but beware of slugs! In early fall cut back the haulm to about 2 in. above the soil, or wait until the foliage dies down naturally; leave the tubers in the ground for 2 weeks for the skins to harden before lifting.

Cut back the haulm and work along the side of each ridge, lifting the potatoes with a fork. Harvest on a dry, sunny day when the soil is moderately moist; leave in the sun for a few hours to dry, then brush off the soil. If the weather is poor, dry them under cloches or on trays indoors. Store healthy tubers in paper or burlap sacks or boxes in a dark, cool, frost-free place. They should keep until spring. Check tubers weekly, removing those that are damaged or diseased.

When harvesting, ensure that all potatoes, however small, are removed from the soil to prevent future problems occurring with pests and diseases.

New potatoes do not store, but can be frozen. Blanch whole in boiling water for 3 minutes. Cool, drain, pack into rigid containers, and freeze. French fries can also be frozen.

Digging up potatoes, Devon, England

PESTS AND DISEASES

Common potato scab shows as raised, corky scabs on the surface of the tuber. It does not usually affect the whole potato and can be removed by peeling. It is common in hot, dry summers, on light, free-draining and alkaline soils. Water well in dry conditions, add plenty of organic matter to the soil before planting, avoid excessive liming or rotating after the soil has been limed for brassicas. Do not put infected potatoes or peelings on the compost pile. Grow resistant cultivars.

Potato blight appears on the leaves as brown patches, often with paler margins. The infection can spread to the stems and through the tuber, making it inedible. The disease spreads rapidly in warm, humid conditions and main crops are more susceptible. Grow resistant cultivars and avoid overhead watering; before the problem appears apply a systemic fungicide every 2 weeks from midsummer. Alternatively, use copper sulfate sprays such as "Bordeaux mixture." Hilling up creates a protective barrier, slowing the infection of tubers. Lift early potatoes as soon as possible and in late summer, cut back the haulms of infected plants just above the ground and burn the infected material or put it in the trash can. Leave tubers in the ground for 2 weeks before lifting.

Potato cyst wireworm ("golden nematode" or "pale eelworm"). Growth is checked and yields can be severely reduced; badly affected plants turn yellow and die. Lift and burn infected plants, rotate crops, and do not grow potatoes or tomatoes in the soil for at least 6 years. Try to grow resistant varieties.

Wireworms are about 1 in. long and golden brown in color. They tunnel into the tubers, making them inedible. They are fairly easy to control. Cultivate the soil thoroughly over winter to expose to the weather and birds, keep crops weed-free, and lift main crops as early as possible. Also rake in a soil insecticide.

Blackleg shows when the upper leaves roll and wilt and the stem becomes black and rotten at the base. The tubers may be rotten. It is more severe in wet seasons; do not plant on waterlogged land. Remove affected plants immediately, burn or put in the trash can. Do not store damaged tubers.

Slugs can tunnel into the tubers; the damage is more severe the longer they remain in the ground.

COMPANION PLANTING

Growing horseradish in large sunken pots near potatoes controls some diseases. Plant with corn, cabbage, beans, and marigolds. Grow with eggplants, which are a greater attraction to Colorado potato beetle. Protect against scab by putting grass clippings and comfrey leaves in the planting hole or trench.

OTHER USES

Potatoes are made into flour and turned into bread. They can be boiled and the starch turned to glucose, which can be fermented to produce strong alcohol, like the poteen made in Ireland. In the past, they have also

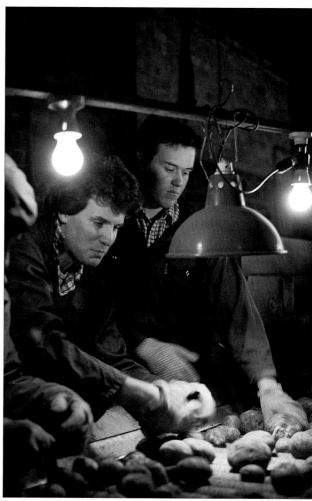

Riddling and sorting potato crop under artificial lights

been a source of starch powder for whitening wigs. The juice of mature potatoes is particularly excellent for cleaning silks, cotton, wool, and even furniture.

MEDICINAL

Potatoes are said to be good for rheumatism. One traditional cure for sciatica and lumbago is to carry a potato in your pocket.

The juice from a raw potato or the water in which potatoes have been boiled is said to relieve gout, rheumatism, lumbago, sprains, and bruises.

Uncooked, peeled, and pounded potatoes are said to make a soothing plaster to scalds or burns when applied cold.

Potatoes contain little fat and provide more potassium pro rata than bananas, while the average potato contains as many calories as most apples or a glass of orange juice and can be eaten by those on a diet.

WARNING

Green potatoes contain the toxic alkaloid solanine, which can cause vomiting and upset stomach. Do not eat green potatoes. Beware that the tomatolike fruits and leaves of the plant are also poisonous.

CULINARY

There are many, many ways of serving potatoes. They can be boiled, steamed, baked, roasted, mashed, sautéed, fried, and cooked au gratin.

In the past, potatoes have been preserved and candied or mashed with butter, sherry, egg yolks, nutmeg, and a little sugar and baked until brown.

Rub the skin from new potatoes under running water and boil for 12 minutes with a sprig of mint. Drain and toss in butter, then eat hot or cold in salads.

Scrape old potatoes; peeling removes much of the vitamin C just below the surface.

Cut potatoes into ½ in. strips, wash in ice-cold water, drain and dry thoroughly. Fry until golden in a shallow frying basket in a pan one third full of oil at 250°F.

The difference between "chips" and "French fries" is their size and the method of cooking. Chips are very thinly sliced and deep-fried in oil. French fries are sliced thickly and were originally cooked in animal fat. Nowadays the only difference is the size.

Microwaving generally retains the flesh color in unusual potatoes.

Mashed Potatoes with Olive Oil

For those on a diet, this at least has less calories than the traditional dish!

5 cups potatoes, peeled
8–10 cloves garlic, unpeeled
8 tablespoons olive oil,
*   preferably extra-virgin*
Salt and freshly ground black
*   pepper*

Put the potatoes and garlic cloves in a pan, cover with water and add salt. Bring to a boil and cook until tender, about 20 minutes, and then drain, reserving the potato cooking liquid. Boil this separately in the pan to reduce to roughly 1 cup. Meanwhile peel the garlic cloves. Mash the potatoes and garlic. Return the pan to a gentle heat and beat in the olive oil and enough potato liquid to give the potatoes the right texture. Season with salt and pepper.

To make the traditional Irish dish called "champ," add ½ cup of cooked and roughly chopped cabbage or springy greens to the above.

Rösti
Serves 4

4 cups waxy potatoes
1 small onion, finely
*   chopped*
½ cup smoked bacon, diced
6–8 tablespoons olive oil
Salt and freshly ground black
*   pepper*

Clean the potatoes and boil them in lightly salted water until just tender. Drain and when cool enough to handle, peel. Shred coarsely.

In a heavy pan, gently sauté the onion and bacon in half the oil. Fold this into the potatoes with the seasoning. Form the potatoes into one big cake. In the same pan heat the balance of the oil and gently slide the potatoes into the pan. Cook over a high heat until the first side is browned. Place a plate over the pan and turn the potatoes onto the plate; then gently slide the cake back into the pan to allow the second side to cook. Serve piping hot.

This classic Swiss dish can be eaten with Emmenthal melted on top (put the browned potatoes, covered with cheese slices, under the broiler for a few minutes).

Rösti

Potato Salad with Goat's Cheese Dressing
Serves 4

The South Americans have excellent ways of cooking potatoes, including this rich salad, which makes a good summer first course.

4 cups potatoes, fairly small
½ red bell pepper, seeded and
*   diced*
1 small onion, peeled and finely
*   chopped*
2 hard-boiled eggs, peeled and
*   diced*
Handful black olives, pitted
2 tablespoons Italian parsley,
*   chopped*

For the dressing.
½ cup well-flavored goat's
*   cheese*
2 cloves garlic, peeled
2 tablespoons yogurt
2 tablespoons lemon juice
1 jalapeño pepper, seeded
¼ teaspoon turmeric
½ teaspoon ground cumin

Potato Salad with Goat's Cheese Dressing

Cook the potatoes in their skins in boiling water until tender, drain, and peel.

Cut into generous dice and put into a serving dish. While the potatoes cook, mix the dressing ingredients in a blender, pureeing until smooth. Combine the potatoes with the red pepper and onion. Add the dressing and toss. Decorate the top with the diced eggs, olives, and parsley.

Spinacia oleracea. Chenopodiaceae

SPINACH

Fast-growing annual, grown for highly nutritious leaves. Hardy. Value: high in iron, beta carotene, and folic acid; rich in vitamins A and C.

Harvest spinach regularly

Spinach is thought to be native to south-west Asia. Unknown to the Greeks and Romans, it was first cultivated by the Persians, was grown in China by the seventh century A.D., and reached Europe around 1100, after its introduction to Spain by the Moors. The prickly-seeded form was known in thirteenth Germany and by the following century it was commonly grown by European monastery gardens. Smooth-seeded spinach was first described in 1522. Its first mention in England comes in William Turner's *New Herball*, in the 16th century: "An herbe lately found and not long in use." The name comes from Old French *espinache*, derived from its Arabic and Persian name.

Children were encouraged to eat spinach because of its effect on Popeye the Sailor. The idea that it contains exceptional levels of iron originated from Dr. E. von Wolf in 1870. His figures went unchecked until 1937, when it was discovered that the iron content was one-tenth that claimed by him—the result of a misplaced decimal point!

VARIETIES

Traditionally there are two main groups. Prickly seeded varieties, which have lobed leaves, are regarded as hardier than the round, smooth-seeded types, which cope better with higher temperatures and are used for summer cropping. Modern cultivars are generally more adaptable. **'America'** has thick deep green leaves for spring sowing. It does not overwinter well. **'Bloomsdale'** (**'Bloomsdale Long Standing'**) is a savoy-leaved spinach with fleshy, tasty leaves. It is cold-tolerant, slow to bolt, and crops over a long period. **'Giant Winter,'** a robust late fall and winter variety, withstands some frost and is highly disease-resistant. **'Medania'** is for summer cropping. It withstands hot, dry weather and is resistant to downy mildew. **'Nordic IV'** is a strong, smooth-leaved variety that shines in midsummer. Fast to grow, slow to bolt, the large leaves are a very dark green. **'Space'** has smooth, dark green leaves and is resistant to downy mildew. Ideal for any season. **'Tyee'** is the most bolt-resistant savoyed spinach. **'Vienna'** is a very early spinach with thick, fully savoyed leaves that hold up well in the garden.

CULTIVATION

Spinach grows best in cool conditions, at temperatures around 60–65°F. It thrives in a bright position, but is better in light shade and moist ground if your garden is hot and sunny.
Zones 3–8.

Propagation
Soak seed overnight to speed up germination. A friend of mine wraps seed in a wet paper towel and places it in a sealed container in the fridge for 5 days before planting. Germination usually takes 5 days. As a cool-season plant, it will not germinate above 86°F.

Sow summer crops every 2–3 weeks from early to late spring for a summer harvest.

Sow in late summer, for cropping in winter until early summer. In mild zones, sow in situ 1 in. apart and ½–¾ in. deep in rows 12 in. apart. When large enough to handle, thin to 6–10 in. It also works as a cut-and-come-again crop.

In colder areas it is better to sow in seed trays or packs for transplanting.

Sow thinly in broad drills the width of a hoe or in rows 4 in. apart. Leave unthinned unless growth is slow, when they can be thinned to 2 in. apart. Plants can be thinned to 4–5 in. apart for larger leaves, though they are more inclined to bolt.

Growing
Spinach needs a rich, fertile, moisture-retentive soil, so where necessary, dig in well-rotted organic matter before planting. On poor soils leaves are stunted, bitter, and prone to bolt. The ideal pH is 6.5–7.5; lime acid soils.

Never allow the soil to dry out. Water regularly before the onset of dry weather and grow bolting-resistant cultivars. Water every 2 weeks with a high-nitrogen liquid fertilizer.

Maintenance
Spring Sow early crops successively.
Summer Keep the soil moist and weed-free. Sow winter crops from late summer.
Fall Protect late crops under cloches, sow cut-and-come-again crops under glass.
Winter Protect winter crops under cloches or fleece, or sow in cold frames.

Protected Cropping
Hardy varieties for winter and early spring cropping are better protected in cold frames, cloches, or under frost fabric.

Container Growing
Spinach is ideal for containers 8–18 in. wide and 12 in. deep. Water regularly in dry weather. Avoid scorching sunshine.

Harvesting and Storing
Harvest from 5 weeks after sowing, cutting the outer leaves first. To harvest as a cut-and-come-again crop, remove the heads 1 in. above the ground and allow them to resprout. Pick off the leaves carefully; the stems and roots are easily damaged. Alternatively, pull up whole plants and resow. Use the leaves fresh, or freeze. They can be washed and stored for up to 2 days in the refrigerator.

Pests and Diseases
Aphids and **slugs** can be troublesome, especially among seedlings. **Downy mildew** appears as yellow patches with fluffy mold on the underside of the leaf. **Bolting** caused by drying out or hot weather is most common cause of failure.

COMPANION PLANTING

Good with beans, peas, corn, and strawberries.

MEDICINAL

Spinach is said to be good for anemia, problems of the heart and kidney, and in low vitality and general debility. Iron is in a soluble form, so any water left after cooking can be cooled and drunk.

Research has shown that those who eat spinach daily are less likely to develop lung cancer. Of all the vegetable juices, spinach juice is said to be the most potent for the prevention of cancer cell formation.

OTHER USES

The water drained from spinach after cooking is said to make good match paper. It was used to make touch paper for fireworks in the 18th and 19th centuries, as paper soaked in it smoldered well.

The leaves of 'Medania' are particularly thick

Spinach is packed with goodness.

CULINARY

Wash leaves thoroughly. Eat immediately after harvesting. Use young leaves raw in salads, lightly cooked, or steamed. Place spinach in a pan without adding water, cover, and stand on moderate heat so the leaves do not scorch.

After 5 minutes, stir and cook over high heat for 1 minute. Drain in a colander and cut with a knife.

Spinach can also be cooked with olive oil, cheese, cream, yogurt, ham, bacon, and anchovies, besides being seasoned with nutmeg, pepper, and sugar. All will bring out the flavor.

Scrambled Eggs with Spinach
Serves 6

12 cups young spinach
2 tablespoons olive oil
Pinch grated nutmeg
Salt and freshly ground black pepper
2 tablespoons butter
12 eggs, lightly beaten with 1 tablespoon heavy cream
1 tablespoon chopped chives

Wash the spinach and remove any tough stalks. Heat the oil in a heavy pan and then wilt most of the spinach, keeping back a couple of handfuls for decoration. Season with nutmeg, salt, and pepper. Set aside and keep warm.

In the same pan, melt the butter and allow to just brown. Over a low flame, pour in the eggs and season. Stir constantly until just set (overcooked scrambled eggs are bad news!). Mound the eggs in the center of individual plates and sprinkle with chopped chives. Arrange the cooked spinach around the outside, and then make another ring with the raw spinach leaves. Serve hot.

Scrambled Eggs with Spinach

Tetragonia tetragonoides (syn. T. expansa). Aizoaceae

NEW ZEALAND SPINACH

Creeping perennial, usually grown as annual for edible leaves. Half hardy. Value: high in iron, beta carotene, and folic acid.

This plant was unknown in Europe until 1771, when it was introduced to the Royal Botanic Gardens at Kew by the great botanist Joseph Banks after his voyage onboard the *Endeavour* with Captain Cook. By 1820 it was widely grown in the kitchen gardens of Britain and France, but it did not appear in New Zealand literature until the 1940s, and there is no evidence of its use by the Maoris. It is unrelated to true spinach, but its leaves are used in a similar manner—hence the borrowed name—though their flavor is milder than that of true spinach. A low-growing perennial with soft, fleshy, roughly triangular, blunt-tipped leaves, about two inches long, it makes an attractive plant for edging and ground cover. It flourishes in hot, dry conditions, without running to seed.

New Zealand spinach is seldom grown by gardeners, yet it is robust and a fine substitute for spinach

CULTIVATION

Propagation

The seed coat is extremely hard and germination is slow unless the seeds are soaked in water for 24 hours before sowing. Sow seeds individually, 1 in. deep in 3-in. pots indoors from mid- to late spring; repot as necessary. Plants are very cold-sensitive and so should be hardened off carefully before planting out once the danger of frost has passed.

Alternatively, sow seed in situ when there is no danger of frost, ½–¾ in. deep in drills about 24 in. apart, thinning to a similar distance between plants. Seeds can also be sown, 2 or 3 per "hill," 24 in. apart, thinning to leave the strongest. Pinch out tips of young plants to encourage bushy growth.

Plants usually self-seed and appear in the same area the following year.
Zones 4–8.

Growing

New Zealand spinach flourishes in an open site on light, fertile soil with low levels of nitrogen, and grows well in dry, poor conditions. It tolerates high temperatures, but is very susceptible to frost.

Keep seedlings weed-free with regular hoeing. Once plants are established, their dense foliage will act as a ground cover and suppress weeds.

Water regularly during dry spells to encourage vigorous growth. It does not bolt in hot weather, but should be watered well to encourage growth. On poor soils, occasional feeding with a half-strength solution of general liquid fertilizer is beneficial, but take care not to overfeed.

The triangular leaves are striking

Maintenance

Spring Sow seed under cover for transplanting once frosts are over.
Summer Keep crops weed-free, and water and harvest as required.
Fall Protect plants to extend the growing season.
Winter Prepare the ground for planting in spring.

Protected Cropping

Protecting with cloches extends the harvesting season in cooler areas before frosts turn the plants into a soggy mess.

Container Growing

Crops can be grown in large containers of soil-based potting mix. Add grit to improve drainage. Water plants well throughout the growing season.

Harvesting and Storing

The first young leaves and shoots are ready to harvest from about 6 weeks after sowing. Pick regularly to maintain a constant supply of young growth and to extend the harvesting

The leaves can be eaten raw.

season, which should last up to 4 months. Young leaves should be used immediately after cutting; they can be stored for 2 days in a plastic bag in the refrigerator or frozen. Wash, blanch for 2 minutes, and allow to cool and drain before packing into plastic bags and placing in the freezer.

CULINARY

The young leaves and shoots are steamed, lightly boiled, and eaten with a pat of butter, or eaten raw in salads. They are better eaten fresh, as the flavor deteriorates rapidly with age.

Cannelloni Stuffed with Chicken and New Zealand Spinach
Serves 4

5 cups fresh New Zealand spinach
2 tablespoons butter
1 red onion, diced
2 tablespoons plain flour
1¾ cups vegetable stock
1 bouquet garni
3 tablespoons heavy cream
Salt and freshly ground black pepper
8 cannelloni shells
2½ cups cooked chicken, diced
½ cup Parmesan, shredded

Wash the spinach in several changes of water, place in a saucepan, and cook for 3 minutes over high heat. Drain thoroughly and chop.

Melt the butter in a heavy pan, cook the onion until golden, and stir in the flour to make a roux. Cook for 1–2 minutes. Stir in the stock, allow to boil, and add the bouquet garni. Season and stir in the cream. Simmer without boiling for 10 minutes.

Meanwhile, boil the cannelloni until al dente and drain, setting aside to cool. Combine the chicken and spinach and half the sauce and season well. Use a large piping bag to stuff each cannelloni shell with the chicken mixture and arrange in a shallow, greased ovenproof dish.

Preheat the oven to 400°F. Reserve 1 tablespoon Parmesan and stir the balance into the remaining sauce. Pour this over the cannelloni and sprinkle with the reserved cheese. Cook for 20 minutes, until the top is browned and the dish hot through. Serve.

Cannelloni Stuffed with Chicken and New Zealand Spinach

PESTS AND DISEASES

New Zealand spinach is very robust but **downy mildew** may be a problem.

COMPANION PLANTING

It is sometimes grown as a "green manure" to improve the soil structure.

Tragopogon porrifolius. Asteraceae

SALSIFY

Also known as Oyster Plant, Vegetable Oyster, Goat's Beard. Grown as biennial for shoots, flower buds, and flowers; annual for cylindrical tapering edible roots. Hardy. Value: contains inulin, turning to fructose in storage; small amounts of vitamins and minerals.

It is difficult to know whether to grow this plant for its delicious roots or to grow it as a fragile ornamental by letting it flower (the flowers are also edible). Its Latin and common names are apt; *tragos* means goat and *pogon*, beard, describes the tuft of silky hairs on the developing seed heads; *porrifolius* means "with leaves like a leek." "Salsify" comes from the old Latin name *solsequium*, from the way the flowers follow the course of the sun.

Salsify is a relatively recent crop. In the thirteenth century it was harvested from the wild in Germany and France. It was not cultivated until the early sixteenth century, in Italian gardens. The English plant collector John Tradescant the Younger recorded it in 1656. It was brought to North America in the late nineteenth century.

VARIETIES

The species *Tragopogon porrifolius* has a thin, creamy-white, tapering taproot up to 15 in. long. It has narrow leaves and long, wandlike stems topped by beautiful dull purple flowers. These are followed by thistle-like seed heads. **'Geante Noire de Russie'** is an extremely long, black-skinned variety with white roots and a superb flavor. **'Giant'** is consistently long-rooted with a delicate taste of oysters. **'Sandwich Island'** is a selected type with strongly flavored roots and smooth skin.

CULTIVATION

Propagation
Always use fresh seed; its viability declines rapidly. Sow as early as possible, from early to midspring. Germination can be somewhat erratic, so it is better to sow 2–3 seeds in hills $^1/_2$–$^3/_4$ in. deep and 4 in. apart with 12 in. between the rows. After germination, when the

Salsify flowers vary from purple to near white.

seedlings are large enough to handle, thin to leave the strongest seedling. Alternatively, sow the seeds in drills and thin to the above spacing. **Zones 5–11.**

Growing
Salsify thrives in an open situation on light, well-drained, stone-free soil which was manured for the previous crop (roots tend to fork when they are grown on freshly manured soil.) On stony or heavy soils, dig a trench about 12 in. deep and 8 in. wide, filling it with finely sieved sandy soil or potting mix and sharp sand to give the roots room to grow. Lighten heavier soils by thoroughly digging over the area the fall before planting, adding well-rotted organic matter and sharp sand. A pH of 6.0–7.5 is ideal; lime acid soils. Before sowing, rake the seedbed to a fine tilth and incorporate a slow-release general fertilizer at 2–3 oz./sq. yd.

Regular watering ensures good-quality roots and, most important, stops bolting in dry conditions. It also prevents roots from splitting, which occurs after sudden rainfall or watering after a period of drought. Salsify should be kept weed-free, particularly during the early stages of growth. Hand weed, as the roots are easily damaged and inclined to "bleed." Alternatively, use an onion hoe or mulch moist soil with a layer of organic matter to stifle weed growth and conserve moisture.

In mild zones, roots can be left in the ground to produce edible shoots or "chards" the following spring. In fall, cut back the old leaves to within $^1/_2$ in. of the soil and hill up to about 5–6 in. In midspring the following year, the shoots are ready to harvest when they appear. On heavier soils, "chards" can be blanched with a covering of hay, straw, or dry leaves at least 5 in. deep when new growth appears in spring. An upturned bucket or flower pots with the drainage holes covered work just as well.

Maintenance
Spring Rake over the seedbed, incorporating general fertilizer. Sow seeds in hills.
Summer Keep the crop weed-free, mulch, and water during dry periods.
Fall Lift crops as required. Cut back the tops and cover those being grown for "chards."
Winter Dig over soil manured for the previous crop. Lift and store crops grown in colder areas.

Container Growing
Salsify can be grown in containers, but it is impractical to produce them in large quantities. However, if you are desperate, fill a large wooden box, tea chest, or plastic drum with sandy,

'Sandwich Island' is the most commonly grown form

Tragopogon dubius, **a relative of the cultivated plant**

COMPANION PLANTING

Salsify grows well with mustard and, planted near carrots, discourages carrot fly.

MEDICINAL

Salsify is said to have an antibilious effect and to calm fevers. In folk medicine it is used to treat gallbladder problems and jaundice.

Salsify seeds, like a giant dandelion clock

free-draining soil or a loam-based potting mix with added sharp sand. Ensure there are sufficient drainage holes. Keep crops weed-free and water regularly.

Harvesting and Storing
Harvest from midfall. Lift as required; protect roots with a layer of straw, hay, or a similar material before severe frosts or snow. They can be lifted in fall and stored in boxes of peat substitute, sand, or sawdust, in a cool, frost-free garage, shed, or cellar. Lift carefully with a garden fork; the roots "bleed" and snap easily.

If you begin lifting and find the crop misshapen, leave the roots in the ground and harvest the shoots and buds the following year. Next time, grow them in sieved soil.

Harvest "chards" in early to midspring: scrape away the soil and cut the blanched shoots when they are 5–6 in. long. Or lift when 6 in. tall, without hilling up, though they are not as tender.

Pests and Diseases
Salsify is usually trouble-free but may suffer from **white blister**, which looks like glistening paint splashes and can distort plants. Spray with Bordeaux mixture and destroy any plants that are badly affected.

Aster yellows cause deformed new growth and the leaf veins or whole leaf become yellow. Control the aster leaf hopper that spreads the disease.

CULINARY

Salsify has a delicate oysterlike flavor and can be cooked in a variety of ways (there is bound to be a recipe that suits you.) Peel after boiling until tender, "skimming" under cold running water as you would a hard-boiled egg.

Cut roots discolor, so drop them into water with a dash of lemon juice, then boil for 25 minutes in salted water with lemon juice and a tablespoon of flour. Drain and skin, toss with melted butter, and chopped parsley and indulge.

Try them with a light mornay sauce, deep-fried or served au gratin with cheese and bread crumbs. Or sauté them in butter and eat them with brown sugar.

Roots can also be baked, pureed, creamed for soup, or shredded raw in salads. They stay fresh in the refrigerator for about a week.

"Chards" can be served raw in salads or lightly cooked. Young flowering shoots can be eaten pickled, raw, or cooked and eaten cold like asparagus with oil and lemon juice. The subtle flavor makes them an excellent hors d'oeuvre.

Pick flower buds just before they open with about 3 in. of stem attached, lightly simmer, and eat when they are cool.

Fried Salsify
Serves 4

3¹/₂ cups salsify, cleaned, topped, and tailed
Vegetable oil, for frying
Lemon wedges, to serve

For the batter:
1 cup flour
1 teaspoon baking powder
1 egg
1 tablespoon olive oil
¹/₂ cup water
¹/₄ teaspoon harissa
¹/₂ teaspoon cumin
¹/₄ teaspoon dried thyme
Salt and freshly ground black pepper

Cut salsify roots in half and boil in salted water for 30 minutes. Rinse under cold water. Peel and cut into 3 in. pieces.

Make the batter: blend all the ingredients in a food processor for 30 seconds.

Heat the oil in a large frying pan. Dip the salsify in the batter and fry in oil until crisp and golden, turning. Keep warm while cooking the remainder. Serve hot with lemon wedges.

Fried Salsify

Salsify in Ham with Cheese Sauce
Serves 4

8 salsify, peeled and trimmed
8 slices cooked ham
2 tablespoons butter
2 tablespoons flour
1 teaspoon Dijon mustard
1 cup milk
4 tablespoons Gruyère, shredded
Pinch nutmeg
Salt and freshly ground black pepper

Preheat the oven to 400°F. Boil the salsify for 5 minutes and drain. Cut into roughly 4 in. lengths. When cool enough to handle, wrap each in a slice of ham and arrange in a greased baking dish.

Melt the butter in a heavy pan and stir in the flour to make a roux. Cook for a minute or two and stir in the mustard. Slowly add the milk and then the Gruyère, and cook until the cheese is melted.

Season with nutmeg, salt, and pepper, and pour over the salsify. Bake for 20 minutes, until browned.

Valerianella locusta (syn. Valerianella olitoria). Valerianaceae

CORN SALAD

Also known as Lamb's Lettuce, Mâche, Lamb's Tongues.
Low-growing, extremely hardy annual grown for edible leaves. Value: good source of beta carotene, vitamin C, and folic acid. Very few calories.

'Jade' growing

In spite of its delicate appearance, corn salad is an extremely hardy plant, particularly valued as a nutritious winter salad crop. Its attractive bright green, rounded leaves have a slightly nutty taste. Its name, corn salad, comes from its regular appearance as a cornfield weed. Depending on the authority, an alternative name, lamb's lettuce, came about because sheep are partial to it, or because it appears during the lambing season.

Gerard wrote: "We know the Lamb's Lettuce as loblollie; and it serves in winter as a salad herb among others none of the worst." He also noted that "foreigners using it in England led to its cultivation in our gardens." It has been popular for centuries in France, where it is known as *salade de prêtre* (as it is often eaten during Lent), *doucette* ("little soft one," referring to the velvety leaves), and *bourcette*, describing their shape. In England it declined in popularity in the 1700s and a nineteenth-century commentator noted, "It is indeed a weed, and can be of no real use where lettuces are to be had." Before the appearance of winter lettuce varieties, corn salad was the main winter salad; it was at one time classified in the same genus.

VARIETIES

There are two forms, the "large" or "broad-leaved" and the darker, more compact "green" type, which is popular in western Europe, but less productive.
'Cavallo' has deep green leaves and crops heavily. 'Elan' is tender and mildew-resistant, as is the extremely robust 'Jade.' 'Large Leaved' is tender and prolific. 'Elan' is very hardy. 'Verte de Cambrai,' a traditional French type, has small leaves and good flavor. 'Verte d'Etampes' has unusual, attractive savoyed leaves. 'Vit' is very vigorous with a mild flavor. 'Coquille' is the most attractive of all varieties.

CULTIVATION

Propagation
Lamb's lettuce can be grown as single plants or cut-and-come-again seedlings. Sow seeds successively from mid- to late spring for summer crops in drills 4–6 in. apart and ½ in. deep, thinning when seedlings

have 3–4 seed leaves to about 4 in. apart. Sow winter crops successively from mid- to late summer.

Seeds can also be sown in broad drills, broadcast, or in seed trays or packs for transplanting. Leave a few plants to bolt, and transplant seedlings into rows. **Zones 4–9.**

Growing

Corn salad flourishes in a sheltered position in full sun or light shade and needs a deep, fertile soil for rapid and continuous growth. It tolerates most soils provided they are not waterlogged. Create a firm seedbed and rake in a slow-release general fertilizer at 1–2 oz./sq. yd. before sowing in spring and summer. Overwintered crops growing on the same site should not need it.

Keep crops weed-free, particularly during the early stages, and water thoroughly to encourage soft growth.

Maintenance

Spring Sow successively.
Summer Continue sowing and harvesting, keep crops weed-free, and water well.
Fall Sow crops under cover. Continue harvesting.
Winter When growth is slower, do not overpick.

Protected Cropping

Although it is extremely hardy, growing corn salad under cloches, polyethylene tunnels, or frost fabric, or in an unheated greenhouse, encourages better quality

Corn salad can fill any space in damp corners of the garden

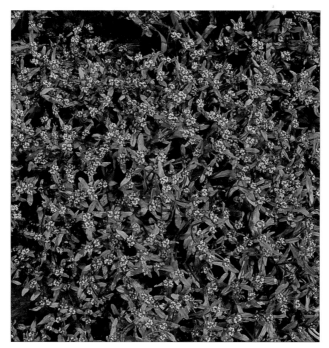

The silver-blue flowers of corn salad are delicate and attractive

and higher productivity. Make the first sowings in early fall.

Container Growing

Can be grown in 10-in. pots of loam-based potting mix with a low fertilizer content. Sow seeds thinly ½ in. deep every 3 weeks from early spring to early summer and again from early to midfall, thinning to leave the strongest seedlings at a final spacing of 4 in. apart.

Keep the potting mix moist when plants are growing vigorously; reduce watering in cooler conditions.

Harvesting and Storing

Harvest seedlings, pick leaves as required, or lift whole plants when they are mature—about 3 months after planting.

Do not weaken by removing too many leaves at one picking. This is particularly important with outdoor winter crops.

Leaves can be blanched for a few days before picking by covering with a box or pot to remove any bitterness.

Young flowers can be eaten in salads.

PESTS AND DISEASES

Some varieties are susceptible to **mildew**. Protect seedlings from **birds** and **slugs**.

COMPANION PLANTING

As plants take up very little space, corn salad is ideal sown between taller crops.

MEDICINAL

With its high beta carotene, vitamin C, and folic acid content, it is regarded by many as a winter and early spring tonic, and is useful when other nutritional vegetables are scarce.

CULINARY

Thinnings can be used in salads. Wash the leaves thoroughly to remove grit and soil. In 17th-century Europe, corn salad was often served with cold, boiled beet or celery. The leaves are used as a substitute for lettuce and combine well with it, also complementing fried bacon or ham and beet. Leaves can also be cooked like spinach.

Corn Salad and Shrimp Salad
Serves 4

A mixture of winter salad leaves, such as corn salad, chicory, and radicchio
Large fresh shrimp, peeled
Toasted sesame seeds

For the vinaigrette:
Lemon juice
Balsamic vinegar
Virgin olive oil
Mustard
Salt and freshly ground black pepper
Fresh herbs—sage, parsley, and chives, chopped

Wash the salad leaves and arrange on individual plates.

Season the shrimp with salt and pepper and coat generously with sesame seeds. (Allow 4 or 5 shrimp per person if they are tiger prawns.) In a heavy-bottomed frying pan, gently cook them, turning after 3 minutes (when golden) to cook the other side. Then arrange on the salad. Make the vinaigrette, dress the salad, and serve.

Vicia faba. Papilionaceae

FAVA BEAN

Also known as Broad Bean, Horse Bean, Windsor. Annual grown for seeds, young leaf shoots, and whole young pods. Value: low protein, good source of fiber, potassium, vitamin E and C.

Thought to have originated around the Mediterranean, the oldest remains of domesticated fava beans have been dated to 6800–6500 B.C. By the Iron Age they had spread throughout Europe. The Greeks dedicated them to Apollo and thought that overindulgence dulled the senses; Dioscorides wrote that they are "flatulent, hard of digestion, causing troublesome dreams."

They may be the origin of the term "bean feast," being a major part of the annual meal given by employers for their staff to make merry. Britain has many folk sayings concerning the sowing date. Huntingdonshire country wisdom states: "On St. Valentine's Day, beans should be in clay," and it was generally accepted that four seeds were sown—"One for rook, one for crow, one to rot, one to grow." Flowers were considered to be an aphrodisiac—"there ent no lustier scent than a bean field in bloom"—while the poet John Clare wrote: "My love is as sweet as a bean field in blossom, bean fields misted wi' dew." Hardy and prolific, they are the national dish of Egypt. An Arab saying goes, "Beans have satisfied even the Pharoahs."

VARIETIES

Fava beans are classified as Dwarf, with small, early-maturing pods that are excellent under cloches or in containers; Longpods, which are also hardy; and Windsors, with broad pods that usually mature later and have a better flavor. There are green- and white-seeded forms among the Longpods and Windsors. **'Aquadulce'** is a reliable hardy Longpod for fall and spring sowing. **'Aquadulce Claudia'** is similar, with medium to long pods and white seeds. Ideal for freezing, it is less susceptible to blackfly. **'Express'** is a fast-maturing early Longpod. Pods are plump and beans tasty. **'Imperial Green Longpod'** produces pods around 15 in. long with up to 9 large green beans. **'Masterpiece Green Longpod'** is a good-quality, green-seeded bean. Freezes well. **'Optica'** is an early, easy-to-grow variety whose gleaming white seeds are well suited for freezing.

'Dreadnought' is an early variety that produces great quantities of white beans. **'Sweet Lorane'** is a delicious small-seeded, prolific bean.

The neatly spaced seeds of fava beans in the pod

Cold-hardy. **'The Sutton,'** a Dwarf variety around 12 in. high, is ideal for small gardens and under cloches. Excellent flavor, very prolific. **'Witkiem Vroma'** is excellent for spring sowing, grows rapidly and has medium-sized pods.

CULTIVATION

Propagation

As they germinate well in cool conditions, fava beans can be sown from mid- to late fall and overwintered outdoors for a midspring crop. Seedlings should be 1 in. high when colder weather arrives. 'Aquadulce' cultivars are particularly suitable.

When the soil is workable, sow every 3 weeks from late winter to late spring for successional cropping.

Plant seeds 2 in. deep in rows or make individual holes with 12 in. in and between the rows. Or grow in staggered double rows, with 9 in. in and between the rows or in blocks 36 in. square with 8–12 in. between plants. Tall plants should be 12–18 in. apart. Sow extra seeds at the end of rows, for use as transplants.
Zones 4–11.

Growing

Fava beans flourish in an open, sunny site but overwintering crops need more shelter. Soils should be deeply dug, moisture-retentive and well drained, having been manured for the previous year's crop. Alternatively, add well-rotted organic matter in late fall before sowing. They need a pH of 6–7, so lime where necessary. Rotate with other legumes.

Rake a granular general fertilizer into the seedbed 1 week before sowing.

Mulch, hoe, or hand weed regularly, especially early on.

Watering should be unnecessary except in drought, but for good-quality crops, plants need 4 gallons/sq. yd. per week from flower formation to harvest end.

Support taller plants with stakes. Planting several staggered rows allows plants to support one another. Dwarf types can be supported with brushwood.

Maintenance

Spring Sow early crops under glass followed by later sowings until late spring.
Summer Harvest from late spring to late summer. Keep crops weed-free and water after flower formation.
Fall Sow outdoor crops for overwintering.
Winter Protect outdoor crops in severe weather.

Protected Cropping

Where plants cannot be overwintered outdoors, sow under cover in pots or boxes from midwinter. Harden off and plant out in midspring. Remove cloches from protected early crops when the beans reach the glass.

Container Growing

Grow dwarf cultivars in containers of low-fertilizer loam-based potting mix at least 8–18 in. wide by 10 in. deep. Sow seeds 2 in. deep and 4–5 in. apart. Water regularly in warm weather, less at other times.

Harvesting and Storing

Pick when the beans begin to show, before the pods are too large (and tough.) Pull with a sharp downward twist or cut with scissors.

Pods harvested at 2–3 in. long can be treated as snap peas and eaten whole, but picking at this stage reduces yields.

Fava beans freeze well, especially green-seeded varieties. Wash, blanch for 3 minutes, freeze in plastic

'Masterpiece Green Longpod' produces a high yield of smaller, thinner beans.

bags or rigid containers. Use within 12 months. Keep them in a plastic bag in the refrigerator for 1 week.

PESTS AND DISEASES

Black bean aphid is the most common problem. Control by pinching off the top 3 in. of stem when the first beans start to form. This also encourages an earlier harvest. **Mice** and **jays** steal the seeds.

COMPANION PLANTING

Plant with summer savory to discourage black bean aphid and among gooseberries to discourage gooseberry sawfly. The flowers are very attractive to bees. Fava beans are a good "nurse" crop for developing corn.

Interplant with brassicas, which benefit from the nitrogen-fixing roots. Dig in plant debris as a "green manure" to increase soil fertility. Seedling beans protect early potato shoots from wind and frost.

CULINARY

Steam or lightly boil beans to eat with ham, pork, and chicken. Eat with sautéed onions, mushrooms, and bacon; dress with tomato sauce, warm sour cream, or lemon butter and dill.

Bissara
Serves 4

An Algerian dish with subtle flavors, this recipe is based on one from the late, great foodie Arto der Haroturian.

3½ cups young fava beans, shelled weight
1 small green chili, chopped
1 teaspoon paprika
1 teaspoon cumin seeds, pounded in a mortar
2 cloves garlic, peeled
8 tablespoons virgin olive oil
Juice of half a lemon
Salt and freshly ground black pepper

Garnish:
A little olive oil, lemon juice, and paprika

Bissara

Boil the beans in lightly salted water until just tender. Drain and place in a food processor, together with the chili, paprika, cumin, and garlic. Puree, slowly drizzling in the oil and lemon juice. Season and pour into a bowl.

Garnish with a little olive oil, lemon juice, and paprika. Serve bissara with warm bread.

Fava Beans with Summer Savory
Serves 4

A dish that reflects the pure tastes of summer.

3 cups young fava beans
2 sprigs and 2 tablespoons (chopped) summer savory
2 tablespoons butter
Salt and freshly ground black pepper

Put the beans into a pan of boiling, salted water with the sprigs of summer savory and cook until just done, about 3–5 minutes. Drain and put the pan back on a gentle heat. Add the butter and toss well as it melts. Season with more summer savory and salt and pepper.

Zea mays. Poaceae

SWEET CORN

Also known as Maize, Corn on the Cob, Indian Corn, Baby Maize, Sweetcorn. Annual grown for kernels of edible seeds. Half hardy. Value: high in carbohydrates and fiber, moderate protein, and B vitamin content.

'Sundance,' an excellent early variety

Wild plants of maize have never been found, but it is believed that the crop was first cultivated in Mexico around 7000 B.C. Primitive types, smaller than an ear of wheat, were found in caves at Tehuacan in southern Mexico dating from around 3500 B.C., yet they were bred by Mayan and Indian farmers almost to the size of modern varieties. Early American civilizations were based on maize, and life for the Aztecs revolved round the milpa or cornfield. Multicolored types with blue, scarlet, brown, and almost black seeds predominated in South America. It became a staple crop in North America after A.D. 800. The first types introduced to Europe in the sixteenth century from Central America were valued for both the "cobs" and the yellow meal. Corn flourished in Spain, France, Italy, the Balkans, and Portugal.

Sweet corn is a sweet form of maize, a starchy crop used for grain and fodder. The yellow-golden varieties are commonly cultivated for the kitchen, but those with multicolored seeds are extremely ornamental. Corn and maize are the third most important cereal in the world, after wheat and rice, and there are more than 500 different by-products. For example: the seeds of corn also provide us with popcorn; starch extracted after milling has been used as laundry starch; and the pith has been used for making explosives and packaging material. Best of all is delicious fresh corn eaten from the cob dripping with butter; take the advice of Edward Bunyard: "The principle of the lathe is adopted in eating them."

VARIETIES

Sweet corn has been developed over centuries and there are many varieties available, as you will see from your seed catalog.

Traditional varieties
'Earliking' is very early, with good-quality cobs. Good for cooler zones. **'Golden Bantam'** is 6 ft. tall with tasty golden cobs that are good for freezing whole. An early, very hardy variety. **'Sweet Chorus'** is very early and ideal for cooler zones and later sowings. Very sweet, tender and tasty. **'Sundance'** matures early and is good for cooler zones. It crops well in poor summers. Seeds are very sweet. **'Silver Queen'** is a late-season type with white kernels. **'Stowell's Evergreen'** is also white and needs a long growing season. Keeps well over a long harvesting period.

Supersweet varieties
These are sweeter and keep their sweetness longer than older varieties. They should not be sown with older types, as there is a danger they will cross-pollinate and lose their sweetness.
   'Honey and Cream' is delicious and has white and

gold seeds. For best results, isolate from other sweet corns. **'Northern Xtra Sweet'** is the earliest bicolor supersweet available. Ears are up to 8 in. long.

Popcorn and ornamental varieties **'Carousel'** reaches 7 ft. tall, producing 4–6 ears per plant, and has tiny red, white, yellow, purple, and blue seeds. Dries well. **'Wampum'** is a new ornamental variety with small kernels and a wide variety of colors.

CULTIVATION

Propagation

Seeds do not germinate when soil temperatures are below 50°F. Better germination and earlier crops are achieved by sowing from midspring under cover in pots or packs. Plant 2–3 seeds 1 in. deep in pots of moist seed potting mix from mid- to late spring, at 55°F. After germination, thin to lcave the strongest seedling. Sweet corn is sensitive to root damage and disturbance, so thin with care, holding the strongest seedling while removing weaker ones.

Male sweet corn flowers

Harden off and plant out once there is no longer any danger of frost.

Plants should be 14 in. apart in and between the rows or spaced 10–12 in. apart in rows 24 in. apart.

To avoid erratic germination, seeds can be pregerminated. Put a few sheets of tissue paper or similar material in the bottom of a seed tray, moisten with water, place seeds evenly over the surface, cover with another layer of moist tissue. Put the tray in a loosely knotted plastic bag in an airing cupboard or warm room. When the seeds swell and tiny rootlets have formed, sow a single seed 1 in. deep in a 3½-in. pot of seed potting mix or sow singly outdoors. Sow a few in pots to replace those that do not germinate outdoors.

Alternatively, sow in situ from late spring to early summer. When the soil is workable, make a block about 48–60 in. comprising 4 ridges of soil about 12 in. high with 14 in. between the top of each ridge. Hill-sow 2–3 seeds in the furrow 14 in. apart each way and thin to leave the strongest seedling.

Cut a square of thin polyethylene slightly larger than the block. Spread it over the furrows, dig a shallow trench around the edge, and weigh the edges down with soil to hold the cover in place. As the seedlings emerge, cut crosses in the cover so they can grow through, or remove it and hill up around the stem bases when plants are 18 in. high.

Alternatively, sow on a level seedbed and protect crops with frost fabric or cloches, which should be removed as soon as the plants become too large.

Supersweet varieties need slightly warmer conditions for germination; soils should be at a minimum of 55°F. Because sweet corn is wind-pollinated, plants are sown

Flower corn, grown for its ornamental and practical value

in blocks for effective germination. The male tassels (flowers) at the top of the plant shed clouds of pollen onto the female tassels or "silks" below. These are clusters of pale green strands on the ends of the cobs which become sticky before pollination and each strand is attached to a single grain. Each must be pollinated, and sowing in a block ensures effective pollination. On a calm day tap the stems to help pollination. Mini varieties can be sown in rows. **Zones 4–10.**

Growing

Sweet corn needs a moisture-retentive, free-draining soil. Dig in plenty of organic matter several weeks before planting, or use ground manured for the previous year's crop. Ideally, the soil should be slightly acid with a pH of 5.5–7.0. Plants need a long, warm growing season to succeed, so grow fast-maturing, early cultivars in cooler zones. The site should be open, sunny, warm, and sheltered from cold winds and frosts.

Rake in a slow-release general fertilizer after transplanting or when preparing the seedbed.

Keep soil moist throughout the growing season. Watering is particularly beneficial when they begin to flower, and when the grains begin to swell. Apply 4 gallons/ sq. yd. per week.

Stake plants when growing on exposed sites.

Sweet corn is shallow-rooted, so take care when hoeing to avoid damaging the roots. It is much better to mulch with a layer of organic matter to suppress weeds and retain moisture. Mulch with black polyethylene on level ground. Do not remove sideshoots (tillers). Hill up to make plants more stable.

Maintenance

Spring Sow seed under cover or outdoors.
Summer Sow seeds; keep crops weed-free and water.
Harvest.
Fall Harvest.
Winter Prepare the ground for next year's crop.

Protected Cropping

When soil temperatures are below 50°F, sow from midspring under cover in pots or packs at 55°F. Harden off and plant out once there is no danger of frost.

Harvesting and Storing

Each plant usually produces one or two ears. Those sown in situ mature later than seed sown indoors.

When ears are ready to harvest, the "silks" wither and turn dark brown. Peel back the leaves and test for ripeness by pushing your thumbnail into a grain: if the liquid runs clear, it is unripe; if it is milky, it is ready to harvest; if it is thick, then it is overmature and unsuitable for eating. To pick, hold the main stem in one hand and twist off the ear with the other.

After pollination the silks begin to turn brown, an indication that the cob is maturing.

Eat or freeze within 24 hours of picking, before the sugars in the seeds convert to starch. Supersweet varieties hold their sugar levels longer.

To freeze, blanch ears for 4–6 minutes, cool and drain, before wrapping singly in foil or plastic wrap and placing in the freezer.

Ears remain fresh for up to 3 days if they are stored in the refrigerator.

Planting in blocks gives higher yields, as plants are wind-pollinated.

PESTS AND DISEASES

Birds can pull up the seedlings and attack the developing ears. **Slugs** attack seedlings. **Smut** appears as large galls on the cobs and stalks in hot dry weather. Cut off and burn immediately, or they will burst open and release a mass of black spores. Burn plants and debris after harvesting and do not grow sweet corn on the site for at least 3 years. **Fruit fly larvae** bore into the growing points of corn seedlings, which then develop twisted and ragged leaves. Growth is stunted and cobs are undersized. Use "treated" seed and rake a granular insecticide into the soil. **Mice** enjoy newly planted seeds, especially supersweet types. Trap, or get a cat.

A well-grown cob, packed full of mature seeds

COMPANION PLANTING

Grow sweet corn with or after legumes. Runner beans can be allowed to grow over sweet corn plants. Intercrop corn with sunflowers, allowing cucurbits to trail through them.

The shade they provide is useful to cucumbers, melons, squashes, zucchini, marrows, and potatoes. Brussels sprouts, kale, Savoy cabbages, rutabaga, and broccoli can be interplanted. Grow lettuce and other salads, string beans, and squash between the crops.

MEDICINAL

Corn is said to reduce the risk of certain cancers, heart disease, and dental cavities. Corn oil is reported to lower cholesterol levels more successfully than other polyunsaturated oils.

In parts of Mexico corn is used to treat dysentery. It is also known in American folk medicine as a diuretic and mild stimulant.

CULINARY

To serve whole, strip off outer leaves, leaving 2–3 in. of stalk on the ear. Pull off "silks." Boil in unsalted water, drain, and eat hot with melted butter.

Roasted corn is a favorite with most children—it tastes wonderfully succulent compared with the sogginess of canned corn.

Deep-fry spoonfuls of a mixture of mashed corn, salt, flour, milk, and egg for 1–2 minutes or until golden brown to make corn fritters.

Seeds are ground, meal boiled or baked, ears can be roasted or boiled or fermented, and maize meal is cooked with water to create a thick mash, or dough.

Tortillas are made by baking in flat cakes until they are crisp.

Dry-milling produces grits, from which most of the bran and germ are separated. Cornflakes are rolled, flavored seeds. Multicolored corn adds color and flavor to sweet dishes and drinks.

Baby corn is particularly decorative: the perfect size for Asian stir-fries, where they combine well with snap peas.

Polenta is made from ground maize.

Barbecued Corn

This is the way to really taste the flavor of corn. Take 1 corn ear for each person. Boil them in salted water for 7–10 minutes and then drain.

Place each in the center of a piece of foil. Use 1 tablespoon butter per corn ear and mix in 1 teaspoon fresh chopped herbs, sea salt, and freshly ground black pepper; spread over the corn ears. Season well and then seal the foil.

Lay the corn on a medium-hot charcoal grill and roast for 20 minutes, turning the cobs once halfway through cooking.

Corn Maque Choux
Serves 4

Cajun cooking has become popular in recent years and this dish reveals the true taste of corn.

1 tablespoon butter
1 large onion, roughly chopped
1 green bell pepper, seeded and diced
4 cups corn, cooked and stripped from the cob
2 tomatoes, peeled, seeded and diced
1/2 teaspoon tabasco sauce

Salt and freshly ground black pepper

Heat the butter in a heavy pan and sauté the onion until softened. Add the pepper and continue cooking for 3–4 minutes. Toss in the corn and the remaining ingredients and, over a low heat, simmer for 10 minutes. Adjust the seasoning and serve.

Succotash
Serves 4

The Native Americans made succotash, and many recipes still exist for it. 'Silver Queen' is a particularly good variety to use for this dish.

3–4 tablespoons unsalted butter
2 cups fava beans, cooked
3 or 4 ears roasted corn, husked

1 1/2 cups string beans, topped and tailed
1 medium red onion, finely chopped
1 cup vegetable stock
1/2 red bell pepper, finely diced
1 beef tomato, peeled, seeded, and chopped
Salt and freshly ground black pepper

Melt the butter in a heavy sauté pan and cook the fava beans, corn, string beans, and onion over a medium heat for about 3 minutes.

Then add the stock and continue cooking for 5 minutes before stirring in the remaining ingredients.

Taste for seasoning, mix thoroughly, and continue cooking for 5 minutes more. Serve hot.

Succotash

Agaricus bisporus and others

MUSHROOMS, EDIBLE FUNGI

Simple organisms growing on decaying substrate or symbiotically with living plants, some with edible fruiting bodies. Half hardy/tender. Value: low in calories, moderate potassium, linoleic and folic acid, carbohydrate, iron, niacin, and B vitamins.

Fungi are extraordinary organisms: lacking both chlorophyll and root systems, they are more akin to molds and yeasts than to traditional vegetable plants. The fleshy mushroom, or bracket, you eat is a fruiting body, dispersing spores in order to reproduce in the same way that plant fruits disperse seeds. Instead of drawing nutrients through roots, however, a fungus is sustained by a network of fine—often microscopic—threads (known collectively as the mycelium.) This can extend over vast distances into rotting wood, soil, or some other preferred medium. To help identify a fungus it is important to know the particular substrate on which it depends, or the higher plant species with which it lives in symbiosis (certain fungi, for example, grow only in the vicinity of specific trees such as birch or oak); when attempting to cultivate any kind of mushroom, you must provide similarly congenial conditions.

However, few of the many thousand fungus genera are amenable to cultivation. Even in nature, fruiting is wildly unpredictable: the organism depends on precise moisture and temperature variables to produce fruiting bodies, and more generally is sensitive to environmental changes such as recent air pollution and high nitrate levels.

Their erratic behavior and mysterious origins—allied with the deadly toxins some contain—have given rise to a "love-hate" attitude toward fungi. Some have been collected as "wild food" since ancient times. The Romans esteemed them as a delicacy and the rich employed collectors to find the most desirable species. However, Gerard, writing in his *Herball*, remained unimpressed: "few . . . are good to be eaten and most of them do suffocate and strangle the eater." John Evelyn advised that all types of mushrooms should be kept well out of the kitchen.

By the late seventeenth century, varieties of *Agaricus* began to be grown in underground caves in the Paris region, in which giant heaps of manure were impregnated with soil taken from areas where field and horse mushrooms grew naturally. For many centuries cultivated mushrooms were a delicacy enjoyed only by the wealthy, and from the eighteenth century most stableyards had a shady corner where there was a mushroom bed. Some garden owners had outhouses converted to provide ideal growing conditions: George IV had a large mushroom house at Kensington Palace in London. In seasons when wild or cultivated crops were plentiful, surplus mushrooms were conserved in the form of sauces and ketchups, and only recently has the role of mushroom sauce in the kitchen been usurped by tomato sauce.

Cultivated *Agaricus* species have remained popular in northern Europe and the English-speaking world, yet elsewhere they are eclipsed by other mushrooms. In Japan, velvet shank, nameko, oyster, and shiitake mushrooms are established as the cultivated varieties, and some of them are slowly becoming popular in other countries.

A number of species are commercially available, some of them to amateur growers, and usually work by inoculating the growing medium with mycelium or "spawn." Home growing of many fungus species is in its infancy, but gaining ground each year. As adventurous gardeners and mushroom eaters increasingly experiment, advances in mushroom cultivation will also help to conserve wild species.

Button mushroom growing in compost

Mushroom gathering has always had a strong following, from the Roman days to 19th-century Russia and France.

SPECIES

The following lists include several of the more common and better-known edible fungi.

Commonly available for home cultivation
These fungi are grown commercially and can occasionally be bought from specialist suppliers as kits, "spawn," or impregnated dowels for inoculating logs. A notable advantage of buying mushrooms in this form is that you are assured of their identity. You should follow suppliers' detailed cultivation instructions carefully to increase the chances of success. Some producers have their own selected strains of these fungi.

Agaricus bisporus (cultivated mushroom, champignon de Paris) has a smooth white to brownish cap and white stem and flesh. Excellent flavor raw and cooked. This accounts for 60 percent of the world's mushroom production. Available as kits or spawn (see "Cultivation"). Commercial growers are developing new races with color variation in the cap: watch out for them in the future as kits for amateur growers.

Flammulina velutipes (enoki, velvet shank, velvet foot, winter mushroom) occurs naturally on dead wood and is grown commercially on sawdust, particularly in Japan. Small tan-yellow caps on dark brown stems. Do not eat stems and wipe or peel off any stickiness from the caps before cooking.

Hericium erinaceus (lion's mane, monkey head) produces large, rounded clusters of icicle-like growths that taste like lobster— delicious fried with butter and onions. Grows in the wild from wounds on living hardwoods such as beech, and can be cultivated on stumps or logs.

Lentinula edodes*/*Lentinus edodes (shiitake) is a small to medium-sized mushroom with light brown stem and pale to dark reddish-brown cap. Documents record this strongly flavored gourmet mushroom being eaten in A.D. 199, and it is the second most important cultivated fungus. In Japan it is grown commercially on logs of chestnut, oak, or hornbeam. Different forms tolerate warmer or colder conditions, and include **'Snowcap,'** a thick-fleshed form with a long fruiting season, grown on large logs, and **'West Wind,'** which is ideal for inexperienced growers, yielding well over a long period.

Oyster mushrooms developing in a growing bag, India

Pholiota nameko (nameko, viscid mushroom) is among the four most important fungi cultivated in Japan. Grows in clusters on tree trunks or wood chips. Orange-brown caps atop paler stems are 2–3 in. in diameter. It is pleasantly aromatic.

Pleurotus (or oyster mushroom) is a genus with a number of distinct species and strains. Popular in Japan and central Europe, they are increasingly available in kit form, or can be grown from plugs of spawn. Eat when small, discarding the tough stem. Sauté in butter until tender, season, then add cream or yogurt. The first two are fairly common in the wild and are also offered in seed catalogs.

P. ostreatus (oyster mushroom) has large fan-shaped caps ranging in color from slate-blue to white and with white or pale straw-colored gills; used coffee grounds (sterilized as the coffee is brewed) are becoming a popular medium for inoculating with the spawn.

P. cornucopiae (golden oyster) has a white stem with a cream cap turning to ocher-brown. Grows on the cut stumps of deciduous trees, usually elm or oak. Other species may be harder to find, and some need warmth to fruit.

P. ergyngii (king pleurotus) has a concave cap, which is whitish to gray-brown. It tastes sweet and meaty and grows in clusters on the decaying roots of plants in the carrot family. It can be grown on chopped straw. ***P. flabellatus*** is an oyster mushroom with pink caps. ***P. pulmonarius*** has brown or gray caps. ***P. samoneus-tramineus*** from Asia is pink-capped. ***P. sajor-caju*** has brown caps.

Stropharia rugosoannulata (king stropharia) is a brown-capped, violet-gilled fungus commonly cultivated in Eastern Europe; it is claimed to be capable of growing in vegetable gardens. It requires a substrate of humus containing rotting hardwood or sawdust. Grow spawn from reputable sources: look-alikes include deadly *Cortinarius* species.

Volvariella volvaceae (Chinese or straw mushroom, paddy straw, padi-straw) has a gray-brown cap, often marked with black, and a dull brown stem. Grown on composted rice straw, it is regarded as an expensive delicacy in China and other Asian countries. Needs high temperatures and humidity to grow well. Harvest when it is immature.

Naturally occurring edible fungi
Many edible species of fungi may be found growing in your garden if it happens to provide the host trees or other conditions that form their natural habitat. In Continental Europe, fungi collected in the wild are often sold in markets; but local pharmacists or health inspectors are on hand to verify that those on sale are edible species.

NEVER EAT A FUNGUS UNLESS FIRST YOU HAVE HAD ITS IDENTITY CONFIRMED BY AN EXPERT.

Agaricus arvensis (horse mushroom) and ***A. campestris*** (field mushroom) are cousins of the cultivated mushroom, found in clusters or rings in grazed or mown grassland. Dome-shaped white "buttons" open to wide caps. Horse mushrooms can grow to soup-plate size with thick, firm flesh smelling of aniseed; the gills are pale grayish-pink darkening to chocolate-brown. Field mushrooms are smaller and rather more delicate in stature, with a "mushroomy" smell; their deep pink gills become dark brown to black at maturity.

Boletus edulis (cèpe, penny bun) grows on the ground near trees, favoring pine, beech, oak, and birch woodlands. The rounded, bunlike brown cap (often covered with a white bloom when young) sits on a bulbous whitish stem—also edible. Tubelike pores (rather than gills) beneath the cap are white, turning dull yellow at maturity. This delicious, fleshy fungus is highly prized in European markets and can be eaten fresh, pickled, or dried. Related species of *Boletus* are also edible.

Cantharellus cibarius (chanterelle) is funnel-shaped; egg yolk–yellow caps, fading with age, are thick and fleshy with gill-like wrinkles running down from the cap's underside and into the stem. Has a mild, peppery aftertaste when eaten raw; excellent flavor cooked. True chanterelles grow on soil in broad-leaved woodland: similar-looking species are highly toxic.

Oyster mushrooms growing on a tree trunk

Hirneola auricula judae, syn. *Auricularia auricula-judae* (Jew's ear, wood ear) looks like a human ear and is date-brown, drying to become small and hard. Found on living and dead elder, beech, and sycamore. Can be dried and reconstituted with water. Popular in Taiwan and China.

Hypholoma capnoides, syn. *Nematoloma capnoides,* is a gilled fungus found growing in clusters on conifer stumps. Caps ¾–2¼ in. diameter are pale ocher with buff-colored edges. Check identity carefully: other *Hypholoma* species are suspect.

Laetiporus sulphureus, syn. *Polyporus sulphureus* (chicken of the woods) is a bracket fungus found on many hardwoods and softwoods, often on sweet chestnut, oak, and beech. Has the flavor of chicken breast and is an orange to sulphur-yellow color. Eat young, but try only a little the first time: it can cause nausea and dizziness in some people. The largest ever found weighed 100 lb.

Langermannia gigantea (giant puffball) can be enormous: large and round with white skin, it sits on the ground like a giant soccer ball. The biggest ever recorded, according to the Guinness Book of Records, was 8 ft. 8 in. in circumference and weighed over 48 lb.! It is found on soil in fields, hedgerows, woodlands, and gardens, often near nettles. Eat when young, while the flesh is pure white; it tastes good sliced, dipped in bread crumbs, and fried. Other related (and smaller) species of puffball are also edible while they remain white all through.

Lepista nuda (blewit, wood blewit, blue-stalk) is medium to large with a light cinnamon-brown to tan cap; the gills and stems are violet

A basket of morel mushrooms

to lavender. It is found in woodlands, parks, and hedges. It can be grown in leaf debris around compost pile. Better eaten young, it is well flavored and particularly good in stews or fried. Never eat raw: cook thoroughly to remove traces of cyanic acid.

Marasmius oreades (fairy ring champignon) is found on lawns in a ring of dark green grass with dying grass in the center. Small with a bell-shaped light tan-colored cap, matching gills and similar stem. Good in omelets. Beware: similar looking species are toxic.

Morchella esculenta (common morel) is a delicious fungus that emerges annually in spring, earlier than most fall-fruiters. The hollow cap has a surface covered in honeycomb-like pits and varies from round to conical in shape. (The many crevices of the cap often harbor dirt and insects—preparing by rinsing in water is advised.) Found on well-drained soils under deciduous trees, particularly in ash and elm woods, in gardens and near old hedges. Other edible species include **M. rotunda,** found on heavier soil, and **M. vulgaris,** on richer soil. Some similar-looking mushroom species are highly toxic.

Sparassis crispa (cauliflower mushroom, brain fungus) has a folded, rounded fruiting body, creamy-white when young, which looks more like a cauliflower than a conventional mushroom. It tastes nutty, with a spicy fragrance. Found at the base of pines and other conifers. As with morels, rinse to remove any debris.

Tuber melanosporum (the Perigord or black truffle), often found in oak woods, is highly desirable and the most valuable truffle. Pigs and trained dogs are used to sniff them out. Commercial growers are now developing truffle-inoculated trees; several closely related species are also edible—I have yet to try them!

CULTIVATION
(of *Agaricus* species)

Propagation
With the traditional commercial methods, indoor crops of *Agaricus* species are more reliable than those grown outdoors. Make a large heap of stable manure, preferably at least 60 in. square, and moisten thoroughly. Cover until temperatures reach 140–160°F, turning once a week until it is crumbly and sweet-smelling. When it reaches that stage, fill boxes, buckets, containers, or trays with a 9–12 in. layer and firm. When the temperature falls to 75°F and the surface is ready for spawning, push golf ball–sized pieces about 1 in. under the surface 12 in. apart. After 2–3 weeks, white "threads" appear on the surface. Spread a 2 in. layer of "casing" made from 2 parts peat substitute to 1 part chalk or ground limestone over the surface and keep it moist. When mushrooms start to appear reduce the temperature to 50–65°.

Two types of spawn are available—fungus-impregnated manure (block spawn) or impregnated rye (grain spawn). Block spawn is easier to use.

Alternatively, buy a bucket or bag of ready-spawned compost or a fungi-growing pack. Do not buy kits that have been in store for a long time, and start the pack into growth within 3 weeks of buying it.
Zones 3–11.

Growing
"Cultivated" mushrooms can be grown inside or outdoors on the lawn or on a manure heap, though crops will be variable. Choose a shady position and enrich the ground with plenty of well-rotted organic matter. On a damp day in spring or fall, "plant" blocks of spawn, about the size of a golf ball, 2 in. below the soil and 12 in. apart. A good crop of mushrooms often appears when spent mushroom compost is used as a mulch around other crops.

Maintenance
Indoor crops can be planted any time of the year. Plant spawn outdoors in spring or fall.

Protected Cropping
Indoor crops grow well in an airy shed, cellar, greenhouse, or cold frame. They do not need to be grown in the dark.

Container Growing
See "Propagation."

Harvesting and Storing
The first "button" mushrooms are ready for harvesting 4–6 weeks after "casing"; it may be another 2 weeks before the next "flush." Harvesting lasts for about 6 weeks. To harvest, twist and pull mushrooms upward, disturbing the compost as little as possible, removing any broken stalks, and filling the holes with "casing."

Mushrooms last in a ventilated plastic bag in the crisper in the refrigerator for up to 3 days.

Most species can be dried. Thread them onto a string and hang them over a radiator or in an airing cupboard, then store in a cool dry place. Reconstitute with water or wine.

After the final harvest, you can use the spent mixture as a mulch; you should never try to respawn for a second crop.

PESTS AND DISEASES

Mushroom fly can be a problem; pick mushrooms when young.

Shiitake mushrooms

MEDICINAL

Edible fungi lower blood cholesterol, stimulate the immune system, and deactivate viruses. Shiitake mushrooms are particularly effective. Jew's ear has been used in herbal medicine for treating sore throats.

WARNING

If you gather wild mushrooms, be certain of their identity before eating. Best of all, collect with an expert. *Those that are highly toxic are often similar to edible species.* **Mistakes can be fatal.**

CULINARY

Fungi should always be eaten fresh as the flavor is soon lost and the quality deteriorates. Avoid washing most kinds: the fruit bodies absorb water, spoiling the texture and flavor. Simply clean the surface by wiping with a damp cloth or brushing off any dirt. Peel only when necessary.

Both caps and stems of *Agaricus* species can be eaten. With some other fungi, stems may be discarded as inedibly tough. Check for any special instructions on preparation: some fungi, for instance, are toxic unless cooked.

Harvested cultivated mushrooms at the "button" stage can be eaten raw, added to salads; more-mature caps can be baked, broiled, or fried whole, or sliced and stir-fried; made into soups, pies, or stuffings; added to stews or the stockpot; or used as a garnish. Other fungi can be prepared in many similar ways. Large fruit bodies can be stuffed.

Try frying in butter and a little lemon juice for 3–5 minutes. Brush with oil and seasoning and grill each side for 2–3 minutes. Add yogurt or cream before serving, or dip in bread crumbs and fry. Garlic mushrooms are especially delicious.

Mushroom Soup
Serves 4

This is particularly satisfying on a cold winter's day. Open-capped cultivated mushrooms make a good alternative to the wild variety.

3/4 stick butter
4 shallots, finely chopped
1 clove garlic, crushed
2 cups field mushrooms, cleaned and sliced
4 cups chicken stock
1 tablespoon all-purpose flour
Dash soy sauce
A little heavy cream
Salt and freshly ground black pepper

Heat half of the butter in a heavy bottomed pan and sauté the shallots until softened; add the garlic and cook for 1 minute more. Add the mushrooms and stir to coat well. Pour in the stock and bring to a boil. Season and cover, simmering for 10–15 minutes, until the mushrooms are cooked. Remove from the heat.

In a separate pan, heat the remaining butter and stir in the flour to make a roux. Cook for 2 minutes and remove from the stove. In a food processor, blend the roux with the soup (this may need to be done in two batches or more). Add the soy sauce and check the seasoning. Garnish with a little heavy cream and serve.

Mushroom Mélange

Grilled Shiitake Mushrooms
Serves 4

Allow 2 mushrooms per person for a first course to be served with Italian bread.

8–12 shiitake mushrooms
6 tablespoons olive oil
1 sprig rosemary
1 tablespoon fresh thyme leaves
2 tablespoons balsamic vinegar
2 tablespoons Barolo wine
1 small onion, finely chopped
4 slices toasted Italian bread
1 tablespoon butter
1 clove garlic, crushed
Salt and freshly ground black pepper

Wash the shiitakes, ensuring the gills are free from dirt. Discard the stems and add to a stockpot. Dry the caps.

Marinate the mushrooms in the oil, rosemary, thyme, vinegar, wine, onion, and seasoning for 30–45 minutes, turning them occasionally.

Broil under a preheated broiler for 5 minutes each side, brushing with the marinade juices. Serve on slices of toasted Italian bread, buttered and rubbed with garlic. Pour a little of the juices over each helping.

Mushroom Mélange
Serves 4

2 cups oyster mushrooms
2 cups shiitake mushrooms
4 tablespoons butter
2 cloves garlic, crushed
2 shallots, finely chopped
4 tablespoons white wine
1/2 cup heavy cream
4 tablespoons shredded Parmesan
Salt and freshly ground black pepper

Wash the mushrooms well and chop them, including the stalks. Melt the butter in a heavy saucepan, add the garlic and shallots, and allow to soften over a gentle heat. Add the mushrooms and stir well. Pour in the wine and the cream and bring to simmering point. Then cover and allow to stew for 15 minutes.

Pour into a greased baking dish, season with salt and pepper, and sprinkle with the Parmesan. Put under a preheated broiler on the highest setting for 3–5 minutes, until the cheese is melted. Serve immediately.

HERBS

Achillea ageratum

ENGLISH MACE

Also known as Sweet Nancy. From the family Asteraceae.

Native of Switzerland, now cultivated in northern temperate countries. This culinary herb is little known and underused.

English mace belongs to the *Achillea* genus, named after Achilles, who is said to have discovered the medicinal properties of the genus. There is no direct historical record of English mace itself apart from the fact it was discovered in Switzerland in 1798.

English mace in spring
Achillea ageratum

SPECIES

Achillea ageratum
English Mace
Hardy perennial.
Ht. 12–18 in. when in flower. Spread 12 in. Clusters of small cream flowers that look very Victorian in summer. Leaves brightish green, narrow, and very deeply serrated. **Zone 6**

CULTIVATION

Propagation
Seed
Sow seed eight weeks before frost. Harden off and plant outdoors when the weather is warm.

Cuttings
This is the best method for the propagation of a large number of plants. Take softwood cuttings in late summer and protect from wilting as they will be very soft. Use the bark-peat mix of potting mix (see p. 591). When well rooted, harden off and plant out in the garden 12 in. apart.

Division
If you require only a few plants it is best to propagate by division. Either divide the plant in early spring—it is one of the first to appear— or in fall. Replant in the garden in a prepared site. In Zones 5 and colder where mace is not hardy, winter plants in a cold frame or cold greenhouse.

Pests and Diseases
Mace, in most cases, is free from pests and disease.

Maintenance
Spring Divide established plants.
Summer Cut back flowers. Take softwood cuttings.
Fall Divide established plants if needed.
Winter Protect or bring inside if needed.

Garden Cultivation
This plant may flourish on heavy soil, but prefers a sunny, well-drained site. It starts the season off as a cluster of low-growing, deeply serrated leaves and then develops long, flowering stems in summer. Cut back after flowering for a fresh supply of leaves and to encourage a second flowering crop. In flower, this plant may need staking in a windy exposed site.

Harvesting
Cut fresh leaves when you wish. For freezing—the best method of preserving—cut before flowering and freeze in small containers.

Pick the flowers during the summer. Collect in small bunches and hang upside down to dry.

Both flowers and leaves dry particularly well.

CULINARY

The chopped leaves can be used to stuff chicken, flavor soups and stews, and sprinkle on potato salads, rice, and pasta dishes. The leaf has a mild, warm, aromatic flavor and combines well with other herbs.

Chicken with English Mace in Foil

Serves 4

4 chicken breasts
2 tablespoons yogurt
2 tablespoons Dijon mustard
Salt and fresh ground black
  pepper
Bouquet garni
Herb oil (or olive oil)
6 tablespoons of chopped
  English mace
Juice of 1 lemon

Preheat the oven to 375°F. Mix the yogurt and mustard together and coat the chicken pieces on all sides. Sprinkle with salt and pepper and herbs. Cut four pieces of foil and brush with herb oil or olive oil. Lay the chicken breasts in the foil and scatter a thick layer of English mace on each piece. Sprinkle with lemon juice. Wrap in the foil, folding the ends very tightly so no juices can escape. Lay the pockets on a rack in the oven, cook for 30 minutes. Serve with rice and a green salad.

OTHER USES

Flowers in dried flower arrangements.

CONTAINER GROWING

For a tall, flowering plant, a terra-cotta pot is most attractive. Make sure it has a wide base to allow for its height later in the season. Use the bark-peat-grit mix of potting soil (see p. 591).

Water regularly throughout the growing season and give liquid food (according to manufacturer's instructions) in the summer months during flowering. Cut back after flowering to stop the plant from toppling over and encourage new growth. As this plant dies back in winter, allow the potting mix to become nearly dry, and winter the container in a cold greenhouse or cold frame.

English mace
Achillea ageratum

Achillea millefolium

YARROW

Also known as Nosebleed, Millefoil, Thousand Leaf, Woundwort, Carpenter's Weed, Devil's Nettle, Mille Foil, Soldier's Woundwort, and Noble Yarrow. From the family Asteraceae.

Yarrow is found all over the world in vacant lots, fields, pastures, and meadows. It is common throughout North America, Europe, and Asia.

This is another very ancient herb. It was used by the Greeks to control hemorrhages, for which it is still prescribed in homeopathy and herbal medicine today. The legend of Achilles refers to this property—it was said that during the battle of Troy, Achilles healed many of his warriors with yarrow leaves. Hence the name, "Achillea."

It has long been considered a sacred herb. Yarrow stems were used by the Druids to divine seasonal weather. The ancient Chinese text of prophecy, *I Ching*, "The Book of Changes," states that 52 straight stalks of dried yarrow, of even length, were spilled to foretell the future instead of the modern way of using three coins.

It was also associated with magic. In Anglo-Saxon times it was said to have a potency against evil, and in France and Ireland it is one of the "Herbs of St. John." On St. John's Eve, the Irish hang it up in their houses to avert illness.

There is an old superstition, which apparently still lingers in remote parts of the United States and Britain, that if a young girl tickles her nostrils with sprays of yarrow and her nose starts to bleed, it proves her lover's fidelity:

"Yarrow away, Yarrow away, bear a white blow? If my lover loves me, my nose will bleed now."

Yarrow *Achillea millefolium*

SPECIES

Achillea millefolium
Yarrow
Hardy perennial. Ht. 1–3 ft., spread 2 ft. and more. Small white flowers with a hint of pink appear in flat clusters from summer to fall. Its specific name, *millefolium*, means "a thousand leaf."
Zone 2

**Achillea millefolium
'Fire King'**
Hardy perennial. Ht. and spread 24 in. Flat heads of rich, red, small flowers in flat clusters all summer. Masses of feathery dark green leaves. An upright habit and a vigorous grower.
Zone 2

Achillea 'Coronation Gold'
Hardy perennial. Ht. 3 ft., spread 2 ft. Large flat heads of small golden flower heads in summer that dry well for winter decoration. Masses of feathery silver leaves.
Zone 3

Achillea 'Moonshine'
Hardy perennial. Ht. 24 in., spread 20 in. Flat heads of bright yellow flowers throughout summer. Masses of small, feathery gray-green leaves.
Zone 3

CULTIVATION

Propagation
Seed

For reliable results sow the very small seed under cool protection in fall. Use either a proprietary seeder or the cardboard trick (see p. 591) and sow into prepared seed or plug trays. Leave the trays in a cool greenhouse for the winter. Germination is erratic. Harden off and plant out in the garden in spring. Plant 8–12 in. apart, remembering that it will spread. As this is an invasive plant, do not sow directly into the garden.

Division

Yarrow is a prolific grower, producing loads of creeping rootstock in a growing season. To stop the invasion, divide by digging up a clump and replanting where required in the spring or early fall.

Pests and Diseases

Yarrow is free from both.

Maintenance

Spring Divide established clumps.
Summer Deadhead flowers, and cut back after flowering to prevent self-seeding.
Fall Sow seeds. Divide established plants.
Winter No need for protection; very hardy plant.

Garden Cultivation

Yarrow is one of nature's survivors. Its creeping rootstock and ability to self-seed ensure its survival in most soils.

It does well in seaside gardens, as it is drought-tolerant. Still, owners of manicured lawns will know it as a nightmare weed that resists all attempts to eradicate it.

Yarrow is the plant doctor of the garden, its roots' secretions activating the disease resistance of nearby plants. It also intensifies the medicinal actions of other herbs and deepens their fragrance and flavor.

Harvesting

Cut the leaves and flowers for drying as the plant comes into flower.

CONTAINER GROWING

Yarrow itself does not grow well in containers. However, the hybrids, and certainly the shorter varieties, can look stunning. Use the bark-peat-grit mix of potting soil (see p. 591) and feed plants with liquid fertilizer during the flowering season, following the manufacturer's instructions. Cut back after flowering and keep watering to a minimum in winter. No variety is suitable for growing indoors.

Salad with Three Wild Herbs

CULINARY

The young leaves can be used in salads. Here is an interesting salad recipe:

Salad with Three Wild Herbs

Equal parts of yarrow, plantain, and watercress
A little garlic
$1/2$ cucumber
Freshly chopped or dried chives and parsley
1 medium, boiled cold potato
Salad dressing consisting of lemon and cream, or lemon and oil, or lemon and cream and a little apple juice

Select and clean herbs. Wash carefully and allow to drain. Cut the yarrow and plantain into fine strips. Cube cucumber and potato into small pieces. Leave watercress whole and arrange in bowl. Add herbs and other vegetables and salad dressing and mix well.

OTHER USES

Flower heads may be dried for winter decoration.

This unassuming plant harbors great powers. One small leaf will speed decomposition of a wheelbarrow full of raw compost.

Infuse to make a copper fertilizer.

WARNING

Yarrow should always be taken in moderation and never for long periods because it may cause skin irritation. It should not be taken by pregnant women. Large doses produce headaches and vertigo.

MEDICINAL

Yarrow is one of the best known herbal remedies for fevers. Used as a hot infusion it will induce sweats that cool fevers and expel toxins. In China, yarrow is used fresh as a poultice for healing wounds. It can also be made into a decoction for wounds, chapped skin, and rashes, and as a mouthwash for

Aconitum napellus

MONKSHOOD

Also known as Friar's Cap, Old Woman's Night-cap, Chariots Drawn by Doves, Blue Rocket, Wolf's Bane, and Mazbane. From the family Ranunculaceae.

Various species of monkshood grow in temperate regions. They can be found on shady banks, in deciduous woodlands, and in mountainous districts. They are all poisonous plants.

One theory for the generic name, *Aconitum*, is that the name comes from the Greek *akoniton*, meaning "dart." This is because the juice of the plant was used to poison arrow tips and was used as such by the Arabs and ancient Chinese. Its specific name, *napellus*, means "little turnip," a reference to the shape of the root. It was the name used by Theophrastus, the Greek botanist (370–285 B.C.), for a poisonous plant.

This plant has been known throughout history to kill both animals and humans. In the 16th century Gerard commented in his *Herball* on its "fair and good bluey flowers in shape like helmet which are so beautiful that man would think they were of some excellent virtue." Appearances should not be trusted. In the 1700s, Miller in his garden dictionary wrote, "Monks Hood was in almost all old gardens and not to be put in the way of children less they should prejudice themselves therewith."

As late as 1993 a British flower seller had to be hospitalized after handling monkshood outside pubs in Salisbury and Southampton.

Monkshood *Aconitum napellus*

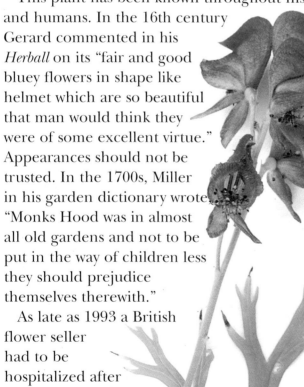

SPECIES

Aconitum napellus
Monkshood
Hardy perennial. Ht. 5 ft., spread 1 ft. Tall slender spires of hooded, light blue-indigo flowers in late summer. Leaves mid-green, palm-shaped, and deeply cut. There is a white-flowered version, *A. napellus* 'Albiflorus,' which grows in the same way. **Zone 4**

***Aconitum napellus* subsp. *napellus Anglicum* Group**
Monkshood
Hardy perennial. Ht. 5 ft., spread 1 ft. Tall slender spires of hooded, blue-lilac flowers in early- to mid-summer. Leaves mid-green, wedge-shaped, and deeply cut. One of a few plants peculiar to the British Isles, liking shade or half-shade along brooks and streams. Probably the most dangerous of all British plants.

Monkshood *Aconitum napellus* **growing with dill**

CULTIVATION

Propagation
Seed
Sow the small seed under protection either in the fall (which is best) or spring. Use prepared seed or plug trays. Cover with perlite. Germination can be erratic, an all-or-nothing affair. The seeds do not need heat to germinate. In spring, when the seedlings are large enough to handle, plant out into a prepared, shady site 12 in. apart. Wash your hands after handling the seedlings; even better, wear thin gloves. The plant takes 2–3 years to flower.

Division
Divide established plants throughout the fall, so long as the soil is workable. Replant in a prepared site in the garden—remember the gloves. You will notice when splitting the plant that the taproot puts out daughter roots with many rootlets. Remove and store in a warm dry place for planting out later.

Pests and Diseases
For obvious reasons this plant does not suffer from pests, and it is usually disease free.

Maintenance
Spring Plant out fall-grown seedlings.
Summer Cut back after flowering.
Fall Sow seeds, divide established plants.
Winter No need to protect. Fully hardy.

Garden Cultivation
In spite of the dire warnings this is a most attractive plant, which is hardy and thrives in most good soils.
  Position it so that it is not accessible. Plant at the back of borders, or under trees where no animals can eat it or young fingers fiddle with it. It is useful for planting in the shade of trees as long as they are not too dense.
  It is important always to teach people which plants are harmful, and which plants are edible. If you remove all poisonous plants from the garden, people will not learn which to respect.

Harvesting
Unless you are a qualified herbalist I do not recommend harvesting.

CONTAINER GROWING

Because of its poisonous nature, I cannot whole-heartedly recommend that it be grown in containers. But if you know you can control the situation, it does look very attractive in a large container surrounded by Heartsease (*Viola tricolor*). Use the bark-peat-grit mix of potting soil (see p. 591), water regularly throughout the summer months. Liquid feed in summer only.

WARNING

The symptoms of *Aconitum* poisoning are a burning sensation on the tongue, vomiting, abdominal pains, and diarrhea, leading to paralysis and death. Emergency antidotes, which are obtainable from hospitals, are atropine and strophanthin.

MEDICINAL

Aconitum is one of the most potent nerve poisons in the plant kingdom and is contained in analgesic medicines to alleviate pain both internally and externally. These drugs can only be prescribed by qualified medical practitioners. Tinctures of monkshood are frequently used in homeopathy.
  Under no circumstances should monkshood ever be prepared and used for self-medication.

CULINARY

None.

Agastache foeniculum

ANISE HYSSOP

Also known as Giant Hyssop, Blue Giant Hyssop, Fennel Hyssop, Fragrant Giant Hyssop. From the family Lamiaceae.

Anise hyssop is a native of North America, the mosquito plant and *A. mexicana* come from Mexico, and *A. rugosa* is from Korea.

There are few references to the history of this lovely herb. According to Allen Paterson, Director of the Royal Botanical Garden in Ontario, it is a close cousin of the bergamots. It is common in North American herb gardens and is certainly worth including in any herb garden for its flowers and scent. The long spikes of purple or lilac flowers are big attractions for bees and butterflies.

SPECIES

Agastache cana
Mosquito Plant
Half-hardy perennial. Ht. 2 ft., spread 1 ft. Pink tubular flowers in the summer with aromatic oval mid-green toothed leaves.
Zone 8

Agastache mexicana
Mexican Giant Hyssop
Half-hardy perennial. Ht. 3 ft., spread 1 ft. In summer whorls of small tubular flowers in shades from pink to crimson. Leaves oval pointed, toothed and mid-green with a eucalyptus scent.
Zone 8

Agastache rugosa
Korean Mint
Hardy perennial. Ht. 3 ft., spread 1 ft. Lovely mauve-purple flower spikes in summer. Distinctly minty scented mid-green oval pointed leaves.
Zone 5

Anise hyssop
Agastache foeniculum

Agastache foeniculum
Anise Hyssop
Hardy perennial. Ht. 2 ft., spread 1 ft. Long purple flower spikes in summer. Aniseed-scented mid-green oval leaves.

CONTAINER GROWING

Not suitable for growing indoors. However, anise hyssop and Korean mint both make good patio plants provided the container is at least 10–12 in. diameter. Use the bark-peat mix of potting soil (see p. 591), and a liquid fertilizer only once a year after flowering. If you feed the plant beforehand, the flowers will be poor. Keep well watered in summer.

CULTIVATION

Propagation

Note: *A. mexicana* can be propagated only by cuttings.

Seed

The small, fine seeds need warmth to germinate: 65°F. Use the cardboard method and artificial heating if sowing in early spring.

Use either prepared seed or plug trays or, if you have only a few seeds, directly into a pot and cover with perlite. Germination takes 10–20 days.

One can also sow outside in the fall when the soil is warm, but the young plants will need protection throughout the winter months.

When the seedlings are large enough to handle, plant in a larger pot using a bark or peat mix of potting soil. In mid-spring, when air and soil temperatures have risen, plant out at a distance of 18 in.

Cuttings

Take cuttings of soft young shoots in spring, when all the species root well. Use 50 percent bark, 50 percent peat mix of potting soil. After a full period of weaning, cuttings should be strong enough to plant out in the early fall.

Semiripe wood cuttings may be taken in late summer; use the same compost mix. After they have rooted, pot them, and winter in a cold frame or cold greenhouse.

Division

This is a good alternative way to maintain a short-lived perennial. In the second or third year divide the creeping roots either by the "forks back-to-back" method, or by digging up the whole plant and dividing.

Pests and Diseases

Since this is an aromatic plant, pests keep their distance. Rarely suffers from disease, although seedlings can **damp off.**

Maintenance

Spring Sow seeds.
Summer Take softwood or semiripe cuttings late season.
Fall Tidy up the plants by cutting back the old flower heads and woody growth. Sow seeds. Protect young plants from frost.
Winter Protect half-hardy species or bring them indoors.

Garden Cultivation

All species like a rich, moist soil and full sun, and will adapt very well to most ordinary soils if planted in a sunny situation. Anise hyssop self-sows readily and can be weedy in the garden.

Anise hyssop, although hardier than the other species, still needs protection below 20°F.

The Mexican half-hardy species needs protection below 26°F.

Harvesting

Flowers

Cut for drying just as they begin to open.

Leaves

Cut leaves just before late spring flowering.

Seeds

Heads turn brown as the seed ripens. At the first sign of the seed falling, pick and hang upside down with a paper bag tied over the heads.

OTHER USES

Anise hyssop, Korean mint, and Mexican giant hyssop all have scented leaves, which makes them suitable for potpourris.

Korean mint tea

Summer fruit cup made with anise hyssop

CULINARY

The two varieties most suitable are:

Anise Hyssop

Leaves can be used in salads and to make refreshing tea. Like borage, they can be added to summer fruit cups. They can also be chopped and used as a seasoning in pork dishes or in savory rice.

Flowers can be added to fruit salads and cups, giving a lovely splash of color.

Korean Mint

Leaves have a strong peppermint flavor and make a very refreshing tea, said to be good first thing in the morning after a night on the town. They are also good chopped up in salads, and the flowers look very attractive scattered over a pasta salad.

Alchemilla mollis

LADY'S MANTLE

From the family Rosaceae.

Lady's mantle is a native of the mountains of America, Europe, and Asia. It is found not only in damp places but also in dry shady woods.

The Arab *alkemelych* ("alchemy") is thought to be the source of the herb's Latin generic name, *Alchemilla*. The crystal dew lying in perfect pearl drops on the leaves has long inspired poets and alchemists, and was reputed to have healing and magical properties, even to preserve a woman's youth provided she collected the dew in May, in full moonlight, alone, naked, and with bare feet as a sign of purity and to ward off any lurking forces.

In the medieval period it was dedicated to the Virgin Mary, hence lady's mantle was considered a woman's protector, nicknamed "a woman's best friend," and was used not only to regulate the menstrual cycle and to ease the effects of menopause, but also to reduce inflammation of the female organs. In the eighteenth century, women applied the leaves to their breasts to make them recover shape after they had been swelled with milk.

It is still prescribed by herbalists today.

Lady's mantle *Alchemilla mollis*

Alchemilla conjuncta
Lady's Mantle Conjuncta Hardy perennial. Ht. 12 in., spread 12 in. or more. Tiny, greenish-yellow flowers in summer. Leaves star-shaped, bright green on top with lovely silky silver hairs underneath. An attractive plant suitable for ground cover, rock gardens, and dry banks. **Zone 3**

SPECIES

Alchemilla alpina L.
Alpine Lady's Mantle Known in the U.S. as Silvery Lady's Mantle. Hardy perennial. Ht. 6 in., spread 24 in. or more. Tiny, greenish-yellow flowers in summer. Leaves rounded, lobed, pale green, and covered in silky hairs. An attractive plant suitable for ground cover, rock gardens, and dry banks. **Zone 3**

Alchemilla mollis
Lady's Mantle (garden variety) Hardy perennial. Ht. and spread 20 in. Tiny, greenish-yellow flowers in summer. Large, pale green, rounded leaves with crinkled edges. **Zone 3**

Alchemilla xanthochlora (vulgaris)
Lady's Mantle (Wild flower variety) Also known as lion's foot, bear's foot, and nine hooks. Hardy perennial. Ht. 6–18 in., spread 20 in. Tiny, bright, greenish-yellow flowers in summer. Round, pale green leaves with crinkled edges. **Zone 3**

CULTIVATION

Propagation
Seed
Why is it that something that self-seeds readily around the garden can be so difficult to raise from seed? Sow its very fine seed in early spring or fall into prepared seed or plug trays (use the cardboard method), and cover with perlite. No bottom heat required. Germination can be either sparse or prolific, taking 2–3 weeks. If germinating in the fall, winter seedlings in the trays and plant out the following spring when the frosts are over, at a distance of 18 in. apart.

Division
All established plants can be divided in the spring or fall. Replant in the garden where desired.

Pests and Diseases
This plant rarely suffers from pests or disease.

Maintenance
Spring Divide established plants. Sow seeds if necessary.
Summer To prevent self-seeding, cut off flower heads as they begin to die back.
Fall Divide established plants if necessary. Sow seed.
Winter No need for protection.

Garden Cultivation
This fully hardy plant grows in all but boggy soils, in sun or partial shade. Seed can be sown in spring where you want the plant to flower. Thin the seedlings to 12 in. apart.
This is a most attractive garden plant in borders or as an edging plant, but it can become a bit of a nuisance, seeding everywhere. To prevent this, cut back after flowering and at the same time cut back old growth.

Early morning dew on
Alchemilla mollis

Harvesting
Cut young leaves after the dew has dried for use throughout the summer. Harvest for drying as plant comes into flower.

CONTAINER GROWING

All forms of lady's mantle adapt to container growing and look very pretty indeed. Use a soil-based potting mix, water throughout the summer, but feed with liquid fertilizer (following manufacturer's instructions) only occasionally. In the winter, the plant dies back; put the container in a cold greenhouse or cold frame, and water only very occasionally. Divide and repot every spring.

MEDICINAL

Used by herbalists for menstrual disorders. It has been said that if you drink an infusion of green parts of the plant for ten days each month it will help relieve menopausal discomfort. It can also be used as a mouth rinse after tooth extraction. Traditionally, the alpine species has been considered more effective, although this is not proven.

CULINARY

Tear young leaves, with their mild bitter taste, into small pieces and toss into salads. Many years ago I heard of a yogurt made with lady's mantle leaves! I wish I had tried it.

OTHER USES
Excellent for flower arranging.
Leaves can be boiled for pale green wool dye and are used in veterinary medicine for diarrhea.

Leaves laid out for drying

Allium

WELSH AND TREE ONIONS

From the family Alliaceae.

These plants are widely distributed throughout the world. The onion has been in cultivation so long that its country of origin is now uncertain, although most agree that it came from Central Asia. The Romans brought it to Europe. The name seems to have been derived from the Latin word *unio*, "a large pearl." In the Middle Ages it was believed that a bunch of onions hung outside the door would absorb the infection of the plague, saving the inhabitants. From this came the scientific recognition that its sulphur content acts as a strong disinfectant. The juice of the onion was used to heal gunshot wounds.

SPECIES

There are many, many varieties of onion (see p. 16); the following information concerns the two that have herbal qualities.

Allium fistulosum
Welsh Onion
Evergreen hardy perennial. Ht. 2–3 ft. Flowers on second year's growth greenish-yellow in early summer. Leaves, green hollow cylinders. This onion is a native of Siberia and extensively grown in China and Japan. The name Welsh comes from "walsch," meaning foreign. **Zone 5**

Welsh onion *Allium fistulosum*

Allium cepa **Proliferum Group**
Tree Onion
Also known as Egyptian Onion, Lazy Man's Onion. Hardy perennial. Ht. 3–5 ft. Small greenish-white flowers appear in early summer. It grows bulbs underground and then, at the end of flowering, bulbs in the air. Seeing is believing. It originates from Canada. It is very easy to propagate. **Zone 5**

CULTIVATION

Propagation
Seed
Welsh onion seed loses its viability within two years, so sow the seed fresh in late winter or early spring under protection, providing a bottom heat of between 60° and 70°F. Cover with perlite.

When the seedlings are large enough, and after a period of hardening off, plant out into a prepared site in the garden at a distance of 9 in. apart.

The tree onion is not grown from seed.

Division
Each year the Welsh onion will multiply in clumps, so it is a good idea to divide them every three years in the spring.

Because the tree onion is such a big grower, it is a good idea to split the underground bulbs every three years in the spring.

Bulbs
The air-growing bulbils of the tree onion have small root systems, each one capable of reproducing another plant. Plant where required in an enriched soil either in the fall, as the parent plant dies back, or in the spring.

Pests and Diseases
The **onion fly** is the curse of the onion family, especially in late spring, early summer. The way to try to prevent this is to take care not to damage the roots or leaves when thinning the seedlings and also not to leave the thinnings lying around, since the scent attracts the fly.

Another problem is **downy mildew** caused by cool, wet falls; the leaves become velvety and die back. Again, too warm a summer may encourage white rot. Burn the affected plants and do not plant in the same position again.

Other characteristic diseases are **neck rot** and **bulb rot**, both caused by a *Botrytis* fungus that usually occurs as a result of the bulbs being damaged either by digging or hoeing.

Onions are prone to many more diseases but if you keep the soil fertile and do not make life easy for the onion fly you will still have a good crop.

Maintenance

Spring Sow the seed and divide three-year-old clumps of Welsh and tree onions. Plant bulbs of tree onions.
Summer Stake mature tree onions to keep them from falling over and depositing the ripe bulbils on the soil.
Fall Mulch around tree onion plants with well-rotted manure. Use a small amount of manure around the Welsh onions.
Winter Neither variety needs protection.

Garden Cultivation

Welsh Onions
These highly adaptable hardy onions will grow in any well-drained fertile soil. Seeds can be sown in spring after the frosts, directly into the ground. Thin to a distance of 9 in. apart. Keep well watered throughout the growing season. In the fall give the area a mulch of well-rotted manure.

Tree Onions
Dig in some well-rotted manure before planting. Plant the bulbs in their clusters in a sunny, well-drained position at a distance of 12–18 in. apart.

In the first year nothing much will happen (unless you are one of the lucky ones). If the summer is very dry, water well.

In the following year, if you give the plant a good mulch of well-rotted manure in fall, it grows to 3–5 ft. and produces masses of small onions.

Harvesting

Welsh onions may be picked at any time from early summer onward. The leaves do not dry well but can be frozen like those of their cousin, chives. Use scissors and snip them into a plastic bag. They form neat rings; freeze them.

The little tree onions can be picked off the stems and stored; lay them out on a rack in a cool place with good ventilation.

CULINARY

Welsh onions make a great substitute for spring onions, as they are hardier and earlier. Pull and use in salads or stir-fry dishes, chop, and use instead of chives.

Tree onions provide fresh onion flavor throughout the year. The bulbils can be pickled or chopped raw in salads (fairly strong), or cooked whole in stews and casseroles.

Pissaladière
Serves 4–6

4 tablespoons olive oil (not extra virgin)
20 tree onions, finely chopped
1 clove garlic, crushed
1 teaspoon fresh thyme, chopped
Salt
Freshly ground black pepper
³/₄ lb. once-risen bread dough
¹/₂–1 cup ripe tomatoes, peeled and sliced
Canned anchovy fillets, drained and halved lengthways
16 large black olives, halved and pitted

Heat the olive oil in a heavy frying pan, add the onions, cover the pan tightly and fry, gently stirring occasionally for 15 minutes. Add the garlic and the thyme and cook uncovered for 15 minutes, or until the onions are reduced to a clear purée. Season to taste and leave to cool. Preheat the oven to 400°F. Roll the bread dough

Pissaladière

directly on a baking sheet into a circle 10 in. diameter. Spread the puréed onions evenly over the dough, put the tomato slices on the onions and top with a decorative pattern of anchovy fillets and olives.

Bake for 5 minutes. Reduce the oven temperature to 375°F and continue to bake for 30 minutes or until the bread base is well risen and lightly browned underneath.

Serve hot with a green herb salad.

OTHER USES

The onion is believed to help ward off colds in winter and also to induce sleep and cure indigestion. The fresh juice is antibiotic, diuretic, expectorant, antispasmodic, and so is useful in the treatment of coughs, colds, bronchitis, laryngitis, and gastroenteritis. It is also said to lower the blood pressure and to help restore sexual potency that has been impaired by illness or mental stress.

CONTAINER GROWING

Welsh onions can be grown in a large pot using a soil-based potting mix, and making sure it does not dry out. Feed regularly throughout the summer with a liquid fertilizer.

Tree onions grow too tall for containers.

Allium schoenoprasum

CHIVES

From the family Alliaceae.

Chives are the only member of the onion group found wild in North America, Europe, and Australia, where they thrive in temperate and warm-to-hot regions. Although one of the most ancient of all herbs, chives were not cultivated in European gardens until the sixteenth century.

Chives were a favorite in China as long ago as 3000 B.C. They were enjoyed for their delicious mild onion flavor and used as an antidote to poison and to stop bleeding. Their culinary virtues were first reported to the West by the explorer and traveler Marco Polo. During the Middle Ages they were sometimes known as rush-leeks, from the Greek *schoinos* meaning "rush" and *parson* meaning "leek."

Chives *Allium schoenoprasum*

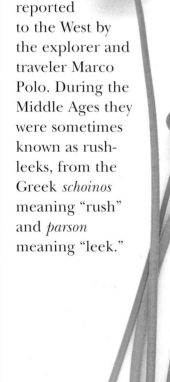

Chives
Allium schoenoprasum

SPECIES

Allium schoenoprasum
Chives
Hardy perennial. Ht. 12 in., spread 18 in. Purple globular flowers early summer. Leaves green and cylindrical. A good culinary herb.
Zone 3

Allium schoenoprasum
fine-leaved
Extra Fine-Leaved Chives
Hardy perennial. Ht. 8 in., spread 12 in. Purple globular flowers early summer. Very narrow cylindrical leaves. Good for culinary usage.
Zone 3

Allium schoenoprasum **white**
White Chives
Hardy perennial. Ht. 8 in., spread 12 in. White globular flowers early summer. Cylindrical green leaves. Effective in a silver garden. Good flavor.
Zone 3

Allium schoenoprasum
'Forescate'
Pink Chives
Hardy perennial. Ht. 8 in., spread 12 in. Pink flowers early summer. Cylindrical green leaves. A cultivar of ordinary chives, its pink flowers can look a bit insipid if planted too close to the purple-flowered variety. Good in flower arrangements.
Zone 3

Garlic chive flower
Allium tuberosum

Allium tuberosum
Garlic Chives (Chinese Chives)
Hardy perennial. Ht. 16 in. White flowers late summer. Leaf mid-green, flat, and solid with a sweet garlic flavor when young. As they get older the leaves become tougher
Zone 3

CULTIVATION

Propagation
Seed
Easy from seed, but they need a temperature of 65°F to germinate, so if sowing outside, wait until late spring for the soil to be warm enough. I recommend starting this plant in plug trays with bottom heat in early spring. Sow about 10–15 seeds per 1 in. cell. Transplant either into pots or into the garden when the soil has warmed.

Division
Every few years in the spring lift clumps (made up of small bulbs) and replant in 6–10-bulb clumps, 6 in. apart, adding fresh compost or manure.

Pests and Diseases
Aphids may be a problem on pot-grown herbs. Wash off gently under the tap or use a liquid horticultural soap. Be diligent, for aphids can hide deep down among the bulbs.

Cool wet falls may produce **downy mildew**; the leaves will become velvety and die back from the tips. Dig up, split, and repot affected plants, at the same time cutting back all the growth to prevent the disease spreading.

Chives can also suffer from **rust**. As this is a serious fungus it is essential to cut back diseased growth immediately and burn it. *Do not compost.* If very bad, remove the plant and burn it all. Do not plant any rust-prone plants in that area.

Maintenance
Spring Clear soil around emerging established plants. Feed with liquid fertilizer. Sow seeds.
Summer Cut back after flowering to encourage new leaf growth.

Fall Prepare soil for next year's crop. Dig up a small clump, pot, and bring inside for forcing.
Winter Cut forced chives and feed regularly.

Garden Cultivation
Chives are fairly tolerant regarding soil and position, but produce the best growth planted 6 in. from other plants in a rich, moist soil and in a fairly sunny position. If the soil is poor they will turn yellow and then brown at the tips. For an attractive edging, plant at a distance of 4 in. and allow to flower. Keep newly transplanted plants well watered in the spring, and in the summer make sure that they do not dry out, otherwise the leaves will quickly shrivel. Chives die right back into the ground in winter, but a winter cutting can be forced by digging up a clump in fall, potting it into a rich mix of potting soil (bark, peat mix, see p. 591), and placing it somewhere warm with good light.

Harvesting
Chives may be cut to within 1 in. of the ground four times a year to maintain a supply of succulent fresh leaves. Chives do not dry well. Refrigerated leaves in a sealed plastic bag will retain crispness for seven days. Freeze chopped leaves in ice cubes for convenience.

Cut flowers when they are fully open before the color fades for use in salads and sauces.

MEDICINAL

The leaves are mildly antiseptic and when sprinkled onto food they stimulate the appetite and promote digestion.

CONTAINER GROWING

Chives grow well in pots or on a windowsill and flourish in a window box if partially shaded. They need regular watering and fertilizing to stay green and succulent. Remember too that, being bulbs, chives need some top growth for strengthening and regeneration, so do not cut away all the leaves if you wish to use them next season. Allow to die back in winter if you want to use it the following spring. A good patio plant, easy to grow, but needs division and repotting each spring.

CULINARY

Add chives at the end of cooking or the flavor will disappear. They are delicious freshly picked and snipped as a garnish or flavor in omelettes or scrambled eggs, salads, and soups. They can be mashed into soft cheeses or sprinkled onto broiled meats. Add to sour cream as a filling for baked potatoes.

COMPANION PLANTING

Chives planted next to apple trees prevent scab, and when planted next to roses can prevent black spot. Hence the saying "Chives next to roses creates posies."

OTHER USES

Chives are said to prevent scab infection on animals.

Chive Butter
Use in scrambled eggs, omelettes, and cooked vegetables and with broiled lamb or fish or on baked potatoes.

1/2 cup butter
4 tablespoons chopped chives
1 tablespoon lemon juice
Salt and pepper

Cream the chives and softened butter together until well mixed. Beat in the lemon juice and season to taste. Cover and cool the butter in the refrigerator until ready to use; it will keep for several days.

Ajuga reptans

AJUGA

Also known as Bugle, Bugle Weed, Babies' Shoes, Baby's Rattle, Blind Man's Hand, Carpenter's Herb, Dead Men's Bellows, Horse and Hounds, Nelson's Bugle, Thunder and Lightning, and Middle Comfrey. From the family Lamiaceae.

A native of Europe, ajuga has naturalized as a lawn weed in parts of North America. It is frequently found in mountainous areas and often grows in damp fields, mixed woodland, and meadows.

Among the many folk tales associated with bugle is the idea that its flowers can cause a fire if brought into the house, a belief that has survived in at least one district of Germany.

SPECIES

Ajuga reptans
Bugle
Hardy evergreen perennial. Ht. 1 ft., spread up to 3 ft. Very good spreading plant. Blue flowers from spring to summer. Oval leaves are dark green with purplish tinge. It is this plant that has medicinal properties.
Zone 3

Ajuga reptans 'Atropurpurea'
Bronze Bugle
Hardy evergreen perennial. Ht. 6 in., spread 3 ft. Blue flowers. Deep bronze-purple leaves. Very good for ground cover.
Zone 3

Ajuga reptans 'Multicolor'
Multicolored Bugle
As *Ajuga reptans*, but ht. 5 in., spread 18 in. Small spikes of blue flowers. Dark green leaves marked with cream and pink. **Zone 3**

CULTIVATION

Propagation
Seeds
Sow the small seed in fall, or spring as a second choice. Cover only lightly with soil. Germination can be slow and erratic.

Division
Ajuga produces runners, each having its own root system. Plant out in fall or spring. Space 2 ft. apart, as a single plant spreads, or 12 in. apart for rapid ground cover.

Pests and Diseases
Nothing much disturbs this plant!

Maintenance
Spring Clear winter debris around established plants. Dig up runners and replant in other areas. Sow seeds.
Summer Control established plants by digging up runners.
Fall Sow seed, dig up runners of established plants, repot using the bark-peat potting mix, and winter in a cold frame, or replant in the garden.
Winter No protection needed.

Garden Cultivation
At close quarters ajuga is very appealing and can be used as a decorative ground cover. It will grow vigorously on any soil that retains moisture, in full sun, and it also tolerates quite dense shade. It will even thrive in a damp boggy area near a pond or in a hedgerow or shady woodland area. Guard against leaf scorch on the variegated variety by growing it in part shade.

Harvesting
For medicinal usage the leaves and flowers are gathered in early summer.

CONTAINER GROWING

Ajuga makes a good outside container plant, especially the variegated and purple ones. Use the bark-peat mix of potting soil (see p. 591). Also good in hanging baskets.

CULINARY

The young shoots of *Ajuga reptans* can be mixed in salads to give you a different taste.

MEDICINAL

An infusion of dried leaves in boiling water is thought to lower blood pressure and to stop internal bleeding. Nowadays it is widely used in homeopathy in various preparations against throat irritation, especially in the case of mouth ulcers.

OTHER USES
In some countries it is gathered as cattle fodder.

SPECIES

Aloe vera
Aloe vera
Tender perennial. Grown outside: Ht. 2 ft., spread 2 ft. or more. Usually grown as a houseplant: Ht. 12 in. Succulent gray-green pointed foliage, from which eventually grows a flowering stem with bell-shaped yellow or orange flowers.
Zone 10

Aloe arborescens 'Frutescens'
Candelabra Plant
Tender perennial. Grown outside: Ht., spread 6 ft. Each stem is crowned by rosettes of long, blue-green leaves with toothed edges and cream stripes. Produces numerous spikes of red tubular flowers in late winter and spring.
Zone 10

Aloe variegata
Partridge-breasted Aloe
Tender perennial.
Ht. 12 in., spread 4 in. Triangular, white-marked, dark green leaves. Spike of pinkish-red flowers in spring.
Zone 10

CULTIVATION

Propagation
Seed
A temperature of 70°F must be maintained during germination. Sow onto the surface of a pot or tray and cover with perlite. Place in a propagator with bottom heat. Germination is erratic: 4–24 months.

Division
In summer gently remove offshoots at the base of a

Aloe vera

ALOE VERA

From the family Aloaceae.

There are between 250 and 350 species of aloe around the world. They are originally native to the arid areas of southern Africa. In cultivation they need a frost-free environment. Aloe has been valued at least since the fourth century B.C., when Aristotle requested that Alexander the Great conquer Socotra in the Indian Ocean, where many species grow.

mature plant. Leave for a day to dry, then pot into 2 parts potting soil to 1 part sharp sand mix. Water and leave in a warm place to establish. Give the parent plant a good liquid feed when returning to its pot.

Pests and Diseases
Overwatering causes rot.

Maintenance
Spring Give containerized plants a good cleaning! Spray the leaves with water. Give a good feed of liquid fertilizer.
Summer Remove the basal offshoots of a mature plant to maintain the parent plant. Repot offshoots if desired.
Fall Bring in pots when there is any danger of frost.
Winter Rest all pot-grown plants in a cool, bright room (minimum temperature 40°F); keep watering to the absolute minimum.

Garden Cultivation
Aloes enjoy a warm, frost-free position—full sun to partial shade—and a free-draining soil. Leave 3 ft. minimum between plants.

Harvesting
Cut leaves as needed, anytime. A plant of more than two years old has stronger properties.

CONTAINER GROWING

Soil mix must be gritty and well drained. Do not overwater. Maintain a frost-free, light environment.

Aloe vera

MEDICINAL

The gel obtained by breaking the leaves is a remarkable healer. Applied to wounds it forms a clear protective seal and encourages skin regeneration. It can be applied directly to cuts and burns, and is immediately soothing.

COSMETIC

Aloe vera is used in cosmetic preparations, in hand creams, suntan lotions, and shampoos.

WARNING

It should be emphasized that, apart from external application, aloes are not for home medication. *Always seek medical attention for serious burns.*

Aloysia triphylla (Lippia citriodora)

LEMON VERBENA

From the family Verbenaceae.

Lemon verbena grew originally in Chile. This crème de la crème of lemon-scented plants was first imported into Europe in the eighteenth century by the Spanish for its perfume.

SPECIES

Aloysia triphylla (Lippia citriodora)
Lemon Verbena
Tender deciduous shrub. Ht. 3–10 ft., spread up to 8 ft. Tiny white flowers tinged with lilac in early summer. Leaves pale green, lance-shaped and very strongly lemon scented.
Zone 8

CULTIVATION

Propagation
Seeds
The seed sets only in warm climates and should be sown in spring into prepared seed or plug trays and covered with perlite; a bottom heat of 60°F helps. Prick out into 3½ in. pots using the bark-peat-grit potting mix (see p. 591). Keep in pots for the first two years before planting specimens out in the garden 3 ft. apart.

Cuttings
Take softwood cuttings from the new growth in late spring. The cutting material will wilt quickly so have everything prepared.
Take semihardwood cuttings in late summer or early fall. Keep in pots for the first two years.

Pests and Diseases
If grown under protection you will have to contend with **whitefly** and **red spider mite**; spray both with a liquid horticultural soap.

Maintenance
Spring Trim established plants. Take softwood cuttings. In warm climates sow seed.
Summer Trim after flowering. Take semi-hardwood cuttings.
Fall Cut back, but not hard. Bring in before frosts.
Winter Protect all winter.

Garden Cultivation
Likes a warm, humid climate. The soil should be light, free draining, and warm. A sunny wall is ideal. It will need protection against frost, wind, and temperatures below 40°F. If left in the ground, cover the area around the roots with mulching material.
In spring give the plant a gentle prune and spray with warm water to help revive it. New growth can appear very late so never discard a plant until late summer. Once buds are evident, remove the dead tips and prune gently to encourage new growth. At the end of the growing season, cut the plant back again.

Harvesting
Pick the leaves any time before they start to wither and darken. Leaves dry very quickly and easily, keeping their color and scent. Store them in a damp-proof container.

CONTAINER GROWING

Choose a container at least 8 in. wide and use the bark-peat-grit mix of potting soil (see p. 591). Place the container in a warm, sunny, light, and airy spot. Water well throughout the growing season and feed with liquid fertilizer during flowering. Then trim the plant to maintain shape, and trim further during the fall. In winter move the container into a cold greenhouse, and allow the potting mix to nearly dry out.

MEDICINAL

A cup of tea made with the leaves is refreshing and has mild sedative properties; it can also soothe bronchial and nasal congestion and ease indigestion. However, long-term use may cause stomach irritation.

CULINARY

Use fresh leaves to flavor oil and vinegar, drinks, fruit puddings, confectionery, apple jelly, cakes, and stuffings. Infuse in finger bowls.
Add a teaspoon of chopped, fresh leaves to homemade ice cream for a delicious dessert.

OTHER USES

The leaves, with their strong lemon scent, are lovely in potpourris, linen sachets, and herb pillows. The distilled oil made from the leaves is an essential basic ingredient in many perfumes.

Althaea officinalis

MARSH MALLOW

Also known as Mortification Root, Sweet Weed, Wymote, Marsh Malice, Mesh-mellice, Wimote, and Althea. From the family Malvaceae.

Marsh mallow is widely distributed from North America to Australia, and from Western Europe to Siberia. It is common to find it in salt marshes and on banks near the ocean.

The generic name, *Althaea*, comes from the Latin *altheo*, meaning "I cure." It may be the althaea that Hippocrates recommended so highly for healing wounds. The Romans considered it a delicious vegetable and used it in barley soup and in stuffing for suckling pigs. In the Renaissance era the herbalists used marsh mallow to cure sore throats, upset stomach, and toothache.

Soft, sweet marshmallow was originally thickened with root of marsh mallow.

SPECIES

Althaea officinalis
Marsh Mallow
Hardy perennial. Ht. 2–4 ft., spread 2 ft. Flowers pink or white in summer. Leaves, gray-green in color, tear-shaped, and covered all over with soft hair. **Zone 3**

CULTIVATION

Propagation
Seed
Sow in prepared seed or plug trays in the fall.
Cover lightly with soil and winter outside under glass. Erratic germination takes place in spring. Plant out, 18 in. apart, when large enough to handle.

Division
Divide established plants in the spring or fall, replanting into a prepared site in the garden.

Pests and Diseases
This plant is usually free from pests and diseases.

Maintenance
Spring Divide established plants.
Summer Cut back after flowering for new growth.
Fall Sow seeds and winter the trays outside
Winter No need for protection. Fully hardy.

Garden Cultivation
Marsh mallow is highly attractive to butterflies. A good oceanside plant, it likes a site in full sun with a moist or wet, moderately fertile soil. Cut back after flowering to encourage new leaves.

Harvesting
Pick leaves for fresh use as required; they do not preserve well.
For use either fresh or dried, dig up the roots of two-year-old plants in fall, after the flowers and leaves have died back.

MEDICINAL

Due to its high mucilage content (35 percent in the root and 10 percent in the leaf), marsh mallow soothes or cures inflammation, ulceration of the stomach and small intestine, sore throat, and pain from cystitis. An infusion of leaves or flowers serves as a soothing gargle; an infusion of the root can be used for coughs, diarrhea, and insomnia.

The pulverized roots may be used as a healing and drawing poultice, which should be applied warm.

CULINARY

Boil the roots to soften, then peel and quickly fry in butter.
Use the flowers in salads, and leaves, too, which may also be added to oil and vinegar, or steamed and served as a vegetable.

DECOCTION FOR DRY HANDS

Soak 1 tablespoon of scraped and finely chopped root in 1 cup of cold water for 24 hours. Strain well. Add 1 tablespoon of the decoction to 2 tablespoons of ground almonds, 1 teaspoon of milk and 1 teaspoon of cider vinegar. Beat it until well blended. Add a few drops of lavender oil. Put into a small screw-top jar. Refrigerate.

Anethum graveolens

DILL

**Also known as Dillweed and Dillseed.
From the family Apiaceae.**

A native of southern Europe and western Asia, dill grows wild in Mediterranean countries and has escaped from gardens in parts of North and South America. The generic name *Anethum* derives from the Greek *Anethon*. *Dill* is said to come from the Anglo-Saxon *dylle* or the Norse *dilla*, meaning to soothe or lull. Dill was found among the names of herbs used by Egyptian doctors 5,000 years ago, and the remains of the plant have been found in the ruins of Roman buildings in Britain.

It is mentioned in the Gospel of St. Matthew, where it is suggested that herbs were of sufficient value to be used as a tax payment—if only that were true today! "Woe unto you, Scribes and Pharisees, hypocrites! for ye pay tithe of mint and dill and cumin, and have omitted the weightier matters of the law."

During the Middle Ages dill was prized as protection against witchcraft. While magicians used it in their spells, lesser mortals infused it in wine to enhance passion. It was once an important medicinal herb for treating coughs and headaches, an ingredient of ointments, and used for calming infants with whooping cough—dill water or "gripe water" is still called upon today. Early settlers took dill to North America, where it came to be known as the "Meeting House Seed," because the children were given it to chew during long sermons to keep them from feeling hungry.

SPECIES

Anethum graveolens
Dill
Annual. Ht. 2–5 ft., spread 12 in. Tiny yellow-green flowers in flattened umbel clusters in summer. Fine, aromatic, feathery green leaves.
All zones

Dill *Anethum graveolens*

CULTIVATION

Propagation
Seed
Seed can be started in early spring under cover, using pots or plug trays. Do not use seed trays, as it does not like being transplanted, and if it gets upset it will bolt and skip the leaf-producing stage.

The seeds are easy to handle, being a good size. Place four per plug or evenly spaced on the surface of a pot, and cover with perlite. Germination takes 2–4 weeks, depending on the warmth of the surrounding area. As soon as the seedlings are large enough to handle, the air and soil temperatures have started to rise, and there is no threat of frost, plant out 9 in. apart.

Garden Cultivation
Keep dill plants well away from fennel, otherwise they will cross-pollinate and their individual flavors will become muddled. Dill prefers a well-drained, poor soil in full sun. Sow mid-spring into shallow drills on a prepared site, where they will be harvested. Protect from wind. When the plants are large enough to handle, thin out to a distance of 8 in. to give plenty of room for growth. Make several small sowings in succession so that you have a supply of fresh leaves throughout the summer. The seed is viable for three years.

The plants are rather tippy, and it may be necessary to provide support. Twigs pushed into the ground around the plant and enclosed with string or raffia will give better results than attempting to stake each plant individually.

Where summers are hot, dill dies out by midsummer. Replant in early fall for a second crop that lasts until severe frost.

Pests and Diseases
Watch out for **aphids** in crowded conditions. Treat with a liquid horticultural soap if necessary. Be warned: **slugs** love dill plants.

Maintenance
Spring Sow the seeds successively for a leaf crop.
Summer Feed plants with a liquid fertilizer after cutting to promote new growth.
Fall (early) Harvest seeds.
Winter Dig up all remaining plants. Make sure all the seed heads have been removed before you compost the stalks, as the seed is viable for three years. If you leave the plants to self-seed they certainly will, and they will live up to their nickname dillweed.

Harvesting

Pick leaves fresh for eating at any time after the plant has reached maturity. Since it is quick-growing, this can be within 8 weeks of the first sowing.

Although leaves can be dried, great care is needed and it is better to concentrate on drying the seed for storage.

Cut the stalks off the flower heads when the seed is beginning to ripen. Put the seed heads upside down in a paper bag and tie the top of the bag. Put in a warm place for a week. The seeds should then separate easily from the husk when rubbed in the palm of the hand. Store in an airtight container and the seeds will keep their flavor very well.

CONTAINER GROWING

Dill can be grown in containers, in a sheltered corner with plenty of sun. However, it will need staking. The art of growing it successfully is to keep cutting the plant for use in the kitchen. That way you will promote new growth and keep the plant reasonably compact. The drawback is that it will be fairly short-lived, so you will have to do successive sowings in different pots to maintain a supply. I do not recommend growing dill indoors—it will get leggy, soft, and prone to disease.

MEDICINAL

Dill is an antispasmodic and calmative. Dill tea or water is a popular remedy for an upset stomach, hiccups, or insomnia; for nursing mothers to promote the flow of milk, and as an appetite stimulant. It is a constituent of gripe water and other children's medicines because of its ability to ease flatulence and colic.

CULINARY

Dill is a culinary herb that improves the appetite and digestion. The difference between dill leaf and dill seed lies in the degree of pungency. There are occasions when the seed is better because of its sharper flavor. It is used as a flavoring for soup, lamb stews, and broiled or boiled fish. It can also add spiciness to rice dishes, and be combined with white wine vinegar to make dill vinegar.

Dill leaf can be used generously in many dishes, as it enhances rather than dominates the flavor of food.

For dill pickles, before it sets seed, add one flower head to a jar of pickled gherkins, cucumbers, and cauliflowers for a flavor stronger than dill leaves but fresher than seeds.

Gravlax—the traditional Scandinavian dish of salmon and dill

Gravlax
Salmon marinated with dill

This is a traditional Scandinavian dish of great simplicity and great merit. Salmon treated in this way will keep for up to a week in the refrigerator.

1½–2 lb. salmon, middle cut or tail piece
1 heaped tablespoon sea salt
1 rounded tablespoon sugar
1 teaspoon crushed black peppercorns
1 tablespoon brandy (optional)
1 heaped tablespoon fresh dill

Have the salmon cleaned, scaled, bisected lengthwise and filleted. Mix remaining ingredients together and put some of the mixture into a flat dish (glass or enamel) large enough to take the salmon. Place one piece of salmon skin-side down on the bottom of the dish, spread more of the mixture over the cut side. Add the second piece of salmon, skin up, and pour the remaining mixture over it. Cover with foil and place a plate or wooden board larger than the area of the salmon on top. Weigh this down with weights or heavy cans. Put in the refrigerator for 36–72 hours. Turn the fish completely every 12 hours or so and baste (inside surfaces too) with the juices.

To serve, scrape off all the mixture, pat the fish dry, and slice thinly and at an angle. Serve with buttered rye bread and a mustard sauce called Gravlaxsas:

4 tablespoons mild, ready-made Dijon mustard
1 teaspoon mustard powder
1 tablespoon sugar
2 tablespoons white wine vinegar

Mix all the ingredients together, then slowly add 6 tablespoons of vegetable oil until you have a sauce the consistency of mayonnaise. Finally, stir in 3 to 4 tablespoons of chopped dill.

Alternatively, substitute a mustard and dill mayonnaise.

OTHER USES

Where a salt-free diet must be followed, the seed, whole or ground, is a valuable replacement. Try chewing the seeds to clear up halitosis and sweeten the breath. Crush and infuse seeds to make a nail-strengthening bath.

Dill vinegar

Angelica archangelica

ANGELICA

Also known as European Angelica, Garden Angelica, and Root of the Holy Ghost. From the family Apiaceae.

Angelica in its many forms is a native of North America, Europe, and Asia. It is also widely cultivated as a garden plant. Wild angelica is found in moist fields and hedgerows in the northeastern and north-central United States and in Canada.

Angelica probably comes from the Greek *angelos*, meaning "messenger." There is a legend that an angel revealed to a monk in a dream that the herb was a cure for the plague, and traditionally angelica was considered the most effective safeguard against evil, witchcraft in particular. Certainly it is a plant no self-respecting witch would include in her brew.

Angelica is an important flavoring agent in liqueurs such as Benedictine, although its unique flavor cannot be detected from the others used. It is also cultivated commercially for medicinal and cosmetic purposes.

SPECIES

Angelica archangelica
Angelica
Biennial and short-lived perennial (about 4 years). Ht. 3–8 ft., spread 3 ft. in second year. Dramatic second-year flower heads late spring through summer, greenish-white and very sweetly scented. Bright green leaves, the lower ones large and bi- or tri-pinnate; the higher, smaller and pinnate. Rootstock varies in color from pale yellowish beige to reddish-brown. **Zone 4**

Angelica sylvestris
Wild Angelica
Also known as Ground Ash, Jack Jump About, Water Kesh. Biennial. Ht. 4–5 ft. White flowers in summer often tinged with pink; smaller than flowers of *A. archangelica*. Lower leaves are large, pinnate, and sharply toothed. Stems often have a purple tinge. Rootstock is thick and gray on the outside.
Zone 7

Angelica atropurpurea
American Angelica (*left*)
Also known as Masterwort, Purple Angelica, and Wild Angelica. Biennial. Ht. 4–5 ft. Flowers resemble those of *A. archangelica*—white to greenish-white, late spring through summer. Leaves large and alternately compound. Rootstock purple. The whole plant delivers a powerful odor when fresh.
Zone 5

Angelica sinensis
Chinese Angelica
Also known as Dang Gui, Women's Ginseng.

CULTIVATION

Propagation
Seed
Angelica can only be grown from seed but, as it loses viability after 3 months, sow preferably when fresh, in the fall. (If for some reason this cannot be done, store in a refrigerator and sow in the spring.) As seedlings do not transplant well, sow in planting position and thin out all but the best plants once germination has occurred. If transplanting is unavoidable, do it when seedlings are small, before the taproots are established.

When planting out or thinning seedlings leave 3 ft. between plants.

If maintaining for another season, mark the spot, as the plant will die back fully during the winter.

If the plant has flowered and seeded, cut back and dig up roots. If you want thousands more angelicas compost the flower head; if not, dispose of it.

Pests and Diseases
Aphids can be removed easily with liquid horticultural soap.

Angelica in seed
Angelica archangelica

Maintenance

Spring Clear ground around existing plants. Plant out fall seedlings. Sow seed.

Summer Cut stems of second-year growth for crystallizing. Cut young leaves before flowering to use fresh in salads or to dry for medicinal or culinary uses. It cannot be stressed often enough that angelica needs plenty of water and if in summer the leaves turn a yellowish-green, it is usually a sign that the plant needs more water.

Fall Seed-sowing time.

Winter No need for protection.

Garden Cultivation

Angelica dislikes hot, humid climates and appreciates a spot in the garden where it can be in shade for some part of every day. But it can be a difficult plant to accommodate in a small garden, as it needs a lot of space. Site at the back of a border, perhaps near a wall where the plant structure can be appreciated. Make sure that the soil is deep and moist. Add well-rotted compost to help retain moisture. Note that angelica dies down completely in winter but green shoots appear quickly in the spring.

Angelica is a biennial plant forming a big clump of foliage in the first summer and dramatic flowers the second, dying after the seed is set. A plant will propagate itself in the same situation if allowed to self-seed. But by cutting back in the fall, and preventing the flower head from seeding, the same plant can be maintained as a short-lived perennial for approximately four years.

Harvesting

Harvest leaves for use fresh from spring onward; for drying, from early summer until flowering. Wild angelica is harvested in early fall.

Pick flowers in early summer for dried flower arrangements.

Collect seeds when they begin to ripen.

Harvest roots for use medicinally in the second fall immediately after flowering and dry.

CONTAINER GROWING

Angelica is definitely not an indoor plant, though if the container is large enough, it can be grown as such. Do not overfertilize and be prepared to stake when in flower. Be wary of the pot toppling over as the plant grows taller.

CULINARY

Young leaves of wild angelica can be used to season salads, and the seeds are used by confectioners in pastry.

Candied Angelica

Angelica is now best known as a decorative confectionery for cakes. Homemade, pale green candied angelica tastes and smells similar to the freshly bruised stem or crushed leaf of the plant.

Angelica stems
Granulated sugar
Water
Sugar for dusting

Choose young, tender, springtime shoots. Cut into 3–4 in. lengths. Place in a saucepan with just enough water to cover. Simmer until tender, then strain and peel off the outside skin. Put back into the pan with enough water to cover and bring to the boil, strain immediately, and allow to cool.

When cool, weigh the angelica stalks and add an equal weight of granulated sugar. Place the sugar and angelica in a covered dish and leave in a cool place for two days.

Put the angelica and the syrup which will have formed back into the pan. Bring slowly to a boil and simmer, stirring occasionally, until the angelica becomes clear and has good color.

Strain again, discarding all the liquid, then sprinkle as much sugar as will cling to the angelica.

Allow the stems to dry in a cool oven (200°F). If not thoroughly dry, they become moldy later.

Store in an airtight container between waxed paper.

Candied angelica

Stewed Fruit

The muscatel flavor of angelica cuts through the acidity of rhubarb or gooseberries.

6 cups rhubarb, in 1-in. pieces
1½ cups angelica stems, in 1-in. pieces
Juice and rind of 1 orange
½ cup water
¼ cup sugar

Place all ingredients in a saucepan, bring to a boil, and simmer for 1 minute (no more or it will turn mushy).

MEDICINAL

Angelica stimulates the circulation. It also has antibacterial and antifungal properties.

Young leaves can be made into a tea, the flavor resembling China tea. Drink last thing at night for reducing tension; also good for nervous headaches, indigestion, anemia, coughs, and colds. The tea made from the root is soothing for colds and other bronchial symptoms made worse by damp, cold conditions.

Externally it is used in bath preparations for exhaustion and rheumatic pain. Crushed leaves freshen the air in a car and help prevent travel sickness.

American angelica can be used much as you would its European relatives, but its most common use is medicinal, for heartburn and flatulence.

Chinese angelica is a blood tonic used in Chinese herbal prescriptions.

WARNING

Large doses first stimulate and then paralyze the central nervous system. The tea is not recommended for those suffering from diabetes. Wild angelica can also be used medicinally, though large doses have the effect of depressing the central nervous system.

Wild angelica resembles wild hemlock (*Conium maculatum*) and several other very poisonous plants. Beware.

Anthriscus cerefolium

CHERVIL

From the family Apiaceae.

Chervil *Anthriscus cerefolium*

Native to the Middle East, southern Russia, and the Caucasus. Cultivated in warm temperate climates where it is now occasionally found growing wild.

Almost certainly brought to Britain by the Romans, chervil is one of the Lenten herbs, thought to have blood-cleansing and restorative properties. It was eaten in quantity in Roman times, especially on Maundy Thursday.

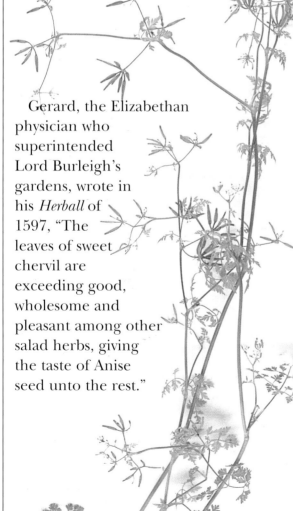

Gerard, the Elizabethan physician who superintended Lord Burleigh's gardens, wrote in his *Herball* of 1597, "The leaves of sweet chervil are exceeding good, wholesome and pleasant among other salad herbs, giving the taste of Anise seed unto the rest."

SPECIES

Anthriscus cerefolium
Chervil
Hardy annual (some consider it to be a biennial). Ht. 1–2 ft., spread 12 in. Flowers, tiny and white, grow in clusters from spring to summer. Leaves, light green and fernlike, in late summer may take on a purple tinge. When young it can easily be confused with several other plants, some of which are poisonous. Be sure to identify it before tasting it.
All zones

Anthriscus cerefolium crispum
Curly-leafed Chervil
Hardy annual. Grows like the ordinary chervil except that, in my opinion, the leaf has an inferior flavor.
All zones

CULTIVATION

Propagation
Seed
The medium-size seed germinates rapidly as the air and soil temperatures rise in the spring, provided the seed is fresh (it loses viability after about a year). Young plants are ready for cutting 6–8 weeks after sowing, thereafter continuously providing leaves as long as the flowering stems are removed.

Seed in prepared plug trays if you prefer, and cover with perlite. Repot to containers with a minimum 5 in. diameter. As a plant with a long taproot, chervil does not like being transplanted, so keep this to a minimum. It can in fact be sown directly into a 5 in. pot, growing it, like mustard and watercress, as a cut-and-come-again crop.

Pests and Diseases

Chervil can suffer from **aphids**. Wash off gently with a liquid horticultural soap. Do not blast off with a high-pressure hose, as this will damage the soft leaves.

Maintenance

Spring Sow seeds.
Summer A late sowing in this season will provide leaves until winter, as it is very hardy. Protect from midday sun.
Fall Protect fall-sown plants for winter use.
Winter Although chervil is hardy in zones 7 and warmer, some protection is needed in subfreezing weather.

Garden Cultivation

The soil required is light with a degree of moisture retention. Plant spacing 9–12 in. Semishade is best, because the problem with chervil is that it will burst into flower too quickly, should the weather become sunny and hot, and be of no use as a culinary herb. For this reason some gardeners sow between rows of other garden herbs or vegetables or under deciduous plants to ensure some shade during the summer months.

Harvesting

Harvest leaves for use fresh when the plant is 6–8 weeks old or when 4 in. tall. Otherwise, freezing is the best method of preservation, as the dried leaves do not retain their flavor.

CONTAINER GROWING

When grown inside in the kitchen, chervil loses color, gets leggy, and goes floppy, so unless you are treating it as a cut-and-come-again plant, plant outside in a large container that retains moisture and is positioned in semishade.

Chervil looks good in a window box, but be sure that it gets shade at midday.

MEDICINAL

Leaves eaten raw are rich in vitamin C, carotene, iron, and magnesium. They may be infused to make a tea to stimulate digestion and alleviate circulation disorders, liver complaints, and chronic catarrh, and fresh leaves may be applied to aching joints in a warm poultice.

CULINARY

It is one of the traditional fines herbes, indispensable to French cuisine and a fresh green asset in any meal, but many people are only now discovering its special delicate parsleylike flavor with a hint of aniseed. This is an herb especially for winter use because it is easy to obtain fresh leaves and, as every cook knows, French or otherwise, "Fresh is best."

Use its leaf generously in salads, soups, sauces, vegetables, and chicken, white fish, and egg dishes.

Add freshly chopped toward the end of cooking to avoid flavor loss.

In small quantities it enhances the flavor of other herbs. Great with vegetables.

OTHER USES

An infusion of the leaf can be used to cleanse skin, maintain suppleness, and discourage wrinkles.

Chervil with broad beans

Armoracia rusticana (Cochlearia armoracia)

HORSERADISH

From the family Brassicaceae.

Native of Europe, naturalized in North America and Britain. Originally the horseradish was cultivated as a medicinal herb. Now it is considered a flavoring herb. The common name means a coarse or strong radish, the prefix "horse" often being used in plant to denote a large, strong, or coarse plant. In the sixteenth century it was known in England as redcol or recole. In this period the plant appears to have been more popular in Scandinavia and Germany, where they developed its potential as a fish sauce. In Britain horseradish has become strongly associated with roast beef.

SPECIES

Armoracia rusticana (Cochlearia armoracia)
Horseradish
Hardy perennial. Ht. 24–35 in., spread infinite! Flowers white in spring (very rare). Leaves large green oblongs. The large root, which is up to 24 in. long, 2 in. thick, and tapering, goes deep into the soil. **Zone 3**

Armoracia rusticana 'Variegata'
Hardy perennial. Ht. 24–35 in., spread also infinite. Flowers white in spring (rare in cool climates). Leaves large with green-cream variegation and oblong shape. Large root as *A. rusticana*; not as good flavor.

Roast beef is traditionally served with horseradish

CULTIVATION

Propagation
Root Cuttings
In early spring cut pieces of root 6 in. long. Put them either directly into the ground, at a depth of 2 in., at intervals of 12 in. apart, or start them off in individual pots. These can then be planted out when the soil is manageable.

Division
If you have a perpetual clump it will need dividing; do this in the spring. Remember, small pieces of root will always grow, so do it cleanly, making sure that you have collected all the little pieces of root. Replant in a well-prepared site.

Pests and Diseases
Cabbage caterpillars may feed on the leaves during late summer. The leaves may also be affected by flea beetles, but these can be treated with rotenone.

Maintenance
Spring Sow seeds. Plant cuttings in garden.
Summer Liquid feed with seaweed fertilizer.
Fall Dig up roots if required when mature enough.
Winter No need for protection; fully hardy.

Garden Cultivation
Think seriously if you want this plant in your garden. It is invasive. Once you have it, you have it. It is itself a most tolerant plant, liking all but the driest of soils, but for a good crop it prefers a light, well-dug, rich, moist soil. Prepare it the fall before with lots of well-rotted manure. It likes a sunny site but will tolerate dappled shade.

If large quantities are required, horseradish should be given a patch of its own where the roots can be lifted and the soil replenished after each harvest. To produce strong, straight use this method from an old gardening book. Make holes 15 in. deep with a crowbar, and drop a piece of horseradish 2–3 in. long with a crown on the top into the hole, crown up. Fill the hole up with good rotted manure. This will produce strong straight roots in 2–3 years; some may be ready in the first year.

Harvesting

Pick leaves young to use fresh, or to dry.

If you have a mature patch of horseradish then the root can be dug up anytime for use fresh. Otherwise dig up roots in fall. Store roots in sand and make sure you leave them in a cool dark place for the winter.

Alternatively, wash, grate, or slice and dry. Another method is to immerse the whole washed roots in white wine vinegar.

COMPANION PLANTING

Grow near potatoes to improve their disease resistance. Be careful it does not take over.

Horseradish root

CULINARY

The reason horseradish is used in sauces, vinegars, and as an accompaniment rather than cooked as a vegetable is that the volatile flavoring oil that is released in grating evaporates rapidly and becomes nothing when cooked. Raw it's a different story. The strongest flavor is from root pulled in the fall. The spring root is comparatively mild. Fresh root contains calcium, sodium, magnesium, and vitamin C, and has antibiotic qualities useful for preserving food.

It can be used grated in coleslaw, dips, pickled beets, cream cheese, mayonnaise, and avocado dips.

The young leaves can be added to salads for a bit of zip.

Make horseradish sauce to accompany roast beef and smoked fish.

Avocado with Horseradish Cream

Fresh horseradish root (approx. 6 in. long); preserved horseradish in vinegar can be substituted (leave out the lemon juice)
1 tablespoon butter
3 tablespoons fresh bread crumbs
1 apple
1 teaspoon yogurt
1 teaspoon lemon juice
Pinch of salt and sugar
1 teaspoon chopped fresh chervil
1/2 teaspoon each of fresh chopped tarragon and dill
3–4 tablespoons heavy cream
2 avocados (ripe) cut in half with the stones removed

Peel and grate the horseradish, melt the butter, and add the bread crumbs. Fry until brown, and add grated horseradish. Remove from heat and grate the apple into the mixture. Add yogurt, lemon juice, salt, sugar, and herbs. Put aside to cool. Chill in refrigerator.

Just before serving, gently fold the cream into the mixture and spoon generously into the avocado halves. Serve with green salad and brown toast.

MEDICINAL

Horseradish is a powerful circulatory stimulant with antibiotic properties.

As a diuretic it is effective for lung and urinary infections. It can also be taken internally for gout and rheumatism.

Grate into a poultice and apply externally to chilblains, stiff muscles, sciatica, and rheumatic joints, to stimulate blood flow.

Its sharp pungency frequently has a dramatic effect and has been known to clear the sinuses in one breath.

WARNING

Overuse may blister the skin. Do not use it if your thyroid function is low or if taking thyroxin. Avoid continuous dosage when pregnant or suffering from kidney problems.

OTHER USES

Chop finely into dog food to dispel worms and improve body tone.

Make an infusion 2 cups water, 1/8–1/4 cup horseradish roots and dilute 4:1. Spray on apple trees to protect against brown rot.

The roots and the leaves produce a yellow dye for natural dyeing.

Slice and infuse in milk for a lotion to improve skin clarity.

Arnica montana

ARNICA

Also known as Mountain Tobacco, Leopards Bane, Mountain Arnica, Wolfsbane, and Mountain Daisy. From the family Asteraceae.

It is found wild in the mountainous areas of Canada, North America, and in Europe, where it is a protected species. Bees love it.

The name arnica is said to be derived from the word *ptarmikos*, Greek for "sneezing." One sniff of arnica can make you sneeze.

The herb was known by Methusalus and was widely used in the sixteenth century in German folk medicine. Largely as a result of exaggerated claims in the eighteenth century by Venetian physicians, it was, for a short time, a popular medicine.

SPECIES

Arnica montana Arnica
Hardy perennial. Ht. 1–2 ft., spread 6 in. Large, single, scented yellow flowers throughout summer. Oval, hairy, light green leaves.
Zone 4

CULTIVATION

Propagation
Seed
Sow the small seed in spring or late summer in either a pot, plug, or seed tray, and cover with perlite. Place trays in a cold frame as heat will inhibit germination. The seed is slow to germinate, even occasionally as long as two years! Once the seedlings are large enough, pot up and harden off in a cold frame.

For reliable germination, collect the seed yourself and sow no later than early fall. After potting up, winter the young plants under protection. They will die back in winter. Plant out in the following spring, when the soil has warmed up, 1 ft. from other plants.

Division
Arnica's root produces creeping rhizomes, which are easy to divide in spring. This is much more reliable than sowing seed.

Pests and Diseases
Caterpillars and **slugs** sometimes eat the leaves.

Maintenance
Spring Sow seeds. Divide creeping rhizomes.
Summer Deadhead if necessary. Harvest plant for medicinal use.
Fall Collect seeds and either sow immediately or store in an airtight container for sowing in the spring.
Winter Note the position in the garden because the plants die right back.

Garden Cultivation
Being a mountainous plant it is happiest in a sandy acid soil, rich in humus, and in a sunny position. Arnica is a highly ornamental plant with a long flowering season. It is ideally suited for large rock gardens, or the front of a border bed.

Harvesting
Pick flowers for medicinal use in summer, just before they come into full flower. Pick in full flower, with stalks, for drying.

Collect leaves for drying in summer before flowering.

Dig up roots of second- or third-year growth after the plant has fully died back in late fall or early winter for drying.

MEDICINAL

Arnica is a famous herbal and homeopathic remedy. A tincture of flowers can be used in the treatment of sprains, wounds, and bruises, and also to give relief from rheumatic pain and chilblains, if the skin is not broken. Homeopathic doses are effective against epilepsy and seasickness, and possibly as a hair growth stimulant. It has also been shown to be effective against salmonella.

WARNING

Do not take arnica internally except under supervision of a qualified herbalist or homeopath. External use may cause skin rash or irritation. Never apply to broken skin.

OTHER USES

Leaves and roots are smoked as herbal tobacco, hence the name Mountain Tobacco.

Artemisia abrotanum

SOUTHERNWOOD

Also known as Lad's Love and Old Man. From the family Asteraceae.

This lovely aromatic plant is a native of southern Europe. It has been introduced to many countries and is now naturalized widely in temperate zones.

The derivation of the genus name is unclear. One suggestion is that it honors Artemisia, a famous botanist and medical researcher, sister of King Mausolus (353 B.C.). Another is that it was named after Artemis or Diana, goddess of the hunt and moon.

In the seventeenth century, Culpeper recommended that the ashes of southernwood be mingled with salad oil as a remedy for baldness.

Southernwood *Artemisia abrotanum*

SPECIES

Artemisia abrotanum
Southernwood
Deciduous or semievergreen hardy perennial. Ht. and spread 40 in. Tiny insignificant clusters of dull yellow flowers in summer. The abundant olive green feathery leaves are finely divided and carry a unique scent.

CULTIVATION

Propagation
Seed
It rarely flowers and sets seeds, except in warm climates.
Cuttings
Take softwood cuttings in spring from the lush new growth, or from semi-hardwood cuttings in summer. Use the bark-peat-grit mix of potting soil (see p. 591). Roots well. It can be wintered as a rooted cutting, when it sheds its leaves and is dormant. Keep the cuttings on the dry side, and in early spring slowly start watering. Plant out 24 in. apart after the frosts have finished.

Pests and Diseases
It is free from the majority of pests and disease.

Maintenance
Spring Cut back to maintain shape. Take cuttings.
Summer Take cuttings.
Fall Trim any flowers off as they develop.
Winter Protect the roots in hard winters with mulch.

Garden Cultivation
Southernwood prefers a light soil containing well-rotted organic material in a sunny position. However tempted you are by its bedraggled appearance in winter (hence the name Old Man). *Never* cut hard back as you will kill it. This growth protects its woody stems from cold winds. Cut the bush hard in spring to keep its shape, but only after the frosts have finished.

Harvesting
Pick leaves during the growing season for use fresh. Pick leaves for drying in midsummer.

CULINARY

The leaves can be used in salads. They have a strong flavor, so use sparingly. It does also make a good aromatic vinegar.

MEDICINAL

It can be used for expelling worms and to treat coughs and bronchial catarrh. A compress helps to treat frostbite, cuts, and grazes.

OTHER USES

The French call it *Garde robe*, and use it as a moth repellent. It is a good fly deterrent, too—hang bunches up in the kitchen—or rub it on the skin to deter mosquitoes.

WARNING

No product containing southernwood should be taken during pregnancy.

Artemisia absinthium

WORMWOOD

Also known as Absinthe and Green Ginger. From the family Asteraceae.

A native of Asia and Europe, including Britain, it was introduced into America as a cultivated plant and is now naturalized in many places. Found on waste ground, especially near the sea in warmer regions.

Legend has it that as the serpent slithered out of Eden, wormwood first sprang up in the impressions on the ground left by its tail. Another story tells that in the beginning it was called *Parthenis absinthium*, but Artemis, Greek goddess of chastity, benefited so much from it that she named it after herself—*Artemisia absinthium*. The Latin meaning of *absinthium* is "to desist from," which says it all.

Although it is one of the most bitter herbs known, it has for centuries been a major ingredient of aperitifs and herb wines. Both absinthe and vermouth get their names from this plant, the latter being an eighteenth-century French variation of the German *wermut*, itself the origin of the English name wormwood.

Wormwood was hung by the door where it kept away evil spirits and deterred nighttime visitations by goblins. It was also made a constituent of ink to discourage mice from eating old letters.

It was used as a strewing herb to prevent fleas, hence:

> *"White wormwood hath seed, get a handful or twaine,*
> *to save against March, to make flea to refrain.*
> *Where chamber is sweeped and wormwood is strewn,*
> *no flea for his life, dare abide to be knowne."*

This extract comes from Thomas Tusser's *Five Hundred Pointes of Good Husbandrie*, written in 1573.

Finally, wormwood is believed to be the herb that Shakespeare had in mind when his Oberon lifted the spell from Titania with "the juice of Dian's bud," Artemis being known to the Romans as Dian or Diana.

Wormwood *Artemisia absinthium*

Artemisia absinthium
Wormwood
Partial-evergreen hardy perennial. Ht. 40 in., spread 4 ft. Tiny, insignificant, yellow flower heads are borne in sprays in summer. The abundant leaves are divided, aromatic, and gray-green in color.
Zone 5

Artemisia absinthium
'Lambrook Silver'
Evergreen hardy perennial. Ht. 32 in., spread 20 in. Tiny, insignificant, gray flower heads are borne in long panicles in summer. The abundant leaves are finely divided, aromatic and silver-gray in color. May need winter protection in exposed sites.
Zone 6

Artemisia pontica
Roman wormwood
Evergreen hardy perennial. Ht. 24 in., spread 12 in. Tiny, insignificant, silver-gray flower heads are borne on tall spikes in summer. The abundant, feathery, small leaves are finely divided, aromatic, and silver-gray in color. This can, in the right conditions, be a vigorous grower, spreading well in excess of 1–2 ft.
Zone 5

Artemisia
'Powis Castle'
Evergreen hardy perennial. Ht. 36 in., spread 4 ft. Tiny, insignificant, grayish-yellow flower heads are borne in sprays in summer. The abundant leaves are finely divided, aromatic, and silver-gray in color.
Zone 6

Left: Artemisia 'Powis Castle'

CULTIVATION

Propagation
Seed
Of the species just mentioned, only wormwood is successfully grown from seed. It is extremely small and best started off under protection. Sow in spring in a prepared seed or plug tray, using the bark-peat-grit mix of potting soil (see p. 591). Cover with perlite and propagate with heat, 60–70°F. Plant out when the seedlings are large enough to handle and have had a period of hardening off.

Cuttings
Take softwood cuttings from the lush new growth in early summer; semihardwood in late summer. Use the bark-peat-grit mix of potting soil.

Division
As they are all vigorous growers, division is a good idea at least every 3 to 4 years to keep the plant healthy, to prevent it from becoming woody, and to prevent encroaching. Dig up the plant in spring or fall, divide the roots, and replant in a chosen spot.

Pests and Diseases
Wormwood can suffer from a summer attack of **aphids**. If it gets too bad, use a liquid horticultural soap, following manufacturer's instructions.

Maintenance
Spring Sow seeds. Divide established plants. Trim new growth for shape. Take softwood cuttings.
Summer Take semihardwood cuttings.
Fall Prune back all the species mentioned to 6 in. off the ground. Divide established plants.
Winter Cover with frost fleece, straw, bark, or anything that can be removed the following spring.

Garden Cultivation
Artemisias like a light well-drained soil and sunshine, but will adapt well to ordinary soils provided some shelter is given. Planting distance depends on spread.
   Wormwood is an overpoweringly flavored plant and it does impair the flavor of dill and coriander, so do not plant nearby.

Harvesting
Pick flowering tops just as they begin to open. Dry.
   Pick leaves for drying in summer.

CONTAINER GROWING

Artemisia absinthium 'Lambrook Silver' and Roman wormwood (*Artemisia pontica*) look very good in terra-cotta containers. Use the bark-peat-grit mix of potting soil. Only feed in the summer; if you feed too early the leaves will lose their silvery foliage and revert to a more green look. In winter keep watering to the absolute minimum and protect from hard frosts.

OTHER USES

It can produce a yellow dye.

Antiseptic vinegar
This vinegar is known as the "Four Thieves" because it is said that thieves used to rub their bodies with it before robbing plague victims.

1 tablespoon wormwood
1 tablespoon lavender
1 tablespoon rosemary
1 tablespoon sage
3 1/2 cups vinegar

Put the crushed herbs into an earthenware container. Pour in the vinegar. Cover the container and leave it in a warm sunny place for two weeks. Strain into bottles with tight-fitting, nonmetal lids. This makes a very refreshing tonic in the bath, or try sprinkling it on work surfaces in the kitchen.

Wormwood vinegar

Moth-Repellent
Wormwood or southern-wood can be used for keeping moths and other harmful insects away from clothes. The smell is sharp and refreshing and does not cling to your clothes like camphor mothballs.

Wormwood moth-repellent

Bug Ban Recipe
2 tablespoons dried wormwood or southernwood
2 tablespoons dried lavender
2 tablespoons dried mint

Mix the ingredients well and put into small sachets.

MEDICINAL

Wormwood was once used to expel worms, but this is no longer considered safe.

WARNING

Not to be taken internally without medical supervision. Habitual use causes convulsions, restlessness, and vomiting. Overdose causes vertigo, cramps, intoxication, and delirium. Pure worm-wood oil is a strong poison.

Artemisia dracunculus

TARRAGON

Also known as Estragon. From the family Asteraceae.

A native of southern Europe, tarragon is now found in dry areas of North America, southern Asia, and Siberia.

Dracunculus means "little dragon." Its naming could have occurred as a result of the shape of its roots, or because of its fiery flavor. Whatever, it was certainly believed to have considerable power to heal bites from snakes, serpents, and other venomous creatures.

In ancient times the mixed juices of tarragon and fennel made a favorite drink for the kings of India.

In the reign of Henry VIII, tarragon made its way into English gardens, and the rhyme "There is certain people, and certain herbs, that good digestion disturbs," could well be associated with tarragon. I love, too, the story that Henry VIII divorced Catherine of Aragon for her reckless use of tarragon.

SPECIES

Artemisia dracunculus
French Tarragon
Half-hardy perennial. Ht. 3 ft., spread 18 in. Tiny, insignificant, yellow flower heads don't set viable seed except in warm climates. The leaves are smooth, dark green, long, and narrow, and have a very strong flavor. **Zone 3**

Artemisia dranunculus dracunculoides
Russian Tarragon
Hardy perennial. Ht. 4 ft., spread 18 in. Tiny, insignificant, yellow flower heads borne in sprays in summer. The leaves are slightly coarser and green in color, their flavor insignificant. This plant originates from Siberia, which also explains why it is so hardy. **Zone 3**

CULTIVATION

Propagation
Seed
Only the Russian variety produces viable seed. A lot of growers are propagating and selling it to the unsuspecting public as French tarragon. If you really want Russian tarragon, sow the small seed in spring, into prepared seed or plug trays, using the bark-peat-grit potting soil (see p. 591). No extra heat is required. When the young plants are large enough to handle, transfer to the garden, 24 in. apart.

Cuttings
Both French and Russian tarragon can be propagated by root or tip cuttings.
Roots: Dig up the underground runners in spring when the frosts are

finished and pull them apart; do not cut. You will notice growing nodules; these will reproduce in the coming season. Place a small amount of root, about 3–4 in., each with a growing nodule, in a 3 in. pot, and cover with compost. Use the bark-peat-grit mix and place in a warm, well-ventilated spot. Keep watering to a minimum. When well rooted, plant out in the garden after hardening off, 24 in. apart.

It is possible to take softwood cuttings of the growing tips in summer. You will need to keep the leaves moist, but the potting mix on the dry side. It works best under a misting unit with a little bottom heat 60°F.

Division
Divide established plants of either variety in the spring.

Pests and Diseases
Recently there has been a spate of **rust** developing on French tarragon. When buying a plant, look for telltale signs—small rust spots on the underneath of a leaf. If you have a plant with rust, dig it up, cut off all foliage carefully, and dispose of the leaves. Wash the roots free from soil, and pot up into fresh sterile soil. If this fails, place the dormant roots in hot water after washing off all the compost. The temperature of the water should be 110–115°F; over 115°F will damage the root. Leave the roots in the hot water for 5 minutes, then replant in a new place in the garden.

Maintenance
Spring Sow Russian tarragon seeds if you must. Divide established plants. Take root cuttings.
Summer Remove flowers.
Fall Pot pieces of French tarragon root.
Winter Protect French tarragon. As the plant dies back into the ground in winter it is an ideal candidate for frost fabric, straw, or a deep mulch.

Garden Cultivation
French tarragon grows best in a warm, dry position, and needs very well-drained soil, especially in winter. It also dislikes humid conditions. The plant should be renewed every 3 years because the flavor deteriorates as the plant matures.

Russian tarragon is fully hardy and will grow in any conditions. There is a myth that it improves in flavor the longer it is grown in one place. This is untrue—it gets coarse. It is extremely tolerant of most soil types, but prefers a sunny position, 2 ft. away from other plants.

Harvesting
Pick sprigs of French tarragon early in the season to make vinegar.

Pick leaves for fresh use throughout the growing season. For freezing it is best to pick the leaves in the midsummer months.

CONTAINER GROWING

French tarragon grows well in containers. Use the bark-peat-grit mix (see p. 591). As it produces root runners, give it room to grow so that it will not become potbound. Make sure the plant is watered, and in the daytime, not at night. It hates having wet roots. Keep feeding to a minimum; overfeeding produces fleshy leaves with a poor flavor. In winter, when the plant is dormant, do not water, keep the soil dry and the container in a cool, frost-free environment. Divide and replant in fresh soil every spring.

CULINARY

Without doubt this is among the crème de la crème of the culinary herb collection. Its flavor promotes appetite and complements so many dishes—chicken, veal, fish, stuffed tomatoes, rice dishes, and salad dressings, and of course is the main ingredient of béarnaise sauce.

Chicken Salad with Tarragon and Grapes
Serves 4–6

1 3-lb. cooked chicken
1¼ cups mayonnaise
¾ cup heavy cream
1 heaped teaspoon chopped fresh tarragon (½ teaspoon dried)
3 spring onions, finely chopped
¾ cup green grapes (seedless)
1 small lettuce
A few sprigs watercress
Salt and pepper

Remove the skin from the chicken and all the chicken from the bones. Slice the meat into longish pieces and place in a bowl.

In another bowl mix the mayonnaise with the cream, the chopped tarragon, and the finely chopped spring onions. Pour this mixture over the chicken and mix carefully together. Arrange the lettuce on a dish and spoon on the chicken mixture. Arrange the grapes and the watercress around it.

Serve with baked potatoes or rice pilaf.

MEDICINAL

No modern medicinal use. Formerly used for toothache. If nothing else is available, a tea made from the leaves is said to overcome insomnia.

Red Orach
Atriplex hortensis var. *rubra*

Atriplex hortensis

ORACH

From the family Chenopodiaceae.

The garden species of orach, *Atriplex hortensis,* originated in Eastern Europe and is now widely distributed in countries with temperate climates. In the past it was called mountain spinach and grown as a vegetable in its own right.

The red form, *Atriplex hortensis* var. *rubra,* is still eaten frequently in Continental Europe, particularly with game, and was used as a flavoring for breads.

The common orach, *Atriplex patula,* was considered a poor man's pot herb, which is a fact worth remembering when you are pulling out this invasive annual weed.

SPECIES

Atriplex hortensis
Orach
Hardy annual. Ht. 5 ft., spread 12 in. Tiny greenish (boring) flowers in summer. Green triangular leaves.
All zones

Atriplex hortensis var. rubra
Red Orach
Hardy annual. Ht. 4 ft., spread 1 ft. Tiny reddish (boring) flowers in summer. Red triangular leaves.
All zones

Atriplex patula
Common Orach
Hardy annual. Ht. 3 ft., spread 12 in. Flowers similar to orach, the leaves more spear-shaped and smaller.

CULTIVATION

Propagation
Seed
If you wish to have a continuous supply of leaves, start off under protection in early spring, sowing the flat seeds directly into prepared plug trays. Cover with perlite. When the seedlings are large enough, and after hardening off, plant out in a prepared site in the garden 10 in. apart.

Pests and Diseases
In the majority of cases this herb is pest and disease free.

Maintenance
Spring Sow seeds.
Summer Cut flowers before they form.
Fall Cut seeds off before they are fully ripe to prevent too much self-seeding.
Winter Dig up old plants.

Garden Cultivation
This annual herb produces the largest and most succulent leaves when the soil is rich. So prepare the site well with well-rotted manure. For red orach choose a site with partial shade as the leaves can scorch in very hot summers. The seeds can be sown in rows 2 ft. apart in spring when the soil has warmed. Thin out to 10 in. as soon as the seedlings are large enough, and replant. Water well throughout the growing season.

As this plant is a very rapid grower, it is as well to do two sowings to ensure a good supply of young leaves. The

Orach
Atriplex hortensis

Orach makes an excellent container plant

Red Orach Soup

2¹/₂ cups sliced potatoes
8 oz. young red orach
* leaves*
4 tablespoons butter
1 clove garlic, crushed
3³/₄ cups chicken stock
Salt and black pepper
4 tablespoons sour cream

Peel the potatoes and cut them into thick slices. Wash the orach and cut up coarsely. Cook the potatoes for 10 minutes in salted water, drain. Melt the butter in a saucepan with the crushed garlic and slowly sweeten; add the red orach leaves and gently simmer for 5–10 minutes until soft (if the leaves are truly young then 5 minutes will be sufficient). Pour in the stock, add the parboiled potatoes and bring to the boil; simmer for an additional 10 minutes. When all is soft, cool slightly then purée in a blender or liquidize. After blending, return the soup to a clean pan, add salt and pepper to taste, and heat slowly (not to boiling). Stir in the sour cream, and serve.

CONTAINER GROWING

The red-leaved orach looks very attractive in containers, provided you don't let it get too tall. Nip out the growing tip and the plant will bush out; do not let it flower. Use the bark-peat potting mix (see p. 591). Keep the plant in semishade in high summer, and water well at all times. If watering in high sun be careful not to splash the leaves as they can scorch, especially the red variety.

MEDICINAL

This herb is no longer used medicinally. In the past it was a home remedy for sore throats,

Red Orach Soup

red varieties look very attractive grown as a hedge. Remove flowering tips as soon as they appear. This will help maintain the shape of the plant.
  If seed is not required, pick the flowers off as soon as they appear. To save the seed, collect before it is fully ripe, otherwise you will have hundreds of orach babies all over your garden and next door.

Harvesting
Pick young leaves to use fresh as required. The herb does not dry or freeze particularly well.

CULINARY

The young leaves can be eaten raw in salads, and the red variety looks most attractive. The old leaves of both species ought to be cooked as they become slightly tough and bitter. It can be used as a substitute for spinach or as a vegetable, served in a white sauce. It is becoming more popular in Europe, where it is used in soups.

Ballota nigra

BLACK HOREHOUND

Also known as Stinking Horehound, Dunny Nettle, Stinking Roger, and Hairy Hound. From the family Lamiaceae.

Black horehound comes from a genus of about twenty-five species mostly native to the Mediterranean region. Some species have a disagreeable smell, and only a few are worth growing in the garden. Black horehound is found on roadsides, hedge banks, and in vacant lots throughout most of America, Europe, and Australia.

Ballota nigra, the black horehound, was originally called *ballote* by the ancient Greeks. It has been suggested that this comes from the Greek word *ballo* which means "to reject," "cast," or "throw," because cows and other farm animals, following their natural instincts, reject it. The origin of the common name is more obscure, it could come from the Anglo-Saxon word *har*, which means "hoar" or "hairy."

SPECIES

Ballota nigra
Black Horehound
Hardy perennial. Ht. 16–40 in., spread 12 in. Purple-pink attractive flowers in summer. The leaves are green and medium-sized, rather like the stinging nettle. All parts of the plant are hairy and have a strong, disagreeable smell and taste.
Zone 4

Ballota pseudodictamnus
Half-hardy perennial. Ht. 24 in., spread 12 in. White flowers with numerous purple spots in summer. Leaves white and woolly. This plant originated from Crete. The dried calyxes look like tiny furry spinning tops; they were used as floating wicks in primitive oil lamps.
Zone 7

Black horehound *Ballota nigra*

CULTIVATION

Propagation
Seed
Sow the seeds directly into the prepared garden in late summer, thinning to 16 in. apart.

Division
Divide roots in mid-spring.

Pests and Diseases
Rarely suffers from any pests or diseases.

HERBS

231

Maintenance

Spring Dig up established plants and divide; replant where required.
Summer When the plant has finished flowering, cut off the deadheads before the seeds ripen, to prevent it from seeding itself in the garden.
Fall Sow seed.
Winter No need to protect.

Garden Cultivation

Black horehound will grow in any soil conditions, although it prefers water-retentive soil. It tolerates full sun or part shade. In the garden, place it in a border. The bees love it, and the flowers are attractive. Make sure it is far enough back so that you do not brush it by mistake because it does stink.

Harvesting

As this is an herbalist's herb, the leaves should be collected before flowering and dried with care.

CONTAINER GROWING

Not recommended, as it has such an unpleasant smell.

MEDICINAL

Black horehound was used apparently in the treatment of bites from mad dogs. A dressing was prepared from the leaves and laid on the infected part. This was said to have an antispasmodic effect.

This is not an herb to be self-administered. Professionals use it as a sedative, anti-emetic, and to counteract vomiting during pregnancy.

Black horehound *Ballota nigra*

Borago officinalis

BORAGE

Also known as Bugloss, Burrage, and Common Bugloss. From the family Boraginaceae.

Borage is indigenous to Mediterranean countries, but has now been naturalized in North America and Northern Europe. In fact, one occasionally finds escapees growing happily on vacant lots.

The origin of the name is obscure. The French *bourrache* is said to derive from an old word meaning "rough" or "hairy," which would only describe the leaf. The herb's pure blue flowers are beautiful and are supposed to have inspired the painting of the robes of the Madonna, and to have charmed Louis XIV into ordering the herb planted at Versailles.

The herb's Welsh name translates as "herb of gladness"; and in Arabic it is "the father of sweat," which we can accept as borage is a diaphoretic. The Celtic word *borrach* means "courage," however, and in this we have an association more credible by far. The Greeks and Romans regarded borage as both comforting and imparting courage, and this belief so persisted that Gerard was able to quote the tag *Ego borage gaudia semper ago* ("I, Borage, bring always courage") in his *Herbal*. It was for courage, too, that borage flowers were floated in stirrup cups given to the Crusaders. American settlers thought highly enough of borage to take the seed with them on their long adventure. Records of it were found in an American seed order of 1631.

Borage *Borago officinalis*

SPECIES

Borago officinalis
Borage
Hardy annual (very occasionally biennial). Ht. 24 in. with hollow, bristly branches and spreading stems. The blue or purplish star-shaped flowers grow in loose racemes from early summer to mid-fall. The leaves are bristly, oval, or oblong. At the base they form a rosette; others grow alternately on either side of the stem. **All zones**

***Borago officinalis* 'Alba'**
White Borage
Hardy annual. Ht. 2 ft. White star-shaped flowers from late spring through summer. Bristly, oval, oblong leaves. Can be used as *B. officinalis*. **All zones**

CULTIVATION

Propagation
Borage is best grown directly from seed in its final position, as it does not like having its long taproot disturbed. But for an early crop it is a good idea to start

the seeds under protection. In early spring sow singly in small pots. Transplant to final position as soon as possible after hardening off, when the seedling is large enough and all threat of frosts is past.

Pests and Diseases
If you are growing borage as a companion plant aphids will not worry you, but if they are becoming a nuisance then spray with liquid horticultural soap.

A form of mildew can make the plant unsightly at the end of the season. At this time of the year it is not worth treating. Dig the plant up and burn it.

Maintenance
Spring Sow seeds. They germinate quickly and plants mature in 5–6 weeks. *Summer* Sow seeds. Look out for flower heads turning into seeds—collect or destroy if you do not want borage plants all over the garden. Deadhead flowers to prolong flowering season. *Fall* As the plants begin to die back, collect up the old plants. Do not till in the flower heads or next year you will have a garden full of unwanted borage. *Winter* Borage lasts until the first major frost, and some years it is the last flowering herb in the garden.

Garden Cultivation
Borage prefers a well-drained, light, rather poor, sandy, alkaline soil, and a sunny position. Sow borage seeds 2 in. deep in mid-spring and again in late spring for a continuous supply of young leaves and flowers. Thin seedlings to 24 in. apart and away from other herbs, as they produce lots of floppy growth.

I have used borage as an exhibit plant at flower shows, and have found that by continuously deadheading the flowers I can maintain a good supply of flowers for longer.

Harvesting

Pick flowers fresh or for freezing or drying when they are just fully opened.

Cut the young leaves fresh throughout summer. They do not dry or freeze very successfully.

Collect seed before the plant dies back fully. Store in a lightproof container in a cool place.

COMPANION GROWING

Borage is a good companion plant. The flower is very attractive to bees, especially good for runner beans and strawberries. Another plus is that borage attracts aphids to itself, thus sparing the other plants. Equally, if planted near tomatoes, it can control tomato worm.

CONTAINER GROWING

It is not suitable for container-growing indoors. However, when planted outside in large containers (like a half barrel), borage can be very effective combined with other tall plants like oxeye daisies, poppies, and bachelor's buttons.

WARNING

Prolonged use of borage is not advisable. Fresh leaves may cause contact dermatitis. Wear gloves when harvesting.

CULINARY

Be brave, try a young leaf. It may be hairy, some would say prickly, but once in the mouth the hairs dissolve and the flavor is of cool cucumber. Great cut up in salads, or with cream cheese, or added to yogurt, or even in an egg salad sandwich. And they give a refreshing flavor to summer cold drinks. Finally, fresh leaves are particularly good to use in a salt-free diet as they are rich in mineral salts. Try them combined with spinach or or added to ravioli stuffing.

The flowers are exciting tossed in a salad, floated on top of a glass of a gin-based drink, or crystallized for cake decoration. Also excellent as garnish for savory or sweet dishes, and on chilled soups.

FACIAL STEAM FOR DRY, SENSITIVE SKIN

Place 2 large handfuls of borage leaves in a bowl. Pour over 6 cups of boiling water. Stir quickly with a wooden spoon. Using a towel as a tent over your head, place your face about 12 in. over the water. Keep your eyes closed and maintain for about 10–15 minutes. Rinse your face with tepid cool water. Use a yarrow infusion dabbed on with cotton balls to close pores.

OTHER USES

Dried flowers add color to potpourris. Children enjoy stringing them together as a necklace. Add to summer flower arrangements.

Borage and cream cheese

MEDICINAL

In the 1980s borage was found to contain G.L.A., gamma linoleic acid, an even more valuable medicinal substance than evening primrose oil. But cultivation problems coincided with a dramatic slump in prices, and blackcurrant pulp provided a cheaper and richer source of G.L.A. Hopes for the future of borage as a commercial crop have diminished recently, but it deserves more medicinal research.

Borage tea is said to be good for reducing high temperatures when taken hot. This is because it is a diaphoretic—inducing sweat—and thus lowering the fever. This makes it a good remedy for colds and flu, especially when these infect the lungs as it is also good for coughs. Both leaves and flowers are rich in potassium and calcium and are therefore good blood purifiers and a tonic.

Borage Tea
Small handful of fresh leaves
2½ cups of boiling water

Simmer for 5 minutes.

Natural Nightcap
3 teaspoons fresh borage leaves
1 cup boiling water
1 teaspoon honey
1 slice lemon

Put the roughly chopped borage leaves into a warmed cup and pour over the boiling water. Cover with a saucer and allow the leaves to infuse for at least five minutes. Strain and add the lemon slice and honey. Drink hot just before going to bed.

Buxus sempervirens

BOX

Also known as Boxwood and Bushtree. From the family Buxaceae.

Variegated box *Buxus sempervirens* 'Elegantissima'

Box is a native plant of Europe, Western Asia, and North Africa. It has been cultivated widely throughout the world and is found in America along the Atlantic coast especially as an ornamental and hedge plant.

The common name, box, comes from the Latin *buxus*, which is, in turn, derived from the Greek *puxus,* meaning "a small box." At one time, boxwoods were widespread in Europe, but the demand for the wood, which is twice as hard as oak, led to extensive felling. Its timber is close-grained and heavy, so heavy in fact that it is unable to float on water. The wood does not warp and is therefore ideal for boxes, engraving plates, carvings, and musical and navigational instruments.

It is not used medicinally now but the essential oil from box was used once for the treatment of epilepsy, syphilis, and hemorrhoids, and also as an alternative to quinine in the treatment of malaria. A perfume was once made from its bark and a mixture of the leaves with sawdust has been used as an auburn hair dye.

When it rains, box gives off a musky smell evocative of old gardens, delicious to most people, but not to Queen Anne, who so hated the smell that she had the box parterres in St. James Park (planted for her predecessors, William and Mary, in the last years of the seventeenth century) torn out.

SPECIES

Buxus balearica
Balearic Box
Half-hardy evergreen. Ht. 6 ft., spread 5 ft. Suitable for hedging in mild areas. Has broadly oval, bright green leaves. Plant as a hedge 15 in. apart.
Zone 8

Buxus microphylla
Small Leaved Box
Hardy evergreen. Ht. 3 ft., spread 5 ft. Forms a dense mass of round-oblong, dark green, glossy leaves. Attractive cultivar 'Green Pillow' is good for formal shaping. Planting distance for a hedge 9 in.
Zone 5

Buxus sempervirens
Common Box
Hardy evergreen. Ht. and spread 15 ft. Leaves glossy green and oblong. Good for hedges, screening, and topiary; plant 18 in. apart.
Zone 5

Buxus sempervirens 'Elegantissima'
Variegated Box
Hardy evergreen. Ht. and spread 3 ft. Good variegated gold-green leaves. Susceptible to scorch in hard winter. Trim regularly to maintain variegation. Very attractive as a center hedging in a formal garden or as specimen plants in their own right. Planting distance for a hedge 15 in.
Zone 6

Buxus sempervirens 'Handsworthiensis'
Handsworth Box
Hardy evergreen. Ht. and spread 10 ft. Broad, very dark green leaves. One of the fast-growing boxes with a dense habit, ideal for hedging or screening. Planting distance for a hedge 18 in.
Zone 5

Buxus sempervirens 'Suffruticosa'
Dwarf Box
Hardy evergreen. Ht. and spread 18 in. Evergreen dark shrub that forms tight dense mass. Slow grower. This is the archetypal edging in a formal herb garden. Trim to about 6 in. in height for hedging. Planting distance for a hedge 9 in.
Zone 5

Buxus wallichiana
Himalayan Box
Tender evergreen. Ht. and spread 6 ft. Slow growing. Produces long, narrow, glossy, bright green leaves. Planting distance for a hedge 15 in.
Zone 5

Box *Buxus sempervirens*

CULTIVATION

Propagation
Cuttings
Box is cultivated from cuttings taken in spring from the new growth. Use a bark-peat-grit mix of potting soil (see p. 591). Keep the cuttings moist but not wet, and in a cool place, ideally in shade. They will take 3–4 months to root. If you have a propagator then they will take 6–8 weeks at 70°F. Use a spray to mist the plant regularly. When rooted, pot the young plants using a soil-based potting mix or plant out, as per the distances mentioned under species.

Alternatively, take semiripe cuttings in summer, using the same potting mix as above. Rooting time is approximately 2 months longer than the softwood cuttings, but only 3–4 weeks longer with heat.

Pests and Diseases
If you notice a white deposit on the leaves, look more closely and you will see that some of the leaves have curled up. Inside, you will find a very small caterpillar. These are very difficult to get rid of. The best way is to give the plant a trim (sweep up the cuttings and dispose of them), then spray with a liquid horticultural soap. Boxwood is subject to many diseases and pests if stressed by poor soil or very hot or cold weather.

Maintenance
Spring Take stem cuttings. Trim fast growers like 'Handsworthiensis.'
Summer Take semiripe cuttings. Trim hedges to promote new growth.
Fall Trim if needed but not hard.
Winter Does not need protection.

Garden Cultivation
The plant is known for its longevity. It is not uncommon for it to live 600 years. Box flourishes on an alkaline soil. But it is very tolerant of any soil provided it is not waterlogged. Box is also fairly tolerant of position, surviving sun or semishade.

Hedges are a frame for a garden, outlining, protecting, and enhancing what they enclose. The preparation of the planting site for hedges is much the same as for the original herb garden.

Because one will be planting the box plants closer together than when planting individual plants, it is important first to feed the soil well by adding plenty of well-rotted manure or garden compost. Width of bed for a boundary hedge should be 2 ft.; for small internal hedges 1 ft. wide. Planting distances vary according to species (see p. 234).

If using common box or Handsworth box, the more vigorous growers, trim in spring and prune at the end of summer/early fall. The slower varieties need a cut only in the summer. In general the right shape for a healthy, dense hedge is broad at the base, tapering slightly toward the top, rounded or ridged but not too flat, to prevent damage from heavy snow.

Left: **Variegated box** *Buxus sempervirens* 'Elegantissima'

CONTAINER GROWING

Box, especially the slow-growing varieties, lends itself to topiary and looks superb in containers. *Buxus sempervirens* 'Elegantissima' looks very attractive in a terra-cotta pot. They are very easy to maintain. Use a soil-based potting soil. Feed with a liquid fertilizer in spring; water sparingly in winter.

OTHER USES
Boxwood is a favorite timber with cabinet makers, wood engravers, and turners because of its nonfibrous structure.

An ornamental mahogany box with boxwood strapping

MEDICINAL

It is advisable not to self-administer this plant; it should be used with caution. Box is used extensively in homoeopathic medicines; a tincture prepared from fresh leaves is prescribed for fever, rheumatism, and urinary tract infections.

WARNING

Animals have died from eating the leaves. All parts of the plant, especially the leaves and seeds, are poisonous. It is dangerous to take internally and should never be collected or used for self-medication. Symptoms of poisoning are vomiting, abdominal pain, and bloody diarrhea.

Calamintha

CALAMINT

From the family Lamiaceae.

Calamintha originated in Europe. It is now well established throughout temperate countries, but sadly it is still not a common plant. Calamint has been cultivated since the seventeenth century. Herbal records show that it used to be prescribed for women.

SPECIES

Calamintha grandiflora
Calamint
Hardy perennial. Ht. 15 in., spread 12 in. Square stems arise from creeping rootstock. Dense swirls of lilac pink flowers appear midsummer to early fall above mint-scented, toothed, oval leaves.
Zone 5

Calamintha grandiflora 'Variegata'
Hardy perennial. As *C. grandiflora* but with cream variegated leaves.
Zone 6

Calamintha nepeta
Lesser Calamint
Perennial. Ht. 12–24 in., spread 12 in. Small purple-white flowers from summer to early fall. Stems and leaves pale gray and covered in fine downy hairs. Its wonderful aromatic scent attracts butterflies and bees.
Zone 5

Calamintha sylvatica subsp. *ascendens* Mountain Balm
Hardy perennial. Ht. 12 in., spread 8 in. Pale purple flowers in dense whorls from late summer to early fall. Leaves mid-green, oval,

Lesser calamint
Calamintha nepeta

finely toothed and mint scented.
Zone 5

CULTIVATION

Propagation
Seed
Sow calamint's fine seeds in spring or fall, either in their eventual flowering position or in trays, covered lightly with perlite. If fall sowing in trays leave them outside to overwinter, covered with a sheet of glass. As germination can be tricky, fall sowing is sometimes more successful because subjecting the seeds to all weathers—thereby giving the hot and cold treatment—can trigger the process (stratification, see p. 590). When the seedlings are large enough to handle, prick out and plant up into pots, using a bark-peat-grit mix of potting soil (see p. 591). Alternatively, plant them directly into the chosen site in late spring after hardening off.

Cuttings
Take cuttings of young shoots in spring. This is an especially good method for the variegated grandiflora. They take easily, but keep in the shade until fully rooted and do not allow to dry out. Plant out in final position when fully hardened off.

Division
Once the plants are established they can be divided in the spring or fall, either by lifting the whole plant or by the double fork method. Replant immediately either into a prepared site or into pots using a bark-peat mix of potting soil. If this method is chosen in the fall, keep in a cold frame all winter.

Pests and Diseases
The leaves are aromatic so this plant is left alone by pests.

Maintenance
Spring Sow seeds. Take cuttings from new growth.
Summer Cut back after first flowering and keep the plant tidy. Give a feeding of liquid fertilizer; this can promote a second flowering.
Fall Sow seeds. Cut back new growth after second flowering.
Winter Protect with mulch in zones 6 and colder.

Garden Cultivation
These plants are indigenous to uplands and like a sunny position in well-drained soil, low in nutrients. The leaves of variegated calamint scorch easily and need some shade.

Harvesting
Leaves
Pick either side of flowering for use either fresh or dried.

CULINARY

The young minty leaves of the lesser calamint can be added to salads and used to make a refreshing tea.

CONTAINER GROWING

Unsuitable for growing indoors, but can look good growing in containers outside. Use a bark-peat-grit mix of potting soil and a container with a diameter no less than 5 in. Variegated calamint looks particularly striking in a terra-cotta pot.

MEDICINAL

Infuse dried leaves as a tea for colic, and as an invigorating tonic.
Use fresh leaves in a poultice for bruises.

Calomeria amaranthoides (Humea elegans)

INCENSE PLANT

From the family Asteraceae.

A native of South Australia, Africa, and Madagascar.

The Latin, *Humea*, is in honor of Lady Hume of Wormleybury. It was changed in 1993 to *Calomeria*.

The incense plant was a favorite of the Victorians, who put it in their front rooms or conservatories.

SPECIES

Calomeria amaranthoides (Humea elegans)
Incense Plant
Tender biennial (sometimes annual). Ht. up to 6 ft., spread 3 ft. Tiny, delicate, coral flower bracts, very numerous on large branches. Large, oblong mid-green leaves.

Warning: Leaves can cause irritation and the same kind of burns as rue. The scent can cause breathing difficulties and when in flower, it has a high pollen count and can trigger asthma attacks.

CULTIVATION

Propagation
Seed
Being a biennial, this is grown from the small seed, which is viable for only a short time. Collect from the plants in the summer, when ripe, and sow immediately into prepared seed or plug trays using the bark-peat potting soil (see p. 591). Leave the seeds uncovered. Overwinter in a cold frame and cover the seed tray with glass or clear plastic. Germination is lengthy and very erratic. Pot seedlings as soon as they appear, taking care not to injure the roots. Grow young plants in a cool, frost-free environment, and keep the roots almost dry through winter. In spring gradually encourage growth by watering and repotting.

Pests and Diseases
As a container-grown plant, it suffers from **aphids** and **red spider mite**. Keep an eye out for these and use a horticultural liquid soap as soon as they appear.

Maintenance
Spring Transplant seedlings from first year. Repot second year's plants.
Summer Feed and water regularly. Collect seeds off second year plants and sow immediately.
Fall Protect first year plants.
Winter Protect plants from frost. Keep watering to the minimum.

Garden Cultivation
Do not plant outside until the night temperature no longer falls below 40°F. Plant in an area protected from the wind; even here, a stake is recommended. It prefers a light soil and a sunny position.

Flowers of the incense plant
Calomeria amaranthoides

Harvesting
Collect flowers for drying in summer. Dry for use in potpourris.

CONTAINER GROWING

The incense plant is very ornamental and is the ultimate potted plant, growing to over 5 ft. It is, however, rarely seen because it needs a good deal of attention and protection.

Use the bark-peat-grit potting soil (see p. 591), and regularly repot and liquid feed throughout its short life until a pot size of 12 in. in diameter is reached. Place in full sun and water through the growing season.

OTHER USES

Use in potpourris.

Calendula officinalis

CALENDULA

Also known as Souci, Marybud, Bulls Eye, Garden Marigold, Holligold, Pot Marigold, and Common Marigold. From the family Asteraceae.

Native of the Mediterranean and Iran. Distributed throughout the world as a garden plant.

This sunny little flower—the "merrybuds" of Shakespeare—was first used in Indian and Arabic cultures, before being "discovered" by the ancient Egyptians and Greeks.

The Egyptians valued the calendula as a rejuvenating herb, and the Greeks garnished and flavored food with its golden petals. The botanical name comes from the Latin *calendae*, meaning the first day of the month.

In India wreaths of calendula were used to crown the gods and goddesses. In medieval times the leaves were considered an emblem of love and used as chief ingredient in a complicated spell that promised a young maiden knowledge of whom she would marry. To dream of Calendula wreaths was a sign of all good things; simply to look at them would drive away evil humors.

During the Civil War, calendula leaves were used by doctors on the battlefield to treat open wounds.

SPECIES

Calendula officinalis
Calendula
Hardy annual. Ht. and spread 24 in. Daisylike, single or double flowers, yellow or orange: from spring to fall. Light green, aromatic, lance-shaped leaves.
All zones

Calendula
Calendula officinalis

CULTIVATION

Propagation
Seeds
Seeds can be sown in the fall under protection directly into prepared pots or singly into plug trays, covering lightly with compost. They can be wintered in these containers and planted out in the spring after any frost, 12–18 in. apart.

Pests and Diseases
Slugs love the leaves of young calendulas. Keep nighttime vigil and pick

them off. In the latter part of the season, plants can become infested with aphids. Treat this in the early stages by spraying with a horticultural soap. Very late in the season, the leaves sometimes become covered with a powdery mildew. Cut off those affected and burn them to prevent spreading.

Maintenance
Spring Sow seeds in garden.
Summer Deadhead flowers to promote more flowering.
Fall Sow seeds under protection for early spring flowering.
Winter Protect young plants.

Garden Cultivation
Calendula is a very tolerant plant, growing in any soil that is not waterlogged, but prefers, and looks best in, a sunny position.

The flowers are sensitive to variations of temperature and dampness. Open flowers forecast a fine day. Encourage continuous flowering by deadheading. It self-seeds abundantly but seems never to become a nuisance. Self-sown seeds normally germinate in autumn and overwinter successfully if temperatures do not go persistently below 32°F. They will flower the following summer.

Do not confuse the calendula or marigold *Calendula officinalis* with the French or African marigolds, which are *Tagetes*. Calendula attracts aphids away from other plants.

Harvesting
Pick flowers just as they open during summer, both for fresh use and for drying. Dry at a low temperature. You can make a colorful oil.

Pick leaves young for fresh use; they are not much good preserved.

CULINARY

Flower petals make a very good culinary dye. They have been used for butter and cheese, and as a poor-man's saffron to color rice. They are also lovely in salads and omelets, and make an interesting cup of tea.

Young leaves can be added to salads.

Sweet Calendula Buns
Makes 18

$1/2$ *cup softened butter*
$1/2$ *cup sugar*
2 eggs
$1/2$ *cup self-rising flour*
1 teaspoon baking powder
2 tablespoons fresh calendula petals

Preheat the oven to 325°F. Put the butter, sugar, eggs, sifted flour, and baking powder into a bowl, and mix together until smooth and glossy. Fold in $1\frac{1}{2}$ tablespoons of calendula petals. Turn the mixture into greased muffin tins or individual cupcake papers. Sprinkle a few petals onto each bun with a little sugar. Bake for approximately 25–30 minutes.

CONTAINER GROWING

Calendulas look very cheerful in containers and combine well with other plants. Well suited to window boxes, but not so in hanging baskets, where they tip over and look sloppy.

Use the bark-peat potting soil (see p. 591). Pinch out the growing tips to stop the plant from becoming too tall and leggy. Deadhead flowers to encourage more blooms.

OTHER USES
There are many skin and cosmetic preparations that contain calendula. Infuse the flowers and use as a skin lotion to reduce large pores, nourish and clear the skin, and clear up spots and pimples.

MEDICINAL

Calendula flowers contain antiseptic, antifungal, and antibacterial properties that promote healing. Make a compress or poultice of the flowers for burns, scalds, or stings. Also useful in the treatment of varicose veins, chilblains, and impetigo. A cold infusion may be used as an eyewash for conjunctivitis and can be a help in the treatment of thrush.

The sap from the stem has a reputation for removing warts, corns, and calluses.

Calendula skin lotion

Carum carvi

CARAWAY

From the family Apiaceae.

Caraway is a native of Southern Europe, Asia, and India and thrives in all but the most humid warm regions of the world. It is commercially and horticulturally cultivated on a wide scale, especially in Germany and Holland.

Both the common and species names stem directly from the ancient Arabic word for the seed, *karawya*, which was used in medicines and as a flavoring by the ancient Egyptians. In fact, fossilized caraway seeds have been discovered at Mesolithic sites, so this herb has been used for at least 5,000 years. It has also been found in the remains of Stone Age meals, Egyptian tombs, and ancient caravan stops along the Silk Road.

Caraway probably did not come into use in Europe until the 13th century, but it made a lasting impact. In the 16th century when Shakespeare, in *Henry IV*, gave Falstaff a pippin apple and a dish of caraways, his audience could relate to the dish, for caraway had become a traditional finish to an Elizabethan feast. Its popularity was further enhanced 250 or so years later when Queen Victoria married Prince Albert, who made it clear that he shared his countrymen's particular predilection for the seed in an era celebrated in England by the caraway seedcake.

No herb this ancient goes without magical properties, of course; caraway was reputed to ward off witches and also to prevent lovers from straying, a propensity with a wide application—it kept a man's doves, pigeons, and poultry steadfast too!

SPECIES

Carum carvi
Caraway
Hardy biennial. Ht. in first year 8 in., second year 24 in.; spread 12 in. Flower white-pinkish in tiny umbellate clusters in early summer. Leaves feathery, light green, similar to carrot. Pale thick tapering root comparable to parsnip but smaller. This plant is not particularly decorative.
Zone 4

Caraway *Carum carvi*

CULTIVATION

Propagation
Seed
Easily grown; best sown outdoors in early fall when the seed is fresh. Preferred situation full sun or a little shade and any reasonable, well-drained soil. For an acceptable flavor it must have full sun.

If growing caraway as a root crop, sow in rows and treat the plants like vegetables. Thin to 8 in. and keep weed-free. These plants will be ready for a seed harvest the following summer; the roots will be ready in their second fall.

Caraway perpetuates itself by self-sowing and can, with a little control, maintain the cycle.

If you want to sow in spring, do it either directly in the garden into shallow drills after the soil has warmed, or into prepared plug trays to minimize harmful disturbance to its taproot when potting up. Cover with perlite. Pot up when seedlings are large enough to handle and transplant in the early fall.

Pests and Diseases

Caraway occasionally suffers from **carrot root fly**. The grubs of these pests tunnel into the roots. The only organic way to get rid of them is to pull up the plants and destroy them.

Maintenance

Spring Weed well around fall-sown young plants. Sow seed.
Summer Pick flowers and leaves.
Fall Cut seed heads. Dig up second-year plants. Sow seeds.
Winter Does not need much protection unless it gets very cold.

Garden Cultivation

Prepare the garden seedbed well. The soil should be fertile, free-draining, and free of weeds, not least because it is all too easy to mistake a young caraway plant for a weed in its early growing stage. Thin plants when well established to a distance of 8 in.

Harvesting

Harvest the seeds in summer by cutting the seed heads just before the first seeds fall. Hang them with a paper bag tied over the seed head or over a tray in an airy place. It was once common practice to scald the freshly collected seed to rid it of insects and then dry it in the sun before storing. This is not necessary. Simply store in an airtight container.

Gather fresh leaves when young for use in salads. They are not really worth drying.

Dig up roots in the second fall as a food crop.

Container Growing

Caraway really is not suitable for growing in pots.

Culinary

When you see caraway mentioned in a recipe it is usually the seed that is required. Caraway seedcake was one of the staples of the Victorian tea table. Nowadays caraway is more widely used in cooking, and in soups, as well as sweet dishes. The strong and distinctive flavor is also considered a spice. It is frequently added to sauerkraut, and the German liqueur Kummel contains its oil along with cumin.

Sprinkle over rich meats—goose, Hungarian beef stew—as an aid to digestion. Add to cabbage water to reduce cooking smells. Add to apple pies, cookies, baked apples, and cheese.

Serve in a mixed dish of seeds at the end of an Indian meal to both sweeten the breath and aid digestion.

Caraway root can be cooked as a vegetable, and its young leaves chopped into salads and soups.

Caraway and Cheese Potatoes
Serves 4

4 large potatoes
1 cup grated Gruyère cheese
2 teaspoons caraway seeds

Preheat the oven to 350°F. Scrub but do not peel the potatoes. Cut them in half lengthwise. Wrap in a boat of foil and sprinkle each half with some of the grated cheese and a little caraway. Bake for 35–45 minutes, or until the potatoes are soft.

Caraway seeds

Caraway and Cheese Potatoes

Medicinal

The fresh leaves, roots, and seeds have digestive properties.

Chew seeds raw or infuse them to sharpen the appetite before a meal, as well as to aid digestion, sweeten breath, and relieve flatulence after a meal. Safe for children.

An infusion can be made from 3 teaspoons of crushed seeds with 1/2 cup of water.

Other Uses

Pigeon fanciers claim that tame pigeons will never stray if there is baked caraway dough in their coop.

Cedronella canariensis (triphylla)

BALM OF GILEAD

Also known as Canary Balm. From the family Lamiaceae.

Although this herb originates from Madeira and the Canary Islands, as indicated by its species name, balm of Gilead is now established in many temperate regions of the world. Many plants have been called balm of Gilead; the common link that they all have a musky, eucalyptus, camphorlike scent.

The Queen of Sheba gave Solomon a balm of Gilead, which was *Commiphora opobalsamum,* an aromatic desert shrub found in the Holy Land. Today this plant is rare and protected, its export prohibited.

The balm of Gilead mentioned in the Bible ("Is there no balm in Gilead; is there no physician there?") was initially held to be *Commiphora meccanensis,* which was an aromatic shrub. However some now say it was oleo-resin obtained from *Balsamodendron opobalsamum,* a plant now thought to be extinct. Whatever is the case, the medicinal balm of Gilead is *Populus balsamifera.* This is balsam poplar, a tree found growing in several temperate countries, which smells heavenly in early summer, while the herb now known as balm of Gilead is *Cedronella canariensis.* This is said to have a similar scent to the biblical shrubs, perhaps the reason for its popular name.

Balsam poplar *Populus balsamifera*

SPECIES

Cedronella canariensis
(triphylla)
Balm of Gilead
Half-hardy perennial, partial
evergreen. Ht. 3 ft., spread 2
ft. Leaves with strong
eucalyptus scent, 3 lobes
and toothed edges, borne
on square stems. Pink or
pale mauve, two-lipped
flowers throughout summer.
Black seed heads. **Zone 10**

CULTIVATION

Propagation
Seed
The fairly small seeds should be sown directly on the surface of a prepared pot, plug, or seed tray. Cover with a layer of perlite.

It is a temperamental germinator so bottom heat of 68°F can be an asset. If using heat remember not to let the compost dry out, and only water with a fine spray when needed. The seedlings will appear any time between 2 to 6 weeks. When two leaves have formed, prick out and plant in position 3 ft. apart.

Cuttings
More reliable than seed. They take readily either in early summer before flowering on new growth or in early fall on the semiripe wood. Use the bark-peat-grit mix of potting soil (see p. 591).

Pests and Diseases
Being aromatic, aphids and other pests usually leave it alone, but the seedlings are prone to **damping-off.**

Maintenance
Spring Sow seeds under protection. In a warm garden a mature plant can self-seed; rub the leaves of any self-seedlings to see if it is balm of Gilead or a young nettle (but don't get stung!). At this stage their aroma is the only characteristic that tells them apart.

Plants overwintered in containers should be repotted if rootbound and given a liquid feed.
Summer Cut back after flowering to keep it neat and tidy, and also to encourage new growth from which late cuttings can be taken.
Fall Take stem cuttings. Collect seed heads.
Winter Protect from frost.

Balm of Gilead
Cedronella canariensis

Garden Cultivation
Balm of Gilead grows happily outside in sheltered positions. Plant in a well-drained soil in full sun, preferably against a warm, wind-protecting wall. The plant has an upright habit but spreads at the top, so planting distance from other plants should be approximately 3 ft.

It is a tender plant that may need protection in cooler climates. If you get frosts lower than 29°F protect the plant for the winter, either by bringing it into a cool greenhouse or conservatory or by covering in a frost fabric.

Harvesting
Pick leaves for drying before the flowers open, when they will be at their most aromatic.

Either pick flowers when just coming into bloom and dry, or wait until flowering is over and collect the black flower heads (good for winter arrangements).

Seeds are ready for extraction when you can hear the flower heads rattle. Store in an airtight container to sow in the spring.

CONTAINER GROWING

Balm of Gilead makes an excellent container plant. A 9–10 in. pot will be required for a plant to reach maturity. Use a free-draining compost with bark and grit.

Feed a mature plant liquid fertilizer monthly throughout summer.

When grown in a conservatory, the scent of the leaves perfumes the air especially when the plant is watered or the sun shining on it. Flowers are long lasting and give a good show during the summer. Keep watering to the absolute minimum in the winter months.

MEDICINAL

Crush the leaves in your hand and inhale the aroma to clear your head.

Rub the leaves on skin to stop being bitten by mosquitoes.

Also said to be an aphrodisiac.

OTHER USES
Dried leaves combine well in a spicy or woody potpourri with cedarwood chips, rosewood, pine needles, small fir cones, cypress oil, and pine oil.

Add an infusion of the leaves to bathwater for an invigorating bath.

Centranthus ruber (Valeriana ruber)

RED VALERIAN

Also known as American Lilac, Bloody Butcher, Bouncing Bess, and Bouncing Betsy. From the family Valerianaceae.

A native of central and southern Europe cultivated widely in temperate climates, this cheerful plant was a great ornament in Gerard's garden, but he described it in 1597 as "not common in England." However, by the early eighteenth century, it had become well known.

SPECIES

Centranthus ruber
Red Valerian
Perennial. Ht. 2–3 ft., spread 18–24 in. Showy red fragrant flowers in summer. They can also appear in all shades of white and pink. Fleshy, pale green, pointed leaves.
Zone 5

CULTIVATION

Propagation
Seed
Sow the small seeds in early fall in seed or plug trays, using the bark-peat-grit mix of potting soil (see p. 591). Cover lightly with soil and leave outside over winter, covered with glass. As soon as you notice it germinating, remove the glass and place in a cold greenhouse. Prick the seedlings out when large enough to handle and pot up using the same mix of soil. Leave the pots outside for the summer, watering regularly until the fall. No need to feed with liquid fertilizer. Plant out 2 ft. apart.

Pests and Diseases
This plant does not suffer from pests or diseases.

Maintenance
Spring Dig up self-sown seedlings and replant if you want them.
Summer Deadhead to prevent self-seeding.
Fall Sow seeds. Plant previous year's seedlings.
Winter A very hardy plant.

Garden Cultivation
Red valerian has naturalized on banks, crumbling walls, and rocks in coastal regions. It is very attractive to butterflies. As an ornamental, it thrives in poor, well-drained, low-fertility soil, and especially in alkaline conditions. It likes a sunny position and self-seeds prolifically.

Harvesting
Dig complete root up in the late fall of the second and third years. Wash and remove the pale fibrous roots, leaving the edible rhizome. If you want to dry this rhizome, cut it into manageable slices (see Drying, p. 609). Pick young leaves as required.

CONTAINER GROWING

Make sure the container is large enough and use a soil-based compost. No need to feed, otherwise you will inhibit its flowers. Position the container in a sunny spot and water regularly.

CULINARY

Very young leaves are eaten in France and Italy. They are incredibly bitter.

Red valerian
Centranthus ruber

MEDICINAL

A drug is obtained (by herbalists only) from the root, which looks like a huge radish and has a characteristic odor. It is believed to be helpful in cases of hysteria and nervous disorders because of its sedative and anti-spasmodic properties.

WARNING

Large doses or extended use may produce symptoms of poisoning. Do not take for more than a couple of days at a time.

"I am sorry to say that Peter was not very well during the evening. His mother put him to bed and made some chamomile tea and she gave a dose of it to Peter, one tablespoon full to be taken at bedtime."
—The Tale of Peter Rabbit, *Beatrix Potter*

Chamaemelum nobile

CHAMOMILE

From the family Asteraceae.

Chamomile grows wild in North America, Europe, and many other countries. As a garden escapee, it can be found in pastures and other grassy places on sandy soils.

The generic name, *Chamaemelum*, is derived from the Greek *Khamaimelon*, meaning "earth apple" or "apple on the ground."

Dyers chamomile
Anthemis tinctoria

SPECIES

Chamaemelum nobile
Roman Chamomile
Also known as Garden Chamomile, Ground Apple, Low Chamomile, and Whig Plant
Hardy perennial evergreen. Ht. 4 in., spread 18 in. White flowers with yellow centers all summer. Sweet smelling, finely divided foliage. Ideal for ground cover. Can be used as a lawn, but because it flowers it will need constant cutting.
Zone 4

***Chamaemelum nobile*
'Flore Pleno'**
Double-flowered Chamomile
Hardy perennial evergreen. Ht. 3 in., spread 12 in. Double white flowers all summer. Sweet-smelling, finely divided, thick foliage. Good for ground cover, in between paving stones and lawns. More compact habit than Roman Chamomile, and combines well with chamomile Treneague.
Zone 4

***Chamaemelum nobile*
'Treneague' (*Anthemis nobile* 'Treneague')**
Treneague Chamomile
Also known as Lawn Chamomile
Hardy perennial evergreen. Ht. 2.5 in., spread 6 in. Nonflowering. Leaves are finely divided and very aromatic. Ideal for ground cover or mow-free lawn. Plant in well-drained soil, free from stones, 4–6 in. apart.
Zone 4

Anthemis tinctoria
Dyers Chamomile
Also known as Yellow Chamomile
Hardy perennial evergreen. Ht. and spread 3 ft. Yellow daisy flowers in the summer. Leaves are mid-green and fernlike. Mainly a dye plant.
Zone 4

Matricaria recutita
German Chamomile
Also known as Scented Mayweed, Wild Chamomile
Hardy annual. Ht. 24 in, spread 4 in. Scented white flowers with conical yellow centers from spring to early summer. Finely serrated aromatic foliage. The main use of this chamomile is medicinal.
All zones

CULTIVATION

Propagation
Seed
Dyers, Roman, and German chamomiles can be grown from seed. Sow onto the surface of a prepared seed or plug tray. Use a bark-peat-grit potting soil (see p. 591). Cover with perlite. Use bottom heat 65°F. Harden off and plant out or repot.

Chamomile *Chamaemelum nobile*

Cuttings
Double-flowered chamomile and Treneague chamomile can only be propagated this way. Take cuttings in the spring and fall from the off-sets or clusters of young shoots. They are easy to grow as they have aerial roots.

Division
All perennial chamomiles planted as specimen plants will benefit from being lifted in the spring of their second or third year and divided.

Pests and Diseases
As all the chamomiles are highly aromatic they are not troubled by pests or disease.

Maintenance
Spring Collect offshoots, sow seeds. Fill in holes that have appeared in the chamomile lawn. Divide established plants. Give a liquid fertilizer feeding to established plants.
Summer Water well. Do not allow to dry out. In the first season of a lawn, trim the plants to encourage bushing out and spreading. In late summer collect flowers from the dyers chamomile and cut the plant back to 2 in. to promote new growth.

Dyers chamomile
Anthemis tinctoria

Fall Take cuttings. Divide if they have become too invasive. Cut back to promote new growth. Give the final feeding of the season.
Winter Use mulches in zones 4 or 5 unless snow cover is reliable.

Garden Cultivation

All the chamomiles prefer a well-drained soil and a sunny situation, although they will adapt to most conditions.

As a lawn plant, chamomile gets more credit than it deserves. Chamomile lawns are infinitely less easy to maintain in good condition than grass lawns. There is no selective herbicide that will preserve chamomile and kill the rest of the weeds. It is a hands-and-knees job.

Prepare the site well, make sure the soil is light, slightly acid, and free from weeds and stones. Plant young plants in plug form. I use a mix of double-flowered and Treneague chamomile at a distance of 4–6 in. apart. Keep all traffic off it for at least 12 weeks, and keep it to a minimum during the first year.

If all this seems daunting, compromise and plant a chamomile seat. Prepare the soil in the same way and do not sit on the seat for at least 12 weeks. Then sit down, smell the sweet aroma and sip a cool glass of wine.

Harvesting
Leaves
Gather in spring and early summer for best results. Use fresh or dry.

Flowers
Pick when fully open, around midsummer. Use fresh or dry. Dyers chamomile flowers should be harvested in summer for their yellow dye.

COMPANION PLANTING

Chamomile has the unique name "Physician's Plant" because, when planted near ailing plants, it helps to revive them. Roman chamomile can be planted next to onions to repel flying insects and improve the crop yield.

Chamomile Infusion

Bring 2 cups of water to a boil. Add a handful of chamomile leaves and flowers. Cover and let it stand for about half a day. Strain.

Spray it onto seedlings to prevent damping-off. If there is any liquid left, pour it on to your compost heap. This acts like an activator for decomposition.

WARNING

When taken internally, excessive dosage can produce vomiting and vertigo.

CONTAINER GROWING

I would not advise growing chamomiles indoors, as they get very leggy, soft, and prone to disease. But the flowers can look very cheerful in a sunny window box. Use chamomile 'Flore Pleno,' which has a lovely double flower head, or the nonflowering chamomile Treneague as an infill between bulbs, with a bark-peat-grit potting soil (see p. 591).

COSMETIC

Chamomile is used as a final rinse for fair hair to make it brighter. Pour $3^{1}/_{2}$ cups of boiling water over one handful of chamomile flowers and steep for 30 minutes. Strain, cover, and allow to cool. It should be poured over your hair several times.

MEDICINAL

German chamomile's highly scented dry flower heads contain up to 1 percent of an aromatic oil that possesses powerful antiseptic and anti-inflammatory properties. Taken as a tea, it promotes gastric secretions and improves the appetite, while an infusion of the same strength can be used as an internal antiseptic. It may also be used as a douche or gargle for mouth ulcers and as an eye wash.

An oil for skin rashes or allergies can be made by tightly packing flower heads into a preserving jar, covering with olive oil, and leaving in the sun for three weeks. If you suffer from overwrought nerves, add five or six drops of chamomile oil to the bath and this will help you relax at night.

Chamomile tea

1 heaping teaspoon chamomile flowers (dried or fresh)
1 teaspoon honey
Slice of lemon (optional)

Put the chamomile flowers into a warm cup. Pour in boiling water. Cover and leave to infuse for 3–5 minutes. Strain and add the honey and lemon, if required. Can be drunk either hot or cold.

OTHER USES

Dyers chamomile can be used as a dye plant. Depending on the chemical blend, its color can vary from bright to olive-brown yellow.

German and double-flowered chamomile are best for herb pillows and potpourri.

Chenopodium bonus-henricus

GOOD KING HENRY

Also known as All Good, Good King Harry, Good Neighbor, Wild Spinach, Lincolnshire Asparagus, and Mercury. From the family Chenopodiaceae.

Good King Henry comes from a genus *(Chenopodium)* that is distributed all over the world and is found growing in all climates. This species *(C. bonus-henricus)* is native to Europe.

Good King Henry was popular from Neolithic times until the last century. Its curious name is not taken from the English king, Henry VIII, as might be expected, but from King Henry IV of Navarre, and to distinguish it from the poisonous Bad Henry *(Mercurialis perennis)*.

In the sixteenth century Gerard observed that Good King Henry grew in untilled places and among garbage near alleys, old walls, hedges and fields, and it still does—colonies of the herb can be found on many historic sites.

SPECIES

Chenopodiaceae, the Goosefoot family, includes 1,500 rather unattractive plants, some of them important edible plants—for example, spinach and beet.

Chenopodium bonus-henricus
Good King Henry Perennial. Ht. 24 in., spread 18 in. Tiny greenish-yellow flowers in early summer. Leaves green and arrow-shaped *(below right)*. Very occasionally a variegated form is found; but the yellow variegation will be difficult to maintain.
Zone 5

Chenopodium album
Fat Hen
Also known as Lambs' Quarters, White Goosefoot, Common Pigweed. Annual. Ht. 2–3 ft. Flowers small, greenish-white, summer to mid-fall. Green lance-shaped leaves. Its seeds have been identified at Neolithic villages in Switzerland and in the stomach of the Iron Age Tollund Man. Rich in fat and albumen, it appears to have been a food supplement for primitive man.
All zones

Good King Henry
Chenopodium bonus-henricus

Chenopodium ambrosioides
American Wormseed, also known as Epazote Annual. Ht. 2–4 ft. Small greenish flowers from late summer to late fall. Green lance-shaped leaves. This is native to tropical Central America. Introduced through Mexico, it has become naturalized as far north as New England. It was introduced into Europe in the 18th century. Epazote was once included in the American pharmacopoeia but is now restricted to folk medicine and mainly used for its essential oil, chenopodium oil, against roundworm and hookworm. Dried leaves are used to season bean dishes in Mexican cooking.
All zones

Warning: Poisonous. Use under strict supervision. It causes deafness, vertigo, paralysis, incontinence, sweating, jaundice, and can be fatal.

CULTIVATION

Propagation
Seeds

Sow the fairly small seeds early in spring in prepared seed or plug trays for an early crop. Use the bark-peat-grit mix of potting soil (see p. 591) and cover with perlite. No extra heat required. When the seedlings are large enough to handle and after hardening off, plant out in the garden 10 in. apart. Can be sown directly.

Division

Divide established plants in the spring. You will find even small pieces will grow.

Pests and Diseases
Does not suffer from these.

Maintenance
Spring Lift and divide established plants. If you wish to grow as an asparagus, blanch the shoots from early spring onward. As they emerge, earth up with soil.
Divide and repot container-grown plants.
Summer Apply liquid fertilizer if a second crop of leaves is required.

Good King Henry makes an interesting addition to salads

Fall Cut back dying foliage and give the plant a mulch of compost.
Winter No need for protection.

Garden Cultivation
Good King Henry will tolerate any soil, but if planted in a soil rich in humus, dug deep, and well drained in a sunny position, the quality and quantity of the crop will be much improved. Sow directly into prepared soil in the garden in late spring in ½ in. drills. Allow 18 in. between rows. Cover the seeds with ¼ in. soil. Germination in warm soil, 10–14 days. When large enough to handle, thin to 10 in. apart.
Keep well watered in dry months. In fall cover beds with a thin layer of manure. Beds should be renewed every 3–4 years.

Harvesting
Allow plants one year to develop before harvesting. From mid-spring the young shoots can be used as raw or cooked greens. They should be cut when they are about 6 in. long. Harvest the flowering spikes as they begin to open. Later in the season gather the larger leaves as a spinach substitute as required. Freeze only when used as an ingredient in a cooked dish.

MEDICINAL

The seeds have a gentle laxative effect, making them suitable relief for a slightly constipated condition, especially in children.
A poultice (or ointment) cleanses and heals skin sores.

WARNING

Sufferers of kidney complaints or rheumatism should avoid medicinal preparations containing extracts from this plant.

CULINARY

The leaves of Good King Henry and fat hen are rich in iron, calcium, and vitamins B_1 and C, and are particularly recommended for anemic subjects.
Like all low-growing leaves, Good King Henry must be washed with great care; the slightest suspicion of grit in the finished dish will ruin the meal. Use 2 or 3 changes of water.

OTHER USES
Good King Henry is a cough remedy for sheep.
The whole plant is used to fatten poultry.
Seed is used commercially in the manufacture of shagreen, an artificially granulated, untanned leather, often dyed green.
The whole plant of fat hen can be used as a red or golden dye *(above)*.

CONTAINER GROWING

Can be grown outside in a large container, in a rich potting soil of a bark-peat-grit mix. Needs to be kept well watered throughout the summer and fed once a week to maintain a supply of leaves. Divide each spring and repot in fresh compost.

Steam flower spikes and toss in butter like broccoli.
Eat young leaves raw in salads. Cook in casseroles, stuffings, soups, and purées and meat pies. They are more nutritious than spinach or cabbage.
Blanch shoots—dip in hot water, rinse immediately under cold water. Cut shoots 6 in. long. Steam or boil very quickly. Peel if necessary. Serve hot with melted butter, or cold with a vinaigrette.
The seed of fat hen can be ground into flour and used to make into a gruel.

Convallaria majalis

LILY OF THE VALLEY

Also known as Our Lady's Tears, Fairy's Bells, May Lily, Ladder to Heaven, and May Bells. From the family Convallariaceae.

Lily of the valley is a native of North America, Canada, and Europe. Introduced throughout the world in moist cool climates.

According to European folk tales, lily of the valley either originated from the Virgin Mary's tears, shed at the foot of the Cross, or from those shed by Mary Magdalen when she found Christ's tomb.

From the Middle Ages onward the flowers have formed the traditional part of a bride's bouquet and are associated with modesty and purity.

In the sixteenth century they were used medicinally and called Convall Lily. The Elizabethan physician Gerard has this amazing recipe: "Put the flowers of May lilies into a glass and set it in a hill of ants, firmly closed for 1 month. After which you will find a liquor that when applied appeaseth the paine and grief of gout."

SPECIES

Convallaria majalis
Lily of the Valley
Hardy perennial. Ht. 6 in., spread indefinite. White, bell-shaped, scented flowers, late spring to early summer. Leaves mid-green in color, oval in shape. There are many attractive forms of this plant. The most striking is 'Vic Pawlowski's Gold,' which has gold stripes running through the leaves. Another is the pink *Convallaria majalis* var. *rosea.*
Zone 4

Lily of the Valley *Convallaris majalis* 'Vic Pawlowski's Gold'

CULTIVATION

Propagation

Seeds
Sometimes self-sows, but the scarlet berries are highly poisonous, so it is far better to propagate by division.

Division
The plant produces crowns on creeping rhizomes. Divide in the fall after the leaves have turned yellow and died back.

Pests and Diseases
Lily of the valley is free from most pests and diseases.

Maintenance
Spring In very early spring, bring pots into the house for forcing.
Summer Do nothing!
Fall When the plant has died back fully dig up the rhizomes for splitting. Pot up crowns for forcing.
Winter No need for protection.

Garden Cultivation
Contrary to its name, it should be grown not in an open valley but in partial shade. Ideal for growing under trees or in woodlands or in the shade of a fence, provided there is not too much competition from other plants.

To get the best flowers, prepare the site well. The soil should be deeply cultivated with plenty of well-rotted manure, compost, or leaf mold. Plant in fall, 6 in. apart, before the frosts make the soil too hard. Place the crowns upright in the prepared holes with the tips just below the soil.

Harvesting
Pick the flowers when in full bloom for drying so that they can be added to potpourri.

CONTAINER GROWING

This plant can be happily grown in pots as long as it is kept in the shade and watered regularly. Use the bark-peat mix of potting soil (see p. 591). Feed with liquid fertilizer only during flowering. In winter let the plant die down, and keep it in a cool place outside.

MEDICINAL

This plant, like the foxglove, is used in the treatment of heart disease. It contains cardiac glycosides, which increase the strength of the heartbeat while slowing and regularizing its rate, without putting extra demand on the coronary blood supply.

Lily of the Valley *Convallaria majalis*

CULINARY

None—all parts of the plant are poisonous.

WARNING

Lily of the valley should be used only as prescribed by a qualified practitioner. All parts of the plant are poisonous.

Coriandrum sativum

CORIANDER

Also known as Chinese Parsley, Cilantro (leaves), Yuen Sai, Fragrant Green, Dhania (seed), Dhania Pattar, and Dhania Sabz (leaves). From the family Apiaceae.

A native of southern Europe and the Middle East, coriander was a popular herb in England up until Tudor times. Early European settlers in America included the seed among the beloved items they took to the New World.

Coriander has been cultivated for over 3,000 years. Seeds have been found in tombs from the twenty-first Egyptian dynasty (1085–945 B.C.). The herb is mentioned in the Old Testament—"when the children of Israel were returning to their homeland from slavery in Egypt, they ate manna in the wilderness and the manna was as coriander seeds"—and it is still one of the traditional bitter herbs to be eaten at the Passover when the Jewish people remember that great journey.

Coriander was brought to Northern Europe by the Romans who, combining it with cumin and vinegar, rubbed it into meat as a preservative. The Chinese once believed it bestowed immortality and in the Middle Ages it was put in love potions as an aphrodisiac. Its name is said to be derived from *koris*, Greek for "bedbug," since the plant smells strongly of the insect.

Coriander *Coriandrum sativum*

SPECIES

Coriandrum sativum
Coriander
Tender annual. Ht. 24 in. White flowers in the summer. The first and lower leaves are broad and scalloped, with a strong, strange scent. The upper leaves are finely cut and have a different and yet more pungent smell. The whole plant is edible. This variety is good for leaf production.

Coriandrum sativum
'Leisure'
Tender annual. Ht. 24 in. As *C. sativum*; whitish flowers in summer; also suitable for leaf production.

Coriandrum sativum
'Morocco'
Tender annual. Ht. 28 in. Flowers white with a slight pink tinge in summer. This variety is best for seed production. **All zones**

CULTIVATION

Propagation
Coriander is grown from seed. Thinly sow its large seed directly into the soil in shallow drills. Lightly cover with fine soil or potting mix, and water. Look for results after a period of between 5 and 10 days. Seed sowing may be carried out as often as required between early spring (under glass) and late fall. When large enough to handle, thin out the

Coriander seeds

Coriander *Coriandrum sativum*

seedlings to leave room for growth.

Sowing into seed trays is not recommended because coriander plants do not transplant well once the taproot is established. If they get upset they bolt straight into flower, missing out the leaf-production stage.

If a harvest of fresh leaves is required, space the plants 2 in. apart; if of seed, 9 in. apart.

Pests and Diseases

Being a highly aromatic plant, coriander is usually free from pests. In exceptional circumstances it is attacked by **aphids**. If so, spray with plain water gently and shake the plant carefully to remove excess water on the leaves, or use a liquid horticultural soap.

Maintenance

Spring Sow seeds.
Summer Sow seeds, cut leaves.
Fall Cut seed heads. Sow fall crop in mild climates. Dig up old plants.
Winter Once the seed heads have been collected, the plant should be pulled up.

Garden Cultivation

Coriander grows best in a light, well-drained soil, a sunny position, and a dry atmosphere. In fact, it is difficult to grow in damp or humid areas and needs a good, dry summer at the very least if a reasonable crop is to be obtained.

Plant out in cool climates when there is no threat of frost, making sure the final position is nowhere near fennel, which seems to suffer in its presence.

When the plant reaches maturity and the seeds set and begin to ripen, the plant tends to loll about on its weak stem and needs staking. On ripening, the seeds develop a delightful orangy scent, and are used widely as a spice and a condiment. For this reason alone, and because the flavor of home-grown seeds is markedly superior to

those raised commercially, coriander deserves a place in the garden. If you live in a mild, frost-free climate, sow in the fall for an over-winter crop; but make sure the plants are in full sunlight.

Harvesting

Pick young leaves any time. They should be 4 in. in height and bright green.

Watch seed heads carefully, as they ripen suddenly and will fall without warning. Cut the flower stems as the seed smell starts to become pleasant. Cover bunches of about six heads together in a paper bag. Tie the top of the bag and hang it upside down in a dry, warm, airy place. Leave for roughly ten days. The seeds should come away from the husk quite easily and be stored in an airtight container. Coriander seeds keep their flavor well.

CONTAINER GROWING

Coriander can be grown in containers inside with diligence or outside on the windowsill or patio, but for a confined space inside it is not the best choice. Until the seeds ripen the whole plant has an unpleasant smell. Also, being an annual it has a short season. The only successful way to maintain it in a pot is to keep picking the mature leaves. However, if you do decide to grow coriander in a container, ensure good drainage with plenty of chippings or broken pot pieces; use a bark-peat potting soil (see p. 591); and do not overwater in the evening. Like many herbs, coriander does not like wet feet.

MEDICINAL

Coriander is good for the digestive system, reducing flatulence, stimulating the appetite and aiding the secretion of gastric juices.

It is also used to prevent grippe caused by other medication such as senna or rhubarb.

Bruised seed can be applied externally as a poultice to relieve painful joints and rheumatism.

CULINARY

The leaves and ripe seeds have two distinct flavors. The seeds are warmly aromatic; the leaves have an earthy pungency.

Coriander seeds are used regularly in the Indian garam masala (a mixture of spices) and in curries. Use ground seed in tomato chutney and ratatouille, and also in apple pies, cakes, cookies, and jam. Add whole seeds to soups, sauces, and vegetable dishes.

Add fresh lower leaves to curries, stews, salads, sauces, and as a garnish. Delicious in salads, vegetables, and poultry dishes. A bunch of coriander leaves with a vinaigrette dressing goes particularly well with hard-boiled eggs.

Mushrooms and Coriander
Serves 2

5 cups button mushrooms
2 tablespoons cooking oil
1 cup dry white wine
2 teaspoons coriander seeds
1 clove garlic
2 tablespoons tomato purée
Salt and pepper
Coriander leaf (cilantro) for garnish

Wipe mushrooms and slice in half. Put the oil, wine, coriander seeds, and garlic in a large saucepan. Bring to a boil and cover and simmer for 5 minutes. Add the mushrooms and tomato purée. Cook for 5 minutes, by which time the vegetables should be tender. Remove the mushrooms and put in a serving dish. Boil the liquid again for 5 minutes and reduce it by half. Pour over the mushrooms. When cool, sprinkle with some chopped coriander leaf (cilantro).

Dianthus

PINKS

Also known as Clove Pink and Gillyflower.
From the family Caryophyllaceae.

The true pinks are derived from *Dianthus plumarius*, a native of Eastern Europe and introduced to Britain in the seventeenth century. From then on, numerous varieties have been cultivated. The wild ancestor of the carnation, *Dianthus caryophyllus*, it is a native of central and southern Europe; both species and their varieties are now cultivated throughout the world.

"Dianthus" comes from the words *dios*, meaning "divine," and *anthos*, meaning "flower," and was coined by Theophrastus, a Greek botanist who lived in 370–285 B.C., alluding to their fragrance and neatness of flower. Both the Romans and Greeks gave pinks a place of honor and made coronets and garlands from the flowers. The strong, sweet clove scent has made it popular for both culinary and perfumery purposes for more than 2,000 years. In the seventeenth century it was recognized that the flowers could be crystallized, and the petals were used in soups, sauces, cordials, and wine, and infused in vinegar.

The Cheddar pink was discovered early in the eighteenth century by Wiltshire botanist Samuel Brewer. It became as famous as Cheddar cheese and is mentioned in all the local guidebooks.

SPECIES

Dianthus armeria
Deptford Pink
Evergreen hardy perennial. Ht. 12–18 in., spread 18 in. Small bunches of little, cerise or pink, unscented flowers in summer. In dull weather the flower closes. Lance-shaped, narrow, dark green leaves.
Zone 5

Dianthus caryophyllus
Clove Pink
Evergreen hardy perennial. Ht. 18–24 in., spread 18 in. Rose or purply-pink flowers, having a spicy sweet scent. Loose mats of narrow, gray-green, lance-shaped leaves. The large-flowered florists' carnations also belong to this species.
Zone 7

Dianthus deltoides
Maiden Pink
Evergreen hardy perennial. Ht. 6 in., spread 12 in. Small cerise, pink, or white flowers are borne singly all summer. Small, narrow, lance-shaped, dark green leaves. Maiden pinks are a lovely spreading plant for rock gardens or gravel paths.
Zone 5

Dianthus gratianopolitanus syn. Dianthus caesius
Cheddar Pink
Evergreen hardy perennial. Ht. 6 in., spread 12 in. Very fragrant, rich pink to magenta, flat flowers are borne singly all summer. Loose mats of narrow, gray-green, lance-shaped leaves. The cheddar pink is very rare and a protected species in the wild, but is grown on many farms as a garden plant.
Zone 5

Dianthus plumarius
Pinks
Evergreen hardy perennial. Ht. 6 in., spread 12 in. Very fragrant white flowers with dark crimson centers borne singly all summer. Loose mats of narrow, gray-green, lance-shaped leaves. These are related to the Cheddar pink and are the origin of the garden pink.
Zone 5

Some old-fashioned garden pinks worth looking for:

Dianthus 'Gran's Favorite'
Fragrant semidouble white flowers with deep purple-red center.

Dianthus 'London Delight'
Fragrant flowers are semidouble and colored lavender laced with purple.

Dianthus 'Mrs. Sinkins'
Heavily scented flower, fringed, fully double, and white.

Dianthus 'Prudence'
Fragrant semidouble flowers, pinkish-white with purple lacing. This variety has a spreading habit.

CULTIVATION

Propagation
Seed
Although pinks can be propagated by seed, they can turn out to be very variable in height, color, and habit. The named forms can only be propagated by cuttings or by layering.

Sow the small seed in the fall when it is fresh, or in early spring, in prepared seed or plug trays; cover with perlite. If sown in the fall the young plants must be wintered under cover. It is critical not to overwater young plants or they will rot off. Allow plenty of air to flow through the greenhouse on warm days—if you open up the cold frame, close it at night. In the spring, when the seedlings are large enough to handle and after a period of hardening off, plant out in the garden about 1 ft. apart.

Cuttings
Stem cuttings can be taken in the spring. Alternatively, heel cuttings can be taken in the early fall (see Softwood Cuttings, p. 592), using the bark-peat-grit potting mix (see p. 591). Again, water the compost before taking the cuttings, then keep the compost on the drier side of moist to help prevent disease.

Division
After flowering, the plants can be dug up and divided.

Layering
In late summer plants can be layered.

Pests and Diseases
The main pest is the red spider mite. Use a liquid horticultural soap and spray at first sign of the pest.

The main disease appears at propagation stage, when the young plants can rot, usually caused by a fungus attack triggered by the compost being too wet. Organically there is nothing one can use to get rid of this; the infected plants must be removed.

Maintenance
Spring Sow seeds. Take stem cuttings.
Summer Deadhead flowers to prolong flowering. Divide after flowering. Layer plants.
Fall Take heel cuttings. Sow seed.
Winter No need for protection.

Garden Cultivation
Pinks prefer a truly well-drained soil, short of organic matter, and a sunny, sheltered site.

They are happy by the ocean or growing in a rock garden. With new varieties being developed all the time, many old pinks and carnations have been lost. But you can still find some excellent specialized nurseries that offer a great range.

Harvesting
Pick flowers when they are open either to use fresh or to crystallize the petals. Dry for potpourris or use for oil or vinegar.

CONTAINER GROWING

All the pinks mentioned here are happy in containers as long as the soil is free-draining; so use the bark-peat-grit mix (see p. 591). They combine well with other plants, and look special on their own. Maiden Pinks look effective in hanging baskets.

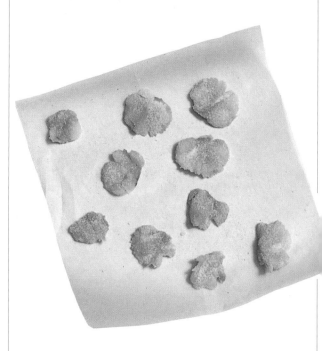

Crystallized dianthus flowers

CULINARY

Infuse the open flowers in almond oil for sweet oil or in wine vinegar for floral vinegar.

If you remove a petal from the flower you will notice that it has a white heel. This must be removed before the petals are added to any food as it is very bitter. Add petals to salads, fruit pies, even sandwiches. Use to flavor sugar and jam, or to make a syrup. Use crystallized flower petals to decorate cakes, cookies, and desserts.

Dissected *Dianthus* flowers showing the white heel

MEDICINAL

A tonic cordial can be made from the flower petals and is even better when combined with white wine! Makes an excellent nerve tonic.

OTHER USES

Add dried petals to potpourris, scented sachets, and cosmetic products.

Digitalis purpurea

FOXGLOVE

Also known as Digitalis, "American" Foxglove, Deadmen's Bells, Dogs Fingers, Fairy Fingers, Fairy Gloves, Fringe Flower, Folksglove, Lion Mouths, Ladiesglove, Purple Foxgloves, Witch's Glove, Gloves of Our Lady, Bloody Fingers, Fairy Caps, and Fairy Thimbles. From the family Scrophulariaceae.

Foxglove grows throughout Europe and in North America, and is a common wildflower in temperate climates throughout the world, seeding freely in woods and hedges.

The principal common name probably derives from the Anglo-Saxon *foxglue* or *foxmusic*, after the shape of a musical instrument. Judging by its other names, it would seem that it was also thought to be a fairy's plant or a goblin's plant, at least in England. Its appearance—its height, the glove shape of the corolla, and the poison of its leaves—seems somehow to suggest its own folklore.

In 1542, Fuchs called it *Digitalis* after the fingerlike shape of its flowers, but he considered it a violent medicine and it was not until the late eighteenth century that William Withering used foxglove tea in Shropshire for dropsy that its reputation as a medicinal herb grew. Commercial production of digitalis now takes place mainly in southeastern Europe.

SPECIES

There are many extremely attractive species and cultivars.

Digitalis grandiflora (Digitalis ambigua)
Yellow Foxglove
Hardy evergreen perennial. Ht. 30 in., spread 12 in. Creamy yellow, downward-pointing, tubular flowers all summer. Smooth, strongly veined leaves.
Zone 4

Digitalis purpurea
Foxglove (wild, common)
Shortlived perennial, grown as a biennial. Ht. 3–5 ft., spread 2 ft. Flowers all shades of pink, purple, and red in summer. Rough, mid- to dark green leaves.
Zone 4

Digitalis purpurea* f. *albiflora
White Foxglove
Shortlived perennial, grown as a biennial. Ht. 3–5 ft., spread 12–18 in. Tubular white flowers all summer. Rough, mid- to dark green leaves.
Zone 4

Foxglove *Digitalis purpurea*

WARNING

Foxgloves are poisonous and should not be eaten or used domestically. Even touching the plant has been known to cause rashes, headaches, and nausea. *Do not use* without medical direction.

White Foxglove *Digitalis purpurea* f. *albiflora*

If you live in a cold climate, zone 6 or colder, protect during the first winter. Use pine boughs, straw, or pine needles. In areas where the soil is damp and cold, it is advisable to lift the plants for the first winter and keep them in a cold frame, replanting the following spring.

Harvesting
This is not advised unless you are an herbalist or a pharmacist.

MEDICINAL

Foxgloves are grown commercially for the production of a drug the discovery of which (a major medical breakthrough) is a classic example of a productive marriage between folklore and scientific curiosity. Foxgloves contain glycosides, which are extracted from second-year leaves to make the heart drug digitalis. For more than 200 years digitalis has provided the main drug for treating heart failure. It is also a powerful diuretic. Although a synthetic form of the drug has been developed, the plant is still grown commercially for the drug industry.

CULTIVATION

Propagation
The seed is very small and fine. Sow in either spring or fall as carefully as possible, using the cardboard method (see p. 591), either directly onto the prepared ground, or into pots or plug trays. Sow on the surface; do not cover with perlite, but with a piece of glass, which should be removed as soon as the seedlings appear. No bottom heat required. Remember,

they will not flower the first season.

Pests and Diseases
Foxgloves, on the whole, are pest- and disease-free.

Maintenance
Spring Sow seeds. Plant out first-year plants.
Summer Remove main flowering shoot after flowering.
Fall Check around second-year plants for self-sown seedlings, thin out if over-crowded, remove if not required. Pot a few in case of an exceptionally hard winter.
Winter In the majority of cases no protection needed.

See Garden Cultivation, below, for the exceptions.

Garden Cultivation
This is one of the most poisonous plants in the flora. Foxgloves will grow in most conditions, even dry exposed sites, but do best in semishade and a moist but well-drained acid soil enriched with leaf mold. The rosettes and leaves are formed the first year and the flower spike the second. The plant then dies but usually leaves lots of self-sown babies nearby. Water well in dry weather and remove the center spike after flowering to increase the size of the flowers on the side shoots.

CONTAINER GROWING

These tall elegant plants do not honestly suit growing in containers. It is possible, but care has to be taken that the plant is not damaged in winds. Use a soil-based compost. Water regularly.

Echium vulgare

VIPER'S BUGLOSS

Also known as Bugles, Wild Borage, Snake Flower, Blue Devil, Blueweed, Viper's Grass, and Snakeflower. From the family Boraginaceae.

This plant originates from the Mediterranean region and is now widespread throughout the Northern Hemisphere, being found on light porous stones on semidry grassland, moorlands, and waste ground. It is regarded as a weed in some parts of America, and to many American farmers this will seem an understatement; they consider it a plague.

The common name, viper's bugloss, developed from the medieval *Doctrine of Signatures*, which ordained that a plant's use should be inferred from its appearance. It was noticed that the brown stem looked rather like a snakeskin and that the seed is shaped like a viper's head. So, in their wisdom, they prescribed it for viper bites, which for once proved right; it did have some success in the treatment of the spotted viper's bite.

SPECIES

Echium vulgare
Viper's Bugloss
Hardy biennial. Ht. 2–4 ft. Bright blue-pink flowers in the second year. The leaves are mid-green and bristly.
All zones

CULTIVATION

Propagation
Seed
Viper's bugloss is easily grown from seed. Start it off in a controlled way in spring by sowing the small seed into a prepared seed or plug tray. Cover the seed with perlite. When the seedlings are large enough to handle, and after a period of hardening off, plant out into a prepared site in the garden, 18 in. apart.

Pests and Diseases
It rarely suffers.

Maintenance
Spring First year, sow seeds; second year, clear around plants.
Summer Second year, pick off flowers as they die so that they cannot set seed.
Fall First year, leave alone. Second year, dig up plants and dispose of. Do not compost unless you want thousands of viper's bugloss plants appearing all over your garden.
Winter No need to protect first-year plant.

Garden Cultivation
This colorful plant is beautifully marked. Sow the seed in spring directly into the garden. It will grow in any soil and is great for growing on dry soils and sea cliffs. With its long taproot, the plant will survive any drought but cannot easily be transplanted except when very young. The disadvantage is that it self-seeds and is therefore invasive.

Harvesting
Gather flowers in summer for fresh use.

CONTAINER GROWING

Because it is a rampant self-seeder, it is quite a good idea to grow it in containers. For the first year it bears only green prickly leaves and is very boring. However, the show put on in the second year is full compensation. Use a soil-based potting mix; no need to feed. Overfeeding

Viper's bugloss *Echium vulgare*

will prohibit the flowering. Very tolerant of drought; nevertheless do water it regularly. Dies back in winter of first year—leave the container somewhere cool and water occasionally.

CULINARY

The young leaves are similar to borage, but they have lots more spikes. It is said you can eat them when young, but I have never attempted it. The flowers look very attractive in salads. They can also be crystallized.

MEDICINAL

The fresh flowering tips can be chopped up for making poultices for treating boils. Infuse lower leaves to produce a sweating in fevers or to relieve headaches.

OTHER USES

At one time, a red coloring substance for dyeing fabrics was extracted from the root.

Equisetum arvense

HORSETAIL

Also known as Mare's Tail, Shave Grass, Bottle Brush, Pewter Wort, Snake's Pie, Fairy Spindle, Paddock's Pipes, Cat's Tail, and Joint Grass. From the family Equisetaceae.

Horsetail *Equisetum arvense*

This plant is a native of the temperate regions, although some species are found in the tropics, where they can grow to a considerable size.

When I first started herb farming I suddenly noticed all these spiky things growing all over the floor of one of my plastic tunnels. Subsequently I discovered it was a very worthy herb, not an invasive weed.

The horsetail is a plant left over from prehistoric times. By the evidence of fossil remains, it has survived almost unchanged since the coal seams were laid. It does not flower, but carries spores as do ferns, to which it is related. The fronds have a harsh feel to them; this is because, uniquely, the plant absorbs large quantities of silica from the soil. The Romans always used horsetail to clean their pots and pans, not just to make them clean but also, thanks to the silica, to make them nonstick. The plant was used in the Middle Ages as an abrasive by cabinetmakers and to clean pewter, brass, and copper, and for scouring wood containers and milk pans.

No plant, having survived so long, could escape myth and magic. This herb has been associated far and wide with various goblins, toads, snakes, and the devil.

SPECIES

Equisetum arvense
Horsetail
Hardy perennial. Ht. 18 in. The plant does not flower. It grows on a thin creeping rhizome producing 8 in. long gray-brown fertile shoots with 4–6 sheaths in spring. The shoots die off and the spores are spread just like ferns. **Zone 4**

CULTIVATION

Propagation
I am not sure that this is necessary, but if you do require a supply of horsetail it may be of merit.

Cuttings
Each piece of horsetail root is capable of reproducing. In summer place small pieces in a seed or plug tray.

Use the bark-peat mix of potting soil (see p. 591). Plant out the following spring when the cuttings are well rooted.

Pests and Diseases
For a plant to have survived so long, it has to be pest- and disease-free.

Maintenance
Spring Make sure the plant is well contained.
Summer Cut back plants that are beginning to die back to stop the spores spreading.
Fall After harvest, cut down to the ground, again to stop the spores spreading.
Winter No protection necessary; very hardy.

Garden Cultivation
If grown in open ground unconfined, horsetail becomes a permanent inhabitant and is only eradicated with great difficulty. Its root systems have been found to extend down a cliff face 40 ft., and breaking the rhizomes stimulates buds on the remainder to sprout and produce more growth.

If horsetail is to be introduced into the garden at all, and to be honest I do not recommend it, it is best confined to a strong container partially sunk into the ground. Leave the rim visible so that the rhizomes cannot penetrate or creep over the top.

Harvesting
The green-brown shoots look almost like miniature Christmas trees and these are the parts that can be collected during the summer months. Dry them.

CONTAINER GROWING

The only sane way to grow horsetail is in a container. But be sure to cut it back in the summer to prevent spread by the spores. No need to feed, and it requires little watering. It can look attractive!

CULINARY

It has been eaten as a substitute for asparagus, but I do not recommend it unless you are stuck on a desert island and there is no other food available.

Horsetail nail strengthener

COSMETIC

Horsetail Nail Strengthener
A simple method of improving easily broken nails is to immerse the finger tips in a decoction made by simmering 2 oz. of dry or fresh herb in $3^3/_4$ cups of water for 20 minutes.

Horsetail Hair Rinse and Tonic
Horsetail provides a good, all-around conditioner and gives the hair a natural shine.

About 8 horsetail stems 6–8 in. long
2 cups of boiling water

Bruise the horsetail stems with a spoon before adding boiling water to make an infusion. Cover and leave until lukewarm, then strain off the liquid. After shampooing and rinsing, pour the infusion over the hair and massage into the scalp. Blot up excess moisture with a towel and comb through your hair. Cover your head with a warm towel and wait for 10 minutes before drying your hair in the usual way.

Horsetail shoots look like miniature Christmas trees

MEDICINAL

This plant is a storehouse of minerals and vitamins, so herbalists recommended it in cases of amnesia and general debility. The tea enriches the blood, hardens fingernails, and revitalizes lifeless hair. Its astringent properties help to strengthen the walls of the veins, tightening up varicose veins, and help guard against fatty deposits in the arteries. It is also useful when white spots occur on the nails, which indicate a calcium imbalance in the body, as the silica encourages the absorption and use of calcium by the body.

WARNING

It is advised that, if you wish to use horsetail, you do so only in consultation with an herbalist.

OTHER USES
Stems have a high silica content and can be used after drying to scour metal and polish pewter and fine woodwork.

The whole plant yields a yellow ocher dye.

Filipendula

MEADOWSWEET

**Also known as Bridewort, Meadow Queen, Meadow-Wort, and
Queen of the Meadow. From the family Rosaceae.**

Meadowsweet can be found growing wild in profusion near streams and rivers, in damp meadows, fens and marshlands, or wet woodlands to 3,300 ft. altitude.

It is a native of Europe and Asia that has been successfully introduced into, and is naturalized in, North America.

The generic name, *Filipendula*, comes from *filum*, meaning "thread," and *pendulus*, meaning "hanging." This is said to describe the root tubers that hang, characteristically of the genus, on fibrous roots.

The common name, meadowsweet, is said to be derived from the Anglo-Saxon word *medesweete*, which owes its origin to the fact that the plant was used to flavor mead, a drink made from fermented honey.

It has been known by many other names. In Chaucer's *The Knight's Tale* it is Meadwort and was one of the ingredients in a drink called "save." It was also known as Bridewort, because it was strewn in churches for festivals and weddings and made into bridal garlands. In Europe it took its name Queen of the Meadow from the way the herb can dominate a low-lying, damp meadow. In America, it became Gravelroot or Joe Pie Weed *(Eupatorium purpureum)*.

In the sixteenth century, when it was customary to strew floors with rushes and herbs (both to give warmth underfoot and to overcome smells and infections), it was a favorite of Queen Elizabeth I. She desired it above all other herbs in her chambers.

The sap contains a chemical of the same group as salicylic acid, an ingredient of aspirin. It was isolated for the first time in the nineteenth century by an Italian professor. When the drug company Bayer formulated acetylsalicylic acid, they called it aspirin after the old botanical name for meadowsweet, *Spirea ulmaria*.

SPECIES

Filipendula ulmaria
Meadowsweet
Hardy perennial. Ht. 2–4 ft., spread 2 ft. Clusters of creamy-white flowers in mid-summer. Green leaf made up of up to 5 pairs of big leaflets separated by pairs of smaller leaflets.
Zone 4

Filipendula ulmaria 'Aurea'
Golden Meadowsweet
Hardy perennial. Ht. and spread 12 in. Clusters of creamy-white flowers in midsummer. Bright golden yellow, divided leaves in spring that turn a lime color in summer. Susceptible to sun scorch.
Zone 4

Filipendula ulmaria 'Variegata'
Variegated Meadowsweet
Hardy perennial. Ht. 18 in. and spread 12 in. Clusters of creamy-white flowers in mid-summer. Divided leaf, dramatically variegated green and yellow in spring. Fades a bit as the season progresses.
Zone 4

Filipendula vulgaris
Dropwort
Hardy perennial. Ht. 2–3 ft., spread 18 in. Summertime clusters of white flowers (larger than meadowsweet). Fernlike green leaves.

CULTIVATION

Propagation
Seed

Sow in prepared seed or plug trays in the fall. Cover lightly with potting soil (not perlite) and winter outside under glass. Check from time to time that the compost has not become dry as this will inhibit germination. Stratification is helpful but not essential. Germination should take place in spring. When the seedlings are large enough to handle, plant out, 12 in. apart, into a prepared site.

Division

The golden and variegated forms must be propagated by division. This is easily done in the fall. Dig up an established plant and tease the plantlets apart; they separate easily. Either replant in a prepared site, 12 in. apart, or, if it is one of the decorative varieties, pot up using the bark-peat mix of potting soil (see p. 591).

Pests and Diseases

Meadowsweet rarely suffers from these.

Maintenance

Spring Sow seeds if required.
Summer Cut back after flowering.
Fall Divide established plants, sow seed for wintering outside.
Winter No need for protection.

Garden Cultivation

Meadowsweet adapts well to the garden, but does prefer sun or semishade and a moisture-retentive soil. If your soil is free-draining, mix in plenty of well-rotted manure and/or leaf mold, and plant in semishade.

Harvesting

Gather young leaves for fresh or dry use before flowers appear. Pick flowers just as they open and use fresh or dry.

MEDICINAL

The whole plant is a traditional remedy for an acidic stomach.

The fresh root is used in homeopathic preparations and is effective on its own in the treatment of diarrhea.

The flowers, when made into a tea, are a comfort to flu sufferers.

Golden meadowsweet
Filipendula ulmaria 'Aurea'

CULINARY

A charming, local vet who made all kinds of vinegars and pickles gave me a meadowsweet vinegar to try. Much to my amazement it was lovely, and combined well with oil to make a different salad dressing, great when used with a flower salad.

I am not a fan of meadowsweet flower fritters so I mention them only in passing. The flowers do however make a very good wine, and add flavor to meads and beers. The flowers can also be added to stewed fruit and jellies, introducing a subtle almond flavor.

CONTAINER GROWING

Golden and variegated meadowsweet look very attractive in containers, but use a soil-based compost to make sure moisture is retained. Position in partial shade to inhibit drying out and prevent sun scorch. The plant dies back in winter so leave it outside in a place where the natural weathers can reach it. If you live in an extremely cold area, protect the container from damage by placing in a cold frame or unheated garage for the winter. Liquid feed only twice during flowering.

OTHER USES

A black dye can be obtained from the roots by using a copper mordant.

Use dried leaves and flowers in potpourris.

Meadowsweet dye

Meadowsweet *Filipendula ulmaria*

Galium odoratum

SWEET WOODRUFF

Also known as New Mowed Hay, Rice Flower, Ladies in the Hay, Kiss Me Quick, Master of the Wood, Woodward, and Woodrowell. From the family Rubiaceae.

This has been introduced and cultivated in North America and Australia, and is a native of Europe. It grows deep in the woods and in hedgerows.

Records date back to the fourteenth century, when woodruff was used as a strewing herb, as bed-stuffing, and to perfume linen.

On May Day in Germany, it is added to Rhine wine to make a delicious drink called "Maibowle."

SPECIES

Galium odoratum
(Asperula odorata)
Sweet Woodruff
Hardy perennial. Ht. 6 in., spread 12 in. or more. White, star-shaped flowers from spring to early summer. The green leaves are neat and grow in a complete circle around the stem. The whole plant is aromatic. **Zone 4**

CULTIVATION

Propagation
Seed
To ensure viability use only fresh seed. Sow in early fall into prepared seed or plug trays, and cover with potting soil. Water in well. Seeds require a period of stratification (see p. 590). Once the seedlings are large enough, either pot or plant out as soon as the young plants have been hardened off. Plant 4 in. apart.

Root Cuttings
The rootstock is very brittle and every little piece will grow. The best time is after flowering in the early summer. Lay small pieces of the root, 1–1½ in. long, evenly spaced, on the soil in a seed tray. Cover with a thin layer of soil, and water. Leave in a warm place, and the woodruff will begin to sprout again. When large enough to handle, split up and plant out.

Pests and Diseases
This plant rarely suffers from pests and diseases.

Maintenance
Spring Take root cuttings before flowering.
Summer Dig up before the flowers have set, to check spreading.
Fall The plant dies back completely in fall. Sow seeds.
Winter Hardy plant.

Garden Cultivation
Ideal for difficult places or underplanting in borders, it loves growing in the dry shade of trees right up to the trunk. Its rich green leaves make a dense and very decorative ground cover, its underground runners spreading rapidly in the right situation.

It prefers a rich alkaline soil with some moisture during the spring.

Harvesting
The true aroma (which is like newly mown hay) comes to the fore when it is dried. Dry flowers and leaves together in early summer.

CONTAINER GROWING

Make sure the container is large enough, otherwise it will become root-bound very quickly. The potting soil should be the bark-peat mix (see p. 591). Only feed with liquid fertilizer when the plant is flowering. Position the container in semishade and do not overwater.

CULINARY

Main ingredients for a modern day May Wine would be a bottle of Rhine wine, a glass of sherry, sugar, and strawberries, with a few sprigs of woodruff thrown in an hour before serving.

MEDICINAL

Not recommended.

Sweet woodruff tea

WARNING

Internal use is not recommended. Consumption can produce symptoms of poisoning, including dizziness, vomiting, and internal bleeding.

Glycyrrhiza glabra

LICORICE

*Also known as Liquorice, Sweet Licorice, and Sweetwood.
From the family Papilionaceae.*

This plant, which is a native of the Mediterranean region, is commercially grown throughout the temperate zones of the world and extensively cultivated in Russia, Iran, Spain, and India. It has been used medicinally for 3,000 years and was recorded on Assyrian tablets and Egyptian papyruses. The Latin name *Glycyrrhiza* comes from *glykys,* meaning "sweet," and *rhiza,* "root."

It was first introduced to England by Dominican friars in the sixteenth century and became an important crop. The whole of the huge cobbled courtyard of Pontefract Castle was covered by topsoil simply to grow licorice. It is sad that Pontefract cakes are made from imported licorice today.

Licorice sticks

SPECIES

Glycyrrhiza glabra
Licorice
Hardy perennial. Ht. 4 ft., spread 3 ft. Pea-like, purple-blue and white flowers borne in short spikes on erect stems in late summer. Large greenish leaves divided into oval leaflets.
Zone 5

CULTIVATION

Propagation
Seed
The seedlings often damp off. In cooler climates the seed tends not to be viable. Root division is much easier.

Division
Divide when the plant is dormant, making sure the root has one or more buds. Place into pots half filled with potting soil. Cover with compost. Water well and leave in a warm place until shoots appear. Harden off, then plant out in early spring or fall. If the latter, winter in a cold greenhouse or cold frame.

Pests and Diseases
Largely pest- and disease-free.

Maintenance
Spring Divide established plants.
Summer Do nothing.
Fall Divide established plants if necessary.
Winter In very cold winters, protect first-year plants.

Garden Cultivation
Licorice needs a rich, deep, well-cultivated soil. Plant pieces of the root, each with a bud, directly into a prepared site 6 in. deep and 3 ft. apart in early spring or in fall if the ground is not frosty.

Licorice does best in long, hot summers, but will need extra watering if your soil is very free draining. It can spread invasively in some conditions. Confine roots with a buried barrier.

Harvesting
Harvest roots for drying in early winter from established three- or four-year-old plants.

CONTAINER GROWING

Never displays as well as in the garden. Use a soil-based potting soil. Feed through the growing season and water until it dies back.

CULINARY

Licorice is used as a flavoring in the making of Guinness and other beers.

MEDICINAL

The juice from the roots provides commercial licorice. It is used either to mask the unpleasant flavor of other medicines or to provide its own soothing action on troublesome coughs. The dried root, stripped of its bitter bark, is recommended as a remedy for colds, sore throats, and bronchial catarrh.

Licorice is a gentle laxative and lowers stomach acid levels, relieving heartburn. It has a remarkable power to heal stomach ulcers because it spreads a protective gel over the stomach wall and in addition it eases spasms of large intestine. It also increases the flow of bile and lowers blood cholesterol levels.

WARNING

Large doses of licorice cause side effects, notably headaches, high blood pressure, and water retention.

Helichrysum italicum

CURRY PLANT

From the family Asteraceae.

This plant is from southern Europe and has adapted well to damper, cooler climates. It is the sweet curry scent of its leaves that has caused its recent rise in popularity.

SPECIES

Helichrysum italicum (angustifolium)
Curry Plant
Hardy evergreen perennial. Ht. 24 in., spread 3 ft. Clusters of tiny mustard yellow flowers in summer. Narrow, aromatic, silver leaves. Highly scented. Planting distance for hedge 2 ft.

Helichrysum italicum 'Dartington'
Curry Plant, Dartington
Hardy evergreen perennial. Ht. 18 in., spread 24 in. Compact plant with clusters of small yellow flowers in summer. Gray-green, highly scented, narrow leaves (half the size of *H. italicum*). Its compact upright habit makes this a good plant for hedges and edging in the garden. Planting distance for hedge 1 ft.

Helichrysum microphyllum
Curry Plant Dwarf
Hardy evergreen perennial. Ht. 12 in., spread 18 in. Clusters of tiny mustard yellow flowers in summer. Narrow, aromatic, silver leaves. Ideal for formal hedging and knot gardens. Planting distance for hedge 1 ft.

Helichrysum italicum subsp. serotinum
Curry Plant
Hardy evergreen perennial. Ht. 24 in., spread 3 ft. Broad clusters of small bright yellow flowers, produced on upright white shoots. Narrow, aromatic, sliver-gray leaves. Planting distance for hedge 2 ft.
Zone 9

CULTIVATION

Propagation
Seed
I have not known *H. italicum* to set good seed. For this reason I advise cuttings.

Cuttings
Take softwood cuttings in spring and semiripe ones in fall.

Pests and Diseases
Pests give this highly aromatic plant a wide berth, and it is usually free from disease.

Curry plant *Helichrysum italicum*

Maintenance
Spring Trim established plants after frosts to maintain shape and promote new growth. Take softwood cuttings.
Summer Trim back after flowering, but not too hard.
Fall Take semiripe wood cuttings.
Winter If the temperature falls below 14°F, protect from frost.

Garden Cultivation
The curry plant makes an attractive addition to the garden, and it imparts a strong smell of curry even if untouched. It is one of the most silvery of shrubs and makes a striking visual feature all year round.

Plant in full sun in a well-drained soil. Do not cut the curry plant as hard back as cotton lavender but it is worth giving a good "haircut" after flowering to keep the larger ones from flopping and maintain the shape of the smaller ones.

If it is an exceptionally wet winter and you don't have a free-draining soil, lift some plants and keep in a cold greenhouse or cold frame.

Harvesting
Pick leaves at any time for fresh use. Pick the flowers when fully open. Dry by hanging in small bunches upside down in an airy place.

CONTAINER GROWING

Dwarf and Dartington curry plants grow happily in large containers (at least 8 in. in diameter). Place in the sun to get the best effect, and do not overwater.

CULINARY

There are not many recipes for the curry plant in cooking, and in truth the leaves smell stronger than they taste, but a small sprig stuffed into the cavity of a roasting chicken makes an interesting variation on tarragon.

Add sprigs to vegetables, rice dishes, and pickles for a mild curry flavor. Remove before serving.

OTHER USES

The bright yellow button flowers add color to potpourris.

Curry plant flowers

Hesperis matronalis

SWEET ROCKET

Also known as Damask Violet and Dame's Violet. From the family Brassicaceae.

This sweet-smelling herb is indigenous to Italy. It can now be found growing wild in much of the temperate world as a garden escapee. The old Greek name *Hesperis* was used by Theophrastus, the Greek botanist (370–285 B.C.). It is derived from *hesperos*, meaning "evening," which is when the flowers are at their most fragrant.

Sweet rocket
Hesperis matronalis

SPECIES

Hesperis matronalis
Sweet Rocket
Hardy biennial; very occasionally it will be a perennial, sending out new shoots from the rootstock. Ht. 2–3 ft., spread 10 in. The 4-petaled flowers are all sweetly scented and come in many colors—pink, purple, mauve, and white—in the summer of the second year. The leaves are green and lance-shaped.
There is a double-flowered form of this plant—*Hesperis matronalis* double. It can only be propagated by cuttings or division and needs a more sandy loam soil than sweet rocket.
Zone 4

CULTIVATION

Propagation
Seed
Sow the seed in the fall in prepared seed or plug trays, covering the seeds with perlite. Winter the young plants in a cold greenhouse for planting out in the spring at a distance of 18 in. apart. Propagated this way it may flower the first season as well as the second.

Pests and Diseases
Flea beetles may bite holes in the leaves, but the damage is mostly cosmetic.

Sweet rocket
Hesperis matronalis

Maintenance
Spring Sow seed outdoors.
Summer In the second year deadhead flowers to prolong flowering.
Fall Sow seed under protection.
Winter No need to protect.

Garden Cultivation
It likes full sun or light shade and prefers a well-drained fertile soil. The seed can be sown directly into a prepared site in the garden in late spring, thinning to 12 in. apart, with an additional thinning to 18 in. later on if need be.

Harvesting
Pick leaves when young for eating. Pick flowers as they open for using fresh or for drying.

CONTAINER GROWING

Sweet rocket is a tall plant. It looks attractive if three or four one-year-old plants are potted together, positioned to make the most of the scent on a summer evening. Use the bark-peat-grit potting mix (see p. 591) and water well in summer months. No need to feed.

CULINARY

Young leaves are eaten occasionally in salads. Use sparingly because they are very bitter. The flowers look attractive tossed in salads. They can also be used to decorate desserts.

OTHER USES

Add dried flowers to potpourris for pastel colors and sweet scent.

Humulus lupulus

HOPS

Also known as Hopbind and Hop vine. From the family Cannabaceae.

Native of the Northern temperate zones, cultivated commercially, especially in northern Europe, North America, and Chile.

Roman records from the first century A.D. describe hops as a popular garden plant and vegetable, the young shoots being sold in markets to be eaten rather like asparagus. Hop gardens did not become widespread in Europe until the ninth century. In Britain the hop was a wild plant and used as a vegetable before it became one of the ingredients of beer. It was not until the sixteenth century that the word hop and the practice of flavoring and preserving beer with the strobiles or female flowers of the *Humulus lupulus* were introduced into Britain by Flemish immigrants, and replaced traditional bitter herbs such as alehoof and alecost.

During the reign of Henry VIII, Parliament was petitioned to prohibit the use of the hop, as it was said that it was a wicked weed that would spoil the taste of the drink, ale, and endanger the people. Needless to say the petition was thrown out. The use of hops revolutionized brewing since it enabled beer to be kept longer.

Hops have also been used as medicine for at least as long as for brewing. The flowers are famous for their sedative effect and were either drunk as a tea or stuffed in a hop pillow to sleep on.

Common hop
Humulus lupulus

Golden hop
Humulus lupulus
'Aureus'

SPECIES

Humulus lupulus
Common Hop
Hardy perennial, a herbaceous climber. Ht. up to 20 ft. There are separate female and male plants. The male plant has yellowish flowers growing in branched clusters. They are without sepals and have 5 petals and 5 stamens. The female plant has tiny, greenish-yellow, scented flowers, hidden by big scales. The scales become papery when the fruiting heads are ripe. These are the flowers that are harvested for beer. The mid-green leaves have 3–5 lobes with sharply toothed edges. The stems are hollow, and are covered with tiny hooked prickles. These enable the plant to cling to shrubs, trees, or anything else. It always entwines clockwise. **Zone 3**

***Humulus lupulus* 'Aureus'**
Golden Hop
Hardy perennial, a herbaceous climber. Ht. up to 20 ft. The main difference between this plant and the common hop is that the leaves and flowers are much more golden, which makes it very attractive in the garden and in dried flower arrangements. It has the same properties as the common hop. **Zone 3**

Common Hop *Humulus lupulus*

CULTIVATION

Propagation

Seed

The best strains for flavoring beer are propagated only by cuttings or division.

Obtain seed from specialized nursery growers. Sow in summer or fall. The seed is on the medium to large side so sow sparingly; if using plug trays, one per cell. Push the seed into the potting soil and cover it with the soil. Then cover the tray with a sheet of glass or polythene, and leave somewhere cool to germinate—a cold frame or cold greenhouse. Germination can be very erratic. If the seed is not fresh you may need to use the hot/cold treatment.

Warning: As the seed will be from wild hops these should not be grown in areas of commercial hop growing, because they might contaminate the crop.

Cuttings

Softwood cuttings should be taken in spring or early summer from the female plant. Choose young shoots and take the cuttings in the morning as they will lose water very fast and wilt.

Division

In the spring, dig up and divide the root stems and suckers of established plants. Replant 3 ft. apart against support.

Pests and Diseases

The most common disease is **hop wilt**. If this occurs, dig up and burn. Do not plant hops in that area again.

Leaf miner can sometimes be a problem. Remove infected leaves immediately.

The golden variety sometimes suffers from **sun scorch**. If this occurs, prune to new growth, and change its position if possible the following season.

Maintenance

Spring Divide roots and separate rooted stems and suckers in spring. Repot container-grown plants.
Summer Sow seed late.
Fall Cut back remaining growth into the ground. Give the plants a good feeding. Bring containers into a cool place.
Winter No need for protection.

Garden Cultivation

For successful plants the site should be sunny and open, and the soil needs to be rich in humus and dug deeply. It is not generally necessary to tie the plants if good support is at hand. A word of warning: you must dominate the plant. Certainly it will need thinning and encouraging to entwine where you want it to go rather than where it chooses. But remember that it dies back completely in winter. Cut the plant into the ground each fall and then give it a good feeding of manure or compost.

The foliage and stems are scratchy. Wear long sleeves and gloves to protect your skin when working with hops.

Harvesting

Pick young fresh side shoots in spring. Gather young fresh leaves as required.

Pick male flowers as required. Pick ripe female flowers in early fall. Dry and use within a few months, otherwise the flavor becomes unpleasant.

CONTAINER GROWING

Hops, especially the golden variety, can look very attractive in a large container with something to grow up. Use a potting soil made up of the bark-peat mix (see p. 591), and feed regularly with a liquid fertilizer from late spring to midsummer. Keep well watered in the summer months and fairly dry in winter. It can be grown indoors in a position with good light such as a greenhouse, but it seldom flowers. Provide some form of shade during sunny periods. During the winter months, make sure it has a rest by putting the pot in a cool place, keeping the compost on the dry side. Repot each year.

OTHER USES

The leaf can be used to make a brown dye. If you live close to a brewery it is worth asking them each fall for the spent hops, which make either a great mulch or a layer in a compost heap.

WARNING

Contact dermatitis can be caused by the pollen of the female flower. Also, hops are not recommended in the treatment of depressive illnesses because of their sedative effect.

MEDICINAL

Hop tea made from the female flower only is recommended for nervous diarrhea, insomnia, and restlessness. It also helps to stimulate appetite, dispel flatulence, and relieve intestinal cramps. A cold tea drunk an hour before meals

Hop pillow

is particularly good for digestion.

It can be useful combined with fragrant valerian for coughs and nervous spasmodic conditions. Recent research into hops has shown that it contains a certain hormone, which accounts for the beneficial effect of helping mothers improve their milk flow.

To make a hop pillow, sprinkle hops with alcohol and fill a small bag or pillowcase with them. It will really help you sleep.

CULINARY

In early spring pick the young side shoots, steam them (or lightly boil), and eat like asparagus. The male flowers can be boiled, cooled, and tossed into salads. The young leaves can be quickly blanched to remove any bitterness and added to soups or salads.

Hyoscyamus niger

HENBANE

Also known as Devil's Eye, Hen Pen, Hen Penny, Hog Bean, Stinking Roger, Symphoniaca, Jusquiamus, Henbell, Belene, Hennyibone Hennebane, Poisoned Tobacco, and Stinking Nightshade. From the family Solanaceae.

This native of Europe has become widely distributed worldwide and is found growing on waste ground or roadsides on well-drained sandy or alkaline soils.

Two famous deaths are attributed to henbane. Hamlet's father was murdered by a distillation of henbane being poured into his ear, and in 1910 Dr. Crippen used hyoscine, which is extracted from the plant, to murder his wife. Every part of the plant is toxic.

Henbane has been considered to have aphrodisiac properties and is the main ingredient in some love potions and witches' brews. It was also placed by the hinges of outer doors to protect against sorcery.

SPECIES

Hyoscyamus niger
Henbane
Annual/biennial. Ht. up to 32 in., spread 12 in. Flowers bloom in summer, are yellow-brown or cream, funnel-shaped, and usually marked with purple veins. Leaves are hairy with large teeth, and the upper leaves have no stalks. The whole plant smells foul.
All zones

Hyoscyamus albus
White Henbane
Annual. Ht. 12 in., spread 12 in. As *H. niger* except flowers are pale yellow marked with violet veins.
All zones

CULTIVATION

Propagation
Seed
Sow the fairly small seeds on the surface of pots or trays in spring, and cover with perlite. Germination 10–15 days. If you want henbane to behave like a biennial, sow in early fall, keeping the soil moist until germination (which can be erratic, but takes about 14–21 days). Winter the young plants in a cold frame or cold glasshouse. Plant out the following spring at a distance of 12 in.

Pests and Diseases
Flea beetle and **Colorado potato beetles** may chew the leaves. Dust with rotenone.

Maintenance
Spring Sow seed.
Summer Deadhead flowers to maintain plant (wear gloves).
Fall Sow seed for second-year flowers.
Winter Protect young plants.

Garden Cultivation
Choose the site for planting henbane with care, because it is poisonous. It will tolerate any growing situation, but shows a preference for a well-drained, sunny site. Sow seeds in late spring. When the seedlings are large enough to handle, thin to 12 in. apart. It can look striking in a mixed border.

Harvesting
Collect seed when the head turns brown and begins to open at the end.

CONTAINER GROWING

Inadvisable to grow such a poisonous plant this way.

MEDICINAL

This plant was used for a wide range of conditions that required sedation. The alkaloid hyoscine, which is derived from the green tops and leaves, is used as a hypnotic and brain sedative for the seasick, excitable, and insane. It is also used externally in analgesic preparations to relieve rheumatism and arthritis. The syrup has a sedative effect in cases of Parkinson's disease.

WARNING

The whole plant is poisonous. Children have been poisoned by eating the seeds or seed pods. Use preparation and dosage strictly only under medical direction.

Hypericum perforatum

St. John's Wort

Also known as Warriors Wound, Amber, Touch and Heal, Grace of God, and Herb of St. John. From the family Clusiaceae.

This magical herb is found in temperate zones of the world in open situations on semidry soils.

Whoever treads on St. John's Wort after sunset will be swept up on the back of a magic horse that will charge round the heavens until sunrise before depositing its exhausted rider on the ground, or so it is said.

Besides its magical attributes, *Hypericum* has medicinal properties and was universally known as the "Grace of God." In England it cured mania; in Russia it gave protection against hydrophobia; and the Brazilians knew it as an antidote to snakebite. St. John's Wort (*wort*, incidentally, is Anglo-Saxon for "medicinal herb") has been used to raise ghosts and exorcise spirits. When crushed, the leaves release a balsamic odor similar to incense, which was said to be strong enough to drive away evil sprits. The red pigment from the crushed flowers was taken to signify the blood of St. John at his beheading, for the herb is in full flower on June 24, St. John's Day.

Division
Divide established plants in the fall.

Pests and Diseases
Largely free from pests and diseases.

Maintenance
Spring Sow seeds.
Summer Cut back after flowering to stop self-seeding.
Fall Divide established clumps.
Winter No need for protection, fully hardy.

Garden Cultivation
Tolerates most soils, in sun or light shade, but it can be invasive in light soils.

Harvesting
Harvest leaves and flowers as required.

Other Uses

The flowers release a yellow dye with alum, and a red dye with alcohol.

Warning

St. John's Wort has sometimes poisoned livestock. Its use also makes the skin sensitive to light.

Medicinal

Oil extracted by macerating the flowers in vegetable oil and applied externally eases neuralgia and the pain of sciatica wounds, varicose veins, ulcers, and sunburn. Only take internally under medical supervision.

Species

Hypericum perforatum
St. John's Wort
Hardy perennial. Ht. 12–36 in., spread 12 in. Scented yellow flowers with black dots in summer. The small leaves are stalkless; covered with tiny perforations (hence *perforatum*), which are in fact translucent glands. This is the magical species. **Zone 3**

Cultivation

Propagation
Seed
Sow very small seed in spring into prepared seed or plug trays, and cover with perlite. Germination is usually in 10–20 days depending on the weather. When the seedlings are large enough to handle and after a period of hardening off, plant out 12 in. apart.

Container Growing

Can be grown in containers, but it is a bit tall so you do need a large clump for it to look effective. Use a soil-based potting mix. Water in the summer months; only feed with liquid fertilizer twice during the growing season, otherwise it produces more leaf than flower.

"Purge me with Hyssop and I shall be clean."
—Psalm 51, verse 7

Hyssopus officinalis

HYSSOP

From the family Lamiaceae.

Hyssop is a native of the Mediterranean region, where it grows wild on old walls and dry banks. It is found as a garden escapee elsewhere in Europe and has been cultivated in gardens for about the last 600 years. It was one of the herbs taken to the New World by the colonists to use in tea, in herbal tobacco, and as an antiseptic.

There has been much back and forth about whether common hyssop is the one mentioned in the Bible. Some say it was oregano or savory. However, present thinking is that hyssop is flavor of the month, especially since it has been discovered that the mold that produces penicillin grows on its leaf. This may have acted as an antibiotic protection when lepers were bathed in hyssop.

The Persians used distilled hyssop water as a body lotion to give a fine color to their skin.

Hippocrates recommended hyssop for chest complaints, and today herbalists still prescribe it.

Hyssop *Hyssopus officinalis*

SPECIES

These are the common hyssops, readily available from nurseries and garden centers.

Hyssopus officinalis
Hyssop
Hardy semievergreen perennial. Ht. 32 in., spread 36 in. Blue flowers from summer to early fall. Small, narrow, lance-shaped leaves, aromatic and darkish green.

Hyssop *Hyssopus officinalis*

Hyssopus officinalis* f. *albus
White Hyssop
Semievergreen hardy perennial. Ht. 32 in., spread 36 in. White flowers from summer to early fall. Small, narrow, lance-shaped leaves, aromatic and darkish green in color.

Hyssopus officinalis* subsp. *aristatus
Rock Hyssop
Hardy, semievergreen, perennial. Ht. 12 in., spread 24 in. Dark blue flowers from summer to early fall. Small, narrow, lance-shaped leaves, aromatic and darkish green.

***Hyssopus officinalis* 'Roseus'**
Pink Hyssop
Hardy, semievergreen, perennial. Ht. 32 in., spread 36 in. Pink flowers from summer to early fall. Small, narrow, lance-shaped leaves, aromatic and darkish green.

Pink hyssop
Hyssopus officinalis 'Roseus'

CULTIVATION

Propagation
Seeds
In early spring sow the small seeds in plug or seed trays under protection, using the bark-peat mix of potting soil. Cover with perlite. If very early in spring, a bottom heat of 60–70°F would be beneficial. When the seedlings are large enough, either repot or transplant into the garden after a period of hardening off. Plant at a distance of 12 in. apart. All varieties can be grown from seed with the exception of rock hyssop, which can only be grown from cuttings. However, if you want a guaranteed pink or white hyssop, cuttings are a more reliable method.

Cuttings
In late spring or early summer, take softwood cuttings from the new lush growth and nonflowering stems.

Pests and Diseases

This genial plant rarely suffers from pests or diseases.

Maintenance

Spring Sow seeds. Trim mature plants. Trim hedges.
Summer Deadhead flowers to maintain supply, trim after flowering to maintain shape. Trim hedges.
Fall Cut back only in mild areas.
Winter Protect in cold, wet winters and temperatures that fall below 23°F. Use frost fabric, straw, etc.

Garden Cultivation

This attractive plant, which has only recently become popular again, likes to be planted in conditions similar to rosemary and thyme, a well-drained soil in a sunny position. The seeds can be sown directly into the ground in very late spring or early summer, when the soil is warm. Thin to 12 in. apart if being grown as specimen plants. If for hedging, 7 in.

As all parts of the plant are pleasantly aromatic and the flowers very attractive, plant it where it can be seen and brushed against. The flowers are also attractive to bees and butterflies. For these reasons hyssop makes a very good hedge or edging plant. Trim the top shoots to encourage bushy growth. In early spring, trim the plant into a tidy shape with scissors. To keep the plant flowering in summer, remove the deadheads. Cut back to 8 in. in fall in mild areas, or trim back after flowering in cold areas. Keep formal hedges well clipped during the growing season.

Harvesting

Cut young leaves for drying in summer. The flowers should be picked during the summer, too, when they are fully opened. The scent is generally improved with drying.

MEDICINAL

An infusion is used mainly for coughs, whooping cough, asthma and bronchitis, and upper respiratory catarrh. It is also used for inflammation of the urinary tract. Externally it can be used for bruises and burns. It was once a country remedy for rheumatism.

COMPANION PLANTING

Grow near cabbages to lure away cabbage whiteflies. Plant near vines to increase yield.

WARNING

Hyssop should not be used in cases of nervous irritability. Strong doses, particularly those of distilled essential oil, can cause muscular spasms. This oil should not be used in aromatherapy for high-strung patients, as it can cause epileptic symptoms. Do not use continuously for extended periods. No form of hyssop should be taken during pregnancy.

Hyssop sugar syrup

CONTAINER GROWING

Hyssop is a lovely plant in containers. It is happy in plenty of sunshine and prefers a south-facing wall. It also likes dry conditions and its tough leaves are not affected by city pollution, making it ideal for window boxes. It is also good on a patio, as the scent is lovely on a hot summer's evening. Give it a liquid feed only during the flowering period. Cut back after flowering to maintain shape.

CULINARY

The flowers are delicious tossed in a green salad. In small amounts, leaves aid digestion of fatty foods but, as they are somewhat pungent, use them sparingly. The herb has a slightly bitter, minty taste and is therefore good flavoring in salads or as an addition to game, meats, and soups, stews, and stuffings. Hyssop is still used in Gascony as one of the herbs in bouquet garni and for flavoring a concentrated purée of tomatoes preserved for the winter. It is used in sausages and also added to fruit pies, $1/4$ teaspoon hyssop being sprinkled over the fruit before the top crust goes on.

When making a sugar syrup for fruit, add a sprig of hyssop as you boil the sugar and water; it adds a pleasant flavor, and the sprig can be removed before adding the fruit.

Basque-Style Chicken
Serves 6

4 bell peppers (2 red, 2 green)
Hyssop olive oil
3 lb. 6 oz. chicken
salt and pepper
5 tablespoons dry white wine
6 onions
4 cloves of garlic
4 medium tomatoes, peeled and roughly chopped
1 bouquet garni with a sprig of hyssop

Deseed and slice the peppers into thin strips. Gently fry them in a small amount of oil until soft. Remove from the pan and put to one side. Joint the chicken and gently fry in oil, turning frequently. Transfer to a casserole, season with salt and pepper, moisten with the wine, and leave over a gentle heat to finish cooking. Slice the onions and peel the garlic cloves, and soften without coloring in the olive oil in the frying pan. Then add the tomatoes, peppers, and bouquet garni, and season. When reduced almost to a cream, turn into the casserole over the chicken and keep on low heat until ready to serve, an additional 20–30 minutes.

Inula helenium

ELECAMPANE

Also known as Allecampane, July Campane, Elicompane, Dock, Sunflower, Wild Sunflower, Yellow Starwort, Elfdock, Elfwort, Horse Elder, Horse Heal, and Scabwort. From the family Asteraceae.

Elecampane originates from Asia, from where, through cultivation, it spread across Western Europe to North America and now grows wild from Nova Scotia to Ontario, from North Carolina to Missouri.

Sources for the derivation of the principal common name, elecampane, and the generic/species name, *Inula helenium*, are not altogether satisfactory, but I have found three possible explanations.

Helen of Troy was believed to be gathering the herb when she was abducted by Paris, hence *helenium*.

Down through the ages the herb was considered as good medicinally for horse or mule as for humans; it was even sometimes called horselene. *Inula* could come from *hinnulus* meaning "a young mule."

Finally, the Romans called the herb *Enula Campana* (Inula of the fields) from which Elecampane is a corruption.

According to the Roman writer Pliny, the emperor Julius Augustus enjoyed elecampane so much he proclaimed, "Let no day past without eating some of the roots candied to help the digestion and cause mirth." The Romans also used it as a candied sweetmeat, colored with cochineal. This idea persisted for centuries, and in the Middle Ages, apothecaries sold the candied root in flat pink sugary cakes, which were sucked to alleviate asthma and indigestion and to sweeten the breath. Tudor herbalists also candied them for the treatment of coughs, catarrhs, bronchitis, and chest ailments. Their use continued until the 1920s as a flavoring in sweets.

I have discovered an Anglo-Saxon ritual using elecampane—part medicinal, part magical. Prayers were sung of the *helenium* and its roots dug up by the medicinal man, who had been careful not to speak to any disreputable creature—man, elf, goblin, or fairy—he chanced to meet on the way to the ceremony. Afterward the elecampane root was laid under the altar for the night and eventually mixed with betony and lichen from a crucifix. The medicine was taken against elf sickness or elf disease.

There is an ancient custom in Scandinavia of putting a bunch of elecampane in the center of a nosegay of herbs to symbolize the sun and the head of Odin, the greatest of Norse gods.

Inula helenium **seed heads**

SPECIES

Inula helenium
Elecampane
Hardy perennial. Ht. 5–8 ft., spread 3 ft. Bright yellow, ragged, daisylike flowers in summer. The leaves are large, oval-toothed, slightly downy underneath, and of a mid-green color. Dies back fully in winter.
Zone 4

Inula hookeri
Hardy perennial. Ht. 30 in. spread 18 in. Yellowish green, ragged, daisylike flowers, slightly scented in summer. Lance-shaped, hairy leaves, smaller than *I. magnifica* and mid-green in color. Dies back fully in winter. **Zone 4**

Inula magnifica
Hardy perennial. Ht. 6 ft., spread 3 ft. Large, ragged, daisylike flowers. Lots of large, dark green lance-shaped rough leaves. May need staking in an exposed garden. This is often mistaken for *I. helenium*—the leaf color is the biggest difference, and on average *I. magnifica* grows much larger. Dies back fully in winter. **Zone 4**

CULTIVATION

Propagation
Seed
The seed is similar to dandelion; when the plant has germinated you can see the seeds flying all over the garden, which should be all the warning you need. Sow on the surface of a pot or plug tray. Cover with perlite. Germination is 2–4 weeks, depending on sowing season and seed viability. Prick out and plant 3–5 ft. apart when the seedlings are large enough to handle.

Root Division
If the plant grows too big for its position in the garden, divide in the fall when the plant has died back. As the roots are very strong, choose the point of division carefully. Alternatively, remove the offshoots that grow around the parent plant; each has its own root system, so they can be planted immediately in a prepared site elsewhere in the garden. This can be done in fall or spring.

Pests and Diseases
It rarely suffers from disease, although if the fall is excessively wet, as the leaves die back, they may suffer from a form of **mildew**. Simply cut back and destroy the leaves.

Maintenance
Spring Sow seed. Divide established plants.
Summer Remove flower heads as soon as flowering finishes.
Fall Cut back growth to stop self-seeding and to prevent the plant from becoming untidy. Remove offshoots for replanting.
Winter The plant dies back, so it needs no protection.

Garden Cultivation
Plant in a moist, fertile soil, in full sun, sheltered from the wind (elecampane grows tall and would otherwise need staking). It can look very striking at the back of a border against a stone wall, or in front of a screen of deciduous trees. In a very dry summer it may need watering.

Elecampane *Inula helenium*

Harvesting
Dig up second- or third-year roots in the fall; they can be used as a vegetable or dried for use in medicine.

The flowers are good in fall flower arrangements and dry well upside down if you cut them just before the seeds turn brown.

CONTAINER GROWING

Elecampane grows too big for most containers and is easily blown over.

CULINARY

Elecampane has a sharp, bitter flavor. Use dried pieces or cook as a root vegetable.

OTHER USES
Your cat may be interested to know that scientific research indicates that elecampane has a sedative effect on mice.

Seeds on a leaf in fall

MEDICINAL

The main use is for respiratory complaints, at one time specifically for tuberculosis. It is still employed in folk medicine as a favorite constituent of cough remedies, and has always been popular both as a medicine and as a condiment.

In America, elecampane oil is used for respiratory, intestinal catarrh, chronic diarrhea, chronic bronchitis, and whooping cough.

A decoction of the root has long been used externally for scabies, herpes, acne, and other skin diseases, hence its country name scabwort.

Recent research shows that the lactines found in the roots are powerful agents against bacteria and fungi.

Elecampane oil

Iris

IRIS

From the family Iridaceae.

All those mentioned are native to the Northern Hemisphere and are cultivated in varying conditions, from dry light soil (orrisroot) to damp, boggy soils (blue flag iris).

The Greek word *iris*, meaning "rainbow" and the name of the Greek goddess of the rainbow, was appended to describe the plant's variable colors. The iris is one of the oldest cultivated plants—it is depicted on the wall of an Egyptian temple dating from 1500 B.C.

In this very large family, three stand out for their beneficial herbal qualities. Orris has a violet-scented root, which has been powdered and used in perfumes since the ancient Egyptians and Greeks. The Latin *Iris* 'Florentina' depicts its association with Florence in the early Middle Ages. It is said to be the fleur-de-lys of French heraldry.

The blue flag iris is the common wetlands plant, native to eastern North America and exported from there to Europe. Employed by the Native Americans and early settlers as a remedy for gastric complaints, it was included in American pharmacopoeia and is still believed in folk medicine to be a blood purifier of use in eruptive skin conditions. Sometimes the plant is known as liver lily because of its purifying effect.

The root of the yellow flag iris, a native of the British Isles, was powdered and used as an ingredient in Elizabethan snuff. It was taken to America and Australia by the earliest settlers.

SPECIES

Iris 'Florentina'
Orrisroot
Also known as Florentine iris. Hardy perennial. Ht. 2–3 ft., spread indefinite. Large white flowers tinged with pale lavender and with a yellow beard appear early to midsummer. Green, sword-shaped leaves. The root stock is stout and rhizomatous with a violet scent. Grows well throughout North America and Europe, except in the warm moist climate of Florida and the Gulf Coast.
Zone 4

Iris germanica
Purple Iris
Also known as garden iris. Hardy perennial. Ht. 2–3 ft., spread indefinite. The fragrant flowers are blue-violet, occasionally white, and form early to midsummer. Leaves are grayish-green and sword-shaped. The root is thickish rhizome. There are many cultivated varieties. It is grown commercially for the rhizomes and, like orrisroot, is used in perfumery and pharmaceutical preparations.
Zone 4

Iris pseudacorus
Yellow Iris (Yellow Flag)
Perennial. Ht. 16 in.–5 ft., spread indefinite. Flowers are bright yellow with radiating brown veins and very slightly scented. They appear early to midsummer. The root is a thick rhizome from which many rootlets descend.
Zone 4

Yellow iris *Iris pseudacorus*

Iris versicolor
Blue Flag Iris
Also known as wild iris. Hardy perennial. Ht. 12–39 in., spread indefinite. Flowers claret-purple-blue in summer. Large, sword-shaped, green leaves. Root large and rhizomatous.

Purple iris *Iris germanica*

CULTIVATION

Propagation
Seed
All the irises produce large seeds, which take some time to germinate and often benefit from a period of stratification. As the seeds are of a good size, sow directly into a 3 in. pot in fall, using a bark-peat-grit mix of potting soil (see p. 591). Water in well, and cover the pots with plastic wrap (to keep mice from eating the seed). Put outside to get the weather. Check that the soil remains damp. If there is any danger of it drying out, stand the container in water. This is especially important for blue and yellow flag irises.

Division
Divide the rhizome roots in late spring or early fall. This suits all the varieties. Replant immediately in a prepared site. Leave 2–3 ft. between plants.

Pests and Diseases
The only major pest is the **iris borer**, which tunnels through the rhizome of orrisroot and purple iris but rarely attacks the yellow or blue flag irises. Dig and discard any rhizomes that show signs of infestation.

Maintenance
Spring Divide roots of mature plants.
Summer Collect the seeds as soon as ripe.
Fall Sow seeds and leave outside.
Winter Fully hardy; no need for protection.

Garden Cultivation
Orris and common iris prefer a well-drained, rich soil and a sunny situation. When planting, make sure that part of the rhizomes is exposed.

Yellow and blue flag irises are marsh-loving plants, ideal for those with a pond or ditch or piece of boggy ground. They grow happily in semishade but need full sun in order to produce the maximum bloom. In deep shade it will not flower at all but will spread quickly by stout underground rhizomes unless you install a barrier or edging.

Harvesting
The full violet fragrance of orris will not be apparent until the roots are two years old. Dig up these rhizomes in fall and dry immediately.

Gather yellow flag flowers and roots for use as a dye, in early summer and fall respectively.

Dig up blue flag roots in fall and dry.

CONTAINER GROWING

These irises grow on strong rhizomes, so make sure that the container is strong enough, large enough, and so shaped that it will accommodate the plant happily and not blow over.

For the bog lovers use more peat than usual in the potting soil mix—75 percent—but put lots of gravel and broken pottery in the bottom of the container to make up for loss of weight. For the dry plants, use a soil-based potting soil. Do not let either soil dry out. They become pot-bound very quickly, so split and repot every year.

WARNING

Always wash your hands well after handling orrisroot, or wear gloves, as it can cause uncontrollable vomiting and violent diarrhea.

Orrisroot used as a fixative in a potpourri

OTHER USES
The violet-scented, powdered root of orris is used as a fresh scent for linen, a base for dry shampoos, a base for tooth powders, in face packs, as a fixative in potpourris, and as a dry shampoo.

Flowers of yellow flag make a weak yellow dye, while the rhizomes yield a pale gray or black dye when used with an iron mordant.

MEDICINAL

Orris and yellow flag are rarely used medicinally nowadays. However, herbalists still use the blue flag as a blood purifier acting on the liver and gall bladder to increase the flow of bile, and as an effective cleanser of toxins. It is also said to relieve flatulence and heartburn, belching and nausea, and headaches associated with digestive problems.

CULINARY

Not really recommended.

Juniperus communis

JUNIPER

From the family Cupressaceae.

Juniper is widely distributed throughout the world and grows either as a shrub or a small tree. It is a native of the Mediterranean region, but also grows in the Arctic, from Norway to the former Soviet Union, in the northern and western Himalayas, and in North America. It is found on heaths, moorlands, open coniferous forests, and mountain slopes.

This widely distributed plant was first used by the ancient Greek physicians, and its use has continued right up to modern days. It was believed to cure snakebites and protect against infectious diseases like the plague.

The English word *gin* is derived from an abbreviation of Holland's *geneva,* as the spirit was first called. This in turn stems from the Dutch *jenever,* meaning "juniper."

SPECIES

Juniper is a conifer, a group of trees and shrubs distinguished botanically from others by its production of seeds exposed or uncovered on the scales of the fruit. True to form, it is evergreen and has needle-like leaves. There are many species and varieties available, *Juniperus communis* being the main herbal species. On the varieties detailed below, the flowers are all very similar: male flowers are very small catkins; female flowers are small, globular, and berrylike, with usually 3–8 fleshy scales. Over a period of three years, these turn blue and then finally black as they ripen.

Irish Juniper
Juniperis communis 'Hibernica'

Juniperus communis
'Compressa'
Juniper Compressa
Hardy evergreen perennial tree. Ht. 30 in., spread 6 in. The leaves are small and bluish-green, sharply pointed, and aromatic. Very slow growing with an erect habit, ideal for rock gardens or containers.
Zone 2

Juniperus communis
'Hibernica' Irish Juniper
Hardy evergreen perennial tree. Ht. 10–15 ft., spread 12 in. Leaves small and bluish silvery-green, sharply pointed, and aromatic. Columnar in shape and with a hint of silver in certain lights. Very slow growing.
Zone 2

Juniperus communis
'Hornibrookii'
Hornibrook Juniper
Hardy evergreen perennial tree. Ht. 20 in, spread 6 ft. Leaves small and darkish green, sharply pointed, and aromatic. A big carpeting plant.
Zone 2

Juniperus communis
Juniper
Hardy evergreen perennial. Ht. 1–25 ft., spread 3–12 ft.—size of the plant very dependent on site. Leaves bright green, sharply pointed, and aromatic.
Zone 2

Juniperus communis
'Prostrata' *Prostrate Juniper*
Hardy evergreen perennial tree. Ht. 8–12 in., spread 3–6 ft. Leaves small and bluish-green, sharply pointed, and aromatic. A smaller carpeting plant.
Zone 2

CULTIVATION

Propagation
Seed

All the species can be propagated by seed. Sow seeds taken from ripe berries in a cold greenhouse or cold frame in early fall. As junipers on the whole are extremely slow growing, it is best to grow the seedlings in a controlled environment for one or two years before planting out in a permanent position in the garden. Start in seed or plug trays; then, when the seedlings are large enough, pot into small pots using a soil-based potting soil. This method is the easiest, but to be sure of the plant's gender and leaf color, taking cuttings is more reliable.

Cuttings

It is quite easy to raise juniper from semihardwood cuttings taken from fresh current growth in spring or fall.

Pests and Diseases

Various rusts attack juniper. If you see small rusty spores on the underside of the leaves, cut the branches out and burn them.

It is typical for junipers to discolor badly in cold weather, and they may look quite dead in severe winters, but they turn green again in late spring.

Maintenance

Spring Set out young plants. Remove any leaders growing incorrectly in late spring/ early summer.
Summer Take semi-hardwood cuttings.
Fall Sow seeds.
Winter Winter young plants in cold frames, or provide added protection.

Garden Cultivation

Juniper likes an exposed sunny site. It will tolerate an alkaline or neutral soil. Both male and female plants are necessary for berry production. The berries, which only grow on the female bush, can be found in various stages of ripeness on the same plant. Their flavor is stronger when grown in warm climates.

To maintain the shape of the juniper, trim with pruning shears to ensure that there is no more than one leader, the strongest and straightest. Do not cut back into old wood or into branches that have turned brown.

Harvesting

Harvest the berries when ripe in late summer. Dry them spread out on a tray, as you would leaves.

CULINARY

Crushed berries are an excellent addition to marinades, sauerkraut, and stuffing for chicken and other game birds. Although no longer generally considered as a spice, it is still an important flavoring for certain meats, liqueurs, and especially gin.

Pork chops with juniper

Pork Chops Marinated with Juniper
Serves 4

Marinade
2 tablespoons olive oil
6 juniper berries, crushed
2 cloves of garlic, crushed
Salt and pepper

Mix the oil, juniper berries, garlic, and seasoning together in a bowl.

4 pork chops
1/4 cup flour
1 cup dry cider

Lay the pork chops in the base of a shallow dish and cover them with the marinade, turning the chops over once to make sure they are covered. Leave for a minimum of 3 hours, overnight if possible. Remove the chops from the marinade, and reserve it. Heat a large frying pan and add the reserved marinade. When hot, add the pork chops and cook over a moderate heat for about 20 minutes, turning the chops regularly. When all traces of pink have gone from the meat, remove from heat, and put the chops on a plate. Return the pan to the heat and stir the flour into the remaining juices. Add the cider and bring to a boil. Return the chops to the sauce in the pan. Heat through slowly, and serve with mashed potatoes and broccoli.

WARNING

Juniper berries should not be taken during pregnancy or by people with kidney problems. Internal use of the volatile oil must only be prescribed by professionals.

MEDICINAL

Juniper is used in the treatment of cystitis, rheumatism, and gout. Steamed inhalations of the berries are an excellent treatment for coughs, colds, and catarrh.

CONTAINER GROWING

Juniper is slow growing and can look most attractive in pots. Use a soil-based potting mix, starting off with a suitable-sized pot, only potting up once a year if necessary. If the root ball looks happy, do not disturb it. Do not overwater but don't let it dry out completely. In cold zones, wrap the container with insulating material to protect the roots during the winter months. Feed during the summer months only with a liquid fertilizer as per manufacturer's guidelines.

Laurus nobilis

Bay

From the family Lauraceae.

Bay is an evergreen tree native to southern Europe and now found throughout the world.

That this ancient plant was much respected in Roman times is reflected in the root of its family name, Lauraceae, the Latin *laurus* meaning "praise," and in its main species name, *Laurus nobilis*, the Latin *nobilis* meaning "famous," "renowned." A bay wreath became a mark of excellence for poets and athletes, a symbol of wisdom and glory. The latin *laureate* means "crowned with laurels" (synonym for bay), hence "poet laureate," of course, and the French *baccalaureate*.

The bay tree was sacred even earlier—to Apollo, Greek god of prophecy, poetry, and healing. His priestesses ate bay leaves before expounding his oracles at Delphi. As large doses of bay induce the effect of a narcotic, this may explain their trances. His temple had its roof made entirely of bay leaves, ostensibly to protect against disease, witchcraft, and lightning. Apollo's son Aesculapius, the Greek god of medicine, also had bay dedicated to him, as it was considered a powerful antiseptic and guard against disease.

In the seventeenth century, Culpeper wrote that "neither witch nor devil, thunder nor lightning, will hurt a man in the place where a bay-tree is." He also wrote that "the berries are very effectual against the poison of venomous creatures, and the stings of wasps and bees."

SPECIES

Laurus azorica
Canary Island Bay
Perennial evergreen tree. Ht. up to 20 ft. Reddish-brown branches, a color that sometimes extends to the leaves.

Laurus nobilis
Bay
Also known as Sweet Bay, Bay Laurel.
Perennial evergreen tree. Ht. up to 26 ft., spread 12 ft. Small, pale yellow, waxy flowers in spring. Green oval berries, turning black in fall. The leaves may be added to stock, soups, and stews and are among the main ingredients of bouquet garni. *L. nobilis* is the only bay used for culinary purposes.
Zone 8

Standard bay tree

Laurus nobilis 'Aurea'
Golden Bay
Perennial evergreen tree. Ht. up to 18 ft. Small, pale yellow, waxy flowers in spring. Green berries, turning black in fall. Golden leaves can look sickly. Needs good protection in winter especially from wind scorch and frosts. Trim in the fall/spring to maintain the golden leaves.
Zone 9

Laurus nobilis f. angustifolia
Willow Leaf Bay
Perennial evergreen tree. Ht. up to 23 ft. Narrow-leafed variety.
Zone 8

Umbellularia californica
Californian Laurel
Perennial evergreen tree. Ht. up to 60 ft. Pale yellow flowers in late spring. Very pungent, aromatic leaves. Can cause headaches and nausea when the leaves are crushed. *Not* culinary.
Zone 7

CULTIVATION

Propagation
Seed
Bay sets seed in its black berries, but rarely in cooler climates. Sow fresh seed on the surface of either a seed or plug tray or directly into pots. Keep warm: 65°F. Germination is erratic, may take place within 10–20 days, in 6 months, or sometimes even longer. Make sure the compost is not too wet or it will rot the seeds.

Cuttings
Not a plant for the fainthearted. When I started propagating over 20 years ago I thought my bay cuttings were doing really well, but a year later not one had properly struck, and three-quarters of them had turned black and died. Out of 100 cuttings only one eventually turned into a tree!

A heated propagator is a great help and high humidity is essential. Use either a misting unit or cover the cutting in plastic and maintain the potting soil or perlite at a steady moisture level. It may be an art, but worth a try. Cuttings are taken in late summer, 4 in. in length.

Bay *Laurus nobilis* **in flower**

Division

If offshoots are sent out by the parent plant, dig them up or they will destroy the shape of the tree. Occasionally roots come with them and these then can be potted up, using the bark-peat-grit mix of potting soil (see p. 591). Place a plastic bag over the pot to maintain humidity. Leave somewhere warm and check from time to time to see if new shoots are starting. When they do, remove the plastic bag. Do not plant out for at least a year.

Layering

Do it in spring. A good method of propagating a difficult plant.

Pests and Diseases

Bay is susceptible to **sooty black spots**, caused by the scale insect, which sticks both to the undersides of leaves and to the stems, sucking the sap. Get rid of them by spraying with a horticultural oil.

Maintenance

Spring Sow seeds. Cut back standard and garden bay trees to maintain shape and to promote new growth. Cut back golden bay trees to maintain color. Check for scale insect and eradicate at first signs. Give container-grown plants a good feeding of liquid fertilizer.
Summer Check that young plants are not drying out too much. In very hot weather, and especially if you live in a city, spray clean, container-

grown plants with water. Propagate by taking stem cuttings or layering in late summer.
Fall Take cuttings of mature plants. Protect container-grown plants and young garden plants. Garden plants can be protected either by covering in straw or bracken, if in a sufficiently sheltered position, or by agricultural fleece.
Winter In severe winters the leaves will turn brown but don't despair: come the spring, it may shoot new growth from the base. To encourage this, cut the plant nearly down to the base.

Garden Cultivation

Bay is shallow-rooted and therefore more prone to frost damage. Also, leaves are easily scorched in extremely cold weather or in strong cold winds. Protection is thus essential, especially for bay trees under two years old. When planting out, position the plant in full sun, protected from the wind, and in a rich well-drained soil at least 3 ft. away from other plants to start with, allowing more space as the tree matures. Mulch in the spring to retain moisture throughout the summer months.

Harvesting

Being evergreen, leaves can be taken all year round. It is fashionable now to preserve bay leaves in vinegars.
Berries are cultivated for use in laurel oil and laurel butter. The latter is a vital ingredient of laurin ointment, which is used in veterinary medicine.

MEDICINAL

Infuse the leaves to aid digestion and stimulate the appetite.

CONTAINER GROWING

Bay makes a good container plant. Young plants benefit from being kept in a container and indoors for the winter in cooler climates. The kitchen windowsill is ideal. Do not water too much, and let the compost dry out in the winter months.
Large standard bays or pyramids look very effective in half barrels or containers of an equal size. Anything in a container will need extra protection in winter from frosts and wind, so if the temperature drops below 25°F, bring the plants in.
To produce a standard bay tree, start with a young containerized plant with a straight growing stem. As it begins to grow, remove the lower side shoots, below where you want the ball to begin. Allow the tree to grow to 8 in. higher than desired, then clip back the growing tip. Cut the remaining side shoots down to about 3 leaves. When the side shoots have grown an additional 4–5 leaves, trim again to 2–3 leaves. Keep repeating this until you have

Bay bouquet garni

a leafy ball shape. Once the shape is established, prune with pruning shears in late spring and again in late summer to maintain it.

OTHER USES

Place in flour to deter weevils. Add an infusion to a bath to relieve aching limbs.

CULINARY

Fresh leaves are stronger in flavor than dried ones. Use in soups, stews, and stocks.

Add leaves to poached fish, like salmon.
Put on the coals of a barbecue.
Put fresh leaves in jars of rice to flavor the rice.
Boil in milk to flavor custards and rice pudding.

Bouquet Garni

I quote from my grandmother's cookbook *Food for Pleasure*, published in 1950: "A *bouquet garni* is a bunch of herbs constantly required in cooking." The essential herbs in a bouquet garni are bay leaf, parsley, and thyme.

Lavandula

LAVENDER

From the family Lamiaceae.

Native of the Mediterranean region, Canary Isles, and India. Now cultivated in different regions of the world, growing in well-draining soil and warm, sunny climates.

Long before the world manufactured deodorants and bath salts, the Romans used lavender in their bath water; the word is derived from the Latin *lava*, "to wash." It was the Romans who first introduced this plant to Britain, and from then on monks cultivated it in their monastic gardens. Little more was recorded until Tudor times when people noted its fragrance and a peculiar power to ease stiff joints and relieve tiredness. It was brought in quantities from herb farms to the London Herb Market at Bucklesbury. "Who will buy my lavender?" became perhaps the most famous of all London street cries.

It was used as a strewing herb for its insect-repellent properties and for masking household and street smells. It was also carried in nosegays to ward off the plague and pestilence. In France in the seventeenth century, huge fields of lavender were grown for the perfume trade. This has continued to the present day.

SPECIES

This is another big family of plants that are eminently worth collecting. I include here a few of my favorites.

***Lavandula angustifolia* (*L. officinalis*)**
Common/English Lavender
Hardy evergreen perennial. Ht. 32 in., spread 3 ft. Mauve-purple flowers on a long spike in summer. Long, narrow, pale, greenish-gray, aromatic leaves. One of the most popular and well known of the lavenders. **Zone 5**

Old English lavender
Lavandula x *intermedia*
'Old English'

***Lavandula angustifolia* 'Alba'**
White Lavender
Hardy evergreen perennial. Ht. 28 in., spread 32 in. White flowers on a long spike in summer. Long, narrow, pale greenish-gray, aromatic leaves. **Zone 5**

***Lavandula angustifolia* 'Bowles' Early'**
Lavender Bowles
Hardy evergreen perennial. Ht. and spread 24 in. Light

blue flowers on a medium-sized spike in summer. Medium-length, narrow, gray-greenish, aromatic leaves. **Zone 5**

***Lavandula angustifolia* 'Folgate'**
Lavender Folgate
Hardy evergreen perennial. Ht. and spread 18 in. Purple flowers on a medium spike in summer. **Zone 5**

***Lavandula angustifolia* 'Hidcote'**
Lavender Hidcote
Hardy evergreen perennial. Ht. and spread 18 in. Dark blue flowers on a medium spike in summer. Fairly short, narrow, aromatic, gray-greenish leaves. One of the most popular lavenders. Often used in hedging, planted at a distance of 12–16 in. **Zone 5**

***Lavandula angustifolia* 'Loddon Blue'**
Lavender Loddon Blue
Hardy evergreen perennial. Ht. and spread 18 in. Pale blue flowers on a medium-length spike in summer. Fairly short, narrow, gray-greenish, aromatic leaves. Good compact habit. There i another variety called 'Loddon Pink'—same size, same height, with pale pink flowers. **Zone 5**

***Lavandula angustifolia* 'Munstead'**
Lavender Dwarf Munstead
Hardy evergreen perennial. Ht. and spread 18 in. Purple-blue flowers on a fairly short spike in summer. Medium length, greenish-gray, narrow aromatic leaves. This is now a common lavender and used often in hedging, planted at distance of 12–16 in. **Zone 5**

Lavender Hidcote *Lavandula angustifolia* 'Hidcote'

Lavandula angustifolia **'Nana Alba'**
Dwarf White Lavender Hardy evergreen perennial. Ht. and spread 12 in. White flowers in summer. Green-gray narrow, short leaves. This is the shortest growing lavender and is ideal for hedges. **Zone 5**

Lavandula angustifolia **'Rosea'**
Pink Lavender Hardy evergreen perennial. Ht. and spread 18 in. Pink flowers in summer. Medium length greenish-gray, narrow, aromatic leaves. **Zone 5**

Lavandula dentata
Fringed Lavender (sometimes called French Lavender) Half-hardy evergreen perennial. Ht. and spread 24 in. Pale blue-mauve flowers from summer to early fall. Highly aromatic, serrated, pale green, narrow leaves. This plant is a native of southern Spain and the Mediterranean and needs protecting in cold damp winters. It is ideal to bring inside into a cool room in early fall as a flowering pot plant. **Zone 10**

Lavandula x *intermedia* **'Dutch'** Lavender Vera Hardy evergreen perennial. Ht. and spread 18 in. Purple flowers in summer on fairly long spikes. Long greenish-gray, narrow, aromatic leaves. **Zone 5**

Lavandula x *intermedia* **'Grappenhall'**
Lavender Grappenhall Hardy evergreen perennial. Ht. and spread 3 ft. Large pale mauve flowers on long spikes in summer. The flowers are much more open than those of other species. Long greenish-gray, narrow, aromatic leaves. **Zone 5**

Lavandula x *intermedia* **'Old English'**
Old English Lavender Hardy evergreen perennial. Ht. and spread 24 in. Light lavender-blue flowers on long spikes. Long, narrow, silver-gray-green, aromatic leaves. **Zone 5**

French lavender *Lavandula stoechas*

Lavandula x *intermedia* **'Seal'**
Lavender Seal Hardy evergreen perennial. Ht. 3 ft., spread 24 in. Long flower stems, mid-purple. Long, narrow, silver-gray-green aromatic leaves. **Zone 5**

Lavandula x *intermedia* **'Twickel Purple'**
Lavender Twickel Purple Hardy evergreen perennial. Ht. and spread 20 in. Pale purple flowers on fairly short spike. Medium length, greenish-gray, narrow, aromatic leaves. Compact grower. **Zone 5**

Lavender Pedunculata *Lavandula stoechas* subsp. *pedunculata*

Lavandula lanata
Woolly Lavender Hardy evergreen perennial. Ht. 20 in., spread 18 in. Deep purple flowers on short spikes. Short, soft, narrow, silver-gray aromatic foliage. **Zone 6**

Lavandula pinnata
Lavender Pinnata Half-hardy evergreen perennial. Ht. and spread 20 in. The flower spikes are a mixture of *L. angustifolia* and *L. stoechas*, purple in color. Leaves are fernlike, gray, and slightly aromatic. Could be easily mistaken for an artemisia. Protect in winter. **Zone 9**

Lavandula stoechas
French Lavender (sometimes called Spanish Lavender) Hardy evergreen perennial. Ht. 20 in., spread 24 in. Attractive purple bracts in summer. Short, narrow, gray-green, aromatic leaves. **Zone 7**

Fringe lavender *Lavandula dentata*

Lavandula stoechas f. *leucantha*
White French Lavender As *L. stoechas* except white bracts in summer.

Lavandula stoechas subsp. *pedunculata*
Lavender Pedunculata Tender evergreen perennial. Ht. and spread 24 in. These attractive purple bracts have an extra center tuft, which is mauve and looks like two rabbit ears. The aromatic leaves are very narrow, gray, and longer than the ordinary *stoechas*. Protect in winter. **Zone 8**

Lavandula viridis
Lavender Viridis Half-hardy evergreen perennial. Ht. and spread 24 in. This unusual plant has green bracts with a cream center tuft. The leaves are green, narrow, and highly aromatic. Protect in winter. **Zone 9**

Lavenders—Small (grow to 18–20 in.)
Lavender Folgate, Lavender Hidcote, Lavender Lodden Pink, Lavender Lodden Blue, Lavender Dwarf Munstead, Dwarf White Lavender, Lavender Twickel Purple.

Lavenders—Medium (grow to 24 in.)
Lavender Bowles, Old English Lavender.

Lavenders—Big (28 in. and above)
Lavender Grappenhall, White Lavender, Lavender Seal.

Half-hardy Lavenders
Fringe Lavender (20 in.), Woolly Lavender (20 in.), Lavender Pinnata (20 in.), French Lavender (20 in.), White French Lavender (20 in.), Lavender Pendunculata (24 in.), Lavender Viridis (20 in.).

CULTIVATION

Propagation
Seed

Lavender can be grown from seed but it tends not to come true to type, with the exception of *Lavandula stoechas*.

Seed should be sown fresh in the fall on the surface of a seed or plug tray and covered with perlite. It germinates fairly readily with a bottom heat of 40–50°F. Winter the seedlings in a cold greenhouse with plenty of ventilation. In the spring, prick out and repot using the bark-peat-grit mix of potting soil (see p. 591). Let the young plant establish a good-sized root ball before planting out in a prepared site in the early summer. For other species you will find cuttings much more reliable.

Cuttings

Take softwood cuttings from nonflowering stems in spring. Root in bark-peat-grit mix of potting soil. Take semihardwood cuttings in summer or early fall from the strong new growth. Once the cuttings have rooted well, it is better to pot them up and winter the young lavenders in a cold greenhouse rather than plant them out in the first

Lavender viridis
Lavandula viridis

winter. In the spring, plant them out in well-drained, fertile soil, at a distance of 18–24 in. apart or 12 in. apart for an average hedge.

Layering

This is easily done in the fall. Most hardy lavenders respond well to this form of propagation.

Pests and Diseases

The flowers in wet seasons may be attacked by **gray mold** (*Botrytis*). This can occur all too readily after a wet winter. Cut back the infected parts as far as possible, again remembering not to cut into the old wood if you want it to shoot again.

There is another **fungus** (*Phoma lavandulae*) that attacks the stems and branches causing wilting and death of the affected branches. If this occurs, dig up the plant immediately and destroy, keeping it well away from any other lavender bushes.

Maintenance

Spring Give a spring haircut. Take cuttings.
Summer Trim after flowering.
Fall Sow seed. Avoid cutting back in autumn—leave the mature stems to overwinter. Protect all the half-hardy lavenders and bring containers inside.

Winter Check seedlings for disease. Keep watering to a minimum.

Garden Cultivation

Lavender is one of the most popular plants in today's herb garden and is particularly useful in borders, edges, as internal hedges, and on top of dry walls. All the species need an open sunny position and a well-drained, fertile soil. But it will adapt to semishade as long as the soil conditions are met, otherwise it will die in winter. If you have very cold winter temperatures, it is worth container growing.

The way to maintain a lavender bush is to trim to shape every year in the spring, remembering not to cut into the old wood as this will not reshoot. After flowering, trim back to the leaves, making sure this is well before the first fall frosts. Otherwise the new growth will be too soft and be damaged. By trimming this way, you will keep the bush neat and encourage it to make new growth, keeping it from becoming woody.

If you have inherited a straggly mature plant then give it a good cut back in fall, followed by a second cut in the spring and then adopt the above routine. If the plant is aged, I would advise that you propagate some of the fall cuts, so that you preserve the plant if all else fails.

Harvesting

Gather the flowers just as they open, and dry on open trays or by hanging in small bunches.

Pick the leaves anytime for use fresh, or before flowering if drying.

Lavender sachets make good presents and can be used as moth repellent.

CONTAINER GROWING

If you have low winter temperatures, lavender cannot be treated as a hardy evergreen. Treated as a container plant, however, it can be protected in winter and enjoyed just as well in the summer. Choose containers to set off the lavender; they all suit terra-cotta. Use a well-drained potting soil—the bark-peat-grit mix suits them well. The ideal position is sun, but all lavenders will cope with partial shade, though the aroma can be impaired.

Feed regularly through the flowering season with liquid fertilizer, following the manufacturer's instructions. Allow the compost to dry out in winter (not totally, but nearly), and slowly reintroduce watering in spring.

CULINARY

Lavender has not been used much in cooking, but as there are many more adventurous cooks around, I am sure it will be used increasingly in the future. Use the flowers to flavor an herb jelly or a vinegar. The flowers can also be crystallized.

Lavender Biscuits

$^1/_2$ cup butter
$^1/_4$ cup sugar
$1^3/_4$ cups self-rising flour
2 tablespoons chopped fresh lavender leaves
1 teaspoon lavender flowers removed from spike

Lavender biscuits

Preheat the oven to 450°F. Cream the sugar and butter together until light. Add the flour and lavender leaves to the butter mixture. Knead well until it forms a dough. Gently roll out on a lightly floured board. Scatter the flowers over the rolled dough and lightly press in with the rolling pin. Cut into small rounds with cutter. Place biscuits on a greased baking sheet. Bake for 10–12 minutes until golden and firm. Remove at once and cool on a wire rack.

Lavender herb jelly

MEDICINAL

Throughout history, lavender has been used medicinally to soothe, sedate, and suppress. Nowadays it is the essential oil that is in great demand. The oil was traditionally inhaled to prevent vertigo and fainting. It is an excellent remedy for burns and stings, and its strong anti-bacterial action helps to heal cuts. The oil also kills diphtheria and typhoid bacilli as well as streptococcus and pneumococcus.

Add 6 drops of oil to bath water to calm irritable children. Place 1 drop on the temple for a headache relief. Blend for use as a massage oil for throat infections, inflammation, skin sores, rheumatic aches, anxiety, insomnia, and depression. The best oil is made from distillation, and may be bought from many shops.

OTHER USES

Rub fresh flowers onto skin or pin a sprig on clothes to discourage flies. Use flowers in potpourri, herb pillows, and linen sachets, where they make a good moth repellent.

Levisticum officinale

LOVAGE

Also known as Love Parsley, Sea Parsley, Lavose, Liveche, Smallage, and European Lovage. From the family Apiaceae.

Lovage *Levisticum officinale*

This native of the Mediterranean can now be found naturalized throughout the temperate regions of the world, including North America, Australia, and Scandinavia.

Lovage was used by the ancient Greeks, who chewed the seed to aid digestion and relieve flatulence. Knowledge of it was handed down to Benedictine monks by the Romans, who prescribed the seeds for the same complaints. In Europe a decoction of lovage was reputedly a good aphrodisiac that no witch worthy of the name could be without. The name is likely to have come from the Latin *ligusticum*, after Liguria in Italy, where the herb grew profusely.

Because lovage leaves have a deodorizing and antiseptic effect on the skin, they were laid in the shoes of travelers in the Middle Ages to revive their weary feet, like latter-day "odor eaters."

SPECIES

Levisticum officinale
Lovage
Hardy perennial. Ht. up to 6 ft., spread 3 ft. or more. Tiny, pale, greenish-yellow flowers in summer clusters. Leaves darkish green, deeply divided, and large toothed.
Zone 3

CULTIVATION

Propagation
Seed
Sow under protection in spring into prepared plug or seed trays and cover with perlite; a bottom heat of 60°F is helpful. When the seedlings are large enough to handle and after a period of hardening off, transplant into a prepared site in the garden 2 ft. apart.

Division
The roots of an established plant can be divided in the spring or fall. Make sure that each division has some new buds showing.

Pests and Diseases
Leaf miners are sometimes a problem. Watch out for the first tunnels, pick off the affected leaves, and destroy them, otherwise broad dry patches will develop and the leaves will start to wither away. To control this, cut the plant right down to the ground, burning the affected shoots. Give the plant a feeding and it will shoot with new growth. The young growth is just what one needs for cooking.

Maintenance
Spring Divide established plants.
Summer Clip established plants to encourage new shoots.
Fall Sow seed in garden.
Winter No need for protection.

Garden Cultivation
Lovage prefers a rich, moist, but well-drained soil. Prior to first planting, dig over the ground deeply and manure well. The site can be either in full sun or partial shade. Seeds are best sown in the garden in the fall. When the seedlings are large enough, thin to 2 ft. apart. It is

important that lovage has a period of dormancy so that it can complete the growth cycle.

Lovage is a tall plant, so position it carefully. It will reach its full size in 3–5 years. To keep the leaves young and producing new shoots, cut around the edges of the clumps.

Harvesting

After the plant has flowered the leaves tend to have more of a bitter taste, so harvest in early summer. I personally believe that lovage does not dry well that and it is best to freeze it (see p. 611).

Harvest seed heads when the seeds start to turn brown. Pick them on a dry day, tie a paper bag over their heads, and hang upside down in a dry, airy place. Use, like celery seed, for winter soups.

Dig the root for drying in the fall of the second or third season.

CONTAINER GROWING

Lovage is fine grown outside in a large container. To keep it looking good, keep it well clipped. I do not advise letting it run to flower unless you can support it. Remember at flowering stage, even in a pot, it can be in excess of 5 ft. tall.

WARNING

As lovage is very good at reducing water retention, people who are pregnant or who have kidney problems should not take this herb medicinally.

CULINARY

Lovage is an essential member of any culinary herb collection. The flavor is reminiscent of celery. It adds a meaty flavor to foods and is used in soups, stews, and stocks. Also add fresh young leaves to salads, and rub on chicken and around salad bowls.

Crush seeds in bread and pastries, sprinkle on salads, rice, and mashed potato.

If using the rootstock as a vegetable in casseroles, remove the bitter-tasting skin.

Lovage Soup
Serves 4

2 tablespoons butter
2 medium onions, finely
  chopped
2¹⁄₂ cups potatoes, peeled and
  diced
4 tablespoons finely chopped
  lovage leaves
2¹⁄₂ cups chicken or
  vegetable stock
Salt and pepper
1 cup milk or cream
Grated nutmeg

Melt the butter in a heavy pan and gently sauté the onions and diced potatoes for 5 minutes until soft. Add the chopped lovage leaves and cook for 1 minute. Pour in the stock, bring to a boil, season with salt and pepper, cover and simmer gently until the potatoes are soft (about 15 minutes). Purée the soup through a sieve or in a food processor and return to a

clean pan. Blend in the milk or cream, sprinkle with a pinch of nutmeg and heat through. Do not boil or it will curdle. Adjust the seasoning. Delicious hot or cold. Serve garnished with chopped lovage leaves.

Lovage and Carrot
Serves 2

3 carrots, grated
1 apple, grated
2 teaspoons chopped lovage
  leaves
2 tablespoons mayonnaise
¹⁄₂ cup plain yogurt
Lettuce leaves
1 onion sliced into rings
Chives

Toss together the grated carrots, apple, lovage, mayonnaise, and yogurt. Arrange the lettuce leaves on a serving dish and fill with the lovage mixture. Decorate with a few raw onions rings, chives, and tiny lovage leaves.

Lovage as a Vegetable

Treat lovage as you would spinach. Use the young growth of the plant stalks and leaves. Strip the leaves from the stalks, wash, and cut the stalks up into segments. Bring a pan of water to a boil, add the lovage, bring the water back to a boil, cover, and simmer for about 5–7 minutes until tender. Strain the water. Make a white sauce using butter, flour, milk, salt, pepper, and grated nutmeg. Add the lovage. Serve and wait for the compliments!

Lovage soup

MEDICINAL

Lovage is a remedy for digestive difficulties, gastric catarrh, and flatulence. I know of one recipe from the west of England—a teaspoon of lovage seed steeped in a glass of brandy, strained, and sweetened with sugar. It is taken to settle an upset stomach!

Infuse seed, leaf, or root and take to reduce water retention. Lovage assists in the removal of waste products, acts as a deodorizer, and aids rheumatism.

Its deodorizing and antiseptic properties enable certain skin problems to respond to a decoction added to bath water. This is made with 1¹⁄₂–2 oz. of rootstock in 2 cups water. Add to your bath.

Lovage, brandy, and sugar settle an upset stomach

Lonicera

HONEYSUCKLE

Also known as Woodbine, Beerbind, Bindweed, Evening Pride, Fairy Trumpets, Honeybind, Irish Vine, Trumpet Flowers, Sweet Suckle, and Woodbind. From the family Caprifoliaceae.

> "Come into the garden, Maud,
> I am here at the gate alone;
> And the woodbine spices are wafted abroad,
> And the musk of the rose is blown."
> —Alfred, Lord Tennyson (1809–1892)

Honeysuckle can also be found growing wild in North America, western Asia, and North Africa, and grows all over northern Europe, including Britain.

Honeysuckle receives its common name from the old habit of sucking the sweet honey-tasting nectar from the flowers. Generically it is said to have been named after the sixteenth-century German physician Lonicer.

Honeysuckle was among the plants that averted the evil powers abroad on May Day and took care of the milk, butter, and cows in the Scottish Highlands and elsewhere. Traditionally it was thought that if honeysuckle was brought into the house, a wedding would follow, and that if the flowers were placed in a girl's bedroom, she would have dreams of love.

Honeysuckle's rich fragrance has inspired many poets, including Shakespeare, who called it woodbine after its notorious habit of climbing up trees and hedges and totally binding them up.

> "Where oxlips and the nodding violet grows quite over-canopied with luscious woodbine . . ."
> —*A Midsummer Night's Dream*

The plant appeared in John Gerard's sixteenth-century *Herball*; he wrote that "the flowers steeped in oil and set in the sun are good to anoint the body that is benummed and grown very cold."

SPECIES

There are many fragrant climbing varieties of this lovely plant. I have only mentioned those with a direct herbal input.

Lonicera x *americana*
Honeysuckle
Deciduous woody vine. Ht. up to 23 ft. Strongly fragrant yellow flowers starting in a pink bud, turning yellow, and finishing with orangish pink throughout the summer. The berries are red, and the leaves are green and oval, the upper ones being united and saucerlike.
Zone 6

Lonicera caprifolium
Deciduous woody vine. Ht. up to 20 ft. The buds of the fragrant flowers are initially pink on opening; they then change to a pale white-pink-yellow as they age, and finally turn deeper yellow. Green oval leaves and red berries, which were once fed to chickens. The Latin species name, *caprifolium*, means "goats' leaf," reflecting the belief that honeysuckle leaves were a favorite food of goats. This variety and *Lonicera periclymenum* can be found growing wild in hedgerows.
Zone 5

Lonicera periclymenum
Deciduous woody vine. This is the taller grower of the two common European

honeysuckles, and reaches a height of 23 ft. It may live for fifty years. Fragrant yellow flowers appear midsummer to mid-fall, followed by red berries. Leaves are oval and dark green with a bluish underside.
Zone 5

Lonicera etrusca
Etruscan Honeysuckle
Semievergreen woody vine. Ht. up to 12 ft. Fragrant, pale, creamy yellow flowers which turn deeper yellow to red in fall and are followed by red berries. Leaves oval, mid-green, with a bluish underside. This is the least hardy of those mentioned here, and should be grown in sun on a south-facing wall, and protected in winter. **Zone 7**

Lonicera caprifolium

Lonicera japonica
Japanese Honeysuckle
Semievergreen woody vine. Ht. up to 33 ft. Fragrant, pale, creamy white flowers turning yellow as the season progresses, followed by black berries. The leaves are oval and mid-green in color. In the garden it is apt to build up an enormous tangle of shoots and best allowed to clamber over tree stumps or a low roof or walls. Attempts to train it tidily are a lost cause. Still used in Chinese medicine today. **Zone 5**

CULTIVATION

Propagation
Seed
Sow seed in fall thinly on the surface of a prepared seed or plug tray. Cover with glass and winter outside. Keep an eye on the soil moisture and only water if necessary. Germination may take a long time; it has been known to take two seasons, so be patient. A more reliable alternative method is by cuttings.

Cuttings
Take from nonflowering, semihardwood shoots in summer and root in a bark-peat-grit mix of potting soil (see p. 591). Alternatively, take hardwood cuttings in late fall, leaving the cuttings in a cold frame or cold greenhouse for the winter.

Layering
In late spring or fall honeysuckle is easy to layer. Do not disturb until the following season when it can be severed from its parent.

Pests and Diseases
Grown in too sunny or warm a place, it can become infested with **aphids**, **caterpillars**, and **red spider mites**. Use a horticultural soap, and spray the pests according to the manufacturer's instructions.

Maintenance
Spring Prune established plants.
Summer Cut back flowering stems after flowering. Take semihardwood cuttings.
Fall Layer established plants. Lightly prune if necessary.
Winter Protect tender species in cold winters.

Garden Cultivation
This extremely tolerant, traditional herb garden plant will flourish vigorously in the most unpromising sites. Honeysuckle leaves are among the first to appear, sometimes midwinter, the flowers appearing in very early summer and deepening in color after being pollinated by the insects that feed on their nectar. Good as cover for an unsightly wall or to provide a rich summer evening fragrance in an arbor.

Plant in fall or spring in any fertile, well-drained soil, in sun or semishade. The best situation puts its feet in the shade and its head in the sunshine. A position against a north or west wall is ideal, or on the shady side of a support such as a tree stump, pole, or pergola. Prune in early spring, if need be. Prune out flowering wood on climbers after flowering.

MEDICINAL

An infusion of the heavy perfumed flowers can be taken as a substitute for tea. It is also useful for treating coughs, catarrh, and asthma. As a lotion it is good for skin infections.

Recent research has proved that this plant has an outstanding curative action in cases of colitis.

Warning: The berries are poisonous. Large doses cause vomiting.

Harvesting
Pick and dry the flowers for potpourris just as they open. This is the best time for scent although they are their palest in color.

Pick the flowers for use in salads as required. Again the best flavor is before the nectar has been collected, which is when the flower is at its palest.

CULINARY

Add flowers to salads.

CONTAINER GROWING

This is not a plant that springs to mind as a good pot plant, certainly not indoors. But with patience, it makes a lovely mop head standard if carefully staked and trained; use an evergreen variety like *Lonicera japonica.* The potting soil should be soil-based. Water and feed regularly throughout the summer and in winter keep in a cold frame or greenhouse and water only occasionally.

OTHER USES
Flowers are strongly scented for potpourris, herb pillows, and perfumery. An essential oil was once extracted from the plant to make a very sweet perfume, but the yield was extremely low.

Honeysuckle flowers in a fresh summer salad

Malva sylvestris

MALLOW

Also known as Billy Buttons, Pancake Plan, and Cheese Flower. From the family Malvaceae.

Native to Europe, western Asia and North America, it can be found growing in hedges, field edges, and on roadsides and vacant lots in sunny situations.

The ancient Latin name given to this herb by Pliny was *malacho*, which was probably derived from *malachi*, the Greek word meaning "to soften," after the mallow's softening and healing properties. Young mallow shoots were eaten as vegetables, and it was still to be found on vegetable lists in Roman times. Used in the Middle Ages for its calming effect as an antidote to aphrodisiacs and love potions. The shape of its seed rather than its flowers suggested the folk name.

SPECIES

Malva sylvestris
Common Mallow
Biennial. Ht. 18–36 in., spread 24 in. Flower, dark pink or violet form, early summer to fall. Mid-green leaves, rounded at the base, ivy shaped at stem.
Zone 4

Malva rotundifolia
Dwarf Mallow
Also known as cheese plant. Annual. Ht. 6–12 in., a creeper. Purplish-pink, trumpet-shaped flowers from early summer to mid-fall. Leaves rounded, slightly lobed, and greenish. North American native.
All zones

Malva moschata
Musk Mallow
Perennial. Ht. 12–32 in., spread 24 in. Rose-pink flowers (sometimes white), summer to fall. Mid-green leaves—kidney-shaped at base, deeply divided at stem—emit musky aroma in warm weather or when pressed. **Zone 4**

CULTIVATION

Propagation
Seed
Sow in prepared seed or plug trays in the fall. Cover lightly with compost (not perlite). Winter outside, covered with glass. Germination is erratic but should take place in the spring. Plant out seedlings when large enough to handle, 24 in. apart.

Cuttings
Take cuttings from firm basal shoots in late spring or summer. When hardened off the following spring, plant out 24 in. apart into a prepared site.

Pests and Diseases
Mallows can catch **hollyhock rust**. There is also a **fungus** that produces leaf spots and a serious black canker on the stems. If this occurs, dig up the plants and destroy them. This is a seed-borne fungus and may be carried into the soil, so change planting site the following season.

Maintenance
Spring Take softwood cuttings from young shoots.
Summer Trim after flowering.
Fall Sow seed.
Winter Hardy enough.

Garden Cultivation
Mallows are very tolerant of site, but prefer a well-drained and fertile soil (if too damp they may well need staking in summer), and a sunny position (though semishade will do). Sow where it is to flower from late summer to spring. Press gently into the soil, 24 in. apart, and cover with a light potting mix. Cut back stems after flowering, not only to promote new growth, but also to keep under control and encourage a second flowering. Cut down the stems in fall.

Harvesting
Harvest young leaves for fresh use as required throughout the spring. For use in potpourris, gather for drying in the summer after first flowering.

CONTAINER GROWING

Musk mallow is the best variety to grow in a large container. It can look very dramatic and smells lovely on a warm evening. Water well throughout the growing season, but feed only twice. Maintain as for garden cultivation. Repot yearly.

CULINARY

Young tender tips of the common mallow may be used in salads or steamed as a vegetable. Young leaves of the musk mallow can be boiled as a vegetable.

Young leaves of the dwarf mallow can be eaten raw in salads or cooked as a spinach.

Musk mallow salad

MEDICINAL

Marsh mallow (*Althaea officinalis*) is used in preference to the mallows (*Malva*) in herbal medicine. However, a decoction can be used in a compress, or in bath preparations, for skin rashes, boils, and ulcers, and in gargles and mouthwashes.

Marrubium vulgare

WHITE HOREHOUND

Also known as Horehound and Maribeum. From the family Lamiaceae.

Common throughout America and Europe, the plant grows wild everywhere from coastal to mountainous areas.

The botanical name comes from the Hebrew *marrob*, which translates as "bitter juice." The common name is derived from the old English *har hune*, meaning "a downy plant."

SPECIES

Marrubium vulgare
White Horehound
Hardy perennial. Ht. 18 in., spread 12 in. Small clusters of white flowers from the second year in midsummer. The leaves are green and wrinkled with an underside of a silver woolly texture. There is also a variegated version. **Zone 4**

CULTIVATION

Propagation
Seed
The fairly small seed should be sown in early spring in a seed or plug tray, using the bark-peat-grit mix of potting soil (see p. 591). Germination takes 2–3 weeks. Prick out into pots or transplant to the garden after a period of hardening off.

Cuttings
Softwood cuttings taken from the new growth in summer usually root within 3–4 weeks. Use the bark-peat-grit mix of potting soil. Winter under protection in a cold frame or cold greenhouse.

Division
Established clumps benefit from division in the spring.

Pests and Diseases
If it is very wet and cold in winter, the plant can **rot** off.

Maintenance
Spring Divide established clumps. Prune new growth to maintain shape. Sow seed.
Summer Trim after flowering to stop the plant from flopping and prevent self-seeding. Take cuttings.
Fall Divide only if it has dangerously transgressed its limits.
Winter Protect only if season excessively wet.

Garden Cultivation
White horehound grows best in well-drained, dryish soil, biased to alkaline, sunny, and protected from high winds. Seed can be sown directly into a prepared garden in late spring, once the soil has started to warm up. Thin the seedlings to 12 in. apart.

Harvesting
The leaves and flowering tops are gathered in the spring, just as the plants come into flower, when the essential oil is at its richest. Use fresh or dried.

CONTAINER GROWING

Horehound can be grown in a large container situated in a sunny position. Use a compost that drains well, and do not overwater. Only feed after flowering, otherwise it produces lush growth that is too soft.

OTHER USES
Infuse the leaf as a spray for cankerworm in trees.
Mix the infusion with milk and put in a dish as a fly killer. Do not spray!

MEDICINAL

White horehound is still extensively used in cough medicine, and for calming a nervous heart. Its property, marrubiin, in small amounts, normalizes an irregular heartbeat. The plant has also been used to reduce fevers and treat malaria.

A Cold Cure
Finely chop 9 small horehound leaves. Mix 1 tablespoon of honey and eat slowly to ease a sore throat or cough. Repeat several times if necessary.

Cough Sweets
4 oz. of fresh white horehound leaves
1/2 teaspoon of crushed aniseed
3 crushed cardamom seeds
1 1/2 cups white sugar
1 3/4 cups moist brown sugar

Put the horehound, aniseed, and cardamom into a cup of water and simmer for 20 minutes. Strain through a filter. Over a low heat, dissolve the sugars in the liquid; boil over medium heat until the syrup hardens when drops are put into cold water. Pour into greased tray. Score when partially cooled. Store in waxed paper.

Horehound cough sweets

Melissa officinalis

LEMON BALM

Also known as Balm, Melissa, Balm Mint, Bee Balm, Blue Balm, Cure All, Dropsy Plant, Garden Balm, and Sweet Balm. From the family Lamiaceae.

Melissa officinalis
Lemon Balm
Hardy perennial. Ht. 30 in., spread 18 in. or more. Clusters of small, pale yellow-white flowers in summer. The green leaves are oval toothed, slightly wrinkled, and highly aromatic when crushed.
Zone 5

Melissa officinalis '**All Gold**'
Golden Lemon Balm
Half-hardy perennial. Ht. 24 in., spread 12 in. or more. Clusters of small, pale yellow-white flowers in summer. The leaves are all yellow, oval in shape, toothed, slightly wrinkled, and aromatic with a lemon scent when crushed. The leaves are prone to scorching in high summer; also more tender than the other varieties. **Zone 6**

Left: **Lemon balm** *Melissa officinalis* and **variegated lemon balm** *Melissa officinalis* 'Aurea'

This plant is a native of the Mediterranean region and central Europe. It is now naturalized in North America and as a garden escapee in Britain.

This ancient herb was dedicated to the goddess Diana, and used medicinally by the Greeks some 2,000 years ago. The generic name, *Melissa*, comes from the Greek word for "bee" and the Greek belief that if you put sprigs of balm in an empty hive it would attract a swarm; if planted near bees in residence in a hive they would never go away. This belief was still prevalent in medieval times when sugar was highly priced and honey a luxury.

In the Middle Ages lemon balm was used to soothe tension, to dress wounds, as a cure for toothache, mad dog bites, skin eruptions, crooked necks, and sickness during pregnancy. It was even said to prevent baldness, and ladies made linen or silk amulets filled with lemon balm as a lucky love charm. It has been acclaimed the world over for promoting long life. Prince Llewellyn of Glamorgan drank Melissa tea, so he claimed, every day of the 108 years of his life. Wild claims apart, as a tonic for melancholy it has been praised by herbal writers for centuries and is still used today in aromatherapy to counter depression.

Melissa officinalis '**Aurea**'
Variegated Lemon Balm
Hardy perennial. Ht. 24 in., spread 12 in. or more. Clusters of small, pale yellow-white flowers in summer. The green-gold variegated leaves are oval, toothed, slightly wrinkled and aromatic with a lemon scent when crushed. This variety is as hardy as common lemon balm. The one problem is that in high season it reverts to green. To maintain variegation keep cutting back; this in turn will promote new growth, which should be variegated. **Zone 6**

Lemon balm *Melissa officinalis* **in flower**

Left: **Variegated lemon balm** *Melissa officinalis* 'Aurea'

CULTIVATION

Propagation
Seed
Common lemon balm can be grown from seed. The seed is small but manageable, and it is better to start it off under protection. Sow in prepared seed or plug trays in early spring, using the bark-peat-grit mix of potting soil (see p. 591) and cover with perlite. Germination takes between 10 and 14 days. The seeds dislike being wet so, after the initial watering, try not to water again until germination starts. When seedlings are large enough to handle, transplant in the garden, 18 in. apart.

Cuttings
The variegated and golden lemon balm can only be propagated by cuttings or division. Take softwood cuttings from the new growth in late spring/early summer. As the cutting material will be very soft, take extra care when collecting it.

Division
The rootstock is compact but easy to divide (fall or spring). Replant directly into the garden in a prepared site.

Pests and Diseases
The only problem likely to affect lemon balm is a form of the **rust virus**; cut the plant back to the ground, and dispose of all the infected leaves, including any that may have accidentally fallen on the ground.

Maintenance
Spring Sow seeds. Divide established plants.
Summer Keep trimming established plants. Cut back after flowering to help prevent self-seeding.
Fall Divide established plants, or any that may have encroached on other plant areas.
Winter Protect plants if the temperature falls below 23°F. The plant dies back, leaving but a small presence on the surface of the soil. Protect with a bark or straw mulch or frost fabric.

Garden Cultivation
Lemon balm will grow in almost any soil and in any position. It does prefer a fairly rich, moist soil in a sunny position with some midday shade. Keep all plants trimmed around the edges to restrict growth and encourage fresh shoots. In the right soil conditions this can be a very invasive plant, but it is more likely to spread by seed than by rhizome.

Harvesting
Pick leaves throughout the summer for fresh use. For drying, pick just before the flowers begin to open when flavor is best; handle gently to avoid bruising. The aroma is rapidly lost, together with much of its therapeutic value, when dried or stored.

CULINARY

Lemon balm is one of those herbs that smells delicious but tastes like school-boiled cabbage water when cooked.
Add fresh leaves to vinegar. Add leaves to wine cups, teas, and beers, or use chopped with fish and mushroom dishes. Mix freshly chopped with soft cheeses.
It has frequently been incorporated in proprietary cordials for liqueurs and its popularity in France led to its name "Tea de France."
It is used as a flavoring for certain cheeses in parts of Switzerland.

Lemon balm with cream cheese

MEDICINAL

Lemon balm tea is said to relieve headaches and tension and to restore the memory. It is also good to drink after meals to ease digestion, flatulence, and colic. Use fresh or frozen leaves in infusions because the volatile oil tends to disappear during the drying process.
The isolated oil used in aromatherapy is recommended for nervousness, depression, insomnia, and nervous headaches. It also helps eczema sufferers.

OTHER USES
This is a most useful plant to keep bees happy. The flower may look boring to you but it is sheer heaven to them. So plant lemon balm around beehives or orchards to attract pollinating bees.

CONTAINER GROWING

If you live in an area that suffers from very cold winters, the gold form would benefit from being grown in containers. This method suits those with a small garden who do not want a takeover bid from lemon balm. Use the bark-peat-grit mix of potting soil. Only feed with liquid fertilizer in the summer, otherwise the growth will become too lush and soft, and the aroma and color diminished. Water normally throughout the growing season. Allow the container to become very dry (but not totally) in winter, and keep the pots in a cool, protected environment. Repot in spring.

Mentha

MINT

From the family Lamiaceae.

The *Mentha* family is a native of Europe that has naturalized in many parts of the world, including North America, Australia, and Japan. Mint has been cultivated for its medicinal properties since ancient times and has been found in Egyptian tombs dating back to 1000 B.C. The Japanese have been growing it to obtain menthol for at least 2,000 years. In the Bible the Pharisees collected tithes in mint, dill, and cumin. Charlemagne, who was very keen on herbs, ordered people to grow it. The Romans brought it with them as they marched through Europe and into Britain, from where it found its way to America with the settlers.

Its name was first used in Greek mythology. There are two versions of the same story: the nymph Minthe was being seduced by Hades, god of the Underworld, and his queen Persephony became jealous. In one version, she turns the nymph into the plant, mint. In the other, Hades himself transforms her into the scented herb.

SPECIES

The mint family is large and well known. I have chosen a few to illustrate the diversity of the species.

Mentha arvensis var. piperascens
Japanese Peppermint
Hardy perennial. Ht. 2–3 ft., spread 24 in. and more. Loose purplish whorls of flowers in summer. Leaves, downy, oblong, sharply toothed, and green-gray; they provide an oil (90 percent menthol), said to be inferior to the oil produced by *M.* x *piperita*. This species is known as English mint in Japan.
Zone 5

Mentha aquatica
Water Mint
Hardy perennial. Ht. 6–24 in., spread indefinite. Pretty purple-lilac flowers, all summer. Leaves soft, slightly downy, mid-green in color. The scent can vary from a musty mint to a strong peppermint. This should be planted in water or very wet marshy soil. It can be found growing wild around ponds and streams.
Zone 5

Mentha x gracilis (Mentha x gentilis)
Ginger Mint
Also known as Scotch Mint. Hardy perennial. Ht. 18 in., spread 24 in. The stem has whorls of small, 2-lipped, mauve flowers in summer. The leaf is variegated, gold-green with serrated edges. The flavor is a delicate, warm mint that combines well in salads and tomato dishes.
Zone 5

Mentha longifolia
Buddleia Mint
Hardy perennial. Ht. 32 in., spread indefinite. Long purple-mauve flowers that look very like buddleia (hence its name). Long gray-green leaves with a musty minty scent. Very good plant for garden borders. **Zone 5**

Above: **Ginger mint**
Mentha x *gracilis* **in summer**

Mentha x piperita
Peppermint
Hardy perennial. Ht. 12–24 in., spread indefinite. Pale purple flowers in summer. Pointed leaves, darkish green with a reddish tinge, serrated edges. Very peppermint scented. This is the main medicinal herb of the genus. There are two species worth looking out for—black peppermint, with leaves much darker, nearly brown, and white peppermint, with leaves green, tinged with reddish brown.
Zone 5

Mentha x piperita f. citrata
Eau de Cologne Mint
Also known as orange mint and bergamot mint. Hardy perennial. Ht. 24–32 in., spread indefinite. Purple-mauve flowers in summer. Purple tinged, roundish, dark green leaves. A delicious scent that has been described as lemon, orange, bergamot, lavender, as well as eau de cologne. This plant is a vigorous grower. Use in fruit dishes with discretion. Best use is in the bath.
Zone 5

Mentha x *piperita* f. *citrata* 'Basil'

Basil Mint
Hardy perennial. Ht. 18–24 in., spread indefinite. Purple-mauve flowers in summer. Leaves green with a reddish tinge, more pointed than eau de cologne mint. The scent is unique, a sweet and spicy mint scent that combines well with tomato dishes, especially pasta.
Zone 5

Mentha x *piperita* f. *citrata* 'Lemon'

Lemon Mint
Hardy perennial. Ht. 18–24 in., spread indefinite. Purple whorl of flowers in summer. Green serrated leaf, refreshing minty lemon scent. Good as a mint sauce, or with fruit dishes. **Zone 5**

Mentha pulegium

Pennyroyal
Hardy semievergreen perennial Ht. 6 in., spread indefinite. Mauve flowers in spring. Bright green leaves, very strong peppermint scent. There is so much to write about this plant, it has its own section (see pp. 296–297).
Zone 6

Mentha requienii

Corsican Mint
Hardy semievergreen perennial. Ground cover, spread indefinite. Tiny purple flowers throughout the summer. Tiny bright green leaves, which, when crushed, smell strongly of peppermint. Suits a rock garden or paved path, grows naturally in cracks of rocks. Needs shade and moist soil.
Zone 8

Mentha spicata

Spearmint
Hardy perennial. Ht. 18–24 in., spread indefinite. Purple-mauve flowers in summer. Green pointed leaves with serrated edges. The most widely grown of all mints. Good for mint sauce, mint jelly, mint julep.
Zone 5

Mentha spicata var. *crispa*

Curly Mint
Hardy perennial. Ht. 18–24 in., spread indefinite. Light mauve flowers in spring. When I first saw this mint I thought it had a bad attack of aphids, but it has grown on me! The leaf is bright green and crinkled, its serrated edge slightly frilly. Flavor very similar to spearmint, so good in most culinary dishes.
Zone 5

Apple mint *Mentha suaveolens*

Left: **Pineapple mint**
Mentha suaveolens 'Variegata'

Mentha spicata var. *crispa* 'Moroccan'

Moroccan Mint
Hardy perennial. Ht. 18–24 in., spread indefinite. White flowers in summer. Bright green leaves with a texture and excellent mint scent. This is the one I use for all the basic mint uses in the kitchen. A clean mint flavor and scent, lovely with yogurt and cucumber.
Zone 5

Mentha suaveolens

Apple Mint
Hardy perennial. Ht. 2–3 ft., spread indefinite. Mauve flowers in summer. Roundish hairy leaves. Tall vigorous grower. Gets its name from its scent, which is a combination of mint and apples. More subtle than some mints, so good in cooking. **Zone 5**

Mentha suaveolens 'Variegata'

Pineapple Mint
Hardy perennial. Ht. 18–24 in., spread indefinite. Mild-scented but it has very pretty cream and green, slightly hairy leaves that look good in the garden. White flowers in summer. Not rampant. Grows well in hanging baskets. **Zone 6**

Buddleia mint
Mentha longifolia

Mentha x *villosa* var. *alopecuroides* Bowles' mint

Bowles Mint
Hardy perennial. Ht. 2–3 ft., spread indefinite. Mauve flowers, round, slightly hairy green leaves, vigorous grower.
Zone 5

Above: **Corsican mint**
Mentha requienii

Pycnanthemum pilosum

Mountain Mint
Hardy perennial. Ht. 3 ft., spread 2 ft. Knotlike white-pink flowers, small and pretty in summer. Leaves long, thin, pointed, and gray-green with a good mint scent and flavor. Not a *Mentha*, so not a true mint. Looks very attractive in a border, and also appeals to butterflies. Any soil will support it provided it is not too rich. Spreads slowly.
Zone 5

Ginger mint
Mentha x *gracilis* **in spring**

CULTIVATION

Propagation
Seed
The seed on the market is not worthwhile—leaf flavor is inferior and quite often it does not run true to species.

Cuttings
Root cuttings of mint are very easy. Simply dig up a piece of root. Cut it where you can see a little growing node (each piece will produce a plant) and place the cuttings either into a plug or seed tray. Push them into the potting soil (bark-peat mix, see p. 591). Water and leave. This can be done anytime during the growing season. If taken in spring, in about two weeks you should see new shoots emerging through the soil.

Division
Dig up plants every few years and divide, or they will produce root runners all over the place. Each bit of root will grow, so take care.

Corsican mint does not set root runners. Dig up a section in spring and divide by easing the plant apart and replanting.

Pests and Diseases
Mint rust appears as little rusty spots on the leaves. Remove them immediately, otherwise the rust will wash off into the soil and the spores spread to other plants. One sure way to get rid of it is to burn the affected patch. This effectively sterilizes the ground.

Another method, which I found in an old gardening book, is to dig up the roots in winter when the plants are dormant, and clean off the soil under a tap. Heat some water to a temperature of 105–115°F and pour into a bowl. Place the roots in the water for 10 minutes. Remove the runners and wash at once in cold water. Replant in the garden well away from the original site.

Maintenance
Spring Dig up root if cuttings are required. Split established plants if need be.
Summer Give plants a haircut to promote new growth. Control the spread of unruly plants.
Fall Dig up roots for forcing. Bring in containers.
Winter Sterilize roots if rust is evident during growing season.

Garden Cultivation
Mint is one of those plants that will walk all over the plot if not severely controlled. Also, mint readily hybridizes itself, varying according to environmental factors. Select a planting site in sun or shade but away from other mints. Planted side by side they seem to lose their individual scent and flavor.

To inhibit spread, sink a large bottomless container (bucket or frame) in a well-drained and fairly rich soil to a depth of at least 12 in., leaving a small ridge above soil level. Plant the mint in the center.

Harvesting
Pick the leaves for fresh use throughout the growing season. Pick leaves for drying or freezing before the mint flowers.

COMPANION PLANTING

Spearmint or peppermint planted near roses will deter aphids. Buddleia mint will attract hoverflies.

OTHER USES

Pick a bunch of eau de cologne mint, tie it up with string, and hang it under the hot water tap when you are drawing a bath. You will scent not only your bath, but the whole house. It is very uplifting (unless you too have a young son who for some reason thinks it is "gross").

Curly mint
Mentha spicata var. *crispa*

Chocolate mint mousse

CULINARY

With due respect to their cuisine, the French are always rude about "mint sauce with lamb;" they reckon it is barbaric. On that side of the Channel they use mint less than other countries in cooking. But slowly, even in France, this herb is gaining favor.

Mint is good in vinegars and jellies. Peppermint makes a great tea. And there are many uses for mint in cooking with fish, meat, yogurt, fruit, and so on. Here is a recipe for chocoholics like me:

Chocolate Mint Mousse
Serves 2

4 squares plain dark chocolate
2 eggs, separated
1 teaspoon instant coffee
1 teaspoon fresh chopped mint, either Moroccan, spearmint, or curly
Whipped cream for decoration
4 whole mint leaves

Melt the chocolate either in a microwave or in a double boiler. When smooth and liquid, remove from the heat. Beat the egg yolks and add to the chocolate while still warm, but not hot. (If the chocolate is still too hot, the eggs may curdle.) Add the coffee and chopped mint.

Leave to cool for 15 minutes. Beat the egg whites (not too stiff) and fold them into the mixture. Spoon into containers. When you are ready to serve put a blob of whipped cream in the middle and garnish with mint leaves.

CONTAINER GROWING (AND FORCING)

Mint is good in containers. Make sure the container is large enough, use a soil-based potting mix, and do not let the soil dry out. Feed regularly throughout the growing season with a liquid fertilizer. Place the container in semishade. Protect the container-grown mint by storing it in a cold frame or unheated basement for winter. Divide and repot each year in early spring.

One good reason for growing mint in containers is to prolong the season. This is called forcing. In early fall dig up some root. Fill a container, or wooden box lined with plastic, with potting soil. Place the root down its length and cover lightly with soil. Water and place in a light, warm greenhouse (even the kitchen windowsill will do). Keep an eye on it, and fresh shoots should sprout within a couple of weeks. This is great for fresh mint sauce for the holidays.

MEDICINAL

Peppermint is aromatic, calmative, antiseptic, antispasmodic, anti-inflammatory, anti-bacterial, antiparasitic, and a stimulant. It can be used in many ways for a variety of complaints including gastrointestinal disorders where anti-spasmodic, anti-flatulent and appetite-promoting stimulation is required. It is particularly useful for nervous headaches, and as a way to increase concentration. Externally, peppermint oil can be used in a massage to relieve muscular pain.

WARNING

The oil may cause an allergic reaction. Avoid prolonged intake of inhalants from the oil, and never use it on babies.

Black peppermint tea

Mentha pulegium

PENNYROYAL

Also known as European Pennyroyal and Pudding Grass. From the family Lamiaceae.

This herb is a native of Europe, including North Africa, and is now widespread in comparable climates.

Pulegium is derived from the Latin *pulex*, meaning "flea," because both the fresh plant and the smoke from the burning leaves were used to exterminate the insect.

Puliol was an old French name for thyme and this plant was designated Royal Thyme, thence *Puliol Royale*, and the corruption Pennyroyal. Today the French name is *Mentha Pouliot*, which reflects this history.

Long ago, the wise women of the village used pennyroyal to induce abortion. It has since been used to facilitate menstruation.

The Elizabethan herbalist John Gerard called it pudding grass. He claimed it would purify corrupt water on sea voyages and that it would cure "swimming in the head and the pains and giddiness thereof."

Creeping pennyroyal *Mentha pulegium*

SPECIES

Mentha pulegium
Pennyroyal
Also known as Creeping Pennyroyal. Semievergreen hardy perennial. Ht. 6 in. A creeper, spread indefinite. Mauve flowers in late spring. Bright green leaves, very strong peppermint scent.
Zone 6

Mentha pulegium 'Upright'
Upright Pennyroyal Semievergreen hardy perennial. Ht. 12 in., spread indefinite. Mauve flowers in late spring. Bright green leaves, very strong peppermint scent.

The American pennyroyal is *Hedeoma pulegioides*, an annual species. It has a similar aroma and usages to the European pennyroyal.

CULTIVATION

Propagation
Seed
Upright pennyroyal can be grown from seed and comes true to species, unlike most mints. The seed is very fine, so sow under protection in prepared seed or plug trays in late spring, then cover with perlite. Germination is 10–20 days. You can leave the plant to become quite well established before planting out in early summer and leave at least

12 in. space between the plants.

Cuttings
Both can be propagated by root cuttings. Unlike ordinary mint, which travels underground, the pennyroyals travel on the surface, and where the plant touches the soil a small root system develops.

Dig up a plant in late spring and divide into small clumps. The miniature root systems are ideal for putting in prepared plug trays with the bark-peat-grit mix of potting soil (see p. 591). Water in well; they will be fully rooted in 4 weeks.

Division
If the plant becomes invasive in the garden, simply remove a section.

Pests and Diseases
Pennyroyal can suffer from **leaf-rotting mildew** if too wet in winter or spring. Pick off any damaged leaves. If the plant is in a container and the weather is mild enough, put it outside and allow the air to get at it. Also, cut back on watering.

Maintenance
Spring Sow seed. Divide established plants.
Summer Cut back after flowering.
Fall Divide plants. Dig up some plants to winter in a cold frame or greenhouse.
Winter Pennyroyal often overwinters on well-drained sites in zones 6 and warmer, but may die out in unusually cold or wet years. Some gardeners simply treat it as an annual.

Garden Cultivation
This mint prefers a rich but free-draining soil in a sunny spot, but—this may seem a contradiction—it does like water in summer, so water freely. The creeping pennyroyal can be grown as aromatic ground cover, but make sure that the ground is very free draining, does not get overwet in winter,

and offers protection from hard frosts.

Harvesting
Pick leaves as required for use fresh. Pick either side of flowering for freezing purposes. Not worth drying.

CONTAINER GROWING

Both pennyroyals are good in containers. When the upright pennyroyal flowers it sends out long branches covered in little circles of mauve flowers. Use the bark-peat-grit mix of potting soil. Feed during flowering with a liquid fertilizer.

MEDICINAL

It has long been considered dangerous to use when pregnant because it is abortive. However, it has now been found that only the oil produced from the plant is active in this way. This oil, which is highly toxic, also leads to irreversible kidney damage. Therefore it should only be prescribed by a professional.

In a hot infusion this herb has always been a favorite remedy for colds as it promotes sweating.

American Pennyroyal, **Hedeoma pulegioides,** *has similar properties and uses. It is also an antispasmodic and calmative, and is used in minor gastric disturbances, flatulence, nausea, headaches, and menstrual pain.*

CULINARY

This mint has a very strong peppermint scent and flavor, so use sparingly in dishes.

It makes a strong mint sauce, and is a good substitute for peppermint in sorbets.

WARNING

Not to be used in pregnancy or if suffering from kidney disease. May cause contact dermatitis. Wear gloves.

An excellent insect repellent, pennyroyal can be used to divert the path of ants, too

OTHER USES

If you rub pennyroyal in the path of an army of ants, it will reroute them.

More practicably, if you grow pennyroyal outside the kitchen door, it will prevent ants entering the house.

If you rub leaves onto bare skin it acts as a very good insect repellent. And if you rub a leaf on a mosquito or horsefly bite, the itch will disappear. I have rubbed it on a wasp sting, and it has brought relief.

Monarda

BERGAMOT

Also known as Oswego Tea, Bee Balm, Blue Balm, High Balm, Low Balm, Mountain Balm, and Mountain Mint. From the family Lamiaceae.

This beautiful plant with its flamboyant flower is a native of North America and is now grown horticulturally in many countries throughout the world.

The species name, *Monarda*, honors the Spanish medicinal botanist Dr. Nicholas Monardes of Seville who, in 1569, wrote a herbal on the flora of America. The common name, bergamot, is said to have come from the scent of the crushed leaf, which resembles the small bitter Italian bergamot orange *(Citrus bergamia)*, from which oil is produced that is used in aromatherapy, perfumes, and cosmetics.

Bee balm or bergamot *(Monarda didyma)* grows wild around Oswego, New York, on Lake Ontario. The Oswego Indians used it for colds and bronchial complaints as it contains the powerful antiseptic thymol. They also made tea from it, hence Oswego tea, which was drunk in many American households, replacing Indian tea, following the Boston Tea Party of 1773.

SPECIES

There are many species and cultivars of bergamot, so I have included some from each of the species.

Monarda 'Beauty of Cobham'
Bergamot Beauty of Cobham Hardy perennial. Ht. 30 in., spread 18 in. Attractive dense 2-lipped pale pink flowers throughout summer. Toothed mid-green aromatic leaves.
Zone 4

Monarda 'Blaustrumpf'
Bergamot Blue Stocking Hardy perennial. Ht. 32 in., spread 18 in. Attractive purple flowers throughout summer. Aromatic, green, pointed foliage.
Zone 4

Monarda 'Cambridge Scarlet'
Bergamot Cambridge Scarlet Hardy perennial. Ht. 3 ft., spread 18 in. Striking rich red flowers through summer. Aromatic, slightly hairy mid-green leaves.
Zone 4

Monarda didyma
Bergamot (Bee Balm Red) Hardy perennial. Ht. 32 in., spread 18 in. Fantastic red flowers throughout summer. Aromatic, mid-green foliage.
Zone 4

Monarda 'Schneewittchen'
Bergamot Snow Maiden Hardy perennial. Ht. 32 in., spread 18 in. Very attractive white flowers throughout summer. Aromatic, mid-green, pointed leaves.
Zone 6

Monarda 'Croftway Pink'
Bergamot Croftway Pink Hardy perennial. Ht. 3 ft., spread 18 in. Soft pink flowers throughout summer. Aromatic green leaves.
Zone 4

Monarda
'Prärienacht'
Bergamot Prairie Night
Hardy perennial. Ht. 3 ft.,
spread 18 in. Attractive
purple flowers throughout
summer. Aromatic, mid-
green, pointed leaves.
Zone 4

CULTIVATION

Propagation
Seed
Only species will grow true
from seed. Cultivars (i.e.,
named varieties) will not.

Sow the very small seed
indoors in the spring on the
surface of either seed or
plug trays or on individual
pots. Cover with perlite.
Germination is better with
added warmth (65°F). Thin
or transplant the strongest
seedlings when large
enough to handle. Harden
off. Plant in the garden at a
distance of 18 in. apart.

Cuttings
Take first shoots in early
summer, as soon as they are
3–4 in. long.

Division
Divide in early spring. Either
grow on in pots, or replant
in the garden, making sure
the site is well prepared with
well-rotted compost.
Planting distance from
other plants 18 in.

Pests and Diseases
Bergamot is prone to
powdery gray mildew. At the
first sign remove leaves. If it
gets out of hand cut the
plant back to ground level.

Young plants are loved
by **slugs**!

Maintenance
Spring Sow seeds of species.
Divide roots. Dig up third-
year-old plants, divide,
and replant.
Summer Take cuttings of
cultivars and species,
if desired.
Fall Cut back to the
ground, and give a good
feed with manure or
compost.
Winter All perennial
bergamots die right back in
winter. In hard winters
protect with a mulch.

Garden Cultivation
Bergamot is a highly
decorative plant with long-
lasting, distinctively fragrant
flowers that are very
attractive to bees, hence
the country name bee balm.

All grow well in moist,
nutrient-rich soil, preferably
in a semishady spot;
deciduous woodland is ideal.
However, they will tolerate
full sun provided the soil
retains moisture. Like many
other perennials bergamot
should be dug up and
divided every three years, and
the dead center discarded.

Harvesting
Pick leaves as desired for use
fresh in the kitchen. For
drying, harvest before the
flower opens.

Cut flowers for drying as
soon as fully opened. They
will dry beautifully and keep
their color.

It is only worth collecting
seed if you have species
plants situated well apart in
the garden. If near one
another, cross-pollination
will make the seed
variable—very jolly provided
you don't mind
unpredictable mixed colors.
Collect the flower heads
when they turn brown.

CONTAINER GROWING

Bergamot is too tall for a
window box, but it can look
very attractive growing in a
large pot, say 14–18 in.
across, or tub, as long as the
soil can be kept moist and
the plant be given some
afternoon shade.

CULINARY

Pick the small flower petals
separately and scatter over a
green salad at the last
moment. Put fresh leaf in
black tea for an Earl Grey
flavor, and into wine cups
and lemonade. The
chopped leaves can be
added sparingly to salads
and stuffings, and can also
be used in jams and jellies.

Pork Fillets with Bergamot Sauce

Serves 2

2 large pork fillets
Salt, black pepper
6 tablespoons butter
2 shallots, very finely chopped
2¹/₂ tablespoons flour
1 cup stock
4 tablespoons dry white wine
3¹/₂ tablespoons chopped
   bergamot leaves
1 tablespoon heavy cream

Preheat the oven to 400°F.
Wash the fillets of pork.
Pat dry, season, and smear
with half the butter.

Roast in a shallow greased
pan for 25 minutes. Allow to
rest for 5 minutes before
slicing. Arrange slices in
warmed serving dish.

Prepare this sauce while
the fillets are in the oven.
Sweat the shallots in half the
butter until soft. Stir in the
flour and cook for about a
minute, stirring all the time.
Whisk in the stock. Simmer
until it thickens, stirring
occasionally. Then slowly
add the wine and 3
tablespoons of the chopped
bergamot. Simmer for
several minutes, then season
to taste. Remove from heat,
stir in the cream, pour over
arranged pork slices,
garnish with remaining
chopped bergamot.

Serve with mashed
potatoes and fresh green
broccoli.

OTHER USES
Because the dried bergamot
flowers keep their fragrance
and color so well, they are
an important ingredient in
potpourris.

The oil is sometimes used
in perfumes, but should not
be confused with the
similarly smelling bergamot
orange.

MEDICINAL

*Excellent herb tea to relieve
nausea, flatulence,
menstrual pain, and
vomiting.*

Myrrhis odorata

SWEET CICELY

Also known as Anise, Myrrh, Roman Plant, Sweet Bracken, Sweet Fern, and Switch.
From the family Apiaceae.

Sweet cicely was once cultivated as a pot shrub in Europe and is a native of this region and other temperate countries.

The Greeks called sweet cicely *seselis* or *seseli*. It is logical to suppose that cicely was derived from them, "sweet" coming from its flavor.

In the 16th century John Gerard recommended the boiled roots as a pick-me-up for people who were "dull." According to Culpeper, the roots were thought to prevent infection by the plague.

In South Wales, sweet cicely is quite often seen growing in graveyards, planted around the headstones to commemorate a loved one.

In the Lake District, sweet cicely was used in puddings and also for rubbing upon oak panels to make the wood shine and smell good.

SPECIES

Myrrhis odorata
Sweet Cicely
Hardy perennial. Ht. 2–3 ft., spread 2 ft. or more. The small white flowers appear in umbels from spring to early summer. The seeds are long, first green, turning black on ripening. The leaves are fernlike, very divided, and smell of aniseed when crushed.
Zone 4

The following plant is called sweet cicely in North America. It is unrelated to the European one, but used in a similar way.

Osmorhiza longistylis
Also known as Anise Root. Perennial. Ht. 18–36 in. Inconspicuous white flowers appear in loose compound umbels in summer. The leaves are oval to oblong and grow in groups of three. The whole plant has an aniseed odor. Its roots used to be nibbled by children for their anise licorice flavor.

CULTIVATION

Propagation
Seed
Sow the seed when ripe in early fall. Use prepared plug or seed trays and, as the seed is so large, sow only one per plug and cover with soil. Then cover the trays with glass and leave outside for the whole winter.

The seed requires several months of cold winter temperatures to germinate. Keep an eye on the compost, making sure it does not dry out. When germination starts, bring the trays into a cold greenhouse. A spring sowing can be

Sweet cicely *Myrrhis odorata*

successful provided the seed is first put in a plastic bag mixed with a small amount of damp, sharp sand, refrigerated for four weeks, and then sown as normal in prepared seed or plug trays. When the seedlings are large enough to handle, which is not long after germination, and after the frosts are over, transplant to a prepared site in the garden, 2 ft. apart.

Root Cuttings
The taproot may be lifted in spring or fall, cut into sections each with a bud, and replanted either in prepared plug trays or directly into a prepared site in the garden at a depth of 2 in.

Division
Divide the plant in fall when the top growth dies down.

Pests and Diseases
Sweet cicely is, in the majority of cases, free from pests and diseases, but subject to **slug** damage in wet years.

Maintenance
Spring Take root cuttings.
Summer Cut back after flowering, to produce new leaves and to stop self-seeding.
Fall Sow seeds. Divide established plants. Take root cuttings.
Winter No need for protection.

Garden Cultivation
It is one of the first garden herbs to emerge after winter and is almost the last to die down, and is therefore a most useful plant.

If you have a light, well-drained, poor soil you may find that sweet cicely spreads all around the garden, and when you try to dig out established plants that the taproot is very long; even a tiny bit remaining will produce another plant. On the soil at my farm, which is heavy clay, it is a lovely plant, however, remaining just where it was planted in

a totally controlled fashion.
The situation it likes best is a well-draining soil, rich in humus, and light shade. If the seed is not wanted for propagation or winter flavoring, the whole plant should be cut down immediately after flowering. A new batch of leaves will soon develop.

Sweet cicely is not suitable for growing in humid areas because it needs a good dormant period before winter to produce its root and lush foliage.

Harvesting
Pick young leaves at any time for fresh use.
Collect unripe seeds when green; ripe seeds when dark brown.
The foliage and seed do not dry or freeze, but the ripe seed stores well in a dry container.
Dig up roots for drying in fall when the plant has died back.

CONTAINER GROWING

As this herb has a very long taproot it does not grow happily in a container. But it can be done. Choose a container that will give the root room to grow, and use the bark-peat mix of potting soil (see p. 591). Place it in a semishady place and keep it well watered throughout the growing season.

MEDICINAL

Many wild plants look very similar to sweet cicely but are highly poisonous. Be sure you have identified a plant accurately before tasting it.

Sweet cicely wine

CULINARY

The root can be cooked as a vegetable and served with butter or a white sauce, or allow to cool and chop up for use in salads. Alternatively, it can be eaten raw, or peeled and grated, and served in a French salad dressing. It is difficult to describe the flavor—think of parsnip, add a hint of aniseed. The root makes a very good wine.

Toss unripe seeds, which have a sweet flavor and a nutty texture, into fruit salads. Chop into ice cream. Use ripe seeds whole in cooked dishes such as apple pie, otherwise use crushed.

The leaf flavor is sweet aniseed. Chop finely and stir in salads, dressings, and omelettes. Add to soups, stews, and to boiling water when cooking cabbage.

Add to cream for a sweeter, less fatty taste. It is a valuable sweetener, especially for diabetics, but also for the many people who are trying to reduce their sugar intake.

When cooking tart fruit, such as rhubarb, plums, gooseberries, or red or black currants, add 2–4 teaspoons of dried sweet cicely. Or, as I do sometimes, mix a handful of large fresh leaves with some lemon balm and add to the boiling water in which the fruit is to be stewed. It gives a delightful flavor and helps to save almost half the sugar needed.

OTHER USES

This is one of the first nectar plants to appear in the spring, so it is valuable to the beekeeper.

Myrtus communis

MYRTLE

From the family Myrtaceae.

Myrtle *Myrtus communis* **in flower**

SPECIES

Myrtus communis
Myrtle
Half-hardy evergreen perennial. Ht. and spread 6–10 ft. Fragrant white flowers from spring to midsummer, each with a dense cluster of golden stamens, followed by dark, purple-black fruits. The leaves are oval, glossy, dark green, and aromatic. **Zone 7**

Myrtle communis '**Variegata**'
Variegated Myrtle
Half-hardy evergreen perennial. Ht. and spread 3–6 ft. Fragrant white flowers from spring to midsummer, each with a hint of pink, and a dense cluster of golden stamens, followed by dark, purple-black fruits. Leaves are oval and dark green with silver variegation, and a pink tinge in fall. **Zone 8**

Myrtle communis subsp. *tarentina*
Tarentina Myrtle
Half-hardy evergreen perennial. Ht. and spread 3–6 ft. Fragrant white flowers from spring to midsummer, each with a dense cluster of golden stamens, followed by dark, purple-black fruits. Leaves are small and oval, dark green, and aromatic. This myrtle is a good hedge in mild areas. Plant 24 in. apart.

Myrtus communis subsp. *tarentina* '**Microphylla Variegata**'
Variegated Tarentina Myrtle
Half-hardy evergreen perennial. Ht. 3 ft., spread 2 ft. Fragrant white flowers from spring to midsummer, each with a hint of pink and a dense cluster of golden stamens, followed by dark, purple-black fruits. Leaves are small, oval, and dark green with silver variegation, and a pink tinge in fall.

I have included the following two because they have only recently been re-classified as *Luma* and are worth looking out for.

Luma chequen
(*Myrtus chequen*)
Half-hardy evergreen perennial. Ht. and spread 30 ft. Fragrant white flowers from spring to midsummer, each with a dense cluster of golden stamens; followed by dark purple-black fruits. The leaves are more oblong with a point at the end: glossy, dark green, and aromatic.

Luma apiculata
'**Glanleam Gold**'
(*Myrtus* '**Glanleam Gold**')
Half-hardy evergreen perennial. Ht. and spread 30 ft. Fragrant white flowers from midsummer to mid-fall, each with a hint of pink and a dense cluster of golden stamens, followed by red fruits, which darken to deep purple as they ripen. Leaves oval, bright green, edged with creamy yellow.

Myrtle comes from a fragrant genus that is widely distributed in warm, temperate, and tropical regions of the world.

Myrtle is a direct descendant of the Greek *Myrtos*, the herb of love. It has been dedicated to Venus and was planted all around her temples. The story goes that Venus transformed one of her priestess called Myrrh into myrtle in order to protect her from an overeager suitor. Also, Venus herself wore a wreath of myrtle when she was given the golden apple by Paris in recognition of her beauty. When she arose out of the sea she was carrying a sprig of myrtle, and to this day it grows very well by the sea, flourishing in the salt air.

Subsequently it was considered an aphrodisiac, and brides carried it in their bouquets or wore wreaths of it at weddings to symbolize love and consistency.

Myrtle *Myrtus communis* **in berry**

Myrtle growing in a hedge

CULTIVATION

Propagation
Cuttings
Take softwood cuttings in spring, semihardwood cuttings in summer. As these are tender plants it is as well to grow them on in pots for the first two years at least. If you live in an area where the winter temperatures fall continuously below 32°F—for variegated varieties 41°F—it would be better to leave them in their pots. Use the bark-peat-grit potting mix (see p. 591) and bring them indoors.

Pests and Diseases
In the majority of cases myrtles are free from pests and diseases, but susceptible to **root rot** from overwatering.

Maintenance
Spring Trim back growth to regain shape. Take softwood cuttings.

Summer Take semi-hardwood cuttings.
Fall Protect from early frosts.
Winter Protect in the winter if you live in a frost area.

Garden Cultivation
This lovely, tender, aromatic shrub will grow in fertile, well-drained soil in full sun. Where your winters are borderline, plant against a south- or west-facing wall to restrict the amount of water it receives from rain, and protect it from the winds. Bring indoors for winter.
   Trim back growth (where possible) to maintain shape in midspring after the frosts have finished.

Harvesting
Pick leaves for sweetness and scent when myrtle is in flower; they can be used dried or fresh.
   Preserve the leaves in oil or vinegar for use in cooking.
   Pick flowers for drying just as they open.

CULINARY

Leaves can be added to pork for the final 10 minutes of roasting, or to lamb when barbecuing. They have a spicy flavor.
   After drying, the berries can be ground and used like juniper as a spice for game and venison.

MEDICINAL

The leaves have astringent and antiseptic properties. Rarely used medicinally, but a leaf decoction may be applied externally to bruises and hemorrhoids. Recent research has revealed a substance in myrtle that has an antibiotic action.

CONTAINER GROWING

This plant, when young, is well suited to containers. Use the bark-peat-grit potting mix. As an evergreen plant, it looks attractive all year round. Place in a cold greenhouse away from central heating. Water in the summer months, and allow the compost to nearly dry out in winter. Watch the watering at all times; if ever in doubt give it less rather than more. Feed with a liquid fertilizer during the flowering period.

OTHER USES

Every part of the shrub is highly aromatic and can be used dried in potpourris.

Myrtle potpourri

Nepeta

CATNIP

**Also known as Catmint, Catnep, Catrup, Catswart, and Field Balm.
From the family Lamiaceae.**

Catnip *Nepeta racemosa*

Native to Europe and east and west Asia, catnip is now naturalized in other temperate zones.

The species name may have derived from the Roman town Nepeti, where it was said to grow in profusion.

The Elizabethan herbalist Gerard recorded the source of its common name: "They do call it *herba cataria* and *herba catti* because cats are very much delighted herewith for the smell of it is so pleasant unto them, that they rub themselves upon it and wallow or tumble in it and also feed on the branches and leaves very greedily."

This herb has long been cultivated both for its medicinal and seasoning properties, and, in the hippie era of the late 1960s and 1970s, for its mildly hallucinogenic quality when smoked.

SPECIES

Nepeta cataria, Nepeta x *faassenii,* and *Nepeta racemosa* are all called catnip, which can be confusing. However the first is the true herb with the medicinal and culinary properties.

Nepeta racemosa (mussinii)
Hardy perennial. Ht. and spread 20 in. Spikes of lavender blue-purple flowers from late spring to fall. Small, mildly fragrant, grayish leaves. Marvelous edging plant for tumbling out over raised beds or softening hard edges of stone flags. Combines especially well with old-fashioned roses.
Zone 4

Nepeta camphorata
Tender perennial. Ht. and spread 24–30 in. Very different from ordinary catnip and very fragrant. Tiny white blooms all summer. Small, silvery gray, aromatic foliage. Prefers a poor, well-drained, dryish soil, not too rich in nutrients, and full sun. However, it will adapt to most soils except wet and heavy.
Zone 8

Nepeta x faassenii
Hardy perennial. Ht. and spread 18 in. Loose spikes of lavender blue flowers from early summer to early fall. Small grayish-green aromatic leaves form a bushy clump.
Zone 4

Nepeta cataria
Catnip
Hardy perennial. Ht. 3 ft., spread 2 ft. White to pale pink flowers from early summer to early fall. Pungent aromatic leaves. This plant is the true herb. In the 17th century, it was used in the treatment of barren women.
Zone 3

CULTIVATION

Propagation
Seed
Sow its small seed in spring or late summer, either where the plant is going to flower or onto the surface of pots, plug, or seed trays. Cover with perlite. Gentle bottom heat can be of assistance. Germination takes 10–20 days, depending on the time of year (faster in late summer). Seed is viable for five years. When large enough to handle, thin the seedlings to 12 in. The seed of *N. camphorata* should be sown in fall to late winter. This seed will usually flower the following season.

Cuttings
Take softwood cuttings from new growth in late spring through to midsummer. Do not choose flowering stems.

Catnip 'Six Hills Giant' *Nepeta* 'Six Hills Giant'

Division
A good method of propagation, particularly if a plant is becoming invasive. But beware of cats! The smell of a bruised root is irresistible. Cats have been known to destroy a specimen replanted after division. If there are cats around, protect the newly divided plant.

Pests and Diseases
These plants are aromatic and not prone to pests. However, in cold, wet winters, they tend to **rot** off.

Maintenance
Spring Sow seeds.
Summer Sow seeds until late in the season. Cut back hard after flowering to encourage a second flush.
Fall Cut back after flowering to maintain shape and produce new growth. If your winters tend to be wet and cold, pot up and winter this herb in a cold frame.
Winter Sow seeds of *Nepeta camphorata*.

Catnip *Nepeta cataria*

Garden Cultivation
The main problem with catnip is the love cats have for it. If you have ever seen a cat spaced-out after feeding (hence catnip) and rolling on it, then you will understand why cat lovers love catnip, and why cat haters who grow it get upset with cat neighbors. The reason why cats are enticed is the smell; it reminds them of the hormonal scent of cats of the opposite sex. With all this in mind, choose your planting site carefully.
Nepeta make very attractive border or edging subjects. They like a well-drained soil, sun, or light shade. The one thing they dislike is a wet winter; they may well rot off.
Planting distance depends on species, but on average plant 20 in. apart. When the main flowering is over, catnip should be cut back hard to encourage a second crop and to keep a neat and compact shape.

Harvesting
Whether you pick to use fresh or to dry, gather leaves and flowering tops when young.

CULINARY

Use freshly picked young shoots in salads or rub on meat to release their mintish flavor. Catnip was drunk as a tea before black tea was introduced into the West. It makes an interesting cup!

MEDICINAL

Nepeta cataria is now very rarely used for medicinal purposes. In Europe it is sometimes used in a hot infusion to promote sweating. It is said to be excellent for colds and flu and children's infectious diseases, such as measles. It soothes the nervous system and helps get a restless child get to sleep. It also helps to calm upset stomachs and counters colic, flatulence, and diarrhea.
In addition, an infusion can be applied externally to soothe scalp irritations, and the leaves and flowering tops can be mashed for a poultice to be applied to external bruises.

COMPANION PLANTING

Planting *Nepeta cataria* near vegetables deters flea beetle.

CONTAINER GROWING

N. x *faassenii* and *N. racemosa* look stunning in large terra-cotta pots. The gray-green of the leaves and the blue-purple of the flowers complement the terra-cotta, and their sprawling habit in flower completes the picture. Use a well-draining potting soil, such as a bark-peat-grit mix (see p. 591). Note: both varieties tend to grow soft and leggy indoors.

OTHER USES

Dried leaves stuffed into toy mice will keep kittens and cats amused for hours.
The scent of catnip is said to repel rats, so put bunches in hen and duck houses to discourage them.
The flowers of *Nepeta* x *faassenii* and *Nepeta racemosa* are suitable for formal displays.

Ocimum basilicum

BASIL

Also known as Common Basil, St. Joseph Wort, and Sweet Basil. From the family Lamiaceae

Basil is native to India, the Middle East, and some Pacific Islands. It has been cultivated in the Mediterranean for thousands of years, but the herb only came to Western Europe in the 16th century with the spice traders and to America and Australia with the early European settlers.

This plant is steeped in history and intriguing lore. Its common name is believed to be an abbreviation of *Basilikon phuton*, Greek for "kingly herb," and it was said to have grown around Christ's tomb after the resurrection. Some Greek Orthodox churches use it to prepare their holy water and put pots of basil below their altars. However, there is some question as to its sanctity—both Greeks and Romans believed that people should curse as they sow basil to ensure germination. There was even some doubt about whether it was poisonous or not, and in Western Europe it has been thought both to belong to the devil and to be a remedy against witches. In Elizabethan times sweet basil was used as a snuff for colds and to clear the brain and deal with headaches, and in the 17th century Culpeper wrote of basil's uncompromising if unpredictable appeal— "It either makes enemies or gains lovers but there is no in-between."

SPECIES

Ocimum basilicum
Sweet Basil
Annual. Ht. 18 in.
A strong scent. Green, medium-sized leaves. White flowers. Without a doubt the most popular basil. Sweet basil comes from Genoa in the north of Italy, hence its local name, Genovese. Use sweet basil in pasta sauces and salads, especially with tomato. Combines very well with garlic. Do not let it flower if using for cooking.
All zones

Ocimum basilicum
'Cinnamon'
Cinnamon Basil
Annual. Ht. 18 in. Leaves olive-brown-green with a hint of purple, highly cinnamon-scented when rubbed. Flowers pale pink. Cinnamon basil comes from

The distinctive leaves of green ruffles basil

Mexico and is used in spicy dishes and salad dressings.
All zones

Ocimum basilicum
'Green Ruffles'
Green Ruffles Basil
Annual. Ht. 12 in. Light green leaves, crinkly and larger than sweet basil. Spicy, aniseed flavor, good in salad dishes and combines well with stir-fry vegetables. But it is not, to my mind, an attractive variety. In fact the first time I grew it I thought its crinkly leaves had a bad attack of

Cinnamon basil *Ocimum basilicum* 'Cinnamon'

aphids. Grow in pots and protect from any frost.
All zones

Ocimum x *citriodorum*
Lemon Basil
Annual. Ht. 12 in. Light, bright, yellowish-green leaves, more pointed than other varieties, with a slight serrated edge. Flowers pale, whitish. Lemon basil comes from Indonesia, is tender in cooler climates, and susceptible to damping-off. Difficult to maintain but well worth the effort. Both flowers and leaves have a lemon scent and flavor that enhance many dishes.
All zones

Ocimum minimum
Bush Basil
Annual. Ht. 12 in. Small green leaves, roughly half the size of sweet basil. Flowers small, scented, and whitish. Excellent for growing in pots on the windowsill. Delicious added whole to green salads; goes well with ricotta cheese.
All zones

Ocimum minimum
'**Greek**'
Greek Basil
(Fine-leaved Miniature)
Annual. Ht. 9 in. This basil has the smallest leaves, tiny replicas of the bush basil leaves but, despite their size, they have a good flavor.
As its name depicts, it originates from Greece. It is one of the easiest basils to look after and is especially good grown in a pot. Use leaves unchopped in all salads and in tomato sauces.
All zones

Ocimum basilicum
'**Napolitano**'
Lettuce-leaved Basil
Annual. Ht. 18 in. Leaves very large, crinkled, and with a distinctive flavor, especially good for pasta sauce. Originates in the Naples region of Italy and needs a hot summer in cooler countries to be of any merit.
All zones

Ocimum basilicum var. *purpurascens*
'**Purple Ruffles**'
Purple Ruffles Basil
Annual. Ht. 12 in. Very similar to straight purple basil (below), though the flavor is not as strong and the leaf is larger with a feathery edge. Flowers are pink. It can be grown in pots or in flowerbeds. Needs full sun for best color.
All zones

Ocimum basilicum var. *purpurascens*
Purple Basil
Annual. Ht. 12 in. Strongly scented purple leaves. Pink flowers. Very attractive plant with a perfumed scent and flavor that is especially good with rice dishes. The dark purple variety that was developed in 1962 at the University of Connecticut represents something of a breakthrough in herb cultivation not least because, almost exclusively, herbs have escaped the attentions of the hybridizers. The variety was awarded the All-American Medal by the nursery growers.
All zones

The many diverse shapes and colors of basil

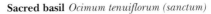

Sacred basil *Ocimum tenuiflorum (sanctum)*

Ocimum basilicum '**Horapha**'
Horapha Basil (Rau Que)
Annual. Ht. 15 in. Leaf olive-purplish. Stems red. Flowers with pink bracts. Aniseed in scent and flavor. A special culinary basil from Thailand. Use the leaves as a vegetable in curries and spicy dishes.
All zones

Ocimum tenuiflorum
(*sanctum*)
Sacred Basil
(Kha Prao Tulsi)
Annual. Ht. 12 in. A small basil with olive-purple leaves with serrated edges. Stems deep purple. Flowers mauve-pink. The whole plant has a marvelously rich scent. Originally from Thailand, where it is grown around Buddhist temples. The Indian-related variety, *sanctum*, is considered kingly or holy by the Hindus, sacred to the gods Krishna and Vishnu. Being held in reverence, it was the chosen herb upon which to swear oaths in courts of law. It was also used throughout the Indian subcontinent as a disinfectant where malaria was present.
All zones

CULTIVATION

Propagation
Seed

All basils can be grown from seed. Sow directly into pots or plug trays in early spring and germinate with warmth. Avoid using seed trays, because basil has a long taproot and dislikes being transplanted. Plugs also help minimize damping-off, to which all basil plants are prone (see below). Water well at midday in dry weather even when transplanted into pots or containers: basil hates going to bed wet. This minimizes the chances of damping-off and will prevent root rot, a hazard when the air temperature is still dropping at night.

Plant out seedlings when large enough to handle and the danger of frost has passed. The soil needs to be rich and well drained, and the situation warm and sheltered, preferably with sun at midday. Basil thrives in hot weather but sulks in cool or cloudy weather. I suggest you plant basil in between tomato plants because:

1. Being a good companion plant, it repels flying insects.
2. You will remember to use fresh basil with tomatoes.
3. You will remember to water it.
4. The situation will be warm and whenever you pick tomatoes you will tend to pick basil, which will encourage bushy growth and prevent it from flowering, which in turn will stop the stems from becoming woody and the flavor of its leaves bitter.

Pests and Diseases
Aphids and **whitefly** may be a problem with pot-grown plants. Wash off with liquid horticultural soap.

Seedlings are highly susceptible to damping-off, a fungal disease encouraged by overcrowding in overly wet conditions in seed trays or pots. It can be prevented by sowing the seed thinly and widely and guarding against an overhumid atmosphere.

Maintenance
Spring Sow seeds in early spring with warmth and watch out for damping-off; plant out around the end of the season. Alternatively, sow directly into the ground after any frosts.
Summer Keep pinching out young plants to promote new leaf growth and to prevent flowering. Harvest the leaves.
Fall Collect seeds of plants allowed to flower. Before first frosts, bring pots into the house and place on the windowsill. Dig up old plants and dig over the area ready for new plantings.

Garden Cultivation
Garden cultivation is only a problem in areas susceptible to frost and where it is not possible to provide for its great need for warmth and nourishment. In such areas plant out after the frosts have finished; choose a well-drained, rich soil in a warm, sunny corner, protected from the wind.

Harvesting
Pick leaves when young and always from the top to encourage new growth.

If freezing to store, paint both sides of each leaf with olive oil to keep it from sticking to the next and to seal in its flavor.

If drying, do it as fast as you can. Basil leaves are some of the more difficult to dry successfully and I do not recommend it.

The most successful course, postharvest, is to infuse the leaves in olive oil or vinegar. As well as being useful in your own kitchen, both the oil and the vinegar make great holiday presents (see Preserving, page 612).

Gather flowering tops as they open in the summer and early fall. Add fresh to salads, dry to potpourris.

CONTAINER GROWING

Basil is happy on a kitchen windowsill and in pots on the patio, and purple basil makes a good centerpiece in a hanging basket. In Europe basil is placed in pots outside houses to repel flies.

Water well at midday but do not overwater. If that is not possible, water earlier in the day rather than later and again do not overwater.

OTHER USES

Keep it in a pot in the kitchen to act as a fly repellent, or crush a leaf and rub it on your skin, where the juice repels mosquitoes.

MEDICINAL

Once prescribed as a sedative against gastric spasms and as an expectorant and laxative, basil is rarely used in herbal medicines today. However, leaves added to food are an aid to digestion and if you put a few drops of basil's essential oil on a sleeve and inhale, it can allay mental fatigue. For those who need a zing, it can be used to make a very refreshing bath vinegar, which also acts as an antiseptic.

CULINARY

Basil has a unique flavor, so newcomers should use with discretion, otherwise it will dominate other flavors. It is one of the few herbs to increase its flavor when cooked. For best results add at the very end of cooking.

Hints and ideas
1. Tear the leaves, rather than chop. Sprinkle over green salads or sliced tomatoes.
2. Basil combines very well with garlic. Tear into French salad dressing.
3. When cooking pasta or rice, heat some olive oil in a saucepan, remove from the heat, add some torn purple basil, toss the pasta or rice in the basil and oil, and serve. Use lemon basil to accompany a fish dish—it has a sharp, spicy lemon flavor when cooked.
4. Add to a cold rice or pasta salad.
5. Mix low-fat cream cheese with any of the basils and use in baked potatoes.
6. Basil does not combine well with strong meats such as goat or venison. However, aniseed basil is very good with stir-fried pork.
7. Sprinkle on fried or grilled tomatoes while they are still hot as a garnish.
8. Very good with French bread and can be used instead of herb butter in the traditional hot herb loaf. The tiny leaves of Greek basil are best for this because you can keep them whole.
9. Sprinkle on top of pizzas.
10. Basil makes an interesting stuffing for chicken. Use sweet basil combined with crushed garlic, bread crumbs, lemon peel, beaten egg, and chopped nuts.

Pesto Sauce
One of the best known recipes for basil, here is a simple version for 4 people.

1 tablespoon pine nuts
4 tablespoons chopped basil leaves
2 cloves garlic, chopped
6 tablespoons sunflower oil or olive oil (not virgin)
¾–1 cup Parmesan cheese

Blend the pine nuts, basil, and chopped garlic until smooth. Add the oil slowly and continue to blend the mixture until you have a thick paste. Season with salt to taste. Stir the sauce into the cooked and drained pasta and sprinkle with Parmesan cheese.

Pesto sauce will keep in a sealed container in the fridge for at least a week. It can also be frozen but it is important, as with all herbs, to wrap the container with at least two thicknesses of plastic wrap to prevent the aroma from escaping.

Pasta with purple ruffles basil

Oenothera

EVENING PRIMROSE

Also known as Common Evening Primrose, Evening Star, Fever Plant, Field Primrose, King's Cure-all, Night Willowherb, Scabish, Scurvish, Tree Primrose, Primrose, Moths Moonflower, and Primrose Tree. From the family Onagraceae.

A native of North America, it was introduced to Europe in 1614 when botanists brought the plant from Virginia as a botanical curiosity. In some areas of North America it is regarded as a weed, elsewhere as a pretty garden plant.

The generic name, *Oenothera*, comes from the Greek *oinos*, "wine," and *thera*, "hunt." According to ancient herbals the plant was said to dispel the ill effects of wine, but both plant and seed have been used for other reasons—culinary and medicinal—by Native Americans for hundreds of years. The Flambeau Ojibwe tribe were the first to realize its medicinal properties. They used to soak the whole plant in warm water to make a poultice to heal bruises and overcome skin problems. Traditionally, too, it was used to treat asthma, and its medicinal potential is still evolving. Oil of evening primrose is currently attracting considerable attention worldwide as a treatment for nervous disorders, in particular multiple sclerosis. There may well be a time in the very near future when the pharmaceutical industry will require fields of this beautiful plant to be grown on a commercial scale.

The common name comes from the transformation of its bedraggled daytime appearance into a fragrant, phosphorescent, pale yellow beauty with the opening of its flowers in the early evening. All this show is for one night only, however. Toward the end of summer the flowers tend to stay open all day long. (It is called evening star because the petals emit phosphorescent light at night.)

Evening primrose
Oenothera macrocarpa

SPECIES

Evening Primrose
Oenothera biennis

Oenothera biennis
Evening Primrose
Hardy biennial. Ht. 3–4 ft., spread 3 ft. Large, evening-scented, yellow flowers for most of the summer. Long green oval or lance-shaped leaves. This is the medicinal herb and the true herb.
Zone 4

Oenothera macrocarpa
Hardy perennial. Ht. 4 in., spread 16 in. or more. Large yellow bell-shaped flowers, sometimes spotted with red, open at sundown throughout the summer. The small to medium green leaves are of a narrow oblong shape.
Zone 4

Oenothera perennis Sundrops
Hardy perennial. Ht. 6–24 in., spread 12 in. Fragrant yellow funnel-shaped flowers; the narrow leaves turn dark red in cold weather.
Zone 4

CULTIVATION

Propagation
Seeds
Sow in early spring on the surface of pots or plug trays, or directly into a prepared site in the garden. Seed is very fine so be careful not to sow it too thickly. Use the cardboard method (see p. 591). When the weather has warmed sufficiently, plant out at a distance of 12 in. apart. Often the act of transplanting will encourage the plant to flower the first year. It is a prolific self-seeder. So once introduced into the garden, it will stay.

Pests and Diseases
This plant rarely suffers from pests or disease.

Maintenance
Spring Sow seed.
Summer Deadhead plants to cut down on self-seeding.
Fall Dig up old roots of second-year growth of the biennials.
Winter No need to protect.

Garden Cultivation
Choose a well-drained soil in a dry, sunny corner for the best results and sow the seeds in late spring to produce flowers the following year. Thin the seedlings to 12 in. apart, when large enough to handle. After the seed is set, the plant dies. It is an extremely tolerant plant, happy in most situations, and I have known seedlings to appear in a stone wall, so be forewarned.

Harvesting
Use leaves fresh as required. Best before flowering.
Pick the flowers when in bud or when just open. Use fresh. Picked flowers will always close and are no good for flower arrangements.

Collect the seeds as the heads begin to open at the end. Store in a jar for sowing in the spring.
Dig up roots and use fresh as a vegetable or to dry.

CONTAINER GROWING

The lower-growing varieties are very good in window boxes and tubs. Tall varieties need support from other plants or stakes. None is suitable for growing indoors.

CULINARY

It is a pot herb—roots, stems, leaves, and even flower buds may be eaten. The roots can be boiled—they taste like sweet parsnips—or pickled and tossed in a salad.

MEDICINAL

Soon this plant will take its place in the herbal hall of fame.
It can have startling effects on the treatment of premenstrual tension. In 1981 at St. Thomas's Hospital, London, 65 women with PMS were treated; 61 percent experienced complete relief and 23 percent partial relief. One symptom, breast engorgement, was especially improved—72 percent of women reported feeling

Evening primrose *Oenothera biennis*

better. In November 1982, an edition of the prestigious medical journal *The Lancet* published the results of a double-blind crossover study on 99 patients with ectopic eczema, which showed that when high doses of evening primrose oil were taken, about 43 percent of the patients experienced improvement of their eczema. Studies of the effect of the oil on hyperactive children also indicate that this form of treatment is beneficial.
True to the root of its generic name, the oil does appear to be effective in counteracting alcohol poisoning and preventing hangovers. It can help withdrawal from alcohol, easing depression. It helps dry eyes and brittle nails, and, when combined with zinc, the oil may be used to treat acne.
But it is the claim that it benefits sufferers of multiple sclerosis that has brought controversy. It has been recommended for MS sufferers by Professor Field, who directed MS research for the U.K. Medical Research Council.
Claims go further—that it is effective in guarding against arterial disease; that the effective ingredient, gami-linolelic acid (GLA), is a powerful anti–blood clotter; that it aids weight-loss (a New York hospital

discovered that people more than 10 percent above their ideal body weight lost weight when taking the oil). It is thought that this occurs because the GLA in evening primrose oil stimulates brown fat tissue. In perhaps the most remarkable study of all, completed in Glasgow Royal Infirmary in 1987, it helped 60 percent of patients suffering from rheumatoid arthritis. Those taking fish oil, in addition to evening primrose oil, fared even better.
The scientific explanation for these extraordinary results is that GLA is a precursor of a hormonelike substance called PGEI, which has a wide range of beneficial effects on the body. Production of this substance in some people may be blocked. GLA has also been found in oil extracted from blackcurrant seed and borage seed, both of which are now a commercial source of this substance.

OTHER USES

Leaf and stem can be infused to make an astringent facial steam. Add to hand cream as a softening agent.

Origanum

OREGANO & MARJORAM

*Also known as Wild Marjoram, Mountain Mint, Winter Marjoram, Winter Sweet, Marjolaine, and Origan.
From the family Lamiaceae.*

For the most part these are natives of the Mediterranean region. They have adapted to many countries, however, and a native form can now be found in many regions of the world under different names. For example, *Origanum vulgare* growing wild in Britain is called wild marjoram (the scent of the leaf is aromatic but not strong, the flowers are pale pink); while in Mediterranean countries wild *Origanum vulgare* is known as oregano (the leaf is green, slightly hairy, and very aromatic, the flowers are similar to those found growing wild in Britain).

Oregano is derived from the Greek *oros* meaning "mountain" and *ganos* meaning

Pot marjoram *Origanum onites*

"joy" and "beauty." It therefore translates literally as "joy of the mountain." In Greece it is woven into the crown worn by bridal couples.

According to Greek mythology, the king of Cyprus had a servant called Amarakos, who dropped a jar of perfume and fainted in terror. As his punishment the gods changed him into oregano, after which, if it was found growing on a burial tomb, all was believed well with the dead. Venus was the first to grow the herb in her garden.

Aristotle reported that tortoises, after swallowing a snake, would immediately eat oregano to prevent death, which gave rise to the belief that it was an antidote to poison.

The Greeks and Romans used it not only as scent after taking a bath and as a massage oil, but also as a disinfectant and preservative. More than likely they were responsible for the spread of this plant across Europe, where it became known as marjoram. The settlers took it to North America, where there arose a further confusion of nomenclature. Until the 1940s, common marjoram was called wild marjoram in America, but is now known as oregano. In certain parts of Mexico and the southern states of America, oregano is the colloquial name for a totally unrelated plant with a similar flavor.

Sweet marjoram, which originates from North Africa, was introduced into Europe in the sixteenth century and was incorporated in nosegays to ward off the plague and other pestilence.

Wild marjoram
Origanum vulgare

SPECIES

Origanum amanum
Tender perennial. Ht. and spread 6–8 in. Open, funnel-shaped, pale pink or white flowers borne above small heart-shaped, aromatic, pale green leaves. Makes a good alpine house plant. Dislikes a damp atmosphere.
Zone 9

Origanum x *applii*
Winter Marjoram
Tender perennial. Ht. 9 in., spread 12 in. Small pink flowers. Very small aromatic leaves which, in the right conditions, are available all year round. Good to grow in a container.
Zone 10

Origanum dictamnus
Ditany of Crete
Tender perennial. Ht. 5–6 in., spread 16 in. Prostrate habit, purplish-pink flowers that appear in hoplike clusters in summer. The leaves are white, woolly, and grow on arching stems. Pretty little plant, quite unlike most of the other origanums in appearance.
Zone 8

Golden marjoram
Origanum vulgare 'Aureum'

Origanum 'Kent Beauty'
Tender perennial. Ht. 6–8 in., spread 12 in. Whorls of tubular pale pink flowers with darker bracts appear in summer on short spikes. Round, oval, and aromatic leaves on trailing stems, which give the plant its prostrate habit and make it suitable for a wall or ledge. Decorative more than culinary.
Zone 8

Origanum laevigatum
Hardy perennial. Ht. 9–12 in., spread 8 in. Summer profusion of tiny, tubular, red-pink-mauve flowers, surrounded by red-purple bracts. Aromatic, dark green leaves, which form a mat in winter. Decorative more than culinary.
Zone 8

Origanum laevigatum 'Herrenhausen'
Hardy perennial. Ht. and spread 12 in. Pink-mauve flowers which develop from deep purple buds in summer. Dark green, aromatic, slightly hairy leaves, with a pink tinge underneath.
Zone 8

Greek oregano *Origanum vulgare* subsp. *hirtum* 'Greek'

Origanum majorana
Sweet Marjoram
Also known as Knotted Marjoram
Tender perennial. Grown as an annual in cool climates. Ht. and spread 12 in. Tiny white flowers in a knot. Round pale green leaves, highly aromatic. This is the best variety for flavor. Use in culinary recipes that state marjoram. The leaf is also good for drying, retaining a lot of its scent and flavor.
Zone 10

Origanum onites
Pot Marjoram
Tender perennial. Ht. and spread 18 in. Pink-purple flowers in summer. Green aromatic leaves that form a mat in winter. Good grower with a nice flavor. Difficult to obtain the true seed; grows easily from cuttings, however.
Zone 8

Origanum rotundifolium
Tender perennial. Ht. 9–12 in., spread 12 in. Prostrate habit. The pale pink, pendant, funnel-shaped flowers appear in summer in whorls surrounded by yellow-green bracts. Leaves are small, round, mid-green, and aromatic. Decorative more than culinary.
Zone 8

Origanum vulgare
Oregano
Also known as Wild Marjoram
Hardy perennial. Ht. and spread 18 in. Clusters of tiny tubular mauve flowers in summer. Dark green, aromatic, slightly hairy leaves, which form a mat in winter. When grown in its native Mediterranean, it has a very pungent flavor, which bears little resemblance to that obtained in the cooler countries.
Zone 4

Origanum vulgare subsp. *hirtum* 'Greek'
Greek Oregano
Hardy perennial. Ht. and spread 18 in. Clusters of tiny tubular white flowers in summer. Gray-green hairy leaves, which are very aromatic and excellent for cooking.
Zone 5

Origanum vulgare 'Aureum'
Golden Marjoram
Hardy perennial. Ht. and spread 18 in. Clusters of tiny tubular mauve-pink flowers in summer. Golden, aromatic, slightly hairy leaves, which form a mat in winter. The leaves have very little flavor.
Zone 5

Compact marjoram
Origanum vulgare 'Compactum'

Origanum vulgare 'Aureum Crispum'
Golden Curly Marjoram
Hardy perennial. Ht. and spread 18 in. Clusters of tiny tubular mauve-pink-white flowers in summer. Leaves, small, golden, crinkled, aromatic, and slightly hairy, which form a mat in winter. The leaves have very little flavor.
Zone 5

Origanum vulgare 'Compactum'
Compact Marjoram
Hardy perennial. Ht. 6 in., spread 12 in. Lovely large pink flowers. Smallish green aromatic leaves, which form a mat in winter, have a deliciously warm flavor and combine well with lots of culinary dishes.
Zone 5

Origanum vulgare 'Gold Tip'
Gold Tipped Marjoram
Also known as Gold Splash
Hardy perennial. Ht. and spread 12 in. Small pink flowers in summer. The aromatic leaves are green and yellow variegated. Choose the garden site carefully: shade prevents the variegation. The leaves have a mild flavor.
Zone 5

Origanum vulgare 'Nanum'
Dwarf Marjoram
Hardy perennial. Ht. 4 in., spread 6 in. White-pink flowers in summer. Tiny green aromatic leaves. It is a lovely, compact, neat little bush, great in containers and at the front of a herb garden. Good in culinary dishes.
Zone 5

CULTIVATION

Propagation
Seed
The following can be grown from seed: *Origanum vulgare, Origanum majorana, Origanum vulgare* subsp. *hirtum* 'Greek.' The seed is very fine, so sow in spring into prepared seed or plug trays. Use the cardboard trick (see p. 591). Leave uncovered and give a bottom heat of 60°F. Germination can be erratic or totally successful. Watering is critical when the seedlings are young; keep the compost on the dry side. As the seed is so fine, thin before pricking out to allow the plants to grow. When large enough, either repot using the bark-peat-grit potting mix (see p. 591), or if the soil is warm enough and you have grown them in plugs, plant into the prepared garden.

Cuttings
Apart from the three species mentioned above, the remainder can only be propagated successfully by cuttings or division.
Softwood cuttings can be taken from the new growing tips of all the named varieties in spring. Use the bark-peat-grit mix of potting soil.

Division
A number of varieties form a mat during the winter. These lend themselves to division. In spring, or after flowering, dig up a whole clump and pull sections gently away. Each will come away with its own root system. Replant as desired.

Pests and Diseases
Apart from occasional **frost** damage, marjorams and oreganos, being aromatic, are mostly pest free.

Maintenance
Spring Sow seeds. Divide established plants.

Take softwood cuttings.
Summer Trim after flowering to prevent plants becoming straggly. Divide established plants in late summer.
Fall Before they die down for winter, cut back the year's growth to within 2½ in. of the soil.
Winter Protect pot-grown plants and tender varieties.

Garden Cultivation
Sweet marjoram and winter marjoram need a sunny garden site and a well-drained, dry, preferably alkaline, soil. Otherwise plant them in containers. All the rest are hardy and adaptable, and will tolerate most soils as long as they are not waterlogged in winter. Plant gold varieties in some shade to prevent the leaves from scorching. For the majority, a good planting distance is 10 in., closer if being used as an edging plant.

Harvesting
Leaves
Pick leaves whenever available for use fresh. They can be dried or frozen, or be used to make oil or vinegar.

Flowers
The flowers can be dried just as they open for dried flower arrangements.

CONTAINER GROWING

The *Origanum* species look great in containers. Use the bark-peat-grit mix of potting soil. Make sure that they are not overwatered and that the gold and variegated forms get some shade at midday. Cut back after flowering and give them a liquid fertilizer feeding.

CULINARY

Marjoram and oregano aid the digestion, and act as an antiseptic and as a preservative.
They are among the main ingredients of bouquet garni, and combine well with pizza, meat, and tomato dishes, vegetables, and milk-based desserts.

Red Mullet with Tomatoes and Oregano
Serves 4–6

4–6 red mullet, cleaned
3 tablespoons olive oil
1 medium onion, sliced
1 clove garlic, chopped
1½ cups tomatoes, peeled and chopped
1 green or red pepper, seeded and diced
1 teaspoon sugar
1 teaspoon chopped fresh oregano or ½ teaspoon dried oregano
Freshly milled salt and pepper
Oil for baking or pan-frying

Rinse the fish in cold water and drain on paper towels. Heat the olive oil in a pan and cook the onion and garlic slowly until golden brown; add the tomatoes, pepper, sugar, and oregano, and a little salt and pepper.

Bring to a boil, then simmer for 20 minutes until thickened.
Bake or fry the fish. Brush them with oil, place in a greased ovenproof dish and cook at a moderately hot temperature, 375°F, for 7–8 minutes. Serve with the sauce.

MEDICINAL

This plant is one of the best antiseptics owing to its high thymol content.
Marjoram tea helps ease bad colds, has a tranquilizing effect on nerves, and helps settle upset stomachs. It also helps to prevent seasickness.
For temporary relief of toothache, chew the leaf or rub a drop of essential oil on the gums. A few drops of essential oil on the pillow will help you sleep.

OTHER USES

Make an infusion and add to bath water to aid relaxation.

Red Mullet with Tomatoes and Oregano

Papaver

POPPY

From the family Papaveraceae

The poppy is widely spread across the temperate zones of the world. For thousands of years grain, poppies, and civilization have gone together. The Romans looked on poppy as sacred to their grain goddess, Ceres, who taught men to sow and reap.

The ancient Egyptians used poppy seed in their baking for its aromatic flavor.

The field poppy grew on Flanders fields after the battles of World War I and became the symbol of Remembrance Day.

SPECIES

Papaver rhoeas
Field Poppy
Also known as Corn Poppy and Flanders Poppy
Hardy annual. Ht. 8–24 in., spread 18 in. Brilliant scarlet flower with black basal blotch from summer to early fall. The mid-green leaf has three lobes and is irregularly toothed.
All zones

Papaver somniferum
Opium Poppy
Hardy annual. Ht. 12–36 in., spread 18 in. Large pale lilac, white, purple, or variegated flowers in summer. The leaf is long with toothed margins and bluish in color. There is a double-flowered variety called peony poppy.
All zones

Papaver commutatum
Ladybird Poppy
Hardy annual. Ht. 12–36 in., spread 18 in. Red flowers in summer, each with black blotch in center. Leaf oblong and deeply toothed. Native of Asia Minor.
All zones

WARNING

All parts of the opium poppy, except the ripe seeds, are dangerous and should be used only by trained medical staff.

CULTIVATION

Propagation
Seed
Sow the very fine seed in fall onto the surface of prepared seed or plug trays, using the bark-peat-grit mix of potting soil (see p. 591). Cover with glass and leave outside for winter stratification. In spring, when seedlings are large enough, plant out into the garden in groups.

Pests and Diseases
Largely pest- and disease-free.

Maintenance
Spring Plant out in garden.
Summer Deadhead flowers to prolong flowering and prevent self-seeding.
Fall Sow seed. Dig up old plants.
Winter No need to protect.

Garden Cultivation
Poppies all prefer a sunny site and a well-drained fertile soil. Sow in the fall in a prepared site; press seed into the soil but do not cover. Thin to 8–12 in. apart. Remove the heads after flowering to prevent self-seeding.

Harvesting
The ripe seeds can be collected from both field and opium poppies, the seed of which is not narcotic. It must however be ripe, otherwise it will go moldy in storage.

CONTAINER GROWING

Use the bark-peat-grit mix of potting soil. Place in full sun out of the wind, and water well during the summer. Refrain from feeding as this will produce lots of soft growth and few flowers.

MEDICINAL

The unripe seed capsules of the opium poppy are used for the extraction of morphine and the manufacture of codeine.

OTHER USES

The oil extracted from the seed of the opium poppy is used not only as a salad oil and for cooking, but also for burning in lamps, and in the manufacture of varnish, paint, and soap.

CULINARY

Sprinkle the ripe seeds on bread, cakes, and cookies for a pleasant nutty flavor. Add to curry powder for texture, flavor, and as a thickener.

Pelargonium

SCENTED GERANIUMS

From the family Geraniaceae.

These form a group of marvelously aromatic herbs that should be grown more. Originally native to South Africa, they are now widespread throughout many temperate countries, where they should be grown as tender perennials.

The generic name, *Pelargonium*, is said to be derived from *pelargos*, a "stork." With a bit of imagination one can understand how this came about: the seed pods bear a resemblance to a stork's bill.

Nearly all the species of scented geraniums (the name is a botanical misnomer) came from the Cape of South Africa to England in the mid-seventeenth century. The aromatic foliage found popularity among Victorians. In the early nineteenth century the French perfumery industry recognized its commercial potential. Oil of geranium is now not only an ingredient of certain perfumes for men, but also an essential oil in aromatherapy.

SPECIES

There are many different scented geraniums. They are very collectable plants. All are tender to frost and can be grown outdoors only in Zone 10.

Pelargonium 'Attar of Roses'
Tender evergreen perennial. Ht. 12–24 in., spread 12 in. Small pink flowers in summer. Trilobed, mid-green leaves that smell of roses.

Pelargonium 'Atomic Snowflake'
Tender evergreen perennial. Ht. 12–24 in., spread 12 in. Small pink flowers in summer. Intensely lemon-scented, roundish leaves with silver-gray-green variegation.

Pelargonium capitatum
Tender evergreen perennial. Ht. 12–24 in., spread 12 in. Small mauve flowers in summer, irregular three-lobed green leaves, rose scented. This is now mainly used to produce geranium oil for the perfume industry.

Pelargonium 'Chocolate Peppermint'
Tender evergreen perennial. Ht. 12–24 in., spread 3 ft. Small white-pink flowers in summer. Large, rounded, shallowly lobed leaves, velvety green with brown marking and a strong scent of chocolate peppermints! This is a fast grower so pinch out growing tips to keep shape.

Pelargonium 'Clorinda'
Tender evergreen perennial. Ht. and spread 3 ft. Large pink attractive flowers in summer. Large rounded leaves, mid-green and eucalyptus-scented.

Pelargonium crispum
Tender evergreen perennial. Ht. and spread 12–24 in. Small pink flowers in summer. Small three-lobed leaves, green, crispy, crinkled, and lemon scented. Neat habit.

Pelargonium crispum 'Peach Cream'
Tender evergreen perennial. Ht. and spread 12–24 in. Small pink flowers in summer. Small three-lobed leaves, green with cream and yellow variegation, crispy, crinkled, and peach-scented.

A variety of scented geraniums

Pelargonium crispum **'Variegatum'**
Tender evergreen perennial. Ht. and spread 12–24 in. Small pink flowers in summer. Small three-lobed leaves, green with cream variegation, crispy crinkled, and lemon scented.

Pelargonium denticulatum
Tender evergreen perennial. Ht. and spread 3 ft. Small pinky-mauve flowers in summer. Deeply cut palmate leaves, green with a lemon scent.

Pelargonium denticulatum **'Filicifolium'**
Tender evergreen perennial. Ht. and spread 3 ft. Small pink flowers in summer. Very finely indented green leaves with a fine brown line running through, slightly sticky, and not particularly aromatic, if anything a scent of balsam. Prone to whitefly.

Pelargonium **Fragrans Group**
Tender evergreen perennial. Ht. and spread 12 in. Small white flowers in summer. Grayish green leaves, rounded with shallow lobes, and a strong scent of nutmeg-pine.

Pelargonium **Fragrans Group** **'Fragrans Variegatum'**
Tender evergreen perennial. Ht. and spread 12 in. Small white flowers in summer. Grayish green leaves with cream variegation, rounded with shallow lobes, and a strong scent of nutmeg/pine.

Pelargonium **'Atomic Snowflake'**

Pelargonium **'Lemon Fancy'** **in flower**

Pelargonium graveolens
Rose Geranium
Tender evergreen perennial. Ht. 24–36 in., spread up to 3 ft. Small pink flowers in summer. Fairly deeply cut green leaves with a rose-peppermint scent. One of the more hardy of this species, with good growth.

Pelargonium **'Lady Plymouth'**
Tender evergreen perennial. Ht. and spread 12–24 in. Small pink flowers in summer. Fairly deeply cut grayish-green leaves with cream variegation and a rose-peppermint scent.

Pelargonium **'Lemon Fancy'**
Tender evergreen perennial. Ht. 12–24 in., spread 12–18 in. Smallish pink flowers in summer. Small roundish green leaves with shallow lobes and an intense lemon scent.

Pelargonium **'Lilian Pottinger'**
Tender evergreen perennial. Ht. 12–24 in., spread 3 ft. Small whitish flowers in summer. Leaves brightish green, rounded, shallowly lobed with serrated edges. Soft to touch. Mild spicy apple scent.

Pelargonium **'Mabel Gray'**
Tender evergreen perennial. Ht. 18–24 in., spread 12–18 in. Mauve flowers with deeper veining in summer. If I have a favorite, this is it: the leaves are diamond-shaped, roughly textured, mid-green, and oily when rubbed and very strongly lemon-scented.

Pelargonium odoratissimum
Tender evergreen perennial. Ht. 12–24 in. spread 3 ft. Small white flowers in summer. Green, rounded, shallowly lobed leaves, fairly bright green in color and soft to touch, with an apple scent. Trailing habit, looks good in large containers.

Pelargonium **'Prince of Orange'**
Tender evergreen perennial. Ht. and spread 12–24 in. Pretty pink-white flowers in summer. Green, slightly crinkled, slightly lobed leaves, with a refreshing orange scent. Prone to rust.

Pelargonium quercifolium
Oak-Leafed Pelargonium
Tender evergreen perennial. Ht. and spread up to 3 ft. Pretty pink-purple flowers in summer. Leaves oak-shaped, dark green with brown variegation, and slightly sticky. A different, spicy scent.

Pelargonium **'Royal Oak'**
Tender evergreen perennial. Ht. 15 in., spread 12 in. Small pink-purple flowers in summer. Oak-shaped, dark green leaves with brown variegation, slightly sticky with spicy scent. Very similar to *P. quercifolium*, but with a more compact habit.

Pelargonium **'Rober's Lemon Rose'**
Tender evergreen perennial. Ht. and spread up to 3 ft. Pink flowers in summer. Leaves grayish-green—oddly shaped, lobed, and cut— with a rose scent. A fast grower, so pinch out the growing tips to maintain shape.

Oak-leafed pelargonium
Pelargonium quercifolium

Pelargonium tomentosum
Tender evergreen perennial. Ht. 12–24 in., spread 3 ft. Small white flowers in summer. Large rounded leaves, shallow lobed, velvet gray-green in color with a strong peppermint scent. Fast grower, so pinch out growing tips to maintain shape. Protect from full sun.

Pelargonium **'Chocolate Peppermint'**

Pelargonium 'Attar of Roses'

CULTIVATION

Propagation

Seed

Although I have known scented geraniums to have been grown from seed, I do not recommend this method. Cuttings are much more reliable for the majority. However, if you want to have a go, sow in spring in a bark-peat-grit potting mix (see p. 591) at a temperature no lower than 59°F.

Cuttings

All scented geraniums can be propagated by softwood cuttings which generally take very easily in the summer. Take a cutting about 4–6 in. long and strip the leaves from the lower part with a sharp knife. At all costs do not tear the leaves off as this will cause a hole in the stem and the cutting will be susceptible to disease, such as blackleg. This is a major caveat for such as *Pelargonium crispum* 'Variegatum.' Use a sharp knife and slice the leaf off, insert the cutting into a tray containing equal parts bark and peat. Water and put the tray away from direct sunlight. Keep an eye on the potting soil, making sure it does not thoroughly dry out, but only water if absolutely necessary. The cuttings should root in 2 to 3 weeks.

Pot into separate pots containing the bark-peat-grit mix of potting soil. Place in a cool greenhouse for the winter, keeping the compost dry and watering only very occasionally. In spring, repot into larger pots and water sparingly. When they start to produce flower buds give a feeding of liquid fertilizer. In early summer pinch out the top growing points to encourage bushy growth.

Pests and Diseases

Unfortunately pelargoniums do suffer from a few diseases.

1. Cuttings can be destroyed by **blackleg virus**. The cutting turns black and falls over. The main cause of this is too much water. Keep the cuttings as dry as possible after the initial watering.

2. **Gray mold** (*Botrytis*) is also caused by the plants being too wet and the air too moist. Remove damaged leaves carefully so as not to spread the disease, and burn. Allow the plants to dry out, and increase ventilation and spacing between plants.

3. **Leaf gall** appears as a mass of small proliferated shoots at the base of a cutting or plant. Destroy the plant, otherwise it could affect other plants.

4. Geraniums, like mint and comfrey, are prone to **rust**. Destroy the plant or it will spread to others.

5. Aphids. Be vigilant. If you catch it early enough, you will be able to control it by spraying with a liquid horticultural soap. Follow manufacturer's instructions.

Maintenance

Spring Trim, slowly introduce watering, and start feeding. Repot if necessary.

Summer Feed regularly. Trim to maintain shape.

Fall Take cuttings. Trim back plants. Bring in for the winter to protect from frost.

Winter Allow the plants to rest. Keep watering to a minimum.

Garden Cultivation

Scented pelargoniums are so varied that they can look very effective grown in groups in the garden. Plant out as soon as there is no danger of frost. Choose a warm site with well-drained soil. A good method is to sink the repotted, overwintered geraniums into the soil. This makes sure the initial compost is correct and makes it easier to dig up the pot and bring inside before the first frost.

Harvesting

Pick leaves during the growing season, for fresh use or for drying.

Collect seeds before the seed pod ripens and ripen in paper bags. If allowed to ripen on the plant, the pods will burst, scattering the seeds everywhere.

CONTAINER GROWING

Scented pelargoniums make marvelous pot plants. They grow well, look good, and smell lovely. Pot as described in Propagation. Place the containers so that passers-by brush against the leaves, releasing their aroma.

CULINARY

Before artificial food flavorings were produced, the Victorians used scented pelargonium leaves in the bottom of cake tins to flavor their desserts. Why not follow suit? When you grease and line the bottom of an 8 in. pan, arrange approximately 20 leaves of either 'Lemon Fancy,' 'Mabel Gray,' or 'Graveolens.' Fill the pan with a cake mix of your choice and cook as normal. Remove the leaves with the lining paper when the cake has cooled. Scented pelargonium leaves add distinctive flavor to many dishes although, like bay leaves, they are hardly ever eaten, being removed after the cooking process. The main varieties used are 'Graveolens,' 'Lemon Fancy,' 'Odoratissimum,' and 'Attar of Roses.'

Geranium Leaf Sorbet

Geranium Leaf Sorbet

*12 scented Pelargonium
  graveolens leaves
6 tablespoons sugar
1¼ cups water
Juice of 1 large lemon
1 egg white, beaten
4 leaves for decoration*

Wash the leaves and shake them dry. Put the sugar and water in a saucepan and boil until the sugar has dissolved, stirring occasionally. Remove the pan from the heat. Put the 12 leaves in the pan with the sugar and water, cover and leave for 20 minutes. Taste. If you want a stronger flavor bring the liquid to a boil again, add some fresh leaves, and leave for an additional 10 minutes. When you have the right flavor, strain the syrup into a rigid container, add the lemon juice and leave to cool. Place in the freezer until semifrozen (approximately 45 minutes)—it must be firm, not mushy—and fold in the beaten egg white. Put back into freezer for an additional 45 minutes. Scoop into individual glass bowls, and decorate each with a geranium leaf.

Rose Geranium Punch

*5 cups apple juice
1 cup sugar
6 leaves of rose geranium
6 drops of green food
  coloring (optional)
4 limes*

Boil the apple juice and sugar and geranium leaves for 5 minutes. Strain the liquid. Cool and add coloring if desired. Thinly slice and crush limes, and add to the liquid. Pour over ice in glasses and garnish with geranium leaves.

Graveolens Geranium Butter

Butter pounded with the leaves makes a delicious filling for cakes and cookies. Spread on bread and top with apple butter.

WARNING

None of the crispums should be used in cooking as it is believed that they can upset the stomach.

Rose Geranium Punch

OTHER USES

In aromatherapy, geranium oil is relaxing but use it in small quantities. Dilute 2 drops in 2 teaspoons of soy oil for a good massage, or to relieve premenstrual tension, dermatitis, eczema, herpes, or dry skin.

Petroselinum

PARSLEY

Also known as Common Parsley, Garden Parsley, and Rock Parsley. From the family Apiaceae.

Parsley in pots

Best-known of all garnishing herbs in the West. Native to central and southern Europe, in particular the Mediterranean region, now widely cultivated in several varieties throughout the world.

The Greeks had mixed feelings about this herb. It was associated with Archemorus, the Herald of Death, so they decorated their tombs with it. Hercules was said to have chosen parsley for his garlands, so they would weave it into crowns for victors at the Isthmian Games. But they did not eat it themselves, preferring to feed it to their horses. However, the Romans consumed parsley in quantity and made garlands for banquet guests to discourage intoxication and to counter strong odors.

It was believed that only a witch or a pregnant woman could grow it, and that a fine harvest was ensured only if the seeds were planted on Good Friday. It was also said that if parsley was transplanted, misfortune would descend upon the household.

SPECIES

Petroselinum crispum
Regular Parsley
Hardy biennial. Ht. 12–16 in. Small creamy white flowers in flat umbels in summer. The leaf is brightish green and has curly toothed edges and a mild taste. It is mainly used as a garnish. **Zone 5**

Parsley *Petroselinum crispum*

Petroselinum crispum var. neapolitannum
Flat-leaved or Italian Parsley
Hardy biennial. Ht. 18–24 in. Small creamy white flowers in flat umbels in summer. Flat dark green leaves with a stronger flavor than regular curly parsley. This is the one I recommend for culinary use.
Zone 5

Petroselinum crispum var. tuberosum
Hamburg Parsley
Also known as turnip-rooted parsley (see also pp. 140–41). Perennial, grown as an annual. Root length up to 6 in. Leaf, green and very similar to French parsley. This variety, probably first developed in Holland, was introduced into England in the early 18th century, but it was only popular for 100 years. The plant is still frequently found in vegetable markets in France and Germany.
Zone 5

Warning: In the wild there is a plant called fool's parsley, *Aethusa cynapium*, which looks and smells a lot like parsley. Do not be tempted to eat it as it is extremely poisonous.

Flat-leaved parsley
Petroselinum crispum 'French'

CULTIVATION

Propagation
Seed
In cool climates, to ensure a succession of plants, sow seedlings under cover only in plug trays or pots. Avoid seed trays because parsley hates being transferred. Cover with perlite. If you have a heated propagator, a temperature of 65°F will speed up germination. It takes 4–6 weeks without bottom heat and 2–3 weeks with. When the seedlings are large enough and the air and soil temperature have started to rise (about mid-spring), plant out 6 in. apart in a prepared garden bed.

Pests and Diseases
Slugs love young parsley plants. There is a fungus that may attack the leaves. It produces first brown then white spots. Where this occurs the whole stock should be destroyed. Get some fresh seed.

Maintenance

Spring Sow seed.
Summer Sow seed. Cut flower heads as they appear on second-year plants.
Fall Protect plants for winter crop.
Winter Protect plants for winter picking.

Garden Cultivation

Parsley is a hungry plant; it likes a good deep soil, not too light and not acid. Always feed the chosen site well in the previous fall with well-rotted manure.

If you wish to harvest parsley all year round, prepare two different sites. For summer supplies, a western or eastern border is ideal because the plant needs moisture and prefers a little shade. For winter supplies, a more sheltered spot will be needed in a sunny position.

The seeds should be sown thinly, in drills 12–18 in. apart and about 1 in. deep. Germination is very slow. Keep the soil moist at all times, otherwise the seed will not germinate.

As soon as the seedlings are large enough, thin to 3 in. and then 6 in. apart. If at any time the leaves turn a bit yellow, cut back to encourage new growth and feed with a liquid fertilizer. At the first sign of flower heads appearing, remove them if you wish to continue harvesting the leaves. Remember to water well during hot weather. In the second year parsley runs to seed very quickly. Dig it up as soon as the following year's crop is ready for picking, and remove it from the garden.

Hamburg or turnip parsley differs only in the respect that it is a root not a leaf crop. When the seedlings are large enough, thin to 8 in. apart. Water well all summer. The root tends to grow more at this time of year, and unlike a lot of root crops, the largest roots taste the best. Lift in late fall, early winter. They are frost resistant.

Harvesting

Pick leaves during first year for fresh use or for freezing (by far the best method of preserving parsley).

Dig up roots of Hamburg parsley in the fall of the first year and store in peat or sand.

CULINARY

Parsley is a widely used culinary herb, valued for its taste as well as its rich nutritional content. Cooking with parsley enhances the flavor of other foods and herbs. In bland food, the best flavor is obtained by adding it just before the end of cooking.

As so many recipes include parsley, here are some basic herb mixtures.

Fines Herbes

You will see this mentioned in a number of recipes and it is a classic for omelets.

1 sprig parsley, chopped
1 sprig chervil, chopped
Some chives cut with scissors
1–2 leaves French tarragon

Chop up all the herbs finely, mix, and add to egg dishes.

Fish Bouquet Garni

2 sprigs parsley
1 sprig French tarragon
1 sprig fennel (small)
2 leaves lemon balm

Tie the herbs together in a bundle and add to the cooking liquid.

Boil Hamburg parsley as a root vegetable or grate raw into salads. Use in soup mixes; the flavor resembles both celery and parsley.

CONTAINER GROWING

Parsley is an ideal herb for containers, it even likes living inside on the kitchen windowsill, as long as it is watered, fed, and cut. Use the bark-peat mix of potting soil (see p. 591). Curly parsley can look very ornamental as an edging to a large pot of nasturtiums. It can also be grown in hanging baskets (keep well watered), window boxes (give it some shade in high summer), and containers. That brings me to the parsley pot, the one with six holes around the side. Do not use it. As I have already said, parsley likes moisture, and these containers dry out too fast; the holes in the side are small and make it very difficult to water, and the parsley has too big a taproot to be happy.

WARNING

Avoid medicinal use during pregnancy. There is an oil produced from parsley, but it should only be used under medical supervision.

MEDICINAL

All parsleys are a rich source of vitamins including vitamin C. They are also high in iron and other minerals, and contain the antiseptic chlorophyll.

It is a strong diuretic suitable for treating urinary infections as well as fluid retention.

Parsley is a well-known breath freshener, being the traditional antidote for the pungent smell of garlic. Chew raw to promote healthy skin.

Use in poultices as an antiseptic dressing for sprains, wounds, and insect bites.

OTHER USES

A tea made from crushed seeds kills head lice vermin. Pour it over the head after washing and rinsing, wrap your head in a towel for 30 minutes and then allow to dry naturally. Equally, the seeds or leaves steeped in water can be used as a hair rinse.

Parsley tea

Phlomis fruticosa

JERUSALEM SAGE

From the family Lamiaceae.

Originates from the Mediterranean region but is now cultivated widely as a garden plant.

The generic name, *Phlomis*, was used by Dioscorides, a Greek physician in the first century whose *Materia Medica* was the standard reference on the medical application of plants for over 1,500 years.

SPECIES

Phlomis fruticosa
Jerusalem Sage
Tender evergreen perennial. Ht. and spread 4 ft. Whorls of hooded yellow flowers in summer. Gray-green oblongish leaves, slightly wrinkled.

Phlomis italica
Narrow-Leaf Jerusalem Sage
Hardy evergreen perennial. Ht. 36 in., spread 30 in. Whorls of lilac-pink flowers in midsummer, borne at the ends of shoots amid narrow, woolly, gray-green leaves.
Both zone 8

CULTIVATION

Propagation
Seeds
Sow the medium-sized seed in the fall either into seed or plug trays and cover with a thin layer of potting soil. Winter in a cold greenhouse or cold frame. Does not need stratification nor heat, just cool temperature. Germination is erratic. When the seedlings are large enough to handle, prick out into pots using the bark-peat-grit mix of potting soil (see p. 591). Plant the young plants into the garden when there is no threat of frosts.

Jerusalem sage *Phlomis fruticosa*

Cuttings
Take softwood cuttings in summer from nonflowering shoots; they root easily.

Division
If an established plant has taken over its neighbor's spot, dig up and divide it in the spring; replant into a prepared site.

Pests and Diseases
In the majority of cases, this is free from pests and disease.

Maintenance
Spring Divide established plants if need be.
Summer Cut back after flowering to maintain shape.
Fall Sow seeds.
Winter Protect outside plants if the winter temperature is persistently below 23°F.

Garden Cultivation
Jerusalem sage is an attractive plant, making a fine mound of gray-furred leaves, proof against all but the most severe winter. A prolific summer flowerer, happy in a dry, well-drained, sunny spot. Cut back each year after flowering (late summer) and you will be able to control and maintain its soft gray dome all year round. Do not trim in the fall as any frost will damage and in some cases kill the plant.

Harvesting
Pick leaves for drying before planting flowers.

OTHER USES
The attractive, slightly aromatic leaves are a nice addition to a potpourri.

CONTAINER GROWING

Jerusalem sage is happy if grown in a large container using a soil-based compost. Resist overfeeding and over-watering as it is a drought-loving plant. Trim back especially after flowering to restrict its rampant growth. Protect during the winter in a cool greenhouse. Keep watering to the absolute minimum.

CULINARY

Although not listed among culinary herbs, the leaves are pleasantly aromatic. In Greece they are collected from the hillside and, once dried and bundled together with other related species, hung up for sale. Dried leaves can be used in stews and casseroles.

Phytolacca americana

POKE

Also known as Red Ink Plant, Pokeweed, Poke Root, Pigeon Berry, Coccum, Indian Poke, and Cancer Root. From the family Phytolaccaceae.

This herbaceous plant is native to the warmer regions of America (especially Florida), Africa, and Asia. It has been introduced elsewhere, particularly in the Mediterranean region.

Its generic name is derived from two Greek words: *phyton,* meaning "plant," and *lac,* meaning "lake," referring to the purple-blue dye that flows from some phytolaccas when crushed.

The herb was introduced to European settlers by the Native Americans, who knew it as *pocan* or *coccum,* and used it as an emetic for a number of problems. It acquired a reputation as a remedy for internal cancers and was called cancer root.

SPECIES

Phytolacca americana
Pokeweed
Hardy perennial. Ht. and spread 4–5 ft. Shallow, cup-shaped flowers, sometimes pink, flushed white and green, borne in terminal racemes in summer. They are followed by round fleshy blackish-purple berries with poisonous seeds that hang down when ripe. Oval to lance-shaped mid-green leaves, tinged purple in fall. There is a variegated form with green and white leaves.

Phytolacca polyandra
Hardy perennial. Ht. and spread 4 ft. Clusters of shallow, cup-shaped, pink flowers in summer, followed by rounded blackish berries with poisonous seeds. Has brilliant crimson stems, oval to lance-shaped, mid-green leaves that turn yellow in summer through fall.
Zone 5

CULTIVATION

Propagation
Seed
Sow the seeds fresh in the fall or spring in prepared seed or plug trays. Cover with perlite. If sown in the fall, winter the young plants in a cold greenhouse or cold frame. In the spring, after a period of hardening off, plant them out in a prepared site in the garden, 3 ft. apart.

Division
The large root can be divided either in fall or spring.

Pests and Diseases
Largely free from pests and diseases.

Maintenance
Spring Sow seeds. Divide established plants.
Summer Cut off the flowers if you do not want berries.
Fall Sow seeds. Divide established plants.
Winter Dies back to the ground; does not usually require protection.

Garden Cultivation
Plant poke in sun or shade in a moist, fertile soil, sheltered from the wind. Despite its poisonous seeds, this plant can look marvelous in a garden.

Harvesting
In some parts of the U.S., poke shoots are gathered and prepared as a spring green, but they can cause upset stomach, so you should do this only if you really know what you are doing. It is better to err on the side of caution and pick some nice fresh sorrel or red orach instead.

Poke *Phytolacca americana*

CONTAINER GROWING

It is a tall plant, and when in berry is sufficiently heavy to unbalance even a large pot. Keep the poisonous berries out of reach of children.

If you choose to try it, use the bark-peat-grit potting mix (see p. 591) and water well during the summer.

MEDICINAL

Herbalists prescribe it for the treatment of chronic rheumatism, arthritis, tonsillitis, swollen glands, mumps, and mastitis.

An extract from the roots can destroy snails. This discovery is being explored in Africa as a possible means to control the disease bilharzia.

WARNING

Poisonous. When handling seeds, roots, or the mature plant, gloves should be worn. It is toxic and dangerous. It should be used only by professionals.

Polemonium caeruleum

JACOB'S LADDER

Also known as Blue Jacket, Charity, Jacob's Walking Stick, Ladder to Heaven, and Greek Valerian.
From the family Polemoniaceae.

This European native species grows sparsely over the whole of the temperate regions of the northern hemisphere. It is not as prolific as some of the other closely related species in America.

It was known to the ancient Greeks as *polemonium*, and the root was once administered in wine in cases of dysentery, toothache, and on the bites of poisonous animals.

The leaf, being divided into many segments, has the appearance of a ladder, hence its common name—"Jacob slept with a stone for a pillow and he dreamed and behold a ladder set upon the Earth and the top of it reached to Heaven and behold the Angels of God ascending and descending on it" (Genesis 28:12).

As late as the nineteenth century, it was known as Valeranae Graecae, or Greek Valerian, and was being used in some European pharmacies. It was predominantly used as an antisyphilitic agent and in the treatment of rabies. To confuse things, the Shakers called it "Abscess" and used it for pleurisy and fevers.

Jacob's ladder
Polemonium caeruleum

SPECIES

Polemonium caeruleum
Jacob's Ladder
Hardy perennial. Ht. and spread 18–24 in. Clusters of attractive, cup-shaped, lavender-blue flowers in summer. The mid-green leaves are finely divided into small lance shapes.
Zone 2

Polemonium caeruleum subsp. caeruleum f. album
White Jacob's Ladder
Hardy perennial. Ht. and spread 18–24 in. Cluster of attractive, cup-shaped, lavender-white flowers in summer. Leaves as *P. caeruleum.*

Polemonium reptans
Greek Valerian
Hardy perennial. Ht. 8–18 in., spread 12 in. Cluster of attractive, cup-shaped, blue flowers in summer. The silver-green leaves are finely divided into small lance shapes. The root of this species is bitter in flavor and is employed as an astringent and as an antidote to snakebites.
Zone 2

Other species worth looking out for (both native to western North America, but not used herbally there):

Polemonium carneum
Hardy perennial. Ht. and spread 18 in. Cluster of attractive, cup-shaped, pink or purple-pink flowers from early summer. Mid-green leaves are finely divided into small lance shapes.
Zone 6

Polemonium pulcherrimum
Hardy perennial. Ht. 20 in., spread 12 in. Cluster of attractive, tubular, blue-purple flowers in summer. The mid-green leaves are finely divided into small lance shapes.
Zone 4

CULTIVATION

Propagation
Seed
For flowering early the following spring, sow the fairly small seeds fresh in fall into a prepared seed or plug tray. Cover with a thin layer of potting soil. Leave in a cool/cold greenhouse over the winter. They will stay in their trays quite happily through the winter, as long as they are kept frost-free. Transplant in spring when the threat of frosts is over and plant directly into the garden, after hardening off, at a distance of 12 in. apart.

For flowering the following season, sow under protection in early spring, or directly in the garden in late spring.

Division
Named varieties must be propagated by division. Divide established plants in the spring. Dig up the whole plant and ease it in half. Replant in a prepared site in the garden.

Pests and Diseases
These plants rarely suffer from pests or disease.

Maintenance
Spring Sow seeds if not sown the previous fall. Divide established plants if need be.
Summer Deadhead flowers. After flowering, cut back to prevent self-seeding.
Fall Sow seeds under protection.
Winter Established plants are hardy and should not need protection.

Garden Cultivation
This lovely, short-lived perennial is not particular about site or soil, although it prefers a rich moisture-retaining soil with an addition of lime. It is not fussy about sun or shade, but looks prettier in the sun. In a long, hot summer, make sure the plant gets plenty of extra water. In an average summer it should not need extra watering.

The fairly short flowering season can be prolonged by deadheading. This is another plant beloved by cats, who seem to take a fancy to the young plants in particular. So if there are cats around, give the young plants some protection.

Harvesting
Cut the flowers just as they open for drying. Dry either in small bunches or individual sprays.

CONTAINER GROWING

Jacob's ladder looks lovely in a container. Use a soil-based compost and do not allow to dry out. Place the container in a semishady location to protect if from overheating in the midday sun. Feed with liquid fertilizer, following manufacturer's instructions, during the flowering period only.

CULINARY

I can find no record of this being used as a culinary herb, and the flowers do not add much flavor when added to salads.

OTHER USES
The dried flowers may not smell, but do look attractive in potpourris.

No longer used for medicinal purposes.

Jacob's ladder growing in a field

Polygonatum x hybridum

SOLOMON'S SEAL

Also known as David's Harp, Jacob's Ladder, Lady's Lockets, Lily of the Mountain, Drop Berry, Seal Root, and Sealwort. From the family Convallariaceae.

A perennial plant that grows in thick woods and thickets in Europe, Asia, and North America.

The plant's generic name, *Polygonatum*, is derived from the Greek *poly*, meaning "many," and *gonu*, meaning "knee joint," or by extension "angle," which refers to the herbs many-jointed rhizome.

King Solomon, wiser than all men, gave his approval to the use of its roots (said to resemble cut sections of Hebrew characters), as a poultice for wounds, and to help heal broken limbs.

In the sixteenth century Gerard cited its contribution in the healing of broken bones, for which the root might be taken internally (in the form of ale) or applied externally as a poultice.

Solomon's seal
Polygonatum x *hybridum*

Polygonatum verticillatum
Whorled Solomon's Seal
Hardy perennial. Ht. 48 in., spread 18 in. The flowers are narrow and bell-shaped, greenish-white in color, and appear in early summer. Its berries are first red, then dark blue. The lance-shaped, mid-green leaves grow in whorls.
Zone 5

SPECIES

Polygonatum biflorum
Solomon's Seal
Hardy perennial. Ht. 12–32 in., spread 1 ft. White, waxy flowers tipped with green hang from arching stems in spring to summer. The berries are bluish-black. The leaves are oval to lance-shaped and mid-green in color.
Zone 4

Polygonatum odoratum
Angular Solomon's Seal
Hardy perennial. Ht. 24 in., spread 12 in. Produces pairs of fragrant, tubular, bell-shaped, green-tipped, white flowers in spring. The berries and leaves are as *P. multiflorum*. A variegated form called *Polygonatum odoratum* 'Varigatum' has creamy white striped leaves. Also a double-flowered one, *Polygonatum odoratum* 'Flore Pleno,' has scented flowers that look rather like ballet dancers' tutus. **Zone 4**

CULTIVATION

Propagation
Seed
Sow fresh seed in fall into prepared seed or plug trays, cover with the potting mix, water in well, then cover with glass and leave outside for the winter. Remove the glass as soon as germination starts in spring. When the seedlings are large enough, plant out in a prepared site. Keep an eye on the watering throughout the first season—before they have developed their creeping rhizomes, young plants dry out quickly.

Division
The plant is best divided just after the stalks die down in fall, although in dampish weather, division and transplanting can be undertaken any time of year. This method is easier and quicker than seeds.

Pests and Diseases
Sawfly caterpillar is a common pest. You will notice that the leaves have clean-cut holes. This will not damage the plant but it can

look unsightly if you have a major attack. Spray with a liquid horticultural soap, at the first sign of invasion. Complete eradication is difficult.

Maintenance
Spring Plant out seedlings.
Summer Make sure the soil does not dry out.
Fall Sow fresh seeds. Divide established plants.

Winter Protect in the event of a prolonged frost below 14°F.

Garden Cultivation
This elegant, graceful plant is sadly becoming scarce. Plant in groups on their own so that the tall and striking arching stems and waxy, green-tipped flowers are shown off to their best. It requires a cool shady situation in fertile, well-drained soil. Dig the soil over before planting with some leaf mold, and each winter top-dress with extra leaf mold.

Harvesting
For medicinal use, dig up and dry the roots of a well-established three-year-old plant in the fall after the foliage has died back.

OTHER USES

The plant has been employed cosmetically to clear freckles and as a skin tonic.

Solomon's seal *Polygonatum biflorum* **in flower**

CONTAINER GROWING

Solomon's seal can be grown in large containers. Use a soil-based compost, and top-dress in fall with well-rotted manure or leaf mold. This will also protect it during winter. Position in semishade and water well throughout the summer. Keep out of reach of children.

WARNING

All parts of the plant are poisonous and should be taken internally only under supervision of a qualified medicinal or herbal practitioner. Large doses can be harmful.

MEDICINAL

The powdered roots and rhizomes make a good poultice for bruises, inflammation, and wounds, and a good wash for skin problems and blemishes.

Native Americans made a tea of the rootstock to take for women's complaints and general internal pains. They also used it as a wash to counteract the effect of poison ivy.

Polygonatum odoratum contains a substance that lowers the level of blood sugar and has long been used in the East for diabetes.

Solomon's seal makes a good skin wash.

Primula veris

COWSLIP

Also known as Our Lady's Bunch of Keys, St. Peter's Keys, Palsywort, Bunch of Keys, Covekeys, Cowflop, Cowstripling, Freckled Face, Golden Drops, Herb Peter, Hot Rod, Long Legs, Nook Maidens, Titsy Totsy, St. Peter's Herb, Paigale, Coweslop, Cowslap, Fair Bells, Fairy Cups, and Keys of Heaven. From the family Primulaceae.

This traditional herb is native to northern and central Europe. It has naturalized elsewhere on porous, calcareous soils, meadows, and pastures, to an altitude of 6,500 feet.

In America the plant that is called cowslip is, in fact, the English marsh marigold *(Caltha palustris)* and is not to be confused with the above.

Cowslip is a corruption of *cowsslop* from the Old English *cu-sloppe*, from the observation that cowslips sprang up in meadows where cows grazed.

The generic name, *primula*, is from the Latin *primus*, meaning "first," after its early flowering in spring. A legend of northern Europe is that St. Peter let his keys to heaven drop when he learned that a duplicate set had been made. Where they fell the cowslip grew, hence the English, French, and German common names Keys of Heaven, Clef de St. Pierre, and Schlusselblumen. The medieval *Regimen Sanitatis Salernitanum* recommended the cowslip as a cure for palsy or paralysis, a cure suggested perhaps by the trembling of its nodding flowers.

It is sadly no longer possible for country folk to go out and collect bushels of cowslip flowers to make cowslip wine. This once-common grassland flower has now become relatively rare, a casualty of improved farming methods, which do not permit long grass and pastures to settle down and develop perennial flora. However, in East Anglia, where it retains the old alternative name *paigale*, it is beginning to reestablish itself on roadside verges and highway shoulders in chalk and limestone areas, away from damaging pesticide sprays.

SPECIES

Primula veris
Cowslip
Hardy perennial. Ht. and spread 6–8 in. Tight clusters of fragrant, tubular, yellow flowers produced on stout stems in spring. Leaves, oval-shaped and mid-green, form a neat clump.
Zone 5

Cowslips are often mistaken for oxlip *(P. elatior)*, which is a hybrid of the cowslip and the primrose *(P. vulgaris)*. The difference between the two is that oxlip have large pale yellow flowers in a one-sided cluster. Cowslip flowers are much deeper yellow and smaller, and there are more in a cluster.

Cowslip *Primula veris*

CULTIVATION

Propagation
Seed
Better sown fresh. Collect the seed heads in early fall when the seeds are slightly succulent. Sow the fairly small seeds onto the surface of a prepared pot, seed, or plug tray. Cover with glass. Put the container somewhere cool, like a cold frame, cold greenhouse, or outside windowsill. Keep an eye on germination, which usually takes 4–6 weeks, and remove glass as soon as the seedlings emerge. If you sow in springtime, they will need cold then warm temperatures to break their dormancy— the frost treatment.

Plant into the final position in the garden when the young plants are large enough to handle, or pot up for a spring display.

Division
Being a primula, cowslips divide easily. The best time for doing this is in the fall. Dig up a clump and tease the plants apart. Replant in situ 6 in. apart or repot. Protect from frost until the roots have come down (this takes 4–6 weeks).

Pests and Diseases
The scourge of all primula plants is the **vine weevil**. I have known them to decimate a complete stock of cowslips in a short time.

Maintenance
Spring Early in the year clear all the winter debris from established plants. Stratify seed if necessary and sow.
Summer Only deadhead if you do not want the seed.
Fall Collect seed. Divide established plants.
Winter No need to protect.

Cowslip wine

Garden Cultivation
Plant cowslips in semishade or sun, in a moist but well-drained soil. They prefer lime soil, but do adapt well. They look better grown in clumps rather than on their own, and are ideal for front of border in a spring garden, or for growing in the lawn, although you will have to mow round them until the seeds have set.

Harvesting
Don't pick or dig up cowslips growing in the wild—they are already rare.

Pick leaves as required to use fresh. Not really worth drying.

Pick flowers as they open to use fresh.

Dig up roots in the fall for drying.

CONTAINER GROWING

Essentially a wild plant, the cowslip does not thrive inside, but is happy in a container on the patio. Use the standard bark-peat potting mix (see p. 591), and do not let it dry out. Position the container where it gets some shade at midday.

WARNING

Some primula species can cause a form of contact dermatitis characterized by a violent vascular eruption on the fingers and forearms. Hypersensitive individuals should avoid these plants.

MEDICINAL

A tea from the flowers is a simple remedy for insomnia, nervous tension, and headaches. Cowslip syrup was a country remedy for palsy and paralysis, hence its alternative name Palsywort.

Cowslip roots are attributed with various medicinal propensities. One, owing to their high saponin content, is to treat whooping cough and bronchitis. Another, attributed to the salicylates present in the root, is to alleviate arthritis.

For this reason, in many old herbals, cowslip roots are called *radix arthritica.*

CULINARY

Use leaves in salads and for meat stuffing. Use flowers in cowslip wine and salads.

Cowslip in salad

Primula vulgaris

PRIMROSE

**Also known as Early Rose, Easter Rose, First Rose, and May-Flower.
From the family Primulaceae.**

This herald of spring is a native of Europe.
The name primrose originates from the old Latin *prima*, meaning "first," and *rosa*, meaning "rose."

The polyanthus, which has been known in gardens since the seventeenth century, probably originates from crosses between colored forms of the primrose and the cowslip.

In the Middle Ages concoctions made from primroses were used as a remedy for gout and rheumatism. The flowers were used in the preparation of love potions. An infusion of the roots was taken for nervous headaches.

SPECIES

Primula vulgaris
Primrose
Hardy perennial. Ht. and spread 6 in. The fresh yellow, sweetly scented flowers with darker yellow centers are borne singly on hairy stems in early spring. Leaves are mid-green and wrinkled. **Zone 6**

Primrose *Primula vulgaris*

CULTIVATION

Propagation
Seed
In summer sow the fresh seed when it is still slightly green and before it turns darkish brown and becomes dry. Sow in a prepared seed or plug tray and cover with perlite. These fresh seeds usually germinate in a few weeks. Either winter in the plug trays, or transplant when the seedlings are large enough and winter in pots for planting out into a prepared site the following spring.

The seed that one gets in seed packets should be sown in the fall or early winter. Do not sow it directly into the ground where it can easily be lost. Water the seeds in; do not cover with potting soil, but with glass or plastic. To help the seeds germinate, leave the trays outside for the winter so that the seeds get the frost (stratification). Sometimes they take two years to germinate from the dry state, so leave the seed trays until the following year if nothing appears in the spring, checking the compost occasionally to make sure it does not dry out. When the seedlings are large enough, plant out in a prepared site in the garden 6 in. apart.

Division
Established clumps (from your own or friends' gardens, not from the wild) can be divided very easily in the fall.

Pests and Diseases
The only major pest to attack the primrose is the

Primrose *Primula vulgaris*

WARNING

Some primula species can cause a form of contact dermatitis, characterized by a violent vascular eruption on the fingers and forearms. Hypersensitive individuals should avoid these plants.

MEDICINAL

Its medicinal use is really in the past, although it is still used occasionally as an expectorant for the treatment of bronchitis. A tisane, which is a mild sedative and good for anxiety and insomnia, can be made from the leaves and flowers.

Primrose tisane

CULINARY

The flowers are lovely in green salads, and they can be crystallized to decorate puddings and cakes.

The young leaves make an interesting vegetable if steamed and tossed in butter.

Primrose salad

vine weevil. Pollinated primrose flowers produce sticky seeds that attract **ants**; they then disperse them around the garden, which is why you sometimes see plants where you least expect them.

Maintenance
Spring Plant out young plants.
Summer Sow fresh seed.
Fall Divide established plants.
Winter Sow dry seed that needs stratification. No need to protect plants; fully hardy.

Garden Cultivation
When planting primroses, bear in mind that their natural habitat is in hedgerows and under deciduous trees, and that therefore they prefer a moist soil and will tolerate heavy soils in semishade. Planted in a very well-sheltered site, they often open early in spring.

If you are growing primroses in a wild garden,

make sure you do not cut the grass until midsummer when the plants will have seeded themselves.

Harvesting
Pick flowers for fresh use anytime. Pick young leaves to use fresh. In summer collect seed for immediate sowing.

CONTAINER GROWING

Primroses can be grown in containers and look very attractive and heartening especially if spring is damp and miserable. Use a soil-based potting mix. Keep the plant well watered and feed only occasionally with liquid fertilizer; once in the spring after flowering is sufficient. This is primarily a wild plant and does not benefit from overfeeding.

Prostanthera

PROSTANTHERA

Also known as Mint Bush. From the family Lamiaceae.

These highly attractive, aromatic shrubs are natives of Australia.

I have fallen in love with these most generous of flowerers. When I was exhibiting one in flower at the Chelsea Flower Show a member of the public fell in love with it in equal measure and tried to liberate it from my display!

I can find no historical references other than in the Royal Horticultural Society's *Dictionary of Gardening*, which states that the generic name, *Prostanthera*, comes from *prostithemi*, "to append," and *anthera*, meaning "anther," the pollen-bearing part of the stamen. This therefore alludes to the appendages usually borne by the anthers.

Prostanthera cuneata

SPECIES

Prostanthera cuneata
Tender shrub. Ht. and spread 2–3 ft. Very attractive white flowers with purple spots that look rather like little orchids; late spring, early summer. Round, dark green, slightly leathery and shiny, mint-scented leaves. Can withstand a minimum temperature of 28°F.
Zone 10

Prostanthera ovalifolia
Tender shrub. Reaches a height and spread of 4 ft. in its native country. Attractive purple flowers appear on short leafy racemes throughout the spring and summer. Dark green aromatic leaves. Can only withstand a minimum temperature of 41°F.
Zone 10

Prostanthera rotundifolia 'Rosea'
Tender shrub. A small tree that reaches a height of 10 ft. in its native country; in cooler climates it is a lot smaller. Pretty mauve-purple flowers in spring that last a long time. The dark green leaves (not as dark as *P. cuneata*) are round and mint-scented. Can only withstand a minimum temperature of 32°F. **Zone 10**

Prostanthera rotundifolia 'Rosea'

Prostanthera incisa
Tender shrub. Reaches a height of 6 ft., spread 5 ft. in its native country; in cooler climates it is a lot smaller. The green leaves are small (but larger than the other species mentioned), oval, and coarsely toothed, with a strong mint scent when crushed. Can only withstand a minimum temperature of 41°F.
Zone 10

CULTIVATION

Propagation
Cuttings
Take cuttings in spring or late summer. Use the bark-peat-grit mix of potting soil (see p. 591). In 8–12 weeks, when the cuttings are well rooted, pot up again using the same mix, and keep in containers for the first year.

Pests and Diseases
Overwatering young plants is a killer.

Maintenance
Spring Take cuttings.
Summer Cut back after flowering only if necessary.
Fall Protect from frosts.
Winter Protect from hard frosts and excessive water.

Garden Cultivation
In cool climates with persistent frosts they are better grown in a container. However if your climate is mild, plant out in the spring in a warm corner, in a lime-free, well-draining soil at a distance of 24–35 in. apart. Rain combined with frost is the killer in winter.

If you want to make a low hedge out of *Prostanthera cuneata*, then plant specimens 18 in. apart.

Harvesting
Pick leaves in the summer after flowering for drying and inclusion in potpourris.

CONTAINER GROWING

This is a real crowd-pleaser when in flower, and even when not, it makes a most attractive aromatic plant. Use the bark-peat-grit mix of potting soil. Keep young plants on the dry side, but water freely in the growing season.

MEDICINAL

I am sure that a plant that gives off as much scent, and has obviously so much oil in the leaf (*P. cuneata*), will one day have some use.

Prunella vulgaris

SELFHEAL

Also known as Carpenter's Herb, Sticklewort, Touch and Heal, All Heal, Woundwort, Hercules' Woundwort, Blue Curl's, Brownwort, and Hock Heal. From the family Lamiaceae.

This herb is found growing wild throughout all the temperate regions of the Northern Hemisphere, including North America, Europe, and Asia. It is found on moist, loamy, well-drained soils, in grassland, pastures, and open woodland, especially in sunny situations. Now introduced into China and Australia.

In strict sixteenth-century adherence to the *Doctrine of Signatures*, whereby it was believed that every plant bore an outward sign of its value to humankind, people noted that the upper lip of the flower was shaped like a hook, and as billhooks and sickles were a main cause of wounds in their agrarian society, they decided that the purpose of the herb was to heal wounds. They also saw the shape of the throat in the flower, which was why it was introduced to treat diseases of the throat such as quinsy and diphtheria, a propensity with a precedent in ancient Greece, where physicians used it to cure sore throats and tonsillitis.

SPECIES

Prunella vulgaris
Selfheal
Hardy perennial. Ht. 2–12 in., spread 6–12 in. Clusters of blue-purple flowers all summer. Oval leaves of a bright green.
Zone 4

CULTIVATION

Propagation
Seed
Sow the small seeds into prepared seed or plug trays in either spring or fall and cover with perlite; no extra heat is required. If a fall sowing, winter the young plants in a cold frame. In spring, when the plants are large enough, plant out 6–8 in. apart.

Division
This plant grows runners that have their own small root systems and is, therefore, easy to divide. Dig up in the spring or fall, and split and replant either in the garden or among grass.

Garden Cultivation
This plant, which is easy to establish, makes a colorful ground cover with attractive flowers. It is happy in full sun to semishade and will grow in most soils, including those that are rather acid,

Selfheal *Prunella vulgaris*

although it does best if the soil is fertile. It can be grown in a lawn, and while the mower keeps its spread and height in check, it will still flower and be much visited by bees and butterflies. However, throughout much of the northern and eastern U.S., it is considered a weed.

Pests and Diseases
In most cases it is free from pests and disease.

Maintenance
Spring Sow seed. Divide established plants.
Summer Cut back after flowering to curtail self-seeding.
Fall Divide established plants. Sow seeds.
Winter No need for protection; fully hardy.

Harvesting
Harvest for medicinal use only. Dry the leaves and flowers.

CONTAINER GROWING

Selfheal can be grown in containers using a soil-based potting mix. However, as it looks a bit insipid on its own, it is better combined with plants like heartsease, poppies, and cowslips.

Water well during the growing season, but only feed liquid fertilizer twice, otherwise it will produce too lush a growth.

MEDICINAL

Used in herbal medicines as a gargle for sore throats and inflammation of the mouth. A decoction is used to wash cuts and to soothe burns and bruises.

Pulmonaria officinalis

LUNGWORT

Also known as Jerusalem Cowslip, Abraham, Isaac, and Jacob, Adam and Eve, Bedlam, Cowslip, Beggar's Basket, Bottle of Allsorts, Children of Israel, Good Friday Plant, Lady's Milk, Lady Mary's Tears, Spotted Mary, Thunder and Lightning, Virgin Mary, Virgin Mary's Milkdrops, Virgin Mary's Tears, Spotted Bugloss, Jerusalem Sage, Maple Lungwort, Spotted Comfrey, and Spotted Lungwort. From the family Boraginaceae.

Lungwort is a native plant of northern parts of the United States and Europe. It has naturalized in many countries in cool climates, where it grows in shady, moist areas and in woodlands. The markings on the leaves were attributed to the Virgin Mary's milk or her tears; however, the generic name, *Pulmonaria*, comes from *pulmo,* meaning "lung," and the common name, Lungwort, conjures up a rather different image—of diseased lungs—to those blotched markings on the leaves. The *Doctrine of Signatures*, which held that all plants must be associated either by appearance, smell, or habit with the disease which they were said to heal, used it for various lung disorders.

SPECIES

Pulmonaria angustifolia
Hardy perennial. Ht. 9 in., spread 8–12 in. Flowers pink, turning to bright blue in spring. Leaves lance-shaped and mid-green with no markings. **Zone 3**

Pulmonaria longifolia
Hardy perennial. Ht. 12 in., spread 18 in. The flowers start pinkish, turning purplish-blue in spring. The leaves are lance-shaped, dark green, and slightly hairy with white spots. **Zone 4**

Lungwort *Pulmonaria officinalis* **in flower**

Pulmonaria officinalis
Lungwort
Semievergreen hardy perennial. Ht. 12 in., spread 24 in. Pink flowers, turning blue in spring. Leaves oval with blotchy white-cream markings on a mid-green, slightly hairy surface. **Zone 6**

Pulmonaria officinalis
'Sissinghurst White'
Semievergreen hardy perennial. Ht. 12 in., spread 18–24 in. White flowers in spring. Leaves white-spotted, mid-green in color, with a pointed oval shape. **Zone 6**

***Pulmonaria rubra* 'Red Start'**
Semievergreen hardy perennial. Ht. 12 in., spread 24 in. Pink-red flowers in spring. The leaves are long ovals, velvety, and mid-green with no markings. **Zone 6**

Pulmonaria saccharata
'Mrs. Moon'
Semievergreen hardy perennial. Ht. 12 in., spread 24 in. Flowers start as pink and turn blue in spring. The green leaves are long pointed ovals with clear, creamy white, variable spots.
Zone 3

Note: The American native Virginian bluebells, **Mertensia virginica,** belong to the same Boraginaceae family as lungwort. The flowers are purple-blue and the leaves lance-shaped. It is excellent for shady places. The foliage dies back very early in fall and leaves a bare patch, so it is not suitable for front of border. Propagate in the same way as the *Pulmonaria.*

Lungwort potpourri

CONTAINER GROWING

Make sure the container is large enough to give the creeping rhizomes a chance to spread and so prevent the plant from becoming potbound too quickly. Use a soil-based potting soil and a frost-hardy container, as these plants do not like coming inside even into a cold greenhouse, where the growth becomes soft and rots off. During the growing season keep the container in a shady spot and water well.

MEDICINAL

Lungwort is a soothing expectorant. The silica it contains restores the elasticity of the lungs. Externally it has been used for healing all kinds of wounds.

CULTIVATION

Propagation
Seeds
Lungwort seldom produces viable seed; increase your stock by division, but watch out in the garden, where it will self-seed erratically.

Division
Divide established plants either after flowering in late spring or in the fall.

Lungwort
Pulmonaria officinalis

Pests and Diseases
Lungwort can suffer from **powdery mildew** when the leaves die back in fall. Simply remove the damaged leaves and dispose of them.

Maintenance
Spring Dig up seedlings that mysteriously appear in odd parts of the garden.
Summer Do nothing.
Fall Divide established plants. Cut back growth.
Winter No need to protect, fully hardy.

Garden Cultivation
This attractive, fully hardy plant prefers a moist but well-drained soil with added leaf mold or well-rotted manure. It is an ideal plant for shady parts of the garden but will tolerate most situations. Plant out 12 in. apart in the fall. Lungwort grows quickly and spreads to provide dense ground cover. Water freely in dry weather.

Harvesting
Pick the leaves after flowering in the summer and dry for medicinal use.

Rosmarinus

ROSEMARY

From the family Lamiaceae.

Rosemary is a shrub that originated in the Mediterranean area and is now widely cultivated throughout the temperate regions. The ancient Latin name means "sea-dew." This may come from its habit of growing close to the sea and the dewlike appearance of its blossom at a distance. It is steeped in myth, magic, and folk medicinal use. One of my favorite stories about rosemary comes from Spain. It relates that originally the blue flowers were white. When the Holy family fled into Egypt, the Virgin Mary had to hide from some soldiers, so she spread her cloak over a rosemary bush and knelt behind it. When the soldiers had gone by she stood up and removed her cloak and the blossoms turned blue in her honor. Also connected to the Christian faith is the story that rosemary will grow for thirty-three years, the length of Christ's life, and then die.

In Elizabethan days, the wedding couple wore or carried a sprig of rosemary as a sign of fidelity. Also, bunches of rosemary were tied with colored ribbon tipped with gold and given to guests at weddings to symbolize love and faithfulness.

Rosemary was burned in sick chambers to freshen and purify the air. Branches were strewn in courts of law as a protection from jail fever. During the plague people used to wear it in neck pouches to sniff as they traveled, and in Victorian times it was carried in the hollow handles of walking sticks for the same reasons.

SPECIES

Rosmarinus officinalis
Rosemary
Tender shrub. Ht. and spread
3 ft. Pale blue flowers in early
spring to early summer and
then sometimes in early fall.
Needle-shaped dark green
leaves are highly aromatic.
Zone 8

**Rosmarinus officinalis var.
albiflorus**
White Rosemary
Tender shrub. Ht. and spread
32 in. White flowers in early
spring to early summer and
then sometimes in early fall.
Needle-shaped dark green
leaves are highly aromatic.
Zone 8

**Rosmarinus officinalis
angustissimus 'Corsican Blue'**
Corsican Rosemary
Tender shrub. Ht. and spread
32 in. Blue flowers in early
spring to early summer and
then sometimes again in early
fall. The needle-shaped dark
green leaves are highly
aromatic. It is much bushier
than the standard rosemary
and has a very pungent scent.
It is lovely to cook with.
Zone 8

Rosmarinus officinalis 'Aureus'
Golden Rosemary
Tender shrub. Ht. 32 in.,
spread 24 in. It hardly ever
flowers, but if it does they are
pale blue. The thin needle
leaves are green splashed with
gold. If you did not know
better you would think the
plant was suffering from
a virus! It still looks
very attractive.
Zone 8

**Rosmarinus officinalis var.
angustissiumus 'Benenden Blue'**
Benenden Blue Rosemary
Tender shrub. Ht. and spread
32 in. Dark blue flowers in
early spring to early summer
and then sometimes again in
early fall. Leaves are fine
needles and dense on the
stem, good aroma.
Zone 8

Prostrate rosemary *Rosmarinus officinalis* Prostratus Group

Miss Jessopp's Upright rosemary *Rosmarinus officinalis* 'Miss Jessopp's Upright'

Rosmarinus officinalis 'Fota Blue'
Fota Blue Rosemary Tender shrub. Ht. and spread 32 in. Very attractive dark blue flowers in early spring to early summer and then sometimes again in early fall. Very well spaced, narrow, needlelike, dark green leaves. The plant has a fairly prostrate habit.
Zone 8

Rosemary officinalis 'Majorca Pink'
Majorcan Pink Rosemary Evergreen half-hardy perennial. Ht. and spread 32 in. Pink flowers in early spring to early summer and then sometimes again in early fall. The needle-shaped dark green leaves are highly aromatic. This is a slightly prostrate form of rosemary.
Zone 8

Rosmarinus officinalis 'Miss Jessopp's Upright'
Miss Jessopp's Upright Rosemary Tender shrub. Ht. and spread 6 ft. Very pale blue flowers in early spring to early summer and then sometimes again in early fall. This rosemary has a very upright habit, making it ideal for hedges (see p. 338). The leaves are dark green needles spaced closely together, making the plant very bushy.
Zone 8

Rosmarinus officinalis 'Primley Blue'
Primley Blue Rosemary (Not "Frimley," which it has been incorrectly called) Tender shrub. Ht. and spread 32 in. Blue flowers in early spring to early summer and then sometimes again in early fall. The needle-shaped dark green leaves are highly aromatic. This is a good, hardy, bushy variety.
Zone 8

Rosmarinus officinalis **Prostratus Group** *(lavandulaceus, repens)*
Prostrate Rosemary Tender shrub. Ht. 12 in., spread 3 ft. Light blue flowers in early spring to early summer and then sometimes again in early fall. The needle-shaped dark green leaves are highly aromatic. This is a great plant for trailing on a wall.
Zone 8

Rosmarinus officinalis 'Roseus'
Pink Rosemary Evergreen half-hardy perennial. Ht. and spread 32 in. Pink flowers in early spring to early summer and then sometimes again in early fall. The needle-shaped dark green leaves are highly aromatic.
Zone 8

Rosmarinus officinalis 'Severn Sea'
Severn Seas Rosemary Evergreen half-hardy perennial. Ht. and spread 32 in. Mid-blue flowers in early spring to early summer and sometimes again in early fall. The needle-shaped dark green leaves are highly aromatic. The whole plant has a slightly prostrate habit with arching branches.
Zone 8

Rosmarinus officinalis 'Sissinghurst Blue'
Sissinghurst Rosemary Tender shrub. Ht. 4½ ft., spread 3 ft. Light blue flowers in early spring to early summer and then sometimes again in early fall. The plant has an upright habit and grows very bushy. The needle-shaped dark green leaves are highly aromatic.
Zone 8

Rosmarinus officinalis 'Sudbury Blue'
Sudbury Blue Rosemary Tender shrub. Ht. and spread 3 ft. Mid-blue flowers in early spring to early summer and then sometimes again in early fall. Good, hardy plant. The needle-shaped dark green leaves are highly aromatic.
Zone 8

Left to right: **White rosemary** *Rosmarinus officinalis* var. *albiflorus*, **Miss Jessopp's Upright rosemary** *Rosmarinus officinalis* 'Miss Jessopp's Upright,' **Pink rosemary** *Rosmarinus officinalis* 'Roseus'

CULTIVATION

Propagation

Seed

Rosmarinus officinalis can, with care, be grown from seed. It needs a bottom heat of 80–90°F to be successful. Sow in the spring in prepared seed or plug trays, using the bark-peat-grit potting soil (see p. 591) and cover with perlite. Once it germinates, be careful not to overwater the seedlings as they are prone to damping-off. Harden off the young plant slowly in summer and repot. Keep it in a pot for the first winter, and plant out the following spring into the required position at a distance of 2–3 ft. apart.

Cuttings

This is a more reliable method of propagation and ensures that you achieve the variety you require.

Softwood: Take these in spring off the new growth. Cut lengths of about 6 in. Use the bark-peat-grit mix of potting soil.

Semihardwood: Take these in summer from the nonflowering shoots, using the same compost as for softwood cuttings.

Layering

Rosemary lends itself to layering, especially as the branches of several varieties hang down. Layer established branches in summer.

Pests and Diseases

Potted rosemaries are subject to aphids, whiteflies, spider mites, mealybugs, and many fungus diseases.

Maintenance

Spring Trim after flowering. Sow seeds of *R. officinalis.* Take softwood cuttings.

Summer Feed container plants. Take semihardwood cuttings. Layer plants.
Fall Protect young tender plants.
Winter Put mulch, straw, or frost fabric around all plants.

Garden Cultivation

Rosemary requires a well-drained soil in a sheltered sunny position. It is frost hardy but in cold areas it prefers to grow against a south- or southwest-facing wall. If the plant is young it is worth giving some added protection in winter. If trimming is necessary, cut back only when the frosts are over; if possible leave it until after the spring flowering. Sometimes rosemary looks a bit scorched after frosts, in which case it is worth cutting the damaged plants to healthy wood in spring. Straggly old plants may also be cut back hard at the same time. Never cut back plants in the fall or if there is any chance of frost, as the plant will be damaged or even killed. On average, despite the story about rosemary growing for thirty-three years, it is best to replace bushes every five to six years.

Harvesting

As rosemary is evergreen, you can pick fresh leaves all year round as long as you are not greedy. If you need large quantities, then harvest in summer and either dry the leaves or make an oil or vinegar.

COMPANION PLANTING

If planted near carrot it repels carrot fly. It is also said to be generally beneficial to sage.

Golden rosemary *Rosmarinus officinalis* 'Aureus'

CONTAINER GROWING

Rosemary does well in pots and this is the preferred way to grow it in cold districts. The prostrate and less hardy varieties look very attractive and benefit from the extra protection offered by a container. Use the bark-peat-grit mix and make sure the potting soil is very well drained. Do not overwater, and feed only after flowering.

HEDGES

Rosemary certainly makes an effective hedge; it looks pretty in flower, smells marvelous, and is evergreen. In fact it has everything going for it if you have the right soil conditions, which must be well drained and carry a bias toward lime. The best varieties for hedges are 'Primley Blue' and 'Miss Jessopp's Upright.' Both are upright, hardy, and bushy. 'Primley Blue' has a darker blue flower and I think is slightly prettier. Planting distance 18 in. apart. Again, if you need eventually to trim the hedge, do it after the spring flowering.

CULINARY

This is one of the most useful of culinary herbs, combining with meat (especially lamb), casseroles, tomato sauces, baked fish, rice, salads, egg dishes, apples, summer wine cups, cordials, vinegars, and oils.

Vegetarian Goulash
Serves 4

2 tablespoons rosemary olive oil
2 medium onions, sliced
1 teaspoon flour
1 tablespoon paprika
1¼ cups hot water mixed
  with 1 teaspoon tomato purée
14-oz. can Italian
  tomatoes
2 4-in. sprigs rosemary
1¼ cups cauliflower sprigs
1¼ cups new carrots, washed
  and cut into chunks
1¼ cups new potatoes,
  washed and cut into halves
½ green capsium, seeded and
  chopped
½ cup sour cream or
  plain yogurt
Salt and freshly ground black
  pepper

Vegetarian Goulash

Preheat the oven to 375°F. Heat the rosemary oil in a flameproof casserole, cook the onion until soft, then stir in the flour and three quarters of the paprika. Cook for 2 minutes. Stir in the water, tomatoes, and rosemary sprigs. Bring to a boil, stirring constantly. Add all the vegetables and the seasonings. Cover and bake for 30–40 minutes. Remove from oven, carefully take out the rosemary sprigs, and stir in the sour cream or yogurt, plus the remaining paprika. Serve with fresh pasta or garlic bread.

OTHER USES

Put rosemary twigs on the barbecue; they give off a delicious aroma. If you have a wood-burning stove, a few twigs thrown onto it makes the house smell lovely.

Rosemary is used in many herbal shampoos and the plant has a reputation as a hair tonic. Use an infusion in the final rinse of a hair wash, especially if you have dark hair, as it will make it shine. (Use chamomile for fair hair.)

Rosemary infusion

MEDICINAL

Like many other essential oils, rosemary oil has antibacterial and antifungal properties, and it helps poor circulation if rubbed into the affected joints.

The oil may be used externally as an insect repellent. It also makes an excellent remedy for headaches if applied directly to the head.

Rosemary tea makes a good mouthwash for halitosis and is also a good antiseptic gargle. Drunk in small amounts it reduces flatulence and stimulates the smooth muscle of the digestive tract and gallbladder and increases the flow of bile.

Put a teaspoon of chopped leaves into a cup and pour boiling water over them; cover and leave it to stand for 5 minutes.

An antiseptic solution of rosemary can be added to the bath to promote healthy skin. Boil a handful in 2 cups of water for 10 minutes.

WARNING

The oil should not be used internally. Extremely large doses of the leaf are toxic, possibly causing convulsions, and can be fatal. Pregnant women should not use it.

Rumex

SORREL

Also known as Bread and Cheese, Sour Leaves, Tom Thumbs, A Thousand Fingers, and Sour Sauce. From the family Polygonaceae.

Sorrel is a native plant of North America, Europe, and Asia. It has naturalized in many countries throughout the world on rich, damp, loamy, acid soils. The generic name, *Rumex*, comes from the Latin *rumo*, "I suck." Apparently, Roman soldiers sucked the leaves to relieve thirst, and their doctors used them as a diuretic.

The name sorrel comes from the old French word *surelle*, meaning "sour." The Tudors considered the herb to be one of the best English vegetables; Henry VIII held it in great esteem. In Lapland, sorrel juice has been used instead of rennet to curdle milk.

Sorrel *Rumex acetosa*

French Sorrel *Rumex scutatus*

SPECIES

Rumex acetosa
Garden Sorrel
Also known as Broad Leafed, Common, and Meadow Sorrel.
Hardy perennial. Ht. 2–4 ft., spread 1 ft. The flowers are small, dull, and inconspicuous; color greenish, turning reddish-brown as the fruit ripens. The mid-green leaves are lance-shaped with 2 basal lobes pointing backward.
Zone 3

Rumex acetosella
Sheep's Sorrel
Hardy perennial. Ht. 6–12 in., spread indefinite (can be very invasive). The flowers are small, dull, and inconspicuous; color greenish, turning brown as the fruit ripens. The mid-green leaves are shaped like a barbed spear. It grows wild on heaths and in grassy places, but is rarely found on chalky soil.
Zone 3

Rumex scutatus
French Sorrel
Also known as Buckler Leaf Sorrel.
Hardy perennial. Ht. 6–18 in., spread 24 in. The flowers are small, dull, and inconspicuous; color greenish, turning brown as the fruit ripens. The mid-green leaves are shaped like squat shields.
Zone 3

CULTIVATION

Propagation
Seed
For an early crop start off under protection in early spring. Sow into prepared seed or plug trays, using the bark-peat potting mix and covering the seeds with perlite. Germination is fairly quick, 10–20 days without extra heat. When the seedlings are large enough and the soil has started to warm up, plant out 12 in. apart.

Division
Sorrel is easy to divide and it is a good idea to divide broad leaf sorrel every other year to keep the leaves succulent. Fall is the best time to do this, replanting in a prepared site.

Pests and Diseases
Slugs and occasionally **leaf miners** attack sorrel, but should cause no problems with established plants. Remove the affected leaves, and put out traps for the slugs.

Maintenance
Spring Sow seed, under protection, in early spring and outdoors from mid-spring.
Summer Cut off flowers to maintain leaf production and prevent self-seeding. In a hot summer, water regularly to keep the leaves succulent.
Fall Divide established plants.
Winter Fully hardy.

Garden Cultivation

This perennial herb likes a rich acid soil that retains moisture in full sun to partial shade. Sow the seeds in late spring into a prepared site. When germinated, thin seedlings out to a distance of 3 in. and finally to a distance of 12 in. apart. Can be grown under cloches to provide leaf throughout the year. The plant tends to run to seed quickly so, to keep the leaves fresh and succulent, remove flower heads as they appear.

In really warm summers or generally warm climates, sorrel leaves tend to become bitter as the season progresses. A mulch will keep the soil cooler and, once the season cools down, the flavor will improve. Grow French sorrel with its smaller leaf, as it is less susceptible.

If sorrel is spreading throughout your garden, simply add some lime to eradicate it. It may need a few applications.

Harvesting

Wear gloves to pick young leaves through-out the growing season for fresh use and for freezing. Sorrel does not dry well.

CONTAINER GROWING

French sorrel makes a good low-growing pot plant. Use the bark-peat mix of potting soil (see p. 591), and make sure the container has room for the plant to spread. It is a very useful culinary herb, so for those with a small garden or who live on an alkaline soil, this makes an ideal container plant. Remember to keep cutting off flowers to keep leaves tender. Water well in the growing season, and feed with liquid fertilizer, especially if you are picking a lot.

French sorrel *Rumex scutatus*

CULINARY

This is an excellent herb with which to experiment. Use sparingly in soups, omelets, fish sauces, and with poultry and pork. It is useful for tenderizing meat. Wrap it around steaks or add pounded leaves to a marinade.

Eat leaves raw in salads, especially French sorrel, but reduce the vinegar or lemon in any accompanying dressing to compensate for the increased acidity.

Cook like spinach, changing the cooking water once to reduce acidity.

A Green Sauce

Wash a handful each of sorrel and lettuce leaves and a handful of watercress. Cook in a little water with a whole peeled onion until tender. Remove the onion and discard. Allow the mushy leaves to cool, then add 1 tablespoon of olive oil, 1 tablespoon of wine vinegar, pepper, and salt. Stir until creamy. Serve with fish or cold poultry.

Sorrel and Lettuce Soup
Serves 4

¹/₂ cup sorrel
¹/₂ cup lettuce
¹/₄ cup flat-leaved parsley
4 tablespoons butter
¹/₂ cup potatoes, peeled and sliced
1 cup chicken stock, heated
4 tablespoons light cream

Wash the sorrel, lettuce, and flat-leaved parsley, pat dry, and roughly chop. Heat the butter in a heavy pan and add the sorrel, lettuce, and parsley. Stew very gently for about 5 minutes, and then add the potato. Mix all together, pour over the heated stock, and simmer covered for 25 minutes. Put in a food processor, or, if you are a purist, through a coarse food mill. Return to the pan and heat gently (do not boil). Swirl in some cream just before serving.

OTHER USES

Sorrel is a good dye plant; with an alum mordant it makes a yellow or green dye.

Use juice of the leaf to remove rust, mold, and ink stains from linen, wicker, and silver.

Sorrel and Lettuce Soup

MEDICINAL

Sorrel is considered to have blood-cleansing and blood-improving qualities in a similar way to spinach, which improves the hemoglobin content of the blood. It also contains vitamin C.

A leaf may be used in a poultice to treat certain skin complaints, including acne.

WARNING

Care has to be taken that sorrel is not used in too great a quantity or too frequently. Its oxalic acid content may damage health if taken in excess. Very large doses are poisonous, causing severe kidney damage.

The herb should not be used medicinally by those predisposed to rheumatism, arthritis, gout, kidney stones, or gastric hyperacidity.

The leaf may cause dermatitis.

Ruta graveolens

RUE

Also known as Herb of Grace and Herbygrass. From the family Rutaceae.

Rue is a native of southern Europe, especially the Mediterranean region, and is found growing in poor, free-draining soil. It has established itself in North America and Australia in similar conditions. It has also adapted to cooler climates and is now naturalized in northern Europe. Rue was known as Herb of Grace, perhaps because it was regarded as a protector against the devil, witchcraft, and magic.

It was also used as an antidote against every kind of poison from toadstools to snakebites. The Romans brought it across northern Europe to Britain, where it did not gain favor until the Middle Ages, when it was one of the herbs carried in nosegays by the rich as protection from evil and the plague. Also, like rosemary, it was placed near the judge before prisoners were brought out, as protection from the pestilence-ridden jails and jail-fever.

It was famous for preserving eyesight and was said to promote second sight, perhaps acting on the third eye. Both Leonardo da Vinci and Michelangelo are supposed to have said that their inner vision had been enhanced by this herb.

SPECIES

CULTIVATION

Propagation
Seed
In spring sow the fine seed using the cardboard trick in prepared plug or seed trays. Use the bark-peat mix of potting soil (see p. 591) and cover with perlite. You may find that a bottom heat of 68°F is helpful. Germination can be an all-or-nothing affair, depending on the source of the seed. Young seedlings are prone to damping-off, so watch the watering, and just keep the compost damp, not wet.

Unlike many variegated plants, the variegated rue will be variegated from seed. When the seedlings are large enough, plant out into a prepared site in the garden at a distance of 18 in.

Cuttings
Take cuttings of new shoots in spring or early summer. Jackman's Blue can only be propagated from cuttings. Use the bark-peat-grit mix of potting soil (see p. 591) for the cuttings; again, do not overwater.

Ruta graveolens
Rue
Hardy evergreen perennial. Ht. and spread 24 in. Yellow, waxy flowers with 4 or 5 petals in summer. Small, rounded, lobed leaves of a green-blue color.
Zone 5

Ruta graveolens 'Jackman's Blue'
Rue Jackman's Blue
Hardy evergreen perennial. Ht. and spread 24 in. Yellow, waxy flowers with 4 or 5 petals in summer. Small, rounded, lobed blue leaves.
Zone 5

Ruta graveolens 'Variegata'
Variegated Rue
Hardy evergreen perennial. Ht. and spread 24 in. Yellow, waxy flowers with 4 or 5 petals in summer. Small, rounded, lobed leaves with a most distinctive cream-white variegation, which is particularly marked in spring, fading in the summer unless the plant is kept well clipped. I have known people mistake the variegation for flowers and try to smell them, which shows how attractive this plant is. Smelling it at close quarters is not, however, a good idea, as this plant, like other rues, can cause the skin to blister.
Zone 6

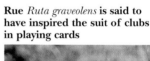

Rue *Ruta graveolens* **is said to have inspired the suit of clubs in playing cards**

Rue Jackman's Blue *Ruta graveolens* 'Jackman's Blue'

WARNING

Handling the plant can cause allergic reactions or phytol-photodermatitis. If you have ever seen a rue burn, it really is quite serious, so do heed this warning.

To minimize this risk, do not take cuttings off the plants either when they are wet after rain or when in full sun, as this is when the plant is at its most dangerous. Wait until the plant has dried out or the sun has gone behind cloud cover; alternatively wear gloves.

Must only be used by medical personnel and not at all by pregnant women, as it is abortive. Large doses are toxic, sometimes precipitating mental confusion, and the oil is capable of causing death.

Pests and Diseases
Rue is prone to **whitefly**, followed by **black sooty mold**. Treat the whitefly with a liquid horticultural soap as soon as the pest appears, following manufacturer's instructions. This should then also control the sooty mold.

Maintenance
Spring Cut back plants to regain shape. Sow seed. Take softwood cuttings.
Summer Cut back after flowering to maintain shape.
Fall The variegated rue is slightly more tender than the other two varieties, so protect when frosts go below 23°F.
Winter Rue is hardy and requires protection only in extreme conditions.

Garden Cultivation
All the rues prefer a sunny site with a well-drained poor soil. They are best positioned away from paths or at the back of beds where people won't brush against them accidentally, especially children, whose skin is more sensitive than adults'. In the spring, and after flowering in the summer (not fall), cut back all the plants to maintain shape, and the variegated form to maintain variegations.

Harvesting
Pick leaves for use fresh when required. No need to preserve.

CONTAINER GROWING

Rue can be grown in containers; use the bark-peat-grit mix of potting soil. Again, position the container carefully so that one does not accidentally brush the leaves. Although it is a drought-tolerant plant, in containers it prefers to be watered regularly in summer. Allow to dry in winter, watering only once a month. Feed plants in the spring with liquid fertilizer, following the manufacturer's instructions.

MEDICINAL

This ancient medicinal herb is used in the treatment of strained eyes and headaches caused by eye strain. It is also useful for nervous headaches and heart palpitations, for treating high blood pressure, and helping to harden the bones and teeth. The anti-spasmodic action of its oil and the alkaloids explains its use in the treatment of nervous digestion and colic. The tea also expels worms.

Variegated rue *Ruta graveolens* 'Variegata'

Rue tea

CULINARY

I seriously cannot believe that people enjoy eating this herb; it is incredibly bitter.

"How can a man grow old who has sage in his garden?"
—Ancient proverb

Salvia

SAGE

From the family Lamiaceae.

This large family of over 750 species is widely distributed throughout the world. It consists of annuals, biennials, and perennials, herbs, subshrubs, and shrubs of various habits. It is an important horticultural group. I have concentrated on the medicinal, culinary, and a special aromatic species.

The name Salvia is derived from the Latin *salveo,* meaning "I save or heal," because some species have been highly regarded medicinally.

The Greeks used it to heal ulcers, consumption, and snakebites. The Romans considered it a sacred herb to be gathered with ceremony. A special knife was used, not made of iron because sage reacts with iron salts. The sage gatherer had to wear clean clothes, have clean feet, and make a sacrifice of food before the ceremony could begin. Sage was held to be good for the brain, the senses, and memory. It also made a good gargle and mouthwash and was used as a toothpaste.

There are many stories about why the Chinese valued it so highly, and in the seventeenth century Dutch merchants found that the Chinese would trade three chests of China tea for one of sage leaves.

Above: **Sage** *Salvia officinalis*

Right: **Purple sage** *Salvia officinalis* 'Purpurascens'

SPECIES

I have chosen only a very few species to illustrate; they are the main ones used in cooking and medicine—with one exception, with which I begin.

Salvia elegans 'Scarlet Pineapple' *(rutilans)*
Pineapple Sage
Half-hardy perennial. Ht. 3 ft., spread 2 ft. Striking red flowers, early fall. The leaves are green with a slight red tinge to the edges and have a glorious pineapple scent. In temperate climates it is basically a houseplant and if kept on a sunny windowsill can be used throughout the year. It can only be grown from cuttings. This is an odd sage to cook with; it does not taste as good as it smells. It is fairly good combined with apricots as a stuffing for pork, otherwise my culinary experiments with it have not met with great success.
Zone 8

Salvia lavandulifolia
Narrowed-Leaved Sage
Also known as Spanish Sage. Hardy evergreen perennial. Ht. and spread 18 in. Attractive blue flowers in summer. The leaves are green with a texture, small, thin, and oval in shape, and highly aromatic. This is an excellent sage to cook with, very pungent. It also makes a good tea. Can only be grown from cuttings.
Zone 5

Salvia officinalis
Sage
Also known as Common Sage, Garden Sage. Hardy evergreen perennial. Ht. and spread 2 ft. Mauve-blue flowers in summer. The leaves are green with a texture, thin and oval in shape, and highly aromatic. This is the best known sage for culinary use. Can be easily grown from seed. There is also a white flowering sage *Salvia officinalis* 'Albiflora,' which is quite rare.
Zone 5

Salvia officinalis broad-leaved *(latifolia)*
Broad-Leaved Sage
Hardy evergreen perennial. Ht. and spread 2 ft. Very rarely flowers in cool climates, if it does they are blue-mauve in color. The leaves are green with a texture, larger than the ordinary sage, with an oval shape and highly aromatic. Good for cooking. Can only be grown from cuttings.
Zone 6

Salvia officinalis 'Icterina'
Gold Sage
Hardy evergreen perennial. Ht. 18 in., spread 30 in. Very rarely flowers in cool climates, if it does they are blue-mauve in color. The leaves are green-gold variegated with a texture, small and oval in shape and aromatic. A mild flavor but equally good to cook with. Can only be grown from cuttings.
Zone 8

Clary sage *Salvia sclarea*

Salvia sclarea
Clary Sage
Hardy biennial. Ht. 2–3 ft., spread 18 in. Colorful flower bracts—blue-purple-lilac with a whitish base in summer. Leaves are often 8–9 in. long, soft green in color, and slightly wrinkled. Easily grown from seed. There is another variety, *Salvia sclarea* var. *turkestanica*, with white flowers tinged with pink.
Zone 4

Salvia officinalis 'Purpurascens'
Purple/Red Sage
Tender evergreen perennial. Ht. and spread 28 in. Mauve-blue flowers in summer. The leaves are purple with a texture, a thin oval shape, and aromatic. Two points to think about: If you clip it in the spring, it develops new leaves and looks really good but flowers only a small amount. If you do not clip it and allow it to flower it goes woody. If you then cut it back it does not produce new growth until the spring, so can look a bit bare. So what to do? There is also a variegated form of this purple sage *Salvia officinalis* 'Purpurascens Variegata.' Both of these can only be grown from cuttings.
Zone 8

Salvia officinalis 'Tricolor'
Tricolor Sage
Tender evergreen perennial. Ht. and spread 16 in. Attractive blue flowers in summer. Leaves are green with pink, white, and purple variegation, with a texture. They are small, thin, and highly aromatic. It has a mild flavor, so can be used in cooking. Can only be grown from cuttings.
Zone 8

CULTIVATION

Propagation
Seed
Common and clary sage grow successfully in the spring from seed sown into prepared seed or plug trays and covered with perlite. The seeds are a good size. If starting off under protection in early spring, warmth is of benefit—temperatures of 60–70°F. Germination takes 2–3 weeks. Pot or plant out when the frosts are over at a distance of 18–24 in. apart.

Cuttings
This is a good method for all variegated species and those that do not set seed in cooler climates. Use the bark-peat mix of potting soil (see p. 591).
Softwood: Take these cuttings in late spring or early summer from the strong new growth. All forms take easily from cuttings; rooting is about four weeks in summer.
Layering: If you have a well-established sage, or if it is becoming a bit woody, layer established branches in spring or fall.

Pests and Diseases
Sage grown in the garden does not suffer much from pests and disease. Sage grown in containers, especially pineapple sage, is prone to **red spider mite**. As soon as you see this pest, treat with a liquid horticultural soap as per the instructions. Plants in damp, heavy soils are subject to **root rots** and often die out in cold winters.

Maintenance
Spring Sow seeds. Trim if needed, and then take softwood cuttings.
Summer Trim back after flowering.
Fall Protect all half-hardy sages, and first-year plants.
Winter Protect plants if they are needed for fresh leaves.

Purple sage *Salvia officinalis* Purpurascens Group and **Gold sage** *Salvia officinalis* 'Icterina'

Garden Cultivation
Sage, although predominantly a Mediterranean plant, is sufficiently hardy to withstand Zone 5 winter without protection, as long as the soil is well drained and not acid, and the site is as warm and dry as possible. The flavor of the leaf can vary as to how rich, damp, etc, the soil is. If wishing to sow seed outside, wait until there is no threat of frost and sow directly into prepared ground, spacing the seeds 9 in. apart. After germination thin to 18 in. apart. For the first winter cover the young plants with frost fabric or a mulch.

To keep the plants bushy prune in the spring to encourage young shoots for strong flavor, and also after flowering in late summer. Mature plants can be pruned hard in the spring after some cuttings have been taken as insurance. Never prune in the fall as this can kill the plant. As sage is prone to becoming woody, replace the plant every four to five years.

Sage bianco *Salvia blancoana* **has a silvery leaf and prostrate habit**

Harvesting

Since sage is an evergreen plant, the leaves can be used fresh any time of the year. In Mediterranean-type climates, including the southern U.S., the leaves can be harvested during the winter months. In cooler climates this is also possible if you cover a chosen bush with frost fabric, as this will keep the leaves in better condition. They dry well, but care should be taken to keep their green color. Because this herb is frequently seen in its dried condition people assume it is easy to dry. But beware, although other herbs may lose some of their aroma or qualities if badly dried or handled, sage seems to pick up a musty scent and a flavor really horrible to taste—better to grow it in your garden to use fresh.

CONTAINER GROWING

All sages grow happily in containers. Pineapple sage is an obvious one as it is tender, but a better reason is that if it is at hand one will rub the leaves and smell that marvelous pineapple scent. Use the bark-peat-grit mix of potting soil (see p. 591) for all varieties, feed the plants after flowering, and do not overwater.

Tricolor Sage *Salvia officinalis* 'Tricolor'

COMPANION PLANTING

Sage planted with cabbages is said to repel cabbage white butterflies. Planted next to vines it is generally beneficial.

OTHER USES

The dried leaves, especially those of pineapple sage, are good added to potpourris.

MEDICINAL

For centuries, sage has been esteemed for its healing powers. It is a first-rate remedy as a hot infusion for colds. Sage tea combined with a little cider vinegar makes an excellent gargle for sore throats, laryngitis, and tonsillitis. It is also beneficial for infected gums and mouth ulcers.

The essential oil, known as sage clary or muscatel oil, is obtained by steamed distillation of the fresh or partially dried flower stems and leaves. It is used widely in toilet waters, perfumes, and soap, and to flavor wine, vermouth, and liqueurs.

CULINARY

This powerful healing plant is also a strong culinary herb, although it has been misused and misjudged in the culinary world. Used with discretion it adds a lovely flavor, aids digestion of fatty food, and being an antiseptic it kills off any bugs in the meat as it cooks. It has long been used with sausages because of its preservative qualities. It also makes a delicious herb jelly, or oil or vinegar. But I like using small amounts fresh. The original form of the following recipe comes from a vegetarian friend of mine. I fell in love with it and have subsequently adapted it to include some other herbs.

Hazelnut and Mushroom Roast
Serves 4

A little sage oil
²/₃ cup long-grain brown rice
1¹/₄ cups boiling water
1 teaspoon salt
1 large onion, peeled and chopped
¹/₄–¹/₂ cup mushrooms, wiped and chopped
2 medium carrots, peeled and roughly grated
¹/₂ teaspoon coriander seed
1 tablespoon soy sauce
¹/₂ cup bread crumbs
1¹/₄ cups ground hazelnuts
1 teaspoon chopped sage leaves
1 teaspoon chopped lovage leaves
Sunflower seeds for decoration
A 2-lb. loaf tin, lined with waxed paper

Preheat the oven to 350°F.
Heat 1 teaspoon of sage oil in a small saucepan and toss the rice in it to give it a coating of oil. Add boiling water and the teaspoon of salt. Stir, and let the rice cook slowly for roughly 40 minutes or until the liquid has been absorbed.

While the rice is cooking, heat 1 tablespoon of sage oil in a medium-sized frying-pan, add the onion, mushrooms, carrots, ground coriander seed, and soy sauce. Mix them together and let them cook for about 10 minutes.

Combine the cooked brown rice, bread crumbs, hazelnuts, sage, and lovage; mix with the vegetables and place the mixture in the prepared loaf tin. Scatter the sunflower seeds on top and bake in the oven for 45 minutes. Leave to cool slightly in the tin. Slice and serve with a homemade tomato sauce and a green salad.

Broad-leaved sage *Salvia officinalis* broad-leaved

WARNING

Extended or excessive use of sage can cause symptoms of poisoning. Although the herb seems safe and common, if you drink the tea for more than a week or two at a time, its strong antiseptic properties can cause potentially toxic effects.

Sambucus

ELDER

Also known as Boun-tree, Boon-tree, Dogtree, Judas Tree, Scores, Score Tree, God's Stinking Tree, Black Elder, Blackberried, European Elder, Ellhorne, and German Elder. From the family Caprifoliaceae.

Elder grows worldwide throughout temperate climates. Its common name is probably derived from the Anglo Saxon *Ellaern* or *Aeld*, which mean "fire" or "kindle," because the hollow stems were once used for getting fires going. The generic name, *Sambucus*, dates from Ancient Greek times and may originally have referred to *sambuke*, a kind of harp made of elderwood. Pipes were made from its branches too, possibly the original Pan pipes. People thought that if you put it on the fire you would see the devil. They believed it unlucky to make cradle rockers out of it, that the spirit of the tree might harm the child. Again, farmers were unwilling to use an elder switch to drive cattle and one folktale had it that elder would only grow where blood had been shed. Planting it outside the back door was a sure way of protecting against evil, black magic, and keeping witches out of the house, which would never be struck by lightning. It was thought that Christ's cross was made of elderwood.

Common elder
Sambucus nigra

Red elder *Sambucus racemosa*

SPECIES

Sambucus canadensis
American Elder
Deciduous hardy shrub. Ht. 5–12 ft. Numerous small white flowers in flat cymes throughout summer. Berries are dark purple in early fall; its compound leaves have long, sharply toothed and bright green leaflets.
Zone 3

Sambucus canadensis 'Aurea'
Golden American Elder
Deciduous hardy shrub. Ht. and spread 12 ft. Creamy white flowers in summer, red fruits in early fall. Large golden yellow leaves.
Zone 3

Warning: All parts of the fresh plant of *Sambucus canadensis* can poison. Children have been poisoned by chewing or sucking the bark. The berries are safe only after being cooked, as are the seeds inside the berries. Always cook berries first.

Sambucus ebulus
Dwarf Elder
Also known as Blood Elder, Danewort, Wild Elder, Walewort.
Deciduous hardy shrub. Ht. 2–4 ft., spread 3 ft. White flowers with pink tips in summer. Black berries in early fall. Its green leaves are oblong, lance-shaped, and toothed around the edges. Dwarf elder grows in small clusters in eastern and central states and in Europe.
Warning: All parts of the plant are slightly poisonous and children should be warned not to eat the bitter berries. It has a much stronger action than its close relative, common elder *(S. nigra)*. Large doses cause vertigo, vomiting, and diarrhea, the latter denoted colloquially as "the Danes," being the origin of Danewort. Nowadays dwarf elder is rarely used and should be taken internally only under strict medical supervision.

Sambucus nigra
Common Elder
Also known as European Elder.
Deciduous hardy shrub. Ht. 20–23 ft., spread 15 ft. Spreading branches bear flat heads of small, star-shaped, creamy white flowers in late spring and early summer. These are followed in early fall by drooping branches of purplish-black juicy berries. The flowers and berries are used in industry for cosmetics, jams, jellies, and liqueurs. The leaves are purgative and should not be taken internally; decoctions have an insecticidal effect. The wood from the adult plant is highly prized by craftsmen.
Zone 5

Sambucus nigra 'Aurea'
Golden Elder
Deciduous shrub. Ht. and spread 20 ft. Flattened heads of fragrant, star-shaped, creamy white flowers from early to mid-summer. Black fruits in early fall. Golden yellow, oval, sharply toothed leaflets.
Zone 5

Sambucus racemosa
Red Elder
Deciduous hardy shrub. Ht. and spread 10–13 ft. Brown bark and pale brown pith. Flowers arranged in dense terminal panicles of yellowish cream. 'Racemosa' refers to the flower clusters. The fruits are also distinct in being red in drooping clusters. It rarely fruits freely. Red-berried elder is native to central and southern Europe. It has naturalized in Scotland, the northern U.S., and Canada. The fully ripe fruits are used medicinally. Bitter tasting, they may be used fresh or dried, and are high in vitamin C, essential oil, sugar, and pectins. Fruits are a laxative and the leaves are a diuretic. This is the most edible and tasty of the elders.
Caution: The seeds inside the berries are poisonous before being cooked.
Zone 3

CULTIVATION

Propagation
Seed
Sow ripe berries 1 in. deep in a pot outdoors. Plant seedlings in semishade in the garden when large enough to handle.

Cuttings
Take semihardwood cuttings in summer from the new growth. Use the bark-peat-grit mix of potting soil (see p. 591) and winter these cuttings in a cold frame or cold greenhouse. When rooted, either pot on or plant out into a prepared site 12 in. apart.
Take hardwood cuttings of bare shoots in fall and replant in the garden 12 in. apart. The following fall lift and replant.

Pests and Diseases
Rarely suffers from pests or diseases.

Maintenance
Spring Prune back golden and variegated elders.
Summer Take semiripe cuttings.
Fall Take hardwood cuttings. Prune back hard.
Winter Established plants do not need protection.

Garden Cultivation
Elder tolerates most soils and *S. nigra* is very good for alkaline sites. They all prefer a sunny position.
Elder grows very rapidly indeed and self-sows freely to produce new shoots 4 ft. long in one season. It is short-lived.
It is important to dominate elder otherwise it will take over your garden. Cut back in late fall, unless it is gold or variegated, when it should be pruned in early spring before growth begins.

Harvesting
Handle flower heads carefully to prevent bruising; spread out to dry with heads down on a fine net without touching one another. Pick the fruits in fall, as they ripen, when they become shiny and violet.

CONTAINER GROWING
Golden varieties of elder can look good in containers, as long as the containers are large enough and positioned to give the plants some shade, to keep the leaves from scorching. Use a soil-based compost. Keep well watered and feed with a liquid fertilizer.

CULINARY

Warning: Berries should not be eaten raw, and the fresh juice should not be used. Be sure to cook first.

Elderflower Cordial
Pick flowers on a dry sunny day, as the yeast is mainly in the pollen.

4 quarts of water
3 cups sugar
Juice and thinly peeled rind of 1 lemon
2 tablespoons of cider or wine vinegar
12 elderflower heads

Bring the water to a boil and pour into a sterilized container. Add the sugar, stirring until dissolved. When cool add the lemon juice and rind, the vinegar, and the elderflowers. Cover with several layers of muslin and leave for 24 hours. Filter through muslin into strong glass bottles. This drink is ready after 2 weeks. Serve chilled.

OTHER USES
Elderflower water whitens and softens the skin and removes freckles.
The fruits make a lavender or violet dye when combined with alum.

Elderflower sorbet

MEDICINAL

Elderflowers reduce bronchial and upper respiratory catarrh and are used in the treatment of hay fever. Externally a cold infusion of the flowers may be used as an eye wash for conjunctivitis and as a compress for chilblains. A gargle made from elderflower infusion or elderflower vinegar alleviates tonsillitis and sore throats. Elderflowers have a mild laxative action and in Europe have a reputation for treating rheumatism and gout. The berries are a mild laxative and sweat inducing. "Elderberry Rob" is traditionally made by simmering the berries and thickening with sugar as a winter cordial for coughs and colds.

Elderberry Conserve
(for neuralgia and migraine)

2 cups elderberries
2½ cups sugar

Boil the elderberries with the least quantity of water to produce a pulp. Pass through a sieve and simmer the juice gently to remove most of the water. Add the sugar and stir constantly until the consistency of a conserve is produced. Pour into a suitable container. Take two tablespoons as required.

Sanguisorba minor

SALAD BURNET

Also known as Drumsticks, Old Man's Pepper, and Poor Man's Pepper. From the family Rosaceae.

This herb is a native of Europe and Asia. It has been introduced and naturalized in many places elsewhere in the world, especially the United States and Britain. Popular for both its medicinal and culinary properties, it was taken to New England by the Pilgrims. It is found in dry, free-draining soil in grassland and on the edges of woodland. The name *Sanguisorba* comes from *sanguis*, meaning "blood," and *sorbere*, meaning "to soak up." It is an ancient herb, which has been grown in this country since the 16th century. Traditionally it was used to staunch wounds. In Tudor times salad burnet was planted along borders of garden paths so the scent would rise up when walked upon.

SPECIES

Sanguisorba minor
Salad Burnet
Evergreen hardy perennial. Ht. 8–24 in., spread 12 in. Produces small spikes of dark crimson flowers in summer. Its soft mid-green leaves are divided into oval leaflets.
Zone 4

Sanguisorba officinalis
Great Burnet
Also known as Drumsticks, Maidens Hairs, Red Knobs, and Redheads.
Perennial. Ht. up to 4 ft., spread 2 ft. Produces small spikes of dark crimson flowers in summer. Its mid-green leaves are divided into oval leaflets.
Zone 4

Salad burnet
Sanguisorba minor

CULTIVATION

Propagation
Seed
Sow the small, flatish seed in spring or fall into prepared seed or plug trays and cover the seeds with perlite; no need for extra heat. If sown in the fall, winter the seedlings under protection and plant out in spring to a prepared site, 12 in. apart. If spring-sown, allow to harden off and plant out in the same way. As an edging plant it should be planted at a distance of 8 in. apart.

Division
It divides very easily. Dig up an established plant in the early fall, cut back any excessive leaves, divide the plant, and replant in a prepared site in the garden.

Pests and Diseases
This herb is mainly free from pests and diseases.

Maintenance
Spring Sow seeds.
Summer Keep cutting to keep it from flowering, if being used for culinary purposes.
Fall Sow seeds if necessary.

Divide established plants.
Winter No protection
needed; fully hardy.

Garden Cultivation

This is a most attractive, soft-
leaf evergreen and is very
useful in both kitchen and
garden. That it is evergreen
is a particular plus for the
herb garden, where it looks
most effective as an edging
plant. It also looks good in a
wild flower garden, where it
grows as happily as in its
original grassland habitat.

The art with this plant is
to keep cutting, which stops
it flowering and encourages
lots of new growth.

With no special require-
ments, it prefers alkaline
soil, but it will tolerate any
well-drained soil in sun or
light shade. It cannot take
extreme summer heat.

Harvesting

Pick young tender leaves
when required. Not
necessary to dry leaves
(which in any case do not
dry well), as fresh leaves can
be harvested all year round.

CONTAINER GROWING

Salad burnet will grow in
containers and will provide
an excellent source of soft
evergreen leaves throughout
winter for those with no
garden. Use a soil-based
potting mix. Water regularly,
but not too frequently; feed
with liquid fertilizer in the
spring only. Do not
overfeed, otherwise the leaf
will soften and lose its cool
cucumber flavor, becoming
more like a spinach. For
regular use the plant should
not be allowed to flower.
Cut back constantly to about
6 in. to ensure a continuing
supply of tender new leaves.

CULINARY

Leaves have a nutty flavor
and a slight taste of
cucumber. The young leaves
are refreshing in salads and
can be used generously—
they certainly enhance
winter salads. Tender young
leaves can also be added to
soups, cold drinks, cream
cheeses, or used (like
parsley) as a garnish or to
flavor casseroles—add at the
beginning of cooking. The
leaves also make an
interesting herbal vinegar.

Salad burnet combines
with other herbs, especially
rosemary and tarragon.
Serve in a sauce with
white fish.

Salad burnet *Sanguisorba minor*

OTHER USES

Because of its high tannin
content, the root of great
burnet can be used in the
tanning of leather.

WARNING

Great burnet should never
be taken in large doses.

This recipe is for an herb
butter, which is lovely with
broiled fish, either cooked
under the grill or on the
barbecue, and gives a
cucumber flavor to the
butter.

1½ tablespoons chopped
*   salad burnet*
1 tablespoon chopped garden
*   mint (spearmint)*
6 tablespoons butter
Salt and black pepper
Lemon juice

Mix the chopped herb
leaves together. Melt the
butter in a saucepan, add
the herbs, and simmer over
very low heat for 10
minutes. Season the sauce
to taste with salt and pepper,
and a squeeze (no more)
of lemon. Pour over
broiled fish.

Salad burnet butter

MEDICINAL

Chewing the leaf assists
digestion. An infusion of
the whole plant is used
for treating hemorrhoids
and diarrhea.

Santolina

SANTOLINA

Also known as Cotton Lavender and French Lavender. From the family Asteraceae.

Santolina chamaecyparissus
Gray Santolina
Half-hardy evergreen shrub.
Ht. 2.5 ft., spread 3 ft.
Yellow button flowers from
midsummer to early fall,
silver coral-like
aromatic foliage.
Zone 7

Santolina is a native of southern France and the northern Mediterranean area, where it grows wild in calcium-rich ground. It is widely cultivated, adapting to warm-to-hot regions of North America and the full spectrum of European and Australian climates, surviving even an eastern Canadian winter on well-drained soil.

The Greeks knew santolina as *abrotonon* and the Romans as *habrotanum,* both names referring to the treelike shape of the branches. It was used medicinally for many centuries by the Arabs. And it was valued in medieval England as an insect and moth repellent and as a cure for intestinal worms.

The plant was probably brought into Britain in the 16th century by French Huguenot gardeners, who were skilled in creating the knot garden so popular among the Elizabethans. Santolina was used largely in low clipped hedges, and as edging for the geometrical beds.

Green santolina Rosmarinifolia
Santolina rosmarinifolia subsp.
rosmarinifolia

Gray santolina
Santolina chamaecyparissus

***Santolina chamaecyparissus* 'Lemon Queen'**
Santolina 'Lemon Queen'
As 'Edward Bowles,' but
with feathery, deep-cut,
gray foliage.
Zone 7

***Santolina pinnata* subsp. *neapolitana* 'Edward Bowles'**
Santolina
Hardy evergreen perennial.
Ht. 2.5 ft., spread 3 ft.
Cream button flowers in
summer. Feathery, deep-cut,
gray-green foliage.
Zone 7

Santolina 'Lemon Queen'
Santolina chamaecyparissus
'Lemon Queen'

Santolina pinnata subsp. neapolitana
Santolina 'Neopolitana'
As 'Edward Bowles.'
Zone 7

Santolina rosmarinifolia subsp. rosmarinifolia 'Primrose Gem'
Green Santolina
Hardy evergreen shrub. Ht. 2 ft., spread 3 ft. Pale yellow button flowers in summer. Finely cut green leaves.
Zone 6

Santolina rosmarinifolia subsp. rosmarinifolia
As 'Primrose Gem.' Bright yellow button flowers in summer. Finely cut, bright green leaves.
Zone 6

Santolina.rosmarinifolia subsp. *rosmarinifolia* Green santolina

CULTIVATION

Propagation
Seed
Although seed is now available, it is erratic and not worth the effort as germination is poor.

Cuttings
Take 2–3 in. soft stem cuttings in spring before flowering, or take semiripe stem cuttings from mid-summer to autumn. They root easily without the use of any rooting compound.

Pests and Diseases
Compost or soil that is too rich will attract **aphids**.

Maintenance
Spring Cut straggly old plants hard back. Take cuttings from new growth.
Summer I cannot stress enough that after flowering the plants should be cut back or the bushes will open up and lose their attractive shape.
Autumn Take semiripe cuttings and protect them from frost in a cold frame or greenhouse.
Winter Protect in only the severest of winters.

Garden Cultivation
This elegant, aromatic evergreen is ideal for the herb garden as a hedging or specimen plant in its own right. Plant in full sun, preferably in sandy soil. If the soil is too rich the growth will become soft and lose color. This is particularly noticeable with the silver varieties.
   Planting distance for an individual plant 18–24 in., for a hedging 12–15 in. Hedges need regular clipping to shape in spring and summer. Do not cut back in the autumn in frosty climates, as this can easily kill the plants. If temperatures drop below

5°F protect with frost fabric or a layer of straw, spruce, or bracken.

Harvesting
Pick leaves and dry anytime before flowering. Pick small bunches of flower stems for drying, in late summer. They can be dried easily by hanging the bunches upside down in a dry, airy place.

CONTAINER GROWING

Santolina cannot be grown indoors; however as a patio plant, a single plant clipped to shape in a large terra-cotta pot can look very striking. Use a bark-peat potting mix (see p. 591). Place pot in full sun. Do not overfeed with liquid fertilizer or growth will be too soft.

CULINARY

Not used in cooking.

MEDICINAL

Although not used much nowadays, it can be applied to surface wounds, hastening the healing process by encouraging scar formation. Finely ground leaves ease the pain of

OTHER USES
Lay in drawers, under carpets, and in closets to deter moths and other insects, or make a herbal moth bag.

Herbal Moth Bag

A handful of wormwood
A handful of spearmint
A handful of santolina
A handful of rosemary
1 tablespoon of crushed coriander

Dry and crumble the ingredients, mix together, and put in a muslin or cotton bag.

Saponaria officinalis

SOAPWORT

Also known as Bouncing Bet, Bruisewort, Farewell Summer, Fuller's Herb, Joe Run by the Street, Hedge Pink. Dog's Clove, Old Maid's Pink, and Soaproot. From the family Caryophyllaceae.

Soapwort, widespread on poor soils in North America, Europe, and Asia, was used by medieval Arab physicians for various skin complaints. Fullers used soapwort for soaping cloth before it went on the stamps at the mill, and sheep were washed with a mixture of the leaves, roots, and water before being shorn.

SPECIES

Saponaria officinalis
Soapwort
Hardy perennial. Ht. 1–3 ft., spread 2 ft. or more. Compact cluster of small pretty pink or white flowers in summer to early fall. The leaf is smooth, oval, pointed, and mid-green in color.
Zone 3

Saponaria officinalis 'Rubra Plena'
Double-Flowered Soapwort
Hardy perennial. Ht. 3 ft., spread 1 ft. Clusters of red, ragged, double flowers in summer. The leaves are mid-green and oval in shape.
Zone 3

Saponaria ocymoides
Soapwort
Hardy perennial. Ht. 1–3 in., spread 16 in. or more. Profusion of tiny, flat, pale pink-crimson flowers in summer. Compact or loose sprawling mats of hairy oval leaves. **Zone 4**

CULTIVATION

Propagation
Seed
Soapwort can be grown from seed. Sow in fall into prepared seed or plug trays and cover with potting soil. Place glass over container and leave outside over winter. Germination usually takes place in spring, but can be erratic. When large enough, plant 24 in. apart.

Cuttings
Softwood cuttings of the nonflowering shoots can be taken from late spring to early summer.

Division
The creeping rootstock is easy to divide in the fall.

Garden Cultivation
Plant it in a sunny spot, in a well-drained, poor soil; rich garden soil makes its already undisciplined habit impossible. Soapwort can become very invasive. Do not plant soapwort around fish ponds because sap onions from the roots can stun fish.

Pests and Diseases
Soapwort is largely free from pests and disease.

Maintenance
Spring Take cuttings.
Summer Cut back after flowering to encourage a second flowering and to prevent self-seeding.
Fall Divide established plants. Sow seed.
Winter Fully hardy.

Harvesting
Pick the leaves when required. Dig up the roots in the fall and dry for medicinal use.

CONTAINER GROWING

S. ocymoides is the best species for container growing. Use a soil-based compost. Water well during the growing season, but only feed twice. In winter keep in a cold greenhouse with minimum watering.

MEDICINAL

It has been used not only for treating skin conditions such as eczema, cold sores, boils, and acne, but also for gout and rheumatism.

OTHER USES

The gentle power of the saponins in soapwort makes the following shampoo ideal for upholstery and delicate fibers.

Soapwort Shampoo
½ oz. dried soapwort root or two large handfuls of whole fresh stems
3 cups of water

Crush the root with a rolling pin or roughly chop the fresh stems. If using dried soapwort, prepare by soaking first overnight. Put the soapwort into an enamel pan with water and bring to a boil, cover, and simmer for 20 minutes, stirring occasionally. Allow to stand until cool and strain through a fine sieve.

WARNING

Do not take internally. It must be prescribed by a qualified herbalist because of the high saponin content, which makes it mildly poisonous.

Satureja (Satureia)

SAVORY

From the family Lamiaceae.

Savory is a native of southern Europe and North Africa, especially around the Mediterranean. It grows in well-drained soils and has adapted worldwide to similar climatic conditions. Savory has been employed in food flavoring for over 2,000 years. Romans added it to sauces and vinegars, which they used liberally as flavoring. (The Ancient Egyptians, on the other hand, used it in love potions.) The Romans also included it in their wagon train to northern Europe, where it became an invaluable disinfectant strewing herb. It was used to relieve tired eyes, for ringing in the ears, indigestion, wasp and bee stings, and for other shocks to the system.

Winter savory *Satureja montana*

SPECIES

Summer savory
Satureja hortensis

Satureja hortensis
Summer Savory
Also known as Bean Herb. Half-hardy annual. Ht 8–12 in., spread 6 in. Small white-mauve flowers in summer. Aromatic leaves, oblong, pointed, and green. A favorite in America, where it is known as the bean herb. It has become widely used in bean dishes as it helps prevent flatulence.
All zones

Satureja coerulea
Purple-Flowered Savory
Semi-evergreen hardy perennial. Ht. 12 in., spread 8 in. Small purple flowers in summer. The leaves are darkish green, linear and very aromatic.
Zone 6

Satureja montana
Winter Savory
Also called Mountain Savory. Semievergreen hardy perennial. Ht. 12 in., spread 8 in. Small white-pink flowers in summer. The leaves are dark green, linear, and very aromatic.
Zone 5

Satureja spicigera
Creeping Savory
Perennial. Ht. 3 in., spread 12 in. Masses of small white flowers in summer. The leaves are lime green and linear. This is a most attractive plant.
Zone 5

CULTIVATION

Propagation
Seed
Only summer and winter savory can be grown from seed, which is tiny, so it is best to sow into prepared seed trays under protection in the early spring, using the cardboard method (see p. 591). The seeds should not be covered as they need light to germinate. Germination takes about 10–15 days—no need to use bottom heat. When the seedlings are large enough, and after a period of hardening off (making quite sure that the frosts have finished), they can be planted out into a prepared site in the garden, 6 in. apart.

Cuttings
Creeping, purple-flowered, and winter savory can all be grown from softwood cuttings in spring, using a bark-peat-grit potting soil (see p. 591). When these have rooted they should be planted out—12 in. apart for creeping savory, 6 in. apart for the others.

Division
Creeping savory can be divided, as each section has its own root system similar to creeping thymes. Dig up an established plant in the spring after the frosts have finished and divide into as many segments as you require. Minimum size is only dependent on each having a root system and how long you are prepared to wait for new plants to become established. Replant in a prepared site.

Pests and Diseases

Being an aromatic plant savory is mostly free from pests and disease.

Maintenance

Spring Sow seed. Take softwood cuttings. Divide established plants.
Summer Keep picking and do not allow summer savory to flower, if you want to maintain its flavor.
Fall Protect from prolonged frosts.
Winter Protect.

Garden Cultivation

All the savories mentioned here like full sun and a poor, well-drained soil. Plant summer savory in the garden in a warm, sheltered spot and keep picking the leaves to keep it from getting leggy. Do not feed with liquid fertilizer, otherwise the plant will keel over.

Winter savory can make a good edging plant and is very pretty in the summer, although it can look a bit sparse in the winter months. Again, trim it from time to time to maintain shape and promote new growth. Creeping savory does not like cold wet winters, or for that matter clay soil, so on this nursery I grow it in a pot (see below). If, however, you wish to grow it in your garden, plant it in a sunny rockery or a well-drained, sheltered corner.

Harvesting

For fresh use, pick leaves as required. For drying, pick those of summer savory before it flowers. They dry easily.

CONTAINER GROWING

All savories can be grown in containers, and if your garden suffers from prolonged cold, wet winters

Savory is an important ingredient in salami

it may be the only way you can grow this delightful plant successfully. Use the bark-peat-grit mix of potting soil. Pick the plants continuously to maintain shape, especially the summer savory, which can get straggly. If you are picking the plants a lot they may benefit from a feed of liquid fertilizer, but keep this to a minimum as they get overeager when fed.

Summer savory, being an annual, dies in winter; creeping savory dies back; the winter savory is a partial evergreen. So, the latter two will need protection in winter. Place them in a cool greenhouse or conservatory. If the container cannot be moved, wrap it up in paper or frost fabric. Keep watering to the absolute minimum.

MEDICINAL

Summer savory is credited with medicinal virtues and is said to alleviate the pain of bee stings if rubbed on the affected spot. Infuse as a tea to stimulate appetite and to ease indigestion and flatulence. It is considered a stimulant and was once in demand as an aphrodisiac.

Winter savory is also used medicinally but is inferior.

CULINARY

The two savories used in cooking are winter and summer savory. The other varieties are edible but their flavor is inferior. Summer and winter savory combine well with vegetables, pulses, and rich meats. These herbs stimulate the appetite and aid digestion. The flavor is hot and peppery, and so should be added sparingly in salads.

Summer savory can replace salt and pepper and is a great help to those on a salt-free diet. It is a pungent herb and until one is familiar with its strength, it should be used carefully. It also makes a good vinegar and oil. The oil is used commercially as a flavoring, as is the leaf, which is an important ingredient in salami.

The flavor of winter savory is both coarser and stronger; its advantage is that it provides fresh leaves into early winter.

Beans with Garlic and Savory
Serves 3–4

1 cup dried haricot beans
1 Spanish onion, peeled
1 carrot, scrubbed and roughly sliced
1 stick celery
3 tablespoons olive oil
1 tablespoon white wine vinegar
1 clove garlic, crushed
2 tablespoons chopped summer savory
2 tablespoons chopped flat-leaved parsley

Soak the beans in cold water overnight or for at least 3–4 hours. Drain them and put them in a saucepan with plenty of water. Bring to a boil slowly. Add half the peeled onion, the carrot and celery, and cook until tender. As soon as the beans are soft, drain and discard the vegetables. Mix the oil, vinegar, and crushed garlic. While the beans are still hot, stir in the remaining half onion (thinly sliced), the chopped herbs, and pour over the oil and vinegar dressing. Serve soon after cooling. Do not chill.

Beans with Garlic and Savory

Skullcap
Scutellaria galericulata

Scutellaria

Virginian skullcap
Scutellaria lateriflora

SKULLCAP

Also known as Helmet Flower, Mad Dog Weed, Blue Skullcap, and Blue Pimpernel. From the family Lamiaceae.

The various varieties of skullcap are natives of different countries. They are found in America, Britain, India, and one grows in the rain forests of the Amazon.

The name *Scutellaria* is derived from *scutella,* meaning a "small shield," which is exactly how the seed looks.

The American Indians used *Scutellaria lateriflora* as a treatment for rabies. In Europe it was used for epilepsy.

SPECIES

Scutellaria galericulata
Skullcap
Hardy perennial. Ht. 6–20 in., spread 12 in. and more. Small purple-blue flowers with a longer spreading lower lip in summer. Leaves bright green and lance-shaped with shallow, round teeth. This plant is a native of Europe.

Scutellaria minor
Lesser Skullcap
As *S. galericulata* except ht. 8–12 in., spread 12 in. and more. Small purple-pink flowers. Leaves lance-shaped with four rounded teeth. Found on wet land.

Scutellaria lateriflora
Virginian Skullcap
As *S. galericulata* except ht. 12–24 in., spread 12 in. and more. Leaves oval and lance-shaped with shallow, round teeth. Native of America.
All zone 5

CULTIVATION

Propagation
Seed
Sow the small seeds in fall into prepared seed or plug trays and cover the seeds with compost. Leave the tray outside under glass. If germination is rapid, winter the young seedlings in a cold greenhouse. If there is no germination within 10–20 days leave alone; the seed may need a period of stratification. In the spring, when the plants are large enough, plant out into a prepared site 12 in. apart.

Root Cuttings
These produce a rhizomatous root from which it is easy to take cuttings. In spring dig up an established clump carefully, for any little bits of root left behind will form another plant. Ensure each cutting has a growing node; place in a seed tray and cover with potting mix. Put into a cold greenhouse to root.

Division
Established plants can be divided in the spring.

Pests and Diseases
Skullcap is normally free from pests and disease.

Maintenance
Spring Divide established plants. Take root cuttings.
Summer Cut back to restrain.
Fall Sow seeds.
Winter. No need for protection, fully hardy.

Garden Cultivation
Skullcap tolerates most soils but prefers a well-drained, moisture-retentive soil in sun or semishade. Make sure this plant gets adequate water.

Harvesting
Dry flowers and leaves for medicinal use only.

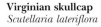

Virginian skullcap
Scutellaria lateriflora

CONTAINER GROWING

This herb can be grown in containers but ensure its large root system has room to spread. Use a soil-based potting mix. Feed only rarely with liquid fertilizer or it will produce too lush a growth and inhibit flowering. Leave outside in winter in a sheltered spot, allowing the plant to die back.

MEDICINAL

The American skullcap is the best medicinal species; the two European species are a little less strong.

It is used in the treatment of anxiety, nervousness, depression, insomnia, and headaches. The whole plant is effective as a soothing antispasmodic tonic and a remedy for hysteria and hydrophobia. Its bitter taste also strengthens and stimulates the digestion.

WARNING

Should only be dispensed by a trained herbalist.

Sempervivum tectorum

HOUSELEEK

Also known as Bullocks Eye, Hen and Chickens, Jupiter's Eye, Jupiter's Beard, Live For Ever, Thunder Plant, Aaron's Rod, Healing Leaf, Mallow Rock, and Welcome-Husband-Though-Never-So-Late. From the family Crassulaceae.

Houseleek *Sempervivum tectorum*

Originally from the mountainous areas of central and southern Europe, now found growing in many different areas of the world, including North America.

The generic name *Sempervivum* comes from the Latin *semper vivo,* meaning "to live for ever." The species name, *tectorum,* means "of the roofs"; there are records dating back 2,000 years of houseleeks growing on the tiles of houses. The plant was said to have been given to man by Zeus or Jupiter to protect houses from lightning and fire. Because of this the Romans planted courtyards with urns of houseleek, and Charlemagne ordered a plant to be grown on every roof. This belief continued throughout history and in medieval times the houseleek was thought to protect thatched roofs from fire from the sky and witchcraft. In the Middle Ages the plant was often called Erewort and employed against deafness. When the settlers packed their bags for America they took houseleek with them.

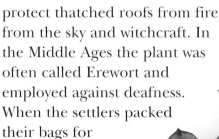

SPECIES

This genus of hardy succulents had 25 species 40 years ago. Now, due to re-classification, it has over 500 different varieties. As far as I am aware, only houseleek has medicinal properties.

Sempervivum tectorum
Houseleek
Hardy evergreen perennial. Ht. 4–6 in. (when in flower) otherwise it is 2 in., spread 8 in. Flowers are star-shaped and pink in summer. The leaves, gray-green in color, are oval, pointed, and succulent.
Zone 4

Some other sempervivum worth collecting:

Sempervivum arachnoideum
Cobweb Houseleek
Hardy evergreen perennial.
Ht. 4–5 in., when in flower, otherwise it is 2 in., spread 4 in. Flowers are star-shaped and pink in summer. The leaves, gray-green in color, are oval, pointed, and succulent. The tips of the leaves are covered in a web of white hairs.
Zone 5

Sempervivum giuseppii
Hardy evergreen perennial. Ht. 3–4 in., when in flower, otherwise it is 1 in., spread 4 in. Flowers star-shaped, pink-red in summer. Leaves, gray-green in color, are oval, pointed, and succulent and grow into a very compact shape. This sempervivum is a vigorous grower.
Zone 7

Sempervivum montanum
Hardy evergreen perennial. Ht. 3–6 in., when in flower, otherwise 2 in., spread 4 in. Flowers star-shaped and deep red in summer. Leaves gray-green in color, oval, pointed, and succulent.
Zone 5

Houseleek *Sempervivum tectorum* **in flower**

CULTIVATION

Propagation
Seed
Most species hybridize readily, so seed cannot be depended upon to reproduce true to type. When you buy seed it often says, "mixture of several species and varieties" on the packet. It can be fun to sow these as long as you do not mind what you get.

The seed is very small, so start off in a seed or plug tray in spring. Sow on the surface. Do not cover except with a sheet of glass. No need for bottom heat. Use the bark-peat-grit potting soil (see p. 591).

Offsets
All the houseleeks produce offsets that cluster around the base of the parent plant. In spring gently remove them and you will notice each has its own root system. Either put straight into a pot, using the bark-peat-grit mix of potting soil, or plant where required. Plant 9 in. apart.

Pests and Diseases
Vine weevil, this scourge of the garden, is very destructive to a number of plants and likes houseleeks. You will know they have been when you see the rosette lying on its side with no roots. See page 606 for methods of destroying the pests.

Maintenance
Spring Sow seeds. Repot or replant offsets.

Summer Collect seeds if required from flowering plants.
Fall Remove offsets if the plant is becoming too invasive, repot for following season's display.
Winter No need for protection.

Garden Cultivation
Basically the soil should be well drained and thin, as they prefer very little to no soil. They will grow anywhere, on weathered rocks and screes and of course rock gardens. Another good place to plant them is between paving stones, or in between other creeping plants like thymes. They can take many years to flower, and when they do they die, but by then there will be many offsets to follow.

Harvesting
Pick leaves to use fresh as required. There is no good way of preserving them.

CONTAINER GROWING

If the Romans could do it, so can we. Houseleeks do look good in containers and shallow stone troughs. The compost must be poor and well drained. Use the bark-peat-grit mix but change the ratio to 50 percent grit, 25 percent peat, 25 percent bark. No need to feed, and do not overwater.

CULINARY

The taste is not recommended.

MEDICINAL

The leaves are an astringent and when broken in half can be applied to burns, insect bites, and other skin problems. Press the juice from the leaf onto the infected part. My son, when he goes on hikes, always has some in his pockets—great for clothes washing—when he gets stung by nettles they are much better than dock when rubbed in.

To soften skin around corns, bind one leaf for a few hours, soak foot in water in attempt to remove corn. Repeat as necessary.

Rarely, if ever, taken internally.

Solidago virgaurea

GOLDENROD

Also known as Woundwort, Aaron's Rod, Cast the Spear, and Farewell Summer.
From the family Asteraceae.

This plant is widely distributed in North America and throughout Europe. It is common from the plains to the hills, but especially where the ground is rich in silica.

Its generic name, *Solidago*, is derived from the Latin word *solido*, which means "to join" or "make whole," a reference to the healing properties attributed to goldenrod.

The plant, originally called Heathen Wound Herb in Britain, was first imported from the Middle East, where it was used by the Saracens, and it was some time before it was cultivated. In Tudor times it was available in London but at a price, its expense due to the fact that it was still available only as an import. Gerard wrote, "For in my remembrance, I have known the dry herb which comes from beyond the sea, sold in Bucklesbury in London for half a crown an ounce," and went on to say that when it was found growing wild in Hampstead wood, no one would pay half a crown for 100 hundredweight of it, a fact that the herbalist felt bore out the old English proverb "Far fetch and dear, bought is best for ladies."

From Culpeper, around the same time, we know that goldenrod was used to fasten loose teeth and as a remedy for kidney stones (which it still is).

Goldenrod *Solidago virgaurea*

SPECIES

Solidago odora
Sweet Goldenrod
Also known as Aniseed-Scented Goldenrod, Blue Mountain Tea.
Perennial. Ht. 2–4ft., spread 2 ft. Golden-yellow flowers on a single stem from midsummer to fall. The green leaf is linear and lance-shaped, and smells like anise.
Zone 6

Solidago nemoralis
Goldenrod
Also known as Dyer's Weed, Field Goldenrod, and Yellow Goldenrod.
Perennial. Ht. 2–3 ft., spread 2 ft. Yellow flowers on large terminals on one side of the panicle. Leaves grayish-green or olive-green.
Zone 3

Solidago virgaurea
Goldenrod
Also known as European Goldenrod. Perennial. Ht. 12–24 in., spread 2 ft. Small yellow flowers from summer to fall. The green leaves are lance-shaped.
Zone 3

***Solidago* 'Goldenmosa'**
Goldenrod
Perennial. Ht. 3 ft., spread 2 ft. Sprays of mimosa-like yellow flowers from summer to fall. Lance-shaped green leaves. Attractive border plant. Has no herbal use.
Zone 4

CULTIVATION

Propagation
Seeds
Sow in plug or seed trays in spring. As seed is fine, sow on the surface and cover with perlite. Germination within 14–21 days without bottom heat. Prick out, harden off, and plant out into prepared site in the garden at a distance of 2–3 ft.

Division
Divide established plants in spring or fall. Dig up the plant, split into required size, half, third, etc., and replant in a prepared site in the garden.

Pests and Diseases
Subject to **powdery mildew** in humid seasons.

Maintenance
Spring Sow seeds.
Summer Enjoy the flowers. If you have rich soil, the plants may become very tall and need support in exposed sites.
Fall Divide mature plants.
Winter No need for protection.

Garden Cultivation
It is an attractive plant and has been taken into cultivation as a useful late flowering ornamental. It is ideal for the herbaceous border, as it spreads rapidly to form clumps.

In late summer, sprays of bright yellow flowers crowd its branching stems among sharply pointed hoary leaves. When planting in the garden, it prefers open conditions and soils that are not too rich and are well drained. It tolerates sun, semishade, and shade, and being a wild plant it can be naturalized in poor grassland.

Sow seed thinly in spring or fall in the chosen flowering position, having

Goldenrod
Solidago 'Goldenmosa'

prepared the site, and cover lightly with soil. When the seedlings are large enough, thin to 12 in. distance apart. (The plant will spread and you may have to do a second thinning.) If sown in the fall, the young plants may in very cold temperatures need added protection. Use a mulch that they can grow through the following spring, or one that can be removed.

Harvesting
Collect the flowering tops and leaves in summer. Dry for medicinal use.

MEDICINAL

Goldenrod is used in cases of urinary and kidney infections and stones, and catarrh. It also helps to ease backache caused by renal conditions because of its cleansing, eliminative action. It is used to treat arthritis.

A cold compress is helpful on fresh wounds because of its anti-inflammatory properties.

Sweet goldenrod is used as an astringent and as a calmative. The tea made from the dried leaves and flowers is an aromatic beverage and can be used to improve the taste of other medicinal preparations. Native Americans applied lotions made from goldenrod flowers to bee stings.

CONTAINER GROWING

Goldenrod can be grown in containers, but being a tall plant, it looks much more attractive in a garden border. Use the bark-peat-grit mix of potting soil (see p. 591) and in the summer give it only liquid fertilizer and water regularly. In winter, as the plant dies back, place the container in a cool airy place protected from frost, but not warm. Keep the compost on the dry side.

Stachys officinalis (Betonica officinalis)

BETONY

Also known as Lousewort, Purple Betony, Wood Betony, Bishop's Wort, and Devil's Plaything. From the family Lamiaceae.

This attractive plant is native to Europe and still found growing wild in Britain. Betony certainly merits inclusion in the herb garden, but is thought by some to be one of the plant world's frauds. There are so many conflicting stories, all of which are well worth hearing. I leave it to you to decide what is fact or fiction.

The Ancient Egyptians were the first to attribute magical properties to betony. In England, by the tenth century, the Anglo-Saxons had it as their most important magical plant, claiming it as effective against the elf sickness. In the eleventh century it was mentioned in the *Lacnunga* as a beneficial medicinal plant against the devilish affliction of the body. Later, Gerard wrote in his *Herbal,* "Betony is good for them that be subject to the falling sickness," and went on to describe its many virtues, one of them being "a remedy against the biting of mad dogs and venomous serpents."

In the eighteenth century it was still considered of use in the cure of diverse afflictions, including headaches and drawing out splinters, as well as being used in herbal tobacco and snuff. Today, betony retains an important place in folk medicine even though its true value is seriously questioned.

We owe the name to the Romans, who called the herb first *Bettonica*

Betony *Stachys officinalis*

Betony *Stachys officinalis*

SPECIES

Stachys officinalis
Betony
Hardy perennial. Ht. 24 in., spread 10 in. Dense spikes of pink or purple flowers end of spring through summer. Square hairy stems bear aromatic, slightly hairy, lobed leaves.
Zone 4

Stachys officinalis '**Alba**'
White Betony
Hardy perennial. Ht. 24 in., spread 10 in. White flowers end of spring through summer. **Zone 4**

CULTIVATION

Propagation
Seed
Grows readily from seed, which it produces in abundance. Sow late summer or spring in planting position and cover very lightly with soil. Alternatively, sow seeds in trays and transplant seedlings into small pots when large enough to handle.

Division
Divide roots of established plants in spring or fall, replant at a distance of

12 in. from other plants. Alternatively pot up using the bark-peat mix of potting soil (see p. 591).

Pests and Diseases
Apart from the occasional **caterpillar**, this plant is pest- and disease-free.

Maintenance
Spring Sow seeds. Divide established plants.
Summer Plant out spring seedlings.
Fall Cut back flowering stems, save seeds, and divide established plants.
Winter No protection needed.

Garden Cultivation
A very accommodating plant, it will tolerate most soils, but prefers some humus. Flourishes in sun or shade, and in fact it will put up with all but the deepest of shade. A wild plant, but it has for centuries been grown in cottage gardens. In the wildflower garden it is a very colorful participant and establishes well either in a mixed bed or in grassland.

It is also excellent for the woodland garden.

Harvesting
Collect leaves for drying before flowering in late spring/early summer. Use leaves fresh either side of flowering.
Pick flowers for drying and for use in potpourris just as they open. Collect through flowering season to use fresh.
Save seed in early fall. Store in dry, dark container.

CONTAINER GROWING

Betony grows to great effect in a half barrel and combines well with other wild flowers such as poppies, oxeye daisy, and chamomile. I do not advise it for growing indoors or in small containers.

Betony *Stachys officinalis* **in flower**

OTHER USES

The fresh plant provides a yellow dye. A hair rinse, good for highlighting graying hair, can be made from an infusion of the leaves.

WARNING

Do not take internally because in any form the root can cause vomiting and violent diarrhea.

Betony makes a good yellow dye

MEDICINAL

Today opinions differ as to its value. Some authorities consider it only as an astringent while others believe it is a sedative.

It is, however, now chiefly employed in herbal smoking mixtures and herbal snuffs. As an infusional powder, it is used to treat diarrhea, cystitis, asthma, and neuralgia. Betony tea is invigorating, particularly if prepared in a mixture with other herbs. In France it is recommended for liver and gallbladder complaints.

Symphytum officinale

COMFREY

Also known as Knitbone, Boneset, Bruisewort, Knitback, Church Bells, Abraham, Isaac-and-Jacob (from the variation in flower color), and Saracen's Root. From the family Boraginaceae.

Native to Europe and Asia, comfrey was introduced into America in the 17th century, where it has naturalized.

Traditionally known as Saracen's root, common comfrey is believed to have been brought to England by the Crusaders who had discovered its value as a healing agent—mucilaginous secretions strong enough to act as a bone-setting plaster, and which gave it the nickname Knitbone.

The Crusaders passed it to monks for cultivation in their monastic herb gardens, dedicated to the care of the sick.

Elizabethan physicians and herbalists were never without it. A recipe from that time is for an ointment made from comfrey root boiled in sugar and licorice, and mixed with coltsfoot, mallow, and poppy seed. People also made comfrey tea for colds and bronchitis.

But times have changed. Once the panacea for all ills, comfrey is now under suspicion as a carcinogen. In line with its common name "Bruisewort," research in America has shown that comfrey breaks down the red blood cells. At the same time, the Japanese are investigating how to harness its beneficial qualities: there is a research study on the high protein and vitamin B content of the herb.

SPECIES

Symphytum 'Hidcote Blue'
Comfrey Hidcote Blue
Hardy perennial. Ht. 20 in., spread 2 ft. Pale blue flowers in spring and early summer. Green lance-shaped leaves. **Zone 5**

Symphytum ibericum
Dwarf Comfrey
Hardy perennial. Ht. 10 in., spread 3 ft. Yellow-white flowers in spring. Green lance-shaped leaves. An excellent ground cover plant, having foliage through most winters. This comfrey contains little potassium and no allantoin, a crucial medicinal substance. **Zone 5**

Symphytum officinale
Comfrey (Wild or Common)
Hardy perennial. Ht. and spread 3 ft. White-purple-pink flowers in summer. This is the best medicinal comfrey and can also be employed as a liquid feed, although the potassium content is only 3.09 percent compared to 'Bocking 14's 7.09 percent. It makes a first-class composting plant, as it helps the rapid breakdown of other compost materials. **Zone 5**

Symphytum x uplandicum
Russian Comfrey
Hardy perennial. Ht. 3 ft., spread indefinite. Pink-purple flowers in summer. Green lance-shaped leaves. This is a hybrid that occurred naturally in Upland, Sweden. It is a cross between *S. officinale*, the herbalist's comfrey, and *S. asperum*, the blue-flowered, prickly comfrey from Russia. A very attractive form is *S. x uplandicum* 'Variegatum', which has cream and green leaves. **Zone 5**

Dwarf Comfrey
Symphytum ibericum

Symphytum x uplandicum 'Bocking 4'
Hardy perennial. Ht. 3 ft., spread indefinite. Flowers nearly violet in color, in spring and early summer. Thick, solid stems. Large green, lance-shaped leaves. Not a particularly attractive plant, but it contains almost 35 percent total protein, the same percentage as in soy beans. Comfrey is an important animal feed in some parts of the world, especially in Africa. Not available in the U.S.

Symphytum x uplandicum
'Bocking 14'
Hardy perennial. Ht. 3 ft.,
spread indefinite. Mauve
flowers in spring and early
summer. Thin stems. Green
oval leaves, tapering to a
point. This variety has the
highest potash content,
which makes it the best for
producing liquid manure.
Not available in the U.S.

Russian Comfrey
Symphytum x *uplandicum*

CULTIVATION

Propagation
Seed
Not nearly as reliable as root
cutting or division. Sow in
spring or fall in either seed
or plug trays. Germination
slow and erratic.

Root Cuttings
Dig up a piece of root, cut
into 1-in. sections, and put
these small sections into a
prepared plug or seed tray.

Division
Use either the double spade
method or simply dig up a
chunk in the spring and
replant it elsewhere.

Pests and Diseases
Sometimes suffers from **rust**
and **powdery mildew** in late
fall. In both cases cut the
plant down and burn the
contaminated leaves.

Maintenance
Spring Sow seeds. Divide
plants. Take root cuttings.
Summer Cut back leaves for
composting, or to use as a
mulch around other herbs
in the growing season.
Fall Sow seeds.
Winter None needed.

Garden Cultivation
Fully hardy in the garden,
all the comfreys prefer sun
or semishade and a moist
soil, but will tolerate most
conditions. The large
taproot can cause problems
if you want to move the
plant. When doing this
make sure you dig up all the
root because any left behind
will reappear later.

Harvesting
Cut leaves with shears from
early summer to fall to
provide foliage for making
liquid feed. Each plant is
able to give four cuts a year
if well fed. Cut leaves for
drying before flowering.
    Dig up roots in fall for
drying.

CONTAINER GROWING

Comfrey is not suitable for
growing indoors, but it can
be grown on a patio as long
as the container is large
enough. Situate in partial
shade and give plenty of
water in warm weather.

CULINARY

Fresh leaves and shoots were
once eaten as a vegetable or
salad, but this is no longer
advised.

LIQUID MANURE
A quickly available source of
potassium for the organic
gardener. One method of
extracting it is to put 14 lb.
of freshly cut comfrey into a
20-gallon tapped, fiberglass
water butt. Do not use metal
as rust will add toxic
quantities of iron oxide to
the liquid manure. Fill up
the butt with rain or
tapwater and cover with a lid
to exclude the light. In
about four weeks a clear
liquid can be drawn off from
the tap at the bottom. Ideal
feed for tomatoes, onions,
gooseberries, beans, and all
potash-hungry crops. It can
be used as a foliar feed.
    The disadvantage of this
method is that the liquid
stinks, because comfrey
foliage is about 3.4 percent
protein, and when proteins
break down they smell.
    An alternative is to bore
a hole into the side (just
above the bottom) of a
plastic dustbin. Stand the
container on bricks, so that
it is far enough off the
ground to allow a dish to be
placed under the hole. Pack
it solid with cut comfrey,
and place something (a
heavy lump of concrete) on
top to weigh down the
leaves. Cover with lid, and in
about three weeks a black
liquid will drip from the
hole into a dish.
    This concentrate can be
stored in a screw-top bottle
if you do not want to use it
immediately. Dilute it 1 part
to 40 parts water, and if you
plan to use it as a foliar
feed, strain it first.

MEDICINAL

*Comfrey has received much
attention in recent years,
both as a valuable healing
herb, a source of vitamin
B_{12} and self-proliferate
allantoin, and as a
potential source of protein.
    Comfrey is also useful as a
poultice for varicose ulcers
and a compress for varicose
veins, and it alleviates and
heals minor burns.*

WARNING

Comfrey is reported to
cause serious liver damage if
taken in large amounts over
a long period of time.

OTHER USES
Boil fresh leaves for golden
fabric dye.
    Comfrey is a good feed for
racehorses and helps cure
laminitis. For curing septic
sores on animals, make a
poultice between clean
pieces of cotton and tie to
the affected places.

Comfrey dye

Tanacetum cinerariifolium (Chrysanthemum cinerariifolium)

PYRETHRUM

From the family Asteraceae.

This plant is native to Dalmatia but is now cultivated commercially in many parts of the world, including Japan, South Africa, and parts of central Europe.

It has been grown for many years for its insecticidal properties. The derivative was originally known as Dalmatian insect powder but is now better known as pyrethrum insecticide. I list the two species to contain this natural insecticide.

SPECIES

**Tanacetum cinerariifolium
(Chrysanthemum
cinerariifolium)**
Pyrethrum daisy
Hardy perennial. Ht. 12–15
in., spread 8 in. White petals
with a yellow center. Leaves
green-gray, finely divided,
with down on the underside.
Zone 6

**Tanacetum coccineum
(Chrysanthemum roseum)**
Painted daisy
Hardy perennial. Ht. 12–24
in., spread 12 in. Large
flower head which can be
white, red, and pink. Very
variable under cultivation.
Native of Iran.
Zone 5

CULTIVATION

Pyrethrum
Tanacetum cinerariifolium

Propagation
Seeds
In spring sow into a
prepared seed or plug tray
and cover with perlite.
Germination is easy and
takes 14–21 days. In late
spring, when the young
plants are large enough and
after a period of hardening
off, plant out into a
prepared site in the garden
6–12 in. apart.

Division
Established clumps can be
dug up in the spring and
divided.

Pests and Diseases
In the majority of cases this
plant is free from pests and
diseases.

Maintenance
Spring Sow seed. Divide
established plants.
Summer Deadhead flowers
to prolong season if not
collecting seed.
Fall Divide established
plants if necessary.
Winter Fully hardy.

Garden Cultivation
Pyrethrum likes a well-
drained soil in a sunny spot;
it is drought tolerant and
fully hardy in most winters.

Harvesting
The flower heads are
collected just as they open
and then dried gently. When
they are quite dry, store
away from light. The
insecticide is made from the
powdered dried flower.

CONTAINER GROWING

This herb is very well suited
to be grown in containers,
especially terra-cotta. Use
the bark-peat-grit potting
mix (see p. 591). Water well
during the summer months,
but use liquid fertilizer
sparingly, otherwise the
leaves will become green
and it will stop flowering.

MEDICINAL

This herb is rarely used
medicinally. Herbalists have
found the roots to be a
remedy for certain fevers.
Recent research has shown
that the flowerheads possess
a weak antibiotic.

OTHER USES

This is a useful insecticide
because it is nontoxic to
mammals and does not
accumulate in the
environment or in the
bodies of animals. It acts by
paralyzing the nervous
system of the insects, and
can kill pests living on the
skin of humans and animals.
Sprinkle the dry powder
from the flowers to deter all
common insects, pests,
bedbugs, cockroaches, flies,
mosquitoes, aphids, spider
mites, and ants.

To make a spray, steep
1 oz. of pyrethrum powder
in 1 oz. of denatured
alcohol and then dilute with
3 gallons water. The solution
decomposes in bright
sunlight, so for maximum
effect and to reduce the risk
to pollinating insects and
bees, spray at dusk.

WARNING

Kills helpful insects and fish.
Wear gloves when
processing flowers for
insecticide use, as it may
cause allergies. When the
active ingredient pyrethrum
is extracted it is toxic to
humans and animals.

Tanacetum balsamita

ALECOST
(COSTMARY)
Other names: Bible Leaf, Sweet Mary, and Mint Geranium. From the family Asteraceae.

Alecost originated in western Asia and by the time it reached America in the seventeenth century, Culpeper wrote of its use in Europe that "Alecost is so frequently known to be an inhabitant of almost every garden, that it is needless to write a description thereof."

Since then, in America it has escaped its garden bounds and grows wild in eastern and midwestern states, while in Europe it has become altogether rare. Only recently has interest revived among propagators as well as horticulturalists who, in the period of twenty years, have reclassified alecost twice, from *Chrysanthemum* to *Balsamita* and now to *Tanacetum.*

The first syllable of its common name, alecost, derives from the use to which its scented leaves and flowering tops were put in the Middle Ages, namely to clarify, preserve, and impart an astringent, minty flavor to beer. The second syllable, *cost,* comes from *kostos,* Greek for "spicy." Literally, *alecost* means "a spicy herb for ale."

The alternative, costmary, by introducing a proper name symbolic of motherhood, conveys another of the plant's traditional uses in the form of a tea.

Religious connotations extend to one other nickname, Bible leaf, which grew out of the Puritan habit of using a leaf of the herb as a fragrant Bible bookmark, its scent dispelling faintness from hunger during long sermons.

SPECIES

Camphor plant *Tanacetum balsamita* subsp. *balsamitoides*

***Tanacetum balsamita
(Balsamita major)***
Alecost (costmary)
Hardy perennial. Ht. 3 ft., spread 18 in. Small white yellow-eyed daisy flowers mid- to late summer. Large rosettes of oval aromatic silvery green leaves.
Zone 5

***Tanacetum balsamita* subsp.
*balsamitoides***
Camphor plant
Hardy perennial. Ht. 3 ft., spread 18 in. Appearance and habit very similar to alecost, but unlike the latter it is not palatable as a culinary herb. Its leaves are an effective moth repellent. **Zone 5**

Alecost *Tanacetum balsamita (Balsamita major)*

CULTIVATION

Propagation
Seed
The seed is fine and thin and cannot be propagated from plants grown in cool climates (the seed not being viable). Obtain seed from a specialist. Sow in spring onto the surface of a seed or plug tray and cover with perlite. Use low warmth to encourage germination, and be patient! The seedlings may emerge in ten days or two months, depending on the freshness of the seed. Repot or plant out into the garden when they are large enough to handle.

Division
The best way to propagate is by division either in spring or fall. Take a portion of the creeping root from an established plant, and either plant out or repot using a bark-peat-grit mix of potting soil (see p. 591). If taking offsets in fall, it is better to winter the pots in a cold frame.

Garden Cultivation
Plant 2 ft. apart and, if possible, in a sunny position. Both alecost and camphor plant will adapt to most conditions, but prefer a rich, fairly dry and well-drained soil. Both species will grow in shade but may fail to bloom. But that is no great loss as the flower is not striking. Both die back in winter.

Pests and Diseases
Leaves of both are aromatic, so pests are not a problem.

Maintenance
Spring Divide established plants. Sow seed if available. Feed established plants.
Summer Plant out seedlings early into permanent positions. Deadhead.
Fall Trim back flowers. Remove offsets from established plants to prevent them encroaching into others' territory.
Winter Tidy up dead leaves; they spread disease if left to rot. Bring in potted-up offsets.

Harvesting
Pick the leaves for fresh culinary use anytime. Both alecost and camphor leaves dry well and retain their sweet aroma. Pick for drying just before flowering for the strongest scent.

The flowers are not worth harvesting for drying.

Only in a warm climate is it worth collecting seeds. Do it when flowers turn brown and center eye disintegrates on touch. Sow the following year (see Propagation).

CONTAINER GROWING
Neither species lends itself to container growing. They grow soft, prone to disease, are untidy when in flower, and tend to be blown over by the wind. If there is no other course, deadhead to prevent from flowering and do not overfeed with liquid fertilizer.

Alecost *Tanacetum balsamita (Balsamita major)*

CULINARY

Use only the alecost leaf and very sparingly, as it has a sharp tang that can be overpowering. Add finely chopped leaves to carrot soups, salads, game, poultry, stuffing, and fruit cakes, or with melted butter to peas and new potatoes. Its traditional value to beer holds good for home brewing.

MEDICINAL

Traditionally in the form of a tea (costmary or sweet Mary tea) to ease the pain of childbirth. It was also used as a tonic for colds, catarrh, stomach upset, and cramps. Rub a fresh leaf of alecost on a bee sting or horse-fly bite to relieve pain.

Alecost with new potatoes

OTHER USES

Both alecost and camphor leaves, which are sweet-scented like balsam, serve to intensify other herb scents and act as an insect repellent. Add to potpourris or to linen bags or with lavender to make nosegay sachets, or infuse to make a final scented rinse for hair.

Fresh or dried leaves of alecost can be added to baths for a fragrant and refreshing soak.

Alecost potpourri

Tanacetum parthenium (Chrysanthemum parthenium)

FEVERFEW

**Also known as Featherfew and Febrifuge Plant.
From the family Asteraceae.**

Feverfew was probably a native of south-east Europe and spread via the Mediterranean to many parts of the world, including North America and Britain. It is an attractive and robust, vigorous plant, and is found growing in the wild on dry, well-drained soils.

Its common name suggests that the herb was used in the treatment of fevers. It is said to be derived from the Latin *febrifugia*, meaning "a substance that drives out fevers." The old herbalists even call it a febrifuge. However, strange as it may seem, the herb was hardly ever employed for the purpose.

Gerard, the Elizabethan herbalist, advised use of the dried plant for "those that are giddied in the head or have vertigo." In the seventeenth century, Culpeper advised its use for pains in the head and colds. In the late eighteenth it was considered a special remedy for a body racked by too much opium. Nowadays it is used in the treatment of migraines.

Feverfew *Tanacetum parthenium*

SPECIES

***Tanacetum parthenium
(Chrysanthemum
parthenium)***
Feverfew
Hardy perennial. Ht. 2–4 ft.,
spread 18 in. White daisylike
flowers from early summer
to early fall. The leaf is mid-
green, and a typical
chrysanthemum shape.
Zone 4

***Tanacetum parthenium*
'White Bonnet'**
Double-Flowered Feverfew
Hardy perennial. Ht. 12 in.,
spread 18 in. Double white
flowers, otherwise as above.
Zone 4

***Tanacetum parthenium*
'Aureum'**
Golden Feverfew
Hardy perennial. Ht. and
spread 8–18 in. Gold-green
leaves that remain colorful
all year. Otherwise as above.
Growth and color make
golden feverfew popular.
Particularly conspicuous
in winter.
Zone 5

CULTIVATION

Propagation

Seeds

Fine, thin, and fairly small, they tend to stick together especially if they get damp. Mix a very small amount of seed with an equally small amount of perlite or dry sand to make sowing easier. Sow very thinly in spring or early fall, directly into pots or plug trays. Cover with a final thin layer of perlite. Germination is usually very rapid, 7–10 days. No need for extra heat. Plant out 12 in. apart, as soon as the seedlings are large enough to handle and hardened off. If sown in fall, the young plants will need to be wintered under protection.

Division

Dig up established clumps in early fall. Ease the plants apart, and either replant directly in the positions required or pot for flowers in late spring. Winter in a cold greenhouse or cold frame. Use the bark-peat potting soil (see p. 591).

Cuttings

Take stem cuttings in the summer, making sure there are no flowers on the cutting material.

Pests and Diseases

Subject to **aphids**, **spider mites**, and many foliage diseases, especially if grown in containers or in humid climates. Golden feverfew can suffer from **sun scorch**; if this occurs, cut back and the new growth will be unaffected.

Maintenance

Spring Sow seeds.
Summer As flowering finishes cut plant back to restore shape, and remove all flowering heads to

Feverfew in sachets makes a good moth repellent

minimize self-seeding.
Fall Divide established clumps. This is the best time for sowing if edging plants are required. Winter young plants in a cold frame.
Winter No need to protect, fully frost hardy.

Garden Cultivation

Feverfew is invasive. It will grow anywhere, but likes best a loam soil enriched with good manure in a sunny position. Seeds can be sown directly into a prepared site in late spring. When the seedlings are large enough to handle, thin to 12 in. apart. Plants often die out in hot summers or cold winters, but reseed themselves.

Harvesting

Pick leaves before the plant flowers; dry if required for use medicinally. Pick the flowers just as they open; dry hanging upside down.

CONTAINER GROWING

Grown indoors, the plants get stretched and leggy. However, in containers outside all the feverfews flourish. Golden feverfew, having the most compact

habit, looks very effective in a hanging basket, tub, or window box. Use the bark-peat mix of potting soil. Keep the plants regularly watered and feed during flowering. Cut back plants after flowering as this will help maintain their shape.

CULINARY

The young leaves of feverfew can be added to salads, but be warned they are very bitter, so add sparingly.

MEDICINAL

That feverfew has a propensity to overcome melancholy has been known by herbalists for centuries. However, its ability to soothe headaches was not given much attention until the 1970s when it was thoroughly investigated scientifically, following claims that it reduced migraines. Many clinical trials were held and results, over a six-month period, showed a 70 percent reduction in migraines, and

43 percent of the patients felt other beneficial side-effects, including more restful sleep and relief from arthritis; 18 percent had unpleasant side effects. Golden and double-flowered forms have not been tested, though experience suggests that they will react similarly.

Eat 3 to 5 fresh leaves between a slice of bread every day to reduce migraines. As mentioned before, this is very bitter, so put the leaves in a sandwich (whole-wheat bread, of course). To make it more palatable, you could add a sprig of mint, marjoram, or parsley. Do *not* eat more.

OTHER USES

A decoction or infusion of the leaves is a mild disinfectant, and the leaves in sachets make a good moth repellent.

WARNING

One side effect associated with taking feverfew is ulceration of the mouth.

Tanacetum vulgare (Chrysanthemum vulgare)

TANSY

Also known as Bachelor's Buttons, Bitter Buttons, Golden Buttons, Stinking Willy, Hind Heel, and Parsley Fern. From the family Asteraceae.

Tansy is a native to Europe and Asia, and it has managed to become naturalized elsewhere, especially in North America. The name derives from the Greek *athanasia*, meaning "immortality." In ancient times it was used in the preparation of the embalming sheets and rubbed on corpses to save them from earthworms or corpse worm.

Tansy *Tanacetum vulgare*

SPECIES

Tanacetum vulgare
Tansy
Hardy perennial. Ht. 3 ft., spread 1–2 ft. and more. Yellow button flowers in late summer. The aromatic leaf is deeply indented, toothed, and fairly dark green.

Tanacetum vulgare* var. *crispum
Curled Tansy
As *T. vulgare* except ht. 24 in. and the aromatic leaf is crinkly, curly, and dark green.

***Tanacetum vulgare* 'Isala Gold'**
Tansy Isala Gold
As *T. vulgare* except ht. 24 in. and the leaf is golden in color.

***Tanacetum vulgare* 'Silver Lace'**
Tansy Silver Lace
As *T. vulgare* except ht. 24 in. and the leaf starts off white flecked with green, progressing to full green. If, however, you keep cutting it, some of the variegation can be maintained.
All zone 3

CULTIVATION

Propagation
Seed
Sow the very small seed in spring or fall in a prepared seed or plug tray and cover with perlite. Germination takes 10–21 days. Plant out 18 in. apart when the seedlings are large enough to handle. If sown in the fall, overwinter under protection.

Division
All species produce root runners, so divide in spring or fall.

Pests and Diseases
Tansy is rarely bothered with pests or disease.

Maintenance
Spring Sow seed. Divide established clumps.
Summer Cut back after flowering to maintain shape and color.
Fall Divide established clumps. Sow seeds.
Winter The plant is fully hardy and dies back into the ground for winter.

Garden Cultivation
Tansy needs to be positioned with care as the roots spread widely. The gold and variegated forms are much less invasive and very attractive in a semishaded border. They tolerate most conditions provided the soil is not completely wet.

Harvesting
Pick leaves as required. Gather flowers when open.

CONTAINER GROWING

Because of its wide-ranging habit, container growing is recommended. Use a soil-based potting mix and a large container, water through the growing season, feed twice during flowering. In winter keep on the dry side in a cool place. Repot in spring.

OTHER USES

Rub into the coat of your dog or cat to prevent fleas.
Hang leaves indoors to deter flies. Put dried sprigs under carpets. Add to insect repellent sachets. Sprinkle chopped leaves and flowers to deter ants and mice.
It produces a yellow-green dye for wool.

MEDICINAL

Can be used by trained herbalists to expel roundworm and threadworm.
Use tansy tea externally to treat scabies, and as a compress to bring relief to painful rheumatic joints.

WARNING

Use tansy only under medical supervision. It is a strong emmenagogue, provoking the onset of a period, and should *not* be used during pregnancy. An overdose of tansy oil or tea can be fatal.

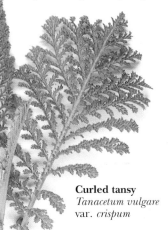

Curled tansy
Tanacetum vulgare var. *crispum*

Taraxacum officinale sativum

DANDELION

Also known as Pee in the Bed, Lions Teeth, Fairy Clock, Clock, Clock Flower, Clocks and Watches, Farmers Clocks, Old Man's Clock, One Clock, Wetweed, Blowball, Cankerwort, Lionstooth, Priests Crown, Puffball, Swinesnout, White Endive, Wild Endive, and Piss-a-beds. From the family Asteraceae.

Dandelion is one of nature's great medicines and it really proves that a weed is only a plant out of place! It is in fact one of the most useful of herbs. It has become naturalized throughout the temperate regions of the world and flourishes on nitrogen-rich soils in any situation to a height of 6,500 ft.

There is no satisfactory explanation why it is called Dandelion, Dents Lioness, Tooth of the Lion in medieval Latin, and Dent de Lion in French. The lion's tooth may be the tap-root, the jagged leaf, or the parts of the flower.

The Arabs promoted its use in the eleventh century. By the sixteenth it was well established as an official drug. The apothecaries knew it as *Herba taraxacon* or *Herba urinari*, and Culpeper called it Piss-a-beds, all referring to its diuretic qualities.

Dandelion *Taraxacum officinale sativum*

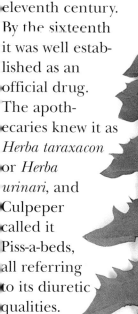

Dandelion
Taraxacum officinale sativum

SPECIES

Taraxacum officinale sativum
Dandelion
Perennial. Ht. 6–9 in. Large, brilliant yellow flowers 2 in. wide, spring to fall. The flower heads as they turn to seed form a fluffy ball (dandelion clock).
Zone 3

Taraxacum kok-saghyz Rodin
Russian Dandelion
Perennial. Ht. 12 in. Similar to the above. Extensively cultivated during World War II: latex was extracted from the roots as a source of rubber.
Zone 3

Taraxacum mongolicum
Chinese Dandelion
Perennial. Ht. 10–12 in. Similar to the above. Used to treat infections.

CULTIVATION

Propagation
Seed
Grow as an annual to prevent bitterness developing in the plant. Sow seed in spring on the surface of pots or plug trays. Do not use seed trays as the long taproot makes it difficult to prick out. Cover with a fine layer of perlite. Germination will be in 3–6 weeks, depending on seed freshness and air temperature. Plant out when large enough to handle.

Root
Sections of the root can be cut and put in either pots, seed or plug trays. Each piece will sprout again, just like comfrey.

Pests and Diseases
Dandelion is rarely attacked by either pest or disease.

Maintenance

Spring Sow seeds for use as a fall salad herb.

Summer Continually pick off the flower buds if you are growing dandelion as a salad crop.

Fall Put an upside-down flower pot over some of the plants to blanch them for fall salads. Sow seed for spring salad crop.

Winter No protection is needed. For salad crops, if temperatures fall below 15°F, cover with agricultural fleece or 3 in. of straw or hay to keep the leaves sweet.

Garden Cultivation

If the dandelion was a rare plant, it would be thought as a highly desirable garden species, for the flowers are most attractive, sweet smelling and a brilliant yellow, and then form the delightful puffballs. Up to that point all is fine. But then the wind disperses the seed all over the garden. And it is very difficult to eradicate when established since every bit of root left behind produces another plant. So, it finds no favor at all with gardeners.

In general, details on how to grow dandelions are superfluous. Most people only want to know how to get rid of them. The easiest time to dig up the plants completely is in the early spring.

Harvesting

Pick leaves as required to use fresh, and flowers for wine as soon as they open fully. Dig up roots in fall for drying.

CONTAINER GROWING

Dandelions do look attractive growing in containers, especially in window boxes, if you can stand neighbors' remarks. The containers will need to be deep to accommodate the long taproot.

CULINARY

Both the leaves and root have long been eaten as a highly nutritious salad. In the last century, cultivated forms with large leaves were developed as a fall and spring vegetable. The leaves were usually blanched in the same way as chicory. Dandelion salad in spring is also considered a blood cleanser, owing to its diuretic and digestive qualities. The leaves are very high in vitamins A, B, C, and D, the A content being higher than that of carrots.

The flowers make an excellent country wine and dandelion roots provide, when dried, chopped, and roasted, the best known coffee substitute.

Dandelion wine

Dandelion and Bacon Salad
Serves 4

1 cup young dandelion
 leaves
4 tablespoons olive or walnut oil
1 tablespoon white wine vinegar
½ cup bacon, diced
1 clove garlic, crushed
1 slice white bread, cubed
Salt and freshly ground pepper
Oil for cooking

Wash and dry the leaves and tear into the salad bowl. Make a vinaigrette using olive oil and vinegar, and season to taste, adding a little sugar if desired. Fry the bacon, crushed garlic, and bread in oil until golden brown. Pour the contents of the pan over the leaves and turn the leaves until thoroughly coated. Add the vinaigrette and toss again and serve at once.

Dandelion and bacon salad

MEDICINAL

It is one of the most useful medicinal plants, as all parts are effective and safe to use. It is regarded as one of the best herbal remedies for kidney and liver complaints. The root is a mildly laxative, bitter tonic, valuable in treating dyspepsia and constipation. The leaves are a powerful diuretic. However, unlike conventional diuretics, dandelion does not leach potassium from the body as its rich potassium content replaces what the body loses.

The latex contained in the leaves and stalks is very effective in removing corns and in treating warts and verrucas. Apply the juice from the plant daily to the affected part.

The flowers can be boiled with sugar for coughs, but honey has a greater medicinal value.

OTHER USES

As an herbal fertilizer dandelion is a good supply of copper. Pick 3 plants completely: leaves, flowers, and all. Place in a bucket, pour over 4 cups of boiling water, cover, and allow to stand for 30 minutes. Strain. This fertilizer will not store.

A dye, yellow-brown in color, can be obtained from the root, and dandelions are excellent food for domestic rabbits, guinea pigs, and gerbils. There is one thing for which they are useless, however—flower arrangements. As soon as you pick them and put them in water their flowers close tight.

Teucrium chamaedrys

WALL GERMANDER

**Also known as Ground Oak and Wild Germander.
From the family Lamiaceae.**

This attractive plant is a native of Europe, and is now naturalized in Britain and other countries in the temperate zone. It is found on dry chalky soils. The Latin *Teucrium* is said to have been named after Teucer, first king of Troy. It is the Ancient Greek word for ground oak, its leaves resembling those of the oak tree.

In medieval times, it was a popular strewing herb and a remedy for dropsy, jaundice, and gout. It was also used in powder form for treating head colds, and as a snuff.

SPECIES

Teucrium fruticans
Tree Germander
Evergreen tender shrub. Ht. 3–6 ft., spread 6–12 ft. Blue flowers in summer. The leaves are aromatic, gray-green with a white underside.
Zone 8

Teucrium chamaedrys L. 'Variegatum'
Variegated Wall Germander
Evergreen hardy perennial. Ht. 18 in., spread 8 in. Pink flowers from midsummer to early fall. The leaves are aromatic, dark green with cream-yellow variegation, small, shiny and oval.
Zone 6

Teucrium x lucidrys
Wall Germander
Evergreen hardy perennial. Ht. 18 in., spread 8 in. Pink flowers from midsummer to early fall. The leaves are dark green, small, shiny, and oval. When rubbed, they smell pleasantly spicy.
Zone 5

CULTIVATION

Propagation
Seed
Sow the small seeds in spring. Use a prepared seed or plug tray and the bark-peat-grit potting soil (see p. 591). Cover with perlite. Germination can be erratic—from 2–4 weeks. When the seedlings are large enough to handle, plant in a prepared site 8 in. apart.

Cuttings
This is a better method of propagating germander. Take softwood cuttings from the new growth in spring, or semihardwood in summer. Ensure compost does not dry out or become sodden.

Division
The teucriums produce creeping rootstock in the spring and are easy to divide. Dig up the plants, split them in half, and replant in a chosen site.

Pests and Diseases
Wall germander hardly ever suffers from pests or disease.

Maintenance
Spring Sow seeds. Take softwood cuttings. Trim established plants and hedges.
Summer Trim plants after flowering, take semi-hardwood cuttings.
Fall Trim hedges.
Winter Protect the variegated form when temperatures drop below 23°F.

Garden Cultivation
Wall germander needs a well-drained soil (slightly alkaline) and a sunny position. It is hardier than lavender and santolina, and makes an ideal hedging or edging plant. To make a good dense hedge, plant at a distance of 6 in. If you clip the hedge in spring and fall to maintain its shape, you will never need to cut it hard back.

It can also be planted in rockeries, and in stone walls, where it looks most attractive. During the growing season it does not need extra water, even in hot summers, nor does it need extra protection in cold winters. The variegated variety is more temperamental, and will require cosseting in the winter in the form of a mulch or frost fabric.

Harvesting
For drying for medicinal use, pick leaves before the plant flowers, and flowering stems when the flowers are in bud.

CONTAINER GROWING

Both wall germander and the variegated form look good in containers. Use the bark-peat-grit mix of potting soil. Only feed during the flowering season. Keep on the dry side in winter.

CULINARY

This plant is occasionally used in the flavoring of liqueurs.

MEDICINAL

Its herbal use today is minor. However, there is a revival of interest, and some use it as a remedy for digestive and liver troubles, anemia, and bronchitis.

Teucrium scorodonia

WOOD SAGE

Also known as Gypsy Sage, Mountain Sage, Wild Sage, and Garlic Sage. From the family Lamiaceae.

This plant is a native of Europe and has become naturalized in the United States and other countries in the temperate zone. There is not much written about wood sage apart from the fact that, like alecost, it was used in making ale before hops were introduced. However, Gertrude Jekyll recognized its value, and with renewed interest in her gardens comes a revival of interest in wood sage.

SPECIES

Teucrium scorodonia
Wood Sage
Hardy perennial. Ht. 12–24 in., spread 10 in. Pale greenish-white flowers in summer. Soft, green, heart-shaped leaves, which have a mild smell of crushed garlic.
Zone 6

Teucrium scorodonia **'Crispum'**
Curly Wood Sage
Hardy perennial. Ht. 14 in., spread 12 in. Pale greenish-white flowers in summer. The leaves are soft, oval, and olive green with a reddish tinge to their crinkled edges. Whenever it is on show it causes much comment.
Zone 6

CULTIVATION

Propagation
Wood sage can be propagated by seed, cuttings, or division. Curly wood sage can be propagated only by cuttings or division.

Seed
Sow the fairly small seed under protection in fall or spring in a prepared seed or plug tray. Use the bark-peat-grit potting soil (see p. 591), and cover with perlite. Germination can be erratic, taking from 2–4 weeks. When the seedlings are large enough to handle, repot and winter under cover in a cold frame. In the spring, after a period of hardening off, plant out in a prepared site in the garden at a distance of 10 in.

Cuttings
Take softwood cuttings from the new growth in spring, or semihardwood cuttings in summer.

Division
Both wood sages produce creeping rootstock. In the spring they are easy to divide.

Pests and Diseases
Wood sages are, in the majority of cases, free from pests and disease.

Maintenance
Spring Sow seeds. Divide established plants. Take softwood cuttings.
Summer Take semi-hardwood cuttings.
Fall Sow seeds.
Winter No need for protection; the plants die back for the winter.

Garden Cultivation
It grows well in semishaded situations, but also thrives in full sun on sandy and gravelly soils. It will adapt quite happily to clay and heavy soils, but not produce such prolific growth.

Harvesting
Pick young leaves for fresh use as required.

CONTAINER GROWING

I have grown curly wood sage in containers. The plain wood sage does not look quite so attractive. Use the bark-peat-grit mix of potting soil, and plant in a large container—its creeping rootstock can too easily become potbound.

Only feed twice in a growing season, otherwise the leaves become large, soft, and floppy. When the plant dies back, put it somewhere cool and keep it on the dry side. Divide and repot every spring.

MEDICINAL

Wood sage has been used to treat blood disorders, colds, and fevers, and as a diuretic and wound herb.

CULINARY

The leaves of ordinary wood sage have a mild garlic flavor. When young and tender, the leaves can be added to salads for variety. But go easy—they are slightly bitter.

Wood sage salad

Thymus

THYME

From the family Lamiaceae.

This is a genus comprising numerous species that are very diverse in appearance and come from many different parts of the world. They are found as far afield as Greenland and western Asia, although the majority grow in the Mediterranean region. This ancient herb was used by the Egyptians in oil form for embalming. The Greeks used it in their baths and as an incense in their temples. The Romans used it to purify their rooms, and most probably its use spread through Europe as their invasion train swept as far as Britain. In the Middle Ages drinking it was part of a ritual to enable one to see fairies, and it was one of many herbs used in nosegays to purify the odors of disease. Owing to its antiseptic properties, judges also used it along with rosemary to prevent jail fever.

Common thyme
Thymus vulgaris

Silver Posie thyme *Thymus vulgaris* 'Silver Posie'

SPECIES

There are so many species of thyme that I am only going to mention a few. New ones are being discovered each year. They are eminently collectable. Unfortunately their names can be unreliable—a nursery might prefer its pet name or one traditional to it, rather than the correct one.

Thymus caespititius (Thymus azoricus)
Caespititius Thyme
Evergreen hardy perennial. Ht. 4 in., spread 8 in. Pale pink flowers in summer. The leaves narrow, bright green, and close together on the stem. Makes an attractive low-growing mound, good between paving stones.
Zone 7

Thymus camphoratus
Camphor Thyme
Evergreen half-hardy perennial. Ht. 12 in., spread 8 in. Pink-mauve flowers in summer, large green leaves smelling of camphor. A beautiful compact bush.
Zone 7

Thymus cilicicus
Cilicicus Thyme
Evergreen hardy perennial. Ht. 2 in., spread 8 in. Pink flowers in summer. The leaves are bright green, narrow, and pointed, growing close together on the stem with an odd celery scent. Makes an attractive low-growing mound, good between paving stones.
Zone 9

Thymus* x *citriodorus
Lemon Thyme
Evergreen hardy perennial. Ht. 12 in., spread 8 in. Pink flowers in summer. Fairly large green leaves with a strong lemon scent. Excellent culinary thyme, combines well with many chicken or fish dishes.
Zone 6

Wild creeping thyme *Thymus polytrichus* subsp. *britannicus*

***Thymus* x *citriodorus* 'Golden King'**
Golden King Thyme
Evergreen hardy perennial. Ht. 12 in., spread 8 in. Pink flowers in the summer. Fairly large green leaves variegated with gold, strongly lemon scented. Excellent culinary thyme.
Zone 6

***Thymus* x *citriodorus* 'Silver Queen'**
Silver Queen Thyme
Evergreen hardy perennial. Ht. 12 in. spread 8 in. Pink flowers in the summer. Fairly large leaves, gray with silver variegation, a strong lemon scent. Excellent culinary thyme.
Zone 6

Thymus Coccineus Group
Creeping Red Thyme
Evergreen hardy perennial, prostrate form, a creeper. Red flowers in summer. Green small leaves. Decorative, aromatic, and good ground cover.
Zone 4

Thymus doerfleri
Doerfleri Thyme
Evergreen half-hardy perennial. Ht. 1 in., spread 8 in. Mauve-pink flowers in summer, gray, hairy, thin leaves, which are mat forming. Decorative thyme, good for rockeries, hates being wet in winter. Originates from the Balkan Peninsula.
Zone 8

***Thymus doerfleri* 'Bressingham'**
Bressingham Thyme
Evergreen hardy perennial. Ht. 1 in., spread 8 in. Mauve-pink flowers in summer. Thin, green, hairy

leaves, which are mat forming. Decorative thyme, good for rockeries, hates being wet in winter.
Zone 8

Thymus 'Doone Valley'
Doone Valley Thyme Evergreen hardy perennial. Ht. 3 in., spread 8 in. Purple flowers in summer. Round variegated green and gold leaves with a lemon scent. Very decorative; can be used in cooking if nothing else is available.
Zone 7

Thymus 'Fragrantissimus'
Orange-Scented Thyme Evergreen hardy perennial. Ht. 12 in., spread 8 in. Small pale pink–white flowers in summer. The leaves are small, narrow, grayish-green, and smell of spicy orange. Combines well with stir-fry dishes, poultry—especially duck—and even treacle pudding.
Zone 6

Thymus herba-barona
Caraway Thyme Evergreen hardy perennial. Ht. 1 in., spread 8 in. Rose-colored flowers in summer. Dark green, small leaves with a unique caraway scent. Especially good in stir-fry and meat.
Zone 4

Thymus 'Peter Davis'
Peter Davis Thyme Evergreen hardy perennial. Ht. 3 in., spread 8 in. Pink-mauve flowers in summer. Thin gray-green leaves,

mild scent. Good in rockeries.
Zone 7

Thymus polytrichus subsp. britannicus
Wild Creeping Thyme Also Mother of Thyme. Evergreen hardy perennial. Ht. 1 in., spread 8 in. Pale mauve flowers in summer. Small dark green leaves, which, although mildly scented, can be used in cooking. Wild thyme has been valued by herbalists for many centuries.
Zone 4

Thymus 'Porlock'
Porlock Thyme Evergreen hardy perennial. Ht. 12 in., spread 8 in. Pink flowers in summer. Fairly large green leaves with a mild but definite thyme flavor and scent. Excellent culinary thyme. Medicinal properties are antibacterial and antifungal.
Zone 4

Thymus pseudolanuginosus
Woolly Thyme Evergreen hardy perennial. Ht. 1 in., spread 8 in. Pale pink–mauve flowers for most of the summer. Gray hairy mat-forming leaves. Good for rockeries and stone paths. Needs excellent drainage, especially in winter.
Zone 7

Thymus pulegioides
Mother-of-Thyme Evergreen hardy perennial. Ht. 3 in., spread 8 in. Pink-mauve flowers in summer. Large round dark green leaves with a strong thyme flavor. Good for culinary uses, excellent for ground cover and good in hanging baskets.
Zone 4

Thymus pulegioides 'Archer's Gold'
Archer's Gold Thyme Evergreen hardy perennial. Ht. 4 in., spread 8 in. Pink-mauve flowers in summer. A mound of green-gold leaves.

Lemon thyme
Thymus x *citriodorus*

Decorative and culinary, it has a mild thyme flavor.
Zone 6

Thymus pulegioides 'Bertram Anderson'
Bertram Anderson Thyme Evergreen hardy perennial. Ht. 4 in., spread 8 in. Pink-mauve flowers in summer. More of a round mound than 'Archer's Gold' and the leaves are slightly rounder with a more even golden look to the leaves. Decorative and culinary, it has a mild thyme flavor.
Zone 6

Thymus pulegioides 'Aureus'
Golden Thyme Evergreen hardy perennial. Ht. 12 in., spread 8 in. Pale pink–lilac flowers. Green leaves that turn gold in summer; good flavor, combining well with vegetarian dishes.
Zone 4

Pink Chintz thyme
Thymus serpyllum 'Pink Chintz'

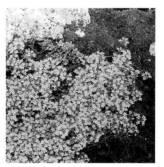

Thymus serpyllum var. albus
White Thyme Evergreen hardy perennial, prostrate form, a creeper. White flowers in summer. Bright green, small leaves. Decorative aromatic and good ground cover.
Zone 4

Thymus serpyllum 'Annie Hall'
Annie Hall Thyme Evergreen hardy perennial, prostrate form, a creeper. Pale pink flowers in summer. Small green leaves. Decorative, aromatic, and good ground cover.
Zone 4

Goldstream thyme
Thymus serpyllum 'Goldstream'

Thymus serpyllum 'Goldstream'
Goldstream Thyme Evergreen hardy perennial, prostrate form, a creeper. Pink-mauve flowers in summer. Green-gold variegated, small leaves. Decorative, aromatic, and good ground cover.
Zone 4

Thymus serpyllum 'Lemon Curd'
Lemon Curd Thyme Evergreen hardy perennial, prostrate form, a creeper. White-pink flowers in summer. Bright green, lemon-scented small leaves. Decorative, aromatic, and good ground cover. Can be used in cooking.
Zone 4

Thymus serpyllum 'Minimus'
Minimus Thyme Evergreen hardy perennial, prostrate form, a creeper. Pink flowers in summer. Tiny leaves, very compact. Decorative, aromatic, and good ground cover. Ideal between pavings and alongside paths. **Zone 4**

Thymus serpyllum 'Pink Chintz'
Pink Chintz Thyme Evergreen hardy perennial, prostrate form, a creeper. Pale pink flowers in summer. Gray-green, small hairy leaves. Decorative, aromatic, good ground cover. Dies out if the soil is too wet in winter.
Zone 4

Thymus serpyllum 'Rainbow Falls'
Rainbow Falls Thyme Evergreen hardy perennial, prostrate form, a creeper. Purple flowers in summer. Small variegated green-gold leaves. Decorative, aromatic, and good ground cover.
Zone 4

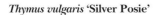

Thymus serpyllum 'Russetings'
Russetings Thyme
Evergreen hardy perennial, prostrate form, a creeper. Purple-mauve flowers in summer. Small green leaves. Decorative, aromatic, and good ground cover.
Zone 4

Thymus serpyllum 'Snowdrift'
Snowdrift Thyme
Evergreen hardy perennial, prostrate form, a creeper. Masses of white flowers in summer. Small round green leaves. Decorative, aromatic, and good ground cover.
Zone 4

Thymus vulgaris
Common (Garden) Thyme
Evergreen hardy perennial. Ht. 12 in., spread 8 in. Mauve flowers in summer. Thin green aromatic leaves. This is the thyme everyone knows. Use in stews, salads, sauces. Medicinal properties are antibacterial and antifungal.
Zone 4

Thymus vulgaris 'Lucy'
Lucy Thyme
Evergreen hardy perennial. Ht. 12 in., spread 8 in. The thyme sometimes does not flower, and if it does, it is a very pale pink flower and not very prolific. The leaves are very small green. Excellent culinary thyme. Medicinal properties are antibacterial and antifungal.
Zone 4

Coccineus thyme *Thymus* Coccineus Group **and Snowdrift thyme** *Thymus serpyllum* 'Snowdrift'

Thymus vulgaris 'Silver Posie'
Silver Posie Thyme
Evergreen hardy perennial. Ht. 12 in., spread 8 in. Pale pink-lilac flower. The leaves have a very pretty gray-silver variegation with a tinge of pink on the underside. This is a good culinary thyme and looks very attractive in salads.
Zone 4

Thymus zygis
Zygis Thyme
Evergreen half-hardy perennial. Ht. 12 in., spread 8 in. Attractive white flowers. Small thin gray-green leaves, which are aromatic. This is an attractive thyme that is good for rockeries. Originates from Spain and Portugal, therefore does not like cold wet winters.

Upright Thymes
Up to 12 in.:
Caespititius, Archer's Gold, Bertram Anderson, Peter Davis.

12 in. and above:
Camphor, Lucy, Lemon, Orange Scented, Golden King, Porlock, Common (Garden), Golden, Silver Posie, Zygis.

Creeping Thymes
Cilicicus, Doerfleri, Bressingham, Doone Valley, Wild Creeping, Woolly, Broad-Leaved, White, Annie Hall, Coccineus, Goldstream, Lemon Curd, Minimus, Pink Chintz, Rainbow Falls, Russetings, Snowdrift.

CULTIVATION

Propagation
To maintain the true plant, it is better to grow the majority of thymes from softwood cuttings. Only a very few, such as common and wild creeping thyme, can be propagated successfully from seed.

Seed
Sow the very fine seed in early spring using the cardboard technique (see p. 591) on the surface of prepared trays (seed or plug), using the bark-peat-grit potting soil (see p. 591) and a bottom heat of 60–70°F. Do not cover. Keep watering to the absolute minimum, as these seedlings are prone to damping-off disease. When the young plants are large enough, and after a period of hardening off, plant out in the garden in late spring/early summer, 9–15 in. apart.

Cuttings
Thymes are easily increased by softwood cuttings from new growth in early spring or summer. The length of the cutting should be 2–3 in. Use the bark-peat-grit mix of potting soil. Winter the young plants under protection and plant out the following spring.

Division
Creeping thymes put out aerial roots as they spread, which makes them very easy to divide.

Silver Posie thyme
Thymus vulgaris 'Silver Posie'

Layering
An ideal method for mature thymes that are getting a bit woody. Use either the strong branch method of layering in early fall or mound layer in early spring.

Pests and Diseases
Being such an aromatic plant it does not normally suffer from pests but, if the soil or compost is too rich, thyme may be attacked by **aphids**. Treat with a liquid horticultural soap. All varieties will rot off if they become too wet in a cold winter.

Maintenance
Spring Sow seeds. Trim old plants. Layer old plants.
Summer Take cuttings of nonflowering shoots. Trim back after flowering.
Fall Protect tender thymes.
Winter Protect containers and only water if absolutely necessary.

Garden Cultivation
Thymes need to be grown in poor soil, in a well-drained bed, to give their best flavor. They are drought-loving plants and will need protection from cold winds and hard and wet winters. Sow seed when the soil has warmed and there is no threat of frost. Thin on average to 8 in. apart.

It is essential to trim all thymes after flowering; this not only promotes new growth, but also stops the plant from becoming woody and sprawling in the wrong direction.

In very cold areas grow it in the garden as an annual or in containers and then winter with protection.

Harvesting
As thyme is an evergreen it can be picked fresh all year round provided you are not too greedy. For preserving, pick before it is in flower. Either dry the leaves or put them in a vinegar or oil.

Annie Hall thyme
Thymus serpyllum 'Annie Hall'

CONTAINER GROWING

All varieties suit being grown in containers. They like a free-draining soil low in nutrients; if grown in a rich soil they will become soft and the flavor will be impaired. Use the bark-peat-grit mix of potting soil; water sparingly, keeping the container bordering on dry, and in winter definitely dry—only watering if absolutely necessary, when the leaves begin to lose too much color. Feed only occasionally in the summer months. Put the container in a sunny spot, which will help the aromatic oils come to the leaf surface and impart a better flavor. Trim back after flowering to maintain shape and promote new growth.

WARNING

Although a medical dose drawn from the whole plant is safe, any amount of the volatile oil is toxic and should not be used internally except by prescription. Avoid altogether if you are pregnant.

CULINARY

Thyme is an aid to digestion and helps break down fatty foods. It is one of the main ingredients of bouquet garni; it is good, too, in stocks, marinades, and stews, and a sprig or two with half an onion makes a great herb stuffing for chicken.

Poached Trout with Lemon Thyme
Serves 4

4 trout, cleaned and gutted
Salt
6 peppercorns (whole)
4 fresh bay leaves
1 small onion cut into rings
1 lemon
1 sprig lemon thyme
1 tablespoon chopped lemon thyme leaves
½ cup white wine
2 tablespoons fresh snipped garlic chives
½ cup (1 stick) butter

Place the trout in a large frying pan. Sprinkle with salt and add the peppercorns. Place one bay leaf by each trout. Put the onion rings on top of the trout, cut half the lemon into slices and arrange this over the trout, add the thyme sprig, and sprinkle with some of the chopped thyme leaves. Pour in the wine and enough water just to cover the fish. Bring it to a boil on top of the stove and let it simmer uncovered for 6 minutes for fresh trout, 20 minutes for frozen.

Mix the remaining chopped lemon thyme and garlic chives with the butter in a small bowl. Divide this mixture into 4 equal portions. When the trout are cooked, lift them out gently and place on plates with a slice of lemon and the herb butter on top. Serve with new potatoes.

MEDICINAL

Thyme has strong antiseptic properties. The tea makes a gargle or mouthwash, and is a remedy for sore throats and infected gums. It is also good for hangovers.

The essential oil is antibacterial, antifungal and used in toothpaste, mouthwash, gargles, and other toilet articles. It can be used to kill mosquito larvae. A few drops added to the bath water helps ease rheumatic pain, and it is used in liniments and massage oils.

Tropaeolum majus

NASTURTIUM

Also known as Garden Nasturtium, Indian Cress, and Large Cress. From the family Tropaeolaceae.

Nasturtiums are native to South America, especially Peru and Bolivia, but are now cultivated worldwide.

The generic name, *Tropaeolum*, is derived from the Latin *tropaeum*, meaning "trophy" or "sign of victory." After a battle was finished, a tree trunk was set up on the battlefield and hung with the captured helmets and shields. It was thought that the round leaves of the nasturtium looked like shields and the flowers like blood-stained helmets.

It was introduced into Spain from Peru in the sixteenth century and reached London shortly afterward. When first introduced it was known as *Nasturcium indicum* or *Nasturcium peruvinum*, which is how it got its common name Indian cress. The custom of eating its petals, and using them for tea and salads, comes from Asia.

Nasturtium Alaska
Tropaeolum majus Alaska Series

SPECIES

Tropaeolum majus
Nasturtium
Half-hardy annual. Ht. and spread 12 in. Red-orange flowers from summer to early fall. Round, mid-green leaves. **All zones**

Tropaeolum majus
Alaska Series
Nasturtium Alaska (Variegated)
Half-hardy annual. Ht. and spread 12 in. Red, orange, and yellow flowers from summer to early fall. Round, variegated leaves. **All zones**

Tropaeolum majus
'Empress of India'
Nasturtium 'Empress of India'
Half-hardy annual. Ht. 8 in., spread 12 in. Dark red flowers from summer to early fall. Round, mid-green leaves. **All zones**

Tropaeolum peregrinum
Canary Creeper
Tender perennial. Climber, ht. 6 ft. Small, bright yellow flowers with 2 upper petals that are much larger and fringed from summer until first frost. Gray-green leaves with 5 lobes. In cool areas, best grown as an annual. **Zone 9**

Tropaeolum polyphyllum
Hardy perennial. Ht. 2–3 in., spread 12 in. or more. Fairly small yellow flowers from summer to early fall. Leaves gray-green on trailing stems. A fast-spreading plant once established. Looks good on banks or hanging down walls. **Zone 8**

Tropaeolum speciosum
Flame Creeper
Tender perennial. Climber, ht. 10 ft. Scarlet flowers in summer followed by bright blue fruits surrounded by deep red calyxes in fall. Leaves green with 6 lobes. This very dramatic plant should be grown like honeysuckle with its roots in the shade and head in the sun.

CULTIVATION

Propagation
Seed

The seeds are large and easy to handle. To have plants flowering early in the summer, sow in early spring under protection directly into prepared pots or cell trays, and cover lightly with compost. Plugs are ideal, especially if you want to introduce the young plants into a hanging basket; otherwise use small pots to allow more flexibility before planting out. When the seedlings are large enough and there is no threat of frosts, plant out into a prepared site in the garden, or into containers.

Cuttings

Take cuttings of the perennial varieties in the spring from the new soft growth.

Pests and Diseases
Aphids and **caterpillars** of cabbage white butterfly and its relatives may cause a problem. If the infestation is light, the fly may be brushed off or washed away with soapy water.

Maintenance
Spring Sow seed early under protection, or after frosts in the garden.
Summer Deadhead flowers to enhance flowering season.
Fall Dig up dead plants.
Winter Plan next year.

Garden Cultivation
Nasturtiums prefer a well-drained, poor soil in full sun or partial shade. If the soil is too rich, leaf growth will be made at the expense of the flowers. They are frost-tender and will suffer if the temperature falls below 40°F.

As soon as the soil has begun to warm and the frosts are over, nasturtiums can be sown directly into the garden. Sow individually 8 in. apart. For a border of these plants sow 6 in. apart. Claude Monet's garden at Giverny in France has a border of nasturtiums sprawling over a path that looks very effective.

Harvesting
Pick the flowers for fresh use only; they cannot be dried.

Pick the seed pods just before they lose their green color (for pickling in vinegar).

Pick the leaves for fresh use as required. They can be dried, but personally I don't think it is worth it.

Nasturtium *Tropaeolum majus*

COMPANION PLANTING

This herb attracts aphids away from vegetables like cabbage and broad beans. It also attracts the hoverfly, which attacks aphids. Further, it repels whitefly, woolly aphids, and ants. Overall it is a good tonic to any garden.

CONTAINER GROWING

This herb is excellent for growing in pots, tubs, window boxes, hanging baskets. Use the bark-peat-grit potting mix (see p. 591). Do not feed, because all you will produce are leaves, not flowers, but do keep well watered, especially in hot weather.

MEDICINAL

This herb is rarely used medicinally, although the fresh leaves contain vitamin C and iron as well as an antiseptic substance, which is at its highest before the plant flowers.

WARNING

Use the herb with caution. Do not eat more than ¹⁄₂ oz. at a time or 1 oz. per day.

CULINARY

I had a group from the local elementary school around the farm to talk about herbs. Just as they were leaving I mentioned that these pretty red flowers were now being sold in supermarkets for eating in salads. When a little boy looked at me in amazement, I suggested he try one. He ate the whole flower without saying a word. One of his friends said, "What does it taste like?" With a huge smile he asked if he could pick another flower for his friend, who ate it and screamed, "Pepper, pepper!" The seeds, flowers, and leaves are all now eaten for their spicy taste. They are also used in salads as an attractive garnish. The pickled flower buds provide a good substitute for capers.

Nasturtium Cream Cheese Dip

¹⁄₂ cup cream cheese
2 teaspoons tender nasturtium leaves, chopped
3 nasturtium flowers

Blend the cream cheese with the chopped leaves. Put the mixture into a bowl and decorate with the flowers. Eat this mixture as soon as possible because it can become bitter if left standing.

Urtica

NETTLE

Also known as Common Nettle, Stinging Nettle, Devil's Leaf, and Devil's Plaything. From the family Urticaceae.

Common nettle *Urtica dioica* **in full flower**

This plant is found all over the world. It is widespread on wasteland, especially on damp and nutrient-rich soil.

The generic name, *Urtica,* comes from the Latin *uro,* meaning "I burn." The Roman nettle *Urtica pilulifera* originally came to Britain with the invading Roman army. The soldiers used the plants to keep themselves warm. They flogged their legs and arms with nettles to keep their circulation going.

The use of nettles in the making of fabric goes back before history. Nettle cloth was found in a Danish grave of the later Bronze Age, wrapped around cremated bones. It was certainly made in Scotland as late as the eighteenth century. The Scottish poet Thomas Campbell wrote of sleeping in nettle sheets in Scotland and dining off nettle tablecloths. Records show that it was still being used in the early twentieth century in Tyrol.

In the Middle Ages it was believed that nettles marked the dwelling place of elves and were a protection against sorcery. They were also said to prevent milk from being affected by house trolls or witches.

Settlers in New England in the seventeenth century were surprised to find that this old friend and enemy had crossed the Atlantic with them. It was included in a list of plants that sprang up unaided.

Before World War II, vast quantities of nettles were imported to Britain from Germany. During the war there was a drive to collect as much of the homegrown nettle as possible. The dark green dye obtained from the plant was used as camouflage, and chlorophyll was extracted for use in medicines.

SPECIES

Urtica dioica
Stinging Nettle
Hardy perennial. Ht. 5 ft., spread infinite on creeping rootstock. The male and female flowers are on separate plants. The female flowers hang down in clusters, the male flower clusters stick out. The color for both is a yellowish green. The leaves are green toothed and have bristles. This is the variety that can be eaten when young.

Urtica pilulifera
Roman Nettle
Hardy perennial. Ht. 5 ft., spread infinite on creeping rootstock. This looks very similar to the common stinging nettle, but its sting is said to be more virulent.

Urtica urens
Small Nettle
Hardy annual. Ht. and spread 12 in. The male and female flowers are in the same cluster and are a greenish-white in color. The green leaves are deeply toothed and have bristles.

Urtica urentissima
Devil's Leaf
This is a native of Timor and the sting said to be so virulent that its effects can last for months and may even cause death.
All zone 3

CULTIVATION

Propagation
Seed
Nettles can be grown from seed sown in the spring. I am sure any of your friends with a garden would be happy to give you a root.

Division
Divide established roots early in spring before they put on much leaf growth, and the sting is least strong.

Pests and Diseases
Rarely suffers from pests and disease—at least not ones that you'd wish to destroy!

Maintenance
Spring Sow seeds, divide established plants.
Summer Cut plants back if they are becoming invasive.
Fall Cut back the plants hard into the ground.
Winter No need for protection; fully hardy.

Garden Cultivation
Stinging nettles are the scourge of the gardener and the farmer and the pest of children in summer, but are very useful in the garden, attracting butterflies and moths, and making an excellent caterpillar food. They will grow happily in any soil. It is worth having a natural corner in the garden where these and a few other wildflowers can be planted.

Harvesting
Cut young leaves in early spring for use as a vegetable.

CULINARY

Nettles are an invaluable food, rich in vitamins and minerals.

In spring the fresh leaves

Nettle soup

may be cooked and eaten like spinach, made into a delicious soup, or drunk as a tea.

Nettle Soup
Serves 4

When cooked, I am pleased to say, nettles lose their sting.

1¼ cups young nettle leaves
¼ cup oil or butter
1 small onion, chopped
1¼ cups cooked potatoes, peeled and diced
3¾ cups of milk
1 teaspoon each fresh sweet marjoram, sage, lemon thyme, chopped
1 teaspoon fresh chopped lovage
2 tablespoons cream
French parsley, chopped optional

Pick only the fresh young nettle leaves, and wear gloves to remove from stalks and wash them. Heat the oil in a saucepan, add the chopped onion and cook until clear. Then add the nettles and cook gently for about 10 minutes. Add the diced potatoes, all the herbs, and the milk and simmer for 10 minutes. Allow to cool, then put all the ingredients into a food processor and blend. Return to a saucepan over gentle heat. Add a swirl of cream to each bowl and sprinkle some chopped French parsley over the top. Serve with French bread.

MEDICINAL

The nettle has many therapeutic applications but is principally of benefit in all kinds of internal hemorrhages, as a diuretic in jaundice, for hemorrhoids, and as a laxative. It is also used in dermatological problems, including eczema.

Nettles make a valuable tonic after the long winter months when they provide one of the best sources of minerals. They are an excellent remedy for anemia. Their vitamin C content makes sure that the iron they contain is properly absorbed.

WARNING

Do not eat old plants uncooked; they can produce kidney damage and symptoms of poisoning. The plants must be cooked thoroughly to be safe.

Handle all plants with care; they do sting.

Nettle rinse and hair conditioner

OTHER USES

Whole plants yield a weak greenish-yellow woolen dye.

Nettles make a good spray against aphids. Pick a bucket full of nettles and pour water over them. Cover the container and allow to soak for a week. Strain the liquid, and put it into a spray. Spray on infected plants.

Nettles have a long-standing reputation for preventing hair loss and making the hair soft and shiny. They also have a reputation for eliminating dandruff.

Nettle Rinse and Conditioner
Use it as a final rinse after washing your hair or massage it into your scalp and comb through the hair every other day. Keep it in a small bottle in the refrigerator.

1 big-handful-size bunch of nettles
2 cups of water

Wear rubber gloves to cut the nettles. Wash thoroughly and put the bunch into an enamel saucepan with enough cold water to cover. Bring to the boil, cover, and simmer for 15 minutes. Strain the liquid into a jug and allow to cool.

Valeriana officinalis

VALERIAN

Also known as All Heal, Set All, Common Valerian, Garden Heliotrope, Cut Finger, Fragrant Valerian, Cat's Valerian, and St. George's Herb. From the family Valerianaceae.

Valerian is a native of Europe and West Asia and is now naturalized in North America. It is found in grasslands, ditches, damp meadows, and close to streams.

The name may come from the Latin *valere*, "to be healthy," an allusion to its powerful medicinal qualities. Or from an early herbalist, Valeris, who first used it medicinally.

Fresh valerian roots smell like ancient leather, but when dried they smell more like stale sweat. In spite of this, valerian is still used to add a musky tone to perfume. Cats and rats are attracted to the smell and the Pied Piper of Hamelin is said to have carried the root. A tincture of valerian was employed in World War I and II to treat shell shock and nervous stress.

COMPANION PLANTING

Planted near other vegetables, it boosts their growth by stimulating phosphorus and earthworm activity.

OTHER USES

Infuse root and spray on the ground to attract earthworms. Add mineral-rich leaves to new compost. Use the root in rat traps.

MEDICINAL

The root is a calmative. Its sedative and antispasmodic effects are of benefit in the treatment of a wide range of nervous disorders and intestinal colic.

Decoct the root or, more effectively, crush 1 teaspoon of dried root and soak in cold water for 12–24 hours. Drink as a sedative for mild insomnia, sudden emotional distress, headaches, intestinal cramps, and nervous exhaustion.

SPECIES

Valeriana officinalis
Valerian
Hardy perennial. Ht. 3–4 ft., spread 3 ft. Pale pink–white flower heads in summer. Leaves deeply toothed.
Zone 4

CULTIVATION

Propagation
Seed
Sow the fairly small seeds in early spring, either in seed or plug trays. Press the seeds into the soil but do not cover, as this will delay germination. When the seedlings are large enough to handle, transplant to the garden at a distance of 24 in. apart.

Valerian *Valeriana officinalis*

Division
Divide the roots in spring or fall. Replant after division in a prepared site.

Pests and Diseases
Valerian is mostly free from pests and disease.

Maintenance
Spring Sow seed. Divide roots.
Summer Cut back after flowering to prevent self-seeding.
Fall Divide establish plants if needed.
Winter A very hardy plant; no need for protection.

Garden Cultivation
Valerian is one of the earliest flowering, tall, wetland plants. As long as its roots are kept cool (which is why it prefers to be near water), it can be grown successfully in almost any garden soil in sun or deep shade. You can sow seeds directly in spring, leaving uncovered, but for a surer result start off in plug trays. When choosing the planting site, remember that cats love the scent.

Harvesting
Dig up complete root in late fall of the second and third years. Wash and remove the pale fibrous roots, leaving the edible rhizome. To dry this rhizome, cut it into manageable slices (see pp. 609–610).

WARNING

Valerian should not be taken in large doses for an extended period of time.

Verbena officinalis

VERVAIN

Also known as Holy Herb, Simpler's Joy,
Pigeon's Grass, Burvine, Wizard's Herb,
Herba Sacra, Holy Plant, European Vervain,
Enchanter's Plant, and Herba the Cross.
From the family Verbenaceae.

This herb is a native of Mediterranean regions. It has now become established elsewhere within temperate zones or, for that matter, wherever the Romans marched.

It is a herb of myth, magic, and medicine. The Egyptians believed that it originated from the tears of Isis. The Greek priests wore amulets made of it, as did the Romans, who also used it to purify their altars after sacrifice. The Druids used it for purification and for making magic potions.

Superstition tells that when you pick vervain, you should bless the plant. This originates from a legend that it grew on the hill at Calgary, and was used to stanch the flow of Christ's blood at the Crucifixion.

In the Middle Ages it was an ingredient in a holy salve, a powerful protector against demons and disease: "Vervain and Dill hinders witches from their will."

Vervain *Verbena officinalis*

SPECIES

Verbena officinalis
Vervain
Hardy perennial. Ht. 2–3 ft., spread 12 in. or more. Small pale lilac flowers in summer. Leaves green, hairy, and often deeply divided into lobes with curved teeth. This plant is not to be confused with Lemon Verbena, *Aloysia triphylla.*
Zone 4

CULTIVATION

Propagation
Seed
Sow the small seeds in early spring in a prepared seed or plug tray. Cover with perlite. No need for extra heat. When the seedlings are large enough, and after a period of hardening off, plant out in a prepared site, 12 in. apart.

Division
An established plant can be divided either in the spring or fall. It splits easily with lots of roots.

Pests and Diseases
If the soil is too rich or high in nitrates, it can be attacked by **aphids**.

Maintenance
Spring Sow seeds. Divide established plants.
Summer Cut back after flowering to stop it from self-seeding everywhere.
Fall Split established plants.
Winter No need for protection; fully hardy.

Garden Cultivation
Vervain can be sown directly into the garden in the spring in a well-drained soil and a sunny position. It is better to sow or plant in clumps because the flower is so small that otherwise it will not show to advantage. But beware its capacity to self-seed.

Harvesting
Pick leaves as required. Cut whole plant when in bloom. Dry leaves or whole plant if required.

CONTAINER GROWING

Vervain does nothing for containers, and containers do nothing for vervain.

MEDICINAL

Vervain has been used traditionally to strengthen the nervous system, dispel depression, and counter nervous exhaustion. It is also said to be effective in treating migraines and headaches of the nervous and bilious kind.

Chinese herbalists use a decoction to treat suppressed menstruation, and for liver problems and urinary tract infections.

CULINARY

Not advisable.

WARNING

Avoid during pregnancy.

Viola tricolor

HEARTSEASE

Also known as Wild Pansy, Field Pansy, Love Lies Bleeding, Love in Idleness, Herb Trinity, Jack Behind the Garden Gate, Kiss Me Behind the Garden Gate, Kiss Me Love, Kiss Me Love at the Garden Gate, Kiss Me Quick, Monkey's Face, Three Faces Under a Hood, Two Faces in a Hood, and Trinity Violet. From the family Violaceae.

Heartsease is a wildflower in Europe and North America, growing on wasteland and in fields and hedgerows.

In the Middle Ages, due to the influence of Christianity and because of its tricolor flowers—white, yellow, and purple—Heartsease was called Trinitaria or Trinitatis Herba, the herb of the Blessed Trinity.

In the traditional language of flowers, the purple form meant memories, the white loving thoughts, and the yellow, souvenirs.

SPECIES

Viola arvensis
Field Pansy
Hardy perennial. Ht. 2–4 in. The flowers are predominantly white or creamy, and appear in early summer. The green leaves are oval with shallow teeth.
Zone 4

Viola tricolor *Heartsease*

Viola lutea
Mountain Pansy
Hardy perennial. Ht. 3–8 in. Single-colored flowers in summer vary from yellow to blue and violet. The leaves are green and oval near the base of the stem, narrower further up.

Viola tricolor
Heartsease
Hardy perennial, often grown as an annual. Ht. 6–12 in. Flowers from spring to fall. Green, deeply lobed leaves.
Zone 4

CULTIVATION

Propagation
Seed
Sow seeds under protection in the fall, either into prepared seed or plug trays or pots. Do not cover the seeds. No bottom heat required. Winter the seedlings in a cold frame or cold greenhouse. In the spring harden off and plant out at a distance of 6 in.

Maintenance
Spring Sow seed.
Summer Deadhead flowers to prolong flowering season.
Fall Sow seed for early spring flowers.
Winter No need to protect.

Garden Cultivation
Heartsease will grow in any soil, in partial shade or sun. Sow the seeds from spring to early fall where they are to flower. Press into the soil but do not cover. Once planted, heartease will self-seed and persist indefinitely.

Harvesting
Pick the flowers fully open—from spring right through until late fall. Use fresh or for drying.

The plant has the most fascinating seed capsules, each capsule splitting into three. The best time to collect seeds is midday, when the maximum number of capsules will have opened.

CONTAINER GROWING

Heartsease look nice in any kind of container. Pick off the dead flowers, as this seems to keep the plant flowering for longer.

CULINARY

Add flowers to salads and to decorate sweet dishes.

MEDICINAL

An infusion of the flowers has long been prescribed for a broken heart. Less romantically, it is also a cure for bed-wetting.

An ointment made from it is good for eczema and acne and also for curing milk rust and cradle cap.

Herbalists use it to treat gout, rheumatoid arthritis, and respiratory disorders. An infusion of heartsease leaves added to bath water has proved beneficial to suffers of rheumatic disease.

Warning: In large doses, it may cause vomiting.

OTHER USES
Cleansing the skin and shampooing thinning hair.

Viola

VIOLET

From the family Violaceae.

There are records of sweet violets growing during the 1st century A.D. in Persia, Syria, and Turkey. It is a native not only of these areas but also of North Africa and Europe. Violets have been introduced elsewhere and are now cultivated in several countries for their perfume.

This charming herb has been much loved for over 2,000 years and there are many stories associated with it. In a Greek legend, Zeus fell in love with a beautiful maiden named Io. He turned her into a cow to protect her from his jealous wife, Juno. The earth grew violets for Io's food, and the flower was named after her.

The violet was also the flower of Aphrodite, the goddess of love, and of her son, Priapus, the god of gardens. The ultimate mark of the reverence in which the Greeks held sweet violet is that they made it the symbol of Athens.

For centuries perfumes have been made from the flowers of sweet violet mixed with the violet-scented roots of orris, and the last half of the nineteenth century saw intense interest in it—acres were cultivated to grow it as a market garden plant. Its main use was as a cut flower. No lady of quality would venture out without wearing a bunch of violets. It was also customary in gardens of large country houses to move the best clump of violets to a cold frame in late fall to provide flowers for the winter.

Common dog violet *Viola riviniana*

SPECIES

Viola odorata
Sweet Violet
Also known as Garden Violet. Hardy perennial. Ht. 3 in., spread 6 in. or more. Sweet-smelling white or purple flowers from late winter to early spring. The leaves are heart-shaped and form a rosette at the base, from which the long-stalked flowers arise. *Viola odorata* is one of the very few scented violets. It has been hybridized to produce Palma violets, with a single or double flower, in a range of rich colors. Recently there has been a revival in interest in this plant, and it is being offered again by specialist nurseries.
Zone 5

Viola reichenbachiana
Wood Violet
Hardy perennial. Ht. 1–8 in., spread 6 in. or more. Pale lilac–blue flowers in early spring. Leaves are green and heart-shaped. The difference between this plant and the common dog violet is the flowering time; there is also a slight difference in flower color.
Zone 5

Viola riviniana
Common Dog Violet
Also known as Blue Mice, Hedging Violet, Horse Violet, and Pig Violet. Hardy perennial. Ht. 1–8 in., spread 6 in. or more. Pale blue–lilac flowers in early summer. Leaves are green and heart-shaped. This violet does not grow runners.

CULTIVATION

Propagation
Seed
The small seed should be sown in early fall in prepared seed or plug trays. Use a soil-based potting soil; I have found violets prefer this. Water in and cover with a layer of compost, and finally cover with a sheet of glass or polyethylene. Put the trays either in a corner of the garden or in a cold frame (because the seeds germinate better if they have a period of stratification, though it will still be erratic). In the spring when the seedlings are large enough to handle, prick out into pots. If grown in cells, allow a period of hardening off. Plant out as soon as temperatures have risen at a distance of 12 in.

Cuttings

These can be taken from the parent plant, with a small amount of root attached, in early spring, and rooted in cell trays, using the bark-peat mix of potting soil (see p. 591). Harden off and plant out into a prepared site in the garden in late spring when they are fully rooted. Water well.

When using runners to propagate this plant, remove them in late spring and replant in a prepared site in the garden, 12 in. apart. Plant them firmly in the ground, making sure that the bases of the crowns are well embedded in the soil; water well.

Runners can be grown on in pots in early fall. Remove a well-rooted runner and plant in a pot of a suitable size (see Container Growing for further information). Overwinter in a cool greenhouse, watering from time to time to prevent red spider mite. Bring into the house in the spring to enjoy the flowers. After flowering, plant out in the garden into a prepared site.

Division

Divide well-established plants as soon as flowering is over in early summer. It is a good idea to plant three crowns together for a better show and as insurance against damage when splitting a crown. Replant in the garden in exactly the same way as for runners.

Pests and Diseases

The major pest for container-grown violets in mild weather is **red spider mite.** A good way to keep this at bay is to spray the leaves with water. If it is persistent, use a liquid horticultural soap (as per manufacturer's instructions).

In propagating violets, the disease you will most likely come across is **black root rot**, which is caused by insufficient drainage in the compost.

Young plants can also be

affected by **damping-off root rot**, which is usually caused by too much water and insufficient drainage.

Maintenance

Spring Take cuttings from established plants. Remove runners and pot or replant in the garden.
Summer Divide well-established plants and replant.
Fall Sow seed. Pot root runners for wintering under cover.
Winter Feed the garden with well-rotted manure.

Garden Cultivation

Violets thrive best in a moderately heavy, rich soil in a semishaded spot. If you have a light and/or gravelly soil, it is a good idea to add some texture—a mulch of well-rotted manure—the previous fall. In spring dig the manure in.

Plant out in the garden as soon as the frosts have finished, allowing 12 in. space between plants. When they become established, they quickly create a carpet of lovely sweet-smelling flowers. There is no need to protect any of the above-mentioned violets; they are fully hardy.

Harvesting

Pick the leaves in early spring for fresh use or for drying.

Gather the flowers just when they are opening, for drying or crystallizing.

Dig up the roots in fall to dry for medicinal use.

CONTAINER GROWING

Violets make good container plants. Use the bark-peat-grit mix of compost. Give them a liquid feed of fertilizer (following the manufacturer's instructions) after flowering. During the summer months, place the container in partial shade. In winter they do not like heat, and if it is too warm they will become weak and fail to flower. So, it is important that they are in a cool place with temperatures no higher than 45°F. There must also be good air circulation, and watering should be maintained on a regular basis.

CULINARY

The flowers of sweet violet are well known in crystallized form for decorating cakes, puddings, ice cream, and homemade sweets. They are also lovely in salads, and make an interesting oil—use an almond oil as base.

The flowers of common and dog violet can also be added to salads and used to decorate puddings. Their flavor is very mild in comparison to sweet violet, but they are just as attractive.

Sweet violet *Viola odorata*

MEDICINAL

Only sweet violet has been used medicinally. Various parts are still used, most commonly the rootstock. It is an excellent, soothing expectorant and is used to treat a range of respiratory disorders such as bronchitis, coughs, whooping cough, and head colds. It also has a cooling nature and is used to treat hangovers.

Made into a poultice, the leaves soothe sore, cracked nipples. Also they have a reputation for treating tumors, both benign and cancerous. Strong doses of the rhizome are emetic and purgative.

The flowers have a reputation for being slightly sedative and so helpful in cases of anxiety and insomnia.

OTHER USES

The flowers of sweet violets are used in potpourris, floral waters, and perfumes.

Zingiber officinale

GINGER

Also known as Stem Ginger, Canton Ginger.
From the family Zingiberaceae.

Freshly dug hand of ginger, Gaylephug, Bhutan

Ginger has been grown in tropical Asia for at least 3,000 years and was one of the first spices brought to Europe along the Silk Road from China. Arab merchants controlled the trade in ginger and other spices for centuries until explorers like Marco Polo reached the Indian Ocean. The Portuguese took ginger to their colonies and the Spaniards introduced it to the New World; in 1547 they exported over 1,000 tons of rhizomes to Jamaica and Mexico, and by the end of the century had a thriving trade with Europe. Fresh ginger is cultivated throughout the tropics and is freely available.

The creeping, branched rhizomes growing near the surface, with pale yellow flesh beneath a thin, buff-colored to dark brown skin, look like knobby fingers and are often referred to as "hands." The stems can grow up to 4 ft. tall, with narrow, lance-shaped leaves; the short-lived flowers are yellow-green and purple, marked with spots and stripes.

VARIETIES

Each center of cultivation has its own forms. Several clones are found in India and three in Malaya. Two found in Jamaica are the high-quality white or yellow form and "flint ginger," with tougher, fibrous rhizomes.

CULTIVATION

Propagation
Propagate in late spring just before growth begins, using sections of rhizomes. Lift parent plants carefully to avoid rhizome damage, shake off the soil and break off sections about 2 in. long with at least one good bud. Dispose of older sections, keeping the young growth, and trim the ends with a sharp knife. Plant, buds uppermost, 2–4 in. deep with 9 in. between rows. Water thoroughly with tepid water after planting.

Maintenance
Spring Plant rhizomes under cover.
Summer Water, feed, and keep weed-free. Maintain high temperatures and humidity.
Fall Lift rhizomes carefully.

Garden Cultivation
Ginger needs an annual rainfall of at least 45 in., high temperatures, and a short dry season for part of the year.

The soil should be rich, moisture-retentive, and free-draining; add well-rotted organic matter where necessary. It is essential that the ground is not compacted and all debris is removed, otherwise the rhizomes become deformed.

Water plants thoroughly during dry periods and keep them weed-free throughout the growing season. In the humid tropics, ginger can be planted at any time.

If rhizomes remain unused, they will sprout and rapidly develop

CULINARY

Ginger is used throughout the world as a flavoring for sweet and savory dishes; it plays a starring role in foods like gingerbread, but is also an integral part of many spice mixes, appearing in cookies, cakes, soups, pickles, marinades, curry powder, stewed fruit, puddings, tea, beer, ale, and wine.

It is the most important spice in Chinese cookery. In Japanese cookery it is used as a side dish called "gari" to accompany sushi. Besides being used fresh, dried, and in powdered form, ginger is pickled, preserved in syrup, candied, and crystallized.

Rhizomes should be lightly scraped or peeled to remove the tough skin before use.

Protected Cropping

Ginger can be grown under cover, but as it needs high temperatures and humidity, this is not normally practical, and for optimum productivity it is better planted outdoors.

As a "novelty crop" under glass, plant the rhizome just below the surface in peat-substitute-based potting soil in a 8 in. pot. Keep it constantly moist, and feed with a liquid fertilizer every 3 weeks during the growing season.

Harvesting and Storing

Younger, tender rhizomes are harvested for immediate use and for preserving; they become more fibrous and pungent with age.

Harvesting can begin from 7 months after planting. Rhizomes for drying should be lifted about 9–10 months after planting.

Fresh "root" can be stored in the refrigerator for several weeks wrapped in paper towels, foil, or any container that allows it to "breathe". It can also be wrapped and frozen.

PESTS AND DISEASES

Soft rot can appear as dark patches at the base of the shoots. To prevent, handle rhizomes with care and avoid waterlogging.

Cultivated ginger flourishing near Transvaal, South Africa

MEDICINAL

Ginger has been used for centuries in Chinese medicine. In Asia fresh ginger is a remedy for vomiting, coughing, abdominal distension, and fever. Many Africans drink ginger root as an aphrodisiac, while in New Guinea it is taken dried as a contraceptive and in the Philippines it is chewed to expel evil spirits.

In the Middle Ages it was believed to possess miraculous properties against cholera. Culpeper in his *Herball* of 1653 says: "It is profitable for old men; it heats the joints and is useful against gout; it expels wind." It can be rubbed on the face as a "rouge," stimulating circulation. Ginger is said to cleanse the body and lower cholesterol; it can be chewed to alleviate sore throats, is a digestive, relieves dyspepsia, colic, and diarrhea, and prevents travel sickness.

Ginger tea

FRUIT

In this section, fruit is defined as plant flesh that we are induced by the plant to eat, in order to distribute its seeds. Included is the closely allied group of nuts, which are in fact the seeds themselves. Presumably the plants are satisfied if a small percentage of the nut seeds are distributed to grow elsewhere.

The fruits covered in the three chapters Orchard Fruits; Soft, Bush, and Cane Fruits; and Tender Fruits are determined by the manner in which we most usually grow them in temperate gardens. Those that require some protection or cover, such as the annual, perennial, and tender fruits, are mostly fruits that are not hardy enough outdoors for the U.K. and northern European gardener, but are achievable in much of the U.S., southern Europe, and Australia. Of course we commonly grow many of these, such as melons, grapes, and even lemons, quite easily with the aid of a greenhouse, in cooler regions. I've also included many exotic tropical and subtropical fruits on sale in supermarkets and abroad which may be grown (or eaten!) out of curiosity and interest. Most of these were once grown and fruited in Victorian stove houses, and can often be fruited at home with a modest heated greenhouse. Failing that, most of these make spectacular, educational, and decorative houseplants. (Please keep in mind, however, the potential final height and size of your humble date palm seedling before you start dreaming of ever ripening a crop!)

The chapter on shrub and flower garden fruits includes those forgotten and unsung heroes that are only called upon in times of shortage and famine, and by those country folk who appreciate the sharp, strong flavors these piquant fruits offer. The potential of these fruits has often been overlooked; many of them are worthy of deliberate cultivation, and with only a little breeding and selection they could become sweet and tender attractions for our delectation. The strawberry today is gigantic and succulent compared to those of two centuries ago; we can only imagine what new fruits we may conjure from nature's raw materials in the future.

ORCHARD FRUITS

When fruits are mentioned, these are probably the first that come to mind: apples, pears, plums, and cherries—the tree-hard or top fruits as they are known. They consist of two main groups: the pome fruits, which are the apple- and pear-like members, and the stone fruits, which are the plums, cherries, peaches, and apricots. The pomes have small seeds in a core around which the "stalk" from immediately behind swells, enclosing them with flesh. The stone fruits have a single seed in a hard shell around which the flesh forms. Both of these groups are related, as they are both members of the *Rosaceae* family. Mulberries and figs come from different families. Nonetheless all are similar in hardiness, size, and manner of cultivation to orchard trees.

Most of these fruits have been cultivated since ancient times. They were nearly all known to the Romans, who spread them throughout their empire. However, much knowledge of their cultivation was then lost during the Dark Ages. The monasteries, and a few noblemen, maintained fruit gardens and orchards, but the common people reverted to farming and cropping from the wild with little interest in fruit cultivation.

Indeed fruits were often seen as poor fare compared to meat, and more suited for animal feed. If it was not for the ease with which many of these fruits could be fermented to make intoxicating beverages, they would probably have been even more neglected. After the Norman conquest of England the new lords proved to be more interested in fruit than the Saxons they had defeated, bringing many of their own improved varieties with them from France. Orchards became more widely planted, and the wealthy vied with each other in collecting the greatest number and variety, and in having the earliest and longest-lasting fruits.

In the sixteenth century, Henry VIII brought many new fruit varieties from the Netherlands and France, and the streets of London became full of homegrown and imported favorites. The impetus of completely different and new fruits from the New World created more interest in horticulture, reviving interest in the old fruits as well as the new discoveries. As old trusted varieties were exported to the colonies, new species and varieties were imported. These produced new varieties, which followed the old abroad at the same time as descendants of the first wave were already returning.

By the Victorian era the number of varieties in cultivation had escalated from a few hundred to many tens of thousands, if you counted local varieties worldwide. The great cities were served by the immense orchards and market gardens that surrounded them. Every gentleman aspired to a house with grounds that would include an orchard at the very least.

In the twentieth century, after the two World Wars, the labor to maintain great gardens and orchards was not available and the land was needed for more basic crops. Orchards were used for cereals and more exciting fruits became available from abroad. The British orchard all but disappeared from many counties. Houses with grounds and orchards were demolished to make way for office buildings at ten to the acre.

However, the green movement, combined with people's increasing awareness of the utility of trees, the value of fruit, and the ecological advantages of permanent culture as opposed to annual crops, has caused a reawakening of interest in orchard fruits. More are now being planted than for nearly a century.

Malus domestica from the family *Rosaceae*

CULINARY AND DESSERT APPLES

Tree up to 33 ft. Life span: medium to long. Deciduous, hardy, sometimes self-fertile.
Fruits: up to 6 in., spherical, green to yellow or red. Vitamin value: vitamin C.

Malus domestica apples are complex selections and hybrids of *M. pumila* with *M. sylvestris* and *M. mitis.* Thus the shape of the fruit varies from the spheres of **'Gladstone'** and **'Granny Smith'** to the flattened buns of **'Bramley'** and **'Mère de Ménage,'** or the almost conical **'Spartan,' 'Golden Delicious,'** and **'Worcester Pearmain.'** The color can be green, yellow, scarlet orange, or dark red to almost purple. The texture can vary from crisp to soft, and they may be juicy or dry, acid or insipid, bitter, bland, or aromatic. All apples have a dent in the stalk end, the remains of the flower at the other, and a central tough core with several brown seeds. These are edible in small amounts, though there is a recorded death from eating a quantity, since they contain small amounts of cyanide.

Granny Smith

The trees will often become picturesque landscape features, particularly when seen in an orchard. They frequently become twisted or distorted when left to themselves. They have soft downy or smooth leaves, never as glossy as pear leaves. The flowers are often pink- or red-tinged as well as snow white.

Apples are native to temperate Europe and Asia. They have been harvested from the wild since prehistory and were well known to the ancient Phoenicians. When Varro led his army as far as the Rhine in the first century B.C., every region had its apples. The Romans encouraged their cultivation, so although Cato had noted only a half dozen varieties in the second century B.C., Pliny knew of three dozen by the first century A.D. The Dark Ages caused a decline in apple growing in Britain and only one pomerium (orchard), at Nottingham, is mentioned in the Domesday book. However, interest increased after the Norman invasion. Costard and Pearmain varieties are first noted in the twelfth and thirteenth centuries, and by the year 1640 there are nearly five dozen varieties recorded by Parkinson. By 1669, Worlidge has the number up to 92, mostly cider apples. *Downing's Fruits*, printed in 1866, has 643 varieties listed. Now we have over 5,000 named apple varieties, representing about 2,000 actually distinguishable clones. Several hundred are easily obtainable from specialty nursery growers, though only a half dozen are grown on a commercial scale.

This sudden explosion in numbers was most probably due to the expansion of the colonies. The best varieties of apple trees from Europe mutated and crossed as they were propagated across North America and Australia, and these then returned to be crossed again. Apples are now grown extensively in every

Orleans Reinette

temperate region around the world. The first apples in North America supposedly were planted on Governors Island in Boston Harbor, but the Massachusetts Bay Company had requested seeds in 1629, and in 1635 a Mr. Wolcott of Connecticut wrote that he had made 500 hogsheads of cider from his new apple orchard.

Golden Delicious

'Spartan'

VARIETIES

Medium to large **'McIntosh,'** first introduced to the U.S. in 1870, has very tender red skin and crisp white flesh with a delicious aroma and a sweet-tart tang. It's a favorite for eating fresh, and also valued for cider and baking. The self-fertile trees bear young and abundantly. The most widely grown apple in the U.S., favored by home gardeners and commercial orchards alike, is the large, tapered **'Red Delicious.'** Solid and crisp, it has a mild, sweet flavor. **'Winesap'** and **'Stayman Winesap'** are old American apples with juicy, firm, yellowish flesh of wonderful winelike flavor that is as good in cooking as it is fresh. The youngster **'Fuji'** was introduced into the United States in 1962, but it's already a firm favorite, thanks to the outstanding honeyed sweetness of its crisp, white flesh. It doesn't need as many hours of winter chill as other varieties, and the fruit takes up to 200 days to mature, so it's popular with gardeners in milder-winter areas. The round, red, sometimes striped **'Jonathan'** is another old American variety, first described in New York

in 1862. Its sprightly, refreshing flavor holds up well in cooking and baking. The huge red fruits of **'Rome'** (also called **'Rome Beauty'**) are excellent for all uses, but they're especially appreciated by cooks, who may only have to peel two or three apples for a pie. A late-season 'McIntosh' type, **'Cortland'** has been a favorite in America for almost a century. It's extremely cold hardy and will tolerate temperatures as low as 40°F. The pure white flesh has a delicious tanginess. **'Liberty'** and **'Freedom'** are part of a new generation of disease-

'Cox's Orange Pippin'

resistant apples bred for carefree vigor. Both are resistant to nearly all major apple diseases and will flourish in the home garden without need or chemical sprays. The oldest variety known and easily available is **'Court Pendu Plat'** (mid-winter, dessert) which may

go back to Roman times. It is still grown because it flowers late, missing frosts. **'Nonpareil'** and **'Golden Pippin'** also come from the 16th century and keep until midspring. However, they are rarely available, though there are a dozen and a half part-descendants all called **'Golden Pippin.' 'Golden Reinette'** (midwinter, dessert) is still popular in Europe and dates from before 1650. The large green **'Flower of Kent'** (1660) has nearly disappeared. This was the apple that prompted Sir Isaac Newton in his discoveries of the laws of motion and gravity. **'Ribston Pippin'** (midwinter, dessert) has one of the highest vitamin C contents and superb flavor. It was bred in 1707 and does not like wet, heavy soils. From 1720 comes **'Ashmead's Kernel,'** one of the best-tasting, late-keeping dessert apples, but it is a light cropper. **'Orleans Reinette'** (midwinter, dessert) has been known since 1776. It is juicy, very tasty, with a rough skin and is not very good on wet, cold sites.

'Bramley's Seedling' (midwinter, culinary) raised in 1809, has one of the highest vitamin C contents of cooking varieties. It grows large, so have it on a more dwarfing stock than others. **'Egremont Russet'** (late fall), bred in 1872, is one of the best russets, a group of apples with scentless, roughened skin, and crisp, firm flesh, which is sweet and tasty but never overly juicy or acid. The ubiquitous **'Golden Delicious,'** so much grown commercially in Europe, is a conical yellow. It actually tastes pretty good when grown at home, but must be waxed for keeping as otherwise it wilts. It was found in West Virginia in 1916. **'Discovery'** was introduced in 1962. It is an early scarlet fruit with creamy white flesh that comes in late summer to early fall. The flowers are fairly frost tolerant and it is scab resistant. It is rapidly dominating the early apple market because it will keep better longer than most other early varieties.

'Egremont Russet'

CULTIVATION

Apples are much-abused trees. They prefer a rich, moist, well-drained loam, but are planted almost anywhere and yet often still do fairly well. What they will not stand is being water-logged, or growing on the site of an old apple tree or near others that have been long established, and they do not thrive in dank frost pockets. Pollination is best served by planting more than three varieties, as many apples are mutually incom-patible, having diploid or triploid varieties with irre-concilable differences in their chromosomes. Crab apples are usually good pol-linators for unnamed trees.

Choosing a Variety
Start your apple orchard with the one you like best to eat, if it can be successfully grown in your area. Then you can branch out and explore the flavors of other varieties, including many old treasures that you'll never find on a supermarket counter. Most apples will grow well in Zones 4 through 8, but some can withstand winter cold as low as −50°F and others will set a good crop in southern California and Phoenix, Arizona. Varieties also differ in their requirements for "winter chill," a period of cold that is vital for a good fruit set. Any trees stocked at your local nursery should thrive in your climate. Disease resistance is the new "watchword" in apple growing. Research stations are working on new releases that combine good-tasting fruit with an ability to shrug off scab, cedar-apple rust,

mildew, and other common apple problems. **'Liberty,' 'Freedom,' 'Red Free,'** and **'Williams Pride'** are some of this new wave of flavorful, disease-resistant introductions.

This distinctive columnar apple tree dominates its container.

Growing in Containers
On very dwarfing stocks apples are easily grown in large pots. They need hard pruning in winter and in summer the lengthening shoots should be nipped out; thus tip-bearing varieties are not really suitable. Special varieties have been developed for containers, which supposedly require little pruning. In cold-winter areas, surround the container with a cylinder of chicken wire or wire fence, and fill it with leaves or straw for insulation.

Maintenance
Spring Weed, mulch, spray seaweed solution monthly.
Summer Thin fruits, summer prune, spray with seaweed solution, apply greasebands.
Fall Use poor fruits first; pick best for storage.
Winter Hard prune, add copious compost, remove mummified fruits.

Propagation
Apple pips rarely make fruiting trees of value; however many of our best varieties were chance seedlings. Apples are grafted or budded onto different rootstocks depending on site and size of tree required. Few grow them from cuttings on their own roots or as standards on seedling stocks as these make very large trees suitable for planting only in grazed meadows. Half-standards are more convenient for the home orchard and these get big enough on M25 stock at about 17 ft. high and 21 ft. apart. At the other extreme, the most dwarfing stock is M27, useful for pot culture, but these midgets need staking all their lives and the branches start so low you cannot mow or grow underneath them. M9 produces a 7-ft. tree, still needing staking but good for cordons. On such very dwarfing stocks the trees do badly in poor soil and during droughts. M26 is bigger, growing to 9 ft., and still needs a stake, but is probably the best for small gardens. It needs 10 ft. on each side. MM106 is better on poor soils, and on good soils is still compact at about 13 ft., needing 15 ft. between trees.

Pruning and Training
Apple trees are often left to grow and produce for years with no pruning other than remedial work once the head has formed. They may be trained and hard pruned

'Golden Delicious'

summer and winter, back to spur systems, on almost any shaped framework, though rarely as fans. For beauty and productivity, apples are best as espaliers; to achieve the maximum number of varieties, as cordons; for ease and quality, as open goblet-pruned small trees. Some varieties, especially many of the earliest fruiters, are tip bearers. These are best only pruned remedially, as hard pruning will remove the fruiting wood. They can be grown on a replacement system as for peaches (see p. 419) but it is hard work. As important as the pruning is the thinning. Removing crowded and congested, damaged and diseased apples improves the size and

Trained apples underplanted with herbs

quality of those remaining and prevents biennial bearing. Thin after the June drop occurs and again twice after, disposing of the rejects to destroy any pests.

Weed, Pest, and Disease Control

Apples are the most commonly grown fruit tree in much of the temperate zone. They have thus built up a whole ecosystem of pests and diseases around themselves. Although they have many problems they still manage to produce enormous quantities of fruit. The commonplace pests require the usual remedies (see pp. 602–607), but apples suffer from some annoying specialties. Holes in the fruits are usually caused by one of three pests. **Codling moth, Oriental fruit moth,** and **apple maggot** tunnel through the fruit, which often causes it to drop when

young. You may see entry holes surrounded by sawdustlike frass. Codling moth is found across the country. Oriental fruit moth is widespread, affecting fruit everywhere except the Midwest, Texas, and some southern states. Apple maggot is a problem mainly in the Northeast and Great Lakes areas. They are controlled by corrugated cardboard band traps, pheromone traps, permitted sprays as the blossom sets, and hygiene. **Cedar-apple rust,** a disease that depends on eastern red cedar and other junipers as an alternative host, causes orange spots on apple leaves and fruits. Plant resistant varieties, or spray with sulfur or copper to control. Many varieties are scab-resistant. If it occurs, it affects first the leaves, then the fruits, and, like brown rot and canker, is spread by mummified apples and dead wood.

'Winston' apples forming a decorative arch

A handy apple store

All of these problems, and mildews, are best controlled by hygiene, keeping the trees vigorous, well watered and mulched, and open pruned. Woolly aphis can be sprayed or dabbed with soft soap or derris. Sticky nonsetting tree bands control many pests all year round.

Harvesting and Storing

Early apples are best eaten off the tree. They rarely keep for long. Most midseason apples are also best eaten off the tree as they ripen, but many will keep for weeks if picked just underripe and stored in the cool. Late keepers must hang on the trees until hard frosts are imminent, then if they are delicately picked and kept cool in the dark they may keep for six months or longer. They are best picked with a cupped hand and gently laid in a tray, traditionally padded with dry straw. (This may mold if dampened so better to use shredded newspaper.) Do not store early varieties with lates, or store either near pears, onions, garlic, or potatoes. The fruits must be free of bruises, rot, and holes, and the stalk must remain attached for them to store well. If apples are individually wrapped in paper they keep longer.

COMPANION PLANTING

Apples are bad for potatoes, making them blight-prone. They are benefited by alliums, especially chives, and penstemons and nasturtiums nearby are thought to prevent sawfly and woolly aphis. Stinging nettles close by benefit the trees and, dried, they help stored fruits keep.

OTHER USES

Apple wood is used for mallet heads, golf clubs, and in engraving. It is delicately scented when burned, and is useful for smoking foods and as fire logs.

'Egremont Russet' apple blossom

CULINARY USES

Apples can be pureed and frozen, juiced and frozen, dried in thin rings, made into cider, or stewed and made into tarts, pies, and jellies, especially with other fruits, which they help set. The juice is delicious fresh and can be frozen for out-of-season use, and made into cider or vinegar. Cooking apples are different from dessert apples: much larger, more acid, and less sweet raw. Most break down quickly when heated, and few retain their texture, unlike most of the desserts. 'McIntosh,' 'Granny Smith,' 'Rome,' and 'Cortland' are excellent for cooking or eating due to their hint of tartness.

Flying Saucers
Serves 1

1 large cooking apple
Approx. 2 tablespoons
  mincemeat
Pat of butter
1 tablespoon sesame seeds
Cream or custard to serve

Wash, dry, and cut the apple in half horizontally. Remove the tough part of the core but leave the outside intact. Stuff the hollow with mincemeat, then pin the two halves back together with toothpicks. Rub the outside with butter and roll in sesame seeds, then bake in a preheated oven at 375°F for 30 minutes or until it "lifts off" nicely. Serve immediately with cream or custard.

Malus pumila from the family *Rosaceae*

CRAB AND CIDER APPLES

Trees up to 33 ft. Life span: long. Deciduous, often self-fertile.
Fruits: ½–3 in., spherical, yellow, green, or red. Value: make tonic
alcoholic beverages.

Crab apples grow wild and have smaller, more brightly colored fruits than cultivated varieties. The fruits make delicious jellies. Cider apples are more like eating and cooking apples, with fruits in-between in size but similarly bitter and astringent. Selected crab apples are grown ornamentally and are useful pollinators for other apples, so they may be found on semidwarfing stocks as small trees. Cider apples were always grown on strong or seedling stock, gaining immense vigor, which they needed to tower above animals grazing underneath.

Crabs have been used since prehistory and doubtless cider has been made for as long.

In the United States, many culinary and dessert apples, including **'McIntosh'** and **'Winesap,'** are also used for cider. True cider apples, including the cold-hardy American varieties **'Centennial,' 'Dolgo,' 'Wealthy,'** and **'Chestnut,'** are interesting for the

VARIETIES

home gardener to experiment with, evoking a rich heritage of homemade apple cider and crab apple jelly, not to mention a bounty of spring blossoms. **'Wealthy,'** raised in 1861 in Minnesota, at its best is a sweet strawberry-flavored variety, soft with creamy flesh, but can be less exciting depending on conditions. **'Prairie Spy,'** raised in 1914, is very sweet with little acidity. It is vigorous and hardy, with firm-fleshed, crisp, and juicy fruits. Many crabs are well-known ornamentals, such as **'John Downie,'** which has long golden-orange fruits, and **'Golden Hornet,'** with bright yellow fruits. Most are mixed hybrids of *Malus pumila* with the native *M. sylvestris,* which has sour, hard, green fruits and is sometimes thorny, and

M. mitis, from the Mediterranean region, which has softer leaves and sweeter, more colored fruits. *M. baccata,* the **Siberian crab**, and *M. manchurica,* from China, are widely planted for their bright red fruits. Cider apples are more improved and closer to *M. domestica* hybrids.

Immature crab apples

CULTIVATION

Tougher than the finer apples, these may be grown almost anywhere not waterlogged or parched. Crab apples are extremely cold tolerant. Most varieties are hardy in Zones 3 through 8, and some will thrive as far north as Zone 2.

Growing under Glass
Neither is happy permanently under glass. They need a winter chill; otherwise they crop badly.

Growing in Containers
Crab apples can be fruited in pots; indeed they often do even in the small pots in which garden centers sell them. Cider apples are shy and less likely to produce heavy crops.

Maintenance
Spring Weed, mulch, and spray seaweed solution.
Summer Keep trees deeply mulched to conserve moisture in soil.
Fall Pick fruit.
Winter Prune, and spread the compost.

Propagation
Although some crabs can be grown from seed, they are not reliable. Named varieties are grafted onto rootstocks suitable for the size and site

Old varieties of cider apples from Sarah Bowen's orchard

'Dabinett'

intended. Neither crab nor cider apple varieties are usually available on the most dwarfing rootstocks, but on more vigorous stock they make large trees.

Pruning and Training
Crab apples are usually worked as half-standards on semidwarfing stock and are only pruned remedially in winter. Cider apples are worked as standards on strong-growing stocks and make big trees. Likewise, cider apples should only be pruned remedially after forming a head.

Weed, Pest, and Disease Control
Although these can suffer from the same problems as dessert and culinary apples, the crops are rarely badly affected. Crab apples are usually remarkably productive whatever care they get. For cider apples many problems such as scab are also mostly irrelevant.

Harvesting and Storing
Crabs can be picked under-ripe for jellying, but you can hang on, as the birds do not go for them as fast as softer fruits. Cider apples are left as long as possible to get maximum sugar and to soften. If they are shaken down they bruise, so the apples are then best pressed immediately, not stored in heaps to soften further before pressing.

COMPANION PLANTING

The plants that benefit dessert and culinary apples (see p. 398) also associate well with these varieties. Both crab and cider apples are often grown in hedgerows and grazed meadow orchards. They seem content with grass underneath.

'Michellin'

OTHER USES

Pressed apple pulp can be dried and stored until late winter for wild bird and livestock food.

Apple cider

CULINARY USES

Crab apples make delicious tart jellies by themselves or mixed with other fruits that have less pectin and do not set so easily. Cider apples are used solely to make cider. They are cleaned, crushed, and pressed and the juice is fermented, often with the addition of wine yeast and sugar. After fermentation, cider may be flat, cloudy, sweet, or sparkling, green or yellow, depending on local taste. Ciders are made from several varieties of apple, to give a blend of acidity, sweetness, and tannin. (Palatable cider can be made from a mixture of dessert and cooking apples.) Some cider is made into vinegar, deliberately.

Crab Apple Jelly
Makes about 7 lb.

12 cups crab apples
Approx. 6 cups sugar

Chop the apples, then simmer them in water to cover until soft. Sieve or strain through a jelly bag and measure the juice. Add three-quarters of the volume in sugar. Return to the heat and bring to a boil, stirring to dissolve the sugar. Boil until the setting point is reached, then skim and pour into warm, sterilized jars. Cover while still hot.

Pyrus communis from the family *Rosaceae*

CULINARY AND DESSERT PEARS

Tree up to 65 ft. Life span: very long. Deciduous, hardy, rarely self-fertile.
Fruits: up to 3 x 7 in. Value: potassium and riboflavin.

'Conference'

Pears very closely resemble, and are related to, apples, but there are no known natural hybrids between them. Pears have a fruit that elongates at the stalk end, which stands proud, whereas an apple's stalk is inset in a dent in the top of the fruit. Some pears, such as **'Conference'** and **'Bartlett,'** will set fruit parthenocarpically (that is, they fruit freely without pollination). However, these fruits are usually not as good as fertilized ones, being misshapen and of course lacking seeds. Pear trees resemble apples but have shiny leaves, more upright growth, and the fat stems usually have a glossier brown hue and more angled buds than apple. Pears on their own roots make very big trees, too big to prune, spray, or pick, and the fruit is damaged when it drops. Pears are thus usually worked on quince roots, which makes them smaller, more compact trees.

'Comice'

Pears are native to Europe and Asia. The first cultivated varieties were selected from the wild in prehistory. The ancient Phoenicians, Jews, and pre-Christian Romans grew several improved sorts; by the time of Cato there were at least a half dozen distinct fruits, Pliny records 41 and Palladius 56. A list of fruits for the Grand Duke Cosmo III, in late medieval Italy, raises the number to 209, and another manuscript lists 232. In Britain in 1640 only five dozen were known. This rose to more than 700 by 1842. In 1866 the American author T. W. Field cataloged 850 varieties. The rapid increase in numbers and quality, from poor culinary pears to fine desserts, was mainly the work of a few dedicated breeders in France and Belgium at the end of the eighteenth century, who selected and bred most modern varieties.

'Durondeau'

VARIETIES

As pears are used more for eating raw than in cooking, and dessert pears can be cooked, but not vice versa, it is not worthwhile growing purely culinary pears. **'Comice'** (late season) is by far the best dessert pear. No other approaches it for sweet, aromatic succulence, and the fruits can reach a magnificent weight. These are very choice and deserve to be espaliered on the best warm wall. **'Bartlett'/ 'Williams' Bon Chretien'** (early to midseason) is widely grown for canning, but is an excellent table fruit—if a bit prone to scab. It is also parthenocarpic as is **'Conference'** (early to midseason). This latter is a reliable cropper on its own and is scab-resistant. Beautiful, light green **'Anjou'** and its ruddy counterpart **'Red Anjou,'** are mild, fine-textured pears with delicate, melting, white flesh. Their fine flavor gets even sweeter a few weeks after picking. Both need a pollinator, and **'Bosc'** is a good one. This golden-brown pear has russeted skin and aromatic, tender white flesh. For low-maintenance gardens, **'Seckel'** is the perfect choice. Its brownish skin and small size may look like nothing special, but this tiny morsel, often called "sugar pear," offers a few bites of spicy-sweet, fine-grained flesh with a mouthwatering aroma. Along with its delicious taste comes an iron constitution: the variety is widely adaptable to almost any conditions, and it's naturally semidwarf, needing no pruning. It bears heavy crops and is less troubled by disease than other varieties. There are hundreds of other pear varieties, many of which are cooking, not dessert, and several species that have more ornamental than edible value: **Birch-leaved Pear**, *P. betulifolia*, **Chinese Sand** or **Duck Pear**, *P. sinensis*, and **Three-lobed-leaved Pear**, *P. trilobata*, are popular.

'Beurre Hardy'

'Lattilac'

CULTIVATION

Dessert pears need a rich, well-drained, moist soil, preferably light and loamy. The blossom and fruitlets need protection from frosts as they flower early in spring. Pollination is best ensured by planting a mixture of varieties. Do not plant deep, as pears are prone to scion rooting, which allows them to make big, less fruitful trees. Most pears will thrive in Zones 5 through 8. Some are more cold-hardy, such as **'Stacey,'** which bears small, sweet fruits after 50°F winters, and will do well as far north as Zone 2. A few varieties are more tender, and best in Zones 6 through 9. The unusual **'Pineapple,'** which has a tropical flavor, is for mild-winter regions, including the Deep South. As with other fruits, read the catalog description to make sure the variety you are considering will do well in your area.

Growing under Glass

Pears appreciate a warm wall but are not easy under glass, as they do not like to get too hot and humid; they are thus difficult to grow in the tropics.

Growing in Containers

Pears have often been fruited in tubs. They are amenable to hard pruning, and so respond better than most other fruits to this and to the cramped conditions of a pot.

Ornamental and Wildlife Value

Why plant an ornamental flowering tree when you can plant a pear? They are just smothered with blossom and buzzing with bees in early spring. Overripe pears that hang on the trees or fall to the ground will attract butterflies as well as wasps and yellow jackets.

Propagation

Pears do not come true from seed, reverting to their unproductive forms. They may root from cuttings and can occasionally be layered, but get too big on their own roots. Normally they are grafted onto quince rootstocks. For heavy, damp soils and for big trees, pear seedling stock was always used, but there is little demand for this nowadays. Pears have been grafted onto apple stocks and even onto hawthorn. As some varieties do not bond readily with quince stock, they are "double-worked," or grafted onto a mutually compatible intergraft on the quince.

Pruning and Training

Grown as trees or bushes, pears can be left to

A pear espalier

'Josephine Malines'

themselves except for remedial pruning. They tend to throw twin leaders, which need rationalizing. Alternatively, they respond better than most fruits to hard winter pruning and are almost as amenable to summer pruning, thus they can be trained to an endless variety of forms. As they benefit from the shelter of a wall, they are commonly espaliered, and are more rewarding for less work than a peach in the same position. There are many specialized training forms for pears in addition to the cordon, espalier, and fan, and equally intricate and specialized pruning methods. Pears will take almost any shape you choose, and you can't go wrong if you then shear almost all long growths off

by three-quarters in summer and in winter. Take care not to let them root from or above the graft, which destroys the benefit of the rootstock.

Weed, Pest, and Disease Control

Pears suffer fewer problems than apples. However, ripening is poor in very cool or hot weather and results in hard or mealy fruits. Leaving the fruit too long on the tree or in storage causes them to **rot** from the inside out. **Pear midge** causes the fruitlets to blacken and drop off; inspection reveals maggots within. These are remedied by the hygienic removal and disposal of affected fruits; running poultry underneath in orchards is as effective. **Fireblight** causes damage resembling scorching. It usually starts from the blossoms. Prune and burn damaged parts immediately, cutting back to clean wood. **Scab** is a problem in stagnant sites. It affects the fruits before the leaves, which is the opposite from apples. Sprays are usually unnecessary with the more resistant varieties. Good open pruning and healthy growth, not overfed with nitrogen, reduce attacks. Always remove all mummified fruits and dead wood immediately. **Leaf blistering** is usually caused by minute mites. These used to be controlled with lime and sulfur sprays before bud burst. Modern soft soap sprays have also proved to be effective.

Maintenance
Spring Weed, mulch, and spray with seaweed solution monthly; protect flowers against frosts.
Summer Thin fruit.
Fall Pick fruit.
Winter Prune hard or not at all; compost heavily.

Harvesting and Storing
Early pears are best picked almost, but never fully, ripe. They should come off when lifted to the horizontal. Left on the tree, they get mealy. Watch them carefully while they finish ripening. They will slowly ripen if kept cool, faster if warm. Late pears should be left until risk of bird damage is too great, and picked with a long-handled fruit picker. Kept in a cool, dark place, late varieties last for months, ripening up rapidly if brought into warmth. Do not wrap them with paper (as one does with apples), and take care not to store the two fruits near each other, as they will cross-taint.

CULINARY USES

Pears are exquisite as dessert fruits and may be used in much the same way as apples, sliced and used in tarts, baked, stewed, or pureed. They are delicious pickled with onions and spices in vinegar.

Pear Islands
Serves 4

4 large pears
1/3 cup superfine sugar
Half bottle sweet Muscat wine
2 tablespoons corn flour
Splash of milk
Dark chocolate to taste

Peel, core, and halve the pears. Dissolve two-thirds of the sugar in the wine over a gentle heat and poach the pears in this syrup. Place the pear halves on a greased baking sheet, dredge with the rest of sugar, and put under the broiler for a minute or two until the tops caramelize. In the meantime, blend the corn flour with a little milk and stir it into the syrup. Return to the heat and cook gently, stirring, until thick. Pour the sauce into a serving bowl, grate some dark chocolate over it, and arrange the pear halves. Serve piping hot or chilled.

'Durondeau'

OTHER USES

The bark contains a yellow dye and arbutin, an antibiotic. The leaves have been used medicinally for renal and urinary infections. The wood is hard and uniform, so loved by carvers. It is beautifully scented.

COMPANION PLANTING

Pears are hindered by grass, so this should not be allowed near them in their early years. However, the pears may be grassed down later, especially if they are situated in heavy and/or damp conditions.

Pear dye

Pyrus from the family *Rosaceae*

PERRY PEARS

Tree up to 65 ft. Life span: very long. Deciduous, rarely self-fertile. Fruits: up to 4 x 3 in., variable, pear-shaped, yellow, brown, or red. Value: make a healthy tonic beverage.

Perry pear fruits are smaller and hardier than their culinary and dessert cousins, while the trees are generally enormous. As these fruits were wanted in quantity for pressing, they were selected for large trees that would stand well above grass and the depredations of stock. The fruits are bitter and astringent, containing a lot of tannin, even though they may often look very appealing. They are pressed for the juice, which ferments to an alcoholic beverage.

Perry pears may have been brought to Britain by the Romans, but they were introduced in force by the Normans. Normandy was by then well established as a perry-growing region and the Normans found parts of the west and midlands of England equally suitable. Many of the original pear orchards would probably still have been planted for perry without the Norman influence, as early pears tended to be unpalatable raw anyway. American colonists certainly did not start off without perry pears. By 1648 a booklet entitled *A Perfect Description of Virginia* describes a Mr. Kinsman regularly making forty or fifty butts of perry from his orchard. Whereas cider has remained a popular drink, perry waned in the nineteenth century, and perry pears are no longer cultivated or available in America.

A mature perry pear tree with a heavy crop of fruit

VARIETIES

There are some 200–300 perry pear varieties known, though these are called by twice as many names, each district having its own local variation. The **'Thorn Pear'** is recorded from 1676 and grows on a very upright tree. Other early varieties such as **'Hastings'** and **'Brown Bess'** could be eaten or made into perry. Later varieties such as **'Holmer'** are more single-purpose and almost inedible. In the 19th century, breeders thought dual-purpose pears would be useful and produced **'Blakeney Red'** and **'Cannock.'** The Huffcap group make very big trees with fruits of a high specific gravity; Rock varieties make even stronger perry, but are still often called Huffcaps.

CULTIVATION

Perry pears are less demanding than culinary or dessert pears and will do quite well in fairly poor soils. They do not like shallow or badly drained sites.

Growing under Glass
These are fairly hardy and will make big trees, so are generally not likely to thrive under glass.

Growing in Containers
Although they would resent it by being short-lived and light-cropping, it should be possible to grow these in large tubs.

Ornamental and Wildlife Value
Perry pears make a mass of flowers and are tall, attractive trees that live for several hundred years, making them very suitable as estate and orchard trees, but too big for most gardens except on modern dwarfing stock. The flowers are good for insects and the fruits are eaten by birds in winter.

Maintenance
Spring Cut grass and spray with seaweed solution.
Summer No maintenance needed.
Fall Cut grass, collect fruits.
Winter Prune and spread compost.

Propagation
Perry pears were often grown from seed or grafted onto stocks grown from pips in order to get large trees. Now they can be had on dwarfing stocks, such as quince, and are more manageable.

Pruning and Training
Once the initial shape is formed, these are only pruned remedially, though care should always be taken to ensure that such large trees are sound.

Weed, Pest, and Disease Control
These suffer the same few problems as dessert and culinary pears, which make little impression on the immense crops. **Fireblight** is a risk, but there is little one can do with such large trees.

Harvesting and Storing
Immense crops are produced; a ton or even two tons per tree is possible, after several decades. One tree in 1790 covered three-quarters of an acre and produced six tons per year. Perry pears do not keep and rot very quickly. Perry is usually pressed from one variety only, with sugar and yeast added. Dessert and culinary pears do not make a perry of any value, but can be made into a pear wine.

COMPANION PLANTING

Young trees were usually cropped between with cereals or hops and then grassed down as they matured, often grazed by geese.

OTHER USES

The wood is useful for carving and, as firewood, scents the room.

A standing cup made of pear wood, dating from the early 17th century

CULINARY USES

Perry pears are not normally very good for eating even when they are cooked, though 'Blakeney Red' was once considered good for baking.

Pressless Perry Wine
Makes approx. 4 quarts

18 cups whole pears, chopped
6 cups sugar
4 quarts water
Approx. 1 teaspoon wine yeast

Boil the water and add the pears. Stir in half the sugar and bring back to a boil, then allow to cool to 7°F before adding the yeast. Seal with a fermentation lock and keep warm for one week, then strain and add the remaining sugar to the liquor. Reseal with the lock and ferment in a warm place until all action has stopped. Siphon off the lees (sediment) and store in a cool place for 3 months, then bottle and store for a year before drinking.

Cydonia vulgaris/C. oblonga from the family *Rosaceae*

QUINCES

Tree up to 20 ft. Self-fertile, deciduous, hardy, long-lived.
Fruits: 2 x 5 in., yellow and fragrant.

'Portuguese' quince blossom

These are small, bushy trees, often twisted and contorted. There are two forms: a lower mounded one with lax branches, more suited to ornamental and wildlife use; and a stiffer, erect type, which bears larger fruits and is better for orchards. The leaves are downy underneath, resembling apple leaves more than pear. They turn a gorgeous yellow in fall. The decorative pink and white flowers resemble apple blossom, but appear singly on short shoots, six to eight inches long, that grow before the flower opens, so they are rarely bothered by late frost. In some varieties the unfurled flower bud looks like an ice-cream cone with strawberry stripes, or a traditional barber's pole. The quinces are hard fruits somewhat resembling pears in shape and color, often covered with a soft down when young, inedible when raw, but delicious and aromatic when cooked. Because they have long been used as rootstocks for pears and other fruits, they are sometimes found as suckers, surviving long after the scion has passed away.

Quinces are old fruits, still much grown in many parts of Europe though originally from Persia and Turkestan. Dedicated by the ancients to the Goddess of Love, they were promulgated by the Roman Empire as one of their favored crops and were well known to Pliny and Columella. In A.D. 812 Charlemagne encouraged the French to grow more, and Chaucer refers to them by the French name, *coines*. Their pulp makes *Dulce de Membrillo* or *Marmelo*—still popular in Portugal and Spain—the origin of the marmalade we now make from citrus fruit.

Japonica quinces (see p. 523) are almost identical to Cydonia

VARIETIES

'Smyrna' is one of the most attractive varieties in flower and fruit, with golden-yellow, pear-shaped fruit that is aromatic and tender. Introduced in 1897, it is still a favorite for desserts, preserves, and jellies. The very old **'Orange'** is a sturdy growing tree with bright yellow fruit that can weigh as much as a pound. **'Champion'** grows 12–15 ft. tall and is cold hardy and reliable.

CULTIVATION

Quinces are hardy in Zones 5 through 10. Their shallow roots grow well in almost any soil. Quinces thrive in moist soil and flourish as waterside specimens. They prefer a warm site, doing badly in cold or exposed places. Plant them at least 10 ft. apart. Normally they will only need staking in their first years of life. They are self-fertile.

Growing under Glass and in Containers

There is little to be gained by growing quinces under glass. They can be grown against a wall with some success and could be grown in pots and taken indoors by those living in harsh climates, but the fruit hardly merits such efforts.

Ornamental and Wildlife Value

Quinces will make excellent small specimen trees as the flowers, fruits, fall colors, and then the knotted branches give year-round interest. The flowers feed beneficial insects while the fruits are relished by birds and other wildlife after all the apples and pears have long gone.

Maintenance

Spring Spray monthly with seaweed solution, weed, and mulch well.
Summer Spray monthly with seaweed solution and weed.
Fall Remove rotten fruit and pick best for storing.
Winter Prune out dead and diseased wood, and add plenty of compost.

Propagation

Quinces can be grown from seed. Better fruits will always result from buying a ready-formed tree of an already named variety.

Pruning and Training

Quinces can be trained but the twisted, contorted growth makes this difficult. They are best grown as bushes or standards, with pruning restricted to removing dead, diseased, and crossing wood. Trees will sucker from the roots, growing into a thicket of branches, but you can cut back the sucker to train the plant as a small tree.

Weed, Pest, and Disease Control

There are no widespread problems for quinces. Even the birds and wasps will ignore the fruits for most of the fall. **Fireblight** may cause the leaves and branch tips to suddenly wilt as if scorched. Cut off affected branches at least 12 in. below the signs of disease.

Harvesting and Storing

Pick the fruits in fall before they drop and keep them in a cool, airy place. Do not store with apples, pears, or vegetables as they may taint.

Quince fruits

COMPANION PLANTING

Like pears and apples, quinces can be expected to benefit from underplantings of chives, garlic, and the pungent herbs.

OTHER USES

The wood is hard and prunings make good kindling. The fruits are excellent room perfumers and can be used as bases for pomanders.

CULINARY USES

Quinces can be made into aromatic clear jelly, jam, or a pulpy cheese that goes well with both sweet and savory dishes. Pieces of quince (if you can hack them off) keep their shape when cooked, adding both texture and aroma to apple and pear dishes.

Quince Cheese
Makes about 4 lb.

6 cups ripe quinces, chopped
1 small orange (unwaxed)
A little water
Approx. 4 cups sugar
1 or 2 drops orange-flower or rose-petal water (optional)

Finely chop the orange and simmer with the quinces, with just enough water to cover them, until they are a pulp. Strain the pulp and add its own volume in sugar. Bring to a boil and cook gently for about 1¹/₂ hours. Add the orange-flower or rose-petal water if desired. Then pot into oiled, warmed bowls, seal, and store for 3 months or more before using. Turn the cheese out of the bowl and slice for serving with cooked meats or savory dishes.

Prunus domestica from the family

PLUMS

Tree 20 ft. Long-lived, deciduous, hardy, slender, thorny, not usually self-fertile. Fruits: ovoid, usually 1–2 in. in any color. Value: rich in magnesium, iron, and vitamin A.

Plums come in more variation than most other fruits. They differ in season, size, shape, color, and taste. We have mixed hybrids, descendants of plums originally selected from fifteen or more different wild species. The European plum, *Prunus domestica*, is thought to be predominantly a hybrid between *P. cerasifera*, the cherry plum or **'Myrobalan,'** and *P. spinosa*, **'Sloe.'** It is a small to medium, slender, deciduous tree with small white blossoms.

The European plum came from Western Asia and the Caucasus. It naturalized in Greece first and then throughout most of the temperate zone. Plum stones were ordered in 1629 for planting in Massachusetts, and plums became widely cultivated in the temperate parts of North America. Some American plums returned to Europe; California, for example, became famous for exporting prunes—late, dark-skinned plums that are dried on the tree.

excellent for eating fresh or for canning and freezing. The very sweet fruits of the **'French Improved'** make it the leading prune plum in California. **'Seneca'** is a wonderful dessert plum, with very sweet, freestone flesh. It is resistant to brown rot. The reliable, early-ripening **'Italian Prune'** is self-fertile, but crops are even larger with a pollinator. **'Empress'** and **'President'** cross-pollinate well. Both are vigorous, upright trees and heavy bearers. Luther Burbank raised a sweet, yellow plum with incomparable flavor called **'The Pearl.'** It is believed to be the result of a cross between a **'Reine Claude'** gage and **'Prune D'Agen,'** an ancient plum brought back to Europe by Benedictine monks returning from the Crusades in Persia.

VARIETIES

There are hundreds of good varieties, which ripen through the season. **'Victoria'** is fully self-fertile, pollinates many others, and is always worth having. It has golden-yellow-fleshed, large, yellow, ovoid fruits, flushed with scarlet. **'Oullin's Gage'** is self-fertile. A plum with a richer, sweeter flavor, it flowers late, missing frosts. Self-fertile **'Stanley'** is a vigorous, spreading tree that gives bumper crops of tender freestone fruit year after year. Originally grown in Missouri, **'Bluefree'** is a good companion to 'Stanley,' which pollinates it well. It bears early and is extremely cold hardy. **'Mount Royal,'** an exceptional pollinator for all European plums, is extraordinarily cold hardy, thriving in northern Wisconsin and Minnesota. Its sweet, meaty fruit is

CULTIVATION

European plums are hardy in Zones 4 through 9. They usually bloom later and ripen later than Japanese plums. Plums like a heavier, moister soil than many other fruits. This means they often may be relegated to cold, damp sites and heavy soils. Even on a shady wall some do well.

Growing under Glass and in Containers
Because of their suscepti-bility to spring frost, brown rot, and wasps, plums are worth growing under glass. However, they would be best confined to large pots so they can spend some time

'Victoria'

outdoors, as they do not relish hot conditions.

Maintenance
Spring Protect blossom from frost; weed, mulch, and spray with seaweed solution.
Summer Put out pest traps.
Fall Remove mummified plums.
Winter Prune if needed.

Propagation
Graft on **'Pixy'** and other new dwarfing stocks, unless you have a big orchard and want immense quantities. Plums can be grown from pits, but take years to fruit and do not come true.

Pruning and Training
Plums make good high standards because, eventually, heavy fruiting branches weep, bringing the fruit down to a skirt. Overladen branches will need propping. Plums are usually grown as a short standard or bush. Leave them alone once a head is formed, except to cut out dead and diseased wood. They can be usefully trained on walls if on dwarfing stock. Plums prefer herringbone, not fan, shapes.

Weed, Pest, and Disease Control
Brown rot may cause spots on fruits that rapidly enlarge, sometimes followed by gray mold. Picking up dropped fruit helps control the disease. Sulfur sprays in summer may be necessary. **Bacterial**

leafspot may disfigure leaves and cause small spots or cracks in fruit. Spray copper after buds open to prevent it. **Apple maggots** may tunnel into fruit. To keep under control, hang red sticky ball traps in trees and collect any dropped fruit. **Plum curculio** may burrow into fruit, leaving small semicircle scars on the skin and causing fruit to drop prematurely. A pyrethrin spray in early spring may help.

Harvesting and Storing
Plums picked underripe for cooking will keep for days, but often have poor flavor compared to plums picked ripe off the tree. Many varieties can be quite easily peeled, and this avoids some of the unfortunate side effects of too many plums.

COMPANION PLANTING

Plant a ground cover of white clover beneath the tree to help control insect pests. Curculios are reportedly kept off by surrounding plum trees with garlic.

OTHER USES

Potent brandy is made from plums in Hungary and in central Europe.

CULINARY USES

Plums can be turned into jam, juice, or cheese, or frozen if pitted first, and are epicurean preserved in plum brandy syrup.

Prunes in Semolina
Serves 4

³/₄ cup dried prunes
¹/₂ cup plum brandy
¹/₂ cup water
3 cups milk
Twist of lemon rind
¹/₂ teaspoon salt
2 heaping tablespoons semolina
2 teaspoons honey
2 medium eggs, separated
Grated nutmeg to taste

Soak the prunes in the brandy and water overnight. Strain off the juice and simmer it down to syrup. Put the fruits and syrup into a baking dish. Boil the milk, lemon rind, salt, and semolina for 10 minutes, stirring continuously. Cool a little, remove the lemon rind, and stir in the honey and egg yolks. Whisk the egg whites and fork them in to the milk mixture. Immediately pour the mixture over the back of a spoon onto the fruit and syrup. Grate nutmeg over the surface and bake in a preheated oven at 400°F for 20 minutes, or until the top starts to brown.
Delicious cold for breakfast or hot for dinner.

Double Victoria
Serves 6–8

2 cups Victoria plums
¹/₆ cup honey
¹/₄ cup flaked blanched almonds

For the sponge:
1 cup sifted self-rising flour
³/₄ cup vanilla-flavored superfine sugar
¹/₂ cup softened butter
2 eggs
Pinch salt

Wash, halve, and pit the plums. Place in a buttered baking dish and drizzle with the honey. Beat together the sponge ingredients with a mixer until creamy and light in color. Dollop the sponge mixture over the fruit, smooth, and garnish with almonds. Bake in a preheated oven at 375°F for 35 minutes, or until golden brown and firm to the touch.

Prunes

Prunus italica from the family *Rosaceae*

GREENGAGES

Tree/bush 13–16 ft. Hardy, long-lived. Fruits: 1–1½ in., green to red.

Greengages are like plums, fruiting in midseason with sweet, green-yellow or golden, lightly scented flesh. The fruits are smaller, firmer, more rounded, and less bloomed than plums. They have a deep crease down one side and frequently russet spotting. The trees are sturdy, not often thorny, and bushier than most plums, though not quite as hardy.

Wild greengages are found in Asia Minor. Possibly introduced to northern Europe by the Romans, they disappeared from cultivation during the Middle Ages and were not reintroduced until 1725. Originally known in France as the **'Reine Claude,'** the first greengage was brought to Britain by, and named after, Sir Thomas Gage, who was fortunate to live where the conditions suit greengages, which need a drier, warmer summer than plums. The original greengage almost always came true from seed, but there are some larger-fruited selections, and also some good crosses between gages and plums.

VARIETIES

The old **'Greengage'** is original, but can be unreliable; an improved seedling is **'Cambridge Gage.'** The **'Transparent Gage'** is another old variety from France and is honeyed in its sweetness. It has almost transparent, golden-yellow flesh and is heavily spotted with red. It fruits in late summer. The true **'Mirabelle'** is very similar, smaller fruited, and of dwarf growth, but is rarely found except in southern France. (Sometimes the yellow Myrobalan plums may erroneously be called Mirabelles to make a sale.) **'Denniston's Superb'** is from the U.S. and is close to the original in flavor, but is larger fruited, hardier, regular cropping, and, most valuable of all, self-fertile. **'Jefferson'** is similar, later, but not self-fertile. **'Reine Claude de Bavay'** possibly has a plum as one parent. It fruits a fortnight or so after the previous varieties, in early fall. It makes a most delicious jam, a touch more acid and tasty if the fruit is picked a week or so early. **'Golden Transparent,'** another hybrid, is a large, round, transparent yellow. It ripens late and needs a wall in most cool areas, but is self-fertile. The tender, juicy **'Imperial Gage'** is a smaller, round, green fruit with a whitish bloom and delicious aroma. It needs a good pollinator or it will set only light crops.

CULTIVATION

Greengages grow best in a warm, sunny climate. They will thrive in Zones 7 through 9. Some varieties have better cold tolerance, such as 'Greengage,' which will flourish to central Iowa. Greengages need a lighter soil than plums but still need it to be rich, moist, and well aerated. They are easiest to tend as standards at least 20 ft. apart. In colder areas they need a wall. Some, such as 'Denniston's Superb,' 'Early Transparent Gage,' 'Jefferson's Gage,' or 'Oullins Golden Gage,' will fruit on a shady wall.

Growing under Glass and in Containers

Greengages, especially the choicer 'Mirabelle' or 'Transparent' varieties, are worth growing in pots, as this is the only way to restrict their growth. They can then be taken under cover for the flowering and ripening periods. Greengages will need a rest in winter.

Ornamental and Wildlife Value

As for plums (see p. 411).

Harvesting and Storing

Picked fully ripe off the tree, greengages are delectable, but do not last, especially if wet. They can be used for jellies or juice, or frozen if pitted first.

Pruning and Training

They are usually grown as low standards or bushes with remedial pruning in late spring once the shape has formed. Overladen branches need propping, but not as much as for plums. As they also tend to irregular bearing, thinning of heavy crops is sensible, but not as effective as for most fruits. Gages are best worked like plums in a herringbone pattern on a wall.

Maintenance

Spring Protect blossom from frost; weed, mulch, and spray with seaweed solution.
Summer Put out pest traps.
Fall Remove mummified fruits.
Winter Prune as needed.

Weed, Pest, and Disease Control

As greengages are so sweet, they suffer particularly from **bird** damage; the buds are attacked as well as the fruits. **Brown rot** and **plum curculio** can cause problems; see plums (p. 411) for treatment. **Wasps** also make a mess of the crop, so be prepared to be ruthless!

Propagation

Gages are usually grafted onto Myrobalan stocks, but newer dwarfing stocks mean that it is easier to fit them onto walls. Cuttings can be taken in late fall with some success and the oldest varieties come nearly true from stones.

COMPANION PLANTING

Greengages benefit from being positioned on the sheltered, sunny side of the larger plums.

OTHER USES

Prunelle (left) is a liqueur from Alsace and Angers, made from Mirabelles. Slivovitsa, an eau-de-vie, comes from the Balkans.

CULINARY USES

They make the best plum jams. True Mirabelle jam is almost apricot flavored, but even better.

Greengage Jam
Makes 4 lb.

4 cups greengages
4 cups sugar
A little water

Wash, halve, and pit the gages. Crack a few pits, extract the kernels, and add these to the fruit. Pour in enough water to cover the bottom of the pan and simmer until the fruit has softened. Add the sugar and bring rapidly to a boil, then carefully skim, jar, and seal.

Prunus species from the family *Rosaceae*

JAPANESE PLUMS AND DAMSONS

Tree/bush up to 16 ft. Long-lived, some self-fertile.
Fruits: 1 in., some vitamin value.

Japanese plums *(P. salicina* and *P. triflora)* are large, conical, orange-red or golden fruits with a mild, sweet flavor. They blossom early and are vulnerable to cold, but they are also more productive and tolerant of a wider range of warm conditions than ordinary plums, so are extensively grown in Australia, South Africa, and the United States. They have shiny, dark twigs, white flowers on bold spurs, and leaves that turn a glorious red in fall.

Damsons *(P. insititia)* bear blue-black fruits, which resemble European plums. They are more oval, with less bloom, and have a sweet, spicy flavor when cooked. Damson trees are compact and are reasonably self-fertile. The **cherry plum** or **'Myrobalan'** *(P. cerasifera)* is less brittle and can be woven into hedges; it is often used as a windbreak. The white flowers open at the same time as the leaves, which are glossier than those of other plums. They are self-fertile. The fruits are yellow, red, or purple, spherical, and a little pointed at the bottom. They have a sweet, juicy, if somewhat insipid, flesh and make good jam.

Damsons come from Damascus, or certainly that region, and were brought to Europe during the Crusades in the twelfth century, supposedly by the Duke of Anjou, after a pilgrimage to Jerusalem. Cherry plums come from the Balkans, Caucasus, and Western Asia and were introduced to Britain in the 16th century. Some of these went to the New World and were interbred with American native species to cope with the harsher climatic conditions. Japanese plums, originally natives of China, were introduced to Japan about 1500 and to America only in 1870. Being rather tender, they have never really expanded into Europe. **American beach plums** *(P. maritima)* and **wild plums** *(P. americana)* have been favorites for jams and jellies since the time of European settlement, and were used by Native Americans long before then. Recently, they have begun gaining popularity in gardens and hedges because of their ornamental blossoms as well as their tasty fruits.

VARIETIES

Wild American plum, also called **Goose**, **Hog**, or **Yellow Plum**, grows in spreading thickets of small, graceful trees with clouds of fragrant, white blossoms in early spring. The abundant red and yellow fruit is only an inch across, but it makes a pleasingly tart nibble and is excellent in jellies and preserves. **'Red Diamond'** is a very cold-hardy variety with juicy, red-purple fruit. Beach plums are likewise small but deliciously sweet. The purple, red, and yellow fruit grows on a thorny shrub that is found on sandy beaches. The large, sweet fruit of **Japanese plums** have made them a favorite in American markets and for home gardeners. **'Black Amber'** has large, almost black fruit with sweet, firm, amber flesh. There are several ornamental forms of cherry plums that may fruit; some have pink flowers, many are purple-leaved.

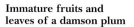

Immature fruits and leaves of a damson plum

A 'Merryweather' damson tree with tansy in foreground

CULINARY USES

Almost all of these fruits are now used culinarily only for jam, jelly, fruit cheeses, wine making, and liqueurs.

Damson Cheese
Makes 5 lb.

6 cups damsons
About 4½–5 cups light brown sugar

Wash the fruit and then simmer until soft with just enough water to prevent burning. Sieve and boil the pulp with three-quarters its own volume of sugar. Cook until the scum has finished rising and the jam is clear. Pot the pulp in warmed oiled bowls and seal.

CULTIVATION

These plums grow well in average, well-drained soil. Beach plum, cherry plum, and American wild plum will also grow in lean soils, and beach plum flourishes in sandy soils. Japanese plum varieties do best in warm climates. They are hardy in Zones 6 through 9, with several varieties thriving in Zone 5 and some low-chill selections doing well in Zone 10. The prolific **'Santa Rosa'** and **'Satsuma'** are hardy in Zones 5 through 9. American plums are extremely tolerant of cold, but less so of heat. Wild plum *(P. americana)* grows well in Zones 3 through 6, and beach plum *(P. maritima)* in Zones 4 through 6. American-Japanese crosses incorporate the cold tolerance of the American parent and the heat tolerance of the Japanese parent, and generally thrive in Zones 4 through 9.

Propagation
Most types do well on Myrobalan stocks, and many on their own roots.

Pruning and Training
As for plums (see p. 411).

Weed, Pest, and Disease Control
Planting disease-resistant varieties will minimize problems. **'AU-Rosa,'** **'Crimson,'** and **'Ozark Premier'** shrug off **brown rot**, **perennial canker**, **black knot**, and **bacterial leaf spot**. **'Redheart,'** **'Homeside,'** **'AU-Amber,'** and **'Santa Rosa'** also show resistance to various diseases. **Birds** will try to beat you to the harvest; netting is a good deterrent.

Harvesting and Storing
Pick plums to be used for cooking before they are completely ripe.

COMPANION PLANTING

A ground cover of white clover beneath the tree will attract beneficial insects.

OTHER USES

As hedges and windbreaks, cherry and beach plums are excellent. Damsons can be planted in sheltered sections.

'Merryweather' damsons with fruit

Prunus armeniaca from the family *Rosaceae*

APRICOTS

Tree up to 20 ft. Hardy, deciduous, self-fertile. Fruits: 1½ x 2 in., yellow-orange. Value: rich in vitamin A and potassium.

This small tree has white flowers (occasionally tinged with pink) very early in spring, well before the leaves emerge. These are spade-shaped and often glossy. The young shoots can also appear glossy as if varnished in red or brown. The leaves are more similar to those of a plum than those of a cherry or peach, and apricot fruits closely resemble some plums, but the pit is more spherical and the flavor distinct. Some think that **'Moorpark,'** one of the most common varieties, is a plumcot (a plum-apricot hybrid).

The first apricots came from China or Siberia, not Armenia, where Alexander the Great found them. The fruits became loved by the Romans, but they never succeeded in transplanting any to northern Europe. Apricots reached Britain in the thirteenth century and were introduced again, more successfully, in the sixteenth. **'Bredase'** may be the oldest variety in cultivation; it closely resembles descriptions of Roman apricots.

'Moorpark' in flower

VARIETIES

Raised in 1830, **'Blenheim'** is a perennial favorite with medium to large, very juicy fruit and sweet, aromatic flavor. It is superb for eating fresh or for canning and drying. **'Perfection'** bears very large fruit of good texture and flavor. Self-fertile **'Stark Tilton'** is a leading commercial variety also good for home gardens. **'Early Golden'** is prolific and does especially well in the South and Southwest. Disease-resistant and cold-hardy varieties from the Harrow Research Station in Canada include **'Harglow,' 'Hargrand,' 'Harlayne,' 'Harogem,'** and **'Harval.' 'Moorpark'** is exquisite; the traditional variety, it ripens a little later.

CULTIVATION

Like most stone fruits, apricots need a cold winter period to rest and warm summers to ripen the fruit. The plants themselves are tough, but the flowers are so early that they are always in danger from frost. The soil should not be heavy nor the site wet. Apricots are generally hardy in Zones 5 through 8, but some, such

as 'Sweet Pit,' are extremely cold tolerant and grow well as far north as Zone 3.

Ornamental and Wildlife Value
Apricots are not noticeable trees, though the flowers are pretty enough. Their earliness makes the flowers useful to bees and beneficial insects.

Growing under Glass and in Containers
Grown under glass, apricots are more sure to crop if allowed a cold resting period, so do not plant in continuously heated greenhouses. A better plan may be to confine them in large pots. Keep these outside unless very cold, bring them under glass for flowering, and take them

'Moorpark' fruits well on a warm wall

back outside again once the weather is warm.

Pruning and Training
The least work is to grow apricots as trees, only removing dead and diseased wood as necessary. Cut out all the dieback until no discoloration is seen. The wood is brittle, so watch for overladen branches and prop or prune early. On walls, build a fan of old wood with fruiting spurs. Prune the frame and any

dieback in late winter, then prune again in summer to restrict the growth.

Weed, Pest, and Disease Control

Apricots are vulnerable to many of the same diseases and pests as peaches. **Canker** and **borers** may plague the tree, but are not always fatal. Oozing sap and interesting formations of hardened resin on branches and possibly trunk are symptomatic of these problems. If you can cut or gouge out the damaged area, do so. Clip off infected branches at least 12 in. below the point of infection. **Aphids**, **scale**, and other **insects** may infest the tree, causing a decline in vigor and possibly a reduction in crop size. Since apricots are so prolific, insect attacks can usually be overlooked.

Propagation

Apricot trees are obtained budded onto suitable rootstocks. Successful trees have been raised from pits.

Maintenance

Spring Cover flowers on frosty nights, weed, mulch, and spray with seaweed solution monthly.
Summer Thin the fruits early, summer prune, and bag fruits against wasps and birds.
Fall Keep weeded and tie in new shoots.
Winter Prune out dieback.

Harvesting and Storing

Apricots ripened on the tree are heavenly, but soon go over. Picked young enough to travel, they never develop full flavor. Thus they are best eaten right away, made into jams, or frozen.

'Alfred' trees espalier-trained after fruiting

CULINARY USES

Apricots make scrumptious jam and can be preserved in brandy and syrup. Unlike the majority of *Prunus* fruits, most apricot kernels are sweet and edible and can be used to make ratafia cookies.

Apricot Sponge
Serves 6–8

2 cups apricots
Pat of butter
Light brown sugar

For the sponge:
$^1/_4$ cup ($^1/_2$ stick) butter
$^1/_3$ cup light brown sugar
1 large egg
$^1/_2$ cup white self-rising flour
A splash of milk
Real vanilla extract

Halve and pit the apricots (score or remove the skin if you prefer) and place in a buttered cake pan, cut side up. Sprinkle with brown sugar. Cream together the butter and sugar, stir in the egg, then fold in the flour—adding the milk if the mixture is stiff—and the vanilla extract. Spoon the sponge mixture over the apricots and cook in a preheated oven at 375°F for about half an hour. When cold, turn out and serve with whipped cream.

COMPANION PLANTING

Do not grow tomatoes, potatoes, or oats near apricots, but they benefit from *Alliums* nearby, especially garlic and chives.

OTHER USES

The wood is brittle, but of use as kindling.

Prunus persica from the family *Rosaceae*

PEACHES

Tree/bush up to 16 x 16 ft. Generally short-lived. Self-fertile, deciduous.
Fruits: 2½–3½ in., yellow, orange, red. Value: rich in vitamin A, potassium, and niacin.

Peach trees are small and resemble willows, with long, lightly serrated leaves. They bloom before the leaves appear. The smaller the flowers, the darker rose colored they are, with the largest being lightest pink. Flowering two weeks later than almonds, they are closely related, the almond having a tough, inedible, leathery skin over a smooth stone. Peach skin has a partition line along which it easily splits. Most peach pits are ribbed or perforated with small holes in the shell. In varieties known as clingstones, the flesh clings to this shell; in others, the freestones, the fruit is free and easier to enjoy without having to tease it off the pit. The flesh may vary from white to yellow; there are even blood peaches with red staining. The texture varies with cultivar, soil, and climate. The skin color can be from dull green through yellows and orange to dark red. The most distinctive feature of peaches is the soft downy fluff on the skin.

The peach was known in the fourth century B.C. to the Greek philosopher Theophrastus, who thought it came from Persia, and so it became named. Early Hebrew writings make no reference to it, nor is there a Sanskrit name, so it seems likely peaches did not reach Europe to any extent until shortly before the Christian period. Dioscorides mentions the peach during the first century, as does Pliny, who states that the Romans had only recently imported it from Persia.

Peaches are, in fact, of Chinese origin. They are mentioned in the books of Confucius from the first century B.C., and can be traced back to the tenth century B.C. in artistic representations. The Chinese still have an immense number of varieties and these were initially spread by seed. The stones produce trees with ease, but of course do not come true. The variability may have accounted for the slow spread to Europe. However, this was more likely to have been because peaches were initially tried in hot countries at too low altitudes. Thus the trees did not get their winter dormancy and would have fruited badly, effectively discouraging further experiments. Pliny indeed mentions that peach trees were taken from Egypt to the island of Rhodes, but this transplantation did not succeed; they were then brought to Italy.

It took until the middle of the sixteenth century for peaches to reach England, and in 1629 a quantity of peach stones was ordered by the governor of the Massachusetts Bay Colony of New England. The peach found its new home in North America highly suitable and spread abundantly. In fact it spread so rapidly through the wild that it was thought to be a native fruit. Peaches spread so widely that they conquered much of South America by Darwin's time. He spotted them on islands in the mouth of the Paraná, along with thickets of similarly fugitive orange trees.

'Rochester' is a prolific fruiter

sight of a good crop of fruits is magnificent. The blossom is wonderful too; peaches in bloom are a joy.

Pruning and Training

Peaches fruit on young shoots; thus it is essential to have plenty of these growths. They are best obtained by a partial pollarding operation late each winter. This makes the pruning more akin to that of black currants than to that of most other tree fruits. Basically the top ends of the higher branches are removed to encourage prolific growth from the lower branches and stubs. This also serves to keep the peach bushes lower and more manageable.

On walls and under cover, peaches are usually fan-trained. Selected young shoots are allowed to spring from a main frame and then tied in to replace the previous growths once those have fruited.

More important than pruning is thinning. Peaches are prone to overcropping, breaking branches, and exhausting themselves. Thin the fruits hard, removing those touching or anywhere near each other. Do this very early and then again later.

Peach tree in a greenhouse

VARIETIES

Grown from a seed in Georgia in 1870, **'Elberta'** and its many selections (including **'Early Elberta,' 'Fantastic Elberta,' 'Com-Pact Elberta,' 'Fay Elberta,'** and others) is the most popular peach in America. The large, yellow fruit has a beautiful blush and juicy, yellow, freestone flesh. It is self-fruitful and makes a good pollinator. **'Red Haven'** is the leader among early peaches. Its offspring, **'Com-Pact Red Haven,'** is better in northern and central regions. **'Hale Haven,'** the parent of **'Red Haven,'** was developed in Michigan and is a peach of exceptional quality. **'Golden Jubilee,' 'Redskin,'** and **'Reliance,'** other favorites of home gardeners and commercial growers, produce a bounty of freestone fruit. Modern, disease-resistant varieties are like those developed at the Harrow Research Station in Canada: **'Harbelle,' 'Harbrite,' 'Harcrest,' 'Harken,'** and others. **'Peregrine'** is a good choice for a bush tree and has yellowish-white flesh of excellent flavor. It is freestone and comes midseason.

CULTIVATION

Peaches ideally need a well-enriched, well-aerated, but moist piece of soil. They prefer open gravelly soils to heavy, and need to be planted at least 20 ft. apart. Peaches grow well in Zones 6 through 9, with some cold hardy varieties thriving in Zone 5. Like apricots, they bloom early and their buds and blossoms are susceptible to frost and cold damage. Late-flowering varieties include **'Jayhaven,' 'Red Haven,' 'Cresthaven,' 'Nectar,'** and **'Emery.'** If they take (peaches do not always), they establish quickly and need no staking after the first year. They need copious quantities of compost annually and mulches are obligatory to ensure the constant moisture they demand. Where they are planted against walls, great care must be taken to ensure adequate water constantly throughout the season or the fruits will split. However, they are quite intolerant of any waterlogging. Peaches also should not be planted near almonds, as the two fruits

may hybridize, resulting in bitter nuts.

Growing under Glass and in Containers

Peaches are often grown under glass where the extra efforts of replenishment pruning and tying in are repaid by gorgeous, succulent, early fruits free from the depredations of birds. The greenhouse must be unheated in winter to give peaches a dormant rest period. More problems occur under cover—the red spider mite can be especially troublesome unless a high humidity is maintained. Peaches are good subjects for large pots as they can take heavy pruning if well fed and watered. Pots enable them to be kept under cover during the winter and through flowering and then brought out all summer, thus avoiding peach leaf curl and frost damage. The flowers must be protected from frosts and so must the young fruitlets. The flowers are more susceptible to frost damage after pollination and the fruitlets likewise for an additional two weeks.

Ornamental and Wildlife Value

The peach is a pleasure to have. The willowy leaves are held well into fall and the

Maintenance
Spring Protect tree from leaf disease with Bordeaux sprays before buds open and blossom. Protect blossoms from frost. Hand-pollinate. Weed, mulch, and spray with seaweed solution monthly.
Summer Thin the fruits early, and often. Protect fruits from birds and wasps.
Fall Remove mummified fruits from the trees.
Winter Prune hard. Spray with Bordeaux mixture.

Propagation
Peaches can be raised from stones, but the results are haphazard and take years to fruit. Budded onto suitable stocks, peaches will normally fruit in their third year. Plum stocks are more resistant to wet, but for warmer, drier conditions, seedling apricot or peach rootstocks are better.

Weed, Pest, and Disease Control
Peaches suffer most losses from **birds** and **wasps**. Small net or muslin bags will

'Peregrine' blossom

protect the crop. **Earwigs** can get inside the fruits and eat the kernel out, but are easily trapped in rolls of corrugated paper around each branch. Protect the bark from **animals**. Peaches are susceptible to myriad diseases. **Brown rot** affects the ripening fruit and causes it to mold; it's worst during wet, humid summers. **Leaf curl**, **leaf spot**, and **powdery mildew** may affect the leaves, thus weakening the leaves if the disease is widespread. Spraying with Bordeaux mixture prevents peach leaf curl if done several times as the buds are opening. **Peach scab** can affect fruits, causing clustered olive green spots near the stem end of the fruit about halfway to maturity. Weekly sulfur sprays will help control brown rot and scab. Other maladies, including **cankers**, **crown gall**, and **viruses**, may besiege your peach trees. Because of these problems, the useful life of peach trees is 10–12 years. Disease-resistant varieties include **'Raritan Rose,' 'Elberta,'** and **'Reliance.'**

Peach jam

Harvesting and Storing
A truly ripe peach is a bag of syrup waiting to burst. If picked underripe, the flesh never develops the full gamut of flavor, or the liquidity. A good peach is a feast, drink and all. As with so many fruits, they are best eaten straight off the tree. They can be picked a few days early if handled with absolute care. Kept cool, they may last. With the slightest bruising, however, they decompose.

COMPANION PLANTING

Peaches are benefited by *Alliums*, especially garlic and chives. Clover or alfalfa leguminous green manures give the richness they need. Nettles nearby are reputedly helpful at preventing the fruit from molding.

OTHER USES

Peach pits are used for making activated charcoal for filters. The wood is brittle, but the prunings make good kindling. In some countries, gluts of peaches are used for feeding the local livestock.

CULINARY USES

Peach jam is more aromatic than plum and a glorious use for the many fruits that never look like ripening intact or early enough. Fruits can be frozen for winter use and retain some texture afterwards. The juice is the nectar of the gods, and peaches will also make excellent chutneys.

Peach Macaroon Cheesecake
Serves 4–6

1 cup macaroons
1 cup vanilla wafers
¹/₃ cup butter, melted
5 cups peaches
¹/₂ oz. gelatin
1 cup cottage cheese
¹/₂ cup yogurt
¹/₄ cup honey or peach jam
Few drops vanilla extract
¹/₂ cup strawberries

Crush the macaroons and wafers and mix with the butter. Press into a cake pan. Peel, slice, and chill the peaches. Simmer the skins and pits in a little hot water, sieve, and dissolve the gelatin in the warm liquid. Beat the cottage cheese, yogurt, honey or jam, and vanilla, then stir in the gelatin. Immediately pour over the cookie crust, chill, and allow to set. Top with strawberries.

Peach Macaroon Cheesecake

Prunus persica from the family *Rosaceae*

NECTARINES

Tree up to 16 ft. Generally short-lived, self-fertile, deciduous.
Fruits: up to 3 in., greenish-yellow/orange and red.
Value: rich in vitamin A, potassium, and niacin, as well as riboflavin and vitamin C.

'Elruge'

In almost every way nectarines are just varieties of peach. However, there are several subtle and fascinating differences. Nectarines are more difficult to grow and are less hardy. The fruits are smaller, on average, than peaches. The flesh is firmer and less melting than a peach and more plumlike, less prone to falling apart while you eat it. Nectarines have a definite, almost peculiar, rich, vinous flavor quite distinct from that of a well-ripened peach. The color of some nectarines also makes them distinguishable from peaches, as many of the older varieties have a greenish or sometimes even a purplish hue over a quite yellowish or greenish ground. Most noticeably, nectarines do not have that downy fuzz on the skin so typical of peaches, but instead are smooth and shiny; indeed they closely resemble a very large, plump plum.

Darwin noted how peach trees occasionally spontaneously produced nectarines, and also the opposite; he even noted the case of a nectarine tree that produced a fruit that was half peach, half nectarine and then reverted to peaches. Despite the peach's long history of cultivation, however, no mention is made of nectarines by pre-Christian authors. Pliny mentions an unknown fruit, a duracina, but the first, if indirect, reference is by Cieza de Leon, who lived in the early sixteenth century and described a Caymito of Peru as being as "large as a nectarine." They were seen growing amongst peaches in Virginia in 1720 and A. J. Downing listed 19 varieties in the U.S. by 1857. Dozens of nectarine varieties are now in cultivation, and travelers also report local varieties of nectarine in most of the world's peach-growing areas, so that their spontaneous emergence is not really a rare phenomenon.

'Early Rivers'

VARIETIES

"Red Gold,' reaching about 15 ft. tall, is a vigorous grower, and an abundant bearer. The sweet flavor of **'Sunglo,'** a 1962 California introduction, is a commercial favorite. **'Goldmine'** is a beauty, with smaller fruits blushed red over a white skin.

CULTIVATION

Nectarines need even better conditions than peaches do. Good water control is critical to keep the fruit from splitting, so thick mulches are obligatory. In any cool region they must be given a wall or extra shelter. Nectarines grow well in Zones 6 through 9, with

'Lord Napier'

some especially cold-hardy varieties, such as **'Hardired,' 'Garden Delight,'** and **'Mericrest,'** thriving in Zone 5. 'Mericrest' is one of the hardiest nectarines, surviving cold as low as −20˚F. It's self-fruitful and a late bloomer, a consideration in areas where capricious spring frosts are a possibility.

Growing under Glass and in Containers

Nectarines are more suited than many plants to culture under glass, preferring warmer conditions than are found in most temperate areas. However, they must be given a cool period of rest each winter or they will be unfruitful, so they can only really be grown in greenhouses unheated through winter. They can be grown in large pots and can fruit successfully, but only if religious attention is given to watering. Hand-pollination is desirable.

Pruning and Training

As for peach (see p. 419).

Propagation

Nectarines sometimes come from peach pits and vice versa. More often they occur when a peach bud produces a sport. Most varieties are budded on suitable stocks as for peaches.

Weed, Pest, and Disease Control

Away from the Pacific coast, **plum curculios** can easily do much damage to their smooth skins. Spray against **peach leaf curl**.

Ornamental and Wildlife Value

Nectarines are attractive, with the long, glossy leaves being held late into the season.

Maintenance

As for peach (see p. 420).

Harvesting and Storing

As for peach (see p. 420).

CULINARY USES

Nectarines can be used in similar ways to peaches, but as their skin is not fuzzy, it is less of a barrier and makes them more toothsome to eat fresh. The firm flesh is also less melting and reduces one's need for a bib to catch half the juice as with a ripe peach. This makes the nectarine a civilized fruit for eating at the table, and this is only enhanced by the succulent vinous flavor.

Nectarine Melba
(All quantities according to taste)

Nectarines
Honey
Vanilla pod
Vanilla ice cream
Frozen raspberries
Bitter chocolate and nutmeg

Halve, peel, and pit one ripe nectarine per person. Poach half of them, those that are the least decomposingly ripe, in a syrup made by gently warming the vanilla pod in the honey. Poach the nectarines very gently until they are tender but not breaking down, then drain and chill well. Create a bed of vanilla ice cream, interspersed with the chilled, riper halves. Lay the poached halves on this base. Crush the frozen raspberries in the drained honey syrup. Chill, then pour over the nectarines followed by a generous grating of bitter chocolate and a hint of nutmeg.

Nectarine Melba

COMPANION PLANTING

As for peach (see p. 420).

OTHER USES

As for peach (see p. 420).

Prunus avium from the family *Rosaceae*

SWEET CHERRIES

Tree up to 33 ft. Long-lived, deciduous, not self-fertile.
Fruits: 1 in., yellow, red, black, rich in riboflavin.

Although described as sweet cherries, some varieties, and particularly wild ones, are not actually sweet. Tall trees, often reaching over thirty feet, with white blossoms, occasionally pink, which are a massive display at about the same time as the peach. The leaves are plumlike with a lengthening and thinning at the tip. Dangling in pairs on long pedicels, the near-spherical fruits hang in groups along the fruiting branches. The flesh is cream or yellow, sweet or bitter, but once ripe is rarely acid.

The wild form native to Europe, known as the bird cherry, gean, or mazzard, is of little value as fruit except in central Europe, where it is used for liqueurs. Mazzards, little improved from the wild version, still survive and have richly flavored black fruits only slightly larger than in the wild. They make good seedling stocks for better varieties, though if left to themselves they can grow to seventy feet or more. Gean or guigne fruits were thought to have softer, more melting flesh, and varieties called **'Bigarreau'** had a crisp texture. Years of continuous selection and cross breeding have given us sweet cherries of mixed parentage. One group, the Duke or Royal cherries, has some Morello blood, which serves to make them tasty and lightly acid as well as generally more hardy.

CULTIVATION

Sweet cherries are very particular to soil and site. They need plentiful moisture at the roots but loathe waterlogging and need a very rich but well-aerated soil. Poor soil conditions can be helped by growing through grass. Sweet cherries flourish in warm, dry climates, but they will also grow in marginal areas. Many varieties will grow in Zones 5 through 7 or 8.

Growing under Glass and in Containers

As the trees get so big and are particular to site and weather, pot cultivation is the most effective way to get cherries. In this way you avoid damage to the flowers from frost or rain and likewise protect the fruits. Do let the trees have a cool dormant period in winter.

VARIETIES

There are countless varieties, but finding combinations compatible for pollination is difficult, so most useful cherries for private orchards are partly self-fertile. **'Bing'** is the quintessential sweet cherry, big, dark, and delicious. The large, spreading tree isn't as prolific as **'Angela'** and other varieties, but it is the standard for flavor. **'Black Tartarian'** also has sweet, thick, tender flesh with rich flavor and its bumper crops are outstanding. **'Van'** is another 'Bing' lookalike, but firmer and short-stemmed. Young trees bear early. Pollinate with **'Bing,' 'Stella,'** or **'Royal Ann,'** an old French variety, which tends to overbear, but this only reduces fruit size, not quality. **'Stella'** is fully self-fertile, a vigorous and upright tree with sweet, dark red fruits. **'Rainer'** is another premier yellow cherry with red blush.

'Stella'

Ornamental and Wildlife Value

Sweet cherries are quite staggering to behold in blossom, as if festooned with snow.

Propagation

Normally budded onto strong-growing rootstocks, which make for big trees, they are now offered on dwarfing stocks such as **'Colt.'** This makes them smaller and easier to constrain. Pits grow, but take years to fruit and get tall.

Pruning and Training

Prune as little as possible after the initial head formation. Any pruning must be done early during the growing season and then only to remove any dead and diseased growth.

Weed, Pest, and Disease Control

Cherries really suffer from **bird** damage, but at least escape the wasps by fruiting early in summer. **Bacterial canker** can kill the tree, and there are several **virus** diseases, but these are only treatable by improving the conditions.

Maintenance

Spring Protect the flowers, weed, mulch, and spray seaweed solution monthly. Prune if necessary.
Summer Protect the fruits from birds with netting

'Royal Ann'

or muslin sleeves.
Fall No maintenance needed.
Winter Remove dead wood.

Harvesting and Storing

Sweet cherries are prone to cracking of the fruit. Moisture or the lack of it at the time the fruit is maturing can ruin a crop. Too little water causes shriveled fruit; too much causes the cherries to swell and split. A thick mulch and irrigation can help with insufficient rainfall, but if a deluge comes when your cherries are ripening, there's nothing much you can do.

COMPANION PLANTING

They are normally grown in grass sward; include clover and alfalfa, to give more fertility. Cherries supposedly suppress wheat and make potatoes prone to blight.

OTHER USES

Cherry wood is much loved by woodworkers and makes a sweet firewood.

Traditional cherry wood and kingwood secretaire

CULINARY USES

Sweet cherries often do not make as good culinary dishes as sour cherries because many lack acidity. Their jams and jellies are better combined with red currant or white currant juice for this reason.

Pickled Cherries
Makes about 3½ lb.

4 cups cherries
1 cup vinegar
2 cups sugar
6 cloves
¾-in. piece fresh ginger, peeled and chopped
Hint of cinnamon

Wash and pit (if desired) the cherries. Dissolve the sugar in the heated vinegar and add the spices. Simmer the cherries in the spiced vinegar for a few minutes, then pack them into warmed jars, and cover with the vinegar. Seal and store.

Eat with pâtés, cold meats, and especially quiches.

Cherry Jam
Makes about 6 lb.

10 cups cherries
3 lemons, squeezed
7 cups sugar

Wash the fruit thoroughly, remove stalks and pits. Put the fruit into a pan with the lemon juice and simmer gently for 30–35 minutes. Warm the sugar and add it to the cherries over a gentle heat and allow the sugar to dissolve. Then bring the jam to a rapid boil and continue boiling until the setting point is reached; this will take about 15 minutes. Test for setting point, remove from the heat, and leave for 5 minutes. Pot and cover. Store in a dry place.

Prunus cerasus from the family *Rosaceae*

SOUR CHERRIES

MORELLO CHERRIES AND OTHERS

Tree up to 27 ft. Long-lived, deciduous, self-fertile.
Fruits: ³/₄ in., crimson to black. Value: rich in vitamin A.

Sour or Morello cherries are similar to sweet cherries, except they are not sweet, so are only useful for culinary purposes. The trees are smaller than sweet varieties, with slightly lax, more twiggy branches and greener foliage that does not have such a red tinge when young. The fruits have shorter stalks, tend to have darker colors, and are more acid.

Sour cherries were selected from *Prunus cerasus* (also known as *P. acida*), which grew wild around the Caspian and Black Seas. In about 300 B.C. sour cherries were known to the Greek Theophrastus and proved so popular with the Romans, who developed at least half a dozen different varieties, that by the time of Pliny, in the first century A.D., sour cherries had already long reached Britain. However, during the Dark Ages, the art of their cultivation was lost and the trees had to be reintroduced to England in the sixteenth century by Henry VIII, who had them brought from Flanders. They were soon adopted by the growers of Kent and by 1640 they had over two dozen varieties. The first cherries to reach the New World, the **'Kentish Red,'** were planted by the Massachusetts colonists.

Fan-trained sour cherry

VARIETIES

Before World War II, more than 50 varieties of Morello and sour cherry were in cultivation, and almost every country had its own wide choice. Now few are grown commercially. **'Montmorency'** is the typical sour cherry for pie—richly flavored with a good tang and firm flesh that doesn't get mushy during cooking. The 15-ft.-tall tree is self-fertile and spreading in habit. **'Early Richmond'** is a heavy producer that ripens more than a week earlier than other sour cherries. The vigorous tree is self-fertile and the fruit is clear, bright red. **'North Star'** is a cross between the English **'Morello'** cherry and the Siberian cherry, which, as you might expect, gives it exceptional cold tolerance. It is cold hardy to –40°F. The natural dwarf tree bows under the weight of the heavy crops of mahogany red fruit. **'Meteor'** is another cross with Russian blood, developed in Minnesota and usually hardy to –50°F. Its tart, bright red fruits are similar to 'Montmorency.'

CULTIVATION

Much the same conditions are needed as for pears, with an increased demand for nitrogen and even more water than needed by sweet cherries. Though the trees will do badly if they are waterlogged, they are more tolerant of poor drainage than sweet cherries. Sour cherries can take quite a bit more winter cold than sweet cherries, but they are much less tolerant of heat. Most varieties thrive in Zones 3

OTHER USES

The prunings make good kindling.

Cherry jam

CULINARY USES

They are primarily a culinary fruit and make fabulous pies, tarts, jams, and cakes.

Black Forest Cake
Serves 6–8

2 cups black cherries
1/3 cup honey
4 tablespoons kirsch
Water

For the sponge:
1/2 cup butter
1/2–3/4 cup light brown sugar
1 cup white flour
2 large or 3 medium eggs
1 heaping teaspoon baking powder
1 heaping teaspoon cocoa powder

For the filling:
2 cups heavy cream
1 heaping teaspoon sugar
1 heaping teaspoon cocoa powder
Vanilla extract
4 squares dark chocolate

Preheat the oven to 325°F. Wash and pit cherries. Dissolve the honey and kirsch in sufficient hot water just to cover the fruits. Simmer till they soften, then strain (keeping the syrup) and chill. Mix the sponge ingredients and divide between three greased cake pans. Bake for about half an hour. Turn out and cool, then soak the sponge cakes in the syrup. Whip the cream, then stir in the sugar, cocoa powder, and vanilla. Build up alternate layers of sponge, cream filling, and fruit. Finish off with a covering of filling and grated chocolate.

'Red Morellos'

through 5, with some hardy in Zone 2.

Growing under Glass and in Containers
Although this would be possible, it would usually be more worthwhile to nurture sweet cherries.

Ornamental and Wildlife Value
Not as elegant or floriferous a tree as the sweet cherry, so less ornamental value. However, sour cherries are well-loved by birds and the early flowers are good for insects.

Propagation and Maintenance
As for sweet cherries (p. 425).

Weed, Pest, and Disease Control
Sour cherries are susceptible to **cracking** like sweet cherries. They may also be bothered by **cherry leaf spot**, **powdery mildew**, and **brown rot**.

Pruning and Training
Sour cherries fruit on younger wood than do sweet cherries and thus they can be pruned harder. However, it is usually more convenient to stick to removing dead, diseased, and congested growths in spring or summer. Usually grown as standards, they are ideal as low bushes for picking and bird protection, although they can also be trained as fans. They will even crop well on cold walls.

Harvesting and Storing
Cut the cherries off the tree rather than risk damage by pulling the stalks. Morellos were one of the first fruits to be stored frozen and are one of the best. They can be frozen without sugaring and retain their flavor superbly.

Companion Planting
As for sweet cherries (p. 425).

Morus nigra and *Morus alba* from the family *Moraceae*

MULBERRIES

Tree up to 30 ft. Long-lived, hardy, deciduous, usually self-fertile.
Fruits: 1½–2¼ in., purple, also red through pink.

Mulberry trees are medium-sized trees with a round domed crown, formed by their habit of having no terminal bud on their overwintering twigs. They can become big, gnarled, and picturesque in advanced old age. The leaves are heart-shaped, toothed, and occasionally lobed, lightly downy underneath but rough on top. The black mulberry *(M. nigra)* fruits are like loganberries, of a blackish dark red through purple when ripe, which stain all they touch. The white mulberry *(M. alba)* fruits are red or pinkish white, and slightly inferior to eat. There is a red mulberry (which can be almost black), native to North America, and several similar species in hotter climates.

Black mulberries are thought to be native to western Asia. Known at least since the time of the Greeks, they failed to become popular until the Roman emperor Justinian encouraged them for the production of silk. The trees appeared all over the empire, and *Morus nigra* was not superseded by *M. alba*, the more productive variety for feeding silkworms, until the sixteenth century. Exceptionally long-lived, the black mulberry may attain some stature; giants found in many parts of the world were planted during the seventeenth and early eighteenth centuries in vain attempts to foster local silkindustries. Some mulberries such as *M. alba* var. *tatarica*, the Russian mulberry, seed freely and become weeds. The red mulberry is native to the northern Missouri region and along the Kansas river system, where it was an esteemed fruit.

White mulberry

Red mulberry

VARIETIES

'Illinois Everbearing' is a favorite for its sweet but tangy blackberry-like taste. 'Downing,' 'Wellington,' 'Black Persian,' and 'New American' all have long, sweet, black fruits. The honey sweet, lavender-white fruit of the *M. alba* variety 'Lavender' are excellent for drying. The **Red Mulberry** *(M. rubra)* has red/black fruits and lovely fall color with bright yellow leaves; it is said to have the preferable fruit. The **White Mulberry** *(M. alba)* has wider leaves and is grown for silkworm fodder, though the fruit is quite edible, often red or pinkish and sweet.

CULTIVATION

Mulberries succeed in any well-drained soil. The tree is so adaptable to even the worst conditions of drought and poor soil that it is the second most common weed tree in New York City. Cold-hardiness of various mulberries varies, but most can be grown in Zones 5 through 8.

Ornamental and Wildlife Value

Mulberries become gnarled and attractively grotesque as they age. The traditional situation is in the middle of a lawn with a circular wooden seat around the trunk. The berries are much appreciated by birds and small children.

Weed, Pest, and Disease Control

No significant pests or diseases bother the trees, other than the usual hazards of **birds** and small **children**.

Maintenance

Spring Cut grass and spray seaweed solution monthly.
Summer Pick the fruits as they ripen and drop.
Fall Cut grass and enjoy the seat occasionally.
Winter Thin and remove dead and diseased growths.

Propagation

Ideally, 10–12 in. cuttings of newly ripened growth with a heel are taken in December. Layering is possible as are (supposedly) whole branch cuttings.

Pruning and Training

Mulberries can be pollarded hard to give the maximum foliage needed for feeding silkworms. If left to themselves, they make congested heads, so thin out twiggy, dead, and diseased growths. Their narrow forks, big heads, and brittle wood mean old trees should be carefully inspected and excess weight removed by a competent tree surgeon.

Harvesting and Storing

Mulberries are aromatic and mouth-watering when fresh and ripe, but decompose rapidly so are really only of use as they drop, and will not store or travel, though they can be frozen. An easy way to harvest the fruit cleanly is to spread several sheets beneath a tree and shake the branches. The ripe fruit will fall like rain.

Mulberry wood tea caddy

COMPANION PLANTING

Mulberries must be grown in a grass sward if there is to be any hope of getting clean fruit. They were one of the traditional trees to support grapevines in ancient times.

OTHER USES

Of course you can try silkworm production, and the foliage is palatable to other animals. The fruits will certainly make dye.

CULINARY USES

The fruits can be made into jams or jellies, though they are usually combined and bulked out with apples, and the wine is an old country favorite.

Mulberry No Fool
Serves 1

Crème fraîche or heavy cream
Honey
A pot of tea
Cookies
A mulberry tree in fruit and a sunny day off

Take a cereal bowl with a large portion of thick cream, and the tea and cookies. Sit peacefully under the mulberry tree, savoring the tea and cookies while waiting for enough fruits to fall to fill your bowl. Then eat them with the cream and honey. In emergencies, canned or fresh fruit of any sort and a patio umbrella can be usefully substituted for the mulberries and tree.

Black mulberry in fruit

Ficus carica from the family *Moraceae*

FIGS

Tree/bush up to 30 x 20 ft.
Hardy, self-fertile. Fruits: pear-shaped,
2 x 4 in., brownish-green.

Fig leaves are large and distinctive, but vary in exact shape with each variety. Although figs are deciduous, young plants tend to be almost evergreen and are then more tender. Figs can be grown as trees or bushes, but are most often trained on walls. Almost all fig cultivars set the fruit parthenocarpically, without actual fertilization. However, some old and mostly inferior varieties in hot climates have female fruiting plants and male caprifigs that are separately and specifically cultivated to produce female fig wasps. These wasps will crawl through the minute end hole into the fruits to pollinate them.

Figs are indigenous to Asia Minor and were one of the first fruits to be brought into cultivation. They thus became an intrinsic part of the diet of the Mediterranean basin long before Classical times, though the Greeks claimed they were given to them by the goddess Demeter. Cato knew of six different figs, and two centuries later, in about A.D. 60, Pliny notes no fewer than 29 varieties! Figs were certainly brought to England by the Romans, as remains have been found, though the plants were not officially introduced until the early sixteenth century. There are over 600 fig species. Many of the varieties that we encounter today are ornamentals such as the **India rubber plant** (*Ficus elastica*), the **weeping fig** (*F. Benjamina*), and the **fiddle leaf plant** (*F. lyrata*).

'Brunswick'

VARIETIES

'**Brunswick**' produces large fruits that are most tasty a couple of days after picking; '**Brown Turkey**' is reliably prolific; '**White Marseilles**' has pale fruits. Planted in San Diego, California, by Franciscan missionaries, '**Black Mission**' is the oldest and still the most popular fig for drying and shipping. The pear-shaped, fine-quality fruits have sweet, red flesh that is excellent fresh, dried, or canned. Self-fertile '**Conadria**' bears heavily in cooler climates.

'Brown Turkey'

CULTIVATION

Varieties vary in hardiness, but even if the tops are lost many will regrow from the roots if these are protected from the frost. Thus figs may be planted a little deep to encourage stooling. Often grown against a wall, they can be cropped in the open in warm areas. **'Brown Turkey'** and **'Celeste'** are cold hardy to Zone 5, but most other figs do best in Zones 8–9 or 10. Some gardeners in cold-winter areas outside of normal hardiness zones dig up their figs and lay them on their sides to winter over, buried under a thick layer of insulating materials. Too much nitrogen will promote abundant undesirable soft growth.

Growing under Glass and in Containers

Figs fruit and ripen much more reliably under glass, and with heat and care three crops a year are possible. Figs can be grown confined in large pots and can make excellent foliage plants for house or patio, though they will need careful watering and training.

Maintenance

Spring Remove frost protection, weed, spray seaweed solution monthly, and thin the fruits.
Summer Protect the fruits carefully from wasps and birds; make layers.
Fall Mulch deeply to protect roots from winter cold.
Winter Prune, take cuttings, protect from frost.

Figs stuffed with mascarpone, glacé mixed peel, a little honey, and brandy to taste are delicious.

Wall-trained fig

Propagation

Layers can be made during summer. Eight-inch well-ripened or old wood cuttings taken during the early winter root, especially if given bottom heat. Seeds produce plants that are unlikely to fruit well.

Pruning and Training

The most fruitful wood is well ripened, short-jointed and sturdy; long soft shoots are unproductive and better removed. Figs can be pruned any time during dormancy, but are best left until growth is about to start in spring.

Weed, Pest, and Disease Control

Fig plants have few problems except **birds** and **wasps**. Weeding must be thorough near the trunks to prevent **rodents** nibbling the bark. Under cover, on walls, or in pots they may suffer from **red spider mites**.

Harvesting and Storing

Most fig varieties bear two crops per year, in early summer and early fall. In some varieties, the first crop is heavy and the second light; in others, the pattern is reversed. In colder areas, any fruits formed in fall for the first crop will probably be killed by cold. In hotter regions figs can be dried and will keep well.

CULINARY USES

Figs are delicious fresh and they can be made into jams, jellies, cheeses, and chutneys.

Savory and Sweet Figs
Serves 4 as a snack or canapé

12 dried figs
1 cup mild hard cheese
Pinch of celery seed
1 shallot
1 square dark cooking chocolate
$^1/_4$ cup marzipan
2 tablespoons sultanas
2 tablespoons raisins
A little Cointreau or other sweet liqueur
Honey

Stuff half the figs with some small chunks of cheese, a sprinkling of celery seeds, and a thin slice of the shallot.

Grate the chocolate and marzipan. Mix in the dried fruit and liqueur, then stuff the remaining figs with this mixture. Smear all the figs with honey, put them in an greased dish, and bake in a preheated oven at 350°F for 10 to 15 minutes. Serve the figs hot or cold.

COMPANION PLANTING

One of the few plants to get on well with rue.

OTHER USES

Figs are known by many for their syrup, administered as a laxative. Also valuable as a food, they contain nearly half their weight in sugar when dried.

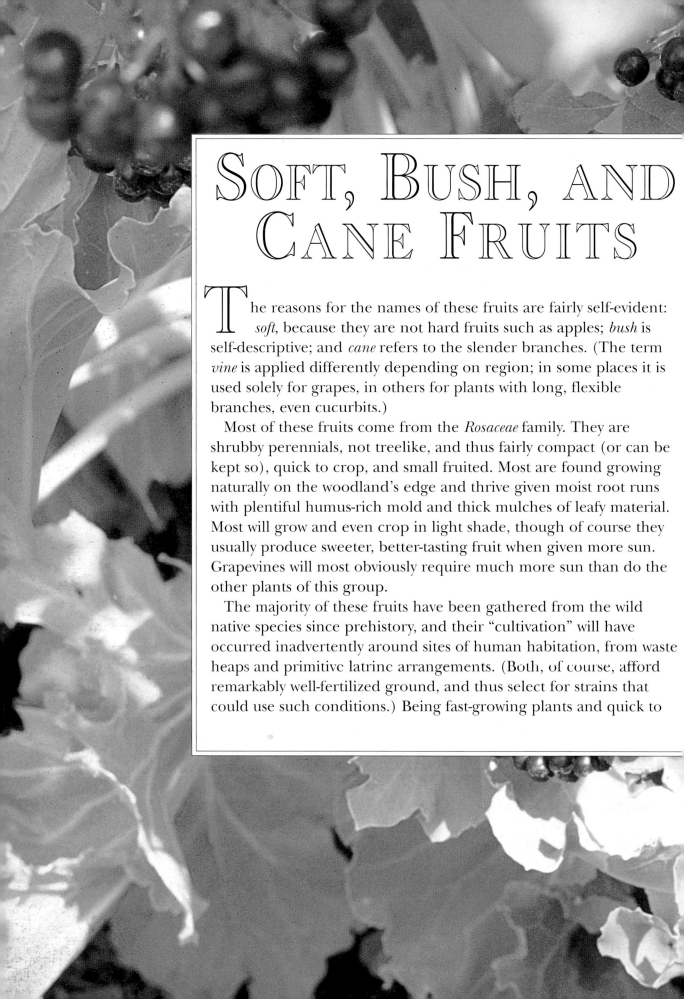

Soft, Bush, and Cane Fruits

The reasons for the names of these fruits are fairly self-evident: *soft*, because they are not hard fruits such as apples; *bush* is self-descriptive; and *cane* refers to the slender branches. (The term *vine* is applied differently depending on region; in some places it is used solely for grapes, in others for plants with long, flexible branches, even cucurbits.)

Most of these fruits come from the *Rosaceae* family. They are shrubby perennials, not treelike, and thus fairly compact (or can be kept so), quick to crop, and small fruited. Most are found growing naturally on the woodland's edge and thrive given moist root runs with plentiful humus-rich mold and thick mulches of leafy material. Most will grow and even crop in light shade, though of course they usually produce sweeter, better-tasting fruit when given more sun. Grapevines will most obviously require much more sun than do the other plants of this group.

The majority of these fruits have been gathered from the wild native species since prehistory, and their "cultivation" will have occurred inadvertently around sites of human habitation, from waste heaps and primitive latrine arrangements. (Both, of course, afford remarkably well-fertilized ground, and thus select for strains that could use such conditions.) Being fast-growing plants and quick to

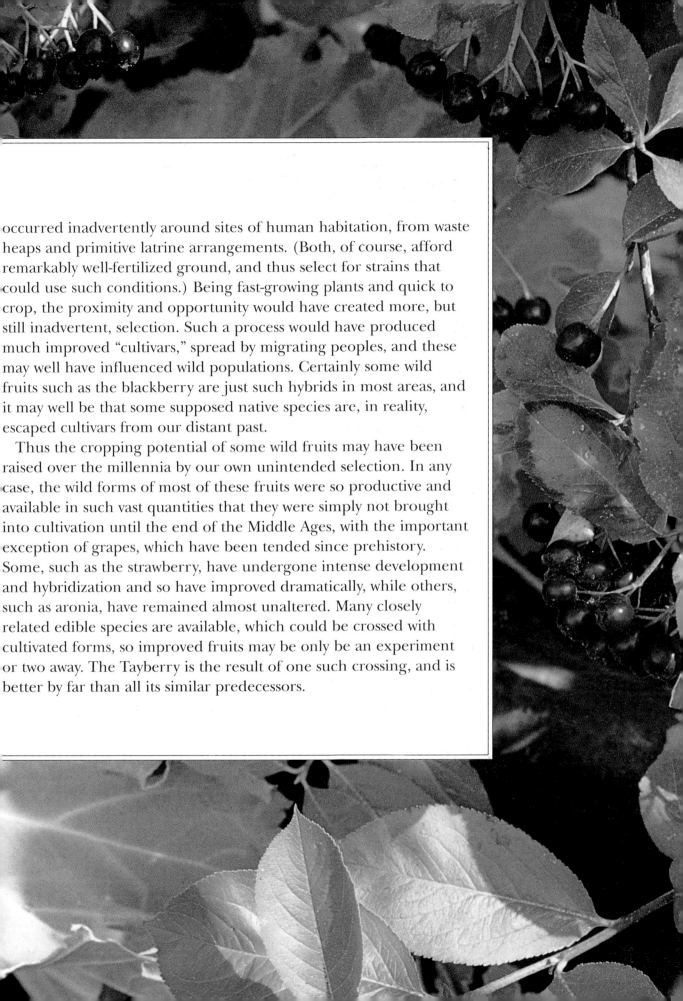

occurred inadvertently around sites of human habitation, from waste heaps and primitive latrine arrangements. (Both, of course, afford remarkably well-fertilized ground, and thus select for strains that could use such conditions.) Being fast-growing plants and quick to crop, the proximity and opportunity would have created more, but still inadvertent, selection. Such a process would have produced much improved "cultivars," spread by migrating peoples, and these may well have influenced wild populations. Certainly some wild fruits such as the blackberry are just such hybrids in most areas, and it may well be that some supposed native species are, in reality, escaped cultivars from our distant past.

Thus the cropping potential of some wild fruits may have been raised over the millennia by our own unintended selection. In any case, the wild forms of most of these fruits were so productive and available in such vast quantities that they were simply not brought into cultivation until the end of the Middle Ages, with the important exception of grapes, which have been tended since prehistory. Some, such as the strawberry, have undergone intense development and hybridization and so have improved dramatically, while others, such as aronia, have remained almost unaltered. Many closely related edible species are available, which could be crossed with cultivated forms, so improved fruits may be only be an experiment or two away. The Tayberry is the result of one such crossing, and is better by far than all its similar predecessors.

Fragaria hybrids from the family *Rosaceae*

June-Bearing
STRAWBERRIES

Herbaceous. 1 ft. Life span: short. Self-fertile. Fruits: up to 2 x 2 in., red, conical.
Value: some vitamin C and half as much iron as spinach.

This most delicious of fruits really needs no introduction. Modern strawberries are hybrids based on *F. chiloensis*, **'Chilean Pine,'** and *F. virginiana*, **'Scarlet Virginian.'** The first contributed larger fruit with a pineapple tang and was brought to Europe in 1712; the latter, first mentioned in Massachusetts in 1621, provides the superior flavor, and is still grown commercially as **'Little Scarlet'** for jam-making. These two were first combined in the nineteenth century, with intensive development since. Every region has its favorite varieties.

VARIETIES

There are far too many to list, and new, improved ones are continually becoming available. Popular U.S. varieties include **'Robinson,'** **'Surecrop,'** **'Guardian,'** **'Sparkle,'** **'Allstar,'** **'Earliglow,'** and **'Lategrow.'**

CULTIVATION

Most strawberry varieties will thrive in Zones 4 through 8. **'Arking'** and some other varieties are suited for southern gardens in Zone 9, and **'Cyclone'** and other cold-tolerant varieties flourish as far north as Minnesota and the Dakotas. All preparation is well repaid. Strawberries need a very rich soil, full of humus, and benefit from slow-release phosphates, such as bone meal. Well-rotted manure or compost will give you better cropping. The more space you give them, the better they will do and the less work they will be; 2 ft. each way is the minimum.

Growing under Glass
They do not like the hot, dry conditions under cover, and these also encourage red spider mites. However, the advantages of protection from birds, prevention of rain damage, and earlier crops mean that they are widely grown under glass and plastic.

Growing in Containers
Many containers, often tower shaped, are sold specifically for strawberries.

The small amount of root run, hot in an aboveground position, and usually dry because of low water-holding capacity, make these poor growing conditions for strawberries. However, strawberries can be grown successfully in pots and containers. They need regular feeding as well as copious automatic watering.

Maintenance
Spring Weed, root first runners, and spray seaweed monthly.
Summer Weed, straw, protect from birds and mold, pick.
Autumn Establish new plants, tidy up the best, eradicate old.
Winter Rake up old leaves, mulch, and compost.

Propagation
While some varieties can be grown from seed, runners are the best choice. These are best taken from quality plants that have been reserved for propagation and deflowered; half a dozen good ones, or many more poor, can thus be had. The first plantlet on an early runner is chosen, pinned or held to the ground—or preferably rooted into a pot of compost for an easier transplantation. Start new beds in late summer or early autumn to allow them to establish; they can then crop well the next summer. Late autumn or spring plantings

Strawberries displayed on a tiered stand

"fluffy." **Verticillium wilt** and **red stele**, which occur occasionally, especially in heavy soils, kill off the plant roots. **Leaf blight**, **leaf scorch**, and **mildew** also may show up. Buy certified virus-indexed plants to avoid bringing in problems.

Harvesting and Storing
June-bearing varieties bear in June or July in most regions, but they ripen as early as April in California and Florida. Strawberries must be used quickly as they only keep for a day or so.

They can be juiced and made into syrup, or made into jams and jellies—the addition of apple or red- or white-currant juice will help with the setting.

OTHER USES

As for everbearing strawberries (see p. 437).

COMPANION PLANTING

Before establishing a new bed, dig in a green manure crop of soybeans to help prevent root rots. Growing borage, any of the beans, or onions nearby reputedly helps strawberry plants.

CULINARY USES

Wimbledon Fortune
Fresh strawberries sprinkled with sugar, cream, a shortbread cookie or two—and you have the treat made famous by tennis.

should be deflowered the first summer to build up their strength for a massive crop the next.

Pruning and Training
Strawberries will become relatively unproductive after three or four years, so in practice, a continual annual replacement of a quarter or a third of the plants is best. Replacing them all every four years or so means years of gluts and years of shortages, as they are all the same age. Strawing up is

essential for clean crops. Do not straw too early—only when the first green fruits are seen swelling. Remove surplus runners regularly.

Weed, Pest, and Disease Control
Major losses are from **birds** and **mold**. Individual bunches can be protected from both with jam jars. Netting is usually obligatory. Mold can be decreased by strawing up and removing fruits that rot, preferably before the mold goes

Fragaria hybrids from the family *Rosaceae*

EVERBEARING
STRAWBERRIES

Herbaceous. 1 ft. Life span: short. Self-fertile. Fruits: up to 2 x 1 in., red, conical.
Value: some vitamin C and half as much iron as spinach.

The everbearing strawberries are just as much a mixture of, and very similar to, June-bearing strawberries, except that they fruit continuously through the fall. In fact they start to set early crops even before the summer varieties, but these are normally removed to ensure bigger crops later when the summer crowd has finished. Some have extremely good flavor, probably due to some *F. vesca* ancestry.

This particular group of strawberries has been improved far more in continental Europe than in America or the U.K. Their development has been parallel to that of the summer strawberries, but with different mixes of species used in the hybridization. Most of the strawberry family are greatly affected by day length, and this group perhaps most of all. Most strawberry varieties respond to a change from their native latitude by producing primarily runners if they move north and fruits if they move south. It would thus seem that any variety would be a perpetual fruiter if cultivated at the "right" latitude, and that perpetual fruiters are really just summer croppers enjoying a warmer latitude than nature intended.

Strawberries do well on window ledges in full sun.

VARIETIES

Developed in the Arkansas Ozarks, the very vigorous **'Ozark Beauty'** bears berries as big as 4 in. across, with good taste for fresh eating, cooking, and freezing. **'Quinault'** has unbelievably big berries, and tasty, too. It produces runners with abandon, which may even fruit before they have grown roots. **'Tristar'** is sweet and good for fresh eating. **'Tribune'** has tarter-tasting berries and is disease-resistant.

CULTIVATION

Everbearers need the same rich, moist conditions as summer strawberries. As they crop for longer and can give higher total yields, they deserve even better treatment. Most varieties grow well in Zones 4 through 8.

Growing under Glass
These are better value grown under glass than summer strawberries, as they use the space productively for longer. They benefit most from such cover at the end of fall. They must have good ventilation or they mold rapidly, and they are

'Aromel'

prone to red spider mite attacks. Either use the commercial predators or suffer.

Growing in Containers
These everbearers are often recommended for growing in containers, as they are productive for far longer than summer fruiters and make better use of limited space. However, they will do much better in the ground, especially if erratic watering is a possibility.

Ornamental and Wildlife Value
Climbing varieties can be trained well over a trellis and can also be quite decorative, especially when in fruit. Their long flowering period makes these plants valuable to insects, and the fruits themselves are enjoyed by both birds and rodents.

Maintenance
Spring Weed, mulch, spray with seaweed solution, and deflower.
Summer Deflower, root some runners, and remove the rest.
Fall Straw up and pick.
Winter Tidy bed, de-runner, plant out in late winter.

Propagation
The everbearing varieties cannot be reliably propagated by seed as they are such mixed hybrids. I have tried! Runners can be rooted in pots in summer and detached. They crop significantly more easily the first year than summer fruiters. This is because when planted out, they have longer to establish before the fruiting commences, whether this happens in the preceding fall, late winter, or even early spring.

Pruning and Training
Everbearers are grown similarly to summer strawberries, but it pays to give them a sunny spot so their later fruits can ripen.

Weed, Pest, and Disease Control
Because they have such a long season, early **moldy** fruits must be rapidly and hygienically removed, or later fruits will suffer exponentially. They are more prone to molds because of humidity. **Bird** damage is less as there are plenty of other attractive fruits around.

Harvesting and Storing
Because the everbearers crop late into fall they are juicier than summer varieties, but not always so sweet, and often rot before ripening.

COMPANION PLANTING

As with other strawberries, they do well with beans and are benefited by onions and borage. Most of all they love a mulch of pine needles.

OTHER USES

Eating strawberries will supposedly whiten your teeth. Strawberry leaves have been used as a tea substitute.

Strawberry tea

CULINARY USES

They can be used just like June-bearing strawberries, but are conveniently fresh from summer until the frosts.

Baked Strawberry Apples
Serves 4

4 cooking apples
2 cups strawberries
A few raisins
A little sugar and butter

Preheat the oven to 375°F. Wash, dry, and core the apples, and smear with butter. Cut a thin slice off one end to ensure they sit flat in a greased baking dish. Setting aside the four best strawberries, eat some and pass the rest through a sieve. Fill the holes in the apples with strawberry puree. Push in raisins to bring the level over the top. Finish with the reserved fruits and a sprinkling of sugar. Bake until the apples are bursting, approximately 20 minutes. Serve hot with custard, cream, or yogurt.

Fragaria vesca semperflorens from the family *Rosaceae*

STRAWBERRIES
ALPINE AND WILD

Herbaceous. 1 ft. Life span: short! Self-fertile. Fruits: up to ½ x 1 in.
Value: some vitamin C.

Alpine strawberries differ from the common garden strawberries in two distinct ways. The fruits and plants are smaller and they do not form runners. The alpines form neat clumps about twelve inches across, with lighter green leaves, and flower all season almost from last to first frost. The other wild (European) strawberries, *F. vesca*, and **'Hautbois,'** *F. elatior*/**moschata**, are more like miniature versions of garden strawberries. With smaller fruits than even the alpines, they do make runners. Indeed some of the wild woodland forms produce only runners and rarely fruit.

'Alexandria'

These wild forms were the earliest strawberries cultivated and are native to Europe, but only north of the Alps. They were thus unknown to the ancient Greeks, and although passing reference is made to them by Roman and early medieval writers, it is as wild, not cultivated fruits. In England the fruits are mentioned during the thirteenth century in the Countess of Leicester's "household roll." By the reign of Henry VIII, the fruit was highly esteemed and cost four pence a bushel. At the same time, the 'Hautbois' strawberry was also popular, especially on the Continent. It was one of the most fragrant of all and made few runners. The species from the Americas arrived during this period, but were considered not as good as these native wild varieties. It was not until the nineteenth century that the natives became superseded by "modern" hybrids.

VARIETIES

Alpines are grown from seed. They are little improved on the true wild form, though yellow- and white-fruited versions are available. **'Baron Solemacher'** is a slightly larger-fruited selection; it needs nearly 2 ft. of space each way. Other fine alpine varieties are **'Rugen,' 'Pineapple Alpine,'** and **'Yellow Alpine.'** All are bushy, runnerless plants that make a neat edging for flower beds. Other regional wild strawberries are also worth growing, or at least picking wild.

'Baron Solemacher'

CULTIVATION

Alpines are easier to grow, needing less richness and moisture than other types of strawberry, though they naturally will do much better given improved conditions. They can be spaced at 12 in. or so apart. Wild strawberries are better grown as ground cover in moist partial shade and allowed to run. Most alpines will grow in Zones 3 through 9.

Weed, Pest, and Disease Control
Alpine and wild species are much tougher plants than conventional varieties and rarely suffer from pests or diseases. The fruits are also less appealing to birds, so they can often be cropped without protection.

Pruning and Training
As with other varieties and species, it is best to replace the entire stock in stages normally running over a three- or four-year period.

Growing under Glass and in Containers
Alpines can be cropped under glass to extend the season, but become more prone to red spider mite.

Culinary Uses

Both alpine and wild strawberries are superlatively fragrant and delicious raw, if fully ripe. Cooking brings out even more flavor, from underripe fruits as well. These are less moist than ordinary strawberries, so they require some water or red currant juice to make jam or jelly.

Alpine Strawberry Tarts

Make individual sweet shortcrust pastries. Smear the insides with butter, then fill each tart with a mixture of both alpine strawberries and strawberry jam (alpine or otherwise). Bake in a preheated oven for 10 minutes or so at 375°F. Cool and top each with cream before serving.

Maintenance
Spring Weed, mulch, and spray thoroughly with seaweed solution monthly.
Summer Pick regularly all through summer.
Fall Remove old, worn-out plants.
Winter Sow seed in pots in cold frame in late winter.

Ornamental and Wildlife Value
Alpines make good ground cover and are more decorative than other strawberries, as they form neat mounds. The long flowering period makes them beneficial to insects.

Harvesting and Storing
They can be picked underripe for culinary purposes. Pick and freeze them until sufficient quantities are gathered; if you shake the frozen fruits in a dry cloth, many seeds can be removed.

Propagation
As true alpines make no runners, they are grown from seed. Sow early for plants to put out in spring. Sometimes the crowns can be successfully divided. The 16th-century poet Thomas Tusser suggested that strawberries should be obtained from the wild:

"Wife, into the garden, and set me a plot
With strawberry roots of the best to be got;
Such growing abroad among thorns in the wood,
Well chosen and picked, grow excellent good."

Companion Planting

Thomas Tusser also said:
"Gooseberries, raspberries, roses all three
With strawberries under do trimly agree."

Other Uses

Traditionally, the leaves of wild strawberries were used for medicinal purposes.

Vaccinium species from the family *Ericaceae*

BLUEBERRIES & HUCKLEBERRIES

Bush 1–15 ft. Life span: medium to long. Deciduous, self-fertile. Fruits: ¼–½ in., spherical blue-black.

Blueberries, huckleberries, or whortleberries, *Vaccinium myrtillus*, are low shrubs native to Europe, found on heaths and moors in acid soils. They have slender, green twigs with myrtlelike leaves and spherical pink flowers followed by blue-black fruits in late summer. Blueberries are a traditional American fruit, with different regions favoring different species, such as **Highbush**, or **Swamp**, and **Rabbiteye Blueberries** in the warmer areas and the **Lowbush**, **Early** or **Low**, **Sweet Blueberry** further north. The **Highbush** is a tall shrub up to fifteen feet, so lower-growing cultivars for garden use have been bred, though commercial growers still prefer the tall ones. Many similar species are used as ornamentals, because in fall the leaves turn to some amazing reds and pinks. The **Rabbiteye Blueberries**, *V. virgatum/ashei* are similar. The **Lowbush Blueberry**, *V. angustifolium*, is different, only about twelve inches high, and is much hardier than the **Highbush**. The berries are large, sweet, and early, so this has been crossed with the **Highbush**.

Huckleberries were once very popular. They would be picked from the wild and taken to market in the towns where they were esteemed for tarts and jellies. They were a staple food to the Scots Highlanders, who ate them in milk and made them into wine. Huckleberries went into oblivion when the better-fruiting blueberries from America became available.

VARIETIES

The early **'Earliblue'** and **'Jersey'** are fairly compact. **'Berkeley'** is a spreader, **'Blue Crop'** more upright. **'Northland'** has long, loose clusters of fruit with a rich flavor. The highbush **'Patriot'** bears tight clusters of large berries with excellent flavor. **'Woodard'** is a Rabbiteye variety for mild areas.

Many other good varieties of blueberries are available. *V. ovatum*, the **Huckleberry** or **Box Blueberry** is a small, attractive, evergreen shrub with tasty berries and can

Huckleberries

be used to make a fruiting hedge. The **Red Huckleberry**, *V. parvifolium*, is a large deciduous shrub that has red fruits. *V. membranaceum*, the **Big Huckleberry**, has big berries, is fairly drought-resistant, and is one of the tastiest of this family. *V. hirsutum*, the **Hairy Huckleberry,** is not very hardy and has hairy fruits.

CULTIVATION

All need planting 5 ft. apart. Many of the species have edible berries. An acid soil suitable for heathers or rhododendrons is essential; a substitute of peat and leaf mold will do. The tall species prefer wetter sites, the dwarfer ones suffer drier, but all crop better with moister positions. They prefer sunny sites, though they will grow in partial shade. Partly self-fertile, they do better if several varieties are grown together. Lowbush varieties grow well in Zones 2 through 6; highbush are for Zones 3 through 8; and Rabbiteye grow only in Zones 7 through 9.

Growing under Glass
They are sufficiently hardy almost anywhere, but glass protection may be worthwhile temporarily while they fruit to prevent losses to birds.

Growing in Containers
Blueberries have to be grown in containers in many areas, as they die on lime soils. Compost for acid-loving plants or a mixture of peat, sand, and leaf mold is essential, as is regular, copious watering with rain or acidic water. In limy areas avoid tap water.

Maintenance
Spring Weed and mulch.
Summer Make layers, pick fruit.
Fall Take suckers and transplant once leaves fall.
Winter Prune if necessary.

Propagation
The species come true from seed but better varieties are layered in summer. Suckers can be detached in winter.

Pruning and Training
Huckleberries and blueberries need little pruning, except to remove dead or diseased growth, best done in winter.

Weed, Pest, and Disease Control
Apart from the usual losses to **birds**, this is a remarkably pest- and disease-free family. Any distress will probably be due to an alkaline soil or lime in the water supply.

Harvesting and Storing
The berries should be picked when fully ripe and easily detached or they are too acid. They may be made into jam, juice, or jelly, or frozen.

Highbush

COMPANION PLANTING

As these are acid-loving, they grow well near heathers.

CULINARY USES

Blueberries and bilberries can be used in pies, tarts, jams, jellies, and syrups. Blueberry cheesecake and blueberry muffins are popular American dishes.

Blueberry Grunt
Serves 4–6

2 cups blueberries
¼ cup sugar
1 teaspoon allspice
1 small lemon
Maple syrup to taste
1 cup white flour
Pinch salt
1½ teaspoons baking powder
¼ cup (½ stick) butter
1 cup half and half

OTHER USES

The leaves were used medicinally. Chewing dried bilberries was a cure for diarrhea and mouth and throat infections.

Simmer the washed blueberries gently with sugar, allspice, and the lemon's juice and grated rind. Add maple syrup to taste. Meanwhile rub the flour, salt, baking powder, and butter into crumbs and blend in enough cream to make a smooth, creamy dough. Carefully spoon the dough on top of the blueberries, cover the pan, and simmer until the crust puffs and sets. Serve with additional maple syrup.

Vaccinium species from the family *Ericaceae*

CRANBERRIES

Bush. Prostrate to 2 ft. Life span: medium to long, Evergreen, self-fertile.
Fruits: up to ³/₄ in., reddish-orange. Value: some vitamin C.

Cranberries are very similar and closely related to blueberries and huckleberries, the most noticeable differences being that cranberries have red berries and are evergreen.

V. oxycoccus, the **cranberry**, is a native of most northern temperate countries and is found on bogs and moorlands. The low-growing, evergreen shrub is tough and wiry with long, sparsely leafed stems. The leaves are longer and thinner than those of the blue-berried *Vaccinium* species. The flowers are tiny, yellow, and pink in early summer, and are followed by the round, red fruits, which are pleasantly acid to taste. The **American Cranberry**, *V. macrocarpon*, is much the same, but larger in size and berry.

The native cranberry has been gathered from the wild in most cool regions by native peoples throughout the Northern Hemisphere. Strangely enough, the British never much liked them, although they are very popular in Sweden.

VARIETIES

Several species of American cranberries are available, including **'McFarlin,'** an old commercial variety that makes an appealing ground cover with its large red berries; **'Ben Lear,'** a Wisconsin clone whose deep red fruit ripens early; **'Pilgrim,'** a fast spreader with small pink flowers; and **'Beckwith,'** a late variety. Apart from those already mentioned, there are several other *Vacciniums* that fall between cranberries and blueberries and have edible berries; *V. floribundum*, the **Mortinia**, is the least hardy and comes from Ecuador but will survive in southern England. It is an attractive evergreen shrub with heavy racemes of rose-pink blooms followed by masses of red berries. From East Asia and Japan comes *V. praestans*, a prostrate, creeping, deciduous shrub with sweet, fragrant, glossy red berries. *V. nummularia* is one of the choicest little evergreens for a mountain cottage.

Cranberry fruit

The evergreen cowberry,
V. nummularia

CULTIVATION

These really need moist, boggy conditions, in lime-free soil and water. The best sites are made on the edge of a river or pond by slowly building up a layer of stones covered with a thick layer of peaty, humus-rich, acid soil. They must be moist but not drowned; they need to stand above the water. Most are small, needing as little as 2–3 ft. each way and even tolerating some light shade. American cranberries will grow well under the proper conditions in Zones 3 through 7.

Growing under Glass
As the usual varieties are hardy, this is only worthwhile for protection from birds. *V. floribundum* and *nummularia* benefit from cool cover and are very beautiful small shrubs.

Growing in Containers
Cranberries have to be grown in containers in many areas as they will die on lime soils. Acid compost or a mixture of peat, sand, and leaf mold is essential, as is regular and copious watering with rain or acidic water. Avoid tap water in limy areas!

Ornamental and Wildlife Value
The berries are loved by wildlife and, being evergreen, the plants will provide good shelter.

Maintenance
Spring Weed, mulch, make the layers.
Summer Keep well watered.
Fall Divide plants and pick fruit before frost.
Winter Protect less hardy species from frost.

Propagation, Pruning, and Training
The species can be grown from seed, by dividing in fall, or they can be layered in spring. Only remedial tidying is required.

Weed, Pest, and Disease Control
Most of the denser-growing species suppress weeds well. They are all pest- and disease-free in most gardens. Grown under glass, they need to be kept cool or they suffer. Any problems are most often due to **lime** in the soil or water. Watering on sequestrated iron chelates will help, but these are not available to organic growers.

Harvesting and Storing
Cowberries are made sour by frosts so must be gathered promptly. In Siberia they were kept under water through the winter, so that they gradually became less acid, and were then eaten in spring.

OTHER USES

The leaves and fruits of most of these berries have been used medicinally in the past.

CULINARY USES

Invariably used for the "sauce," but also in tarts and pies and added to many other dishes.

Cranberry Sauce
Makes about 7 lb.

2 cups cranberries
4½ cups apples
Approx. 8 cups sugar

Wash the fruits, chop the apples, and simmer both with enough water to prevent burning. Once the apples are soft, strain and add 1 cup of sugar to each cup of liquid.

Bring the liquid back to a boil, stirring to dissolve the sugar. Cook briefly, skim, and pour into sterile warmed jars. Seal at once. Serve with roast turkey.

COMPANION PLANTING

They are acid-loving and enjoy similar conditions, root bacteria, and fungi as rhododendrons and azaleas so can be used as ground cover between these.

Coralling cranberries on the surface of a bog in Massachusetts

Ribes sativum from the family *Grossulariaceae*

RED CURRANTS & WHITE CURRANTS

Shrub 7 ft. Life span: long. Deciduous, self-fertile.
Fruits: $1/2$–$3/4$ in., globular, glossy red or white.

Red currants are reliable, productive plants we rarely notice except when translucent, glossy red berries festoon the branches. Otherwise they are insignificant, similar to flowering red currant, *R. sanguineum,* which has such prolific pink tassels in early spring. (This sets inedible fruits occasionally.) White currants are varieties selected without the color and with their own flavor. I find that the whites crop slightly less extravagantly than reds and are culinarily useful.

Red currants, *R. sativum* and *R. rubrum,* are native European fruits. They were not cultivated by the Romans. They gained garden notice in the 16th century when they rapidly became a stalwart of the cottager's garden. Long-lived, they often survive, neglected and unproductive, whereas, given a good site and bird protection, they produce prodigiously. Surprisingly little-known in much of Europe and the U.S., they are popular in Scandinavia and Russia.

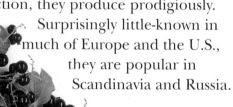

VARIETIES

The superior **'Red Lake,'** developed at the University of Minnesota, bears compact clusters of dark red berries. **'Cherry Red'** is one of the heaviest bearing as well as hardiest red currants. It is beautiful in a hedge or wildlife garden. **'Wilder Red'** has sprightly red berries over a long season. **'White Grape'** and **'White Versailles'** are hardy white currants.

CULTIVATION

Red and white currants are hardy as far north as Zone 3; **'Cherry'** and **'Red Lake'** will grow in Zone 2. Red currants respond best to a cool, well-mulched soil. They do not need conditions as rich as black currants or raspberries and will grow in partial shade. However, the berries are sweeter grown in the sun. The main requirement is protection from birds.

'White Versailles'

Without thorough netting, all else is useless, as these are the bird food supreme.

Weed, Pest, and Disease Control

The only major threat to the crop is the **birds**. **Minor sawfly caterpillar** attacks sometimes occur but do little damage. Berries left to ripen fully **mold** in damp weather unless protected. The leaves regularly pucker with red and yellow blotches from the **leaf blistering aphis**, though surprisingly this does not affect the yield. Indeed these leaves are removed wholesale, with aphids on board, during summer pruning.

Pruning and Training

These are the most easily trained and forgiving of plants. No matter how you misprune them, they respond with new growth and ample fruit. Red currants can be made to take any form—cordon, goblet, fan, or espalier—and moreover are quick to regrow. They will fruit best on a permanent framework with spurs and need every shoot, except leaders, cut back in summer and again harder in winter. Growing in good conditions, red currants can be trained over large walls, including north-facing ones. Moderately pruned as goblet bushes, they need to be at least 6 ft. apart. As cordons they can be grown two to the yard.

Propagation

The easiest of all plants to root from fall cuttings.

Maintenance

Spring Weed, mulch, and spray seaweed solution monthly.
Summer Pick fruit as required. After midsummer, prune.
Fall Take cuttings once leaves fall.
Winter Cut back hard to spurs on frame.

'Wilson's Longbunch'

Growing under Glass and in Containers

This can be worthwhile if you want pristine berries over a longer season or have no space for bushes. They do not want to get too hot!

Harvesting and Storing

Currants can be picked from early summer as they color, for use as garnishes, adding to compotes, and for the most acid jellies. Ripening continues into late fall in dry years when the fruits become less acid and tasty raw. Being seedy, the fruit is conveniently stored juiced and frozen. Similarly, currants are better as jelly rather than jam. Dry, cool berries keep very well.

OTHER USES

Once popular with apothecaries, as they could be stored for months packed fresh and dry into sealed glass bottles and were thus available as "vitamin pills" in bleak late winter and spring when fresh fruit and vegetables became scarce. The juice of red currants must be the best edible red dye you could want.

COMPANION PLANTING

Red currants may benefit from nettles nearby, but the fruit picker will curse. *Limnanthes douglassii* is the best companion and ground cover once the bushes are well established.

CULINARY USES

Red currants are immensely useful because of their color and acidity. They add deep red to everything and their juice makes other fruit jellies set. Red currant juice adds tartness and flavor to other juices and can be used in many sweet and savory dishes.

White currant juice is a substitute, if not an improvement, for lemon juice, and makes even more delicious jellies.

Mint Sauce Supreme
Makes about 2 lb.

2 cups white currants
Approx. 2 cups sugar
1/2 cup fresh mint leaves, finely shredded

Simmer the white currants until soft, then strain, or simply juice. Add the same volume of sugar to the juice and slowly bring to a boil. Skim and remove from the heat. Stir in the finely shredded mint and bottle in warm sterile jars. Cover immediately. This is the sauce for spring lamb roasts, for yogurt dips, and for barbecue glazes.

Ribes grossularia from the family *Grossulariaceae*

GOOSEBERRIES

**Bush up to 5 ft. Life span: long. Deciduous, self-fertile. Fruits: up to 1 in., oval, green to purple.
Value: some vitamin C.**

Gooseberries you find in the shops are green bullets; for culinary use, there is nothing like the meltingly sweet, well-ripened dessert varieties. Compared to other *Ribes*, gooseberries have bigger, hairy berries and sharp thorns. They are easy to grow but often handicapped by being grown as a stool. Given attention and good pruning, large, succulent berries can be had, in almost any color and with delicious flavor, which can range from a clean, acid-sweet taste to a deep and vinous plumness.

Unnoticed by classical writers but a European native, the gooseberry, *Ribes grossularia*, is first mentioned in purchases for the Westminster garden of King Edward I in 1276. They became popular almost solely in Britain, and by the nineteenth century there were hundreds of varieties and countless clubs whose members vied to grow larger fruits, achieving berries the size of small eggs. The wild relation is found in rocky terrain as a small shrub, variable in berry color, size, and in habit of growth, with some being inconveniently lax. American gooseberries/ Worcesterberries are derived from *R. divaricatum*. They have smaller berries and are resistant to the American mildew disease that can damage European varieties.

Worcesterberries

VARIETIES

Almost thornless **'Welcome'** produces large crops of sweet-tart light green fruits that turn pinkish red. **'Poorman'** has the largest fruit of any American variety, and the plant is mildew-resistant. I love **'Langley Gage'** (midseason), which has divine, bite-sized, syrupy sweet, translucent white globes hanging in profusion. **'Early Sulphur'** (very early) has golden-yellow, tasty berries. For a substantial, dark olive-green, strongly flavored, large berry, choose **'Gunner'** (mid). **'Leveller'** (mid) is a heavy cropper, and has delicious yellow-green fruits. The **Worcesterberry** is even meaner-thorned with smaller black berries more like black currants. *R. hirtellum*, the **Currant Gooseberry**, is another edible species with small reddish fruits.

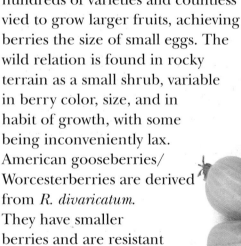

'Langley Gage' in flower

CULTIVATION

Gooseberries love rich, moist, loamy soil and do not like hot, dry, sandy sites or stagnant air, doing better with a breeze. Gooseberries do well in Zones 4 through 7 or 8.

Growing under Glass and in Containers
Gooseberries are so hardy and thorny they need no protection. They can be potted, but are easier in the ground.

Ornamental and Wildlife Value
The bushes are drab, the flowers inconspicuous, and the berries not brightly colored—the ideal landscaping plant to go with modern buildings!

Maintenance
Spring Weed, mulch, spray seaweed solution monthly.
Summer Thin and pick fruit, and watch out for the hazards of sawfly and mildew.
Fall Take cuttings.
Winter Prune hard.

Propagation
Gooseberries are propagated by 1-ft.-long cuttings. Disbud the lower end to prevent suckers.

Pruning and Training
Often misgrown as a stool with many shoots directly from the ground, gooseberries are better hard pruned to spurs on a goblet-shaped frame with a short leg. I leave the pruning until late winter so that the thorns protect the buds from the birds, which perversely delight in disbudding gooseberries. To get larger berries or more varieties in a confined space, gooseberries may easily be grown as vertical cordons, fans, or even standards.

Weed, Pest, and Disease Control
American mildew is the worst problem, burning tips and felting fruits with a leathery coat that dries them up. Hygiene, moist roots, hard pruning, and good air circulation reduce the damage. Sodium bicarbonate sprays and sulfur-based ones (which burn some varieties) are available to organic growers. Occasionally, often in the third year or so after planting, gooseberries suffer damage from **sawfly caterpillars**. First appearing as a host of tiny holes in a leaf, they move onto stripping the bush. However, vigilance and early action prevent serious damage.

Harvesting and Storing
Gooseberries do not have as much bird appeal as many fruits and can even be had unripe without protection. Birds and wasps do steal them once they're ripe; otherwise the fruits mellow and will hang on until late summer if protected from such pests and damp.

COMPANION PLANTING

Tomatoes and fava beans nearby are reputed to aid them, and I always grow them with *Limnanthes douglasii* as ground cover.

OTHER USES

Gooseberries make a powerful wine much like that of the grape.

CULINARY USES

Picked small and green, they make the most delicious acid jams and tarts—which turn red if overcooked. As they ripen they become less acid and fuller-flavored for dessert purposes. Ripe fruits for cooking combine well with red currants to keep up the acidity, and are often jellied to remove the tough skins and seeds.

Gooseberry Fool
Serves 4

2½ cups ripe green
  gooseberries
Approx. ⅓ cup honey
  or sugar
1 cup heavy cream
Dark chocolate and
  nutmeg to garnish

If the gooseberries are soft, press them through a sieve. If not, warm very carefully until soft first, or freeze and defrost first. Add sweetening to the puree to taste, and cool. Immediately before serving, whip the cream and fold into the puree. Garnish with grated dark chocolate and nutmeg.

Ribes nigrum from the family *Grossulariaceae*

BLACK CURRANTS

Bush 5 ft. Life span: short. Deciduous, self-fertile.
Fruits: up to ¹/₂ in., black, spherical. Value: very rich in vitamin C.

Black currants are quite different from the other types of *Ribes*, though they are often bundled in with red currants. They fruit on young wood, not old, and have dark purple, almost black, berries with a most distinct and unforgettable aroma that is similar to that of the aromatic foliage and stems.

These, like other *Ribes*, seem to have been unknown to the ancient Greeks or Romans and were used only medicinally, as quinsy berries, for curing colds and throat problems, until the sixteenth century. Then they became more popular as a garden crop and are now very widely grown commercially in Europe, but not so much in the U.S. Their rise in fame was due to their very high vitamin C content, and probably also due to the fact that sugar, needed to make this naturally sour fruit palatable, became available more cheaply. The native plants can occasionally be found in wild wet areas of northern Europe and Asia, but are now more likely to be garden escapees. Improvement has been made mostly by selection rather than producing hybrids with other *Ribes*, though the **Josta** is a good example of what is possible.

VARIETIES

New varieties such as **'Ben Sarek'** (midseason), **'Ben Lomond'** (late), and **'Ben More'** (very late) are numerous and generally more productive, with better disease resistance, than old favorites. **'Laxton's Giant'** (mid) is still one of the biggest. The **Josta** berry is a much larger hybrid, more like a thornless gooseberry. Some American species have been esteemed, such as the fragrant, bright-yellow-flowered **Buffalo Currant** or **Golden Currant**, *R. aureum/odoratum*, which is also used as the stock for standard

'Ben More'

gooseberries. *R. americanum,* **'American Black Currant,'** has yellowish flowers and inferior fruit, but turns glorious colors in fall. Heavy-bearing **'Consort'** has unique, musky-sweet black fruit that is good for all uses. It is hardy to –30°F.

CULTIVATION

Black currants revel in rich, moist ground, the richer the better, and similarly respond to heavy mulching. They do not mind light shade. Late varieties are usually chosen to avoid frost damage during their flowering period. European black currants *(R. nigrum)* grow best in the Northeast and Northwest, where summers aren't too hot and brutal, generally in Zones 4 through 7 or 8. American varieties are heat-tolerant, cold-tolerant, and drought-tolerant, and do well as far north as Zone 2.

Growing under Glass and in Containers
The bushes prefer to be cool so they are not happy for long under cover. They can be grown and fruited successfully in large pots.

Maintenance
Spring Weed, mulch, spray seaweed solution monthly.
Summer Protect and pick fruits.
Fall Take cuttings.
Winter Prune back hard and compost heavily.

Propagation
There are no easier cuttings. As black currants are best grown as a stool, the main requirement is for multiple shoots from ground level. Thus cuttings have all buds left on, and new bushes are planted deeper than is the standard practice for almost every other subject.

Pruning and Training
In order to provide as much young fruitful wood as possible, the optimum pruning is to remove annually all shoots from a one-third segment of the stool. The lazy and less effective way is just to cut back one-third total—preferably of three or more—of the bushes once every three years.

Weed, Pest, and Disease Control
Weeds must be kept from encroaching on the stool, but rarely germinate there because of the intense shade. **Mildew** is aggravated by stagnant air and dry roots; hygienic pruning and vigorous growth is usually sufficient redress.

Harvesting and Storing
Unlike European varieties, American black currants lose much of their flavor when cooked. Black currants will keep for several days once picked as they are so firm and tough-skinned.

'Ben Lomond'

COMPANION PLANTING

Nettles nearby benefit black currants.

OTHER USES

The leaves have been used as tea for medicinal and tonic purposes and dried currants likewise, especially for throat infections.

CULINARY USES

The currants have too little liquid to simmer down on their own, so they need water or other juices. Add red currant juice to make black currant jams and dishes more pleasantly acid. Jelly is easier work than jam as despriging the berries is tedious.

Bob's Cunning Black Currant Jam
Makes about 6½ lb.

6 cups black currants
2 cups red currants
A little water
Approx. 8 cups sugar

Desprig the best quarter of the black currants and set aside. Simmer the rest with the red currants and just enough water to cover, until they are soft. Strain, reserving the juice. Cover the pulp with water, boil up again, and strain off another lot of juice. Measure the combined juices, add reserved black currants and two-thirds of the juice's volume in sugar. Bring to a boil, stirring until the sugar has dissolved. Boil briefly, skim, and pour into warm sterilized jars. Cover the jars immediately.

Aronia melanocarpa from the family Rosaceae

CHOKEBERRIES

Bush up to 7 ft. Life span: medium. Deciduous, self-fertile.
Fruits: ½ in., spherical, black. Value: very rich in vitamin C.

With a name like chokeberry you can be sure the fruits are astringent and sour raw, though fine cooked and sweetened. They are hard, red, ripening to purple or almost lustrous black. They closely resemble black currants in appearance and even in taste, though are more acid and almost pine-flavored, making them a useful substitute where black currants may not be grown, such as in some parts of their native U.S. The bushes are easy to grow, reliable, highly productive, and compact, with a height and spread of about five feet. White, hawthorn-like flowers and brilliant fall leaf colors make this a most decorative fruit bush.

Distantly related to the pear and *Sorbus* genus, these berries came from eastern North America in 1700. They were relished by native Americans who would mix the dried fruits with others to make "cakes" for winter storage, but it was the fall coloring that recommended them to European plantsmen. The Royal Horticultural Society Award of Merit was eventually granted in 1972, but for their ornamental appeal rather than their taste. They are a fruit with great potential. I'm sure they would do better if called the tastyberry!

Unripe chokeberries have a strong and sour taste.

VARIETIES

Aronia melanocarpa is available as bushes for fruit production and is self-fertile. It has exceptionally good fall leaf coloring. *A. arbutifolia*, the **Red Chokeberry**, also has good fall color and produces red berries that were eaten by Native American children for their aroma rather than for their taste. There is also a more erect form.

CULTIVATION

Chokeberries are easy and do well on any reasonable soil other than very shallow chalk or in very boggy ground. Naturally they will respond to better conditions by becoming larger and more prolific, and are happier with well-mulched peaty conditions. The bushes need to be 7 ft. apart for effective cropping, but possibly closer for massed displays of berries and fall color. *A. melanocarpa* grows well in Zones 3 to 7; *A. arbutifolia*, which tends to form colonies, is less cold hardy and does best from Zone 6 through Zone 9.

Maintenance

Spring Weed, mulch, and spray with seaweed solution.
Summer Net to keep birds off and pick the fruit.
Fall Prune out dead and diseased growths and take cuttings.
Winter Mulch with compost and straw, leaf mold, or bark.

Propagation

The species come true from seed but named varieties are best reproduced from early fall cuttings or division.

Pruning and Training

They can tend to sucker, turning them into a stool, but cultivation is easier if

COMPANION PLANTING

No good or bad companions are yet recognized as they have been little cultivated. I grow mine in a bed with rhubarb and sea kale.

OTHER USES

The berries can be used for an edible dye and I can vouch for their being a high-vitamin self-service food for my poultry, who head for them whenever they get out.

they are kept to a single stem. Pruning is mostly remedial, removing suckering, low-growing, congested, and diseased growths. I suspect chokeberries would be good trained on wires or a wall—they would certainly be most decorative.

Weed, Pest, and Disease Control

Other than the usual hazards of choking **weeds** and losses to the **birds**, these plants are remarkably free from problems. One reason chokeberries are coming into cultivation is that they are as good a source of vitamin C as black currants, but also more productive, with none of the potential problems of disease.

Growing under Glass and in Containers

There seems no need to grow chokeberries under glass, as they thrive outdoors and are of little value fresh, only tasty once preserved. However, it is worth growing them in a container if you need a rich source of vitamin C and have no garden space available.

Ornamental and Wildlife Value

The tough reliability, the profusion of spring flowers, immense quantities of glossy black berries and the color of the fall leaves make this

an essential plant for any area, ornamental or wild, especially if you like birds.

Harvesting and Storing
Chokeberries ripen in midsummer but the flavor improves if they are left to hang. They will need good bird protection. The best and only sensible means of storage is turning them into preserves.

Chokeberries ripening on the bush

CULINARY USES

They can be used in the same way as black currants and indeed taste similar, if more piney and aromatic. However their preserve goes better with savory dishes in the manner of cranberry jelly.

Chokeberry Preserves

4 cups chokeberries
2 cups white currants or red currants (if white unavailable)
1 small lemon
Water
Approx. 4 cups sugar

Thoroughly wash the berries and currants, chop the lemon, and simmer all three with just sufficient water to cover. Simmer until soft, then sieve out the skins and pips, measure the juice, and return it to the pan with three-quarters of its volume in sugar. Bring to a boil. Skim well, then pot in small jars. Store for six months before use. Serve with ham steak, new potatoes, and peas.

Rubus idaeas from the family *Rosaceae*

RASPBERRIES

Bush/vine. Life span: short. Deciduous, self-fertile. Fruits: up to 1 in., red, yellow, black, conical.
Value: valuable amounts of vitamin C, riboflavin, and niacin.

Although many have described the strawberry as the finest fruit, others consider the raspberry to be as good, if not better. However, these exquisite berries are much less common by far, because the fruits perish so rapidly. Strangely, they are also little grown as garden fruits primarily, although they are among the easiest to care for and cultivate.

Raspberries vary considerably in size and are usually red, with black and yellow sorts also sometimes encountered. In good varieties, the conical fruit pulls off the plug easily, leaving a hole. Some are less easy to pick and the berries may be damaged in the extrication as they are very soft and thin-skinned.

Their young shoots are usually green but soon turn red or brown as they grow. Eventually the canes reach three to ten feet high. They are often bristly and occasionally thorny. Individually the canes are short-lived, springing from a suckering root system one year to die the following year after fruiting. The root systems could spread perpetually, though they most often fade away from virus infections. The flowers are small, usually white, with the fruitlet visible in the middle once the petals fall. While the flowers are usually unscented, the leaves have a slight fragrance. This is more pronounced in the North American wild species *Rubus odorata,* which has a resiny smell to the stems, though the pale reddish-purple flowers remain scentless. (Another, *R. deliciosus* has large, roselike flowers, which are deliciously perfumed.)

R. idaeus raspberries are native to Europe and Asia in hilly areas, heaths, and on the edge of woodlands, especially those with acid soils. They are found growing wild in northern Scandinavia and have long been gathered. Seeds and debris from the plants have been found preserved in the remains of the prehistoric lake villages of what is now Switzerland. Strangely, like other northern temperate fruits, raspberries went unrecorded by the classical writers. The Romans were such ravenous gourmands that it seems unlikely they did not eat these delightful fruits when colonizing cooler, wetter lands than their own. Perhaps because these were gathered from the wild in such profusion they needed no mention, being considered commonplace. Raspberries are included in the practical poetry of Thomas Tusser and noted by Gerard in the sixteenth century. It seems that at that time the fruit of the closely related bramble was considered far superior, and raspberries were used more for medicinal and tonic purposes. There are many similar and wild species that are enjoyed in other temperate countries.

'Autumn Bliss'

VARIETIES

There are many *Rubus* species closely resembling raspberries and others much like brambles or blackberries. Some are so interesting they have been included as a separate group with wineberries (see pp. 462–463). In North America, red and yellow raspberries, descended from *R. strigosa* but similar to European raspberries, are grown, as are black raspberries, **Blackcaps**, *R. occidentalis*, which are less hardy and have fewer, stouter canes, more given to branching. The **Rocky Mountain Raspberry**, *R. deliciosus*, is large fruited and delicious, but a shy fruiter.

Raspberries can be summer or fall cropping. **'Autumn Bliss'** is a good variety

specifically for fall fruiting. As to choice, the "new" varieties are soon replaced by others at a great rate and no list can be complete. **'Cumberland,'** introduced before 1900, is the largest of the blackcap types, with glossy, juicy, firm berries of superb taste, excellent for all uses. **'Black Hawk'** is another exceptional blackcap type, with big crops even in hot, dry weather. **'Latham'** is the standard for spring-bearing red raspberries; the fruits often reach an inch in size. **'Boyne'** has dark red berries similar to 'Latham,' but better flavored. **'Royalty'** is a cross of mixed parentage that looks like a purple-colored black raspberry, but tastes like a red one. **'Jewel'** is the most disease-resistant of the black raspberries and its abundant fruits are highly flavored. **'Heritage'** is an everbearer that produces dark red berries in a moderate summer crop followed by a better fall crop until frost.

CULTIVATION

Raspberries can be grown in most soils, but they do considerably better given plentiful moisture and a rich neutral or acidic soil, or at least copious quantities of compost and very thick mulches. With hot, dry summers and wetter falls the fall-fruiting varieties can be much more productive, especially on drier sites. Summer-fruiters need a moist site, and do not mind quite heavy shade. Most raspberry varieties will grow in Zones 4 or 5 through 8. Black varieties generally do best in cooler areas; reds are more heat tolerant. **'Dorman Red'** is a good red variety for the South, in Zones 7 through 9; **'Cumberland,'** a black variety, will also grow in Zone 9.

Growing under Glass
Being mostly very hardy, raspberries need no protection. Under cover, however, providing they are

A raspberry seedling

Yellow raspberries

kept cool and airy, they can produce good crops and benefit immensely from the bird protection.

Growing in Containers
I have fruited raspberries in large pots. They resent it and do not crop well or flourish as they really need a bigger, cooler root run.

Ornamental and Wildlife Value

Cultivated raspberries are not very ornamental themselves and the fruit does not last long enough to be called a display! Some of the species are more decorative, and scented, so are worth considering, but are nowhere near as productive as modern fruiting varieties. The birds adore raspberries and will get to them anywhere, so raspberries are good in wild gardens. However, you have a duty to others to eradicate the berries when they become virus-infected. The flowers are very beneficial to bees and other insects.

Maintenance (Summer Fruiters)

Spring Weed, mulch heavily, spray seaweed solution at monthly intervals.
Summer Protect and pick fruit, thin shoots.
Fall Cut out old canes and tie in the new.
Winter Add copious quantities of compost.

Maintenance (Fall Fruiters)

Spring Weed, mulch heavily, spray seaweed solution monthly, and thin the shoots as they emerge.
Summer Tie in canes.
Fall Protect and pick the fruit.
Winter Cut all canes to the ground and add copious compost to soil.

Propagation

Varieties are multiplied by transplanting any piece of root with a bud or young cane in the fall. Pot-grown ones may be planted in spring. Summer fruiters should not be cropped the first year but built up first; fall fruiters may be cropped if they were well established early the previous fall. I have found that seed can provide very vigorous and productive, if variable, plants, but it is a better plan to buy new, named cultivars.

Pruning and Training

Too lax to be left free, they are best restrained by growing between pairs of wires or winding the tips around horizontal ones. Alternatively, they can be grown as tripods, with three well-spaced stools being joined to an apex. Pruning for summer raspberries is done in fall; remove all old canes that have fruited or died and fix the new ones in place, selecting the biggest and strongest at about 5 in. apart. (It helps to prethin these when the shoots emerge in early summer.) Fall fruiters are easier still: just cut everything to the ground in late winter. (Prethinning the canes in spring is again quite advantageous.)

Raspberries—training canes

A spray of raspberry flowers

Japanese wineberry (see pp. 462–463), a raspberry/blackberry hybrid

Weed, Pest, and Disease Control

Weeding must be done carefully because of their shallow roots. Thick mulching is almost essential. **Birds** are the major cause of lost crops—no protection, no fruit! The **raspberry beetle** can be controlled with hygiene and mulching (methodically rake thick mulches aside in winter to allow birds to eat the pupae) or the use of permitted sprays if necessary. These maggots are rarely a problem with fall fruiters. **Virus diseases** may appear, mottling the leaves with yellow and making the plants less productive. Replacing the stock and moving the site is the only practical solution, but wait until the yields have dropped. **Interveinal yellowing** is a reaction to alkaline soils; seaweed solution sprays with added magnesium sulfate are a palliative. Compost and mulching provide the most effective cure.

Harvesting and Storing

Pick gently, leaving the plug behind; if the berry won't come off easily, don't force it! They do not keep for long if they are wet, and less still if warm. The best way to preserve them is to cut the fruiting stalks with scissors and do not touch the fruits. They must be processed or eaten within a matter of hours, as they are one of the least durable fruits. Those sold commercially are the toughest—and obviously also the least meltingly sumptuous!

COMPANION PLANTING

They reputedly benefit from tansy, garlic, or marigolds, and strawberries may be grown close by but not underneath them. Do not grow potatoes nearby as they will then become more prone to blight.

OTHER USES

Raspberry canes are bristly if not thorny. They have little strength or heat value but can be useful for wildlife shelters. I find short lengths, bundled together, then "Swiss rolled" in newspaper and jammed into a cut-open plastic bottle, will make superb dry but airy ladybug hibernation quarters, which I hide in evergreen shrubs. Raspberry leaves and fruits have been used medicinally, and have often traditionally been used as a tea.

Raspberry tea

Interwoven raspberry canes are easy to net and need no wires.

CULINARY USES

Raspberries make wonderful juices, jellies, drinks, and sorbets. They are often combined with red currant juice to add tartness. Their wine is delicate and beautifully colored. Raspberries can be frozen, but have poor texture afterward.

Kitty Topping's Raspberry Conserve
Makes about 4 lb.

4 cups freshly picked raspberries
4 cups superfine sugar

Pick fresh raspberries and hurry straight to the kitchen. Wash them and immediately heat them in a covered pan, rapidly but gently, swirling the pan to prevent sticking and burning. Once most berries have softened, but before they break down totally, add the same measure of prewarmed sugar. Stir while heating. One minute after you are absolutely sure all the sugar has completely dissolved, pour into small, heated jars and seal. Keep in a cool place and use quickly once opened, as the aim of this recipe is the stunning flavor, not keeping quality. Be sure to use freshly picked fruit!

Rubus fruticosus from the family *Rosaceae*

BLACKBERRIES

BRAMBLES AND DEWBERRIES

Bush/vine. Life span: medium to long. Deciduous, self-fertile.
Fruits: up to ³/₄ in., black, drupe. Value: rich in vitamin C.

Even without its glistening blackberries, the native bramble is known to everyone for the long, arching and scrambling stems armed with vicious thorns. What may be appreciated more by the picker than the walker is that the fruits vary widely from plant to plant. In fact there is no single bramble or blackberry, but hosts of them. These have occasionally been crossed deliberately, and often inadvertently, with each other and with other *Rubus,* and then again with other garden escapees. Although in some remote areas the stocks remain as several distinct but variable species, they may nevertheless have been altered in prehistory by unconscious human behavior, as has also been suggested for raspberries (see p. 452). Certainly now, any blackberry found near enough to human habitation to be picked is highly likely to be a hybrid. And those nearby will probably be different. Just by looking at the fruits or the flowers in any area you will usually see great diversity.

The common brambles have fernlike leaves, thin purple or green stems, white or light purple flowers, and small, hard berries. A better and recognizable type of wild blackberry is *Rubus ulmifolius*, which has strong-growing, plum-colored branches with five-lobed leaflets, which are very light on the underside. It is not self-fertile.

An improved form of this blackberry, *bellidiflorus*, is grown ornamentally for its pink double flowers. *Rubus caesius*, the **dewberry**, is another distinctive species with three-lobed leaflets on long, thin, creeping, almost tendril-like stems, which can form large mats. The dewberry is smaller than most blackberries, with fruits containing fewer drupelets that break up as you pick them. These come earlier in summer than the blackberries and do not have the same shiny glossiness, but are more matte, with a whitish bloom similar to a plum's.

Blackberry remains have been found in many of the earliest European habitations and have been an important fall crop since before recorded history. They were known to the ancient Greeks, as much for the herbal properties of their leaves as for the fruits. They have always grown in great profusion in woods and hedges, on heaths and moorlands, and indeed on every site as soon as it has been vacated by humans. So much fruit has always been available free that brambles have never been cultivated on a large scale and even the markets were satisfied by gleaning the wild crop. More recently there has been some breeding, with improved varieties such as **'Dirkson Thornless'** and **'Chester.'** Most work has gone into producing thornless and large-fruited varieties, in effect neglecting flavor, so many people prefer to pick the wild berries rather than to use cultivated sorts. Certainly there has been more interest in the development of hybrids with other *Rubus*. The North American dewberries, which derived from *R. Alleghaniensis*, were introduced to Europe. They are less vigorous and larger-fruited than the natives, but have unfortunately also proved more tender. Other introductions have been more successful. The **'Himalayan Giant'** is an exceptionally vigorous variety that has encroached on the wild populations in Britain. Strangely enough, the thornless **'Oregon Cutleaf'** blackberry is not American, as formerly thought, but an old English variety of *R. laciniatus*, or **Parsley-leaved Blackberry**. It has bigger fruits, is nearly evergreen, and comes almost true from seed. It was discovered in Surrey in 1770.

'Oregon Thornless'

VARIETIES

'Hull Thornless' and **'Black Satin Thornless'** bear large, flavorful, sweet fruits, good for fresh eating or preserving. Both yield about half as much as thorned varieties. **'Darrow'** has long, good-quality berries in abundant crops; it is less cold hardy than other varieties and may be damaged where there is not deep snow cover. **'Chester'** is another thornless variety with very sweet fruit. It is probably the most productive of the thornless types. **'Navaho'** has very small berries, but many believe they have the best taste of any blackberry. **'Shawnee'** bears heavily over a long period of several weeks, offering large, tasty, firm berries.

'Ashton Cross'

CULTIVATION

The whole bramble family are gross feeders and love rich, moist soils. They will crop in a light shade but are sweeter in the sun. Their cultivation and control is more like a pitched battle—if you give way they will take over your garden. Each stem arches over, grows down, and roots from the tip to form a new stool of stems. Heavy dressings of compost and thick mulches will keep up the yields. Blackberries grow well in Zones 5 to 8. As with other fruits, some varieties (such as **'Dirksen,'** to Zone 10) are adapted to warmer climates; others (including **'Illini Hardy,'** which tolerates −23°F) thrive in cool areas. Select a variety that is suited to your region.

Growing under Glass and in Containers

They are so easy outside it would be bizarre to grow them under cover. Blackberries do not like the cramped conditions pots afford, and as most of them are thorny they are seldom grown this way. The thornless ones are still too vigorous to thrive in any reasonable pot.

Ornamental and Wildlife Value

The fruiting species are all delightful in flower, with a mass of blossom in early summer. There are also many ornamental varieties and species, though most are too vigorous for modern gardens. Their vast quantity of blossom is valuable for bees and other insects, and the fruit is an immense feast for wildlife, fattening up the bird population for the winter. The thicket of the bushes makes a snug, dry home for many small creatures, from ladybugs and beetles to small rodents and birds.

Maintenance

Spring Weed, mulch, and spray seaweed solution.
Summer Tie in new shoots.
Fall Root tips or cut off; pick fruit.
Winter Prune and add copious amounts of compost.

Weed, Pest, and Disease Control

Remarkably tough and reliable, blackberries pose few problems. Even the birds find it hard to eat them as fast as they are produced. Weeds can get into the stool but rarely succeed for long, as the brambles are so vigorous a weed themselves.

Propagation

Seedlings come up everywhere, but are variable. The tips readily root and form new plants in the few weeks at the end of summer and into fall. At this time, make sure the tips go into pots of compost if you want extra plants, or cut them off if not.

Pruning and Training

Blackberries can fruit on wood older than one year old and the canes do not always die, as with raspberries. However, the new wood is better and carries fewer pests and diseases, so it is best to cut all the old and dead wood out and tie in the new. The canes are much longer and carry heavier loads than raspberries, so strong supports are necessary. The young canes need tying in during summer. If new plants are not needed they are best detipped in late summer to stop them from rooting wherever they hit the ground.

Harvesting and Storing

Traditionally blackberries are picked as they ripen, from late summer until Michaelmas, or the first frost, when the devil was supposed to have spat on them and made them sour. They are unusable red but turn soft to the touch as they blacken. The berries are fairly tough-skinned, and can travel well and last longer than raspberries if picked dry and not so overloaded that they pack down. They are best used as soon as possible or frozen; the spoiled texture when they defrost is no problem if they are to be used in cooking anyway.

COMPANION PLANTING

Blackberries benefit from tansy or stinging nettles nearby, and they are a good companion and sacrificial crop for grapevines.

Blackberry flowers and fruits

CULINARY USES

Blackberries are often too sour to eat raw, but once cooked they are much tastier and do not have such a deleterious effect on one's insides. They make excellent jams. but as they are rather seedy, the jelly is more often made. Frequently apples are included in blackberry dishes, especially jams and jellies, to aid setting and also because the flavors combine so lusciously. Blackberry wine is made by country folk everywhere, and the berries used to be added to wines and spirits to give a distinctive color, such as with the Red Muscat of Toulon.

Bob's Blackberry and Apple Pancake Supreme
Serves 4

*Approx. 1 cup pancake
  batter
1 cup blackberries
Golden syrup to taste
Water
Tablespoon of corn flour
A little milk
2 apples
Pat of butter
Sugar, lemon juice, lots of cream
  or yogurt*

Prepare the pancake batter and set aside. Wash the blackberries and simmer with golden syrup until soft. Strain, reserving the juice, and keep the fruit warm. To the juice add enough water to make ¾ cup, return to the heat, and bring to a boil. Mix the corn flour with a little milk, pour it into the boiling blackberry juice, stirring all the time, and cook until the juice thickens. Set aside.

  Peel, core, and chop the apples into chunks. Heat them rapidly with a little butter until they start to crumble at the edges, then remove from the heat and keep warm. Next preheat the broiler and a frying pan. Oil the pan. Once it is smoking, pour in all the pancake batter. As the bottom sets, but while the top is still liquid, take the pan off the heat, rapidly spoon in apple chunks and blackberry blobs, and drizzle in the sauce. Swirl slightly so that the liquid batter blends a little but does not mix or cover completely. Sprinkle sugar generously over the top, then add lemon juice and put under the broiler. Serve as soon as the top has caramelized. This goes well with yogurt or cream.

Bob's Blackberry and Apple Pancake Supreme

OTHER USES

Brambles make a secure and quick barrier to many four-legged animals and two-legged rats. There are few in the world who will try to come over or through a fence or hedge clothed in any of this thorny bunch. 'Himalayan Giant' is so big and tough it will stop almost anything between the size of a rabbit and that of a tank! The prunings are vicious but do burn well and fiercely.

Rubus hybrids from the family *Rosaceae*

LOGANBERRIES

BOYSENBERRIES AND TAYBERRIES

Bush/vine. Life span: medium. Deciduous, mostly self-fertile.
Fruits: 2 x ³/₄ in. Value: some vitamin C.

Tayberries

The loganberry resembles a blackberry in manner of growth, but the fruits are more like raspberries: cylindrical, dull red, and firm, with a more acid flavor than either, making them sour raw but exquisite cooked. Boysenberry fruits are sweeter, more blackberry-like, larger, and reddish-purple. They can be savored raw with cream but also make the celebrated jam. The tayberry is bigger and sweeter than either, with an aromatic flavor. When fully ripe, the enormous loganberry-like fruits are dark wine-red or purple and nearly three times the size of most other berries.

Loganberries were reputedly a hybrid of American dewberry and raspberry, raised by a Judge Logan of California in 1882. Introduced to Britain in 1897, loganberries have remained the supreme culinary berry for nearly a century. The boysenberry has a similar history. It is believed to be another hybrid dewberry but in fact is probably a youngberry x loganberry. It is not as hardy as other hybrids and does better in a warmer site than the rest. The **Medana Tayberry** was developed by the Scottish Crop Research Institute, which crossed the Oregon blackberry **'Aurora'** with a tetraploid raspberry to produce this excellent fruit. It is outstandingly the best of all hybrids so far.

VARIETIES

There are several varieties and many other similar hybrids. The **Thornless Loganberry** is often thorny; the fruit does not pull off the plug easily, but it is a very heavy cropper and has a good flavor. The totally thornfree **'L654'** is better picking but is not quite as productive. I similarly find the **Thornless Boysenberry** not as good a cropper as the thorned. There is now a thornfree **Tayberry**. The **Tummelberry** is like a late tayberry. The **Marionberry** and the **Youngberry** have the habit and appearance of blackberries but the fruits have more flavor. The **Youngberry**, sometimes called the **Young Dewberry**, is available as a thornless version. The **Black Loganberry** is a New Zealand variety; it has cylindrical, tapering fruits, and is slow to establish and crop. The **Black Raspberry** is close to the **American Black Raspberry**, *R. occidentalis*, in habit and fruit. The **Laxtonberry** has a round, raspberry-like fruit and is not self-fertile. The **Veitchberry** is a blackberry crossed with a fall-fruiting raspberry, more mulberry-like, with a later fruiting season than that of other hybrids, and large sweet fruits.

Thornless loganberries

CULTIVATION

The hybrids all need much the same cool conditions and rich moist soils. The boysenberry will cope with drier sites and indeed prefers some shelter. They are generally quite happy on a cool shady wall if they have a moist root run. These berries grow well in Zones 5 through 9, but need protective winter mulch and may die back where temperatures dip below –50°F.

Growing under Glass and in Containers
They prefer cool, shady positions and find the dry heat under glass too much and become prone to pests such as red spider mite. Generally needing a bigger, cooler root run than can be afforded in a pot, they will resent the confinement, sulk, and crop poorly.

Maintenance
Spring Weed, mulch, and spray seaweed solution at monthly intervals.
Summer Protect and pick fruit; tie in new canes.
Fall Root tips in pots or cut them off.
Winter Cut out old canes and tie in the new. Add copious compost.

Propagation
As these are hybrids, they will not come true from seed, though interesting results may be had. Tips can be rooted in late summer and early fall and occasionally the roots can be successfully divided.

Pruning and Training
They grow much like blackberries but can have more brittle canes, like raspberries, so care must be taken when bending them. They mostly fruit on young

wood, which dies and is cleared completely after the second year. Canes may produce again a third year, as blackberries might, but are usually unproductive, so annual replacement of all the old by new is generally considered a better policy.

Weed, Pest, and Disease Control
The only common major problem is **bird** losses, which are high, as these plants mostly crop after the summer fruits, but before the wild blackberries. **Weeds** choking the stool can reduce their vigor more than with blackberries.

Tayberries

Boysenberries

COMPANION PLANTING

Tansy, marigolds, and alliums are all beneficial.

OTHER USES

These canes will make good additional barriers with fences and hedges.

CULINARY USES

Generally best flavored when fully ripe, these fruits are not very acid and benefit from the addition of red currant juice to many recipes. Varieties from which the plug is not easily removed, or which even detach a thorny stalk with the fruit, are best used by straining or juicing them first. These fruits make excellent jams, jellies, tarts, and pies. The juices are delicious as drinks and make wonderful sorbets.

Summerberry Squash
Makes about 4 pints

4 cups mixed berries
2 cups red currants
2 cups sugar
3 1/2 cups water

Wash the fruits and simmer them down with half the water until soft, then strain. Cover the fruit pulp with the rest of the water, bring almost to boiling, and strain again. Combine the strained juices and the sugar, heating gently if necessary to make sure the sugar dissolves completely. Cool, then pour into plastic bottles when cold and freeze until required. Defrost and dilute with water to taste.

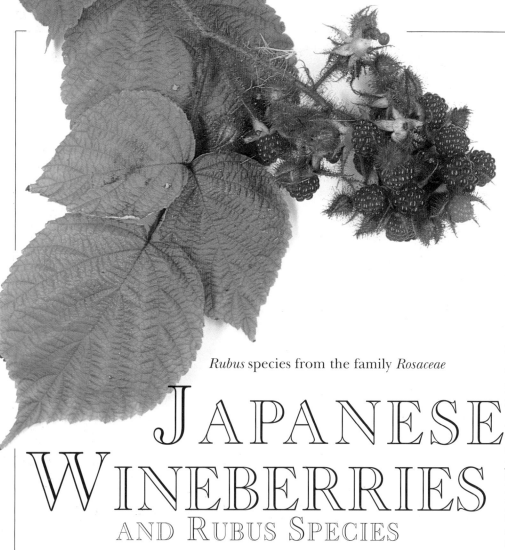

There are no named varieties of any of these species, though there is some variation in leaf and fruit color so there is scope for improvement. *R. leucodermis*, **Blackcap**, has thorny, bluish stems with light green leaves, white underneath, on a medium-sized bush, small white flowers and purple-black sweet fruits with a plumlike bloom. Yellow- and red-fruited forms occur in its native northwest America. Another, *R. parviflorus*, the **Thimbleberry**, has large, fragrant, white flowers on strong, thornless stems and large, flattened, insipid, red berries. *R. parvifolius*, the **Australian Bramble**, was fruited in England in 1825 and has small, pink, tasty, juicy berries. The **Salmonberry**, *R. spectabilis*, has maroon red flowers on prickly erect stems and acid orange-yellow fruits. Apparently Native Americans ate the cooked young shoots. *R. arcticus*, the **Arctic** or **Crimson Bramble**, has amber-colored fruits that are said to taste of pineapple. Very unusual is the **Rock** or **Roebuck Bramble**, *R. saxatilis*, which grows just like strawberry plants, and is eaten in much the same way. The Russians used to distill a spirit from the berries.

Rubus species from the family *Rosaceae*

JAPANESE WINEBERRIES
AND RUBUS SPECIES

Bush/vine. Life span: medium to long. Deciduous, self-fertile.
Fruits: variable. Value: some vitamin C.

Rubus phoenicolasius, the Japanese wineberry, is the best of the vast raspberry/blackberry clan. This delicious and highly ornamental cane fruit resembles a vigorous raspberry covered with russet bristles and thorns. Unlike blackberries, these prick rather than jab so are more pleasant to handle and pick. The fruits are smaller than blackberries, orange to cherry red, and they are generally far more palatable.

Japanese wineberries are not a hybrid but a true species coming from north China and Japan. They certainly do come true, as you will find when they appear all over the garden after the birds spread the seed. Introduced to Britain around 1876, Japanese wineberries were considered worth cultivating and won a First Class Certificate from the Royal Horticultural Society in 1894. During the century since, however, they have not proved popular except with children of all ages who are lucky enough to find them.

CULTIVATION

Although they will grow almost anywhere, the biggest berries come from plants growing in rich, moist soil well enriched with compost and leaf mold. They will grow in moderate shade or full sun and are self-fertile.

Best grown on a wire fence or wired against a wall, in the manner of blackberries, they need a spacing of at least 10 ft. apart and wires to at least 7 ft. in height. Like most fruits, they do best when grown in well-mulched, clean soil, but will still produce grown in grass. Wineberries thrive in Zones 6 through 8, and can be grown in milder areas of Zone 5.

Growing under Glass

These are mostly so easy to grow outside that there is little advantage to having them under glass except to extend the season.

Growing in Containers

Growing them in pots will shorten their life and give greatly reduced yields.

Ornamental and Wildlife Value

Japanese wineberry leaves are a striking light green, with russet bristled stems, bright orange-red fruits, and a star-shaped calyx left over afterward. They are highly decorative—probably the best fruiting plant to train against a whitewashed wall or up a pole for all-year-round interest and color. Their value to wildlife is as immense as that of the whole clan.

Maintenance

Spring Weed, mulch, and spray seaweed solution.
Summer Protect and pick fruit; tie in canes.
Fall Pick the fruit and tie in canes.
Winter Cut out old canes, tie in the new, and add copious quantities of compost.

Propagation

These are species, so they come true from seed and the tips can be layered in late summer and early fall. Remove the old canes and tie in the new each fall. Plants have a long life if cared for. Prune out any infections early.

Weed, Pest, and Disease Control

Choking and climbing **weeds** such as nettles and bindweed must be well controlled. There are no major problems other than the **birds**.

Harvesting and Storing

Japanese wineberries are one of the most delicious of all fruits eaten fresh and also in quantity, though they will keep for a while in the cool of a refrigerator.

COMPANION PLANTING

Tansy, garlic, and French and pot marigolds are all potential good companions.

OTHER USES

Their dense growth and prickly bristles make them attractive but impenetrable informal boundaries.

CULINARY USES

Very valuable as garnishing for sweet and savory dishes and simply eating off the plant. Some berries can be frozen to add to mixed fruit compotes. Japanese wineberry jelly does not set, but forms a treacly syrup, ideal to accompany ice cream.

Wineberry Ripple
Serves 6

4 cups Japanese wineberries
Approx. 2 cups sugar
4 cups vanilla ice cream

Freeze a few berries for garnishing. Simmer the rest until soft with just enough water to prevent sticking. Strain and measure the juice. Thoroughly dissolve three-quarters of the juice's volume in sugar in the warm juice. Allow to cool completely. Once cooled, layer scoops of ice cream with the syrup, pressing it all down into a new container. Freeze the new block and then scoop as required, garnishing with the frozen berries.

A cluster of Japanese wineberries

Vitis vinifera from the family *Vitaceae*

GRAPES

Vine up to any height. Life span: long. Deciduous, self-fertile.
Fruits: 1 in., ovoid, white, black, red. Value: generally beneficial.

These scrambling vines have smooth, peeling, brown stems, large lobed leaves, and bunches of grapes in fall. The flowers are so insignificant they are rarely noticed, but are white, yellow, or green, and sweet-scented. The leaves color well in fall; red-berrying varieties tend to turn red and white ones yellow.

Grapes have been with us since biblical times; Noah planted a vineyard. The Egyptians show full details of vineyards and wine-making in relics from 2440 B.C. The Romans spread vines all over Europe until, in the first century A.D., Emperor Domitian protected his home market and ordered the extirpation of the grape from Britain, France, and Spain. Two centuries later, Emperor Probus restored the vine, and long after the Roman Empire collapsed the monasteries kept vineyards going. European settlers arrived in America to find wild grapes (mainly *Vitis labrusca*, but also including other species such as *V. riparia*, *V. vulpina*, and others) of much vigor and rich flavor growing commonly as weeds. In California and Mexico, Franciscan monks planted European grapes, which soon succumbed to *phylloxera* root aphids and the extremes of climate. By grafting European wine grape varieties to hardy American rootstocks, they were finally able to establish successful vineyards of familiar fruit. The **'Concord,'** a superior variety introduced in 1843, has the distinctive "grapey" flavor we recognize from bottled grape juice. Hybrids such as the table grape **'Thompson's Seedless,'** combine the delectable fruit of the Europeans with the disease resistance, hardiness, and tolerance for humidity of the American species.

Boskoop Glory

VARIETIES

Specific grapes for growing under glass or for wine-making are recommended in the next sections. Choose your grape varieties with care, to be sure of getting a good match for your climate. As with other fruits, look for varieties that are resistant to any diseases prevalent in your area. Diseases vary from one region to another; before you plant, do some research to find out what might be problematic.

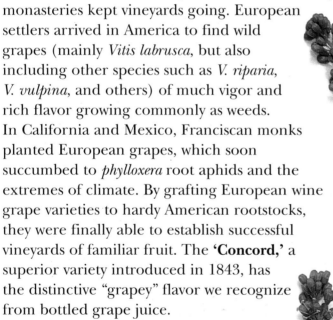

CULTIVATION

American grapes, such as **'Concord,' 'Niagra,'** and **'Catawba,'** thrive in Zones 4 through 8, depending on variety. Most have superior cold-hardiness. They thrive in the Northeast, Northwest, and Central states. European grapes, such as **'Chardonnay'** and **'Zinfandel,'** are best for areas with a very long, warm growing season and mild winters, generally Zones 7 through 9. American-European hybrids, including **'Himrod'** and the popular pink-red **'Reliance,'** combine the best of both. The fruit may be winey or grapey, but the vines have improved cold tolerance. They can be grown in Zones 4 through 9. Muscadines, including the old favorite **'Magnolia,'** do best in humid, hot summers, and thrive in Zones 7 through 9.

Growing under Glass and in Containers

Grapes can be successfully grown in containers in a greenhouse. They are moved outside for winter chilling and brought into the heated greenhouse for an early start. Grapes in containers bear less abundantly than those planted in the open ground and need careful watering, feeding, and pruning.

Maintenance
Spring Weed, mulch, and spray with seaweed solution at monthly intervals.
Summer Tie in and later nip out ends of shoots.
Fall Protect; pick the fruit.
Winter Prune back hard.

Propagation
Grapes can be easily grown from cuttings rooted in damp sand. European

Netting is essential to keep birds off the grapes.

varieties must be grown on American roots to avoid the fatal *phylloxera*.

Pruning and Training
See sections on pages 467, 469, and 471.

Weed, Pest, and Disease Control
Many pests and diseases attack grapes, but take heart: not all are severe in every year. See section on pages 470–71.

Harvesting and Storing
Kept cool and dry, the grapes hang on the vines well. Cut bunches with a stalk, place the stalk in a bottle of water, and keep the grapes in a cool, dry cellar for weeks. The less they are handled the better they will keep.

COMPANION PLANTING

Traditionally grown over elm or mulberry trees, grapevines are benefited by blackberries, sage, mustard, and hyssop growing nearby and inhibited by cabbages, radish, Cypress spurge, and even by laurels.

'Strawberry Grape'

CULINARY USES

The best are excellent dessert fruits. They are easily juiced and the juice can be frozen for year-round use. They make good jellies and any surplus can be used for wine.

Love Nests
Per person

*Individual meringue shell
Approx. 6 large table grapes, preferably muscat*

Marzipan, apricot preserves, crème fraîche or whipped cream, and dark chocolate

Peel and seed all but one grape per portion and fill each with a pellet of marzipan. Smear the meringue bases with apricot preserve, then a layer of cream. Press in the filled grapes, cover with more cream, top with grated black chocolate and the perfect grape. Serve the nests immediately.

Vitis species from the family *Vitaceae*

GRAPE SPECIES

Vine. Life span: long-lived. Deciduous, sometimes self-fertile.
Fruit: up to ¾ in., in bunches, red or black

There are hundreds of true grapes, or *Vitis* species, which are mostly ornamental climbing vines. (Very closely resembling them are the *Ampelopsis* and *Parthenocissus*, of which the most common are known as **Virginia Creepers**. These resemble grapevines and even form bunches, which are not edible.) These *Vitis* species are much grown for their covering capacity as they soon hide eyesores, and for their spectacular fall color. The fruits are often considered a bonus, but offer different and exciting flavors.

Although the *Vitis vinifera* varieties are almost exclusively used for commercial purposes and wine making, there are countless other *Vitis* species grapes eaten throughout the world, and have been since time immemorial. Their blood has also influenced the *V. vinifera* varieties on many occasions. These are but a few.

VARIETIES

Vitis aestivalis, the **Summer, Bunch,** or **Pigeon Grape** is from North America. It has heart-shaped leaves, downy underneath, scented flowers, and early black grapes. It was first seen in Europe in 1656. *V. labrusca*, the **Plum, Skunk,** or **Fox Grape,** is another first brought to Europe in 1656. Its young shoots are covered in down and the leaves are thick, dark green on top, aging to pink underneath. The fruits are rounded, blackish-purple, and have a distinctive musk or fox flavor which some dislike. I enjoy it but not in wine! It has given rise to several good cultivars such as '**Concord.**' *V. vulpina* is similar, with glossy leaves. Both have sweet-scented flowers. *V. rotundifolia* is the **Muscadine** or **Southern Fox Grape**, widely used for wine in the South. It produces only half a dozen large fleshy grapes per cluster, usually black or coppery purple, though there are cultivated local white varieties. The **Winter, Chicken** or **Frost Grape** berry, *V. cordifolia*, is very hardy and does well on lime soils. The dark purple fruit has to be frosted before it is edible and is used for wine. Some local cultivated

Grapes on the vine

varieties have sweeter, tastier, red or black fruits.

V. riparia is the high-climbing **Riverbank Grape** from North America, with large, glossy, deeply lobed leaves and big panicles of male flowers that smell most distinctly and sweetly of mignonette. The fruits are black or amber and very acid. *V. coignetiae* comes from Japan and Korea. It has enormous leaves up to 1 ft. across. It is strong-growing and the leaves turn crimson and scarlet in fall so it is much used ornamentally, but the black grapes with a bloom are not very tasty. *V. davidii*, once called **Spinovitis** because it has spines on the shoots, stems, and leaves, was brought from China for its glorious, rich crimson, fall coloring. It also has edible black fruits. *V. californica* was originally cultivated by the Pueblo Indians. It must have been good because, to quote Sturtevant, "The quantity of the fruit that an Indian will consume at one time is scarcely credible."

CULTIVATION

Overrich conditions should be avoided. For most, a warm site is better, but they do not like warm winters and do best with some chilling in winter.

Growing under Glass
The freedom from frost, rain, and birds is valuable, but vines grown under glass become more susceptible to pests and mildew.

Growing in Containers
The species do not enjoy cramped conditions, but they can be grown in large pots. This shortens their life and gives a small crop, but conveniently controls their vigor, allowing many to be grown in a small area.

Ornamental and Wildlife Value
These are of the highest value as ornamentals and are useful for quick screens and coverings, though they can be too vigorous for small gardens unless hard pruned. Their bountiful flowers and fruit make them very good for wildlife gardens.

Maintenance
Spring Weed, mulch, and spray seaweed monthly.
Summer Tie in shoots, protect fruit, cut off tips.
Fall Pick fruit.
Winter Prune well.

Propagation
As these are species they can be grown from seed. Ripe wood cuttings, taken in late fall, are best, and budding or grafting is possible.

Weed, Pest, and Disease Control
As these are species, they are generally resilient to most of the common grape pests and diseases. However, **birds** are still as much, if not more, of a problem.

CULINARY USES

Most of these grapes are too small and pippy or sour to be used raw as dessert. They are best juiced or turned into jellies. The strong flavor of some, such as the Fox Grape, can make them unsuitable for wine.

Grape Jelly
Makes approx. 4 lb.

5–6 cups grapes
Approx. 4 cups sugar

Simmer the grapes with just enough water to keep them from sticking. When they are soft, strain and measure the liquid. Add the same amount of sugar to the juice and bring to a boil, skim until clear, bottle into hot jars, and seal.

Pruning and Training
See also sections on Table Grapes and Wine Grapes. There are many ways to prune grapes and many subvariations, enough to fill a book on their own. The species are best treated much as regular vines which, left to themselves, often produce rank growth and nearly exhaust themselves with overcropping. For ornamental purposes that is no problem. However, for fruit they are best hard pruned and trained on a wall on wires about $1\frac{1}{2}$ ft. apart. The main framework is formed in the first years, covering the wires with stems that are furnished with fruiting spurs. There-after, these shoot each spring and a flower truss appears between the third and fifth leaf. After another three or four leaves, each shoot is tipped, as are any replacements as they come. It is essential to thin the number of bunches, leaving no more than two per yard run of cane. In winter, all shoots are cut back to one bud out from each spur, except for that of the leaders.

COMPANION PLANTING

Species grapevines are probably benefited by blackberries, sage, mustard, and hyssop growing nearby and they are inhibited by cabbages, radishes, Cypress spurge, and laurels.

OTHER USES

Grapevine prunings make great kindling and attractive wreaths.

Vitis vinifera, V. labrusca, and *V. rotundifolia* from the family *Vitaceae*

TABLE GRAPES

Vine. Life span: exceptionally long-lived.
Fruits: up to 1 in., oval or round, any color.

Grapes with the best flavor, size, and succulence for fresh eating may be American or European varieties or hybrids. American grapes are "slipskin," their skins sliding easily from the fruit pulp. You can eat the skin or not, as you choose. Europeans have the skin and pulp firmly attached. American varieties have a familiar grapey flavor, and some have a hint of "foxiness," a slight musk that many people like and others find distasteful. If you like the taste of a commercial grape juice, you'll like American grapes, which are the basis of that product. European grapes are often very sweet and have a winey flavor. Although European varieties are most often used for wine, those with a milder flavor are also used as table grapes. Hybrids of these species may share the qualities of either parent.

VARIETIES

The green, sweet **'Thompson Seedless'** is a favorite for fresh eating, although red **'Flame Seedless'** is giving it stiff competition. Both are European varieties that do well in home gardens. **'Tokay'** is another red European with sweet, crisp flesh. **'Emperor'** has large purple or red fruit with fine flavor. The diminutive seedless light green grapes of **'Perlette'** are wonderful for dessert. European Muscat varieties, such as **'Muscat Hamburg'** and **'Muscat Ottonel,'** have large, green-amber fruit with intense aroma. Among the American varieties, **'Concord'** is always a staple. **'Niagra,'** which began as a chance seedling of 'Concord,' is the most popular white hybrid. **'Candace'** is a seedless red variety with superior grapey flavor. It is moderately resistant to black rot. **'Steuben,'** a hybrid, has very large, purple-black fruit with sweet-tangy flavor. **'Schuyler,'** another popular hybrid, is highly disease resistant. **'Himrod'** and the related **'Interlaken Seedless'** are two seed-free varieties with crisp, sweet, table-grape flavor and superb cold-hardiness. Among the smoky-flavored muscadines, the self-fertile varieties **'Albermarle,' 'Dixie Red,' 'Dearing,'** and **'Magnolia,'** are all excellent.

CULTIVATION

Amenable to almost any soil, they do not require rich conditions. Soil must be well drained for grapes to succeed. If your soil is heavy and wet, build raised beds, incorporating plenty of compost and rotted manure and sand to lighten the soil. Grapes are generally easy to grow and bear quickly after planting, often the following year. Be sure to choose a variety that is well suited to the particular conditions and climate of your garden.

Growing in Containers
Grapes resent a confined root system and need careful watering and pruning to be grown successfully in containers. The container limits their usually rampant growth. Several varieties can go into a greenhouse too small for one planted in the ground.

Warm sun is needed to ripen the grapes.

Ornamental and Wildlife Value
Well-pruned vines in pots or trained on walls are very decorative. The framework is easy to manipulate, so almost any form can be achieved as long as all fruiting wood is kept at roughly the same level and in the light.

Maintenance
Spring Spray with seaweed solution.
Summer Prune back tips, thin bunches, and spray with seaweed solution.
Fall Pick the fruits.
Winter Prune.

Pruning and Training
The vine framework is formed over the first years, covering the wires with main stems furnished with fruiting spurs. Thereafter, these shoot each spring and a flower truss appears between the third and fifth leaf. After another three or four leaves, each shoot is tipped, as are any replacements as they come. It is essential to thin the number of bunches, leaving no more than two per yard run of cane. In winter, shoots are all cut back to one bud out from each spur. In pots, vines are grown vertically or wound as spirals around a central supporting post.

Weed, Pest, and Disease Control
Grapes can suffer many problems but usually still produce. If the air is too humid when grapes are ripening they may **mold**. If they are kept too dry before then, they get **mildew** and **red spider mite**. However, the permitted sprays and usual remedies work well with most problems. See pages 470–471 for more about diseases.

Harvesting and Storing
Cut bunches when ripe, using scissors to snip the stem. Be careful of wasps when reaching for clusters. Muscadine varieties ripen over a long period; most others ripen all at once.

Vines in a pot need a central vertical support.

'Muscat Hamburg'

COMPANION PLANTING

Grow French marigolds underneath the vines to deter whitefly.

OTHER USES

Pieces of old vine, detached when pruning, make good supports for climbers in pots.

CULINARY USES

The dessert fruit par excellence, their juice is delicious and freezes well.

For wine making, the flavor and high sugar content will go well in combination with outdoor grapes, which have lower sugar and higher acidity.
Just eat them as they come, sun-warmed.

Vitis vinifera from the family *Vitaceae*

WINE GRAPES

Vine. Life span: long-lived. Deciduous, self-fertile.
Fruits: up to 1 in. Some vitamin value.

'Miguel Torres'

Wine grapes are as sweet, or more so, than table varieties. They have been bred to produce many small bunches rather than large berries, and this suits the vine's natural habit. The grapes are every bit as tasty, just smaller, and if you don't want the wine, the juice is still valuable. They are hardier than dessert grapes and are cropped commercially.

Although wine is predominantly produced in the Mediterranean region and areas with a similar climate, vineyards have been and are successful in many cool regions. The wines are usually light whites, but new hybrids now produce reds as well. European grapes are the standard for wine making, and are grown in multitude by California vineyards. But many American varieties and American-European hybrids also produce a fine-flavored wine. Vineyards in New York State and other cold regions attest to the superior cold-hardiness of these strains, and the wines they produce are frequently awarded in national competitions.

VARIETIES

The classic wine grapes such as **'Cabernet,' 'Chardonnay'**/ **'Pinot Blanc,' 'Pinot Noir,'** and even **'Riesling'** are not suitable for cooler regions. **'Mueller Thurgau'**/**'Riesling Sylvaner'** is much planted for its excellent white wine, but mildew can be a problem, **'Seyve Villard 5/276'** is a white hybrid. It is more reliable but lacks the character, so often both are grown. **'Siegerrebe'** is a light cropper of rosé berries, which add flavor to blander grapes. The hybrids are by far the best croppers and most disease-resistant; **'Seibel 13053'** and **'Marshall Joffre'** produce masses of dark black bunches. The **'Strawberry Grape'** and **'Schuyler'** produce well and easily, but their flavor is not to everyone's taste. Among the cold-hardy varieties, **'Catawba'** and **'Champanelle'** are excellent. The coppery-red 'Catawba,' widely grown in New York and Ohio vineyards, is the top variety for American wine and juice.

CULTIVATION

Rich soils should be avoided, as vines will grow excessively. Obviously the warmer and sunnier the better: wires and supports should ideally run north–south, to give sun on both sides of each row.

Growing in Containers
Although crops are light they can be grown in pots; see page 469.

Maintenance
Spring Weed and spray with seaweed solution monthly.
Summer Thin and tie in new shoots; tip after flowering.
Fall Protect fruit and pick when ripe.
Winter Prune back hard.

Weed, Pest, and Disease Control
Generally grapes are gratifyingly easy to grow. **Viruses** are the most dreaded, because there is no cure. Keep an eye on your vines for potential problems, and treat them before they overwhelm the plants. **Japanese beetles** can turn leaves into lace in a matter of days. Tap them off into a jar of ammonia. **Black rot**, which dots the leaves with rusty spots and turns the fruit into hardened "mummy berries," can be controlled by sulfur sprays throughout the season. Removing any affected fruits or leaves will help, too.

'Pinot Blanc'

'Chilean Riesling'

'Chilean Cabernet-Sauvignon'

Botrytis bunch rot softens the berries and causes them to turn brown. As with black rot, remove infected parts and apply sulfur sprays. **Downy** and **powdery mildew** are common, especially where air circulation is restricted. Prune for better ventilation and apply sulfur sprays.

Pruning and Training

There are many different ways of treating vines outside. They can be grown with a permanent framework, high or low, with benefits from air circulation or heat from the ground. Strong posts and wires up to shoulder height are probably best, so the fruit is borne high up enough to avoid soil splash. Thus the bottom wire should not be less than 1 ft. high. A modified form of Guyot pruning is often used instead of spur pruning. A short leg reaches to the bottom wire and supports a strong shoot, or two, of last year's growth tied down horizontally to fruit from the buds along its length. Two replacements are allowed to grow from the leg and all other new shoots there are removed. Fruiting shoots are nipped out a few leaves after the flower truss, as with other methods.

Harvesting and Storing

When the fruit has finally ripened enough, but before losses to the birds and mold have mounted, pick the bunches. A dry day after a rainy period gives cleaner bunches. Cut out moldy bits as you go and press as quickly as possible for juice for drinking or for white wine. White wines can be made from black grapes; only certain Teinturier grapes have red juice. With most varieties the color only comes from fermenting the skin. In red wines, the grapes are fermented whole, merely mashed. The juice is pressed from the pips and skins later.

COMPANION PLANTING

Asparagus is sometimes grown with the vines in France.

Vineyards by the Moselle in Germany

OTHER USES

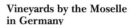

The vine prunings make good kindling. Big stems are often made into corkscrew handles.

Harvesting 'Pinot Blanc' grapes in Baden, Germany

CULINARY USES

The juice is one of the most satisfying drinks. It can be used from the freezer throughout the year and is useful as a sweetener. The wine may be even better.

Fruit Salad Soup
Serves as many as you like

Chop and slice finely as many fruits as are available and serve in copious grape juice with cream or yogurt and macaroons.

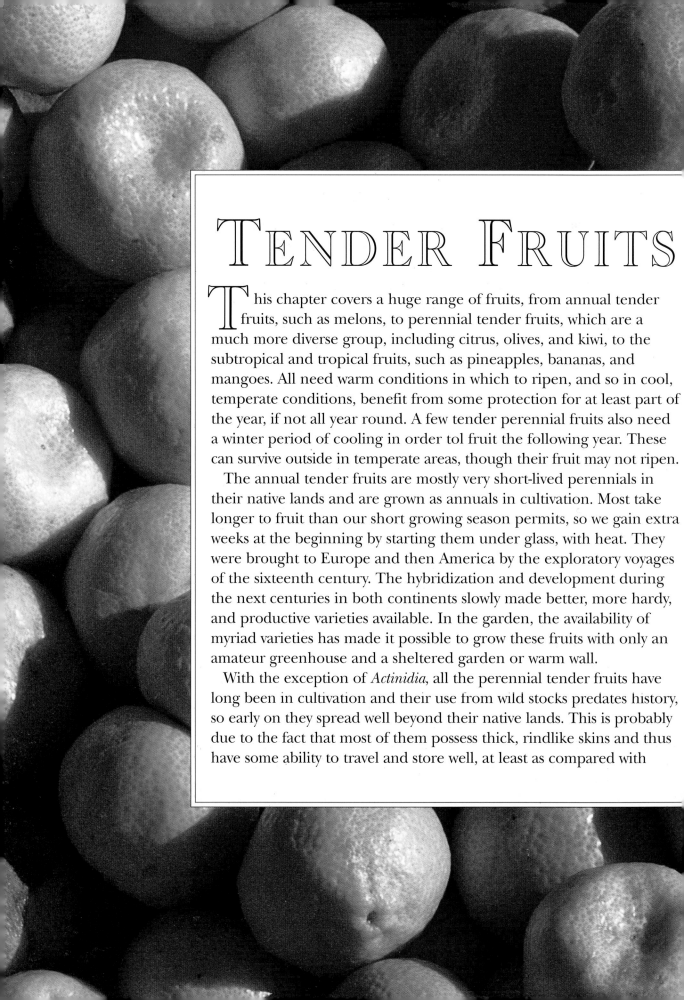

TENDER FRUITS

This chapter covers a huge range of fruits, from annual tender fruits, such as melons, to perennial tender fruits, which are a much more diverse group, including citrus, olives, and kiwi, to the subtropical and tropical fruits, such as pineapples, bananas, and mangoes. All need warm conditions in which to ripen, and so in cool, temperate conditions, benefit from some protection for at least part of the year, if not all year round. A few tender perennial fruits also need a winter period of cooling in order tol fruit the following year. These can survive outside in temperate areas, though their fruit may not ripen.

The annual tender fruits are mostly very short-lived perennials in their native lands and are grown as annuals in cultivation. Most take longer to fruit than our short growing season permits, so we gain extra weeks at the beginning by starting them under glass, with heat. They were brought to Europe and then America by the exploratory voyages of the sixteenth century. The hybridization and development during the next centuries in both continents slowly made better, more hardy, and productive varieties available. In the garden, the availability of myriad varieties has made it possible to grow these fruits with only an amateur greenhouse and a sheltered garden or warm wall.

With the exception of *Actinidia*, all the perennial tender fruits have long been in cultivation and their use from wild stocks predates history, so early on they spread well beyond their native lands. This is probably due to the fact that most of them possess thick, rindlike skins and thus have some ability to travel and store well, at least as compared with

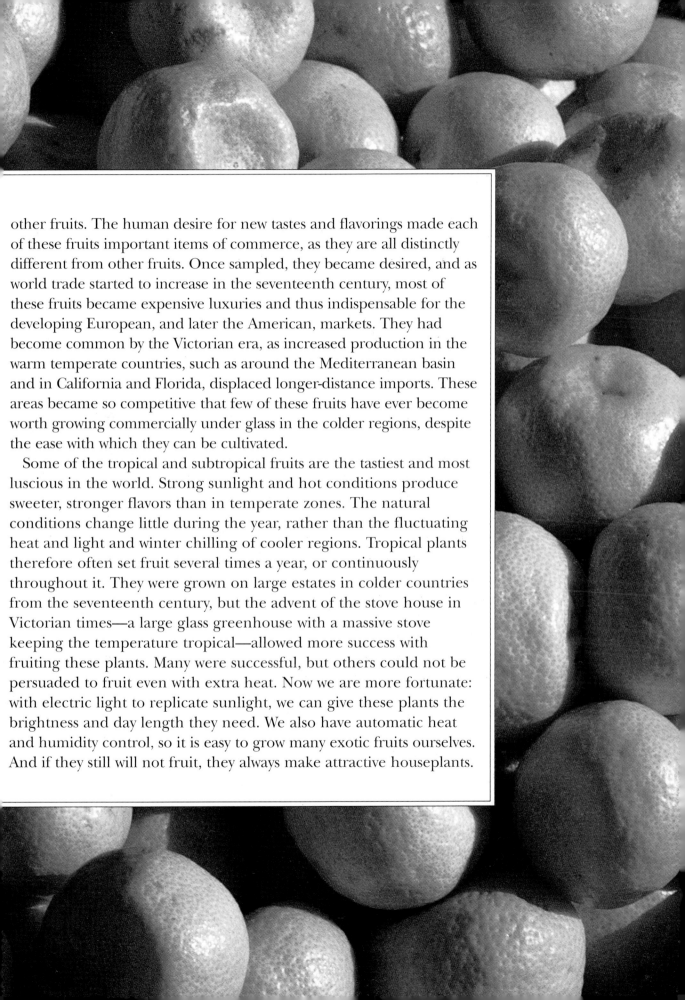

other fruits. The human desire for new tastes and flavorings made each of these fruits important items of commerce, as they are all distinctly different from other fruits. Once sampled, they became desired, and as world trade started to increase in the seventeenth century, most of these fruits became expensive luxuries and thus indispensable for the developing European, and later the American, markets. They had become common by the Victorian era, as increased production in the warm temperate countries, such as around the Mediterranean basin and in California and Florida, displaced longer-distance imports. These areas became so competitive that few of these fruits have ever become worth growing commercially under glass in the colder regions, despite the ease with which they can be cultivated.

Some of the tropical and subtropical fruits are the tastiest and most luscious in the world. Strong sunlight and hot conditions produce sweeter, stronger flavors than in temperate zones. The natural conditions change little during the year, rather than the fluctuating heat and light and winter chilling of cooler regions. Tropical plants therefore often set fruit several times a year, or continuously throughout it. They were grown on large estates in colder countries from the seventeenth century, but the advent of the stove house in Victorian times—a large glass greenhouse with a massive stove keeping the temperature tropical—allowed more success with fruiting these plants. Many were successful, but others could not be persuaded to fruit even with extra heat. Now we are more fortunate: with electric light to replicate sunlight, we can give these plants the brightness and day length they need. We also have automatic heat and humidity control, so it is easy to grow many exotic fruits ourselves. And if they still will not fruit, they always make attractive houseplants.

Physalis species from the family *Solanaceae*

GROUND CHERRIES

CAPE GOOSEBERRIES AND TOMATILLOS

Herbaceous. Life span: annual or short-lived perennial. Fruits: up to 2½ in., yellow to purple in papery husk. Value: rich in vitamin C.

'Chinese Lantern'

The *Physalis* are all distantly related to tomatoes, peppers, eggplants, and potatoes. Their best-known member is the perennial **Chinese Lantern**, or **Bladder Cherry**, *P. franchetii/alkekengi*, which has straggling stems, heart-shaped leaves, inconspicuous flowers, and bright orange, papery lanterns surrounding a red, edible, but unpalatable fruit. The more palatable species are similar. The **Ground Cherry**, **Strawberry Tomato,** or **Cossack Pineapple**, *P. pruinosa*, is low-growing, up to knee level, and has small, green fruits ripening to dirty yellow. Sweet and acid, they are vaguely pineapple-flavored. *P. peruviana*, the **Cape Gooseberry**, **Ground,** or **Winter Cherry**, is taller (three feet) with yellower fruits. Both fruits are enclosed in papery husks similar to, though duller than, those of the **Chinese Lantern**. Another similar fruit is the **Tomatillo** or **Jamberry**, *P. ixocarpa*, which is perennial, with much larger green or purplish berries filling the husk.

The first *Physalis* to be commonly eaten seems to be have been *P. alkekengi*, which was known to the Greek Dioscorides in the third century A.D., and was gathered from the wild. The annual *P. pruinosa*, which grows wild in North America, was popular with Native Americans and, apparently, also with Cossacks. It was introduced to England in the eighteenth century, but never caught on. The perennial **Cape Gooseberry**, *P. peruviana*, comes from tropical South America and became an important crop for the settlers on the Cape of Good Hope at the beginning of the nineteenth century. *P. ixocarpa*, the **Tomatillo** or **Jamberry**, comes from Mexico, but has become popular in many warm countries, as it fruits easily and reliably and makes good sauces and preserves. Improved versions are now being offered for greenhouse culture elsewhere.

VARIETIES

No varieties of any species are widely available except for *P. ixocarpa*, which has an improved form, **'New Sugar Giant,'** with fruits up to 2½ in. across, yellow or green instead of the usual purple. Many other *Physalis* species are cultivated locally in warm countries, but seed or plants are rarely available.

Cape gooseberries

Leaves and fruit of the Cape gooseberry

CULTIVATION

Members of this genus are all best started under cover and planted out. They all prefer a rich, light, warm soil and a sunny position. Little support is really necessary, though they do flop.

Growing under Glass
All the family give sweet fruits grown under glass and present no major problems; indeed they seem to be designed for it.

Growing in Containers
P. pruinosa is easily grown in pots. The larger *Physalis* can be grown likewise, but do not do quite as well, preferring a bigger root run. The decorative *P. alkekengi* is worth having in a pot just for the show it provides.

Ornamental and Wildlife Value
Most of the productive species are nowhere near as attractive as their more ornamental cousin, the **Chinese Lantern**. They have small value to wildlife, though the flowers are popular with insects.

Maintenance
Spring Sow indoors and plant out once hardened off.
Summer Support lax plants.
Fall Pick fruits once fully ripe; discard husks.
Winter Protect the roots of perennials well for another season.

Propagation
Normally grown from seed, the perennial varieties can be multiplied by root cuttings or division in the spring. Start them off early and pot up regularly to build up a large root system.

Pruning and Training
They need little attention other than tying in the lax growths and clearing away the withered stems after cropping. The roots of perennial varieties can get through mild winters under protection for earlier crops the following year.

Weed, Pest, and Disease Control
They are remarkably pest- and disease-free. The **Tomatillo** is especially useful as it can be used much like a tomato, but can ripen as early in cool conditions and does not suffer blight as tomatoes may.

Harvesting and Storing
The fruits must be fully ripe to be edible. They can hang on the plant until required, as they are rarely attacked by pest, disease, or bird. The husk is inedible and must be removed.

COMPANION PLANTING

There are no known companion effects.

OTHER USES

The ornamental Chinese lanterns can be dried for winter decoration and have been used medicinally.

CULINARY USES

Most *Physalis* berries are relatively tasteless and insipid raw but make delicious preserves, sauces, and tarts. The **Cape gooseberry** often tastes best on first acquaintance. In South Africa, it is used for Tippari jam or jelly. The **Tomatillo** is a favorite in salsa and other Mexican dishes.

Tippari Jelly
Makes about 4 lb

4 cups Cape gooseberries
A *little water*
Approx. 4 cups sugar

Remove the husks from the fruit and boil them with just enough water to prevent the fruit from sticking. Strain the juice and add its own volume in sugar. Simmer until fully dissolved, skim off scum, then jar and seal.

Cucumis melo from the family *Cucurbitaceae*

MELONS

Herbaceous vine. Life span: annual. Self-fertile but requires assistance as separate male and female flowers. Fruits: 2–10 in. spheres or ovoids, whitish-cream to green, netted or smooth. Value: rich in vitamins A and C, niacin, and potassium.

Melons belong to a very wide family of tender, trailing, annual vines, much resembling cucumbers in habit. They have broad leaves, softly prickled stems, and small yellow flowers, followed by fruits that can be any size from small to very large, round or oval. Melons are characterized by a thick, inedible rind covering succulent, melting flesh, which encloses a central cavity and a battalion of flat, pointed oval, whitish seeds.

The tasty, sweet, aromatic melons we know were apparently unknown to the ancients. They certainly grew similar fruits, but these seem to have been more reminiscent of the cucumber. Pliny, in the first century A.D., refers to the fruits dropping off the stalk when ripe, which is typical of melons, but they were still not generally considered very palatable. To quote Galen, the philosopher-physician, writing in the second century A.D., "the autumn (ripe) fruits do not excite vomiting as do the unripe." By the third century A.D., they had become sweeter and aromatic enough to be eaten with spices, and by the sixth and seventh centuries they were distinguished from cucumbers. The first reference to really delicious, aromatic melons comes in the fifteenth and sixteenth centuries, probably as the result of hybridization between many different strains. The seeds were left wherever humans ventured. Christopher Columbus returned to the New World to find melons growing aplenty where his previous expedition had landed and eaten the odd meal of melons, liberally discarding the seeds. Likewise, both deliberately and inadvertently, melons have reached most warm parts of the globe and are immensely popular crops for the home garden in many countries.

VARIETIES

There are countless varieties, hundreds if not thousands, and many more go unrecorded world-wide. Most of those that are available, either as seed or commercially, fall into three or four main groups. **Cantaloupe** varieties usually have orange flesh. The fruits tend to be broadly ribbed, often with a scaly or warty rind, but not netted. The flesh is sweet and aromatic. A good typical variety is **'Charentais.'** They are the hardiest—well, least tender—of the

Honeydew melon

An Ogen variety of melon

Galia melon growing intertwined with cucumber

CULTIVATION

Melons are not difficult as long as their particular requirements are met. They need continuous warmth, greater than that needed for tomatoes, peppers, or eggplants, and must have a much higher humidity. The soil must be rich, very well drained, and moist. Melons should be planted in the sunniest spot in the garden. They must have plenty of space for their wide-ranging vines, and good air circulation to prevent disease problems. Don't plant melons until the soil has thoroughly warmed, to at least 70°F. You can plant seeds early indoors in pots, about two to four weeks before planting outside. In cooler climates with shorter growing seasons, you can speed up soil warming by anchoring a piece of black plastic in the melon patch a few weeks before you plant. Keep the plastic around the young plants for a week or two after they sprout, removing it to water. If you plant seeds directly in the garden, put them in mounded hills, which improves drainage and helps warm the soil. Once plants are growing well, mulch deeply to preserve water.

Growing under Glass
Cold greenhouses can produce light crops, heated ones far more. A cold frame or curtained area in the greenhouse is better still, and the ease of providing extra warmth and humidity more than makes up for the diminished light. A cold frame set on a hotbed, or with soil-warming cables, in a greenhouse or polytunnel can produce an impressive crop. Indoors, pollination is advisable as a precaution.

Growing in Containers
Melons are one of the easiest plants to crop well in a large pot, providing they are kept warm, watered well, and fed regularly with a liquid feed. I even grow them successfully in bags of fresh grass clippings topped off with a bucketful of sieved garden compost to seal in the heat and smell. The seed is sown directly in a mound of sterile compost set on top of that and covered with a plastic bottle cloche. The bag stands in my polytunnel, a self-contained mini hotbed. When the plant is

melons and **'Sweetheart'** is one of the most reliable. **Ogen** melons are an Israeli strain. These resemble a much-improved but more tender **Cantaloupe**. The fruits are smooth, broadly ribbed, and yellow when ripe, with very sweet, green, aromatic flesh. **Muskmelons** are netted or nutmeg melons and have distinct netting, lighter in color and raised from the yellow or green rind. These are the typical hothouse melons—large oval or round fruits with very sweet and aromatically perfumed flesh from green to orange. A good old variety is **'Blenheim Orange.'** Winter melons are round to oval, yellow or green, smooth or with a leatherlike surface and hard yellow flesh that is not very sweet or perfumed. Often called **Honeydews**, these are long-keeping, up to a month or so, thus they are popular in commerce.

'Sweetheart' melons in net supports

A Cantaloupe variety of melon

growing, the bottle is reversed to make a useful watering funnel.

Ornamental and Wildlife Value

These are not really very decorative plants, but can impress with their luxurious growth. The scent of ripening melons is heavenly. The fruits are well liked by rodents and birds, making these useful for the wild garden in warmer countries.

Maintenance

Spring Plant as soon as soil warms, nip out tip after four true leaves, reduce excess number of fruits, spray with seaweed solution weekly, and mist frequently.
Summer Spray with seaweed solution weekly, water frequently, and support swelling fruits.
Fall Continue as for summer.

Melons are highly suited to growing in pots.

Winter Melons can be grown throughout the year if sufficient heat is maintained.

Propagation

Melons are normally started from seed, which does not come true when self-saved unless you are very careful, as cucurbits are promiscuous cross-pollinators. The seed needs warm, moist conditions to start and the plants need continuous warm, rich, humid conditions. Avoid the roots making a tight ball in the pot, but do not overpot. The stems can be layered or even taken as soft cuttings to continue the season.

Weed, Pest, and Disease Control

The worst melon pests are striped and spotted **cucumber beetles**, which spread bacterial wilt as they move from leaf to leaf and plant to plant. Floating row covers and determined hand picking may help; rotenone is a last resort. **Squash vine borers** also attack melons, burrowing into the stem so that it wilts past the point of entry. **Downy** and **powdery mildew** are common in humid or rainy weather. Remove any infected leaves or branches to prevent the melons from losing sweetness to the mold.

Harvesting and Storing

Their perfumed, aromatic sweetness and luscious, melting texture make them divine when ripened to perfection—though too often they are taken young to travel and are then not sweet, but woody and never well perfumed. For sybarites, they really must be ripened on the vine until they are dropping—the nets are not there to support but to catch the fruits! Once they are ripe enough to scent a room, the fruits should be chilled before eating to firm the flesh and then removed from the refrigerator a short while before serving to allow the perfume to emerge fully.

COMPANION PLANTING

Melons like to ramble under sweet corn or sunflowers, enjoying their shelter and dappled shade. They also get along with peanuts, but do not thrive near potatoes. Morning glory seed sown with melons is said to improve their germination. Most of all, melons need the same hot, humid conditions as cucumbers, and there seems little problem with their pollinating each other. However, there might be if you want to save seed.

OTHER USES

Melons accumulate a great deal of calcium in their leaves, which makes them especially useful for worm compost. The empty shells make good slug traps. *Cucumis melo dudaim,* **Queen Anne's Pocket Melon,** is grown for its strong perfume, but the flesh is insipid.

Muskmelon with flower and fruit

CULINARY USES

Quintessentially a dessert fruit, melons are nevertheless most often served as a starter in the place of savory dishes and are exquisite as chunks combined with Dolcelatte cheese and wrapped in ham. Melons can be made into jam or chutney, added to compotes, and used as bowls for creative cuisine.

Melon Sundae
Quantities to taste

Ripe melon
Vanilla ice cream
Toasted flaked almonds
Sultanas
Honey
Dark chocolate
Glacé cherries

Remove balls of melon with a spoon. Layer these in sundae glasses with scoops of vanilla ice cream, almonds, and sultanas. Then add the melon juice thickened with honey. Top with grated dark chocolate and a glacé cherry.

Melon chutney

Melon sundae

Citrullus lanatus/vulgaris from the family *Cucurbitaceae*

WATERMELONS

Herbaceous vine. Life span: annual. Self-fertile. Fruits: variably large, green.
Value: rich in vitamins and minerals; a serving contains more iron than spinach.

Watermelons are scrambling, climbing vines. Their leaves are darker, more blue-green, hairy, and more fernlike than melon leaves; the flowers are similar, small and yellow. Watermelon fruits vary in size from small to gigantic, from light to dark green or yellow in color. The thin, hard rind is packed with red flesh, embedded in which are small, dark seeds. Eating the very juicy flesh is like drinking sweet water.

This productive and nutritious, thirst-quenching fruit comes from Africa and India, but was first mentioned by botanists and travelers in the sixteenth century. The fruit became widely cultivated, but it appears to have been little improved until it reached North America. There it was developed to produce examples weighing over 100 pounds and many varieties with different colored flesh, rind, or seed. These included a subgroup with ornamental "painted," "engraved," or "sculptured" seeds.

A spray of watermelon leaves

VARIETIES

'Charleston Gray' is long, oval, and light-green-skinned with crisp red flesh. 'Sugar Baby' is round, darker green, and with very sweet red flesh, but needs an early start for maximum sweetness. 'Sweet Heart Seedless' and 'Honey Red Seedless' are other small-sized varieties popular for the home garden. 'Moon and Stars' is an heirloom variety with a beautiful spangled rind; 'Yellow Baby' is a yellow-fleshed mini. I have unexpectedly grown good fruits from seed saved from tasty, ordinary, unnamed supermarket varieties.

CULTIVATION

Warm, well-aerated, but moist soil is needed. Although copious water is needed at the roots to swell the large fruits, watermelons prefer less humid conditions than melons or cucumbers. They also do not need the same high degree of fertility, and thrive in any reasonable, sandy soil, as they benefit from watering as much as from feeding. Watermelons were once only grown in southern gardens, because the huge fruits took so long to mature. With today's modern small-fruited varieties, gardeners in cooler climates with 65 days or more of warm weather can also enjoy growing their own. There are even bush cultivars, such as 'Bush Baby,' for gardens short on space.

Growing under Glass
This is absolutely essential anywhere other than in a location with hot summers.

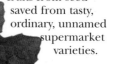

The vines do not mind light shade but need warmth and prefer a drier atmosphere than melons or cucumbers —although they do better with them than with the *Solanums.* They need plenty of space; grow them a yard apart. Provide support and train them up if space is limited, but always keep the fruits well supported.

Growing in Containers

Watermelons can be grown in big pots, although they resent the restricted root run and lack of aeration. Be sure to use an open, gritty compost; ensure that regular watering and feeding are maintained throughout the season.

Maintenance

Spring Sow as soon as warm conditions can be maintained; spray with seaweed solution weekly. *Summer* Spray with seaweed solution weekly and straw under swelling fruits. *Fall* Remove old vines. *Winter* Save the seeds for spring sowing.

Propagation

These are readily started from seed. Watermelons are not as easy to layer as melons. They will prefer clay pots to plastic ones and react very badly to overwatering or to compaction of the compost.

Pruning and Training

The plants are best allowed to ramble. If they are trained up anything, provide support for the immensely heavy fruits. On the ground,

they are best laid on straw to keep them clean.

Weed, Pest, and Disease Control

Wilt, carried by cucumber beetles, may cause problems; remove affected parts of the plant or control severe outbreaks with rotenone. Soil-borne **anthracnose** can be problematic; choose resistant cultivars such as **'Paladin.'** Very prone to attack by **red spider mite** under glass, so commercial predators should be introduced early before a major attack starts. Although watermelons like it as warm as melons, a similar degree of humidity under glass will aggravate these attacks.

Harvesting and Storing

Watermelons are ripe when they sound taut and "hollow" to a tap from the knuckle. If really ripe and well grown, they split open as soon as the knife bites. However, if left intact, they will keep for a week.

A good watermelon curry with chili, turmeric, and cilantro powders, cumin seeds, and lime juice is traditionally made in Rajasthan.

COMPANION PLANTING

Watermelons do not object to potatoes, as melons do, and may run among the plants to advantage in warm countries.

OTHER USES

The closely related *Citrullus colocynthis*, **Colocynth**, **Bitter Gourd**, is like a small, intensely bitter watermelon. It is used medicinally and occasionally pickled or preserved after many boilings.

Young watermelon plants growing in an old freezer

CULINARY USES

Watermelons are best eaten fresh. Their seeds may be eaten—they are oily and nutritious. The pulp can be made into conserves, or reduced to make a sugar syrup.

Watermelon Ices
All quantities to taste

Watermelon
Melted chocolate
Grated desiccated coconut

Freeze bite-sized cubes of watermelon on a wire rack. Once they are frozen solid, dip each quickly in cooling melted chocolate, sprinkle with grated coconut, and freeze again. Serve nearly defrosted, but still just frozen.

Citrus species from the family *Rutaceae*

LEMONS, ORANGES
AND OTHER CITRUS FRUITS

Tree/bush up to 25 ft. Life span: medium to long. Evergreen, self-fertile.
Fruits: variable size, orange, green, or yellow. Value: rich in vitamin C.

Lemon

Citrus fruits of the *Rutaceae* family are small, glossy-leaved evergreens with green stems that are occasionally thorny, especially in the leaf axils. Typical of this family, the leaves have glands that secrete scented oil. The small, white, star-shaped flowers are intensely and similarly perfumed, and are followed by the well-known fruits, which take up to a year to ripen. These swell to a size that ranges from that of a cherry to a human head, depending on the species.

They are yellow or orange with light-colored flesh inside a tough, bitter, and scented peel. The flesh is sweet or sour, always juicy, and segmented. Each **Orange** piece may contain a few small seeds.

Originally from China and Southeast Asia, some species and closely interrelated cultivars have been in cultivation since prehistory. They moved slowly westward to India and then on to Arabia and then to the Mediterranean countries. The ancient Greeks seem not to have been aware of any citrus. The Romans knew the citron, which was recorded in Palestine in the first century A.D., but probably arrived several centuries before. The citron was widely planted in Italy in the second and third centuries, becoming especially popular near Naples.

The Romans were such gourmands that they would hardly have failed to notice a delight such as an orange. These did not reach Arabia until the ninth century. It was recorded as growing in Sicily in A.D. 1002 and was grown in Spain at Seville, still famous for its oranges, while it was occupied by the Moors in the twelfth century. It is said St. Domine planted an orange in Rome in the year 1200, and a Spanish ship full of the fruits docked at Portsmouth, England, in 1290; the Queen of Edward I received seven. These were probably bitter oranges, as many believe the sweet orange did not reach Europe until later. First seen in India in 1330, the sweet sort was first planted in 1421 at Versailles; another planted in 1548 in Lisbon became the "mother" of most European sweet orange trees and was still living in 1823.

The lemon reached Egypt and Palestine in the tenth century and was cultivated in Genoa by the mid-fifteenth century. The new fruits were soon spread around the warmer parts of Europe, and then farther afield with the voyagers of the fifteenth and sixteenth centuries. Columbus must have scattered the seeds as he went, for they are recorded as growing in the Azores in 1494 and the Antilles in 1557. They had reached orchard scale in South America in 1587 and by then Cuba was covered with them. They are now mainly grown in California, Florida, Israel, Spain, and South Africa, though every warm to tropical area produces its own and more.

Pink grapefruit

VARIETIES

The various types are of obscure parentage and were probably derived by selection from a distant common ancestor. *Citrus aurantium* is the **Seville, Bitter,** or **Sour Orange**. Too sour to eat raw, this is the best for marmalade and preserves and was the first sort to arrive in Europe. *C. sinensis* is the **Sweet Orange,** often known by the variety such as **'Valencia Late,' 'Jaffa,'** which is large, thick-skinned, and seedless, or the nearly seedless and finest-quality **'Washington Navel.' Blood Oranges**, such as the **'Maltese,'** are sweet oranges with a red tint to the flesh.

C. limon is the lemon. The fruits are distinctly shaped yellow ovoids with blunt nipples at the flower end and the characteristic acid taste. The most common are **'Lisbon,' 'Eureka,'** and **'Villafranca'**; the hardiest and most convenient for a conservatory is the compact **'Meyer's Lemon.'**

C. aurantifolia is the lime. This makes a smaller tree of up to 12 ft. The small green fruits do not travel well and are mainly consumed locally or made into a concentrate. Limes offered for sale are

The beautiful flowers of the 'Valencia Late' orange

Lemon 'Lisbon'

often small, unripe lemons, given away by the nipple, which a true lime does not have. Alternatively, they may be the similar *C. limetta,* **Sweet Lime,** which is insipidly sweet when ripe. True limes are grown mostly from seed and will require near-tropical conditions.

C. paradisi is the grapefruit. Not as acid as a lemon, it is relished for breakfast by many. It may be a hybrid of the **Pomelo** or **Shaddock,** *C. grandis,* which is similar but coarser. **'Marsh's Seedless'** is the most common kind of grapefruit, with greenish-white flesh; but some prefer the Texan varieties with pink flesh.

C. reticulata is the **Mandarin, Satsuma, Tangerine,** or **Clementine**. These names are confused and interchanged for several small, sweet, easily peeled, and segmented kinds of small orange. *C. medica* is like a large, warty lemon and is now mainly produced in a few Mediterranean countries for making candied peel. There are many other citrus species and hybrids, **Uglis, Ortaniques,** and **Tangelos,** to name but a few. The **Kumquat** is not a citrus, but belongs to the similar genus *Fortunella.* The fruits are very like small, yellowish, tart oranges, and are especially good for making preserves.

Kumquats

CULTIVATION

Citrus need a warm, rich, moist soil, well aerated, and never badly drained. They are all tender, though lemons and oranges have, despite the odds, been grown successfully outdoors in favorable positions on warm walls in southern England, and even cropped in some years. In warm countries they are spaced about 15–20 ft. apart each way and are in their prime at ten years old. Trees with fruits of orange size will give a crop of about 500 each winter; small fruits, such as lemons, will crop more than 500; while big fruits, such as grapefruits, will crop less. Lemons, oranges, and other citrus are hardy only in Zones 9 and 10, or where temperatures stay above 12–15°F. Trifoliate orange (*Poncirus trifoliata*) can stand more cold, surviving in sheltered areas as cold as Zone 5.

Growing under Glass
Frost-free protection in winter is necessary in northern countries. Citrus do not like being under glass all year round. They are much happier outdoors in summer and enjoy a rest in fall. Thus they are best

A grove of 'Jaffa' oranges growing in Kos, Greece

grown in large containers and moved under glass only for the frosty months, the months that they flower and crop. Limes and grapefruits are among the least hardy types and need more heat than the others.

Growing in Containers

This is ideal for citrus, as it keeps them compact and makes it easy to give them winter protection indoors. They must have a well-aerated, well-drained, but rich compost.

Ornamental and Wildlife Value

Very decorative in leaf, flower, and fruit, all of which have a wonderful scent, these are ideal subjects for a sunroom and for a warm patio in the summer.

Maintenance

Spring Prune, spray with seaweed solution weekly, and move outdoors.
Summer Prune, spray with seaweed solution weekly.
Fall Prune, spray with seaweed solution weekly.
Winter Prune, move indoors, and pick the fruit.

Propagation

Commonly, commercial plants are grafted or budded, often on *Poncirus* stock to dwarf them. Cuttings can be taken. I find some succeed quite easily in every batch. Seedlings are slow to bear fruit and may not be true; however, citrus seeds occasionally produce two seedlings, one being a clone copy of the original plant and the other normal. Seedlings are often more vigorous and longer lived than worked plants, which may offset their slow development.

Pruning and Training

Once these have grown tall enough, they are best cut back hard to form a neat cone or globe shape. Regularly remove and/or shorten straggly, unfruitful, diseased, and long shoots, cutting back hardest before growth starts in spring. They generally need no support until they are in fruit, when heavy crops may even cause the branches to bend severely and tear.

Weed, Pest, and Disease Control

All kinds of pests bother these plants under glass, but when they go out for the summer most of the problems disappear. The usual remedies work and soft soap sprays may also be useful against scale insects, which can particularly bother citrus, especially if ants are about to farm them. Bad drainage will kill them more rapidly than cold weather will!

Harvesting and Storing

Usually picked too young so they can travel, they are of course best plucked fresh off the tree and fully ripe. They do not all ripen at once and picking may continue over many weeks. The rind contains the bitter oil that can be expressed to give a zest to cooking.

Carved lime wood is from *Tilia* **species rather than** *Citrus.*

The beautiful Citrus Allée at the Villa Carlotta, northern Italy

COMPANION PLANTING

In warm countries citrus are benefited by growing aloes, rubber, oak, and guava trees nearby. However, they are also said to be inhibited by *Convolvulus* or possibly by the *Ipomoea* species.

Citrus cuttings are easy to grow in pots.

OTHER USES

The leaves, flowers, and fruits, especially of *C. bergamia*, the bergamot, are used in perfumery. The empty shells of the fruits make slug traps if dried. *Citrus/Poncirus trifoliata* is hardier than the others and heavily thorned; it is used as a hedge in mild regions.

CULINARY USES

The fruits can be juiced—much of the world's crop is consumed this way—or made into jams, jellies, or marmalade. The peel is often candied or glacéed. Small amounts of lemon juice prevent freshly prepared fruits and vegetables from oxidizing and give a delightful, sharp, clean taste to most things, savory or sweet. The Victorians grew the seeds for the young tender leaves to add to salads. The peels are often used for liqueurs and flavorings.

Orange Sorbet
Serves 4

4 large unwaxed oranges
Mace
Sugar
Egg white
Parsley sprigs

Cut the tops off the oranges and scoop out the contents. Freeze the lower shells to use as serving bowls. Strain the juice from the pulp and measure it. Simmer the chopped tops of the oranges with the pulp and a small piece of fresh mace in half as much water as you have juice, then strain and add half the juice's measure in sugar. Once it has dissolved, mix this sweetened water and the juice and partially freeze. Take it from the freezer and beat vigorously, adding one beaten egg white per 1 lb. of mixture, refreeze, then repeat the beating. Serve, partially thawed, in the reserved shells with a garnish of parsley.

Lemon jam

Orange flower water lends a wonderful perfume to the bath.

Orange Sorbet

Olea europaea from the family *Oleaceae*

OLIVES

Tree up to 33 ft. Life span: long. Evergreen, self-fertile.
Fruits: up to 1 in., ovoid, green to black. Value: rich in oils.

Cultivated olive trees are gnarled and twisted with long, thin, dark leaves, silvered underneath, though the wild species are bushier with quadrangular stems, rounder leaves, and spines. The inconspicuous, sometimes fragrant, white flowers are followed by green fruits that ripen to brown or blue-purple-black, and occasionally ivory white, each containing a single large stone.

Found wild in the Middle East, olives have long been cultivated. They were among the fruits promised to the Jews in Canaan. According to Homer, green olives were brought to Greece by Cecrops, founder of Athens. They were certainly the source of its wealth. By 571 B.C., the olive had reached Italy and in the first century A.D. Pliny records a dozen varieties grown as far as Gaul (France) and Spain. These are still the major producing areas; olives are also grown in California, Australia, and China.

Olive branch and leaves

VARIETIES

There are up to several dozen varieties of olive grown commercially in different regions, but usually only unnamed species are available. **'Queen Manzanillas'** are the biggest of the green pickling olive varieties.

CULTIVATION

Olives grow well in arid sites that will not support much else. They are generally hardy only in Zones 9 and 10. They may also grow in Zone 8 but are unlikely to fruit. They prefer a well-drained, light, lime-based soil. They will grow, but rarely fruit well, outside Mediterranean climatic regions. The small, strong trees need little support.

Growing under Glass
It is worth growing olives in big pots so that they can be brought in for winter and put outside in summer. If kept indoors, it must not be too hot or humid.

Growing in Containers
Olives make good subjects for containers, though they are unlikely to be very productive. They must have a free-draining compost and then are fairly trouble-free.

Ornamental and Wildlife Value
Very attractive shrubs, these are worth having even if they never fruit, and they probably won't. The flowers are beneficial to insects, and some are fragrant. They are dense evergreens, making good shelter, and the fruits are rich in oils, so these are useful plants for wild gardens.

Maintenance
Spring Prune and spray with seaweed solution monthly.
Summer Spray with seaweed solution monthly.
Fall Spray with seaweed solution monthly.
Winter Take indoors or protect from frost.

Propagation
Seeds may not come true, though they are often used, and the resulting plants can be slow to come into fruit. Cuttings with a heel can be taken in late summer, but like the seeds need bottom heat to ensure success. Grow seedlings on for a year or two in large pots before planting out—they get tougher as they get bigger.

Pruning and Training
As olives bear on the previous year's growth, they must have only remedial pruning to remove the dead and diseased or crossing branches. This is best done in late winter or early spring. They can be trained as fans on walls for the extra protection. If the tops are frosted, they can still come again from the root and can be cut back very hard or pollarded. Old trees often throw suckers as replacements.

Weed, Pest, and Disease Control
Olives have very few problems in private gardens, though **scale insects** can bother them occasionally. Protection from **frost** and good drainage are more important.

A ripe green olive

Nets are suspended below the olive trees to catch the ripe fruit.

Harvesting and Storing
In the Mediterranean region the trees bear fruit when they are about eight years old. They produce about 60 lb. of fruit each, which reduces to about a quarter to half that weight in oil. The green fruits are ones picked unripe and pickled; the black fruits are ripe and ready for pressing for oil or preserving. The oil that is squeezed out without heat or excess pressure is called extra virgin (an interesting concept, rather typical of Latin thinking). Cheaper grades are produced by heating or adding hot water to the mass.

COMPANION PLANTING

Oaks are thought to be detrimental to olive trees.

OTHER USES

The oil has many industrial as well as culinary uses. Much is used in cosmetics and perfumery, and it was once burned in lamps.

CULINARY USES

The oil is used in many ways—in Mediterranean countries it is used in preference to animal fats—and the fruits are added to various dishes. The fruits are also eaten as savory accompaniments pickled in brine, often stuffed with anchovy or pimento, or dried. If beaten to a paste, olives will make a delicious savory spread.

Olive Bread
Makes 1 loaf

4 cups all-purpose flour
1 packet dried yeast
Water
¹/₄ cup black olives, pitted
Olive oil
Poppy seeds

Mix the flour and yeast with enough water to form a dough. Knead and allow to rise until it is half as big again. Knead again and work in the olives. Rub the dough with olive oil; place it in an oiled loaf pan to rise again with a sprinkling of poppy seeds. Once it has risen to half its size again, put it in a preheated oven at 425°F for 20 minutes or until brown on top. Serve as an entrée with a crisp green salad and a sharp dressing.

Actinidia chinensis/deliciosa from the family *Actinidiaceae*

KIWI FRUIT

OR CHINESE GOOSEBERRY

Vine up to 30 ft. or more. Life span: medium. Deciduous, some not self-fertile.
Fruits: up to 2 in., flattened ovoid, brown, hairy. Value: very rich in vitamin C.

Kiwis, whole and sliced

The kiwi fruit or Chinese gooseberry is the best-known member of a small number of deciduous clambering and twining shrubs closely related to camellias. The kiwi has large, hand-sized, heart-shaped leaves, downy underneath, on softly bristled stems. The flower is like a small, poorly developed rose, off-whitish and fragrant. The brown, furry fruits are thin-skinned and firm with luscious green pulp containing many tiny black seeds around the center.

These were not known in the West until the end of the nineteenth century, when they were introduced from Japan and East Asia, more for their use as decorative climbers than for their fruits. Though now commonly known as kiwi fruit, they are not native to New Zealand, but were introduced there in the early years of the last century and became more popular as a fruit when greenhouse growers needed to look for alternative crops to their oversubscribed tomato market. Recent breeding has developed self-fertile varieties. A dwarf, shrubby form would be handy.

Leaf and flower of the kiwi vine

VARIETIES

A. chinensis/deliciosa **'Hayward'** is the most widely available but is not self-fertile, so it needs planting with a male. **'Blake'** is very high yielding (up to 200 lb. per vine is claimed). It is self-fertile and needs protection for the lower stems in cold regions.

A. arguta, the **Siberian Kiwi** or **Tara Vine**, is very vigorous with deeply toothed leaves and fragrant, triple, white flowers with purple anthers, followed by green, sweet, slightly insipid fruits. The copious sap is drinkable. An improved self-fertile variety, **'Issai,'** is available, which has hairless fruits. **'Ananasnaja,'** a Russian variety, is a female that bears large, firm fruit with sweet, spicy taste.

A. kolomikta is very attractive with large, oblong leaves. The single, white flowers are sweetly perfumed and followed by long, yellowish, sweet berries. This is less vigorous than the other species and is thus more useful for cramped, modern gardens. It tolerates shade well. **'Arctic Beauty'** has both male and female plants. Its green fruits are the size of a very big grape, with excellent flavor right off the vine. It has survived cold as low as −40°F. There are many more sweet edible species.

CULTIVATION

Kiwis require a warm site, preferably against a wall, as their young growths and flowers are easily damaged by late frosts. They need rich, loamy soil and strong supports. Kiwis are extremely rampant growers that need frequent, hard cutting back to keep the vine in control. Be sure the fence or trellis on which they grow is exceedingly sturdy. *A. chinensis* is cold hardy only to 10°F, Zones 7 through 9; *A. arguta* grows in Zones 4 through 7. They will grow, but not crop, in shade. Some of the early varieties, such as **'Hayward,'** are female only and require one male to be planted to every half dozen females. Modern varieties are self-fertile, though they may perform better if planted with others to cross-pollinate.

Growing under Glass
If crops are wanted, kiwis have to be grown under glass to give them the warmth and long season they require. However, they take up a lot of space. They like similar conditions to tomatoes, so the two could possibly be grown together.

Growing in Containers
These are too vigorous to be confined for long in a pot and are never likely to be very productive in one.

Maintenance
Spring Prune and tie in; spray with seaweed solution monthly.

The kiwi vine needs good support and training.

Kiwi fruit makes a soothing lip balm.

Summer Prune and tie in new shoots.
Fall Cut back sideshoots to shorter stubs.
Winter Pick the fruit—if you are lucky.

Propagation
The species can be grown from seed, but varieties are grown from half-ripe summer or hardwood fall cuttings rooted with bottom heat in a frame.

Pruning and Training
The fruits are borne on sideshoots. Unless these are left there are no fruits, so these must not be hard pruned, but may be shortened. Kiwis need regular, hard, pruning to stay in bounds. You can cut the new growth back to 4 or 5 buds once a month in summer. Kiwis must be well trained or they form an unruly thicket; therefore give them plenty of space. Old shoots die, so tie in replacements in spring. Good supports are necessary for these vigorous plants.

Weed, Pest, and Disease Control
There seem to be no major problems with these fruits.

Harvesting and Storing
The fruits ripen late; hang well with protection against frosts from the elements, ideally under glass.

COMPANION PLANTING

There are no known companion effects.

OTHER USES

These plants are useful for covering old trees and other eyesores.

CULINARY USES

Kiwis can be eaten raw or made into juices, jellies, and jams and are much liked for decorating other dishes, usually sweet but occasionally savory. They contain an enzyme that breaks down gelatin, so should not be used to make jelled desserts. This enzyme can also tenderize meat.

Kiwi Meringue Pie
Serves 4

4 individual meringue bases
Green gooseberry jam or
  preserve
Crème fraîche
4 kiwi fruits
Toasted chopped nuts
Glacé cherries

On each meringue base build a thick layer of jam, then a layer of crème fraîche covered with very thin, overlapping slices of peeled kiwi. Top with nuts and a cherry or two.

Passiflora from the family *Passifloraceae*

PASSION FRUIT

Herbaceous vine up to 3 ft. Life span: short. Semi-deciduous, self-fertile. Fruits: from 1 in. to 4 in., spherical to cylindrical, yellow, orange, red, brown, black, or green.
Value: rich in vitamin C.

Passion fruit are a family of perennial climbers with tendrils, deeply lobed leaves, amazing flowers, and peculiar fruits. These vary in size, from that of a cherry to that of a coconut, and in color, coming in almost any shade from yellow to black. They are usually thick-skinned with a juicy, acid, fragrant, sweet pulp inside, almost inseparable from the smooth, black seeds. The passion fruit *Passiflora edulis* is the most widely grown species. It has white or mauve flowers fragrant of heliotrope, and purple-black fruits that are best when "old" and wrinkled.

Passion fruit are native to America and were first recorded in Europe in 1699. The flowers caused quite a stir in European society, with many contemporary Christians claiming that they were a sign of Christ's Passion (the Crucifixion): The three stigmas represented the nails, the central column the scourging post, the five anthers the wounds, the corona the crown of thorns, the calyx the halo, the ten petals the faithful apostles, and the tendrils the whips and scourges of His oppressors. These delightful climbers, with their stunning flowers and delicious fruits, have now become popular in most warm countries. They are often grown in sunrooms and in pots on patios for the flowers rather than the fruits.

Passion fruit and leaves

VARIETIES

Passiflora edulis is the tastiest variety and hardy enough to survive in a frost-free greenhouse. Improved varieties such as **'Crackerjack'** are available. The **'Giant Granadilla,'** *P. quadrangularis,* needs more-tropical conditions, but can produce fruits weighing many pounds; these are often used as vegetables in their unripe state. *P. laurifolia* is the **'Water Lemon'** or **'Yellow Granadilla,'** much esteemed in Jamaica. *P. incarnata* **'Maypops'** comes from eastern

Banana passion fruit

North America. It has attractive creamy flowers, ornamental, three-lobed leaves, and tasty yellow fruits. It is not self-fertile and spreads by underground runners. It can survive outdoors, as it comes again from the roots. *P. caerulea* is the hardiest, with blue flowers and orange fruits which may be edible but are not palatable, even after boiling with sugar. Dozens of edible-fruited passion flowers are grown locally, such as *P. antioquiensis,* with yellow, banana-shaped fruits; *P. foetida,* the goat-scented passion flower; *P. mixta* **'Curuba di Indio';** and *P. ligularis,* said by connoisseurs to be the most delicious.

The passion fruit and its extraordinarily beautiful flowe

CULTIVATION

A humus-rich, moist soil and a sheltered position on a warm wall suit hardier varieties, with thick mulches to protect their roots. However, most of these plants are happier under cover. Most passion fruit grow only in Zones 8 through 10, but *P. incarnata* is hardy to Zones 6 through 10.

Growing under Glass
For edible fruit production, and to grow most of the more tender varieties, glass is essential. Fortunately, they can also be grown in pots, making them less rampant and allowing some to be put outside for the summer.

Growing in Containers
Surprisingly, such rampant climbers take fairly well to pot culture, but require a lot of watering. They will crop in pots and, indeed, this is one of the better ways of growing them, so they can be taken indoors for winter. They need an open, free-draining, rich compost, and regular feeding.

Ornamental and Wildlife Value
Among the most attractive of all climbers in flower, foliage, or when festooned with fruits.

Maintenance
Spring Tie in new growth; spray with seaweed solution monthly.
Summer Tie in growths; spray with seaweed solution monthly.
Fall Pick fruits after a long, hot summer.
Winter Prune before frosts and protect roots or take pots inside.

Propagation
Passion flowers can all be grown from seed, which can give good results, for they are still relatively unimproved and most are true species. Propagate good varieties from heel or nodal cuttings in midsummer if they are given bottom heat.

Pruning and Training
Pruning is remedial, removing dead and surplus growth. Strong wires are needed, as these are quite vigorous and productive.

Weed, Pest, and Disease Control
Passion flowers tend to form rather dense stools, which means they are prone to **weed infestations**, which make the crown damp and short-lived.

Harvesting and Storing
Best to ripen the fruit on the vine until they drop, though picked young for transport they keep well. As they ripen they will shrivel, appearing old and wrinkled, and the flavor is then at its best.

Passion fruit vines are highly decorative and provide a dazzling splash of color.

OTHER USES

The empty shells make good slug traps for the garden.

Passion fruit in flower

CULINARY USES

Thirst-quenching raw, passion fruit are made into a juice that is a popular drink in many countries, much like orange juice and squash are in others. They can be made into jams, liqueurs, and sorbets.

Passion Fruit Sorbet
Serves 4–6

12 ripe passion fruit
Approx. $\frac{1}{2}$ cup sugar
Mint sprigs

Scoop out the fruit pulp and seeds and sieve. Discard the seeds. To the juice, add half its volume in water and the same of sugar, stir until the sugar has dissolved, and freeze. Partially thaw and beat vigorously, then refreeze. Serve partially thawed, scooped into glasses, and decorated with mint sprigs.

Punica granatum from the family *Lythraceae*

POMEGRANATES

Bush up to 14 ft. Life span: medium. Deciduous, self-fertile.
Fruits: up to 3 in., spherical, orange. Value: little.

Pomegranates have coppery young leaves that yellow in fall; glorious orange or red, camellia-like blooms; and orange fruits with a rough nipple and thin, leathery rind. Inside they have bitter yellow pith and are stuffed with seeds embedded in pink, sweet pulp. They are infuriating to eat. Natives of Persia, pomegranates were cultivated in ancient Egypt and other Mediterranean countries. Some are now grown in California. Because they are easily transported, they were widely known in early times, even in colder countries where they would not fruit.

Pomegranate flowers are dazzling in full bloom.

OTHER USES

They grow densely enough to be used for hedges in warm countries. A dye is made from the fruit peel. The peel and the bark are used as native cures for diarrhea and dysentery.

Weed, Pest, and Disease Control, and Companion Planting
Pomegranates suffer from few problems and no companion effects have been noted.

VARIETIES

Iraq is said to have the best pomegranates, large with perfumed flesh and almost seedless. **'Wonderful'** is a Californian variety. **'Nana,'** a dwarf cultivar, is decorative and very small, rarely coming above knee height.

Immature pomegranates and leaves

CULTIVATION

They will grow and flower outdoors but seldom set a crop in most of the U.S., even on a warm wall. They prefer well-drained, limy soil. The plants are hardy in Zones 8 through 10, and may survive in a sheltered location in Zone 7.

Growing under Glass
This is the only way to have a crop in cooler areas. They need intense heat in summer to ripen and are more manageable in pots.

Growing in Containers
Pomegranates are easily grown in pots, especially the dwarf variety, **'Nana.'**

Maintenance
Spring Spray with seaweed solution; prune outdoor specimens.
Summer Keep hot to ripen the fruits.
Fall Keep hot to ripen the fruits.
Winter Prune indoor specimens in early winter.

Propagation
By seed, layering, or half-ripe summer cuttings using bottom heat.

Pruning and Training
They can be fan-trained but are easiest allowed to grow out as a bush from the wall. Old, diseased, and weak wood is best pruned out in late spring. Prune indoor specimens in early winter and give them a reduced temperature for a few weeks afterward.

Harvesting and Storing
They travel very well, keeping for weeks, so are easy to distribute.

CULINARY USES

The juice is used for drinks, syrup, conserves, and fermenting.

Pomegranate Pastime

Sit down under a shady tree with your ripe pomegranate. Cut open the rind, pick out the seeds individually with a pin, and eat the pulp. The seed may be swallowed or spit out.

Diospyros kaki from the family *Ebenaceae*

PERSIMMONS

*Tree/bush up to 20 ft. Life span: medium. Deciduous.
Fruits: 2–3 in., round, orange-red. Value: minor.*

Persimmons have lustrous, dark green leaves. The flowers are drab and the fruits look like large orange tomatoes. Japanese persimmons were first seen in 1776. Extremely popular in Japan and China, they are now grown on the French Riviera and in California. Other persimmons are eaten locally in hot countries.

CULTIVATION

Persimmons are hardy, but need a well-drained soil and warmth to produce passable fruit. Japanese persimmons can be grown in Zones 8 through 10. **'Saijo'** is unusually hardy and may survive in Zone 6. American persimmons are more cold tolerant and thrive in Zones 5 through 10.

Growing under Glass
They need glass protection in northern Europe to extend the season long enough to ripen good fruits.

Growing in Containers
Persimmons are better in borders than pots, though these will do. Thin out the fruits to 10 in. apart, otherwise they overcrop and will not swell.

Maintenance
Spring Weed and spray with seaweed solution.
Summer Disbud if over-vigorous.
Fall Cut off fruit and store until ripe.
Winter Dress with compost and copious amounts of straw.

Propagation
By seed or grafting for the better varieties.

Japanese persimmons

Pruning and Training
The branches split easily and are not easily trained. Only remedial pruning is needed, so plant at about 20 ft. apart. Thin the fruits to get bigger ones.

Weed, Pest, and Disease Control
There are few common pests or diseases, though a **fungus** has been known to kill wild trees in America.

Harvesting and Storing
Cut rather than pick to retain the short pedicel. This way they keep better. Store cool and dry until ripe—up to four months, as they are best when somewhat shriveled. When soft, they lose the astringency that makes unripe persimmons mouth-puckering and rather disgusting.

COMPANION PLANTING

No companion effects have been noted.

OTHER USES

The fruits are successfully used as pig food.

VARIETIES

Diospyros kaki is the **Japanese Persimmon**. There are many varieties from the East. **'Fuyu'** is a nonastringent, smooth-textured fruit. Self-fertile **'Saijo'** is a very old Japanese variety with small, conical, very sweet fruit. *D. virginiana* is the **American Persimmon**, which has smaller, redder fruits and crops as far north as the Great Lakes. **'Meader'** is an American persimmon variety selected in New Hampshire by Elwyn Meader.

CULINARY USES

Persimmons are eaten fresh, dried, or candied, but rarely cooked.

Percinnammons
Serves 4

4 soft, ripe persimmons
Ground cinnamon
Apricot conserves
Cream
4 glacé cherries

Peel the fruit and cut in half. Dust each half with cinnamon, cover with conserves, and top with cream and a cherry.

Eriobotrya/Photinia japonica from the family *Rosaceae*

LOQUATS

JAPANESE MEDLARS OR PLUMS

Tree/bush up to 33 ft. Life span: medium to long. Evergreen.
Fruits: up to 2 in., pear-shaped, orange. Value: minor.

Loquats have very large, leathery, corrugated leaves, woolly-white underneath, and fragrant, furry, yellowish flowers. The fruits are orange and pear-shaped with one or more big brown-black seeds and sweet, acid, chewy pulp.

First reported in 1690, these were imported from Canton to Kew Gardens in London in 1787. Widely cultivated in the East, they are now popular in the Mediterranean countries and in Florida.

VARIETIES

'Advance' is a small tree and a good pollinator. 'Champagne' has white-fleshed, golden fruits. 'Gold Nugget' is late season.

CULTIVATION

Any reasonable soil and a warm, well-drained site will suffice. They will crop only under glass or in countries with warm winters. Loquats grow in Zones 7 through 10.

Growing under Glass
As they flower in fall and the fruits ripen in late winter and spring, loquats need to be grown under glass if they are to fruit in any location that does not have a warm winter.

Loquats ripening on the tree

Growing in Containers
Loquats make big shrubs, so they are usefully confined in large pots.

Propagation
Loquats can be grown from fresh seed, or layers, or soft-wood cuttings taken in spring with bottom heat.

Ornamental and Wildlife Value
Very architectural plants with a lovely scent, they will also make good shelter for birds and insects.

Weed, Pest, and Disease Control
Few problems with these.

Maintenance
Spring Prune if needed, spray with seaweed solution, and pick fruit.
Summer Move outdoors for the summer.
Fall Bring indoors.
Winter Protect outdoor plants from frosts.

Pruning and Training
Only remedial pruning is needed. They are best trained on a wall and allowed to grow out from it or grown as bushes in pots. Trim back any dead and diseased growths in spring.

Harvesting and Storing
The fruits need warmth and protection to ripen in late winter/early spring, so they must be grown under glass in cold countries.

COMPANION PLANTING

These are dense evergreens that will kill off any plants grown underneath.

OTHER USES

These shrubs make tall and attractive screens in countries with warmer climes.

CULINARY USES

Loquats are eaten raw, stewed, or as jams or jellies. They are made into a liqueur in Bermuda.

Loquat Jam
Makes about 5 lb.

3 cups loquats
Approx. 4 cups sugar

Wash and pit the loquats, then simmer until soft with just enough water to prevent burning. Measure and add three-quarters of the volume in sugar. Stir to dissolve the sugar, then bring to a boil. Skim and pot in sterilized jars. Store in a cool place.

Opuntia ficus-indica/dillenii from the family *Cactaceae*

PRICKLY PEARS

BARBERRY FIGS

*Herbaceous, up to 7 ft. Life span: medium to long. Evergreen, self-fertile.
Fruits: 2–3½ in., ovoid, red, yellow. or purple. Value: minor.*

These are typical cacti, with round or oval, thick, fleshy pads covered with tufts of long and short spines. The flowers are large (2–3 inches) and yellow, with numerous petals, stamens, and filaments. These are followed by red, yellow, or purple, prickly, oval cylinders, which are the fruits. Under the skin the flesh is very acid and sweet.

These are natives of the Americas where they have long been used. They have naturalized in the Mediterranean basin and almost every hot, dry country, even flourishing on the lava beds of Sicily.

CULTIVATION

Opuntia need a well-drained, open, limy soil and a warm position. They are remarkably hardy, for cacti. Several survive outside at the Royal Botanic Gardens at Kew in England, and I have had them for many years in eastern England. Cold hardiness depends on the species. Many thrive in Zones 5 through 10.

Growing under Glass
This is necessary if fruits are to be produced, and you will also need extra artificial light.

Growing in Containers
Providing the pots are large and free-draining, prickly pears can be grown this way.

Ornamental and Wildlife Value
Very decorative and quite a conversation piece in a garden.

Pruning and Training
No pruning is required. When the pads become heavy they may need propping up.

Weed, Pest, and Disease Control
Weed control needs to be good, as these are nasty to weed between. Slugs and

Prickly pears thrive in arid areas.

snails may develop a taste for the pads.

Maintenance
Spring Keep weed-free.
Winter Protect outside plants during coldest weather.

Propagation
These can be grown from seed, but are slow. Detached pads or pieces root easily and are much quicker.

Harvesting and Storing
This is a thorny task. Wrap a piece of bark around to pick the fruit, which will keep for several days. The peel is best skinned off completely before the fruit is eaten.

COMPANION PLANTING

I grow them outside in front of evergreen hedges of leylandii and holly. They have survived, but unfortunately, have never fruited.

VARIETIES

Opuntia maxima is very similar to *Opuntia*. There is also a spineless variety, rarely available.

CULINARY USES

Prickly pears are usually eaten raw in place of drink and are occasionally fried or stewed. The red varieties will stain everything.

OTHER USES

After ensilaging or pulping with salt, prickly pears make a useful animal feed.

Ananas comosus from the family *Bromeliaceae*

PINEAPPLES

Herbaceous, 3 x 3 ft. Life span: short-lived, perennial. Fruits: average 4 x 8 in., dull orange or yellow.
Value: rich in vitamins C and A.

Pineapples need little description; they are the most distinctive of fruits—there is nothing else like them. They are Bromeliads, like many houseplants. They resemble common garden yuccas, nearly cylindrical with a tuft of narrow, pointed leaves emerging from the top. The skin of the fruit is green to yellow, with many slightly raised protuberances. Wild species have serrated, thorny-edged leaves and set seed. Modern cultivars are seedless, with smoother leaves and smaller fruits; those of traditional varieties weighed up to twenty pounds.

Cultivated and selected from the wild by the people of Central America for thousands of years, the fruits were sensational in 1493 to the crew of Columbus. The first fruit, surviving the voyage back, was regarded as nearly as great a discovery as the New World itself. Pineapple motifs appeared, sometimes distorted, throughout European art—often as knobs on pew ends. By 1550 pineapple was being preserved in sugar to be sent back to the Old World as an exotic, and profitable, luxury. By the end of the sixteenth century pineapples had been spread to China and the Philippines and were naturalizing in Java, and soon after were colonizing the west coast of Africa. An enterprising Mr. Le Cour of Holland succeeded in growing them under glass in 1686 and was supplying plants to English gardeners in 1690. Within a few years there was a craze for pineapples, with noblemen's gardeners growing them under glass on deep hotbeds of horse dung and the waste from leather production as far north as Scotland. The Victorians raised the cultivation of pineapples to a high level with the regulated heat from steam boilers.

Pineapple fields in Hawaii

VARIETIES

There have been hundreds of varieties, but most have disappeared as a few commercial cultivars monopolized trade. Pineapples are now grown most intensively in Hawaii, but also in Australia, Malaysia, and South Africa. **'Smooth Cayenne,'** or **'Kew Pine,'** was widely grown for many years, but connoisseurs preferred **'Queen'** and **'Ripley.'** Long gone is the favorite British hothouse variety **'Enville.'**

Pineapples grow on a central stem, which rises out of the crown of the fruit.

CULTIVATION

A tropical plant, the pineapple is happiest in Hawaii. It needs very high soil and fairly high air temperatures; high humidity during the growing season except when ripening; as much light as possible; and a very rich, open, fibrous compost in quantity. On plantations pineapples have about a square yard of ground each, so generous pots are required! Never let them chill below 70°F or "cook" above 90°F.

Ornamental and Wildlife Value

They are easy to root and grow as houseplants, but require lots of heat and care to fruit well.

Maintenance

Spring Pot up cuttings and mature plants.
Summer Root cuttings or crowns.
Fall Tidy plants for the winter.
Winter Keep warm!

Propagation

Suckers from healthy plants are best, fruiting in a year and a half or so. Gills, the shoots produced at the base of the fruit, seeds, and even stem cuttings can be used, but take longer to grow and fruit. The crown from a fruit is easily rooted; cut it off whole with a thin shoulder, pry off the shoulder, and pull off the lower withered leaves individually. Root over heat in a gritty compost. Keep the foliage moist in a plastic bag, but be careful of mold.

Pruning and Training

Young plants rooted in summer need potting up in spring, growing on for a year and repotting the following spring to fruit that summer or fall. Repot annually, and remove superfluous shoots and fruited stumps if you have any. If happy, pineapples may grow and produce for five to ten years.

Weed, Pest, and Disease Control

The main pests are white scale and mealybugs, controlled by sprays of soft soap or commercial predators.

COMPANION PLANTING

A secret of success is apparently to grow them with a light top dressing of banana skins.

HARVESTING AND STORING, CULINARY USES

Picked underripe and kept cool, they can be stored for several weeks. They make tasty jam, delicious juice and are best-known canned. Although a fruit, they add sweetness and texture to many savory dishes, from Chinese to curries, and can even be fried with ham.

Pineapple-baked Ham
Serves 4

1 canned ham
1 large pineapple
Garlic (optional)

Carefully empty the meat from the can in one piece. Extract the pineapple from its skin, first slicing off the top shoulder. Leave the skin intact. (Slice and chill the pineapple flesh for dessert, cutting out the tough central core.) Insert the ham in the hole created, pin the shoulder back on to seal, and bake for at least an hour in a preheated oven at 400°F. (Garlic lovers may rub the ham over before insertion.) To serve, turn the pineapple on its side to cut circles of ham with a pineapple rind. Serve with pureed sweet corn and baked sweet potatoes.

Musa species from the family *Musaceae*

BANANAS

Tree/herbaceous plant, 10–30 ft. and nearly as wide. Life span: perpetual as vegetative clones but sterile. Fruits: up to 12 in., green to yellow or red. Value: nutritious and rich in starch.

Banana plants form herbaceous stools of shoots like small trees. Each enormous shoot unfurls sheaths of gigantic, oblong leaves up to fifteen feet long. A mature shoot disgorges one flower stalk, which hangs down under its mighty bunch of many "combs" or "hands" of bananas. The hands point upward, sheltered by succulent, purple bracts the size of plates, along the length of the stalk, and a mass of male flowers adorns the end. One bunch can hold about a dozen combs, each with over a dozen fingers. Bananas are the most productive food crop, giving about forty times the yield of potatoes. The fruits are green, ripening yellow, sweet, notoriously shaped, and unforgettably scented.

The Ancient Egyptians had the culinary Abyssinian banana *(Musa ensete),* but early travelers from Europe soon discovered sweeter, more edible bananas in most tropical and semitropical regions. The hardiest, the smaller Chinese banana was brought from the East Indies for cultivation in the Canary Islands by 1516—and, it has been suggested, was introduced to the Americas from there, but evidence of indigenous bananas discounts this. Most cultivated bananas are probably descendants of *M. sapientum, M. acuminata,* and *M. balbisiana,* wild bananas thought to come from eastern Asia and Indo-Malaysia. *Musa maculata* and *M. rosacea* descendants are popular in parts of Asia, and worldwide there exist many other species. In prehistoric cultivation, seed-bearing species were replaced by selected hybrids with big, seedless fruits propagated vegetatively. These superior sorts multiplied and by the nineteenth century there were countless local varieties of bananas in most hot countries. Many of these have now been lost and replaced by a few high-yielding commercial cultivars.

VARIETIES

Common cultivars are **'Robusta,' 'Lacatan,'** and **'Gros Michel,'** the latter pair being old varieties that survived the Panama disease that destroyed many. However, they are tall and need hot, moist conditions such as those of Jamaica, where **'Gros Michel'** was introduced in 1836. The **'Chinese Banana'** *(M. cavendishii),* also known as **'Dwarf'** or **'Canary Island Banana,'** is hardier, smaller, and particularly tasty, with shorter, delicate fruits, making it widely grown for domestic use, and well suited for greenhouse culture. A new, medium-sized and more productive hybrid, **'William,'** is taking over commercially.

Plantains are separate varieties, possibly descendants of *M. paradisiaca,* larger and slightly horn-shaped. Plantains are most often used for cooking, not dessert purposes; thus cooking bananas are sometimes referred to as plantains.

The author's Abyssinian banana, which thrives outside in Norfolk, England

CULTIVATION

In warm enough climates bananas need a rich, quite heavy, deep, well-drained soil with copious moisture. Freedom from strong winds is also essential. The smallest varieties are usually planted about 10 ft. apart; the larger proportionately more.

Growing under Glass and in Containers
In cooler climates the Canary/Chinese/Cavendish is best, as it is very compact and fruits at less than 10 ft. high. Keep the temperature above 65°F in winter and under 85°F in summer. Potted plants can go out for summer.

Maintenance
Spring Pot up or top dress; thin and root suckers.
Summer Top dress and thin suckers.
Fall Cut fruits, remove old shoots, and thin suckers.
Winter Keep warm.

Banana trees need large pots, so growing them in the ground under cover is best.

Propagation
Some ornamental and inferior varieties grow from seed. The best edible plants are bits of rhizome with a bud or sterile hybrids, propagated by suckers. Viable buds will resemble enormous, sprouting bulbs. They root easily in a gritty compost over heat in a moist atmosphere.

HARVESTING AND STORING, CULINARY USES

Bananas are best matured off the tree and kept in a warm room. Most are at their best when yellow. They can be dried, made into flour, or fermented to produce a sweet liqueur.

In hot countries, bananas are a staple food, being used as a vegetable and a source of flour, as well as a fruit.

Banana Custard Pie
Serves 4

6 oz. vanilla wafers
1/3 cup butter
1 tablespoon strawberry jam
1 1/4 cups milk
1 tablespoon honey
1 tablespoon cornstarch
Dash of vanilla extract
3 or 4 bananas, sliced and chilled
Grated nutmeg

Crush the wafers and mix with most of the butter. Press into a pie dish and freeze. Spread the frozen surface with the remaining butter and the jam, and refreeze. Heat the milk and honey, mix the corn starch with a drop of water and the vanilla, then pour the hot milk onto the flour mixture. Return to the heat, stirring continuously, until thickened, then allow to cool. Put chilled banana slices into the cooled custard, mix together, and pour into the cookie shell. Top with nutmeg and chill until ready to serve.

Pruning and Training
Bananas fruit continuously if growing happily. A stem will flower and fruit in about a year and a half. Only one main shoot and a replacement are allowed; all others should be removed, and once the main shoot has fruited it is cut out. The clump or stool may live as long as a human being, but is replaced commercially every dozen years or so.

Weed, Pest, and Disease Control
No major problems for private gardeners.

The medium-sized hybrid 'William' is becoming popular.

OTHER USES

Often used in beauty preparations and shampoos (below). The foliage will provide good animal fodder.

Phoenix dactylifera from the family Arecaceae

DATE PALMS

Tree 80 x 20 ft. Life span: as long as a human being.
Fruits: just under 1 x 2 in., blue, brown, or yellow.
Value: rich in vitamins A, B$_1$, and B$_2$, and some B$_3$.

Date palms are tall trees with ferny leaves, the russet dead leaf bases protecting the trunk. Separate male and female plants are required for fruiting, which is prolific. Each tree annually bears several bunches of three or four dozen strings, each string carrying two or three dozen d the total weight being up to 150 pounds.

Dates have been cultivated in the Middle East for at least 4,000 years and all wild forms have disappeared. They have always been one of the staple foods of the Arab peoples, much of whose lives were centered around the oases where the palms were found.

Fresh dates

A date palm laden with unripe fruit

donkeys and camels, **'Farayah'** a choice, long blue.

CULTIVATION

One of the few crops to revel in very hot, dry places, date palms still need irrigation to fruit well but can use brackish water. Date palms can be grown only in Zones 9 and 10.

Growing under Glass and in Containers
They are well suited to indoor life, though they may find it too humid with other fruits, and they get too big and need too much heat to produce good fruit. Date palms are easy to distribute as the small rootballs will transplant with ease.

Ornamental and Wildlife Value
Choice ornamentals, they are popular in hotter climates both with people and wildlife. Birds love the fruits.

Propagation
For choice fruit, offshoots or suckers have to be potted up; however, for ornamental use, seedlings are easily germinated but grow slowly. Large trees are easily transplanted with small root balls. One male palm will be needed to every fifty females.

OTHER USES

The palms have their sap extracted for sugar or fermenting. They may also be used as lumber.

VARIETIES

Numerous local varieties exist. **'Deglet Noor'** is from North Africa and is the world's most popular variety. **'Saidi'** is the common date, **'Fardh'** is favorite in Arabia, **'Weddee'** a feed date for

HARVESTING AND STORING, CULINARY USES

Soft dates are partly dried, pitted, and pressed into cakes, then exported all over the world. Semisoft dates are those we see at Christmas. Dry dates are hard and ground to a flour, commonly found only in Arab markets. Dates can be used in cakes, cookies, and candies and with curries and savory dishes. They are also made into wine.

Stuffed Date Chocolates

28 dates
1 8-oz. package real
marzipan
5 squares of dark
chocolate
Powdered sugar

Pit the dates and stuff with marzipan. Dip in melted chocolate and cool on a tray dusted with powdered sugar.

Monstera deliciosa from the family *Araceae*

CERIMANS
SWISS CHEESE PLANTS

Herbaceous vine, may ramble or climb to over 40 ft.
Life span: appears perpetual and invulnerable.
Fruits: about 1 x 9 in., green. Value: some vitamin C.

Cerimans are among the most common and enduring house plants, somehow surviving hostile conditions in dark, dry rooms the world over. The leaves are dark green, large, scalloped, and curiously, have natural holes in them, presumably to let tropical winds pass with less damage. In its native habitat it is an epiphytic climber, rambling on the forest floor and climbing up vigorously, clothing the trees and throwing down masses of aerial roots. It is a close relation of the arum lily and the flowers are similar. The long, conelike spadix fruit, or ceriman, is green, cylindrical, and leathery with tiny, hexagonal plates for skin. The flesh is sweet and richly flavored, resembling a cross between a pineapple and banana. It is absolutely delicious if completely ripe, otherwise the texture is spoiled by spicules and it is inedible.

Cerimans are native to Central America, but have been spread worldwide for their attractive leaves and amazing durability. This fruit was discovered in Mexico and was originally known as the Mexican breadfruit. It became known as the "shingle plant" and classed as *Philodendron pertusum*, then *Monstera acuminata*, and now as *M. deliciosa*, but is known worldwide as the Swiss cheese plant. In 1874 the fruits were exhibited before the Massachusetts Horticultural Society. The fruits are as delicious as the name suggests, but the spicules make unripe fruits unpleasant, so they have never become widely popular.

A distinctive Swiss cheese plant

CULTIVATION

One of the most enduring and robust plants discovered, but will fruit only if given warmth and moisture. It does not need as much bright light as most tropical fruits, and has been grown successfully under glass in most countries.

Ornamental and Wildlife Value
Superb ornamental value almost anywhere frost-free.

Growing under Glass and in Containers
Ideally suited to almost any treatment. For fruits, give better conditions, copious watering, and misting.

Propagation, Pruning, and Training
They can be air-layered or easily rooted from cuttings. They are happiest climbing up a stout, rough-barked tree or log, or wired on a wall.

HARVESTING AND STORING, CULINARY USES

When the fruit is ripe the inside appears to swell and the leathery skin plates loosen up; they can be easec off like tiny buttons. Then the flesh can be eaten off the stem. Try it with care— the tiny spicules of calcium oxalate irritate some people's throats but appear harmless. Do not worry about the spicules if you eat only ripe fruits—many people regularly enjoy them Cerimans are used only as dessert fruit and are widely popular in native markets.

Fruit of the Swiss cheese plant

OTHER USES

The vines make a good, quick-growing screen in warm regions.

Persea americana from the family *Lauraceae*

AVOCADO PEAR

Evergreen tree or shrub. Tender. Value: very rich in vitamin E, average fat content, high in monounsaturated fatty acids.

This subtropical tree from Central America was originally introduced to Europe by the conquistadores and has since been planted in many parts of the world. Its anglicized name is a corruption of the Aztec word *ahuacatl*, which was used to describe both its fruit and the testicle. There are three main races: Guatemalan fruits are large with a warty skin, Mexican ones are small, and large, smooth-skinned types come from the West Indies. All have been hybridized, producing hundreds of cultivars suitable for Mediterranean to tropical climates.

VARIETIES

'Ettinger' (Mexican x Guatemalan) produces oblong fruit with bright green, shiny skin. 'Fuerte' (Mexican x Guatemalan) is the most common cultivar, producing large fruit with green, textured skin. 'Hass' (Guatemalan) is self-fertile, the skin dark purple when it is mature.

CULTIVATION

Avocados flourish in shelter and sunshine.

The ideal soil is a slightly acid, moisture-retentive, free-draining loam. Improve sandy or clay soils by adding organic matter.

Temperatures should be between 68–82°F with humidity greater than 60 percent all year round. Some can withstand temperatures down to 48–58°F. Allow 20 ft. between the trees and the rows. In exposed areas, plant windbreaks to prevent damage.

During the growing season, apply 3 lb. 4 oz. to 4 lb. 6 oz. of general fertilizer in 2 or 3 doses. Mulch around the base to suppress weeds. Water during times of drought. until trees are established.

Shape young trees to ensure a balanced crown. Remove diseased, damaged, or crossing branches after fruiting. They withstand hard pruning. Plant several cultivars with overlapping or simultaneous flowering periods to produce fruit.

Growing under Glass

Grow in a greenhouse, maintaining moderate temperatures and humidity according to the origin of the cultivar.

Flowers and fruit are rarely produced in cool temperate zones due to low light intensity and reduced daylight hours.

Growing in Containers

Repot young plants as the compost becomes congested with roots. Every 2–3 years repot established plants into a pot one size larger, using a loam-based potting mix with moderate fertilizer levels. Top-dress in the intervening years by removing and replacing the top 2–3 in. of potting mix in spring. Apply a general fertilizer every 2–3 weeks when plants are actively growing.

Water as the compost surface dries out. Reduce watering in winter and do not feed.

In spring, prune side branches to encourage bushy growth. Containerized plants can be placed outdoors in summer in a warm, sheltered position when there is no danger of frost. During winter, they need a light, cool position with temperatures no lower than 60°F.

A cluster of fruits in South Africa, ripe and ready for harvest and the increasingly demanding export market

An avocado orchard in Transvaal, South Africa

Maintenance
Spring Repot containerized plants.
Summer Feed, harvest, and water as necessary.
Fall Bring containerized plants indoors in cool temperate zones.
Winter Reduce watering and stop feeding avocados grown under glass.

Propagation
Avocados are propagated from seed, although the seedling may not come true (more reliable results are obtained professionally by grafting named cultivars onto disease-resistant rootstocks). Choose healthy seeds, cut ½ in. from the pointed end, and dip the wound in fungicide. Sow in a 6-in. pot of moist potting mix, with the cut end just above the surface. Germinate in a greenhouse or propagator, or place the pot in a clear plastic bag, lightly knot the end, and put in a bright position away from direct sunshine at 70–80°F.

When the fourth leaf appears, remove the bag and leave the plant for 2 weeks to acclimatize. Do not force the stone from the roots; allow it to rot away. Repot as the potting mix becomes congested with roots; when they outgrow 12–16 in. pots, plant out into their final positions.

Harvesting and Storing
Seed-raised trees fruit after 5 to 7 years; grafted plants take 3 to 5 years.

Remove fruit carefully using hand pruners. Discard damaged fruit. They are ready for eating if slightly soft when pressed. If unripe, store for a few days.

PESTS AND DISEASES

Use resistant rootstocks against avocado root rot. Those grown indoors may be attacked by whitefly: use sticky traps, the predator *Encarsia formosa*, or soft soap. Control red spider mite by maintaining humidity, and

Avocados for sale, Costa Rica

remove mealybugs by dabbing them with a paintbrush dipped in denatured alcohol.

OTHER USES

The pulp of avocados makes an ideal natural ingredient for face masks and for skin moisturizers.

CULINARY USES

Coat cut surfaces with lemon or lime juice to prevent discoloration. Avocado is delicious simply with olive oil and vinaigrette. The flavor also blends well with shrimp, crabmeat, and other seafood, or grapefruit and pineapple. Try it with bacon in a sandwich, or made into a fine salad. To make guacamole, bake and then mash avocados with chilies, onions, and garlic and serve with tortillas.

Cold Avocado Soup
Serves 2

This is a welcome alternative to vichyssoise.

Puree 2 avocados, peeled and pitted, with 1 cup of crème fraîche or low-fat yogurt combined with heavy cream. Gently heat 3½ cups chicken stock and stir in the avocado puree, gently heating: do not boil.

Season with salt and freshly ground black pepper, and a judicious squeeze or two of lemon juice to accent the flavor. Decorate with a dollop of yogurt and sprinkle with fresh chives.

Avocado Mousse
Serves 4

Oded Schwartz gives this unusual dessert recipe in Reader's Digest's *Fast and Fresh Cooking*.

1 cup heavy cream
1 tablespoon sugar
1 teaspoon orange-blossom water
2 avocados
2 tablespoons runny honey
3 tablespoons Grand Marnier
Grated rind and juice of 2 limes
Mint, to garnish

Whip the cream until stiff and add the sugar and orange-blossom water. Chill well. In the meantime, scoop the pulp from the avocado shells and puree with all the remaining ingredients except for half of the lime rind.

Transfer to a mixing bowl and stir in the whipped cream. Serve in individual glass bowls and decorate with the remaining rind and a sprig of mint.

Nutrition
Avocados are high in protein, vitamin B complex, and vitamin E, and have low carbohydrate levels and no cholesterol.

Avocado Mousse

Cyphomandra betacea (syn. *C. crassicaulis*) from the family *Solanaceae*

TAMARILLO

***(Tree Tomato) Woody perennial grown as annual shrub or tree. Half hardy.
Value: rich in beta carotene, vitamin E; moderate levels of vitamin C.***

This fast-growing small evergreen tree has large, heart-shaped leaves, clusters of caramel-scented white flowers, and attractive fruits. The fruits are also delicious, with a distinctive, intense flavor. Native to the foothills of the Andes in Peru and surrounding countries, it was introduced to several tropical and subtropical countries as a garden fruit tree during the nineteenth century. In the 1960s commercial production began in New Zealand, but already in the 1920s they had developed cultivars with large, attractive, crimson fruits and given them the name "tamarillo."

VARIETIES

Most so-called cultivars have arisen as a result of grower selection. As plants are easy to grow from seed, any with different characteristics are often named. Because of this they do not have official cultivar status. Yellow-skinned types do not have dark pigment around the seeds and the flesh retains its yellow pigmentation after cooking. **'Amberlea Gold,'** a medium-sized, yellow-skinned variety, is moderately tasty. **'Bold Gold'** is a large yellow variety of inferior taste.

'Goldmine,' with golden skin sometimes blushed red, is an exceptionally sweet type. **'Oratia Red'** has large fruit with deep red skin enclosing moderately sweet, well-flavored flesh. **'Red Beau'** is oval-shaped, with red skin and an excellent flavor. **'Red Delight'** is a large, round red-skinned type with moderate flavor.

CULTIVATION

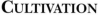

Tamarillo is an excellent fruit tree for small gardens in warm temperate zones. It can also be grown under glass in colder areas.

Tamarillo flourishes in moisture-retentive, free-draining soil, and benefits from mulching in spring. Water during dry periods.

Growing under Glass
Tamarillos need bright, frost-free conditions in a greenhouse, or can be overwintered by the window in a cool room at 45°F.

Indoors, restrict ventilation and maintain high temperatures and humidity; tapping fully open flowers ensures pollination. By late summer, first-year plants are about 3 ft. and should produce 5 to 8 fruits. At the same time remove cuttings to provide the following season's plants. During the growing season

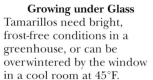
A well-grown tamarillo can crop very heavily. Mature fruit on tree in New Zealand

feed every 2 weeks with a high-potash fertilizer.

To keep the plants for the next season, cut the main branches back after harvest to a single bud. Flowers are carried on the current season's growth, so maintaining a large, woody framework of branches is unnecessary. Alternatively, repropagate annually from cuttings.

In spring, prune larger trees back to a bud to keep them within their allotted space, and remove and replace the top 3 in. of potting mix.

Reduce watering in cool winter conditions and keep the soil slightly moist.

Growing in Containers
Tamarillos are ideal for growing in containers. They grow rapidly, so repot regularly, using loam-based potting mix with moderate fertilizer levels. If you intend to keep the plant for several years, add a third part of perlite or sharp sand to the mix to improve drainage. Stand plants outdoors in a sheltered, sunny position once the danger of frost has past. If leaf scorch occurs in direct sunshine, move the plant into dappled shade.

Outdoors, the self-fertile flowers are pollinated by bees. Bring plants indoors before the first frosts and place in a sunny position for the fruits to ripen.

Maintenance
Spring Repot before the compost becomes congested with roots.
Summer Water and feed; place containerized plants outdoors.
Fall Bring indoors before the first frosts.
Winter Water sparingly.

Propagation
Take stem cuttings in late summer, each with 2 leaves, from the current season's growth; trim below the bottom leaf joint, dip in rooting compound, and insert in a gritty, open

Tree tomatoes are a common feature in gardens in parts of South America. This one grows in Columbia.

potting mix. Place in a propagator or bright, warm position away from direct sunlight at 68°F. Cuttings root after 3 to 4 weeks; pot them individually using a loam-based potting mix with added perlite or sharp sand to improve drainage. Overwinter under glass or indoors in a light, frost-free position at 45°F. Pinch out the growing point early to encourage development of 4–6 side branches from the base.

Weed, Pest, and Disease Control
Tamarillos are very prone to **whitefly**. Use the predatory wasp *Encarsia formosa*, sticky traps, or spray with soft soap.

Control **aphids** with soft soap and red spider mite by maintaining humidity.

Harvesting and Storing
In fall, fruits continue to swell and are ready for picking when brightly colored, but may not be fully ripe until midwinter. Pick them at the point where the stem naturally breaks, about 2 in. above the fruit. The crop ripens over several weeks.

Companion Planting
Plant French marigolds *(Tagetes)* alongside to deter whitefly.

CULINARY USES

Tamarillos are ripe when soft to the touch. Blanch in boiling water for 3 minutes, then plunge into cold water. The skins peel off easily if you start at the stem. Do not eat without removing the skin—it is very bitter.

Use them in salads. Pureed, they make a cheesecake topping or can be used in pies. Eat with chicken, lettuce, cottage cheese, cold meat, and fish. Add to pasta or make jams. They can be kept in a refrigerator for about 2 weeks or can be cooked and frozen.

Tamarillo Chutney
Makes about 2 jars

Serve this garlic-flavored, deep purple, hot relish with fried foods, roast duck or pork, or ham. Its lush texture and intense taste make a little go a long way.

4 large tamarillos, peeled
¼ cup sugar
½ teaspoon cinnamon
⅛ teaspoon cloves
1 tablespoon peanut or corn oil
4 large garlic cloves, chopped
2 small jalapeño or serrano chili peppers, seeded and minced
2 medium onions, roughly diced

1 large tart apple, peeled and diced
½ teaspoon salt
2 tablespoons cider vinegar

Slice the tamarillos lengthwise, then across into half-rounds. Combine them in a bowl together with the sugar, cinnamon, and cloves.

Heat the oil in a flameproof casserole, then stir in the garlic, chilies, and onions and cook over a low heat for about five minutes. Add the apple, tamarillo mixture, salt, and vinegar and stir over a moderate heat for about 15 minutes. The mixture should thicken slightly and the apples should be tender.

Cool, then cover and chill. This keeps for up to two weeks and freezes well.

Banana and Tamarillo Puree
Makes about 2 jars

This is a simple, all-purpose recipe, which can be used in a variety of ways: spooned over fresh or cooked fruit, vanilla pudding, or rice pudding; spread in sandwiches or between cake layers; layered with whipped cream or crème fraîche as a *parfait*; or blended with light cream cheese for a delicious brunch.

2 large tamarillos, peeled
6 tablespoons lemon juice
2 medium bananas, peeled and sliced
⅓ cup sugar

Slice the tamarillos, then toss them in a bowl with the lemon juice, bananas, and sugar. Allow to stand for 30 minutes. Puree the fruit in a food processor or blender until smooth. Scrape the mixture into a small pot, then bring to a boil, stirring. Cool, then cover and refrigerate.

Mangifera indica from the family *Anacardiaceae*

MANGO

Tree, variable size. Life span: as long as a human being. Fruits: variable in size, flat ovoids, green/yellow or red. Value: rich in vitamins A, B, and C.

Medium to large trees, with luxuriant masses of narrow leaves, these carry fruits that weigh anything from a few ounces to a couple of pounds. They have an inedible, tough skin, and an enormous, flat pit to which the fibrous flesh adheres.

Mangoes are native to India and exist there in countless variety. Doubtless early Europeans came across them, but they were first recorded by a Friar Jordanus in about 1300. Mangoes have now spread to most hot regions, including Florida.

VARIETIES

India's favorite varieties are **'Alphonso'** and **'Mulgoa.'** The West Indies prefer **'Bombay'** (**'Peters'**) and **'Julie.'** American varieties include anthracnose-resistant **'Keitt'**; the Hawaiian standard, **'Haden'**; small, purple-skinned **'Manzanillo'**; and the fall-ripening **'Brooks Late.'**

CULTIVATION

Mangoes want a hot, dryish climate and deep, well-drained, rich soils. Excessive rain spoils pollination. They want exceptionally deep and wide planting holes dug about 30 ft. apart. Mangoes will thrive only in Zone 10.

A well-developed mango tree in the sunshine of St. Lucia

Growing under Glass and in Containers

As they are large when fruitful, the greenhouse would have to be big. They may be grown in pots for ornamental use but fruiting success seems unlikely.

Propagation

Mangoes raised from seed are often polyembryonic, giving several seedlings. Some are near-clones of the original, and some produce poor fruits with stringy texture and a turpentine taint! The best varieties are grafted or layered and will bear in about four years.

HARVESTING AND STORING, CULINARY USES

Mangoes soften and turn yellow, red, or purple as they ripen. Picked unripe, they travel well and are fine for culinary use. They are messy to eat raw! They are widely used for jams, pickles, chutneys, and preserves.

Mango Chutney
Makes about 2 lb.

2 lb. green mangoes
$^3/_4$ cup salt
2 cups vinegar

12 garlic cloves, peeled and
   chopped
$^1/_2$ cup sultanas
$^1/_4$ cup almonds, blanched
   and chopped
$^1/_4$ cup dates, chopped
3-in. piece fresh ginger, chopped
2 teaspoons hot chili powder
$2^1/_4$ cups brown sugar

Peel, pit, and chop the mangoes, sprinkle with salt, and keep cool overnight. Rinse and drain thoroughly. Mix all the ingredients except the sugar and simmer for several hours till soft. Add the sugar, bring to a boil, and bottle in clean sterilized jars. Store for six months before use.

Pruning and Training

Remedial pruning of thin and poor growth is necessary once a head has formed, plus root pruning if the tree persists with strong, unfruitful growth.

OTHER USES

The seeds have been boiled and eaten in famines. The wood is poor but used for packaging crates and firewood.

Carica from the family *Caricaceae*

PAPAYAS
PAWPAWS

Herbaceous, up to 20 ft. Life span: very short.
Fruits: up to 12 x 6 in.
Value: rich in papain.

Papayas (also known as pawpaws) are small herbaceous "trees" that resemble palms as they are unbranched with ornate, acanthus-like foliage clustered on top and up to fifty green "melons" underneath. There are male, female, and hermaphrodite plants. The fruits uncannily resemble melons, turning yellow-orange as they ripen. The flesh is usually pink with a central hole full of small round seeds and can weigh up to five pounds.

Although it is indigenous to Central America, the papaya has rapidly spread to every warm country. Seeds were sent to Nepal as early as 1626 from the East Indies.

VARIETIES

'Solo' is a commercial dwarf, but most papayas are local varieties selected from seed, which vary considerably. Grow them from fruit you like. *Carica candamarcensis*, or the **Mountain Papaya**, is hardier with coarser leaves and smaller fruit, which have blunt ridges and an applelike aroma. They are too acid to eat raw, but good cooked or as jam.

CULTIVATION

Papayas prefer deep, humus-rich soil, and should be planted about 10 ft. apart. They need support while young. You should eliminate most males and replace the whole lot every

A papaya tree in fruit

five years. Papayas are successful only in Zone 10.

Growing under Glass and in Containers
They are practical for tall, heated greenhouses and are highly ornamental, so they are worth growing as pot plants, but they do not fruit well easily.

Ornamental and Wildlife Value
Their foliage is very attractive and they're so easy to grow.

Propagation
Variable from seed; usually grown by sowing several to a hole and eliminating the poorest seedlings. (Only one male is needed to fifty females, but in fact they can only be differentiated when flowering.) Fruiting occurs within a year.

CULINARY USES

Papayas are in season all year, and unripe ones keep for many days. Eaten as dessert or cooked as a side dish, papaya is delicious, especially the first time. However, most important, the fruit and leaves contain papain, which tenderizes meats that are cooked with them.

Papaya
Breakfast Juice
Serves 2

1 ripe papaya
Juice of 1 small lime
Honey or sugar to taste

Scoop out the flesh and sieve out the seeds of the papaya. Add lime juice and sweetener and puree. Serve immediately in frosted glasses with sugared rims.

OTHER USES

Papain is used medicinally and for chewing gum.

Psidium and *Acca* from the family *Myrtaceae*

GUAVAS

& FEIJOAS

Tree 10–30 ft. Life span: short.
Fruits: 2–3 in., yellow or red.
Value: very rich in vitamin C.

Guavas are small trees or spreading shrubs with leathery leaves. The bark peels off the smooth, ruddy branches in flakes. The fruits are round, ripening from green to yellow or red, full of acid yellow or red pulp, and many hard, round seeds.

Native to tropical America, guavas soon became popular the world over and were grown in orangeries.

Feijoa leaves

VARIETIES

There are many species of guavas. *P. guajava* is the commonest, with yellow fruits. Many varieties of it are pyriferum, bearing somewhat pear-like fruits, which are a little acid and better for cooking. Some varieties are pomiferum, bearing apple-shaped fruits, which are thought better. For dessert, gourmets choose *P. cattleianum*, the **Strawberry Guava**. This has a reddish-purple, plum-size, sweeter fruit on a hardier, shaggy-barked tree. *P. araca*, *P. montanum*, *P. pigmeum*, and *P. polycarpon* are all reputed to be more delicious still. *Acca sellowiana* (Feijoa) is so similar as to be a variety of guava. It is smaller, with crimson and white flowers and fragrant fruit. It is almost hardy and not self-fertile, and grown in California. Feijoas are rich sources of iodine.

The pineapple guava flower

Guava fruit on the tree

CULTIVATION

Any good soil and a sunny site is all they require. In a warm climate they are normally planted at about 15 ft. apart. Tropical guavas thrive in Zone 10; strawberry guava in Zones 9 and 10. Feijoas are more tolerant of cold and will grow in Zones 8 through 10, and possibly in Zone 7.

Growing under Glass and in Containers
Feijoa is most reliable, the **Strawberry Guava** next, but all guavas are easily grown under glass and/or confined in pots. They can be put outdoors during the warmer months of the year.

Propagation, Pruning, and Training
Propagate by seeds for the species but also by suckers, layers, or grafts for better varieties. Some plants occasionally produce seedless fruits: note these and propagate from them. Nip out top shoots to promote bushiness, otherwise prune only remedially.

OTHER USES

The heavy wood is used for agricultural implements. The leaves and bark are a native cure for dysentery.

Sliced, ripe guava fruit

HARVESTING AND STORING, CULINARY USES

Guavas are best fresh off the tree, or picked early, as they soften. They are good for dessert, and cooked as tarts, jam, and of course the jelly.

Guava Jelly
Makes about 4 lb.

2 lb. guavas, washed and chopped
Juice of 1 large lemon
Approx. 4 cups sugar

Simmer the guavas for two hours with a little water. Strain, measure, and bring back to a boil. Add the same volume of sugar and the lemon juice, bring back to a boil, pour into warmed sterilized jars, and seal.

Artocarpus from the family *Moraceae*

BREADFRUIT
AND JACKFRUITS

Trees up to 90 ft. Life span: medium.
Fruits: up to 8 in. diameter, leathery balls. Value: mostly starch.

Both breadfruit and jackfruit are attractive, tall trees with large, deeply incised leaves. From the branch ends hang green, round to ovoid fruits, which have a thin, warty rind and are white and starchy within. Some have about 200 fleshy edible seeds or more, some have none.

Breadfruits are native to the Pacific and East Indies; jackfruits come from the Asian mainland and Indian subcontinent. They were first noted in the voyages of the sixteenth century and soon taken to other hot regions, but never proved really popular. Breadfruit plants being taken to the West Indies played a part in the famous 1787 mutiny on the *Bounty*. When the water supply ran low, water was given to the valuable cargo before the crew.

VARIETIES

Artocarpus communis (incisa or altilis) is the **Breadfruit** proper, bearing a remarkable resemblance, once cooked, to bread. From the West Indies comes the bread-nut tree, which, when cooked, is claimed to rival a new loaf in both taste and texture. *A. integrifolia (heterophylla)* is the **Jackfruit** or **Jakfruit**. The fruit is much bigger, weighing up to 65 lb. These largest of fruits strangely spring from

Breadfruit and leaves

older branches and directly from the trunk. When ripe they have a strong odor of very ripe melon. *A. odoratissima*, the **Johore Jack,** is smaller and esteemed for its sweetness and flavor.

CULTIVATION

Any reasonable soil and site in a hot and moist climate. They grow in Zone 10.

Growing under Glass and in Containers
The size of the fruiting tree makes it impractical to grow these in pots or under glass except for ornamental value.

Propagation, Pruning, and Training
They can be propagated by seed, but the best varieties come only by root suckers or by layering. Little pruning is required except remedial.

Harvesting and Storing
Breadfruit is eaten fresh after cooking, but used to be stored in pits where the pulp was fermented to make a nauseous soft "cheese," which would keep for several years.

COMPANION PLANTING

The jackfruit tree is often used to support **pepper** (*Piper nigrum*) and as a shade tree for coffee plantations.

CULINARY USES

Breadfruit are usually eaten roasted, boiled, or fried as a vegetable. The edible seeds are often preferred, when they occur. Jackfruit are eaten in the same way and have a stronger flavor. Breadfruits can be dried and ground to a flour.

Baked Breadfruit
Serves 2

Bake a breadfruit in a preheated oven at 375°F, until you can push a knife through it easily. Extract the pulp, seeds and all, and serve with curry or a savory sauce.

OTHER USES

Jackfruit wood is like mahogany, valuable and useful. A yellow dye for clothing is extracted from the wood in India and the east. Breadfruit wood is light and used for box manufacture, and in Hawaii for surfboards.

Breadfruit leaf

Durio zibethinus from family *Malvaceae/Bombacaceae*

DURIANS
CIVET FRUIT

*Tree 100 ft. Life span: fairly long. Fruits: about
10 x 8 in., ovoid, green to yellow.
Value: a little protein, a little fat; one-quarter
to one-third is fat and starch.*

This is an infamous fruit, banned from airlines and loathed by most people on first acquaintance. It has an aroma similar to that of an overripe Gorgonzola cheese in a warm room. The flavor was long ago described as "French custard passed through a sewer pipe." The texture is like that of blancmange or custard, and the sweet flavor delicious and addictive. Once bravely tasted, the durian is unforgettable and "the sensation is worth a voyage to the East."

The trees are very large and upright with leaves not dissimilar to those of a peach. The fruits are round to ovoid, very large, weighing up to ten pounds, green initially, yellowing as they ripen, with a long stalk. They are covered in short, sharp spikes and resemble some brutal medieval weapon. The pulp is white with up to a dozen big seeds.

Durians come originally from Malaysia and spread to Southeast Asia in prehistoric times. Widely grown all over the region, they have never managed to become more than a curiosity elsewhere.

VARIETIES

Local varieties exist with variation in size, shape, and flavor, but no widespread commercial clones are available.

Durian fruits taste delicious, but smell revolting!

CULTIVATION

The large trees need a deep, heavy soil to secure them, but they are not too difficult to please. They will grow in Zone 10.

Propagation, Pruning, and Training
Seeds, if fresh, germinate in about a week and come nearly true. Only remedial pruning work is necessary.

Growing under Glass and in Containers
Their size and their need for heat and moisture make them difficult. They may make good pot specimens if fresh seed can be obtained.

Ornamental and Wildlife Value
Attractive trees in their native climate.

OTHER USES

Durians help you get a train compartment all to yourself. They are also reputed to be an aphrodisiac.

The Durian tree has a truly majestic stature.

HARVESTING AND STORING, CULINARY USES

Durians must be eaten fresh and they quickly spoil due to a chemical change (the aroma gets worse!). They are best eaten raw but may be made into ice cream or jam, or juiced and drunk with coconut milk. The large, fleshy seeds are boiled or roasted and eaten as nuts.

Durian Delight
Serves 6

1 cup unsweetened
   durian puree
1/2 cup honey
1 1/4 cups yogurt
1 cup heavy cream
Dash of vanilla extract

Mix the ingredients and beat till smooth. Partially freeze, beat again, and repeat two or three times before freezing firm. Keep well sealed until just before eating!

Annona from the family *Annonaceae*

CHERIMOYAS

CUSTARD APPLES AND SOURSOPS

Tree up to 20 ft. Life span: short.
Fruits: variable in size, green, and scaly.

A family of small trees, known as custard apples or soursops, from the flavor and texture of the better fruits. Many have aromatic leaves and/or fragrant flowers. Despite the varying appearance of each species, the common names are often swapped or confused in different countries. The flesh is usually white, sweet, and acid, with up to thirty black seeds embedded in it and covered with a thin rind, which breaks off like scales when ripe.

Natives of the Americas, they are most popular there but have spread to other tropical and warm zones. They are grown in Madeira and the Canary Islands for the European trade.

OTHER USES

Corossol tea, shown above, was traditionally made from the leaves of *A. muricata*.

HARVESTING AND STORING, CULINARY USES

Picked underripe they keep for up to a week or so. They are usually eaten raw or used to flavor drinks and ices.

VARIETIES

Anona squamosa is the true **'Custard Apple'** or **'Sweet Sop'** and is most common in the West Indies. *A. cherimolia* is the **'Cherimoya.'** This is deciduous and more hardy, growing at high elevations in the hotter areas. The leaves are deliciously scented and downy underneath; the flowers are fragrant, fleshy, green and yellow; the fruit resembles a small artichoke with a banana/pineapple flavor. *A. muricata*, or **'Soursop,'** is evergreen with leaves that smell of black currants and large (up to 8 lb.) green fruits with soft spines in ridges and a sourer taste. *A. reticulata* is the **'Bullock's Heart,'** so-called because of its ruddy color. It has a firm, sweet, yellow pulp. Numerous other species are grown all over the Americas.

CULTIVATION

They will thrive in poor soils but give better crops with better treatment and prefer dryish, hilly conditions. They will grow in Zone 10.

Growing under Glass and in Containers

The cherimoya is worth growing even if it never fruits and custard apples are probably worth trying. Soursops may not crop, but all are good value as pot specimens.

A cherimoya tree will grow well in a pot.

A ripening cherimoya fruit

Propagation, Pruning, and Training

They grow from seed, but best varieties are budded. Only remedial pruning and nipping out is required.

Soursop Sorbet
Serves 6

2 cups sugar
1 large ripe soursop
3-in. piece crystallized ginger

Dissolve the sugar in 2 cups of boiling water and chill. Squeeze the juice from the soursop pulp and strain. To each cupful add half a cup of sugar syrup. Partly freeze, beat, and refreeze. Repeat twice. After the final beating, mix in the chopped ginger.

Averrhoa carambola from the family *Oxalidaceae*

CARAMBOLAS

Tree up to 35 ft. Life span: medium. Fruits: up to 2 x 6 in. Cylindrical, star-shaped in cross section, yellow. Value: sugar, some oxalic acid.

Averrhoas are small trees with delicate, pinnate (walnutlike) foliage. A profusion of sprays of little white or pinkish flowers is followed by huge quantities of yellow, cylindrical, star-shaped fruits with five prominent angles, which weigh down the branches.

Natives of Indonesia and the Moluccas, averrhoas are still mostly grown in Southeast Asia and the Indian subcontinent. However, because of their decorative value, and being quite robust, they are now exported and appear almost everywhere.

The distinctive, star-shaped carambola fruit

VARIETIES

Carambolas are variable in taste. Some are much better than others, though they are all juicy. I have eaten them from European supermarkets, when they tasted like yellow soap, and also fresh, when they were amber and a joy. *Averrhoa bilimbi* or **'Billings'** are similar, resembling gherkin cucumbers, but are used more as vegetables and in curries, and for a popular jam.

CULTIVATION

Adaptable to most warm, moist climates, and any reasonable, well-drained soil, they fruit prolifically. They will grow in Zone 10.

Ornamental and Wildlife Value
Burdened with yellow fruit, they are impressive.

Growing under Glass and in Containers
Carambolas are pretty plants, so make good specimens. If they fruit they will put on a terrific show.

Propagation
Usually they are grown from seed, but better varieties are grafted. Only remedial pruning is needed.

The delicate sprays of the flowers are very attractive.

They travel fairly well if picked just underripe, and then keep for a week or two. Carambolas are more often used for making jelly and preserves than as dessert fruits. Their star shape makes excellent decorative garnishes in compotes and fruit salads. **'Billings'** are used for pickles and preserves and Billings jam is made after soaking overnight and straining to remove the acid bitterness. The flowers of both species were once made into conserves.

Camaranga or Carambola Jam
Makes about 4 lb.

2 lb. carambolas
4 cups white sugar

Cut the fruit up into finger-thick pieces and discard the sharp edges. Do not discard the seeds, as they improve the flavor of the jam. Add water to cover them and boil until the pieces are softening—about 15 minutes should be sufficient. Add the sugar and bring to a boil again for another 15 minutes, then bottle and seal.

OTHER USES

Carambola juice removes stains from linen and can be used for polishing brass. 'Billings' also polishes brass.

Achras sapota/Manilkara zapota from the family *Sapotaceae*

SAPODILLAS

OR SAPOTA, NASEBERRIES, BULLY TREES, CHIKKUS

Tree 14–52 ft. Life span: medium.
Fruits: about 2½ in., rounded, brown.

Sapodilla is a medium to big tree with glossy leaves. The fruit is a large, round berry with a rough, brown skin over luscious pulp similar to a pear's, containing a core with up to a dozen seeds much like an apple's—black, shiny, and inedible. The tree's milky sap can be tapped in the same way as rubber. Once collected, it is coagulated with heat and the sticky mass produced is strained out and dried to form chicle gum. Still mostly grown in its native region of Central America, sapodilla is also found wild in the forests of Venezuela. Sapodillas were more extensively planted when chicle gum started to be used for a booming new commodity—chewing gum. Now it is an important crop for Mexico and Central American countries. The naseberry is Jamaica's national fruit.

Fruit on the sapodilla tree

VARIETIES

Local varieties are cultivated for fruit, but there is little commercial demand, as it must be eaten absolutely ripe. However, there is a big demand for chicle gum; varieties selected for sap production can yield up to 6½ lb. of gum per year.

CULINARY USES

Perfectly ripened, they are considered a superb dessert fruit. The fruits keep up to a month or more in a cold refrigerator.

Chewing Gum

4 oz. each of chicle gum, glucose, powdered sugar, caramel paste
1 cup sugar
Spearmint or mint flavoring to taste

Melt the gum carefully in a double boiler. Meanwhile boil ½ cup water and the sugar and glucose to exactly 255°F. Remove from the heat, add the caramel, and boil again. Off the heat, mix the syrup into the melted gum, beating steadily and briskly. Add the flavoring and pour onto a cold surface thickly coated with powdered sugar. Roll flat. When cold, cut into strips, wrap, and label.

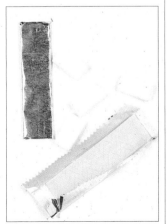

CULTIVATION

Sapodilla prefers very hot, moist climates with rich soil. They will grow in Zone 10.

Propagation, Pruning, and Training

Propagate by seed or preferably by grafting for better varieties. Only remedial pruning work seems necessary.

Growing under Glass and in Containers

The trees are variable in size and unlikely to crop well under glass, but they are attractive so should make good specimen pot plants.

Ornamental and Wildlife Value

Sapodilla has very attractive foliage and the fruits are enjoyed by wildlife.

Harvesting and Storing

Best finally ripened off the tree, when the fruit softens and mellows in a few days to a treacly, gummy consistency. Left on the tree, the fruits become veined with milk, which makes them too acid until bletted like medlars (see p. 522).

COMPANION PLANTING

Sapodilla trees are normally grown for the first five years with underplanted legume crops.

OTHER USES

Sapodilla wood is hard and durable, so it is used for handles and tools.

Nephelium lappaceum and *N. chinensis/litchi* from the family *Sapindaceae*

RAMBUTANS & LITCHIS

Tree up to 60 ft. Life span: medium to long. Usually not self-fertile; male and female flowers often on separate trees. Fruits: 1–2 in.,

Rambutan or ramtum trees are large and spreading, with pinnate leaves, and festooned with hairy, chestnut-like conkers. These fruits are apricot-sized, covered with red or orange-yellow, soft spines like tentacles. Underneath the skin the flesh is wrapped around the single, inedible, brown seed. The flesh is sweet, acid, almost like pineapple with a hint of apricot—it is a shame there is so little of it, as it is one of the best fruits I've ever tried.

Very similar yet more perfumed are litchis (or "litchees," "lychees"). These have a prickly, crackly shell and grow on a smaller tree.

Originally from the Malay archipelago, rambutans are greatly appreciated in Southeast Asia where they are often grown in gardens, but, surprisingly, have never proved popular anywhere else. Litchis have long been a Chinese specialty, so they followed the Chinese to many other suitable areas, such as Florida.

VARIETIES

Many different varieties of rambutan and litchi are grown in their regions. The '**Pulassan**,' *Nephelium*

mutabilechryseum, is another species, native to Java. It is similar but covered with warts instead of tentacles. *N. longana*, the '**Longan**,' is popular in southern China. It is smaller, brownish-yellow, and nearly smooth-skinned, with similar chewy flesh.

CULTIVATION

They need tropical conditions. Litchis prefer lower humidity, rambutans more. They will grow in Zone 10.

Growing under Glass and in Containers
Sadly they are too large. They may possibly do as pot specimens for foliage, but are unlikely to fruit.

Ornamental and Wildlife Value
The fruit is exceptionally attractive to birds and bats.

Propagation and Weed, Pest, and Disease Control
They come nearly true from seed, but the best varieties are budded. **Bird** and **bat** damage is a severe problem.

Harvesting and Storing
Both will ripen if picked early off the tree, so they are often found in temperate country shops.

Litchis have tiny, soft spines

CULINARY USES

Litchis are often preserved in syrup or dried to perfumed "prunes." All the fruits are superb desserts.

Litchis are often used to close a Chinese meal.

Litchi Sundae
Serves 4–6

4 cups litchis
2 cups vanilla ice cream
¼ cup blanched toasted almonds
Nutmeg
¼ cup brown sugar
4–6 glacé cherries

Peel and pit the litchis, then chill them. Layer the fruit in tall glasses with ice cream and almonds and top with a flourish of nutmeg, sugar, and a cherry.

Garcinia mangostana from the family *Clusiaceae (Guttifereae)*

MANGOSTEEN

Tree 45 ft. Life span: long. Fruits: 2½ in., round, brownish. Value: small amounts of protein, mineral matter, and fat; about one-seventh sugar and starch.

The trees are small to medium-sized, cone-shaped, and have large, leathery leaves somewhat like a lemon's. The fruits are round, purplish-brown, about apple size, with a rosette of dead petals around the stalk and an odd flower-shaped button on the other end. If you cut the rind around the fruit's circumference, the top can be lifted off to reveal about half a dozen kernels of melting white pulp, tasting something like grape and strawberry, tart and sweet, almost syrupy, and chewy. There is a seed contained in many kernels, which is not eaten.

Mangosteens are natives of Malaya and were described by Captain Cook in 1770 in detail, and with delight. They were introduced to Ceylon (now Sri Lanka) in 1800 and were successfully fruited in English greenhouses in 1855. Widely held to be the world's most delicious fruit, they may be found in gardens in every tropical area, but are nowhere grown on a commercial scale.

Mangosteen trees

Ripe mangosteens

VARIETIES

There are many local varieties and also close relations, most of which are found in the East Indies. *Garcinia cambogia* has a smaller, yellow-pulped, yellow fruit. *G. cowa* is the **Cowa-Mangosteen**. Bigger, ribbed, and apricot-colored, it is generally too acid for dessert but makes good preserves. Another, *G. indica*, the **Cocum, Conca,** or **Kokum**, has a sour, purple pulp used to make a vinegar, and the seeds are pressed for cocum oil. *G. dulcis* is a yellow-fruited variety found in the Moluccas. *G. morella* is common in Southeast Asia and provides an orange-red resin, gamboge.

CULTIVATION

Mangosteens need deep, rich, well-drained soil, a sheltered site, shade when young, a hot, moist climate. They will grow in Zone 10.

Growing under Glass and in Containers
If it could be done in England in the mid-19th century, it can be done now.

Propagation
They are slow and unreliable from seed. They are then slow-growing, reaching only to the knee after two or three years. The best varieties are layered.

COMPANION PLANTING

Mangosteens benefit from light shade, especially when young, preferring tropically bright but not direct light, so they are planted in the shade of taller trees.

HARVESTING AND STORING, CULINARY USES

Use a ladder to climb up and pick mangosteens, as they bruise if they fall. They can be picked unripe and kept for a few days.

Mangosteen Ecstasy
If you are fortunate enough to have a mangosteen, just eat it!

OTHER USES

The thick rinds are rich in tannic acid and dyes.

TRAVELER'S TALE TROPICAL FRUITS

There are many more fruits the inveterate traveler may come across in tropical and semi-tropical countries. Some of these are of more practical or commercial interest, such as the spices, while others are of such purely local interest they are rarely recorded. Many may be unpalatable by "modern" standards, or they may be delicious but hard to cultivate. As we move into a homogenized world of mass consumption, the numbers of varieties of even popular fruits are declining. Quaint, difficult, and unusual fruits have already disappeared from all but local native markets and botanic and private gardens. If you travel far off the beaten track, you may come across the following, and others—but, when choosing to taste them, do not rely on my identification.

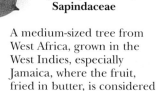

Tamarind pods

Blighia sapida, **Akee, Sapindaceae**

A medium-sized tree from West Africa, grown in the West Indies, especially Jamaica, where the fruit, fried in butter, is considered excellent fare. The fruits are bright red, heart-shaped pods, which burst to reveal three glossy, black seeds the size of peas sitting in a yellowish cup, which is the tasty bit. The seeds are inedible, the pink flesh highly poisonous, and even the edible bit is poisonous if under- or overripe. One wonders how this ever became popular!

Borassus flabellifer, **Borassus** or **Palmyra palm, Palmaceae**

A tall palm like a date palm but with shorter, fan-shaped leaves. It is widely distributed in the drier regions of Africa and Asia. The fruits contain much sap. This is also tapped from the trunk for boiling down into sugar or for fermenting.

Aberia gardneri, **Ceylon Gooseberry, Bixineae**

Native to what is now Sri Lanka, this is a small, shrubby tree with large, purple-brown, round berries mostly used for making jams and preserves. Closely related is *A. caffra,* the **Kai, Kau,** or **Kei Apple** of South Africa, which is yellow and so acid it is used as a pickle, omitting the vinegar.

Baccaurea dulcis/Pierardia motleyana, **Rambeh** or **Rambei, Euphorbiaceae**

Found in Malaysia, especially Sumatra, and China, this has long, hanging bunches of large, yellow berries that are reputedly sweet-tasting, juicy, and luscious.

Bactris/Guillielma utilis, **Peach Nut** or **Pewa, Palmaceae**

A native of Central America, similar to a date palm, this has fruits like large dates. Usually cooked in salted water before eating, they taste of chestnuts. The best varieties are seedless. Other relations are the **Prickly Palm,** *B. major,* and the **Tobago Palm,** *B. minor.*

The Borassus or Palmyra palm

Carissa grandiflora,
Natal Plum, Apocynaceae

This and *Carissa carandas* are large, thorny shrubs used as hedges in Natal. They have purple, damson-like fruits tasting of gooseberry that are widely used for tarts and preserves. *C. carandas*, which is also used for pickling, prefers drier areas.

The exotic Natal plum

Chrysophylum cainito, **Star Apple, Sapotaceae**

Noted by Cieza de Leon in Peru in 1532–1550, this is a large evergreen tree with purple-brown "apples," which, when cut through, have a star shape in the middle with about half a dozen shiny, brown seeds in a sweet/acid pulp.

Coccoloba uvifera, **Seagrape, Polygonaceae**

A colonizer of tropical shores, this is a very salt-tolerant, small evergreen shrub or tree found from Florida to Venezuela. The "grapes" are up to half an inch across, mild, and sweet. They are eaten raw or jellied. The wood is hard and takes a polish well. It is often used as hedging or for good windbreaks.

Eugenia caryophyllus,
Cloves, Myrtaceae

Cloves are the dried flower buds of this Indonesian tree. Other *Eugenia* species such as the **Malay Apple,** *E. Malaccensis,* the **Rose Apple,** *E. Jambos,* and, the **Surinam Cherry,** *E. uniflora,* have edible fruits varying from yellow to red or purple. They are eaten raw and made into jams and liqueurs in tropical and subtropical countries.

Mimusops elengi, **Sapotaceae**

This large East Asian tree has fragrant flowers. The 1-in. yellow berries are eaten when ripe and an oil is expressed from the seed. Other *Mimusops* are also grown for their similar fruits. *M. elata* of Brazil is the **Cow Tree.** Its apple-sized fruits contain a whitish latex that resembles milk when fresh, and is drunk with coffee, but soon congeals to a glue.

Pimenta dioica, **Allspice, Pimento, Myrtaceae.**

This small, evergreen West Indian tree has pea-sized berries that are dried unripe for their mixed spice flavor.

Piper nigrum, **Pepper, Piperaceae**

Black and white pepper are the unripe and ripe (and de-corticated) seeds of this Indian climbing vine.

Spondias, **Spanish, Hog,** or **Brazilian Plum, Anacardiaceae**

Distantly related to cashews and pistachios, the *Spondias* have edible fruits, most of them only when made into preserves, but some are eaten raw. They are purple to yellow, resembling a plum with a central "stone." The stone of the **Spanish Plum,** *Spondias purpurea,* is eaten by some people.

Black and white peppercorns, allspice, cloves, and cardamoms

Tamarindus indica, **Tamarind Tree, Caesalpiniaceae**

This large, handsome tree has brown pods containing very acid pulp used for beverages and in chutneys, curries, and medicine.

Vanilla planifolia,
Orchidaceae

Vanilla is the fruit of an orchid that is native to Central America but is mostly grown in Madagascar. The beanlike pods are cured and dried for flavoring.

Zizyphus jujuba, **Jujube, Chinese Date, Rhamnaceae**

An East Indian native, this reached China and was improved to dessert quality. In China it is popular dried or preserved in syrup. Jujubes resemble large, yellowish or reddish cherries with thick, tough skin, a hard kernel, and a pithy, acid pulp, rich in vitamin C. The thorny, shrubby trees survive in cooler climates and have been in Mediterranean countries since biblical times. *Z. vulgaris,* a native of the Middle East, is similar but less agreeable. *Z. lotus* is like a sweet olive and is thought to be the lotus Odysseus had trouble with.

This banana tree from the Canary Islands thrives in the author's garden.

SHRUB AND FLOWER GARDEN FRUITS

WILD GARDEN FRUITING TREES & SHRUBS

Many of our familiar garden and countryside plants also bear fruit. Some of these are edible and can add variety and nutritional range to the diet. But first, I must insist that you never eat anything you are not sure of. Have it identified as safe by an expert on the spot. Also you must realize that although the fruits of some plants, such as yew, may not themselves be harmful, the foliage and seeds are deadly if ingested in quantity. Various parts may also be an irritant to some people.

However, such paranoid exclamations aside, there are many familiar plants that have edible, if not actually delicious, fruits. Although they might not seem at first glance very attractive or be popular with many of us today, some of these were once greatly esteemed by native peoples, and others were part of the country fare of our not-so-distant predecessors. With a little care and attention, these plants can provide us with fresh and unusual dishes, far exceeding in vitamins and flavor those made from the tired and flabby fruits usually offered for sale.

The plants at the beginning of this chapter are all excellent garden subjects, worthy of anyone's attention, which incidentally bear edible fruit. Some of the other plants with edible fruits are not attractive enough, or grow too big, for most gardens, but are of interest or value to insects or birds, and are more often planted in larger, public or wildlife gardens.

The ideal picturesque garden, often called the cottage garden, is typified these days by extravagant species at flower shows with odd mixtures of flowers, half of them out of season, grown elsewhere in pots and jammed full, with a camouflage of bark. The true cottager's garden was indeed a mixture of plants, but all with a purpose—to provide medicines, herbs, flavorings, fruits, and, last of all, flowers.

Fruiting trees and shrubs can be easily cultivated with other plants underneath, and they were the backbone of a true cottage garden. A mixture of plants that were found to grow happily together for both production and ornament was sensible, as it produced a mixed ecology and there were rarely pest or disease problems. In addition, the plants grown in flower, shrub, and wild gardens are often innately more reliable than those especially cultivated for fruits, as they are closer to the wild forms, with natural pest and disease resistance.

The biggest handicap for some of these plants has probably been their very attractiveness. If they had been a little less pretty, they might have been developed further for their fruits and have remained part of our diet. Few of them are palatable raw, at least not to most people's taste, and all are better made into jams, jellies, and preserves, but they have appealing and interesting flavors and are of inestimable value to the adventurous gourmet or those wishing to expand their dietary range. And for those interested in breeding, they offer plenty of opportunity for rapid improvement toward bigger, tastier, and better fruits.

Amelanchier canadensis from the family *Rosaceae*

JUNEBERRIES

SNOWY MESPILUS, SHADS, SWEET/GRAPE PEARS

Tree/bush up to 20–30 ft. Life span: medium. Self-fertile.
Fruits: ½ in., round, purple-black, rich in vitamin C.

Amelanchiers look beautiful covered in white blossoms.

The amelanchiers are small, deciduous trees or shrubs tending to suckering growth, most noticeable when totally covered with white blossoms. The fruits are purplish, spherical, and about pea-size, but can be larger.

A. *canadensis* is the best species and a native of North America. Though there are relatives in Asia and Europe, these are not as palatable. A. *vulgaris* grows wild in European mountain districts and was long cultivated in England, as much for the flowers as the fruits.

VARIETIES

Amelanchier canadensis was a favorite fruit of Native Americans. It was adopted by the French settlers and became **Poires** in Canada and **Sweet** or **Grape Pear** in the U.S. It has small purple berries that are sweet and tasty. A. *alnifolia*, or **Western Service Berry**, is larger and found wild in Oregon and Washington.

CULTIVATION

Amelanchiers do best in moist but well-drained, lime-free soil. They are slow-growing, and some species tend to sucker. Most species grow in Zones 3 through 8.

Propagation, Pruning, and Training

Sow seeds fresh for the species, but graft choice varieties in April onto *Sorbus aucuparia* stock. They may need to have suckers removed, otherwise prune only remedially.

Growing under Glass and in Containers

They are so hardy that they hardly seem worth the space under cover. They could be delightful small specimens in pots.

Weed, Pest, and Disease Control

No particular problems affect these tough plants.

A spray of juneberries and leaves

CULINARY USES

They can be eaten raw, but are better as jams or tarts, or dried like raisins.

Snowy Mespilus
Sponge Cakes
Makes about 10

2 oz. each butter,
powdered sugar, and white
self-rising flour
1 large or 2 small eggs
Dash of vanilla extract
Splash of milk
4 oz. dried amelanchier
berries

Cream the butter and sugar, beat in the egg and vanilla, fold in the sifted flour, then add enough milk to make a smooth mixture. Stir in the berries; pour into greased paper cups. Stand the cups on a baking sheet and bake in a preheated oven at 375°F for 20 minutes or until firm.

OTHER USES

Can be used as rootstocks for pome fruits.

Berberis vulgaris from the family *Berberidaceae*

BARBERRIES
MAHONIAS, OREGON GRAPES

Bush up to 14 x 14 ft. Life span: short.
Fruits: under ½ in., white, yellow, scarlet, purple, or black.

The *Berberis* family contains hundreds of small- to medium-sized, spiny shrubs that have masses of berries in many colors. The leaves of most deciduous varieties turn bright shades in fall and the wood is usually yellow.

Various species are found all over the world. Our common barberry is now seldom relished, but was once widely popular. Indeed the settlers in Massachusetts grew so many that in 1754 the province had to forbid further planting.

VARIETIES

Berberis vulgaris is the **Common Barberry**, which once existed in a host of local forms and colors. One found in Rouen was seedless. Other species are enjoyed all over the world: *B. darwinii* is popular; *B. buxifolia*, the **Magellan Barberry**, is large and said to be the best raw or cooked. *Mahonia* is now a separate genus, but is very similar in many ways, only lacking the spines and having pinnate leaves. The flowers are yellow, usually scented, and the blue-black berries of *M. aquifolium* were made into preserves as Oregon grapes.

A cluster of Oregon grape holly

CULTIVATION

They will grow anywhere not bone-dry or waterlogged, even tolerating salt spray. Most will grow in Zones 6 through 9, with some species and varieties hardy to Zone 3.

Growing under Glass and in Containers
They are hardy enough not to need protection, but do make good plants in containers.

Ornamental and Wildlife Value
Some ornamental varieties are very attractive, though not as productive of berries, which are exceedingly well liked by birds. Most varieties are excellent when used for wildlife gardens.

Propagation, Pruning, and Training
The species grows from seed, layered, or grafted. They can usually be cut to the ground and will recover.

Barberry flowers

WEED, PEST, AND DISEASE CONTROL, COMPANION PLANTING

Barberries are an alternate host for wheat rust, so care should be taken not to plant them near wheat.

OTHER USES

They make good hedges and game cover. They were once used for a yellow dye.

HARVESTING AND STORING, CULINARY USES

The berries can be pickled in vinegar, preserved in sugar or syrup, candied, or made into jam. The leaves were once used as a seasoning.

Colonel Flowerdew's
Bengal Chutney
Makes about 3 lb.

6 cups grated apple
½ cup dried barberries
½ cup mustard seed
1¼ cups brown sugar
¼ cup corn syrup
¼ cup chopped onions
¼ cup chopped garlic
¼ cup chopped fresh ginger
¼ cup salt
1 tablespoon cayenne pepper
2 cups vinegar

Mix all the ingredients and simmer until soft, about 2–3 hours. Bottle in small jars for 6 months.

Mespilus germanica from the family *Rosaceae*

MEDLARS

Tree up to 30 ft. Life span: medium. Self-fertile.
Fruits: 1–2 in., green to russet.

Medlars resemble pear trees but are smaller, have bigger leathery leaves, single, large, white flowers, and fruits like giant, distorted rose hips. The brownish-green fruits have a rough "leafy" end, which shows the seed chambers. Medlars seldom ripen fully on the tree in cool regions and were eaten "bletted"—stored until the point of decomposition. The taste is somewhat like that of rotten pear and they are now disdained.

Originally from Persia, medlars became naturalized over much of Europe. Theophrastus mentions them in Greece in 300 B.C. and Pliny refers to the Romans having three sorts. Once very popular, they are now planted infrequently.

Medlar flower and leaves

VARIETIES

There are only a few left. Generally the bigger the tree, the larger the fruit tends to be. **'Dutch'** and **'Monstrous'** are the largest, **'Royal'** and **'Nottingham'** the tastiest and smaller. The seedless **'Stoneless'** has disappeared.

CULTIVATION

Medlars are obliging and will grow in most places, generally preferring a sunny spot in a lawn or grass.

Medlar trees are beautiful in their fall colors.

Medlars are hardy in Zones 6 through 10.

Growing under Glass and in Containers
The tree is hardy, so it is a waste to grow it under cover, but the twisted framework and general attractiveness make it a good specimen plant for pot growing.

Ornamental and Wildlife Value
Pretty flowers, large leaves, and gorgeous fall golds make this a delightful specimen tree, with a twisted and contorted framework for winter interest.

Propagation, Pruning, and Training
Medlars can be grown from seed, but are usually grafted on pear, quince, or thorn stock. They are best pruned only remedially, as they fruit on the ends of the branches.

Weed, Pest, and Disease Control
Medlars rarely suffer from any problem.

HARVESTING AND STORING, CULINARY USES

The fruits should be left on the tree until winter and then stored in a cool, dry place until they soften (blet). The pulp was once popular raw, mixed with liqueur and cream, but is better jammed or jellied.

Medlar Fudge
Makes about 4 lb.

2 lb. medlars
1 large or 2 small lemons
3 cloves
2 cups apple cider
Approx. 2¹/₂ cups light brown sugar
Honey or maple syrup to taste, cream and macaroons to serve

Wash and chop the fruit, add the cloves and cider, and simmer until the fruit is soft. Sieve and measure the pulp. Add three-quarters of its volume in sugar and bring back to a boil, then bottle and seal. When ready to serve, whip the fruit cheese with honey or maple syrup until soft, spoon into bowls, and top with whipped cream and broken macaroons.

Chaenomeles japonica from the family *Rosaceae*

JAPONICA QUINCES

*Shrub up to 10 x 10 ft. Life span: short. Self-fertile.
Fruits: 1–2 in., round, green/red/yellow.*

A tangled mass of dark, occasionally thorny branches covered with red, white, orange, or pink blossom in early spring. This is followed later in the year by hard, roundish fruits, green flushing red or yellow.

Often just called japonica, this shrub arrived in Europe from Japan as late as 1800. It was rapidly accepted and is now widely planted in many varieties and hybrids, for its flowers, not the fruits. There is opportunity for developing a better culinary or even a dessert form.

CULTIVATION

Hardier than **Cydonia quinces**, these are easy almost anywhere, even on shady walls. They thrive in Zones 4 through 9 or 10.

Growing under Glass and in Containers
Tough and unruly plants, they are better outdoors. However, I've found them dependable in pots to force for early flowers.

Ornamental and Wildlife Value
The displays of early flowers and long-lived fruit are exceptional, making these valuable shrubs.

Propagation, Pruning, and Training
Unlikely to come true from seed. Better varieties are easily layered or can be grafted. Winter cuttings may take; softwood cuttings are better but trickier. The shrubs have a congested form and are best left alone or tip pruned in summer to control their size. I weave young growths like basketwork to produce a tight surface that can be clipped.

Weed, Pest, and Disease Control
Other than **weeds** and **congestion**, they have no common problems.

Japonica quince flowers provide a marvelous splash of color.

VARIETIES

The botanical *C. japonica* has orange flowers, and true japonica is *C. speciosa*. **'Texas Scarlet'** is a dense, spreading shrub with 3-in. fruit. **'Thornless Cameo'** has double flowers in a beautiful shade of peach. The fruits of **'Toyo Nashiki'** are as big as apples. *C. cathayensis*, is larger, with green fruits up to 6 in. long.

OTHER USES

Chaenomeles make good, sturdy hedges.

HARVESTING AND STORING, CULINARY USES

Inedible—impenetrable anyway—until cooked, when they have an aromatic scent similar to but different from Cydonia quinces. They can be used for tarts, baked or stewed, or made into cheese or jelly.

Japonica Jelly
Makes about 8 lb.

*4 lb. chaenomeles fruits
Approx. 8 cups sugar*

Chop the fruit and simmer in 10 cups of water until tender, then sieve and measure the pulp. Add 1 cup of sugar per 1 cup of pulp and return to the heat. Bring to a boil, bottle, and seal. Will keep for 3 months.

Arbutus unedo from the family *Ericaceae*

STRAWBERRY TREE
CANE FRUIT, ARBUTE

Tree up to 20 ft. Life span: long. Fruits: about 1 in., spherical, red.

Arbutus unedo is a small evergreen tree often with gnarled, shedding bark, rich brown underneath. It has white, heather-like flowers in late fall as the previous year's crop of spherical fruits ripens. These are stubbily spiky, resembling litchis. The pulp is really no good raw, especially in cool regions, but may be better in warmer climes.

Arbutus unedo is native to the Mediterranean. The ancient Greek Theophrastus knew it was edible, but three hundred years later, the Roman Pliny did not regard it as worth eating. Ever since, it has been planted for its beauty but not really for the fruit, which have remained undeveloped. I gather the descriptive name *unedo* means "I eat one only."

A colorful display of fall fruit on the tree

Strawberry tree leaves and fruit

VARIETIES

The ordinary **Killarney Strawberry Tree** is commonest and in few varieties; **'Rubra'** has pink flowers and abundant fruits. Other species are *A. canariensis*, whose berries are made into sweetmeats, and *A. menziesii.* **'Madrona,'** from California, has cherry-like fruits that are said once to have been eaten. .

CULTIVATION

A. unedo prefers a mild climate or a warm site. It grows well in Zones 7 and 8. Although acid-loving, it does not mind some lime, but does better in a leaf-mold-rich woodland or acid soil. The other species are not as compliant.

Ornamental and Wildlife Value
One of the most highly prized, small, ornamental evergreens. Of slight value to wildlife, though the flowers are handy for insects late in fall.

Weed, Pest, and Disease Control
Few problems occur.

Growing under Glass and in Containers
So ornamental it is worth having under cover, but only if confined in a pot. Be careful to use rainwater.

Propagation, Pruning, and Training
Seed of the species comes true, layers are possible, and winter cuttings may take. The strawberry tree needs little pruning and usually recovers if cut back hard.

OTHER USES

The hard, tough wood is turned into carved souvenirs of Killarney, especially small cudgels.

HARVESTING AND STORING, CULINARY USES

Harvested a year after the flowers, the fruits are made into sweets, liqueurs, and sherbets, but never eaten raw.

Killarney Strawberry Surprise
Serves 6

1½ cups graham cracker crumbs
½ cup (1 stick) butter
¼ cup strawberry jam
1 cup strawberries
2 tablespoons gelatin
1 large cup hot water
Killarney strawberries (arbutus fruits) to garnish

Mix the cracker crumbs with most of the butter. Press into a tart dish and chill. Once set, rub the cookie crust with the rest of the butter, line with half the jam, then fill with strawberries. Dissolve the gelatin and the rest of the jam in a cup of hot water, then cool. Pour the jelly over the fruit, swirl and chill. Garnish with Killarney strawberries and serve with cream.

Viburnum trilobum from the family *Caprifoliaceae*

HIGHBUSH CRANBERRIES

Shrub 14 ft. Life span: relatively short. Fruits: 1 in., round, scarlet.

A large, spreading shrub with maplelike leaves that give good fall color, and scarlet, glossy, translucent berries in midsummer, very similar to the European guelder rose.

Viburnum is an immense genus of many species, some of which have berries that were once considered highly edible. The guelder rose (snowball tree, whitten, water elder, *V. opulus*) is now forbidden fruit and as children we were warned how dangerous it is. Though the foliage is poisonous, the fruit was cooked and eaten by the poor for millennia. A native European fruit, it thrives in wet soils and damp hedgerows. Similar conditions suit most species.

VARIETIES

V. trilobum, **Highbush Cranberry**, which is very similar to *V. opulus*, is one of several edible wild North American species; *V. lentago* (**Sweet Viburnum, Nannyberry,** or **Sheepberry**) has sweet black berries; *V. nudum* (**Naked Viburnum** or **Withe Rod**) is similar, with a deep blue berry; *V. prunifolium* (**Black Haw**) is sometimes good enough even to eat raw.

Unripe fruit

The elegant flower of the highbush cranberry

Growing under Glass and in Containers
Tough individuals, these are mostly hardy and need no glass, though other viburnums may be grown in pots so that their scented flowers may be enjoyed.

Ornamental and Wildlife Value
Most viburnums are grown for their pretty or scented flowers. The berrying sorts are often as decorative and both fruit and flowers are very useful for attracting insects and birds.

Propagation, Pruning, and Training
Species come true from seed but are slow. Most varieties can be layered and some will strike from hardwood cuttings taken in winter.

Weed, Pest, and Disease Control
No common problem other than **weeds** and **bird** losses.

CULTIVATION

Very easy to please. Most species do best in moist, humus-rich soil. Highbush cranberry is hardy to Zone 3.

OTHER USES

The berries are used to make a spirit in Scandinavia. The bark of the black haw is a source of medicinal drugs.

HARVESTING AND STORING, CULINARY USES

The berries are not eaten raw, save occasionally after frost, but can be made into sharp-tasting jams and jellies.

American Highbush Chutney
Makes about 2½ lb.

1½ lb. highbush cranberries
1¼ cups distilled vinegar
4 oz. each currants, sultanas, raisins, sugar
½ oz. salt
2 teaspoons cinnamon
2 teaspoons allspice
Pinch of nutmeg

Wash the fruits and then remove each of the stalks. Simmer with enough water to prevent burning until soft. Add in the vinegar and the other ingredients and simmer until the chutney thickens. Jar and store for 3 months.

Fuchsia from the family *Onagraceae*

FUCHSIA

Semi-herbaceous shrub, to 7 x 7 ft. Life span: short.
Fruits: ½ in., round/oval, purple-black.

**Fuchsia
flower and leaves**

This gloriously flowered plant needs little description, and most of us must have noticed the roundish oval, purple fruits it occasionally sets. As I have always searched for new fruits from far places, I was amused when I first saw fuchsia jelly and learned that I had overlooked these berries that are so close at hand, often edible, and as delicious as many from distant shores.

The first fuchsia was recorded in 1703. Over the following century a few species arrived in Britain from South America with little remark, but in 1793 James Lee astutely launched his *F. coccinea*, the first with impressive flowers, and took the world by storm. Other species were introduced from New Zealand and now there is an amazing range of colors and forms of hybrids of many species.

A mixture of royal ferns and fuchsia forms this rich Irish hedge.

HARVESTING AND STORING, CULINARY USES

Some are tasty raw, but all are best jellied or in tarts.

Fuchsia Jelly
Makes about 4 lb.

2 lb. fuchsia berries
Approx. 4 cups sugar
Juice of 1 lemon

Simmer the berries with sufficient water to cover. Once they have softened, sieve and measure. Add the same volume of sugar and the lemon juice. Bring back to a boil, then jar.

VARIETIES

Fuchsia species *corymbiflora* and *denticulata* were eaten in Peru and *F. racemosa* in Santo Domingo. Fuchsia clubs and societies often have jelly competitions. There appears to be no known poisonous variety— and I have tried many. As they are all bred for flowers, the berries are neglected and should be easily improved—there is enough variety to start with! *F. magellanica* is the hardiest, but rarely fruits.

CULTIVATION

Most fuchsias are hardy only on Zones 9 and 10, but *F. magellanica* may survive in Zone 7 if deeply mulched in winter. Even many less hardy species can be grown in cold regions if the roots are well protected, as fuchsias usually spring again from underground to flower and fruit. Make backup plants to be safe and keep these indoors. Fuchsias are amenable to almost any soil but prefer a sunny site.

Propagation, Pruning, and Training
Seed produces mixed results; cuttings are easy to train to any shape. Control growth by nipping out tips in summer; cut back in winter.

Ornamental and Wildlife Value
Appealing to hummingbirds.

Growing under Glass and in Containers
One of the ideal plants for a cool or heated greenhouse. Can be grown for many years in large pots.

Weed, Pest, and Disease Control
They suffer from common pests requiring the usual remedies (see pp. 602–607).

OTHER USES

Fuchsias are used as hedges in mild regions.

Pinus pinea from the family *Pinaceae*

PINENUTS
PIGNONS, PINONS, PINOCCHI

Tree up to 80 ft. Life span: long. Evergreen, self-fertile.
Fruits: up to ¹/₂ in. long, ivory-white seeds inside a cone.
Value: high in minerals and oils.

Pine cones (above) contain the edible kernels (left).

Pinenuts are more nuts than fruits, as we eat the seed and not the surrounding part (in this case, the cone), but they are softer than true nuts. Most pine kernels come from the stone or umbrella pine. It is an attractive, mushroom-shaped tree with glossy, brown cones that expand in the sun and drop the seeds. Each is in a tough skin that needs to be removed before it is eaten.

The stone pine is indigenous to the Mediterranean region. Loved by the ancient Greeks, it was dedicated to the sea god Poseidon. The kernels of other species are eaten almost anywhere they grow.

Ornamental and Wildlife Value
Very attractive if the space is available. Pine kernels will provide excellent food for many species of birds.

Weed, Pest, and Disease Control
Pines need companion bacteria and fungi, so do better if soil from around another pine is used to inoculate new sites.

Pruning and Training
Pines are best left well alone.

Propagation
They can be grown from seed or grafted (with skill).

VARIETIES

Pinus cembroides is a native of North America and has pea-sized kernels that taste delicious roasted. *P. pinea* grows happily in northern regions, but without enough sun the cones do not ripen. *P. cembra*, the **Arolla Pine**, is native to central Europe and Asia, and the seeds are a staple food in Siberia. *P. gerardiana*, **Gerard's Pine**, comes from the Himalayas. *P. edulis*, from Mexico, is the best variety, but unlikely to fruit in Britain. Likewise the **Araucaria Pine** or **Monkey Puzzle Tree**, *A. araucana*, which has edible kernels and grows but rarely fruits in cooler climates (see p. 559).

The **Parana Pine**, *A. angustifolia*, from South America, is not hardy and is too big for greenhouse culture.

CULTIVATION

Stone pines will need shelter to fruit in cold regions. They prefer to grow in sandy soils and acid conditions, and are hardy to Zone 8.

Growing under Glass and in Containers
Most pines grow too large unless confined and are unlikely to crop. *P. canariensis*, however, is a particularly pleasing indoor pot plant.

A Colorado pine, Arizona

OTHER USES

Pines are a source of turpentine and resin.

HARVESTING AND STORING, CULINARY USES

Pine nuts are roasted and salted in the same way as peanuts, and also used in marzipan, sweets, salads, and soups.

Pinon Truffle Salad
Quantities to taste

Pine kernels
Butter
Truffles
Walnut oil
Vinegar
Lettuce

Gently fry the kernels in butter until light brown. Remove from the heat; add finely sliced truffles, oil, and vinegar. Cool the mixture and toss it with clean, dry lettuce leaves.

The brightly colored Mexican stone pine flower and needles

Rosa from the family *Rosaceae*

ROSE HIPS

Clambering shrub up to 30 ft. Life span: short to medium. Usually self-fertile. Fruits: up to 1 in., ovoid, red, yellow, or purplish-black. Value: very rich in vitamin C.

There can be no one who does not know roses, and few who have never nibbled at the acid/sweet flesh of a rose hip. These are so rich in vitamin C that they were collected on a massive scale during World War II for rose-hip syrup for expectant mothers and babies. Rose stems are commonly thorny with a few exceptions such as the divine **'Zéphirine Drouhin.'** The deciduous leaves vary from glossy to matte, the flower color is any you want save black or blue, though wild roses are almost all white or pink. The **'Eglantine'** rose leaves smell of apples after rain.

Rose hips and flowers are eaten in countries all over the world. The brier or dog rose, *Rosa canina*, and eglantine or sweetbrier, *R. rubiginosa*, are natives of Europe and temperate Asia. Their fruits have been eaten by country folk since time immemorial, but are now regarded with some disdain. However, eglantine sauce was made at Balmoral Castle from sweetbrier hips and lemon juice and was considered good enough for Queen Victoria. Roses are bred for flowers, not for their hips, so most varieties have small hips. However, a little selective breeding could produce hips as large as small apples within a few generations.

VARIETIES

The **'Brier'** and **'Eglantine'** rose hips are the commonest varieties used for hips, though *R. rugosa*, the **'Rugosa Rose,'** offers larger hips, so is more rewarding. *R moyesii* has large flask-shaped hips and *R. omiensis* has pear-shaped, yellow and crimson fruits that ripen early. *R. spinosissima/pimpinellifolia*, the **'Scotch'** or **'Burnet Rose,'** is another European native, often found in maritime districts. It has a very sweet, purplish-black fruit.

A spray of roses and leaves

Ripe rose hips are a glorious re

CULTIVATION

Most roses prefer heavy soil. Roses vary in cold hardiness, depending on species, but they are typically not assigned to particular hardiness zones because so many other factors affect their survival.

Propagation
Some species can be grown from seed. Cuttings taken in early fall are reliable for many varieties and most species.

Ornamental and Wildlife Value
Roses are *the* garden plant. At least one or more can fit into almost any garden anywhere to good effect.

Growing under Glass and in Containers
Only tender roses such as *R. banksiae* are happy under glass. Hardier varieties tend to become soft and drawn and suffer from pests. They must be kept moist at the roots, well ventilated, and shaded against scorch.

Maintenance
Spring Weed, mulch heavily, and spray with seaweed solution often.
Summer Deadhead regularly, watch for aphids.
Fall Take cuttings.
Winter Cut back or tie in.

Pruning and Training
This requires a chapter on its own just to list the methods. Basically, for most roses, plant them well apart, prune as little as possible, and wind in growths rather than prune. Reduce tall hybrid bushes by a third to a half in height with hedge trimmers annually in late winter.

Weed, Pest, and Disease Control
Roses suffer from a host of common diseases, but providing they are growing reasonably well, the only real threat to flower and hip production is **aphids**. Control these with jets of water and soft soap.

A mixture of immature and ripe hips

COMPANION PLANTING

Underplantings of alliums, especially garlic or chives, help deter blackspot and pests. Parsley, lupines, mignonette, and lavender are beneficial; catnip and *Limnanthes douglassii* are good ground cover underneath roses.

OTHER USES

Strong-growing roses such as *R. rubiginosa*, *R. spinosissima*, or **'The Queen Elizabeth'** make excellent hedges. The flower petals are dried for potpourri and used medicinally and in confectionery and perfumery.

A bowl of rose hip potpourri

HARVESTING AND STORING, CULINARY USES

The berries need to ripen fully on the bush before being eaten raw, but are best taken before they soften for culinary use. All seed hairs must be removed! Hips can be made into jellies, preserves, and the famous syrup. The flower petals may be used as garnishes, preserved in sugar or syrup, used for rose-water flavoring, honeys, vinegars, and conserves, pounded to dust for lozenges, and make good additions to salads. The leaves of *R. canina* have been used for tea (in desperation, one suspects).

Rose Hip Tart
Serves 6

For the pastry:
2 cups self-rising flour
²/₃ cup butter
1 large egg yolk
¹/₄ cup brown sugar
Pinch of salt
Splash of water

For the filling:
2 cups rose hips
²/₃ cup brown sugar
¹/₄ cup honey
¹/₃ cup chopped stem ginger preserved in syrup
¹/₂ teaspoon cinnamon
Sprinkling of sugar and grating of nutmeg

Preheat the oven to 350°F. Rub together the ingredients for the pastry, making it a little on the dry side, and use it to line a tart dish. Wash, top, tail, and halve the rose hips, extract every bit of seed and hairy fiber, rinse, and drain. Mix with the sugar, honey, cinnamon, and ginger and spoon on top of the pastry. Decorate with pastry cutouts and sprinkle with sugar and nutmeg before baking for half an hour, or until the pastry is light brown on top.

Cornus mas from the family *Cornaceae*

CORNELIAN CHERRY, SORBET

Tree/bush up to 25 ft. Life span: medium to long. Deciduous, self-fertile.
Fruits: ½ in., ovoid, red.

Cornelian cherry fruits resemble small, red cherries but are generally too sour to eat raw, except for the occasional better one. The trees or large bushes are tall, deciduous, densely branched, and suckering, common in hedgerows and old grasslands. The stems are grayish and the leaves are oval, coming to a point with noticeable veins. The flowers are primrose yellow and appear in small clusters early in spring before the leaves.

The Cornelian cherry is one of a genus of about a hundred mostly small, shrubby plants up to ten feet high, but ranging from creeping sub-shrubs to small trees. One of the two species native to Europe and western Asia, *Cornus mas* was once widely cultivated and rated very highly, though now it is rarely eaten even by country folk. There are species from North America and the Himalayas and it seems a shame they have not been cross-bred for better fruits. The Cornelian cherry really is a fruit that has stalled in development and probably would not take much more work to improve immensely.

found in Louisiana, is said to be very good. The berries of *C. suecica* used to be gathered by Native Americans, who froze them in wooden boxes for winter rations. *Cornus kousa chinensis* comes from China via Japan and is a smaller tree than *C. mas*. The flowers are grayish-purple, backed by immense pale bracts, the fruits are more strawberry-like and juicy with better flavor. This species needs a moist, acid soil. *C. macrophylla* and the tenderer *C. capitata* come from Asia and the Himalayas and are eaten raw and made into preserves in India. *C. canadensis* (*Chamaepericlymenum canadense*), **Bunchberry** or **Dwarf Cornel**, is a different type altogether. A lime hater more resembling a soft dwarf raspberry in manner of growth, it has white flowers on low, soft shoots with vivid red fruits. These are pleasant enough, if tasteless, and can be added to summer puddings.

The distinctive primrose-yellow flowers of the Cornelian cherry

VARIETIES

'Redstone' and **'Russian Giant'** produce better crops than the common species. The variety *C. mas macrocarpa* has somewhat larger fruits and is still available. There used to exist many other improved forms, now apparently lost. In France and Germany there are records of several varieties of sorbets, as they were called— one that had a yellow fruit, some with wax-colored fruits, white fruits, and even one with a fleshy, rounded fruit. Other cornus such as *C. stolonifera*, the **Red Osier**, and *C. amomum*, **Kinnikinnik**, are found in North America and are edible. The former was eaten more in desperation than for pleasure; the latter,

The flowers of the Cornelian cherry appear before the leaves in spring.

CULTIVATION

C. mas is easy to grow almost anywhere but prefers calcareous soil. Some species need acid conditions. They are among the most reliable of shrubs, requiring little attention. They are cold hardy to Zone 5.

Maintenance
Spring Cut back ornamental-stemmed varieties, weed, mulch, and spray with seaweed solution.
Summer Make layers.
Fall Preserve fruit for winter.
Winter Take cuttings or suckers and prune.

Growing under Glass and in Containers
They are hardy, so are hardly worth growing under glass unless you wish to force them for their early flowers. They will grow well in pots.

Ornamental and Wildlife Value
Many species are liked particularly for their fall color and some species and varieties are grown for their brightly colored stems. The flowers are early, benefiting insects, and birds and rodents love the berries. One of the best "backbone" shrubs of a wild garden.

Propagation
The species come true from seed with some variation, but are slow. Suckers taken in fall are best, hardwood winter cuttings may take, but layering is more sure.

Pruning and Training
Generally only remedial pruning is needed—though, as these plants sucker, some root pruning may become necessary. Ornamental colored-stem varieties are best sheared to ground level in early spring.

Weed, Pest, and Disease Control
No common problems bother these tough plants.

OTHER USES

Cornus sanguinea, the **Cornel Dogwood**, **Dogberry**, or **Pegwood**, is a common European relation, not really edible, though the fruits were once used for oil and in brewing. *C. alba* varieties tolerate wet or dry situations and can be used to reinforce banks. Dogwoods grow stiff and straight, so they were once used for arrows.

HARVESTING AND STORING, CULINARY USES

In Germany the fruits were sold in markets to be eaten by children (who presumably liked them). They were widely made into tarts, confectionery, and sweetmeats, even used as substitutes for olives. In Norway the flowers were used to flavor spirits and in Turkey the fruits were used as flavoring for sherbets. It is noticeable that fruits vary on different bushes and some are more palatable raw than others.

Sorbet Sorbet
Serves 4

4 cups cornelian cherries
1 small lemon
Approx. 2¹/₂ cups sugar
2 medium egg whites

Wash the fruits, slit the cherries, chop the lemon, and simmer until soft, just covered with water, in a deep pan. Strain and measure the liquid, then dissolve just less than 1 cup of sugar per cup of liquid. Bring back to a boil, cool, and partially freeze. Remove from the freezer and beat, adding one beaten white of egg for every two cups of sorbet. Repeat the freezing and beating once more before freezing until required.

Crataegus azarolus from the family *Rosaceae*

HAWTHORN AND AZAROLE

Tree/bush up to 25 ft. Life span: long. Deciduous, self-fertile.
Fruits: up to 1 in., roundish, usually orange.
Value: rich in vitamins C and B complex.

The azarole is a more palatable relation of the well-known hawthorn and is cultivated in many of the Mediterranean countries for its cherry-sized fruits. These are usually yellow to orange, but can occasionally be red or white. They are larger than a hawthorn haw and have an apple-flavored, pasty flesh with two or three tough seeds. Small, spreading trees or large shrubs, these are typical of the thorn genus, with clusters of large, white flowers that do not have the usual family scent.

Characteristic yellow azarole fruits on the tree

The thorn family are remarkably hardy, tough plants for wet, dry, windswept, or even coastal regions. They are survivors, and various species can be found in almost every part of the world, many of which bear similar small, edible, applelike fruits. Native to North Africa, Asia Minor, and Persia, the azarole, *C. azarolus,* may be the mespile anthedon about which the Greek Theophrastus wrote. More popular in the Latin countries, it was brought to Britain in 1640. In 1976 it got an award of merit from the Royal Horticultural Society, but it has never really caught on, probably because other more floriferous varieties and species were readily available.

Red azarole fruits

VARIETIES

The azarole is the more productive of the species and is grown commercially for flavoring liqueurs. It is probably the best choice for a tree for preserves. The Armenian *C. tanacetifolia,* the **Tansy-leafed Thorn** or **Syrian Hawberry,** is another good choice. The berries are almost relishable raw as a dessert and have an aromatic apple flavor, which is surprising, as they also closely resemble small yellow apples. They are pale green to yellow, with slight ribs like a melon, and a tassel of "leaves" at the end. The **Common Hawthorn** or **Quickthorn Haw**, *C. monogyna,* has one seed and is edible but not at all palatable, so is seldom eaten, save by curious children. Reputedly it was eaten raw when fully ripe by Scots Highlanders. The fruits are dark red and hang in immense festoons in autumn. The flowers have a sweet perfume when new, but go fishy as they age— on some trees more than others. Equally common, *C. oxycantha/laevigata* is very similar, usually with dark red flowers. There are several edible North American species. *C. tomentosa,* **Black Thorn** or **Pear Thorn**, has hard, orange-red, pear-shaped fruits; *C. flava* has yellow fruits; *C. douglasii* is a better species with small but sweet, black berries with yellow flesh. One identified as *C. coccinea* (now *mollis, sub mollis, pedicellata,* or *intricata*) was very popular with Native Americans, who dried the large scarlet or purple fruits for winter use. Sometimes these fruits were mixed together with chokecherries and service berries before they were dried and pressed into cakes for storage.

A hawthorn or May bush in full flower

CULTIVATION

The thorns are all extremely easy to please and require little skill or attention. They tend to lean when in the open. Hawthorns, including red azarole, are generally hardy to Zone 5, and some can take even more extreme cold. The black hawthorn (*C. douglasii*) is found in the wild from Alaska to California and east into Minnesota.

Growing under Glass and in Containers
Because they are so hardy they do not need protection, but several of the ornamental varieties can be grown in pots for forcing to produce early flowers.

Ornamental and Wildlife Value
The shows of blossom and masses of bright fruits make these an excellent choice for larger shrub borders and informal gardens.

Propagation
This is more difficult than for many fruits. The haws need stratifying for winter and a year before sowing the next spring, and may also produce mixed offspring unless they are from a true species grown far from any others. Cuttings are difficult, so choice

'Paul's Double Scarlet' hawthorn in flower

varieties are best obtained budded in May or grafted in April onto common stock.

Maintenance
Spring Weed, mulch, and spray with seaweed monthly.
Summer No maintenance.
Fall Collect fruits before the birds do.
Winter Prune if necessary.

Pruning and Training
Very little is needed. Do not overthin the branches, as thorns will naturally have a congested head.

Weed, Pest, and Disease Control
Thorns rarely suffer badly from problems, though they are occasionally defoliated by caterpillar attacks.

OTHER USES

Thorns make the best and most traditional hedge with a trimmed surface like fine tweed. The wood is heavy and hard and will burn with a good heat.

CULINARY USES

The flowers of common hawthorn once made a heady liqueur or wine. The young leaves and buds, known to school-children as "bread and cheese," had a nutty taste and made a welcome addition to salads. We are now told that both are slightly poisonous. However, the berries of azarole, common thorn, and especially the Armenian or Syrian, will make excellent preserves, wines, and jellies.

Hedge Jelly
Makes about 6 lb.

4 cups haws
3 cups crab or cooking apples
1 cup elderberries
Approx. 6 cups sugar

Wash the fruits, chop the apples, and simmer the fruits together, just covered with water, for about 2 hours, until softened. Strain and measure the liquid. Add the same volume of sugar to the liquid and bring back to a boil. Skim off the scum, jar, and seal.

Sorbus aucuparia from the family *Rosaceae*

MOUNTAIN ASH
ROWAN, WHITEBEAM, AND SERVICE BERRIES

Tree up to 50 ft. Life span: short. Deciduous, self-fertile. Fruits: up to ½ in., spherical, scarlet, in clusters. Value: very rich in vitamin C and pectin.

Mountain ashes or rowans are most attractive, small trees with distinctive, pinnate leaves, dark green above, lighter underneath. They have big heads of foamy, cream flowers like elderflowers, but smell unpleasant. In fall the branches bend under massive clusters of bright red to scarlet berries, which would hang through the winter if the birds did not finish them so quickly. The Latin name *aucuparia* means "bird catching," and refers to the fruit's early use as bait.

The *Sorbus* family is large and includes dwarf shrubs and large trees. They are spread all over the world and the majority are quite hardy. They color richly in fall and are widely grown for their attractive shows of fruits, also in yellow and white. Many new ornamental species were introduced from China during the nineteenth century, but little advance has been made in fruit quality since *S. aucuparia edulis* (*moravica* or *dulcis*) was first introduced in about 1800.

Sorbus is a native tree.

VARIETIES

Sorbus aucuparia, the **Rowan** or **Mountain Ash**, has scarlet berries that birds love and that are generally too sour and bitter for our tastes. There are many other ornamental species and varieties, for example *S. aucuparia xanthocarpa*, which has yellow fruits. However, the common rowan is still the frequent favorite choice from the genus and much planted in metropolitan areas. The best variety by far for the gourmand is *edulis* which has larger,

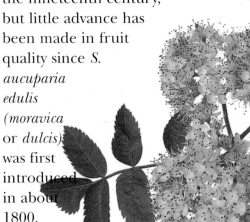
Rowan flowers and leaves

sweeter fruits carried in heavy bunches. *S. aria*, the **Whitebeam,** has similar red berries to a rowan and they were once eaten and used for wine. *S. domestica*, the **Service Tree**, is a native of Asia Minor and was also once widely liked, but is now less common. It has smaller clusters of larger fruits of a brownish green, resembling small pears. They need to be bletted like medlars (see p. 552) before they are edible. There were once pear-shaped and apple-shaped versions; the flavor and texture were improved after a frost and they were commonly sold in London markets. In Brittany they were used to make a rather poor cider. The **Wild Service** or **Chequer Tree**, *S. torminalis*, has smaller, still harder fruits, that would pucker even the hungriest peasant's mouth, but were once eaten by children.

Fruits on the wild service tree

A mountain ash tree covered in berries

CULTIVATION

Mountain ashes are tolerant of quite acid soils and do not like alkaline soils, protesting by being short-lived. They generally prefer drier to wetter sites but, strangely, are commonly seen growing naturally by mountain streams and in wet, hilly country. Most mountain ash species are cold hardy to Zone 5, with *S. acuparia* being hardy to Zone 3.

Growing under Glass and in Containers
They are hardy and rather too large for growing inside. They can be grown, and fruited, in pots if only a small crop is desired.

Ornamental and Wildlife Value
Almost all the species and varieties are very attractive to us in flower and fruit, turning glorious shades of crimson in fall, but most unfortunately do lack a sweet scent. Rowans are valuable to the birds and insects and are pollinated by flies and midges.

Maintenance
Spring Weed, mulch, and spray with seaweed solution.
Fall Pick fruits before the birds get them.
Winter Prune as necessary.

Propagation
Seed from the species may come true if the tree is isolated, but it must be stratified over winter first. Cuttings are rarely successful, so selected forms are budded in midsummer or grafted in early spring onto seedling rootstocks.

Pruning and Training
Pruning should be only remedial once a good head has formed, but watch for overladen branches and prop in time. The strongly erect growth of young trees can be bent down and into fruitfulness: pull them down gently with weights tied near the ends.

Weed, Pest, and Disease Control
Apart from bird losses, and being rather short-lived on alkaline soils, the members of this genus need little care and rarely suffer problems. They are thus well liked for planting.

OTHER USES

Rowan bark was used in dyeing and tanning. The wood is strong and was used for handles. Service wood is tough and resists wear well. The berries of the wild service tree, *S. torminalis*, were also used medicinally.

Rowan berries in fall

Mountain Ash Jelly

HARVESTING AND STORING, CULINARY USES

Rowan berries make a delicious jelly, almost like marmalade, which goes well with venison, game, and fatty or cold meats. They can be used in compotes, preserves, and syrups, and are sometimes added to apple dishes to liven them up. They have been used for fermenting and distilling liquor, and in emergencies the dried berries have been ground into meal to make a substitute for bread. Service fruits were used traditionally in quite similar ways.

Mountain Ash Jelly
Makes about 4 lb.

2 lb. firm ripe rowan
berries
1 small lemon
Approx. 4 cups sugar

Wash and stem the berries, add the chopped lemon and 2 cups of water and simmer until soft, about 1 hour. Strain and add 1 cup of sugar to each cup of liquid. Bring back to a boil, skim, and jar.

Prunus species from the family *Rosaceae*

SLOES AND BIRD CHERRIES

Tree/bush up to 30 ft. Life span: medium. Deciduous, self-fertile.
Fruits: up to 1 in., ovoid, single pit, red to black. Value: rich in vitamin C.

Closely related to orchard plums and cherries, the wild *Prunus* species remain tough, hardy alternatives for difficult spots or wild gardens. Sloes are the fruits of the blackthorn, *P. spinosa*, which is a medium-sized shrub, many-branched, very thorny, with blackish bark. The fruits are black ovoids with a bloom that resembles plums, and hard, juicy, green flesh that is usually far too astringent to eat raw. However, like many children, I forever searched for a sweeter one.

Sloes are native to Europe, North Africa, and Asia. The pits have been found on the sites of prehistoric dwellings, so they have long been an item of diet. They may be one of the ancestors of the damson and some of their "blood" has probably gotten into many true plums. The bird cherry is a native of Europe and Asia, especially grown in the north of England. The sixteenth-century herbalist Gerard claimed it was in "almost every hedge." Many ornamental *Prunus* species were later introduced in the eighteenth and nineteenth centuries; *P. maritima* was introduced by Farrer in 1800.

Sloe berries and leaves

Ripe sloe berries have a sharp, bitter taste.

VARIETIES

Prunus padus, the **Bird Cherry** or **Hag Berry**, is a small tree with white, fragrant flowers in late spring; the double-flowered form, *P. padus plena*, is more heavily almond-scented. The leaves and bark smell of bitter almonds and contain highly poisonous prussic acid. The **Sand Cherry** (*P. besseyi*) is an American species native to the Great Plains and the Great Lakes region. It has shiny, silvery green, leathery leaves and bears small, sweet, purplish-black fruits in abundance. **Hansen's Bush Cherry** is an improved form of this wild fruit, good for wildlife gardens and with attractive red fall color. Another North American species is *P. virginiana*, the **Choke Cherry**. This is a tall shrub with glossy green leaves and variable red to purplish-black berries. *P. simonii*, the **Apricot Plum,** from China, has large, attractive, red and yellow, scented fruits.

CULTIVATION

Sloes and bird cherries are very hardy—*P. padus* is cold hardy to Zone 4; *P. besseyi* to Zone 2—and good for making windbreaks. They like an exposed site and thrive on quite poor soil. Do mulch these heavily; water well while establishing on very sandy soils as these hold little water.

Growing under Glass and in Containers

Most of these are hardy and not tasty enough to merit space under cover.

Ornamental and Wildlife Value

All *Prunus* are good at flowering time, but few are worth space in most small, modern gardens. They are of more use to the wild garden, as the flowers are early, benefiting insects, while the fruits are excellent winter fare for birds and rodents.

Pruning and Training

Minimal pruning is required. As hedges, blackthorn should be planted at forty-five degrees, staggered in two or three close rows, each laid in opposite directions. Most species can be trained as small trees.

Flowers and leaves of the bird cherry tree

Maintenance

Spring Weed, mulch, spray with seaweed solution.
Summer Prune if any pruning is needed.
Fall Protect fruits from the birds.
Winter Pick fruits.

Propagation

The species usually come true from seed. Choicer varieties have been developed for ornamental use and must be budded in summer or grafted in spring. Cuttings do not take.

Weed, Pest, and Disease Control

These wildest members of the *Prunus* family suffer least from pests or diseases.

Blackthorn bush in flower

CULINARY USES

Sloe berries are much used for liqueurs, especially gin-based ones, and to add color to port-type wines. All over Europe they are fermented for wine or distilled to a spirit. In France the unripe sloes are pickled like olives. They can be made into juice, syrup, or jelly. Bird cherries have been used in much the same way but are inferior. The American species are used similarly. The apricot plum seems strangely underrated.

Sloe Gin

Sloes
Brown sugar or honey
Peeled almonds
Gin, brandy, or vodka

Wash and dry the sloes and prick each several times. Pack the sloes loosely into bottles. To each bottle add $3/4$ cup brown sugar or honey and a couple of almonds, then fill with gin (or brandy or vodka). Let sit for several months before drinking.

OTHER USES

Sloes are good hedging plants. Their leaves were formerly used to adulterate tea. Bird cherries do well in a hedge. Their wood is hard and used for carving and especially liked for rifle butts. Sloe bark was once used for medicinal purposes.

Bird cherry blossom

VERY WILD FRUITS

A Hottentot fig in flower

There are many other edible, if not palatable, fruits in gardens and parks, just waiting for breeders to improve them. What could be more gratifying and worthy than to present the world with new and improved fruits that can be grown in almost anyone's backyard? The following are a few of the many that are occasionally eaten by some, but are not widely used. Please remember *not* to eat anything unless you are 100 percent sure of it and you have had it identified on the spot by an expert!

Flower and leaves of the Hottentot fig

Asimina/Annona triloba, Pawpaw, Annonaceae

Pawpaw is a bottle-shaped fruit. Closely related to the papaya, it is much hardier; it is found as far north as Michigan and New York. A large, attractive, long-leafed, suckering bush, it is pest-resistant with fragrant, purple flowers. It prefers moist, not wet soils. Cultivars include **'Sunflower,' 'Sweet Alice,' 'Zimmerman,' 'Taylor,'** and **'Mary Foos Johnson.'** Male and female plants are needed; pollination is by flies. The fruits vary from 2–6 in. long, are green, ripening yellow to bronze, with yellow pulp, big brown seeds, and a resinous flavor, best cooked. They are slow-growing, slow-bearing, and long-lived. Zones 5 to 8.

Carpobrotus edulis, Hottentot Fig, Aizoaceae

This resembles the mesembryanthemums, with which it was once classed. Native to South Africa, it is a low-growing succulent, found wild in maritime southwest England and southern Europe. Large, magenta, or occasionally yellow, flowers are followed by small, figlike fruits, which can be eaten raw or cooked, pickled or preserved. The fleshy, triangular leaves can be eaten as salads as can those of the similar *Mesembryanthemum crystallinum.* Zones 9 and 10.

Ceratonia siliqua, Carob Tree, Leguminosae

The Locust Bean or St. John's Bread is an edible, purple-brown, beanlike pod that tastes so much like chocolate it can be ground up and used as a substitute. The seeds are not eaten, but are so exact in size and weight they were used for weighing gold and were the original "carat." This tree is native to the Mediterranean region, and preserved pods have been found at Pompeii. Nowadays the pods are used as animal feed. Zones 9 and 10.

Elaeagnus umbellata, Autumn Olive, Elaeagnaceae

A strong-growing, spreading, deciduous shrub from Asia with fragrant, yellow flowers and small, orange or red berries used like red currants or dried to "raisins." Many species in this genus bear edible fruits, and most of these have fragrant flowers. *E. commutata,* the **Silver Berry**, has pasty, silver berries and silver leaves. *E. angustifolia,* **Oleaster** or **Wild Olive,** has sweet berries, and is still popular in southeastern Europe. Zones 5 to 9.

Akebia quinata, Lardizabalaceae

A hardy climber from China with attractive, five-lobed leaflets, and scented, chocolate-purple flowers in two sizes. These are followed by weird little purple sausage fruits, surprisingly edible—sweetish but pasty and insipid. This needs a warm spot to ripen the fruits, which have a yellowish pulp full of black seeds. *A. trifoliata/lobata* is similar. Zones 5 to 9.

Hovenia dulcis, Japanese Raisin Tree, Rhamnaceae

I remember having this as a child. Resembling brown, candied angelica, the "fruit" is the dried, swollen flower stalk from behind the pea-sized seed of a small, attractive, Asian tree with glossy foliage. Zones 7 to 9.

Pods hanging from the carob or locust tree

Humulus lupulus,
Hop, Cannabidaceae

The common hop in flower

I have to include this strange fruit or I will never be forgiven by my beer-swilling compatriots! A rampant climber closely related to cannabis, this is a hardy native of southern Europe with maplelike leaves. Twining stems produce drooping, green-yellow, aromatic flower clusters that enlarge as they set. These are boiled to add their bitter, aromatic flavor to good ale and make it beer. The youngest shoots can be eaten in the manner of asparagus in early spring. Zones 4 to 8.

Rhus glabra,
Scarlet Sumac, Vinegar Tree, Anacardiaceae

This small, easily grown, hardy shrub was introduced to the U.K. from North America in 1622. It is often grown for its spectacular foliage, which turns scarlet in fall. However, it can produce masses of fruits if both males and females are grown, and these were once eaten by Native Americans and children. They have a sour taste and were used as a substitute for vinegar and in teas. Dried and crushed, they were sprinkled over meat and fatty dishes as a seasoning. Some other members of the *Rhus* family have apparently had their fruits or foliage eaten, but as they are closely related to poison ivy, *R. toxicodendron*, great caution is advised! Zones 4 to 8.

Taxus baccata,
Yew, Taxaceae

The foliage is deadly without cure, the seed may be poisonous—but for centuries children have eaten the red, fleshy aril. However, it is advisable not to try this one. Zones 6 to 9.

Yucca filamentosa,
Adam's Needle, Agavaceae

A well-known, spiky, garden perennial, this flowers occasionally in Britain and rarely sets fruit. This can be as large as a peach in the plant's homeland, south-western North America. Native Americans were fond of the fruit fresh or dried and ate the flower buds roasted or boiled. Zones 5 to 9.

Hippophae rhamnoides,
Sea Buckthorn, Elaeagnaceae

Often grown as an ornamental for its silver leaves, this tall, thorny shrub produces acid, orange-yellow fruits if both sexes are planted. The fruits are too sour for most tastes, but have been eaten in famines and by children and are apparently widely collected in Russia, as they are very rich in vitamin C. They are used as a sauce with fish and meat in France, and in central Europe they are made into a jelly that is eaten with fish or cheese. Zones 4 to 9.

Tilia species,
Lindens, Tiliaceae

These enormous, well-known trees have sweet sap that was formerly boiled down to sugar. The fruits were once ground into a "chocolate," but this never caught on. Can be grown to Zone 4, depending on species.

Smilacina racemosa,
Treacle Berry, False Solomon's Seal, Convallariaceae

This delectable, herbaceous garden plant has scented, foamy white flowers followed by apparently edible, sweet, red berries. One of the best unknown fruits! Zones 3 to 7.

Harvesting linden flowers

Gaultheria procumbens,
Checkerberry, Teaberry, Ericaceae

A low-growing, evergreen native of North America with white flowers and red berries, needing moist, acid soil and partial shade. The berries are odd raw, but can be cooked for jellies and tarts and were once used to flavor chewing gum. *G. humifusa* was also used, as was *G. shallon*, another taller, shrubbier version with great clusters of purple berries, which were eaten dried by Native Americans. Zones 4 to 7.

Colorful checkerberries and leaves

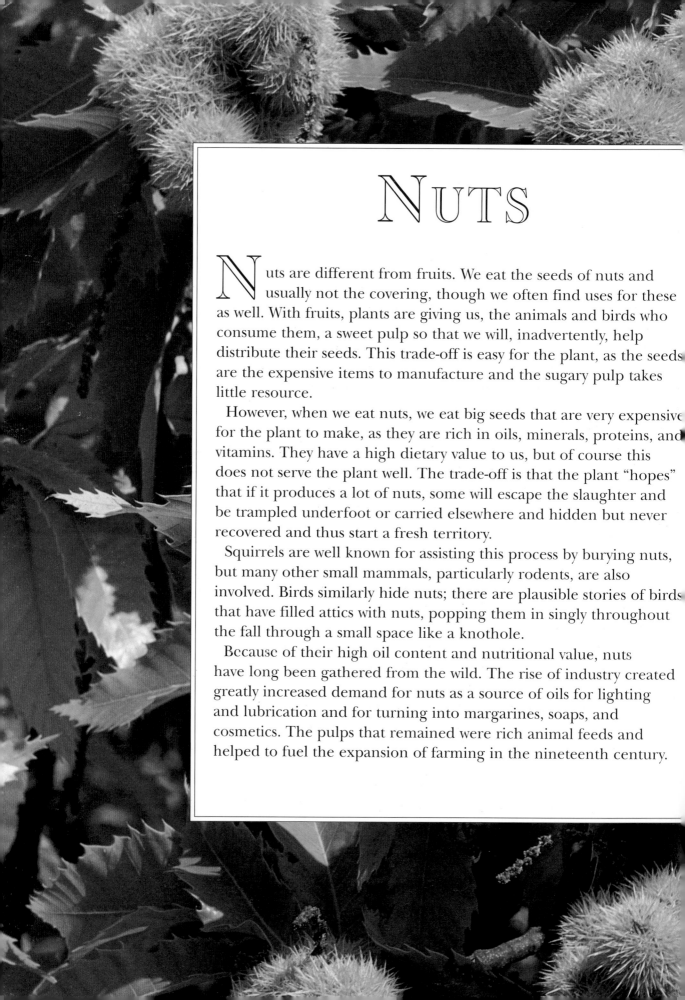

NUTS

Nuts are different from fruits. We eat the seeds of nuts and usually not the covering, though we often find uses for these as well. With fruits, plants are giving us, the animals and birds who consume them, a sweet pulp so that we will, inadvertently, help distribute their seeds. This trade-off is easy for the plant, as the seeds are the expensive items to manufacture and the sugary pulp takes little resource.

However, when we eat nuts, we eat big seeds that are very expensive for the plant to make, as they are rich in oils, minerals, proteins, and vitamins. They have a high dietary value to us, but of course this does not serve the plant well. The trade-off is that the plant "hopes" that if it produces a lot of nuts, some will escape the slaughter and be trampled underfoot or carried elsewhere and hidden but never recovered and thus start a fresh territory.

Squirrels are well known for assisting this process by burying nuts, but many other small mammals, particularly rodents, are also involved. Birds similarly hide nuts; there are plausible stories of birds that have filled attics with nuts, popping them in singly throughout the fall through a small space like a knothole.

Because of their high oil content and nutritional value, nuts have long been gathered from the wild. The rise of industry created greatly increased demand for nuts as a source of oils for lighting and lubrication and for turning into margarines, soaps, and cosmetics. The pulps that remained were rich animal feeds and helped to fuel the expansion of farming in the nineteenth century.

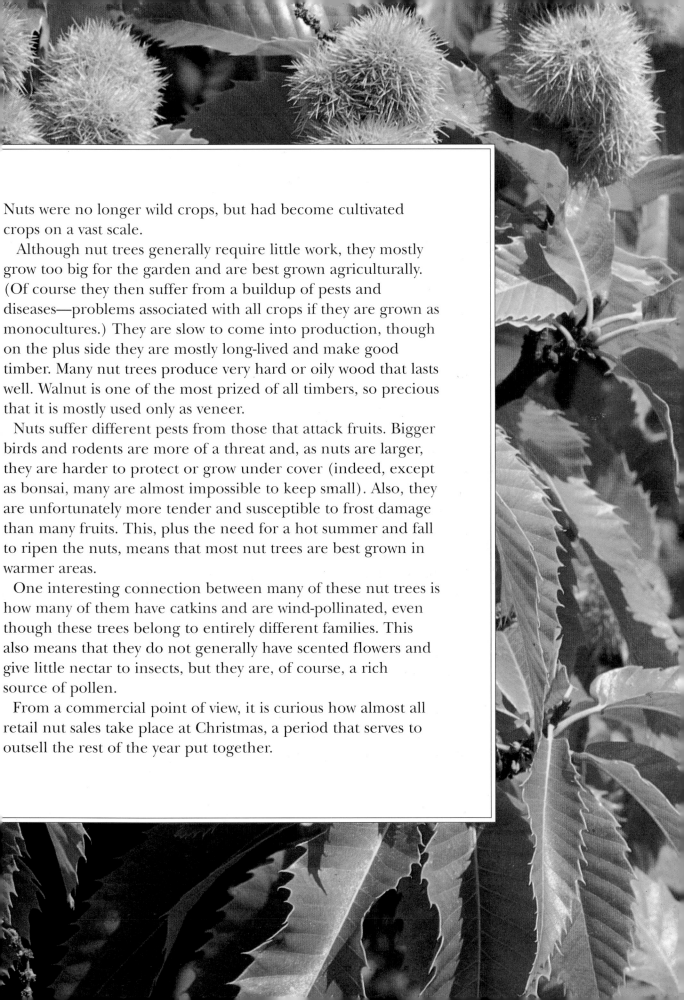

Nuts were no longer wild crops, but had become cultivated crops on a vast scale.

Although nut trees generally require little work, they mostly grow too big for the garden and are best grown agriculturally. (Of course they then suffer from a buildup of pests and diseases—problems associated with all crops if they are grown as monocultures.) They are slow to come into production, though on the plus side they are mostly long-lived and make good timber. Many nut trees produce very hard or oily wood that lasts well. Walnut is one of the most prized of all timbers, so precious that it is mostly used only as veneer.

Nuts suffer different pests from those that attack fruits. Bigger birds and rodents are more of a threat and, as nuts are larger, they are harder to protect or grow under cover (indeed, except as bonsai, many are almost impossible to keep small). Also, they are unfortunately more tender and susceptible to frost damage than many fruits. This, plus the need for a hot summer and fall to ripen the nuts, means that most nut trees are best grown in warmer areas.

One interesting connection between many of these nut trees is how many of them have catkins and are wind-pollinated, even though these trees belong to entirely different families. This also means that they do not generally have scented flowers and give little nectar to insects, but they are, of course, a rich source of pollen.

From a commercial point of view, it is curious how almost all retail nut sales take place at Christmas, a period that serves to outsell the rest of the year put together.

Prunus dulcis/amygdalus from the family *Rosaceae*

ALMONDS

*Tree up to 20 ft. Life span: short. Deciduous. Fruits: 2 in., pointed oval, in brown skin.
Value: rich in protein, calcium, iron, vitamins B_2 and B_3, and phosphorus.*

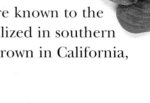

Almond trees resemble and are closely related to peaches, with larger, light pink blossoms appearing before long, thin leaves. Flowering a fortnight earlier than peaches, they are often affected by frost. The wild varieties sometimes have spiny branches. The almond fruit has tough, inedible, leathery, greenish-brown, felted skin with a partition line along which it easily splits. The skin peels off a smooth, hard stone, full of small holes that do not penetrate the shell, containing the single, flat, pointed oval seed.

Originally from the Middle East, almonds were known to the ancient Hebrews and Phoenicians. Long naturalized in southern Europe and western Asia, they are now widely grown in California, South Africa, and south Australia.

Almond blossom

VARIETIES

Prunus dulcis dulcis is the **Sweet Almond**, *P. dulcis amara*, the **Bitter Almond**. The former is the much-loved nut; the latter is used for producing oil and flavorings and is too bitter for eating. It contains highly poisonous amounts of prussic acid. The variety **'Texas'** is especially tasty roasted and salted. Self-fruitful **'Hall's Hardy'** is a beautiful tree with a cloud of pale pink flowers and heavy crops of nuts. **'Nonpareil'** is the leading commercial variety.

CULTIVATION

Almonds want well-enriched, well-aerated, light soil, and to be at least 10 ft. apart. They need no staking after the first year. They want copious quantities of compost and mulches. Usually grown as a bush, they can be planted against walls. They should not be planted near peaches, as they may hybridize, resulting in bitter nuts. Hand-pollination is recommended. They are not usually self-fertile, so several trees should be planted together. Almonds can be grown in Zones 6 through 9. Like the related peach trees, almonds have a tendency to bloom early, which can be problematic in areas with unpredictable late spring weather. **'Hall's Hardy'** is reliable in Zone 5.

Growing under Glass

Almonds are rarely grown under glass because the necessary extra efforts of replenishment pruning and tying in are not usually well rewarded. The greenhouse must be unheated in winter to give them a dormant rest period.

Growing in Containers

Almonds can be grown in large pots, as they can take heavy pruning if well fed and watered. Pots enable them to be kept under cover during winter and through flowering and then brought out all through the summer, thus avoiding peach leaf curl and frost damage. The flowers must be protected from frosts and so too must the young fruitlets.

Ornamental and Wildlife Value

The almond is a real beauty—the fruiting tree as much as the many ornamental varieties.

Propagation

Almonds can be raised from stones, but take years to fruit and may produce a mixture of sweet and bitter fruits. Peach rootstocks are better.

Maintenance

Spring Protect blossoms from frost, hand-pollinate, weed, mulch, and spray with seaweed solution monthly.
Summer Thin fruits early.
Fall Remove ripe and mummified fruits from the trees.
Winter Prune hard; spray with Bordeaux mixture.

Pruning and Training

Almonds fruit on young shoots, like peaches, but need to carry more fruits, so the trees are not pruned as hard. Commercially, every third year or so a few main branches are cut back hard and the top end of the remaining higher branches is removed to encourage prolific growth from the lower branches and stubs. This is best done in late winter, though it may let in silver leaf disease. It also keeps the bushes lower and more manageable. On walls and under cover, almonds may be fan trained, as for peaches (see p. 419). Thinning the fruits is not essential, but prevents biennial bearing.

A grove of almond trees

OTHER USES

The wood is hard and makes good veneers; the oil is used in cosmetics.

Almonds ripening on the tree

Weed, Pest, and Disease Control

Earwigs can get inside the fruits and eat the kernel, but are readily trapped in rolls of corrugated paper around each branch. Protect the bark from **animals** such as rabbits and deer. Although we think of them as nuts, not fruits, almonds are closely related to peaches and susceptible to some of the same diseases, including brown rot, borers, and **peach leaf curl. Shot hole fungus** and **navel orange worm** can also cause problems.

Harvesting and Storing

Once the nuts start to drop, knock them down, peel, and dry. Commercially they are hulled, but the nuts will keep better intact. They can be stored in dry salt or sand for long periods.

COMPANION PLANTING

Almonds are benefited by alliums, especially garlic and chives. Clover or alfalfa and stinging nettles are also reputedly helpful.

CULINARY USES

The nuts are left with the brown skin on, or are blanched to provide a cleaner-tasting product. They may be eaten raw, cooked, or turned into a milk.

Almond Milkshake
Quantities to taste

Almond milk
Ice-cold whole milk
Grated nutmeg

To one part almond milk add approximately seven parts milk, mix well, and top with the grated nutmeg.

Carya species from the family *Juglandaceae*

PECAN AND HICKORY NUTS

Tree up to 100 ft. Life span: medium to long. Deciduous, partly self-fertile. Fruits: up to 2 in., green-skinned, hard-shelled nuts. Value: rich in oils and vitamins B_1 and B_2.

Pecans are very large, fast-growing trees with pinnate leaves, male catkins, and insignificant flowers followed by pointed, rounded,

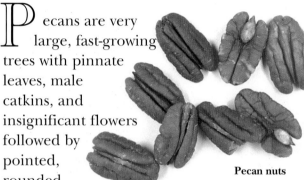

Pecan nuts

cylindrical fruits. These have a leathery skin that peels off to reveal a reddish, smooth shell enclosing the walnutlike kernel. Hickories are similar, though not as large in tree or fruit, with nonaromatic leaves and peeling bark, while the pecan has gray, resinous leaves. Hickories also prefer more humid conditions than pecans.

These are natives of North America and have been long enjoyed by Native Americans. They are grown in Australia, but rarely crop well elsewhere, though they are widely grown for their timber. The first trees were introduced to Britain in 1629.

VARIETIES

Carya illinoensis is the **pecan**, a fruit much like a walnut in most ways save that the reddish shell is smooth, not embossed. The trees grow up to 70 ft. high. Hickories are similar to pecans, with more flattened nuts, and the trees grow half as big again, which is pretty big. The **Shellbark Hickory**, *C. laciniosa/ alba*, and *C. ovata*, the **Shagbark Hickory**, are the more popular and productive sorts. American breeders have developed many good varieties of hickories. The shagbarks **'Wurth,' 'Yoder,'** and **'Wilcox'** are good producers of flavorful, easily cracked nuts. **'Missouri Mammoth'** and **'Keystone'** are excellent shell barks, with nutmeats that crack clean of the shell. The pecan **'Desirable'** has large nuts with thin shells that crack cleanly; pollinate it with **'Stuart.' 'Mohawk'** bears very large pecans with very thin shells that crack into halves for fancy baking needs. **'Cape Fear,' 'Cheyenne,'** and **'Choctaw'** are other good cracking and tasty pecans. **'Hican'** is a pecan and hickory hybrid with hickory flavor but a thinner shell; **'Burton'** is a worthy variety.

CULTIVATION

Plant pecans in deep, rich, moist soil; hickories tolerate a range of soils but do best in rich, well-drained sites. Pecans thrive in Zones 6 through 9, hickories in Zones 3 through 8.

Immature pecans growing on the tree

The pointed, cylindrical pecan fruit contains the edible kernel.

Growing under Glass and in Containers

There is little practical possibility of getting these huge trees under cover. They resent being confined in pots and are unlikely to crop, though they may make good bonsai subjects.

Ornamental and Wildlife Value

Given a suitable setting, these are large, attractive trees with decorative foliage that turns a rich yellow in fall.

Maintenance

No maintenance needed.

Propagation

Normally grown from seed, they are best pot-grown and then planted out as soon as possible in their final site, as they do not like to be transplanted. They are slow to establish and then fast-growing. Improved varieties are grafted or budded on seedling stock.

Pruning and Training

No pruning and training are required. Large specimens need staking for the first few years, as they are slow to take.

Harvesting and Storing

Ripe fruits are knocked down from the tree, husked (if the husk has not dropped off already), and dried. They do not store as well as walnuts, though they may keep up to a year if they are stored in a cool, dry place. Commercially they are hulled before storage and will keep up to two years at 5°F.

WEED, PEST, AND DISEASE CONTROL, COMPANION PLANTING

Disease is usually not a factor in drier areas, but in the humid Southeast, scab can be troublesome. Choose disease-resistant cultivars such as **'Candy'** and **'Caddo.'** Black and yellow aphids may also inflict damage. A healthy tree will usually shrug off such attacks. Birds and squirrels will compete for the nuts.

OTHER USES

Hickories are planted for their tough, elastic timber and are renowned as fuel for smoking foods. The bark was once used for a yellow dye.

CULINARY USES

Pecan nuts taste a lot like mild, sweet walnuts and to my taste are preferable. They are used raw or cooked in savory and sweet items, especially cakes and ice cream. Pecan pie is a legendary dessert. Hickory nuts are used similarly and can be squeezed to produce nut milk or oil.

Pecan Pie
Serves 4–6

6 oz. shortcrust pastry
¹⁄₄ cup shelled pecans
3 oz. brown sugar
2 large eggs
1 cup golden syrup
1 oz. maple syrup
¹⁄₂ teaspoon vanilla extract
¹⁄₄ teaspoon salt

Roll out the pastry and line a wide, shallow pie dish. Bake blind, weighed down with dried peas or the like, at 375°F for 20 minutes or until cooked. Cool and fill the crust with pecans, arranged aesthetically. Beat together the other ingredients until the sugar is dissolved and pour over the crust carefully without disturbing the nuts, which may float. Bake at 450°F for 10 minutes, then reduce the temperature to 350°F and cook for another 30 minutes. Cool and chill well before serving in slices with whipped cream.

Juglans species from the family *Juglandaceae*

WALNUTS

Tree 135 ft. Life span: long. Deciduous, partially self-fertile.
Fruits: up to 2 in., green sphere enclosing nut. Value: rich in oil; the husks contain much vitamin C.

Walnuts are slow-growing, making massive trees up to 135 feet eventually, with aromatic, pinnate foliage, silvery bark, insignificant female flowers, and male catkins. All parts have a distinct sweet, aromatic smell. The fruits have a green husk around the nut, enclosing a kernel wrinkled like a brain.

Juglans regia, the common or Persian walnut, is native to western Asia. Introduced to the Mediterranean basin before the 1st century B.C., it became an important food in many regions and was also grown for timber. The Carpathian strain, from the mountains of Poland, is similar to the Persian walnut, but more cold hardy. The black walnut, *J. nigra*, comes from northeast America. It is even bigger than the common walnut and widely grown for timber. The nuts are large, very hard to crack, and a valuable dietary source of phosphorus.

"The wife, the dog and the walnut tree, the more you beat them the better they'll be" is advice that puzzles many. It is not to encourage fruitfulness, but rather to give the walnut a damaged bark that then produces a more valuable distorted grain in the timber. (As to wife or dog, I suggest attention and treats probably develop better relationships with either.)

Growing under Glass and in Containers

Huge trees, these can hardly be housed. I have a fifteen-year-old bonsai, but I doubt that it will ever fruit!

Ornamental and Wildlife Value

Very attractive and sweetly aromatic trees, they grow too big for most small gardens. They are very valuable to wildlife, especially rodents, squirrels, and birds.

Maintenance

No maintenance needed.

The fruit of the Persian walnut opens as it ripens.

VARIETIES

Named varieties of common walnuts include **'Franquette,'** once popular as a commercial variety on the West Coast, and slow to leaf out in spring so less susceptible to frost damage. **'Chandler'** bears large nuts with light-colored meats on a smaller tree. **'Ambassador'** is a Carpathian variety with plump, well-flavored kernels and heavy crops. **'Thomas Black'** is an excellent black walnut with large, thin-shelled nuts. There are several named varieties available from the U.S. They can grow half as high again as common trees, up

to 150 ft. Another American species, the **White Walnut** or **Butternut**, *J. cinerea*, introduced in 1633, is grown for timber and ornamental use.

CULTIVATION

Walnuts prefer a heavy, moist soil. **Black walnuts** thrive in Zones 4 through 8, **Persians** in 5 through 9, and **Carpathian** in 3 through 9. As pollination is difficult, it is best to plant several together. The old saying

Walnut catkin

Propagation
The species can be grown from seed, but are slow. Improved varieties are grafted or budded, and still take a decade to start to fruit, finally maturing after a century. They are best started in pots and moved to their final site while still small, as they resent transplanting.

Pruning and Training
Walnuts must be pruned only in fall, as they bleed in spring. Minimal pruning is required, but branches become massive, so remove badly positioned ones early. They need no stake after the first years.

The common walnut tree

Weed, Pest, and Disease Control
There are few problems. **Late frosts** damage them, otherwise they are slow, reliable croppers, each averaging 150 lb. annually.

Harvesting and Storing
The nuts are knocked down and the sticky staining peel is removed before drying. Ripe nuts will drop, but squirrels will get them before you do. Walnuts can then be stored for up to a year.

COMPANION PLANTING

Varro, in the 1st century B.C., noted how sterile the land near walnut trees was. Walnut leaves and roots give off exudates that inhibit many plants and prevent their seeds from germinating. The American species are more damaging than the European and they are particularly bad for apples, *Solanaceae, Rubus,* and many ornamentals.

CULINARY USES

Walnuts may be eaten either raw or cooked, often in sweets or cakes, and go particularly well with coffee or chocolate. They yield an edible, light oil. The young fruits may be pickled before the stone forms.

Walnut Aperitif

Young green walnuts
Brandy
Red wine
Sugar as required

Wash and prick enough nuts to fill a wide-necked bottle. Fill with brandy, seal, and store in a cool, dark place. After a year, decant the brandy into another bottle, refill the original bottle with red wine, and reseal. After another year, decant the wine into the brandy, refill the walnut bottle with wine, and reseal. After another year, decant again, fill the walnut bottle with granulated sugar, and reseal. After a year (making four in total), discard the nuts and add the sugar syrup to the wine and brandy. Serve in sherry glasses before meals.

OTHER USES

The foliage and husks have long been used as brown dyes and the oil as a hair darkener and for paints. The wood has always been valued for veneers and gun stocks, the more gnarled the better. Walnut trees were often planted near stables and privies, as their smell was thought to keep away flies. The walnut sap has traditionally been boiled to produce sugar.

Corylus species from the family *Corylaceae*

HAZELNUTS AND FILBERTS

Tree/bush up to 20 ft. Life span: medium to long. Deciduous, partially self-fertile. Fruits: up to 1 in., pointed round, or oblong oval, brown nuts. Value: rich in oils.

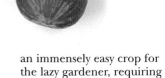

These are shrubby trees, typical of woods and thickets, with dark stems, leaves rounded to a point, and magnificent, yellow catkin male flowers in early spring. The gorgeous, carmine-red, female flowers are tiny, sea-urchin-like tentacles that protrude on warm days. The nuts are a pointed round or oblong oval. Hazelnuts have a husk around the base, while filberts (full-beards) are completely enveloped by the husk. The shell is thin and the kernel sweet. Wild hazels are *Corylus avellana*, but, being wind-pollinated, these have often been influenced by *C. colurna*, Turkish filberts or Barcelona nuts, also known as "cobs," and *C. maxima*, or filberts.

Hazelnuts of wild species were known in ancient times and filberts were introduced by the Romans from Greece. Pliny claims they came there from Damascus. The Romans may have brought filberts to Britain, but they were not noticed officially until introduced in 1759. Cob nuts were introduced earlier, in 1582, and the American hazelnut, *C. americana*, a similar, smaller nut with a thicker shell and heart-shaped leaves, arrived in 1798. Any appellation no longer signifies true breeding, as these all became interbred during the nineteenth century, giving us most of our current varieties.

Immature hazelnuts

VARIETIES

I adore **Red-skinned Filberts**; they are certainly small and fiddly, with tight, russet husks, but they are so delicious. Filberts are grown commercially in the Pacific Northwest. **'Barcelona,'** popular in commercial orchards and home gardens, bears very large nuts that self-husk and are easy to crack out. Pollinate with **'Duchilly,'** which bears large, long nuts. **'Ennis'** is a recent introduction for European filbert from Oregon State University. It has excellent flavor and produces more nuts and fewer "blanks" (empty nutshells) than older varieties. For the best flavor, however, you can't beat the wild hazelnut.

CULTIVATION

Hazels thrive in stony, hilly ground or well-drained, loamy soil and will tolerate heavy, damp soils. Hazels need no support and are best planted severally to ensure pollination. They are an immensely easy crop for the lazy gardener, requiring even less effort than most.

Growing under Glass and in Containers

There seems no reason to grow them under cover and I suspect they would not like it anyway. They survive in pots quite well, looking attractive but seldom cropping.

Ornamental and Wildlife Value

These are not generally noticed, save when their catkins make a welcome display. The **Twisted Hazel** is attractively distorted and deformed and still crops well. The hazels will support many life forms, both large and small, and are also excellent plants for wild or native gardens.

Maintenance

No maintenance needed.

Propagation

These can be grown from seed but do not come true. Layering or grafting is possible, but root suckers are best, detached in fall and potted up or planted in situ or a nursery bed for a year before their final move.

Pruning and Training

Traditionally hazels were grown on a low, flat, cartwheel frame. They are probably best trained to spurs on goblets, but are often left to be bushes or thickets. It is worth keeping them on a single trunk, uncongested, and removing the suckers, to prevent losing any of the nuts.

Weed, Pest, and Disease Control

Weedy growth underneath makes it hard to find nuts, so hazels are best planted in grass or mulched. In gardens they suffer few problems on a scale sufficient to damage crops, other than the attentions of **birds**, **rodents**, **children**, and especially **squirrels**.

Male and female hazel flowers

Harvesting and Storing

The nuts can be eaten a little unripe, but have to be fully ripe to keep. Ideally they should be allowed to fall off, but many are stolen by wildlife. They need to be husked and dried to keep well, though I never dehusk my red-skinned filberts. They will keep best, and for years, if packed in salt.

COMPANION PLANTING

Truffles can be grown on their roots.

OTHER USES

Hazels make good hedges and windbreaks. The foliage is eaten by many animals, including cows. The stems are tough and flexible, so they are good for baskets and hurdles, and forked branches make divining rods. The wood is used for smoking fuel and I smoke cheese with the shells.

CULINARY USES

Hazelnuts of all varieties are used in savory dishes, but more often in sweet dishes and confections. They are used for liqueurs and can be squeezed to express a light, edible oil.

Hazelnut Macaroons
Makes about 12

½ cup hazelnuts
½ cup light brown sugar
1 egg white
Drop of vanilla extract
Whipped cream to serve

Grind three-quarters of the nuts in a food processor, then add the other ingredients and cream them together. Pour rounds of the mix onto parchment paper on a baking sheet, place the remaining nuts on top, and bake for 15 minutes at 350°F. Serve sandwiched with whipped cream.

Hazel growing in the wild

Castanea sativa from the family *Fagaceae*

CHESTNUTS
CHINESE AND
SWEET

Tree up to 120 ft. Life span: long. Deciduous, rarely self-fertile. Fruits: 2 in., prickly burrs containing two or three nuts. Value: rich in oils.

Chestnuts make beautiful trees. They have very large, serrated-edged leaves. The male flowers are long, yellow catkins, different from walnut or hazel catkins, as they are divided like pearls on a string. The fruits are brownish-russet, softly spiny burrs usually containing three brown nuts with thin, tough, leathery shells, flattened on one side and pointed.

Sweet chestnuts are native to the Mediterranean region. They were highly valued by the Romans for food and timber and became widely distributed. They fruit well only after hot summers, but are still capable of reaching a large size, so they have been planted for timber and were often coppiced. The major exporter of these nuts has always been Spain, though most southern European countries have their own production, as chestnuts have become a staple food. Madeiran nuts are said to be the biggest and traditionally served to sustain the peasants for months each year.

Sweet chestnut leaves and ripening fruit

VARIETIES

C. dentata was the **American Sweet Chestnut**, with smaller, richly flavored, sweeter nuts, but has been almost wiped out by a fungus, chestnut blight. Now American growers are breeding hybrids from the resistant *C. mollissima*, the **Chinese Chestnut**. Chinese-American crosses are taller than the Chinese species—they may reach 90 ft.—and include **'Dunstan,'** which bears in three or four years after planting. **'Revival'** is a third-generation Chinese-American hybrid with very large, sweet nuts from which the brown membrane is easily removed. **'Layeroka'** is a Chinese-American hybrid and early ripening. Other *Castanea* species are widely grown and the delicious nuts eaten with appreciation all around the world.

CULTIVATION

Chestnuts are far too big for most gardens, rapidly reaching 100 ft. or even more. They thrive in light, well-drained loam or light, dry, sandy soil. Chinese and European chestnuts and their hybrids are hardy in Zones 5 through 8. They need no staking after the first year or so. If nuts are required rather than timber, plant on the sunny side of woodlands or windbreaks, ideally of yew or holm oak.

Maintenance
No maintenance needed.

Ornamental and Wildlife Value

Sweet chestnuts make statuesque trees and the large leaves color well in fall. The nuts are often rather too useful to wildlife.

Growing under Glass and in Containers

Far too big to grow under glass, they resent being confined in a pot and they are unlikely to ever fruit in one.

Harvesting and Storing

The nuts will drop when ripe, or they can be beaten down, the husks then removed and dried. They will keep for a year in cool, dry conditions; longer if totally dried first.

Propagation

They can be grown from seed and are fast-growing but still slow to fruit. The best varieties are budded or grafted.

The elegant shape of the sweet chestnut tree

Weed, Pest, and Disease Control

In America, chestnut blight wiped out the best species; so far this is no problem elsewhere. Rodents, birds (especially rooks and pheasants), and squirrels soon take the nuts.

Pruning and Training

Minimal pruning is required and is best tackled in winter. Chestnuts get very large, so care must be taken to remove unsound branches.

COMPANION PLANTING

Chestnuts are considered healthier when they are grown near oak trees.

The brown chestnut is contained within a tough, leathery shell.

CULINARY USES

Chestnuts are not eaten raw, but are delicious roasted. They are made into *marrons glacés* (crystallized chestnuts), ground into flour, and then made into porridge, puddings, breads, cakes, muffins, and tarts, and they are also much used for savory dishes such as pâtés and in stuffing for meats. Sweet chestnuts are even made into liqueurs.

Chestnut Amber
Serves 4

1 cup chestnuts
1¼ cups milk
1 lemon, peel and juice
1 vanilla pod
⅓ cup bread crumbs
2 tablespoons butter
¼ cup superfine sugar
2 eggs, separated
1 quantity piecrust made from
 ¾ cup flour, ⅓ stick butter
 and water to mix

Roast the chestnuts for 20 minutes, cool, and remove the skins. Simmer gently, with sufficient water to cover, until tender, then drain and sieve to a puree. Simmer the milk with the lemon peel and vanilla pod for 15 minutes, then strain over the bread crumbs. Blend the butter and half the sugar, mix in the egg yolks and lemon juice, and stir in the pureed chestnuts, bread crumbs, and milk. Line a deep dish with the piecrust and fill with the mixture. Bake at 400°F for 25 minutes, or until firm and brown. Whisk the egg whites to a stiff froth, add a teaspoon of sugar, whisk again, and spoon on top of the pie. Sprinkle with more sugar and then return to the oven until the meringue turns a delicious amber.

OTHER USES

The wood is durable, but has "shakes" or splits in it. Often used for rough or external timber, such as coffins and hop poles, it makes a poor firewood but superior charcoal. The nuts were traditionally used for fattening pigs.

Pistacia vera from the family *Anacardiaceae*

PISTACHIOS

Tree up to 30 ft. Life span: medium. Deciduous, not self-fertile.
Fruits: 1 in., pointed oval nuts. Value: rich in oil.

Pistachios are small, tender trees with gray bark and gray-green, slightly downy, pinnate leaves. The male and female flowers are borne on separate trees in the wild, but some cultivated varieties may be unisexual. It is hard to tell, as the flowers are inconspicuous though carried in panicles, which later become masses of small, pointed red fruits. These have a thin, green husk covering the thin, smooth, twin-shelled nut, housing a small, oval, green kernel that has a most appealing taste, especially after roasting and salting.

Pistachios are natives of the Middle East and Central Asia and have been cultivated since ancient times. They were grown in Italy in the late Roman period but were not introduced to Britain until the sixteenth and seventeenth centuries and then never proved hardy enough. The seed was distributed by the U.S. Patent Office in 1854 and the trees proved successful in California and other mild-climate states, where the nuts are now produced in quantity, rivaling the output of the Mediterranean and Turkey.

VARIETIES

'**Kerman**' is a female plant that bears heavy clusters of excellent nuts, up to 50 lb. per tree. It can be single- or multi-trunked and is beautiful ornamental. Pollinate with '**Peters,**' a male, nonfruiting variety.

Pistacia terebinthus, the **Cyprus Turpentine Tree** or **Terebinth,** is not hardy. The whole plant is resinous with nuts that start coral red, ripening to brown, and have edible, oily kernels, also green and pointed but smaller. It was used as a pollinator for pistachios *(P. vera),* as these shed pollen too early to fertilize themselves. Thus most seedling pistachios became hybrids of these two species. This has prevented much improvement of the pistachio nut. *P. lentiscus* is the evergreen **Mastic Tree.** The nuts yield edible oil, but this tree is grown mainly for the resin obtained from bark incisions, used in turn for chewing gum and medicines.

Pistachio trees are grown in warm, arid countries for their edible nuts (above).

A spray of pistachios and leaves

CULTIVATION

Pistachios are not particular as to soil. In warmer countries they are useful for growing on poor, dry, hilly soil where other nuts will not thrive. Their greater value commercially also encourages this. Pistachios need a period of moderate cold to produce well. They are cold hardy to about 15°F and reliable in Zone 9 and possibly Zone 8. One male staminate tree is needed for six female pistillate trees, but as the pollen is shed early it needs to be saved in a paper bag until the pistils are receptive.

Growing under Glass and in Containers
Pistachios have been grown under glass and they make very attractive shrubs in large pots. However, good provision must be made for their pollination.

Ornamental and Wildlife Value
In warm countries or on a warm wall these are not unattractive, small trees. Pistachio nuts are readily taken by birds and mammals.

Maintenance
Spring Put out pots or uncover trees, weed, mulch, spray with seaweed solution.
Summer Water plants in pots regularly but minimally.
Fall Gather nuts if the summer has been hot.
Winter Bring in pots or protect trees.

Propagation
Although better varieties could be grown, pistachios seem to lack development. Continual cross-hybridization with terebinths has prevented improvement, but means that nuts come as true as their parents, which is not claiming a lot. Better varieties can be layered, budded, or grafted.

Pruning and Training
Only remedial pruning is required and this is best done in midsummer. They can be trained against walls and are best fan-trained initially, then allowed to grow out to form a bush.

Weed, Pest, and Disease Control
No common pests or diseases are a problem for pistachios in garden cultivation, though under glass and on a warm wall they may suffer **red spider mite** attacks.

Harvesting and Storing
As these hang severally on panicles, they can be cut off to be dried and husked. They are best stored in their shells, which open automatically if they are roasted.

OTHER USES

P. terebinthus was long ago cultivated for producing terebinth, the resin that oozes from the tree, and later turpentine. The wood is dark red and hard and used in cabinet making.

CULINARY USES

Pistachios can be eaten raw, but are most commonly roasted and salted, the shelling being left to the purchaser. They are much used as a coloring and flavoring for a wide range of foods, some savory, and many sweet, including nougat and ice cream.

Pistachio Ice Cream
Serves 6

2 large egg yolks
³/₄ cup. honey
1 teaspoon vanilla extract

2 cups cream
¹/₂ cup shelled pistachios
Natural green food coloring
Candied lemon slices and glacé cherries to taste

Whisk the egg yolks, honey, vanilla, and half the cream. Scald the remaining cream in a double boiler, add the egg mixture, and stir until the mixture thickens. Remove from the heat, cool, chill, then partially freeze. Remove from the freezer, beat vigorously, and freeze again. Repeat, but after the second beating mix in the nuts and coloring, then freeze again. Partially defrost before serving the ice cream scooped into glasses, garnished with lemon slices and cherries.

Anacardium occidentale from the family *Anacardiaceae*

CASHEWS

Tree up to 40 ft. Life span: medium.
Semi-evergreen. Fruit: up to 3 in. long.
Value: kernels are nearly half fat
and one-fifth protein.

Cashews are medium-sized, spreading trees with rounded leaves related to pistachios. The cashew comes attached underneath the bottom of the much larger and peculiar fruits, cashew apples, which are juicy and astringent. The nut is gray or brown, ear-shaped, and contains a white kernel within the acrid, poisonous shell.

Indigenous to South America, cashews were planted in the East Indies by the sixteenth century and are now grown in many tropical regions, especially India and eastern Africa.

VARIETIES

Other cashews are eaten: *A. humile*, the **Monkey-nut**, and *A. nanum* are from Brazil and have similar nuts. *A. rhinocarpus* is the **Wild Cashew** of Columbia and British Guyana.

CULTIVATION

Cashews grow in Zone 10 and will thrive in any reasonable soil.

A cashew tree in Kenya

Growing under Glass and in Containers
Plants dwarfed by large pots could probably be grown in a hot greenhouse or conservatory, if the seed could be found.

Ornamental and Wildlife Value
Cashews make interesting subjects for a collection or botanical garden.

Propagation
They are normally grown from seed, but this is difficult to obtain.

Pruning and Training
Only remedial pruning is necessary.

Weed, Pest, and Control
No problems are known. The trees exude a gum obnoxious to insects, which was used in bookbinding.

Harvesting and Storing
Once the nuts are picked from underneath the fruits, they have to be roasted and shelled, which, despite mechanization, is labor-intensive. This is because all the shell must be removed, as it contains an irritant in the inner membrane around the kernel, though this is rendered harmless by heat.

OTHER USES

The shells of the nuts contain an oil used industrially. The "apples" are then fermented to make a liquor. The sap makes an indelible ink.

CULINARY USES

Cashew nuts are popular raw, that is, already partially roasted, or roasted and salted. They are used in many sweet and savory dishes and can be liquidized to make a thick sauce. Cashews are fermented to make wine in Goa.

Cashew Tarts
Makes 12

1 cup marzipan
A little powdered sugar
1/2 cup cashew nuts
1/4 cup honey
1 teaspoon vanilla extract
A little milk
Glacé cherries

Roll the marzipan as pastry and form individual "crusts" in a tray dusted with powdered sugar. Puree the other ingredients, adding just enough milk to ensure success. Pour into the crusts, set a cherry in each, and chill them to set.

Macadamia ternifolia from the family *Proteaceae*

MACADAMIAS
OR QUEENSLAND NUTS

Tree up to 60 ft. Life span: medium. Semi-evergreen.
Fruits: up to 1 in., gray-husked nuts. Value: over 70% fat.

Macadamia trees are densely covered with narrow, glossy dark green leaves. The tassels of whitish flowers are followed by strings of small, hard, roundish, pointed nuts in grayish-green husks. The kernel is finely flavored and of exquisite texture.

These nuts, despite the Greek-sounding name, are natives of northeastern Australia. Not widely appreciated, they are mostly consumed in the United States from plantations in Hawaii, where *M. intergricolia* is the species grown commercially. They were introduced to Ceylon, now Sri Lanka, in 1868.

The distinctive foliage of the macadamia tree

VARIETIES

'Mauka' and 'Wiamanola' are two fine varieties with buttery rich flavor.

Propagation
They are propagated by seed, but as they are usually sold roasted and salted this may be difficult to find.

Pruning and Training
Only remedial pruning is necessary and they will form bushy trees.

Harvesting and Storing
The shells are very hard to crack, so the bulk crops are collected mechanically and taken to factories to be husked, shelled, roasted, and salted before packaging and storing, when they will keep for up to a year or so.

CULTIVATION

Macadamia nuts prefer tropical or subtropical, moist conditions. They are hardy in Zones 9 and 10. They are not particular as to soil and thrive at medium elevations.

Growing under Glass and in Containers
If the seed could be obtained they might be grown under glass, in pots to con-strain growth, though it is doubtful they would crop.

Ornamental and Wildlife Value
They are attractive trees, but too tender for growing successfully outside subtropical zones.

CULINARY USES

Most macadamia nuts are eaten roasted and salted, but they are also used in certain baked goods and confectionery.

Macadamia Slice
Serves 8–10

½ cup macadamia nuts
Powdered sugar
1 cup marzipan
2 teaspoons apricot jam
¼ cup chopped candied peel

Rinse and dry the macadamia nuts if they are salted. Dust a rolling board with powdered sugar and roll out the marzipan thickly. Coat thinly with jam and cut into three equally shaped pieces. On one piece spread a layer of nuts and peel, then place one third of marzipan on top, sticky side down. Smear the top with jam and add another layer of nuts and peel. Then put the last third on top (also sticky side down). Carefully press and roll this sandwich flatter and wider until the nuts almost push through. Trim, cut into small portions, and sprinkle the mixture with powdered sugar before presenting.

Cocos nucifera from the family *Arecaceae*

COCONUTS

Palm up to 90 ft. Life span: medium to long.
Evergreen, not usually self-fertile. Fruits: 12 in. plus, green-brown, oval
husk containing the nut. Value: 65% oil.

These attractive palms, so typical of dreamy, deserted islands, are spread by their floating, oval-husked nuts. The thick, fibrous husk is contained in a rind and itself encloses a thick-shelled, oval nut with a hollow kernel that is full of milk when underripe.

Venerated in the islands of the Pacific as a sacred emblem of fertility, coconuts are distributed and known around the world.

VARIETIES

The **King Coconut** of Ceylon is esteemed for its sweet juice. The **Dwarf Coconut, Nyiur-gading**, of Malaysia has small fruits, but crops when young and at only about a few feet high. The **Maldivc Coconut** is small and almost round; the **Needle Coconut** of the Nicobar Islands is triangular and pointed.

The King Coconut

CULTIVATION

Coconuts thrive by the sea in moist, tropical heat and rich, loamy soils and are planted about 33 ft. apart. They are suitable only in Zone 10, but they are interesting to grow from seed as houseplants.

Growing under Glass and in Containers

These are very attractive, easy plants to start with, rapidly outgrowing most places. The **Dwarf Coconut** may fruit, given good conditions, in only four years—thus while still small enough to stay indoors!

Ornamental and Wildlife Value

Very attractive trees, these can be used for indoor display until they grow too large.

Propagation

Ripe nuts that are laid on their side and barely covered with compost will germinate readily in heat.

Pruning and Training

Dead leaves need removing.

Harvesting and Storing

The nuts are used as they drop.

A coil of coir rope in Sri Lanka

COMPANION PLANTING

Coconuts are often grown in alternate rows with rubber trees, and with cacao while young. Climbing peppers, *Piper nigrum*, are grown up the coconut trunks.

OTHER USES

The trunks are used as timber, the leaves for thatch, the husk is coir, used for ropes and matting. The sap makes sugar or is fermented to toddy or distilled to arrack. Dried nuts are copra, used for oil for cosmetics, soaps, and detergents. The pressed waste is animal food.

CULINARY USES

The milk is drunk fresh or fermented. The nut is eaten raw or cooked, often as dried, shredded coconut.

Coconut Cookies
Makes about 10

1 egg white
1 1/3 cup powdered sugar
3/4 cup dried coconut
Glacé cherries
Crystallized angelica

Beat the egg white until stiff, then beat in the sugar and coconut. Spoon blobs of the mixture onto parchment paper on a baking sheet. Garnish each with a cherry and angelica and bake at 350°F for 15 minutes, or until they start to brown.

Bertholletia excelsa from the family *Myrtaceae*

BRAZIL NUTS

PARA OR SAVORY NUTS

Tree up to 100 ft. Life span: long. Semi-evergreen.
Fruits: up to 6 in., brown, spherical shell containing many nuts.
Value: 65% fat and 14% protein.

The Brazil nut tree enjoys a
warm tropical climate.

These are tall handsome trees found on the banks of the Amazon and Orinoco Rivers. They have large, laurel-like leaves and panicles of white flowers, which drop brown, spherical bombs with thick, hard cases. These need to be smashed to reveal inside a dozen or more nuts shaped like orange segments, each with its own hard shell enclosing the oval, brown-skinned, sweet, white kernel.

Natives of Brazil, these are still mainly produced there and also in Venezuela and Guyana. They are grown ornamentally in other countries such as Ceylon, but rarely on a commercial scale.

Pruning and Training
These need no special attention, but are slow. They are often not cultivated, but are gathered from the wild, as they take fifteen years to start fruiting.

Propagation
The nuts can be started off in heat, but actually take months to germinate.

OTHER USES

The oil expressed from the kernels is used industrially; the bark once caulked ships.

VARIETIES

Many consider the **Sapucaya Nut** superior; it is similar, though it comes from a different tree, *Lecythis zabucajo*.

CULTIVATION

Brazil trees thrive in deep, rich, alluvial soil in tropical conditions. They will grow in Zone 10.

Ornamental and Wildlife Value
Very attractive trees, but too large and requiring too much heat and warmth for widespread use.

Growing under Glass and in Containers
These can be grown from seed and kept dwarfed in containers, making interesting specimens, but are unlikely ever to fruit.

Harvesting and Storing
The individual nuts are obtained by cracking the spherical containers, which are sealed with wooden plugs. Inside their shells the nuts will keep for up to two years.

CULINARY USES

Most often Brazil nuts are eaten raw at Christmas time, but they are also widely used in cooking and baking.

Treacly Brazil Pie
Serves 6
1 quantity piecrust made with
* 1 1/2 cups flour, 3/4 stick butter*
* and water to mix*
1/3 cup Brazil nuts
1/3 cup bread crumbs
1/3 cup corn syrup
Juice and shredded rind of
* 1 lemon*
Whipped cream to serve

Roll out three-quarters of the piecrust and line a pie dish with it. Use dried peas to weigh it down, and bake blind at 375°F for 10 minutes. Remove the peas and put a layer of nuts around the base. Mix the other ingredients together and pour on top. Decorate with strips of piecrust and then bake for 20 minutes at 375°F. Serve the pie with whipped cream.

Arachis hypogaea from the family *Leguminosae*

Peanuts

GROUNDNUTS OR PEANUTS

Herbaceous, 2 ft. Life span: annual. Self-fertile.
Fruits: ½ in. small oval seeds. Value: rich in oil, protein. and vitamins B and E.

Peanuts are always known and used as nuts, although they are in fact the seeds of a tropical, pea-like, annual plant. After pollination of the yellow "pea" flower, the stalk lengthens and pushes the seed pod into the ground, where it matures. The light brown husks shell easily to reveal a few red-skinned, whitish-yellow seeds.

Natives of tropical America, peanuts were brought to Europe in the sixteenth century and remained curiosities until the nineteenth. Useful for oil, animal feed, and "nuts," they are now grown worldwide.

Growing under Glass and in Containers
Peanuts are good subjects for greenhouses, or in large pots, which can be kept under cover at the start and end of the season and put out on the patio during the summer months.

COMPANION PLANTING

Peanuts have been grown with rubber and coconuts.

OTHER USES

Peanut oil is used industrially.

VARIETIES

Spanish Bunch or **Virginia** varieties average fewer kernels than the better **Valencia** varieties, which have up to four. **Mauritius** peanuts are believed to be of superior quality.

Ornamental and Wildlife Value
Too pea-like to be attractive, they have curiosity value. The seeds are only too valuable to wildlife!

Pruning and Training
These require no care. The old, runnering varieties were more difficult.

Weed, Pest, and Disease Control
On a garden scale these are problem-free, save for **rodent** thefts.

Harvesting and Storing
The pods are dug in fall, thoroughly dried, and shelled before storing. Commercially the bulk is pressed for oil and feedcake.

Propagation
Sow in pots in heat for growing on in large pots to fruition, or planting out in favorable areas. In warm countries they are grown outdoors, sown 3 in. deep, about 2 ft. apart each way.

CULTIVATION

Peanuts prefer loose, dryish, sandy soil. They need a long season of warmth to mature, and thus do best in southern gardens. Northern gardeners can choose earlier varieties and start the seeds indoors a month before the last spring frost date, to get a head start on the season. They are normally grown on ridges to make digging the crop easier.

CULINARY USES

Peanuts are commonly roasted and salted, and are much used in baking and candy, savory sauces, and for their butter and edible oil. They should be kept dry until required.

Roasted Peanuts
Makes 2 lb.

4 cups peanuts, shelled weight
4 cloves garlic
6–8 canned anchovy fillets
3 tablespoons oregano

Boil the peanuts for two minutes, slip off their skins, then dry the nuts. Process the garlic, anchovies, and oregano. Coat the peanuts with this mixture and roast in the oven at 350°F for 10 minutes or so. Stir and cool.

OTHER NUTS

Araucaria araucana,
Monkey Puzzle or **Chile Pine, Auracariaceae**
These well-known trees, with spiny, overlapping, dark green leaves festooning the long, tail-like branches, rarely fruit in the U.K., it seems, as they are usually planted singly. Where they have been planted severally, they reportedly set seed and the nuts were shed most years. In Chile the seeds are eaten raw, roasted, or boiled. Closely related trees are also grown in Brazil and in Australia. Zones 8 to 10.

Castanospermum australe,
Moreton Bay Chestnut, Leguminosae
These poisonous Australian nuts are relished by native Australians, who leach them in water before drying and roasting the nuts to render them edible. Zones 9 and 10.

Coffea arabica,
Coffee, Rubiaceae
Small evergreen trees, which once grew wild in Arabia and are now cultivated in most hot countries. Coffee "beans" are seeds from the cherrylike berries, roasted to oily charcoal, then leached with hot water. Zone 10.

Cyperus esculentus,
Tiger Nut, Cyperaceae
Also called **Ground-almond** or **Chufa**, this is not a nut at all but the edible, underground rhizome of a small, perennial, grasslike sedge. It is grown in dry, sandy soils in western Asia and Africa. Zones 9 and 10.

An open, ripe cocoa pod showing the beans and flesh

Fagus sylvatica,
Beech, Fagaceae
A well-known tree that can reach 100 ft. and chokes out everything underneath with heavy, dry shade. Although parts of the tree are poisonous and have been used medicinally, an edible oil can be extracted from the seeds, and seeds have been eaten raw and roasted to make "coffee." In sheer desperation, beech sawdust has been boiled, baked, and mixed with flour to make "bread." Far too large for most gardens! The **American Beech**, *F. grandiflora*, is similar. Zones 5 to 7.

Ginkgo biloba,
Maiden Hair Tree, Ginkgoaceae
This "prehistoric" plant is grown ornamentally for the strange, leathery, fan-shaped leaves, which turn bright yellow in the fall. Fruits resemble unpleasant-smelling, yellowish plums. In the Far East the seeds, which resemble round, vaguely fishy almonds, are eaten, especially by the Chinese at weddings. Zones 4 to 9.

Ripe coffee beans on bushes in Costa Rica

Myristica fragrans,
Nutmeg, Myristiceae
These nuts are natives of the Moluccas Islands in Indonesia and are commercially grown in few other places save Grenada in the West Indies. The trees reach 60–70 ft. and have fruits resembling apricots or peaches which split, like almonds, revealing a nut surrounded by a reddish yellow aril. This is the spice mace. Inside the thin shell is the brown nutmeg kernel that rattles when ripe. If still alive, they will germinate in heat after three months or so. Zone 10.

Pterocarya fraxiniflora,
Caucasian Wing-nut, Juglandaceae
Native to the Caucasus and Persia and introduced to Britain in 1782, these are strong-growing relations of the walnut. They have large, nonaromatic, pinnate leaves, catkins, and small, edible nuts surrounded by semi-circular wings. They are hardy, though sustain some dieback after hard frosts, and succeed in damp places. They could be improved, perhaps by crossing with other species such as the **Japanese Wing-nut**, *P. rhoifolia*, or the large-fruited Chinese *P. stenoptera*. Zones 6 to 9.

Theobroma cacao,
Cacao, Sterculiaceae
The cocoa beans are fermented, dried, and ground to make chocolate. The trees, which are small natives of the Americas, are now mainly grown in West Africa. The melonlike pods are green, ripening to red or yellow. They spring directly out of the trunk and main branches of the tree after the delightful pink flowers. Zone 10.

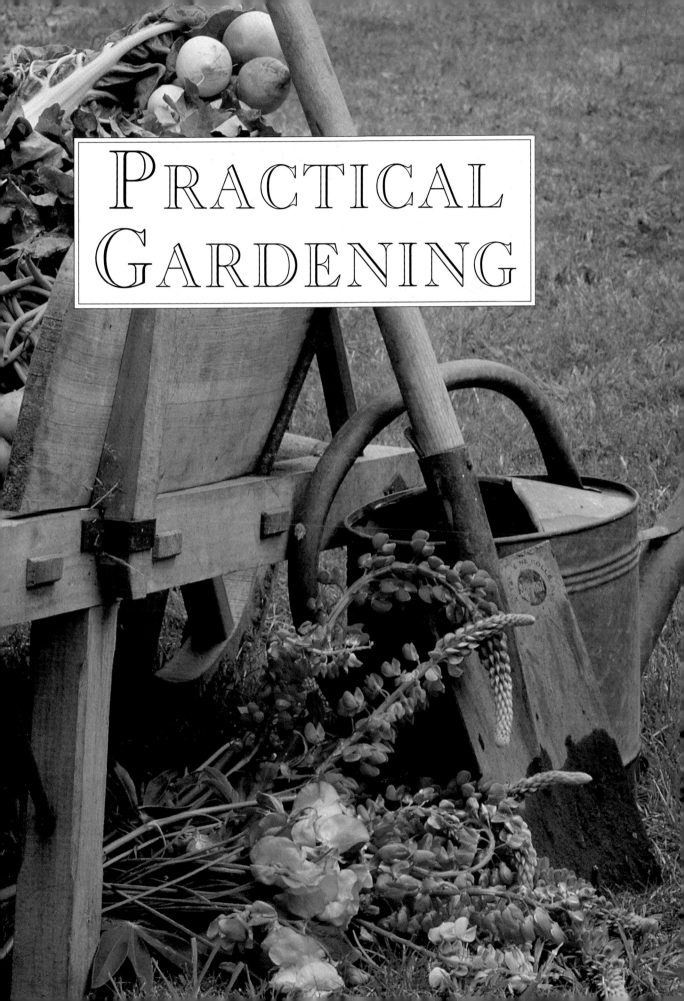

PRACTICAL GARDENING

PLANNING YOUR VEGETABLE GARDEN

Is there a more glorious site for a garden than the foot of the Alps?

Several factors determine the planning and layout of a vegetable garden and the species that can be grown:
• the locality and climatic conditions
• the size and shape of the plot
• the number of people to be supplied with vegetables
• the duration of cropping
• the skill of the gardener, and the time available for maintaining the plot
• whether the vegetables are intended for use when fresh, stored, or both

It is a good idea to list the vegetables you like, then decide how and where they can be grown to achieve the best results. In large gardens a vast range and volume of tasty vegetables can be produced using crop rotation and protected cropping to extend the growing season. Smaller sites allow fewer opportunities for self-sufficiency, but it is still possible to grow a good selection or experiment with unusual varieties. Even the tiniest gardens, balconies, or yards are suitable, particularly with the use of containers, while areas surrounded by buildings sometimes create favorable microclimates for tender vegetables such as okra. Protected cropping provides further opportunities to defy the cold weather.

Before preparing a planting plan it is important to be aware of the advantages and disadvantages of the site, considering everything from aspect and shelter to soil quality and drainage. Choose a design that suits your site and taste: traditionally, plots were planned in beds and rows, but you may prefer the *potager* (or "edible landscape") developed by the French, or the raised bed system, which is ideal for intensive small or large-scale cropping. It is essential to provide the best possible growing conditions for optimum production, and the old saying "the answer lies in the soil" is particularly relevant to vegetable growing.

Accurate timing is also a prerequisite. A cropping timetable should make full use of the ground all year round. It is advisable to plan backward from the intended harvesting date to work out when crops should be sown. There is little advantage in having a garden full of vegetables that are cheap and plentiful in the market; it is far better to plan your cropping dates for times when they are scarce and expensive.

Site and Soil
Most vegetables are short-term crops, which are harvested before they reach maturity. To achieve the necessary rapid growth, the ideal site is warm and light with good air circulation. This is particularly important for the fertilization of wind-pollinated crops such as corn, and to discourage pests and diseases, which flourish in still conditions. However, it is worth noting that strong winds can reduce plant growth by up to 30 percent.

On a gently sloping site facing the sun, the soil warms faster in spring than in other aspects, making such an area perfect for early crops.

It is more difficult to work the soil on steeper slopes, especially if machinery is being used: crops should be planted across rather than down the slope to reduce the risk of soil erosion during heavy rain. On very steep slopes the ground should be terraced.

A sloping site is ideal for early crops.   **Kitchen garden (opposite)**

ORNAMENTAL VEGETABLE GARDENS

Small fruiting gourd—attractive as well as edible

Conditioned to believe that vegetables are functional, and flowers beautiful, many people fail to appreciate the splendor and bounty of a vegetable plot with its contrasting colors, forms, and textures, neatly framed by well-kept paths.

The traditional design for a vegetable garden is based on a system of rows (see p. 584). Large kitchen gardens were formerly attached to a "great house," with the gardeners' task to cultivate a wide range of crops and supply the household with vegetables throughout the year. By way of contrast, most gardeners now have smaller gardens, and the basis for what they grow and how they grow it is more a matter of choice than necessity. This provides them with the opportunity to grow vegetables for their ornamental values as well as utilitarian ones. For the same reasons, it may also be preferable to grow small quantities of a wider range of cultivars.

Color

Vegetables are not only eaten for their flavor and nutritional value but add welcome color to a meal. Consider the range of color and tonal variation in a salad; it is generally greater than the range of flavors.

There are tones of green in lettuce, chicory, and cucumber, yellow in bell peppers, purple in beets and leaf lettuce, and red in tomatoes. For centuries, only the French potager capitalized on this display of colors, but vegetables are at last more often used as design elements in ornamental planting. Vegetables in the flower border have in recent years become a familiar sight.

The contrasting red and green foliage of ruby chard is sumptuous, as is beet 'Bull's Blood,' while purple- or yellow-podded string beans and the mauve leaves of cabbage 'Red Drumhead' create their own exotic magic. Red-skinned onions like 'Red Baron' and the red-leaved lettuce 'Lollo Rosso' are equally stunning. Squashes impress with their bold shapes and color (just look at 'Turk's Turban'), while tomatoes like the golden 'Yellow Perfection' and striped 'Tigrella' delight the eye. Flowers and fruits add other color accents.

Form

A good many vegetables have appealing foliage or a distinctive habit. The bold architectural leaves and sculptured form of globe artichokes are prized by garden designers, and a "teepee" of scarlet runner beans or trailing cucurbits makes a dramatic focal point. Members of the onion family, leeks, and chives have spiky, linear leaves, which contrast well with the rounded shapes of lettuce and the feathery, arching growth of carrot tops. Celery and Brussels sprouts naturally have a distinguished upright habit. Perhaps the most unusual of all is 'Rubine,' the purple Brussels sprout, which when planted as a single specimen in a container looks like an angular, alien sculpture.

Texture

The different colors and forms of vegetable foliage are underlined by their texture. Consider the solidity of a compact cabbage head, wreathed in glaucous, puckered leaves, or the soft, billowing effect created by the dissected leaves of fennel or asparagus foliage. Exploiting such contrasts provides a foliage display as interesting as a herbaceous border. Even after harvest the impact remains; the tall dried stems of corn look wonderful when frosted on a winter's day, and the rustling sound as the wind blows through their dead leaves brings life to a desolate garden.

Vegetables as "Bedding Plants"

Many vegetables are grown as annuals and, as each crop matures and is harvested, the appearance of the vegetable garden changes. Often, the only constant elements are the framework of paths and hedges and long-lived perennial crops.

Such intensively grown crops are easier to maintain when grown in a formal pattern, as this provides the ideal opportunity to arrange crops in brightly colored, bold patterns or emphasize their subtle qualities. Brightly

colored chard, lettuce, or kale, or the shimmering foliage of carrots can be used to provide a foliage display rivaling any bedding.

Vegetables that have run to seed look particularly spectacular; lettuces are upright and leafy, beets display their red-veined leaves and bold flower spikes, while onions and leeks produce symmetrical globes of flowers, which are invaluable for attracting pollinating insects. Some gardeners allow a few plants to go to seed to enjoy such effects, but would you be daring enough to create a planting scheme featuring vegetables in their later stages?

One approach to creating a "bedding" scheme is to group together plants with a similar life span, for a long-term display. Alternatively, with skillful planning, it is possible to plant crops taking different times to reach maturity, filling any gaps with suitable vegetables after harvest, to retain the impact of the design. The time scale can vary, with radishes taking a mere five weeks, and sprouting broccoli and winter cabbages remaining in the ground for several months. The rapid changeover of these annual crops means that plant colors as well as flavors are constantly changing within the scheme.

Perennial vegetables such as asparagus, globe artichoke, and rhubarb can be grown in separate beds or used as permanent feature plants within the design. In smaller or irregularly shaped gardens, crop rotation allows a wide range of annual design patterns and planting arrangements.

The Potager

Their love of food and appreciation of aesthetics motivated French gardeners to create the *potager*, or ornamental vegetable garden, with a more obvious visual appeal than the

Globe artichoke flowers are prime examples of attractive vegetables.

English kitchen garden. Simple, formal, geometric shapes such as four square-shaped raised beds dissected by straight paths form a permanent structure, enlivened with a succession of vibrantly colored leafy crops chosen for their culinary and visual qualities.

Vegetables are placed according to their height and habit, larger vegetables forming centerpieces and smaller ones making up the rows. Climbing vegetables growing over ornamental tripods, arches, or stakes provide height, and the whole area can be screened by trellis and include vegetables in containers.

To maintain the symmetry, harvest plants with an eye to pattern: work evenly from both ends and from the center, or cut every other plant to keep the coverage balanced as far as possible. Make full use of successional cropping so that the soil is always utilized and the pattern maintained.

Random Systems

Scattering vegetables individually or in groups among ornamental borders is becoming more popular. They should be planted according to their ultimate height with lower plants near the front of the border, using brightly colored vegetables strong enough to stand up to their brightly colored neighbors. Grow purple-podded climbing string beans through shrubs instead of clematis, runner bean 'Painted Lady' instead of sweet peas, and purple-leaved cabbage alongside nasturtiums. Mini vegetables can be grown in window boxes or hanging baskets; try tomato 'Tumbler,' or grow climbers as trailing plants.

The only requirement for successful growth of vegetables among ornamentals is adequate soil or compost fertility, which can easily be maintained with well-prepared soil and careful feeding.

PLANNING YOUR HERB GARDEN

Herbs are so versatile that they should appeal to anyone: a cook, a lover of salads, or someone just wanting to enjoy the rich scents of plants and watch the butterflies collecting nectar from the flowers. And there are herbs for every space; they will grow in a window box or in a pot on a sunny window ledge; and some can be grown indoors as houseplants as well as outside in gardens, small or large. The best way to grow herbs is the organic way. Quite apart from the fact that if you use natural products, the soil remains clean and free from chemical pollutants, in organic herb gardens there is no chance of contaminating a plant before you eat it. Organic methods also attract bees and other insects to the garden, which in turn helps maintain the healthy natural balance of predator and pest.

CONDITIONS

As herbs are basically wild plants tamed to fit a garden, it makes sense to grow them in conditions comparable with their original environment. This can be a bit difficult, for they come from all over the world. As a general rule, the majority of culinary herbs come from the Mediterranean and prefer a dry sunny place. But herbs really are adaptable and they do quite well outside their native habitat, provided you are aware of what they prefer.

Back row, left to right: **Eau de Cologne Mint**, *Mentha* x *piperita* f. *citrata*, **English Mace**, *Achillea ageratum*, **Scented Pelargonium 'Mabel Gray,' Orange-scented Thyme** *Thymus* 'Fragrantissimus'; front row, left to right: **Creeping Savory**, *Satureja spicigera*, **Chives**, *Allium schoenoprasum*, **Lady's Mantle Conjuncta**, *Alchemilla conjuncta*, **Curry Plant Dartington**, *Helichrysum italicum* 'Dartington.'

CHOOSING THE SITE

Before planning your site, it is worth surveying your garden in detail. Start by making a simple plan and mark on it north and south. Show the main areas of shade—a high fence, a neighboring house and any high trees, noting whether they are deciduous or evergreen. Finally, note any variations in soil type—wet, dry, heavy etc. Soil is one of the most important factors and will determine the types of herb you can grow. For different soil types, see pp. 578–579.

USE

Next, decide what you want from your herb garden. Do you want a retreat away from the house? Or an herb garden where the scents drift indoors? Or do you want a culinary herb garden close to the kitchen door?

STYLE

Then think about what shape or style you want the garden to take. Formal herb gardens are based on patterns and geometric shapes. Informal gardens are a free-for-all, with species and colors all mixed together. Informal gardens may look unplanned, but the best have been well planned. This is worth doing even if it is just to check the final height and spread of the plant. It can be misleading buying plants from a garden center—they are all neat, uniform, and fairly small, and it is well worth investigating and trying to visualize their mature size.

The plants have to be accessible, either for using fresh or to harvest, so paths are a good idea. They also introduce patterns to the design and can help to define its shape. For convenience, herbs should be no more than 30 in. from a path, and ideally the beds no more than 3–4 ft. wide. If they are more than 4 ft. wide, insert stepping stones to improve access.

LAYING PATHS

There are a number of choices of materials you can use for paths.

Grass
A grass path is quite easy to achieve and looks very attractive. Another plus point is the minimal cost. Make it at least as wide as your lawn mower, otherwise you will be cutting it on your hands and knees with shears. It is a good idea to edge the path either with wood, metal, or, more attractively, with bricks, laid on their side end to end. Disadvantages to this kind of path are that it needs mowing and will not take heavy traffic.

Gravel
Gravel paths really do lend themselves to being planted with herbs. Be sure to prepare them well otherwise a water trap will form, and the plants would be better off being aquatic.

First remove the topsoil carefully. Then dig out to a depth of 12 in., putting the soil to one side. It is advisable to put a wooden edge between the soil of the garden or lawn and the new path. This will keep the soil from falling into the path, and keep the edge neat. Fill the newly formed ditch with 6 in. rough stone. Mix the topsoil with peat, bark, and grit in the ratio 3:1:1:1, and put this mix on top of the rough stone to a depth of 3 in. Finish with 3 in. of fine gravel. There are many colors of gravel available and most large garden centers stock a good range, or if you have a quarry nearby, it is worth investigating that as a source.

Roll the path before planting. Herbs that will grow happily in gravel are creeping or upright thymes, winter savory, and pennyroyal. The disadvantage of gravel is that you will find that weeds will recur, so be diligent.

Bricks

Paths made out of bricks have become very fashionable. There is now a subtle range of colors available, and varied and original patterns can be created. For standard-size bricks, dig out to a depth of 4 in. As with the gravel path, include a wooden edge. Spread 2 in. of sharp sand over the base; level and dampen. Lay the brick on top of the sand in the desired pattern, leaving a ⅛–¼ in. gap between the bricks. Settle them in, using a mallet or a hired plate vibrator.

If you wish to plant the path with herbs, you might want to leave out one or two bricks, filling the gaps later with potting mix and planting them when the path has settled. When the whole path has been laid, spread the joints with a mix 4:1 of fine dry sand and cement, and brush it in. The mixture will gradually absorb the moisture from the atmosphere, setting the brick.

Planning your planting

Paving stones

These can take up a lot of space and are expensive to lay over a large area. Garden centers now stock a large range in various colors and shapes. Also try suppliers of building materials—you may get a better deal, especially if you require large quantities. Paving stones are ideal for the classic checkerboard designs and the more formal designs.

If you want the paving stones to lie flush with the ground, dig out the soil to the depth of the slab plus 2 in. Put 2 in. of sharp sand onto the prepared area, level off, and lay the slabs on top, tapping them down, and making sure they are level. If the chosen area is already level and you want the slabs to be proud, then lay them directly in position with only a small layer of sand underneath.

ALTERNATIVE PLANTING

Raised beds

If your soil is difficult, or if you wish to create a feature in the garden, raised beds are a good solution. Also, plants in raised beds are easier to keep under control and will not wander so much around the rest of the garden. Finally, they are more accessible for harvesting and stand at a good height for those in wheelchairs.

The ideal height for a raised bed is between 12 in. and 30 in. If you raise it over 3 ft. high you will need some form of foundation for the retaining walls, to prevent them keeling over with the weight of the soil. Retaining walls can be made out of old railway ties (which are not as cheap as they used to be), logs cut in half, old bricks, or even red bricks—leave the odd one out and plant a creeping thyme in its place.

For filling a 1-ft. raised bed, the following ratios are ideal. First put a layer of rough stone on top of the existing soil to a depth of 3 in., followed by a 3-in. layer of gravel, and finally 6 in. of topsoil mix—made up of 1 part peat, 1 part bark, 1 part grit or sharp sand, and 3 parts topsoil.

Lawns

Many herbs are excellent ground cover and can make a fragrant lawn, but beware of planting too large an area to begin with. It can be an error costly in both time and money. Small areas filled with creeping herbs give great delight to the unsuspecting visitors who, when walking over the lawn, discover a pleasant aroma exuding from beneath their feet!

It may sound repetitious, but it is worth saying that preparing your site well is the key to a good garden. Given a typical soil, prepare the site for the lawn by digging the whole area out to a depth of 12 in. and then prepare in exactly the same way as for the raised bed: 3 in. rough stone, 3 in. fine gravel, 6 in. topsoil mix—this time, 1 part peat, 2 parts sharp sand, 3 parts topsoil. Apart from chamomile, other plants that can be used for an herb lawn are Corsican mint, *Mentha requinni*, planted 4 in. apart, or creeping thymes—see pages 375–377 for varieties—and plant them about 9 in. apart.

HERB GARDENS

The designs for six herb gardens included on the following pages can be adhered to religiously, or adapted to meet your personal tastes, needs, and of course the space you have available in your garden.

It is with this last requirement in mind that I have specifically not included the exact size of the garden in the design and instead have concentrated on the shape, the overall layout and the

relationship between plants. I hope these plans give you freedom of thought and some inspiration.

FIRST HERB GARDEN

When planning your first herb garden, choose plants that you will use and enjoy. I have designed this garden in exactly the same way as the one at my herb farm. Much as I would love to have a rambling herb garden, I need something practical and easy to manage, because the nursery plants need all my attention.

It is also important that the herbs are easy to get at, so that I can use it every day. By dividing the garden up into four sections and putting paving stones around the outside and through the middle, it is easy to maintain and provides good accessibility.

For this garden, I have chosen a cross section of

herbs with a bias toward culinary use, because the more you use and handle the plants, the more you will understand their habits. There is much contradictory advice on which herb to plant with which, but many of these are old wives' tales.

There are only a few warnings I will give: Do not plant dill and fennel together, because they intermarry and become

fendill, losing their unique flavors in the process. Equally, do not plant dill or coriander near wormwood as it will impair their flavor. Also, different mints near each other cross-pollinate and over the years will lose their individual identity. Finally, if you plan to collect the seed from lavenders, keep the species well apart.

Aside from that, if you like it, plant it.

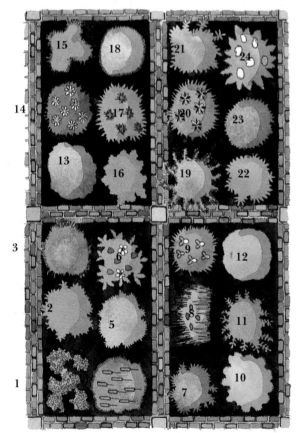

1	**Parsley**	*Petroselinum crispum*
2	**Pineapple Mint**	*Mentha suaveolens* 'Variegata'
3	**Fennel**	*Foeniculum vulgare*
4	**Lavander Munstead**	*Lavandula angustifolia* 'Munstead'
5	**Greek Oregano**	*Origanum vulgare* subsp. *hirtum* 'Greek'
6	**Alpine Strawberry**	*Fragaria vesca*
7	**Purple Sage**	*Salvia officinalis* 'Purpurascens'
8	**Chives**	*Allium schoenoprasum*
9	**Heartsease**	*Viola tricolor*
10	**Golden Curly Marjoram**	*Origanum vulgare* 'Aureum Crispum'
11	**Salad Burnet**	*Sanguisorba minor*
12	**Lemon Thyme**	*Thymus* x *citriodorus*
13	**Garden Thyme**	*Thymus vulgaris*
14	**Roman Chamomile**	*Chamaemelum nobile*
15	**Rock Hyssop**	*Hyssopus offinialis* subsp. *aristatus*
16	**Buckler Leaf Sorrel**	*Rumex scutatus*
17	**Bergamot**	*Monarda didyma*
18	**Curry Plant, Dartington**	*Helichrysum italicum* 'Dartington'
19	**Rosemary**	*Rosmarinus officinalis*
20	**Borage**	*Borago officinalis*
21	**Variegated Lemon Balm**	*Melissa officinalis* 'Aurea'
22	**Apple Mint**	*Mentha suaveolens*
23	**Winter Savory**	*Satureja montana*
24	**Chervil**	*Anthriscus cerefolium*

HERB BATH GARDEN

This garden may seem a bit eccentric to the conventionally minded, but when my back is aching after working in the nursery, and I feel that unmentionable age, and totally exhausted, there is nothing nicer than lying in an herb bath and reading a good book.

The herbs I use most are thyme, to relieve an aching back; lavender, to give me energy; and eau-de-cologne to knock me out. Simply tie up a bunch of your favorite herbs with string, attach them to the hot water tap and let the water run. The scent of the plants will

invade both water and room. Alternatively, put some dried herbs in a muslin bag and drop it into the bath.

Remember when planting this garden to make sure that the plants are accessible. Hops will need to climb up a fence, a pole, or over a log. Again, quite apart

from the fact that the herbs from this garden are for use in the bath, they make a very aromatic garden in their own right. Position a seat next to the lavender and rosemary so that when you get that spare five minutes, you can sit in quiet repose and revel in the scent.

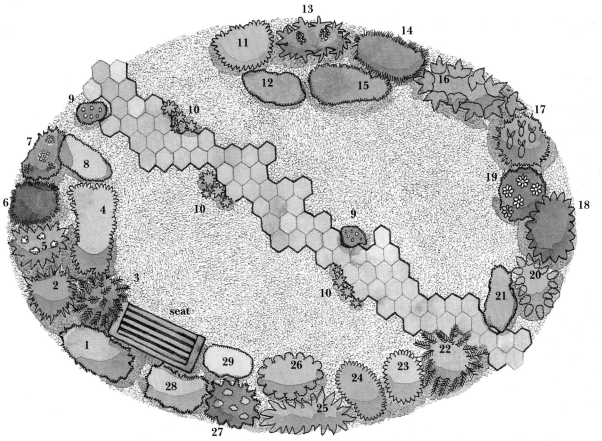

1   **Lavender Seal** *Lavandula* x *intermedia* 'Seal'
2   **Lemon Verbena** *Aloysia triphylla*
3   **Benenden Blue Rosemary** *Rosmarinus officinalis* 'Benenden Blue'
4   **Gold Sage** *Salvia officinalis* "Icterina"
5   **Valerian** *Valeriana officinalis*
6   **Bronze Fennel** *Foeniculum vulgare* 'Purpureum'
7   **Tansy** *Tanacetum vulgare*
8   **Golden Lemon Thyme** *Thymus* x *citriodorus* 'Golden Lemon'
9   **Double-Flowered Chamomile** *Chamaemelum nobile* 'Flore Pleno'
10 **Houseleek** *Sempervivum tectorum*
11 **Peppermint** *Mentha* x *piperita*
12 **Orange-Scented Thyme** *Thymus* 'Fragrantissimus'
13 **Meadowsweet** *Filipendula ulmaria*
14 **Green Fennel** *Foeniculum vulgare*

15 **Pennyroyal** *Mentha pulegium*
16 **Hops** *Humulus lupulus*
17 **French Lavender** *Lavandula stoechas*
18 **Bay** *Laurus nobilis*
19 **Roman Chamomile** *Chamaemelum nobile*
20 **Lemon Balm** *Melissa officinalis*
21 **Porlock Thyme** *Thymus* 'Porlock'
22 **Prostrate Rosemary** *Rosmarinus officinalis* Prostratus Group
23 **Golden Marjoram** *Origanum vulgare* 'Aureum'
24 **Eau de Cologne Mint** *Mentha* x *piperita* f. *citrata*
25 **Comfrey** *Symphytum officinale*
26 **Lady's Mantle** *Alchemilla mollis*
27 **Yarrow** *Achillea millefolium*
28 **Lavender Grappenhall** *Lavandula* x *intermedia* 'Grappenhall'
29 **Silver Posie Thyme** *Thymus vulgaris* 'Silver Posie'

WHITE HERB GARDEN

This garden gave me great pleasure to create. For me, it is an herb garden with a different perspective.

It has a row of steps going from the road to the front door of the house. Either side of the steps is a dwarf white lavender hedge. In spring, before the lavender and just before the lily of the valley are in flower, the sweet woodruff gives a carpet of small white flowers. This is the start of the white garden, which then flowers throughout the year through to autumn. It is a most attractive garden with a mixture of scents, foliage, and flowers.

This planting combination can easily be adapted to suit a border. Even though it is not a conventional herb garden, all the herbs can be used in their traditional way. The garlic chives with baked potatoes, the horehound for coughs, the chamomile to make a soothing tea, and the lavender to make lavender bags or to use in the bath.

The great thing about a garden like this is that it requires very little work to maintain. The hedge is the only part that needs attention—trim in the spring and after flowering in order to maintain its shape.

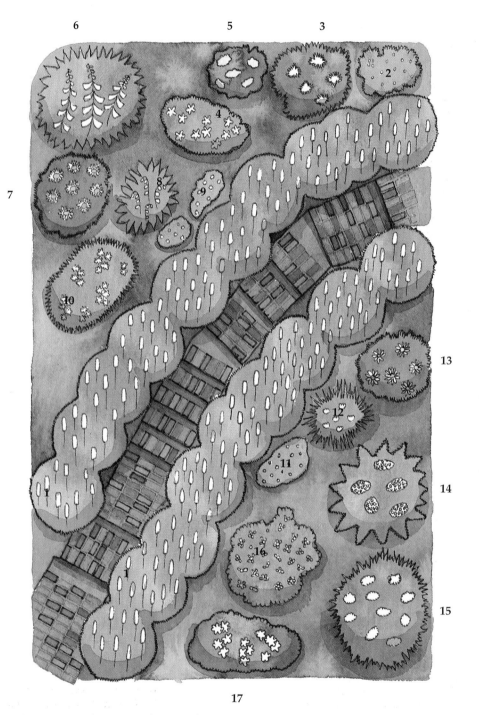

1	**White Lavender (dwarf)**	*Lavandula angustifolia* 'Nana Alba'
2	**Sweet Woodruff**	*Galium odoratum*
3	**Bergamot Snow Maiden**	*Monarda* 'Schneewittchen'
4	**Jacob's Ladder (white)**	*Polemonium caeruleum* subsp. *caeruleum* f. *album*
5	**Yarrow**	*Achillea millefolium*
6	**Foxgloves (white)**	*Digitalis purpurea* f. *albiflora* (POISONOUS)
7	**Roman Chamomile**	*Chamaemelum nobile*
8	**Lily of the Valley**	*Convallaria majalis* (POISONOUS)
9	**White Thyme**	*Thymus serpyllum* var. *albus*
10	**White Hyssop**	*Hyssopus officinalis* f. *albus*
11	**Snowdrift Thyme**	*Thymus serpyllum* 'Snowdrift'
12	**Garlic Chives**	*Allium tuberosum*
13	**Pyrethrum**	*Tanacetum cinerariifolium*
14	**Sweet Cicely**	*Myrrhis odorata*
15	**Valerian**	*Valeriana officinalis*
16	**White Horehound**	*Marrubium vulgare*
17	**Prostanthera**	*Prostanthera cuneata*

COOK'S HERB GARDEN

The best site for a culinary herb bed is a sunny area accessible to the kitchen. The importance of this is never clearer than when it is raining. There is no way that you will go out and cut fresh herbs if they are a long way away and difficult to reach.

Another important factor is that the sunnier the growing position, the better the flavor of the herbs. This is because the sun brings the oils to the surface of the

leaf of herbs such as sage, coriander, rosemary, basil, oregano and thyme.

The cook's herb garden could be grown in the ground or in containers. If

in the ground, make sure that the site is very well drained. Position a paving stone near each herb so that it can be easily reached for cutting, weeding, and

feeding, and also to help contain the would-be rampant ones, such as the mints.

Alternatively, the whole design could be adapted to be grown in containers. I have chosen only a few of the many varieties of culinary herb. If your favorite is missing, either add it to the design or substitute it for one of my choice.

1   **Ginger Mint** *Mentha* x *gracilis*
2   **Chervil** *Anthriscus cerefolium*
3   **Coriander** *Coriandrum sativum*
4   **French Parsley** *Petroselinum crispum* 'French'
5   **Chives** *Allium schoenoprasum*
6   **Corsican Rosemary** *Rosmarinus officinalis* 'Corsican Blue'
7   **Garden Thyme** *Thymus vulgaris*
8   **Angelica** *Angelica archangelica*
9   **Fennel** *Foeniculum vulgare*
10 **Winter Savory** *Satureja montana*
11 **Greek Basil** *Ocimum minimum* 'Greek'
12 **Buckler Leaf Sorrel** *Rumex scutatus*
13 **Bay** *Laurus nobilis*
14 **Sweet Cicely** *Myrrhis odorata*

15 **Garlic** *Allium sativum*
16 **Greek Oregano** *Origanum vulgare* subsp. *hirtum* 'Greek'
17 **French Tarragon** *Artemisia dracunculus*
18 **Lovage** *Levisticum officinale*
19 **Chives, Garlic** *Allium tuberosum*
20 **Lemon Balm** *Melissa officinalis*
21 **Moroccan Mint** *Mentha spicata* var. *crispa* 'Moroccan'
22 **Dill** *Anethum graveolens*
23 **Parsley** *Petroselinum crispum*
24 **Lemon Thyme** *Thymus* x *citriodorus*
25 **Sweet Marjoram** *Origanum majorana*

SALAD HERB GARDEN

Herbs in salads make the difference between boring and interesting; they add flavor, texture and color (especially the flowers).

Included in the design is a selection of salad herbs and salad herb flowers. There are two tall herbs in the middle, chicory and red orach (blue and red), which are planted opposite each other. Also, I have positioned the only other

tall plant—borage—on the outside ring, opposite the chicory so that the blue flowers together will make a vivid splash. To make access easy, there is an inner ring of stepping stones.

The herbs chosen are my choice and can easily be changed if you want to include a particular favorite. Remember to look at the heights; for instance, do not plant angelica in the outside

circle because it will hide anything in the inner circle. Equally, in the inner circle make sure you do not plant a low-growing plant next to a tall, spreading herb because you will never find it.

This whole design can be incorporated in a small garden or on the edge of a vegetable garden to give color throughout the growing season. As the

majority of these herbs are annuals or die back into the ground, the fall is an ideal time to give the garden a good feed by adding well-rotted manure. This will encourage lots of leaves from the perennial herbs in the following season, and give a good kick start to the annuals when they are planted out in the following spring.

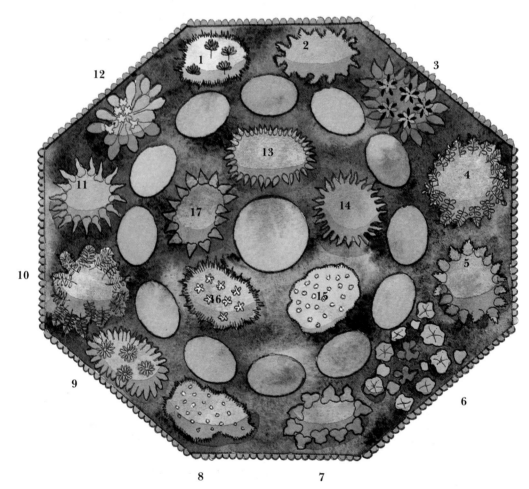

1	**Chives** *Allium schoenoprasum*	10	**French Tarragon** *Artemisia dracunculus*
2	**Caraway** *Carum carvi*	11	**Salad Rocket** *Eruca vesicaria* subsp. *sativa*
3	**Borage** *Borago officinalis*	12	**Cowslips** *Primula veris*
4	**Salad Burnet** *Sanguisorba minor*	13	**Spearmint** *Mentha spicata*
5	**French Parsley** *Petroselinum crispum* French	14	**Chicory** *Cichorium intybus*
6	**Nasturtium** *Tropaeolum majus*	15	**Lemon Thyme** *Thymus* x *citriodorus*
7	**Buckler Leaf Sorrel** *Rumex scutatus*	16	**Garlic Chives** *Allium tuberosum*
8	**Hyssop** *Hyssopus officinalis*	17	**Red Orach** *Atriplex hortensis* var. *rubra*
9	**Pot Marigold** *Calendula officinalis*		

MEDICINAL HERB GARDEN

I would like this garden, not just for its medicinal use, but for the tranquillity it would bring. The choice of herbs is not only for internal use but for the whole being. I can imagine sitting on the seat watching the dragonflies playing over the pond.

Some of the herbs included are certainly not for self-administration, for instance blue flag iris, but this is a beautiful plant and would look most attractive with the meadowsweet and the valerian. Chamomile, peppermint, dill, and lemon balm are easy to self-administer with care as they all make beneficial teas. One should not take large doses just because they are natural, as some are very powerful. I strongly advise anyone interested in planting this garden to get a good herbal medicine book, see a fully trained herbalist, and always consult your doctor about a particular remedy.

1	**Blue Flag Iris** *Iris versicolor*	12	**Feverfew** *Tanacetum parthenium*
2	**Meadowsweet** *Filipendula ulmaria*	13	**Heartsease** *Viola tricolor*
3	**Valerian** *Valeriana officinalis*	14	**Lemon Balm** *Melissa officinalis*
4	**Horseradish** *Armoracia rusticana*	15	**Garlic** *Allium sativum*
5	**Sage** *Salvia officinalis*	16	**Peppermint** *Mentha x piperita*
6	**Lady's Mantle** *Alchemilla mollis*	17	**Fennel** *Foeniculum vulgare*
7	**Rosemary** *Rosmarinus officinalis*	18	**Pot Marigold** *Calendula officinalis*
8	**Dill** *Anethum graveolens*	19	**Seal Lavender** *Lavandula x intermedia* 'Seal'
9	**Roman Chamomile** *Chamaemelum nobile*	20	**Garden Thyme** *Thymus vulgaris*
10	**White Horehound** *Marrubium vulgare*	21	**Houseleek** *Sempervivum tectorum*
11	**Comfrey** *Symphytum officinale*		

PLANNING YOUR FRUIT GARDEN

Planning your fruit garden means deciding your priorities—what do you want most? A little thought beforehand can save you a lot of wasted effort and ensure you actually get what you are after. With vegetables and bedding plants we have the luxury of burying our mistakes annually; with our trees and bushes we need to be more certain.

Although many of us get our garden fortuitously, with our house, we usually have quite a wide choice of what we actually do with it, though it is rare that we make radical changes. However, if we spend as much time and effort planning and remaking the garden as we do on decorating and furnishing the rest of our home, it will turn out to be a fine place!

Obviously the soil, climate, large trees, buildings, and the rest of the hard landscape have to be worked around. But with skill and know-how, and modern materials, we can have almost any fruit we desire. Which fruits we actually choose to grow must depend on our budget as much as our climate. Obviously growing fruit in the open garden is easiest and cheapest, but a heated greenhouse allows for growing many more.

I think the first criterion for choosing fruit must be taste. After all, if you are growing for yourself, there is no point having poorly flavored varieties or ones that are widely available commercially. Go for those

Apples grown as single-tier espaliers

with flavor and sweetness even if they are poor croppers. If you find you especially like a particular kind, you can always grow more.

Freshness is invaluable and one's own fruits are the most truly fresh. It makes sense to choose fruits and varieties that are best eaten straight off the plant and thus rarely found in stores. Likewise dessert types are preferable to cooking varieties as we eat them with all their vitamins and flavor while culinary fruits lose some in the cooking.

Of course growing your fruit yourself guarantees freedom from unwanted chemical residues, and applying plentiful compost will ensure a good internal nutritional balance in the fruit. However, when choosing fruits, bear in mind that their dietary value

can vary as much with variety as with type or growing conditions. For example, **'Golden Delicious'** apples contain a third or less vitamin C than **'Ribston Pippin,'** while **'Laxton's Superb'** has only one-sixth!

Economy must always be considered. Fruit growing requires higher investment initially than vegetables but

running costs are lower. Similarly, soft fruit plants are cheaper than tree fruits individually, but require netting from birds in many areas. For maximum production, tree fruits produce as much weight from fewer plants per acre and usually require less maintenance, but are slower to crop and live longer.

Dwarf peaches in a courtyard garden

Likewise vine fruits and cordons require more posts, ties, and wires than trees or bushes. Any form of greenhouse or cover is costly, requiring upkeep, and of course heating uses much expensive energy.

The seasonal implications, and the time taken to maintain different fruits need to be considered, although in general fruit requires much less labor per yield than vegetable production. Initially the preparation and planting are heavy demands on time and energy, but afterward the workload is light, for the amateur if not for the professional. Fruit trees and bushes generally need mulching, thinning, picking, and pruning, which are all light tasks and can be done upright in pleasant conditions. Growing the fruit is only half the battle though. After picking we need to process and store the fruit, and this takes more time than the growing! Don't plan to grow fruits that mature just when you go away on vacation!

Apples trained over interlocking arches leading to an apple tunnel

ORNAMENTAL FRUIT GARDENS

Trained fruit trees and bushes that can be bought in a host of interesting and architectural forms, such as espaliers and fans, create interest out of season as the framework of the plants is revealed. Attention to the appearance of the supports is essential as they are also exposed for much of the time. Neatness and uniformity are thus of the greatest moment. Pergolas can look as beautiful clothed in grapevines as they do with any climber and even a fruit cage can be fashioned ornamentally from the right materials.

It is important in a fruit garden to allow for lots of light and air, more than perhaps might be necessary for a shrub garden. Wide paths aid such design and can be made of turf where traffic is light. Gravel is the next choice for practicality and economy, and concrete or stone paving stones where the area is small or budget large.

More color and interest—with benefit to the main planting—is obtained by having companion plants to provide shelter, ground cover, flowers for nectar and pollen for the beneficial insects, and sacrificial plants that give up their fruits that others may not be eaten. Vegetables, however, are not easily mixed in. They do not grow well surrounded by vigorous competitors such as fruiting plants. Most of the culinary herbs can be grown to advantage and use.

Wildlife Fruit Gardens

Although these may be as stylized and neat as any purely decorative garden, an accurate description of many so-called wild gardens is "unkempt." Indeed the term is often used to justify total neglect.

However, if the aim is truly to provide more and better habitats for endangered native flora and fauna, then neglect is not enough. A wild garden needs to be managed so that we maximize the number and forms of life supported. The more fruiting and berrying plants we include, the more wildlife we attract, and we need to ensure other basic necessities for wild creatures.

The fruit helps immensely, but shelter for nesting and hibernation, water, and peace are also required. Dense briars, shrubs, and evergreens are mandatory, but do ensure the gardener can still gain access. Paths should be maintained to permit various tasks, but of course excess traffic will soon drive away most creatures.

Many garden soils are too rich for the more appealing wildflowers. To establish these it is frequently necessary to start them in pots and plant them out into sites prepared by removing the sod. Thus they should be kept away from the fruiting plants that require richer conditions.

Flowering espalier pear on the garden wall of a country house

ORCHARDS

Orchards are devoted to the production of top or tree fruits, most frequently (privately and commercially) for apples, pears, and plums. Other fruits are less common, being widely grown only in suitable areas—for example cherries are rarely grown in wetter maritime regions, but are common in drier zones such as Kent, in England.

Orchards were always turfed over for convenience and soil preservation, though recent practice has been for bare cultivation, but this has been shown to be irresponsible. Initially weed-free conditions must be maintained in the orchard, but in general the preservation of bare soil is counterproductive. Most home orchard fruits will be best with a heavy mulch, ground cover or companion plants, or a grass lawn.

For comfort and least cost, private orchards are still customarily planted with standard or half-standard trees on strong rootstocks. Though more intensive plantings with more dwarfing stock are more productive, they also require much more pruning and training and are difficult to mow underneath!

Grass clippings are an excellent mulch if put on in thin layers, and are a good fertilizer if returned to the lawn. However orchards, and indeed most other lawns, should not be composed solely of grasses, as these compete strongly for resources in the topmost layers and do not contribute much to the mineral levels. Include clovers, alfalfa, and chicory seeds in your sowing mixture. Special blends are now available ready mixed.

Traditionally orchards

Mistletoe growing on an old apple tree in a cider orchard

were combined with grazing livestock. Though no longer done on a commercial scale, the practice is still useful for amateurs. Running chickens underneath adds interest and fertility and almost guarantees freedom from most pest problems. (Cynics might add "especially if you don't overfeed them!") Ducks control slugs and snails better than hens and do not scratch and damage so much, and the drakes do not crow so they are preferable from that point of view. Geese are superb lawn mowers, converting grass into fertilizer and eggs, as well as being the most noisy watchdogs. Be warned though, as geese may damage young plants with

thin bark if they are hungry.

Other forms of livestock are more dangerous to the home orchard. I suggest that no four-legged herbivorous animals are allowed anywhere near valued plants unless each is individually and securely fenced and protected.

Orchards are also an enticement to two-legged pests, and it has long been established best practice to surround them with a thick, impenetrable hedge of thorny plants such as quickthorn or blackthorn. This and a narrow verge of long grass and native plants simultaneously provide a good background ecology to help control all the other pests of the orchard.

A fence or wall does not contribute in the same way, and is usually more expensive and surmountable.

Groves of almonds, olives, oranges, and lemons

SITE, SOIL, PREPARATION, AND PLANTING

Commercial strawberry growing on polyethylene

Most old gardening books started off with instructions to make a garden on a well drained, south-facing slope of rich loamy soil. If only we always had this option! We usually have to take what we can get. And as we get small gardens with modern houses, we rarely have much choice of positioning.

SITE

Shelter is the most important aid we can give our plants—good hedges, fences, windbreaks, warm walls, cloches, plastic sheets, and even old drapes on frosty nights. But be careful not to overdo it and make the area stagnant. Drainage is occasionally necessary to prevent waterlogging, as few plants survive for long with drowning roots. But for most gardens, water is more often a problem in its absence. Growing on raised mounds is preferable to draining away the water in areas with dry summers.

SOIL

For most crops, a neutral to slightly acid soil with moderate fertility and organic matter content is ideal. There are basically four types of soil.

Chalk or Limestone Soil

This soil tends to be light and very well drained. But its inability to hold moisture can cause problems in a hot summer. It is alkaline in character and it is sometimes difficult to lower its pH level, so some plants become stunted and leaves turn yellowish in color, because the minerals, especially iron, become locked away. If you find the plants are not thriving, try a raised bed where you can introduce the soil you require.

Clay Soil

This soil is made up of tiny particles that stick together when wet, making the soil heavy. When dry, they set rock hard. Because it retains water and restricts airflow around roots, it is often known as a "cold soil." It may have a natural reserve of plant food, but even so it is better to work compost, sharp sand, and horticultural grit into the top layer, as this will help get the plant established and improve drainage. If you continue to do this every year, it will gradually become easier to cultivate.

Loam Soil

This soil is a mixture of clay and sand. It contains a good quantity of humus and is rich in nutrients. There are various types of loam: heavy, which contains more clay than loam and becomes wet in winter and spring; light loam, which has more sand

Sinking tree stake to support fruit tree

Young pear and apple trees protected by a hedge

than clay; and medium loam, which is an equal balance of clay and sand.

Sandy Soil
This is a very well-drained soil, so much so that plant foods are quickly washed away. A plus point is that it warms up quickly in the spring, so it is ideal for early crops. For hungry plants you will need to build the soil up with compost to help retain moisture and stop the leaching of nutrients. Plants such as the Mediterranean herbs will thrive on this soil.

Soil Acidity and Alkalinity
The natural acidity of the soil must be taken into account. Find out whether your soil is acid or alkaline using a reliable soil-testing kit, available from any good garden center. Soil acidity and alkalinity is measured on a pH scale ranging from 0 to 14; 0 is the most acid and 14 the most alkaline.

Acid soils (0–6.5 pH), on a sliding scale from acidic to nearly neutral, include sphagnum moss peat, sandy soil, coarse loam soil, sedge peat, and heavy clay. Alkaline soils (7.7–14 pH) tend to contain chalk or lime and are of a fine loam.

A reading that approaches either end of the pH scale indicates that the soil will tend to lock up the nutrients necessary for good growth. If it is very acid, you will need to add lime in the late fall to raise the pH. Fork the top 4 in. of the soil and dress with lime. Clay soils need a good dressing, but be careful not to over-lime sandy soils. It should not be necessary to do this more than once every 3 years unless your soil is very acid. Never add lime at the same time as manure, garden compost, or fertilizer, as a chemical reaction can occur that will ruin the effects of both. As a general rule, either add lime 1 month before, or 3 months after manuring, and 1 month after adding fertilizers. If the soil is alkaline, dress it every fall with well-rotted manure to a depth of 2–4 in., and dig over in the spring.

Soil pH also influences the number and type of beneficial soil-borne organisms and the incidence of pests and diseases; worms dislike a low pH, but leatherjackets and wireworms are usually more common in acid conditions, as is the fungal disease clubroot.

Some plants and plant families have quite specific pH requirements; others are more tolerant. On the whole, we have unwittingly selected plants that grow happily in the average, mildly acid to slightly alkaline soils most of us have. Herbs generally do best in a soil between 6.5 and 7.5 pH (fairly neutral).

Fruit cage mulched with leaf mold

A few fruits such as blueberries need acid conditions. They resent lime in the soil and need to be cultivated in pots of ericaceous potting mix and watered with rain, not ground water. Brassicas benefit from a slightly alkaline soil to reduce the risk of clubroot.

PREPARATION

The more you plan in advance and the more carefully you prepare the site, the better the results and the more pitfalls avoided. Always work out plans on paper. Draw a map of existing features and plan how you will fit in the new. For vegetables, plan your rotation (see p. 582). For fruits and perennial herbs, imagine walking around after five years when all the plants have grown up.

A good soil structure can be easily damaged by cultivating when it is excessively wet or dry and by using heavy machinery— even walking on wet soil causes compaction and smearing. To reduce the impact, lay a plank on the soil to disperse the weight. Once the soil is under cultivation, aim to stick to the path rather than tread on the soil.

Eliminating Weeds

If you do this at the start, you will not have the hassle of trying to remove quack grass, bindweed, or ground elder. Weeds do not emerge until the spring, and continue well into the season. If you wish to get rid of them successfully, it is best to cover the plot with black plastic the previous fall. Dig a shallow trench around the area and bury the sides of the plastic in it to keep it secure. Starved of light, the weeds will eventually give up. This will take until the following spring, so if you do not like the sight of the black plastic, position a few paving stones (taking care not to make any holes because the weeds will find them and come

Potatoes are good groundbreaking crops.

Double digging and filling a trench with green manure

through), cover the plastic with bark, and place terra-cotta pots planted up on top of the stones.

If you do not have the patience, use a weed killer instead. There are *no* organic weed killers but you can use ammonium sulfamate, which is sold as white crystals in hardware shops. Read the instructions carefully, dissolve it in water and spray the weeds. It is effective against most perennial plants, so be careful not to get it on any you wish to keep. You will notice the difference in about 1–2 weeks, but it is not safe to plant for 2–3 months. However, it is safer than modern weed killers, both for the environment and for us, because as the plants die down the ammonium sulfamate breaks down to ammonium sulfate, which is a fertilizer used by gardeners. So, despite the fact that this is not totally organic, it is beneficial in the end. But even this process does take time. There is no shortcut to eradicating weeds.

Soil Cultivation

The soil structure essential for successful growth is created by incorporating different materials into the soil: well-rotted compost improves moisture and nutrient retention, creates an open structure, and aerates the soil; sharp sand helps drainage; and "green manures" improve the structure.

Digging is the most important method of cultivation prior to planting. In the vegetable garden it is an annual event. On heavier soils in cooler climates fall digging is beneficial as the winter frosts that follow help to break down these wet, sticky soils into a workable tilth. Sandy soils can be lightly forked over and it is advisable to cover them with compost or green manure to reduce the loss of nutrients during the winter rains, or to leave the digging until spring. No matter what type of soil you have, it is beneficial to lay a good layer of well-rotted manure or garden compost over the surface in winter and dig it in the following spring.

Single digging consists of cultivating the soil to about 12 in., a good spade's depth and the average rooting zone of many plants. Double digging is used on poorly drained and previously uncultivated land. It encourages deep rooting and promotes rapid drainage. "Double" refers to the depth of cultivation, some 18–24 in. deep or approximately two spades' depth. When double digging, it is important to ensure that the topsoil and subsoil are not mixed.

There should be no need to add extra fertilizers to the soil if it has been well-prepared. Too much fertilizer causes lank, soft, disease-prone growth.

If necessary, in the vegetable garden you can gradually improve the soil by planting a groundbreaking crop such as potatoes or Jerusalem artichokes. Potatoes are good for this because they need a number of cultivations to "hill up" and cover the tubers, thus preventing weeds from becoming established. Potatoes also produce large, leafy tops, blocking the light that is so essential for the germination of many weeds.

PLANTING

If this is a new garden, and you are planting fruit trees and bushes, herbs, or perennial vegetables, it is worth laying the plants out on top of the prepared ground first, walking around, and getting an overall view. Make any changes to the design now rather than later. For details on buying plants, see page 593.

For trained, tall, and lax subjects, the stakes or supports must be in place beforehand, and for trees and bushes they must be strong enough to do the job and must last for a reasonable number of years. It is false economy to be stingy with these, as it will be hard to correct when the plants are grown.

Remember that once the planting is done, the future is determined. So do a good job and don't skimp on the digging or preparation of the ground. Dig a planting hole: bigger is always better! Mix in garden compost with the soil. Do not bury plants too deeply. Almost all of them should be planted at the same depth as they have grown. For grafted fruit trees, do not bury the rootstock. Keep their roots in their respective and different layers. Do not force them doubled up into a cramped hole, and never pack them all down in a flat layer unless they grew like that. Gently pack soil around roots, filling and firming as you go. It is better to overfirm! Then attach the support if needed.

AFTERCARE

For fruit trees and bushes, herbs, and perennial vegetables, use a mulch to retain moisture and suppress weeds. Try a thick layer of organic matter or a plastic sheet or carpet mulch.

In the fruit garden, whatever the final goal, do not allow a weed or grass within a circle as wide as the tree or bush is high for three years.

Good watering in dry spells is absolutely crucial! For long-term plants, water regularly for three years.

Raking in lime

CROP ROTATION

Rotation is a system whereby groups of vegetables are grown on a different section of the plot each year, maintaining the balance of soil nutrients for successive crops. Growing crops in this way avoids the buildup of pests and diseases, assists in weed control, and prevents the soil from deteriorating.

For crop rotation to be effective, a large area of ground is required, particularly when controlling soil-borne pests and diseases. White rot (which attacks the onion family), clubroot (which damages members of the cabbage family), and potato cyst wireworm remain dormant in the soil for many years and can survive on any weeds that are relatives. This makes good husbandry just as vital as crop rotation.

Planning

Before planting, first list the vegetables you want to grow and group them together according to their botanical relationship. Allocate each group to a plot, then compile a monthly cropping timetable for each space. The four rotational groups are as follows:

Legumes
Fava bean
Pea
Runner bean
String bean

Onion family
Bulb onion
Garlic
Leek
Scallion
Shallot

Carrot and tomato families
Bell pepper
Carrot
Celery
Parsnip
Potato
Tomato

Brassicas
Cabbage
Cauliflower
Radish
Rutabaga
Turnip

Next, allocate each rotation group to a plot of land ("plot A," etc.), and draw up a month-by-month timetable for each space. The example below fully utilizes the land and provides continuity of cropping. As space becomes available, plant the crops due to follow immediately: for example, Brussels sprouts and leeks cleared in early spring should be followed by peas, scallions, and lettuce. Crops may come from different groups, which means that rotation from one plot to another is a gradual process, rather than a wholesale changeover on a set date.

	Year 1	Year 2	Year 3	Year 4
Plot A	*Legumes* Fava bean Pea Runner bean String bean	*Onion family* Bulb onion Garlic Leek Scallion Shallot	*Carrot and tomato families* Bell pepper Carrot Celery Parsnip Potato Tomato	*Brassicas* Cabbage Cauliflower Radish Rutabaga Turnip
Plot B	*Onion family* Bulb onion Garlic Leek Scallion Shallot	*Carrot and tomato families* Bell pepper Carrot Celery Parsnip Potato Tomato	*Brassicas* Cabbage Cauliflower Radish Rutabaga Turnip	*Legumes* Fava bean Pea Runner bean String bean
Plot C	*Carrot and tomato families* Bell pepper Carrot Celery Parsnip Potato Tomato	*Brassicas* Cabbage Cauliflower Radish Rutabaga Turnip	*Legumes* Fava bean Pea Runner bean String bean	*Onion family* Bulb onion Garlic Leek Scallion Shallot
Plot D	*Brassicas* Cabbage Cauliflower Radish Rutabaga Turnip	*Legumes* Fava bean Pea Runner bean String bean	*Onion family* Bulb onion Garlic Leek Scallion Shallot	*Carrot and tomato families* Bell pepper Carrot Celery Parsnip Potato Tomato

GROWING SYSTEMS

Vegetable gardens can be laid out in a huge variety of ways and the individual crops grown using different techniques. Select methods that suit your needs and the space available in your garden. Major paths between beds should always be wide enough for a wheelbarrow; access paths can be narrower. equidistant spacing of plants in and between the rows. Plants may be set in staggered rows, creating a diagonal pattern. Pathways between the beds are slightly wider than those on the row system, but closer plant spacing means that more plants are grown per square yard and their growth and

Bed system, with paths separating each

further incorporated by worm activity. Worms are recommended for intensive vegetable production and are particularly advantageous in wetter climates.

Random Planting
Vegetables can be grown as "edible bedding plants" scattered among flowering plants and borders in the ornamental garden. Swiss chard, cabbage 'Ruby Ball,' beetroot 'Bull's Blood,' fennel, and Brussels sprout 'Rubine' are particularly pleasing. See also page 565.

The Potager
This is the French tradition of planting vegetables in

Row of good-looking ball-headed cabbages

Rows
Traditionally, vegetables are grown in long straight rows, with plants close together within the rows, and paths to allow access. This has some drawbacks. Competition between plants for space in a row means that much of the plants' extension growth is into the pathways, causing leafy vegetables like cabbages, cauliflowers, and lettuces to produce oval "hearts" rather than round ones.

Beds
These are effectively multirow systems, with

shape is more uniform. Close spacing ensures that weed growth is suppressed in its later stages and the soil structure remains intact, because there is less soil compaction when pathways are further apart.

Raised beds should be about 30 in. wide so that it is easy to reach into the center without overbalancing. After initial double digging and the addition of organic matter, they will not be walked on, allowing a good soil structure to form. Layers of well-rotted compost added annually will be

Potagers can look extremely pleasing

formal beds; a practical and visually pleasing display. See also page 565.

Long-term Crops
Perennial vegetables such as asparagus are difficult to incorporate into a crop rotation program. For this reason, they are often grown on a separate, more permanent site for several years before being replaced.

Sowing for Continuity
The greatest challenge is to have vegetables ready for harvest throughout the year.

sowing. Careful selection of cultivars also helps to achieve continuity; growing both rapidly maturing and slow-growing types extends the cropping period. The season for many root vegetables such as parsnips can be lengthened by growing a portion of the crop for eating fresh and the remainder for storage. These can slowly be eaten over the winter period.

Successional Sowings
It is usually quick-maturing crops that are prone to gluts and gaps, often bolting and

seed when the first true leaves of the previous sowing begin to emerge.

Intercropping
Spaces between slow-growing crops can be used as a seedbed for vegetables such as brassicas that will later need to be transplanted into permanent positions at wider spacings. This is only successful where the competition for moisture, nutrients, light, and space is not too great. This can be partially solved by growing them between rows of deep-rooted crops, so that the roots are in different levels of the soil. To achieve this it may also be necessary to space crops a little further apart than the usual spacings. Radishes sown on the same day as parsnips will have germinated, grown and been harvested before the parsnips have fully developed, achieving the maximum possible yield, covering the soil with vegetation and suppressing weed growth. This intercropping requires some flexibility in the cropping plan.

Catch Crops
These are rapidly maturing vegetables, including radishes, lettuces, and salad onions, all of which can be grown before the main crop is planted. Catch cropping is

useful when growing tender crops such as tomatoes, sweet corn, and courgettes, which cannot be planted until the risk of late frost is well past.

Extending the Season
The season for vegetables can be extended by growing them under cover at the beginning or end of their natural season; sowing early under cover hastens maturity while protection later in the season extends the cropping period. See also pages 588–589 and 599.

Pot-raised Plants
Raising plants in pots or modules is useful for those that are frost tender and allows plants to mature while the ground is cleared of earlier crops. This saves time and space and gives more control over the growth and development of young plants. Brassicas, lettuces, leeks, and onions can be grown in this way.

"The Hungry Gap"
Few vegetables mature from late winter to early sping—a period often referred to as "the hungry gap." Careful planning allows this gap to be bridged; spring cauliflower, winter cabbage, celeriac, kale, and leeks can all be grown for harvesting during this period.

Runner beans interplanted with a row of lettuces

Some, such as asparagus, have only a short harvesting period, while vegetables like cabbage, cauliflower and lettuce are available at almost any time, provided that there is successional

becoming inedible. To avoid this, sow sufficient seed for your needs a little and often, so that if something goes wrong, the problem is only a small one. a good guide is to sow a patch of

Vegetables in a random system, with aster, gladioli, and plum

POLLINATION AND COMPANION PLANTING

Almost all of our fruiting plants require their flowers to be pollinated. Pollination usually occurs naturally, without intervention, but for some fruits, a few vegetables, and many plants grown under glass, you can improve the rate of pollination and thus fruit set. Many fruits are self-fertile and can set by pollinating themselves, but crop better if cross-pollinated. Some, such as figs, have varieties that produce fruit parthenocarpically, without pollination, thus they are often seedless. A few fruits such as 'Conference' pears are partly parthenocarpic—if not pollinated by another variety their fruits are different and oddly shaped.

Some plants do not have male and female flowers on the same plant, so we have to grow a nonfruiting male to pollinate every half dozen or so females. Kiwis and grapevines are good examples. For convenience, varieties that carry both sexes have been bred.

Some fruit trees, many nuts, and sweet corn are wind-pollinated, while other plants are pollinated by bees and other insects. Under cover, none of these natural pollinators exist and we have to assist. A rabbit's tail, a cotton ball, or piece of wool lightly touched on each flower should suffice. We can lure more insects to help by growing attractant companion plants and this can also add a bit of color and life as well. Commercial tomato growers even buy cardboard nests of bumble bees to pollinate for them.

Outdoors early in the year there are few insects around and for the earliest flowerers pollination is risky. Hand-pollination is effective but tedious. It is better to ensure insect pollination by increasing the numbers. Planting companion plants as attractants helps; taking up beekeeping makes an enormous improvement.

It is well worth getting to know the pollination requirements of fruit trees. To pollinate each other, not only do varieties have to be compatible, they also have to be flowering at the same time. All good catalogs have a choice of suitable cross pollinators indicated. When in doubt, the wild species is often the best pollinator for most of its varieties. Alternatively, simply plant more varieties. This is especially true for a few fruits that are not good pollinators themselves. For example the apples **'Cox's Orange Pippin'** and **'Bramley's Seedling'** never crop together, but if you add a **'James Grieve,'** all three fruit.

COMPANION PLANTING

Companion planting is of immense benefit to most edible plants, as it brings in and supports pollinating and predatory insects, and maintains them throughout the rest of the year. Aim at having a continuity of flowers throughout the year as it is these that provide nectar and honey for the bees, hoverflies, and other

Limnanthes douglasii with **gooseberries**

beneficial insects we want to encourage. Of particular usefulness is *Limnanthes douglasii*, the poached egg plant, which is a low-growing, self-seeding, weed-suppressing, hardy annual. It is especially beneficial under gooseberries and soft fruit. *Phacelia tanacetifolia*, *Convolvolus tricolor*, pot marigolds, and clovers are all very good for beneficial insects.

Other plants can be good companions to our plants by repelling pests. French marigolds are one of the strongest, and their smell will keep aphids out of a greenhouse. Planted around the garden, they disorient pests sniffing for their quarry. Other insect repellents include the herbs tansy, pennyroyal, nasturtiums, stinging nettle, hyssop, wormwood, and southernwood. Fragrant herbs such as hyssop, thyme, marjoram, and parsley also

Chives flourishing under apples

help maintain garden health.

Alliums are valuable companions. Their smell deters many pests, yet their flowers attract beneficial insects. They seem to help protect the plants they grow with from fungal attack. Garlic and chives are the easiest to grow and use in quantity at the base of almost all fruit trees and bushes.

Many companion plants help access nutrients and make them available for our fruiting plants. Clovers, lupins, and other leguminous plants are especially good, as they fix nitrogen from the air and the surplus will feed our crops. *Alfalfa/lucerne* is exceptionally deep rooted and brings up minerals from depths other plants cannot reach. It should be included in the seed mixture for orchard and wild garden swards. Similarly a few thistles and docks can be tolerated in those areas for the same purpose. Clovers and chicory should be included whenever grass is seeded, as the sward produced will be richer and lusher.

In grass at the base of trees, dense shrubs, and hedges, bulbous spring-flowering plants can be fitted in with no difficulty. These areas can remain uncut till the bulbs' foliage dies down, and their flowers will be rich sources of pollen and nectar for the earliest pollinators and predators. Some ivy in the hedges provides late flowers for insects in fall before they hibernate.

Ground-cover plants provide habitats for ground beetles and many other useful creatures, but may also harbor slugs, snails, and overwintering pests. On the whole it is better to keep such habitats as far as possible from soft fruit and seedbed. Particular plants that help or hinder others are noted with individual crop entries.

This attractive garden of herbs enjoys the semishade of a peach tree.

CONTAINER CULTURE

Growing in containers is an ideal technique for fruits and vegetables that might otherwise be difficult, enabling you to control the size of the plant and the conditions in which it is kept. Almost all herbs can be grown in containers. The individual plant entries give details of the best size of container for each crop and where to place it to receive the ideal growing conditions. This section provides more general information and advice on container growing.

ADVANTAGES OF CONTAINERS

With attention to feeding and watering, almost any plant can be coaxed to grow in a container. Where room is limited, containers offer an alternative to ground space. They can also offer different conditions from those found in the ground. Tomatoes and cucumbers have long been grown under glass in containers to prevent any contact with disease-infected soil. If you have a chalky soil, lime-hating plants can be grown in containers of ericaceous potting mix and watered with rainwater.

Portable containers allow you to respond to weather conditions, moving plants outdoors once spring frosts end, and putting them under shelter again at the onset of colder weather.

For large fruit plants, a container cramps the root system, preventing them from growing too large or too quickly. Allied with pruning, this allows us to dwarf plants we would find too large to handle. Often this restriction is resented by the plant and, perversely, may result in earlier

fruiting. The fruits may not be prolific, but a selection of containers can give several different varieties in a space otherwise occupied by one, allowing greater variety and a longer season.

Vegetables most suited to container culture are either rapidly maturing crops such as mini beets, carrots, lettuces, radishes, and scallions, or dwarf varieties of bush or climbing vegetables, including eggplants, beans, cucumbers, peas, peppers, and tomatoes, as these need little support. Deep-rooted vegetables like sprouts, main-crop carrots, and parsnips can be grown in containers at least 18 in. deep.

CHOOSING A CONTAINER

Choose the container to suit the plant. If it is a tall plant, make sure the container has a base wide enough to prevent it from toppling over, even outside in a high wind. For vegetables, the chance of successful cropping is improved with large containers; they allow for a greater rooting depth, dry out slowly, and provide adequate anchorage for crops that need staking.

Plastic containers (with drainage holes) are more moisture-retentive than those of wood or terra-cotta, but the latter are preferred by some plants such as citrus.

If using unconventional containers—old watering cans, sinks, a half beer barrel—make sure they have drainage holes and gravel or broken pots in the bottom of the container to keep the holes from clogging up.

Herbs can suit hanging baskets, but the position is crucial. They dislike high wind and full sun all day.

Also, they are mostly fast growers, and if too cramped or over- or underwatered they will drop their leaves.

POTTING MIXES AND FERTILIZERS

Choosing the right potting mix is essential for healthy plants. Potting mixes for containers are either loam-based (soil-based) or loamless.

John Innes

This is loam-based and includes chemicals. On the plus side, it stays richer in nutrients longer, making feeding less critical; it holds water well and is a stable potting mix for a large, long-term plant. If it does dry out, it takes up water easily. The biggest problem is that it is easy to overwater.

There are usually three different grades of potting mix, though some manufacturers combine No. 1 and No. 2. No. 1 is for growing rooted cuttings, No. 2 for seedlings, and No. 3 for final potting. The numbers indicate the amount of nutrients. You must choose the correct one for the job. Loam-based composts are generally ideal for vegetables and fruits in containers, and organic matter can be added if required. This is not a good potting mix for hanging baskets, because it is heavy when wet.

Homemade Soil-based Mix

If you wish to make a soil-based potting mix of your own try this reliable recipe.

4 parts good weed-free garden topsoil
3 parts well-rotted garden compost
3 parts moist peat
1 part horticultural sharp sand

Multipurpose Potting Mix

This is usually peat-based with added chemicals. The bags are light and the potting mix is clean and easy to use. On the negative side, you will need to feed regularly as nutrients are soon depleted; also the potting mix is light, so watch out that large plants do not fall over. The most frequent problem is that it takes up water poorly if it dries out.

Homemade Bark, Peat, Grit Mix

This is ideal for many herbs as well as some fruits and vegetables. The open mix helps prevent overwatering; the bark retains water, which protects against under-watering and keeps the potting mix open to help absorb water if ever it dries out completely. It is suitable for containers and hanging baskets alike. Another plus is that you know what nutrients are in it, so you will be able to feed in a balanced way.

Alternative Potting Mixes

Peat-free composts are increasingly available as we become aware of the need to conserve our diminishing peat fields. They are generally made of coir, a by-product of coconuts, or composted bark. Coir is very free-draining, so some composts include a jelly that retains water, releasing it gradually. Coir compost is light, so there may be a stability problem with tall or large plants. A final drawback—the nutrients are soon depleted, so you will need to feed from the start.

Composted bark has similar drawbacks if used straight, with no peat or soil: watering and nutrient loss. If the bark has not been composted for long enough, it can leach the nutrients and starve the plants. However, mixed with peat or soil, bark is a great asset.

Fertilizers

Liquid seaweed contains small amounts of nitrogen, phosphorous, potassium, and it is also rich in trace elements. It not only makes a good soil feed but, as the elements are easily taken in by the plant, can also be sprayed on as a foliar feed.

Calcified seaweed contains calcium, sodium, magnesium, and numerous trace elements. It is ideal for adding to seed potting mix. Use according to manufacturer's instructions.

MAINTENANCE

Most plants need moist soil but drown if waterlogged and wilt if dry. Water stress due to drought, even for short periods, can greatly reduce the potential productivity of plants. If you cannot maintain consistent watering, install an automatic system of irrigation. It is best to water containers in the early morning or the evening, especially in summer, as this reduces the amount lost through evaporation.

Repotting into a larger container helps provide new nutrients, but this may become difficult with larger plants. The alternatives are top-dressing with an enriched mix of compost and organic fertilizer, or feeding little and often with a diluted liquid feed such as seaweed, or comfrey and nettle extract.

Maintenance Calendar

Spring Repot perennial plants if necessary (look for roots protruding from the bottom of the container). Use a pot the next size up. Carefully remove the plant from its old pot. Clean it up, removing any weeds and dead leaves. Place gravel or other drainage material in the bottom of the container, and keep the potting mix sweet by adding a tablespoon of granulated charcoal. As soon as the plant starts producing new growth or flowers, start feeding regularly with liquid feed. Prune fruits as needed.

Summer Keep a careful eye on the watering; make sure the pots do not dry out fully. Move some plants out of the midday sun. Deadhead any flowers on herbs. Feed with liquid feed, on average once a week. Remove any pest-damaged leaves. Prune fruits as needed.

Fall Cut back the perennial herbs. Weed containers and at the same time remove some of the top compost and re-dress. Bring any tender plants inside before the frosts. Start reducing the watering. Prune fruits as needed.

Winter Protect all container-grown plants from frosts. If possible, move them into a cold greenhouse or garage. If the weather is very severe, cover the containers in a layer of burlap. Keep watering to a minimum. Prune fruits as needed.

Back row, left to right: **Lungwort** (*Pulmonaria officinalis*), *Prostanthera rotundifolia*, **Variegated Box,** (*Buxus sempervirens* 'Elegantissima'), **Rosemary Benenden Blue** (*Rosmarinus officinalis* 'Benenden Blue'), **Box** (*Buxus sempervirens*); front row, left to right: *Prostanthera rotundifolia* 'Rosea,' **Golden Curly Marjoram** (*Origanum vulgare* 'Aureum Crispum'), **Rue Jackman's Blue** (*Ruta graveolens* 'Jackman's Blue'), **Old Warrior** (*Artemisia pontica*)

PROPAGATING AND BUYING PLANTS

One of the great joys of gardening is propagating your own plants. Success is dependent on adequate preparation and the care and attention you give in the critical first few weeks. This section provides general instructions for the main propagation methods. Individual guidelines are given under each plant entry. Where space and time are short, or for larger perennial plants such as fruit trees and bushes, it may be easier to buy your plants.

SEED

Most vegetables, annual herbs, and annual fruits are usually grown from seed. There is a huge range of seed available from seed catalogs, or you can save your own. Seed is not always advisable for perennials, particularly fruits; a fruit seedling will not fruit until mature, which may be quick for some but takes many decades for most trees. Until the fruit is produced there is usually no way of telling what it will be like—and it may not be very good. Most of the best varieties will not come true from seed.

Seed can be sown outside, either directly where it is to mature or into a seedbed for transplanting. Starting off seeds in a greenhouse or on a windowsill gives you more control over the warmth and moisture, and enables you to begin propagating earlier in the season.

Types of Seed

Seeds are usually bought as packets of individual "naked" seeds; but vegetable seeds in particular may be available in other forms.

Pelleted seeds are coated in a ball of clay, which moistens and disintegrates in the soil. They are easy to handle and sow at precise spacings, reducing the need for thinning. Sow at a depth of about twice their diameter and keep the soil moist but not waterlogged until germination.

Seed tapes and sheets are individual seeds encased at the correct spacing in tapes or sheets of tissue paper or gel. These substances are soluble when placed in moist soil. Tapes and sheets are quick to use and are precisely spaced so there is no need for thinning.

Primed seeds are in the first stages of germination and are used for those that are hard to germinate or need high germination temperatures, such as cucumbers. They arrive by mail in plastic packages to prevent moisture loss and are pricked out into pots or trays on arrival.

Preparation of Seed

Most seeds need air, light, particular temperatures, and moisture to germinate. Some have a long dormancy, and some have hard outer coats and need a little help to get going. Here are two techniques. See individual plant entries for when to use these techniques.

Scarification
If left to nature, seeds that have a hard outer coat would take a long time to germinate. To speed up the process, rub the seed between two sheets of fine sandpaper. This weakens the coat of the seed so that moisture needed for germination can penetrate.

Stratification (vernalization)
Some seeds need a period of cold (from 1 to 6 months) to germinate. Mix the seed with damp sand and place in a plastic bag in the refrigerator or freezer. After 4 weeks, sow on the surface of the compost and cover with perlite.

Sowing Outside

In an average season the seed should be sown in mid- to late spring after the soil has been prepared and warmed. It is simplest to sow directly where the plants are to mature, and this is best for plants that resent root disturbance, such as many root vegetables. Alternatively, you can use a seedbed if you need the space seedlings are to occupy for something else, and to save space, as small plants are not at their final spacing until they mature.

Before starting, check your soil type (see pp. 578–579), making sure that the soil has sufficient food to maintain a seedbed. Dig the bed over, mark out a straight line with a piece of string secured tightly over each row, draw a shallow drill, $^{1}/_{4}$–$^{1}/_{2}$ in. deep (according to seed size), using the side of a fork or hoe, and sow the seeds thinly. Sow larger seeds individually. If your soil is sticky clay, give the seeds a better start by adding a fine layer of sharp sand along the drill. Do not overcrowd the bed, otherwise the seedlings will grow leggy

Misting unit

and weak and be prone to disease. For more precise details of seed spacing see individual plant entries.

Protected Sowing
Sowing under cover is expensive and often labor-intensive, yet it allows seeds to be sown whatever the weather. It is most often used in cooler climates for tender crops that cannot be planted out until there is no longer any danger or frost.

Start with a thoroughly cleaned container. Old potting mix also provides ideal conditions for damping off, fungi, and sciarid flies, so remove any spent compost from the greenhouse or potting shed.

Potting Mix
It is best to use a sterile seed potting mix. Ordinary garden soil contains many weed seeds that could easily be confused with the germinating seed. The best potting mix for most seed sowing is 50 percent propagating bark, 50 percent peat-based seed potting mix. However, for plants that prefer a freer draining potting mix, or for those that need stratification outside, a 25 percent peat-based seed potting mix, 50 percent propagating bark, 25 percent horticultural grit mix is ideal. And if you are sowing seeds that have a long germination period, use a soil-based seed potting mix.

Sowing in Seed Trays
Fill a clean seed tray with compost to $^1/_2$ in. below the rim and firm with a flat piece of wood. Do not press too hard, as this will over-compress the potting mix and restrict drainage, encouraging damping off disease and attack by sciarid flies.

The gap below the rim is essential, as it prevents the surface-sown seeds and compost being washed over the edge when watering.

Water the prepared tray using a fine rose on the watering can so as not to disturb the seed. Do not overwater. The potting mix should be damp, not soaking. After an initial watering, water as little as possible, but never let the surface dry out. Once the seed is sown, lack of moisture can prevent germination and kill the seedlings, but too much excludes oxygen and encourages damping-off fungi, and root rot.

Sowing Methods
There are three main methods, the choice dependent on the size of the seed. They are, in order of seed size, fine to large:
1 Scatter on the surface of the potting mix, and cover with a fine layer of perlite.
2 Press into the surface of the potting mix, either with your hand or a flat piece of wood the size of the tray, and cover with perlite.
3 Press down to one seed's depth and cover with potting mix.

The Cardboard Trick
When seeds are too small to handle, you can control distribution by using a thin piece of card cut to 4 in. x 2 in. and folded down the middle. Place a small amount of seed into the folded card and gently tap it over the prepared seed tray. This technique is especially useful when sowing into pack trays (see below).

Sowing in Pack (Module) Trays (Multicell Trays)
These packs are a great invention. The seed can germinate in its own space, get established into a strong seedling, and make a good rootball. When potting on, the young plant remains undisturbed and will continue growing. This is very good for plants like cilantro, which hate being transplanted and tend to bolt if you move them. Another advantage is that the problem of overcrowding is cut to a minimum, and

damping-off disease and sciarid fly are easier to control. Also, because seedlings in packs are easier to maintain, planting out or potting on is not so critical.

Packs come in various sizes; for example, you can get trays with very small holes of $^1/_2$ in. x $^1/_2$ in. up to trays with holes of $1^1/_4$ in. x $1^1/_4$ in. To enable a reasonable time lapse between germination and repotting, the larger are recommended.

Prepare the potting mix and fill the tray right to the top, scraping off surplus mix with a piece of wood level with the top of the holes. It is better not to firm the potting mix down. Watering in (see Sowing in Seed Trays) settles the mix enough to allow space for the seed and the top-dressing of perlite.

The principles of sowing in packs are the same as for trays. Having sown your seed, label the trays clearly with the name of the plant and the date.

Sowing in Pots
Multisowing in pots speeds the growth of root and bulb vegetables. Sow up to six seeds (two for beets) into a 3–4-in. pot, leave the seedlings to develop and then transplant the potful of plants, allowing extra space within the rows. Thinning is not needed. This technique works well for beets, cauliflower, turnips, kohlrabi, leeks, and onions.

Fluid Sowing
This is useful when weather and soil conditions make germination erratic. Seeds germinated under ideal conditions are sown, protected by a carrier gel. To germinate the seeds, place some moistened paper towels in the base of a plastic container. Scatter the seeds evenly on the surface, cover with a lid or plastic wrap and keep at 70°F. When the rootlets are about $^1/_4$ in. long, they are ready to sow. Wash

them into a fine mesh strainer. Mix carrier gel from half-strength fungicide-free wallpaper paste, scatter the seeds in the paste, and mix. Pour into a clear bag, cut off a corner and force the mixture through the hole. Cover the seeds with soil or vermiculite.

Seed Germination
Seeds need warmth and moisture to germinate. In a cold greenhouse, a heated propagator may be needed in early spring for seeds that germinate at warm to hot temperatures. In the house you can use a shelf near a radiator (never on the radiator), or a warm linen closet. Darkness does not hinder the germination of most seeds, but if you put your containers in a linen closet check them daily. As soon as there is any sign of life, place the trays in a warm light place, not in direct sunlight.

Hardening Off
When large enough to handle, prick out seed tray seedlings and pot up individually. Allow them to root fully. Test pack tray seedlings by giving one or two a gentle tug. They should come away from the cells cleanly, with the rootball. If they do not, leave for another few days.

When the seedlings are ready, harden them off slowly by leaving the young plants outside during the day. Once weaned into a natural climate, plant them directly to where they will mature.

Seed Storage and Viability
Once seed is harvested from the plant, it begins to deteriorate; even ideal storage conditions can only slow down the rate of deterioration. Viability (the ability to germinate) usually declines with age. Always use fresh seed, or store in cool, dark, dry conditions (definitely not the corner of the greenhouse) in airtight containers.

CUTTINGS

Taking cuttings is the best way to propagate many fruiting plants and nonflowering herbs. This may be the only way to reproduce a particular variety or cultivar that will not come true from seed. For successful softwood cuttings it is worth buying a heated propagator, which can be placed in a greenhouse or on a shady windowsill. For successful semi-ripe, hardwood and root cuttings, a shaded cold frame can be used. For specific details, see the individual entry.

Softwood Cuttings

Softwood cuttings are usually taken between spring and midsummer, using the new, lush, green growth. To produce successful rooting material from herbs, prune the plant vigorously in winter to encourage new growth, and take cuttings as soon as there is sufficient growth.

Prepare a pot, seed tray, or packs with cutting potting mix—50 percent bark, 50 percent peat. Firm the compost to within 1 in. of the rim. Collect the cuttings in small batches in the morning. Choose sturdy shoots with plenty of leaves. Best results come from nonflowering shoots with the base leaves removed. Cut the shoot with a knife, not scissors. Place the cutting at once in the shade in a plastic bag or a bucket of water; softwood cuttings are extremely susceptible to water loss.

To prepare the cutting material, cut the base of the stem 1/4 in. below a leaf joint, to leave a cutting of roughly 4 in. long. If the cutting material has to be under 4 in., take the cutting with a heel. Remove the lower leaves and trim the tail that is left from the heel. Trim the stem cleanly before a node, the point at which a leaf stalk joins the stem. Remove the leaves from the bottom third of the cutting with a knife, leaving at least 2 or 3 leaves on top.

Make a hole in the potting mix and insert the cutting up to its leaves. Do not overcrowd the container or include more than one species, because quite often they take different times to root. Label and date the cuttings clearly, and only water the potting mix from above if necessary. Keep out of direct sunlight in hot weather. If it is very sunny, heavy shade is best for the first week.

Place in a heated or unheated propagator, or cover the pot or container with a plastic bag supported on a thin wire hoop (to prevent the plastic from touching the leaves), or with an upturned plastic bottle with the bottom cut off. If you are using a plastic bag, turn it inside out every few days to stop excess moisture from condensation from dripping onto the cuttings. Spray the cuttings with water every morning for the first week. Average rooting time is 2–4 weeks. The cutting medium is low in nutrients, so give a regular foliar feed when the cutting starts to root. Harden off the cuttings gradually when they are rooted. Bring them out in stages to normal sunny, airy conditions. Repot them

Fruit trees at a nursery

using a prepared potting mix once they are weaned. Label and water well after transplanting. About 4–5 weeks after transplanting, when the plant is growing away, pinch out the top center of the young cutting. This will encourage the plant to bush out, making it stronger as well as fuller. Allow to grow on until a good-sized rootball can be seen in the pot, then plant out.

Semihardwood or Greenwood Cuttings

These are usually taken from shrubby herbs such as rosemary and myrtle toward the end of the growing season (from midsummer to midfall). Use basically the same method as for softwood cuttings, but the potting mix should be freer-draining. Make the mix equal parts peat, grit, and bark. Once the cuttings have been inserted in the compost, place the pot, seed tray, or packs in a cold greenhouse or cold frame, not in a propagator, unless it has a misting unit.

Average rooting time for semihardwood cuttings is 4–6 weeks. If the fall is exceptionally hot and the potting mix or cuttings seem to be drying out, spray once a week. Begin the hardening off process in the spring after the frosts. Give a foliar feed as soon as there is sufficient new growth.

Hardwood Cuttings

Taken mid- to late fall in exactly the same way as softwood cuttings, but with a freer-draining potting mix of equal parts peat, grit, and bark. Keep watering to the absolute minimum. Winter in a cold frame or greenhouse. Average rooting time be as long as 12 months. For hardwood cuttings of hardy fruits,

Young fruit plants in containers

A plastic bag to retain moisture

push cuttings into a slit trench lined with sharp sand in moist ground, firm well, and keep them weed-free and protected from drying winds—a cloche is usually advantageous.

Root Cuttings

This method of cutting suits plants with creeping roots, such as bergamot, comfrey, horseradish, lemon balm, mint, soapwort, and sweet woodruff. Dig up some healthy roots in spring or fall. Fill a container with cutting potting mix—50 percent bark, 50 percent peat—firmed to within 1 in. of the rim. These cuttings lend themselves to being grown in packs. Water well. Cut $1\frac{1}{2}$–3 in. lengths of root that carry a growing bud. For comfrey and horseradish, simply slice the root into sections, $1\frac{1}{2}$–3 in. long, using a sharp knife to give a clean cut through the root. Make holes in the potting mix with a dibble. If using pots or seed trays these should be 1–$2\frac{1}{2}$ in. apart. Plant the cutting vertically. Cover with a small amount of potting mix and a layer of perlite level with the top of the container. Label and date. Average rooting time is 2–3 weeks. Do not water until roots or top growth appears. Then apply liquid feed. Slowly harden off the cuttings when rooted. Repot cuttings in seed trays and pots in a potting mix once they are hardened off. Label and water well after transplanting. About 2–3 weeks after transplanting, when you can see that the plant is growing, pinch out the top center of the young cutting. This will encourage the plant to bush out, making it stronger as well as fuller. Allow to grow on until a good-sized rootball can be seen in the pot. Plant out in the garden when the last frosts are over.

LAYERING

Layering is a process that encourages sections of plant to root while still attached to the parent. Bay, rosemary, sage, and other evergreens suit this method. Blackberries root their tips anywhere they can in fall, and many plants will root where they touch the ground to form natural layers, which easily detach with roots in fall.

To layer a plant, cultivate the soil around it during winter and early spring by adding peat and grit to it. In spring trim the leaves and sideshoots of a young, low vigorous stem for 4–24 in. below its growing tip. Bring the stem down to ground level and mark its position on the soil. Dig a trench at that point. Roughen the stem at the point where it will touch the ground, and peg it down into the trench, then bend the stem at right angles behind the growing tip, so that it protrudes vertically. Return the soil to the trench to bury the stem. Firm in well and water. Keep the soil moist, especially in dry periods. Sever the layering stem from its parent plant in fall if well rooted, and 3–4 weeks later nip out the growing tip from the rooted layer to make plant bush out. Check that the roots are established before lifting the layered stem. If necessary, leave for another year. Replant either in open ground or in a pot. Label and leave to establish.

A swollen graft point on a fruit tree

GRAFTING

Some fruit plants are only propagated by grafting or budding small pieces onto more easily grown rootstocks. Often this is done with special rootstocks simply to influence growth or to get the maximum number of plants from limited material. Budding and grafting techniques, although essentially simple, are profoundly difficult to master without a lot of practice and are beyond the scope of this book.

BUYING PLANTS

Buying fruit, vegetable, and herb plants has the advantage of ease and speed over growing them yourself, but is relatively costly and incurs a high risk of importing weeds, pests, and diseases along with the plants, especially with pot-grown specimens.

To fill an average garden with plants does not require an immense investment, but it is still quite enough to warrant care and budgeting. For fruit, specialist mail order nurseries usually provide a greater choice, and are often cheaper than most local suppliers. Get several catalogs and compare them before ordering, and do so early.

For fruit trees and shrubs bare-rooted plants are easier to inspect than pot-grown ones for signs of health or disease. The root systems on well-grown, bare-rooted trees are usually more extensive than those of pot-grown plants. Furthermore, for larger growing trees, there is the danger of pot-grown specimens being root bound. However, for most smaller subjects, container-ized plants from reputable suppliers are convenient and give good results.

Vegetables may be available pregrown as seedlings, at the stage when they require pricking out; as plugs with three or four true leaves, which may need growing on; or as plants that are quite large (sold in strips or multi-packs, like bedding plants) and should be transplanted directly on arrival.

MAINTAINING THE GARDEN

Trained 'Catillac' pear tree

To ensure that plants are productive and the crops are of high quality, vegetables, herbs, and fruit need careful nurturing and diligent husbandry. Vegetables require more constant attention than either herbs or fruit. However, all plants benefit from regular checking, so that any problems can be spotted early. For watering, see pages 596–597; for pests and diseases, see pages 602–607.

PLANTING OUT

Plants that have been germinated or grown as cuttings in a greenhouse will need to be planted out after hardening off. The timing depends on the prevailing weather and soil conditions. All plants suffer a check in their growth rate after transplanting, caused by inevitable root disturbance and by the change in environment to a cooler site. Younger plants tend to recover rapidly while older ones take longer. To reduce stress, ensure there is plenty of water available, transplant on an overcast day into moist soil, and provide shelter from strong sunshine until plants are established.

PLANT SUPPORTS

These should be positioned before they are required by the plants. Plants growing tall without a support can be damaged or suffer a check in growth. Select a support according to the plant being grown. Peas climb with tendrils, preferring to twine round thin supports such as chicken wire or spindly twigs, while runner beans hug poles or stakes. Vegetables without climbing mechanisms need to be tied to stakes with garden twine in a loose figure-eight loop, positioning the stake on the windward side of the plant. Fruit trees trained against a flat surface need strong wires to which the branches can be tied.

PRUNING FRUIT TREES

We prune for two reasons: to remove diseased, damaged, or ill-placed growth, and to channel growth into fruit production. We may also prune to reduce the size of a plant as it becomes too large for the space available.

Excessive pruning, especially at the wrong time, is counterproductive. In general, pruning even moderate amounts from a tree or bush in fall and winter stimulates regrowth, proportionately as much as the amount removed. This is useful when the plant is young and we wish to form the framework by stimulating the growth of young, vigorous replacement shoots.

However such fall and winter pruning is not so suitable for more mature fruiting plants whose structure is already formed and from which we wish to obtain fruit. Most respond much better to summer pruning, which is cutting out three-quarters of every young shoot, except the leaders. This redirects growth and causes fruit bud production on the spurs, or short sideshoots to form. These may be further shortened and tidied in the winter but then, as only a little is removed, vigorous regrowth is avoided.

Although it may seem complicated, pruning is easy once you've done it a few times. Use clean pruning shears, sterilized with alcohol (rarely use a saw), and cover large wounds with a good sealant to prevent water from getting in.

Training the Basic Shape

The majority of perennial woody fruiting plants can be trained and pruned to make a permanent framework that carries spurs, preferably all over. Growing just one such single stem, branch, or cordon on a weak rootstock allows us to squeeze many varieties into the same space as one full-sized tree. Such single-stemmed cordons do not produce very much fruit, especially as they are hard to support if they reach more than head height. Sloping these cordons serves to make them longer without going too high.

Growing two, three, or more branches is a better compromise. These can be arranged as espaliers (in tiers), fans (radiating from the center), or gridirons of almost any design. However, for the vast majority of trees and bushes, the actual shapes most commonly employed are the expanding head, and the open bowl or goblet arrangement, on top of a single stem or trunk.

This bowl shape maximizes the surface area of fruiting growth exposed to the sun and air. To achieve it the main leader is removed from the middle and the branches trained as a bowl with a hollow center open to the sky. The number of main stems is customarily about five or six, which divide from the trunk and redivide to form the walls of the goblet. The stem or trunk may be short, as is common with gooseberries, or taller, which is often more convenient.

Where the branches of a tree divide from the trunk on a short trunk they are termed bushes; at waist to shoulder height they are called halfstandards; and they are standards where they start higher still. Bushes, especially those on the more dwarfing stocks, tend to be too low to mow underneath but can always be mulched

Raspberries before pruning (top), and after (below)

A wall of Morello cherries

instead. Halfstandards grow large, depending on stock, and are tall enough to mow underneath. Full standards make very big specimens and are only usually planted in parks and meadows.

Young unformed plants, maidens, cost less than trained forms. It is very satisfying to grow your own espalier or gridiron from a maiden, but the result will depend on your skill and foresight.

Renewal Pruning

Some fruits need pruning on the renewal principle. Whole branches or shoots are removed at a year or two old, after they have fruited. Summer raspberries are typical, the old shoots being removed at ground level as the young are tied in. Grapevines can be constrained to two young branches emerging from the trunk, replaced each year. Peaches on walls also have young shoots tied in

and old fruited ones removed. Black currants have a third of growths from the ground removed annually.

Timing

A few plants are pruned only at certain times of year. Hollow-stemmed, tender, and evergreen plants are pruned in spring once the hardest weather is over and *Prunus* are pruned in summer, as otherwise they are prone to disease.

FERTILITY AND WATER MANAGEMENT

Plants have varying nutrient requirements according to the species. All need sufficiently fertile soil and water to grow and yield well. Fruits are not usually as demanding as many vegetable crops; this is because they are mostly perennial. Growing in open ground, they make extensive root systems, which find the water and nutrients required. Annual and short-lived crops generally need much more attention to soil fertility and water provision because they have limited root systems. Plants in containers similarly require much care, and because of the confinement also readily suffer from any excess.

SOIL FERTILITY

Soil fertility is the source of essential nutrients needed for healthy growth. There is no precise definition of a fertile soil, but ideally it has the following characteristics: a good crumb structure; plenty of humus and nutrients; good drainage, moisture-retentive; and a pH that is slightly acid to neutral. Nutrients are absorbed in solution by the roots and transported through the plant's system. The major elements include nitrogen, phosphorus, potassium, calcium, magnesium, and sulfur. Minor, or trace, elements include iron, manganese, boron, zinc, copper, and molybdenum. These are needed in minute quantities yet are still essential.

Nutrients are present in the soil as a result of the weathering processes on the mineral particles and the chemical breakdown or decay of organic matter and humus by bacteria and other microorganisms. These release nutrients in a form available to plants. To function effectively they must have an open, well-drained soil with adequate supplies of air and water. Extra nutrients in the form of compost and fertilizer may be needed to provide sufficient nutrients to sustain healthy growth.

Fertility is best provided organically from materials that slowly convert to a usable form in the soil. Well-rotted farmyard manures; good compost; seaweed meal; hoof and horn meal; blood, fish, and bone meal; bone meal; and fish emulsions are all suitable.

If mineral shortages are suspected, then ground rock dusts provide cheap, slow-release supplies; potash, phosphate, magnesium (dolomitic) limestone, calcified seaweed, and lime are all widely available, cheap, and pleasant to apply. Wood ashes are extremely valuable to most fruiting plants. Seaweed extracts sprayed on the foliage can give rapid relief of mineral deficiencies.

Bulkier materials such as well-rotted manure and compost also provide much humus, which is essential for the natural fertility of the soil, its water-holding capacity and its buffering action (preventing the soil being too acid or alkali). The humus content is conserved by minimal cultivation and refraining from soluble fertilizers.

More humus can be provided by growing green manures. These occupy the soil when other plants are dormant or if parts of the plot are empty throughout winter. Nutrients and water that would have leached away are combined with winter sunlight to grow dense covers of hardy plants. These also protect the soil surface from erosion and rain impaction. When the weather warms up, green manures are incorporated in situ by digging in or composting under a plastic sheet, or are removed and added to the compost heap.

Organic mulches such as well-rotted manures, composted shredded bark, leaf mold, mushroom compost, straw, or peat are all advantageous to most plants. They rot down at the soil surface, aiding fertility and humus levels, and suppress weeds if they are thick enough, but most

Freshly dug clay lumps will break up as weathering occurs.

Freshly dug clay/loam soil

important, they conserve soil moisture.

Careful rotation in the vegetable plot can aid fertility. Plant "hungry" crops such as celery, leeks, and members of the cabbage family, which require plenty of nitrogen, after peas, beans, and other legumes, which fix nitrogen from the atmosphere using nitrogen-fixing bacteria in swollen nodules on their roots and release nitrogen into the soil.

WATERING

Vegetables and fruits crop to their full potential only when water is plentiful. Yields are reduced when plants suffer from drought stress. The soil is a plant's reservoir and different soils are able to retain different levels of water. Clays retain water very efficiently, loams have a good balance between drainage and water retention, and sandy soils are very free-draining.

Water is lost from both the soil and the leaves of plants, and this loss is most rapid on hot, sunny days with drying winds. It is vital to reduce the loss of water from soil by:
• regularly incorporating well-rotted organic matter into the soil, to increase its moisture-holding capacity.
• deep cultivation to open up the soil and encourage deeper rooting. This allows plants to draw water from a greater soil depth.
• covering the surface with an organic or inorganic mulch such as well-rotted manure or black plastic to prevent moisture loss from the surface and upper layers.
• improving drainage on waterlogged soil; a high water table restricts root development, making plants prone to stress during drought. By improving the drainage system and lowering the water table, the roots are encouraged to penetrate to a greater depth, thereby leaving them more drought-tolerant.
• removing weeds, which compete with other plants for water. They should be removed at seedling stage.
• reducing plant density, particularly on dry, exposed sites, to allow each plant to draw water from a greater volume of soil.
• providing shelter, especially on exposed sites. Reducing wind speed reduces moisture loss from the soil and plants.
• being careful with accurate timing and frequency of application. Most plants have critical periods when adequate water supplies are very important for successful development and cropping.

Critical Watering Periods
Water before it is too late; if a plant is wilting it is already suffering badly!

Seeds and Seedlings
Water is essential for seed germination and rapid seedling development. Seedbeds should be moist, not waterlogged. Water seedlings using a fine rose on a watering can to provide a shower of tiny droplets and prevent plant damage.

Transplants
Plants often suffer from transplanting shock due to root damage after being moved, and the effects are more pronounced if the soil is dry. Water plants gently after moving them to settle moist soil around the roots. Water woody plants until they have been established for up to three years, particularly evergreens, which cannot drop their leaves when under stress and so survive dormant.

Fruiting Crops
Fruits and vegetables with edible fruits, such as peas, beans, and tomatoes, have two critical periods for water availability once they have established: when flowering (to aid pollination and fruit set) and when the fruit begins to swell.

Leaf and Root Crops
These need a constant water supply throughout their cropping life.

Methods of Watering
It is vital to maintain rapid growth in the growing season, particularly in annual plants, otherwise plant tissues can harden and growth can be affected. Growth check in cauliflowers can cause young plants prematurely to form a small, poorly developed curd, while other annuals will "bolt."

Always water thoroughly, soaking the soil to a reasonable depth. It is bad practice merely to wet the soil surface. This draws the roots up to form a surface mat while much is wasted by evaporation. A good soaking descends and draws the roots after it, thus they become deeper and more able to find other soil moisture on their own.

If you bury a length of hosepipe with the roots of a tree you can inject the water right where it is needed during the critical first few years. Likewise a pot or funnel pushed in nearby is a useful aid.

When time is limited and cash more abundant, it is wise to invest in automatic watering equipment. Drip feeds and seeping hoses allow a constant and even supply of water close to the roots without the gardener's constant attention, and soon repay the investment. Overhead sprinklers are extremely inefficient, as only about 20 percent of the water ever reaches the plant.

Mulching
Once the winter rains have drenched the soil, a mulch prevents the moisture from evaporating. Any mulch helps, but the looser and thicker the better. Less than 2 in. is ineffective, and initial applications always pack down, so be prepared to add more after a few months.

When organic material for mulching is in short supply, inorganic ones may be used. Sharp sand and gravel make excellent moisture-retaining mulches and are cheap and sterile.

Grass clippings are an excellent mulch, if applied in thin layers—though if applied too thickly in wet conditions they may make a nasty mess. Clippings provide a rich source of nitrogen and encourage soil life. They soon disappear and need replenishing. Continuous applications slowly make the soil less alkaline and more acid, which is often advantageous.

GROWING IN GREENHOUSES

There is no substitute for walk-in cover, which is more valuable if heated and frost-free, and even more so if kept warm or even hot. If maintained as warm as a living room all year round, many exotic fruits and vegetables become possible in cooler zones, from oranges to eggplants. And it is not only summer crops that benefit. Lettuce, spinach, and other hardy winter salads produce more tender, better-quality crops in an unheated greenhouse than outside.

Exotics such as passion-fruits are best grown under cover, as they may not crop otherwise. Heat ripens the fruit and also the wood, which may not ripen outdoors in cooler areas. Some plants take many months to crop each year and without cover they would never ripen before frosts come. Extra warmth and shelter allows us to have tender or delicate plants that would not survive in the open, but it also means we can have the same crop earlier than if grown outdoors—for example, strawberries or tomatoes.

Often it is best to grow plants in containers that are to go under cover, as this allows for more variety in the same area, though each plant will necessarily yield less than if it was in the ground. Containers not only control the vigor of the plants but also make them portable so they can be moved under cover and outside as convenient. This suits many fruits such as the citrus, which really prefer to be outside all summer but need frost protection in winter. By contrast, many varieties of grapevine are best under cover for an early start and for ripening, but need to be chilled in winter to fruit well.

This is why some plants are difficult. They need hot summers and warm falls and also cold winters to go dormant. Without dormancy they do not ripen wood or fruit well and often just fade away. It is quite easy to chill a greenhouse in a cold area for the couple of months required, but not of course if other tender plants are kept there also.

The other requirement may be for extra light. Many plants need more light than can be had in winter through dirty glass. The physical barrier reduces light intensity by half. Fortunately, artificial lights are cheap to install and run—compared to heating anyway. Some plants are very demanding; not only do they want more light and heat but they want enough hours of complete darkness every night as well. This requires blinds to exclude daylight and light from any nearby streetlights, too! Similarly, some plants find bright light too intense and need shading.

Fortunately most exotics are remarkably easy to grow. The biggest problems are usually the cost of heating and the eventual size of the plants.

Hygiene in the Greenhouse
Greenhouses should be cleaned annually in winter: wash thoroughly with disinfectant to kill overwintering eggs and fungal spores. If you have space, before introducing a new plant to the greenhouse, keep it in quarantine for a few weeks to prevent new problems being introduced.

Grapevine growing in a sunroom

PROTECTED CROPPING

Many crops need protecting at some point in their life. In some cases they need protecting from the elements, to provide conditions more conducive to growth; they may also need protecting from predators such as birds and rodents.

Protection from the Elements

A few simple structures can extend the growing season in spring and fall, accelerate growth, and increase productivity.

Cold frames are ideal for raising seedlings or hardening off plants before transplanting outdoors. The lack of height limits the

floating film are flexible covers that can be laid immediately over the crop or suspended on hoops as "floating mulches." As the plants grow they are forced upward. Frost fabric is lightweight, soft-textured spun polypropylene, which lasts for a year if it is kept clean, or sometimes longer if cared for. It is ideal for frost protection and for forcing early crops. Many crops, especially vegetables, can be grown under this, from sowing to harvesting, and it is an effective barrier against pests and diseases. More light and air can penetrate through this than

Frost fabric protecting newly planted corn

Cloches protecting spinach

crops that can be grown in them. Cloches of glass or plastic are easily moved to provide shelter to those individual plants or small groups that need it most. Low polyethylene tunnels are like small cloches, are cheap, portable, and versatile, but are of limited use because of their flimsiness and lack of height. Crop covers and

through plastic film. Plastic film is usually perforated with minute slits or holes for ventilation, but the crop may overheat on sunny spring days. The film is laid directly over the plants; as they grow, the flexible material is pushed upward, splitting open the minute slits and increasing ventilation. It is often used in the early stages of growth.

Plastic netting has a very fine mesh, filtering the wind and providing protection, but has little effect on raising temperature. It lasts for several seasons.

As many of these materials are manufactured in long, narrow rolls, the most effective way to use them is to grow crops in long, narrow strips. Insect-pollinated crops like zucchini, squash, cucumbers, and tomatoes should have the covering removed or opened as the crop develops.

Protection from Predators

Fruit cages are cover with netting. They are necessary to protect soft fruit in areas with many birds. The most troublesome birds, such as blackbirds, can be excluded with coarse 1-in. mesh, while smaller, insectivorous birds such as wrens can still gain access. If all the net is wire, squirrels and rodents can also be stopped. If a finer mesh, down to about $1/2$ in. is used, then bees can still enter but large moths and butterflies are excluded.

Fruit cages have other uses. The netting itself makes a more sheltered environment enjoyed by the plants. Light frosts are kept off, and chill

winds are reduced. In very hot regions, denser netting gives welcome shade and cooler conditions.

A fruit cage can even be reversed in principle to enclose all of a small garden and to confine ornamental seed- and insect-eating, but hopefully not inadvertently fruit-eating, birds. On a more prosaic level, it is practical to grow plants on a tall leg and then run chickens underneath for their excellent pest control. If you have chickens, they can be running in the cage during most of the year when the plants are not in fruit.

Fruit cages can be handcrafted from secondhand materials or easy custom-made ones are available. In areas of high wind, obviously, the most substantial materials have to be used. Permanent sides of wire mesh and a light net laid on wires for the roof are most practicable. Make sure you can remove the roof net easily if snows are forecast, as a thick layer on top will break most cages.

Most fruit cage plants are natives of the woodland's edge and do not mind light shade, but few of them relish stagnant air, so do not overcrowd them.

WEED CONTROL

Any plant that grows in a place where it is not wanted is described as a weed. Weeds compete with crops for moisture, nutrients, and light, acting as hosts to pests and diseases, which can then spread to crops.

TYPES OF WEED

Knowledge of a weed's life cycle enables the gardener to control weeds effectively.
• Ephemeral weeds germinate, flower, and seed rapidly, producing several generations each season and copious quantities of seed.
• Annual weeds germinate, flower, and seed in one season.
• Biennial weeds have a life cycle spanning two growing seasons.

• Perennial weeds survive for several years. They often spread through the soil as they grow, producing many new shoots and setting seed. New plants sprout from tiny fragments of root, rhizome, or bulbils in the soil.

METHODS OF CONTROL

There are four main methods of weed control: manual, mechanical, mulching, and chemical. Wherever possible, keep the garden weed-free, and if germination occurs, remove weeds immediately, before they flower and produce seed. The old saying "One year's seed is seven years' weed" is, unfortunately, scientifically proven.

Complete elimination of weeds from an area before planting is invariably worthwhile and is much easier than trying later to weed among the plants (see pp. 580–581).

Manual Weeding
Digging, forking, hoeing, and hand weeding, are often the only practical ways to eradicate weeds in confined spaces.

Digging cultivates the soil to a depth of at least 12 in. Soil is turned over, burying surface vegetation and annual weeds. Perennial weeds should be removed separately and not buried among the surface vegetation.

Forking cultivates the soil around perennial weeds

before they are lifted by hand. If this is undertaken carefully, roots can be removed without breaking them into sections and forming new plants.

Hoeing prevents weed seeds from germinating, reduces moisture loss, and minimizes soil disturbance. Hoeing is best undertaken in dry weather and the blade should penetrate no deeper than $\frac{1}{2}$ in.

Hand weed in dry weather when the soil is moist so that weeds are easily loosened from the soil; try to remove the whole plant. Remove weeds from the site to prevent them from rerooting.

Mechanical Weed Control
Machines with revolving rotary tines, blades, or

Couch weeds flourishing among cabbages

cultivator attachments are useful for preparing seedbeds and can also be used to control annual weeds between rows of vegetables. They should be employed carefully to avoid root damage. When clearing the ground of perennial weeds, the blades simply slice through the roots and rhizomes. While this increases their number initially, several sessions over a period of time should gradually exhaust and eventually kill the plants. This is only viable when there is plenty of time.

Biological Weed Control

Mulching is the practice of covering the soil around plants with a layer of organic or inorganic material to suppress weeds, reduce water loss (see also p. 597), and warm the soil. Choose your material carefully; straw harbors pests such as vine weevil and flea beetle and contains weed seeds, but is effective as an insulating layer over winter. It also draws nitrogen from the soil in the early stages of decay. Using rotted material like well-rotted farm manure or spent hops avoids this problem.

Organic mulches are also limited where crops need to be hilled up—a process that disturbs the soil. Inorganic materials like plastic sheeting, though effective, are unattractive, but can at least be hidden beneath a thin layer of organic mulch.

Inorganic mulches suppress weeds and prevent seeds from germinating. They also conserve soil moisture by slowing evaporation; plastic films are the most effective for this purpose. They keep trailing crops clean. White plastic mulches hasten growth and ripening by reflecting light onto leaves and fruit; black plastic mulches warm the soil in spring. Sheet mulches are most effective when applied before the crop is planted,

and the young plants are then planted through small holes in the sheet.

Organic mulches improve soil fertility and conserve its structure by protecting the surface from heavy rain and from being walked on, encouraging earthworm activity, and adding organic matter and nutrients to the soil. They insulate the soil, keeping it cooler in summer and warmer in winter. Weeds that push their way through are easily removed. For effective weed control organic mulches should be about 4 in. deep, to block out the light.

In general, organic mulches improve soil fertility as they decay, while inorganic mulches are more effective against weeds, as they form an impenetrable barrier.

Chemical Weed Control

Choose and use herbicides with extreme care and ensure they are suitable for the weeds to be controlled. FOLLOW THE MANUFACTURER'S INSTRUCTIONS CAREFULLY.

• Residual herbicides form a layer over the soil, killing germinating weeds and seedlings.

• Contact herbicides kill only those parts of the plant that they touch. They are effective against annual weeds and weed seedlings, but not against established plants.

• Systemic or translocated herbicides are absorbed by the foliage, traveling through the sap system to kill the whole plant, including the roots. Glyphosate is often the active ingredient. Individual weeds can be "spot treated" using such herbicides in gel or liquid form.

Several chemical weed-control methods have been developed for use with vegetables and other edible plants, but no single chemical is suitable for all crops. This gives the grower three options: stock a range of chemicals and change

the type regularly; use chemicals only as a last resort; or grow organically. For edible plants the latter is almost invariably the best.

Using and Storing Herbicides Safely

Always wear adequate protective clothing, such as face mask, goggles, rubber gloves, and old waterproof clothes when mixing herbicide. Dilute herbicide according to manufacturer's instructions, and never mix different chemicals together. Never dilute chemicals in a confined space, as they may give off toxic fumes.

As for mixing, always wear the specified protective clothing when applying herbicide. Follow the manufacturer's instructions carefully and use only as recommended on the product label. Do not apply herbicide in windy conditions; nearby plants may suffer serious damage. Do not apply herbicide in very hot, still conditions when there is a high risk of spray traveling on warm air currents. If you are using a watering can to apply chemicals, ensure that it is obviously labeled and do not use it for any other purpose.

Store chemicals in the original containers with the labels well secured so that the contents can be identified. Mark the container with the date of purchase, so that you know how long it has been stored. Never store dilute herbicide for future use. Always store in cool, frost-free, dark conditions, out of the reach of children and animals, in a locked cupboard in a workroom or shed.

Thoroughly wash protective clothing, sprayers, mixing vessels, and utensils after use. Never use the same sprayer, mixing vessels, and utensils for other types of chemical such as fungicides. The results could be disastrous!

GRASS MANAGEMENT

Under woody perennial plants such as fruit trees and bushes, the most convenient ground cover is usually grass. Grass competes vigorously, especially if kept closely mowed as a lawn. However, it is simple to maintain, ornamental, hygienic, and prevents worse weeds. The clippings themselves are a free source of mulching material and can contribute much fertility to our plants.

Grass is most productive of useful clippings when it is cut often and not too closely. Long grass grows more quickly, is more drought-resistant and suppresses weeds better than closely cropped grass. Cut your grass regularly and frequently with slightly greater height of cut, and the longer, more vigorous grass will soon choke out most weeds.

When sowing grass, it is sensible to include clovers in the grass seed mix, as they have the advantage of fixing nitrogen from the air to aid the grasses. A clover grass mixture also stays greener for longer in hot, dry summers and, if left to flower, the clovers attract bees and other beneficial insects.

Providing you are not growing ericaceous plants or fine bowling green grasses, you should lime all your sod every fourth year, even if you have lime in the soil. Most grasses slowly become acid in the topmost layer; this encourages mosses and acid-loving weeds. If such weeds—daisies, for example—are increasing, you need to add more lime, up to a couple of handfuls per square yard per year. You probably also need to raise the height of your cut. If weeds that like wet acid soils, such as buttercups, appear, then lime is desperately needed, and probably better drainage as well.

PEST AND DISEASE CONTROL

The control of pests and diseases is done to preserve the yield or appearance of our crops, but we must ensure that the costs incurred do not outweigh the gains. Herbs suffer from few pests and diseases and in fact many can be used to protect other crops (see pp. 586–587). For the home gardener, usually the main cause of loss of crops is the weather. There is very little we can do to make the sun come out, the wind stop, or the rain fall.

The second cause of loss is probably the gardener. We all leave action until too late, skimp on preparation and routine tasks, put plants in less than optimum positions, and then overcrowd them as well. What we must remember is that our plants "want" to leaf, flower, and crop. They are programmed as tightly as any computer. If we give them the right input, they must produce the right output.

Raspberry damaged by raspberry beetle

PREVENTING PROBLEMS

Organic gardeners avoid the use of artificial chemicals, relying on good management and natural predators to control pests and diseases, while working to create an environment in which they are unlikely to occur. If we give plants the right conditions, then they are healthy and vigorous enough to shrug off pests and disease. Healthy plants grow in a well-suited site and soil, with shelter and water when they are small, and are not overfed. Excess fertilizer makes plants flabby and prone to problems.

Natural Defenses

The most effective way to control pests is to persuade others to do it for you. The natural ecology always controls them in the long run. We can help it quickly reach a balance of more ladybugs, thrushes, and frogs with fewer aphids, snails, and slugs. Our allies require shelter, nest sites, food, water, and companion plants. If we provide these they increase in number and the pests decrease.

Timing can help. For example, late raspberries usually escape the attentions of their fruit maggot. Having many fruits that ripen at the same time also reduces damage. When successive plants ripen they are picked clean by small numbers of pests, which are overwhelmed by a glut, as may be the gardener!

Check plants daily if possible. Instant eradication is often the best remedy:

Scab on apple fruit ('Golden Delicious')

remove the affected part of the plant or wipe off the pest or disease, as with aphids.

General Hygiene

Plant debris is a logical host for pests and diseases, particularly during winter, allowing them to survive in preparation for reemergence and reinfection the following year. Clean your greenhouse and equipment regularly. Dispose of organic matter immediately; compost healthy material and get rid of infected plants by burning or placing in the trash can. Buy plants from a reputable source and, if possible, keep them in quarantine for a while before introducing them to the greenhouse.

Winter is the time to disinfect plant supports such as bamboo canes, which are hollow and often split with age, creating crevices that form suitable sites for fungi and insect eggs to overwinter. These can be sprayed or dipped in disinfectant.

Cultural Practices

Always use sterilized compost for seed sowing and potting. Seedlings are particularly vulnerable, especially when sown under cover. Sow seeds thinly, do not irrigate with stagnant or cold water, and ventilate the greenhouse, but avoid chilling plants or seedlings and do not allow compost to become waterlogged. Promote rapid germination and continuous growth to reduce the risk of infection at the time when seedlings and young plants are at their most vulnerable. Inspect plants regularly, particularly if a variety is prone to certain problems. Grow pest- and disease-resistant cultivars when possible. Rotate vegetable crops and always keep the garden weed-free. Handle plants with care, particularly when harvesting, as this is a common cause of infection. Regularly check stored crops, as rot spreads rapidly in a confined space.

CONTROL METHODS

Barriers and Traps

The simplest method of protection is to use a barrier to prevent pests or disease from reaching the plant—netting stops birds and frost fabric stops many insects.

On fruit trees, traps of cardboard, carpet, or old burlap can be made by rolling strips around trunk or stem. These attract pests, which hide within and can be dislodged in winter. Non-setting sticky bands applied to aluminum foil wrapped tightly around trunk, branch, or stem stop pests from climbing up and down. Remember to paint the support as well.

Sticky traps can be bought to lure flying pests to them with pheromone sex attractant "perfumes." Others use the smell of the fruit or leaf to entice the pest to a sticky end. Jars of water with lids of foil containing pencil-sized holes trap wasps when baited with fruit juice or jelly.

Organic Sprays

Soap spray kills most small insect pests by suffocation and is remarkably safe for us and the environment. People used to employ ordinary soap flakes, but improved soft soaps are now sold specifically for this use. Bordeaux mixture is an old-fashioned fungicide. It is wholly chemical, made from copper sulfate and lime, and can be used by organic gardeners in moderation.

Rotenore and pyrethrum are insecticides made from plant products. They are the strongest allowed to organic gardeners and degrade fast, but kill pests immune to soft soap. Spray at night when the bees have gone home.

Carrots covered with fleece to protect from carrot fly

Biological Controls

Many predators are now available commercially. Apart from *Bacillus thuringiensis*, the bacterial control for caterpillars, few are effective outside the greenhouse. Most pesticides (with the exception of insecticidal soaps and pirimicarb) kill predators and so should be avoided. Particularly useful are *Phytoseiulus persimilis*, the predatory mite that controls two-spotted or red

Silver foil and other bird-scaring devices over cabbages

spider mite and *Encarsia formosa*, a parasitic wasp, controlling greenhouse whitefly. Biological control methods are expensive compared to chemical alternatives, and nearly all need warm temperatures to be efficient.

Chemical Controls

Before using any chemicals, it is worth considering the following. Many chemicals are toxic and can be harmful to humans, pets, and wildlife. Chemicals may remain in soil and plant tissue for long periods, affecting predators. Many pests and diseases can develop a resistance to chemicals that are used persistently for long periods, rendering controls less effective. Applying a range of chemicals can overcome this.

Always follow instructions with regard to safety, mixing, and application. Apply chemicals in still, overcast conditions, in the early morning or evening. Protect surrounding plants. Clean equipment after use. Dispose of unwanted chemicals according to manufacturer's recommendations. DO NOT POUR THEM DOWN THE DRAIN.

SOIL-BORNE PESTS

Cutworms

These gray-green caterpillars, approximately 2 in. long, appear from late spring until early fall. They burrow into root crops eating through stems at soil level.

Plants grown under cover seem less prone to damage, and heavy watering in early summer often kills young caterpillars. To control them, incorporate a soil insecticide such as diazinon and chlorpyrifos or water pirimiphos-methyl into the top 2 in. of soil.

Cutworms

Cabbage Root Fly

These white larvae, approximately $\frac{1}{3}$ in. long, are found from late spring to midfall. They feed on the roots of brassicas just below soil level, stunting growth and causing plants to wilt, seedlings to die, and tunnels to appear in root crops. As a preventive measure, grow under frost fabric. To control them, place a 5-in. collar of cardboard, plastic, or the like around the plant base. Or incorporate an insecticide such as chlorpyrifos and diazinon or pirimiphos-methyl into the top 2 in. of soil.

Carrot Root Fly

These creamy-white maggots, about $\frac{1}{3}$ in. long, appear from early summer until midfall. They are a common problem with carrots, but can also affect other umbelliferous plants. Larvae burrow into the roots, causing stunted growth and reddish-purple coloration of the foliage.

Sow thinly and lift crops in late summer or in early fall. Place a barrier 24 in. high around crops or cover with frost fabric when young. If plants are badly affected, pull them up and destroy them. Large herbs should overcome attacks, so just pick off dead leaves and boost with a liquid seaweed feed. A chemical control is to incorporate a soil insecticide such as

pirimiphos-methyl into the top 2 in. of the soil.

Leatherjackets

These gray-brown, wrinkled grubs can be up to $1\frac{1}{2}$ in. long. They eat through roots and stems of young plants just below soil level. Most crops are vulnerable, including Brussels sprouts, cabbage, cauliflower, and lettuce. To discourage them, ensure the soil is well drained and dig over the ground in the early fall, especially if it has been fallow in the summer. The problem is often worse on new sites and usually diminishes with time. A chemical solution is to water vulnerable plants with piriphos-methyl and

Carrot root fly

treat soil with diazinon and chlorpyrifos.

NEMATODES (WIREWORMS)

Potato Cyst Wireworm

These white to golden-brown, pinhead-sized cysts are found on roots in midsummer. Each can contain up to 600 eggs, which can remain dormant in the soil for up to six years. Potatoes and tomatoes are affected, with

weak and stunted growth, small fruits and tubers, and yellow foliage, with the lower leaves dying first, followed by premature death of the plants.

Rotate crops and grow resistant varieties. Do not grow potatoes or tomatoes on site for at least 6 years.

Cabbage root fly

Stem and Bulb Eelworm

These are microscopic pests that live inside the plant and move around on a film of moisture; most active from spring to late summer. The symptoms are weak, stunted growth, swollen bases on young plants, and later stems that thicken and rot. They affect a wide range of young plants from spring until late summer, particularly leek, onion, shallot, and chives.

Rotate crops, practice good hygiene and management, and destroy infected crops. Do not grow potatoes or tomatoes on infected soil for at least 6 years, and any other vulnerable crops on the site for at least 4 years.

Leatherjackets

SLUGS

Slimy, with tubular-shaped bodies up to 4 in., from creamy-white through gray to jet-black and orange, slugs are voracious feeders, making circular holes in plant tissue; damaged seedlings are usually killed. They tend to feed at night. Slugs are more of a problem on wet sites and clay soils; keep the soil well drained and weed-free. Remove all crop debris. Grow less susceptible cultivars. Remove slugs by hand at night and destroy them. Create a barrier of grit, sand, soot, or eggshells around plants or cut a 4-in. section from a plastic bottle

Potato cyst wireworm

foliage to collapse; seedlings are usually killed. A wide range of plants are attacked, particularly root

Dead potatoes after potato cyst wireworm attack

and place it as a "collar" around plants. Make traps from plastic cartons, half-buried in the ground and filled with milk or beer, or lay old roof tiles, newspaper, or lettuce leaves on the ground and hand pick from underneath. Attract natural predators like toads to the garden or use biological controls. Chemical controls include applying aluminum sulfate in the spring as the slug eggs hatch and using slug pellets, which contain metaldehyde.

WIREWORMS

These are thin, yellow larvae, pointed at each end, about 1 in. long. They make holes in the roots and tubers, and can cause

crops and potatoes. Symptoms appear from spring until midsummer. More of a problem on newly cultivated soil, wireworms usually disappear after 5 years; avoid planting root crops until the sixth year. Dig root crops as soon as they mature. Cultivate the ground thoroughly before planting and mix chlorpyrifos and diazinon into the top 2 in. of soil.

SOIL-BORNE DISEASES

Clubroot

A soil-borne fungus that can remain in the soil for up to 20 years, it causes leaves to yellow and

Wireworm

discolor, wilting rapidly in hot weather; the roots display swollen wart-like swellings and become distorted. All members of the *Brassicaceae* family are vulnerable. Clubroot is worse on acid soils, so lime to raise the pH and improve the drainage. Practice strict crop rotation, hygiene, and good management. Grow your own plants, or at least purchase from a reputable source. Raise plants in pots. Rutabaga 'Marian' has good resistance to clubroot. For a chemical control, dip the roots of transplants in a fungicidal solution such as thiophanate-methyl. Dig and dispose of affected plants immediately, and do not compost.

Common Scab

This fungus causes superficial damage to the underground parts of affected plants. Rough brown lesions appear on the surface of roots and tubers. It is more severe on alkaline soils and in dry summers. Common scab affects mainly potatoes, but can be found on radishes,

beet, rutabaga, and turnips. Avoid liming, do not grow potatoes on soil recently used for brassicas, apply organic matter, and irrigate thoroughly in dry weather. Grow resistant potato cultivars like 'Russian Banana.' Rotate crops.

Root Rot

This fungus is difficult to eradicate. It attacks beans and peas, causing shriveled, yellowing leaves, stems, and pods; roots rot and stems rot at the base. Plants collapse. Practice a minimum 3-year crop rotation; remove and burn infected plants. Sow seed treated with fungicide, or water seedlings with a copper-based fungicide.

Stem Rot

This fungus is difficult to eradicate. It attacks eggplant and tomato, causing yellow-brown cankerous lesions with

Clubroot

black dots in and around the lesions, at soil level. Remove and burn infected plants and debris, disinfect anything that comes into contact with diseased material, including hands. After planting apply a fungicide such as captan to the bottom 4 in. of the stem, repeating 3 weeks later.

White Rot

This fungus is almost impossible to eradicate. Common on onions and leeks, it also attacks chives and garlic, causing discolored, yellowing leaves, which die slowly. Roots rot and plants fall over, covered with a white feltlike mold. Do not grow susceptible crops for 8 years after infection. Remove and burn infected plants; don't compost any debris. Apply a fungicide such as thiophanate-methyl to seed drills when sowing.

AIRBORNE PESTS

Aphids

These are dense colonies of winged and wingless insects, from pale-green through pink to green-black. They attack soft tissue on a wide range of plants, including brassicas, beans and peas, lettuces, potatoes, and root crops. Shoot tips and young leaves become distorted; they leave a sticky coating on lower leaves, often accompanied by a black, sooty mold. Pinch the growth tips from fava beans, destroy alternative hosts, and take care not to overfeed with high nitrogen fertilizers. Treat small infestations by squashing or, on sturdy plants, washing off with a jet of water; spray with soft soap, rotenore, pyrethrum-based insecticide; encourage natural predators like lacewings, ladybugs and their larvae, and small birds. On larger woody perennials these are more

of an annoyance than a problem.

Cabbage Caterpillars

These are small, hairy, yellow and black caterpillars up to 2 in. long. Voracious feeders, they eat holes in the leaves and in severe cases leave plants totally defoliated. They attack all brassicas, and are a problem from late spring to fall. Inspect plants regularly, squash eggs or caterpillars as they are found, pick off caterpillars, and grow crops under frost fabric or fine netting. Alternatively, spray regularly with rotenore, pyrethrum, or permethrin when eggs are first seen.

Cabbage Whitefly

These small, white-winged insects are usually found on the leaf underside. Clouds of insects fly up when leaves are brushed. Young leaves pucker and have a sticky coating and a black mold. Whitefly attack all leafy brassicas. They can survive severe winter weather and are seen all year round. Remove and burn badly infected plants immediately after cropping. Spray with insecticidal soap or pyrethrum-based sprays, dimethoate or malathion; concentrate on the leaf underside.

Pea Thrips

These small, white to black-brown or yellow-bodied insects, usually on the leaf underside, are commonly known as "thunder flies." They cause distorted pods with a silvery sheen; peas fail to swell. The insects are often found on peas and also on fava beans. Remove and burn badly infected plants. Spray with malathion or a similar insecticide just as the plants start to flower.

White rot on maturing onion crop

Vine Weevils

The adult weevil is dark gray and beetlelike, $1/2$ in. long, with a very long snout. It takes rounded pieces out of leaves, but the most harm is done by the grubs, which are up to the same size with a gray-pink body and brown head. They destroy the roots of many plants. Adults can be trapped in rolls of corrugated cardboard, in bundles of sticks, or under saucers, where they hide in the daytime. The grubs can be destroyed by watering on the commercially available predatory nematode.

Leaf Miners

These grubs are sometimes a problem on lovage, wild celery, certain sorrels, and various mints. They eat through the leaf, creating winding tunnels in the

leaves that are clearly visible. Pick off the affected leaves as you see them. If left, the tunnels will extend into broad dry patches and whole leaves will wither away.

AIRBORNE DISEASES

Blight

This fungus infects leaves, stems, and tubers and is worse in wet seasons. Severe epidemics led to the Irish potato famine. In mid-summer, brown patches appear on the upper and lower leaf surfaces, ringed with white mold in humid conditions; leaves become yellow and fall prematurely. In humid climates, the fungus spreads rapidly over the foliage and stems, which quickly collapse. Tubers show dark, sunken patches. The fungus attacks

Aphids

potatoes, tomatoes, and closely related weeds. Remove and burn badly infected plant tops in late summer, avoid overhead watering, and use resistant cultivars. Do not store infected tubers. In wet seasons spray with fungicide before the disease appears. Spray in summer with copper-based fungicide or mancozeb, and repeat at regular intervals as soon as symptoms reappear.

Botrytis
This fungus infects flowers, leaves, and stems, and usually enters through wounds. Discolored patches appear on stems, which may rot at ground level; flowers and leaves become covered with woolly, gray fungal growth. It causes shadows on unripe tomato fruit called "ghost spot." Soft-leaved plants are particularly vulnerable, including fava beans, brassicas, lettuces, potatoes, and tomatoes. Maintain good air circulation, handle plants with care to avoid injury, and remove infected material. If you wish to use chemicals, spray with thiophanate-methyl or carbendazim as soon as the disease symptoms are seen; remove and burn badly infected plants.

Downy Mildew
This is a fungus that infects leaves and stems, overwintering in the soil or plant debris. It causes discolored, yellowing leaves, which have gray or white moldy patches on the lower surface; plants often die slowly in the fall. Attacks brassicas, including weed species, lettuce, spinach, peas, and onions. Avoid overcrowding, remove and burn badly infected plants, and maintain good air circulation. Spray with zineb, mancozeb, or

Cabbage caterpillar

copper-based fungicide when the first symptoms appear.

Powdery Mildew
This common fungal disease can occur when the conditions are hot and dry, and the plants are overcrowded. Prevent it by watering well during dry spells, following the recommended planting distances, and clearing away any fallen leaves in the fall. Adding a mulch in the fall or early spring also helps. If your plant does suffer, destroy all the affected leaves before spraying with elder if regulations permit.

Blight

Rust
Plants affected by rust should be dug up and thrown away. Alternatively you can, in the fall, put straw around the affected plant and set it on fire; this will sterilize the soil and the plant.

PESTS AND DISEASES UNDER COVER
Red Spider Mite
The spider mites like hot, dry conditions and can become prolific in a greenhouse. Look out for early signs such as speckling on the upper surfaces of the leaves. Another telltale sign is cobwebs. At first sight, either use a spray of horticultural soap, or the natural predator *Phytoseiulus persimilis*, but not both.

Scale Insects
These are often noticeable as immobile, waxy, brown-yellow, flat, oval lumps gathered on the backs of leaves or on stems. These leaves also become covered with sticky, black, sooty mold. Rub off the scales gently before the infestation builds up, or use a horticultural liquid soap.

Whitefly
It is essential to act as soon as you see the small white flies, either by introducing the natural predator *Encarsia formosa*, or by spraying with horticultural soap.

OTHER PESTS
Birds
Birds damage many fruits and some vegetables. Netting is the answer. If the whole plant cannot be enclosed or moved under cover then protect each fruit or bunch with waxed paper or netting bags. Things that flash, such as pieces of foil, all work to

keep birds away, but only for a short time. Scarecrows rarely work at all!

Ants
A minor problem on their own, they farm aphids and scale insects, making these more of a threat. Put out some sugar, watch where

Botrytis

they take it home, then pour boiling water down their hole.

Wasps
Wasps are valuable allies early in the year, when they control caterpillars and other pests. Later they turn to fruit and need trapping with jars (see p. 603). Dusting them with flour enables you to follow them home so the nest can be destroyed with derris dust puffed in the entrance as they all return in the evening.

Rabbits
Only netting the area will keep rabbits out. In case they get in, have a plank ramped against the fence so they are not trapped inside and eat even more. If the perimeter cannot be secured, surround or wrap each plant in wire netting.

HARVESTING AND STORING

One of the pleasures of a productive garden is picking your produce and cooking or eating it fresh. However, there are myriad means of storing many crops, thus extending the season, and avoiding unmanageable gluts. See also details under the individual crops.

WHEN TO HARVEST

Vegetables

While the majority of vegetables are not harvested until they reach maturity, others, like some lettuces, are harvested while semimature and others still, such as arugula, are harvested while juvenile. Some vegetables, again like lettuce, cannot be stored for long and so must be harvested and eaten fresh. Many other leafy vegetables, such as Brussels sprouts and sprouting broccoli, are hardy, surviving outdoors in the ground in freezing conditions. The flavor of Brussels sprouts even improves immeasurably after they have been frosted. Some root vegetables with a high moisture content are easily damaged in winter, even when protected by the soil. This is usually caused by rapid thawing after a period of cold weather. Carrots, parsnip, and rutabaga are exceptions; they are very hardy and can be left in free-draining soils until required. In wet soils these crops would suffer winter loss by slug damage and rotting.

Herbs

Herbs can be harvested from very early on in their growing season. This encourages the plant to produce vigorous new growth and allows the plant to be controlled in shape and size. Most herbs reach their peak of flavor just before they flower. Snip off suitable stems early in the day before the sun is fully up, or even better on a cloudy day (provided it is not too humid.) Cut whole stems rather than single leaves or flowers. Always use a sharp knife, sharp scissors, or pruning shears, and cut lengths of 2–3 in. from the tip of the branch, this being the new, soft growth. Do not cut into any of the older, woody growth. Cut from all over the plant, to leave it looking shapely. Pick herbs that are clean and free from pests and disease. If herbs are covered in garden soil, sponge them quickly and lightly with cold water (not hot, as this will draw out the oils prematurely). Pat dry as quickly as possible. Keep each species separate, so that they do not contaminate each other.

Most annual herbs can be harvested at least twice during a growing season. Cut them to within 4–6 in. of the ground, and feed with liquid fertilizer after each cutting. Give annuals their final cut of the season before the first frosts; they will have stopped growing some weeks before.

In the first year of planting, perennials will give one good crop; thereafter it will be possible to harvest two or three times during the growing season. Do not cut into the woody growth unless deliberately trying to prevent growth; again, cut well before frosts. There are of course exceptions: sage is still very good after frosts, and both thyme and golden marjoram (with some protection) can be picked even in midwinter.

Pick flowers for drying when they are barely open. Seed should be collected as soon as you notice a change in color of the seed pod; if, when you tap the pod, a few scatter on the ground, it is the time to gather them. Seeds ripen very fast, so watch them carefully.

Roots of herbs are at their peak of flavor when they have just completed a growing season. Dig them throughout the fall as growth ceases. Lift whole roots with a garden fork, taking care not to puncture or bruise the outer skin.

Individual herbs laid out for drying

Wash them to remove the soil. Cut away any remains of top growth and any fibrous offshoots. For drying, cut large, thick roots in half lengthwise and then into smaller pieces for ease.

Fruit

Without a doubt most fruits are best, and certainly are enjoyed most, when they are plucked fully ripe off the tree or vine. Only a few, such as melons, are improved by chilling first. The majority are tastiest fresh and warmed by the sun. Some, such as pears, have to be carefully nurtured until they are fully ripe, and need to be picked early and brought to perfection, watched daily, in a gently warm, not too dry, dim room. Medlars are similarly picked early and are then ripened, or bletted, to the point of rotting.

The best date for picking will vary with the cultivar, the soil, the site, and the season, and can only be determined by experience as these factors all vary considerably. Of course, it will generally remain much the same in relation to other fruits nearby, which are also subject to the same conditions; that is, in a late year, most fruits are late.

On any tree, the sunny side ripens first. Fruit will also ripen earlier where extra warmth is supplied, so that growing sites next to a wall, window, chimney, or vent, or close to the soil, are good places for finding early fruits. Likewise, when all the rest have gone, you may find some hidden in the shade.

If you want to store fruits

for home use, they need to be picked at just the right stage. Most fruits store best when picked just underripe. They may keep much longer if picked even younger, but this is at the cost of flavor and sweetness.

STORAGE CONDITIONS

Vegetables

Vegetables overwintering in the ground in mild-winter zones need additional protection. This can be provided by spreading a layer of loose straw or hay over them to a depth of 8 in. and covering with plastic sheet. While this is labor-saving, crops stored in this way are susceptible to attack by pests and diseases throughout the winter.

The traditional method for storing root vegetables is in a clamp or "pie." Low mounds of vegetables are laid on a bed of loose straw up to 8 in. thick. The top and sides of the mound are covered with a similar layer of straw, and then with a 6-in. layer of soil or sand. Clamps can be made outdoors on a well-drained site or under cover in a shed; for extra protection outdoors, they can be formed against a wall or hedge. If crops are to be stored for a long period, find a site that receives as little sunlight as possible during the winter. Although storage conditions are very similar to those in the ground, harvesting from a clamp is much easier. However, losses from rodent damage and rotting can be high.

The length of time that vegetables may be stored depends on the type and cultivar as well as the storage conditions. When traditional methods are used, the main cause of deterioration is moisture loss from plant tissue; for instance, beets and carrots dry out very rapidly. Fungal infection of damaged tissue is a common problem; onions and potatoes

bruise very easily. Vegetables intended for storage should be handled carefully; only store those that are disease-free, check them regularly, and immediately remove any showing signs of decay.

Fruits

Although we occasionally store some fruits, such as pears, for a period to improve their condition, mostly we store fruit to extend the season, so that we can enjoy them for as long as possible.

To be stored, all fruit must be perfect. Any blemish or bruise is where molds start. Choose varieties that are suitable for storing—many early croppers are notoriously bad keepers!

Common, long-keeping fruits such as apples and quinces can be stored at home for months, or even up to a year. The major problems, apart from the molds, are shriveling due to water loss and the depredations of rodents and other big pests. A conventional store is too large for most of us and the house or garage is too warm, too cold, or too dry. Broken freezers and refrigerators make excellent, compact stores. They are dark, keep the contents at the same constant temperature, and will keep out night frosts easily. Most useful of all, they are rodent-proof.

Some ventilation is needed and can be obtained by cutting holes in the rubber door or lid seal. If condensation occurs it usually indicates insufficient ventilation, but too much draft will dry out the fruits. The unit can stand outdoors; in a shed it is out of sight and better protected against the cold, but may then get too warm.

When putting fruits in storage it is usually best to allow them to chill at night in trays and load them into the storage space in the morning when they have dried off but before they

Parsley stored in a bag for freezing, together with ice cubes for convenience

have warmed up again. Similarly, it is helpful to chill and dry off the fruits initially by leaving the container open on cold, dry nights and closing it during the day for a week or two after filling.

Most fruits are best removed from storage some time before use, so any staleness can leave them. Care should be taken not to store early and late varieties together, or any that may cross-taint. Obviously it is not a good idea to site your storage in the same place as strong-smelling things such as onions, paint, or creosote. Likewise, although straw is a convenient litter, if it gets damp it taints the fruit. Shredded newspaper is safer, though it also has a slight odor. Dried stinging nettles are said to be good but dangerous to handle.

Always inspect stored fruits regularly. They can go bad very quickly. Remember, if only one in ten goes bad every month, you have to start with two trays just to have one tray left after six months. So don't store fruit long just for the sake of it; store what you will use.

DRYING

Vegetables

Peas and beans can be harvested when almost mature and dried slowly in a cool place. Either lift the whole plant and hang it up

or pick off the pods and dry them on a tray or newspaper. Beans can be collected and stored in airtight jars until needed. They will need soaking for 24 hours before use. Storage areas should be frost-free. Chilies, green peppers, garlic, and onions can be hung indoors where there is good air circulation. Peppers, tomatoes, and mushrooms can be cut into sections and sun-dried outdoors if conditions allow, or in the gentle heat of a linen closet or above a radiator.

Herbs

The object of drying herbs is to eliminate the water content of the plant quickly and, at the same time, to retain the essential oils. Herbs need to be dried in a warm, dark, dry, and well-ventilated place. The faster they dry, the better the aromatic oils are retained. Darkness helps to prevent loss of color and unique flavors. The area must be dry, with a good air flow, to hasten the drying process and to discourage mold.

Suitable places for drying herbs include: a linen closet; loft space immediately under the roof (provided it does not get too hot); in the oven at a low temperature and with the door ajar (place the herbs on a piece of brown paper with holes punched in it and check

Grape vines growing in a greenhouse

regularly that the herbs are not overheating); a plate-warming compartment; a spare room with the drapes shut and the door open. The temperature should be kept at 70–90°F.

Herb leaves should always be dried separately from each other, especially the more strongly scented ones. Spread them in a single layer on trays or slatted wooden racks covered with muslin or netting. Place the trays or racks in the drying areas so that they have good air circulation. Turn the herbs over by hand several times during the first two days.

Roots require a higher temperature—from 120–140°F. They dry more quickly and easily in an oven and require regular turning until they are fragile and break easily. Seed should be dried without any artificial heat and in an airy place. Almost-ripe seed heads can be hung in paper bags (plastic causes them to

sweat) so the majority of seeds will fall into the bag as they mature. They need to be dried thoroughly before storing, and the process can take up to two weeks.

An alternative method for flowers, roots, or seed heads is to tie them in small bundles of 8 to 10 stems. Do not pack the stems too tightly together. Then hang them on coat hangers in an airy, dark room until they are dry.

The length of drying time varies from herb to herb and week to week. The determining factor is the state of the plant material. If herbs are stored before drying is complete, moisture will be reabsorbed from the atmosphere and the herb will soon deteriorate. Leaves should be both brittle and crisp. They should break easily into small pieces but should not reduce to a powder when touched. The roots should be brittle and dry right through. Any soft-ness or sponginess means they

are not sufficiently dry and, if stored, will rot.

It is possible to dry herbs in the microwave, but easy to overdry and cook the leaves to the point of disintegration. Small-leaved herbs such as rosemary and thyme take about 1 minute, while the larger, moist leaves of mint dry in about 3 minutes. Add a couple teaspoons of water to the microwave during the process.

Herbs lose their flavor and color if not stored properly. Pack the leaves or roots, not too tightly, into a dark glass jar with an airtight screw top. Label with name and date. Keep in a dark cupboard; nothing destroys the quality of the herb quicker at this stage than exposure to light.

After the initial storing, check on the jars regularly for several days. If moisture starts to form on the inside of the container, the herbs have not been dried correctly. Return them to the drying area and

allow more drying time.

Most domestic herb needs are comparatively small so there is little point in storing large amounts for a long time. The shelf life of dried herbs is only about one year, so it is sufficient to keep enough just for the winter.

If you have large, dark jars, thyme and rosemary can be left on the stalk. This makes it easier to use them in casseroles and stews and to remove before serving.

Fruit

Many fruits can be dried if they are sliced thinly and exposed to warm, dry air. Sealed in dark containers and kept cool and dry, they keep for long periods to be eaten, dried or reconstituted, when required. However, in much of North America, the air is too humid and drying is not quick enough, not helped by the low temperatures in these regions. Solar-powered dryers—simply wire trays under glass—with good

Red currants preserve well

ventilation, allow fruit to be dried to a larger extent, but in high humidity regions the fruit may still get moldy before it dries.

Slicing the fruit thinly and hanging the pieces, separated by a space of at least half their own diameter, on long strings over a cooking range provides the dry warmth and ventilation needed to dry most within a day or two, or even just overnight for the easier ones, such as apple.

Oven-drying with artificial heat is risky as it can cook the fruit. It is possible, however, if the temperature is kept down and the door kept partly open. It may be convenient to finish off partly dried samples in the cooling oven after you have finished baking. The dying heat dries fruit well with little risk of caramelizing.

FREEZING

Vegetables

Only the best-quality vegetables should be frozen, and they should always be thoroughly cleaned and carefully packed. Vegetables should be fast-frozen. Most freezers have a fast-freeze switch, and keep the freezer door closed during freezing. Do not open the freezer door regularly or leave it open longer than necessary. Many vegetables need to be blanched before freezing, and others need to be shredded, pureed, or diced, or frozen when young. See under individual vegetables for details.

Herbs

Freezing is great for culinary herbs as color, flavor, and the nutritional value of the fresh young leaves are retained, and it is quick and easy. It is far better to freeze herbs such as fennel, dill, parsley, tarragon, and chives than to dry them.

Pick the herbs and, if necessary, rinse with cold water, and shake dry before freezing, being careful not to bruise the leaves. Put small amounts of herbs into labeled, plastic bags, either singly or as a mixture for bouquet garnis. Either have a set place in the freezer for them or put the bags into a container, so that they do not get damaged with the day-to-day use of the freezer.

There is no need to thaw herbs before use; simply add them to the cooking as required. For chopped parsley and other fine-leaved herbs, freeze the bunches whole in bags and, when you remove them from the freezer, crush the parsley in its bag with your hand.

Another way to freeze herbs conveniently is to put finely chopped leaves into an ice-cube tray and fill them with water. The average cube holds 1 tablespoon chopped herbs and 1 teaspoon water. The flowers of borage and leaves of variegated mints look very attractive frozen individually in ice cubes for drinks or fruit salads.

Fruits

Most fruits freeze easily with little preparation. Obviously only the best are worth freezing, as few fruits are improved by the process! Most fruits turn soggy when defrosted, but they are still packed full of sweetness, flavor, and vitamins and are well worth having for culinary use, especially in tarts, pies, sauces, and compotes. A mixture of frozen fruits is marvelous if it is partially defrosted so the fruits retain their frozen texture, like pieces of sorbet, served with cream.

For most fruits, merely putting them in sealed freezer bags or boxes is sufficient. However, they then tend to freeze in a block. If you freeze them loose on wire racks or a greased cookie sheet, they can be packed afterward and will stay separate. Fruits that are cut or damaged need to be drained first or, if you have a sweet tooth, they can be dredged in sugar, which absorbs the juice, before freezing them.

Stone fruits are best pitted before freezing, as the pit can give an almond taint otherwise. The tough skins of fruits such as plums are most easily removed after freezing and before use. Carefully squeeze the frozen fruit under very hot water, and the skin should slip off.

Fruits lose value slowly in the freezer. The longer they are frozen the less use they are nutritionally.

JUICING

Not all fruits can be juiced, but the majority can be squeezed to express the juice, or heated or frozen to break down the texture and then strained. Sugar may be added to taste as it improves the color, flavor, and keeping qualities. When the juice remains unheated, honey may be substituted, though it has a strong flavor of its own. Sweet juices such as apple can be mixed with tart ones like plum.

Fruit juices may be drunk as they are or diluted with water, added to cocktails, and used in cooking. Grapes are the easiest to press and the most rewarding; they are best crushed first to break the skins. Most currants and berries can be squeezed in the same way. Apples and pears must be crushed first and then squeezed; they will go through the same juicing equipment as grapes, but more slowly than the more juicy fruits.

Pulpy, firm fruits such as blackcurrants and plums are best simmered with water until they soften, then the juice can be strained off. If you repeat the process and add sugar to the combined juices you also have the basis for jellies. Raspberries, strawberries, and fruits with similar delicate flavors are best frozen and then defrosted and strained, to obtain a pure juice unchanged by heating.

Suitable equipment for processing large amounts of fruit is widely available if the quantities are too large for kitchen tools.

Commercially juices are passed through microfine filters or flash pasteurized. At home they will ferment rapidly in the warm, last longer if kept cool in the refrigerator, and keep for months or years frozen.

OILS, VINEGARS, AND PRESERVES

HERB OILS

These can be used in salad dressings, marinades, sauces, stir-fry dishes, and sautéing. To start with, you need a clean glass jar, large enough to hold 2 cups, with a screw top.

Basil oil

This is one of the best ways of storing and capturing the unique flavor of basil.

1/3 cup basil leaves
2 cups olive or sunflower oil

Pick over the basil, remove the leaves from the stalks, and crush them in a mortar. Pound very slightly. Add a little oil and pound gently again. This bruises the leaves, releasing their own oil into the olive oil. Mix the leaves with the rest of the oil, pour into a wide-necked jar and seal tightly. Place the jar on a sunny windowsill. Shake it every other day, and, after 2 weeks, strain through muslin into a decorative bottle and add a couple of fresh leaves of the same basil. This helps to identify the type of basil used and also looks fresh and enticing. Label.

Adapt for dill, fennel (green), sweet marjoram, rosemary, and garden or lemon thyme.

Bouquet garni oil

1 tablespoon sage
1 tablespoon lemon thyme
1 tablespoon Greek oregano
1 tablespoon French parsley
1 bay leaf
2 cups olive or sunflower oil

Break all the leaves and mix them together in a mortar, pounding lightly. Add a small amount of the oil to mix well, allowing the flavors to infuse. Pour into a wide-necked jar with the remaining oil. Cover and leave on a sunny windowsill for 2–3 weeks. Either shake or stir the jar every other day. Strain through muslin into an attractive bottle. If there is room, add a fresh sprig of each herb used.

SWEET OILS

Good with fruit dishes, marinades, and desserts. Use almond oil, which combines well with scented flowers such as pinks, lavender, lemon verbena, rose petals, and scented geraniums. Make as for savory oils above. Mix 4 tablespoons of torn petals or leaves with 2 cups almond oil.

SPICE OILS

Ideal for salad dressings, they can be used for sautéing and stir-frying too. The most suitable herb spices are: coriander seeds, dill seeds, and fennel seeds. Combine 2 tablespoons of seeds with 2 cups olive or sunflower oil, having first pounded the seeds gently to crush them in a mortar and mixed them with a little of the oil. Add a few of the whole seeds to the oil before bottling and labeling. Treat as for savory oils and store.

HERBAL VINEGARS

These can be used in gravy and sauces, marinades, and salad dressings. A time-saving recipe follows:

2 cups white wine vinegar
4 large sprigs herb

Pour off a little vinegar from the bottle and push in 2 sprigs of herb. Fill with the reserved vinegar if necessary. Reseal the bottle and leave on a sunny windowsill for 2 weeks. Change the herb sprigs for fresh ones and the vinegar is ready to use.

Seed vinegar

Make as for herb vinegar, but the amounts used are 2 table-spoons of seeds to 2 1/2 cups white wine or cider vinegar. Dill, fennel, and coriander seeds make good vinegars.

Floral vinegar

Made in the same way, these are used for fruit salads and cosmetic recipes. Combine elder, nasturtiums, sweet violets, pinks, lavender, primrose, rose petals, rosemary, or thyme flowers in the following proportions:

10 tablespoons torn flower heads or petals
2 cups white wine vinegar

Pickled horseradish

Wash and scrape the skin off a good-sized horseradish root. Mince in a food processor or shred it (if you can stand it!). Pack into small jars and cover with salted vinegar made from 1 teaspoon salt to 2 cups cider or white wine vinegar. Seal and leave for 4 weeks before using.

SAVORY HERB JELLY

Use the following herbs: sweet marjoram, mints (all kinds), rosemary, sage, summer savory, tarragon, and common thyme.
Makes 2 12-oz. jars

6 cups tart cooking apples or crab apples, roughly chopped, cores and all
3 3/4 cups water
2 cups sugar
2 tablespoons wine vinegar
2 tablespoons lemon juice
1 bunch herbs, approx. 4 tablespoons chopped herbs

Put the apples into a large pan with the bunch of herbs and cover with cold water in a preserving pan. Bring to a boil and simmer until the apples are soft, roughly 30 minutes. Pour into a jelly bag and drain overnight.

Measure the strained juice and add 3 1/2 cups sugar to every 2 cups fluid. Stir over gentle heat until the sugar has dissolved. Bring to a boil, stirring, and boil until setting point is reached, roughly 20–30 minutes. Skim off the surface scum and stir in the vinegar and lemon juice and the chopped herbs. Pour into jars, seal and label before storing.

SWEET JELLIES

Follow the above recipe, omitting the vinegar and lemon juice, and adding 1 cup water. The following make interesting sweet jellies: bergamot, lavender flower, lemon verbena, scented geranium, and sweet violet.

PRESERVES

Chutneys and pickles are a traditional method of preserving, and the perfect solution to harvest-time gluts in the fruit and vegetable gardens. Some recipes with regional and personal variations such as piccalilli, pickled onions, and mango chutney have become legendary. Others, like runner bean chutney are reserved for small-scale production. They are the ideal accompaniment for cold meats, pies, and other traditional fare, and are one of the best ways to maximize the variety and flavor from home-grown produce.

Coriander chutney
Makes 2 1-lb. jars

6 cups cooking apples, pared, cored, and sliced
2 cups onions, peeled and roughly chopped
2 cloves garlic, peeled and crushed
1 red and 1 green bell pepper, seeded and sliced
3³/₄ cups red wine vinegar
2¹/₄ cups soft brown sugar
¹/₂ tablespoon whole coriander seeds
6 peppercorns and 6 allspice berries tied securely in a piece of muslin
¹/₄ cup root ginger, peeled and sliced
2 tablespoons cilantro leaves, chopped
2 tablespoons mint, chopped

Combine the apples with the onions, garlic, and bell peppers in a large, heavy stockpot. Add the vinegar and bring to a boil, simmering for about 30 minutes until all the ingredients are soft. Add the brown sugar and the muslin bag of seeds and berries. Then add the ginger. Heat, gently stirring all the time, until the sugar has dissolved, and simmer until thick; this can take up to 60 minutes. Stir in the chopped cilantro and mint and spoon into hot, sterilized jars. Seal and label when cool.

FRUIT JELLIES AND JAMS

These preserve the fruit in sugar gel. Jelly is made from the juice only, without the seeds and skins, while jam is made with and often also contains whole fruits or pieces thereof. A conserve is expensive jam, usually implying more fruit and less sugar or filler.

Almost any fruit can be made into jam or jelly, and many fruits are only palatable if so treated. The fruit is cooked to the point when the cells break up so that the juices run. The juice is then turned to a gel with sugar, which acts as a preservative as well. Most fruits need to have up to their own weight of sugar added to them to make a setting gel.

With jellies, the juice is often augmented with the squeezings of the fruit pulp reheated with some water. This thinner part then needs proportionately more sugar to set. Jellies are made from the strained juice and these washings, so they set clear and bright and are appreciated by many as there are no seeds. It is easy to pick and prepare fruits for jelly as the odd sprig, hard or underripe fruit, or bit of leaf will be strained out.

Many prefer the textures (and the nutritional value) of jams with the seeds and skins. But these require much more careful picking and preparation.

White sugar is usually used for making jams and jellies, unless a strong flavor is required. Honey is not really successful as the flavor is strong and it goes off when heated as much as is needed for jam. Concentrated juices can add too much flavor. The amount of fruit can be increased and the sugar decreased if your technique is good and you can eat the jam quickly!

Ideally, simmer down the fruit with the absolute minimum of water, strain if it is for jelly, add the sugar, bring to a boil, skim off any scum, and jar in sterile conditions. Hot jars and clean lids put on immediately improve results. Store, once cold, in a dark, cool place.

Some fruits are difficult to set, particularly strawberries in a wet year. Adding chopped apples to the jelly fruits or their puree to the jams will supply the pectin needed to make any jam set. Extra acidity to bring out the piquant flavor of some jams is often achieved using lemon juice. White-currant juice is a good substitute and red currant even better, especially where the color is also an advantage. Adding white- or red-currant juice also aids the setting of difficult jams. Their flavor is so tart yet mild that their jellies make good carriers for more strongly flavored fruits in shorter supply, especially for raspberries and cherries.

A tip: it is quicker and easier to make four 5-lb. batches of jam than one 20-lb. batch—and the result is better. Large batches have a low heating and evaporating surface compared to their volume and take much longer to process so the fruit degrades more.

Basil oil, coriander seed vinegar, and coriander oil all make delicious additions to the cupboard.

NATURAL DYES

Herbs, vegetables, and fruits have been used to dye cloth since the earliest records. In fact, until the nineteenth century and the birth of the chemical industry, all dyes were "natural." Then the chemical process, offering a larger range of colors and more guaranteed results, took over. Now, once again, there is a real demand for more-natural products and colors, which has resulted in a revival of interest in plants as a dye source.

Herbs offer the widest range of dyes, and the most common dyeing herbs are listed in the dye chart below. You will notice that yellows, browns, and grays are predominant. Plenty of plant material will be required, so be careful not to overpick in your own garden. To begin with, keep it simple. Pick the flowers just as they are coming out, the leaves when they are young and fresh and a good green; dig up roots in the fall and cut them up well before use.

Few vegetables contain plant juices with residual colors; all must be used with a mordant and the color varies according to the type used. There are three particularly worth trying. Juices of beets, although notorious for staining skin, produce drab brown or fawn when used for dyeing. The papery brown skins of onion bulbs are needed in large quantities for dyeing and produce colors ranging from pale yellow to a copper brown; although bold, these colors tend to fade rapidly when exposed to light. The "flags" or foliage of leeks produce yellow and dull brown pigments.

Apple, pear, and cherry barks yield dyes in shades of yellow, as do the roots and stems of berberis, while reddish-yellows come from pine cones. Walnuts stain everything they touch and need no mordant to help fix their dye, which can be obtained from the roots, leaves, and husks. Elder bark with an iron mordant gives a black dye; the leaves with an alum mordant give a green dye; and the berries produce shades of purple, blue, and lilac, often used as hair dyes. Rowan berries give a black dye, plums and sloes a blue dye, and their bark yields a red-brown colorant, while junipers give an olive brown.

FABRIC

Any natural material can be dyed, but some are more tricky than others. It just takes time and practice. The following sections explain the techniques connected with dyeing wool, the most reliable and easiest of natural materials. Silk, linen, and cotton can also be dyed, but are more difficult.

PREPARATION

This is a messy and fairly lengthy process, so protect all areas. Best of all, keep it away from the home altogether. Some of the mordants used for fixing dye are poisonous, so keep them well away from children, pets, and food.

The actual dyeing process is not difficult, but you will need a few special pieces of equipment, and space.

1 large stainless steel vessel, such as a preserving can (to be used as the dye bath)

HERB DYE CHART

Common Name	Botanical Name	Part Used		Mordant	Color
Comfrey	*Symphytum officinale*	Leaves and stalks	Alum		Yellows
Chamomile, Dyer's	*Anthemis tinctoria*	Flowers	Alum		Yellows
Chamomile, Dyer's	*Anthemis tinctoria*	Flowers	Copper		Olives
Elder	*Sambucus nigra*	Leaves	Alum		Greens
Elder	*Sambucus nigra*	Berries	Alum		Violets/purple
Goldenrod	*Solidago canadensis*	Whole plant	Chrome		Golden yellows
Horsetail	*Equisetum arvense*	Stems and leaves	Alum		Yellows
Juniper	*Juniperus communis*	Crushed berries	Alum		Yellows
Marigold	*Calendula officinalis*	Petals	Alum		Pale yellow
Meadowsweet	*Filipendula ulmaria*	Roots	Alum		Black
Nettle	*Urtica dioica*	Whole plant	Copper		Grayish-green
St. John's Wort	*Hypericum perforatum*	Flowers	Alum		Beiges
Sorrel	*Rumex acetosa*	Whole plant	Alum		Dirty yellow
Sorrel	*Rumex acetosa*	Roots	Alum		Beige/pink
Tansy	*Tanacetum vulgare*	Flowers	Alum		Yellows
Woad	*Isatis tinctoria*	Leaves	Sodium dithionite, ammonia		Blues

1 stainless steel or enamel bucket and bowl
1 pair of tongs (wooden or stainless steel; to be used for lifting)
1 measuring jug
1 pair rubber gloves essential for all but Jumblies—"Their heads are green and their hands are blue, And they went to sea in a sieve."
Mortar and pestle
Thermometer
Water; this must be soft, either rainwater or filtered
Scales

Dyeing comprises four separate tasks: preparation of the material (known as scouring); preparation of the mordant; preparation of the dye; and the dyeing process

PREPARATION OF THE MATERIAL

Prepare the wool by washing it in a hot solution of detergent or a scouring agent in order to remove any grease. Always handle the wool gently. Rinse it several times, squeezing (gently) between each rinse. On the final rinse add ¼ cup of vinegar.

PREPARATION OF THE MORDANT

Mordants help "fix" the dye to the fabric. They are available from drugstores or dye suppliers. The list below includes some of the more common. Some natural dyers say that one should not use mordants, but without them the dye will run very easily.

Alum: Use 1 oz. to 1 lb. dry wool

This is the most useful of mordants, its full title being potassium aluminum sulfate. Sometimes potassium hydrogen tartrate, cream of tartar, is added (beware! this is not the baking substance) to facilitate the process and brighten the color.

Iron: Use ⅛ oz. to 1 lb. dry wool

This is ferrous sulfate. It dulls and deepens the colors. It is added in the final process after first using the mordant alum. Remove the wool before adding the iron, then replace the wool and simmer until you get the depth of color required.

Copper: Use ½ oz. to 1 lb. dry wool

This is copper sulfate. If you mix with 1 cup of vinegar when preparing the mordant it will give a blue-green tint to colors. WARNING: Wear gloves—copper is poisonous.

Chrome: Use ½ oz. to 1 lb. dry wool

This is bichromate of potash and light-sensitive, so keep it in the dark. It gives the color depth, makes the colors fast, and gives the wool a soft, silky feel. WARNING: Wear gloves—chrome is poisonous.

Dissolve the mordant in a little hot water. Stir this into 4 gallons of hot water at 122°F. When thoroughly dissolved, immerse the wet, washed wool in the mixture. Make sure it is wholly immersed. Slowly bring to a boil and simmer at 180–200°F for an hour. Remove it from the heat, then take the wool out of the water and rinse.

PREPARATION OF THE DYE

No two batches of natural dye will be the same. There are so many variable factors—plant variety, water, mordant, immersion time.

The amount of plant material required for dyeing is variable. A good starting ratio is 1 lb. of mordanted wool in skeins to 1 lb. plant material.

Chop or crush the plant material. Place it loosely in a muslin or nylon bag and tie the bag securely. Leave it to soak in 4 gallons of soft, tepid water overnight. Slowly bring the water and herb material to a boil. Reduce the heat and simmer at 180–200°F for as long as it takes to get the water to the desired color. This can take between 1 and 3 hours. Remove the pan from the heat, remove the herb material, and allow the liquid to cool to lukewarm.

DYEING PROCESS

Gently add the wool to the dye mixture. Bring the water slowly to a boil, stirring it occasionally with the wooden tongs. Allow it to simmer for another hour, then remove the pan from the heat and leave the wool in the dye bath until it is cold, or until the color is right. Remove the wool with the tongs and rinse in tepid water until no color runs out. Give it a final rinse in cold water. Dry the skeins of wool over a rod or cord, away from direct heat. Tie a light weight to the bottom to stop the wool from kinking during the drying process.

THE YEARLY CALENDAR

This calendar gives general guidelines for a garden in a fairly temperate zone. But as any gardener knows, you cannot be precise. Each year is different, wetter, windier, hotter, drier, colder. So use this calendar as a general guide, and check with the specific entry for each plant for more detailed information.

MIDWINTER

Look back over the previous year, at successes and mishaps, and plan for the following season. Think about any structural changes and order seeds and plants. Keep an eye out for any weather damage in the garden, checking especially after heavy frost, snow, and gales.

Vegetables
Prepare cropping plants. Lime fall-dug plots if necessary. Place early seed potatoes in shallow boxes with "eyes" up, and store in a light, frost-free place. Toward the end of the month, plant out shallots if the soil is moist enough.

Under cover, sow radishes and carrots in growing bags or in the borders of a cold greenhouse; sow lettuce for growing under cloches, and leeks.

Herbs
This is one of the quietest months. Keep an eye on the degrees of frost and protect tender herbs with an extra layer of frost fabric or mulch if necessary.

With a little bit of protection in the garden,

Vines sprouting in spring from woody stock

bay, hyssop, rosemary, sage, winter savory, thyme, lemon thyme, chervil, and parsley can be picked.

Start parsley seed with heat. Outside, if not sown in the fall, sow sweet cicely, sweet woodruff, and cowslip, to enable a period of stratification. Force chives, mint, and tarragon in boxes in the greenhouse.

Keep watering of containers to a minimum. Clean old pots to be ready for the spring "pot up."

Fruit
Make a health and hygiene check and examine each plant in your care for pests, diseases and dieback. Check stores and remove and use any fruits starting to deteriorate before they go bad and infect others.

LATE WINTER

As the days lengthen, and if the weather is not too unpleasant, this is a good time to tidy up before the busy season starts. If you want to get an early start in the garden and you have prepared a site the previous fall, cover the soil now with black polyethylene. It will warm

up the soil and force any weeds.

Vegetables
Sow fava beans, early peas, and spinach. Sow early-maturing cabbage and cauliflowers in pots from the middle of the month on. "Chit" main-crop potatoes. Sow cabbages, carrots, lettuces, and radishes under cloches or under row covers.

Herbs
With a little bit of protection in the garden, bay, hyssop, rosemary, sage, winter savory, thyme, lemon thyme, chervil, and parsley can be harvested. Chives start to come up if they are under protection, and mint can be available if forced.

Start borage, dill, and parsley seeds with heat, and sow chervil in a cold greenhouse.

Herbaceous perennial herbs, including chives, lemon balm, pot marjoram, mints, oregano, broad-leaved sorrel, and tarragon, can be divided now, as long as they are not too frozen and are given added

Ladybugs on black currants

protection after replanting.

As the containers have been brought in for the winter, new life may be starting. Dust off and slowly start watering.

Outside, check to be sure that any dead or decaying herbaceous growth is not damaging plants. Check for wind and snow damage.

Fruit
Check stores and remove and use any fruits starting to deteriorate before they go bad and infect others. Spread a good layer of compost or well-rotted manure under and around everything possible and add a good layer of mulch, preferably immediately after a period of heavy rain.

Lime most grassy areas one year in four, more often on acid soil, but not among ericaceous plants or lime-haters! Once the ground becomes workable, plant out hardy trees and shrubs that missed the fall planting. Sow the very earliest crops for growing under cover. Ensure good weed control, hoeing every two weeks or adding extra mulches on top.

Do major pruning work to trees and bushes missed earlier or damaged in winter (but not stone fruits or evergreens). Prune fall-fruiting raspberries to the ground.

Spray everything growing with diluted seaweed solution at least once a month, and anything with deficiency symptoms more often. Spray peaches and almonds with Bordeaux mixture to protect against peach-leaf curl.

Examine each plant in your care for pests, diseases, and dieback. Apply sticky bands and inspect the sacking bands on apple trees, and others if they suffered from many pests.

Check straps and stakes after gales. On still, cold nights protect the blossoms and young fruitlets from frost damage with net curtains, plastic sheeting, or newspaper.

EARLY SPRING

Gradually uncover tender plants outside and look for hopeful signs of life. Give them a gentle tidying up.

Vegetables
Plant onion sets in prepared ground. Sow beet, cabbage, carrots, parsnip, lettuce, and main-crop peas.

Plant lettuce under cloches or in plastic tunnels, and sow scallions in growing bags in an unheated greenhouse for early crops. Sow early cabbages and cauliflowers under glass for transplanting later.

Herbs
Herbs available for picking include angelica, lemon balm, bay, chives, fennel, hyssop, mint, parsley, peppermint, pennyroyal, rue, sage, savory, sorrel, and thyme.

Toward the end of the month, start borage, fennel, coriander, sweet marjoram, rue, and basil seeds with heat. In a cold greenhouse sow chervil, chives, dill, lemon balm, lovage, parsley, sage, summer savory, and sorrel. Outside in the garden sow chervil, chives, parsley (cover with cloches), chamomile, tansy, caraway, borage, and fennel.

Check seeds that have been left outside from the previous fall for stratification. If they are starting to germinate, move them into a cold greenhouse.

Take root cuttings from mint, tarragon, bergamot,

chamomile, hyssop, tansy, sweet woodruff, and sweet cicely. Divide mint, tarragon, wormwood, lovage, rue, sorrel, lemon balm, salad burnet, camphor plant, thyme, winter savory, marjoram, alecost, horehound, and pennyroyal. This is a good time to start mound layering on old sages or thymes.

Clean up all the pots and trim old growth to maintain shape. Start liquid feeding with seaweed. Repot if necessary. Pot up new plants into containers for display later in the season.

In the garden, clear up all the winter debris, fork the soil over, and give a light dressing of bonemeal. If your soil is alkaline, and you gave it a good dressing of manure in the fall, now is the time to dig it well in.

Remove black polyethylene, weed, and place a cloche over important sowing sites a week before sowing to raise the soil temperature and keep it dry.

When major frosts are over, you can cut lavender back and into shape. This is certainly advisable for plants two years old and older. Give them a good mulch. Equally, sage bushes of two years and older would

benefit from a trim, but not hard back. Cut back elder and rosemary, neither of which minds a hard cutting back. Transplant the following if they need it: alecost, chives, mint, balm, pot marjoram, sorrel, horehound, and rue.

Fruit
Continue to spread a good layer of compost or well-rotted manure under and around everything possible. Spread wood ashes under and around plants, giving priority to gooseberries and culinary apples. Plant out evergreen and the more tender hardy plants. Protect them from frost and wind the first season. Sow plants grown under cover or for later planting out.

Maintain good weed control by hoeing every two weeks or adding extra mulch on top. Cut the grass at least every two weeks, preferably weekly, returning the clippings or raking them into rings around trees and bushes.

Spray everything growing with diluted seaweed solution at least once a month, and anything with deficiency symptoms more often. Spray peaches and almonds with Bordeaux

Comfrey 'Goldsmith' nestling in a shady corner makes an attractive border plant.

mixture against peach-leaf curl. Do a health and hygiene check on each plant in your care for pests, diseases, and dieback.

Prune back tender plants and evergreens. Protect the new growth against frost afterward. Pollinate early-flowering plants and those under cover by hand. On still, cold nights protect the blossoms and young fruitlets from frost damage with net curtains, plastic sheet, or newspaper.

MIDSPRING

This is the main period for sowing outdoors, as soon as soil conditions permit. It is also now possible to prune back to strong new shoots the branches of any shrubs that have suffered in winter.

Vegetables
Dig plots occupied by winter greens and prepare for leeks; plant main-crop potatoes, cabbages, and cauliflowers (sown under cover in early spring). Do additional sowings of beet, radishes, spinach, carrots, cauliflower, main-crop peas, fava beans, and parsnips. Sow iceberg lettuce, scallions, and sea kale. From late April, sow winter cauliflower, Savoy cabbage, kale, and broccoli into seedbeds. Transplant cabbages and cauliflowers sown in nursery beds in February. Pinch out the growing tips of flowering fava beans.

Tomatoes sown and pricked out in early spring should be transferred to a cold frame and hardened off. Sow squashes and corn. Prepare greenhouse borders or growing bags for tomatoes.

Herbs
Herbs available for picking include: angelica, balm, bay,

borage, caraway, chervil, chives, fennel, hyssop, lovage, pot marjoram, mints, parsley, pennyroyal, peppermint, rosemary, sage, winter savory, sorrel, thyme, tarragon, and lemon thyme.

Start basil seeds with heat. In a cold greenhouse sow borage, chervil, cilantro, dill, fennel, lemon balm, lovage, pot marjoram, sweet marjoram, sage, summer savory, winter savory, sorrel, buckler leaf sorrel, horehound, rue, bergamot, caraway, and garden thyme. Outside in the garden sow parsley, chives, hyssop, caraway, and pot marigold. Prick out the previous month's sown seeds and repot, or harden off before planting out.

Take softwood cuttings of rue, mint, sage, southernwood, winter savory, thymes, horehound, lavender, rosemary, cotton lavender, and curry. Take root cuttings of sweet cicely, fennel, and mint. Divide pennyroyal, chives, lady's mantle, salad burnet, and tarragon.

You should be able to put all containers outside now; keeping an eye on the watering and feeding. In the garden, if all the frosts have finished, the following will need cutting and pruning into shape: bay, winter savory, hyssop, cotton lavender, lavenders, rue especially variegated rue, southernwood, and thymes.

Fruit

Ensure good weed control, hoeing weekly or adding extra mulch on top. Cut the grass at least weekly, returning the clippings or raking them into rings around trees and bushes. Sow plants grown under cover or for later planting out. Plant out more tender hardy plants under cover or with protection.

Spread a good layer of mulch under and around everything possible, and spread wood ashes under and around fruit trees, giving priority to gooseberries and culinary apples. Spray everything growing with diluted seaweed solution at least once a month, and anything with deficiency symptoms more often.

Water all new plants established within the previous twelve months whenever there has been little rain. Deflower or defruit new plants to give them time to establish. Pollinate plants under cover by hand. Tie in new growths of vines and climbing plants. Make a health and hygiene check weekly and examine each plant in your care for pests, diseases, and dieback. On still, cold nights protect the blossoms and young fruitlets from frost damage with net curtains, plastic sheet, or newspaper. Make layers of difficult subjects.

Prepared seedbed with a measuring rod for spacing rows

LATE SPRING

Vegetables

Sow string and runner beans, Chinese lettuce, carrots, zucchini, outdoor cucumbers, lettuce, turnips, spinach, and parsley. Plant out celeriac, celery, corn, and summer cabbage. Harvest asparagus, fava beans, cauliflowers, peas, radish, and spinach. Earth up potatoes. Under cover, transplant eggplants, outdoor cucumbers, tomatoes, peppers, and corn.

Herbs

Everything should be growing quickly now. The annuals will need thinning; tender and half-hardy plants should be hardened off under a cold frame or by a warm wall. A watch must be kept for a sudden late frost; basil is especially susceptible. Move container specimens into bigger pots or top-dress with new compost.

Nearly all varieties of herbs are available for picking. Outside, keep sowing cilantro, dill, chervil, parsley, sweet marjoram, basil, and any other annuals you require to maintain crops. Prick out and repot or plant out any of the previous month's seedlings.

Take softwood cuttings of marjorams, all mints, oregano, rosemarys, winter savory, French tarragon, and all thymes. Containers should now be looking good. Keep trimming to maintain shape; water and feed regularly. In the garden, trim southernwood into shape.

Cut second-year growth of angelica for candying. Cut thyme before flowering to dry.

Fruit

Maintain good weed control. Sow plants grown

under cover or outdoors. Plant out tender plants under cover or with protection. Pollinate plants under cover by hand. Cut the grass at least every two weeks, preferably weekly, returning the clippings or raking them into rings around trees and bushes.

Water all new plants established within the previous twelve months, especially whenever there has been little rain. Deflower or defruit new plants. Spray everything growing with diluted seaweed solution at least once a month, and anything with deficiency symptoms more often.

Examine each plant twice weekly for pests, diseases, and dieback. Tie in new growths of vine and climbing plants. On still, cold nights, protect the blossoms and young fruitlets from frost damage with net curtains, plastic sheet, or newspaper. Make layers of difficult subjects. Protect almost every ripening fruit from the birds.

EARLY SUMMER

Vegetables

Sow string and runner beans, Chinese lettuce, carrots, zucchini, outdoor cucumbers, lettuce, turnips, spinach, and parsley. Transplant celery, summer cabbage, and tomatoes. Harvest asparagus, fava beans, cauliflowers, calabrese, peas, radish, spinach, and turnips. Under cover, transplant eggplant and corn; pollinate tomato plants.

Herbs

This is a great time in the herb garden. All planting is now completed. Plants are beginning to join up so that little further weeding will be needed. Many plants are now reaching perfection.

All herbs are available fresh. Outside in the garden

sow basil, borage, chives, cilantro, dill, fennel, sweet marjoram, summer savory, winter savory, and any others you wish to replace or keep going.

With all the soft new growth available this is a very busy month for cuttings. Make sure you use material from nonflowering shoots. Take softwood cuttings of all perennial marjorams, all mints, all rosemary, all sage, variegated lemon balm, tarragon (French), and all thymes. Also divide thymes and layer rosemary.

Plant up annual herbs such as basil and sweet marjoram into containers to keep near the kitchen. If you must plant basil in the garden, do it now. Nip out the growing tips of this year's young plants to encourage them to bush out.

Trim cotton lavender hedges if flowers are not required and to maintain their shape; clip box hedges and topiary shapes as needed. A new herb garden should be weeded thoroughly to give the new plants the best chance.

Cut second-year growth of

angelica for candying. Cut sage for drying.

Fruit
Maintain good weed control. Plant out the tender plants or move them out for summer. Cut the grass at least every two weeks, preferably weekly, returning the clippings or raking them into rings around trees and bushes. Raise the height of cut of your mower. Spray everything growing with diluted seaweed solution at least once a month, and anything with deficiency symptoms more often.

Water all new plants established within the previous twelve months especially whenever there has been little rain. Examine each plant twice weekly for pests, diseases, and dieback.

Start summer pruning. This applies to all red and white currants, gooseberries, and all trained apples and pears. From one third of each plant, remove approximately half to three-quarters of each new shoot, except for leaders. Prune grapevines back to three or

five leaves after a flower truss. Tie in new growths of vine and climbing plants.

Also begin fruit thinning. To do this, remove every diseased, decayed, damaged, misshapen, distorted, and congested fruitlet. This applies to all apples, pears, peaches, apricots, quality plums, dessert grapes, gooseberries, figs, and especially to trained forms. Compost or burn rejected fruitlets immediately. Of course usable ones, such as the larger gooseberries, may be consumed.

Take softwood cuttings if you have a propagator. Make layers of difficult subjects. Protect almost every ripening fruit from birds.

MIDSUMMER

Vegetables
Sow final crops of beet, carrots, lettuce, turnips, spinach, and parsley. Sow scallions, spring cabbage, and sea kale for overwintering. Sow keeping onions in a seedbed for transplanting the following spring. In colder zones, plant leeks sown in cold frames in winter. Remove basal suckers from early trench

celery, water well, and earth up.

Under cover, harvest cucumbers and tomatoes regularly to encourage further fruiting, and pinch out the growing point when each stem contains about 5 or 6 trusses of fruit.

Herbs
The season is on the wane, the early annuals and biennials are beginning to go over. It is already time to think of next year and to start collecting seeds. Take cuttings of tender shrubs as spare shoots are available.

All herbs can be harvested fresh. Outside in the garden sow chervil, angelica (if seed is set), borage, cilantro, dill, lovage, and parsley. Take softwood cuttings of wormwood, scented geraniums, lavenders, and the thymes. Layer rosemary. Keep an eye on watering of containers as the temperatures begin to rise.

Cut all lavenders back after flowering to maintain their shape. If this is the first summer of the herb garden and the plants are not fully established, it is important to make sure they do not dry out, so water regularly. Once established, many are tolerant of drought.

Back row: **Curly wood sage** *Teucrium scorodonia* 'Crispum'; **Lawn Chamomile** *Chamaemelum nobile* 'Treneague'; front row: **Variegated Meadowsweet** *Filipendula ulmaria* 'Variegata'; **Houseleek** *Sempervivum tectorum*; **Dwarf Marjoram** *Origanum vulgare* 'Nanum'

Harvest and dry lemon balm, horehound, summer savory, hyssop, tarragon, thyme, and lavender. Use lavender and rosemary for dying and potpourris. Harvest seed of caraway and angelica.

Fruit

Maintain good weed control. Cut the grass at least every two weeks, preferably weekly, returning the clippings or raking them into rings around trees and bushes. Raise the height of cut of your mower. Spray everything growing with diluted seaweed solution at least once a month, and anything with deficiency symptoms more often. Water all new plants established within the previous twelve months, especially whenever there has been little rain. Examine each plant in your care for pests, diseases, and dieback. Tie in new growths of vines and climbing plants.

Continue summer pruning. For red and white currants, gooseberries, and all trained apples and pears, from the second third of each plant remove approximately half to three-quarters of each new shoot, except for leaders. Prune grapevines back to three or five leaves after a flower truss. Black currants may have a third to half of the old wood removed after fruiting. Stone fruits are traditionally pruned now to avoid silver-leaf disease.

Continue to thin fruits as in June. Take softwood cuttings if you have a propagator, and root tips of the black and hybrid berries. Protect almost every ripening fruit from the birds.

LATE SUMMER

Vegetables

Sow turnips for spring "greens" and Japanese onions for overwintering in mild zones. Sow spring cabbage in nursery rows. To prevent wind-rock in fall and winter, draw soil around the stems of winter greens, particularly Brussels sprouts, kale, and broccoli. Earth up trench celery. Harvest main-crop onions, ensuring that the bulbs' outer skins are well ripened before storing. Under cover, harvest cucumbers and tomatoes regularly, and self-pollinate tomatoes.

Herbs

Traditionally a time for holidays, this is also a time to harvest and preserve many herbs for winter use. Collect and dry material for potpourris, and collect seeds for sowing next year.

All herbs are available fresh. In the garden or greenhouse sow angelica, cilantro, dill, lovage, parsley, winter savory. Take softwood cuttings of bay, wormwood, rosemary, the thymes and lavenders, scented geraniums, balm of Gilead, pineapple sage, and myrtles.

Protect your fruit from birds!

If you are going away, make sure you ask a friend to water your containers for you. Give box, cotton lavender, and curry their second clipping and trim any established plants that are looking unruly. Maintain watering of the new herb garden and keep an eye on mints, parsley, and comfrey, which need water to flourish. There is no real need to feed if the ground has been well prepared, but if the plants are recovering from a pest attack they will benefit from a foliar feed of liquid seaweed.

Harvest thyme, sage, clary sage, marjoram, and lavender for drying. Pick the mints and pennyroyal to freeze. Gather basil to make

a basil oil. Collect the seed of angelica, anise, caraway, cilantro, cumin, chervil, dill, and fennel.

Fruit

Maintain good weed control. Plant new strawberry plants, if you can get them. Cut the grass at least once every two weeks, preferably weekly, returning the clippings or raking them into rings around trees and bushes. Lower the height of cut of your mower. Spray everything that is growing with diluted seaweed solution at least once a month, and anything that has deficiency symptoms more often. Water all new plants established within the previous twelve months, especially whenever there has been little rain. Sow green manures and winter ground cover on bare soil that is not mulched; grass down orchards. Check for

Apart from being beautiful, butterflies are a useful addition to the garden.

pests, diseases, and dieback, and apply sticky bands and sacking bands to apple trees, and to others if they suffer from many pests.

Finish summer pruning. For red and white currants, gooseberries, and all trained apples and pears, for the last, unpruned third of each plant, remove approximately half to three-quarters of each new shoot, except for leaders. Prune grapevines back to three or five leaves after the fruit truss.

Thin fruits as in summer. Protect almost every ripening fruit from the birds. Root the tips of the black- and hybrid berries.

EARLY FALL

Vegetables
Order seed catalogs for the following year. In mild zones, plant out spring cabbages into permanent positions. Sow spinach for harvesting in spring. Lift main-crop carrots, beets, and potatoes, and store in a cool, dark place: later sowings may be left in the ground. Earth up celery before severe frosts. Lift tomato plants with fruits still attached and store; ripen on straw under cloches or in the greenhouse. Wrap green fruits in paper and store in the dark.

Plant thinnings from late-sown salads in frames or under cloches to provide crops during winter. Lettuces reaching maturity should be covered with cloches or frames; sow further crops in a cold frame. Fall is a good time to lay drains through waterlogged sites.

Herbs
Basil should be taken up and leaves preserved. Line out semiripe cuttings of box, cotton lavenders, etc., in cold frames, under cloches, or in polyethylene tunnels for hedge renewal in the spring.

Herbs that can be picked fresh include: lemon balm, basil, bay, borage, caraway, chervil, chives, clary sage, fennel, hyssop, pot marigold, marjoram, the mints, parsley, pennyroyal, peppermint, rosemarys, sages, winter savory, sorrels, and the thymes. Outside in the garden or greenhouse sow angelica, chives, cilantro, parsley, and winter savory. Take softwood and semiripe cuttings of rosemary, the thymes, tarragon, the lavenders, rue, the cotton lavenders, the curry plants, and box. Divide bergamot.

At the beginning of the month give the shrubby herbs their final clipping (bay, lavender, etc.). Do not leave it until too late or frost could damage the new growth. Put basil into the greenhouse or kitchen. Top-dress bergamots if they have died back. If lemon verbena is to be kept outside, make sure it is getting adequate protection. Toward the end of this month take in all containers, and protect tender plants like bay trees, myrtles, and scented geraniums. Harvest dandelion (roots), parsley, marigold, clary sage, and peppermint for drying or freezing. Collect seed of angelica, anise, caraway, chervil, and fennel.

Fruit
Maintain good weed control. Plant out pot-grown specimens and those that can be dug with a decent rootball or moved with little disturbance. Cut the grass at least once every two weeks,

'Malling Jewel' raspberries

preferably weekly, returning the clippings and fallen leaves or raking them into rings around trees and bushes. Sow green manures and winter ground cover on bare soil that is not mulched; grass down orchards. Spray everything that is growing with diluted seaweed solution at least once a month, and anything that has deficiency symptoms more often.

Make a health and hygiene check for pests, diseases, and dieback. Apply sticky bands and sacking bands to apple trees, and to others if they suffer from many pests. On still, cold nights protect ripening fruits from frost damage with net curtains, plastic sheet, or newspaper. Protect first the tops then the stems and roots of more tender plants before frosts come. Bring tender plants in pots indoors or protect them. Take cuttings of plants as they start to drop their leaves. Prune early fruiting raspberries and hybrids, and black currants and other plants as they start to drop their leaves. Protect almost every ripening fruit from the birds. Root the tips of the black- and hybrid berries.

MIDFALL

Vegetables
Lift potatoes, beet, and carrots for storing. Tie onions onto ropes when the skins have thoroughly ripened. Transplant lettuces sown in summer to a well-

Alpine strawberries and thyme on a low bank

Winter trap

drained, protected site to overwinter in mild zones. Plant root cuttings of sea kale in pots of sand and leave them in a sheltered place until the spring. Cut down asparagus foliage as it turns yellow. Tidy up the vegetable plot, removing all plant debris. Double dig, adding organic matter, and lime if necessary.

Sow lettuce in greenhouse borders or growing bags for cutting in the spring. Continue harvesting green tomatoes, storing in a dark, frost-free place to ripen. Clear growing bags used for cucumbers, peppers, and tomatoes in the summer and replant with winter lettuce.

Herbs

The best time in all but the coldest areas to plant hardy perennial herbs.

Basil, bay, borage, chervil, fennel, hyssop, marigold, marjoram, parsley, rosemary, sage, winter savory, sorrel, and the thymes can all be picked fresh. Sow parsley seed with heat. In the garden sow catnip, chervil, wormwood, chamomile, fennel, and angelica.

Take softwood and semiripe cuttings of bay, elder, hyssop, cotton lavender, southernwood, lavenders, the thymes, curry, and box. Take root cuttings of tansy, pennyroyal, the mints, and tarragon. Divide alecost, the marjorams, chives, lemon balm, lady's mantle, hyssop, bergamot,

camphor plant, lovage, sorrel, sage, oregano, and pennyroyal.

Start reducing the watering of containers. Clear the garden and weed it well. Cut down the old growth and collect any remaining seed heads. Cut back the mints, trim winter savory and hyssop. Give them all a leaf mold dressing. Dig up and remove the annuals, dill, cilantro, borage, summer savory, sweet marjoram. and the second-year biennials, parsley, chervil, rocket, etc. Protect with cloches or frost fabric any herbs to be used fresh through the winter, like parsley, chervil, lemon thyme, salad burnet. Dig up some French tarragon and pot up in trays for forcing and protection.

Check the pH of alkaline soil every third year. Dress with well-rotted manure to a depth of 2–4 in. and leave the digging until the following spring. Dig over heavy soils; add manure to allow the frost to penetrate.

Fruit

Ensure good weed control. Plant out bare-rooted hardy trees and bushes if soil is in good condition and they are dormant. Cut the grass at least once every two weeks, preferably weekly, collecting the clippings with the fallen leaves or raking them into rings around trees and bushes. Spray everything that is growing with diluted seaweed solution at least once a month, and anything that has deficiency symptoms more often.

Check plants for pests, diseases, and dieback. Replenish the sticky bands and inspect the sacking bands on apple trees and others if they suffered from many pests. Check straps and stakes before the gales. On still, cold nights protect ripening fruits from frost damage with net curtains, plastic sheet, or newspaper.

Take cuttings of hardy plants as they start to drop

Espalier-trained peaches on a redbrick wall

their leaves. Prune early-fruiting raspberries and hybrids, and black currants and other plants as they start to drop their leaves. Protect first the tops, then the stems and roots of more tender plants before frosts come. Check stores, remove and use any fruits starting to deteriorate before they go bad and infect others. Protect almost every ripening fruit from the birds.

LATE FALL

Vegetables

In mild zones, sow fava beans, and round-seeded peas in the open: protect with cloches if necessary. Remove dying leaves from winter greens, allowing air to circulate between plants. Check stored vegetables regularly and remove any showing signs of decay. Use those that are slightly damaged immediately.

Sow green manure. Lift and store crowns of endive as well as sea kale.

Herbs

The days are getting shorter and frosts are starting. Planting of hardy herbaceous herbs can continue as long as soil remains unfrozen and in a workable condition.

Basil, bay, hyssop, marjoram, mint, parsley, rosemary, rue, sage, and thyme are available to pick fresh. Sow the following so that they can get a good period of stratification: arnica (old seed), sweet woodruff, yellow iris, poppy, soapwort, sweet cicely, hops (old seed), and sweet violet. Sow in trays, cover with glass and leave outside in a cold frame or corner of the garden where they cannot get damaged.

Cut back on all watering of container-grown plants.

'Bedford Giant' blackberry

Runner bean 'Painted Lady' climbing a decorative frame

EARLY WINTER

Vegetables

Plan next year's rotation of vegetables, ordering seeds as soon as possible. Prepare a seed-sowing schedule. Dig and store rutabaga and late-sown carrots. If heavy falls of snow or prolonged frosts are forecast, lift small quantities of vegetables such as celery, leeks, and parsnips and store under cover in a cool, easily accessible place. Finish digging before the soil becomes waterlogged. On clay soils, spread sand, old potting compost or well-rotted leaf mold on the surface and dig in as soon as conditions are favorable, allowing the frost to break down the soil. Sow green manures on sandy soils or cover with compost to reduce leaching.

Herbs

Bay, hyssop, marjoram, oregano, mint (forced), parsley, chervil, rosemary, rue, sage, and thyme are all available for picking fresh.

In the garden, remove all the dead growth that falls into other plants and add more protective layers if needed. Wrap any terra-cotta or stone ornaments in burlap if you live in extremely cold conditions.

Bring bay trees in if the temperature drops too low. Keep an eye on the plants you are forcing in the greenhouse.

Fruit

Maintain good weed control by hoeing or mulching. Plant out bare-rooted hardy trees and bushes if the soil is in good condition and they are dormant. Collect the fallen leaves and use them for leaf mold or rake them in rings around trees and bushes.

Examine plants for pests, diseases, and dieback. Replenish the sticky bands and inspect the sacking bands on apple trees and others if they suffered from many pests. Check straps and stakes before the gales.

Spread a good layer of compost or well-rotted manure under and around everything possible, preferably after heavy rain. Prune late-fruiting trees and bushes as their leaves fall, and do major work to trees and bushes (but not to stone fruits or evergreens). Check stores and remove and use any fruits starting to deteriorate before they go bad and infect others.

Give them all a prune, so that they go into rest mode for the winter. This is the time for the final tidying up in the garden. Cut back the remaining plants, lemon balm, alecost, and horehound, and give them a dressing of leaf mold. Give the elders a prune. Dig up a clump of mint and chives, put them in pots or trays and bring them into the greenhouse for forcing for winter use.

Fruit

Keep on top of weeds. Plant out bare-rooted hardy trees and bushes if the soil is in good condition and they are dormant. Cut the grass at least once every two weeks, collecting the clippings with the fallen leaves or raking them into rings around trees and bushes. Check plants for pests, diseases, and dieback. Replenish the sticky bands and inspect the sacking bands on apple trees, and on others if they suffered from many pests.

Check straps and stakes before the gales. Spread a good layer of compost or well-rotted manure under and around everything possible, preferably after a period of heavy rain. On still, cold nights protect ripening fruits from frost damage with net curtains, plastic sheet, or newspaper. Protect first the tops, then the stems and roots of more tender plants before frosts come.

Take cuttings of hardy plants as they start to drop their leaves. Prune late fruiting raspberries, hybrid berries, currants and vines, trees, and bushes as the leaves fall. Check stores, remove and use any fruits starting to deteriorate before they go bad and infect others. Protect almost every ripening fruit from the birds.

A covering of frost on a vegetable garden

GLOSSARY

Analgesic A substance that relieves pain.
Annual A plant completing its life cycle from germination to seed in one growing season.
Antidote A substance that counteracts or neutralizes a poison.
Aromatherapy The use of essential oils in the treatment of medical problems and for cosmetic purposes.
Astringent A substance that contracts the tissues of the body, checking discharges of blood and mucus.

Base dressing An application of organic matter or fertilizer, applied to the soil prior to planting or sowing.
Bed system A method of planting vegetables in close blocks or multiple rows.
Beta carotene The orange-yellow plant pigment and precursor of vitamin A, which protects against certain cancers and heart disease.
Biennial A plant completing its life cycle in a two-year period.
Blanch To exclude light from leaves and stems and prevent development of green coloration. In the culinary sense, to immerse in boiling water for the removal of skin or color, often as a preparation for freezing.
Bolt To flower and produce seed prematurely.
Brassica A member of the cabbage family *(Brassicaceae).*
Broadcast To scatter granular substances such as seeds, fertilizer, or pesticide evenly over an area of ground.
Bulb A modified plant stem, with swollen leaves acting as a storage organ.
Bulbil A small bulb rising above the ground in the axil of a leaf or bract.

Capping A crust forming on the surface of soil damaged by compaction, heavy rain or watering.
Carminative A substance that allays gastrointestinal pain and relieves flatulence and colic.
Chitting Pregermination of seeds before sowing. The same term is used for sprouting potatoes.
Clamp A structure made of earth for storing root vegetables outdoors.
Cloche A small portable structure, often made of plastic or glass, used to protect early crops grown outdoors.
Cold frame A low-lying rectangular unheated structure, with a glass or plastic lid.
Compost Decomposed organic material used as soil conditioner, mulch, potting, or seed-sowing medium.
Cultivar A contraction of "cultivated variety," a group of cultivated plants that retain desirable characteristics when propagated.

Damp down To wet the floors and benches in a greenhouse in order to increase humidity and lower high temperatures.
Deciduous Plants that lose leaves at the end of the growing season and redevelop them the following year.
Decoction An extract of an herb (when the material is hard and woody, i.e., root, wood, bark, nuts) obtained by boiling a set weight of plant matter in a set volume of water for a set time.
Diuretic A substance that increases the frequency of urination.
Dormancy Temporary cessation of growth during the dormant season.

Emetic A substance that induces vomiting.
Essential oil A volatile oil obtained from a plant by distillation, and having a similar aroma to the plant itself.
Evergreen Plants retaining their leaves throughout the year.

F₁ Hybrid First-generation plants obtained by crossing two selected pure-breeding parents to produce uniform vigorous offspring.
Fanging A term to describe the forking of a root vegetable.
Fertilizer A chemical or group of chemicals applied to the soil or plants to provide nutrition.
Floating mulch (floating cloche) Sheets of flexible lightweight material placed over plants to provide protection.
Fluid sow A method for sowing germinated seeds into the soil using a carrier gel.
Folic acid Part of the vitamin B complex, found in leafy vegetables. Deficiency of folic acid causes anemia.
Friable Used to describe soil with a crumbly, workable texture, capable of forming a tilth.
Frost fabric Lightweight, woven polypropylene cover used for crop protection.
Fungicide Chemical used for the control and eradication of fungi.

Genus A taxonomic classification used to describe plants with several similar characteristics.
Germination The chemical and physical changes that take place as a seed starts to grow.
Green manure A rapidly maturing, leafy crop grown for incorporation into the soil to improve its structure and nutrient levels.
Growing bag A bag of compost used as a growing medium.

Half hardy Plants that tolerate low temperatures but not frost.
Harden off To acclimatize plants gradually, enabling them to withstand cooler conditions.
Hardy Plants that can withstand frost without protection.
Haulm The foliage of plants such as potatoes.
Heart up The stage at which leafy vegetables, like cabbage and lettuce, swell to form a dense cluster of central leaves.
Heavy soil A soil with a high proportion of clay particles, prone to waterlogging in winter and drying in summer.
Herbaceous Relating to plants that are not woody and that die down at the end of each growing season.
Herbicide A chemical used to control and eradicate weeds.
Hill up To draw the soil around the base for support or to cover a plant for the purpose of blanching.
Homeopathy A system of medicine based on the supposition that minute quantities of a given substance, such as that of a medicinal plant, will cure a condition that would be caused by administering large quantities of the same substance.
Humus The organic decayed remains of plant material in soils.
Hybrid A variety of plant resulting from the crossing of two distinct species or genera.

Infusion Made by pouring a given quantity of boiling water over a given weight of soft herbal material (leaves or petals) and steeping.
Inorganic Term used to describe fertilizers made from refined, naturally occurring chemicals, or artificial fertilizers.
Insecticide Chemical used to eradicate insects.

Inulin An easily digestible form of carbohydrate.

John Innes compost Loam-based growing medium made to standardized formulas.

Leaching The downward washing and loss of soluble nutrients from topsoil.
Leaf A plant organ containing chlorophyll essential for photosynthesis.
Leaf mold Decaying leaves.
Legume The bean and pea family which enrich the soil with bacterial nodule on their roots.
Lime Calcium compounds used to raise the pH of the soil.
Loam The term used for a soil of medium texture.

Main crop The largest crop produced throughout the main growing season. Also used to describe the cultivars used.
Mordant A substance used in dyeing which, when applied to the fabric to be dyed, reacts chemically with the dye, fixing the color.
Mulch A layer of organic or inorganic material laid over the ground that controls weeds, protects the soil surface, and conserves moisture.

Nematacide Chemical used for the control and eradication of nematodes (wireworms).
Neutral Soil or compost with a pH value of 7, which is neither acid nor alkaline (see pH).
Nutrients Minerals that are essential for plant growth.

Organic Term used to describe substances that are derived from natural materials. Also used to denote gardening by encouraging the life in the soil and without the use of harmful chemicalsl.

Pan A layer of compacted soil that is impermeable to water and oxygen, and impedes root development and drainage.
Perennial A plant that survives for three or more years.
Perlite Expanded volcanic rock. It is inert, sterile, and has a neutral pH value.
pH A measure of acidity or alkalinity. The scale ranges from 0 to 14, and is an indicator of the soluble calcium within a soil or growing medium. A pH below 7 is acid, and above, alkaline.
Pinch out To remove the growing tip of a plant to induce branching.
Pot on To move a plant into a larger pot.
Prick out To transfer seedlings, from a seedbed or tray, to another pot, tray, or seedbed.
Propagation The increase of plant numbers by seed or vegetative means.

Radicle A seedling root.
Rhizome A fleshy underground stem that acts as a storage organ.
Root The part of the plant that is responsible for absorbing water and nutrients and for anchoring the plant into the growing medium.
Root crops Vegetables grown for their edible roots, like carrot and parsnip.
Runner A trailing shoot that roots where it touches the ground.

Salve A soothing ointment.
Saponin A substance that foams in water and has a detergent action.
Seed A ripened plant ovule containing a dormant embryo, which is capable of forming a new plant.

Seed leaves or *cotyledons* The first leaf or leaves formed by a seed after germination.
Seedling A young plant grown from seed.
Sets Small onions, shallots, or potatoes used for planting.
Shoot A branch, stem, or twig of a plant.
Shrub A plant with woody stems, branching at or near the base.
Sideshoot A branch, stem, or twig growing from a main stem of a plant.
Species A taxonomic classification of similar closely related plants.
Spore The reproductive body of a nonflowering plant.
Stale seedbed method A cultivation technique whereby the seedbed is created and subsequent weed growth is removed before crops are sown or planted.
Stamen The pollen-producing part of the plant.
Stem The main axis of a plant, from which lateral branches appear.
Stigma The part of a pistil (the female organs of a flower) that accepts the pollen.
Subsoil Layers of less fertile soil immediately below the topsoil.
Sucker A stem originating below soil level, usually from the plant's roots or underground stem.
Systemic or *translocated* A term used to describe a chemical that is absorbed by a plant at one point and then circulated through its sap system.

Taproot The primary anchoring root of a plant, usually growing straight down into the soil. In vegetables this is often used for food storage.
Tender Plant material that is intolerant of cool conditions.
Thinning The removal of seedlings or shoots to improve the quality of those that remain.
Thymol A bactericide and fungicide found in several volatile oils.
Tilth The surface layer of soil produced by cultivation and soil improvement.
Tincture A solution that has been extracted from plant material after macerating in alcohol or alcohol/water solutions.
Tisane A drink made by the addition of boiling water to fresh or dried unfermented plant material.
Top-dressing The application of fertilizers or bulky organic matter to the soil surface, while the plants are in situ.
Topsoil The upper, usually most fertile layer of soil.
Transpiration The loss by evaporation of moisture from plant leaves and stems.
Transplant To move a plant from one growing position to another.
Tuber A swollen underground stem used to store moisture and nutrients.

Variety Used in the vernacular to describe different kinds of plant. Also used in botanical classification to describe a naturally occurring variant of a plant.
Vegetative Used to describe parts of a plant that are capable of growth.
Vermifuge A substance that expels or destroys worms.
Vulnerary A preparation useful in healing wounds.

Weathering Using the effect of climatic conditions to break down large lumps of soil into small particles.
Wind-rock Destabilizing of plant roots by wind action.

FURTHER READING

Bio-dynamic Gardening J. Soper, Souvenir Press, 1983

Collins Guide to the Pests, Diseases & Disorders of Garden Plants S. Buczacki & K. Harris, Collins, 1981

Complete Book of Herbs Lesley Bremness, Dorling Kindersley, 1988

Complete Herbal Culpeper, J. Gleave & Son, 1826

Complete Know and Grow Vegetables J. K. A. Bleasdale, P. J. Salter et al, OUP, 1991

Complete New Herbal, The Richard Mabey, ed., Penguin, 1988

Complete Cookery Course Delia Smith, BBC Books, 1982

Contained Garden K. Beckett, D. Carr & D. Stephens, Frances Lincoln, 1982

Diagnosis of Mineral Deficiencies in Plants HMSO, 1943

Domestication of Plants in the Old World D. Zohary & Maria Hopf, Oxford Science Publications, 1994

Dye Plants and Dyeing J. & M. Cannon, Herbert Press/Royal Botanic Gardens, Kew

Early Garden Crops F. W. Shepherd, RHS, 1977

Encyclopedia of Garden Plants and Flowers R. Hay, ed., Reader's Digest, 1978

Encyclopedia of Herbs and Herbalism Malcolm Stuart, ed., Black Cat, 1979

Encyclopedia of Medicinal Plants Roberto Chiej, Macdonald, 1984

Encyclopedia of Organic Gardening HDRA/DK, 2001

English Gardener, The William Cobbett, 1833

English Man's Flora, The Geoffrey Grigson, Paladin, 1975

Evening Primrose Oil Judy Graham, Thorsons, 1984

Food for Free Richard Mabey, Fontana/Collins, 1972, 1975

Four-Season Harvest E. Coleman, Chelsea Green, 1992

Gardener's Dictionary Philip Miller, 1724

Gardening on a Bed System P. Pears, Search Press/Henry Doubleday Research Association, 1992

Gardening without Chemicals J. Temple, Thorsons, 1986

Good Fruit Guide L. D. Hills, Henry Doubleday Research Association

Growing Under Glass K. A. Beckett, RHS/Mitchell Beazley, 1992

Handbook of Insects Injurious to Orchard and Bush Fruits E. A. Ormerod, Simpkin, Marshall, Hamilton & Co., 1898

Herb Book, The John Lust, Bantam, 1974

Herb Book, The Arabella Boxer & Philippa Black, Octopus, 1980

Herb Gardening at Its Best Sal Gilbertie with Larry Sheehan, Atheneum/smi, 1978

Herball John Gerard, 1636; Bracken Books, 1985

Herbs for Health and Cookery Clair Loewenfeld & Philippa Black, Pan, 1965

Herbs in the Garden Allen Paterson, Dent, 1985

Hillier's Manual of Trees and Shrubs David & Charles

Hints for the Vegetable Gardener Gardenway Publications, 1990

History and Social Influence of the Potato R. N. Salaman, CUP, 1949

Jane Grigson's Vegetable Book J. Grigson, Penguin, 1988

Kitchen Garden: A Historical Guide to Traditional Crops D. C. Stuart, Hale, 1984

Maison Rustique, or the Country Farm Estienne, C. Liebault, 1570

Modern Herbal A M. Grieve, Peregrine, 1976

Month by Month Guide to Organic Gardening Lawrence D. Hills, Thorsons 1983

Nutritional Values in Crops and Plants Werner Schuphan, Museum Press, 1965

Organic Bible Bob Flowerdew, Kyle Cathie, 2001

Organic Gardening R. Lacey, David & Charles, 1988

Organic Growing for Small Gardens J. Hay, Century, 1985

Organic Plant Protection R. B. Yepsen, ed., Rodale, 1976

Oriental Vegetables: The Complete Guide for Garden & Kitchen J. Larkcom, John Murray, 1991

Ornamental Kitchen Garden, The Geoff Hamilton, BBC Books, 1990

Oxford Book of Food Plants Peerage Books, 1969

Pelargoniums Derek Clifford, Blandford, 1958

Planning the Organic Herb Garden Sue Stickland, Thorsons, 1986

Plant and Planet Anthony Huxley, Allen Lane, 1974

Plant Finder 2002–3, The Dorling Kindersley, 2002

Plant Physiological Disorders ADAS, HMSO, 1985

Plants from the Past David Stuart & James Sutherland, Viking, 1987

Pruning of Trees, Shrubs & Conifers George E. Brown, Faber & Faber, 1972

Queer Gear: How to Buy & Cook Exotic Fruits & Vegetables M. Allsop & C. Heal, Century Hutchinson, 1986

RHS Encyclopedia of Gardening C. Brickell, ed., Dorling Kindersley

RHS Gardeners' Encyclopedia Oxford Press, 1951

Salad Garden, The J. Larkcom, Frances Lincoln, 1984

Science and Fruit Long Ashton Research Station, University of Bristol, 1953

Seeds Jekka McVicar, Kyle Cathie, 2001

Soil Conditions and Plant Growth Sir John Russell, Longmans 8th edition, 1954

Sow and Grow Vegetables B. Salt, MPC, 1995

Sturtevant's Edible Plants of the World U. P. Hendrick, ed., Dover Publications, 1972

Successful Organic Gardening G. Hamilton, Dorling Kindersley, 1987

Treatise on Gardening William Cobbett, 1821

Trees and Bushes of Britain and Europe Oleg Polunin, Oxford University Press, 1976

Tropical Planting & Gardening H. F. Macmillan, Malayan Nature Society, 1991

UK Green Growers' Guide, The S. G. Lisansky, S. Robinson, J. Coombs, CPL Press, 1991

Vanishing Garden, The Christopher Brickell & Fay Sharman, John Murray, 1986

Vegetable Garden Displayed, The J. Larkcom, RHS, 1992

Vegetable Varieties for the Garden J. R. Chowings & M. J. Day, RHS/Cassell, 1992

Vegetables R. Phillips & M. Rix, Pan Macmillan, 1993

Vegetables of South East Asia G. A. L. Herklots, Allen & Unwin

Vegetarian Cookbook, The Sarah Brown, Dorling Kindersley, 1984

Weed Control Robbins, Crafts & Raynor, McGraw Hill, 1942

Your Kitchen Garden George Seddon, Mitchell Beazley, 1975

SEED SOURCES

When importing plants and seeds, both American and Canadian consumers must obtain an import permit and a phytosanitary certificate from the exporting country. In the U.S., visit **www.aphis.usda.gov** *and in Canada, visit* **www.inspection.gc.ca**

In both cases, there are restrictions under CITES (Convention on International Trade in Endangered Species of Wild Fauna and Flora) of importing endangered plants.

Artistic Gardens/
Le Jardin du Gourmet
P.O. Box 75
St. Johnsbury Center, VT
05863-0075
Tel: (802) 748-1446
www.artisticgardens.com

B & T World Seeds
Paguignan 34210
Aigues Vives, France
Tel: 011 33 0 4 68 91 29 63
www.b-and-t-world-seeds.com

Bountiful Gardens
18001 Shafer Ranch Road
Willits, CA 95490-9626
Tel: (707) 459-6410
www.bountifulgardens.org

The Cook's Garden
P.O. Box C5030
Warminster, PA 18974
Toll-free: 1-800-457-9703
www.cooksgarden.com

Dixondale Farms
P.O. Box 129-6129
Department WP05
Carrizo Springs, TX
78834 6129
Tel: (877) 367-1015
www.dixondalefarms.com

Ed Hume Seeds
P.O. Box 73160
Puyallup, WA 98373
Tel: (253) 435-4414
www.humeseeds.com

eSeeds.com Ltd.
335-916 West Broadway
Vancouver, BC V5Z 1K7
www.eseeds.com
E-mail: service@eseeds.com

Evergreen Seeds
P.O. Box 17538
Anaheim, CA 92817
Tel: (714) 637-5769
www.evergreenseeds.com

Hole's
101 Bellerose Drive
St. Albert, AB T8N 8N8
Toll-free: 1-888-884-6537
Tel: (780) 419-6800
www.holesonline.com

Johnny's Selected Seeds
955 Benton Avenue
Winslow, ME 04901
Toll-free 1-800-879-2258
Tel: (207) 861-3901
www.johnnyseeds.com

Mapple Farm
129 Beech Hill Road
Weldon, NB E4H 4N5
Tel: (506) 734-3361

Nourse Farms, Inc.
41 River Road
South Deerfield, MA 01373
Tel: (413) 665-2658
www.noursefarms.com

Pinetree Seeds
P.O. Box 300
New Gloucester, ME 04260
Tel: (207) 926-3400
www.superseeds.com

Plants of the Southwest
3095 Agua Fria Road
Santa Fe, NM 87507
Toll-free: 1-800-788-7333
Tel: (505) 438-8888
www.plantsofthesouthwest.com

Richters Herb Specialists
357 Highway 47
Goodwood, ON L0C 1A0
Tel: (905) 640-6677
www.richters.com

Salt Spring Seeds
Box 444, Ganges P.O.
Salt Spring Island, BC
V8K 2W1
Tel: (250) 537-5269
www.saltspringseeds.com

Seeds of Change
P.O. Box 15700
Santa Fe, NM 87506
Toll-free: 1-888-762-7333
www.seedsofchange.com

Seeds of Diversity Canada
P.O. Box 36, Station Q
Toronto, ON M4T 2L7
Toll-free: 1-866-509-7333
www.seeds.ca

Seeds West Garden Seed
317 14th Street N.W.
Albuquerque, NM 87104
Tel: (505) 843-9713
www.seedswestgardenseeds.com

Vegetable Seed Warehouse
410 Whaley Pond Road
Graniteville, SC 29829
Fax: (803) 232-1119
www.vegetableseedware
house.com

Vesey's Seeds Ltd.
Box 9000
Charlottetown, PEI C1A 8K6
Toll-free: 1-800-363-7333
www.veseys.com

Wood Prairie Farm
49 Kinney Road
Bridgewater, ME 04735
Toll-free: 1-800-829-9765
www.woodprairie.com

INDEX

NORTH AMERICAN HARDINESS ZONES

North American gardeners are given guidance through a system of zones, of which zone 0 is the Arctic and zone 11 the southernmost part of the continent. A plant may be hardy to zones 7–9, which means you can leave it outdoors all winter if you live in Texas, but not if you live in Manitoba. Both countries recently revised their zone systems—the U.S. in 1990, Canada in 2000—to incorporate changes in climate and advances in data collection. The key to using the zone system is simple: know the minimum winter temperature of your area and check the hardiness rating of plants before purchasing them. For more details, American gardeners should go to *www.usna.usda.gov/Hardzone/index.html* and Canadians can visit *http://sis.agr.gc.ca/cansis/nsdb/climate/hardiness/intro.html*

Hardiness Zones and Average Minimum Winter Temperature Range

Zone	Temperature (°F)	Examples of Cities in This Zone	Temperature (°C)
1	below −50°F	Fairbanks, Alaska; Resolute, Nunavut	below −46°C
2	−50°F to −40°F	Pinecreek, Minnesota; Lloydminster, Alberta	−46°C to −40°C
3	−40°F to −30°F	Tomahawk, Wisconsin; Sidney, Montana; Dauphin, Manitoba	−40°C to −34°C
4	−30°F to −20°F	Minneapolis/St. Paul, Minnesota; Sherbrooke, Quebec	−34°C to −29°C
5	−20°F to −10°F	Mansfield, Pennsylvania; Sackville, New Brunswick	−29°C to −23°C
6	−10°F to 0°F	St. Louis, Missouri; Lebanon, Pennsylvania; Windsor, Ontario	−23°C to −18°C
7	0°F to 10°F	Little Rock, Arkansas; Griffin, Georgia, Victoria, B.C.	−18°C to −12°C
8	10°F to 20°F	Dallas, Texas; Gainesville, Florida; Chilliwack, B.C.	−12°C to −7°C
9	20°F to 30°F	Houston, Texas; Fort Pierce, Florida; Brownsville, Texas	−7°C to −1°C
10	30°F to 40°F	Miami, Florida; Victorville, California; Coral Gables, Florida	−1°C to 4°C
11	above 40°F	Honolulu, Hawaii; Mazatlan, Mexico	above 4°C

ACKNOWLEDGMENTS

The authors and publisher wish to thank the following for permission to quote recipes: Onion and Walnut Muffins—*Hudson Valley Cookbook* by Wally Malouf; La Gasconnade—*Goose Fat & Garlic* by Jeanne Strang; Mrs. Krause's Pepper Hash—*Pennsylvania Dutch Country Cooking* by William Woys Weaver; Risotto with Artichokes—*The River Café Cookbook* by Rose Gray and Ruth Rogers; Pelecing Peria—*Indonesian Food and Cookery* by Sri Owen; Chayote in Red Wine and Creamed Chinese Artichokes—*The Vegetable Book* by Jane Grigson; Tzimmes—*Russian Cooking* by Olga Phklebin.

Photography key

A–Z	A–Z Botanical Collections
BAL	The Bridgeman Art Library
CT	Christine Topping
GPL	The Garden Picture Library
HSI	Holt Studios International
JF	John Fielding
MG	Michelle Garrett
OSF	Oxford Scientific Films
PH	Photos Horticultural
SM	Sally Maltby

Pages 1–13 as follows: 1 MG; 2 Jekka McVicar; 3 SM; 5 GPL (Mayer/Le Scanff); 6 *background* (GPL (Brigitte Thomas); 7 Glasgow Museums, Art Gallery Kelvingrove; 8 *background* GPL (Mayer/Le Scanff); *bottom left* PH; 9 *top* Bridgeman Art Library (Chris Beetles Ltd.); 10–11 *background* CT; *bottom right* SM; 12–13 *background* GPL (Bob Challinor)

Pages 14–193, all food photography by Michelle Garrett; all other photography by Sally Maltby, except for the following: 14 *top right* PH; *bottom left* HSI (Bob Gibbons); 15 *top right* HSI (Sylvestre Silver) 16 *left* SM; *top right* JF; *middle right* JF; 17 *top right* JF; *bottom right* JF; 18 *top* PH; *bottom* GPL (Gary Rogers); 20 JF; 21 *top* PH; *bottom* A–Z (Anthony Cooper); 22 *bottom right* PH; 23 *top left* GPL (John Glover); *top right* GPL (Michael Howes); *bottom middle* PH; 24 *top right* MG; 25 A–Z (Rosemary Greenwood); 26 *bottom middle* (PH); 27 *top left* HSI (Irene Lengui); 28 *top right* Roger Phillips; 30 *top right* GPL (John Glover); *bottom right* HSI (Nigel Cattlin); 31 *top left* PH; *bottom right* GPL (Michael Howes); 32 *top right* HSI (Rosemary Mayer); *bottom right* HSI Nigel Cattlin); 34 *bottom middle* PH; 36 *bottom middle* GPL (Brian

Carter); 37 *top left* GPL (Lamontagne); 38 *top right* GPL (David Askham); *bottom middle* GPL (Gary Rogers); 39 *top* A–Z (Elsa M. Megson); 40 *bottom left* PH; *bottom right* PH; 41 *top left* PH; *bottom right* GPL (Joanne Pavia); 43 *middle left* GPL (John Glover); *bottom right* JF; 44 *top left* GPL (Michael Howes); *bottom right* GPL (Brian Carter); 45 *top left* JF; 46 *bottom left* PH; *bottom right* PH; 47 *top left* JF; 48 *bottom right* PH; 49 *top left* JF; 50 *top right* PH; *bottom right* GPL (John Glover); 51 *top left* PH; 52 *top right* PH; 53 *top right* GPL (Gary Rogers); *bottom left* GPL (Brian Carter); 54 *top left* HSI (Andy Burridge); *bottom right* PH; 56 *top right* PH; 57 *top right* MG; *bottom left* GPL (Juliette Wade); *bottom right* PH; 58 *top right* PH; 60 *bottom left* JF; 61 *bottom left* JF; 62 *bottom left* GPL (John Glover); 63 *right* HSI (Nigel Cattlin); 64 *top left* GPL (Michael Howes); *bottom right* GPL (John Baker); 66 *bottom right* GPL (John Glover); 67 *top right* HSI (Nigel Cattlin); 68 *top right* HSI (Nigel Cattlin); 69 *bottom left* SM; 70 *top right* GPL (Juliette Wade); *bottom left* PH; *bottom right* GPL (Lamontagne); 72 *bottom right* HSI (Nigel Cattlin); 73 *top left* HSI (Nigel Cattlin); 74 *top right* JF; *bottom right* JF; 75 *top left* GPL (Mayer/Le Scanff); 76 *left bottom left* GPL (John Glover); 76 *left*

GPL (Lamontagne); *right* JF; 77 *top left* PH; 78 *bottom* HSI (Richard Anthony); 80 *bottom left* OSF (Denni Brown); *bottom right* OSF (Denni Brown); 81 *top left* OSF (Harry Fox); 82 *bottom left* OSF (Sean Morris); 83 *top right* PH; 84 *top right* GPL (Michael Howes); *bottom* PH; 86 *top right* Natural History Photographic Agency (Brian Hawkes); *bottom left* GPL (Neil Holmes); *bottom right* PH; 87 *bottom left* GPL (David Askham); 89 *top left* PH; *top right* SM; *bottom* PH; 90 *bottom middle* GPL (Mel Watsom); 91 *top right* GPL (J. S. Sira); *bottom left* GPL (Neil Holmes); 92 *top right* GPL (Gary Rogers); *bottom left* GPL (Rex Butcher); 94 *bottom left* GPL (Brigitte Thomas); 95 *bottom left* GPL (Joanne Pavia); 96 *top right* JF; 97 *top right* OSF (Mike Slater); *bottom left* GPL (Marianne Majerus); 98 *top left* MG; 99 **top right** GPL (John Glover); 100 *top right* PH; 101 *bottom left* PH; 102 *top left and bottom right* GPL (Michael Howes); *bottom left* MG; 104 *top left* HSI (Nigel Cattlin); *bottom left* GPL (Michael Viaro); 105 *top left* HSI (Richard Anthony); *bottom left* HSI (Nigel Cattlin); 106 *bottom left* HSI (Bob Gibbons); 107 *top middle* GPL (John Glover); *bottom left* HSI (Nigel Cattlin); 108 *bottom left* HSI (Nigel Cattlin); 109 *top left* HSI (Inga Spence); 110 *bottom left* PH; 112 *bottom* right HSI (Nigel Cattlin); 113 top left PH; 114 bottom right JF; 115 top left GPL (Mayer/Le Scanff); middle left GPL (John Glover); 116 top right PH; bottom left PH; 117 top right GPL (Lamontagne); bottom left GPL (Michael Howes); 119 bottom right Roger Phillips; 120 top right A–Z (Bjorn Svensson); 121 top left J. Allen Cash Ltd.; 122 x 3 HSI (Nigel Cattlin); 124 middle left PH; bottom right HSI (Bob Gibbons); 125 top right JF; 126 top left GPL (Sunniva Harte); bottom right GPL (John Glover); 127 bottom right GPL (Juliette Wade); 128 top right JF; 129 bottom left GPL (Lamontagne); 131 top right HSI (Nigel Cattlin); 132 bottom right HSI (Mary Cherry); 134 top right OSF (Waina Cheng); 135 top left PH ; 136 bottom left HSI (Dick Roberts); 137 bottom right HSI (Richard Anthony); 138 top right OSF (G. I. Bernard); bottom left PH (ACM); 140 top right A–Z; 141 bottom left PH; 142 top left MG; bottom right HSI (Nigel Cattlin); 143 x 2 HSI (Nigel Cattlin); 144 bottom right GPL (Neil Holmes); 145 top GPL (Brian Carter); bottom PH; 146 top left GPL (Gary Rogers); 147 top right GPL (Lamontagne); 148 top left PH; top right GPL (John Glover); 150 top right GPL (Michael Howes); bottom left GPL (Chris Burrows); 151 top left GPL (Michael Howes); bottom right GPL (Steven Wooster); 152 top left PH; 153 middle HSI (Nigel Cattlin); 154 bottom left PH; 155 top right MG; bottom left PH; bottom right GPL (David Askham); 157 middle PH; 158 top left PH; 159 bottom right PH; 160 top right HSI (Bob Gibbons); 161 bottom left PH; 163 middle MG; 164 top right HSI (Nigel Cattlin); bottom left PH; 165 top left HSI (Rosemary Mayer); 166 top right GPL (Vaughan Fleming); 167 bottom left PH; 169 top right GPL (Elizabeth Strauss); middle right GPL (Marie O'Hara); bottom left HSI (Nigel Cattlin); 170 top left HSI (Willem Harinck); middle right PH; 171 top right GPL (Michael Howes); bottom left HSI (Primrose Peacock); 172 top right HSI (Andy Burridge); 174 top right PH; 175 top right JF; bottom left GPL (Michael Howes); 176 bottom left GPL (Lamontagne); 177 top left A–Z (F. Collet and U. Lund); bottom left JF; 178 top right HSI (Jean Hall); bottom right PH; 179 top left OSF (Stan Osolinski); top right HSI (Jean Hall); 180 top left JF; 181 top middle OSF (Geof Kidd); bottom left PH; 182 bottom right PH; 183 top left PH; 184 top right PH; 185 top right PH; bottom left OSF (G. A. Maclean); 186 top right and bottom left HSI (Nigel Cattlin); 189 top right HSI (Nigel Cattlin); bottom left GPL (Christel Rosenfeld); 190 top left HSI (P. Karunakaran); bottom right GPL (Vaughan Fleming); 191 top right GPL (Mayer/Le Scanff); 192 top right MG

Pages 194–389 all food photography by Michelle Garrett and all other photography by Jekka McVicar and Sally Maltby, except for the following: 220 bottom left Roger Phillips; 250 courtesy of Rowden Garden; 349 SM; 388 top right HSI (Richard Anthony); 389 x 2 HSI (Nigel Cattlin)

Pages 390–623 as follows:
390–1 SM; 392–3 background H. Angel; bottom right SM; 394 SM; 395 top right J. Hurst; top left and bottom SM; 396 CT; bottom PH; 397 top right CT; bottom CT; top left SM; 398 top SM; bottom left CT; bottom right MG; 399 MG; 400 top right SM; bottom left J. Hurst; 401 top left J. Hurst; right J. Hurst; bottom left MG; right MG; 402 SM; 403 SM; 404 top right A. Blake; bottom left CT; 405 center SM; top MG; bottom MG; 406 top right HSI; bottom CT; 407 top MG; bottom Christie's Images; 408 top right CT; bottom GPL; 409 bottom left H. Angel; right MG; 410 top left CT; right PH; 411 top left A. Blake; top right MG; center Photos International; bottom right SM; 412 Photos International; 413 MG; 414 SM; 415 top left J. Hurst; top right MG; bottom right GPL; 416 CT; 417 top right MG; bottom left GPL; 418 SM; 419 top left CT; bottom right GPL; 420 top right MG; bottom left CT; 421 MG; 422 top right PH; bottom left SM; 423 top left John Glover; right MG; 424 top CT; bottom PH; 425 top right Christie's Colour Library; bottom left CT; bottom right MG; 426 center SM; bottom left H. Angel; 427 top left PH; top right MG; bottom right MG; 428 top right PH; bottom SM; 429 top right Christie's Colour Library; right MG; bottom left H. Angel; 430 top right SM; bottom right SM; center right CT; 431 top PH; center right MG; bottom J. Dixon; 432–3 x 3 SM; 434 CT; 435 top left H. Angel; top right MG; bottom left GPL; bottom left SM; 437 MG; 438 top SM; bottom PH; 439 top left PH; top right MG; bottom right MG; 440 SM; 441 bottom left PH; top right MG; bottom right MG; 442 H. Angel; 443 top left PH; bottom right H. Angel; top right MG; 444 left CT; top right SM; bottom right MG; 445 top CT; left SM; bottom MG; 446 bottom SM; top right PH; 447 bottom SM; top left CT; top right MG; 448 SM; 449 top left PH; bottom PH; top right MG; center MG; 450 top right SM; bottom left CT; 451 top left SM; right SM; bottom MG; 452 top left PH; top right CT; bottom right SM; 454 top PH; left CT; right SM; 455 top CT; right MG; bottom right MG; left MG; 456 SM; 457 PH; 458 SM; 459 MG; 460 top A. Blake; bottom left PH; center PH; bottom MG; 462 SM; 463 bottom left SM; right MG; 464 top right SM; bottom CT; 465 top CT; bottom left SM; bottom right MG; 466 bottom left CT; top right SM; 467 bottom left CT; top right MG; 468 SM ; 469 top right CT; bottom left SM; right SM; center SM; 470 Janet Price; 471 top right MG; bottom right MG;

bottom left Janet Price; center Janet Price; 472–3 NHPA; 474 top right GPL (John Glover); bottom right CT; 475 top left CT; right PH; 476 SM; 477 top left CT; top right SM; bottom left PH; right PH; 478 SM; 479 MG; 480 top G. W. Lennox; bottom CT; 481 top left SM; center right SM; bottom left Peter Knab; bottom right MG; 482 SM; 483 top left CT; bottom left CT; top right SM; bottom right J. Hurst; 484 top right H. Angel; bottom left Christie's Images; bottom right SM; 485 top SM; center right SM; bottom MG; 486 top right CT; bottom MG; 487 top PH; bottom MG; 488 top SM; bottom CT; 489 top SM; bottom left CT; bottom MG; 490 bottom left SM; top PH; bottom right PH; 491 top right PH; center GPL (J. S. Sira); bottom right MG; 492 top H. Angel; bottom left SM; right MG; 493 top PH; bottom right MG; 494 center CT; bottom right MG; 495 top SM; bottom right CT; 496 top right H. Angel; bottom left SM; 497 top right A–Z (D. C. Clegg); bottom right MG; 498 top SM; bottom right CT; 499 top left CT; bottom left CT; right SM; bottom right SM; 500 top SM; left A–Z (G. A. Matthews); right MG; 501 top PH; right CT; bottom right SM; 502 middle MG; bottom right HSI (Nigel Cattlin); 503 top left HSI (Nigel Cattlin); middle right HSI (Inga Spence); 504 bottom left HSI (Duncan Smith); 505 top left HSI (Nigel Cattlin); 506 top left SM; center right MG; bottom right MG; bottom left G. W. Lennox; 507 top MG; bottom left CT; bottom right G. W. Lennox ; 508 top left SM; bottom right MG; center MG; top left H. Angel; bottom left GPL (Steven Wooster); 509 center right MG; bottom right SM; bottom left G. W. Lennox; 510 bottom right MG; 511 top right MG; middle right MG; 513 bottom MG; 514 top SM; bottom MG; 515 center left SM; bottom right MG; 516 SM; 517 top left CT; bottom CT; top right SM; 518–9 CT; 520 top right PH; bottom MG; 521 center Bjorn Svensson; bottom left GPL (Aary Rogers); bottom right MG; 522 top MG; bottom right MG; center SM; bottom center CT; 523 top left SM; center GPL (Brigitte Thomas); bottom right MG; 524 top GPL (J. S. Sira); center SM; bottom right MG; 525 center A–Z; bottom left SM; bottom right MG; 526 center H. Angel; top right SM; bottom right MG; 527 top left SM; top right A–Z (Maurice Nimmo); bottom left A–Z (Andrew Brown); bottom right A–Z (Leslie J. Borg); 528 top right PH; bottom SM; 529 top left PH; center right MG; bottom right SM; 530 left CT; bottom right Botanical Collection (T. G. J. Rayner); 531 top left PH; bottom right SM; 532 top PH; bottom GPL (J. S. Sira); 533 top PH; bottom left A–Z (Maurice Nimmo); bottom right SM; 534 top A–Z (Andrew Brown); bottom left CT; bottom right PH; 535 top left PH; top right SM; bottom H. Angel; 536 top PH; bottom SM; 537 top left GPL (Christopher Fairweather); top right H. Angel; bottom left PH; bottom right MG; 538 top H. Angel; bottom H.

Angel; center A–Z (Glenis Morre); 539 top GPL (Sunniva Harte); center GPL (Mayer/ Le Scanff); bottom PH; 540–1 PH; 542 top SM; bottom A–Z (Malcolm Richards); 543 top A-Z (Jiri Loun); bottom A-Z; bottom right MG; 544 top SM; bottom A–Z (Irene Windridge); 545 top SM; right MG; bottom MG; 546 top SM; bottom A–Z (Peter Hallett); 547 top CT; center PH; bottom MG; 548 top SM; bottom SM; 549 top left CT; bottom left CT; top right MG; bottom right MG; 550 top SM; bottom A–Z (Elsa Megson); 551 top right A–Z (Geoff Kidd); bottom right A–Z (John Klegg); 552 top SM; bottom A–Z (Michael Ward); 553 top A–Z (Michael Ward); bottom MG; 554 top left SM; top right MG; bottom A–Z (Alan Gould); 555 center SM; bottom MG; 556 top SM; center A–Z (John Pettigrew); bottom left A–Z (John Pettigrew); bottom right MG; 557 A–Z; center SM; bottom MG; 558 top SM; bottom SM; 559 top HSI (Inga Spence); bottom HSI (Nigel Cattlin); 560–1 GPL (Mayer/ Le Scanff); 562 top left HSI (Nigel Cattlin); bottom PH; 563 GPL (Gary Rogers); 564 top GPL (Marie O'Hara); 565 top right GPL (Gary Rogers); 566 SM; 567 Jekka McVicar; 568–9 SM; 570 SM; 571 SM; 573 PH (Ryton Hydra HDRA Organic Garden); 574 top H. Angel; bottom H. Angel; 575 H. Angel; 576 HSI (Nigel Cattlin); 577 top J. Hurst; bottom Sue Cunningham; 578 top H. Angel; bottom HSI (Rosemary Mayer); 579 top J. Hurst; bottom J. Hurst; 580 bottom PH; 581 top left PH; bottom right A–Z ; 582–3 PH (Ryton Hydra HDRA Organic Garden); 584 top right A–Z (Anthony Cooper); middle left HSI (Richard Anthony); bottom right PH; 585 middle left GPL (Marijke Heuff); bottom right A–Z (Martin Stankewitze); 586–7 CT; 588–9 Derek St. Romaine; 590–1 SM; 592 top right CT; bottom left CT; 593 top left SM; top right CT; bottom right H. Angel; 594 CT; 595 top left SM; bottom SM; right J. Hurst; 596 bottom left A–Z; bottom right (Nigel Cattlin); 597 top left PH; 598 HSI (Nigel Cattlin); 599 top right A–Z (D. W. Bevin); middle left PH; 600–1 HSI (Nigel Cattlin); 602 HSI (Nigel Cattlin); 603 top right PH; bottom HSI (Nigel Cattlin); 604 top right HSI (Duncan Smith); middle right HSI (Len McLeod); bottom left A–Z (D. W. Bevin); bottom right HSI (Nigel Cattlin); 605 top left HSI (Nigel Cattlin); top right HSI (Nigel Cattlin); middle left HSI (Nigel Cattlin); bottom right A–Z (Margaret Sixsmith); 606 top right HSI (Andy Burridge); bottom right PH; 607 top left HSI (Nigel Cattlin); top right HSI (Nigel Cattlin); bottom left HSI (Nigel Cattlin); 608 MG; 609 MG; 610 Ardea London; 611 CT; 612–3 MG; 614–5 SM; 616 top H. Angel; bottom SM; 617 Jekka McVicar; 618 A–Z; 619 Jekka McVicar; 620 top CT; bottom SM; 621 top PH; bottom CT; 622 top left SM; top right J. Hurst; bottom CT; 623 top GPL (Juliette Wade); bottom PH